Handbook of
Adolescent Psychology
(PGPS-142)

Pergamon Titles of Related Interest

Apter/Goldstein YOUTH VIOLENCE: Programs and Prospects
Feindler/Ecton ADOLESCENT ANGER CONTROL: Cognitive–Behavioral Techniques
Goldstein/Hersen HANDBOOK OF PSYCHOLOGICAL ASSESSMENT
Hersen THE CLINICAL PSYCHOLOGY HANDBOOK
Liebert/Sprafkin/Davidson THE EARLY WINDOW: Effects of Television on
Children and Youth, 2nd Edition
Santostefano COGNITIVE CONTROL THERAPY WITH
CHILDREN AND ADOLESCENTS

Related Journals
(Free sample copies available upon request)

CHILD ABUSE AND NEGLECT
CHILDREN AND YOUTH SERVICES REVIEW
JOURNAL OF CHILD PSYCHOLOGY AND PSYCHIATRY

Contents

Part IV: Specific Disorders

Part V: Special Topics

Preface and Acknowledgements

Surprising as it may seem, it is only in the past decade or so that adolescence has received the proper empirical attention that it so rightly deserves. Although there is a folklore of what adolescence is all about, a careful reading of the pages that follow clearly indicates that very few of the original notions about this intriguing developmental period have ever been validated in any scientific fashion whatsoever. More remarkable than this is that prior to this century, adolescence, as a milestone in an individual's life, was given practically no scrutiny at all.

When we first undertook the task of outlining the contents for the *Handbook of Adolescent Psychology*, we were most struck by how this area of study has developed because it previously was examined elsewhere from a primarily psychoanalytic stance. We therefore endeavored to present a balanced perspective by examining the data from a variety of theoretical frameworks and by including the input from many disciplines, such as psychology, sociology, psychiatry, education, and rehabilitation. We also made an effort to consider the unique psychological problems of the adolescent from the physical, maturational, familial, moral, intellectual, and vocational perspectives.

Our handbook is divided into five major sections. The first, Introduction, surveys the historical perspectives of adolescence and provides a general overview. The second, Theoretical Models, provides five unique frameworks for which many critical questions still need to be posed and for which some are beginning to receive answers. The third part involves an examination of General Issues, such as physical development and maturation, social interactions and adjustment, sexuality, family and environment, morals and values, intellectual growth, and research issues. In the fourth part, Specific Disorders, we survey seven pathological conditions, several of which have their genesis in adolescence. Finally, in part five, Special Topics, we evaluate cross-cultural perspectives, the handicapped adolescent, adolescent pregnancy and marriage, educational influences, and career planning.

Many people have contributed their time and talents to this handbook. First, of course, we thank our gracious contributors from diverse disciplines who agreed to share their expertise with us. Next, we extend our gratitude to our technical helpers, Jenifer Brander, Judith A. Lorenzetty, Louise E. Moore, and Mary H. Newell. Finally, we express our sincere appreciation to Jerome B. Frank, our editor, who has reinforced us in many of our endeavors over the years. We certainly appreciate his good cheer and hearty encouragement in the light of the usual and unusual delays that typify our editorial work.

PART I
Introduction

CHAPTER 1

Historical Perspectives

Lori A. Sisson, Michel Hersen, and Vincent B. Van Hasselt

Most writings portray the concept of adolescence as relatively recent in the history of civilization (Aries, 1962; Demos & Demos, 1969). However, the notion of adolescence has early roots in the scholarly works of the ancient Greeks (see Grinder, 1973, for a succinct review). For example, Plato and Aristotle recognized a hierarchy of developmental events (differentiated stages of socialization) and attached special significance to the growth of "reasoning" during the transitional period between childhood and adulthood. They were struggling mainly to resolve the philosophical dilemmas associated with the nature of reality and, in this context, set forth views on how to reach maturity. They considered the adolescent to be unstable and impressionable. Therefore, both Plato and Aristotle emphasized the role of education (especially mathematics and abstract sciences) during adolescence. Aristotle also recognized the importance of practical experience with the physical world. The philosophers agreed that the external, material environment might prevent full realization of potential or attainment of maturity and recommended shielding young people from its effects or at least carefully controlling their exposure to possible corrupting events.

The advances made by the early Greeks were

obscured for centuries by the myopic culture of medieval Europe. Phillippe Aries (1962) has conducted an extensive review of medieval art, language, arms, crafts, and games to determine views of childhood at that time. His findings are presented in an authoritative treatise, *Centuries of Childhood: A Social History of Family Life.*

Information from a number of sources indicates that medieval society generally had no concept of children as uniquely different from adults. From the time children were able to function without the constant care of an adult, they became adults themselves. They dressed like adults and shared in the work and play of adults as early as they were able.

Evidence for this has been found in artwork: Childhood was not a theme until the 12th century. When children did begin to appear as subjects in paintings, they were portrayed as tiny renditions of adults, with their physical size being the only characteristic distinguishing them. Aries (1962) also notes that the word "child" was used the way many people use "lad" or "son" today.

As the medieval church became more influential, new views about children evolved. The physical weakness of children was thought to reflect their innocence and divine purity. Grinder (1973) has called attention to Aries' (1962) citation of the following caption from a 17th century engraving:

> This is the age of innocence, to which we must all return in order to enjoy the happiness to come which is our hope on earth; the age when one can forgive anything, the age when hatred is unknown, when nothing can cause distress; the golden age of human life, the age which defies Hell, the age when life is easy and death holds no terrors, the age to which the heavens are open. Let tender and gentle respect be shown to these young plants of the Church. Heaven is full of anger for whosoever scandalizes them. (p. 19)

The Platonic and Aristotelian belief in the necessity of a pristine environment for socialization was revived. It was felt that children should be shielded from imperfections in the adult world in order to preserve innocence, promote morality, and enhance the likelihood of healthy development. In addition, children were often subjected to strict discipline designed to promote virtuous behavior. In stressing the innocence of childhood, the Church gave children a central role in families and distinguished this stage of development from all others (Aries, 1962).

Appreciation of the unique nature of childhood was accompanied by the practice of educating children in special institutions. Thus, schools were developed in the 16th and 17th centuries. According to Aries (1962), the first schools began educating children at age 9 or 10, and education continued until about age 25. Education, then, prolonged childhood for as long as 2½ decades, which is in marked contrast to earlier times. Initially, individuals of all ages studied together. Later, those with beards were separated, leaving children from about the ages of 10 to 19 together.

Finally, during the 18th and 19th centuries, the regularization of annual cycles of promotion, the preference for education via a sequence of classes, and the development of teaching systems for small, homogeneous student groups resulted in increasing correspondence between age, peer groups, and material presented. This differentiation may be the first hint of a realization that the extended childhood period may include substages characterized by different behaviors and needs (Grinder, 1973).

Also in the 18th and 19th centuries, books for young people appeared that described the years from 12 to adulthood as tumultuous ones due to susceptibility to a variety of social influences and development of sexual interest. Authors of such books as *How to Be a Man* and *Papers for Thoughtful Girls* warned that failure to resist social pressures and to control passions and sexual urges would have detrimental consequences later in life (see Demos & Demos, 1969). On a more positive note, this period was also described by Jean Jacques Rousseau (1762/1966) as one in which the individual showed great energy and curiosity that ultimately led to the acquisition of knowledge.

ADOLESCENCE IN NORTH AMERICA

Although the stage of childhood was recognized in the 13th century (and an extended childhood with special characteristics was recognized subsequently), the concept of adolescence was not introduced in North America until 1880 (Aries, 1962; Demos & Demos, 1969; Kett, 1977). It appears to have reflected the social changes that were occurring on this continent toward the latter part of the 19th and beginning of the 20th centuries (Bakan, 1972).

Prior to the Industrial Revolution and the move toward urbanization in this country, the family functioned as a comprehensive economic unit. Most work took place in and around the home. Reminiscent of medieval times, children often shared adult tasks. They were needed to help tend the livestock and harvest the crops. Even during the early years of industrialization, children were important as a source of cheap labor. Thus, childhood could be viewed as an apprenticeship period that terminated in full work responsibilities even before puberty.

However, several factors led to the segregation of children and adults (Adams & Gullotta, 1983; Bakan, 1972; Coleman et al., 1974). First, advancements in technology and mechanization eliminated the need for children in the labor market. By 1914, most states had passed laws prohibiting the employment in industry of children under 14 years of age and limiting the hours of employment for older youths. Second, compulsory-education laws, evolving from social and religious views of children as needing guidance and control, kept young people in school and further removed them from the adult world and workplace. Moreover, a changing and increasingly complex society required more and more years of formal education. Third, youth organizations, such as the YMCA, were formed to assist young people in filling their free time constructively. Clubs and activities were thought to counter the wide range of corrupting influences that accompanied the new urban life. Finally, special legal protection for juveniles set them off as being at a special age and reconfirmed society's perception of children as needing special attention, guidance, and family and community support.

As the roles of children and parents became more separate, the passage from childhood to adulthood became ambiguous and prolonged. It has been hypothesized that, to a large extent, young people have coped with this ambiguity by creating their own rituals and culture (Hareven, 1982). The invention of the concept of adolescence by psychologist G. Stanley Hall (1904) was in part a response to this phenomenon, as well as an attempt to understand the tasks, transitions, and experiences encountered by youth—no longer children but not yet adults—and their families.

SCIENTIFIC STUDY
OF ADOLESCENCE

Description and Popularization of Adolescence

The scientific study of adolescence, which began as the 20th century opened, gave legitimacy to the growing lay perception of adolescence as a special stage of development occurring between childhood and adulthood.

There can be little doubt that G. Stanley Hall was the primary early figure who provided the impetus for study in this area. His monumental two-volume treatise, *Adolescence: Its Psychology, and Its Relations to Physiology, Anthropology, Sociology, Sex, Crime, Religion, and Education*, appeared in 1904 and had profound effects upon the study of adolescence and the treatment of adolescent problems for some 25 years. He lived at a time when scientific inquiry in the social sciences was just beginning to take place, leading to new syntheses about human development. Hall, in particular, was influenced heavily by the increasingly popular biological evolutionary perspective. Although Hall's theory will be detailed in a later chapter, a brief over-

view will help place the study of adolescence in historical perspective.

In what is called a psychological *theory of recapitulation*, Hall believed that each individual retraces the history of humanity (phylogeny) in his or her own course of development (ontogeny). Therefore, each person, beginning in childhood, lives through preprogrammed periods: (a) animal-like primitivism, (b) savagery, (c) barbarism, and (d) maturity (which reflects a more civilized nature). In recapitulation theory, adolescence corresponds to the period when the human race was in a turbulent, transitional stage. Hall described adolescence as a period both of upheaval, suffering, passion, and rebellion against adult authority and of physical, intellectual, and social change. "Storm and stress" were popularized by Hall as adjectives describing adolescence.

Whereas childhood was thought to be completely dominated by instinct, susceptibility to environmental influences was thought to be a hallmark of adolescence (Grinder, 1973). In fact, the adolescent period was particularly significant because the provision of appropriate educational experiences would, according to Hall, create the potential for internalization of character traits that were believed to be genetically transmissible to offspring.

Although the recapitulationist interpretation of adolescent storm and stress quickly became obsolete with new knowledge, and the idea of inheritance of acquired personality traits was criticized severely, elements of Hall's approach to adolescence have had long-lasting effects. For example, through his writings and lectures, Hall encouraged parents, educators, and scientists to record the course of children's growth and development and to recognize adolescence as a crucial period of physical, intellectual, and social change (Adams & Gullotta, 1983). In addition, Hall's conceptualization of adolescence as a period of storm and stress has received widespread acceptance among many of those who since have studied this period of development (Grinder, 1973).

Sigmund Freud introduced psychoanalytic theory to North America in the early 1900s. As Hall's contemporary, Freud also was affected by the post-Darwinian consciousness of evolution and also gave strong support to the storm and stress interpretation of adolescence. Hall, however, focused on the relationship between biological and psychological forces during adolescence to the exclusion of developmental events during infancy and childhood, whereas Freud held that personality growth was nearly complete by the end of the fifth year of life.

Nevertheless, Freud dealt briefly with adolescence in his *Three Essays on the Theory of Sexuality (1953)*. He viewed this period as the culmination of a series of changes destined to give infantile sexual life its final, normal form. According to Freud, earlier resolution of childhood conflicts between instinctual demands and ego mechanisms are disrupted at puberty when maturation of the external and internal sexual organs bring new sexual tension. This increased inner turmoil leads to feelings of guilt, anxiety, isolation, and confusion as well as to behaviors that vacillate widely between extremes of egocentrism and altruism, dependence and independence, and rebelliousness and affirmation. Freud's authoritative presentation of an intriguing theory promoted a large following among not only psychologists but also philosophers, educators, and novelists. Today, few persons in North America are unfamiliar with his ideas.

Psychoanalytic theory is directly applied to adolescence in the modern writings of Peter Blos (1972) and reflected in the Neo-Freudian conceptualizations of Erik Erikson (1959; 1968).

A quarter of a century after Hall and Freud presented their theories of adolescence, Margaret Mead described her studies of primitive cultures in Samoa (1950) and New Guinea (1953). Her observational research showed that young people in primitive societies appeared to make the transition from childhood to adulthood with relative ease. Therefore, Mead concluded that stress and alienation are not universal characteristics of adolescence driven by biological forces. Instead, she proposed that the stormy nature of adolescence was merely a "cultural invention." Through popular lectures, books, and films, Mead aroused societal interest in cultural and environmental factors that influence the behavior of adolescents.

Following this lead, numerous writers have addressed aspects of the social system in North America in terms of its effects on adolescent behavior (see Adams & Gullotta, 1983). In particular, a rapidly changing and unsettled society (Goodman, 1956), inadequate education and socialization in schools (Friedenberg, 1965), and the influence of peer groups (Coleman, 1961) were implicated as factors contributing to characteristic adolescent behavior patterns.

The Empirical Study of Adolescence

Hall, Freud, Mead, and other early scholars can be credited with popularizing the concept of adolescence. However, their theories, assumptions, and generalizations were obtained by reading the diaries of adolescents, interrogating youth about their feelings, and observing young people's behavior. Although important in establishing hypotheses about adolescent behavior, these methods are subject to bias, lack of standardization, and the effects of extraneous factors, all of which can lead to erroneous conclusions.

It has not been until recently that data-based, controlled, research studies of the adolescent period have appeared. As Adams and Gullota (1983) have pointed out, until the 1970s, only five universities in North America offered doctoral programs in adolescent psychology, and fewer than 2% of research articles on human behavior published each year used adolescents as subjects. Although 20 years ago there was just one specialty journal serving as a publication outlet for research on adolescence, today there are five: *Adolescence, Journal of Adolescence, Journal of Early Adolescence, Journal of Adolescence and Youth,* and *Youth and Society.*

Several important empirical investigations have helped clarify the question of a biological versus an environmental basis for adolescent behavior. If adolescence is a biological phenomenon, it should be a universal and uniform period of life. Hall and Freud subscribed to this notion. However, as we have already noted, Margaret Mead objected to this viewpoint based on her studies of adolescents in primitive societies. Even within North America, adolescent behavior apparently varies with a number of variables, particularly social class.

First, a longitudinal study of adolescent boys conducted by Offer and Offer (1975) has challenged the historical belief that adolescence is inevitably a period of storm and stress. Only 21% of the boys in the Offer and Offer study manifested significant and continuous behavior problems, unhappiness, and distrust of adults. An additional 35% exhibited periodic conflicts. In contrast, many youths (23%) were found to progress through the adolescent period in a smooth and steady manner. The remainder of the sample failed to fit any of these descriptive categories. Collateral measures showed that family discord and crisis, poor communication between parent and child, and low income generally marked children in turmoil. Interestingly, those boys who showed uncomplicated adjustment to adolescence were generally from stable, intact families.

Second, Hollingshead (1949) and Havighurst (Havighurst, Bowman, Liddle, Matthews, & Pierce, 1962) have conducted comprehensive investigations specifically designed to determine the effects of social class on adolescent behavior. In these studies, adolescents selected from a wide range of social class backgrounds contributed information about a number of social factors (e.g., formation of cliques, leisure activities, school attendance, sex, marriage, etc.). Both research projects found that adolescent behavior patterns differed predictably according to social class. Adolescent boys and girls from lower socioeconomic levels were more likely to drop out of school, show aggressive maladjusted tendencies, engage in delinquency, and marry early. Later, these youths were frequently judged to be less competent and often found it difficult to obtain employment. Thus, it appears that disadvantaged youths find growing up a more difficult and stressful experience than their middle-class peers.

Third, social-learning theorist Albert Bandura has extended this research by conducting studies to pinpoint the environmental events that cause certain behaviors said to characterize adolescence (Bandura, 1969, 1973; Bandura, Ross, & Ross, 1963; Bandura & Walters, 1959). Bandura is perhaps most well-known for his work on aggression in children. Careful laboratory investigations have repeatedly shown that children imitate the behavior of others, especially influential adults, entertainment heroes, and peers. For example, when children watched unusually aggressive behavior in a real-life model, or a model in a film or cartoon, many of their subsequent responses were accurate imitations of the aggressive acts (Bandura, Ross, & Ross, 1963).

Further work has shown that a number of factors in the home may contribute to aggressive behavior in children and adolescents. Aggressive boys have been found to have parents who use physical punishments, encourage their sons to exhibit aggression outside the home, and receive vicarious enjoyment from their sons' aggressive escapades. Children may learn aggression by modeling the behavior of a punishing parent, and they may be reinforced for aggressive behavior by parental attention to reports of aggression toward peers (Bandura & Walters, 1959).

Bandura and other social-learning theorists have provided convincing empirical evidence that adolescence is continuous with childhood and adulthood in that the same principles of learning are applicable to all stages of development. In sum, the data from these and other controlled investigations highlight the importance of recognizing social and environmental conditions likely to influence adolescent behavior. In the chapters that follow, the importance of these conditions will be demonstrated again and again.

DEFINITION OF ADOLESCENCE

Although adolescence has been a growing concern to Western society for the past century, we have seen that there appears to be no universal agreement about the characteristics that distinguish it as a developmental phase. Similarly, there are a number of perspectives on when the period begins and ends. As defined by the *Webster's New Collegiate Dictionary* (1977), adolescence refers to the "process of growing up" or to the "period of life from puberty to maturity." But for most people, adolescence is simply an uncomfortable intermediate state between being a child and being an adult (Rice, 1984). This conception is aptly reflected in Garrison and Garrison's (1975) description of adolescence as an in-between period:

> There is a fairly distinct time during which the individual cannot be treated as a child, and actually resents such treatment. Yet this same individual is by no means fully mature, and cannot be classed as an adult. During this transition from childhood to adulthood, therefore, the subject is referred to as an adolescent. (p.6)

The move to empirical research with adolescents has required more precise inclusionary criteria for subjects. For this purpose, adolescence has been tied to an age span, with the starting age varying from 10 to 13 and the concluding age varying from 19 to 21, depending on whose definition we apply (see, for example, Ramsey, 1967).

Another early approach that continues to receive widespread acceptance today denotes the adolescent by the occurrence of physical changes. In this definition, adolescence commences when the reproductive organs begin to change in late childhood and terminates with the maturation of the reproductive system (Douvan & Gold, 1966).

A more recent sociological approach to defining this period also recognizes the onset of puberty (sexual maturity) as a starting point, but turns to social criteria for determining its end (Lambert, Rothschild, Altland, & Green, 1978). Sociological indices of adulthood include participating in such adult activities as voting, drinking, marrying, finishing one's education, achieving independence, and demonstrating "mature" behavior.

It has been argued that definitions based solely on chronological age or development of reproductive capacity seem too simple and inflexible for many practical purposes (Garrison & Garrison, 1973; Rice, 1984). The 23-year-old parent who abuses or neglects his or her young child presents behaviors that make many reluctant to use the term "adult." Further, such definitions may create false beliefs about young people at various ages (Adams & Gullotta, 1983). This concern is especially relevant in modern society, where sexual maturity is occurring at rather young ages (Petersen & Taylor, 1980), and affluence has allowed individuals to extend their carefree years well into the second and sometimes the third decade of life (Garrison & Garrison, 1975; Johnstone & Rosenberg, 1968).

On the other hand, the intuitively appealing strategy of relying on social criteria to mark the end of adolescence and beginning of adulthood creates additional definitional problems. In particular, what exactly are the behavioral traits that characterize maturity? In addition, society's perspective on adolescents is likely to change as social conditions change (Adams & Gullotta, 1983). For example, during periods of war, chronological definitions of who is and is not an adolescent are changed according to military needs. The individual who is encouraged

to remain an adolescent due to job scarcity in his or her city may be welcomed into the employment world in another.

We do not hope to offer an immediate and acceptable answer to the dilemma of establishing a precise definition of adolescence. Instead, we are content to alert the reader to some problems inherent in defining the term and defer to the expertise of various theoreticians and researchers as they more completely address definitional issues from their perspectives.

THE FUTURE OF ADOLESCENCE

Our review of the history of adolescence indicates that, in spite of definitional problems, the concept has been unequivocally accepted by both the general public and the scientific community as a developmental stage in its own right. The likelihood that interest in this area will continue to expand is quite high. This prediction is based on several considerations.

First, although current popular opinion is that the number of young people in America is decreasing, recent U.S. Bureau of the Census data indicate a general trend of ever-expanding numbers of persons in the 15–24 age range (reported in Adams & Gullotta, 1983). In addition, we have already alluded to the fact that the age-boundaries of adolescence are unclear, and these probably will extend both downward and upward over the coming years. This will further increase the number of individuals termed adolescent. Younger children are developing reproductive capacities and engaging in social and other behaviors once thought to be the exclusive province of adolescents (e.g., dating, drug use, and running away), whereas the complexity of adult responsibilities demands longer and longer periods to develop necessary coping skills. The more adolescents there are, the more likely it is that their issues, characteristics, and problems will come to the attention of others.

Second, the development of educational programs and outlets for research on adolescents will no doubt encourage professional and scientific attention to this group. Current convictions that mental health problems of adults may have their roots in childhood and adolescence further serve to focus attention on this age period. Hopefully, increased activity in this area will result in better understanding of behavior exhibited by both youths and members of older generations.

Third, adolescence frequently has been identified with rebellion, sexual promiscuity, delinquency, and other behaviors that easily capture the casual interest as well as intense concern of lay persons and professionals alike. Although it is not clear that the incidences of these problems in the adolescent population are rising (Rutter, 1979), these behaviors will continue to be exhibited by a portion of youths.

Rapidly changing societal conditions, which create new social environments for successive generations, will ensure different behaviors and attitudes among children than among their parents and other adults. This, in turn, will promote occasional misunderstanding and conflict between the generations (Rice, 1984).

Increased premarital sexual activity, pregnancy, and contraceptive use among adolescents may well reflect changing attitudes of society as a whole (Rutter, 1979). However, sexual behavior creates unique problems for young people who may lack the education and experience to cope with adult consequences. Finally, juvenile delinquency does appear to be increasing, and extensive work in this area has already begun in the fields of psychology and psychiatry.

Fourth, numerous industries have been built around this age group. We now have secondary schools and institutions of higher education, medical programs, sports and recreational services, movie theaters, and clothing stores that are designed to capture the interest and support of adolescents. To many businesses, adolescence has been identified as a meaningful age period because it constitutes a rich source of potential customers. Their continued investment in the adolescent age group will be maintained because of interest in self-preservation.

REFERENCES

Adams, G. R., & Gullotta, T. (1983). *Adolescent life experiences.* Belmont, CA: Brooks/Cole.

Aries, P. (1962). *Centuries of childhood: A social history of family life.* New York: Vintage.

Bakan, D. (1972). Adolescence in America. In J. Kagan & R. Coles (Eds.), *Twelve to sixteen: Early adolescence.* New York: Norton.

Bandura, A. (1969). *Principles of behavior modification.* New York: Holt, Rinehart and Winston.

Bandura, A. (1973). *Aggression: A social learning analysis.* Englewood Cliffs, NJ: Prentice-Hall.

Bandura, A., Ross, D., & Ross, S. A. (1963). Imitation of film-mediated aggressive models. *Journal of Abnormal and Social Psychology, 67,* 3011–3020.

Bandura, A., & Walters, R. H. (1959). *Adolescent aggression.* New York: Ronald.

Blos, P. (1972). The child analyst looks at the young adolescent. In J. A. Kagan & R. Coles (Eds.), *Twelve to sixteen: Early adolescence.* New York: Norton.

Coleman, J. S. (1961). *The adolescent society.* New York: Free Press.

Coleman, J. S., Bremner, R. H., Clark, B. R., Davis, J. B., Eichorn, D. H., Griliches, Z., Kett, J. G., Ryder, N. B., Doering, Z. B., & Mays, J. M. (1974). *Youth: Transition to adulthood.* Chicago: University of Chicago Press.

Demos, J., & Demos, V. (1969). Adolescence in historical perspective. *Journal of Marriage and the Family, 31,* 632–638.

Douvan, E., & Gold, M. (1966). Model patterns in American adolescence. In L. M. Hoffman (Ed.), *Review of child development research* (Vol. 2). New York: Russell Sage.

Erikson, E. (1959). *Identity and the life cycle.* New York: International Universities.

Erikson, E. (1968). *Identity: Youth and crisis.* New York: Norton.

Freud, S. A. (1953). *Three essays on the theory of sexuality* (Vol. 7). London: Hogarth Press.

Friedenberg, E. Z. (1965). *The dignity of youth and other atavisms.* Boston: Beacon.

Garrison, K. C., & Garrison, K. C., Jr. (1975). *Psychology of adolescence* (7th ed.). Englewood Cliffs, NJ: Prentice-Hall.

Goodman, P. (1956). *Growing up absurd.* New York: Vintage.

Grinder, R. E. (1973). *Adolescence.* New York: Wiley.

Hall, G. S. (1904). *Adolescence: Its psychology, and its relations to physiology, anthropology, sociology, sex, crime, religion, and education* (Vols. 1 & 2). New York: Appleton-Century-Crofts.

Hareven, T. K. (1982). American families in transition. In F. Walsh (Ed.), *Normal family processes.* New York: Guilford.

Havighurst, R. J., Bowman, P. H., Liddle, G., Mathews, C. V., & Pierce, J. V. (1962). *Growing up in River City.* New York: Wiley.

Hollingshead, A. B. (1949). *Elmstown's youth.* New York: Wiley.

Johnstone, J. W., & Rosenberg, L. (1968). *Understanding adolescence: Current developments in adolescent psychology.* Boston: Allyn and Bacon.

Kett, J. F. (1977). *Rites of passage: Adolescence in America 1790 to the present.* New York: Basic.

Lambert, B. G., Rothschild, B. F., Altland, R., & Green, L. B. (1978). *Adolescence: Transition from childhood to maturity.* Monterey, CA: Brooks/Cole.

Mead, M. (1950). *Coming of age in Samoa.* New York: New American Library.

Mead, M. (1953). *Growing up in New Guinea.* New York: New American Library.

Offer, D., & Offer, J. (1975). *From teenage to young manhood.* New York: Basic.

Peterson, A., & Taylor, B. (1980). The biological approach to adolescence: Biological change and psychological adaptation. In J. Adelson (Ed.), *Handbook of adolescent psychology*. New York: Wiley.

Ramsey, C. E. (1967). *Problems of youth*. Belmont, CA: Dickinson.

Rice, F. P. (1984). *The adolescent: Development, relationships, and culture*. Boston: Allyn and Bacon.

Rousseau, J. J. (1966). *Émile* (B. Foxley, Trans.). New York: Dutton. (Original work published 1762)

Rutter, M. (1979). *Changing youth in a changing society*. London: Nuffield Provincial Hospitals Trust.

Webster's new collegiate dictionary. (1977). New York: G. & C. Merriam.

PART II

Theoretical Models

CHAPTER 2

Developmental Theories

John Paul McKinney and Juliet Vogel

Developmental theories of adolescence fall into two broad categories: psychosocial–developmental theories and cognitive–developmental theories. Two theorists, Erikson and Piaget, have been selected as the primary focus of a chapter on developmental theories because each describes the organization of behavior in a way that highlights its progressive unfolding. Subsequent theories in each area have been selected for their elaboration of developmental concepts.

PSYCHOSOCIAL DEVELOPMENT

Erikson's Work: History and Development

Erikson – The Theorist

The terms a theorist uses to describe his or her own unique way of perceiving and construing development come from a complex interplay between the theorist and his or her own personal history. Elkind (1979) calls this theoretical substructure the theorist's "child sense," which, he says ". . . refers to a special insight into children and or about childhood that has roots in the investigator's personal history and

which is then given expression in a particular line of research and mode of theoretical construction" (p. 1). Elkind goes on to suggest that each person's own childhood is characterized by a unique blend of setting, mood, character, or theme that seems to permeate childhood as a whole for the person. It is from the vantage point of that theme or mood that the researcher or, in this case the theorist, views children and childhood generally. His or her constructs about development will be flavored by that "child sense."

In the case of Erikson, the reader does not have to go far to understand the "child sense" that characterizes the theorist's constructs or what personal historical facts infuse that "child sense." In his paper, Autobiographical Notes on the Identity Crisis, Erikson (1970) is very explicit about the personal origin of that construct for which he is best known and with which, more than any other concept, he advanced the understanding of adolescence. For the adolescent psychologist, it is a happy coincidence that Erikson's concept of identity—in one sense, the cornerstone of his whole theory—is also the psychosocial task of adolescence.

In describing the circumstances of his life that led to the formulation of the identity construct,

Erikson (1970) first mentions his own adolescence as an "artist" ("a way of life rather than a way of making a living," p. 741). A life style of late adolescence in many areas and eras, this *Wandershaft* was, according to Erikson, well institutionalized in early 20th-century Europe. With a passing identity as an artist, coupled with a romantic attachment to "a peasant's nature," Erikson describes his own identity confusion.

> The trouble was, I often had a kind of work disturbance and needed time. *Wandershaft* under those conditions meant neurotic drivenness as well as deliberate search, even as today dropping out can be a time of tuning in, or of aimless negativism. (p. 742)

Suggesting that the negative aspects of his own identity confusion might easily be labeled "borderline," he argues that it was precisely this sort of diagnosis to which he later gave a developmental perspective in his clinical work and in his theory.

A second element in Erikson's personal history that informed his child sense was his role as a stepson. He comments on the importance of the fact that his biological father had abandoned his mother before Erikson was born. Later, when Erikson was 3, his mother married a German pediatrician. Erikson, born a Dane who would grow tall and blond, lived among German children. At puberty, his sense of being different heightened. He was considered a "goy" in the Jewish community but was a "Jew" to his German classmates. He took refuge in the fantasy that he was a foundling with "real" parents who were much better.

This "stepson" theme is repeated by Erikson in his writing about identity. He saw his relationship to Freud as influenced by his stepson identity. Always feeling that he did not quite belong (Erikson was not a physician, nor did he have any formal training other than a Montessori teacher's diploma after gymnasium until he met the circle around Freud in Vienna), he felt somehow like the "favored stepson" who would be taken in and accepted regardless.

Erikson's theory was first outlined in his now famous work, *Childhood and Society* (1950). His major contribution to psychoanalytic thought was in seeing the psychology of the developing child in a social context. Erikson has been less concerned with intrapsychic forces in develop-

ment and more concerned with the resolution of a set of tasks or crises that, if successfully mastered, can provide the individual with the foundation for new developmental levels of social relations. Thus, he proposed his eight psychosocial stages of development.

In describing this relationship between self and society, Erikson (1968) wrote, "In fact, the whole interplay between the psychological and the social, the developmental and the historical, for which identity formation is of prototypal significance, could be conceptualized only as a kind of *psychosocial* relativity" (p. 23).

Erikson's theory of development was stated in *Childhood and Society* (1950), and has been elaborated in his voluminous writing since then. From the point of view of the student of adolescence, the main sources are *Identity: Youth and Crisis* (1968) and *Identity and the Life Cycle* (1959), as well as Erikson's psychobiographical works, *Young Man Luther* (1958) and *Gandhi's Truth* (1969).

In *Identity: Youth and Crisis*, Erikson said that his theory was based on the principle of epigenesis, a term he borrowed from the biological study of early life and the geological study of rock formations. In both cases the principle refers to differentiation and diversification of a formerly undifferentiated entity as the result of external influences. Erikson put it this way:

> Somewhat generalized, this principle states that anything that grows has a ground plan, and that out of this ground plan the parts arise, each part having its time of special ascendancy, until all parts have arisen to form a functioning whole. (p. 92)

Identity, and its epigenetic development, is the backbone of Erikson's theory. The development of identity is Erikson's way to describe ego consistency from one developmental period to the next; it is seen as the primary, albeit not exclusive, task of adolescence. Initially, the concept of identity was used to refer to ego identity, but later the concept was meant to incorporate both a self (or object) component as well as an ego (or process) aspect. Erikson's (1959) inclusion of the self paid homage to the importance of societal influences:

> One could argue that it may be wise in matters of the ego's perceptive and regulative dealings with its self to reserve the designation "ego"

for the subject, and to give the designation "self" to the object. The ego, then, as a central organizing agency, is during the course of life faced with a changing self which, in turn, demands to be synthesized with abandoned and anticipated selves. This suggestion would be applicable to the *body ego*, which could be said to be the part of the self provided by the attributes of the organism, and, therefore, might more appropriately be called the *body self*; it would also concern the ego ideal as the representative of the ideas, images, and configurations, which serve the persistent comparison with an ideal self; and finally, it would apply to what I have called ego identity. What could consequently be called the *self-identity* emerges from all those experiences in which a sense of temporary self-diffusion was successfully contained by a renewed and ever more realistic self-definition and social recognition. *Identity formation thus can be said to have a self-aspect, and an ego aspect.* (p. 149)

The crisis of adolescence (i.e., the task of identity achievement) is preceded in Erikson's theory by several other stages in the epigenetic unfolding of the human person. In all he describes eight stages.

Basic trust vs. basic mistrust is the task of infancy during which the child learns the correspondence between his or her own inner needs and the predictability of a nurturing environment. It is during this period that, as waking hours increase, the child comes to match an increasing familiarity with the outer world with inner expectations. Erikson (1950) refers to a "constant tasting and testing of the relationship between inside and outside . . . " (p. 248). This growing trust is in part the result of a parental relationship that both responds with sensitivity to the needs of the child and simultaneously provides a firm guide to the limitations set by social and cultural standards. The resulting sense of trust is the basis of a later sense of identity.

During the second stage, *autonomy vs. shame and doubt*, the toddler develops a sense of him or herself as a separate person and as possessing a will of his or her own. (Erikson, 1950, uses this term "sense of" to include ". . . ways of *experiencing* accessible to introspection; ways of *behaving*, observable by others; and unconscious *inner states* determinable by test and analysis" p. 251.) Again, as in the first stage of trust vs. mistrust, outer control must be present and reassuring. It is at this stage that the child either experiences autonomy and freedom of choice,

within firmly established limits, or else turns the urge to manipulate against him or herself and develops a precocious conscience with a corresponding feeling of shame and doubt.

The third stage, *initiative vs. guilt*, is characterized by another set of achievements, including the ability to plan, undertake, and execute activities. This is in addition to the earlier accomplishment of autonomy and is based primarily on the motive to be active and self-initiating, whereas the earlier stage was based more on the need to be simply defiant or, at least, independent. One danger in the growth toward initiative can lie in the potential for experiencing guilt over the choice of conquests or the aggressive means chosen to pursue one's goals. The developing sense of moral responsibility can tyranically become an overstrict superego unless the child has appropriate adult role models, as well as peers with whom he or she can cooperate in the planning and executing of activities.

The period of the school-age child comprises the stage of *industry vs. inferiority*. The child's social world expands beyond the family as the child enters the world of school with its social comparison with peers. The child must learn to be productive, to do rather than to take. The child must now acquire mastery over the impersonal world of the tools that will be required to enter later into the world of adulthood. In the process, the child must also learn to work beside and in cooperation with peers. Failure at this stage results in a feeling of inadequacy, including feeling inferior to one's peers, or, at the other extreme, an overidentification of one's self in terms of what one can produce, a restricted identity, based solely on one's work.

The stage that is our immediate concern, however, namely *identity vs. identity confusion*, is the central task of adolescence. The sense of continuity with previous experience and a hope for the future are the crux of the adolescent's task of identity formation. Erikson (1950) says,

The integration now taking place in the form of ego identity is, as pointed out, more than the sum of the childhood identifications. It is the accrued experience of the ego's ability to integrate all identifications with the vicissitudes of the libido, with the aptitudes developed out of endowment, and with the opportunities offered in social roles. The sense of ego identity, then, is the accrued confidence that the inner sameness and continuity prepared in the past are matched by the sameness and continuity of one's meaning for others, as evidenced in the tangible promise of a "career." (p. 261)

Three periods of adult development follow the stage of identity vs. identity confusion. *Intimacy vs. isolation* is the task of young adulthood, during which those youth who have already established their identities can work toward intimacy with the other sex. Erikson is not limiting his use of the word "intimacy" to mean merely sexual relations, although that is certainly an element. He is rather referring to a more general psychological intimacy. He also maintains that those who are not yet sure of their identities shy away from this sort of intimacy, whereas those who are more sure look for this intimacy "in the form of friendship, combat, leadership, love, and inspiration" (Erikson, 1959, p. 95).

The psychosocial conflict of middle adulthood is *generativity vs. stagnation*. The desire to produce and care for offspring is, in Erikson's theory, the hallmark of this stage. This same wish or drive may be directed not only to the production and nurturing of the next generation, but also to other altruistic and creative endeavors that require in their own way a kind of parental care. The antithesis of this activity is the stagnation of self-indulgence.

Integrity vs. despair is the task of old age. Erikson (1959) refers to the maintainance of integrity in old age as "the fruit of the seven stages:"

> Only he who in some way has taken care of things and people and has adapted himself to the triumphs and disappointments of being, by necessity, the originator of others and the generator of things and ideas—only he may gradually grow the fruit of the seven stages. I know no better word for it than *integrity*. (p. 98)

For each of the psychosocial stages, Erikson emphasizes that the healthy resolution is a balance between poles rather than an extreme experience of one of them. For example, he postulates that the resolution of basic trust vs. mistrust involves the "experience of a mutual regulation of . . . increasingly receptive capacities with the maternal techniques of provision . . ." (Erikson, 1950, p. 147). The resolution of autonomy vs. shame and doubt involves a balance as well. While the child learns to exercise his or her own will, an outer control is necessary to prevent free choice from turning into anarchy, stubbornness, and intolerance. Later, a balance between industry and inferiority prevents both a permanent sense of inadequacy, as well as, at the other extreme, an identity based solely on one's productivity.

So it is with all of the psychosocial stages, including identity vs. identity diffusion. The development of a personal identity is based on the integration, as noted above, of all previous identifications with both internal endowments and aptitudes based on environmental opportunities. To overidentify with a particular element in one's repertoire of experiences would be as much a hindrance to the achievement of identity as would an inability to identify at all.

Contemporary Issues

An Empirical Approach to the Study of Identity: Identity Statuses

Research dealing with identity in adolescents had emanated almost exclusively from the notion of identity statuses as conceptualized by Marcia (1966). In his early formulation, Marcia represented Erikson's two polar resolutions of the identity crises, namely *identity achievement* and *identity diffusion*, as statuses in which an adolescent might find him or herself with respect to some issue of major importance. Initially, Marcia focused on the issues of occupation and religious and political ideology.

Besides achievement and diffusion, Marcia adds the statuses of *moratorium* and *foreclosure* to embrace all the possible positions an adolescent might take on these three important issues. Each of the four statuses is defined for any given individual in terms of crisis (i.e., a decision-making period) and commitment (i.e., personal investment). For example, Identity Achievers are those who have experienced a decision-making period and have then committed themselves to occupational and/or ideological goals. Those in the Identity Diffusions status may or may not have experienced a crisis, but in any case are not committed to any goal. Adolescents identified as Moratoriums are currently experiencing a period of decision-making and have not yet committed themselves. Finally, Foreclosures have committed themselves to ideological and occupational goals, but have not experienced any crisis or period of decision making; rather, their commitment is based on parental expectations.

The traditional measure of identity statuses, and the one on which most subsequent work has been based, is Marcia's (1966) Identity Status Interview. The basic interview has been modified by others to include domains other than ideology and occupation. For example, Grotevant, Thorbecke, and Meyer (1982) extended the interview to include three interpersonal domains: friendships, dating, and sex roles. Waterman (1982) and Grotevant and Cooper (1981) have used coding schemes that allow for independent ratings of crises and commitment in the various domains.

Subsequent measures of identity have included the Q-sort methodology (Mallory, 1983), various paper and pencil measures (Adams, Shea, & Fitch, 1979; Constantinople, 1969; Grotevant & Adams, 1984; Rasmussen, 1964; Simmons, 1970, 1973; Spiesman et al., 1983), and an incomplete sentence test (Marcia, 1966). The relative advantages and disadvantages of the various methods have been treated in recent papers (Adams, 1985; Craig-Bray & Adams, 1985; Grotevant, 1985). Reviews of research on the identity statuses (Bourne, 1978; Marcia, 1980; Waterman, 1982) have documented the theoretical richness of this conceptualization of identity.

Among the personality correlates of the identity statuses, Marcia (1980) has summarized the research and identified the following: (a) anxiety (Moratoriums are most anxious and Foreclosures least); (b) self-esteem (Identity Achievers and Moratoriums have higher self-esteem than Identity Diffusions and Foreclosures; the latter two are also more likely to change their stated view about themselves in response to feedback, whether positive or negative); (c) authoritarianism (Foreclosures score higher); (d) moral reasoning (Identity Achievers and Moratoriums, typically score highest, that is, they score at the post-conventional level whereas the other two statuses are more likely to be at the conventional and preconventional level); (e) autonomy (Identity Achievers and Moratoriums score highest); (f) cognitive styles (no general IQ differences across the four statuses; however, when stressed, Identity Achievers do best and Foreclosures do worst on a concept attainment task).

Criticism of Erikson's Theory and Marcia's Elaboration

Although Erikson's stages of psychosocial development are theoretically rich, they are not completely unambiguous (Maddi, 1972). His figurative language and rich literary description may in part be responsible for the fact that there has been little large-scale empirical testing of his hypotheses, except for those surrounding the stage of identity vs. identity diffusion.

The theory also has been criticized for what some believe to be a masculine bias, particularly in Erikson's dealing with the stage of identity vs. identity diffusion. Douvan and Adelson (1966) have observed that identity in boys may be related to occupational choice and achievement, but that for girls it is related to issues of relationships. From that point of view, it may be more reasonable to expect that for females the stage of identity vs. identity diffusion will occur in conjunction, rather than prior to, the stage of intimacy vs. isolation. Gilligan (1982) makes the case even stronger and inclusive of the other stages as well:

> For the female, Erikson (1968) says, the sequence is a bit different. She holds her identity in abeyance as she prepares to attract the man by whose name she will be known, by whose status she will be defined, the man who will rescue her from emptiness and loneliness by filling "the inner space." While for men, identity precedes intimacy and generativity in the optimal cycle of human separation and attachment, for women these tasks seem instead to be fused. Intimacy goes along with identity, as the female comes to know herself as she is known, through her relationships with others.
>
> Yet despite Erikson's observation of sex differences, his chart of life-cycle stages remains unchanged: identity continues to precede intimacy as male experience continues to define his life-cycle conception. (p. 12)

The criticisms of Marcia's elaboration of Erikson's theory center around a number of issues. First, the developmental sequence of the identity statuses remains unclear both theoretically and empirically, and it is even unclear whether each of the statuses is indeed a stage. Other criticisms have addressed the difficulty in administering and scoring the original interview and the fact that judgments made across all identity domains tend to be global and miss the fact that identity can be multifaceted.

Grotevant (1985) and Craig-Bray and Adams (1985) have called for new methodologies that focus on other aspects of the identity dimension. In this way, the richness of Erikson's theorizing will better be exploited in our understanding of adolescence. An example of relevant work is the development of the concept of "engagement style" by McKinney and his associates (McKinney, 1980; McKinney and Moore, 1978; Hotch, 1979).

A Possible Dimension of the Study of Identity: Engagement Style

The separation of subject and object at each cognitive stage of development has been outlined by Elkind (1967). A similar paradigm can be proposed for differentiating the sense of self as subject (agent) versus sense of self as object (patient) at each psychosocial stage. This duality is explicit in Erikson's discussion of the differentiation of identity formation as involving an ego aspect (sense of self as agent) and a self-aspect (sense of self as patient), as discussed previously. The relative salience in one's self-definition of agency versus patient has been labeled "engagement style" (McKinney, 1980, 1981).

At each stage, an increased interaction between self and environment leads to an increased awareness of oneself as both subject and object or as both agent, acting on the environment, and patient, responding to environmental changes resulting from one's agency.

The infant's sense of *trust* implies an understanding that his or her active behavior (agency) will lead to predictable changes in the social environment and to predictable effects on him or her (patience).

> The simplest and earliest modality is "to get", not in the sense of "go and get", but in receiving and accepting what is given; and this sounds easier than it is. For the groping and unstable newborn's organism learns this modality only as he learns to regulate his readiness to get with the methods of a mother who, in turn, will permit him to coordinate his means of getting as she develops and coordinates her means of giving. The mutuality of relaxation thus developed is of prime importance for this first experience of friendly otherness: . . . the baby also develops the necessary ground work to *get to be* the giver, to "identify" with her. (Erikson, 1959, p. 58)

Autonomy results when one's independent behavior (agency) leads to positive rewards (patience), encouraging further independence rather than leading to shame (i.e., being seen by others before one is prepared, which would block further agency). Erikson says (1959) that, "The matter of mutual regulation between adult and child now faces its severest test. . . . This

stage, therefore, becomes decisive for the ratio between love and hate, for that between cooperation and willfulness, and for that between the freedom of self-expression and its suppression" (p. 68).

In the same way, *industry* develops when one's active efforts (agency) result in predictable effects of others on the individual (patience) and are not thwarted by feedback that suggests inferiority (i.e., a negative comparison with others, and seeing oneself as an inferior object). For Erikson, industry develops in part via an appropriate balance between play and work, that is, between doing for its own sake and doing as a means to an end. The latter occurs when the process (agency) is more important than what happens to the person as a result (patience).

In early adolescence, the individual experiences an increase in self-consciousness (seeing oneself primarily as object or patient). Erikson (1950) suggests that the continuity of self that worked well for the younger child is brought into question because of the relatively sudden rapid growth, as well as because of the maturation of the genitals and the consequent awakening of sexual drives. It is for these reasons also that the early adolescent becomes self-conscious (Costanzo & Shaw, 1966). Nor could the self-consciousness occur without the necessary cognitive growth that makes the adolescent capable of the formal logic needed to see himself as an object (i.e., from the point of view of others).

The narcissistic cognitive consequences of this transition have been outlined by Elkind (1967) as twofold: an overgeneralization of one's thoughts and concern to other people (imaginary audience) and an undergeneralization of one's feelings ("it could only happen to me"—personal fable). An overemphasis on patience on the one hand (everyone is looking at me) and an overemphasis on agency on the other (I am unique in the way I feel and behave) are both modes of separation and individuation. There needs to be an appropriate balance between the two. This balance holds equally true for optimal psychosocial development. Integration requires both subjectivity and objectivity, agency and patience. The establishment of identity during adolescence requires the overcoming of these extremes, or rather their integration.

The construct of "engagement style" (agent vs. patient) has been recently explored by McKinney (1980, 1981), McKinney and Moore (1978), and Hotch (1979). It was predicted in one study (McKinney, 1980) that during adolescence subjects would demonstrate a decrease in agency. This hypothesis was based on the fact that: (a) adolescents experience an increase in self-consciousness coincident with the onset of puberty; (b) their rapid and asynchronous physical changes draw their attention to their bodies (themselves as objects); (c) the development of formal logic provides them with a new level of decentering that allows them to take the position of another, thus seeing themselves as objects among objects.

The hypothesis of a decrease in agency (or an increase in patience) at early adolescence was confirmed in two separate communities, especially for boys (See Figure 2.1.). It would appear that the separation/individuation of early adolescent boys is that of a patient, not an agent. It seems obvious that this separateness needs to be overcome for the individual to resolve the succeeding stage of intimacy versus isolation. The existence of a less dramatic trend toward

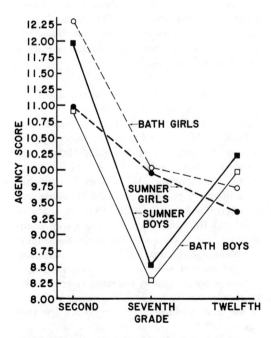

Figure 2.1. Agency scores for boys and girls in grades 2, 7, and 12 in two communities: Bath, Michigan and Sumner, Washington.

decreased agency for early adolescent girls supports the view that there are sex differences in identity formation, with early adolescent girls showing less separateness than boys.

Gilligan (1982) observes that Erikson had grappled with the integration of separateness and "the adult ethic of taking care." She complains:

> But when he charts a developmental path where the sole precursor to the intimacy of adult love and the generativity of adult work and relationships is the trust established in infancy and where all intervening experience is marked as steps toward autonomy and independence, then separation itself becomes the model and the measure of growth. (Gilligan, 1982, p. 98)

It is also possible to see Erikson's stages, not as unmitigated steps toward independence and autonomy and away from caring, but rather as developmental psychosocial crises (i.e., encounters between the self and social environment in which the self strives towards new levels of agency and can be responsive to resulting environmental changes). Not to strive for greater agency would doom the individual to a life of patience, that is, separate. The same separateness would occur if one accomplished only that new level of agency without the development of patience or response to environmental changes.

From this point of view, it appears that agency is the antithesis of patience and social interaction requires an interplay between the two.

Future Directions

Clearly one area of needed theorizing and research is that of gender differences in the dynamics of identity development. Gilligan (1977, 1982) and Lyons (1983) have provided both direction and some data along this line, although this need has been recognized at least since Douvan and Adelson (1966) demonstrated in their interviews the very real differences between the styles adolescent boys and girls used in defining themselves.

It is clear, too, that identity statuses, despite the great richness of this approach, provides only one perspective on identity. For too long it has been *the* perspective. Future approaches will include new methodologies as well as fresh theorizing about such other dimensions as agency, caring and nurturance, and other domains of identity achievement. In the theory of Bakan (1966), agency is contrasted with communion; that is, separateness, individuation, and personal striving are contrasted with connectedness, nurturance, and sharing. In McKinney's (1980) formulation of engagement style, the two poles of agency and patience are both seen as ways of being separate or isolated. Communication rests on a balance between the two extremes, for example, speaking and being spoken to, loving and being loved. Identity achievement, in the sense that it is a truly psychosocial achievement, dealing with the commerce between the individual and his or her social world, is based on a balance between doing and being done to (i.e., between agency and patience). In many respects, this balance appears analogous to the assimilation–accommodation balance in the cognitive task of adaptation as formulated by Jean Piaget. We turn now to that developmental theory.

COGNITIVE DEVELOPMENT

Piaget's Work: History and Development

During the past 20 years, the work of Jean Piaget has provided the starting place for most psychologists' discussions of adolescent thinking. This is the case for even those psychologists who disagree with Piaget's views.

Piaget: An Adolescent Scientist

Piaget's characterization of the adolescent as an emerging scientist fits his own youth. As with Erikson, his "child sense," which can be traced to his own adolescence, was influential in his choice of theoretical concerns. Piaget was born in Neuchatel, Switzerland, in 1896. His development as a young scientist has been described by Vidal (1984). At the age of 10, Piaget published his first paper, a brief observation of an albino sparrow. This paper was published to prove to the curator of the local natural history museum the seriousness of Piaget's interest in nature so that the young Piaget could get access to the museum's collection.

During the next 4 years, Piaget spent considerable time working under the supervision of the museum's curator on projects involving the classification of mollusks. Piaget published his first papers on mollusks at ages 13 and 14. These works showed concern with systematic classification but focused on the concrete—characteristics that, according to Vidal, reflected the style of Piaget's mentor and not simply lack of readiness for formal thought. Vidal traces the increasing abstractness of Piaget's scientific contributions during his adolescence, relating this to environmental influences as well as cognitive maturation.

At age 16, Piaget visited his godfather, who decided that Piaget's interests were too narrowly focused on biology and decided to teach him philosophy, which, together with biology, was to remain one of Piaget's central interests throughout his life.

Vidal describes that at the age of 15, Piaget, who had been sent to religion classes by his religious mother, but who also had been influenced by his father's skeptical attitude, was struck by the difficulty of reconciling biology and religion. During the years between 16 and 18, Piaget's interests in philosophy grew, and his writing included philosophical discussions relating science and religion. Much later in his life, Piaget (Inhelder & Piaget, 1955/1958) gave as an example of adolescent egocentrism with its overestimation of the power of one's own abstract thought processes that an adolescent "taken with philosophy, dedicated himself to no less a task than the reconciliation of science and religion" (p. 344).

Piaget's Problem: Genetic Epistemology and the Representation of Knowledge

At the age of 21, Piaget received his doctorate in biology. After a brief period of studying psychology in Zurich, Piaget went to Paris where he worked in the school that Alfred Binet had set up as a laboratory. While interviewing children there, Piaget developed the idea that was to determine his life's work—that the study of children's thinking might provide a way to answer philosophical questions about the origins of knowledge (Elkind, 1975). Thus, Piaget considered himself to be a genetic epistemologist whose primary goal in studying cognitive development was to reach a better understanding of the philosophical basis for knowledge (see Piaget, 1970).

In one of his earliest books, Piaget (1927/1960) discussed "the Problem of Knowledge," the problem of how the developing individual comes to construct an understanding of the external world, and the related problem of the evolution of accepted scientific and common-sense beliefs about the nature of the world:

We propose . . . to inquire into the relations existing between the mind of the child and the external world. This should lead us into the very heart of the Problem of Knowledge. . . . If we examine the intellectual development of the individual or of the whole of humanity, we shall find that the human spirit goes through a certain number of stages, each different from the other, but such that during each, the mind believes itself to be apprehending an external reality that is independent of the thinking subject. . . . This being so, two points of view are possible in the study of intellectual evolution. The first of these is to choose a system of reference and agree to call "external reality," reality such as it is conceived to be during one of the stages of mental evolution. Thus, it would be agreed upon to regard as the external world reality as it is postulated by contemporary science, or contemporary common-sense. From this point of view, the relations of child thought to the external world would, in fact, be its relations to the universe of our existing scientific thought taken as the norm. In each explanation given by a child it would be possible to determine the part played by the activity of the subject and the part played by the pressure of objects, the latter being, by definition, objects as we now conceive them to be. And this would be Psychology. . . .

Or else, the attempt to regard any system of reference as absolute can be abandoned. Contemporary common-sense or even contemporary science may be regarded as stages among other stages, and the question as to the true nature of external reality left open. And this would be Theory of Knowledge: this would be to place oneself above all the types of mentality that characterize the various stages of human development, and to seek to define the relations of the mind to reality without any preconceived notions as to what is mind and what is reality. (pp. 237–238)

Piaget reached the decision to study the psychological problem of the relationship between the developing individual's understanding of the world and the accepted scientific wisdom of the individual's times. It was his expressed hope, however, that this venture would lead to better understanding of the more general issue of the historical development of what is accepted as scientific understanding of reality:

For our part, we shall confine ourselves to psychology, to the search, that is, for the relations between child thought and reality as the scientific thought of our times conceives it. . . .

But . . . it may very well be that the psychological laws arrived at by our restricted method can be extended into epistemological laws arrived at by the analysis of the history of the sciences . . . [that] it will be possible to establish between our conclusions and those of epistemological analysis a relation of particular case to general law. (pp. 238–240)

In this early discussion, Piaget not only specified the primary aim of his studies of cognitive development, but also expressed his concern about the relativity of knowledge. Ironically, one of the criticisms of Piaget's theory of formal operational thinking is that it does not take into account the development in late adolescence or early adulthood of the ability to appreciate the relativity of knowledge, an issue that will be discussed further below.

Piaget's Theory of Formal Operational Thinking

Piaget's primary discussion of adolescent reasoning is the volume by Inhelder and Piaget (1955/1958). He also included summaries in two overviews of his theory (Piaget, 1970; Piaget & Inhelder, 1966/1969). Several other useful discussions of his theory are available (Flavell, 1963, 1977; Ginsburg & Opper, 1979; Neimark, 1975).

For Piaget, there are both functional invariants, which characterize all of cognitive development, and stage-specific aspects of cognition. The process of equilibration is considered basic to all cognitive development. Equilibration includes both a tendency toward a greater equilibrium between the knowing organism and the environment and a tendency toward greater stability of the organization of the individual's cognitive structures. Progress toward equilibrium with the environment is achieved through the complementary processes of assimilation and accommodation. Thus, the individual always deals with the environment using existing modes of knowing or cognitive structures, which Piaget labels assimilation. At the same time, the environment constantly puts pressure on the individual to modify modes of knowing or cognitive structures in order to better fit environmental demands; this process is labeled accommodation.

With development comes not only a proliferation of cognitive structures and increasing coordination of these structures, but periodic changes in the overall organization of cognitive structures and in the nature of the mode of knowing. In Piagetian theory, there are three stages of cognitive development, each characterized by the emergence of a new type of cognitive structure or mode of knowing.

During the *sensory–motor* stage, approximately the first 1½ years, the infant knows about the world in terms of his or her own actions on it, such as sucking, grasping, and visual following. During this period, the infant only gradually comes to construct an understanding that objects have an existence in time and space separate from the infant's activity on them.

During the second stage, labeled the stage of *representational intelligence*, the child develops symbolic processes, such as the use of language and images to stand for attributes of concrete objects and events. This period is divided into two subperiods. During the first, preoperational period, which lasts from 1½ or 2 years until about 7 years, symbolic processes tend to be tied to specific, static contexts, and manipulations of symbols do not form a coherent, logical system. This period is viewed as a transition into true representational logic or concrete operational thinking.

Concrete operational thinking is characteristic of the period from approximately 7 to 11 years. During this period, the child first becomes capable of using operational thinking (i.e., mental manipulations that form coherent, logical systems and are characterized by reversibility). Two types of operations become available: operations involving classes (e.g., joining two classes) and operations involving relations. Operations involving classes may be reversed by an inverse operation, which Piaget also refers to as negation. Piaget uses the terms reciprocity and compensation to refer to reversibility involving relations. Reciprocity and compensation are indicated by the understanding that for every relationship there is a reciprocal relationship (e.g., if $A > B$, then $B < A$) and by ability to coordinate two dimensions and note that a change in one dimension may compensate for a change in another (e.g., change in width compensates for change in height when liquid is poured from a short, fat container to a taller, skinnier container).

The final stage of cognitive development, the *formal operational* stage, begins around age 12. Piaget divides this stage into a transitional period, lasting from approximately 11 to between 14

and 15 years, and a period of consolidation, beginning around age 14 or 15. Inhelder and Piaget (1955/1958) discuss formal operational thinking in terms of a qualitative description of the new acquisitions of this period and in terms of the logico–mathematical structures that they propose as a formal description of the structure of reasoning.

The qualitative description of formal operational reasoning includes at least four overlapping key acquisitions:

1. The adolescent or adult is able to reason about abstract propositions that are not tied to concrete objects or images, something with which children have difficulty. Flavell (1984) uses the example from Osherson and Markman (1975) that adolescents and adults typically can appreciate the necessary validity of the statement that a concealed solid-color chip "either is green *or* it is not green," but younger children will typically say that the statement cannot be evaluated without seeing the chip.

2. The formal operational reasoner can consider reality as a subset of what is possible, using propositional statements to generate possibilities that have not been encountered in reality and using hypothetico–deductive reasoning. In contrast, the concrete operational child can think about possibilities only in terms of extensions of their concrete experiences and thus are tied to inductive reasoning.

3. The formal operational individual can use "second-order" thinking or operations on operations. The individual can thus evaluate the relationship between two relationships. For example, the ability to reason about proportions, which involves the comparing of two ratios, is an ability cited by Inhelder and Piaget as emerging during this period. Similarly, a concrete operational thinker can classify events simultaneously on two dichotomous dimensions, but a formal operational thinker can then classify the possible outcomes of the classification to determine which outcomes would be consistent with an abstract proposition.

4. The formal operational thinker is able to use a more fully integrated and coordinated logic than the concrete operational reasoner. Thus, the formal operational reasoner can systematically generate all possible combinations of a set of variables (e.g., systematically figuring out all of the ways that five chemicals can be combined). He or she also understands that to eval-

uate the effects of one variable experimentally, it is necessary to isolate that variable by holding all others constant (e.g., holding constant the weight on the end of a pendulum when evaluating the effect of the pendulum's length on its frequency of oscillation). Finally, the formal operational thinker can coordinate the two types of reversibility that are characteristic of concrete operations. For example, the concrete operational thinker can deal with a balance scale by adjusting the weights on the two sides or the distances of the weights from the fulcrum but cannot deal with the two characteristics simultaneously; the formal operational thinker can learn this complex coordination.

Piaget's logico–mathematical model for formal operational reasoning includes two components, (a) the complete combinatorial scheme and (b) the INRC group.

There are 16 binary operations that comprise the complete combinatorial scheme. These binary operations specify all possible relationships between two propositions that may each be either true or false. To use Neimark's (1975) example, mammals may be classified as bipedal (walking on two legs) or not bipedal, represented by B and $\overline{B}$, and as herbivores that eat only plants (H) or nonherbivores ($\overline{H}$). Simultaneous classification on the basis of these two characteristics into one of the four categories of

BH, B$\overline{H}$, $\overline{B}$H, $\overline{B}\overline{H}$, is a concrete operational skill.

For each of the characteristics, one may also state as a proposition that the characteristic is true or false, and one can use a logical operator to form compound propositions about the relationships between two propositions. For example, the statement, "If a mammal is bipedal, then it is a herbivore" specifies an implication relationship in which a value of "true" for the first proposition implies a value of "true" for the second proposition. Of the four possible conditions that might exist, BH, $\overline{B}$H, and $\overline{B}\overline{H}$ are consistent with statement, but B$\overline{H}$ is not. Thus, the observation of any case of B$\overline{H}$ makes the statement false. As Table 2.1 indicates, there are 16 possible logical relationships between two propositions.

According to Piaget, the use of the complete combinatorial scheme both involves and forms the basis for the characteristics of formal operational thinking specified previously: (a) propositional thinking; (b) considering reality as a subset of what is possible and using hypothetico-deductive reasoning; (c) second-order reasoning (i.e., the ability to classify the results of a classification); and (d) the ability to generate the 16 binary operations outlined in Table 2.1.

According to Piaget, there are four types of transformations that can lead from one ele-

Table 2.1. The Combinatorial System

NAME	SYMBOL	COMBINATION*	NAME OF COMPLEMENT	SYMBOL	COMBINATION
Complete affirmation	(p*q)	BH + $\overline{B}$H + B$\overline{H}$ + $\overline{B}\overline{H}$	Negation	(ϕ)	
Incompatibility	(p/q)	B$\overline{H}$ + $\overline{B}$H + $\overline{B}\overline{H}$	Conjunction	(p·q)	BH
Disjunction	(pvq)	BH + $\overline{B}$H + B$\overline{H}$	Conjunctive negation	($\overline{p}\cdot\overline{q}$)	$\overline{B}\overline{H}$
Implication	(p⊃q)	BH + $\overline{B}$H + $\overline{B}\overline{H}$	Nonimplication	(p·$\overline{q}$)	B$\overline{H}$
Reciprocal implication	(q⊃p)	BH + B$\overline{H}$ + $\overline{B}\overline{H}$	Negation of reciprocal implication	($\overline{p}\cdot$q)	$\overline{B}$H
Equivalence	(p⊊q) or (p=q)	BH + $\overline{B}\overline{H}$	Reciprocal exclusion or exclusive disjunction	(pvvq)	$\overline{B}$H + B$\overline{H}$
Affirmation of p	p[q]	BH + B$\overline{H}$	Negation of p	$\overline{p}$[q]	$\overline{B}$H + $\overline{B}\overline{H}$
Affirmation of q	q[p]	BH + $\overline{B}$H	Negation of p	$\overline{q}$[p]	B$\overline{H}$ + $\overline{B}\overline{H}$

*Note. to shift from property combinations to propositional combination, B = p, $\overline{B}$ = $\overline{p}$, H = q, $\overline{H}$ = $\overline{q}$, + = v.

Note. From "Intellectual Development during Adolescence" by E. D. Neimark, 1975, in *Review of Child Development* (p. 592) edited by F. D. Horowitz, E. M. Hetherington, S. Scarr-Salapatel, & G. M. Siegel, Chicago: University of Chicago Press. Copyright 1975 by the University of Chicago. Reprinted by permission.

ment to another of the combinatorial system described in Table 2.1. As a set, these four transformations have the property of a mathematical group. The four types of transformations are labelled: identity (I), negation (N), reciprocity (R), and correlativity (C). A more detailed description of the INRC group is provided by Inhelder and Piaget (1955/1958) and is summarized by Neimark (1975). The major application of the INRC group to the actual reasoning of adolescents is to situations analyzed as requiring coordination of the two types of reversibility, negation and reciprocity (e.g., dealing simultaneously with the roles of weight and distance on a balance). Piaget (1972) states:

> Generally speaking the group [INRC] structure intervenes when the subject understands the difference between the cancelling or undoing of an effect (N in relation to I) and the compensation of this effect by another variable (R and its negation C) which does not eliminate but neutralizes the effect. (p. 6)

Contemporary Issues

The portion of Piaget's theory dealing with adolescent reasoning, although highly influential, has attracted considerably less attention than his discussions of earlier development. On the basis of a review of the literature carried out in 1973, Neimark (1975) concluded that Piaget's theory was the only theory of the development of adolescent thought available, but that there was a scarcity of data relevant to evaluating Piaget's description of reasoning during this period. Since Neimark's review, far more data concerning adolescent reasoning have become available (see reviews by Braine & Rumain, 1983, and Keating, 1979), there has been increasing agreement on problems with Piaget's theory of formal operational thinking, and new theories of cognitive development have been proposed that attempt to deal with these problems (e.g., Case, 1978, 1985; Fischer, 1980; Pascual-Leone, 1976, 1980).

Criticisms of Piaget's Theory

Four problems with Piaget's description of formal operational reasoning as a universal, final stage of cognitive development will be discussed. Attempts to deal with these issues play major roles in theories proposed as alternatives to Piagetian theory. This list of issues is not exhaustive. For a discussion of further issues, see Keating (1979).

The four problems are:

1. Numerous studies have failed to find universal incidence of formal operational thinking among adolescents and adults. Thus, fewer than 60% of college students succeed on some formal operational tasks. Further, several other adult groups show far lower incidents of formal operational thinking than do college students, with such groups including those with little education, members of non-Western cultures, and the aged (see reviews by Neimark, 1975, 1981). In addition, even late adolescents show substantial intraindividual variability when tested on a range of formal operational tasks patterned after those used by Inhelder and Piaget (Martorano, 1977).

Piaget (1972) addressed the issue of poor performance on formal reasoning tasks by many adolescents and adults. He suggested that in situations that do not provide optimal cognitive stimulation, the emergence of formal operational thinking may be delayed until ages 15 to 20 years, when the individual is most likely to receive advanced schooling or vocational training. Piaget also suggested that even though the underlying cognitive structures are general and not tied to specific content, people may display their most advanced reasoning in their areas of expertise, familiarity, and interest. Thus, the initial tasks that he and Inhelder employed may have been biased toward populations with formal training in science.

Neimark (1981) proposes a different explanation, that the nonuniversal incidence of formal operations may be an artifact of the ambiguous instructions of most formal operational tasks, and that this may be particularly likely to cause problems for individuals with field-dependent cognitive styles. She notes that groups with relatively low incidence of formal thought are also ones likely to be field-dependent, and that there is limited evidence directly linking cognitive style and formal reasoning. Neimark suggests that the best way to obtain unbiased evaluation of formal thinking is to elicit optimal performance by providing explicit information about the goal of the task, the means available for reaching the goal, and the criteria to be used for evaluating performance. In addition, for tasks that may be unfamiliar, a demonstration of appropriate performance is recommended.

2. At the same time that the evidence led to questioning of the universality of formal operational thinking, some psychologists were questioning the adequacy of Piaget's description of this stage as the final stage of mature reasoning. Influential early contributions to this discussion were made by Perry (1970) and Riegel (1972).

Based on a longitudinal study of Harvard undergraduates' views of their experience as college students, Perry (1970) and his associates concluded that during the college years, students show considerable development in their views concerning the nature and origin of knowledge. Perry (1970) sees his work as building on Piaget's description of formal operational thought, but believes that by studying people older than 15, he has been able to observe developmental processes not examined by Piaget. Perry's work will be discussed in more detail in the next section.

Riegel (1972) criticized Piaget's work on more theoretical and philosophical grounds. He argued that although Piaget's emphasis on the complementary processes of assimilation and accommodation provide a dialectical foundation for his theory, Piaget's characterization of the advanced stages of reasoning failed to take into account dialectical issues of the interaction between psychic activities and cultural–historical conditions.

Although they argued from different perspectives, both Riegel and Perry stressed the need to take into consideration the contextual dependency of knowledge, and Perry argued that the ability to do so might develop after the developments described by Inhelder and Piaget (1955/1958).

3. Studies have found that formal reasoning tasks based on those used by Inhelder and Piaget differ substantially from each other in difficulty (e.g., Martorano, 1977). This kind of decalage cannot be explained directly by a theory, involving one unitary logical structure as the basis for performance on all of the tasks. To account for such decalage, either performance factors separate from logical structures need to be invoked, or the stage theory needs to be revised.

4. Several individuals have pointed out problems with Piaget's logical models, including ambiguities and paradoxes in his discussion of the propositional logic involved in the use of the complete combinatorial scheme. A summary of major issues in these criticisms is provided by Braine and Rumain (1983). They conclude that although Piaget's logical system is badly flawed, there is a formally similar system that might provide Piagetians with an adequate basis for a theory of formal operations, and that without such a formal system, "claims about the formal operational stage are left without any theoretical foundation" (p. 316). Alternatively, neo-Piagetian theories build on Piaget's qualitative description of adolescent and adult thought, but not on his mathematico-logical model.

New Theories: General Issues

Recently, there has been a proliferation of new theories of cognitive developments (e.g., see Sternberg, 1984a). There also has been growing interest in characterizing the development during adolescence and early adulthood of views concerning the nature and origins of knowledge (Kitchener & King, 1981; Perry, 1970, 1981).

Many current theories adopt an information-processing perspective, drawing analogies between humans and computers and attempting to describe the sequence of processes involved in performing a task and/or the nature of representation of knowledge involved. Such approaches dominate current views of adult cognition. Siegler (1983) has provided an overview of general information-processing models and their applications to studying development.

There is considerable debate about acceptance or rejection of the concept of stages. Neo-Piagetian stage theorists have attempted to avoid the problems with Piagetian stages by revising the concept of stages (Fischer, 1980) or by redefining the basis for stage transitions in terms of information-processing constructs (Case, 1985; Pascual-Leone, 1980). The majority of theorists adopting an information-processing perspective, however, reject the concept of stages (e.g., Brainerd, 1983; Siegler, 1979). One advantage of the neo-Piagetian stage theories over current nonstage alternatives is that the stage theorists provide coherent sets of hypotheses concerning differences between adolescent reasoning and other reasoning. Nonstage theorists have investigated processes that might change during adolescence (see review by Keating, 1979) and have pointed out the importance of generally wider experience and knowledge basic to older individuals compared to younger ones (e.g., Chi, 1978). So far, however, the nonstage theorists have attempted little synthesis of issues concerning adolescent reasoning.

Two examples of recent theories will be discussed, Perry's work on the development of views concerning knowledge, and Fischer's (1980) neo-Piagetian stage theory. Fischer's theory was selected because it presents a differentiated view of development during adolescence. However, it is also typical of recent theories in terms of having a far stronger empirical base for the descriptions of earlier periods.

Perry's Work: Adolescent Views of the Origins of Knowledge

As noted previously, Perry (1970) proposed a theory of the intellectual and ethical development of college students. Perry described a sequence of nine positions through which students progress; the positions may be divided into four groups. In the initial positions, labeled *dualism*, students consider knowledge to be absolute and possessed by authorities, so that the student's job is to learn the "right answers" from the professors. Gradually, students come to accept the existence and legitimacy of multiple perspectives. Initially, the acceptance of *multiplicity* leads students to see no way of evaluating and choosing between perspectives, so that all views seem equally valid. In later positions, the students recognize that perspectives exist within a larger context and must be considered in relation to that context. With this *contextual relativism* comes the ability to evaluate ideas. "Ideas can then be considered as contextual, relativistic, and better or worse, rather than right or wrong" (Perry, 1981, p. 88).

The magnitude of the shift represented by relativism is a major one. This comparison of interpretations and thought systems with one another introduces *metathinking*, the capacity to examine thought, including one's own.

> Theories become, not "truth", but metaphors or "models," approximating the order of observed data or experience. Comparison, involving systems of logic, assumptions, and inferences, all relative to context, will show some interpretations to be "better," others "worse," and many worthless. Yet, even after extensive analysis there will remain areas of great concern in which reasonable people will reasonably disagree. (Perry, 1981, p. 88)

Finally, in developments that have more to do with identity than with views concerning the nature of knowledge, the most mature students make *commitments* to particular views and roles, while acknowledging that other individuals might make different choices.

Perry (1970) notes the relevance of his work to the issue of adolescent egocentrism raised by Inhelder and Piaget (1955/1958), who comment that adolescents frequently overestimate the power of their own abstract thought processes and must come to decenter from this position. Perry proposes that it may be the further development of relativism that allows the putting of one's own ideas as well as those of others into a framework permitting evaluation.

Several researchers have developed scales based on Perry's work, although little attempt has been made to cross-validate these scales (King, 1978). Studies have generally found progression through his positions in the college years, although there is infrequent reaching of the final positions reflecting commitment (see King, 1978; Perry, 1981). Progression with age has been observed even when subjects in all age groups (ranging from high school students to PhD candidates) perform well on Piagetian formal reasoning tasks (Kitchener & King, 1981).

Perry (1970) hypothesized that two factors are likely to contribute to college students' progress through his positions: (a) exposure to college course work that stresses comparison of theories and evaluation of evidence rather than simply learning of correct answers, and (b) exposure to a heterogeneous peer group with diverse values. That components of the college experience rather than age per se are important is indicated by a study by Strange cited by King (1978) comparing traditional-age and older college freshmen and seniors.

A question raised by this work is the nature of developmental change necessary to develop a framework within which one can compare broad theories, including theories and assumptions about the basis of knowledge. It is interesting that Piaget, who was so concerned with the relativity of knowledge, left to others the discussion of how mature reasoners come to grapple with this issue.

Fischer's Skill Theory

Fischer (1980) has proposed a theory to characterize the development of skills from infancy until adulthood. He believes that his framework can be used to understand diverse skills, including both scientific concepts and social cognition.

For Fischer, the basic unit of cognition is a skill of controlling a source of variation in one's behavior. The stage-like component of development is characterized by shifts in the complexity of skills an individual could develop given maximum environmental support and opportunity for learning. The upper boundary of the skills that can be constructed is labeled the optimal level; it can be conceptualized in terms of limits on the individual's information-processing capacity. Because most skills are not developed to the optimal level, asynchronies in performance are expected. Indeed, by adolescence the potential for both interindividual and intraindividual variability in performance is enormous.

Fischer proposes a sequence of 10 optimal levels divided into three tiers of sensory-motor, representational, and abstract skills, respectively. Ages for the three tiers correspond roughly to the ages for Piaget's sensory-motor, representational, and formal operational stages. Although the labeling of the tiers follows Piagetian theory, the structures assumed within the tiers do not. Each tier contains four levels; the highest level of each of the first two tiers is also the lowest level of the next tier.

At the first level of a tier, a *skill* is a single set, or the ability to control a single source of variation, whether on a sensory-motor level (e.g., being able to track an object visually), a representational level (e.g., understanding that balls bounce), or an abstract level (e.g., being able to state a general definition for the operation of addition). The second level within a tier involves the coordination of two single skills or sets into a *mapping*. The third level within a tier involves coordinating two mappings into a *system*: Two or more skills or sets are each differentiated into a least two components, and there is a complex integration of these differentiated skills or sets. Finally, the highest level involves coordination of a *system of such systems*; this type of complex structure forms the basic cognitive unit for the first level of the next tier.

Levels 6 and 7 are the last two levels of the representational tier; Level 7 is also the first of the abstract tier. *Level 6–representational systems* first can be seen around age 6 for middle-class children and continues to be developed and consolidated during the elementary school years. Mastery of standard Piagetian conservation tasks, by differentiation of two characteristics of one array (such as height and width) and coordination with the same two characteristics of a second array, meets criteria for use of a representational system. Also meeting the criteria is the ability to solve and explain on a concrete level simple arithmetic problems, such as $2+5=7$.

Level 7–single abstractions first are used around age 10 or 11. They involve the coordination of a system of level 6 systems. Thus, the preadolescent can give a general explanation of the principle of conservation that is not tied to specific conservation problems and can give a general definition of an arithmetic operation, such as addition, and then show how the general definition can be applied to specific examples (see illustration in Table 2.2.).

Level 8–abstract mappings emerges around age 15; it is shown in the ability to explain the relationship between two abstract concepts. For example, the adolescent can learn to explain the relationship between addition and multiplication on an abstract level. (See Table 2.2.)

Level 9–abstract systems requires the coordination of two differentiated abstracts sets. For example, the individual can explain the relationship between dissimilar arithmetic operations, such as addition and division, in terms of relationships on two differentiated dimensions (see Table 2.2.). Based on the limited amount of data from late adolescents collected by Fischer and his associates, Fischer (personal communication) considers that there is beginning to be evidence consistent with the emergence of Level 9 around age 18 or 19.

Finally, *Level 10–general principles* require the ability to relate two abstract systems (e.g., explaining general principles that specify how addition, subtraction, multiplication, and division are all interrelated) (see Table 2.2.). Fischer proposes that Level 10 reasoning is necessary for the most advanced views of the nature of knowledge identified by Perry (1970) and Kitchener and King (1981). This level allows comparisons of two abstract systems within the framework of a higher order frame of reference. Fischer states that, "With this attainment, and with the requisite environmental support or stimulation, individuals can presumably construct a fully mature organization of identity, morality, or political ideology" (Fischer, Hand, & Russell, 1984, p. 53).

Fischer predicts that when a new optimal lev-

Table 2.2. Examples of Each Cognitive Level

LEVEL	CHARACTERISTIC STRUCTURE	EXAMPLES FROM ARITHMETIC STUDY
6	Representational systems: coordination of several aspects of two or more representations	Calculation and explanation of concrete arithmetic problems $9+7=16$ $3\times8=24$
7	Single abstractions (which are systems of representational systems): coordinations of two or more systems to form an intangible category	General definitions of arithmetic operations: "Subtraction is when you take one number away from another number, and you end up with a smaller number called the difference."[a]
8	Abstract mappings: coordination of two or more abstractions in a simple relation	General relations of two similar arithmetic operations: "Addition and multiplication are similar operations. Both combine numbers to produce a larger number, but the numbers are combined in different ways—by single units in addition and by groups of numbers in multiplication. Multiplication is really addition repeated a specific number of times.[a]
9	Abstract systems: coordinations of several aspects of two or more abstractions in a complex relation	General relations of two dissimilar arithmetic operations: "Addition and division are opposite operations in two ways. Addition increases by single units, while division decreases by groups of units. The fact that one increases and the other decreases is one way addition and division differ, and the manner in which they increase or decrease by units or groups is the other way they differ. Repeated addition might be used to express a division problem like $32\div8=4$. Eight added four times yields 32, so we know there are four eights in 32."[a]
10	Single principles (which are systems of abstract systems): coordinations of two or more systems to form an overarching framework or theory	Principles unifying the four arithmetic operations: "Addition, subtraction, multiplication, and division are all operations, which means that they all transform by either combining or separating numbers and doing so either in groups or one number at a time. There are relationships between all possible pairs of operations. Some pairs are closely related, and others are more distantly related . . . (elaboration explaining the pairs, as diagrammed in the table below)."[a]

	Unit	Group
Increase	Addition	Multiplication
Decrease	Subtraction	Division

Note. The arithmetic concepts deal with positive whole numbers only.
[a]In each of these cases, the person can not only give the definition but also apply it appropriately to specific arithmetic problems, as illustrated for Level 9.
Note. From "The Development of Abstraction in Adolescence and Adulthood" by K. W. Fischer, H. H. Hand, and S. L. Russell, 1984, in *Beyond Formal Operations* (pp. 43–50) edited by M. Commons, F. A. Richards, & C. Armon, New York: Praeger. Copyright 1984 by Dare Association, Inc., and Praeger Publishers. Reprinted by permission.

el is reached, individuals will show a spurt in performance on tasks at that level of complexity if tested under conditions that provide both environmental supports and opportunities for learning. Spontaneous performance without these supports, however, should be far more variable.

Fischer (1980; Fischer et al., 1984) also proposes rules for describing how skill structures can be transformed into new ones within a level or as a transition to the next level. He also discusses simplification strategies for using transformations within a lower level as a way of mimicking skills at a higher level.

When Fischer presented his theory in 1980, he had empirical support for the earlier levels, but had no data using his methods of analysis for the abstract tier. Since that time, three studies have been carried out by Fischer and his associates to investigate Levels 7 and 8 (Hand & Fischer, 1981; Kenny, 1983; Lamborn, 1985). On the basis of these studies, as well as work carried out from other orientations, Fischer concludes that there is clear support for discontinuities (i.e., shifts in the upper limits on cognitive abilities) at ages 10–12 years and 14–16 years, consistent with his descriptions of Levels 7 and 8. He considers that there is definite evidence for some type of cognitive development beyond age 16, but that there is not yet strong evidence for the type of discontinuities needed for specifying clear levels or stages (Fischer & Silvern, 1985).

Fischer's theory is appealing because it provides differentiation of levels of abstract reasoning within adolescence and young adulthood. It also deals with both intra- and interindividual unevenness in performance. In addition, his approach to the diagnosis of level of reasoning involves eliciting an individual's best performance, a strategy consistent with recent suggestions by others (including the recommendations of Neimark, 1981, discussed previously).

Although highly suggestive, Fischer's description of adolescent reasoning needs to be applied more widely before its usefulness will be clear. There are several potential problems.

First, as Flavell (1984) has pointed out, the operationalization of Fischer's constructs is not always obvious, nor is it clear that structural constructs are truly equivalent when applied across different content domains. This problem is not unique to Fischer's theory, but rather is a general problem for the new stage theories that require analysis of diverse tasks into comparable structural components (for example, see the comments about Case's theory by Flavell, 1978, 1984).

Second, although Fischer and his associates have developed structured interviews around specific tasks to test reasoning within the abstract tier, for at least some of these tasks, appropriate probing and scoring of the interviews remain difficult. This problem does not seem to be a necessary outgrowth of the theory. It should be possible to develop tests with constrained answers that would permit diagnosis of skills at an abstract level. For example, Fischer (1980) suggests that the ability to solve most analogies is a Level 7 skill. Presumably, analogies of varying degrees of complexity, such as those described by Sternberg (1984b), could also be analyzed within Fischer's framework.

Third, and related to the previous problem, is that the test procedures currently used involve subjects' giving verbal explanations and, thus, are highly dependent on verbal ability. It should be possible to develop nonverbal tasks that could be analyzed according to Fischer's framework.

In summary, Fischer's theory provides a promising framework for analyzing adolescent reasoning, including addressing whether there are distinct shifts in structure of reasoning in late adolescence. How useful this framework will actually be, however, remains to be determined.

Future Directions

On both theoretical and empirical levels, there is a need for comparisons of the post-Piagetian approaches to studying cognitive development. Comparisons of the newer theories are beginning to appear (e.g., Flavell, 1984). However, more are needed, particularly comparisons dealing with adolescent reasoning. It would also be useful to have more synthesis of the characteristics of adolescent reasoning from an information-processing perspective.

Analyses of tasks from more than one theoretical perspective would be helpful. For example, Siegler (1981) has provided analyses of rules children and adolescents apply in trying to solve several of Inhelder and Piaget's formal reasoning tasks. His procedures involve careful task and skill analyses, as is required by Fischer's theory. It is not obvious, however, what skill levels from Fischer's perspective would be required to use the rules inferred by Siegler, nor whether the data that allow inferences about Siegler's rules would be sufficient to provide a diagnosis of Fischer's skill levels.

In general, there is a need for more data concerning reasoning in adolescence. Most discussions of current issues in cognitive development focus on periods prior to adolescence, because the bulk of the research available still concentrates on these earlier periods.

Particularly useful would be evidence showing whether there are distinct stage-like shifts in the reasoning that develops after age 16, and whether reasoning structures beyond those available in early to mid-adolescence are necessary for the highest levels of reasoning about the bases of knowledge described by Perry (1970). If distinct levels of thinking corresponding to Fischer's Levels 9 and 10 can be identified, it would be useful to examine the relationship between their use on an impersonal task, such as one concerning mathematical concepts, and on tasks that involve reflecting on one's own values and self-definition.

In Perry's work on the development of college students, the subject matter analyzed was the students' views of their college experiences. Thus, Perry's examples of contextual relativism involve analyzing one's owns experiences and values and placing them in a larger context, and his examples of developmental change involve fundamental shifts in self-definition. It is likely that such shifts require more than cognitive ability to see that two abstract systems can be compared. The kind of reasoning described by Fischer as Level 10-use of systems might be necessary for use of the most sophisticated version of contextual relativism described by Perry, but might well not be sufficient for it.

SUMMARY

Two theories of the developmental psychology of adolescence and some contemporary elaborations of these theories have been presented. In many respects, these two "grand" theories of development deal with similar phenomena. Whereas Erikson has conceptualized development as a continuous interchange between the individual and his or her social space, Piaget sees adaptation, the primary intellectual process, as developing via a balance between assimilation and accommodation. Both theories stress individuation, but not at the expense of integration. Moreover, in each of these theories, adolescence is seen in the context of those stages that have gone before. Erikson's notion of an epigenetic principle of development, in which each stage rests on the accomplishments of the earlier stages, can be seen as equally true of Piaget's theory of cognitive development. Finally, although each of these theorists has dealt with only one broad aspect of human behavior, both attempt to encompass the entire lifespan.

Erikson's theory of psychosocial development has expanded on psychoanalytic psychology by emphasizing the development of ego and the interaction of the individual and the social environment. Although his position is rich in theoretical detail, it has been left to others to test empirically. The work of Marcia and his colleagues has been seminal in this regard. Yet, it is clear that their early work is in need of further refinement and elaboration. Several identity researchers have called for the exploration of domains of identity other than the traditional areas of occupation and ideology, and others have argued for the development of new measures. It is undoubtedly in these directions that Erikson's powerful and elaborate notions of identity formation in adolescence will become even more powerful and useful to theorists and researchers in adolescent psychology.

Piaget's work has provided the starting place for most current discussions of adolescent reasoning, even though there is increasing agreement on some of the problems with Piaget's description of formal operational thinking. New theories of cognitive development have included discussions of reasoning in adolescence, although there continues to be more empirical work on younger children. Thus, the usefulness of the newer characterizations of adolescent reasoning largely remains to be shown. Two of the questions raised by recent work are: (a) Are there stages of reasoning that first appear in late adolescence and early adulthood? and (b) Must individuals develop these types of reasoning before being able to compare theories, reach an appreciation of the relativity of knowledge, and reflect on the place of their own values in a larger context?

Acknowledgements—The authors acknowledge with gratitude the constructive criticism provided by Professor Kurt Fischer, University of Denver and Professor Edith Neimark, Rutgers University.

REFERENCES

Adams, G. R. (Chair). (1985, April). *Identity development from adolescence to adulthood: Advances in conceptualization and methodology.* Symposium presented at the meeting of the Society for Research in Child Development, Toronto.

Adams, G. R., Shea, J., & Fitch, S. A. (1979). Toward the development of an objective assessment of ego-identity status. *Journal of Youth and Adolescence, 8*, 223–237.

Bakan, D. (1966). *The duality of human existence: An essay on psychology and religion.* Chicago: Rand McNally.

Bourne, E. (1978). The state of research on ego identity. A review and appraisal. Part I. *Journal of Youth and Adolescence, 7*, 223–252.

Braine, M. D. S., & Rumain, B. (1983). Logical reasoning. In P. H. Mussen (Ed.), *Handbook of child psychology* (Vol. 3, pp. 263–340). New York: Wiley.

Brainerd, C. J. (1983). Working-memory systems and cognitive development. In C. J. Brainerd (Ed.), *Recent advances in cognitive-developmental theory; Progress in cognitive development research* (pp. 167–236). New York: Springer-Verlag.

Case, R. (1978). Intellectual development from birth to adulthood: A neo-Piagetian interpretation. In R. S. Siegler (Ed.), *Children's thinking: What develops?* Hillsdale, NJ: Erlbaum.

Case, R. (1985). *Intellectual development: Birth to adulthood.* Orlando, FL: Academic Press.

Chi, M. (1978). Knowledge structures and memory development. In R. W. Siegler (Ed.), *Children's thinking: What develops?* (pp. 73–96). Hillsdale, NJ: Erlbaum.

Constantinople, A. (1969). An Eriksonian measure of personality development in college students. *Developmental Psychology, 1*, 357–372.

Costanzo, P. R., & Shaw, M. E. (1966). Conformity as a function of age level. *Child Development, 37*, 967–975.

Craig-Bray, L., & Adams, G. R. (1985, April). Different methodologies in the assessment of identity: Congruence between self-report and interview techniques. In G. R. Adams (Chair), *Identity development from adolescence adulthood: Advances in conceptualization and methodology.* Symposium presented at the meeting of the Society for Research in Child Development, Toronto.

Douvan, E., & Adelson, J. (1966). *The adolescent experience.* New York: Wiley

Elkind, D. (1967). Egocentrism in adolescence. *Child Development, 38*, 1025–1034.

Elkind, D. (1975, August). Piaget. *Human Behavior, 4*, 24–39.

Elkind, D. (1979, September). *Child sense and child development research.* Paper presented at American Psychological Association Convention, New York.

Erikson, E. H. (1950). *Childhood and society.* New York: Norton.

Erikson, E. H. (1958). Young man Luther: *A study in psychoanalysis and history.* New York: Norton.

Erikson, E. H. (1959). Identity and the life cycle. *Psychological Issues.* New York: International Universities Press (whole no. 1).

Erikson, E. H. (1968). *Identity: Youth and crisis.* New York: Norton.

Erikson, E. H. (1969). *Gandhi's truth: On the origins of militant nonviolence.* New York: Norton.

Erikson, E. H. (1970). Autobiographic notes on the identity crisis. *Daedalus, 99*, 730–759.

Fischer, K. (1980). A theory of cognitive development: The control and construction of hierarchies of skill. *Psychological Review, 87*(6), 477–531.

Fischer, K. W., Hand, H. H., & Russell, S. (1984). The development of abstractions in adolescence and adulthood. In M. L. Commons, F. A. Richards, & C. Armon (Eds.), *Beyond formal operations: Late adolescent and adult cognitive development* (pp. 43–73). New York: Praeger.

Fischer, K. W., & Silvern, L. (1985). Stages and individual differences in cognitive development. *Annual Review of Psychology, 36*, 613–648.

Flavell, J. H. (1963). *The developmental psychology of Jean Piaget.* Princeton, NJ: Van Nostrand.

Flavell, J. H. (1977). *Cognitive development.* Englewood Cliffs, NJ: Prentice-Hall.

Flavell, J. (1978). Comments. In R. S. Siegler (Ed.), *Children's thinking: What develops?* (pp. 97–105). Hillsdale, NJ: Erlbaum.

Flavell, J. (1984). Discussion. In R. J. Sternberg (Ed.), *Mechanisms of cognitive development* (pp. 187–209). New York: Freeman.

Flavell, J. (1985). *Cognitive development* (2nd ed.). Englewood Cliffs, NJ: Prentice-Hall.

Gilligan, C. (1977). In a different voice: Women's conception of self and of morality. *Harvard Educational Review, 47*, 481–517.

Gilligan, C. (1982). *In a different voice: Psychological theory and women's development.* Cambridge, MA: Harvard University Press.

Ginsberg, M., & Opper, S. (1979). *Piaget's theory of intellectual development* (second edition). Englewood Cliffs, NJ: Prentice-Hall.

Grotevant, H. (1985, April). Assessment of identity development: Where are we and where do we need to go. In G. R. Adams (Chair), *Identity development from adolescence to adulthood: Advances in conceptualization and methodology.* Symposium presented at the meeting of the Society for Research in Child Development, Toronto

Grotevant, H. D., & Adams. G. R. (1984). Development of an objective measure to assess ego identity in adolescence: Validation and replication. *Journal of Youth and Adolescence, 13*, 419–438.

Grotevant, H. D., & Cooper, C. R. (1981). Assessing adolescent identity in the areas of occupation, religion, politics, friendship, dating, and sex roles: Manual for administration and coding of the interview. *JSAS Catalog of Selected Documents in Psychology, 11*, 42. (Ms. No. 2295)

Grotevant, H. D., Thorbecke, W., & Meyer, M. S.

(1982). An extension of Marcia's Identity Status Interview into the interpersonal domain. *Journal of Youth and Adolescence, 11,* 33–47.

Hand, H. H., & Fischer, K. W. (1981). *The development of concepts of intentionality and responsibility.* Paper presented at the biennial meetings of the Society for Research in Child Development, Boston.

Hotch, D. F. (1979). *Separating from the family: A study of perceptions of home-leaving in late adolescence.* Unpublished doctoral dissertation, Michigan State University, East Lansing.

Inhelder, B., & Piaget, J. J. (1958). *The growth of logical thinking from childhood to adolescence* (A. Parsons & S. Milgram, Trans.). New York: Basic Books. (Original work published 1955)

Keating, D. P. (1979). Thinking processes in adolescence. In J. Adelson (Ed.), *Handbook of adolescent psychology* (pp. 211–246). New York: John Wiley & Sons.

Kenny, S. (1983). *The development of abstract reasoning skills in an arithmetic domain.* Paper presented at the 1983 meeting of the Society for Research in Child Development, Detroit.

King, P. M. (1978). William Perry's theory of intellectual and ethical development. In L. Knefelkamp, C. Widick, & C. A. Parker (Eds.), *New directions for student services, No. 4. Applying new developmental findings* (pp. 35–52). San Francisco: Jossey-Bass.

Kitchener, K. S., & King, P. M. (1981). Reflective judgment: Concepts of justification and their relationship to age and education. *Journal of Applied Developmental Psychology, 2,* 89–116.

Lamborn, S. (1985, April). *Adolescents' understanding of honest and kind interactions.* Paper presented at the biennial meetings of the Society for Research in Child Development, Toronto.

Lyons, N. P. (1983). Two perspectives: On self, relationships, and morality. *Harvard Educational Review, 53,* 125–145.

Maddi, S. R. (1972). *Personality theories: A comparative analysis* (rev. ed.). Homewood, IL: Dorsey Press.

Mallory, M. E. (1983). *Longitudinal analysis of ego identity status.* Unpublished doctoral dissertation, University of California at Berkeley.

Marcia, J. E. (1966). Development and validation of ego identity status. *Journal of Personality and Social Psychology, 3,* 551–558.

Marcia, J. E. (1980). Identity in adolesence. In J. Adelson (Ed.), *Handbook of adolescent psychology.* New York: Wiley.

Martorano, S. (1977). A developmental analysis of performance on Piaget's formal operations tasks. *Developmental Psychology, 13,* 666–672.

McKinney, J. P. (1980). Engagement styles (agent vs. patient) in childhood and adolescence. *Human Development, 23,* 192–209.

McKinney, J. P. (1981). The construct of engagement style: Theory and research. In H. Lefcourt (Ed.), *Research with the locus of control construct: Vol. 1. Assessment methods.* New York: Academic Press.

McKinney, J. P., & Moore, D. D. (1978, August). *Sex differences in agency.* Paper present at the meeting of the American Psychological Association, Toronto.

Neimark, E. D. (1975). Intellectual development during adolescence. In F. D. Horowitz, E. M. Hetherington, S. Scarr-Salapatek, & G. M. Siegel (Eds.), *Review of child development research* (Vol. 4, pp. 591–594). Chicago: University of Chicago Press.

Neimark, E. D. (1981). Toward the disembedding of formal operations from confounding with cognitive style. In I. Sigel, E. Brodzinsky, & R. Golinkoff (Eds.), *Piagetian theory and research: New directions and applications.* Hillsdale, NJ: Erlbaum.

Osherson, D. N., & Markman, E. M. (1975). Language and the ability to evaluate contradictions and tautologies. *Cognition, 2,* 213–226.

Pascual-Leone, J. (1976). Metasubjective problems of constructive cognition: Forms of knowing and their psychological mechanism. *Canadian Psychological Review, 17,* 110–125.

Pascual-Leone, J. (1980). Constructive problems for constructive theories: The current relevance of Piaget's work and a critique of information—processing simulation psychology. In R. H. Kluwe & M. Spade (Eds.), *Developmental models of thinking* (pp. 263–296). New York: Academic Press.

Perry, W. G., Jr. (1970). *Forms of intellectual and ethical development in the college years: A scheme.* New York: Holt, Rinehart and Winston.

Perry, W. G., Jr. (1981). Cognitive and ethical growth: The making of meaning. In A. J. Chickering (Eds.), *The modern American college* (pp. 76–138). San Francisco: Jossey-Bass.

Piaget, J. (1960). *The child's conception of physical causality* (M. Gabain, Trans.). Totowa, NJ: Littlefield Adams. (Original work published 1927).

Piaget, J. (1970). Piaget's theory. In P. H. Mussen (Ed.), *Carmichael's manual of child psychology* (pp. 703–732). New York: Wiley.

Piaget, J. (1972). Intellectual development from adolescence to adulthood. *Human Development, 15,* 1–12.

Piaget, J., & Inhelder, B. (1969). *The psychology of the child.* (H. Weaver, Trans.) New York: Basic Books. (Original work published 1966)

Rasmussen, J. E. (1964). The relationship of ego identity to psychosocial effectiveness. *Psychological Reports, 15,* 815–825.

Riegel, L. (1972). Dialectic operations: The final period of cognitive development. *Human Development, 16,* 346–370.

Siegler, R. S. (1979). Children's thinking: The search for limits. In G. J. Whitehurst & B. J. Zimmerman (Eds.), *The foundations of language and cognition* (pp. 83–113). New York: Academic Press.

Siegler, R. S. (1981). Development sequences within and between concepts. *Monographs of the Society for Research in Child Development, 46,* (2, Serial no. 189).

Siegler, S. S. (1983). Information processing approaches to development. In P. H. Mussen (Ed.), *Handbook of child psychology* (Vol. 1, pp. 129–211). New York: Wiley.

Simmons, D. D. (1970). Development of an objective measure of identity achievement status. *Journal of Projective Techniques and Personality Assessment, 34,* 241–244.

Simmons, D. D. (1973). Further psychometric correlates of the Identity Achievement Scale. *Psychological Reports, 32,* 1042.

Spiesman, J. C., White, K. M., Costos, D., Houlihan, J., & Imbasciati, C. (1983). *An objective instrument for assessment of Erikson's developmental conflicts.* Paper presented at the meeting of the American Psychological Association, Los Angeles, CA.

Sternberg, R. J. (Ed.). (1984a). *Mechanisms of cognitive development.* New York: Freeman.

Sternberg, R. J. (1984b). Higher-order reasoning in postformal operational thought. In M. L. Commons, S. A. Richards, & C. Armon (Eds.), *Beyond formal operations: Late adolescent and adult cognitive development* (pp. 74–91). New York: Praeger.

Vidal, F. (1984). The development of the young Piaget: Case materials against Utopian psychology. In M. L. Commons, F. A. Richards, & C. Armon (Eds.), *Beyond formal operations: Late adolescent and adult cognitive development* (pp. 28–40). New York: Praeger.

Waterman, A. S. (1982). Identity development from adolescence to adulthood: An extension of theory and a review of research. *Developmental Psychology, 18,* 341–358.

CHAPTER 3

Biological Theoretical Models of Adolescent Development

Maryse Richards and Anne C. Petersen

The defining characteristic of adolescence is change. During this period of life marking the transition from childhood to adulthood, the young person experiences change in every domain of individual development and in every social context important to the growing adolescent. The first change that occurs for many young people is the biological change of puberty. Indeed, some definitions of adolescence attribute to puberty the beginning of this phase of life.

In this chapter, we first describe the biological changes that comprise puberty. Next we describe current theories and knowledge about the relationship of pubertal change to other aspects of development.

THE NATURE
OF PUBERTAL CHANGE

Several aspects of puberty are important for understanding its role in development. First, it is a near universal experience; every person experiences the physical transformations by age 20 or so, unless there is some serious endocrine disorder. The generality of puberty as an aspect of adolescence makes it a convenient and fairly reasonable explanation for various adolescent phenomena.

Second, puberty is a gradual *process* and not an event, involving more or less continuous change over time from a physically immature organism to a mature one with full reproductive potential (Grumbach, Grave, & Mayer, 1974a). The fact that it occurs gradually over several years, rather than happening all at once, has implications for other aspects of development. The hormonal system needed to produce pubertal change actually develops prenatally. Functioning of the system, however, is suppressed in almost all individuals from shortly after birth until about 7 years of age, when the system is gradually released from suppression and hormone increases begin. Figure 3.1 portrays the process of pubertal change from the perspective of the endocrine system.

Third, the hormonal changes of puberty involve at least three endocrine systems. Each of these systems influences different aspects of pubertal growth, thus contributing to asynchrony among aspects. The maturation of the

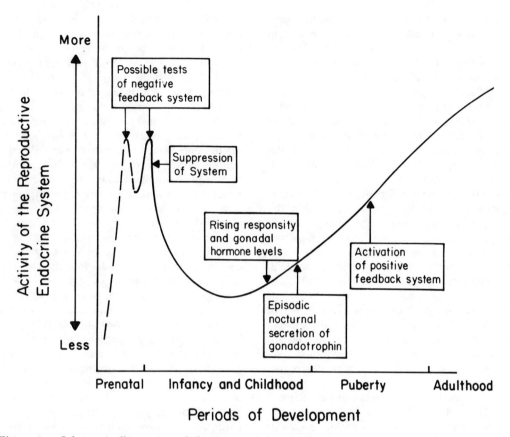

Figure 3.1. Schematic illustration of changes in the endocrine system. (From: "Pubertal Development as a Cause of Disturbance: Myths, Realities, and Unanswered Questions" by A. C. Petersen, 1985, *Genetic, Social, and General Psychology Monographs, 111*, p. 206. Copyright 1985 by the Helen Dwight Reid Educational Foundation. Reprinted by permission.)

adrenal hormone system is commonly referred to as *adrenarche* and is the first system to begin maturing. Changes in the gonadal endocrine system are initiated by *gonadarche* or *pubarche*. Finally, *menarche*, seen only in girls, marks a point in the development of the endocrine changes related to the menstrual cycle.

Increasing levels of estrogens, androgens, and progestins characterize pubertal endocrine change. The concentrations of each of these hormone groups increase during puberty, with more androgens in boys and more estrogens and progestins in girls. These endocrine changes begin quite early in the pubertal process, with increases in some hormones beginning as early as age 7 (Grumbach, Roth, Kaplan, & Kelch, 1974b).

Eventually, increasing hormone levels lead to

the changes in physiology and appearance that we commonly associate with puberty. These changes begin, on the average, at age 11 in girls and at age 12½ in boys (Tanner, 1962) and include the development of secondary sex characteristics as well as changes in height, weight, and several physiological functions. The most prominent secondary sex characteristics include penis and testicle development in boys, breast development and changes in the labia and vagina in girls, and axillary (underarm) hair and pubic hair growth in both sexes. Other changes include the initiation of beard growth in boys and the increased growth of hair on other parts of the body in both boys and girls. In addition, the apocrine (sweat) glands, particularly those under the arm, begin to produce a characteristic odor, and the activity of the sebaceous (oil) glands increases, sometimes leading to a temporary overproduction of oil, which results in acne.

Rapid gains in height and weight occur at this time, with girls usually beginning their growth spurts about $1^1/_2$ to 2 years prior to boys. The growth pattern typically involves a spurt that is associated with an increased rate of bone growth, followed by slower but continuing growth. Growth ceases when the ends of the growing bones reach and fuse with the joints, leaving no room for further growth.

The development of secondary sex characteristics is due primarily to increasing levels of the estrogens and androgens. The most potent androgen is testosterone; similarly, the most potent estrogen is estradiol. Testosterone is responsible for the growth of the penis, prostate, and seminal vesicles in boys, as well as the development of body hair in both sexes. Pubic hair tends to appear concurrently with the growth of the penis, but axillary hair generally appears when pubic hair growth is relatively well advanced. A sequential maturation of testosterone receptors may explain this growth differential (Brook, 1981).

Breast development results from an increase in estradiol levels and the maturation of estradiol receptors. Estradiol also promotes growth of the uterus and vagina and the development of the accessory vaginal exocrine glands. Menarche occurs when critical levels of estradiol are attained, among other factors. Although menarche may be considered an event, it occurs about midway through the process leading to the development of the mature menstrual cycle. It is most likely that hormones begin fluctuating in a cyclic way until they attain levels sufficient to initiate bleeding (Petersen, 1979). Menarche typically marks the beginning of monthly bleeding, although it is not uncommon for bleeding to be irregular at first. After menarche, early cycles are usually anovulatory (i.e., no egg is produced). Without ovulation, young women are infertile. Although fewer data are available, it is assumed that adolescent males also pass through a phase of infertility.

The adolescent growth spurt occurs through a synergism between the steroids and growth hormones, assuming other endocrine functions are operating normally (Aynsley-Green, Zachmann, & Prader, 1976; Tanner, Whitehouse, Marubin, & Resele, 1976). Growth in the vertebral column and in the width of the shoulders and hips is caused primarily by sex steroids. In contrast, growth of the long bones such as those in the legs is largely growth-hormone-dependent. Voice deepening, which is particularly marked in males, appears to be due to testosterone secretion. Striking changes in body composition, which include lean body mass, skeletal mass, and body fat, as well as body fat distribution, occur at puberty and are related to sex hormones. Estrogens affect the feminine pattern of fat distribution, whereas endogenous testosterone secretion appears to limit this pattern in males. The male-female difference in muscle development and strength appears to be caused in part by different levels of, and tissue receptivity to, testosterone; different patterns of exercise in males and females tend to exacerbate differences due to hormones.

As shown in Figure 3.2, there is a typical sequence to these various changes of puberty. Following the initial increases in endocrine levels, breast and genital development are usually the first somatic manifestations of puberty. The time of fastest growth in height occurs relatively late in the process; another late event, menarche, typically occurs after the time of peak velocity in growth. On the average, the entire process takes about 4 years for an individual child.

There are, however, rather large individual differences in the timing and sequence of these various changes (Eichorn, 1974; Tanner, 1972). For example, although breast growth is usually the first visible pubertal change in girls, in some, pubic hair appears earlier than breast growth. There are even greater individual differences in the amount of time required for pubertal maturation. In some individuals, the entire set of pubertal changes occurs within a relatively short period of time, with the changes in various characteristics occurring in a nearly synchronous fashion; in others, the pubertal process can extend over several years. Finally, the age at which the somatic changes of puberty first appear varies widely among both boys and girls.

Because of variations in the timing of puberty and the rapidity of maturation, somatic changes can occur anywhere between the ages of 9 and 19 among normal young people in the United States today. It is unlikely, however, that those individuals who become pubertal at age 9

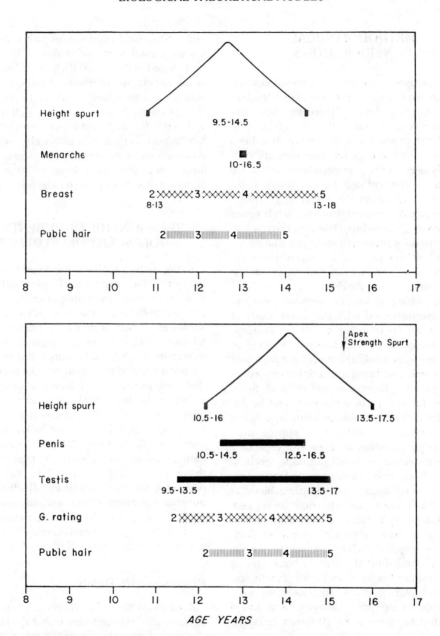

Figure 3.2. Schematic sequence of events at puberty for an average girl (upper) and boy (lower). (From: "Sequence and Tempo in the Somatic Changes in Puberty" by J. M. Tanner, in *The Control of the Onset of Puberty* (p. 460) edited by M. M. Grumbach, G. D. Grave, & F. E. Mayer, 1974, New York: Wiley. Copyright 1974 by John Wiley & Sons. Reprinted with permission.)

would be still pubertal at age 19. Furthermore, some changes in males, such as increases in height or in the distribution of body hair, can continue into the early 20s.

In summary, puberty is a universal process involving dramatic changes in size, shape, and appearance. It, more than any other change during adolescence, signals impending adult status. Once a young person looks like an adult, adult behavior and motivations are typically expected. Thus, biological change stimulates or elicits change on a number of other dimensions.

METHODOLOGICAL CONSIDERATIONS

Our description of puberty demonstrates that although we know a great deal about the biological aspects of puberty, there are, nevertheless, areas where information is yet needed. One of the problems until recently has been endocrine methodology (cf. Petersen, 1979). It has only been in the past decade or so that we have had convenient and accurate assay methods that could detect the rather large differences in hormones differentiating adult males and females. Prior to this, detecting the low levels of hormones present in early pubertal development had been impossible. Nevertheless, the assessment of hormone functioning in adolescents remains a scientific challenge.

The multiple problems of hormone measurement have interfered with the direct study of hormonal effects on other aspects of development. Hormones can be detected in blood or serum, urine, and saliva, but may not represent the hormone level being utilized; hormones are bound by other hormones and utilized differently by different parts of the body and by different individuals. Although urine and saliva are somewhat less difficult to sample than blood, large quantities of urine and especially saliva are needed to detect hormone levels in children. Many endocrinologists prefer the precision of blood assays, yet sampling blood is intrusive and unacceptable to some young people. Additionally, hormone levels fluctuate from causes other than pubertal development. Various types of cycles, such as the menstrual cycle in women and diurnal cycles in both women and men, alter the hormonal state. Finally, external and internal factors, such as stress, food and drug consumption, activity, and mood state affect hormone levels (Petersen & Taylor, 1980).

We also do not fully understand the processes that "turn on" or "turn off" pubertal maturation, although recent research on precocious puberty has made exciting headway here (e.g., Cutler et al., 1983; Grumbach et al., 1974a). Research is beginning to identify endocrine markers and processes, and normative data for physical change are beginning to accumulate. Nevertheless, classifications such as precocious puberty or delayed puberty typically remain quite crude, often relying on parental identifica-

tion and clinical information rather than systematic examination and diagnosis by a physician skilled with pubertal change. Knowledge of the normal distributions of pubertal change may not yet be widely available to physicians. Parents are likely to be even less well informed and to rely for judgment about their children on recollections of their own pubertal growth, their observations of their children's peers, and information in the media. None of these sources of information have proven to be reliable.

RELATIONSHIP OF PUBERTY TO ADOLESCENT DEVELOPMENT

Today, many surveys of adolescents—particularly those focusing on difficulties such as suicide, depression, and eating disorders—suggest that psychological problems increase during the adolescent years (Conger & Petersen, 1984; Johnson, 1982; Petersen & Craighead, 1986). An examination of such information has frequently led scientists and practitioners alike to conclude that these increases are linked to physical maturation in the individual. Pubertal change has often been considered a primary determinant of this process and the resultant behavioral problems (e.g., Kestenberg, 1968). Biological explanations have been invoked to explain everything from juvenile unrest to suicide. In particular, the increases in and fluctuations of pubertal hormones have been assigned a leading explanatory role. We shall consider the validity of attributing these effects solely and directly to the biological changes of puberty.

Psychoanalytic Theory

A common theme in theories of adolescent psychological development is that the biological changes of puberty present a major adaptive task for the individual and, in particular, for the individual's personality (Blos, 1962; A. Freud, 1946; S. Freud, 1905/1953; Hamburg, 1974; Kestenberg, 1967a, 1967b, 1968). Historically, these theories have been developed by psychoanalytic scholars.

Initial psychoanalytical formulations emphasized, almost exclusively, a psychological adaptation to an upsurge in the "drives." Sigmund Freud (1905/1953) postulated that the central stimulus to development in adolescence stems from a marked increase in the sexual drive (or "libido") at puberty. Freud believed that some type of sex hormone was stimulating this increase in sex drive. In his third essay on sexuality, "The Transformations of Puberty," he wrote: "It must suffice us to hold firmly to what is essential in this view by the sexual processes: The assumption that substances of a peculiar kind arise from the sexual metabolism" (Freud, 1905, p. 82). He went on to propose that the type of sexual excitement thought to emerge with puberty possesses the character of tension. This feeling of tension can cause both unpleasurable and pleasurable sensations, to which a person must and will adapt in various ways. These adaptations then form the basis of personality development during adolescence.

Anna Freud (1946, 1958) consolidated this view and integrated it with the perspective that psychological upheaval in adolescence results inevitably and universally from drive development at puberty. Thus, to her, adolescence involves a normative developmental disturbance (A. Freud, 1969). From her perspective, drive development was viewed as producing a "relatively strong id" that "confronts a relatively weak ego," resulting in increased instinctual anxiety, heightened conflict over impulse expression, intensified defenses against impulses, greater affective lability, and psychologically regressive behavior (A. Freud, 1946). This high degree of psychological conflict and stress was perceived to exist in all adolescents as an invariant and necessary feature of psychological development. More recently, Kestenberg (1967a, 1967b, 1968) proposed a similar position, hypothesizing direct relationships of pubertal changes in hormone processes to phases of psychological development.

Other psychoanalytic scholars have linked pubertal change with changes in interpersonal attachments during adolescence. It has been proposed that with the increased sex drive accompanying puberty, affectional bonds to parents become intensely sexualized, reactivating unresolved and disruptive oedipal fantasies (Blos, 1962; A. Freud, 1958; S. Freud, 1905/ 1953). Because the resolution of the oedipal complex is rarely completed by the initiation of latency (about age 6), residuals of these feelings are thought to emerge in adolescence in the form of unconscious fantasies and impulses. This unconscious stimulation by old oedipal

feelings is thought to produce anxiety in the adolescent, leading to the emergence of new ego defenses against the strong emotional ties to parents. Sexual and affectional strivings are first turned inward and invested in the self and then in persons outside the family, most typically in peers (A. Freud, 1969). Before this reinvestment of libido in people external to the family is completed, the child experiences intrapsychic turbulence. Thus, adolescents are tossed about emotionally by their own biologically enhanced internal sexual drives and impulses, and the resultant conflict with the taboos against directly expressing them to parents. In addition, the initial attempts at expressing them indirectly to acquaintances of the opposite sex may feel awkward and frightening to the adolescent and may be rejected by peers. Anna Freud (1958) proposed that certain defenses (namely, intellectualization and asceticism) become particularly prominent during adolescence as a response to this emotional upheaval and, at the same time, are inconsistently employed, thus creating the picture of psychological turbulence and erratic behavior.

Blos (1962), another psychoanalytic theorist, described the changes in adolescent attachments as initially motivated by similar underlying hormonal changes and the subsequent physical changes, but he focuses on a different aspect of the attachment. The process of psychologically individuating and separating from the parents is a life-long one, but, according to Blos, with the emergence of an adult physiology, the process becomes intensified at adolescence. The drive to separate and individuate pushes the child to redefine his or her familial relations by turning away from family members and turning toward individuals outside the family. The vicissitudes of this significant force, and the child's particular ways of coping with it, can produce psychological unrest and growth, and may be expressed by varying degrees of troubling behavior.

Social and Cultural Theories

Scholars have written about the role of puberty in adolescent development from other than the psychoanalytic perspective presented above. One major alternative has focused on the importance of pubertal change as a determinant of social status (e.g., Meyer, 1982; Opler,

1971). For example, in many societies, pubertal markers are used to signify attainment of adult status (Paige & Paige, 1982). In our own society the status change is not so direct, but it is evident that adult size and appearance (and presumably reproductive maturity) lead to expectations for more mature behavior (Jones & Bayley, 1950; Mussen & Bouterline-Young, 1964; also see Conger & Petersen, 1984, for a review).

The shift in social status, which is triggered by pubertal change, has many different cultural meanings. In many societies it signifies changes in sexuality, familial and nonfamilial relations, and in what constitutes appropriate recreational and productive activities (Mead, 1962; Muensterberger, 1975). Feelings about the maturing child held by older members of the society are expected to shift as issues of competition with, replacement by, and separation from the pubescent individual come to the fore. For example, with puberty, the young boy becomes capable of doing the same tasks and fulfilling the same roles previously held by older male relatives. The postpubescent girl with her sexually mature body will elicit responses from others that are different and more sexualized than those she experienced as a child.

"Rites of passage" often help the individual and the society to cope with these changes; they also appear to fulfill multiple functions within a culture (Conger & Petersen, 1984). Rites of passage are culturally defined rituals and customs that acknowledge the change from one phase of life to another (e.g., birth, puberty, marriage, death). They emphasize both the division of the life course into biologically and socially meaningful segments and the continuity or interconnectedness of life (e.g., Muensterberger, 1975). Rites of passage or initiation rituals function to aid the younger generation in attaining adult status and prerogatives. They validate for the individual, as well as other members of the society, that the individual is about to enter a new phase of life that includes a new reproductive capacity and new social expectations. As such, these rituals stress the psychosexual development of the initiates, their new capacities and strivings, and the ambivalent responses of the older generation. These puberty rites often involve seclusion, food and movement restrictions, and, at times, intense pain and fear. After a final celebration, often involving a feast, the initiate enters the community as a young adult.

Although concepts such as rites of passage have been carefully investigated by anthropologists, they have not been widely applied to the study of adolescence within our culture. Beliefs about puberty and the behavior we link with adolescence appear to have been more strongly influenced by the psychoanalytic than the anthropological and sociological perspectives. Attributions are typically made to changes in the individual and are viewed as a result of a change in the physical state, which, in turn, causes a change in the psychological state. The influence of the social context is usually ignored.

These attributions are somewhat understandable, given the co-occurrence of the two changes: (a) hormonal increases and the resulting physical changes and (b) behavioral changes. But the existence of two similar developmental trends within a group does not demonstrate their co-occurrence within individuals. Furthermore, even if both sets of changes occur in an individual at about the same time, it does not necessarily mean that one caused the other. Further evidence would be needed to establish that such a correlation results from a direct and universal causal link between hormones and adolescent behavior, and not from some other factor related to both of these.

The theoretical perspectives on the role of puberty in adolescent disturbance, discussed below, reflect a more current set of formulations. The psychoanalytic and sociocultural paradigms have provided the foundation for these more contemporary views of pubertal effects on adolescent psychological functioning. However, significant subsequent contributions have transformed our thinking about the relationship of puberty to adolescence.

CONTEMPORARY THEORIES AND RESEARCH EVIDENCE

The relationships between pubertal maturation and psychological development can be considered in two broad categories or models (Petersen & Taylor, 1980). The *Direct Effects Model* attributes certain psychological effects directly to physiological sources. With this model, nonbiological influences, such as historical change and cultural values, are either ignored or considered to be unimportant. Changes in psychological states and phases of psychological development are believed to be linked directly to pubertal changes in hormone levels (Kestenberg, 1968). Similarly, increases in sexual and aggressive impulses are considered to be direct effects of fluctuating hormone levels (A. Freud, 1946, 1958).

A second set of models, called *Mediated* (or *Indirect*) *Effects Models,* proposes that the psychological effects of puberty are mediated by complex relations of intervening variables or are moderated by contextual factors (Petersen & Taylor, 1980). The intervening variables consist of psychological factors, such as level of ego development, whereas the contextual factors are those that are exogenous to the personality, such as sociocultural contexts and socialization practices. Figure 3.3 displays both models. These two groupings of basic models represent relatively opposing views of the relationship of pubertal change to adolescent psychological functioning. A review of the research testing these competing hypotheses is presented below.

Direct Effects of Hormones and Pubertal Status

Although it is a commonly held belief that pubertal change directly affects behavior, little evidence to support this notion has been provided to date. The methodological difficulties with hormone research, as discussed previously, have impeded research examining hormone effects. Current collaborative studies (e.g., Sonis, Klein, Blue, Comite, & Cutler, 1983; Susman, Nottleman, & Blue, 1983) should produce some clarification about direct hormonal effects.

One recent study (Udry, Billy, Morris, Groff, & Raj, 1985) of sexual behavior does provide evidence that hormones have more powerful direct effects than does the social stimulus value of secondary sex characteristics. The measures of hormones may be better than those of pubertal status in this research, thereby confounding adequacy of measure with variance attributable to constructs. Nonetheless, this study does provide important preliminary support for direct hormonal effects on sexual behavior in adolescence.

Although hormones stimulate the somatic changes of puberty, the two levels of change are distinct, both in physiological aspects and in the extent to which changes are visible. In large part because of the relative ease of assessment, there is a great deal more research on the psychological and behavioral correlates of pubertal status, as indicated by visible somatic changes, than on hormone–behavior relations in puberty. Although previous research has reported some associations between pubertal status and behavior, these are less pervasive and reliable than is commonly believed (cf. Petersen & Taylor, 1980, for a review).

In our own analysis of correlates or direct ef-

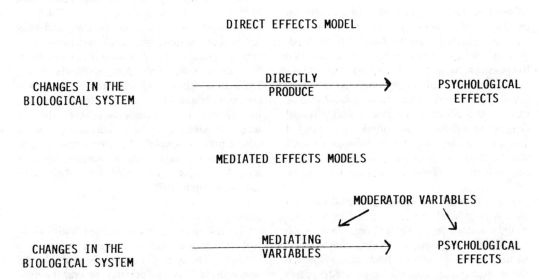

Figure 3.3. The direct effects and mediated effects models.

fects of pubertal status, we have found few significant direct associations (e.g., Crockett & Petersen, in press; Petersen, 1983; Petersen & Crockett, 1986), although we have not yet examined all the domains in which associations might be expected. Furthermore, the effects that we and others (e.g., Blyth, Simmons, & Bulcroft, 1983; Simmons, Blyth, Carlton-Ford, & Bulcroft, 1982) find are with variables that are more proximal to pubertal change, such as body image and feelings of attractiveness. Dating and heterosocial behavior are also related to pubertal status in many analyses in our study as well as in that of Simmons and Blyth (in press).

One factor that may limit the effects of pubertal change is the strong social effect of spending large amounts of time with same-aged peers in school. In our society, we have no rites linked to pubertal change, and we segregate children by chronological age. Although maturational age might potentially be more relevant to the individual than chronological age, our society does not recognize it in any structural way. In fact, it is almost as if we deliberately ignore the physical changes and their impact on the individual and on society. In contrast, experiences during the school-aged years are strongly structured by grade in school. Therefore, a model that includes the social mediation of pubertal change seems appropriate.

The Mediated Effects of Puberty

The Mediated Effects Model of puberty on psychological development is, by its nature, more complicated than the Direct Effects Model. There are many more ways to conceptualize the phenomena with the Mediated Effects Model. According to this perspective, social–situational and individual factors may moderate or mediate the effects of hormones and physical change on behavior and other psychological variables. Moderating factors enhance or limit direct effects, whereas mediating factors interact with direct effects (cf. Petersen & Taylor, 1980).

The Mediated Effects Model integrates a focus on the individual, as represented by psychoanalytic theory (e.g., Kestenberg, 1968), with a focus on the society, as represented by most sociological (e.g., Meyer, 1982) and some anthropological (e.g., Paige & Paige, 1982) writers

to provide greater prediction and understanding of adolescent development and disturbance. This perspective also assumes an interaction between the developing individual and social factors (e.g., Lerner & Busch-Rossnagel, 1981; Sameroff, 1975). Ethologists who take this perspective (e.g., Weisfeld, 1979) focus on the common features of adolescence, relative to pubertal change, across cultures. Developmentalists who take this perspective (e.g., Petersen, 1985; Petersen & Taylor, 1980) focus on the common features of adolescence, relative to pubertal change, across individuals within a culture.

Interactionists note aspects of adolescent development that co-occur with pubertal change. For example, early in adolescence many young people develop the capacity to think abstractly, often termed formal operational thought (e.g., Elkind, 1974; Keating, 1980). This capacity affects the way that young people perceive, understand, and experience puberty as well as other adolescent phenomena. Aspects of the social environment also affect the experience of puberty. For example, social control of sexual behavior has implications for the meaning of pubertal changes to adolescents (Petersen & Boxer, 1982). In general, changes in those aspects of the social system linked to puberty will affect the nature of the puberty–behavior relationship. This interactionist perspective, as will be demonstrated, provides a useful framework for examining the research on puberty and adolescence.

Some mediating factors that have been found to be important are *gender* (Petersen, 1983; Tobin-Richards, Boxer, & Petersen, 1983) and *social norms*, both general and local, regarding deviance in timing and appearance (Petersen, 1983; Rierdan & Koff, 1985; Tobin-Richards et al., 1983). In addition, and consistent with the notion that variables from multiple levels of analysis may interact with pubertal effects, other researchers have found that certain small pubertal effects may be amplified if they occur in conjunction with certain social changes, such as school transitions (e.g., Simmons, Blyth, Van Cleave, & Bush, 1979).

General Social Norms

General social norms have been found to be particularly pervasive with regard to deviance in timing. The effects of timing are multiple and hence should be studied from several theoretical perspectives. The first has to do with timing as a developmental issue (Neugarten, 1969, 1979). This perspective is based on the idea that individuals have "social clocks" involving a sense of when certain life events should occur; during various periods of the life course, people may feel themselves to be "off-time" or "on-time." Being off-time may cause one to be perceived by self and others as socially deviant (Clausen, 1975). The relatively strong need for conformity characteristic of young adolescents (Berndt, 1979; Costanzo & Shaw, 1966) contributes to the salience of deviance in pubertal timing.

Another approach to timing effects has to do with what Petersen and Taylor (1980) call the *stage termination* perspective. Differences between early and late pubertal developers may be a function of the amount of time available for the completion of the psychological development of latency before puberty (Peskin, 1973; Peskin & Livson, 1972). Alternatively, the additional time for the developmental tasks of adolescence provided by early pubertal development may, by the end of adolescence, profit the early developers (Peskin, 1973; Peskin & Livson, 1972). This conceptualization permits the test of specific hypotheses. Although the focus of this research has been on ego development, other experiences and their developmental correlates (e.g., cognitive development or middle childhood play activities) also could be considered.

A third perspective, which integrates aspects of the first two, focuses on the importance of pubertal change for social status (e.g., Meyer, 1982; Opler, 1971). The attainment of an adultlike body is seen as introducing significant changes in the meanings of social roles for the adolescent and for the adults and peers who share the adolescent's world. Socially shared expectations, responses, and fantasies associated with this stage of physical maturation are viewed as influencing the adolescent's social prestige, role behaviors, social adaptation, and self-concept. Thus, it is hypothesized that a young adolescent with a mature body will experience a different environment and that this experience will then influence his or her psychological functioning in a manner quite different from a same-aged peer whose body still appears childlike. For example, significant others may react differently to pubertal boys and girls

as they mature physically, stimulating a shift in socially shared aspects of their self-concepts. The visual and apparent changes of puberty have been found to influence patterns of family interaction (Hill, 1980; Lynch, 1981; Steinberg, 1981; Steinberg & Hill, 1978) and to alter peer relations (Savin-Williams, 1979), particularly with regard to patterns of intimacy (Douvan & Adelson, 1966) and heterosocial behavior (Crockett & Petersen, in press; Simmons et al., 1979).

Support for the effects of general social norms on puberty and adolescent development have emerged through two analyses from our own research. We considered two questions: (a) What are the effects of timing on body image and feelings of attractiveness? (b) Do individuals with extremely deviant timing have more adjustment problems? We expected that the groups likely to have the most difficulty are early maturing girls and late maturing boys.

The data for early maturing girls have been examined more completely thus far in our research. These girls typically began to menstruate in the fifth grade and often were distressed about this change (Petersen, 1983). Almost half of these girls failed to report menarche to their interviewers until much later in the study, at which time the dates they gave came closer and closer to the dates reported by their mothers. They often did not even tell their mothers when they first began menstruating, unlike later maturing girls, who almost always told their mothers immediately. Instead the early girls told no one, with some manifesting rather bizarre behavior in their attempts to conceal their menstruation. They displayed many behaviors, as reported vividly by their mothers, that suggested that they were attempting to deny their advanced pubertal status. One illustrative example is the girl who would not wear a bra but instead insisted on wearing several layers of T-shirts and sweat shirts, all to conceal the presence of breasts. In analyses of both boys and girls, we (Petersen & Crockett, 1985) found that early maturers reported more psychopathology and moodiness and poorer emotional tone.

Consistent with our results are recent findings by Rierdan and Koff (1985). Studying sixth-through ninth-grade girls, they found that off-time girls (postmenarcheal sixth graders and premenarcheal ninth graders) displayed the highest levels of depression. Additionally, these same off-time groups indicated the greatest degree of intent to commit self-harm and the highest scores on an anorexia nervosa inventory.

General social norms may also mediate the effects of pubertal development on psychological development in ways other than on timing. Social norms about what is considered attractive appear to be a significant force. During adolescence, a person's overall self-evaluation or self-image is strongly related to viewing one's body as attractive, and this association is stronger for females than it is for males (e.g., Kavrell & Jarcho, 1980; Lerner & Karabenick, 1974). A sex difference in general body image satisfaction emerges in early adolescence, with females feeling less satisfied (e.g., Rosenberg & Simmons, 1975; Tobin-Richards et al., 1983). Additionally, more positive attributions are made about attractive relative to unattractive women, while attractiveness does not differentiate attributions about men to the same degree (e.g., Hill & Lando, 1976).

Weight has been found to be particularly important to a girl's sense of her own attractiveness and to her perceptions of her body (Faust, 1983; Simmons et al., 1983; Tobin-Richards et al., 1983). The heavier a girl is, or perceives herself to be, the more dissatisfied she is with both her weight and her figure. A strong cultural value to be tall and slim may contribute to these feelings and self-perceptions (Faust, 1983).

This strong cultural pressure appears to mediate the effects of pubertal development on psychological well-being. Simmons and colleagues (1983) report that early developers are significantly less satisfied with their weight compared to late developers. When weight is controlled for, the difference in reported satisfaction disappears. Consistent with Simmons' findings, our data indicate that as girls mature physically, they become increasingly more dissatisfied with their weight and perceive themselves as more overweight. Boys do not share these negative perceptions and feelings.

Local Social Norms

Evidence for local social norms has been found in one analysis thus far. We have found community differences in girls' responses to pubertal changes related to weight gain (Tobin-Richards, Petersen, & Boxer, 1983). For our study we randomly sampled two suburban school districts, both similar in social class. Boys from both communities and girls from one community reported similar satisfaction with their weight and feelings of attractiveness. (See Figure 3.4.)

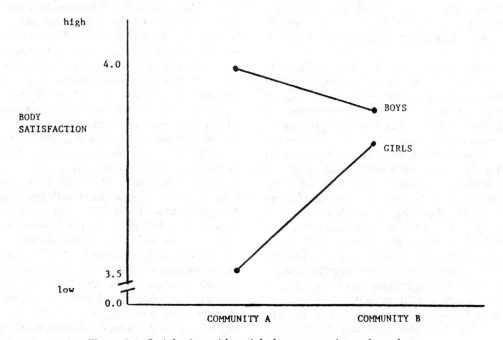

Figure 3.4. Satisfaction with weight by community and gender.

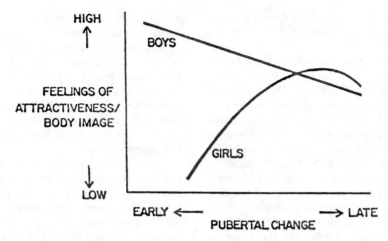

Figure 3.5. The model describing the relationship of pubertal change to body image and feelings of attractiveness. (From: "Early Adolescents' Perceptions of their Physical Development" by M. H. Tobin-Richards et al., in *Girls at Puberty: Biological and Psychosocial Perspectives* (p. 137) edited by J. Brooks-Gunn & A. C. Petersen, 1983, New York: Plenum. Copyright 1983 by Plenum Publishing Corp. Reprinted by permission.)

In the other community, however, girls were dissatisfied with their weight, felt that they were overweight, and perceived themselves as unattractive. These differences persisted even when we controlled for actual weight in our analyses. These girls, like many others in our society, hold standards of thinness that are unrealistic for postpubertal young women. We also noted that these girls were less active in sports and other school activities compared to the girls from the other community and compared to the boys (Browning, 1983). Not only does this mean that they were less likely to be getting regular exercise, but, more importantly, it also means that they had fewer experiences through which to develop their identities and senses of self; instead, they focused excessively on appearance. We think that these results have implications for understanding the recent increases in such eating disorders as anorexia nervosa and bulimia.

Gender Effects

The differential norms related to gender also constitute a very important factor influencing responses to pubertal change. As discussed previously, effects of both general social and local social norms differ for boys and girls. For boys, pubertal change tends to be experienced positively (Tobin-Richards et al., 1983). The re-

lationship between pubertal change and self-perceptions is linear, with early maturing boys having the highest body image, feelings of attractiveness, and self-image generally. Late maturing boys are lowest on these dimensions, with boys of average timing falling in between.

For girls the picture is entirely different. It is the girls who are maturing at about the same time as everyone else who feel most attractive and positive about themselves. Late maturers have just slightly less positive self-views. As we have described, early maturing girls score *much* lower on these dimensions. These contrasting patterns are shown in Figure 3.5. For girls the pattern was consistently obtained for all indicators of pubertal change except breast development, in which a pattern more similar to that seen in boys was observed; that is, more breast development was seen as positive.

Two culturally valued ideals in body shape may be influencing the young adolescent girl's feelings about herself. The positive attitudes associated with more advanced breast development contrasts with the ideal of a prepubertal look. The full-bodied, large-breasted, "sexy" look representative of the figures displayed in both popular and pornographic media emphasize a more mature body, with particular focus on large breasts. This may explain why a girl with breast development tends to feel more positive about her physical self than a girl who is more flat-chested (Tobin-Richards et al., 1983).

Interestingly, little research has been conducted on breast development. Based on exploratory research, Rosenbaum (1979) concluded that because of the relative absence of visibility and mobility of female genitalia, breasts occupy an inordinate degree of psychic space for adolescent girls. Interviews with adolescent girls reveal that all body parts, except for breasts, are desired to be small and unobtrusive, and that big breasts are valued for their appeal to boys. Rosenbaum writes, "Thus, breasts were seen as the most consciously sexualized body parts, symbols of the maturing sexuality of the girl" (p. 245). Young adolescent girls, particularly premenarcheal seventh-grade girls, appear to be more preoccupied with breast development than postmenarcheal seventh-grade girls, as demonstrated in the premenarcheal group producing figure drawings with more explicit breasts (Rierdan & Koff, 1980).

Additional support for this concern was the sex difference found in our research on a Body Image Scale item, "When others look at me they must think that I am poorly developed"; girls tend to endorse this item more than boys (Tobin-Richards et al., 1983). Once breasts have developed and there is no more concern as to whether or not this development will ever occur, and a girl becomes accustomed to her "endowment," this preoccupation probably diminishes considerably. There is some evidence, though, that a cultural preoccupation with breasts never allows a woman to become completely unaware of her breast shape and size relative to cultural ideals (Ayalah & Weinstock, 1979).

Physical maturation in girls, not containing the same meaning as for boys, may elicit a more sexualized response from others in the broader social context. This response, perhaps unconscious, may be enacted with restrictions on the pubertal girls' freedoms, with parents becoming concerned with protecting their daughters (Block, 1978; Katz, 1979). It has been suggested that sexual maturity is, at this time, more a concern than a joy to parents (Brooks-Gunn & Matthews, 1979). In addition, parents' personal responses to their young adolescent's physical development may be mediated by their life-cy-

cle position and experience of aging (Rossi, 1980). As adolescents become more adultlike in appearance, parents may be more likely to identify with their offspring. This enhanced similarity between parent and child, triggered by the adultlike appearance of the child, may stimulate new feelings of competition, envy, and attraction in the parent, all of which can cause discomfort and anxiety, in both the younger and older generations.

These differences between boys and girls cannot be explained simply by the earlier pubertal maturation of girls, because the patterns of the relationships are entirely different and are not a simple transposition over time. In other words, for boys, a straight line describes the pattern, with earlier maturers doing better and later maturers worse. For girls, it is being in the middle, where most of their peers are, that is best.

We asked several questions of the young adolescents to try to understand their feelings about pubertal change and heard repeatedly from girls that they did not want to be different from others. We know from other research that conformity to peers peaks during the early adolescent years (e.g., Berndt, 1979; Costanzo & Shaw, 1966). Conformity may explain the effect that we see in girls for pubertal timing, particularly because of the greater salience of appearance to girls (Tobin-Richards et al., 1983) and because of the greater risk for girls of deviance due to early maturation.

For girls who are experiencing the events of puberty, the social support of a peer group may serve as an especially important buffer in accommodating to the changes of their bodies. One of the adolescent girls in our study, who perceived herself to be early in her development, responded to the question of how she felt about having gotten her period by saying: "Well, I suppose I felt more grown up. I also felt a little embarrassed." When asked why, she said: "Well, I knew that barely any of my friends had it and it was just kinda embarrassing, even though you know you can't tell if someone has their period. You feel different inside around your friends, like a little self-conscious" (Tobin-Richards et al., 1983).

One other puberty-related effect may support the conformity explanation. Simmons, Blyth, and their colleagues (1979) have found that girls, but not boys, who change from elementary to junior high school show decreases in self-esteem. The same decrease occurs later when these girls change from junior to senior high school (Simmons, Blyth, Carlton-Ford, & Bulcroft, 1982). Therefore, the authors suggest that the earlier stress of school change does not help to "inoculate" girls against the same kinds of changes subsequently. Instead, they are once again susceptible, perhaps with an anaphylactic effect involving *increased* sensitivity.

These findings suggest how pubertal development affects psychological health. School change typically occurs prior to seventh grade, the same age at which most girls are mid- to late-pubertal (Petersen & Crockett, in press); in contrast, most boys at this age are still prepubertal. Therefore, girls must begin dealing with several simultaneous changes, whereas boys typically need to deal with only school change. These results may contain important implications for preventive interventions. The well-being of young adolescents, particularly girls, may be enhanced if they remain in elementary school during this period when so much else is changing.

Another hypothesis emerging from our research is that cohort-related pubertal behavior may be initiated by the group of young people becoming pubertal (Petersen, 1985). There is a period—in our study this happened by the spring of sixth grade—when a majority of adolescents in the birth cohort became at least mid-pubertal (see Figure 3.6). We might compare this phenomenon with the "tipping effects" discussed in the contexts of racial populations in neighborhoods or of gender stereotyping of occupations. For example, once there is a "critical mass" of women in a job, it becomes known as women's work. We think that a similar thing happens in becoming pubertal. Once there are enough adolescents in a cohort who are pubertal, the entire cohort begins engaging in "pubertal behavior," regardless of pubertal status. This phenomenon is seen especially in the transmission of behavior from primarily pubertal girls to primarily prepubertal boys during seventh grade.

Pubertal behavior is that which is stereotypically thought normative among pubertal adolescents and which increases during the period from sixth to eighth grades. Some examples are dating, preoccupation with the opposite sex, talking on the telephone, and increased conflict with parents. With these variables, our research supports grade-related but not puberty-related

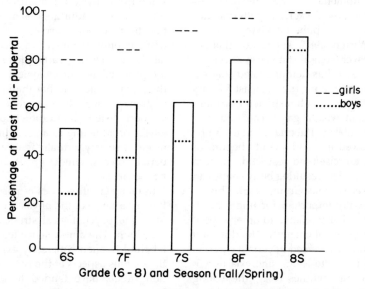

Figure 3.6. Percentages of young adolescents who are at least midpubertal, by grade and season. (From: "Pubertal Development as a Cause of Disturbance: Myths, Realities, and Unanswered Questions" by A. C. Petersen, 1985, *Genetic, Social, and General Psychology Monographs, 111,* p. 214. Copyright 1985 by the Helen Dwight Reid Educational Foundation. Reprinted by permission.)

changes, except that early maturers are more likely to be among the group doing these things first (Crockett & Petersen, in press). Considering a broader range of variables, several cognitive, psychological, and social variables increase during the early adolescent years, but again these increases are grade-related and not linked to pubertal status (Crockett & Petersen, in press; Kavrell & Petersen, 1984; Petersen, 1983; Petersen & Crockett, 1986).

SUMMARY AND FUTURE DIRECTIONS

There is little evidence to support the belief of a strong and direct causal role of puberty in adolescent behavior, particularly disturbed behavior. Instead, more evidence supports a Mediated Effects Model (Petersen, 1985; Petersen & Taylor, 1980), consistent with a theoretical perspective positing interaction between the individual and the social context. We note, however, that the paucity of evidence for direct effects may be more related to inadequate methods than to true lack of relationships. Over the next decade we will be able to speak more definitively about pubertal effects.

Traditionally, puberty has been viewed as unidirectionally influencing psychological and behavioral phenomena. Recently, however, exciting work has linked exercise patterns, nutritional intake, and pubertal changes (e.g., Frisch, 1983; Warren, 1983), suggesting that behavioral and psychological status can affect puberty. This research has demonstrated that extensive exercise or training (i.e., at least 5 hours a day), in combination with restricted nutritional intake (to limit weight gain), can influence the process of puberty. Pubertal change can be reversed or slowed if it had already begun, or delayed if the exercise/food restriction pattern precedes puberty. The resulting body shape can be altered as well (Brooks-Gunn, 1985). This research is especially important for understanding the role of puberty relative to other experiences or developmental changes. The direction of influence may be reversed in certain cases so that psychological states (e.g., anorexia nervosa) and behavioral routines (e.g., the young professional dancer's regimen) can directly affect the pubertal process.

The fact that all adolescents go through puberty remains extremely important. Because all adolescents, except those who are ill, experience puberty, there is no variation on this dimension to be related to other variables. It would be a logical error, therefore, to conclude that pubertal change is an inconsequential event in life. Adolescence marks the transition from childhood to adulthood, and the physical manifestations of mature appearance are often taken as evidence of adulthood.

The *social stimulus value* of pubertal change is extremely important. Adult size and shape serve as the signal of adult status and lead to expectations that the adult-appearing person will behave like an adult. The risk here is that the adult-appearing individual is probably immature psychologically, socially, and cognitively (cf. Petersen, 1982, 1985; Petersen & Crockett, 1986). Our culture does not prepare or allow individuals to be more fully mature in all ways, except for the physical, until many years have passed from the time of puberty. Thus, adolescents are in an odd position of appearing as adults but not having the developmental maturity to cope with adultlike expectations. Young people experience pressure to behave the way adults do—in both the healthy and unhealthy ways—but usually lack the experience that facilitates the development of healthy, mature behavior.

Currently in our society there is no single, culturally shared acknowledgement of the transition from physical immaturity to physical maturity. Instead, adulthood is marked by graduation from school, marriage, of attainment of a first job, often as much as a decade after pubertal change. During early adolescence, children are grouped by chronological age or grade in the school system, rather than by physical maturation. Hence, there is no culturally bound support system to aid the child with the challenges of adjusting to a very different body. In fact, our society virtually ignores the whole pubertal process, almost pretending that it does not occur.

In many cultures, rites of passage emphasize the importance of the physical changes and validate the psychological stress attached to the transition. The ambivalence felt about a pubertal child is often concretely expressed through the various aspects of the rites. Although initiation rituals have tended to be discussed in terms of the psychological benefits accrued by the older generation (Muensterberger, 1975), an equally valid argument could be made for the benefits accrued by the younger generation. Many, if not most, of these initiation rites involve a trial or ordeal of some type, that, when passed, signifies to the society and the successful initiate that he or she is capable of enduring the challenges of adulthood. Second, these rites often involve pain or discomfort. We could argue that this functions partially to express in a concrete form the psychological pain of the transition. Third, these rites are frequently undergone in the company of other same-sex peers who are manifesting similar pubertal development. Thus, the culture provides a support group of peers who may render the ordeal less noxious. Last, a community-sponsored celebration often follows the successful completion of the rituals. This may function to express the positive side of the ambivalence about the transition. The new young adult can then partake of the socially sanctioned excitement and pleasure associated with a new body and the new adult status. In summary, these rites of passage acknowledge the significance of the change in its multifaceted qualities and thus, creates an important, effective support for the child.

Why do we as a society blatantly ignore pubertal development? What purpose does the lack of acknowledgement serve? One obvious answer is that as a society we need to keep young people out of the labor force for as long as possible both because there are too few jobs available and because the level of specialization in many fields is so great that many years of education are required (e.g., Kett, 1977). This promotes great delay in the attainment of adulthood. Thus, it serves the society best to try to ignore the fact that children become physical adults years before they are recognized as social adults. It could be argued that rites of passage at this age would have no meaning because no adult status is attained.

A second reason for the lack of socially shared acknowledgement of physically mature status may have to do with attitudes towards adolescent sexuality. On the one hand, we provide inadequate sex education for adolescents out of fear that discussion will promote sexual behavior. On the other hand, sexual messages to adolescents are abundantly provided in movies, on MTV, and in our obsession with youthful looks in advertisements. There is a long interval between the attainment of a sexually mature body and complete cultural permission to engage in a sexual relationship within marriage. Thus, it could be argued that pubertal rites during early

adolescence would have no meaning because no change in culturally approved sexual status occurs. Although both of these arguments provide reasonable explanations for why there is no recognition of mature physical status in our society today, both arguments serve the interests of the adults and the larger economic community more than they do the pubertal adolescent. Indeed, the costs to adolescents may be great.

Pubescent adolescents, especially off-time adolescents, might gain psychologically from community recognition of their physical status change. Pubertal adolescents could participate in a brief series of activities involving education about the physical changes, including an opportunity to talk with a group of same-sex children of the same physical age about the feelings and thoughts stimulated by puberty, perhaps as a retreat. Upon return to the community, a dinner shared with families and friends could celebrate the transition.

Although a rite of passage of this sort would not carry the same meanings for status change in productive, recreational, and sexual activities as it does in more primitive cultures, it would serve to validate the importance of the physical changes for the young adolescent and acknowledge the stress involved with change. It would create peer group support that may be badly needed, especially by early or late developers. Particularly strategies for special groups could be shared; for example, early developing girls could be encouraged to minimize the number of other changes experienced at the same time. Additionally, community recognition might benefit parents who could also use each other for support in facing their child's inevitable growth and change.

Although puberty rites would not eradicate the disjunction of socially derived expectations and opportunities with the physical transformation of puberty, these rites would acknowledge the importance and the strain of these changes for the child, the family, and, to a lesser extent, the community. This acknowledgement might function in itself as an important support, particularly for those who face unusual stress associated with puberty.

Acknowledgements—The work described in this chapter was supported by grants MH 30252/38142 to A. Petersen. We gratefully acknowledge the assistance of Pamela Sarigiani.

REFERENCES

Aynsley-Green, A. M., Zachmann, M., & Prader, A. (1976). Inter-relation of the therapeutic effects of growth hormone and testosterone on growth in hypopituitarism. *Journal of Pediatrics, 89,* 992.

Ayalah, D., & Weinstock, I. J. (1979). *Breasts: Women speak about their breasts and their lives.* New York: Summit Books.

Berndt, T. J. (1979). Developmental changes in conformity to peers and parents. *Developmental Psychology, 15,* 608–616.

Block, J. H. (1978). Another look at sex differentiation in the socialization behaviors of mothers and fathers. In J. Sherman & F. Denmark (Eds.), *Psychology of women: Future directions of research* (pp. 31–87). New York: Psychological Dimensions.

Blos, P. (1962). *On adolescence: A psychoanalytic interpretation.* New York: The Free Press.

Blyth, D. A., Simmons, R. G., & Bulcroft, R. (1983, August). Puberty, achievement, and self-esteem among black and white adolescents. In R. Lerner (Chair), *The effects of pubertal timing on achievement and self-image.* Symposium conducted at the meetings of the American Psychological Association, Anaheim, CA.

Brook, C. G. (1981). Endocrinological control of growth at puberty. *British Medical Bulletin, 37,* 281–285.

Brooks-Gunn, J. (1985, August). *Being an early or late maturer: Does it matter?* Paper presented in a symposium entitled Growing Up Female and Liking It sponsored by the Personal Products Company (Johnson & Johnson), Washington, DC.

Brooks-Gunn, J., & Matthews, W. S. (1979). *He and she.* Englewood Cliffs, NJ: Prentice-Hall.

Browning, M. M. (1983). *Children's experience in two junior high schools.* Unpublished manuscript, University of Chicago Press.

Clausen, J. A. (1975). The social meaning of differential physical and sexual maturation. In S. E. Dragastin & G. H. Elder (Eds.), *Adolescence in the life cycle: Psychological change and social context* (pp. 25–47). Washington, DC: Hemisphere.

Conger, J. J., & Petersen, A. C. (1984). *Adolescence and youth: Psychological development in a changing world* (3rd ed.). New York: Harper & Row.

Costanzo, P. R., & Shaw, M. E. (1966). Conformity as a function of age level. *Child Development, 37,* 967–976.

Crockett, L. J., & Petersen, A. C. (in press). Pubertal status and psychosocial development: Findings from the Early Adolescence Study. In R. M. Lerner & T. T. Foch (Eds.), *Biological-psychosocial interactions in early adolescence: A life span perspective.* Hillsdale, NJ: Erlbaum.

Cutler, G. B., Comite, F., Rivier, J., Vale, W. E., Loriaux, D. L., & Crowley, W. F. (1983). Pituitary desensitization with a long-acting luteinizing-hormone-releasing hormone analog: A potential new treatment for idiopathic-precocious puberty. In J. Brooks-Gunn & A. C. Petersen (Eds.), *Girls at puberty: Biological and psychosocial perspectives* (pp. 89–102). New York: Plenum Press.

Douvan, E., & Adelson, J. (1966). *The adolescent experience.* New York: Wiley.

Eichorn, D. H. (1974). Asynchronizations in adolescent development. In S. E. Dragastin & G. H. Elder, Jr. (Eds.), *Adolescence in the life cycle: Psychological change and social context* (pp. 81–96). Washington, DC: Hemisphere.

Elkind, D. (1974). Recent research on cognitive development in adolescence. In S. E. Dragastin & G. H. Elder, Jr. (Eds.), *Adolescence in the life cycle: Psychological change and social context* (pp. 49–61). Washington, DC: Hemisphere.

Faust, M. S. (1983). Alternative constructions of adolescent growth. In J. Brooks-Gunn & A. C. Petersen (Eds.), *Girls at puberty: Biological, psychological, and social perspectives* (pp. 105–125). New York: Plenum Press.

Freud, A. (1946). *The ego and the mechanisms of defense.* New York: International Universities Press.

Freud, A. (1958). Adolescence. *Psychoanalytic Study of the Child, 16,* 225–278.

Freud, A. (1969). Adolescence as a developmental disturbance. In G. Caplan & S. Lebovici (Eds.), *Adolescence: Psychosocial perspectives* (pp. 5–10). New York: Basic Books.

Freud, S. (1953). *A general introduction to psychoanalysis* (J. Riviere, Trans.). New York: Permabooks. (Original work published 1905)

Frisch, R. E. (1983). Fatness, puberty, and fertility: The effects of nutrition and physical training on menarche and ovulation. In J. Brooks-Gunn & A. C. Petersen (Eds.), *Girls at puberty: Biological and psychosocial perspectives* (pp. 29–49). New York: Plenum Press.

Grumbach, M. M., Grave, G. D., & Mayer, F. E. (Eds.). (1974). *The control of the onset of puberty.* New York: Wiley.

Grumbach, M. M., Roth, J. C., Kaplan, S. L., & Kelch, R. P. (1974). Hypothalamic–pituitary regulation of puberty: Evidence and concept derived from clinical research. In M. M. Grumbach, G. D. Grave, & F. E. Mayer (Eds.), *Control of the onset of puberty* (pp. 115–166). New York: Wiley.

Hamburg, B. A. (1974). Early adolescence: A specific and stressful stage of the life cycle. In G. V. Coelho, D. A. Hamburg, & J. E. Adams (Eds.), *Coping and adaptation* (pp. 101–124). New York: Basic Books.

Hill, J. P. (1980). The family. In M. Johnson (Ed.), *Toward adolescence: The middle school years.* Chicago: National Society for the Study of Education (distributed by the University of Chicago Press).

Hill, M. K., & Lando, M. A. (1976). Physical attractiveness and sex-role stereotypes in impression formation. *Perceptual and Motor Skills, 43,* 1251.

Johnson, C. (1982). Anorexia nervosa and bulimia. In T. J. Coates, A. C. Petersen, & C. Perry (Eds.), *Promoting adolescent health: A dialog on research and practice* (pp. 397–412). New York: Academic Press.

Jones, M. C., & Bayley, N. (1950). Physical maturing among boys as related to behavior. *Journal of Educational Psychology, 41,* 129–148.

Katz, P. (1979). The development of female identity. *Sex Roles, 5,* 155–178.

Kavrell, S. M., & Jarcho, H. (1980, September). *Self-esteem and body image in early adolescence*. Paper presented at the annual meeting of the American Psychological Association, Montreal.

Kavrell, S. M., & Petersen, A. C. (1984). Patterns of achievement in early adolescence. In M. L. Maehr & M. W. Steinkamp (Eds.), *Women in science* (pp. 1-35). Greenwich, CT: JAI Press.

Keating, P. P. (1980). Thinking processes in adolescence. In J. Adelson (Ed.), *Handbook of adolescent psychology* (pp. 211-246). New York: Wiley.

Kestenberg, J. (1967a). Phases of adolescence with suggestions for a correlation of psychic and hormonal organizations. Part I: Antecedents of adolescent organizations in childhood. *Journal of the American Academy of Child Psychiatry, 6*, 426-463.

Kestenberg, J. (1967b). Phases of adolescence with suggestions for a correlation of psychic and hormonal organization. Part II: Prepuberty, diffusion, and reintegration. *Journal of the American Academy of Child Psychiatry, 6*, 577-614.

Kestenberg, J. (1968). Phases of adolescence with suggestions for a correlation of psychic and hormonal organization. Part III: Puberty growth, differentiation, and consolidation. *Journal of the American Academy of Child Psychiatry, 7*, 108-151.

Kett, J. F. (1977). *Rites of passage: Adolescence in America 1790 to the present*. New York: Basic Books.

Lerner, R. M., & Busch-Rossnagel, N. A. (1981). Individuals as producers of their development: Conceptual and empirical bases. In R. M. Lerner & N. A. Busch-Rossnagel (Eds.), *Individuals as producers of their development: A life-span perspective* (pp. 1-36). New York: Academic Press.

Lerner, R. M., & Karabenick, S. A. (1974). Physical attractiveness, body attitudes, and self-concept in late adolescence. *Journal of Youth and Adolescence, 3*, 7-16.

Lynch, M. E. (1981). *Paternal androgyny, daughters' physical maturity level, and achievement socialization in early adolescence*. Unpublished doctoral dissertation, Cornell University, Ithaca, NY.

Mead, M. (1962). *Sex and temperament in three primitive societies*. New York: New American Library.

Meyer, J. W. (1982, December). *Cultural links between gender roles and identity*. Paper presented at a conference on Pubertal and Psychosocial Change, sponsored by the Social Science Research Council Subcommittee on Child Development in Life-Span Perspective, Tucson.

Muensterberger, W. (1975). The adolescent in society. In A. H. Esman (Ed.), *The psychology of adolescence*. New York: International University Press.

Mussen, P. H., & Bouterline-Young, H. (1964). Personality characteristics of physically advanced and retarded adolescents in Italy and the United States. *Vita Humana, 7*, 186-200.

Neugarten, B. L. (1969). Continuities and discontinuities of psychological issues into adult life. *Human Development, 12*, 121-130.

Neugarten, B. L. (1979). Time, age, and the life-cycle. *American Journal of Psychiatry, 136*, 887-894.

Opler, M. K. (1971). Adolescence in cross-cultural perspective. In J. G. Howells (Ed.), *Modern perspectives in adolescent psychiatry* (pp. 152-179). Edinburgh: Oliver & Boyd.

Paige, K. M., & Paige, J. M. (1982). *The politics of reproductive ritual*. Berkeley: University of California Press.

Peskin, H. (1973). Influence of the developmental schedule of puberty on learning and ego development. *Journal of Youth and Adolescence, 1*, 273-290.

Peskin, H., & Livson, M. (1972). Pre- and postpubertal personality and adult psychological functioning. *Seminars in Psychiatry, 4*, 343-353.

Petersen, A. C. (1979). Hormones and cognitive functioning in normal development. In M. A. Wittig & A. C. Petersen (Eds.), *Sex-related differences in cognitive functioning: Developmental issues* (pp. 189-214). New York: Academic Press.

Petersen, A. C. (1982). Developmental issues in adolescent health. In T. J. Coates, A. C. Petersen, & C. Perry (Eds.), *Promoting adolescent health: A dialog on research and practice* (pp. 61-72). New York: Academic Press.

Petersen, A. C. (1983). Menarche: Meaning of measures and measuring meaning. In S. Golub (Ed.), *Menarche* (pp. 63-76). New York: D. C. Heath.

Petersen, A. C. (1985). Pubertal development as a cause of disturbance: Myths, realities, and unanswered questions. *Genetic, Social, and General Psychology Monographs, 111*, 205-232.

Petersen, A. C., & Boxer, A. (1982). Adolescent sexuality. In T. J. Coates, A. C. Petersen, & C. Perry (Eds.), *Promoting adolescent health: A dialog on research and practice* (pp. 237-253). New York: Academic Press.

Petersen, A. C., & Craighead, W. E. (1986). Emotional and personality development in normal adolescents and young adults. In G. Klerman (Ed.), *Suicide and depression among adolescents and young adults* (pp. 19-52). New York: American Psychiatric Press.

Petersen, A. C., & Crockett, L. (1985). Pubertal timing and grade effects on adjustment. *Journal of Youth and Adolescence, 14*, 191-206.

Petersen, A. C., & Crockett, L. (1986). Pubertal development and its relation to cognitive and psychosocial development in adolescent girls: Implications for parenting. In J. Lancaster & B. Hamburg (Eds.), *School-age pregnancy and parenthood: Biosocial dimensions* (pp. 147-175). Hawthorne, NY: Aldine Press.

Petersen, A. C., & Taylor, B. (1980). The biological approach to adolescence: Biological change and psychological adaptation. In J. Adelson (Ed.), *Handbook of adolescent psychology* (pp. 117-155). New York: Wiley.

Rierdan, J., & Koff, E. (1980). The psychological impact of menarche: Integrative vs. disruptive changes. *Journal of Youth and Adolescence, 9*, 49-58.

Rierdan, J., & Koff, E. (1985). Timing of menarche and initial menstrual experience. *Journal of Youth and Adolescence, 14*, 237-244.

Rosenbaum, M. (1979). The changing body image of the adolescent girl. In M. Sugar (Ed.), *Female adolescent development* (pp. 234-252). New York: Brunner/Mazel.

Rosenberg, F., & Simmons, R. G. (1975). Sex differences in the self-concept in adolescence. *Sex Roles: A Journal of Research, 1,* 147–159.

Rossi, A. S. (1980). Life-span theories in women's lives. *Signs, 6,* 4–32.

Sameroff, A. (1975). Transactional models in early social relations. *Human Development, 18,* 65–79.

Savin-Williams, R. (1979). Dominance hierarchies in groups of early adolescents. *Child Development, 50,* 923–935.

Simmons, R. G., & Blyth, D. A. (in press). *Moving into adolescence: The impact of pubertal change and school context.* Hawthorne, NY: Aldine.

Simmons, R. G., Blyth, D. A., Carlton-Ford, S., & Bulcroft, R. (1982, December). *The adjustment of early adolescents to school and pubertal transitions.* Paper presented at a conference on Pubertal and Psychosocial Change sponsored by the Social Science Research Council Subcommittee on Child Development in Life-Span Perspective, Tucson.

Simmons, R. G., Blyth, D. A., & McKinney, K. L. (1983). The social and psychological effects of puberty on white females. In J. Brooks-Gunn & A. C. Petersen (Eds.), *Girls at puberty: Biological and psychosocial perspectives* (pp. 229–272). New York: Plenum Press.

Simmons, R. G., Blyth, D. A., VanCleave, E. F., & Bush, D. M. (1979). Entry into early adolescence: The impact of school structure, puberty, and early dating on self-esteem. *American Sociological Review, 44,* 948–967.

Sonis, W., Klein, R., Blue, J., Comite, F., & Cutler, G. (1983, April). *Social competence and behavior problems in children with precocious puberty.* Paper presented at the meeting of the Society for Research in Child Development, Detroit.

Steinberg, L. D. (1981). Transformations in family relations at puberty. *Developmental Psychology, 7,* 833–840.

Steinberg, L. D., & Hill, J. (1978). Patterns of family interactions as a function of age, the onset of puberty, and formal thinking. *Developmental Psychology, 14,* 683–684.

Susman, E. J., Nottleman, E. D., & Blue, J. H. (1983, April). *Social competence, mood, and behavior problems in normal adolescents.* Paper presented at the meeting of the Society for Research in Child Development, Detroit.

Tanner, J. M. (1962). *Growth at adolescence.* Oxford: Blackwell Scientific Publications.

Tanner, J. M. (1972). Sequence, tempo, and individual variation in growth and development of boys aged twelve to sixteen. In J. Kagan & R. Coles (Eds.), *Twelve to sixteen: Early adolescence* (pp. 1–24). New York: Norton.

Tanner, J. M. (1974). Sequence and tempo in the somatic changes in puberty. In M. M. Grumbach, G. D. Grave, & F. E.Mayer (Eds.), *Control of the onset of puberty* (pp. 448–470). New York: Wiley.

Tanner, J. M., Whitehouse, R. H., Marubin, E., & Resele, L. F. (1976). The adolescent growth spurt of boys and girls from the Harpenden Growth Study. *Annual for Human Biology, 3,* 109–126.

Tobin-Richards, M. H., Boxer, A. M., & Petersen, A. C. (1983). Early adolescents' perceptions of their physical development. In J. Brooks-Gunn & A. C. Petersen (Eds.), *Girls at puberty: Biological and psychosocial perspectives* (pp. 127–154). New York: Plenum.

Tobin-Richards, M. H., Petersen, A. C., & Boxer, A. M. (1983, April). *The significance of weight to feelings of attractiveness in pubertal girls.* Paper presented at the meeting of the Society for Research in Child Development, Detroit.

Udry, J. R., Billy, J. D. G., Morris, N. M., Groff, T. R., & Raj, M. H. (1985). Serum androgenic hormones motivate sexual behavior in adolescent boys. *Fertility and Sterility, 43,* 90–94.

Warren, M. P. (1983). Physical and biological aspects of puberty. In J. Brooks-Gunn & A. C. Petersen (Eds.), *Girls at puberty: Biological and psychosocial perspectives* (pp. 3–28). New York: Plenum Press.

Weisfeld, G. E. (1979). An ethological view of human adolescence. *The Journal of Nervous and Mental Disease, 167,* 38–55.

CHAPTER 4

Psychodynamic Models

Howard Lerner

The development of psychoanalytic theory over the past century can be viewed in a broad theoretical context as part of a major scientific revolution that began in the middle of the 19th century. As Blatt and Lerner (1983) observe, developments in mathematics involved the realization that the conception of the universe based on Euclidean geometry and rectilinear Cartesian coordinates was only one among a number of alternative ways of its being construed. With the development of nonEuclidean geometry and new concepts of curvilinearity, it became possible to understand the universe in a number of equally valid ways. These advances contributed to the growing realization that the experience and conception of reality is influenced by the relative position and assumptions of the observer.

In philosophy, there was an increasing awareness that nature was not simply observed, but rather constructed based upon the nature of a particular vantage point. These developments had major epistemological implications in that the conceptualization of multiple and relative perspectives carried with it the meaning that surface and manifest appearance of phenomena could no longer simply be accepted as valid or the only way of comprehending reality. There

was an important recognition that to understand phenomena, one had to identify the structure and organizing principles that underlie surface manifestations of phenomena. The emphasis on internal structure became, according to Foucault, a major cultural epistomology of the 20th century.

The concept of internal, underlying structure and with it the search for an identification of the inherent principles of organization that define the relationships among elements and their potential transformations in hierarchical organized systems has had a significant influence on the physical and biological sciences as well as the humanities. According to Blatt and Lerner (1983):

> Despite this emphasis on internal structure in numerous fields throughout the twentieth century, a large segment of American psychology and psychiatry still maintain an exclusive interest in manifest behavior and overt symptomatology. There have been notable exceptions, of course, and these exceptions have made major contributions to the understanding of some of the structural principles inherent in human behavior. These notable exceptions include the Gestalt analyses of perception, contemporary approaches to cognitive processes including the work of Piaget and Werner, and psychoanalytic theory. (pp. 87–88).

Blatt and Lerner (1983) further note that efforts in the human sciences to investigate the principles of structural organization that underlie manifest behavior must include a consideration of two central dimensions that are fundamental to the human condition: (a) the person's capacity for complex symbolic activity and (b) a recognition of the importance of the complex interpersonal matrix within which we evolve and exist. These factors are unique to the human condition and must be accounted for in understanding the underlying structural principles and factors that integrate multiple perspectives of different observations of manifest behavior. It is of historical interest that the emergence of structuralism corresponds with the concept of childhood as a separate stage of life, the concept of development stages, and ultimately, in the 20th century, with the phenomenon of adolescence.

HISTORY AND DEVELOPMENT

Psychoanalytic theory is not a static body of knowledge; rather it is in a state of constant evolution (Easer, 1974). Historically, psychoanalytic theory has evolved from an early concentration on the identification of the instincts and their development, to a focusing on the characteristics, synthesis, and functions of the ego, to a contemporary interest in the early mother-child dyad and its decisive impact upon ego development and object relations. The comparatively recent integration of a systematic psychology of the self, a broadened psychodynamic developmental theory, and a modern object-relations theory into the mainstream of psychoanalytic theory is now providing the conceptual basis for a more comprehensive and phenomenological clinical theory. This evolution is in concert with a theoretical movement away from an "experience-distant" metapsychology couched in a mechanistic natural science framework of impersonal structures, forces, and energies to a more "experience-near" clinical theory primarily concerned with the representational world as a core focus (Stolorow & Atwood, 1979). Contemporary psychoanalytic theorists and researchers are progressively appreciating the complex interactions among early formative relationships, the developmental level and quality of internal structures (including thought processes and defensive organization),

the internal representational world, and the nature of ongoing interpersonal relationships and the ways they are internalized and become part of the personality.

Recently, many of what were once regarded to be quintessential tenets and propositions of psychoanalytic theory have been drastically reformulated. Whereas instinct theory and later ego psychology were once the conceptual nucleus of psychoanalytic theory, psychoanalysis has increasingly become a developmental psychology of self and object relations. The shift from classical psychoanalytic drive psychology to the emergence of developmental theory, self-psychology, and object-relations theory into the mainstream of psychoanalytic thought is part and parcel of the "widening scope of psychoanalysis" (Stone, 1954). It is associated with a theoretical and treatment interest in more disturbed patients extending beyond an exclusive focus on the intricacies of neurotic conditions, so lucidly articulated by Freud. Paralleling this change is the view that the instinctual drives of sex and aggression are but one aspect of experience that must be integrated with other dimensions, whether they be of internal or environmental origin.

Within contemporary psychoanalytic thought, one notes a confluence of attachment theory (Bowlby, 1969), cognitive theory (Piaget, 1954; Werner, 1948), and traditional ego psychology (e.g., Hartmann, 1958; Rapaport, 1967), all within a developmental framework (Mahler, Pine, & Bergman, 1975). The major contemporary thrust within psychoanalytic theory is on the development of a differentiated, cohesive, and integrated representational world that is seen as developing within the context of a maternal or primary matrix, termed by Winnicott (1965) "a holding environment." The primary caretaking agent, in turn, is seen as the mediator of psychological organization and structure formation.

In keeping with these developments, psychoanalysis or psychoanalytic psychotherapy is increasingly being conceptualized object relationally as a therapeutic matrix within which the therapist is viewed as the mediator of organization (Winnicott, 1965). Clinicians are directing greater attention to the specific and unique nature of the therapeutic situation, the treatment relationship, and communicative transactions as a database. In turn, broadened meaning is being attributed to transference and countertransference phenomena—there is a greater emphasis in treatment on the "here and now" rather than the "there and then" (Gill, 1982).

Psychology of the Self

Kohut (1971, 1977), in a series of major publications has laid the theoretical foundation for a systematic psychoanalytic psychology of the self. In a paper with significant diagnostic implication, Tolpin and Kohut (1980) distinguished between more classical neurotic psychopathology and what they termed pathology of the self. Unlike neurosis, which is presumed to originate in later childhood and at a time where there is self-other differentiation and when the various agencies of the mind (id, ego, superego) have been firmly established, self-pathology begins in early childhood and at a point when psychic structures are still in formation. Self-pathology stems from the absence of a cohesive sense of self; symptoms occur when an insecurely established self is threatened by dangers of psychological disintegration, fragmentation, and devitalization. Unlike the neurotic patient, who develops a transference neurosis in which the therapist is experienced as a new edition of the parents and thus an object of libidinal and aggressive urges, patients with self-pathology develop a treatment relationship in which the therapist is used to correct or carry out a function that should be managed intrapsychically; that is, the therapist becomes a "self object." What interpretation is to the classical treatment of the neurosis, empathy is to the treatment of self disorders, termed narcissistic conditions.

Developmental Theory

A second major advance in psychoanalysis has been the elaboration of an empirically based, dynamic, developmental theory. Mahler (1971) and her colleagues (Mahler et al., 1975) have carefully observed children and their caretakers and have described the steps in what they term the separation-individuation process. First is the infant's differentiation or "hatching" from a symbiotic fusion with the mother. Next comes the period of the infant's absorption in his or her own autonomous functioning to the near exclusion of the mother (practicing subphase). Then, there is the all-important period of rapprochement, in which the child, precisely because of a more clearly perceived state of separateness from the mother, is prompted to redirect attention back to the mother, often in provocative ways. Finally, the child acquires a primitive sense of self, of individual identity, and of object constancy.

Object Relations Theory

A third major advance within psychoanalytic theory is modern object-relations theory. Object-relations theory, or object-relational thinking (Guntrip, 1974) does not constitute a singular organized set of concepts, principles, or formulations or a systematized theory. Rather, it represents a broad spectrum of thought that historically and collectively has taken the form of a movement or line of conceptual development within psychoanalysis.

An understanding of the development of object relations has been proposed by Blatt (1974), who integrated the psychoanalytic theories of Jacobson (1964), Mahler et al. (1975), A. Freud (1965), and Fraiberg (1969) with the cognitive-developmental theories of Piaget and Werner. According to Blatt and Lerner (1983), the formulations of the cognitive-developmental psychologists about the child's development of cognitive schemas have been based primarily on the study of children in states of relative quiescence in which the child responds primarily to inanimate objects. Psychoanalytic theorists advance formulations of development of cognitive-affective structures based on the investigation of children in states of relative comfort and discomfort within personal relationships (Wolff, 1967) expressed primarily in terms of concepts of the self and others.

According to psychoanalytic theorists such as Mahler, Jacobson, and Anna Freud, the representations of self and of others are initially vague and diffuse, and develop gradually to become consistent, relatively realistic representations of actual people and events. Based initially on pleasurable and unpleasurable experiences of frustration and gratification, the child begins to develop stable representations of the self and of others and to establish enduring investments and affective commitments. During the earliest state, representations of the self, the object, and interpersonal experience is merged, nondifferentiated, affectively charged sensorimotor experience of pleasure or nonpleasure. During these early stages of what Mahler terms autism and symbiosis, the infant is in a state of undifferentiated fusion and attachment to the mother. Gradually, the infant begins to perceive need satisfaction as coming from the maternal object, and there is a shift from the internal experience of pleasure to an awareness of a need-satisfying object. Initially, the external object is recognized primarily in terms of its anaclitic need-gratifying functions and actions. Slowly, the child becomes able to differentiate representations of him or her self and of others. With development, representations of self and of self in relationship to objects become more stable, constant, and, increasingly, particularly during adolescence, integrated into a sense of identity.

Within object-relations theory, the concept, object representation, has served as a superordinate construct. Defined broadly, object representation refers to the conscious and unconscious mental schemata, including cognitive, affective, and experiential dimensions of objects encountered in reality (Blatt, 1974). Beginning within an interpersonal matrix as vague and variable sensorimotor experiences of pleasure and nonpleasure, these schemata develop into increasingly differentiated, consistent, and relatively realistic representations of the self and the object world. Earlier forms of representations are based more on action sequences associated with the gratification of needs; intermediate forms are based on specific perceptual features; and higher forms are more symbolic and conceptual. Whereas these schemata evolve from and are intertwined with the developmental internalization of object relations and ego functions, the developing representations provide a new organization of templates for experiencing object relations.

Formulations derived from contemporary psychoanalytic theory are beginning to provide a phenomenologically based, experience-near, and clinically relevant theoretical model that can contribute to a fuller understanding of the multiple dimensions of personality development in adolescence. The development of the psychoanalytic theory of adolescence has in many ways paralleled the development of psychoanalytic theory in general, with an early emphasis on drives, followed by an increasing focus on ego development and object relations. Early psychoanalytic theory emphasized innate drives of sex and aggression that were held to unfold in predetermined ways. These were expressed in a sequence of universal psychosexual stages (oral, anal, phallic) with specific bodily zones of conflict and pivotal stages of development (e.g., the Oedipus complex). Esman (1975) offers the following comment on Sigmund Freud's (1905/1957) essay on the theory of sexuality and the transformations of puberty:

> Freud's argument is couched in terms of his libidinal theory; i.e., that the sexual drive is powered by a type of energy which he calls "libido," and that it undergoes a developmental course in which, after a succession of childhood ("pregenital") stages, it achieves its mature culmination in "genital primacy." Freud analogizes this development to the flow of a great stream, in which the various pregenital aims of sexuality (oral pleasure, voyeurism, sadism, etc.) are tributaries which, flowing into the mainstream, make their contributions in the form of "foreplay" and some of the secondary aspects of the sexual act. Puberty is, he suggests, the critical point at which all these tributaries merge to form the great river of adult genital heterosexuality. (p.11)

Ernest Jones (1922) advanced the first recapitulation theory of adolescent development, which he saw as a reexperiencing of the first 5 years of life. According to Jones, "the general law . . . that adolescence recapitulates infancy, and that the precise way in which a given person will pass through the necessary stages of development in adolescence is to a very great extent determined by the form of his infantile development" (p.23). Instinct theory, coupled with the recapitulation hypothesis, gave rise to what may be considered the psychoanalytic "storm and stress" model of adolescence.

In her early writings, Anna Freud (1958) emphasized instinctual anxiety at puberty. She observed the pubescent ego's dread of the instincts, deriving from that time in early development when the ego is in the process of separating from an undifferentiated id. At puberty, when the ego is threatened by the upsurge of instincts, the adolescent reverts back to, or regresses to the primitive level of dread of the instincts. In this view, regression is seen as one of several defenses the adolescent relies on to sustain the id-ego differentiation and to ensure the permanence of the ego against the storm of the drives stirred up at puberty.

Anna Freud (1965) was instrumental in the development of ego psychology. Her book *The Ego and the Mechanisms of Defense* is regarded as a classic. In terms of adolescence, Anna Freud emphasized the impact of puberty on ego organization. In her paper on adolescence (1958), she further developed the hypothesis of adolescence as a period of normative "storm and stress":

> I take it that it is normal for an adolescent to behave for a considerable length of time in an inconsistent and unpredictable manner; to fight his impulses and to accept them; to ward them off successfully and to be overrun by them; to love his parents and to hate them; to revolt against them and to be dependent on them; to be deeply ashamed to acknowledge his mother before others and, unexpectedly, to desire heart-to-heart talks with her; to thrive on imitation of and identification with others while searching unceasingly for his own identity; to be more idealistic, artistic, generous, and unselfish than he will ever be again, but also the opposite: self-centered, egoistic, calculating. Such fluctuations between extreme opposites would be deemed highly abnormal at any other time of life. At this time they may signify no more than that an adult structure of personality takes a long time to emerge, that the ego of the individual in question does not cease to experiment and is in no hurry to close down on possibilities. (p.221)

The writings of Erik Erikson (1950, 1964, 1978) have had an enormous influence on the field. While Anna Freud emphasized the interface between the developing ego and the drives, Erikson's formulations on development stress the interaction between the ego and the environment in the form of "normative crises"— nodal points in development that determine the outcome of subsequent developmental stages. Erikson's concept of ego identity and the experience of adolescents in maintaining and promoting a sense of personal identity is a classic psychoanalytic formulation of the adolescent process.

Recently, the contributions of Blos (1979) have greatly influenced the psychoanalytic theory of adolescence with an important shift in emphasis from instinct theory and ego psychology to object relations. Blos furthers the recapitulation hypothesis in his view of adolescence as essentially a second individuation process, an opportunity for the individual to definitively resolve conflicts dating back to the first individuation phase at the end of the 3rd year of life. According to Blos, regression is imperative in permitting the individual this "second chance." Regression in this case is seen as nondefensive in the service of development. By recapitulating and reworking previously internalized, early conflictual relationships, the young adolescent is free to form new, nonincestuous relationships. The adolescent ego is strong enough to handle this task due to the maturation that has occurred during the previous stage of latency. According to Blos (1979):

> Discounting the assumption of a fundamental enmity between ego and id, I came to the conclusion that the task of psychic restructuring by regression represents the most formidable psychic work of adolescence. Just as Hamlet, who longs for the comforts of sleep but fears the dreams that sleep might bring, so the adolescent longs for the comforts of drive gratification, but fears the reinvolvements of infantile object relations. Paradoxically, only through regression, drive and ego regression, can the adolescent task be fulfilled. (p. 164)

Blos (1979) adds that this nondefensive regression frequently evokes anxiety; when the anxiety becomes unmanageable, secondary defensive measures are activated. It is under these circumstances that one sees the erratic, tumultuous behavior associated with adolescence; that is, when youngsters have to resort to extreme behaviors to guard against regressive dissolution.

Recently, a number of authors have questioned Anna Freud's storm and stress model of adolescent development. According to Offer (1969):

> Studies of normal populations that exhibit little behavioral disequilibrium might eventually lead to the concept that adolescence as a period of growth can be undergone without serious disruptions between the generations or between the adolescent and his former identity. The transition to adulthood may be accomplished gradually, but accomplished all the same. Our findings emphatically suggest that a state of inner turmoil need not be the password of adolescence. (p. 1129)

Masterson (1968) also, from a more psychoanalytic perspective, takes issue with the storm and stress model. According to Masterson, extreme turmoil is indicative of disturbance and the need for treatment.

CONTEMPORARY ISSUES

With the integration of a systematic psychology of the self, a modern object-relations theory, a developmental perspective into the mainstream of psychoanalysis, and a shift in emphasis within psychoanalytic theory, new models of personality formation and development are beginning to appear. Whereas earlier models were derived from theories of instinct and ego development, these newer models issue from theories of structure and structure formation in development. These latter views start from the proposition that development involves the growth and differentiation of psychological functions that crystallize into more stable psychological structures. Psychic conflict can occur among these various structures and can lead to psychopathology, as conceptualized in earlier models. However, in addition, the structures themselves can be pathological as a result of incomplete or arrested development. These conceptual advances have facilitated the introduction of a developmental perspective in which major attention is accorded the role of pivotal interpersonal relationships on structure formation.

Concepts of adolescent development as the result of psychic conflict and unconscious strivings gave rise to theoretical and clinical efforts aimed at identifying the basic drives, the prevailing modes of defense, and the interaction between the two as manifest in the development of character traits and neurotic symptoms. Concepts of adolescent development predicted on structure formation, by contrast, prompt inquiry focused on the nature and quality of the structures themselves, the degree to which they have been internalized, and their developmental vicissitudes.

Adolescence is an inordinately complex and passionate developmental stage, especially in terms of the interplay between childhood and adult psychodynamics, as well as in demands unique to the transition of adulthood. Based on the contributions of Greenspan (1979, 1981), Anna Freud (1965), and Sugarman, Bloom-Feshbach, and Bloom-Feshbach (1980), a developmental structuralist approach focused on the multiple lines or dimensions of adolescent de-

velopment will be advanced. First, important terms will be defined. Second, a number of pertinent dimensions of adolescent development will be outlined. Third, the complex interdigitation between these lines of development through the major substages of adolescence toward synthesis and, with it, the transition to adulthood, will be presented.

Greenspan's developmental structuralist approach evolved out of a complex integration of research data and theoretical propositions regarding infant development. Nevertheless, his emphasis on integration and use of adaptation as an organizing theme make his framework ideally suited for conceptualizing adolescent development and a nidus for applying the most recent developments in psychoanalytic theory to understanding the complexity of adolescent development. According to Greenspan (1979, 1981), the developmental structuralistic approach focuses on how an individual organizes experience at each stage of development. Experience is conceptualized broadly to encompass affective experience as well as experience with the inanimate and impersonal world. The organization of experience is regarded as the final common pathway for multiple determinants of behavior (environmental, biological, etc.). It can be studied in relation to specific lines of development, such as interpersonal relationships, cognition, and moral development.

The developmental structuralistic approach is based on two fundamental assumptions (Greenspan, 1981). The first assumption involves the notion that the organizational capacity of the individual progresses to higher levels as the individual matures; that is, phase-specific higher levels of development assume an ability to organize an increasingly broad and more complex range of experience into stable patterns. The organizational level of experience can be delineated along a number of dimensions including age or phase appropriateness, range and depth, stability, and personal uniqueness. The second major assumption of the developmental structuralist approach is that for each stage of development there are particular characteristic *tasks* that the individual must accomplish before advancing to the next stage of development. This assumption suggests that certain *types* of experience must be organized by means of the structures available to the individual for development to proceed.

In keeping with the formulations of Sugarman et al. (1980), adolescence will be conceptualized as a developmental stage rather than a period of life. This viewpoint deemphasizes chronology and regards adolescence as a qualitatively new developmental level involving specific tasks that must be mastered in the series of developmental increments that mark the course of the human life cycle (Levinson, 1978). Entrance and departure from adolescence is assessed in terms of the adolescent's resolution of the various demands of this developmental stage.

Several different tasks have been proposed as overarching issues for resolution by the adolescent. Anna Freud (1965) has emphasized the psychosexual line of development, focusing on biological maturation in the adolescent as creating the need to rework and finally resolve the oedipal conflict as a prerequisite to the integration of gender identity. Erikson (1964) proposes the achievement of ego identity as the superordinate demand of adolescence. Cognitive theorists, such as Piaget (1954), emphasize the cognitive transition from concrete to formal operations characteristic of adolescence. Formulations from object-relations theory and developmental psychoanalysis emphasize the revision of self and object representations and the separation-individuation process as core to adolescent development (Jacobson, 1964; Mahler et al., 1975). Adolescence is conceptualized as a second individuation stage (Blos, 1979) during which the rival of separation conflicts leads to the resolution of parental dependency and the achievement of more genuine autonomy. According to Sugarman et al. (1980), structural emphases focus on the attainment of ego autonomy and superego maturity, which facilitates a balance between drive-dominated wishes and needs on the one hand and the demands of the external world (A. Freud, 1958) on the other. Under the rubric of structural development, Sugarman and Jaffe (in press) propose a developmental line for transitional phenomena that foster the internalization of core self-regulatory functions that, in turn, facilitate adaptation to increasingly complex internal and external demands. Finally, formulations involving moral development (Kohlberg & Gilligan, 1972) stress the adolescent transition from conventional to postconventional morality.

The broad scope of psychological functions subsumed under these multiple dimensions speaks to the complexity of adolescent development. In keeping with a developmental-structural point of view, the major task of adolescence will be seen as *synthesis*—specifically, the integration of the various dimensions or developmental lines of development (psychosexual, psychosocial, cognitive, etc.). These various dimensions of development are conceptualized as salient aspects of psychological functioning that are transformed over time and are shaped by both maturation and experience. Although actual development is multifaceted and extremely complex, the dimensions of development are considered separately for heuristic and conceptual reasons. These dimensions are interdependent and interdigitate in complex and not fully understood ways. Although these dimensions are relatively discrete during early development, they become more integrated with maturation and experience. Adolescence is that stage in which integration occurs in the form of a definitive sexual identity and character structure that is relatively stable and consistent across situations and along a dimension of time.

In what follows, the major psychological dimensions of adolescent development will be considered from a developmental-structural perspective. The developmental thrust toward synthesis will be emphasized both in the normal course of events and when this process miscarries, resulting in psychopathology. Contributions from theory, clinical practice, and academic psychology will be brought to bear to understand these dimensions or lines of development.

The Psychosexual Dimension: Drives and Bodily Experience

There is a consensus among most psychoanalytic theorists and clinicians that many of the major psychosexual passions and conflicts of the first 5 years of life are rekindled and reworked during adolescence. As Sugarman et al. (1980) note, despite the continuum in sensual experience (Klein, 1976) suggested in Freud's theory of psychosexual development, there are important qualitative differences between adolescent and prepubertal sexuality. A metamorphosis of the body, combined with growing cognitive capacities, intersects with hormonal secretions, menstruation, or the discharge of semen (Lidz, Lidz, & Rubenstein, 1976) to impact on the adolescent in concrete bodily manifestations—changing sexual status "feels" different. The core issue among psychoanalytic thinkers concerns the relative impact of puberty on the adolescent's stability and equilibrium. The traditional psychoanalytic formulation derived from drive theory asserts that normal, healthy puberty is a necessary time of psychological regression, anxiety, and inner turmoil grounded in the recapitulation and final resolution of infantile conflicts and object relations. An alternative point of view, derived from research on nonclinical populations, is that puberty and adolescence is not normatively tumultuous, but is rather a milestone in an essentially smooth and continuous course of development (Diamond, 1983). The effects of actual somatic changes at puberty on psychological experience have given rise to two models of sexual development. One view posits the development of secondary sex characteristics, specifically menarche and emissions, as disruptive to the adolescent's sense of self, thereby triggering the storm and stress associated with adolescence. Another view, in contrast, asserts that secondary sexual maturation serves a stabilizing, integrative function in that pubertal growth provides an explanation for the disquieting but invisible hormonal changes that precede the blossoming of secondary sexual characteristics.

The metamorphosis of the body (Sugarman et al., 1980), and with it clear sexual and gender distinctions, is a defining characteristic of adolescent development. Integrating these changes, which are brought about according to an autonomous biological timetable, within the self, the family, and the peer group can be extremely problematic. Precocious or delayed puberty can pose a significant developmental interference (Nagera, 1970) which interacts with other developmental dimensions. This is a period in which the adolescent makes the transition from self-love to love of another. A complicating factor is that sexual and affectional feelings must be distinguished and separated for those of the same sex, whereas they are fused for those of the opposite sex. Early sexual relationships among adolescents often have a narcissistic theme and involve crushes on a partner that is like oneself or one's ideal self. According to Lidz et al. (1976), the object of identification (same-sex parent) and the object of love (target of love, opposite-sex parent) are not well differentiated.

Rekindled oedipal desires and with them the reactivation of preoedipal ties to the mother are regarded by many psychoanalytic thinkers as the most significant aspect of adolescent development. The adolescent is confronted with the need to reexperience the repressed sexual passions of latency while maintaining the incest taboo. According to Laufer (1976), the core developmental function of adolescence revolves around the establishment of a final sexual organization that must include the physically mature genitals. The three developmental tasks of adolescence postulated by Laufer—change in relationship with the parents, peers, and in attitude toward the body—are subsumed within this main developmental function. This investigator contends that the resolution of the Oedipus complex fixes what is termed the "central masturbation fantasy," the content of which contains various regressive satisfactions and significant sexual identifications. The fate of this fantasy, which is thought to be universal, occurs within the context of mature genitals, which places additional stress upon an already precariously stabilized defensive organization. Sexual acting out, drug ingestion, and bingeing can be seen as ways in which some disturbed adolescents attempt to integrate regressive, symbiotic fantasies with mature genitality.

Many adolescents manifest what Lidz et al. (1976) define as an "anaclitic syndrome"—unable to master the essential separation tasks of early and middle adolescence, they desperately seek to establish new, all-encompassing, dependent relationships that are doomed to fail because of the intensity of the needs involved. Some individuals approach middle adolescence feeling empty, lonely, and depressed. Consequently, they turn to casual sexual activity, drugs, and episodic compulsive bingeing to counter apathy and loneliness. One hospitalized adolescent girl had a history of fleeing the inevitable doubts, anxieties, and feelings of loneliness associated with adolescence by prematurely attaching herself to exclusive male relationships and by using sexuality as a conduit to physical closeness and fusion needed to feel secure and cohesive. Lidz et al. (1976) depict poetically the sense of acute neediness:

> Supplies that do away with the unbearable sense of emptiness are, insofar as possible, substituted for a supplier; food that can be

gorged is sought instead of a feeder; the sexual act replaces a lover; a body to hold through the dark and fearful night replaces a person; and drugs are found to be a more reliable source of comfort than a living object. (p. 340)

In this case, the parents' inability to establish reasonable limits or provide patterns for identification seriously hampered their daughter's development. Within her family matrix, the parents were either inadequately internalized or the internalized parental objects themselves were inadequate. As a result, the achievement of object constancy (a differentiated self from object), a firm ego identity, and a mature capacity for intimacy without regressive refusion of self with other had been vitiated, leaving the girl dependent on external objects as substitutes for regressive longings for the mother. Accompanying these longings were a sense of self as passive, unlovable, helpless, weak, and depleted.

Interestingly, despite a history of sexual promiscuity, this girl reported that she did not masturbate and in fact had psychotic experiences when she attempted to masturbate. It seems that the anxiety engendered by the temporary regression involved in masturbation induced the fear that she might not be able to reestablish her previous level of functioning. Although masturbation can be seen as promoting development through "trial action" by which autoerotic activity helps integrate regressive fantasies as part of the achievement of genital dominance, in this case, the regressive pull of pregenital wishes undermined genitality and interfered with the ability to utilize masturbation and its accompanying fantasies as "trial action." For this girl, sexual activity and eventual psychosis were the only solutions available in her effort to integrate the contents of her "central masturbation fantasy" within the context of genitality. In the face of these contradictory regressive and progressive demands, she felt ultimately helpless and passive. This culminated in a renunciation of her ability to control her body or the sensations emanating from it. In her own words:

I realize there's a chance in relationships to get hurt, I got hurt a lot—it doesn't matter anymore—I knew I'd find someone I really loved. Once you have sex with someone you become dependent on them. I wanted to be with Shawn all the time. I'm a nobody without him . . . I need him . . . I'm very dependent on him, he takes care of me, I'm not ready to be responsible for myself.

The reactivation of preoedipal object ties to the mother at puberty, coupled with the need to loosen that ambivalent, infantile tie, set the groundwork for an intense, desperate turning to men in a highly sexualized way. In this case, sexual activity had many meanings and served many psychosexual functions, not the least of which were a defense against regressive incestuous strivings. Sexuality also served as a defense against separateness and as an attempt to merge with a need-satisfying, empathically responding, mirroring other in a total and complete way. Also, while she was in the maelstrom of a psychotic decompensation, sexual promiscuity served to relieve unbearable tension and to stave off dysphoric feelings and psychotic experience. Her sexual activity, indiscriminate drug ingestion, and eating binges may be characterized by their immense orality. In talking about the meaning of love, she said " . . . it means having someone to look after you who really cares—when they offer to do things for you, to walk you home, buy presents, pay attention to you . . . to be taken care of."

There is a compelling consensus within the psychoanalytic clinical literature, particularly the growing literature on the borderline adolescent, that the establishment of gender identity and the working through of psychosexual issues is problematic for many adolescents. It is not unusual clinically to see sexuality both over-infused with aggressive fears and oral longings. It should be noted that the very fears and longings that can lead to precocious sexual activity in some adolescents can be manifested through avoidance, constriction, and massive inhibition in others.

The question remains, however, whether puberty triggers drive regression and inner turmoil, as suggested by many psychoanalytic clinicians and theorists (the storm and stress model), or whether it is simply a nodal point in an essentially smooth course of development, as suggested by research on normal adolescents. Both questionnaires and projective tests were used by Diamond (1983) to examine the conscious and unconscious experiences of regression, anxiety, and self-image across the stages of puberty in 74 seventh- and eighth-grade girls. Pubertal age, determined by both menstrual status and by the subjects' self-ratings on Tanner's Pubertal Age Scale, were used to define groups. Regression in both personality structure and drives was measured using multiple objective and projective measures.

Diamond's (1983) results support a model of development marked by regression in psychosexual level and in aspects of psychological functioning, but without the storm and stress described in the clinical literature. Specifically, Diamond (1983) reports that menarche triggers regression to preoedipal modes of object relations, with a marked increase in oral nurturant longings for the fantasized "good mother." Regression also occurred in areas of psychological functioning, particularly in the postmenarcheal adolescent's difficulty maintaining a concept of the "mother" as a whole and benevolent object. There were no differences between the prepubertal and pubertal girls in anxiety or overall self-image. According to Diamond (1983), puberty triggers drive and ego regression in normal girls. However, the healthy girl's ego, combined with the sense of inner security provided by the fantasy of the "good" mother, modulates the disruptive impact of this regression and protects the normal girl against the storm and stress described in the clinical literature.

The Psychosocial Dimension: Strivings for Ego Identity

Whereas more classical psychoanalytic theorists have stressed the role of psychosexuality in adolescent development from an intrapsychic perspective, Erikson (1950, 1964, 1978), in a series of influential papers and books, has stressed the importance of the broader social context of the adolescent. In concert with the task of integrating psychosexual changes, Erikson notes that the adolescent is also confronted with the difficult task of assessing society, assimilating those values that appear sensible, and finding a place within society. To do so, according to Erikson, is to develop a sense of identity, a sense of who he or she is as a unique individual across situations and through historical time, and a sense of self-sameness (consistency). Erikson suggests that adolescence is a time of life when there is a simultaneous demand to achieve commitments to physical inti-

macy, to decisive occupational choice, and to psychosocial definition—all central to components of adult role identity.

Staples and Smarr (1980) assert that:

> The various identifications must be worked out and consolidated into forms that simultaneously satisfy certain internal and external needs. They must be internally consistent with each other and with the moral value system that is chosen. Social roles must be adopted that are consistent with the predominant identifications and which provide a fulfilling lifestyle for these identifications and value systems. Moreover, these social roles must also provide reality testing of those values and be compatible enough with them. (p. 485)

Adolescence is a stage of poignant encounters with adult role models outside the family who can potentially serve as important alternatives to or modulators of parental identifications. The process of ego identity formation facilitates the resolution of both preoedipal and oedipal ambivalences through relatively conflict-free identifications with role models. Finding these role models may foster more positive identifications with the parent of the same sex.

Identity formation may be viewed as combining the adolescent's sense of uniqueness, an unconscious striving for continuity of experience, and a solidarity with group ideals (Sugarman et al., 1980). According to Erikson (1968), "Identity in this connection, has a claim to recognition as the adolescent ego's most important accomplishment" (p.211). The formation of ego identity may be formulated intrapsychically as a process that results in the integration of self and object representations with actual interpersonal behavior. As Erikson (1950) notes:

> Ego identity is . . . more than the sum of the childhood identifications. It is the accrued experience of the ego's ability to integrate all identifications with the vicissitudes of the libido, with the aptitudes developed out of endowment and with the opportunities offered in social roles. (p.261)

Identity formation can also go awry. Difficulties disengaging from the parents and parental identifications can take the form of either precocious, wholly positive imitations of parental models without the self-testing and societal questioning that mature identity requires or the equally compulsive negative identity and wholesale rebellion against parents and society that can easily be found by declaring who one is not. Often, revolt against parents and society is matched by unquestioned conformity to the peer group. In this regard, the peer group can be seen as a transitional phenomenon between the nuclear family and integration with social norms and values.

An important outcome of identity in late adolescence is the synthesis of a stable and integrated character structure. During the early and middle phases of this stage, there is considerable variability and nonintegration of various self-representations and an absence of a definitive defensive structure and a predominant central dynamic concern. Many theorists and clinicians draw a distinction between "identity diffusion" and "identity confusion." Often, precocious character formation and a precipitous foreclosure of identity are not just defensive attempts to stave off regression and a loss of self-definition. They can also be an adaptive effort to deal with "identity diffusion—a splitting of self-images, a loss of center, and a dispersion" (Erikson, 1968). Whereas identity confusion is often a normative aspect of identity formation, identity diffusion is more malignant and involves a fundamental loss of clarity and definition as to who one is. It is not unusual for some disturbed adolescents to exhibit identity confusion in regard to gender identity.

Identity confusion manifested along the psychosocial dimension is illustrated in the following case of an 18-year-old, white male who was the youngest of three children in a wealthy, intact suburban family. After he dropped out of college, hospitalization was recommended because of his tendency to steal, connive, or resort to impulsive acts in order to avoid feeling empty, inadequate, and nonmasculine. Although behavioral and interpersonal problems were apparent as early as age 9, serious difficulties involving self-mutilation, polymorphous perverse sexual activities, drug abuse, and many arrests for forging checks began after his unsuccessful attempt to attend college.

Bill presented a somewhat effeminate, exceptionally well-dressed and well-groomed appearance and wore a small gold earring in his left ear. Concerning his major problems he stated that: "I keep trying to succeed and I just don't," "I hate hard work," "I have a terrible fear of the unknown," and "I don't know where I live emotionally." Behind exhibitionistic displays of bravado about his bisexuality and ability to please a woman, Bill reported feelings of low self-esteem, bodily defectiveness, an inability to tolerate discomfort, a fear of rejection, strong dependence on and rage at his father, and an inability to experience emotions. He claimed that "the trouble is, my emotions are not connected. I go through life physically and intellectually, but without feeling." He stated that he learned how to act angry, for example, by watching others, but that he rarely experienced anger. He asserted that he presents himself to the world "in images and facades."

Bill's mother described him as ". . . a delight from the very beginning . . . the child mothers dream of . . . he would go to sleep happy and wake up happy." Bill "loved people . . . was flirtatious and even at a very early age, women were charmed by him." He never developed peer relationships and complained about being bullied and that people took advantage of him. He was characterized as a loner and as effeminate.

During early adolescence, Bill became involved with neighborhood boys whom he recalls stripping him and tying him to a post and then spanking him with branches. Although repulsed by his "friends," he smiled as he spoke about his suffering and seemed, in a perverse way, to enjoy describing it. He was introduced to alcohol by these friends and several times they abandoned him drunk in the street. He said that his parents did not interfere because they knew he needed friends.

There was little constructive interaction between Bill and his parents, who viewed him as a child, fearful of eliciting his "temper tantrums." Bill viewed his father as the ideal business tycoon and as "a stingy cocksucker who denies me the essentials." This adolescent does not meet many of Kernberg's (1976) criteria that distinguish a normal identity crisis from a more pathological identity confusion: the capacity to experience guilt and concern and a genuine wish to be reparative, the capacity for establishing lasting nonexploitative relationships, and a consistently expanding and deepening set of values regardless of whether in conformity or opposition to the prevailing culture. Normal adolescents, in contrast to the present case example, are thought to exhibit an internal consistency between values, behavior, and relationships to others.

The Cognitive Dimension: The Emergence of Formal Operations

The cognitive dimension underlies and inter-acts with other dimensions, particularly the ego structural dimension, in important and com-plex ways; nevertheless, it will, for conceptual purposes, be considered separately. Many at-tempts have been made to integrate formula-tions from cognitive psychology with drive the-ory (Wolff, 1960), ego psychology (Greenspan, 1979), and more recently with object-relations theory (Basch, 1981; Lerner & Lerner, in press; Sugarman & Jaffe, in press).

An important transformation in cognitive de-velopment takes place during adolescence. In Piagetian theory (Inhelder & Piaget, 1958) this shift is from concrete to formal operations. As Piaget (1954) notes, the principle of formal oper-ations involves the real versus the possible (Greenspan, 1979). According to Sugarman et al. (1980):

> During the stage of concrete operations, the child is increasingly able to think in terms of complex classes of things and to make linked statements about them. Formal operational thinking allows the adolescent to progress from combining the properties of objects into classes to combining classes into classes. The adolescent can, thereby, have access to a com-plete system of all possible combinations (Rich-mond, 1970). This system can be used to solve problems, to generate hypotheses, and to inte-grate identifications. Reversibility of thinking develops. That is, formal operations reverse the possible and the real. . . . Such reversibili-ty frees adolescents from the constraints of concrete reality. With formal operations [ado-lescents] can act on representations of reality rather than on reality itself. (p. 483)

According to Greenspan (1979), three devel-opments characterize this fundamental reorien-tation in cognition: (a) adolescent thinking be-comes hypothetico-deductive in nature; (b) this thinking involves propositions rather than con-crete events; (c) adolescent thinking is capable of isolating variables and of examining all possi-ble combinations of variables (Flavell, 1963). In that formal operational thinking in general and hypothetico-deductive thought in particular pro-ceed from the possible to the real, they resem-ble scientific reasoning; that is, the implications of a statement are considered and then tested against reality. The capacity to think in terms of

propositions rather than in concrete, observable events frees the adolescent from the constraints of immediate content and affords greater intel-lectual mobility and flexibility. The isolation of variables and the investigation of all possible combinations permits the adolescent to organ-ize his or her examinations into a coherent pat-tern a priori and then perform all relevant com-binations. Greenspan (1979) states:

> The ability to consider cognitively all possible combinations marks the final equilibrium state in development. The system can take account of all possible events on the external boundary of the ego without altering its structure. Formal operations thus have a high degree of flexibili-ty. (p. 212)

The transformation of thinking from concrete to formal operations enhances adaptation in a number of ways. In contrast to the concrete-operational child, the adolescent manifests in-creased freedom in dealing with wishes, af-fects, and object relations—in that both the real and the possible can be considered. Fantasy can become an adaptive and creative modality. Af-fect-drenched issues, such as sex, rage, death, and the meaning of life, can be considered in the abstract; all possibilities and consequences can likewise be considered; and the internal world takes on the quality of a real place. The thinking of adolescents takes on a "what if" quality. As Greenspan (1979) notes, "It is not just that the events of puberty produce an in-tense rekindling of oedipal and preoedipal is-sues; it is also that the new cognitive abilities permit the adolescent the freedom to experi-ence a wider range of internal issues" (p. 212). These cognitive changes facilitate a quantum leap in self-awareness for the adolescent. The internal world can be considered in a proposi-tional sense as not necessarily real—reality and fantasy can be distinguished, thought is freed from action (e.g., anger does not lead to killing, sexual feelings do not lead to incest). The ado-lescent can experience his or her internal world in a more reflective and flexible manner because an appreciation of the possible significantly re-duces the fearful aspects of internal stimuli.

The shift from concrete to formal operations facilitates identity formation by affording the adolescent the cognitive capacities to organize and integrate the representations of the past with those of the present and the future. According to Greenspan (1979):

> The new capacity to organize a number of variables into one system, if operating at the internal boundary, may, from a cognitive perspective, be what makes identity formation possible. The higher level of equilibrium possible—the increase in the field of application, mobility, permanence, and stability—permits the adolescent to conserve more discordant variables than ever before in an interrelated system. (p. 214)

Although the transformation from concrete to formal operations enhances adaptive capacities, it also can go awry. The pressure to move from a world of observable, concrete reality to a world of potential reality often leads to an upsurge in cognitive egocentrism. Sugarman et al. (1980) point out that adolescents exhibit "a failure to distinguish between the ego's new and unpredicted capacities and the social or cosmic universe to which they are applied. . . . The adolescent goes through a phase in which he attributes an unlimited power to his own thoughts" (p. 345). According to Piaget (Inhelder & Piaget, 1958), succeeding levels of egocentrism are relinquished through a gradual process of "decentration" (i.e., the ability to shift from one aspect of a situation to another in a flexible, balanced fashion).

During the stage of concrete operations, the child gradually comprehends his or her own viewpoint more complexly in that different viewpoints can be considered to be held by different individuals and that different perspectives result. With the emergence of formal operations, the final form of egocentrism is relinquished with the awareness not only of the independent existence of objects, but also the independence of his or her own cognitive processes from the environment. As Blatt (1983) states:

> With this reflective self-awareness and appreciation of the nature of his own thought processes, as well as the viewpoints of others, the child can develop genuine social reciprocity in which he can maintain his own subjectivity while appreciating the subjectivity of others and differentiating it from more objective dimensions of reality. (p. 298)

The interaction of cognitive egocentrism with the new capacity to reverse the real and the possible can give rise to serious cognitive difficulties and behavioral problems in adolescence. Erlich (1976) has illustrated the centrality of the cognitive dimension in the phenomenon of adolescent suicide. He suggests that suicidal preoccupations and acts may result from the interaction of two necessary but not sufficient conditions: (a) intense longings for symbiotic bliss and maternal union and (b) specific proneness to vacillation and mixing of cognitive levels of concrete and formal operations. According to Erlich, "This regressive-progressive interplay between the two areas may lead to the concrete and actual treatment of death as the symbolic expression of union with the mother" (p. 268). Seen in this way, the transition between concrete and formal operations predisposes the adolescent to treat abstract ideas concretely. The fantasy of maternal reunion through death is acted upon in a direct, concrete fashion (Sugarman et al., 1980).

The Objective Relations Dimension: Separation–Individuation and Underlying Representations

Blos (1979) has stated that: "we can recognize a thread in psychic restructuring that winds through the entire fabric of adolescence. This unrelenting component is manifest with equal pertinacity in preadolescence and late adolescence. It is conceptualized . . . as the second individuation process of adolescence" (pp. 141–142). Blos formulates the second individuation process as essential to adolescent development in terms of providing the adolescent with an opportunity to finally resolve conflicts dating back to the first individuation phase at the end of the 3rd year of life. Both periods of individuation share a heightened vulnerability of the personality organization, an urgency for psychic restructuring in concert with the maturational surge forward, and, if the process should miscarry, the development of psychopathology. What is seen in infancy as "hatching" from the symbiotic orbit of the mother becomes in adolescence the "shedding of family dependencies, the loosening of infantile object ties in order to become a member of society at large, or simply, of the adult world" (Blos, 1979, p. 142). In order to relinquish these early infantile object ties (preoedipal attachments) to the parents, the adolescent must be able to regress—to reexperience infantile longings and passions with a view toward mastery and relinquishment.

The need to achieve separation is crucial to fostering independence and to permit freedom in seeking more mature object relations. What is particularly distinctive of adolescence, according to Blos (1979), is that it is the "only period in human life during which ego and drive regression constitute obligatory components of normal development. Adolescent normative regression operates in the service of development. Regression as a defense mechanism operates alongside regression in the service of development" (p. 153). The losses accompanying the second individuation process are regarded as a central determinant of the grief reactions and moodiness so often attributed to adolescents. Further, what Blos (1979) terms "action language" as distinguished from more verbal symbolic communication characterizes regressed states associated with this process. Also, Blos (1979) observes a return to "body language" in adolescence, which he sees as a somatization of affects, conflicts, and drives. This phenomenon is responsible for the numerous physical complaints and malaise associated with adolescent turmoil and exemplified by anorexia, bulimia, and obesity. The core conflict of activity versus passivity is evoked in an attempt to regulate what is often perceived as painful tension states. On the other hand, resistance to normative regression during adolescence, either through withdrawal or pseudomaturity, is regarded as an impediment to development and a prognostic indication of later difficulties with separation and the internal regulation of self-esteem.

In order to initiate the momentum toward individuation, many adolescents polarize their world, experiencing others as either idealized or devalued (Sugarman et al., 1980). Often, idealized peer group members, same-sexed friends, or celebrities or antiheroes serve as replacements of deidealized parents. Peers, nonfamilial adults, and often older siblings take on increasingly important and structurally formative roles during this period.

The second individuation period is thought to be somewhat different for males than females. Normative development demands that the adolescent boy identify with his father or a father figure. This task may be problematic because it involves relinquishing an anaclitic attachment to the mother. The adolescent boy is caught between the Scylla of being overwhelmed by pre-oedipal passions and dependency needs on the mother and the Charybdis of rekindled oedipal desires. Competition for the mother's love is managed by an identification with the aggressor, that is, through a strong identification with the father. Thus, according to theory, the father is represented in idealized form in the ego ideal which, in turn, is seen as a prime regulating agency for self-esteem and mood states. Thus, a problematic father-son relationship carries with it the risk that the adolescent male will suffer chronically low self-esteem, uncertainty, and restlessness.

Difficulties of the second individuation process for females are thought to be somewhat different because the mother remains the central identificatory object. Similar to the male, however, the female fears maternal engulfment and the painful sense of a loss of autonomy. Further, her reawakened oedipal passions evoke competition with mother and necessitate relinquishment of the "incestuous object" (Sugarman et al., 1980). The desire to please father is in conflict with sexual feelings and the need to displace her oedipal desires onto male peers.

The reorganization and structuralization of self and object representations during the second individuation phase can easily miscarry and result in serious psychopathology. Masterson (1972) postulates that parental reward for dependency and rejection of autonomy strivings during the first rapprochement substage of separation-individuation are recapitulated during the second individuation phase of adolescence and result in a failure to integrate split self-representations. This original failure in synthesizing object representations interferes with the achievement of object constancy. Consequently, such adolescents are extremely vulnerable to separation and the experience of what Masterson (1972) terms abandonment depression.

Although the second individuation process is a relative concept (Blos, 1979), the reorganization and restructuralization of self- and object representations both impact on and parallel cognitive maturation and have a profound impact on identity formation. The growing representational capacity, facilitated by differentiating from the parents, allows greater flexibility in dealing with both internal and external stimulation and provides a template for more complex interpersonal relationships.

The developmental gains ushered in by the second individuation phase facilitate the formation of new representational structures that interdigitate with a hierarchical model suggested by Greenspan (1979). At the foundation are the developmentally earliest self- and object representations. The evolution of new representational systems from concrete-somatic to increasingly abstract and verbal forms permits greater flexibility in regulating the vicissitudes of drive and affective experience and actual interpersonal relationships. The new representational capacities at each successive stage of development are integrated with preceding representations to form a hierarchically organized, developmentally based system of self- and object representations.

A successful negotiation of the second individuation process during adolescence will be characterized by a state of whole-object relatedness and object constancy consistent with a high degree of differentiation between self and other. In terms of ego identity, an enhanced representational capacity facilitates a personality structure that can assimilate a broad scope of internal and external experiences, integrate them over time and space without major accommodations, and maintain a high level of object constancy despite fluctuations in external situations and/or internal states.

The Structural Dimension: Ego Development

The traditional psychoanalytic view of normal adolescent development holds that puberty initiates a prolonged period of storm and stress, marked by an ebb and flow of shifting regressions and progressions in drive and ego organization until late adolescence. At this time, a process of synthesis and integration occurs that engenders a relatively stable ego and character organization, marking the transformation of adolescence into adulthood. Only in recent years have psychoanalytic clinicians and theorists questioned this view, advancing evidence indicating that the turmoil-fraught adolescent is not necessarily normative and that most adolescents negotiate this stage without major disruptions of personality organization.

The fact that, normatively speaking, adoles-

cent unrest and turmoil is rare does not minimize the stresses of adolescent development. Rather, it suggests that most adolescents bring to bear a system of defenses and coping skills that enable them to successfully negotiate these stresses. Nevertheless, many adolescents bring to this period a fragile ego, or what is termed "ego weakness," that brings additional burdens to the process of individuation and the establishment of more intimate and mature interpersonal relationships.

The structural dimension of adolescent development refers especially to ego development; that is, a complex and multifaceted set of psychological functions based upon interactions among innate constitutional givens, maturational forces, and experiential influences. This dimension includes the innate and developmental strengths and weaknesses of cognitive structures and of drive and affect modulating structures such as defenses. Under optimal conditions, when these functions operate effectively, they facilitate adaptation and further development by freeing the adolescent for age-appropriate tasks not related to conflict. Where there is ego weakness, regardless of etiology, there is either a diffusion or severe inhibition of drives and affects. There may be more pervasive regressions that impinge on cognitive structures, and the vulnerable adolescent confronted with such threats to structural integrity may break down, manifesting an acute psychotic episode.

Affect tolerance is an important aspect of structural dimension. Although the affects of "normal adolescents" can be labile, they differ in both quantity and quality from the emotional expression of more disturbed borderline or psychotic adolescents. More pathological expressions of affect tend to be less differentiated and articulated (Sugarman et al., 1980). The level of development and structural integrity of the defensive organization represents an important aspect of affect tolerance and expression. Some adolescents rely on more "primitive" or less developed modes of defense, such as splitting, in which self and others are seen in global, highly polarized, black and white terms. Because of a tenuous defensive organization, many adolescents are frightened of being overwhelmed by emotional sweeps and are unable to use emotions as signals or indicators. These adolescents tend to take a passive stance in relationship to affects, as if these feelings just happen without any rhyme or reason. In conjunction with a predominance of negative feelings, affects tend to be externalized or projected, hence leaving the adolescent feeling "empty" or bored.

The use of language rather than action for communication implies a developmental advance in ego structure. The prolonged use of action or what Blos (1979) describes as an "action language" suggests a reliance on the environment as a tension regulator. This orientation works against the process of internalization and against modifications within the self that are seen, under optimal conditions, as more adaptive. The use of action either through acting out or excessive eidetic imagery, at the expense of language, is referred to by Blos as adolescent "concretization, . . . a private language . . . which has no communal reference and remains idiomatic in character, comparable to a private dialect" (p. 283). This action language, often manifested through delinquent or self-destructive acts, frequently represents a condensation of perceptual, cognitive, affective, and dynamic determinants. According to Blos (1979):

> Concretization implies, by its very nature, a continued and tenacious dependency on the environment. The silent mastery of tension through thought, fantasy, recollection, anticipation—briefly, through processes that are the result of internalization—appears inadequately and electively developed in these cases. (p.285)

The dependency on action to regulate internal tension is indicative of ego weakness or ego undifferentiation in which there is a blurring of boundaries between perceptions, affects, and cognitions, that is, a confusion between the internal and external, the subjective and objective.

The Moral Dimension: Superego and Ego Ideal

Psychoanalysis and cognitive psychology have both made important contributions to a theory of moral development that may lead to a synthesis of viewpoints (Greenspan, 1979). Whereas psychoanalytic theory involves moral development in psychosexual drive states, cognitive psychology is primarily concerned with moral judgment. Consequently, the scope of cognitive theory is narrower than the formulations derived from psychoanalysis. Psychoanalytic inquiry has focused on moral development in terms of the socialization process and the progressive internalization of standards that modulate potentially disruptive drives. On the other hand, Piagetian theory has focused on the role of higher cognitive processes and role-taking ability in normal judgment.

Working within a Piagetian framework, Kohlberg and Gilligan's (1972) research on moral judgment indicates that adolescence marks a crucial transition from the conventional morality of preadolescence to the postconventional morality of adulthood. Conventional morality is defined by global conformity to a valued social order. Postconventional morality, according to Kohlberg and Gilligan (1972), involves the formation of autonomous moral principles that have validity separate from the groups that hold them and independent from the adolescent's identification with the group. Seen from this perspective, the attainment of postconventional morality is inextricably contingent upon the achievement of formal operations (Sugarman et al., 1980).

Psychoanalytic theorists have approached moral development from the perspective of transformation and consolidation of the superego during adolescence (Blos, 1979; Jacobson, 1964). According to theory, during adolescent development, external changes in relationship to the parents are paralleled by internal changes in the superego in terms of a revival of oedipal and preoedipal conflicts. It is thought that these changes exert a disruptive and destabilizing effect on self-regulation and self-esteem. Sigmund Freud (1923/1957) described the superego as a precipitate of the ego, consisting of identifications with the mother and father and reactions against them. The function of the superego was seen as the repression of the Oedipus complex. According to Freud, functions involving self-judgment, prohibitions and injunctions, moral censorship, a sense of guilt, and social feelings and identifications are all subsumed under the superego. Freud (1923/1957) conceptualized the ego ideal as function of the superego, a vehicle "by which the ego measures itself, which it emulates, and whose demand for ever greater perfection it strives to fulfill" (p. 65). According to Freud, the ego ideal is a precipitate of the child's early relationship with the parents and an expression of admiration of the perfection that was attributed to the parents by the child.

Adolescence is a time of particular stress upon and reorganization of the superego, including the ego ideal, because of the simultaneous upsurge in sexuality, and with it a revival of oedipal conflicts and a strict enforcement of the incest taboo. Blos (1979) observes a decrease in superego efficiency during early adolescence as a result of separating from the parents and their corresponding representations. Modulating the impact of the superego at this time is a crystallization of the ego ideal in the form of identifications with idealized images of the parents and the parents' own ideals.

In summary, six psychological dimensions of development have been delineated that, according to psychoanalytic theorists, clinicians, and researchers, must be synthesized by the adolescent in order to make the transition into adulthood. The organization of drives and bodily experience, the emergence of formal operations, the reorganization of underlying self and object representations, ego development, and a revision of the adolescent's conception of morality and ideals are all modified, reworked, and restructured into a hierarchically organized and synthesized ego identity (Erikson, 1968). Successfully navigating this "adolescent passage," as Blos (1979) defines it, leads to the adolescent taking psychological ownership of his or her own body and thoughts and hence marks the consolidation of a coherent adult personality structure. Although these dimensions interrelate in complex ways, they have been outlined separately for conceptual and heuristic reasons. Such an approach clarifies our particular state of understanding and highlights the often striking discreteness of these dimensions when psychopathology or developmental disturbance interrupts the most salient task of adolescence— *synthesis.*

FUTURE DIRECTIONS

The more recent contributions of the object-relations theorists, developmental psychoanalysts, and self-psychologists have led to a broadened view of traditional psychoanalytic concepts that is beginning to be applied to adolescents. An important aspect of these developments within psychoanalytic theory and allied disciplines is a shift from an almost exclusive emphasis on mental functioning on a metapsychological level of conceptual abstraction to an interest in experiencing (Lichtenberg, 1979), conceptualized in what Mayman (1976) terms a "middle-level language" that focuses on subjective meanings, intentions, aims, and motives emerging from cognitive-emotional schemata (Klein, 1976) of the representational world (Sandler & Rosenblatt, 1962).

These contemporary developments indicate an emerging emphasis in psychoanalytic thought on the experiential dimension and the inclusion of a phenomenological point of view (Blatt & Lerner, 1983). Phenomenological considerations, that is, a focus on subjective experience and personal meanings, supplement Freud's biological, drive-discharge model. A central issue facing contemporary psychoanalysis is whether "psychoanalytic theory [can] conceptualize the individual's total experience, his [or her] sense of the world of people and things actual and illusory" (Lichtenberg, 1979, p. 376). Psychoanalytic concepts now include in addition to an interest in the vicissitudes of drive and functions of the ego, a concern with early formative mother-child interactions and their impact on the development of object relations and narcissism. Illustrative of this conceptual shift toward a phenomenological point of view are two additional lines or dimensions of development that focus on the development of self—transitional objects and narcissism.

Transitional Objects

In recent years, the work of D.W. Winnicott has received increasing attention both within and outside of psychoanalytic thought. Combining the dual roles of pediatrician and psychoanalyst, Winnicott brought a distinctive "poetic evocation of child development and maternal experience in an individual language difficult to link with other approaches" (Dare, 1976). His clinical work with children and regressed patients led him in a remarkably evocative way to verbally conceptualize what is pre- or nonverbal and, eschewing technical jargon, to sensitively describe experience that is blindingly familiar to all. For example, his term "ordinary devoted mother" immediately evokes meaning, precisely because it is colored by personal experience. Winnicott's formulations, particularly concerning transitional objects, omnipotence, and self-development all have important implications for understanding adolescent development.

Winnicott's keen observations express an appreciation of the solipsistic nature of the child's experience and the profound disruptions to narcissistic equilibrium induced by "too much" or "not enough" responding on the part of the caring object. It is in describing the infant's experience of adapting to a shared reality through the transition from absolute to relative dependence that Winnicott's most original contributions reside. The natural unfolding of the infant's growth potential, including developing cognitive and affective structures within a facilitating environment, makes possible a dawning awareness of maternal care and the need for it. In turn, the "not me" gradually becomes separate from the "me," a capacity for objectivity is attained, and an active participation in a world where objects can be experienced as permanent in time and space is achieved. At this nodal point, gradual nontraumatic failures of maternal adaptation to the infant's needs becomes a crucial aspect of "good-enough" mothering and a determinant of the growing infant's capacity to internalize the mother's caring functions and, in turn, to regulate his or her own self-experiences.

The transition from absolute to relative dependence and the acceptance of a "not-me" world, that is, a world outside of the self, corresponds to Freud's notions concerning the transition from the pleasure principle to the reality principle, that is, from a need-gratifying to an adaptive orientation. Winnicott (1951/1958) describes the child's earliest experiences of decentration and efforts to bridge the gap between fantasy and reality:

> Part of the life of the human being . . . is an intermediate area of experiencing, to which inner reality and external life both contribute. . . . I am here staking a claim for an intermediate state between a baby's inability and his growing ability to recognize and accept reality. I am therefore studying the substance of illusion, that which is allowed to the infant, and which in adult life is inherent in our religion, and yet becomes the hallmark of madness when an adult puts too powerful a claim on the credulity of others. (p. 233)

The illusion Winnicott refers to is the illusion of omnipotence. Without it, " . . . it is not possible for the infant to begin to develop a capacity to experience a relationship to external reality or even to form a conception of external reality" (Winnicott, 1951/1958, p. 233). From earliest infancy, according to Winnicott, there is " . . . something, some activity or sensation in between the infant and the mother." It is in this in-between area or "space" that fantasy and reality join and omnipotence is experienced. This space is an area in which the inner and outer worlds overlap in such a way that what the infant discovers in the outer, "not-me" world, he or she also creates. Thus, the illusion of omnipotence is to some degree retained, and the result of the reality principle can be coped with in potentially enjoyable and realistic ways.

Winnicott further articulated this area of illusion as "potential space." His deceptively simple and direct clinical observations led him to the remarkable discovery of the child's first "not me" possession, that is, the "transitional object." Winnicott traced the transitional object to very early forms of relating and playing. The significance attributed to the child's first possession is graphically captured by Winnicott (1951/1958):

> If we study any one infant, there may emerge some one thing or some phenomena—perhaps a bundle of wool or the corner of a blanket . . . that becomes vitally important to the infant for use at the time of going to sleep, and is a defense against anxiety, especially anxiety of depressive type. Perhaps some soft object or other type of object has been found and used by the infant and this then becomes what I am calling a transitional object. This object goes on being important. The parents get to know its value and carry it around when traveling. . . . I suggest that the pattern of transitional phenomena begins to show at about 4–5 to 8–12 months. Purposely, I leave room for wide variations. (p. 233)

The relationship of the infant to the transitional object is marked by several qualities, including a decrement in omnipotence, a relationship in which the object is only changed by the infant, and a relationship in which the object becomes a target for love and hate. The transitional object, according to Winnicott (1951/1958), takes on a reality of its own, combining the qualities of being paradoxically created and discovered.

> It is fate for us to be gradually allowed to be decathected, so that in the course of years it becomes not so much forgotten as relegated to

limbo . . . . It is not forgotten and it is not mourned. It loses meaning, and this is because the transitional phenomena have become diffused, have become spread out over the whole intermediate territory between "inner psychic reality" and "the external world as perceived by two persons in common," that is to say, over the whole cultural field. (p. 233)

Recently, Sugarman and Jaffe (in press) asserted that multiple developmental transitions occur throughout the life cycle and that transitional phenomena are psychologically called upon and used to "regain inner-outer equilibrium at each phase." In keeping with Winnicott's formulations, transitional phenomena are conceptualized as adaptive mechanisms that are used throughout the life span. In this context, the transitional object is considered to be a type of transitional phenomenon that is specific to a particular developmental period. A core premise is that equilibrium between the individual and the environment is promoted through the internalization of key self-regulatory functions. Transitional phenomena are seen as central aspects of this process, because they foster internalization. As a consequence, the "self-representation becomes increasingly differentiated and integrated through a series of internalizations" (Sugarman & Jaffe, in press).

In essence, Sugarman and Jaffe demonstrate how the transitional object facilitates the modulation of tension created by internal and external stresses in development. These authors focus on four nodal points of development—(a) symbiosis, practicing, and rapprochement; (b) the oedipal phase; (c) latency; and (d) adolescence. According to Sugarman and Jaffe (in press):

> The specific nature of transitional phenomena will differ at each stage due to maturational and developmental shifts in cognitive functioning, libidinal focus, affect organization, and the demands of the environment. The level of cognitive maturity is of particular importance in determining and delimiting the manifest forms of transitional phenomena.

Benson (1980; Benson & Pryor, 1973) has noted that what he calls narcissistic guardians become more abstract the higher the developmental stage. We suggest that this finding may be understood easily by recognizing that the manifest forms of transitional phenomena parallel cognitive functioning (i.e., from concrete to abstract). The blanket is chosen by the toddler to serve as a transitional object, not only for its tactile and olfactory qualities but also because the cognitive level of the toddler allows for a concrete tangible object. With the advanced cognitive capabilities of the oedipal stage and latency, the child turns to more abstract, less tangible objects as imaginary companions. Finally, adolescence with its emergence of formal operational thinking ushers in even more abstract transitional phenomena, such as new philosophies and life goals. These observations have led some scholars to characterize the adolescent as a philosopher (e.g., Kohlberg & Gilligan, 1972).

With the emergence of formal operations, transitional phenomena during adolescence become increasingly abstract and ideational in nature. In early adolescence, the key self-regulatory functions are facilitated by symbolic representations of the youth culture, such as career aspirations, rock music, and literature—phenomena valued by the peer group and conduits for separating from more infantile object-ties to the parents. In contrast to the transitional objects of earlier stages, the transitional phenomena of adolescence are more abstract, ideational, depersonified, and less animistic. They are also increasingly coordinated with reality. Rather than the concrete fantasy representation, such as the imaginary companion of the preceding stage, it is the "ideas, the cause, the role or the symbol which has value" for the adolescent.

Transitional phenomena for adolescence, whether they be clothes, records and rock groups, athletic teams, esoteric religions and philosophies, or social and political causes, are thought to promote the internalization of core regulatory functions. These functions include narcissistic regulation in terms of sustaining self-esteem, drive regulation, superego integration, ego functioning, and object-relations development. Through the use of abstract transitional phenomena, the adolescent along each dimension of internalization is better able to synthesize discrepant events in his or her experience. Representational capacities evolve in tandem and become more complex because more alternative solutions and choices can be conserved simultaneously.

Narcissism

One of the most lively debates in contemporary psychoanalysis and dynamic psychology revolves around the concept and the very nature of narcissism and its role in normal development, in psychopathology, and in the treatment process. Freud's use of the term narcissism left many areas of ambiguity that subsequent investigators have attempted to clarify. Clinically, Freud referred to narcissism as a sexual perversion in terms of treating one's own body as a sexual object or as a basis for a homosexual object choice in seeking a body like one's own. Developmentally, narcissism refers to a phase of libidinal development in the self. Object relationally, narcissism refers to either a type of object choice in which aspects of the self predominate or to the absence of object relations. In terms of energy concepts, Freud used the concept of narcissism to refer to self-esteem and to fluctuations in self-esteem as the ego/self is narcissistically invested or cathected. Freud also used narcissism to refer to an infantile mode of thinking, which is magical and omnipotent.

The most widely used definition of narcissism was offered by Hartmann (1950): "the libidinal investment of the self." Hartmann's contributions and later elaborations by Jacobson (1964) distinguished the concepts of (a) self as person, (b) ego as structure, and (c) self- and object representations as subsystems within the structural schema. Some recent attempts at definitional reformulation have involved a dispensing with the energy model and with it the concept of libido. Stolorow (1975) offers a functional definition of narcissism in terms of the "structural cohesiveness, temporal stability and positive affective coloring of the self-representations" (p. 174). Psychological functioning is seen as narcissistic to the degree that it serves to establish and maintain such cohesiveness, stability, and positive affective coloring of the self-representations.

Kohut (1971), in his earlier formulations, retained the energy metaphor but used it differently. According to Kohut (1971), narcissism is not defined as the "target" of the libido (i.e., self versus object), but rather as the "quality" of the libido that determines whether or not it is narcissistic. For Kohut, libido is narcissistic when it involves "idealizing" or "self-aggrandizing" features; that is, if an attachment, either of the self or an object, serves idealization or self-aggrandizement, then that attachment is narcissistic. This formulation is in keeping with Kohut's clinical observation that patients with narcissistic disturbances, rather than withdraw-

ing their interest from objects, tend to relate to objects in highly disparate and intense ways. Such disparate attachments can be understood in terms of the individual's needing the object to stabilize and bolster a threatened self as a result of a defect or an arrest in structural development.

Most authors implicate self-esteem in formulations of narcissism (Kernberg, 1976; Kohut, 1971). Jacobson (1964), in particular, has drawn relationships among ego ideal formation, narcissism, and self-esteem. According to Jacobson, self-representations are optimally and progressively based on accurate representations of the real and not the fantasized self, because they gradually develop out of appropriately accurate perceptions of past and present experiences. By contrast, the ego ideal is based on the wished-for "potential self"—the idealized self as it would like to be in the future. The ego ideal serves the function of holding up to the ego an idealized edition of the self-representation to strive for. It is out of this development matrix that self-representations and ego ideal formation gradually evolve in tandem and that a cognitive-affective schema or attitude toward the self develops. It is in the nature of the "ideal self" subsumed by the ego ideal that will influence the level of self-esteem as well as the libidinal investment of the self (i.e., narcissism).

Several theorists have attempted to formulate the relationship between narcissism and object relations (Jacobson, 1964; Kernberg, 1976; Kohut, 1971, 1977; Modell, 1968; Schafer, 1968). Schafer (1968) relates positive narcissism to the development of positive self- and object representations that arise from relatively positive experiences in infancy and childhood. Conversely, disturbances in narcissism involve primarily negative self- and object representations, which leads to the defensive expenditure of psychic energy for protection and for gaining satisfaction through revenge. Modell (1968) and Mahler et al. (1975) observe that whereas the self emerges from a kind of merger with the object, paradoxically, it is only through the progressive separation of self from object that mature object relations develop. According to Modell (1968), "the awareness of the self as a discrete and beloved entity . . . may enable the individual to accept the fact that objects in the external world are separate and can be lost and destroyed" (p. 59). Individuals lacking a coherent, stable, harmonious sense of self, as Kohut (1977) observes, cannot tolerate the separateness of the object. These individuals need the object for psychological survival, that is, survival of the self.

Basic to approaching narcissism in adolescence is a view emphasized by Kohut (1971) that narcissism is not opposed to object love, it is not relinquished when another is loved; narcissism is rather altered or transformed as development proceeds. According to this view, there are immature and mature manifestations of narcissism, and healthy and pathological forms. Advances in the capacity to love another suggests advances in narcissism. As one can see, the developmental transformations of narcissism during adolescence are crucial in that, by the very nature of the process, the libidinal or narcissistic investment in the self is heightened owing to the pressure to disengage from earlier infantile object ties. With a host of developmental imperatives superimposed on narcissistic challenges, there is a tendency toward narcissistic object choices or withdrawal from objects into a pseudo-sense of self-sufficiency, as well as a resorting to defensive grandiosity and omnipotence to bolster self-esteem. These manifestations are often fueled by the emergence of formal operational thought that leads to a quantum, almost magical leap in possibilities.

Some investigators trace the impact and transformations of narcissism in terms of separate strands or developmental lines (Spruiell, 1975; Tyson, 1983). Particular developmental lines that have been identified and that are pertinent to adolescence include: self-constancy, self-esteem, and omnipotence. According to Spruiell (1975), transformation of narcissism parallels transformations in object relations. In adolescence, this transformation is organized around the acquisition of an adult body image, is catalyzed by the first romantic love relationship, and massively reorganizes psychic equilibrium in terms of developmental advances in erotic self-love, a taming of omnipotence, and a more adaptive regulation of self-esteem.

Self-constancy is a complicated concept that concerns the continuity of the self or identity over time. It requires the ability to maintain self-intactness in interaction with others, as well as the capacity to sustain an image of one's self that integrates different affectively toned "good" and "bad" self-representations. The

attainment of self-constancy serves as an inner support, nourishing the adolescent's sense of safety, autonomy, and mastery, just as does the constant representation of the parents and significant others.

As Sugarman and Jaffe (in press) note, the ability to develop and sustain enduring self-esteem is a crucial vicissitude of adolescence. As parental limitations and imperfections become increasingly scrutinized under the need to relinquish infantile object ties, the adolescent's confidence and competence are severely tested. During early adolescence, self-esteem based upon striving for perfection is equalized through idealistic values, idealization of other, and symbols of the adolescent subculture that help maintain a sense of perfection and are independent of the parents. As Benson (1980) notes, fantasies of career aspirations serve as narcissistic guardians that promote a continuity of self-worth and mastery. An increase in narcissism during middle adolescence is considered adaptive and brings with it the opportunity for genuine creativity in art, writing, acting, and music that is invariably embellished with narcissism.

Fantasies of omnipotence, according to Tyson (1983), play an important role in the course of development as well as in pathological states. Mahler et al. (1975) trace the gradual decrease in age-appropriate feelings of grandeur and omnipotence from about the 15th month of infancy: "the repeated experience of relative helplessness punctures the toddler's inflated sense of omnipotence" (p. 213). The adaptive aspects of optimally implementing omnipotence in infancy (Winnicott, 1951/1958) and nontraumatically relinquishing it during development include: (a) recognition and tolerance of differentiation and separation from primary love objects; (b) reassurance that expressions of aggression do not result in the loss of objects; (c) the recognition that idealized primary and secondary objects are not omnipotent themselves; and, finally, with these advances, (d) a protection from a "basic depressive mood" (Mahler, 1968)—a mood that can lead to intense regressive yearnings to restore a state of narcissistic well-being. According to Tyson (1983):

> If identification with the presumed omnipotence of the object has not taken place, then to the extent that feelings of omnipotence and

power remain important in the person's narcissistic equilibrium and depend on the loved one for their persistence and potency, there exists a vulnerability to narcissistic injury in that area, by disappointment in or loss of the object. (p. 212)

Typically, adolescents who clinically exhibit omnipotence or grandiosity do so to fend off deflating feelings of low self-esteem and self-regard. In a compensatory fashion, they may have a compelling need to be treated as special, a craving to be admired, and an alienating sense of entitlement.

Adolescents whose sense of self lacks coherence, stability, positive affective coloring, and harmony often defend against this narcissistic vulnerability and accompanying feelings of depletion and low self-esteem by constructing what Winnicott (1965) terms a "false self." Winnicott conceptualized the false self as serving a self-protective function in order to hide the "true self" by means of compliance with external demands. Some forms of eating-disordered adolescents (Lerner, 1983) or male imposters (Kaplan, 1984) manifest false selves. The origin of the false self, according to Winnicott, resides in the infant's seduction into a compliant relationship with a nonempathic care-taking agent. When the parent substitutes something of him or herself for the infant's "spontaneous gestures," the infant experiences traumatic disruptions of his or her developing sense of self and accompanying omnipotence. When such impingements are a core feature of the parent-child relationship, the infant will attempt to defend him or herself by developing a second or reactive personality organization (false self). The false self vigilantly monitors and adapts to the conscious and unconscious needs of the parent and in so doing provides a protective exterior behind which the true self is afforded the privacy it requires to maintain its integrity. The false self, as such, is a caretaker self that manages life so that an inner self might not experience the threat of annihilation resulting from excessive pressure on it to develop according to the needs of another person.

SUMMARY

New orientations in psychoanalytic theory involving the emergence and elaboration of object relations theory, self-psychology, and developmental psychoanalysis have converged into a phenomenological point of view and a developmental structural perspective that intersects both with more traditional psychoanalytic formulations and with other disciplines, including cognitive, developmental, and social psychological theories. Whereas traditional psychoanalytic propositions are being questioned, and core concepts such as developmental lines, thought processes, defenses, and the impact of formative object relations on psychological structure formation are being re-conceptualized, these new developments are being applied to our understanding of adolescence and the developmental process. This review has sought to integrate these recent developments in theory and to advance a more phenomenological, developmental structure point of view. Anna Freud's concept of developmental lines was expanded beyond the psychosexual track to include multiple dimensions of adolescent development, which is consistent with recent theoretical advances, research findings, and clinical phenomena.

The emergence of a phenomenological, developmental structural point of view in psychoanalytic theory has resulted in a broadening scope of psychoanalytic inquiry to include an interest in more severe forms of psychopathology, an interest in specifying the mutative factors in the therapeutic process, an interest in very early, preverbal development, and an interest in the development of concepts of self and other, that is, the representational world. These contemporary developments have had a profound impact on clinical practice, theory, and research, all of which bear directly on our understanding and treatment of adolescence.

REFERENCES

Basch, M. (1981). Psychoanalytic interpretation and cognitive transformation. *International Journal of Psycho-Analysis, 62*, 151–175.

Benson, R. (1980). Narcissistic guardians: Developmental aspects of transitional objects, imaginary companions, and career fantasies. *Adolescent Psychiatry, 8*, 253–264.

Benson, R., & Pryor, D. (1973). When friends fall out: Developmental interference with the function of some imaginary companions. *Journal of the American Psychoanalytic Association, 21*, 457–473.

Blatt, S. (1974). Levels of object representation in anaclitic and introjective depression. *Psychoanalytic Study of the Child, 29*, 107–157.

Blatt, S. (1983). Narcissism and egocentrism as concepts in individual and cultural development. *Psychoanalysis and Contemporary Thought, 6*, 291–303.

Blatt, S., & Lerner, H. (1983). Psychodynamic perspectives on personality development. In M. Hersen, A. Kazdin, & A. Bellack (Eds.), *The clinical psychology handbook* (pp. 87–106). New York: Pergamon.

Blos, P. (1979). *The adolescent passage.* New York: International Universities Press.

Bowlby, J. (1969). *Attachment and loss* (Vol. 1). New York: BasicBooks.

Dare, C. (1976). Psychoanalytic theories. In M. Rutter & L. Hersou (Eds.), *Child psychiatry: Modern approaches.* Oxford, England: Blackwell.

Diamond, M. (1983). The transition to adolescence in girls: Conscious and unconscious experiences of puberty. Unpublished doctoral dissertation, University of Michigan.

Easer, R. (1974). Empathic inhibition and psychoanalytic technique. *Psychoanalytic Quarterly, 43,* 557–580.

Erikson, E. (1950). *Childhood and society.* New York: Norton.

Erikson, E. (1964). *Insight and responsibility.* New York: Norton.

Erikson, E. (1968). *Identity: Youth and crisis.* New York: Norton.

Erikson, E. (1978). *Life history and historical moment.* New York: Norton.

Erlich, S. (1978). Adolescent suicide: Maternal longing and cognitive development. *The Psychoanalytic Study of the Child, 33,* 261–277.

Esman, A. (1975). *The psychology of adolescence.* New York: International Universities Press.

Flavell, J. (1963). *The developmental psychology of Jean Piaget.* Princeton, NJ: Van Nostrand.

Foucault, M. (1970). *The order of things: An archaeology of human sciences.* London: Tavistock.

Fraiberg, S. (1969). Libidinal object constancy and mental representation. *The Psychoanalytic Study of the Child, 24,* 9–47.

Freud, A. (1958). Adolescence. *The Psychoanalytic Study of the Child, 13,* 261–277.

Freud, A. (1965). Normality and pathology in childhood. New York: International Universities Press.

Freud, S. (1957). Three essays on the theory of sexuality. In J. Strachey (Ed. and Trans.), *The standard edition of the complete psychological works of Sigmund Freud.* London: Hogarth Press. (Original work published 1905)

Freud, S. (1957). The ego and the id. In J. Strachey (Ed. and Trans.), *The standard edition of the complete psychological works of Sigmund Freud.* London: Hogarth Press. (Original work published 1923)

Gill, M. (1982). *Analysis of transference* (Vol. 1). New York: International Universities Press.

Greenspan, S. (1979). *Intelligence and adaptation.* New York: International Universities Press.

Greenspan, S. (1981). *Psychopathology and adaptation in infancy and early childhood.* New York: International Universities Press.

Guntrip, H. (1974). Psychoanalytic object relations theory: The Fairbairn-Guntrip approach. In S. Arieti (Ed.), *American handbook of psychiatry* (Vol. 1). New York: Basic Books.

Hartmann, H. (1958). Comments on the psychoanalytic theory of the ego. *The Psychoanalytic Study of the Child, 5,* 74–96.

Hartmann, H. (1950). *Ego psychology and the problem of adaptation.* New York: International Universities Press.

Inhelder, B., & Piaget, J. (1958). *The growth of logical thinking from childhood to adolescence: An essay on the construction of formal operational structures.* New York: International Universities Press.

Jacobson, E. (1964). *The self and the object world.* New York: International Universities Press.

Jones, E. (1948). Some problems of adolescence. In E. Jones (Ed.), *Papers on psychoanalysis.* London: Bailliere, Tindall & Cox (Original work published 1922)

Kaplan, L. (1984). *Adolescence: The farewell to childhood.* New York: Simon and Schuster.

Kernberg, O. (1976) *Borderline conditions and pathological narcissism.* New York: International Universities Press.

Klein, G. (1976). *Psychoanalytic theory: An exploration of essentials.* New York: International Universities Press.

Kohlberg, L., & Gilligan, C. (1972). The adolescent as a philosopher: The discovery of the self in a postconventional world. In J. Kagan & R. Coles (Eds.), *Twelve to sixteen: Early adolescence.* New York: Norton.

Kohut, H. (1971). *The analysis of the self.* New York: International Universities Press.

Kohut, H. (1977). *The restoration of the self.* New York: International Universities Press.

Laufer, M. (1976). The central masturbation fantasy, the final sexual organization, and adolescence. *The Psychoanalytic Study of the Child, 31,* 297–316.

Lerner, H. (1983). Contemporary psychoanalytic perspectives on gorge-vomiting. *International Journal of Eating Disorders, 3,* 47–64.

Lerner, P., & Lerner, H. (in press). Contributions of object relations theory toward a general psychoanalytic theory of thinking: A revised theory of thinking. *Psychoanalysis and Contemporary Thought.*

Lichtenberg, H. (1979). Factors in the development of the sense of the object. *Journal of the American Psychoanalytic Association, 27,* 375–386.

Lidz, T., Lidz, R., & Rubenstein, R. (1976). An anaclitic syndrome in adolescent amphetamine addicts. *The Psychoanalytic Study of the Child, 31,* 317–348.

Mahler, M. (1968). *On human symbiosis and the vicissitudes of individuation: Vol. 1 Infantile psychosis.* New York: International Universities Press.

Mahler, M. (1971). A study of the separation-individuation process and its possible application to borderline phenomena in the psychoanalytic situation. *The Psychoanalytic Study of the Child, 26,* 403–424.

Mahler, M., Pine, F., & Bergman, A. (1975). *The psychological birth of the human infant.* New York: Basic Books.

Masterson, J. (1968). The psychiatric significance of adolescent turmoil. *American Journal of Psychiatry, 124,* 240–268.

Masterson, J. (1972). *Treatment of the borderline adoles-*

cent: A developmental approach. New York: Wiley.

Mayman, M. (1976). Psychoanalytic theory in retrospect and prospect. *Bulletin of the Menninger Clinic, 40*, 199–210.

Modell, A. (1968). *Object love and reality*. New York: International Universities Press.

Nagera, H. (1970). Children's reactions to the death of important objects: A developmental approach. *The Psychoanalytic Study of the Child, 25*, 360–400.

Offer, D. (1969). *The psychological world of the teenager*. New York: Basic Books.

Piaget, J. (1954). *The construction of reality*. New York: Basic Books.

Rapaport, D. (1967). *The collected papers of David Rapaport* (M. Gill, Ed.). New York: Basic Books.

Richmond, P. (1970). *An introduction to Piaget*. New York: Basic Books.

Sandler, J., & Rosenblatt, B. (1962). The concept of the representational world. *The Psychoanalytic Study of the Child, 17*, 128–145.

Schafer, R. (1968). *Aspects of internalization*. New York: International Universities Press.

Spruiell, V. (1975). Narcissistic transformation in adolescence. *International Journal of Psychoanalytic Psychotherapy, 4*, 518–535.

Staples, H, & Smarr, E. (1980). Bridge to adulthood: Years from eighteen to twenty-three. In S. Greenspan & G. Pollock (Eds.), *The course of the life cycle: Psychoanalytic contribution toward understanding personality development* (Vol. II, pp. 477–496). Washington, DC: National Institute of Mental Health.

Stolorow, R. (1975). Toward a functional definition of narcissism. *International Journal of Psycho-analysis, 56*, 179–185.

Stolorow, R., & Atwood, G. *Faces in the clouds*. New York: Jason Aronson.

Stone, L. (1954). The widening scope of implications for psychoanalysis. *Journal of the American Psychoanalytic Association, 2*, 567–594.

Sugarman, A., & Jaffe, L. (in press). A developmental line of transitional phenomena.

Sugarman, A., Bloom-Feshbach, J., & Bloom-Feshbach, S. (1980). The psychological dimensions of borderline adolescents. In J. Kwawer, H. Lerner, P. Lerner, & A. Sugarman (Eds.), *Borderline phenomena and the Rorschach test*. (pp. 469–494). New York: International Universities Press.

Tolpin, M., & Kohut, H. (1980). The disorders of the self: Psychopathology of the first year of life. In S. Greenspan & G. Pollock (Eds.), *The course of the life cycle: Psychoanalytic contribution toward understanding personality development* (Vol. 1). Washington, DC: National Institute of Mental Health.

Tyson, R. (1983). Some narcissistic consequences of object loss: A developmental view. *Psychoanalytic Quarterly, 51*, 205–224.

Werner, H. (1948). *Comparative psychology of mental development*. New York: International Universities Press.

Winnicott, D. (1958). Transitional objects and transitional phenomena. In D. Winnicott (Ed.), *Collected papers: Through pediatrics to psychoanalysis*. New York: Basic Books. (Original work published 1951)

Winnicott, D. (1965). *The maturational processes and the facilitating environment*. London: Hogarth Press.

Wolff, P. (1960). The developmental psychologies of Jean Piaget and psychoanalysis. *Psychological Issues*, Monograph 5.

Wolff, P. (1967). Cognitive considerations for a psychoanalytic acquisition. In R. Holt (Ed.), *Motives and thought* (pp. 300–343). New York: International Universities Press.

CHAPTER 5

Learning

Alan M. Gross and Renée B. Levin

The study of learning has long played an important part in the understanding of personality (Rachlin & Logue, 1983). In the 1920s, Pavlov produced an analogue of human neuroses by exposing dogs to increasingly difficult discriminations (Pavlov, 1927). The discriminations were between a circle and an ellipse; the ellipse was made to look increasingly like the circle. As the discrimination became more complex, the dogs barked, squealed, whined, trembled, bit and tore at the apparatus, and lost the ability to make even simple, previously mastered discriminations. Pavlov and the psychologists of his day used these findings to support the role of learning in human behavior.

The relevance of laboratory-based learning theory for understanding human behavior has been based on three assumptions (Rachlin & Logue, 1983). The first assumption, that human behavior is at least to some degree learned, is well-accepted. The second assumption, that experiments performed in the laboratory setting can have relevance for the real world, is often challenged, especially by ethologists who argue for the importance of studying an organism's behavior in the "natural" environment. This assumption continues to be controversial. However, laboratory experiments do allow for tighter

control of critical variables than is possible in the "natural" environment, and findings from the laboratory have been successfully applied to natural settings. The third assumption also involves the generality of laboratory experiments. The notion that data from nonhuman subjects are relevant for humans has been the target of much criticism. Learning theorists are aware that there are differences between species and between situations; however, they have chosen to study some of the many aspects of learning that do seem to be constant across species and across situations. General laws of learning certainly have their biological limits, but within these limits, these laws do exist and can be studied.

What then is the contribution of learning theory to adolescent psychology? Learning theory provides a paradigm for the examination of human responding that emphasizes empiricism. According to learning theorists, both stimuli and responses are objective empirical events that can be observed and measured. Unlike many traditional approaches to the study of personality, in which internal events are frequently targeted as the critical variables for study, learning theory focuses solely on observable, operationally definable phenomena.

Minimizing the reliance on hypothetical constructs and inferred mental states increases the ease with which behavioral scientists can reliably test hypotheses and behavioral predictions.

Learning theorists also suggest that behavior is controlled by the environment. Attempts to alter responding involve modifying environmental conditions that support and maintain the target responses. Maladaptive, as well as adaptive, behaviors are conceptualized in terms of maintaining or eliciting stimuli (Franks & Abrams, 1980). This view differs considerably from traditional personality theories in which behavior is believed to stem from internal conditions.

Viewing behavior as a function of the environment brings additional and important new dimensions to the study of human responding in general and adolescent psychology in particular. Unlike many theoretical orientations, this perspective emphasizes the flexibility of human responding. That is, people are capable of learning new behavior throughout the entire life cycle. This point of view is in contrast with the traditional perspectives in which it is believed that the foundation for an individual's behavioral style occurs during a relatively limited developmental period.

Up to this point, we have spoken of learning theory as if it were one unified approach. Naturally, the picture is not quite that simple. This chapter will begin by briefly tracing the work of a few of the important figures in the field and by defining basic terminology. Next, there will be a discussion of some contemporary issues within the area. Finally, we will consider self-control, a future direction for learning theory.

HISTORY AND DEVELOPMENT

John Broadus Watson is considered the father of behaviorism (Rychlak, 1981). He called himself a "behaviorist" because of his emphasis on observable behavior. In the course of his research with animals, Watson decided that his observations could be divided into two categories: (a) those that could be verified by other psychologists (his observations of overt behavior) and (b) those that could not be verified (his observations of the conscious states of animals). Furthermore, Watson insisted that introspection, a technique for observing mental events in which the mind is said to reflect on its own contents, had no place in psychology. Rather, Watson asserted that psychology should rely on observations of overt behavior.

Classical Conditioning

Although Watson is considered the father of behaviorism, he drew heavily on the work of Ivan Petrovich Pavlov, a Russian physiologist. Pavlov (1927) explicated an important paradigm within learning theory that is known by several names: classical conditioning, Pavlovian conditioning, or respondent conditioning. Pavlov was studying the salivation reflex in dogs. As a physiologist, he was interested in examining the physiological reflexes that occurred following the presentation of food. Pavlov found, however, that as the dogs became familiar with the experimental situation, they would begin to salivate and secrete stomach acids as soon as he entered the room and prior to the presentation of food. To study these anticipatory secretions, Pavlov isolated a dog from as many extraneous stimuli as possible; he then sounded a tuning fork, and immediately thereafter he fed the dog. Pavlov repeated these tone and food pairings several times, each time measuring the dog's salivation. Initially, the dog salivated only after the food was placed in its mouth. Gradually, the dog came to salivate earlier and earlier in the procedure until eventually it salivated prior to the presentation of food but subsequent to the sounding of the tone.

This paradigm is the basic model for classical conditioning: the pairing of an initially neutral or conditioned stimulus (CS), in this case the tone, with an unconditioned stimulus (US), that is, one that already elicits a response, in this case the food. Eventually, the CS comes to elicit a conditioned response (CR), in this case the salivation, which is very much like the unconditioned response (UR), again in this case the salivation. Pavlov referred to this new stimulus–response relationship as "conditioning."

This model has been used to explain the development of many human behaviors, as well as the development of anticipatory salivation in dogs. It is particularly useful for describing the development of phobias or irrational fears. For example, a young adolescent may be afraid of staying overnight away from home. Perhaps as a child this individual became ill on several occasions while away from home. Several pairings of the CS (staying overnight away from home) with the US (getting sick) resulted in the development of a CR (anxiety regarding staying overnight away from home). Another example of the development of a phobia through classical conditioning might involve a young adolescent's fear of doctors. In the past, such an individual has received painful shots from the doctor. Several pairings of the CS, in this case the doctor, with the US, a painful shot, resulted in the development of a CR, fear of the doctor.

Just as the fears of these adolescents may be explained on the basis of the classical conditioning paradigm, so does the paradigm suggest a treatment for these fears. The treatment is based on an aspect of classical conditioning known as extinction.

Let us now return to Pavlov and his dog. Once he had produced the CR of salivation to a tone (CS), Pavlov ran a series of trials in which he presented the tone but did not follow it with food (US). He found that following such a series of trials, the CS (the tone) lost its capacity to elicit the CR of salivation. Elimination of the CR through unpaired presentations is referred to as extinction. In the example of the youngster who fears visiting her physician, an extinction treatment would involve repeated visits in which she did not experience aversive stimulation (e.g., shots).

Although the extinction of a classically conditioned response is a simple matter in the laboratory, it is not always as straightforward in applied settings. Asking patients to expose themselves to stimuli that evoke strong fear responses may be viewed as unnecessarily harsh. More frequently, a graduated extinction procedure is employed. Patients are gradually exposed to increasingly powerful conditioned stimuli in the absence of occurrence of the unconditioned stimulus. In the case of the adolescent who is afraid to stay overnight away from home, the teenager could be taught a relaxation response. Then, she would be given a series of exercises involving exposure to increasingly more threatening versions of the conditioned stimulus. For example, an early exercise might be to pack some things for staying overnight at a friend's house. While doing this exercise, the youngster would practice the relaxation technique. Once this exercise could be accomplished without experiencing anxiety, the ado-

lescent would then progress to the next step. Eventually, she would be able to stay overnight away from home without experiencing anxiety.

Another term related to classical conditioning is stimulus generalization. Stimulus generalization is the process whereby the CR generalizes to other stimuli that are related to the CS. That is, stimuli similar to the original CS come to elicit the CR. This observation is an important one because it begins to demonstrate how generality of behavior develops. In the case of the youngster who is afraid to stay overnight away from home, she might become afraid of spending the evening at a friend's home or of eating dinner at a friend's home because these stimuli are similar to the original CS of staying overnight at a friend's home.

Operant Conditioning

Although classical conditioning can account for a variety of human behaviors, there are many for which the explanation is insufficient. Another type of conditioning, known variously as instrumental conditioning, instrumental learning, or operant conditioning, is used to explain the development of most other human behaviors. The earliest researcher associated with this form of conditioning was an American, Edward L. Thorndike, who did research with kittens in puzzle boxes (Watson, 1978). Each box had a unique "solution" that, when learned, enabled the hungry kitten to leave the box and obtain food. The tasks that the kitten had to learn involved pulling strings, turning buttons, and pressing levers. Initially, the kitten would manifest a frenzy of activity, pawing in all directions and trying to squeeze through the bars of the box. During much excessive activity, the kitten would fortuitously paw the appropriate string, button, or lever, and the door would open. On subsequent trials, the extraneous or unsuccessful behaviors gradually decreased. Eventually, the kitten, when placed in the puzzle box, would immediately perform the appropriate behavior and escape from the box. Thorndike referred to this learning process as trial-and-error learning. Across trials, the number of errors and the time needed to escape decreased. In other words, the kittens became more efficient in their approach to escaping from puzzle boxes. On the basis of this research, Thorndike observed that a behavior that produces positive consequences has an increased probability of recurring, whereas a behavior that produces negative consequences has a decreased probability of recurring.

Thorndike referred to this observation as the Law of Effect. According to the Law of Effect, an adolescent who receives much praise from her family for studying hard and getting good grades is likely to continue to study hard. Conversely, a teenager who is punished for "speaking back" to his parents may cease arguing with them. In terms of treatment, it is possible to increase desirable behaviors by rewarding them and to decrease undesirable behaviors by punishing them.

We have now considered two early behaviorists, Watson and Thorndike. Watson emphasized the importance of viewing observable behavior as the subject matter for psychology. Thorndike began to formulate laws of behavior. However, Thorndike's Law of Effect requires some inferences. A behavior that produces a pleasant consequence has an increased probability of recurring, yet one must infer what pleasant means. This conceptual difficulty was eliminated by Burrhus Frederic Skinner. Skinner firmly opposed any attempt to fill in the gaps between observed events with inferred variables (Hall & Lindzey, 1970). Utilizing principles derived from precise experimentation, Skinner argued for tighter definitions. He promoted the concept of functional analysis (i.e., an analysis of behavior in terms of behavior-consequence relationships). From Skinner's viewpoint, there was no need to talk about mechanisms operating within the organism. Although he recognized the importance of Thorndike's Law of Effect, he suggested a revision designed to eliminate the ambiguity created by the use of the terms *pleasant* and *unpleasant* events. He stated that the basic principle defined by the Law of Effect would be better represented by simply describing the relationship that existed between a behavior and the consequence it produced.

Skinner replaced the Law of Effect with the concepts of reinforcement and punishment. A positive reinforcer is any stimulus that when delivered contingent on the occurrence of a behavior increases the future probability of that behavior. For example, if giving money to a youth contingent on the occurrence of mowing the lawn increases the probability that the adolescent will mow the lawn in the future, then money is a reinforcer.

Reinforcement

Reinforcers support a large majority of human behavior. This is especially evident in the behavior of adolescents. The responses of teenagers seem to be dominated by behavior designed to produce pleasurable consequences. Self-indulgent and self-centered are terms often employed by adults when describing their adolescent child. It is reported that teenagers only want to do what pleases them. Staying up late, visiting with friends, watching television, and eating snack foods appear to take priority over studying, doing chores, consuming well-balanced meals, and getting a good night's sleep. Clearly, most adults, if given the opportunity, would prefer to lead an existence in which most of their behavior resulted in immediate reinforcement. Adult responding, however, requires delay of gratification. Appropriate adult behavior is more a function of long-term consequences (i.e., weekly or monthly pay checks).

Parents frequently encourage behavior patterns in their teenage children in which the youngster behaves in a manner designed to produce immediate reinforcement. Although parents want their teenage children to finish their homework before viewing television, they frequently do not make this a regular requirement. By giving in to the demands (requests, nagging, noncompliance) of their adolescent they are reinforcing what they will eventually label typical adolescent behavior.

At this point, there is no completely adequate general theory of reinforcement; however, it does seem that no stimulus is intrinsically reinforcing, and the effectiveness of a stimulus as a reinforcer depends on many factors (Zeiler, 1978). For example, when a teenager acts up in class, the teacher's negative attention may serve to reinforce his disruptive behavior (i.e., increase the likelihood that it will recur). In another situation, perhaps with his girlfriend, such negative attention will not be reinforcing.

There are four main factors that determine the effectiveness of reinforcers: contingency, immediacy, magnitude, and deprivation (Miller, 1975). In terms of contingency, for a reinforcer to be most effective, it must be delivered only following the occurrence of a target behavior. If the reinforcer is available for a variety of responses, it will be difficult for the individual to discriminate the relationship between his behavior and the consequences it produces. Similarly, if the reinforcer is delivered noncontingently, it will not be effective. Thus, if parents give an adolescent everything he or she desires, regardless of his or her behavior, it is unlikely that a gift from the parents will be an effective reinforcer for the adolescent. It is critical that the relationship between the response and the reinforcer be made clear.

The effectiveness of a reinforcer is also influenced by how closely in time it follows the occurrence of a behavior. The more immediate the reinforcer, the easier it is for the individual to make the correct response–reinforcer discrimination. For example, if you want to increase the frequency with which a teenager does the dishes, this behavior should be reinforced on a daily rather than a weekly basis. In addition, the more reinforcement given after a response, the more effective it will be. What adolescent would mow the neighbor's lawn for 10 cents? However, for $10, he might be much more willing. Finally, the more the person is deprived of the reinforcer, the greater the effect it will have. Thus, money is likely to be a more effective reinforcer for the poor inner-city youngster than for the wealthy youngster from the suburbs.

Premack (1959) suggested a particular way for viewing the reinforcement value of various activities. According to Premack's principle, people engage in a variety of activities that hold different degrees of interest for the individual. Theoretically, for any person, these activities could be rank-ordered from most to least preferred. Obviously, the order would be different for each person. A given activity can be used to reinforce those activities of lesser, but not of greater, value. In other words, a high-probability behavior when made contingent on the occurrence of a low-probability behavior will increase the frequency of the low-probability behavior. Thus, if an adolescent prefers going to the movies to mowing the lawn, going to the movies could be used to reinforce mowing the lawn. The reverse—using mowing the lawn to reinforce going to the movies probably would not work. The order of value of different activities is not necessarily constant.

Reinforcement is a potent tool for behavior development or change. However, reinforcement can only strengthen behaviors that al-

ready occur. To develop complex behaviors, shaping, or a process of successive approximations, must occur. At first, a very rough approximation of the ultimate behavioral goal will be reinforced. Gradually, closer and closer approximations must be performed before reinforcement will be delivered. For example, when an adolescent learns to drive, he or she does not master the task all at once. Rather, the skill is attained through a series of successive approximations.

Punishment

The second basic principle of operant conditioning is punishment. A punisher is any stimulus event that when made contingent upon the occurrence of a behavior decreases the future probability of that behavior. For example, if being grounded contingent on smoking in the house decreases the probability that an adolescent will smoke in the house in the future, then being grounded has served as a punisher. As with reinforcers, what serves as a punisher for one individual may not serve as a punisher for another. As with effective use of reinforcing stimuli, punishers are more effective if they are delivered immediately, if they are of large magnitude, if they are not overused, and if they are delivered contingent upon each occurrence of the target response.

Avoidance and Escape

A problem associated with the use of punishment is that the treatment mediator (the individual administering the contingency) may become a discriminative stimulus. In his or her presence, subjects will learn that the performance of the target behavior will result in aversive consequences. Thus, the individual who is the target of a punishment procedure may not stop performing the inappropriate response, but rather he or she may learn to emit the response when the punishing agent is not present. In other words, the individual may learn an avoidance response.

Avoidance and escape are basic principles of operant conditioning. In escape conditioning, an individual learns to perform a response that results in the termination of an aversive stimulus. The elimination of aversive stimulation results in the strengthening of the escape behavior. This paradigm is also referred to as negative reinforcement. The term negative reinforcement is employed because it is the removal, rather than the presentation, of the consequence stimulus that increases the probability of the response. Nagging behavior is frequently maintained by a negative reinforcement contingency. For example, adolescents often nag their parents when they fail to receive a desired response to a request. Parents generally consider this to be extremely aversive behavior. By acquiescing to their child's request, a parent can terminate this aversive stimulus (their child stops nagging). The fact that acquiescing resulted in the successful escape from aversive stimulation increases the likelihood that parents will display this behavior in future similar situations. It is also important to note that parental compliance acts as a positive reinforcer for their child's nagging behavior.

Another example of how negative reinforcement shapes the behavior of adolescents and their parents involves compliance to parental requests. Teenagers are generally asked by their parents to perform a wide variety of household chores. These include cleaning one's room, taking out the garbage, cutting the lawn, doing the dishes, and feeding the dog. All too often when a parent makes a request, their youngster ignores it or complains that he or she cannot do it at that time. If the parent does not force the issue, the task will not be completed. However, prompting the response often leads to conflict. Rather than argue following a request, many parents will not require their child to complete it. Although a parent may avoid an argument by doing the task himself (negative reinforcement), the teenager's noncompliant behavior is reinforced (ignoring parental commands results in the youngster being allowed to continue to engage in a preferred activity). It is this negative reinforcer trap that inadvertently results in many problematic parent–child maladaptive behavior patterns.

As noted in our discussion of punishment, individuals who administer aversive consequences for specific behaviors become discriminative stimuli. Similar to what occurs during a punishment condition, escape conditioning leads to avoidance. That is, individuals learn to avoid the occurrence of an aversive event. In the example cited above, parents who are negatively reinforced for submitting to their child's nagging behavior may learn to avoid this situation by decreasing the frequency with which they refuse their youngster's requests.

Extinction

Another important operant conditioning concept is referred to as extinction. Extinction involves withholding reinforcers that previously followed the occurrence of a given behavior. This procedure results in a decrease in response rate. For example, if an adolescent's disruptive classroom behavior results in attention from the teacher, such attention may be acting as the reinforcer maintaining the behavior. Failing to deliver this reinforcer contingent on the occurrence of disruptive behavior will lead to a decrease in that disruptive behavior. This tool is a powerful one for changing behavior. Sometimes, however, it is inadvertently used in an incorrect fashion. For instance, teachers may fail to provide attention for appropriate classroom behavior, thus extinguishing such behavior.

When an extinction procedure is applied, it sometimes produces a phenomenon known as an extinction burst. An extinction burst involves either an increase in response frequency or an increase in response intensity. For example, most teenagers have a history of success in obtaining parental compliance to their commands. On occasions when they are unsuccessful (reinforcement is withheld), they often display temper outbursts. It is important to note that extinction bursts are related to a youngster's reinforcement history. Temper outbursts do result in intermittent reinforcement—parental compliance. As noted earlier, the negative reinforcer trap provides an explanation for why parents respond incorrectly to their child's inappropriate behavior.

An extinction burst is generally brief in duration. Although it does not always occur, if it does, it takes place at the beginning of an extinction trial. It is imperative that the patient be warned of the possibility of an extinction burst and cautioned against abandoning the extinction regime. This caution is particularly critical due to a phenomenon known as Humphreys' paradox.

According to Humphreys' paradox, extinction occurs more rapidly when a response has been rewarded constantly than when there has been an intermittent schedule of reinforcement. Consider a boy whose girlfriend always accepts when he asks her for a date. Suddenly, she starts turning him down, explaining that she is no longer interested in dating him. Possibly feeling quite crushed, the young man is likely to stop asking this particular girl for a date. On the other hand, consider a boy whose girlfriend sometimes accepts his requests for dates and sometimes refuses. If this young woman decides she is no longer interested in this young man, it will likely take considerably longer before she stops receiving requests for dates. Behavior that has been intermittently reinforced is more resistant to extinction than behavior maintained on a continuous reinforcement schedule. Such increased resistance is due to the increased difficulty involved in discriminating changes in the response–reinforcer relationship.

Differential Reinforcement and Discrimination Training

Frequently, reinforcement and extinction are employed to modify behavior. Differential reinforcement involves reinforcing one response while extinguishing other responses. Two or more different responses are involved; one is reinforced, whereas the other(s) is (are) extinguished. In a classroom, for instance, a teacher may ignore (extinguish) a student's disruptive behavior and praise (reinforce) her studying behavior.

It is also the case that differential reinforcement can be involved in the development of inappropriate behavior. All too often, good behavior goes unnoticed. Inappropriate behavior is disruptive and results in attention. Parents may fail to observe the lengthy list of good behavior their youngster displays each day (i.e., being on time, courteous, helpful). If, however, their adolescent forgets to complete a chore, parents will call attention to this failure. This pattern results in no reinforcement for appropriate behavior and reinforcement for inappropriate behavior. Prompting parents to change this pattern is usually the first step in a family behavior-therapy program.

Like differential reinforcement, discrimination training also involves both reinforcement and extinction. A stimulus is any physical event or object in the environment that is related to an individual's behavior. An individual discriminates among two or more stimuli when he or she can learn to respond in different ways or with different rates to each of the stimuli. This discrimination ability develops through the reinforcement of a response in the presence of one stimulus and the extinction of the same response in the presence of another stimulus. For example, an adolescent may learn that it is ac-

ceptable to use slang expressions with his friends but not with his parents. Slang usage is reinforced by his friends but extinguished by his parents. Thus, discrimination training consists of reinforcing a response in the presence of a particular stimulus and extinguishing that same response in the presence of a different stimulus.

The stimulus that is associated with reinforcement is referred to as the S^D, whereas the stimulus that is associated with extinction is referred to as S^Δ. The S^D precedes the response and cues the individual that reinforcement will be given for that response. Similarly, the S^Δ precedes the response and provides the opposite information. Discriminated behavior exists when an individual is more apt to make a given response in the presence of the S^D than in the presence of the S^Δ. The influence that the S^D and the S^Δ have over the discriminated behavior is referred to as stimulus control.

Discrimination training differs from differential reinforcement in that differential reinforcement involves two or more different responses and only one stimulus, whereas discrimination training involves only one response but two or more different stimuli. Discriminated responding is critical for successful behavior. What is adaptive in one stimulus setting would be maladaptive in another. For example, the teenager who fails to discriminate between a football game and a classroom and behaves the same way in both situations will have a difficult time.

The S^D often becomes a conditioned reinforcer. That is, through its consistent association with reinforcement, the discriminative stimulus acquires reinforcement value. There are two classes of reinforcers: primary reinforcers and secondary or conditioned reinforcers. A primary reinforcer is any reinforcer that periodically loses its effectiveness as a consequence of satiation, but later regains it after a time of deprivation (Miller, 1975). The prototypic primary reinforcer is food. In contrast, a conditioned reinforcer is any reinforcer that loses its effectiveness both through satiation and as a function of the number of unpaired presentations to the person (Miller, 1975). Thus, a conditioned reinforcer gains its power from association with other reinforcers. A frequently encountered conditioned reinforcer is money. Money acquires its reinforcing power from its association with other reinforcers such as food. Praise, attention, affection, and approval are also considered to be powerful conditioned reinforcers.

A frequent concomitant of discrimination training is generalization or the occurrence of a discriminated response in the presence of a new stimulus. The more the new stimulus is like the S^D, the more likely it is that generalization will occur. Generalization is critical in any behavior-change program. Without generalization, each situation would require new learning. Generalization helps to facilitate adaptation to new situations. If an adolescent is given assertiveness training, the ultimate goal is for him or her to generalize this training so that he or she can be assertive with other people in addition to the therapist.

Reference has been made to intermittent versus continuous reinforcement. In the natural environment, continuous reinforcement (CRF) schedules, or reinforcement for each response, are unusual. Rather, behaviors are more frequently reinforced on occasion or on an intermittent reinforcement schedule. There are a number of types of intermittent reinforcement schedules, each of which leads to a different characteristic pattern of responding. Skinner (Ferster & Skinner, 1957) devoted much effort to studying various reinforcement schedules, and he demonstrated their differing effects.

Reinforcement Schedules

There are four basic types of intermittent reinforcement schedules: fixed ratio (FR), variable ratio (VR), fixed interval (FI), and variable interval (VI). On an FR schedule, the individual's behavior is reinforced after completion of a fixed number of responses. After each reinforcement, there is a pause before responding resumes. In a programmed study book, the student must complete a fixed number of questions before being reinforced by the opportunity to move on to the next unit. Upon completion of this fixed number of questions, there will be a pause before the student starts the next segment.

In contrast to the FR schedule, a VR schedule involves reinforcing the individual's behavior after a variable number of responses have been emitted. The prototypical VR schedule is illustrated by a slot machine. Following a varying number of responses (placing a coin in the machine), the individual's behavior will be reinforced by the winning of money. FR and VR

schedules lead to equally rapid rates of response, but the VR schedule does not produce a pause after reinforcement; consequently, the VR schedule leads to the higher overall response rate. Ratio schedules of reinforcement lead to higher rates of responding than does CRF. In addition, they help avoid satiation and are more resistant to extinction. A disadvantage to ratio schedules is the possibility of "ratio strain" (i.e., when the ratio is so large that reinforcement is not delivered frequently enough to maintain responding).

In contrast to ratio schedules, which involve reinforcement after a certain number of responses, interval schedules involve reinforcement after a certain amount of time. On an FI schedule, a fixed amount of time must pass before the individual's behavior will be reinforced. The first response made after the allotted time elapses will be reinforced. An FI schedule results in a pause after reinforcement followed by an increase in the rate of responding until a high rate is reached just prior to the end of the interval. This pattern is referred to as scalloping, due to the appearance of the cumulative record produced by graphing responses against time. An example of an FI schedule can be seen in the study behaviors of students. Studying increases as exams approach. Following an examination and reinforcement in the form of high grades, studying behavior decreases. However, a new rise in studying will not be displayed again until another exam approaches. With a VI schedule, varying lengths of time must elapse before a response will be reinforced. Like the VR schedule, the VI schedule does not produce a pause after reinforcement. The teenage girl whose boyfriend lives in another state may constantly check the mail for a letter from him. After varying intervals of time, her checking behavior will be reinforced by a letter.

The critical difference between ratio and interval schedules is who controls how quickly the individual's behavior will be reinforced—the individual or someone else. With the ratio schedules, the individual determines the speed of reinforcement. With interval schedules, the individual does not have this control.

For approximately 20 years, Skinner's operant-conditioning theory dominated all other learning theories in the United States. It continues to exert a strong influence; however, this viewpoint has not been without its critics. Skinner's insistence that the effect of consequences is direct, mechanical, and automatic, and further that this effect need not be mediated by conscious ideas has been criticized by cognitive psychologists.

Social-Learning Theory

Bandura's social-learning theory, which is a type of cognitive behaviorism, gained prominence in the late 1960s (Franks & Abrams, 1980). Like other behaviorists, social-learning theorists accept the prohibition against invoking psychodynamic "inner causes" of disturbed behavior. However, they do emphasize the role of cognitive–symbolic functioning in acquiring new behaviors and in regulating the frequency and occasions of their occurrence. Social-learning theory examines learning, motivation, and reinforcement of social behavior in terms of cognitive events mediating the impact of external events. For example, the importance of reinforcement contingencies is considered to be how the individual views them rather than their objective parameters.

Traditional theories of learning attached much importance to learning by direct experience through the application of reinforcement contingencies to practiced responses. The shaping of complex behavior chains through successive approximation was very important. Social-learning theory accepts shaping principles; however, it tends to view the role of rewards in this process as providing information about the best response in a given situation and as providing incentive motivation for a given behavior due to its anticipated reward. Extremely important in the social-learning view is modeling or observational learning.

Social-learning theory added observational learning to the principles of classical and operant conditioning. However, the importance of observational learning has long been recognized (Whitehurst, 1978). Plato talked about the need for good models in the development of human behavior, and Aristotle noted that people learn their earliest lessons through observation. In addition to classical and operant conditioning, observational learning is another means of acquiring new behavior patterns, both adaptive and maladaptive.

According to Bandura (1969), much learning occurs not through direct experience and its consequences, but rather through vicarious experience. Further, Bandura asserts that virtually all learning that results from direct experience can occur on a vicarious basis by observing the behavior of others and its consequences for them. Thus, the young adolescent who observes an older sibling being punished for smoking cigarettes may be less likely to do so. Conversely, the young adolescent who observes an older sibling being rewarded for good grades is apt to strive for this same goal.

Modeling

Modeling is a process through which observers acquire new behaviors. In addition, it can inhibit behaviors an observer has previously learned, or it can disinhibit behaviors that were previously suppressed. For example, a youth who has grown up in a family with poor table manners may be shamed into inhibiting these behaviors when she goes to a camp for the summer where the girls try to use proper eating etiquette. However, when she returns home at the end of the summer, she rapidly returns to her prior table manners. This phenomenon is known as disinhibition.

Bandura has differentiated two aspects of modeling referred to as acquisition and performance. Frequently, an individual will learn to do something through observation of a model (acquisition), yet will never actually engage in this behavior (performance). For example, teenagers may acquire behaviors from watching television that they never actually perform.

One need only look at the dress styles, language, and ideology of most teenagers to see the influence of peer models. Youngsters are exposed daily to peers who are rewarded for displaying typical teen behaviors. In these settings, imitation produces immediate social reinforcement. For example, the ninth grader who imitates the dress style of an upper classman will receive much social attention from his classmates at school.

Television and film are another powerful source of models for teenagers. Children and adolescents are bombarded with a television diet that includes heros who display numerous maladaptive behaviors. Attractive models can be seen being rewarded for abusive drinking, smoking, reckless driving, and drug abuse.

The verbal behavior of teenagers is also greatly influenced by models. Children and adolescents are continually using new words and phrases that are not heard in the home environment. Few parents attempt to teach their children to describe fun things as "totally awesome" and unpleasant events as something that "grosses me out." A youth will hear a new word or phrase at school or on television and then use it in conversation with peers. This verbal response results in attention from friends. In many instances, this reinforcement may take the form of another child beginning to employ this expression.

Although it is tempting to attribute many of the undesirable adolescent behaviors (e.g., alcohol abuse, smoking) to peer and television models, it is important to note that most youngsters' first exposure to many of these responses comes from the model provided by their parents. Children see their parents drink to alleviate stress, use violence in attempts to discipline, or smoke cigarettes for pleasure. Moreover, parents who model behaviors they subsequently forbid their children to perform also set the stage for conflict. For example, the youngster who is reprimanded by school officials for smoking cigarettes will argue with his parents about why it is not permissable for him to smoke and it is acceptable for dad to exhibit that behavior.

When the influence of models on the behavior of adolescents is discussed, all too frequently the focus is on bad behavior. However, a wide variety of appropriate behaviors may be learned from models. Social skills and dating skills can be acquired from observing peer models. Parents also model many important social behaviors. Cooperation, kindness, understanding, caring, honesty, and trust are just a few of the qualities that children begin to acquire through observing their parents.

Modeling is an important concept in the discussion of learning. Models provide the opportunity for adolescents to acquire rapidly numerous behaviors. However, it must be remembered that the learning principles discussed earlier (reinforcement, punishment, extinction) play the major role in determining whether imitated behavior is supported. The adolescent who is not reinforced (extinction) for his imitation of a response learned from a model will not continue to display that response.

Having explained the basic concepts of learning theory, it may be useful to provide an illus-

tration of how these processes might be employed in the analysis of behavior. Carl is a 19-year-old college student at a large midwestern university. Carl's dormitory advisor is concerned about him and suggests that he talk with a counselor at the university counseling center. The focus of this concern involves Carl's apparent discomfort with women and lack of dating skills. In fact, Carl has complained to a number of hall residents about his inability to find a girlfriend.

An interview with Carl reveals that he is an only child. He attended a male boarding school through junior and senior high school. Carl reported that there were few opportunities to date while in high school. Although there were occasional dances held at his school, there were few additional opportunities to spend time with female peers. Upon arriving at college, Carl made a number of attempts to date. He reported that every time he asked a woman for a date she refused. Some of these refusals involved rude behavior on the part of the woman. Recently, he has given up trying to meet potential dating partners.

Although only a small portion of material is presented, this case illustrates a number of the processes described earlier. Carl went to an all-boy school from age 12 to 19. In the absence of women, there would be few opportunities for Carl to observe models (observational learning) who displayed appropriate heterosexual dating skills. This situation would increase the difficulty for Carl of learning these behaviors. Carl's attempts to obtain dates were not successful. That is, requesting date behaviors were not reinforced (extinction) or in some instances were followed by aversive stimulation (punishment). Responses that do not result in reinforcement or produce punishment decrease in frequency of occurrence. Behaviors that consistently result in aversive stimulation generally lead to avoidance responding. In this instance, women may have become discriminative stimuli indicating that approach responses will be punished. Thus, Carl has learned to avoid approaching women and asking for dates. Moreover, although he has been rejected by very few women, this discriminative stimulus has generalized to all women. Finally, his schedule of reinforcement for approaching girls (continuous punishment or extinction) has led him to expect failure following almost all approach responses.

The example presented illustrates how a behavioral-learning theorist might conceptualize Carl's problems. As stated earlier, the emphasis of learning theory is that behavior is a function of the environment. Once response–consequence relationships are identified, the behavior analyst may then develop a plan to alter the individual's environment and attempt to program new behaviors. In the above case, Carl might be given social-dating skills training. Such training would involve having Carl observe models demonstrate appropriate dating behaviors. Carl would then rehearse these responses in a controlled setting and receive feedback and praise for his performance. Upon mastering these behaviors, he would be shaped or gradually required to try these responses in a nonthreatening environment (e.g., friend's party, dorm activity). Eventually, Carl would be encouraged to seek a date on his own. The development of appropriate social skills increases the likelihood that he will be successful. Lastly, it is assumed that a successful date will reinforce dating behavior and help him to discriminate that date requesting results in intermittent reinforcement.

CONTEMPORARY ISSUES

Discrimination and Generalization

In order for learning theory to contribute to our ability to predict and control human behavior, it must be able to account for both the general and specific response patterns people display. One problem inherent in the application of learning-theory concepts to practice is seen in attempts to account for what at times appears to be inconsistent behavior patterns. In the example provided previously it was suggested that Carl's social problems (avoidance of dating) were a result of his feeling uncomfortable around female peers. However, if we probed more deeply, it would become apparent that although this is a general tendency, there are numerous instances in which Carl displays no anxiety while in the presence of young women. For example, he may be anxious when introduced to women at a fraternity party, but be completely at ease with a similar group of peers in a classroom discussion.

Two concepts briefly discussed earlier are imperative to this analysis: discrimination and generalization. Discrimination is any difference in responding in the presence of different stimuli. Generalization is the spread of the effects of reinforcement (or of other operations, e.g., punishment, extinction) in the presence of one stimulus to other stimuli that differ from the original stimulus along one or more stimulus dimensions. Discrimination is the process that accounts for a specific stimulus-response relationship, and generalization is the process that explains why individuals display the same behavior across a variety of similar stimuli.

In the analysis of the behavior of adolescents, there are numerous examples of what parents consider to be unexplainable behavioral inconsistencies. A frequently cited dilemma involves youngsters who are reported as regularly displaying appropriate behavior in one setting and exhibiting inappropriate behavior in other similar situations. This is illustrated by the child who behaves appropriately in the home environment but gets into mischief in school and other social settings. These parents ask why the child's good behavior does not carry over (generalize) to other situations.

The stimulus conditions in the home environment are particular to that setting. Parents establish a system of rewards and punishers for their child's behavior around the house. That is, they create a specific set of response–consequence relationships. Successful application of these contingencies will result in the youth's learning that the performance of certain behaviors will be rewarded and the performance of other responses will be punished. The circumstances of this situation make it such that the dominant stimulus cues (parents) for these behaviors are limited to a very specific environment. Thus, it would be predicted that the adolescent will discriminate these contingencies and his behavior will be subject to stimulus control. Because the behaviors of interest have been primarily reinforced in one specific setting, it is unreasonable to expect to see response generalization.

Similar learning situations exist outside the home. In most cases, the dominant stimuli involve the adolescent's peer group. Unfortunately, for parents, the behaviors that are heavily reinforced by peers are not always those encouraged by parents. In this situation, once again, the youth makes an accurate discrimination concerning response-consequence relationships and behaves very differently from the way he does in the stimulus setting involving his parents.

Although such discriminated responding may result in the youngster's emitting inappropriate behaviors in school (which result in him being sent to the principal's office), it probably results in a much larger magnitude of reinforcement than the adolescent would obtain if he refrained from emitting these responses. For example, acting out in class is rewarded by attention from a number of peers on a continuous reinforcement schedule. It is also the case that acting out is detected inconsistently by teachers so that any aversive consequences it might produce only occur on an intermittent basis.

Discriminated behavior such as that described in this example is a very adaptive skill. It allows the individual to maximize reinforcement and minimize aversive stimulation. Although this may be disconcerting to parents, it is a strength whose existence provides the basis for promoting desired behavioral performance. That is, teaching adolescents to discriminate that there are a number of contingencies associated (immediate and long-range consequences) with each behavior may facilitate the desired behavioral generalization.

Discrimination and stimulus control can account for why the good behavior of adolescents does not always generalize. The particular quality of the stimulus conditions under which these behaviors are often acquired makes it unreasonable to expect generalization to occur without prompting. It is important to note, though, that there is a great deal of generalized responding seen in the behavior of adolescents. General response styles are visible in their interactions with peers and with adults. However, even in these general stimulus classes, discriminated behavior exists (e.g., a boy learns that physical horsing around is rewarded by most but not all of his male friends).

Discrimination and generalization are two processes that help account for the robust quality of human behavior. Generalization of responding from one stimulus setting to other similar settings provides for adaptive flexibility in responding. Discrimination skills lead to specialized performance and maximization of reinforcement. Historically, learning theorists have been most concerned with discriminated operants and stimulus control. They have developed procedures for fostering discrimination skills so that individuals could be more successful in their daily functioning (e.g., treatment designed to learn new discriminations, such as date requests, will not always result in aversive consequences). Moreover, it was believed that the variability of stimuli that exist in learning situations would result in generalization of the new response to other stimulus settings. Clinical experience, however, reveals that generalization does not occur automatically and it must be programmed (Stokes & Baer, 1977).

Parents of adolescents often expect the good behavior of their children to generalize across an infinite variety of stimulus settings. When this fails to occur, they often view this as a baffling problem. Learning theory offers a valuable tool for analyzing these behavior patterns. What may appear to many as incongruous behavior is easily accounted for in terms of discriminated behavior and stimulus control.

FUTURE DIRECTIONS: SELF-MANAGEMENT

Implicit in the learning-theory analysis of behavior is the notion of control (Skinner, 1953). Learning theory suggests that behavior is a function of the environment. The principles of behavior suggest relationships between responses and stimuli. Empirical validation of these concepts requires the manipulation of stimuli to which the behavior is believed to be related. When an independent variable can be controlled, a means of controlling the behavior of which it is a function is discovered (Skinner, 1953).

A large technology of behavior change has been developed from the principles of behavior. The effectiveness of these procedures is well documented. For the most part, these programs have focused on teaching someone (parent, teacher, therapist) to use the principles of learning theory to identify the response–consequence relationships associated with a target behavior. Once this has been completed, an attempt is made to foster behavior change through environmental manipulation. For example, parents who want to alter the study habits of their teenage daughter might be told to arrange her environment such that the opportunity to watch television becomes contingent upon the completion of her homework.

The dominant approach of behavior modification has relied on using a treatment mediator. However, given that the principles and procedures of learning theory are well established, it seems reasonable to speculate that individuals could be taught to apply these laws to their own behavior. In the case of adolescents, the shift away from reliance on external agents would be particularly advantageous. When significant others control the treatment contingencies, they often miss a great deal of behavior. Therefore, the desired response may not be consistently reinforced (Kazdin, 1975). Those who administer the contingencies may become discriminative stimuli. This results in the child's performing the target behavior only in the presence of the individual who delivers the rewards. Moreover, when children control their own behavior, adults can spend more time teaching other skills (O'Leary & Dubey, 1979). Additionally, it has been suggested that teaching children to control their own behavior might result in stronger maintenance effects than those observed when contingencies have been administered by external agents.

As a behavior-change strategy, self-control training has generally involved teaching children to monitor a target behavior (self-monitoring), to evaluate whether they have performed to criterion (self-evaluation), and to reward themselves for the performance of the target response (self-reinforcement). The vast majority of studies conducted on the effectiveness of self-control training with children and adolescents have concluded that youngsters can be taught to control their own behavior (Gross & Drabman, 1982; Gross & Wojnilower, 1984).

Closer examination of this research area raises a number of important questions for learning theorists. Virtually all attempts to teach children self-control have involved teaching the youngsters to self-administer a program that therapists, teachers, or parents would apply if they assumed the role of primary-treatment mediators. Gross and Wojnilower (1984) also point out that virtually all of these studies are confounded by environmental sources of control. More importantly, however, these investigations failed to examine whether the youngsters acquired a working knowledge of learning theory. In the absence of the ability to functionally analyze one's own behavior such that the individual can subsequently arrange his or her environment to support specific behaviors, it is not possible to say that an individual has displayed self-control behavior.

An exception to this approach to self-management training can be found in the work of Gross and his colleagues. Gross, Brigham, Hopper, and Bologna (1980) taught predelinquent youths, aged 11–15, a course in behavior modification. The youngsters were required to read 10 lessons on the principles and procedures of behavior analysis and to complete study guides and quizzes on each unit. Additionally, the youngsters were required to conduct a self-change project and a behavior-modification project to alter another person's behavior. It was reported that the youths were able to learn the fundamentals of behavioral technology and to successfully alter their own as well as another person's behavior. Learning these behavior-change skills was associated with a reduction in delinquent behavior. Moreover, unlike many youngsters who respond negatively to attempts by external agents to alter their behavior, the youngsters in this investigation displayed a large degree of enthusiasm for the procedure. The children indicated that participation in the training program resulted in learning skills that increased their success in both social and academic situations. Gross (1983) and Gross, Magalnick, and Richardson (1985) have also reported using this approach to increase medication compliance in youngsters with diabetes.

These studies by Gross represent a departure from traditional children's self-control training. He has argued that teaching the fundamentals of behavior analysis in combination with practical experience in the application of the associated techniques may provide youngsters with a set of readily generalizable management skills. Providing this general working knowledge may not only allow children to alter their own behavior, but also may enable them to modify the behavior of others who may serve as cues for inappropriate responding. Although these studies are preliminary attempts, they do suggest a self-control training approach that more closely approximates the goal of teaching children to manage effectively their behavior and environment.

The interest in self-management demonstrated by learning theorists reflects a concern for greater emphasis being given to the reciprocal nature that exists between an organism and its environment. That is, not only does the environment influence behavior, but behavior alters the environment. Recognizing the importance of environmental influences will in all likelihood increase the personal influence a youngster has over his or her environment. Youngsters who are aware of the role played by others in their attempts to modify their own behavior will have a stronger chance of arranging the environment to support their efforts than will youths who merely know how to self-monitor, self-evaluate, and self-reinforce. Thus, an issue of the future for learning theorists is to teach youngsters to identify and manipulate response–environment relationships.

SUMMARY

Learning theory has long played an important role in the understanding of human behavior. That role can be traced from Pavlov, Watson, and Thorndike to Skinner and Bandura. Within this perspective, adolescence can be viewed as a time of much learning. Learning theory offers explanations of adolescent behavior and suggests ways of modifying that behavior when necessary. Three major learning paradigms that were delineated are classical conditioning, operant conditioning, and observational learning. Learning-theory concepts of generalization and discrimination were discussed in an attempt to illustrate how learning theory can account for the individuality of response styles. Finally, self-control training was suggested as a future direction for learning-theory research and practice.

REFERENCES

Bandura, A. (1969). *Principles of behavior modification*. New York: Holt, Rinehart & Winston.

Bandura, A. (1971). Vicarious and self-reinforcement processes. In R. Glaser (Ed.), *The nature of reinforcement* (pp. 228–278). New York: Academic.

Ferster, C., & Skinner, B. F. (1957). *Schedules of reinforcement*. New York: Appleton-Century-Crofts.

Franks, C., & Abrams, D. B. (1980). Behavior therapy. In A. E. Kazdin, A. S. Bellack, & M. Hersen (Eds.), *New perspectives in abnormal psychology* (pp. 440–459). New York: Oxford University Press.

Gross, A. M. (1983). Self-management training and medication compliance in young diabetics. *Child and Family Behavior Therapy, 4*, 47–55.

Gross, A. M., Brigham, T. A., Hopper, R., & Bologna, N. C. (1980). Self-management and social skills training: A study with predelinquent and delinquent youth. *Criminal Justice and Behavior, 7*, 161–184.

Gross, A. M., & Drabman, R. S. (1982). Teaching self-recording, self-evaluation, and self-reward to non-clinic children and adolescents. In P. Karoly & F. H. Kanfer (Eds.), *Self-management and behavior change: From theory to practice* (pp. 285–313). Elmsford, NY: Pergamon.

Gross, A. M., Magalnick, L., & Richardson, P. (1985). Self-management training with families of insulin-dependent diabetic children: A long term controlled investigation. *Child and Family Therapy, 7*, 35–50.

Gross, A. M., & Wojnilower, D. A. (1984). Self-directed behavior change in children: Is it self-directed? *Behavior Therapy, 15*, 501–514.

Hall, C. S., & Lindzey, G. (1970). *Theories of personality*. New York: Wiley.

Kazdin, A. E. (1975). *Behavior modification in applied settings*. Homewood, IL: Dorsey.

Miller, L. K. (1975). *Principles of everyday behavior analysis*. Monterey, CA: Brooks/Cole.

O'Leary, S. C., & Dubey, D. R. (1979). Applications of self-control procedures by children: A review. *Journal of Applied Behavior Analysis, 12*, 449–465.

Pavlov, I. P. (1927). *Conditioned reflexes*. London: Oxford University Press.

Premack, D. (1959). Toward empirical behavior laws: I. Positive reinforcement. *Psychological Review, 66*, 219–233.

Rachlin, H., & Logue, A. W. (1983). Learning. In M. Hersen, A. E. Kazdin, A. S. Bellack (Eds.), *The clinical psychology handbook*. Elmsford, NY: Pergamon.

Rychlak, J. F. (1981). *Introduction to personality and psychotherapy* (2nd ed). Boston: Houghton Mifflin.

Skinner, B. F. (1953). *Science and human behavior*. New York: Free Press.

Stokes, T. F., & Baer, D. M. (1977). An implicit technology of generalization. *Journal of Applied Behavior Analysis, 10*, 349–367.

Watson, R. I. (1978). *The great psychologists* (4th ed). Philadelphia: Lippincott.

Whitehurst, G. J. (1978). Observational learning. In A. C. Catania & T. A. Brigham (Eds.), *Handbook of applied behavior analysis: Social and instructional processes*. New York: Irvington.

Zeiler, M. D. (1978). Principles of behavioral control. In A. C. Catania & T. A. Brigham (Eds.), *Handbook of applied behavior analysis: Social and instructional processes*. New York: Irvington.

CHAPTER 6

A Phenomenological Approach to Adolescence*

Constance T. Fischer and Richard J. Alapack

There is no phenomenological, existential, or humanistic adolescent psychology, at least not in the sense of a comprehensive collection of studies and opinions. The title of this chapter was worded with that fact in mind. What phenomenological psychology has to offer the field of adolescent psychology at present is an *approach*—a way to look at phenomena, to see with a different vision, one that preserves the uniquely human character of the subject matter.

This chapter will briefly introduce phenomenological psychology. After that, the first half of the chapter will be devoted to a phenomenological study of one kind of adolescent relationship, that of first love. The study illustrates how a phenomenological approach can address "what it's like" to live through an experience, can evoke the unitary nature of experience, can preserve the simultaneously limited and open character of experience, and can evoke the relation of concrete phenomena to the meaning of human existence. Next, the chapter presents a

briefer, more abstract phenomenological characterization of a presumably related aspect of adolescence, namely sexuality. The third substantive section of the chapter provides an overview of one phenomenological theory of development. Finally, the three sections are contrasted with our traditional natural science approach to adolescence.

PHENOMENOLOGICAL PSYCHOLOGY

A century ago science was thought of as an enterprise through which *the* mathematical, physical, causal truths of our earth, and of our life on it, would be discovered. Today, scientists and philosophers alike acknowledge that what we see as facts depends on the particular questions we ask, on the history of our interest in the subject matter, on our theoretical background, and on the methods with which we study the subject. We are also increasingly

---

*The section on first love is a presentation of work by Richard J. Alapack; the section on sexuality was written by Constance T. Fischer.

aware that these factors inevitably occur within historical, cultural, economic, social times, and that these help to shape what we see as facts. In short, facts as discovered by humans necessarily are fashioned in part by the human context. Phenomenology addresses that context.

Early in the present century, two German philosophers, Edmund Husserl (1913/1968, 1954/1970) and Martin Heidegger (1927/1962) developed philosophical foundations that would encourage scientists and theoreticians to take into account the ways in which we co-constitute—co-author—our perceptions of the world, both as individuals and as scholars.

When psychologists apply philosophical phenomenology to their domain, they begin with life situations, rather than with test scores, laboratory experiments, or with variables such as "anxiety" or "intelligence." They allow the person's situation as lived to become apparent through direct observation and/or through the person's description. The lived situation is addressed as a structural unity—as simultaneously shaping as well as being shaped by relations with the world, and as simultaneously physical, biological, and psychological.

When we look at instances in everyday life, without "benefit" of theories, constructs, or experimental variables, we also find that whatever we experience is always within a temporal context—one of a living past, of things that are givens in the present, and of a future that is relatively open.

In their pursuit of baseline human ways of experiencing the world, phenomenologists have found that spontaneous descriptions also refer to goals and choices, and to feelings, emotions, thoughts, and actions. Again, putting aside current theories, the phenomenological researcher would look at the descriptions and ask what about them was essential to, say, an adolescent's "being in love." Although any one aspect could be looked at independently of the others, from a pretheoretical stance, no one aspect is more essential than any of the others, and hence none should be posed as an explanation of the other. For example, a youngster may throw a pillow angrily; we then can speak of the behavior and of the emotion, but these are abstractions from a unitary moment, not separate variables one of which causes the other.

Phenomenological psychologists study events (in this instance throwing a pillow angri-

ly) before their vision is formed by theory and technology, in particular, before the unitary experience is analyzed into parts. The problem with partitive analysis is that we too often forget that it was we who broke the phenomenon down, and that we then treat the parts as though they were real, separate entities with causal force. For example, we might say that anger caused the youngster to throw the pillow, or that throwing the pillow was a sign of anger. The problem with such constructions is that they lose sight of the participating, partially responsible person.

It may be helpful for the reader to think of phenomenology etymologically: the study of (ology) how things appear to us (phenomena). Concomitantly, phenomenology is the study of what our experience of our worlds tells us about humanness. In addition to asking, "What is this person's lived world in this situation?" the phenomenological psychologist asks, "And how does that inform us about what is universally human?" That is, what does this phenomenon (e.g., being anxious or angry) tell us about being human? Perhaps that humans always care about what is happening to them, that they are always on their way toward personal destinations, that their stances contribute to their futures.

In North America, the word phenomenological also has a legitimate history of simply referring to an individual's own perspective or personal experience. However, as indicated above, in the European tradition and in the largely North American school of psychology as a human science (Giorgi, 1970), phenomenological also refers to a systematic study of the ways we live/experience our worlds and to what that study says about the nature of being human. Phenomenologically oriented psychologists usually also are concerned with existential issues—the value and choice dimensions inherent in being finite and yet faced with open futures. Similarly, phenomenological practitioners share humanistic psychologists' interests in maximizing people's growth and enjoyment of life.

Phenomenological psychology has addressed the major interests of psychology in considerable detail. Examples are: theoretical foundations (Giorgi, 1970), empirical research (de-Rivera, 1981; Giorgi, 1985), psychotherapy (Barton, 1974; Fischer & Fischer, 1983), psychopathology (deKonig & Jenner, 1982), psychological assessment (Fischer, 1985), and developmental psychology (Knowles, 1986). The foregoing references are primarily to work conducted at Duquesne University, which is the major center for phenomenological psychology in the United States. For references to that program and to other phenomenological efforts, see Misiak and Sexton (1973) and Fischer and Fischer (1983). For a broad range of the writing and research done at Duquesne, the reader is referred to four volumes edited by Giorgi and colleagues (1971, 1975, 1979, 1983), the *Duquesne Studies in Phenomenological Psychology*. The international *Journal of Phenomenological Psychology* publishes both theoretical and research articles.

The Psychology Departments at Seattle University and Georgia State University also are explicitly phenomenological. Phenomenology is strongly represented in the Psychology Department at the University of Dallas. There are strong phenomenological components in the Departments of Education at the Universities of Alberta, Cape Breton, and Michigan. The journals, *Human Development* and *Phenomenology and Pedagogy* publish phenomenological and related theory and research.

A PHENOMENOLOGICAL STUDY: ADOLESCENT FIRST LOVE

Phenomenological Research

In general, phenomenological researchers try to put aside, for the moment, what is already known about something, for example, adolescent first love. They acquire descriptions of how the phenomenon is lived by individuals and, sometimes, of how it appears to observers. They then attempt to characterize what is essential to all occasions and to do so in language that retains both the mutuality of the discerned constituents and the ambiguity and flow of the phenomenon. The resulting accounts are understood as always unfinished in that they remain subject to consideration of additional instances, to reflection by other researchers, and to expression by different authors.

This kind of qualitative research is ideal for indicating productive parameters for quantitative study. Natural-science methods also can test the generalizability of qualitative findings. On the other hand, the life-world meanings of

quantitative results can be explored via qualitative research (see Fischer, 1984).

The empirical qualitative dissertations conducted at Duquesne University first study lifeworld phenomena and then attempt to integrate those findings with normative data and presentations from other theoretical perspectives. Among completed dissertations pertinent to developmental and adolescent psychology are: Becker's (1973) *A Phenomenological Explication of Friendship: As Exemplified by Most Important College Women Friends*; Benswanger's (1975) *An Empirical–Phenomenological Study of Inhabited Space in Early Childhood*; Brennan's (1971) *Being in a Family: An Exploratory Phenomenological Study*; and Wolfe's (1980) *An Empirical–Phenomenological Study of the Best Friend Relationship Between Preadolescent Boys*. Dissertations in process include: Robert Bodnar's on *Children's Imaginary Companions*; Irene Calhoun's on adolescents *Not Doing What One's Parents Want*; Ann Johnson's on *Children's Concepts of Gender Difference*; Janice Knapp's on *Reconciliation Fantasies of Children of Divorce*; and Rebecca Miles' on *The Psychological Unfolding of the Transformation of Self–Other Relationships at Menarche*. At Rhodes University in South Africa, Mudaly (1984) completed a dissertation on adolescents' experiences in youth homes. Other phenomenological studies include Everhart's (1983) ethnographic account of *Reading, Writing, and Resistance: Adolescence in a Junior High School*, and Wolf's (1981) phenomenological study of adolescent's perception of drug abuse.

Phenomenological researchers are differently attuned to the drama of life events, and they choose different lengths for their reports. (For examples of one-page phenomenological research reports, see Fischer, 1971 and 1984.)

For his analysis of adolescent mutual first love, Richard Alapack (1984) has gathered accounts for over 10 years from students in his adolescent psychology course at Saint Jerome's College (Waterloo, Ontario). He has asked them to describe, usually in writing, "the relationship you experienced with the first person you truly loved." Results are based on descriptions of heterosexual love. However, other work has led Alapack to believe that essentially the same structure holds for same-gender love. Alapack has continuously revised his findings in light of new protocols and qualifications arising in the course of his research. His analyses are unusually rich and alive. They evoke both what the experience is like for individuals and what that implies about human existence at a general level.

The Structure of the Adolescent First-Love Relationship *

Two adolescents meet, ready to risk flowing out to each other, ripe to love in a new way. Time stops. Two alien, hitherto egocentric, worlds collide, rebound, pause, then expand to embrace and include each other. Time begins afresh. Their lives, rapt in one another, are galvanized by the intense collision. "We're together alone," they say, "we two against the world." A new *egoisme à deux* has emerged—their first love. The following essential characteristics differentiate this relationship from other intense personal–sexual involvements.

Absolutes

Adolescent first love is experienced as absolute. Listen to some typical expressions: "There's nothing I wouldn't do for you!" "I love everything about you." "We'll never part." "I can't get enough of you." "Nothing else matters as much as you do." "Our love is everything and everlasting." The relationship is splashed with a sense of being omnipresent and eternal.

Uniqueness

The specialness of the first love creates a conviction that the experience is unique. Descriptions include: "Nobody has ever loved like we love." "This kind of thing has only happened to us." "Look what everyone else is missing." "We are God's chosen ones, picked at perfect prime." The experience of first love is suitably captured by the Latin term, *sui generis.*

Perfection

The adolescent experiences the first love as flawless. Spontaneous exclamations bespeak the experience: "My one and only true love!" "My pure love!" "It's heavenly!" One male wrote: "The feeling of loving Diane, and of knowing that Diane was in love with me, was

---

*This section is an adaptation of a study by Alapack (1984).

the closest thing there could be to heaven. Nothing has come closer yet." A female stated succinctly, "My being had been brushed with meaning." In contrast to the ambiguous imperfection of mature adult love, the first-time love is as close to perfect as possible.

Togetherness

The word "ours" dominates the experience. It's our music, our poet, our spot, our moon. Any event, song, concert, movie, game, although common property to the world, is special because it is "ours." This togetherness veers toward exclusiveness. "We did everything together. It seemed like we were the only ones in the world living. If parents or peers saw you alone, they might ask, "Where's your other half?" The couple creates a love cocoon within which their most important self-validating needs or desires are gratified. The cocoon protects the fledgling and delicate relationship from external, intrusive influences. The relationship is strengthened because it is nourished from within itself, but the exclusiveness also sows seeds of potential dependent possessiveness.

Idealism

Devoid of the practical exigencies and ambiguities of adulthood, adolescent first love is a haven wherein the youngsters in effect postpone facing the stark indifference of the world. The first love is dream-laden with an accent on openness, wonder, and possibility. The perfect spot of Camelot and of Don Quixote's Impossible Dream are fit images of this rampant idealism.

Innocence

Adolescent first love happens on the innocent side of life. It teams with feelings and thoughts of respect and sacrifice. Although the relationship is sexually expressive, genital behavior is not essential to it. The relationship as relationship is central:

> I had her on a pedestal, and respected her too much to defile.
> An absence of flirtation marked our relationship. Our unspoken intention was to share and communicate with a whole person, not only with a sexual other. We never profaned our love. Even our physical touches felt sacred.
> They'll ruin us if we let them, if they think we go to bed together, let them think that even

though we don't; it's their filthy minds and lives, not ours. We did go to bed together once. We listened to music all night and laid in bed half-naked, kind of feeling around at each other, too awed to do anything more. It was exquisite.

Communication

A cardinal characteristic of adolescent first love is sharing. The eyes speak, blending with and yielding to the spoken word. The partners seem to always have something to say to each other, especially words about feelings, thoughts, and plans. Interaction is not a matter of turning out the lights and getting physical. Not infrequently, after spending several hours together, one last phone call is needed to utter that new insight that flashed in the interval between the good night kiss and the present moment.

In talking and sharing, the partners carve out a common language and cultivate a common ground. They do not interact, they commune. The nascent acts of undressing each other's mind occur in love letters, in poetry, in words that trustingly trickle off the lips—risk-talk. Each learns the pristine lessons of what it means to be vulnerable to the other person.

Emotional Connection

Communication, which flows and unveils, is heartfelt. The adolescent first-love relationship is a veritable delivery room of unprecedented emotions. "With her," wrote one fellow, "I came to explore my new depths; the feelings she called up came from places that hadn't been before." One begins to enjoy and suffer through emotions that one has only read about in books, or that one believed were the privileged fare of heroes and heroines: possessiveness and jealousy; deep thrill and tenderness; the "astonishing discovery, not only that pain can be lived with and gotten over with in time, but that the pain softens us, makes us more sympathetic." First-love partners unlock doors for each other to the inchoate experiences of empathy, generosity, and reciprocity.

Reciprocal Involvement

The reciprocity is rudimentary, but the first-love partners live out the give-and-take that is so vital to loving. Accent is not merely on togetherness, but upon the hyphen between the "I" and the "Thou." In the speaking–listening

dialectic, not only are two separate worlds revealed, but "our world" is created.

> I lived always with her image before me. Without her I was my old self. That old self wasn't me anymore. I was now the one who was in love with her and shared as much as I could. From her and with her I learned how to share a life.

Orientation to a Future

Born along with the love bond is, in the apt phrase of Steinbeck (1972), a "sharp appetite for the future" (p. 524). The partners begin to imagine, to plan for, and, at times, actually to build a common future. Within the relationship, each comes to understand a history that is unique, separate from one's own. In meeting the other's family, and seeing the other's place within that family, the foundation is laid both for recognizing the other as other and for painting a possible future. Motherhood and fatherhood become concrete possibilities, not just abstract notions. The partners share dreams and fantasies about the home they would build, the family they would raise, the careers they would pursue, and the ways in which they might deepen their sexual–spiritual bond. They are at the first stage of understanding the gravity and the beauty of commitment.

Consistency with One's Roots

This special someone with whom the adolescent envisions a future tends to be someone compatible with his or her family background and central values. Most likely Mom and Dad welcomed the partner into their home, approved the relationship, and even blessed plans for the future. A special bond frequently develops between the individual and the parents of his or her counterpart. Often the fondness grows to the point of greeting each other with the endearing terms, "Mom," "Dad," "Son," or "Daughter."

Structural Elaboration of the Meaning of First Love

First love happens within our contemporary middle-class North American culture. It does not happen automatically or inevitably. Not everyone experiences it during chronological adolescence, nor is it the exclusive prerogative of the young or of heterosexual individuals. First-time lovers are as unique as humanly possible.

Some do not love until they are 30 or 40 years old, or until after they are divorced. Others might never experience it. This report speaks to the adolescent in us all and to the first-love phase of any major sexually toned mutual attachment. Although first love is an actual, observable phenomenon, it is also a metaphor, inherently undatable.

Whenever the relationship happens, it is neither accidental nor caused. A ripeness is requisite if one is to notice the epiphany of the other's entrance into one's world; a readiness is necessary if one is to respond to the appeal in the other's eyes. But although the individual might be anticipating the other, or actively searching to find the other, he or she lacks both the power to make the other appear and the control to make that other come to one. The other must come of his or her own desire. If that person flows out to one in trust and with risk, and if one flows back meeting the other, then they might know the fulfillment that is first love.

The Discovery Side of Adolescent First Love

An advantage of experiencing a first-love relationship is the great discoveries about life that it affords. The discoveries are about self and world in their dialectical unity. The three reflections that follow—Coming Out, Informing Presence, and Orienting Presence—are thoroughly interrelated.

Coming Out. "What kind of man will I grow to be?" "Will I ever develop into a woman?" "Will I be capable of truly loving? Or will I only selfishly care that another might love me?" Voiced or unspoken, these questions haunt the person who feels unseasoned and unsure about his or her loving capabilities. The answers to these questions can be discovered within a relationship that is experienced as intensely special. The first-love relationship is precisely that nesting ground from which emerges one's unique style of manhood or womanhood:

> Until him, I felt as though I was in soft focus, waiting for someone to come along to sharpen the image, and to draw me out. Suddenly I found myself evolving into a woman.
>
> Before we met I felt lonely and not as big as the other guys. I remember riding my bicycle over and over around the block, strangely tangled up inside, and languishing in the dol-

drums. Then she softly but forcefully said, "Come to me." In responding I found my vitality.

The first-love couple comprises an authentic psychospiritual debutant/debutante.

Informing Presence. First love not only calls one out, but informs one, shapes one's nascent sense of self. The following excerpts depict the movement from nebulous confusion to a sense of direction:

> She set standards which challenged me. Or rather, life itself, through our relationship, tested my strength and courage. I struggled. Then I began to believe in myself.
>
> Suddenly I didn't feel like a backward, shy, plump tomboy anymore. It was the first time that I had been singled out as desirable.
>
> I doubted that I was an attractive person. No one except my parents had ever told me so. Incredibly I had won this beauty by being gentle, understanding, and caring.

The first love who catalyzes one's life becomes a foundational referent, influentially powerful and long-lasting.

Orienting Presence. The relationship also orients one in his or her lived world, spatially and temporally. Finding a structure to replace the sense of being rudderless and bewildered is revealed in the following:

> Before I met him, my life felt like many mismatched pieces of a jigsaw puzzle strewn over the floor. Nothing seemed to be fitting together properly. I was frustrated, befuddled, and mostly lonely. He somehow put into focus a horizon of possibilities, expectations, and promises.
>
> During physical education I would walk on my hands around the gym. That's how topsy turvey was my world then. Somehow my world was stabilized by the way she would press back when kissing me goodnight. For the first time I could see a pattern to life.

The French word, *sens,* which means both "meaning" and "direction," best expresses the meaning of the first love as an orienting or alchemizing presence.

The Painful Side of First Love

Within the context of first love, we grow psychospiritually as we deal with pain. Hard but valuable lessons learned about relating include the necessity of giving up infantile illusions about boundless love and the realization that everything is not under one's control. If the neophyte love is to grow into a steadfast bond, strong enough to support a long-term future, then this painful shift from a self-centered to an other-centered orientation must occur and persist. Below are some empirical variations of this painful side, here mostly having to do with the demise of the relationship.

The Experience of Loss Within the Marriage of First-Love Partners. More than a few first-love couples do marry. For them, the painful crisis occurs either when one or both have to face their aloneness or find their own bearings, or when the magical beginning wears on the imperfect edge of everyday life. Take the situation in which a young couple has to square their idealistic vision with the hard fact of a stillborn son. Suppose they have to deal with the loss of innocence in the shape of an extramarital affair, drug addiction, or a suicide attempt. The couple, with the resiliency to face the pain of disappointment and disenchantment, can deepen their bond and parlay its specialness into an authentic intimacy. Pain that is not endured honestly tends to lead to a relationship fraught with bitterness, cynicism, hostility, cruelty, or despair. A popular alternative is divorce.

Loss at the Breakup of the First-Love Relationship. For those many relationships that do not lead to marriage, a breakup occurs. The more truly reciprocal the relationship, the more it is a mutual loss, a genuine death experience for both parties, requiring grief work through the same structural issues that Freud (1917/1963) clarified about mourning and melancholia in the face of any death.

If the relationship is balanced in reciprocal desire, then it is as painfully grief-laden for the one who must end the relationship as it is for the one who is rejected. For the one who could not, or would not, foresee the ending, the breakup comes as a cruel, precipitous shock, leaving a gaping hole and a myriad of unanswered questions: "Why did she all of a sudden stop loving me?" "What did I do that was so wrong?" "Did I abuse the privilege of loving him?"

The painful burden of the one who lives, seemingly endlessly, with rehearsed words of parting, is the knowledge that he or she will hurt that precious other, that other whom he or she had tamed and by whom one has been tamed (Saint-Exupery,1971). Some excerpts expressing the pain of the adolescent who instigates the ending: "How can I hurt him?" "What is wrong with my love? Why can't I deliver my promise of everlasting?" "Am I making a terrible mistake?"

Breakup of Unbalanced First Loves. The demise of an unbalanced relationship particularly crushes the weaker or overdependent partner. Instead of witnessing the dynamics of grief work, we see desperate reactions: the "slump" of losing interest in school, extracurricular activities, family relations, and peer interactions, as well as depression, physical illness, even severe disorientation and suicide attempts.

The following are ways of evading the hurt that the relationship has ended, either in fact or in meaning.

Parrying the Loss of Meaning. One way to postpone grief work is to ward off admitting that the relationship has changed in meaning—spoiled by the dimming of its vital spark, eroded by jealousy or possessive smothering, choked in the rarefied atmosphere of dwelling on a pedestal. Some refuse to see the changes; others delay the act of separation: "I'll put it off until tomorrow." "I've got lots of time to end this. I live one day at a time." The procrastination is often rooted in special significances known to the person alone. Suppose the young Catholic girl has "lost" her virginity to her first love. She might believe that she "has to" marry him even though the relationship has gone stale. Her counterpart, believing that he "took" her virginity, might also believe that he cannot now discard her. External circumstances can also contribute to warding off the ending. The most significant is family involvement. Pressure is strong to stay in the relationship so that one does not have to loosen the many ties between families.

Carrying the Torch. Remaining "hung up" on an "old flame" after an actual parting avoids grief work too. To "carry the torch" is to seek a duplication of the first love in any subsequent relationship, constantly to compare new partners with that special someone. Carrying the torch is a good-faith/bad-faith act in that one accepts the ending in fact, but leaves its meaning unresolved.

The most prevalent condition that makes carrying the torch possible is when the first love stays good and pure until the end. Stunned by the unanticipated loss, the person is left tied to good memories, with nothing to fault or regret except the ending itself. Until the individual assumes responsibility for undoing the first relationship, he or she keeps seeking a duplicate. Sometimes the search takes the form of finding someone with whom he or she can work out the issue, and the first love is finally finished. Other times, the person keeps chasing a paradise lost, treating new partners unfairly for not being true traces. Or he or she may carry the torch into a marriage. If one is haunted by questions of what to do if the old love returns, doubts may create jealousy; moreover, the spouse would experience the futility of trying to compete with a live ghost.

The most touching stories, few but not rare, are those of young people who, at the zenith of their first love, lost their partner through a physical death. How easy to carry the torch for someone, absent in body, but still remembered as perfect! In this instance, one must struggle to resist the temptation to enshrine the lost love.

On the Rebound. A partner who is left feeling manipulated, exploited, or betrayed tends to engage in one or another of three styles of rebounding. One style is to *withdraw*. When the ending rips into the person's trust, he or she tends to be suspiciously reserved. The cliche applies: "Once burnt, twice shy." The end of a destructive first love is a "natural" time in life to be vigilent—careful not to become too vulnerable, cautious not to commit too soon.

A second style of rebounding is to play the *tyrant*. In an attitude of revenge, the individual acts out on new partners the "games" played on him- or herself. Steeled against another pain, the person teases or punishes the new other for his or her own hurts.

Remaining a *victim* is the third style. The person continues a pattern, finding someone who will render hurt in an old familiar way—someone who will feed the same lines, someone who will toy with him or her like a puppet, someone who will cooperate in rendering love another bridge to burn.

Theoretical Reflections

To this point we have evoked the phenomenon of first adolescent love, depicted its structure, and illuminated its general meanings. We will now situate that relationship along the developmental spiral road (Alapack & Alapack, 1984) and place it within a more comprehensive whole. What calls out first love? On what basis is it differentiated from any other romantic involvement?

Ontological Revolution

To Kierkegaard (1844/1980) the human is a "synthesis of psyche and body sustained by spirit" (p. 43). He described the growth process as movement from a state of innocence, when the spirit is still dreaming and sensual desire is present only in premonition, to a coming-to-consciousness. The awakening of sexuality/spirituality provokes anxiety—the vanguard of a crisis. One either faces the crisis and makes a qualitative leap into authentic freedom and selfhood or succumbs, in some form, to despair.

This initial adolescent crisis about the possibilities of the self, and about separation from one's family of origin, has been called the developmental *ontological revolution* (Alapack, 1984). Boelen (1978) describes this metamorphosis as a movement to a new level of existence—beyond the dependent level of the child and beyond the technical–functional level of the juvenile, to a truly personal level. Born with the awakening of the "personal self" is the "discovery of primordial wonder" and the "multidimensional presence to the world"—an expansion horizontally, vertically, and in depth.

Until the ontological revolution, the growing youngster is subsumed within the network of three overlapping rings: family, peer group, and adult authorities (teachers, coaches, clergy, etc.). With the realization that one is a unique self, a part of but also apart from that threefold network of relationships, the adolescent ceases to be a "satellite" to it (Keen, 1970). The ontological revolution is the turning point in life from the collective fusion of childhood dependence to the independence of the singular self, on the way to the community of mature dependence in intimacy, parenthood, worker solidarity, and friendship.

The ontological revolution jars the narrow, taken-for-granted view of self and world. In a nascent way, and at the lived level, the adolescent begins to ask the Kantian question: What are the conditions that make something possible? and the Husserlian question: What are the foundations, the roots, the genesis of phenomena? and the Heideggerian question: Can I be an aware shepherd of Being? In Erikson's (1982) phraseology, the adolescent experiences a new desire for "fidelity" to someone or some cause or ideal beyond self.

When the adolescent begins to write poetry or songs or starts to keep a diary or commits himself or herself to causes, these signs of having entered into the revolution are also signs of readiness to flow out to one's first love. Similarly, the carnival of affections and kaleidoscope of images, with which first love teams, opens the adolescent to the One, the Good, the True, the Beautiful, and the Tragic.

First Love: An Infinite Relationship

Granted that first love is grounded in a developmental ontological revolution, what distinguishes it from other love involvements? First love is infinite (Alapack, 1975; Levinas, 1979), that is, not just a fantasy based upon projection of wishes, but a *relationship* more substantial than imagination could concoct.

Simply stated, an infinite relationship goes beyond self, and is other-centered and relationship-constellated; a finite relationship is self-centered. Discussion of the infinite, and then description of some finite relationships, will cast the infinity of first love into sharp relief.

Infinite Relationship. The signs of first love clearly reveal that it pivots both around the partner as a real other and around the shared relationship. The meaning of first love is neither a mere fantasy projection nor a correlate of one's needs or intentions. In Levinas' (1969) language, the other "overflows" one's "ideals" or images. As Levinas writes, "He at each instant undoes the form he presents" (p. 66). There is always more to this inexhaustible richness than what meets one's eyes. The other comes as an epiphany who shines with his or her own kind of light, radically separate and outside oneself. Levinas (1969) is fond of speaking about the "gleam of exteriority in the eye of the other" and of the "transcendence in the face" (p. 84). The other also brings new, surprising sights and sounds for one's life, if one can let go of sedimented

meanings to look at the other and to listen. One can see that the other's richness is inexhaustible.

Finite Situations. First love is distinct from infatuation. When one instead falls in love with love, he or she is dazzled by the exciting idea of romance. The person with whom one is enamored matters little. Rather, the infatuated person veers toward the image of that person—toward what filters through the distorting lenses of one's desires. Although one might secretly compose poems or love letters, he or she might take no action to encounter the other. Even if one should dare to speak, he or she would not tell the other of one's great affection. Most often, such admiration occurs at a distance. Although one might feel lovesick about the other, she or he could never blow a hole through one's heart with grief.

The following are descriptions of finite interactions. "Having a boyfriend was a status symbol. To be liked by a boy, and to be popular at school were more important to me than my boyfriend." "Dating her was my form of insurance against being alone." "My life revolved around having that one special boy who made *me* feel special." "When our relationship ended, I discovered that he had been using me for our swimming pool, our snowmobile, and my body." In such finite interactions, the other whom one allegedly loves is more accurately designated as an extension of oneself. His or her reality pales beneath his or her representation for one. The other's face is encompassed by one's ideas, and the other's voice is muffled by one's intentions. One wants the other to admire one and/or to gratify one's sexual urges. In brief, the finite other shines in the "borrowed light" (Levinas, 1969) of one's desires for social prestige and self-esteem.

In brief, a finite conjunction is an ad hoc situation of self-appeasement and bilateral adjustment. It lasts until the new wears off, the conquest is made, or the pleasure traded. An infinite relationship is a potentially enduring situation of both self-realization and mutual coordination.

Comment

Even as Alapack continues to revise this study, he has undertaken related investigations: on the meaning of leaving home (1984), on adolescent love relationships with socially disapproved persons ("The Outlaw Relationship," 1975), and on young person/older person romantic relations (in press). It is through this kind of systematic study that a phenomenological psychology of adolescence can develop.

In the meantime, the above effort has illustrated the power of phenomenological research to evoke both the lived world of the individual and general themes of human existence. Alapack's structural analysis helps us to see the adolescent's world—an ever-progressing network of relations with persons, environment, and self. We see both the power of that network on the adolescent *and* the adolescent's continual choosings. Later, as we reflect on implications for educational and social policy, and for the meaning of other relationships, we can be in fairly direct touch with this one aspect of adolescence (first-love relations). We are not left to hypothesize about what scientific measurements have to do with actual lives. Nor do we have to try to add variables together to come up with a sense of the whole; a structural description *is* such an account.

A PHENOMENOLOGICAL UNDERSTANDING OF SEXUALITY

The transition between childhood and adulthood, which we call adolescence, is said to begin with the appearance of secondary sex characteristics and the advent of reproductive capacity. Changed sexual status is an essential aspect of adolescence. Yet, aside from psychoanalytic theory, we do not have a foundational psychology of sexuality for adolescents, nor a satisfactory one for adults. Indeed, we can not achieve it with our traditional research approach alone.

Natural Science Influence

Most studies reported in adolescent psychology journals and textbooks automatically include sex as a *variable*, thereby perpetuating expectations of sex differences. With our reticence to acknowledge science's contribution to values and to social reality, we have perpetuated many aspects of the status quo. Although reported research and textbook illustrations now frequently include members of different classes

and races, the work of feminist psychology is slow to appear in adolescent psychology writings. Gender-biased language (the generic "he") is still prevalent. Reports of more females now choosing careers over marriage are presented as results of social forces, which social scientists presumably merely observe.

The strongest natural-science influence, however, has been a residual reductionistic, deterministic orientation—in this case reducing sexuality to a biological force. Chapters on sexuality continue to focus on physiology and then on controlling its force in social situations. Many texts continue to explain that teenage boys have stronger drives than girls, and that they often "cannot help themselves." Research on homosexuality stresses efforts to locate the source of the "problem" within gene structure and hormonal variation. What with males being regarded as the sexually oriented gender, male homosexuality is mentioned, although lesbianism rarely is. A final example of the reductive impact of natural science is the way in which the word sex is used to refer indiscriminately to biological designation, gender-role identification, reproduction, interpersonal attraction, erotic arousal and activity, and intercourse. Even now, biological designation often is assumed to determine gender role. Similarly, adolescents are not informed that arousal can be a state in itself, that it is not necessarily a biological need or a drive pressing for culmination in orgasm.

A PHENOMENOLOGICAL APPROACH TO SEXUALITY

A phenomenological approach to the sexual dimension explores moments in persons' lives that they experience as involving sexuality. Reflection on such moments led to the following preliminary comprehension by this chapter's first author (Fischer).

From the beginning, humans' life energy is bodily grounded and is both sensually and outwardly oriented. The growing child develops and differentiates sources and targets of pleasure, danger, and power. In adolescence, vitality (life energy, desire) becomes sexual in that the possibilities of *affecting/being-affected* now include a genital/erotic arousal and orgasmic culmination. From now on, sensuousness, danger, and power are toned by one's sexual body and by societal attitudes toward sexuality. There is a heightened sense of difference from and sameness with others in regard to these possibilities.

Arousal is not only physiological, but also simultaneously psychological—arousal of the possibilities of bridging or of maintaining separateness through control, affirmation, or subordination. Arousal can take the form of going forth to the mystery of the other or the Other, toward transcendence of the separate self, and toward union—interpersonal or spiritual. In contrast, arousal also can move toward possession or destruction of the other. For example, rape most often is not so much an erotic expression as it is an effort toward power. In another variation, mass arousal of vitality in its sexually toned form can occur, for example, at a basketball game, where the fans participate in the dramatic, bodily play with power and its danger of subordination.

That there are such variations of sexual vitality can, of course, be confusing to adults as well as to adolescents. The adolescent, however, is living with a recently changed body—one that sometimes seems to have a life of its own. One can be captivated by another's sexually toned potential for affecting/being-affected, for enhancing one's nascent similarities and differences, and for affirming both individuality and the possibility of union. In short, meanings of being a body for self and for others change. Concomitantly, the meanings of participating, mastering, and of letting go change. All of these meanings develop in the context of societal attitudes.

Our contemporary society genitalizes sexuality. That is, as a society, we seem to be fascinated with vitality when it is closest to its initial sexual form—the introduction of genital/erotic arousal and expression, definition of feminine and masculine sexuality in terms of differences, and the sexual transformation of sensuality, danger, and power. Similarly, we seem to celebrate first love's narcissistic captivation as though it were a standard for later years, rather than being a developmental form.

Adult vitality is inevitability sexually toned, and yet, not even in adolescence, is it necessarily reducible to genitality or eroticism. Sexuality is at once personal/bodily/interpersonal/societal. Freud notwithstanding, sexual energy is not the founding life force, but rather is a post-pubertal transformation, a particular toning, of vitality (cf. Dillon, 1980).

From this perspective on sexuality, we can more readily redesign what we misguidedly refer to as sex education in the schools. For the most part, these courses present information about reproduction and hygiene, although parents fear that their adolescents are learning the "how to" of eroticism and intercourse. Too rarely does either set of adults help the youngster to integrate so-called sex education diagrams with personal and interpersonal longings, family values, and so on.

A more useful curriculum might be one drawn from life. A life development course could occur throughout one's schooling. For the postchildhood transitional years, it might include, for example, open descriptions of sexuality within individuals' lives across all ages. Such description could help young people to see that sexuality is not a phenomenon belonging to their generation exclusively, that genitality does not require orgasmic fulfillment, that all relations are bodily-toned, and that "sexual preferences" are indeed preferences—all with attendant repercussions. Youngsters could begin to see that their confusions are, for the most part, accurate perceptions of life's ambiguities and multiple possibilities. They could begin to see connections between interpersonal responsibility now and in their later years. Perhaps they could see that sexuality is inextricably intertwined with the rest of daily life, part of the fabric of existence, but not an underlying force.

Indeed, Alapack's life-world study revealed that, contrary to much theory and popular assumption, genital sexuality was not commonly a major focus for the first-love adolescent. Of course, in certain other adolescent relationships, it certainly is (e.g., Alapack, in press). However, from both of these studies (first love and sexuality), it seems that contemporary emphasis on burgeoning genitality in adolescence could profitably give way to exploration of adolescent interpersonal relations and their role in the moral and existential development of individuals and of society.

Not surprisingly, Knowles' (1977, 1986) independent phenomenological theory of human development, presented next, also lends itself to reflection on the importance of adolescence for responsive, fulfilling, responsible adult growth.

A PHENOMENOLOGICAL APPROACH TO HUMAN DEVELOPMENT

There are a few European phenomenological treatments of adolescence (Beets, 1964, 1968; Buytendyk, 1966). Unfortunately, they have not been translated into English. Van den Berg's (1961) *The Changing Nature of Man*, which is available in English, describes how it was historically possible for adolescence to first appear in the 18th century. Knowles' work, below, may be the only formal phenomenological developmental psychology theory published in English.

Readers who are not familiar with Erik Erikson's theory of human development as well as with phenomenological philosophy may wish to read the following segment just for a general sense of its themes.

Richard Knowles (1977, 1986), a psychologist at Duquesne University, has attempted an integration of Erikson's (1963, 1968) theory of human development with themes from Heidegger's (1927/1968) philosophy. The following characterization is drawn primarily from Knowles' 1986 book. Knowles respects Freud's exploration of the body's and of childhood's importance for development. He affirms Erikson's expansion of the Freudian vision to include both social context and stages of continuing adult development. However, Knowles has found that Freud's emphasis on biological forces and Erikson's emphasis on ego, although valid and fruitful, neglect what could be called "selfhood." Knowles uses the latter term to remind us of the open-endedness of our personal futures. That is, we are not simply shaped by events. We also take up those events in terms of our goals and values as well as our histories. To highlight this dimension of life, Frankl (1969) introduced the term "noological" (referring to existential meaning) to accompany the "biological" and "psychological" realms, and van Kaam (1981) proposed the "transcendent" to accompany the "vital" and "functional" aspects of human life.

Knowles acknowledges that Heidegger did not intend for his philosophical writings to be applied to everyday actual existence. Nevertheless, like other psychologists and psychiatrists seeking ways to take into account those aspects of being human that transcend body and reaction, Knowles has applied some aspects of Heidegger's reflections directly to psychology. Of particular importance is Heidegger's characterization of our finding ourselves *already involved* in our world, always in a temporal manner. Heidegger referred to this feature of being human as *Care*. We are always *in relations with* ourselves, others, and the world. We are always ahead of ourselves, on our way to the possible, even as we are restrained by the *facticity* of the past and the apparently predefined character of the present.

Although each of these temporalities is an essential aspect of human involvement, Knowles emphasizes *existentiality*—the open-endedness of existence that requires that we *co-author* our own futures. That co-authoring occurs in the present, where we are susceptible to a particular mode of coping with everyday existence—one that Heidegger called *fallenness*. He was not passing moral judgment here, but rather was pointing to a fundamental characteristic of being human. That is, we lose sight of our existentiality and of the inevitability of death as we fall into an attitude of getting things done, of classifying and manipulating, all the while assuming that things have static, given natures. Western science idealizes this mode, which Heidegger referred to as *inauthentic*, when we are unmindful of our own thing-ifying.

Knowles takes up Erikson's stages of development, and reviews for each what Erikson says explicitly about the relations among body (biological, vital realm), ego (psychological, including calculative, realm), and the social realm (other persons, the world). Knowles contributes "self" to this schema, characterizing it as the realm of the possible and noological. Knowles traces the mutual influence (co-constitution) of the individual and his or her world. He discusses each of the developmental crises (e.g., trust versus mistrust in the oral stage) first in terms of facticity—the condition one finds oneself in by virtue of history and unchosen constraints. The virtue of each stage, which Erikson also notes as that stage's contribution to society, Knowles elaborates as an essential strength for the developing individual (self). Knowles emphasizes that the virtues are all future-oriented—which probably is why psychology, with its emphasis on past and present determinants, has not directed much attention to this important aspect of Erikson's theory.

Knowles also traces the ego/cognitive concerns for each developmental stage (for infancy, consistency and prediction). Finally, in a major innovation, for each stage, Knowles differentiates the developmental crisis in accordance with the temporal moment (given past, cognized present, existential future). The virtues are thereby delineated in a manner rich with implications for adult life. Trust, for example, may be differentiated as bodily (prepersonal, unreflective), interpersonal (trust based on cognition and predictability), and existential (allowing vulnerability, based on bodily and interpersonal trust, as well as on the virtue, hope). Consonant with Erikson, Knowles regards the tasks of each new stage as opportunities for continued development of prior achievements. The virtues, in particular, are never finished; one is always in the process of hoping, of becoming faithful, and so on. Knowles' presentation of the virtues is enhanced by his empirical phenomenological research based on descriptions of phenomena such as being hopeful and being faithful.

The adolescent, according to an Eriksonian perspective, faces the crisis of identity versus role confusion, with fidelity being the related virtue. The crisis arises, of course, in the face of new possibilities presented by the beginnings of genitality and related bodily maturity (facticity). In the ego mode, the adolescent more or less cognitively identifies himself or herself in terms of, or against, existing models, types, and norms. The adolescent relates to the social world through and against ideologies. Knowles goes on to make a particular contribution to our understanding of adolescence in his presentation of the fallen modes, which arise first in this stage: fanaticism on one hand and faintheartedness on the other.

In fanaticism, one closes off the ambiguous future through a forced certainty, which seeks to define one's identity once and for all. One becomes devoted, without question, to a cause, group, or person (e.g., cults and rock groups). In faintheartedness, the ambiguity, uncertainty, and risk of life are avoided through remaining half-sure and half-hearted, as in adolescent cynicism, and being above it all or dismayed by it all. The mode of fallenness is an ordinary condition, but continuing development requires that it give way, that one bring identity and commitments into question, that one be present to the open-endedness of the world and others. One comes to know oneself gradually through repeated vacillations in quests for certainty and in spontaneous openness to difference, commitment, questioning, and reaffirmation. Knowles' analysis powerfully reminds us that the adolescent's struggles are not merely adolescent.

In actuality, the crisis of identity is intertwined with the next crisis in the Eriksonian schema, the crisis of intimacy versus isolation and self-absorption. Knowles reminds us that committed, loving relations involve a rhythm of forgetting and remembering oneself. Again, presence to the other person as being both different and evolving allows for the possibility of a loving, open relationship, whereas the fallen, calculative mode of relating allows only for affiliation through manipulation or sentimentality. Most of the self-help books today seem to "fall" into this mode, for example, telling us how to get what we want from others, how to create an image, how to be sexy. Togetherness and solitariness (the clique, singles bars) are inauthentic modes insofar as they are lived out without awareness of choice.

Especially in a chapter on commitment, Knowles stresses the existential–phenomenological theme that even though we find ourselves confronted with facticity (such as a changing body), it is we who take up those givens in our own ways. We are never totally determined by givens, but co-constitute their impact for our lives. A major, more original, significance for adolesence of Knowles' developmental psychology is that it helps us to be present to the young person's particular developmental tasks while respecting these tasks as still being unfinished in authentic adult life.

Perhaps readers have sensed connections among the earlier sections on first love and on sexuality with Knowles' developmental theory. We are reminded of Knowles' characterization of fallenness as we witness the adolescent's minidimensional but exaggerated assumptions of the loved one; we are reminded of the foundations of idealism and fidelity as we witness the adolescent's first new, postchildhood love commitment. We see how adolescent senses of pleasure, danger, and power are now sexually toned, but always within multiply motivated relationships.

NATURAL SCIENCE AND
ADOLESCENT PSYCHOLOGY

Natural Science Psychology

The phenomenological approach addresses the life-world—the world as it is lived and shaped by people. However, psychology traditionally has chosen instead to address underlying causes of behavior, in the manner of the natural sciences. To help the reader appreciate the historical differences between approaches, the following is a characterization of natural science psychology as it applies to this chapter. First, however, it should be noted that the critique and criticism below often are also made in-house by nonphenomenological psychologists. The authors of this chapter are also fully aware that it is easier to find shortcomings and limitations than it is to provide revisions. Phenomenological psychology's own emerging body of knowledge is subject to critique and criticism from within and without. The insights of the two approaches can, and should, be integrated.

In the late 1800s, persons interested in the relations between mind and matter successfully extended to psychology the exciting European laboratory experiments in physics. Professors who were interested in psychology argued about whether it should retain its ties with philosophy and be identified as a uniquely human science (Geisteswissenschaft) or should join the physical sciences (Naturwissenschaften). As it happened, we modeled our discipline after the natural sciences, thereby largely bypassing whatever content was unique to humans (e.g., hope, love, intentionality) in favor of whatever was physically visible and hence measurable.

We now design research in terms of operationally defined variables, manipulate these variables, measure outcomes, and conduct statistical analyses. Although in our theories we know better, in practice, as we measure outcomes of manipulation, we are encouraged to think in terms of cause and effect. Quantitative research, of course, is valid in its own right and obviously can be very useful. However, when we fail to acknowledge the primacy of the life-world, from which the research variables were derived, too often we act as though the variables are real, separate, and causal. We thus de-velop a science of variables in lieu of a science of human life as it is lived.

Adolescent Psychology

A review of textbooks and journals on adolescence quickly reveals the impact of our natural science approach. We note artificial classifications. For example, child development and child psychology courses and textbooks usually are separate from presentations of adolescence. Adolescents are regarded as a separate population. We have tended to think in terms of fairly exclusive categories: child/adolescent/adult. Adult development, which does not break neatly into subcategories by age, remains inadequately studied.

Scientific psychology has supported our everyday inclination to categorize when we want to make sense of things, in this instance exaggerating the separateness of adolescents. Science and society have placed this group in separate educational facilities (junior- and senior-high schools), labeled its members teenagers, and pronounced (albeit with dissension) that adolescence in our times is an inherently troubled stage.

Textbooks on adolescence begin with publically observable criteria for defining their subjects: age and puberty. Textbooks then break down their subject matter into seemingly separate, although presumably interacting, parts. There are chapters on theories of adolescence, on cognitive development, moral development, sexual development, social relations, social deviance and pathology, and education and career options. Each chapter reviews research, which inevitably is quantitative. There are straight statistical presentations: "35% of white subjects and 23% of black subjects had never gone steady during the previous 3 years." There are correlational data: "Teachers' grades were rather highly correlated with achievement test scores for disadvantaged students and black students, but only minimally correlated with achievement test scores for advantaged students and white students." And there are semiexperimental data: "2,062 subjects in grades 6 through 12 rated themselves on a 7-point semantic differential scale. The self-concept ratings were factor-analyzed and four factors emerged: (a) achievement–leadership, (b) congeniality–sociability, (3) adjustment, and (d) sex-appropriateness of the self-concept." Such findings provide food for thought about adolescent life. However, we are left to wonder just what these data point to in the actual lives of these people.

Much of the remaining content of many textbooks on adolescence strikes the authors of this chapter as superficial. The texts are reminiscent of seventh-grade health books' statements of the obvious: "By now you have noticed that your body has been changing." Textbooks at both college and public school levels typically contain equally gratuitous photos of young people dating, being at school, and socializing in groups. Both sets of textbooks purport to present facts from a value-free scientific perspective. Nevertheless, there is an "establishment" aura, for example, in the assumption that adolescent rebellion is a symptom that precludes it from also being a viable political critique. An integration of phenomenological studies, such as those presented in this chapter, with data in current textbooks would provide much more stimulating and challenging material. Part of the challenge would be to acknowledge the inevitable participation of context and values in any scholarly enterprise, whether it be data from the life-world or the laboratory.

There are very few sources that address adolescents' experiences directly. An exception is Goethals' and Klos' (1970) book, *Experiencing Youth: First-Person Accounts*. Other textbooks occasionally and effectively evoke adolescents' experience by including quotations or brief case studies. Unfortunately, these life-world excerpts are presented along side of, but not integrated with, theories and statistics or are intended to illustrate their validity. From a phenomenological perspective, we see that we instead could begin with life-world events and reported experiences and from there develop both studies and theories. In the meantime, having begun with measurement, we have developed a construct of adolescence, but we do not yet have a psychology of adolescents.

SUMMARY

Phenomenological psychology offers a framework for studying how people live their worlds, develop through them, and simultaneously shape and are shaped by those worlds. Phenomenology has not accomplished a full-bodied psychology of adolescence. However, it does offer an invitation through which such a psychology could be pursued. It offers phenomenological foundations, qualitative research methods, and some empirical studies and theoretical presentations. This chapter sampled the latter two offerings through three presentations: a qualitative study of the adolescent first-love relationship, an understanding of sexuality, and a theoretical expansion of Erikson's developmental theory.

As the reader saw, the samples were not "cut and dried" and indeed would be difficult to summarize. Phenomenology's invitation is not an offering of "bottom-line" clarity, but rather, an invitation to respectfully explore the ambiguities, holistic complexity, and richness of existence. The three presentations thus also implied that staying in touch with life as lived necessarily means also being in touch with contexts. In phenomenological studies, the interests and values of social scientists are (and should be) more evident than is usually the case, and the co-authoring of lives by social/cultural settings remains more readily available for reflection.

The sexuality section of the chapter included examples of how sedimented theory inevitably shapes what we see. This is true, of course, for phenomenology as well as for mainstream psychology. In this instance, a critique, followed by some concrete suggestions for sex education, illustrated the practical utility of a phenomenological approach.

Above all, though, when the life-world is the object of study, we remain closer to the human context and find ourselves mindful of existential choice as well as of unchosen contingencies, both of which guide our lives. Reflecting on the three presentations in this chapter, we can see hints of a continuity of this existential dimension across developmental stages. Phenomenological studies remind us that these stages are not just phases that happen to us or that we "go through" passively or reactively.

A human science psychology acknowledges the power of givens (e.g., chronological age, health, family background). Hence, it respects and utilizes the natural science research practices and data that throw light on such aspects of life. Because humans take up these givens in personally meaningful ways, however, a phenomenologically grounded human science does not adopt the standard of explanation in terms of prediction and control. Instead, it sets a standard of understanding, in terms of anticipation and influence.

In short, phenomenological psychology: (a) takes into account that science, including the psychology of adolescence, is a human enterprise shaped by our times and by psychologists; (b) looks first, as much as is possible, at life events, initially putting aside theories and experimental manipulation; (c) preserves the unitary character of phenomena and understands that their distinguishable aspects imply one another; (d) acknowledges that in concert with the givens of a situation, people co-create meanings and futures; and (e) through its empirical qualitative research studies, provides access to individuals' worlds in their own right. Phenomenological psychology offers an invitation to develop a psychology of adolescents as well as a psychology of adolescence.

REFERENCES

Alapack, M. C. L., & Alapack, R. J. (1984). The hinge of the door to authentic adulthood: A Kierkegaardian inspired synthesis of the meaning of leaving home. *Journal of Phenomenological Psychology,15*, 45–69.

Alapack, R. J. (1975). The outlaw relationship: An existential phenomenological reflection upon the transition from adolescence to adulthood. In A. Giorgi, C. T. Fischer, & E. L. Murray (Eds.), *Duquesne studies in phenomenological psychology* (Vol. 1, pp. 182–205). Pittsburgh, PA: Duquesne University Press.

Alapack, R. J. (1984). Adolescent first love. In C. M. Aanstoos (Ed.), *Studies in the social sciences: Vol. 23. Exploring the lived world: Readings in phenomenological psychology* (pp. 101–117). Carrollton: West Georgia College.

Alapack, R. J. (in press). The outlaw relationship as an intertwining of two identity crises: A phenomenological/psychotherapeutic reflection upon female awakening at late adolescence and male rejuvenation at mid-life. *Journal of Phenomenological Psychology*.

Barton, A. (1974). *Three worlds of therapy: Freud, Jung, Rogers*. Palo Alto, CA: National Press Books.

Becker, C. S. (1973). *A phenomenological explication of friendship: As exemplified by most important college women friends*. Unpublished doctoral dissertation, Duquesne University, Pittsburgh.

Beets, N. (1964). *Lichaamsbeleving en seksualiteit in de puberteit* [*The experience of body and sexuality in adolescence*]. Utrecht, the Netherlands: Bijleveld.

Beets, N. (1968). *Jeugd en welvaart* [*Youth and prosperity*]. Utrecht, the Netherlands: Bijleveld.

Benswanger, E. (1975). *An empirical–phenomenological study of inhabited space in early childhood*. Unpublished doctoral dissertation, Duquesne University, Pittsburgh.

Boelen, B. (1978). *Personal maturity: The existential dimension*. New York: Seabury.

Brennan, J. F. (1971). *Being in a family: An exploratory phenomenological study*. Unpublished doctoral dissertation, Duquesne University, Pittsburgh.

Buytendyk, F. J. J. (1966). *Jeugd in protest?* [*Youth in protest?*]. Tilburg, the Netherlands: MSC Drukkerij.

deKonig, A., & Jenner, F. (Eds.). (1982). *Phenomenology and psychiatry*. London: Academic Press.

deRivera, J. (Ed.). (1981). *Conceptual encounter: A method for the exploration of human experience*. Lanham, MD: University Press of America.

Dillon, M. C. (1980). Merleau-Ponty on existential sexuality: A critique. *Journal of Phenomenological Psychology, 11*, 67–81.

Erikson, E. H. (1963). *Childhood and society*. New York: Norton.

Erikson, E. H. (1968). *Identity: Youth and crisis*. New York: Norton.

Erikson, E. H. (1982). *The life cycle completed*. New York: Norton.

Everhart, R. (1983). *Reading, writing, and resistance: Adolescence in a junior high school*. Boston: Routledge & Keegan Paul.

Fischer, C. T. (1971). Toward the structure of privacy: Implications for psychological assessment. In A. Giorgi, W. F. Fischer, & R. vonEckartsberg (Eds.), *Duquesne studies in phenomenological psychology* (Vol. 1, pp. 149–163). Pittsburgh: Duquesne University Press.

Fischer, C. T. (1984). A phenomenological study of being criminally victimized: Contributions and constraints of qualitative research. *Journal of Social Issues, 40*, 161–177.

Fischer, C. T. (1985). *Individualizing psychological assessment*. Monterey, CA: Brooks-Cole.

Fischer, C. T., & Fischer, W. F. (1983). Phenomenological–existential psychotherapy. In M. Hersen, A. E. Kazdin, & A. S. Bellack (Eds.), *The clinical psychology handbook* (pp. 489–505). Elmsford, NY: Pergamon.

Frankl, V. E. (1969). *The will to meaning*. New York: New American Library.

Freud, S. (1963). Mourning and melancholia. In *General psychological theory* (pp. 164–179). New York: Collier Books. (Original work published 1917)

Giorgi, A. (1970). *Psychology as a human science: A phenomenological approach*. New York: Harper & Row.

Giorgi, A. (Ed.). (1985). *Phenomenology and psychological research*. Pittsburgh: Duquesne University Press.

Giorgi, A., Barton, A., & Maes, C. (Eds.). (1983). *Duquesne studies in phenomenological psychology* (Vol. 4). Pittsburgh: Duquesne University Press.

Giorgi, A., Fischer, C. T., & Murray, E. (Eds.). (1975). *Duquesne studies in phenomenological psychology* (Vol. 2). Pittsburgh: Duquesne University Press.

Giorgi, A., Fischer, W. F., & vonEckartsberg, R. (Eds.). (1971). *Duquesne studies in phenomenological psychology* (Vol. 1). Pittsburgh: Duquesne University Press.

Giorgi, A., Knowles, R., & Smith, D. L. (Eds.). (1979). *Duquesne studies in phenomenological psychology* (Vol. 3). Pittsburgh: Duquesne University Press.

Goethals, G. W., & Klos, D. S. (1970). *Experiencing youth: First-person accounts* (2nd ed.). Toronto: Little, Brown.

Heidegger, M. (1962). (J. Macquarrie, E. Robinson, Trans.). *Being and time*. New York: Harper & Row. (Original work published 1927)

Husserl, E. (1968). *Ideas: General introduction to pure phenomenology* (W. R. B. Gibson, Trans.). London: Allen & Unwin. (Original work published 1913)

Husserl, E. (1970). *The crisis of European sciences and transcendental phenomenology: An introduction to phenomenological philosophy* (D. Carr, Trans.). Evanston, IL: Northwestern University Press. (Original work published 1954)

Keen, E. (1970). *Three faces of being: Toward an existential clinical psychology*. New York: Appleton-Century-Crofts.

Kierkegaard, S. (1980). *Concept of anxiety*. Princeton, NJ: Princeton University Press. (Original work published 1844)

Knowles, R. T. (1977). Suggestions for an existential–phenomenological understanding of Erikson's concept of basic trust. *Journal of Phenomenological Psychology*, 7, 183–194.

Knowles, R. T. (1986). *Human development and human possibility: Erikson in the light of Heidegger*. Lanham, MD: University Press of America.

Levinas, E. (1969). *Totality and infinity*. Pittsburgh: Duquesne University Press.

Misiak, H., & Sexton, V. (1973). *Phenomenological, existential, and humanistic psychology: A historical survey*. New York: Grune & Stratton.

Mudaly, B. S. (1984). *The life-world of youth in children's homes*. Unpublished doctoral dissertation, Rhodes University, Grahamstown, South Africa.

Saint-Exupery, A. (1971). *Le petit prince*. New York: Harcourt, Brace, & World.

Steinbeck, J. (1972). *East of Eden*. New York: Bantam Books.

van den Berg, J. H. (1961). *The changing nature of man: Introduction to a historical psychology*. New York: Norton.

van Kaam, A. (1981). Explanatory charts of the science of foundational formation. *Studies in Formative Spirituality*, 2, 132.

Wolf, B. M. (1981). The struggling adolescent: A social–phenomenological study of adolescent substance abuse. *Journal of Alcohol and Drug Education*, 26 (3), 51–61.

Wolfe, J. (1980). *An empirical–phenomenological study of the best friend relationship between preadolescent boys*. Unpublished doctoral dissertation, Duquesne University, Pittsburgh.

PART III

General Issues

CHAPTER 7

Pubertal Processes: Their Relevance for Developmental Research

J. Brooks-Gunn

As Havinghurst (1952) noted years ago, psychological development may be profitably studied by examining both the biological changes of the body and the expectations of society. Both biological and social role change demand that the individual respond or adapt to that change. Interestingly, major transitional points in the social life tend to co-occur with changes in reproductive biology (Rossi, 1980). However, this co-occurrence does not necessarily imply a causal relationship between the two. Models of direct causal links between biological and psychological adaptation have been replaced by more interactive models in which the social events that co-occur with biological events are studied simultaneously in order to understand the role of each upon psychological adaptation (Brooks-Gunn & Petersen, 1983; Petersen & Taylor, 1980). Few studies have been designed in which changes in both types of events are explored.

From a developmental perspective, early adolescence is an ideal life phase in which to study the interface between social and biological changes. The pubescent child must incorporate the rapid physical changes and the ultimate attainment of reproductive maturity into his or her self-image, as well as adjust to the social demands made by others as physical maturity progresses.

The current literature on developmental aspects of puberty focuses on four themes. The first involves charting the course of *pubertal processes*, paying particular attention to the multidimensional nature of puberty, interindividual variation in the timing of events, and intraindividual variation in the timing, onset, and duration of different processes. Indeed, the title of this chapter reflects such a perspective; puberty is a set of processes, not just one process. The *psychological effect* of pubertal events constitutes the second theme. Most of the developmental literature focuses on maturational timing. Less often studied, but just as important, is the question of the *psychological significance* of puberty to the adolescent and to others, such as parents, teachers, and peers. Finally, possible mediating effects of *social factors* upon the relationship between maturational timing or status and psychological adaptation are studied. Contextual features or environmental demands may affect how the pubescent child responds to physical changes. In Lerner's (1985) terms, one may study the goodness of fit between an individual's maturational course and the expectations of a particular context. Or, in Bronfenbrenner's terms (1985), the interaction of person and environmental characteristics may be studied. The person's characteristics under study may be the pubertal processes themselves or the timing of these processes. Various environmental characteristics have been studied, including peer groups (Magnusson, Strattin, & Allen, 1986), variations in school composition (middle school versus junior high school; Simmons, Blyth, & McKinney, 1983), and athletic participation (Brooks-Gunn & Warren, 1985a; Gargiulo, Attie, Brooks-Gunn, & Warren, 1985).

In this chapter, literature related to these four themes will be reviewed. More comprehensive treatments of these topics are available (Brooks-Gunn, 1984; Brooks-Gunn & Petersen, 1983, 1984; Brooks-Gunn, Petersen, & Eichorn, 1985; Lerner & Foch, 1986; Petersen & Taylor, 1980).

PHYSICAL CHANGES OF PUBERTY

Physical changes associated with puberty have been described in great detail in the medical literature, especially with regard to body hair, breast and penis development (Marshall & Tanner, 1969; Tanner, 1974), growth velocity (Bock et al., 1973; Faust, 1977; Thissen, Bock, Wainer, & Roche, 1976), bone age on X-ray (Cheek, 1974; Forbes, 1975), and hormonal changes (Grumbach, Grave, & Mayer, 1974; Styne & Grumbach, 1978). Five longitudinal studies, four in the United States and one in England, have provided the bulk of information on growth and maturation (Malina, 1978). From a psychosocial perspective, however, multiple indices of physical growth have not been studied as extensively. This is due in part to the difficulties inherent in studying measures of physical status outside of medical settings, the necessity for prospective studies, and the reluctance of parents and teachers to allow pubertal studies to be conducted in school systems.

Developmentalists have not concentrated upon pubertal events for other reasons as well. In an attempt to move away from biological deterministic models, they have concentrated upon social and psychological events. Even when physical status has been included as a measure in early adolescent psychological research, it is often conceptualized either as a time-bounded variable or as a unidimensional one. Rate changes, asynchronies, or changes in status or timing have not been explored across the adolescent period (Brooks-Gunn & Warren, 1985b).

In order to understand the psychological effects of puberty, it is necessary to examine some of the various physical parameters related to maturation. Eight physical parameters associated with puberty will be reviewed briefly. These comprise three anthropomorphic measures (height, weight, bone age) and five secondary sexual characteristics (breast, body and pubic hair, and penile, testicular, and menarcheal development). Current methods for measuring each and interrelationships of various pubertal measures to one another will be discussed. (See Brooks-Gunn & Warren, 1985b for a more extensive discussion of these issues as well as a discussion of the relevance of each measure for maturational timing and status research and the usefulness of each measure for psychological research in general.) It is beyond the scope and is not the purpose of this review to provide a comprehensive look at growth and maturation; the reader is referred to several excellent reviews for such information (Eveleth & Tanner, 1976; Grumbach et al., 1974; Malina, 1978; Petersen & Taylor, 1980; Tanner, 1975).

Before turning to specific pubertal changes, a brief look at the timing of these changes is in order. The sequences for boys and girls are illustrated in Figures 7.1 and 7.2 (Marshall & Tanner, 1970). These schematics only outline the general process of puberty, as intraindividual and interindividual variations in the onset and duration of each event are large. In girls, breast and pubic hair growth begin, on the average, between 9 and 11 years of age. The apex of the height spurt occurs shortly thereafter, as the secondary sexual characteristics continue to develop. Menarche occurs fairly late in the sequence, and after the peak height velocity (PHV). For boys, the genitals begin to develop

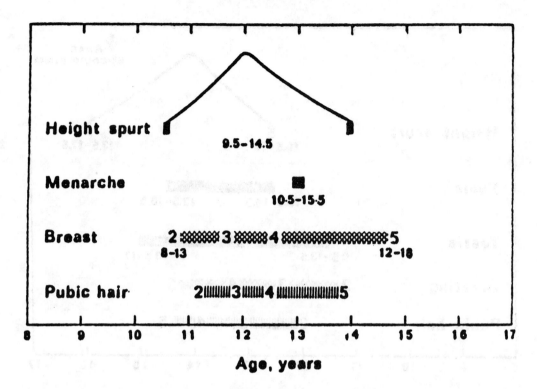

Figure 7.1. The developmental course of four pubertal processes for girls (From: *Growth at Adolescence* (p. 36) by J. M. Tanner, 1962, Oxford, England: Blackwell Scientific. Copyright 1962 by Blackwell Scientific. Reprinted with permission).

around age 11, with the testis developing before the penis. Pubic hair follows. The apex of the height spurt occurs late in the sequence, around 13 to 14 years of age.

Anthropomorphic Measures

Skeletal Maturity

Based on epiphyseal fusion of different bone centers and osseus maturation, bone status has been extensively studied (Styne & Grumbach, 1978). During the course of sexual maturation and as a direct result of the secretion of gonadal hormones, the epiphyseal cartilage plates become progressively obliterated. There is resultant fusion of the shafts and epiphyseal ossification centers, at which time linear growth ceases. Radiographs are made of the hand and wrist and compared to norms published in the Greulich and Pyle *Atlas* (1959) or the more recent norms of Tanner and Whitehouse (1975).

Skeletal maturity is related to secondary sexu-

al characteristics, peak height velocity, and menarche (Roche, Wainer & Thissen, 1975; Tanner, Whitehouse, Marubin, & Resele, 1976). It closely correlates with menarche, but is of little value in predicting when the secondary sex characteristics will develop (Marshall, 1974). At most stages of sexual development the variations in skeletal and chronological age differ very little from each other (Marshall, 1974). Correlations between skeletal age and the pubertal indices are typically higher for girls than boys (Malina, 1978; Marshall, 1974). For example, in one study, the correlation between PHV (peak height velocity) and skeletal age was .34 for boys and .74 for girls (Marshall, 1974).

Height

The most common anthropomorphic measure is standing height. Typically, changes in height over age are assessed using curve-fitting techniques (Bock et al., 1973; Thissen et al., 1976). In addition, maximum velocity and age at the peak of the growth spurt are examined

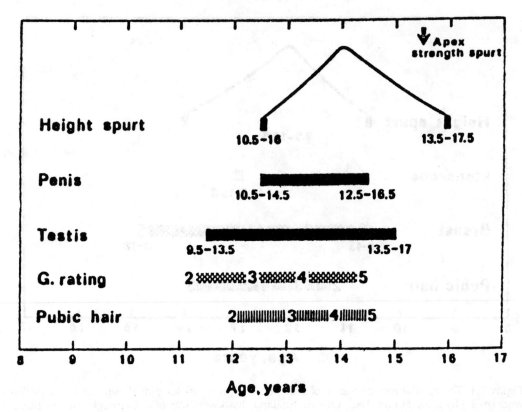

Figure 7.2. The developmental course of four pubertal processes for boys (From: *Growth at Adolescence* (p. 30) by J. M. Tanner, 1962, Oxford: Blackwell Scientific. Copyright 1962 by Blackwell Scientific. Reprinted with permission).

(Malina, 1978; Faust, 1977). The interest in velocity changes necessitates charting a child's height from middle childhood onwards—for girls, from age 8 or 9, and for boys, from age 9 or 10. Because 5 or 6 years of data collection are often not feasible, information on velocity is more likely to be collected for boys than for girls, as the former reach PHV later than the latter do.

The growth spurt typically occurs between Tanner Stages 1 and 3 for girls and Tanner Stages 4 and 5 for boys. The peak of the spurt occurs on the average 2 years earlier for girls than for boys (Faust, 1977; Tanner, 1962). PHV is moderately related to other pubertal indices.

Weight and Body Fat

Weight, like height, increases through pubertal growth, with a weight spurt around the time of peak height velocity (Malina, 1978; Parizkova, 1976; Tanner & Whitehouse, 1976). Much

less is known about the weight than the height spurt, and peak velocities typically are not charted. (See, as an exception, Tanner & Whitehouse, 1976.) Thus, weight is represented as an absolute, as a ratio related to height, or as a percentile. Percentile ratings take into account age and height, because weight increases with both during childhood and adolescence. Thus, absolute weight is not a good measure of physical growth (without taking into account height). Absolute weight or ideal weight using percentiles is used in most studies.

Rapid weight gain also is associated with an accumulation of body fat in girls and with increased muscle mass in boys (Tanner, 1962, 1972, 1975). The increases occur throughout sexual maturation, with the most rapid rise in body fat typically occurring in Tanner Stages 4 and 5 and in muscle circumference in Tanner Stages 3 and 4 (Gross, 1984). Figures 7.3 and 7.4 illustrate these relationships.

Body fat may be measured by examining skinfold thickness, percentage of body fat to total weight, or hydrostatic weighing. Measurement of skinfolds are made on one side of the body at four sites—biceps, triceps, iliac crest, and the subscapula area. The sum of these four skinfolds can be read off a table adjusted for sex and age (Durnin & Womersley, 1974; Merrow, 1967; Wilmore & Behnke, 1970; Young, Sipin, & Rose, 1968). Body fat also may be estimated from weights and heights, using the equation of Mellits and Cheek (1970). The Mellits–Cheek formula has been criticized because of the sample from which the formula was derived and the failure of many to consider the error term in the prediction equation (Billewicz, Fellowes, & Hyt-

ten, 1976; Johnston, Roche, Schnell, & Wettenhall, 1975).

Secondary Sexual Characteristics

The progression of secondary sexual characteristics has been carefully documented by Tanner (1962, 1975, 1978). For girls, changes in breast and body hair development, and for boys, body hair, changes in facial hair, voice lowering, penis development, and testicular volume have been examined. Data are most complete for pubic hair development in both sexes, breast development in girls, and penile development and testicular volume in boys. The sexual maturation stages will be discussed

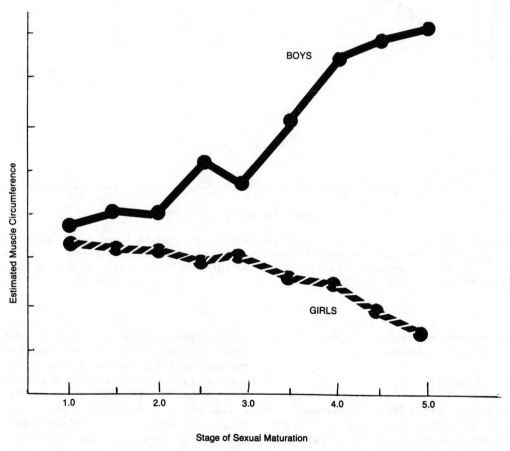

Figure 7.3. The relation of muscle circumference and pubertal developmental stage for boys and girls (From: Patterns of maturation: Their effects on behavior and development by R. T. Gross in *Middle Childhood: Development and Dysfunction*, p. 55, edited by M. D. Levine and P. Satz, 1984. Baltimore, MD: University Park Press).

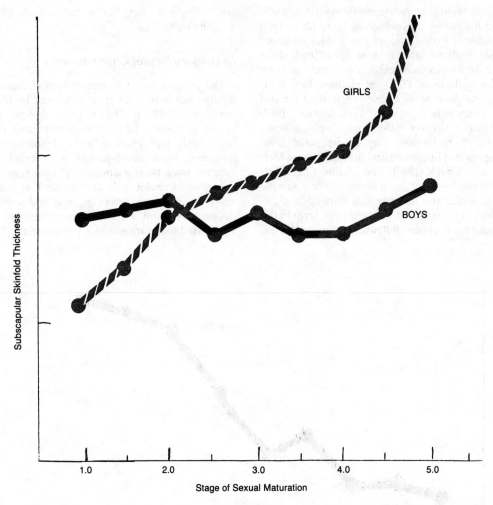

Figure 7.4. The relation of body fat (skinfold thickness) and pubertal developmental stage for boys and girls (From: Patterns of maturation: Their effects on behavior and development by R. T. Gross in *Middle Childhood: Development and Dysfunction*, p. 56, edited by M. D. Levine and P. Satz, 1984. Baltimore, MD: University Park Press).

first, followed by a brief presentation for each pubertal event separately.

Sexual Maturation Stage

Following Reynolds and Wines (1948, 1951), Marshall and Tanner (1969, 1970) devised a system for rating the amount of growth in breasts and pubic hair for girls and in the penis and pubic hair for boys. This system superimposes stages upon a continuous process, as Tanner has noted. Such a system allows for classification of an individual's amount of growth as well

as for comparison across cohorts and with other pubertal processes. Thus, the Tanner Stages, as they are often termed, do not represent qualitative changes, but a characterization of quantitative change. Schematic drawings and written explanations of the five stages of development are presented in Figure 7.5 for girls (breast and pubic hair growth) and Figure 7.6 for boys (penile and pubic hair growth). Stage 1 is prepubertal and State 5 postpubertal.

Typically the adolescents' development is rated by a pediatrician or nurse-practitioner during a physical examination. Other measurement techniques have been developed, given the reluctance of some adolescents to have a physical examination, feelings of parents, and school concerns. In one, nude photographs of the child are taken (front and profile positions). Sexual maturation ratings made from photographs are fairly reliable, although some difficulties arise when using black and white rather than color pictures (Petersen, 1976). However, photographs may be as objectionable to school personnel, parents, and adolescents as are physical examinations (and perhaps even more

so). Another approach is to ask adolescents or parents to rate current physical development using photographs or schematic drawings of the five sexual maturation stages. These attempts have been successful in medical and school settings and correlate well with nurse-practitioner ratings (Brooks-Gunn, Warren, Russo, & Gargiulo, in press; Duke, Litt, & Gross, 1980; Morris & Udry, 1980).

For example, in our study, correlations between physician ratings, Tanner ratings, and self-ratings were .82 and higher for 11- to 13-year-old girls. Another technique for assessing

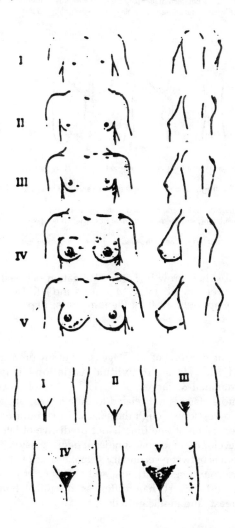

BREASTS

Please circle the stage your daughter currently is in.

  I. No breast development.

  II. The first sign of breast development has appeared. This stage is sometimes referred to as the breast budding stage. Some palpable breast tissue under the nipple, the flat area of the nipple (areola) may be somewhat enlarged.

  III. The breast is more distinct although there is no separation between contours of the two breasts.

  IV. The breast is further enlarged and there is greater contour distinction. The nipple, including the areola, forms a secondary mound on the breast.

  V. Mature Stage. Size may vary in the mature stage. The breast is fully developed. The contours are distinct and the areola has receded into the general contour of the breast.

PUBIC HAIR

Please circle the stage your daughter currently is in.

  I. No pubic hair.

  II. There is a small amount of long pubic hair chiefly along vaginal lips.

  III. Hair is darker, coarser, and curlier and spreads sparsely over skin around vaginal lips.

  IV. Hair is now adult in type, but area covered is smaller than in most adults. There is no pubic hair on the inside of the thighs.

  V. Hair is adult in type, distributed as an inverse triangle. There may be hair on the inside of the thighs.

Figure 7.5. The five pubertal stages for breast and pubic hair growth (From: "Variations in the pattern of pubertal changes in girls" by W. A. Marshall & J. M. Tanner, 1969, *Archives of Disease in Childhood, 44,* p. 291. Copyright 1969 by British Medical Association. Reprinted by permission).

PENIS AND SCROTUM

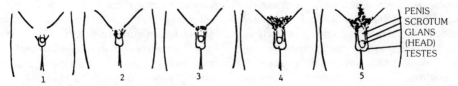

Stage 1: The infantile state that persists from birth until puberty begins. During this time the genitalia increase slightly in overall size, but there is little change in general appearance.

Stage 2: The scrotum has begun to enlarge, and there is some reddening and change in texture of the scrotal skin.

Stage 3: The penis has increased in length and there is a smaller increase in breadth. There has been further growth of the scrotum.

Stage 4: The length and breadth of the penis have increased further and the glans has developed. The scrotum is further enlarged, and the scrotal skin has become darker.

Stage 5: The genitalia are adult in size and shape. The appearance of the genitalia may satisfy the criteria for one of these stages for a considerable time before the penis and scrotum are sufficiently developed to be classified as belonging to the next stage.

PUBIC HAIR

Stage 1: There is no true pubic hair, although there may be a fine velus over the pubes similar to that over other parts of the abdomen.

Stage 2: Sparse growth of lightly pigmented hair, which is usually straight or only slightly curled. This usually begins at either side of the base of the penis.

Stage 3: The hair spreads over the pubic symphysis and is considerably darker and coarser and usually more curled.

Stage 4: The hair is now adult in character but covers an area considerably smaller than in most adults. There is no spread to the medial surface of the thighs.

Stage 5: The hair is distributed in an inverse triangle as in the female. It has spread to the medial surface of the thighs but not up the linea alba or elsewhere above the base of the triangle.

Figure 7.6. The five pubertal stages for penile and pubic hair growth (From: "Validation of a self-administered instrument to assess stage of adolescent development" by N. M. Morris and J. R. Udry, 1980, *Journal of Youth and Adolescence, 9,* pp. 275–276. Copyright 1980 by Plenum Press. Reprinted with permission).

pubertal growth is to ask parents to rate their adolescents' physical status. In the 10 schools with which we have worked, this procedure was accepted, whereas the self-rating procedure was not. Mothers rated their daughters' pubertal stages as reliably as the adolescent girls themselves (Brooks-Gunn & Warren in press-a).

Finally, students may be asked how much they have developed using an interview or questionnaire format rather than giving them schematic drawings of nude figures (Petersen et al., 1985). This procedure also correlates with physician ratings, although not as highly as the ratings of schematic drawings (Brooks-Gunn et al., in press).

The duration of any stage is not easily predicted, and large individual variations exist (Marshall & Tanner, 1969, 1970). Age of entry into a stage is not related to duration or rate of progression through the stages. Thus, information taken at one time is not predictive of later development to any significant degree. Asynchronies between secondary sexual characteristics are common. The timing and sequence of pubic and axillary hair differ, as do pubic hair, breast, and penile growth.

Hair Growth

The development of hair involves pubic, axillary, and facial hair, all of which show somewhat different developmental progressions.

Hair growth may be related to androgen secretion, in part from the adrenal gland. An as yet unidentified pituitary adrenal androgen-stimulating hormone has been hypothesized to account for hair growth (Grumbach, Richards, Conte, & Kaplan, 1977). Pubic rather than axillary body or facial hair development is most frequently studied.

Breast Development

Breast development is believed to be influenced by the secretion of estrogen, specifically estradiol from the ovary. Other contributing factors may be hormones secreted by the anterior pituitary gland, such as prolactin. Also indicative of increased estrogen secretion is the increase in body fat and menarche (Warren, 1983). Like hair growth, breast development is ultimately controlled by a pituitary–adrenal hormone, in this case one stimulating estrogen (Grumbach et al., 1977). Breast development is typically assessed using the Tanner staging method discussed earlier.

Testicular and Penile Development

Growth of the testes is usually the first sign of puberty in the male; it occurs about 6 months later than secondary sexual development in girls, which usually begins with breast development. In general, a longitudinal measurement of greater than 2.5 cm in a testis is compatible with pubertal testicular enlargement. The testicular volume index (length × width of right testis and length × width of left testis/2) and testicular volume measured by comparison of testes with ellipsoids of known volume correlate with stages of puberty (Styne & Grumbach, 1978). Typically, penile development is measured using Tanner stages (see Figure 7.6).

The maturation of the male phallus usually correlates closely with pubic hair development as both are under androgen control. However, pubic hair, phallus, and testes development are classified separately. Genital development proceeds faster than growth of pubic hair.

The timing of these pubertal events relative to the growth spurt in boys is substantially different from that in girls. Whereas girls usually show acceleration of linear growth at the onset of puberty and reach peak height velocities relatively early in the pubertal process, boys more typically reach their peak height velocities

when genital and pubic hair ratings are at Tanner stage 4 or 5.

Menarche

Menarche, or the onset of menstruation, occurs relatively late in the maturational sequence, typically after the peak growth spurt, between Tanner Stages 4 and 5, and in the middle of the fat/weight spurt (Marshall & Tanner, 1969). The events that initiate normal puberty development and culminate in menarche and normal cyclicity in girls are not well understood. Research suggests that the events are probably initiated in the central nervous system (CNS), which releases the toxic inhibitory control of gonadotropin luteinizing hormone (LH) and follicle stimulating hormone (FSH) secretion from the pituitary.

Puberty is marked by a rise in FSH secretion, nocturnal spurting of gonadotropins, and finally enhanced release of FSH, and later LH, in response to intravenous luteinizing releasing hormone (LRH). The pattern of LRH stimulation also appears to be important, as intermittent LRH injections can initiate puberty in humans (Styne & Grumbach, 1978; Swerdloff, 1978; Valk, Corley, Kelch, & Marshall, 1980). Full maturity of the CNS hypothalamic–pituitary–gonadal unit in the female is marked by the development of an adult pattern of episodic release of gonadotropins and eventually in normal menstrual cyclicity (Grumbach et al., 1974; Styne & Grumbach, 1978).

Self-reports of menarche are quite accurate, across all birth cohorts and ages (Garn, 1980). However, around the time of menarche, a few girls may misreport menarche. In one study of 50 girls called every 10–12 weeks to see if they had begun to menstruate, 2 said they had begun, but, upon a subsequent interview, stated that they had not (Brooks-Gunn & Ruble, 1982a). In another study of 87 junior-high-school students, 89% of the mothers and daughters agreed as to the girls' menarcheal status. Six girls denied menarche had occurred when it had (according to the mother), and three did not know or declined to say, although their mothers said it had not occurred (Petersen, 1983). Menarcheal age reports are less reliable; some individuals often "round off" to the nearest year (Marshall, 1984). Even then, correlations between actual and recalled ages are about .40, from 4 to 19 years later (Bergsten-Brucefors, 1976; Damon et al., 1969).

Summary

One of the major lessons to be learned from the English and American growth studies is that puberty is a series of correlated events, not a unitary process. In addition, any one measure will not accurately represent an individual's current status. No particular measure will necessarily characterize pubertal status better than another. Indeed, the choice of a particular measure depends on the purpose of the study, the feasibility of obtaining accurate measures, and the importance of distinguishing between biological processes and the social significance of the event.

MATURATIONAL TIMING

Life-Span Development

Life-span developmentalists have proposed that age-graded, history-graded, and nonnormative influences may affect the course of development (Baltes, 1968; Baltes & Reese, 1984). Age-graded means all normative age-related factors.

Petersen and Crockett (1985) have suggested that at least four age-graded factors are relevant to the study of early adolescence; these are chronological age, biological age, cognitive age, and grade in school. The first reflects amount of life experience; the second, maturation (in the case of adolescence, pubertal age); the third, intelligence or cognition; and the fourth, the amount one has learned academically and socially. Thus, maturation is only one normative factor for which timing effects may be studied.

In several of the papers in a special issue of the *Journal of Youth and Adolescence* (Brooks-Gunn, Petersen, & Eichorn, 1985), the relative effects of different age-related factors are examined within a timing framework. For example, Petersen and Crockett's work (1985) suggests that, when maturational timing and grade are examined, grade-in-school effects are much larger than timing effects. Because the adolescents' social world is organized by grade in school rather than by pubertal development, the primacy of the former should not surprise us. On the other hand, this does not mean that maturation has no influence on behavior, but

does suggest the need to embed pubertal timing effects within a larger framework.

Another approach to the study of grade and maturational timing not unrelated to the life-span perspective has been taken by Blyth, Simmons, and Zakin (1985). In their work, the interaction of grade, school transitions, and pubertal timing has been studied. They have found, for example, that early-maturing sixth-grade girls find the transition to middle school more difficult than on-time or late-maturing sixth-grade girls or than early-maturing sixth graders not moving to middle school. This fine-grained individual difference approach suggests that maturational timing may be especially potent at a specific juncture for a subgroup of children defined by their maturational timing—in this case, sixth graders leaving elementary school.

The life-span perspective also has made a major contribution to our understanding of timing effects by the introduction of the notion of on-time and off-time events. Neugarten (1979), in particular, has discussed how the life cycle is perceived in terms of a set of norms about what events should occur, as well as when they should occur. The "social clock," which is internalized by individuals, identifies life phases and expected life transitions. Events that are off-time, occurring earlier or later than anticipated, may result in a crisis for the individual (Neugarten, 1969; Neugarten & Hagestad, 1976). Critical to this notion is the importance of the individual's perception of timeliness, as well as actual timelines. That is, an event may be perceived to be on-time or off-time depending on a variety of factors, such as one's referent group, the cohort in which one finds herself, the importance to the individual of being in phase, and an individual's perception of the range of on-time. For example, late-maturing female adolescent athletes are more likely to perceive themselves as being on-time, rather than late-maturing nonathletic peers. In part, these differences are due to the fact that more athletes have delayed menarche than do nonathletes; the athlete's peer group influences her perception of timeliness (Gargiulo et al., 1985).

Psychological Effects

Early Results
The facts that not all children go through pubertal development at the same time and that children are aware of their actual stage of devel-

opment vis-à-vis their peers have intrigued psychologists for the past 40 years. The Berkeley, Oakland, and Fels growth studies have explored the effects of early and late maturation upon individuals' social adaptation in adolescence and beyond. Specifically, early maturing boys seemed to have an advantage relative to late maturers in many aspects of social–emotional functioning. In the Oakland Growth Study, for example, early maturing boys were seen as more relaxed and attractive to adults and more attractive and popular with their peers than were the late maturers (Jones, 1965; Jones & Bayley, 1950). In late adolescence, early maturing boys were more likely to be leaders and to display more adult behavior than were late maturers (Clausen, 1975; Mussen & Jones, 1957). Finally, differences in social functioning were still seen when the subjects reached adulthood (Clausen, 1975). In contrast, the Berkeley Guidance Study found that early maturation had detrimental as well as positive behavioral correlates. Peskin (1967) found that early-maturing males were more somber, temporarily more anxious, and more submissive around the time of puberty, whereas this was not the case for the late maturers.

The growth studies produced more divergent findings for girls than for boys with regard to timing of maturation. Early maturation does not seem to be as much of a social advantage for girls as for boys. For example, Jones and Mussen (1958) reported that the early-maturing girls in the Oakland Growth Study were not likely to be popular or to be in leadership positions, although this relationship was later found to be mediated by social class. In the Berkeley Guidance Study, early-maturing girls displayed significantly more diminished sociability and unrest in adolescence than late-maturing girls. These negative effects had disappeared by the time the girls had reached adulthood (Peskin, 1973). And, in an early study conducted by Faust (1960), being average for age was more desirable in grade 6, whereas being advanced was more prestigious in grades 7 and 8.

Recent Research *

Many investigators have focused on timing effects for girls, because the earlier data were so inconsistent. A large range of psychosocial domains have been studied—familial relationships, parent–adolescent interaction, peer relationships, heterosocial behavior, sexuality, psychopathology, school adjustment, self-esteem, body image, eating problems, and deviant behavior (Brooks-Gunn & Petersen, 1984). The diversity is laudable, in that it provides a way of identifying the domains in which timing effects are found. For example, pubertal timing effects for girls seem to be quite prevalent for social deviancy and body image, with early maturers exhibiting poorer body images and more social deviancy than later maturers (Brooks-Gunn, Petersen, & Eichorn, 1985).

Family relationships are affected by maturational status also. Early maturing girls in seventh grade were less likely to participate in family activities and less influenced by their parents. In addition, their parents were less accepting of them (Hill, Holmbeck, Marlow, Green, & Lynch, 1985). Two other studies, using different family relationship scales than the Hill study, do not report timing effects (Brooks-Gunn & Warren, in press-b; Petersen & Crockett, 1985). However, the finding that early-maturing girls may not participate in the family as much as later developing girls speaks to the possibly greater influence of peers on early maturers. Magnusson, Strattin, and Allen (1986), in an analysis of a sample of Swedish Adolescent girls, find early-maturing girls to have more older friends than late-maturing girls. In addition, those early maturers with more older friends were most likely to exhibit socially deviant behavior (see Figure 7.7). Because these effects were seen at age 16, it is possible that maturational timing effects may persist, at least through the adolescent years. The Oakland and Berkeley growth studies report maturational timing effects through adulthood for boys.

Pubescent children may seek friends who are similar in physical status, such that early maturers would have more early-maturing friends, even controlling for grade in school or age. In one study, best friends were perceived to be more physically similar than other friends by fifth-, sixth-, and seventh-grade girls (Brooks-Gunn, Samelson, Warren, & Fox, 1986).

In brief, early maturation seems to be a disadvantage or to have no effect for girls but to be an advantage for boys. However, these effects are

---

*A special issue of the *Journal of Youth and Adolescence* (Brooks-Gunn, Petersen, & Eichorn, 1985) presents the recent research on the psychological effects of maturational timing; a more in-depth discussion of this topic may be found there.

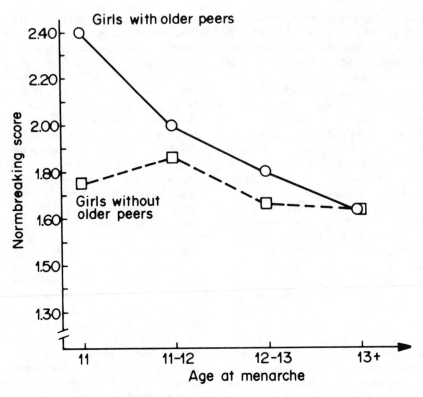

Figure 7.7. Relation between norm breaking and menarcheal age for girls with and without older friends (From: "Relation between Expected Peer Sanctions for Norm Breaking and Menarcheal Age for Girls with and without Older Friends" by D. Magnusson, H. Strattin, and V. L. Allen, 1985, *Journal of Youth and Adolescence, 50*, p. 276. Copyright 1985 by Plenum Press. Reprinted with permission).

measure-specific, are often not as strong as grade effects and may or may not be long-lasting.

Conceptual Models

Several conceptual models concerning pubertal timing effects have been developed. Petersen and Crockett (1985) have looked at deviance and stage termination hypotheses. The *deviance* hypothesis states that early and late maturers differ from on-time maturers because of their status, being socially deviant compared to their peer group. Early-maturing girls and late-maturing boys would be at risk for adjustment problems because they constitute the two most deviant groups in terms of maturation. Another hypothesis is the *stage termination* hypothesis which states that early maturation interrupts

the developmental tasks of middle childhood. Girls, especially those maturing early, would be most affected by timing if this hypothesis is correct. The Petersen and Crockett findings (1985) support both, at least to some degree, for girls.

Another set of hypotheses was proposed by Blyth et al. (1985) to account for the effects of pubertal development in different school contexts. All three are related to the salience of potential reference standards or groups for body image. The authors find strong support for a cultural ideal of thinness hypothesis as influencing body image and, to a lesser extent, a school transitions hypothesis.

In brief, these approaches allow for the refinement of possible explanatory models, as well as a comparison of alternative hypotheses. Of interest is the fact that most models are interactive, in that both biological and social factors are taken into account.

PSYCHOLOGICAL MEANING OF PUBERTAL PROCESSES

Distinct from the maturational timing literature is that focusing on the psychological response to pubertal change. In the former case, the effect of one's maturation relative to a referent group or a norm is of interest; in the latter case, the psychological effects of physical growth or the significance of a physical event, independent of when it occurs, is studied. Much less is known about the meaning of puberty to the individual than about the effects of variance in the timing of maturation (Brooks-Gunn, 1984). The paucity of research is in part due to the fact that pubertal change was believed to be a negative experience or, at the very least, something not to be discussed. Societal changes, including more universal health education, an earlier age of intercourse, national advertising of personal products for women, and a more open attitude about discussing reproduction in certain segments of society, have made it possible to question adolescents directly about the significance of puberty to them.

The significance of various pubertal events will be reviewed. (See Brooks-Gunn, 1984, for a more complete discussion.) Because events may have different meaning, they are considered individually. For example, physical changes that may be observed by others (e.g., breast growth) may possibly have more of an effect than changes not as easily observed (e.g., pubic hair). Events that are more directly linked to sexuality may mean something different to the pubescent child than events not as indicative of sexuality (e.g., breast development versus the growth spurt or penile growth versus pubic hair growth).

Menarche

In the last decade, the psychological significance of menarche has been studied quite extensively, as illustrated by edited volumes (Brooks-Gunn & Petersen, 1983; Golub, 1983) and reviews (Greif & Ulman, 1982). One of the primary questions has to do with to what extent menarche elicits anxiety, may be considered traumatic, and/or has integrative positive aspects. The adult psychoanalytic literature has addressed all three possibilities. The event was most often characterized as anxiety-producing and disgusting, although it was thought to have

beneficial effects by some (Blos, 1962; Deutsch, 1944; Kestenberg, 1967). Research on adolescents' experience of menarche rather than adults' recollections is more relevant. Menarche heralds increases in social maturity, peer prestige, self-esteem, heightened self-awareness of one's body and self-consciousness (Garwood & Allen, 1979; Koff, Rierdan, & Jacobson, 1981; Koff, Rierdan, & Silverstone, 1978; Simmons, Blyth, & McKinney, 1983). Thus, menarche seems to be related to social maturity.

However, when examining emotional feelings, somewhat ambivalent reactions to menarche are reported. Typically, girls describe both positive and negative feelings—excited and pleased, scared and upset (Petersen, 1983; Whisnant & Zegans, 1975). In one study that interviewed girls about how they felt right after menarche occurred (within 2 to 3 months), 20% gave only positive, 20% negative and 20% mixed emotions such as "felt same" or "felt funny" (Ruble & Brooks-Gunn, 1982). One third indicated they were not scared or upset, indicative perhaps of denial or negative premenarcheal expectations. Using less direct measures of emotional reactions, such as projective techniques, approximately one third of girls are somewhat scared or upset and one half pleased or happy (Petersen, 1983). The most negative responses are found using a sentence completion task starting with the phrase "Ann just got her period for the first time" (Rierdan & Koff, 1984).

Thus, girls tend not to be extremely negative, although the percentage reporting any negative feelings at all is related to the type of technique used to elicit responses. Girls may be more reluctant to discuss negative feelings in interviews. At the same time, projective techniques may elicit girls' feelings about the event in general, not their specific reaction to the event for themselves. For example, adult and adolescent females report that women in general experience more severe symptoms than they themselves experience (Brooks, Ruble, & Clarke, 1977).

The psychological meaning of menarche seems to vary as a function of contextual factors. The most robust findings are that girls who are early and girls who are unprepared for menarche report more negative experiences at menarche than on-time or prepared girls (Brooks-Gunn & Ruble, 1982a; Koff, Rierdan, & Sheingold, 1982). In addition, not being prepared seems to have long-term effects, as adult and late adolescent females who remember being unprepared report more severe menstrual symptoms, more negative attitudes about menstruation, and more self-consciousness (Ruble & Brooks-Gunn, 1982; Koff, Rierdan, & Sheingold, 1982; Logan, 1980). Being unprepared typically is related to lack of information from the mother, because the mother is still the primary source of information about menarche for the majority of girls in the United States today (Brooks-Gunn & Ruble, 1982a).

Familial contextual features also have been examined. For example, girls have been asked whether or not their fathers knew about their menarche. Girls whose fathers were not told about menarche are more likely to report negative attitudes and severe menstrual symptoms than those who report that their fathers knew about their menarche (Brooks-Gunn & Ruble, 1980; Brooks-Gunn, in press). This question—fathers' knowledge of their daughters' menarche—might be a proxy for familial openness in discussing physical or sexual issues, which in turn relates to a less negative attitude about one's body and/or a less negative menarcheal experience. Families from different cultural or religious subgroups also may prepare girls differently for menarche, or at the very least may provide varied amounts of information to girls (Abel & Joffe, 1950). For example, the menstrual flow has different salience for the three major religious groups in this country (Brooks-Gunn, 1985; Paige, 1974).

Discussion about menarche also may vary with respect to the peer group. Girls almost never discuss menarche with boys, but do have extensive exchanges with girl friends (Brooks-Gunn & Ruble, 1982a; Brooks-Gunn et al., 1986). Even with girl friends, reluctance to discuss menstruation occurs immediately after menarche: Premenarcheal girls expect to tell more girl friends than they actually tell. In one study, only one quarter tell anyone other than their mothers when they reach menarche. Their reluctance to discuss the event lasts for about 6 months; by that time approximately 80% of the girls in our study had talked to their girl friends. Thus, little information transmission seems to occur immediately following menarche, although later on, friends share stories about symptoms and negative attitudes (Ruble & Brooks-Gunn, 1982). Girls also may select friends based on their perceived similarity with respect to menarche (Brooks-Gunn et al., 1986).

Breast Development

Like menarche, breast development is linked culturally to childbearing as well as to sexuality. Unlike menarche, it is observed by others and may be an event that is frequently commented upon. Almost no information is available on the meaning of breast development. In one study, 120 fifth- and sixth-grade girls were surveyed. Breast development was ascertained by maternal ratings of schematic representations of the five Tanner stages, and psychological adaptation was measured using scales from the Self Image Questionnaire for Young Adolescents (Petersen, Schulenberg, Abramowitz, Offer, & Jarcho, 1984). Girls with more advanced breast growth had higher scores on the adjustment, body image, and peer relation scales and rated marriage and children as more important than less advanced girls. More physically mature girls had higher scores in both grades, although the differences were only significant for the fifth graders. Similar results were found using a measure of perceived timing of breast development (Brooks-Gunn, 1984).

Whether such effects are due to the sexual meaning of breast development to girls themselves, actions of others, a press for more grown-up behavior, or some combination of these is not known. In order to begin an exploration of the meaning of breast development to others, these same girls were asked a series of questions about direct comments made to them about their breast development. When asked about whether or not they had ever been teased about breast development, one third said they had been. Being teased was related to pubertal growth. Only 6% of those who had no breast development had been teased versus 50% who were in Tanner Stage 3. Those who were teased reported that one or two persons on the average had done so, with the most frequent teasers being mothers, fathers, and female peers. When asked to indicate how they felt when teased, 8% reported being upset, 22% embarrassed, and 20% angry. None were pleased (Brooks-Gunn, 1984). As expected, then, others do comment about a girl's breast development, starting with the onset of breast buds. Many girls are embarrassed or angry, suggesting that they do not interpret these comments as positive.

Hair Growth

Another pubertal event that is not as easily observed as breast development but occurs at approximately the same is pubic hair growth. While it is private like menarche, hair growth does not carry the sexual and reproductive meaning that menarche does. In the study that was just mentioned, mothers also rated their daughters' pubic hair development using schematics of the five Tanner stages. No relationships were found between psychological functioning and hair growth for any measure or for either grade. In fact, when covariate analyses were performed, breast, but not pubic, hair growth accounted for the relationship between physical status and psychological functioning (Brooks-Gunn, 1984).

Ejaculation

Very little is known about the meaning of pubertal changes to boys. It is believed that the occurrence of ejaculation, or spermarche, is as significant for boys as menarche is for girls. In a pilot study, 13 midadolescent boys were interviewed with regard to their emotional reactions to the event, informational sources, and extent of peer discussion following the event (Gaddis & Brooks-Gunn, 1985). First, emotional reactions to ejaculation were not very negative, although two thirds of the sample did report being a little scared, comparable to studies of girls' reactions to menarche (Petersen, 1983; Ruble & Brooks-Gunn, 1982). Positive responses were stronger than negative ones. Second, none of the boys were totally unprepared prior to the event. Third, although all boys were a little prepared, few sources were mentioned. Indeed, adolescent males may have more information about menarche than ejaculation, given the pervasiveness of health education classes and the treatment of menarche in these classes (Clarke & Ruble, 1978). Finally, these boys, all of whom had had an ejaculation, were extremely reluctant to discuss the experience with parents or peers. None had talked to peers about their own experiences, although all joked about it. This secrecy may be in part due to spermarche's

link to masturbation, a relationship that does not exist for menarche.

Meaning of Puberty to Others

Although a great deal has been written about possible effects of pubertal growth upon family members and peers (Blos, 1979; Erikson, 1968; A. Freud, 1958), little research has been forthcoming. The exception is the work of Hill, Steinberg, and their colleagues (Steinberg, 1981; Steinberg & Hill, 1978; Hill et al., 1985). The Hill and Steinberg work focused on parent-son interactions during early adolescence that were altered during the period of physical change. For example, mothers and sons both interrupted each other more as physical change progressed. At the end of pubertal growth, mothers' interruptions declined and a corresponding increase in maternal diffidence was seen. Not surprisingly, the mothers lost influence over their sons at the end of puberty. In contrast, fathers did not become more submissive as their sons developed but instead became more dominant.

A recent study of parents and daughters examined parental acceptance, family rules, involvement in family activities, parental influence, and disagreement over rules in families with daughters in seventh grade. The mother-daughter but not the father-daughter relationship was related to menarcheal status. Specifically, changes in relations occurred just after menarche and 12 months after menarche, with girls becoming less involved in family activities, and parents having less influence over them.

Summary

It is clear that the psychological significance of puberty is determined by many factors. First, the maturational indices under study are of critical importance. The adolescent's reaction may in part be determined by distinctions that are made among events, such as public versus private, relevance for adult sex roles, perceived links to sexuality, familial acceptance of discussion, and so on. Second, contextual cues influence psychological reactions to puberty; research to date has focused on preparation, maturational timing, and, to a lesser extent, family and peer factors. Third, others' responses to pubertal change have begun to be explored. The meager findings suggest that physical changes act as a stimulus to others for a change in behavior; of particular importance is the fact that parents may expect more socially mature behavior from the developing adolescents and that peer groups may change as a function of physical growth.

CONTEXTUAL INFLUENCES: PERSON AND ENVIRONMENT INTERACTIONS

Lerner (1985) has stressed the importance of reciprocal relations between the environment and the organism, in order to understand how adolescent maturational change and psychological development are linked. He has outlined three ways in which the adolescent may act as a producer of his or her own environment. The adolescent may influence his or her development "as a consequence of constituting a distinct stimulus to others, for example, through characteristics of physical and/or behavioral individuality." Pubescent adolescents may elicit different responses from others based on their physical status, maturational timing, or attractiveness. For example, physically attractive adolescents of both sexes are perceived more positively than their less attractive peers (Sorell & Nowak, 1981). Feedback from significant others influences the adolescent's psychological development: More adjustment problems are seen in physically unattractive than attractive adolescents (Lerner & Lerner, 1977).

Adolescents also may "produce their own development as a consequence of their capabilities as a processor of the world" (e.g., in regard to cognitive structure and mode of emotional reactivity; Lerner, 1985). For example, girls who report being prepared for menarche subsequently have a more positive experience (Ruble & Brooks-Gunn, 1982).

Finally, adolescents may shape and/or select their contexts or environments. One of the most obvious examples is the selection of peers; we have found that the best friends are more similar in maturational status than other friends—or at least are perceived as similar (Brooks-Gunn et al., 1986). Magnusson et al. (1986) have found that early maturers with older friends act differently than those with few or no older friends (see Figure 7.7).

Another example is our work with adolescents in two contexts, dance and nondance schools. Because the dance student must maintain a relatively low body weight, it was expected that being a late maturer (who is often leaner than an on-time maturer) will be more advantageous to the dancer than to the student who is not required to meet a weight standard (Brooks-Gunn & Warren, 1985a). More adolescent dancers than nondancers were late maturers (55% versus 29%). The dance students weighed less and were leaner than the comparison sample and had more eating problems and lower impulse control. Late-maturing students weighed less, were leaner, and had lower eating scores than on-time maturers, with these differences being more pronounced in the dance than nondance students. In addition, the on-time dancers had higher psychopathology, perfection, and bulimia scores and lower body-image scores than did the later maturing dancers.

These findings suggest that a goodness of fit exists between the requirements of a particular social context and a person's physical and behavioral characteristics. In addition, they suggest that those dancers who are more successful in keeping their weight low delay their menarche (Brooks-Gunn & Warren, 1985a, Brooks-Gunn, 1986). Dancers with delayed menarche are different physically: They weigh much less than on-time dancers, a condition that is adaptive within the dance context. In addition, late maturers seem to have greater control over eating, which may in part account for their lower weight. These differences in turn may affect the later maturers' behavior and self-expectancies.

Though the on-time maturing dancers are thin by almost any standards, they are average weight for dancers. That the on-time dancers may be at a relative disadvantage, at least in terms of their weight, is reflected in their negative body images and feelings about their weight. With regard to behaviors related to weight, they have higher scores on dieting and bulimia scales, suggesting that food is highly salient. However, they have lower oral control scores than later maturers, suggesting that they may be less successful in restraining themselves. They may be exhibiting the cycle of binging and restraining described by others in nonathletic samples. Psychologically, they are less emotionally healthy, which may be a consequence of not meeting the expectations of their profession and of realizing that they are less likely to enter a national company after high-school graduation than are their late-maturing counterparts (Hamilton, Brooks-Gunn, & Warren, 1986). This premise is predicated on the fact that on-time dancers rate dance to be as important to them as do late-maturing dancers.

In brief, maturation may have different meaning, depending on the context in which it occurs. For dancers, who must maintain a low weight in order to perform, being on-time (and heavier) is a disadvantage. For girls for whom weight is not an issue, being on-time is not perceived negatively. In a similar vein, the development of breasts and menarche seem to affect athletes negatively, which is not true of non-athletic adolescents (Gargiulo, Brooks-Gunn, Attie, & Warren, 1985).

CONCLUSIONS

In brief, the role of pubertal processes in the development of the young adolescent is being studied from a variety of perspectives, with multidisciplinary approaches, using a number of methodologies. Simplistic views of unidirectional effects of puberty upon behavior, static conceptualizations of pubertal processes, and differing effects of puberty upon psychosocial functioning are being replaced. Perhaps most important is the emphasis on the effects of changes in pubertal status and timing upon the individual, and the possible interactions between pubertal processes and environmental characteristics upon behavior. Such a developmental perspective has been absent from much of the earlier work.

Acknowledgements—The support of the W. T. Grant Foundation and the National Institutes of Health for the preparation of this chapter is greatly appreciated. Dr. Michelle P. Warren's collaboration on research reported here and her comments on the medical aspects of the chapter are deeply appreciated. Rosemary Deibler is to be thanked for her help in manuscript preparation.

REFERENCES

Abel, T., & Joffe, N. F. (1950). Cultural background of female puberty. *American Journal of Psychotherapy, 4*, 90–93.

Baltes, P. B. (1968). Longitudinal and cross-sectional sequences in the study of age and generation effects. *Human Development, 11*, 145–171.

Baltes, P. B., & Reese, H. W. (1984). The life-span perspective in developmental psychology. In Lamb, M. E., & Bornstein, M. H. (Eds.), *Developmental psychology: An advanced textbook*. Hillsdale, NJ: Erlbaum.

Bergsten-Brucefors, A. (1976). A note on the accuracy of recalled age of menarche. *Annals of Human Biology, 3*, 71.

Billewicz, W. Z., Fellowes, H. M., & Hytten, C. A. (1976). Comments on the critical metabolic-mass and the age of menarche. *Annals Human Biology, 3*, 51–59.

Blos, P. (1962). *On adolescence: A psychoanalytic interpretation*. New York: Free Press.

Blyth, D. A., Simmons, R. G., & Zakin, D. F. (1985). Satisfaction with body-image for early adolescent females: The impact of pubertal timing within different school environments. *Journal of Youth and Adolescence, 14*, 207–225.

Bock, R. D., Wainer, H., Petersen, A. C., Thissen, D., Murray, J., & Roche, A. F. (1973). A parameterization for individual human growth curves. *Human Biology, 45*, 63–80.

Bronfenbrenner, U. (1985, May). *Interacting systems in human development. Research paradigms: Present and future*. Paper presented for the Society for Research in Child Development Study Group. Ithaca, NY: Cornell University.

Brooks, J., Ruble, D. N., & Clarke, A. (1977). College women's attitudes and expectations concerning menstrual-related changes. *Psychosomatic Medicine, 39*, 288–298.

Brooks-Gunn, J. (1984). The psychological significance of different pubertal events to young girls. *Journal of Early Adolescence, 4*(4), 315–327.

Brooks-Gunn, J. (1985). The salience and timing of the menstrual flow. *Psychosomatic Medicine, 47*, 363–371.

Brooks-Gunn, J. (in press). Delayed menarche as a sample case of the study of biobehavioral interaction. In R. Lerner & T. T. Foch (Eds.), *Biological-psychosocial interactions in early adolescence: A life-span perspective*. Hillsdale, NJ: Erlbaum.

Brooks-Gunn, J., & Petersen, A. C. (Eds.). (1983). *Girls at puberty: Biological and psychosocial perspectives*. New York: Plenum.

Brooks-Gunn, J., & Petersen, A. C. (1984). Problems in studying and defining pubertal events. *Journal of Youth and Adolescence, 13*(3), 181–196.

Brooks-Gunn, J., Petersen, A. C., & Eichorn, D. (1985). Time of maturation and psychosocial functioning in adolescence. *Journal of Youth and Adolescence, 14*(3/4).

Brooks-Gunn, J., & Ruble, D. N. (1980). Menarche: The interaction of physiology, cultural and social factors. In A. J. Dan, E. A. Graham, & C. P. Beecher (Eds.), *The menstrual cycle: A synthesis of interdisciplinary research* (pp. 141–159). New York: Springer.

Brooks-Gunn, J., & Ruble, D. N. (1982a). The development of menstrual-related beliefs and behaviors during early adolescence. *Child Development, 53*, 1567–1577.

Brooks-Gunn, J., & Ruble, D. N. (1982b). Developmental processes in the experience of menarche. In A. Baum & J. E. Singer (Eds.), *Handbook of psy-

chology and health (Vol. 2, pp. 117–147). Hillsdale, NJ: Erlbaum.

Brooks-Gunn, J., Samelson, M., Warren, M. P., & Fox, R. (1986). Physical similarity of and disclosure of menarcheal status to friends: Effects of grade and pubertal status. *Journal of Early Adolescence, 6*(1), 3–14.

Brooks-Gunn, J., & Warren, M. P. (1985a). Effects of delayed menarche in different contexts: Dance and nondance students. *Journal of Youth and Adolescence, 14*(4), 285–300.

Brooks-Gunn, J., & Warren, M. P. (1985b). Measuring physical status and timing in early adolescence: A developmental perspective. *Journal of Youth and Adolescence, 14*(3), 163–189.

Brooks-Gunn, J., & Warren, M. P. (in press-a). Convergent validity of mother and daughter ratings of pubertal development. *Child Development.*

Brooks-Gunn, J., & Warren, M. P. (in press-b). Genetic and environmental influences: Contributions to delayed puberty. *Annals of Human Biology.*

Brooks-Gunn, J., Warren, M. P., Rosso, J., & Gargiulo, J. (in press). Validity of self-report measures of girls' pubertal status. *Child Development.*

Cheek, D. B. (1974). Body composition hormone, nutrition, and adolescent growth. In M. M. Grumbach, G. D. Grave, & F. E. Mayer (Eds.), *Control of the onset of puberty* (pp. 424–442). New York: Wiley.

Clarke, A. E., & Ruble, D. N. (1978). Young adolescents' beliefs concerning menstruation. *Child Development, 49*, 231–234.

Clausen, J. A. (1975). The social meaning of differential physical and sexual maturation. In S. E. Dragastin & G. H. Elder, Jr. (Eds.), *Adolescence in the life cycle: Psychological change and the social context.* New York: Halsted.

Damon, A., Damon, S. T., Reed, R. B., & Validian, I. (1969). Age at menarche of mothers and daughters with a note on accuracy of recall. *Human Biology, 41*, 161–175.

Deutsch, H. (1944). *The psychology of women* (Vol. 1). New York: Grune & Stratton.

Duke, P. M., Litt, I. F., & Gross, R. T. (1980). Adolescents' self-assessment of sexual maturation. *Pediatrics, 66*, 918–920.

Durnin, J. V. G. A., & Wormersley, J. (1974). Body fat assessed from total body density and its estimation from skinfold thickness: Measurement on 481 men and women aged 16 to 72 years. *British Journal of Nutrition, 72*, 77–97.

Erikson, E. H. (1968). *Identity: Youth and crisis.* New York: Norton.

Eveleth, P. B., & Tanner, J. M. (1976). *Worldwide variation in human growth.* London: Cambridge University Press.

Faust, M. S. (1960). Developmental maturity as a determinant in prestige of adolescent girls. *Child Development, 31*, 173–186.

Faust, M. S. (1977). Somatic development of adolescent girls. *Monographs of the Society for Research in Child Development, 42* (Serial No. 169).

Forbes, G. B. (1975). Puberty: Body composition. In S. R. Berenberg (Ed.), *Puberty, biological and psychosocial components.* Leiden: Stenfert Kroese.

Freud, A. (1958). Adolescence. In R. S. Eissler et al.

(Eds.), *Psychoanalytic study of the child* (Vol. 13). New York: International Universities Press.

Gaddis, A., & Brooks-Gunn, J. (1985). The male experience of pubertal change. *Journal of Youth and Adolescence, 14*, 61–69.

Gargiulo, J., Attie, I., Brooks-Gunn, J., & Warren, M. P. (1985, April). *Girls dating behavior as a function of social context and maturation.* Paper presented at a symposium on "Love and Sex in Early and Middle Adolescence" at the biennial meeting of the Society for Research in Child Development, Toronto.

Garn, S. M. (1980). Continuities and change in maturational timing. In O. Brim & J. Kagan (Eds.), *Constancy and change in human development* (pp. 113–162). Cambridge: Harvard University Press.

Garwood, S. G., & Allen, L. (1979). Self-concept and identified problem differences between pre- and post-menarcheal adolescents. *Journal of Clinical Psychology, 35*, 528–537.

Golub, S. (Ed.). (1983). *Menarche.* Lexington, MA: Lexington Books.

Greif, E. B., & Ulman, K. J. (1982). The psychological impact of menarche on early adolescent females: A review of the literature. *Child Development, 53*, 1413–1430.

Greulich, W. W., & Pyle, S. I. (1959). *Radiographic atlas of skeletal development of the hand and wrist* (2nd ed.) Stanford, CA: Stanford University Press.

Gross, R. T. (1984). Patterns of maturation: Their effects of behavior and development. In M. D. Levine & P. Satz (Eds.), *Middle childhood: Development and dysfunction.* Baltimore, MD: University Park Press.

Grumbach, M. M., Grave, D., & Mayer, F. F. (Eds.). (1974). *Control of the onset of puberty.* New York: Wiley.

Grumbach, M. M., Richards, H. E., Conte, F. A., & Kaplan, S. A. (1977). Clinical disorders of adrenal function and puberty: An assessment of the role of the adrenal cortex in normal and abnormal puberty in man and evidence for an ACTH-like pituitary adrenal androgen stimulating hormone. In M. Serio (Ed.), *The endocrine function of the human adrenal cortex, Serono Symposium.* New York: Academic Press.

Hamilton, L., Brooks-Gunn, J., & Warren, M. P. (1986). Nutritional intake of female dancers: A reflection of eating problems. *International Journal of Eating Disorders, 5*(5), 925–934.

Havinghurst, R. (1952). *Developmental tasks and education* (2nd ed.). New York: McKay.

Hill, J. P., Holmbeck, G. N., Marlow, L., Green, T. M., & Lynch, M. E. (1985). Menarcheal status and parent–child relations in families of seventh-grade girls. *Journal of Youth and Adolescence, 14*(4), 301–316.

Johnston, F. E., Roche, A. F., Schnell, L. M., & Wettenhall, N. B. (1975). Critical weight at menarche: Critique of a hypothesis. *American Journal of Diseases of Children, 129*, 19–23.

Jones, M. C. (1965). Psychological correlates of somatic development. *Child Development, 36*, 899–911.

Jones, M. C., & Bayley, N. (1950). Physical maturing among boys as related to behavior. *Journal of Educational Psychology, 41*, 129–148.

Jones, M. C., & Mussen, P. H. (1958). Self-conceptions, motivations, and interpersonal attitudes of early- and late-maturing girls. *Child Development, 29,* 491–501.

Kestenberg, J. (1967). Phases of adolescence with suggestions for correlations of psychic and hormonal organizations, II: Prepuberty, diffusion, and reintegration. *Journal of the American Academy of Child Psychiatry, 6,* 577–614.

Koff, E., Rierdan, J., & Jacobson, S. (1981). The personal and interpersonal significance of menarche. *Journal of the American Academy of Child Psychiatry, 20,* 148–158.

Koff, E., Rierdan, J., & Sheingold, K. (1982). Memories of menarche: Age, preparation, and prior knowledge as determinants of initial menstrual experience. *Journal of Youth and Adolescence, 11,* 1–9.

Koff, E., Rierdan, J., & Silverstone, E. (1978). Changes in representation of body image as a function of menarcheal status. *Developmental Psychology, 14,* 635–642.

Lerner, R. M. (1985). Adolescent maturational changes and psychosocial development: A dynamic interactional perspective. *Journal of Youth and Adolescence, 14,* 355–372.

Lerner, R. M., & Foch, T. T. (Eds.). (in press). *Biological–psychosocial interactions in early adolescence: A life-span perspective.* Hillsdale, NJ: Erlbaum.

Lerner, R. M., & Lerner, J. V. (1977). Effects of age, sex, and physical attractiveness on child–peer relations, academic performance, and elementary school adjustment. *Developmental Psychology, 13,* 585–590.

Logan, D. D. (1980). The menarche experience in twenty-three foreign countries. *Adolescence, 15,* 247–256.

Magnusson, D., Strattin, H., & Allen, V. L. (1986). Differential maturation among girls and its relation to social adjustment in a longitudinal perspective. In D. L. Featherman & R. M. Lerner (Eds.), *Life span development* (Vol. 7, pp. 135–172). New York: Academic.

Malina, R. M. (1978). Adolescent growth and maturation. Selected aspects of current research. *Yearbook of physical anthropology* (Vol. 21, pp. 63–94). Washington, DC: American Anthropological Association.

Marshall, W. A. (1974). Interrelationships of skeletal maturation, sexual development and somatic growth in man. *Annals of Human Biology, 1,* 29–40.

Marshall, W. A. (1984). Puberty. In F. Falkner and J. M. Tanner (Eds.), *Human growth. 2: Postnatal growth* (pp. 141–181). New York: Plenum.

Marshall, W. A., & Tanner, J. M. (1969). Variations in the pattern of pubertal changes in girls. *Archives of Disease in Childhood, 44,* 291–303.

Marshall, W. A., & Tanner, J. M. (1970). Variations in the pattern of pubertal changes in boys. *Archives of Disease in Childhood, 45,* 13–23.

Mellits, E. D., & Cheek, D. B. (1970). The assessment of body water and fatness from infancy to adulthood. *Monographs of the Society for Research in Child Development, 35,* 12.

Merrow, S. B. (1967). Triceps skin-fold thickness of Vermont adolescents. *American Journal of Clinical Nutrition, 20,* 978.

Morris, N. M., & Udry, J. R. (1980). Validation of a self-administered instrument to assess stage of adolescent development. *Journal of Youth and Adolescence, 9,* 271–280.

Mussen, P. H., & Jones, M. C. (1957). Self-conceptions, motivations, and interpersonal attitudes of late- and early-maturing boys. *Child Development, 28,* 243–256.

Neugarten, B. L. (1969). Continuities and discontinuities of psychological issues into adult life. *Human Development, 12,* 121–130.

Neugarten, B. L. (1979). Time, age and life cycle. *American Journal of Psychiatry, 136,* 887–894.

Neugarten, B. L., & Hagestad, G. O. (1976). Age and the life course. In R. H. Binstock, & E. Shanas (Eds.), *Handbook of aging and the social sciences.* New York: Van Nostrand Reinhold.

Paige, K. E. (1974). The curse: Possible antecedents of menstrual distress. In A. A. Harrison (Ed.), *Explorations in psychology.* Monterey, CA: Brooks/Cole.

Parizkova, J. (1976). Growth and growth velocity of lean body mass and fat in adolescent boys. *Pediatric Research, 10,* 647–650.

Peskin, H. (1967). Pubertal onset and ego functioning. *Journal of Abnormal Psychology, 72,* 1–15.

Peskin, H. (1973). Influence of the developmental schedule of puberty on learning and ego functioning. *Journal of Youth and Adolescence, 2,* 273–290.

Petersen, A. C. (1976). Physical androgyny and cognitive functioning in adolescence. *Developmental Psychology, 12,* 524–533.

Petersen, A. C. (1983). Menarche: Meaning of measure and measuring meaning. In S. Golub (Ed.), *Menarche* (pp. 63–76). New York: Heath.

Petersen, A. C., & Crockett, L. (1985). Pubertal timing and grade effects on adjustment. *Journal of Youth and Adolescence, 14,* (3), 191–206.

Petersen, A. C., Crockett, L., Tobin-Richards, M., & Boxer, A. (1985). *Measuring pubertal status: Reliability and validity of a self-report measure.* Unpublished manuscript.

Petersen, A. C., Schulenberg, J. E., Abramowitz, R. H., Offer, D., & Jarcho, H. D. (1984). A Self-Image Questionnaire for Young Adolescents (SIQYA) and validity studies. *Journal of Youth and Adolescence, 13*(2), 93–111.

Petersen, A. C., & Taylor, B. (1980). The biological approach to adolescence: Biological change and psychological adaptation. In J. Adelson (Ed.), *Handbook of adolescent psychology* (pp. 117–155). New York: Wiley.

Reynolds, E. L., & Wines, J. V. (1948). Individual differences in physical changes associated with adolescence in girls. *American Journal of Disease in Childhood, 75,* 329–350.

Reynolds, E. L., & Wines, J. V. (1951). Physical changes associated with adolescence in boys. *American Journal of Disease in Childhood, 82,* 529–547.

Rierdan, J., & Koff, E. (1985). Timing of menarche and initial menstrual experience. *Journal of Youth and Adolescence, 14*(3), 237–244.

Roche, A. F., Wainer, H., & Thissen, D. (1975). The RWT method for the prediction of adult stature. *Pediatrics, 56,* 1026–1033.

Ross, G. T., Vande Weile, R. L., & Frantz, A. G. (1981). The ovaries and the breasts. In R. H. Williams (Ed.), *Textbook of endocrinology* (6th ed., p. 355). Philadelphia, PA: W. B. Saunders.

Rossi, A. S. (1980). Life-span theories in women's lives. *Signs, 6,* 4–32.

Ruble, D. N., & Brooks-Gunn, J. (1982). The experience of menarche. *Child Development, 53,* 1557–1566.

Simmons, R. G., Blyth, D. A., & McKinney, K. L. (1983). The social and psychological effects of puberty on white females. In J. Brooks-Gunn & A. C. Petersen (Eds.), *Girls at puberty: Biological and psychosocial perspectives* (pp. 229–272). New York: Plenum.

Sorell, G. T., & Nowak, C. A. (1981). The role of physical attractiveness as a contributor to individual development. In R. M. Lerner & N. A. Busch-Rossnagel (Eds.), *Individuals as producers of their own development: A life-span perspective* (pp. 389–446). New York: Academic.

Steinberg, L. D. (1981). Transformations in family relations at puberty. *Developmental Psychology, 17,* 833–840.

Steinberg, L. D., & Hill, J. P. (1978). Patterns of family interaction as a function of age, the onset of puberty, and formal thinking. *Developmental Psychology, 14,* 683–684.

Styne, D. M., & Grumbach, M. M. (1978). Puberty in the male and female: Its physiology and disorders. In S. S. C. Yen & R. B. Jaffe (Eds.), *Reproductive endocrinology, physiology, pathophysiology, and clinical management.* Philadelphia: Saunders.

Swerdoloff, R. S. (1978). Physiological control of puberty. *Medical Clinics of North America, 62,* 351–366.

Tanner, J. M. (1962). *Growth at adolescence.* Springfield, IL: Charles C Thomas.

Tanner, J. M. (1972). Sequence, tempo, and individual variation in growth and development of boys and girls aged twelve to sixteen. In J. Kagan & R. Coles (Eds.), *Twelve to sixteen: Early adolescence.* New York: Norton.

Tanner, J. M. (1974). Sequence and tempo in the somatic changes in puberty. In M. M. Grumbach, G. D. Grave, & F. E. Mayer (Eds.), *Control of the onset of puberty* (pp. 448–470). New York: Wiley.

Tanner, J. M. (1975). Growth and endocrinology of the adolescent. In L. Gardner (Ed.), *Endocrine and genetic diseases of childhood* (2nd ed., pp. 14–64). Philadelphia: Saunders.

Tanner, J. M. (1978). Physiological control of puberty. *Medical Clinics of North America, 62,* 351–366.

Tanner, J. M. et al. (1975). *Assessment of skeletal maturity and prediction of adult height.* London: Academic.

Tanner, J. M., & Whitehouse, R. H. (1976). Clinical longitudinal standards for height, weight, height velocity, weight velocity and the stages of puberty. *Archives of Disease in Childhood, 51,* 170–179.

Tanner, J. M., Whitehouse, R. H., Marubin, E., & Resele, L. F. (1976). The adolescent growth spurt of boys and girls of the Harpenden growth study. *Annals of Human Biology, 3,* 529–542.

Thissen, D., Bock, R. D., Wainer, H., & Roche, A. F. (1976). Individual growth in stature. A comparison of four growth studies in the U. S. A. *Annals of Human Biology, 3,* 529–542.

Tobin-Richards, M., Boxer, A., & Petersen, A. C. (1983). Early adolescents' perceptions of their physical development. In J. Brooks-Gunn & A. C. Petersen (Eds.), *Girls at puberty: Biological and psychosocial perspective* (pp. 127–154). New York: Plenum.

Valk, T. W., Corley, K. P., Kelch, R. P., & Marshall, J. C. (1980). Hypogonadotropic hypogonadism: Hormonal response to low dose pulsatile administration of gonadotropin-releasing hormone. *Journal of Clinical Endocrinology and Metabolism, 51,* 730–738.

Warren, M. P. (1983). Physical and biological aspects of puberty. In J. Brooks-Gunn and A. C. Petersen (Eds.), *Girls at puberty: Biological and psychosocial perspectives* (pp. 3–28). New York: Plenum Press.

Whisnant, L., & Zegans, L. (1975). A study of attitudes toward menarche in white middle-class American adolescent girls. *American Journal of Psychiatry, 132,* 809–814.

Wilmore, J. H., & Behnke, A. R. (1970). An anthropometric estimation of body density and lean body weight in young women. *American Journal of Clinical Nutrition, 23,* 267.

Young, C. M., Sipin, S. S., & Rose, D. A. (1968). Density and skinfold measurements: Body composition of preadolescent and adolescent girls. *Journal of the American Dietetic Association, 53,* 25.

CHAPTER 8

Social Interactions and Adjustment

Jeffrey A. Kelly and David J. Hansen

Social interactions are an everyday occurrence for individuals of all ages. Children, adolescents, and adults regularly encounter social situations in which they must, or they choose to, interact with others. Social interactions are necessary for successful functioning at home, at school, at work, and at social activities. Thus, individuals need to be able to interact socially with a variety of people in a variety of social situations, including family, friends, acquaintances, coworkers, employers, as well as other individuals encountered in the community.

Social interaction is important psychologically for several reasons. Effective social interaction is important for eliciting social and nonsocial reinforcement from the environment and also for preventing the loss of current reinforcement (Kelly, 1982). For instance, effective social interaction helps an individual initiate and maintain interpersonal relationships that provide social support and reinforcement. In addition, effective social interaction may be necessary to obtain goals that are not social in nature, such as in a job interview. Finally, effective social interaction skills, such as assertiveness, may prevent

the loss of current reinforcement when others seek to take advantage of an individual.

Social interactions occur on an everyday basis throughout the life span, and social interaction skills are necessary for effective and rewarding functioning in interpersonal situations. For youths, social interactions and relationships are clearly necessary for social development and may be related to adjustment and well-being (cf. Combs & Slaby, 1978; French & Tyne, 1982; Hartup, 1982, 1983).

The purpose of this chapter is to examine the influence of social interactions on adjustment during adolescence. First, we will explore the development of social interactions from childhood through adolescence, the relationship of social interactions and adjustment, and the functions of social interactions in the adolescent years. Next, contemporary issues related to social interactions and adjustment in adolescence will be addressed, including possible mechanisms for learning social interaction skills, the literature on loneliness and on conduct-disordered social behavior in adolescence, and the intervention approaches used to remediate social-interaction skill deficits. Finally, future directions for further exploration of the impact of social interaction on adjustment in adolescence are suggested.

HISTORY AND DEVELOPMENT

Much change takes place in the type of social interactions that occur from childhood through adolescence. Social interactions progress from the minimal social interaction of infancy, which may be as simple as a smile, to complex interactions such as those involved in dating during adolescence. As individuals develop, their primary targets for social interaction, the settings where social interactions take place, and the functions social interactions may serve, vary greatly. In order to understand the basis for social skills in adolescence, we should first consider social interactions in childhood.

Social Interactions in Childhood

Infants exhibit many behaviors that appear to be social in nature, such as crying "for attention," smiling, grasping, and babbling. However, during the first few months of life, neonates exhibit little interactive social behavior (Hurlock, 1972; LaBarba, 1981). The most early signs of attachment are actually indiscriminate as the infant seeks stimulation, not attention, from various environmental sources. However, by about 3 months, infants display social behavior and respond differentially to people and objects, and by about 7 months, infants develop special attachments, generally to a mother or mothering figure, and possibly to others as well (Ambron, 1975). By 2 years children show an increasing interest in adults and other children and cooperate in routine activities and social activities such as play (Hurlock, 1972). Thus, in a relatively short period, infants develop into individuals actively participating in and initiating social interactions.

During early childhood, most time is spent with the family in a social role that might best be described as "supervised or subordinate" (de Armas & Kelly, in press). As the child matures, interactions with individuals outside of the family increase. However, the social role of children when in situations outside the home, such as daycare, is also usually very supervised. The most notable change in interactions is that there is an increase in time spent with other children.

As children between the ages of 2 and 6 years spend increasing amounts of time with other children, their social-interaction skills increase, especially with children of similar age. Social interactions among children consist primarily of play behavior, which is an extremely important and common form of social interaction (Moore, Evertson, & Brophy, 1974); research has demonstrated a relationship between effective, reinforcing play skills and popularity with peers, as well as a relationship between the absence of play skills and social isolation (Gottman, Gonso, & Rasmussen, 1975; Hartup, Glazer, & Charlesworth, 1967).

The child's increasing ability to interact with peers is reflected in his/her changing pattern of play behavior. Children's initial play behavior with peers during the early preschool years often takes the form of parallel play. For instance, children may engage in play activity by themselves, and other children may be present and also engaging in play activity, but there is not any intentional sharing or interaction. As children mature, it becomes more common for them to play together, especially in unstructured activities such as sharing or exploring materials; several children may engage in cooperative play, which is distinguished from parallel play primarily by the amount of influence a play partner has on a child's activities (Ambron, 1975). For instance, children may share playthings, make friends, organize games such as "tag," and cooperatively play with each other.

Many preschool children develop imaginary companions with whom they interact, and it has been suggested that the creation of imaginary companions illustrates the importance of play and fantasy for the preschool child's development of the skills required in interpersonal relationships (Ambron, 1975). In addition, young children often engage in sociodramatic play, which combines play and fantasy. For example, children may play "house" or "school," acting out various social roles and thereby learning methods for interacting with others (Hurlock, 1972).

Through play-based social interaction, preschool age children are able to establish one-to-one relationships with peers. The establishment of such relationships is one of the most significant advances for the preschool child. These early friendships are often with other children similar in age and sex (Hartup, 1982).

After children begin elementary school, further changes in social-interaction patterns take place. For example, the circle of friends gradually widens, children become members of peer groups, and group games become more common (Hurlock, 1972). Through social interactions with peers, the child learns "prosocial" behavior, such as what is acceptable and what is not, sharing and helping, and how to interact "kindly and fairly," continuing the socialization that began in the home (Damon, 1983).

During later childhood, social-interaction patterns continue to change. In particular, social interactions become more complex and reciprocal. For example, Hurlock (1972) outlined several patterns of social behavior in late childhood: susceptibility to social approval and disapproval, oversensitivity, suggestibility and contrasuggestibility, competition, sportsmanship and cooperation, responsibility, social discrimination and prejudice, and sex antagonism.

Childhood Social Interactions and Adjustment

A number of investigations have addressed the impact of childhood social interactions and relationships on adjustment. Research interest in social interactions with peers during childhood has been increased by findings that a child's social interactions within the peer group are related to later adjustment (Bierman & Furman, 1984; French & Tyne, 1982; Kagan & Moss, 1962, 1983). Several negative outcomes of inadequate or insufficient social interaction in childhood have been reported, with the most serious outcome being predisposing the child to autism or childhood schizophrenia (Roff, Sells, & Golden, 1972). Other correlates of poor social interaction in childhood include poor academic achievement (Buswell, 1953), social avoidance and mistreatment by peers (O'Conner, 1972), avoidance of group activities (Emmerich, 1966; Olpin & Kogan, 1969), adolescent delinquency (Roff et al., 1972), and dropping out of high school (Barclay, 1966; Ullman, 1957).

Patterns of childhood social interactions have been shown to predict adult life adjustment. Children with deficient social interactions are disproportionately represented in adult psychiatric populations (Cowen, Pederson, Babigian, Izzo, & Trost, 1973; Kohn & Clausen, 1955; Roff, 1963), military bad-conduct discharges (Roff, 1961), and adult suicides (Stengel, 1971). In the Cowen et al. (1973) study, information such as IQ, grades, attendance, and peer ratings was collected on individuals in the third grade. Eleven years later, following graduation from high school, the best predictor of adult mental health status, as indicated by community mental health records, was the peer rating.

Kagan and Moss (1983) followed the psychological development of 71 individuals from birth through early adulthood (i.e., 19 to 29 years old). They found that social interaction anxiety during ages 6 to 10 was a moderately good predictor of similar adult characteristics, as were sex-role interests, dependency, aggression, and achievement. Thus, if social interaction anxiety is present in a youth it is likely to continue throughout the individual's life and have long-term, stable effects on interpersonal functioning.

It should be noted that these findings are often derived from correlational evidence, and it is difficult to determine whether inadequate social interactions are the cause of later adjustment difficulties. However, numerous studies demonstrate a moderate to strong relationship between inadequate social interactions and later maladjustment. In this context, it is disturbing that between 5% and 15% of elementary school students experience significant social-relationship problems (French & Tyne, 1982), and that many children appear to go through school with few friends or no friends (Gronlund, 1959).

The results of the studies on the relationship of social interaction in childhood and later adjustment suggest that normal development requires social interaction (Conger & Keane, 1981); adequate functioning in social interactions can thus be viewed as a prerequisite for adjustment (Kelly, 1982). Because opportunities for peer interaction are probably necessary for a child to develop social skills, initial deficits in social skills may limit the opportunity for interaction and, consequently, further limit the development of social skills (Combs & Slaby, 1978). Children deficient in social-interaction skills may then be hindered throughout their lives in the development of interaction skills that are required for effective interpersonal functioning.

Social Interactions in Adolescence

As children grow, one of the most significant developmental changes is the emergence of new social interaction patterns. During adolescence, individuals are exposed to new social-interaction situations and need different social-interaction skills than those required in earlier childhood interactions (Grinder, 1978). In fact, the shift from childhood to adolescence is marked by change in many aspects of social life (Damon, 1983). In their relationships with parents, siblings, and same-sex and other-sex peers, teenagers must interact with others differently than during childhood. During adolescence, peer relations become more intense and extensive, family relations are altered, and the adolescent begins to encounter many new demands and expectations in social-interaction situations. For instance, adolescents may begin dating, working with others in a part-time job, or spending time with peers without adult supervision (de Armas & Kelly, in press).

Several developmental changes serve to alter the manner in which adolescents interact with family and peers. These include more advanced cognitive, verbal, and reasoning abilities, and the changes associated with puberty (de Armas & Kelly, in press). In addition, many of the developmental tasks of adolescence involve relationships and require new, and more complex, interpersonal skills (Hartup, 1982). The developmental tasks of adolescence that relate to social development include (Damon, 1983; Douvan & Adelson, 1966; Havighurst, 1972; Rice, 1978):

1. Participating in social and extracurricular activities.
2. Becoming and perceiving oneself as part of a peer group.
3. Establishing caring, satisfying relationships with same-sex and other-sex persons.
4. Moving from the same-sex interests and playmates of middle childhood to other-sex concerns and friendships.
5. Learning sex-appropriate behavior.
6. Practicing dating patterns and skills that contribute to personal and social development, and eventually to mate selection and marriage.
7. Becoming more independent, responsible, confident, and adultlike in many different social interaction situations.

As a result of developmental changes and demands, several striking changes occur in peer interactions during adolescence. One change is that the nature and meaning of friendships evolves. During adolescence, the trend, which began in childhood, toward greater mutuality continues and is fostered by new interpersonal needs (Damon, 1983). For instance, the desire for close friends increases, as adolescents turn to their peers for support formerly provided by the family (Douvan & Adelson, 1966). The adolescent tends to desire close, caring relationships with peers for the purpose of sharing mature affection, thoughts, concerns, and common interests, and to desire friends who are loyal, trustworthy, intimate, and who demonstrate potential for positive regard, admiration, and similarity (Bigelow, 1977; Bigelow & LaGaipa, 1975; Gallatin, 1975; Grinder, 1978; Rice, 1978). However, as their number of acquaintances broadens, adolescents are more aware of the importance of belonging to a group; by midadolescence, many teenagers also strive to be accepted by members of a clique or peer group that they admire (Rice, 1978). These changes in the nature and meaning of friendship make it crucial for the teenager to have the social interaction skills to intensely interact with individuals, as well as to be socially effective in group situations. It is important for youths to maintain contact with other youths at this age, as age-appropriate behaviors are continuously changing and individuals need to be aware of social expectations.

Another change, which is very different from adolescents' previous experiences, is that some of the adolescent's peer relations become sexual in nature, and this sexuality begins to influence many of the adolescent's peer encounters with both sexes (Damon, 1983). As a result of increased interest in heterosexual interactions, dating becomes a desirable activity and is, in fact, one of the major social activities of adolescence (Grinder, 1978). Dating may range from casual meetings to "going steady" and becoming engaged to be married. Dating involves a series of new demands, expectations, and complex behaviors from the initial request for a date to the final parting (e.g., the good night kiss) and the decision to call or not call again. As are other social skills, the skills required in dating are clearly complex behaviors that are not part of most adolescents' repertoires and are a source of significant anxiety for many teenagers (Arkowitz, Hinton, Perl, & Himadi, 1978).

Social Interaction Skills

Because of the new social demands placed on them, adolescents must develop or refine a variety of social-interaction skills (e.g., Kelly, 1982). Conversational skills, such as asking questions, using appropriate self-disclosure and speech acknowledgers, and talking about high-interest-content topics, must be refined and expanded in order to make same-sex and other-sex friends and to become part of a peer group. In addition, assertiveness skills, such as expressing praise or giving compliments and making and refusing requests, are needed for effective interactions with friends and peer groups and for effectively gaining independence and responsibility from parents.

Dating and heterosocial skills, such as asking an individual for a date, as well as appropriate social behaviors to exhibit on a date, are new skills that are clearly needed during adolescence. In addition, as adolescents seek more independence from parents and seek employment or part-time employment, even job-interview skills, including making positive self-statements about past experiences, education, hobbies, or interests, may be necessary.

Functions of Social Interactions during Adolescence

It has been noted that the complex social skills that are needed for competent, successful social interactions with other people are certainly among the most important skills that a youth must learn (Combs & Slaby, 1978). For instance, talking with friends is one of the most popular ways for adolescents to spend their leisure time (Hurlock, 1973), and an adolescent's conversational ability is related to socialization and social acceptance (Damon, 1983; Hartup, 1982). An individual who is unable to successfully interact with others may be prone to problems in interpersonal relationships or, indirectly, to problems in school, occupational, and social activities. Thus, effective social interactions during adolescence are important for adjustment, as they are necessary for an adolescent to make friends, become part of a peer group, develop heterosocial relationships, and become an independent, socially competent individual.

Hartup (1983) has pointed out that peer interaction "is not a superficial luxury to be enjoyed by some children and not by others, but is a necessity in childhood socialization" (p. 220). Peer social interactions take on increasingly important roles in the socialization process as youths grow older (French & Tyne, 1982) and are believed to make several significant contributions to the development of youths. For instance, the regulation of aggressive behavior, sexual socialization, the development of cognitive and social skills, and the development of moral judgment and social values are believed to be influenced by peer interactions (French & Tyne, 1982; Hartup, 1983). Hartup (1982) has observed that, although popular myth suggests that peer pressure is undesirable, evidence indicates that peer influence serves important functions and contributes more to constructive socialization than to deviance. Several functions of social interactions can be addressed.

Regulating Aggressive Impulses. The regulation of aggressive impulses is one of the most commonly cited effects of social interaction among young people. Hartup (1983) stated that there is evidence that children master their aggressive impulses within the context of peer interactions, rather than within the family, the school, or through television. Socialization is facilitated by experiences in which rough play escalates into aggression and then deescalates into play (Hartup, 1983). As individuals become older, the regulation of aggression continues to be fostered by interaction with peers, through both the opportunity to deal with situations that provoke aggression and by observing how peers deal with situations that provoke anger. For instance, a teenager may learn that assertive behavior, as opposed to aggressive behavior, is a useful method for dealing with a "bully," after observing another teenager effectively use assertive behavior.

Obtaining Emotional and Social Support, and Gaining Independence. Interactions with peers and a peer group facilitate an adolescent's transition from relying on the family to gaining relative independence and new patterns of expectations and responsibility (Grinder, 1978). Friends and peer groups provide support for teenagers as they encounter new demands and responsibilities and provide instruction and modeling in how to deal with these demands and responsibilities. For example, through peer involvement, teenagers may see how their friends handle their parents' demands and thereby learn skills for dealing with their own parents.

Providing Settings for Experimentation with New Thoughts, Emotions, and Behaviors. Interaction with peers provides adolescents with the opportunity to explore and refine their improving cognitive, verbal, and reasoning abilities. A peer group especially facilitates such experimentation because the other individuals are undergoing similar development and also desire to expand these abilities. Through conversation, discussion, and debate with peers, as well as through observation of peers, teenagers have the opportunity to develop their vocabulary and verbal abilities, and to refine and expand their cognitive and reasoning abilities.

Social interaction with peers also provides the opportunity to experience emotions and express feelings. Teenagers may experience love and caring for same-sex and other-sex peers and may develop skills for dealing with and expressing such emotions that prepare them for experiencing such feelings as adults (Douvan & Adelson, 1966). In addition, peer interactions help adolescents refine their skills for dealing with and expressing anger and negative emotions.

The social-interaction situations encountered by adolescents are also useful for furthering the development of a variety of social behaviors. For instance, assertiveness skills, such as giving and receiving compliments, making and refusing requests, and "standing up for rights," may be fostered in peer interactions. Similarly, through social interactions, adolescents may refine conversational skills that will also be important as adults.

Developing Sexual Attitudes, Interests, and Sex-Role Behaviors. Adolescence brings about a tremendous increase in heterosexual interests and social relationships (Grinder, 1978). There is little doubt that sexual attitudes and sex-role behaviors are primarily shaped through peer interactions (Hartup, 1983), and during adolescence there is much opportunity to develop and refine sexual attitudes and interests and to experiment with sexual behaviors.

Dating is one of the major social activities of adolescents (Grinder, 1978). Surveys of adolescents demonstrate that dating serves many purposes: entertainment, companionship, sexual stimulation, enhancing reputation and popularity, assertion of independence, experimentation (sexual in particular), and mate selection (Grinder, 1966; Husbands, 1970; Rice, 1978). Douvan and Adelson (1966) have pointed out that, as an integral part of the courtship to marriage sequence, dating is the closest phenomenon in America to a rite of passage. Dating facilitates mate selection by providing the opportunity to learn and refine the skills required in heterosexual interactions.

Developing Moral Judgment and Social Values. The quantity and quality of peer relations are believed to be related to a youth's moral development (Hartup, 1983). Hartup stated that the authoritarian nature of most adult–child interactions does not provide youths with the opportunity to view moral rules as changeable and subjective, yet the peer group is not usually authoritarian and provides the social reciprocity necessary to further moral development.

There are little empirical data to support the notion that the amount of peer interaction is associated with advanced moral development, but there is more evidence that the quality of peer interaction is associated with advanced moral development (Hartup, 1983). For instance, Keasey (1971) found that youths who belonged to many clubs and social organizations had higher moral judgment than youths belonging to few organized groups. Keasey (1971) also reported that self-reports of leadership functions, peer ratings of leadership, peer friendship nominations, and teacher ratings of leadership and popularity were all positively related to level of moral judgment.

The development of values and behavioral norms is also fostered through social interaction, especially through participation in a peer group (Grinder, 1978). By experiencing the values and norms of a peer group, the adolescent is able to evaluate the perspectives of others while developing his or her values and attitudes.

Improving or Maintaining Self-Esteem through Strategic Interactions. The term strategic interactions has been used to describe the nature of those adolescent social interactions that serve to acquire, conceal, or reveal information in an indirect manner (Damon, 1983; Elkind, 1983; Goffman, 1969). Elkind (1983) stated that adolescents, in contrast to most adults, engage in strategic interactions to maintain or enhance their self-esteem. For instance, Elkind uses the example of telephoning others. Among children and adults, this is usually done for communication, to give or get information. However, for adolescents, telephoning and being telephoned are indices of status, popularity, and peer group affiliation and therefore contribute to an adolescent's self-esteem. Additional strategic interactions include attracting and rejecting friends and demonstrating sexual appeal through acquiring dates and engaging in sexual activity.

Damon (1983) also pointed out that social interactions enhance an adolescent's sense of self, because adolescents "stage" social interactions and exhibit an increase in self-consciousness and a sense of "planfulness" during social interactions. Because adolescents may consciously use social interactions for enhancement of the self, social interactions often become more planned, strategic, and cautious (Damon, 1983). However, by the onset of adulthood most individuals no longer use social interactions in this manner to enhance self-esteem (Damon, 1983; Elkind, 1983).

CONTEMPORARY ISSUES

To this point, we have noted that adolescence entails exposure to new social-interaction situations, occupying new roles within social interactions, and developing social skills different from those needed earlier in childhood. If relationships during adolescence serve functions that promote the individual's adjustment and independence, it becomes important to examine more closely the mechanisms through which teenagers naturalistically learn social behavior and to consider the possible origins of relationship difficulties, such as loneliness, social anxiety, and the learning of socially inappropriate behavior.

The Learning of Social Behavior: Possible Mechanisms

From a cognitive–behavioral perspective, one can posit the existence of several factors that operate to facilitate, or to hinder, the development of social-interaction skills during adolescence. These factors include: (a) the presence of appropriate social skill models; (b) the consequences and reinforcement patterns associated with an adolescent's social responding; (c) exposure to, and personal participation in, peer social activities; and (d) more cognitively based self-statements and attributional processes.

Observational Learning

Most research on the observational learning of social behavior has studied the effect of models on the conduct of preschool- and grade-school-age children (Bandura & Walters, 1963). Experimental investigations of naturalistic social-skill modeling among adolescents are quite uncommon in the literature. However, there are several reasons to suspect that social modeling is of particular importance during the teenage years. Many investigators have noted that adolescents are oriented to peer groups and are likely to imitate the conduct of their age mates (Hurlock, 1973). Style of dress, hairstyles, musical interests, speech and language use, activities, and values are among the socially relevant characteristics that teenagers appear to learn, in part, by exposure to peer models.

Undoubtedly, teenagers learn methods of handling social relationships by observing and imitating peers. For example, double-dating and group dating are common in early adolescence and midadolescence and permit teenagers to learn heterosocial skills by modeling from peers. Interestingly, the frequency of group dating appears to decrease in late adolescence, perhaps coinciding with the time that many teenagers have had sufficient exposure to dating models to comfortably exhibit heterosocial skills with fewer models present. As we will discuss shortly, adolescents who report good social adjustment are more likely to have a history of exposure to multiple social skill models.

Reinforcement Contingencies

From a behavioral perspective, one would surmise that individuals who exhibit successful social adjustment have a repertoire of social strategies or skills capable of producing reinforcing interpersonal outcomes (Kelly, 1982). For example, an adolescent will be more apt to initiate conversations, join in peer social activities, assert views or opinions, ask another person to date, and engage in other social initiations if he or she has a history of reinforcement for such behavior. To the extent that the teenager learns and uses appropriate social skills in situations where they will be reinforced, successful relationships are also likely to be formed.

To question of *which* social behaviors will be reinforced by others has not yet been well explored with adolescent populations. There is evidence that adolescents find certain conversational topics—including music; the activities of friends; television, movies, and radio; and school events—higher in reinforcement value than other conversational topics (Bradlyn et al., 1983). Thus, adolescents who converse about high-interest themes may elicit greater peer reinforcement than those who talk about low-interest topics. Presumably, characteristics of the peer group in which a teenager seeks acceptance also determine the specific social behaviors that will be reinforced by members of that group. The social skills reinforced by members of a school science club are perhaps different than those skills positively valued by a group of teenagers engaged in delinquent activities; social behavior reinforced by teenage males may be different than that reinforced by females.

Social Activity Participation

If adolescents can gain social-relationship skills through observation of skilled models and as a result of achieving reinforcing outcomes in social-interaction situations, we would assume that participation in peer activities is a necessary precursor for naturalistic skill learning to occur. The adolescent who engages in few activities with peers will have reduced opportunities to observe and interact with skillful models; the isolated teenager would also have fewer opportunities to practice various social behaviors and to learn which skills will be reinforced with whom and under what circumstances.

Cognitive–Affective Processes

There exists the stereotype that adolescence is a period characterized by frequent periods of moodiness, introspective rumination, and worries. At least some recent research suggests this portrayal may be relatively accurate. Csikszentmihalyi and Larson (1984) recently examined the behavioral, cognitive, and affective characteristics of normal adolescents by asking them to make self-monitoring notations whenever a

"beeper" unit that each adolescent carried sounded. The beeper sounded at random intervals throughout the day and night. The investigators found that the adolescents recorded frequent shifts in mood, frequent periods of rumination over relationships and identity, and more time spent alone than with others.

There are many reasons why cognitive and affective patterns might influence the social adjustment of adolescents. Because teenagers are called upon to function in new roles with other people, uncertainty and conflict concerning new social-role expectations are likely. If teenagers rely considerably on feedback from others concerning their attractiveness and acceptability, they may be more sensitive to rejection cues, perceived or genuine, that foster cognitively mediated social anxiety. Other factors that have been identified as contributors to the social adjustment of adolescents include: (a) acceptance of physical, maturational change; (b) physical attractiveness; (c) the ease with which an adolescent gains independence of the parental family; (d) acceptance by a peer social group; and (e) the development of cognitive self-appraisals of competence in social interactions. (See Havighurst, 1972, for a discussion of these issues.) To the extent that an adolescent is successful in social relationships, we would expect the development of positive patterns of self-appraisal; if a teenager encounters frequent negative outcomes in relationships, the presence of negative self- and other-appraisals, and the presence of social anxiety or inhibition, would be more likely.

To summarize, a social-learning analysis would suggest that the experience of an adolescent (including exposure to socially skilled models, opportunities for social interaction practice, predictable and reinforcing outcomes for social initiations, and cognitive, anticipatory, and self-talk patterns) influences the adequacy and type of peer relationships that will be developed. As suggested earlier, interaction difficulties experienced by adolescents are often transitory in nature, reflecting the normal awkwardness that is likely to occur in new social roles, especially during a period of maturational–developmental change. On the other hand, some adolescents experience more longstanding patterns of social maladjustment, perhaps extending from childhood through adolescence and into adult life (Kagan & Moss, 1983).

In order to understand how relationship difficulties affect adjustment and to identify the nature of these difficulties, we will next review research on two of the more common types of interaction difficulties observed in adolescents: loneliness and socially inappropriate or conduct-disordered behavior.

Loneliness and Social Isolation in Adolescence

The prevalence of reported loneliness, shyness, and social anxiety among adolescents appears to be rather high. Zimbardo (1977) found that over 50% of a sample of seventh and eighth graders label themselves as overly shy, whereas Arkowitz et al. (1978) report that 31% of older adolescents in a survey sample indicate heterosocial interactions (social interactions with different-sex persons) as problematic. Other investigators have suggested that social anxiety, shyness, and social inhibition affect from 11.5 to 50% of adolescents (Borkovec, Stone, O'Brien, & Kaloupek, 1974; Bryant & Trower, 1974). Although such survey data demonstrate that inadequate social relationships are a concern of many teenagers, less is known about the severity of these difficulties, the frequency that relationship problems are a transient concern versus a long-standing developmental pattern, and the degree to which teenagers are able to overcome social anxiety or inhibition, on their own, through increased exposure to naturally occurring social interactions. Surveys almost certainly "capture" both those adolescents experiencing transient, normal social self-consciousness and those with more serious relationship deficits (de Armas & Kelly, in press).

Research investigating correlates of adolescent loneliness and social isolation has focused on several factors that seem to contribute to these interaction difficulties. To date, investigators have identified certain social-skill, social-participation, and cognitive–attributional characteristics of lonely adolescents.

Skill Deficits

Adolescents may encounter difficulty establishing satisfactory peer relationships because they lack the social skills needed to initiate interactions, converse easily with others, and handle peer interactions such as dating. If a teenager lacks appropriate, peer-valued social skills, the adolescent would presumably achieve fewer positive outcomes in social interactions and would be likely to avoid interactions requiring skills he or she has not yet mastered.

Support for the notion that lonely adolescents lack appropriate social skills has been found in several studies. Jones, Hobbs, and Hockenbury (1982) compared the performance of college students reporting high loneliness with those reporting low loneliness based on the UCLA Loneliness Scale during 14-minute dyadic interactions. Videotapes of the conversations revealed that, compared to low-loneliness students, high-loneliness students asked their partners fewer conversational questions, made fewer partner references, showed less attention to their partners, and more often changed conversation topics away from topics initiated by the partner.

Other investigators, studying the social behavior of heterosocially anxious and infrequently dating students in role-play situations, have established the presence of such skill deficits as extended silences, affective "flatness," speech dysfluencies, less reinforcing conversational content, and more frequent negative-opinion statements (Bander, Steinke, Allen, & Mosher, 1975; Curran, 1977; Heimberg, Madsen, Montgomery, & McNabb 1980; Kupke, Hobbs, & Cheney, 1979; Twentyman & McFall, 1975). Although most of this research has been done with older adolescent college students, similar skill deficits have also been identified among socially deficient younger teenagers (Christoff et al., in press; Franco, Christoff, Crimmins, & Kelly, 1983).

Social Participation Deficits

Adolescents reporting themselves to be lonely, shy, or socially anxious appear to participate less often than their nonlonely counterparts in peer social activities. For example, lonely adolescents report dating less often, spending more time alone, and participating in fewer extracurricular activities than other teenagers (Brennan, 1982). In addition, measures of social participation have been shown to increase following interventions intended to alleviate excessive shyness (Christoff et al., in press; Franco et al., 1983).

Although the notion that lonely, isolated adolescents participate less often in peer activities than nonlonely adolescents seems intuitively obvious, at least one study has not found social-participation deficits among lonely teenagers. Jones (1981) reported that lonely and nonlonely students do not differ in the *frequency* of their self-monitored social interactions, but instead differ in the reported *quality* of the interactions, with lonely students reporting less warmth and intimacy associated with their social contacts. This finding suggests that cognitive processes, or how the individual labels self and others, are also important in understanding adolescent loneliness.

Cognitive–Attributional Factors

Jones, Freeman, and Goswick (1981) conducted a project to investigate the attributional styles of lonely and nonlonely adolescents. In the study, Jones et al. asked students, varying in degree of self-reported loneliness, to engage in 15-minute "get-acquainted" conversations with one another. Following the interaction, the conversants completed measures assessing how attractive and skillful they regarded their partner and completed measures of attraction and esteem as they thought their *partner* would answer. Jones et al. did not find that lonely students were evaluated negatively by their conversational partners, but did find that lonely individuals attributed more negative characteristics to their partners. Lonely females rated their conversational partners lower in honesty and affection and held the partners in lower esteem than did nonlonely females; lonely males reported liking their partners less following the conversation than did their nonlonely counterparts. As a result of these findings, Jones et al. suggest that shy, lonely individuals may have a negative social outlook that interferes with the formation of relationships. The origins of such possible attitudinal negativism are unclear. On one hand, a tendency to develop negative social attributions might be a defensive consequence of unsuccessful past efforts to develop relationships; on the other hand, negative attitudes toward others may serve as antecedents responsible for certain relationship problems.

Several investigations have examined the social problem-solving capabilities of adolescents experiencing relationship difficulties relative to teenagers with good social adjustment. In separate projects, Platt, Spivack, Altman, Altman, and Peizer (1974) and Horowitz, French, and

Anderson (1982) asked adolescents with a range of social and emotional adjustment disorders to verbalize how they would handle social conflicts with others in a problem-solving assessment paradigm. Ratings of the subjects' solutions to hypothetical social-conflict situations revealed that, compared to their better adjusted counterparts, socially maladjusted adolescents exhibited poorer social problem-solving skills. This suggests that adolescents with relationship difficulties may be relatively unable to generate, and know how to act upon, effective solutions to social conflicts with others.

Loneliness and Social Isolation: Some Conclusions

Survey-based research suggests that loneliness is a relatively frequent problem or concern among adolescents. As noted earlier, occasional feelings of loneliness, isolation, and awkwardness are probably normal and "self-correcting" for many teenagers. Among more seriously lonely adolescents, researchers have established the presence of social-skill deficits, cognitive–attributional and social "outlook" problems, and social participation infrequency that may contribute to, or maintain, interpersonal adjustment difficulties. Although investigators have examined these characteristics separately, they may interact with each other to create insufficient relationships. For example, a teenager who has failed to master effective social skills may then develop negative cognitions concerning self and others and participate little in social activities with peers. Alternatively, social inactivity may be an antecedent responsible for inadequate social-skill learning and deficient social problem-solving abilities; mastery of social skills and problem-solving likely requires adequate experience and practice dealing with others.

This leads to another issue relevant to conceptualizing certain social interaction problems. Terms like loneliness, shyness, or social inhibition are global descriptors that seem to involve not only a teenager's objective frequency of interactions, but also his or her subjective evaluation of their quality. If the self-reported problem of loneliness has multiple antecedents (e.g., poor social skills, negative cognitive appraisals of self or others, infrequent activities with others), we might expect that adolescents can feel lonely for different reasons and require different forms of intervention if the difficulties are sufficiently serious. Thus, some interventions seek to teach lonely adolescents new social skills (Filipczak, Archer, & Friedman, 1980; Franco et al., 1983; Jones et al., 1982); other interventions focus on more cognitively based factors (Christoff et al., in press); still others attempt to gradually expose the individual to safe, planned, practice social interactions (Arkowitz et al., 1978).

Conduct-Disordered Social Behavior in Adolescence

As we have discussed, some adolescents experience adjustment difficulties because they are unable to establish satisfactory social relationships. However, other teenagers may encounter adjustment problems because they have learned to engage in socially inappropriate activities that bring them into conflict with schools, community authorities, or the court system. In some cases, the activities might involve minor status offenses; in other cases, the activities may reflect more serious predelinquent patterns.

A comprehensive review of teenage conduct disorders and delinquency is beyond the scope of this chapter. However, in addition to "molar" theories concerning the causes of teenage antisocial behavior, some investigators have recently examined cognitive and social-skill characteristics of adolescents who engage in delinquent and predelinquent behavior. Their findings suggest that social-relationship skill deficits may characterize not only adolescents who have difficulty establishing peer relationships, but also those who are susceptible to antisocial peer influence as well.

Skill Deficits and Conduct Disorders

From a perspective emphasizing social-learning factors, a teenager would be more likely to engage in antisocial behavior with peers if he or she (a) lacked the social skills needed to engage comfortably in sanctioned, appropriate peer activities, (b) had difficulty resisting the influence of antisocial peers, and (c) was unable to problem-solve effectively in situations requiring good social judgment. In essence, this model proposes that some adolescents engage in socially unacceptable behavior because they lack the skills necessary to develop more appropri-

ate patterns of conduct. In addition to insufficient learning of appropriate skill behaviors, the conduct-disordered adolescent may have also learned antisocial activities by the same general mechanisms we discussed earlier (i.e., learning of delinquent patterns from socially deviant skill models, attaining reinforcement by engaging in socially unsanctioned activities, and so on).

The notion that certain delinquent behavior patterns are associated with social-skill deficits has received empirical support. Freedman, Rosenthal, Donahue, Schlundt, and McFall (1978) constructed a measure of role-playing social skill and social problem-solving items termed the Adolescent Problems Inventory (API). Items on the API describe a range of interpersonal problem situations that, if mishandled, could cause the individual to get in trouble with peers or the law. Freedman et al. found, across several different samples, that delinquent teenagers provided less competent, less skilled responses to the API items than matched, nondelinquent, and socially well adjusted peers. This pattern indicates that conduct-disordered adolescents exhibit deficits in social and problem-solving skills and suggests that these deficits may contribute to the development of delinquent behavior patterns.

Further indirect support for the conceptualization that conduct-disordered teenagers have deficient social skills is found in the rather large number of studies that have (a) established social-skill inadequacies in a group of delinquent adolescents, (b) provided those adolescents with training in social skills or social problem-solving, and (c) obtained evidence of skill acquisition and/or improved adjustment following the intervention. The focus for these intervention projects had included: (a) improved conversational skills (Hansen, St. Lawrence, & Christoff, 1984; Maloney et al., 1976; Minkin et al., 1976); (b) appropriate assertiveness, rather than aggression or passivity, when confronted by an unreasonable antagonist (Ollendick & Hersen, 1979; Pentz, 1980); and (c) improved social problem-solving skills (Sarason & Sarason, 1981). In the Sarason and Sarason project, students in a high school with a high rate of delinquency and dropout were taught general social skills, social skills for handling peer conflicts, and problem-solving skills. The students who received training to improve their social relationships not only exhibited those skills during role-playing and other assessments, but also had fewer school absences, reduced rates of tardiness, and fewer behavior problems through a 1-year follow-up period than did students in an untreated control group.

Conduct disorders and delinquency are complex phenomena that almost certainly have multiple determinants. However, there is evidence that at least some adolescents with such adjustment problems exhibit deficits in their social-interaction skills. Thus, just as difficulties like loneliness, friendlessness, and social anxiety can be due to an adolescent's skill deficits, certain patterns of antisocial and unsanctioned behavior may also be due to the absence of more appropriate interaction skills. We will next briefly review the types of interventions that have been used most often to improve the social relationships of skills-deficient adolescents.

Intervention Approaches

Earlier, it was noted that teenagers with poor social relationships have been found to exhibit deficits in their behavioral social skills, their extent of participation in peer social activities, and their cognitive problem-solving skills. In parallel fashion, interventions to improve the relationships of socially maladjusted adolescents have also focused on the same three areas. The interventions can be categorized as those emphasizing social-skills training, increased exposure to peer social interaction, or social problem-solving.

Social-Skills Training

Social-skills training interventions assume that individuals may fail to establish appropriate, successful relationships because they lack the behavioral competencies needed to handle social interactions effectively. Thus, adolescents unable to meet and talk with one another may be in need of conversational-skills training, those with date-related difficulties may benefit from heterosocial-skills training, and those who deal with antagonists either overly passively or aggressively might benefit from training in assertiveness.

Regardless of the type of social skill identified as deficient, skills-training interventions generally utilize a "package" of behavioral techniques (including instruction, modeling, behavior rehearsal or practice, and feedback) to

intensively teach the adolescent to handle role plays or simulations of social situations that he or she presently cannot handle well (Kelly, 1982). Attention is directed towards improving the individual's verbal skills in the role plays, as well as nonverbal skills and overall social "style." As the adolescent becomes behaviorally proficient in handling role-played enactments of problematic situations, he or she is gradually encouraged to use the same skills in real life. By using new and more effective social skills, the adolescent will presumably be better able to handle those social interactions that had previously been difficult. This method of intervention has been used with adolescents exhibiting shyness and poor conversational skills (Christoff et al., in press; Franco et al., 1983; Hansen et al., 1984), unassertiveness (Rhodes, Redd, & Berggren, 1979), and disruptiveness (Filipczak et al., 1980).

Increased Social Exposure

Because adolescents may experience social-interaction difficulties due simply to insufficient exposure and participation in peer activities, fostering greater exposure to peer interactions represents another form of intervention used to promote better relationships. Social-exposure training has been most widely used to reduce heterosocial (date-related) anxieties (Arkowitz et al., 1978). In projects conducted by Arkowitz and his colleagues, date-anxious individuals were assigned to have repeated practice dates with one another. The practice dates, always with another student who also reported heterosocial anxiety, were structured as low-key and for practice only, thereby allowing participants to become desensitized to date-related anxieties through nonthreatening, nonevaluative practice socializing. Arkowitz et al. (1978) report positive outcomes with this exposure-based approach, although it would appear best suited to adolescents who already have adequate social skills to interact effectively with others. For teenagers with severe social-skill deficits, direct training of social skills may also be needed (de Armas & Kelly, in press).

Social Problem-Solving Training

A number of interventions have sought to teach adolescents with peer-relationship difficulties more effective social problem-solving skills, either as a sole focus of intervention or in combination with social-skills training (Christoff et. al., in press; Sarason & Sarason, 1981; Spivack & Levine, 1963). Although specific training methods vary somewhat across projects, subjects are presented with scenarios describing a social problem or conflict and are asked to verbalize how they would handle it. The adolescent is then taught, usually by instruction, modeling, practice, and feedback, to explicitly follow a number of steps in order to solve the problems described in each scenario. These steps include: (a) identifying a specific goal (e.g., what the adolescent wants to see happen in the situation); (b) generating or brainstorming multiple possible solutions to bring about that goal; (c) evaluating each potential solution for feasibility and effectiveness; (d) selecting a solution strategy as best; and (e) elaborating those actions needed to implement the solution selected as best (see D'Zurilla & Goldfried, 1971).

The rationale for this training is that adolescents with poor social adjustment lack the cognitive problem-solving skills to handle social conflicts, dilemmas, and difficulties. It seeks to address these deficits by making overt the steps needed to solve social problems effectively and encouraging the adolescent to engage in active problem-solving when confronted by difficult interaction situations.

FUTURE DIRECTIONS

As we have seen, social relationships in adolescence serve a variety of functions important to a teenager's adjustment, independence, and well-being. Effective relationship skills permit an adolescent to make friends, participate in peer activities, develop heterosocial relationships, gain independence from the parental family, and view himself or herself as a competent, socially attractive individual.

We doubt that social interactions develop easily, smoothly, and without anxiety for most adolescents. To varying degrees, at various times, and in various situations, most teenagers probably experience relationship difficulties, anxieties, and uncertainties. Although there has been a great deal of descriptive attention given to the function of social relationships in adolescence, there is a need for much more empirical research on the nature of effective social interactions during this developmental period.

Although researchers have studied behavioral correlates of popularity among young children

(Foster & Ritchey, 1979; Gottman et al., 1975), little empirical study has been given to identifying correlates of popularity among teenagers. For example, does a well-adjusted adolescent have a large network of friends with whom she or he spends a great deal of time, or is it more important to have one or perhaps several close, intimate friendships? It is possible to identify young adolescents who are likely to otherwise encounter significant, enduring relationship problems, and can we provide early intervention to prevent later social maladjustment? How can school activities be structured so as to provide natural opportunities for socially unskilled teenagers to develop greater social competencies, and is it possible to transform what have been clinical skills-training interventions into more extensive programs that can be incorporated into school curricula to assist socially deficient adolescents?

For the most part, questions such as these have received little attention. However, to understand what social factors give rise to successful adolescent adjustment and to develop effective treatment and prevention programs will require additional empirical research on the social behavior of "essentially normal" adolescents.

Finally, the topic of this chapter is social interactions and adjustment. Some adjustment difficulties, including loneliness and anxiety in interpersonal situations, can be related rather directly and logically to an adolescent's social relationship problems or skill deficits. Other adjustment difficulties, such as delinquency, have only recently been conceptualized in terms of the individual's skill deficits. There remains a need to explore whether still other common adjustment problems of adolescents—including, for example, depression, drug abuse, and alcoholism—may result in part from social-relationship inadequacies. To the extent that social-skill factors make an adolescent susceptible to difficulties like these, intervention efforts to improve relationships may also help us treat or prevent other problems.

SUMMARY

During adolescence, teenagers confront a range of interpersonal situations that are either new to the individual or that require the use of social skills different than those expected when the person was a child. In addition, because adolescents are oriented toward peers and are sensitive to peer evaluation, relationships take on special importance during this developmental period. From a social-learning perspective, one would expect that adolescents acquire relationship skills as a result of exposure to skilled models, opportunities for participation in social activities, and reinforcement of social behavior; one would further expect that, as a result of these experiences, adolescents develop positive or negative cognitive appraisals of themselves and others.

Research has identified social-skill deficits, social participation infrequency, and social problem-solving deficits among adolescents with interpersonal adjustment difficulties. Most interventions to improve the quality of adolescents' peer interactions have focused on skills training in one or more of these areas. Although results of these interventions are promising, there remains the need to better investigate the nature of adolescent social relationships and the manner in which relationships affect adjustment.

REFERENCES

Ambron, S. R. (1975). *Child development*. San Francisco: Rinehart.

Arkowitz, H., Hinton, R., Perl, J., & Himadi, W. (1978). Treatment strategies for dating anxiety in college men based on real-life practice. *Counseling Psychologist, 7,* 41–46.

Bander, K. W., Steinke, G. V., Allen, G. J., & Mosher, D. L. (1975). Evaluation of three dating-specific treatment approaches for heterosexual dating anxiety. *Journal of Consulting and Clinical Psychology, 43,* 259–265.

Bandura, A., & Walters, R. H. (1963). *Social learning and personality development*. New York: Holt, Rinehart, and Winston.

Barclay, J. R. (1966). Sociometric choices and teacher ratings as predictors of school dropouts. *Journal of School Psychology, 4,* 40–44.

Bierman, K. L., & Furman, W. (1984). The effects of social skills training and peer involvement on the social adjustment of preadolescents. *Child Development, 55,* 151–162.

Bigelow, B. J. (1977). Children's friendship expectations: A cognitive–developmental study. *Child Development, 48,* 246–253.

Bigelow, B. J., & LaGaipa, J. J. (1975). Children's written descriptions of friendships: A multidimensional analysis. *Developmental Psychology, 11,* 857–858.

Borkovec, T. D., Stone, N. M., O'Brien, G. T., & Kaloupek, D. G. (1974). Evaluation of a clinically relevant target behavior for analogue outcome research. *Behavior Therapy, 5,* 503–511.

Bradlyn, A. S., Himadi, W. G., Crimmins, D. R., Christoff, K. A., Graves, K. G., & Kelly, J. A. (1983). Conversational skills training for retarded adolescents. *Behavior Therapy, 14,* 314–325.

Brennan, T. (1982). Loneliness at adolescence. In L. Peplau & D. Perlman (Eds.), *Loneliness: A source of current theory, research, and therapy* (pp. 269–290). New York: Wiley-Interscience.

Bryant, B. M., & Trower, P. E. (1974). Social difficulty in a student sample. *British Journal of Educational Psychology, 44,* 13–21.

Buswell, M. M. (1953). The relationship between social structure of the classroom and academic success of pupils. *Journal of Experimental Education, 22,* 37–52.

Christoff, K. A., Scott, W. O. N., Kelley, M. L., Schlundt, D., Baer, G., & Kelly, J. A. (in press). Social skills and social problem-solving training for extremely shy young adolescents. *Behavior Therapy*.

Combs, M. L., & Slaby, D. A. (1978). Social skills training with children. In B. B. Lahey & A. E. Kazdin (Eds.), *Advances in child clinical psychology*, (Vol. 1, pp. 161–206). New York: Plenum.

Conger, J. C., & Keane, S. P. (1981). Social skills intervention in the treatment of isolated or withdrawn children. *Psychological Bulletin, 90,* 478–495.

Cowen, E. L., Pederson, A., Babigian, H., Izzo, L. D., & Trost, M. A. (1973). Long term follow-up of early detected vulnerable children. *Journal of Consulting and Clinical Psychology, 41,* 438–446.

Csikszentmihalyi, M., & Larson, R. (1984). *Being adolescent: Conflict and growth in the teenage years*. New York: Basic Books.

Curran, J. P. (1977). Skills training as an approach to the treatment of heterosexual social anxiety. *Psychological Bulletin, 84,* 140–157.

Damon, W. (1983). *Social and personality development: Infancy through adolescence*: New York: Norton.

de Armas, A., & Kelly, J. A. (in press). Social relationships in adolescence: Skill development and training. In J. Worell & F. Danner (Eds.), *Adolescent development: Issues for education*. New York: Academic Press.

Douvan, E., & Adelson, J. (1966). *The adolescent experience*. New York: Wiley.

D'Zurilla, T. J., & Goldfried, M. R. (1971). Problem solving and behavior modification. *Journal of Abnormal Psychology, 78,* 107–126.

Elkind, D. (1983). Strategic interactions in early adolescence. In W. Damon (Ed.), *Social and personality development: Essays on the growth of the child* (pp. 434–444). New York: Norton.

Emmerich, W. (1966). Continuity and stability in early social development. II. Teacher's ratings. *Child Development, 37,* 17–27.

Filipczak, J., Archer, M., & Friedman, R. M. (1980). In school social skills training: Use with disruptive adolescents. *Behavior Modification, 4,* 2.

Foster, S. L., & Ritchey, W. L. (1979). Issues in the assessment of social competence in children. *Journal of Applied Behavior Analysis, 12,* 625–638.

Franco, D. P., Christoff, K. A., Crimmins, D. B., & Kelly, J. A. Social-skills training for an extremely shy young adolescent: An empirical case study. *Behavior Therapy, 14,* 568–575.

Freedman, B. J., Rosenthal, L., Donahue, C. P., Schlundt, D., & McFall, R. M. (1978). A social behavioral analysis of skill deficits in delinquent and nondelinquent adolescent boys. *Journal of Consulting and Clinical Psychology, 46,* 1448–1462.

French, D. C., & Tyne, T. F. (1982). The identification and treatment of children with peer-relationship difficulties. In J. P. Curran & P. M. Monti (Eds.), *Social skills training: A practical handbook for assessment and treatment* (pp. 280–308). New York: Guilford.

Gallatin, J. E. (1975). *Adolescence and individuality.* New York: Harper & Row.

Goffman, E. (1969). *Strategic interaction.* Philadelphia: University of Pennsylvania Press.

Gottman, J. M., Gonso, J., & Rasmussen, B. (1975). Social interaction, social competencies and friendship in children. *Child Development, 46,* 709–718.

Grinder, R. E. (1966). Relations of social dating attractions to academic orientation and peer relations. *Journal of Educational Psychology, 57,* 27–34.

Grinder, R. E. (1978). *Adolescence* (2nd ed.). New York: Wiley.

Gronlund, N. E. (1959). *Sociometry in the classroom.* New York: Harper & Brothers.

Hansen, D. J., St. Lawrence, J. S., & Christoff, K. A. (1984, November). *Group conversational skills training with psychiatric inpatient children and adolescents.* Paper presented to the 18th Annual Association for the Advancement of Behavior Therapy Meeting, Philadelphia.

Hartup, W. W. (1982). Peer relations. In C. B. Kopp & J. B. Krakow (Eds.), *The child: Development in a social context* (pp. 514–575). Reading, MA: Addison-Wesley.

Hartup, W. W. (1983). Peer interaction and the behavioral development of the individual child. In W. Damon (Ed.), *Social and personality development:* Essays on the growth of the child (pp. 220–233). New York: Norton.

Hartup, W., Glazer, J., & Charlesworth, R. (1967). Peer reinforcement and sociometric status. *Child Development, 38,* 1017–1024.

Havighurst, R. J. (1972). *Developmental tasks and education.* New York: McKay.

Heimberg, R. G., Madsen, C. H., Montgomery, D., & McNabb, C. E. (1980). Behavioral treatments for heterosocial problems: Effects on daily self-monitored and role-played interactions. *Behavior Modification, 4,* 147–172.

Horowitz, L. M., French, R., & Anderson, C. A. (1982). The prototype of a lonely person. In L. A. Peplau & D. Perlman (Eds.), *Loneliness: A sourcebook of current theory, research, and therapy* (pp. 183–206). New York: Wiley-Interscience.

Hurlock, E. B. (1972). *Child development.* New York: McGraw-Hill.

Hurlock, E. B. (1973). *Adolescent development.* New York: McGraw-Hill.

Husbands, C. T. (1970). Some social and psychological consequences of the American dating system. *Adolescence, 5,* 451–462.

Jones, W. H. (1981). Loneliness and social contact. *Journal of Psychology, 113,* 295–296.

Jones, W. H., Freeman, J. E., & Goswick, R. A. (1981).

The persistence of loneliness: Self and other determinants. *Journal of Personality, 49,* 27–28.

Jones, W. H., Hobbs, S. A., & Hockenbury, D. (1982). Loneliness and social skill deficits. *Journal of Personality and Social Psychology, 42,* 682–689.

Kagan, J., & Moss, H. A. (1962). *Birth to maturity: A study in psychological development.* New York: Wiley.

Kagan, J., & Moss, H. A. (1983). *Birth to maturity: A study in psychological development* (2nd ed.). New Haven, CT: Yale University Press.

Keasey, C. B. (1971). Social participation as a factor in the moral development of preadolescents. *Developmental Psychology, 5,* 216–220.

Kelly, J. A. (1982). *Social-skills training: A practical guide for interventions.* New York: Springer.

Kohn, M., & Clausen, J. (1955). Social isolation and schizophrenia. *American Sociological Review, 20,* 265–273.

Kupke, T. E., Hobbs, S. A., & Cheney, T. H. (1979). Selection of heterosocial skills. I. Criterion-related validity. *Behavior Therapy, 10,* 327–335.

LaBarba, R. C. (1981). *Foundations of developmental psychology.* New York: Academic Press.

Maloney, D. M., Harper, T. M., Braukmann, C. J., Fixsen, D. L., Phillips, E. L., & Wolf, M. M. (1976). Teaching conversation-related skills to predelinquent girls. *Journal of Applied Behavior Analysis, 9,* 371.

Minkin, N., Braukmann, C. J., Minkin, B. L., Timbers, G. D., Timbers, B. J., Fixsen, D. J., Phillips, E. L., & Wolf, M. M. (1976). The social validation and training of conversational skills. *Journal of Applied Behavior Analysis, 9,* 127–139.

Moore, N. V., Evertson, C. M., & Brophy, J. E. (1974). Solitary play: Some functional considerations. *Developmental Psychology, 10,* 830–834.

O'Conner, R. D. (1972). The relative efficacy of modeling, shaping, and combined procedures. *Journal of Abnormal Psychology, 79,* 327–334.

Ollendick, T. H., & Hersen, M. Social skills training for juvenile delinquents. (1979). *Behaviour Research and Therapy, 17,* 547–554.

Olpin, M., & Kogan, K. L. (1969). Child meets child: Social interaction between school-age boys. *Perceptual Motor Skills, 28,* 751–754.

Pentz, M. A. W. (1980). Assertion training and trainer effects on unassertive and aggressive adolescents. *Journal of Counseling Psychology, 27,* 76–83.

Platt, J. J., Spivack, G., Altman, W., Altman, D., & Peizer, S. B. (1974). Adolescent problem-solving thinking. *Journal of Consulting and Clinical Psychology, 43,* 787–793.

Rice, F. P. (1978). *The adolescent: Development, relationships, and culture.* Boston: Allyn and Bacon.

Rhodes, W. A., Redd, W. H., & Berggren, L. (1979). Social skills training for an unassertive adolescent. *Journal of Clinical Child Psychology,* 18–21.

Robins, L. (1966). *Deviant children grow up.* Baltimore: Williams & Wilkins.

Roff, M. (1961). Childhood social interactions and young adult bad conduct. *Journal of Abnormal and Social Psychology, 63,* 333–337.

Roff, M. (1963). Childhood social interaction and young adult psychosis. *Journal of Clinical Psychology, 19,* 152–157.

Roff, M., Sells, S. B., & Golden, M. M. (1972). *Social adjustment and personality development in children*. Minneapolis: University of Minnesota Press.

Sarason, I. G., & Sarason, B. R. (1981). Teaching cognitive and social skills to high school students. *Journal of Consulting and Clinical Psychology, 49*, 908–918.

Spivack, G., & Levine, M. (1963). *Self-regulation in acting-out and normal adolescents* (Report to National Institute of Mental Health, M-4531). Washington, DC: United States Public Health Service.

Stengel, E. (1971). *Suicide and attempted suicide*. New York: Penguin.

Twentyman, C. T., & McFall, R. M. (1975). Behavioral training of social skills in shy males. *Journal of Consulting and Clinical Psychology, 43*, 384–395.

Ullman, C. A. (1957). Teachers, peers, and tests as predictors of adjustment. *Journal of Educational Psychology, 48*, 257–267.

Zimbardo, P. G. (1977). *Shyness*. Reading, MA: Addison-Wesley.

CHAPTER 9

Adolescent Sexuality

Sol Gordon and Jane F. Gilgun

At a time when sexual identity and role-taking are major developmental tasks, the adolescent is confronted with conflicting values, messages, and injunctions about sex. Most adolescents manage quite well, although they often are subject to periods of vulnerability. For many, parents and other adults are important sources of information and emotional support, and they leave adolescence adequately prepared to assume adult roles. On the other hand, contemporary attitudes toward sexuality contribute to needless hurt and vulnerability among young people. Customs guiding sexual behavior and methods of transmitting sexual information are notable problematic issues related to adolescence.

Adults usually do not know how to talk to adolescents about sex, and adolescents are left on their own. Though most are sexually active to some degree, they often know surprisingly little. Because of lack of information, hundreds of thousands of young people have intercourse without contraceptive protection. As a result, as many as 40% of today's 14-year-old girls can expect to be pregnant by age 20 ("Forty percent," 1985). This is an alarming trend, fostered by an ambivalent governmental policy toward adolescent sexuality, which results in lack of contraceptive information and services (Jones et al., 1985). Governmental policy, of course, reflects the ambivalence of American society.

Peer support mitigates some of the difficulty inherent in testing and adapting to a heterosexual script of sexual conduct. Slumber parties and bull sessions serve important roles in adolescent sexual socialization. Many adolescents, however, are burdened by the expectations of this script. Performance fears for boys and mixed messages for girls are examples. When an adolescent begins to suspect that he or she may have a homosexual orientation, the expectations of the heterosexual script often delay the stabilization of sexual orientation into adulthood and beyond. Whether heterosexual or homosexual, however, the sexual developmental tasks of adolescence are problematic. Often the causes of these difficulties are related to how we are educating our youth. Without some examination of our sexual socialization practices and without some changes in these practices, we will continue to pay a high price, both in monetary and human terms.

An argument can be made that adolescent sexual abuse, adolescent sex offenses, and juvenile prostitution of both boys and girls are related to contemporary sexual socialization practices. Similarities between the heterosexual script and the conduct of individuals who are involved in these proscribed behaviors are not likely merely to be coincidental with or unconnected to the customs of the larger culture.

HETEROSEXUAL BEHAVIOR

During the past 15 years, the percentage of adolescent women experiencing sexual intercourse has increased substantially. Among 15- to 19-year-olds, the increase has been from 30% in 1971, to 43% in 1967, to 50% in 1979, according to a series of studies conducted at Johns Hopkins University (Zelnik & Kantner, 1980). Males were included in these studies in 1979. At that time, 77% of the males aged 17 to 19 stated that they had experienced intercourse at least once. Though the gap is closing, males tend to be more sexually experienced at earlier ages than females. Black adolescent women are more likely to be sexually active than whites, with 66% of black women and 47% of white adolescent women reporting intercourse at least once (Zelnik & Kantner, 1980). Of those who were sexually active, age at first intercourse was 16.2 overall, 16.4 for white women and 15.5 for black women (Zelnik & Kantner, 1980). These figures are very similar to a study of adolescent sexual behavior in two suburban Chicago schools (Ostrov, Offer, Howard, Kaufman, & Meyer, 1985).

Among the younger adolescents, the most recent data are from Ostrov et al. (1985). These and earlier investigations show that from 5% to 17% of girls 15 and under have had sexual intercourse, whereas among boys the same age, the range is from 19% to 38% (Gilgun, 1984; Jessor & Jessor, 1975; Ostrov et al., 1985; Sorensen, 1973; Vener & Stewart, 1974).

Oral sex has increased substantially among adolescents since the first studies by Kinsey 40 years ago (Newcomer & Udry, 1985). Many adolescents who have not had intercourse report having given or received oral sex. Sorensen (1973) calls these individuals "experienced beginners." In a sample of 10th, 11th, and 12th graders (Newcomer & Udry, 1985), 25% of the males and 15% of the females who reported not having intercourse reported having oral sex. Moreover, 29% of the boys and 17% of the girls reporting no experience in intercourse had ex-

perienced oral sex in a study of 10- to 15-year-olds (Gilgun, 1984).

These data and others document what Broderick and Rowe (1968) have called the "heterosexual continuum among adolescents" (p. 100). Introduction into sexual intimacy is usually gradual, with an order of events. Necking precedes petting and petting precedes fellatio and cunnilingus, which can, but often doesn't, precede intercourse. Many adolescents, however, experience oral sex after having what many think is "the real thing."

Significant proportions of adolescents have sexual experiences outside of this "heterosexual continuum" through masturbation and same-sex behaviors. Most boys experience ejaculation for the first time at about age 12 or 13, as Bell, Weinberg, and Hammersmith (1981) found in their study of sexual preference. Masturbation, genital contact with same-sex or other-sex partner, and during sleep are the circumstances under which ejaculation occurs. In the study conducted by Bell et al. (1981), more heterosexual than homosexual males reported their first sexual encounter to be with other males, if looking and parallel masturbation are included. If genital touching only is considered, more homosexual than heterosexual males reported their first sexual encounter to be with males. More heterosexual males than homosexual reported first ejaculation during sleep. By age 19, both the heterosexual and homosexual men in the Bell et al. study reported having masturbated.

Unlike the heterosexual male, the heterosexual female in the Bell et al. (1981) report had much less same-sex experience than the homosexual female. In fact, the researchers found that adolescent female heterosexuals are less sexually active than homosexual peers. Fewer heterosexuals than homosexuals reported orgasm during sleep and masturbation before age 19. However, of those who reported these behaviors, there was no difference in their ages when the behaviors began. Heterosexual female adolescents, however, did report sexual behavior with other females, but much less same-sex behaviors than did heterosexual male peers.

Both male and female adolescents frequently report feelings of sexual arousal toward members of their sex, whether or not the feelings are accompanied by sexual behavior. Same-sex feelings either with or without same-sex behaviors sometimes lead to what clinicians have called "homosexual panic," where individuals who are predominantly heterosexual—or will be when their sexual orientation stabilizes—become fearful they are gay or lesbian.

The young person needs to know that sometimes sexual identity doesn't stabilize until adulthood. Until then, sexual orientation may fluctuate, though fluctuation appears to be more common among adolescents who in adulthood come to accept themselves as homosexuals. When the young person reaches adulthood and finds that he or she has sexual relations with members of the same sex much more than with the other sex and/or finds sex with members of the same gender more satisfying and meaningful than heterosexual relations, then homosexuality may be the predominant sexual orientation. Some sex educators believe that in sexual behavior many people have majors and minors.

Sexual Scripts

Just as there appear to be major differences in male and female adolescent experiences of same-sex behavior, so there are differences in how members of each gender experience first intercourse. Differences in male and female socialization, or social learning, appear to account for these differences (Gagnon & Simon, 1973). Role prescriptions for males appear to be more clear-cut than for females (Carns, 1973; Gagnon & Simon, 1973; Gilgun, 1984), although occasionally adolescent females are reported to be under pressure from female peers to "lose their virginity." Sorensen's (1973) survey of adolescents aged 13 to 19 showed major disparities between the male and female experience of first intercourse. More females than males reported guilt, fear, and hurt, whereas many more males reported feeling happy and satisfied. In general, about twice as many boys as girls reported positive feelings about sexual interaction. For many, then, the experience of first intercourse is grim.

Eastman (1972), in his study of undergraduate men and women, reported similar findings. He interpreted these differences as having to do with females' greater difficulty "in integrating premarital intercourse with their total sexuali-

ty" (pp. 24–25). Carns (1973) found that women are less pressured by same-sex peers to engage in intercourse than men are. Also, women are given less approval than men when they do so. Some girls do experience same-sex pressure. When this occurs, losing one's virginity is seen as a way of gaining adult status.

This double standard of sexual behavior shows itself in other ways. Young males tend to tell more of their male peers about their sexual activity than females tell female peers. In fact, it may be true that, although their female partners rarely achieve orgasm, the boys get their orgasms 3 days later when they tell the other guys about it. Females tend to tell one or two very close girlfriends, sometimes excitedly and happily, but frequently as a way of working out feelings of guilt and of being used (Carns, 1973). Guilt and confusion are compounded when sexual intercourse does not lead to going steady, which the girl often expects. Few things are more devastating to a girl than to be ignored the next day by the boy with whom she shared what she thought were sexual intimacies the night before.

Discrepancies in male–female scripting cause a great deal of confusion as adolescents work out their sexual identities and roles. By the time a girl has reached adolescence, she has learned to link sexual intercourse with love. She often rationalizes her sexual behavior by telling herself she was swept away by love. Study after study has shown that young females, much more than young males, report being in love as a primary reason they became sexually active (Cassell, 1984). Many more females than males engage in intercourse with partners they love and would like to marry. Other possible reasons for engaging in sex include giving into male pressure, gambling sex will be a way to get a boyfriend, curiosity, and sexual appetite not related to loving and caring.

Boys know girls have been socialized into a love ethic. They also know the pressure many feel to have a boyfriend. "You would if you loved me" and "If you really loved me, you'd have sex with me" are two classic male lines that show how well males understand female thinking on sex and love. Girls who are able to say, "If you really loved me, you wouldn't put such pressure on me," indicate understanding of male motivation (cf. Gordon, 1979).

It is obvious that young people are not being helped to understand how they can tell when they're really in love. This probably is due to myths like, "If you think you're in love, you are" and "Love is blind." Mature love, however, gives the person energy. Mature love motivates the person to become the best possible partner for the other. The well-being of the other is just a little bit more important than the well-being of the self. In mature love, people talk to each other about differences between them, although they may have heated arguments before coming to an understanding. They can spend a whole day together without television and find it fantastic. Immature love is exhausting. Violence is always a sign of immature and conflicted forms of love (Gordon & Gordon, 1983). Finally, sex is never a test of love. Young people need to learn that, in a marriage, sex is number nine on a list of ten most important parts of a marriage. Respect for each other and a sense of humor and playfulness are at the top of the list (cf. Gordon & Gordon, 1983). It is a safe gamble that if adults began giving young people these messages, there would be less confusion and exploitation among adolescents as they work out their sexual identities and roles.

Because this egalitarian view of love is not conveyed, exploitation and courtship violence are very common. Girls do not necessarily know that boys have motives other than love for wanting intercourse. Girls do not seem to understand male sexual socialization. Most fail to understand the pressure boys are under to prove themselves to be men. Because of this pressure, boys more than girls have sexual intercourse with partners for whom they have little or no feeling. Boys often are encouraged to misrepresent their feelings (Gordon, 1979), and they risk losing touch with or becoming insensitive to their own feelings of caring and love. Girls are at risk for being used and for learning not to trust males.

Males, then, are socialized to take control of sexual behavior. Two other factors support the ethic of male control. One is the tendency for both sexes to assume that it is the male role to take the initiative in the continuum of heterosexual behaviors (Gagnon & Simon, 1973; Laws, 1980; Nass, Libby, & Fisher, 1981). In a recent empirical study, Gilgun (1984) found that a small minority of her sample of 10- to 15-year-olds expected the girl to take the initiative in

heterosexual behaviors. More than half the sample thought the boy should take the lead in heavy petting, defined as touching the female below her waist, while two thirds of the girls and more than half of the boys said either sex should take the initiative in intercourse. There are discrepancies by sex in terms of thinking on initiative, but clearly the girl is much less frequently considered the initiator.

A second factor in support of male control in heterosexual interactions is age. Surveys show, as does everyday observation, that the male partner is almost never younger than the female, whereas the female often is 1 to 3 years younger than the male (Furstenberg, 1976; Sorensen, 1973; Zelnik & Kantner, 1977). With age comes a degree of authority. For many adolescent girls, going out with "an older man" gives her status. With the older male–younger female couple, the male has more authority over the female than vice versa. In short, he's the boss.

The male sexual script is interpreted by some males to mean they have permission to be sexually aggressive without having to be concerned about female consent. The relationship of male sexual aggression to the consent of the young female to have intercourse or other sexual experiences has received little research attention, although there is interest in male sexual aggression in dating. In research on adolescents, consent may be assumed. Sorensen (1973), for example, one of the few who described the circumstances of first intercourse, did not discuss consent, although he noted that "many sexually inexperienced girls" received "immediate and direct" pressure from "would-be" male partners (p. 156). He reported that pressure often succeeded in persuading girls to have intercourse. He did not note that consent might be problematic under these circumstances.

Furstenberg (1976) found that more than three-quarters of his pregnant, mostly black adolescent respondents believed a girl should be 18 or older when she begins to have intercourse. This belief and their pregnancies point to an obvious contradiction. When asked why most girls have intercourse, the majority chose the answer "inability to resist pressure from the male" (p. 45). Though Furstenberg (1976) observed that this answer could be obscuring genuine consent, he also stated that girls sometimes believed the male would leave them if they didn't have intercourse. The majority left once the girl became pregnant.

Having and keeping a boyfriend are powerful motivators for girls to engage in intercourse. Particularly when other life choices are restricted, some adolescent girls may see having a boyfriend as one of the few viable ways to achieve status. Among girls who are runaways or live in group homes, most of whom have suffered severe deprivation, the pressure to have a boyfriend is high. Many will do almost anything for a boy, and some are classic doormats. When a girl is driven to achieve status through having a boyfriend, she is at risk for putting aside her own beliefs regarding the timing and circumstances of participation in sexual activities.

Not only do girls experience pressure to have a boyfriend and pressure from some boys to engage in intercourse, but they often experience male physical aggression. The male sexual script appears to include widespread social support for coercive behavior (Burt, 1980, 1983; Korman & Leslie, 1982; Malmuth, Haber, & Feshbach, 1980). For example, more than half a sample of male college students stated there is likelihood they would rape a woman if they were assured they would not be punished (Malmuth et al., 1980). Male perceptions of the rape victim indicate that they, in general, consider the act less of a trauma than do females (Malmuth et al., 1980). Korman and Leslie (1982) suggested the existence of a "reward structure" for male sexual aggression.

Most adolescent girls do not seem to know that men receive social support for being sexually aggressive. Studies of college women and men substantiate the degree of male sexually aggressive episodes during dating (Kanin, 1957; Kanin & Parcell, 1977; Kirkpatrick & Kanin, 1957; Korman & Leslie, 1982). Between one-fourth and one-fifth of the women reported forceful male attempts at intercourse. Threats of and instances of physical violence ranged from 3% to 8%. In a study of college men, 25% stated they had attempted to force intercourse on a woman to the point where she screamed, pleaded, and cried for him to stop (Kanin, 1969).

Many boys may not like the male sexual script or may not be able to follow it. Those who have rejected the injunction that males must be sexually experienced to be real men, and who have peace of mind about it, are probably rare. More common are boys who follow the script, but feel conflicted. Also common are boys who feel humiliated and isolated from peers because they do not demonstrate sexual prowess. Many adolescents feel conflicted and inferior because of the sexual scripts they are expected to follow. Increasingly, young people are asking, "Is it ok not to have sex?" Some have sex because they think they are supposed to. This reflects the degree of pressure young people have to be sexually active.

Contraceptive Use

Despite the pressure young people feel to be sexual, they often are not taught how to prevent pregnancy and how to be sexually responsible. Numerous reports have indicated that adolescents need information about birth control and ready access to free or inexpensive contraceptives. This generally is not available in the United States. As a result, the rates of adolescent pregnancy, abortion, and childbearing are much higher in the United States than in most industrialized nations with similar rates of adolescent sexual activity (Jones et al., 1985).

The American teenage abortion rate is as high or higher than the combined birth and abortion rates in Canada, England, Wales, Sweden, and the Netherlands. The other nations are characterized by a tolerance for teenage sexual activity, general openness to sexuality, and government policies that support sex education and contraception education in the school and readily available free or inexpensive contraceptives. In short, these countries have accepted the fact of adolescent sexual activity. Further, they have developed specific policies geared toward the prevention of adolescent pregnancy and abortion.

Few American adolescents learn about contraception in sex-education classes. Some learn from parents, but most learn from peers, who are the sources, not only of misinformation, but often of attitudes that foster the development of sexual exploitation for boys and "doormatism" for girls. Not coincidentally, American adolescents use contraceptives inconsistently, poorly, or not at all. For example, 35% of the sexually active adolescent women surveyed by Zelnik and Kantner (1980) always used contraceptives and 26% never used it. The remainder used it sporadically. Not only are the inconsistent and never users running a serious risk of pregnancy, but the always users are also. About 14% of them had been pregnant at least once. This is not a contradictory statement; the most common form of birth control was withdrawal, notoriously unreliable. The always users, then, frequently use unreliable methods. By contrast, in countries that are providing contraceptive services, the pill is most frequently used. And the pill, of course, is highly reliable. In the United States, the use of the pill and the IUD declined by 50% between 1976 and 1979, whereas the use of rhythm and withdrawal increased by 86%. The decline in the use of the most effective methods has resulted in an almost 5% increase in the number of pregnancies reported by adolescents who always use contraceptives. Clearly, for American adolescents, the only solution to the 1.3 million pregnancies and 600,000 abortions per year is the development of policies and programs that work so well in other countries.

Because there is differential access to information and to contraceptives, there is differential use of contraception. In an environment unsupportive of the need for contraceptive information and services, four factors have been linked to adolescent contraceptive use in the United States: (a) level of commitment to the well-being of the partner, (b) self-acceptance as a sexual person, (c) parents as sources of sexual information, and (d) plans for the future that have social and familial support.

A relationship where there is commitment and caring is characterized by contraceptive use. The male often plays a decisive role. Males are most likely to be concerned about birth control when they feel a commitment to the other person. Then, they are willing to discuss birth control, either use it themselves or encourage the girlfriend to obtain it, and are cooperative in its use. Ironically, couples who run the greatest risk of pregnancy are those involved in casual encounters. Under conditions of noncommitment, males simply do not think about birth control, trust to luck, or assume that the female has taken care of it. Scales and Beckstein (1982) consider these behaviors to characterize male self-centeredness, where the focus is on his satisfaction and not on protection of the female from pregnancy. When ego-centeredness interferes with contraceptive use and pregnancy results, adolescent males have an easy out. They

can abandon the girl, and most do. Not yet known is the degree of guilt, if any, these males experience. If there is guilt, then unprotected intercourse can be considered self-destructive for the male as well as for the female.

In order for intercourse to take place without contraception, the female, of course, has a part to play. Growing evidence suggests that female ambivalence about sexuality dovetails with male nonconcern about contraception. Lindemann (1974) wrote that many young women are ambivalent about their sexuality. Contraceptive use forces a redefinition of the self as a sexual being. Young females have to grapple with the notion of "Nice girls don't." In an environment as ambivalent about their sexuality as they are, young females usually have no one with whom to work through their conflicts. When they are not able to overcome this sex-typed prescription for their behavior, they feel guilty and conflicted about seeking contraceptives. The ability to discuss contraception with prospective partners also is limited.

Young women who are struggling to define themselves sexually may at times deny their sexual interests. Thus, they may have intercourse under "romantic and spontaneous" conditions, with no planning for contraception. Being swept away by passion is the rationalization used to blot out the injunction "Nice girls don't." Conflicted young women often look to the male for the decision to have intercourse. If he behaves as if being sexual is all right, then she thinks it may be acceptable (Cassell, 1984).

Female self-centeredness, fostered by the heterosexual script, also seems to play a part in unprotected intercourse. Some adolescent women are so focused on pleasing the male—which they think is the proof of their self-worth—that they lose sight of what is in their best interest. One study found that the female noncontraceptor was primarily concerned with whether the male loved her, whether he would enjoy himself, what he would think of her, and what others would think of her if they knew she was sexually active (Cvetkovich & Grote, 1980). In this report, noncontracepting females routinely expressed fears of pregnancy only when directly questioned. Common answers were, "Oh yes, that, too," "I didn't think of it until later," and "Not until my period was late."

Sexually active young females who use contraceptives tend to reject traditional sex-typed prescriptions, such as "Nice girls don't." They believe that "Nice girls do—use contraception." They accept themselves as sexual, and they seek contraceptives and use them in a pre-planned way (e.g., Goldsmith, Gabrielson, Gabrielson, Mathews, & Potts, 1972; Gordon, Scales, & Everly, 1979; Lindemann, 1979). They usually are involved in a long-term relationship, have discussed contraception with their boy-friends, and have egalitarian views toward female–male relationships.

The source of this self-acceptance appears to be parents. Many investigations have shown that when parents are the primary sex educators of their children, the children tend to post-pone sexual activity until adulthood. Those who do not postpone sexual activity use contra-ceptives more often and more consistently than those who do not (Fox, 1981; Gordon et al., 1979). Noncontraceptors more frequently cite peers as the source of sexual information. Non-contraceptors outnumber contraceptors three to one (Zelnik & Kantner, 1980). As members of this society, adults have to take some responsi-bility for the risks to which adolescents are sub-jected when they become sexually active.

What is tragic about these facts is that so much nonuse of contraception is preventable. The recent study of the major industrialized na-tions, discussed previously, underscores this point. In the United States, sex education in the schools (and in the home) are great experiments that have not been attempted. Evidence of the effectiveness of sex education in the schools, combined with availability in reducing adoles-cent pregnancy, abortion, and childbearing, has been obtained in research conducted by Jones et al. (1985).

What fails to distinguish contraceptors from noncontraceptors is plans for the future. Most adolescents, whether contraceptors or not, whether sexually active or not, whether white or members of minority groups, have plans for the future. For almost all of them and for their families, pregnancy is upsetting and often con-sidered a tragedy. Families go into mourning for what might be the curtailment or end of their hopes for the child. Certainly, for most of these families, there eventually is acceptance and ac-commodation made for the pregnancy—when they don't choose abortion, which many do not. The infants are usually warmly received. Once the children are born, the young mothers typically return to school and continue to plan for their futures. Most, however, drop out of school and abandon their plans, often because of lack of childcare, and, for many blacks and other minorities, because they have difficulty seeing how they will ever find a meaningful job in a world that appears—and often is—hostile to them. In short, many adolescents, even before they become pregnant, feel defeated by racial and class discrimination, which shows itself to them through lack of meaningful opportunity.

Postponers

Postponers represent a sizeable portion of ad-olescents. More than half of the white and a third of the black 15- to 19-year-old women have not initiated intercourse. By age 17, slightly less than half of the white males and about 40% of the black males have not had intercourse (Zelnik & Kantner, 1980). By age 19, these per-centages decrease to 23% and 20% respectively.

There are many different types of adolescents who postpone having intercourse. Those who plan on going to college tend to postpone more than those who plan on getting married after high school (Jessor & Jessor, 1975; Miller & Si-mon, 1974). Drinking, drug-taking, and truancy are associated with some segments of the sexu-ally active population, according to Jessor and Jessor (1975), who consider these behaviors, along with intercourse during high school, as part of a general pattern of deviance from social norms. Church attendance was related to post-ponement of intercourse among whites (Jessor, Costa, Jessor, & Donovan, 1983; Jessor & Jessor, 1975; Miller & Simon, 1974), but not among a sample of middle- and lower-class black adoles-cent women from a southern Christian tradition (Roebuck & McGee, 1977). These young wom-en considered themselves religious, and many were sexually active.

Postponers appear to be less dependent on peers and more involved with their families than sexually active adolescents, who, typically, are strongly peer-identified. Dependence on male peers is strongly associated with sexual behavior among boys (Jessor et al., 1983; Miller & Simon, 1974; Scales & Beckstein, 1982). How-ever, dependence on female peers is not asso-ciated with sexual activity for girls (Miller & Si-mon, 1974). Girls who obtain their sexual infor-mation from adolescent boys, however, tend to be more sexually active than girls who have other sources of information.

A negative self-concept may influence postponement of sexual activity. Yet, it also seems to be a causative factor in the sexual behavior of some adolescents. Many sexually active young people are motivated to be sexual because of feelings of inadequacy. This is true for girls as well as boys. Seeking out sex is a way of seeking assurance of self-worth. Some girls are socialized to believe that their sex is one of the few ways they can feel worthwhile. Ironically, sex motivated primarily by the need for reassurance usually results in exploitation and an increase rather than a decrease in a sense of inadequacy.

On the other hand, virgins were differentiated from nonvirgins in a 9-year follow-up on research begun in 1970 on high school students on measures of feelings of inadequacy (Jessor et al., 1983). On follow-up, subjects were between 23 and 25 years old. Virgins were more likely to report feelings of being less competent in interpersonal relationships and of being less physically attractive than nonvirgins. Feelings of inadequacy, then, can cut both ways in relation to sexual behavior. The direction of causality is not clear: Does lack of sexual activity result from or cause feelings of inadequacy? In the Jessor et al. (1983) follow-up, however, virgins had attained higher educational and occupational levels and reported more closeness to parents and more church attendance than nonvirgins.

Sexual Behavior and Vulnerability

If one grand generalization can be made about young people, it is that vulnerable adolescents are the most prone to engage in irresponsible sexual behavior. Adolescents who feel inadequate and inferior, who are without opportunities for meaningful education and work, and who feel compelled to prove something to themselves through sex, are at greatest risk. These youngsters often have been physically, sexually, and/or emotionally abused. Many have been socially abused; racism and sexism have limited their access to opportunities that some segments of the population take for granted. It is not coincidental that members of minority groups use contraceptives less frequently and have higher rates of pregnancy than members of nonminority groups. Minorities, in general, simply have less access to information and services. Such youngsters are made vulnerable through social policy, which might not be intended to hurt young people, but which does in its consequences. Irresponsible behavior involves risk-taking that could lead to pregnancy, sexually transmitted diseases, and psychological trauma. Irresponsible behavior is often exploitative, as when boys misrepresent their feelings to persuade girls to have sex with them. Boys who believe sexual intercourse or making a girl pregnant are proof of masculinity and virility are as vulnerable as the girls who might respond to them.

Adolescent vulnerability is not necessarily indefinite. The period can last for days or weeks at a time at different periods. Most adolescents manage quite well without major trauma. Although it is important to proceed with an awareness of vulnerability, adolescence is not a disease. Sexual intercourse, however, can be a health hazard for adolescents. They simply are too young and too vulnerable to engage in sex. Only exceptional adolescents engage in sex responsibly, with love and caring.

Adolescents have many worries about sex. More often than not their anxiety is related to being liked, to being like everyone else, to making friends, and to having interesting things to do. In the sexual area, worries are often concerns about being normal. Specifically, they focus on:

- Am I sexually attractive?
- Will I grow more?
- Is my penis/vagina too small (or oddly shaped)?
- Why am I so slow in developing (pubic hair, breasts, hips, deep voice, shaving, getting my period, etc.)?
- Will anyone ever love me?
- Is it normal not to have sex?

When sexual intercourse is used to prove they are normal, adolescents are running a great risk of being hurt or being hurtful.

Sex education at home and at school can go a long way to help adolescents be less vulnerable. Less than 10% of all adolescents are getting a comprehensive sex education (Kirby, Alter, & Scales, 1979). One study showed that almost all parents (95%) and their children (76%) thought parents should be the primary sex educators of their children, and that schools should provide backup (Alexander & Jorgensen, 1983). Schools and parents, however, rank lower than peers and literature as sources of sex education in several studies of adolescent sources of information (Thornburg, 1981). The peak years when most sexual concepts are learned are ages 12 and 13, the early stages of puberty. Accuracy of information was found to be fairly high for some topics in a study of early adolescents. However, information on homosexuality, masturbation, seminal emission, contraception, and ejaculation was likely to be distorted (Thornburg, 1981).

Besides needing information, adolescents also require education in values. It is hard to imagine sex education without values. In the home and in the school, the most sensible values to be taught are those of the democratic society in which we live. Equality of all persons, freedom from coercion and exploitation, the right to respect and to a sense of dignity are some of the values of a democratic society. The sex education that makes the most sense, then, is a moral education, where the young person can acquire the highest aspirations of our democratic society (Gordon, 1984).

Being moral takes into account the points of view of others and respects divergent points of view. Being moralistic implies dogmatism and authoritarianism. In a moral sex education, young people would be taught that it is wrong to exploit others and to allow someone to exploit them. The central tension in American democracy has to do with the question, "How can I exercise my individual liberty without interfering with the liberty of another?" This is a fundamental question that would be addressed in a moral sex education. A moral sex education would state that most organized religions believe it is better for young people to wait until adulthood before they have intercourse, at least until they move out of their parents' house. A moralistic position would state, "If you have sexual intercourse before marriage, you'll go to hell." By depriving individuals of the freedom to debate, test, and choose, dogmatism interferes with individual liberty and moral development (Gilgun & Gordon, 1983).

This is not to say that adults should never state their opinions to adolescents. An adolescent who is exploitative or involved in a violent relationship would need the authoritative guidance of an adult. "I can't tell you what to do" is not a helpful response. The adolescent often needs an alternative point of view. Whether exploited or exploiting, the adolescent will benefit from knowing how others view the behavior. Besides empathy, adolescents often need to know about limits (i.e., when behavior is not acceptable because of possible injury to self or other).

Besides being vulnerable to feelings of inadequacy and exploitation, young sexually active people are vulnerable to pregnancy and sexually transmitted diseases (STDs). More than 1 million girls become pregnant each year, and about 600,000 give birth. Induced and spontaneous abortions account for half or more of these pregnancies. Herpes, chlamydia, and a host of other diseases are rampant among sexually active adolescents, many of whom have never heard of the diseases. Some STDs, like chlamydia, have no symptoms but can cause sterility. Gonorrhea also is a leading cause of sterility among adolescents. The second highest incidence rate among all groups is in the 15- to 19-year-old group (Phillips, 1984). One quarter of the 1 million reported cases of gonorrhea occurs in the 10 to 19 age group. Besides sterility, gonorrhea can lead to ectopic pregnancies. It has been identified as a major unmet health need among adolescents.

Adolescent suicide recently has been identified as a serious public health problem. Trouble with parents, school failure, and breakup of love relationships are the most common reasons for suicide attempts among adolescents (Berman, 1985; Paluszny, 1984). Suicide has become the third leading cause of death among adolescents. Adolescents, who often are not able to think about the future in terms adults would call realistic, are vulnerable to "the forevers." That is, they think that how they feel now is how they will always feel. Berman (1985) quoted a 14-year-old girl who said, "If I died, I wouldn't hurt as much as I do now" (p. 124). Sex education is not likely to be a panacea for adolescent suicide. However, if more adolescents could be helped to see themselves as being worthy human beings, regardless of whether or not they have a boyfriend or girlfriend, this might mitigate some of the suffering. Adolescents often do not realize that people can fall in love more than once.

Although sexual intercourse is a health hazard for adolescents, they often have strong sexual drives that they need help understanding and channeling. They must be taught alternatives to sexual intercourse. The increase in oral sex discussed above indicates that many are learning that sexual gratification does not have to mean sexual intercourse. Discussion of consensual oral sex is a logical component of a sex education program, whether parents or teachers (or both) are the educators.

Another alternative to intercourse is masturbation. Even today, many youngsters are taught that it is wrong and nasty. Some males believe that rape and sex with a prostitute are preferable to masturbation. There is a countervailing trend, however, to these avataristic prejudices. Masturbation to orgasm is not only beginning to be seen as a developmental milestone for adolescents and a preparation for adult sexual intercourse, but it is being thought of as contributing to a sense of well-being throughout the life span. It used to be that something was wrong with married adults who masturbated. Not anymore. Many married adults masturbate and have frequent sexual intercourse. Many forms of sex therapy teach women how to masturbate as one step toward becoming orgasmic with partners. Male sex therapy often includes masturbation, as often to retard ejaculation as to bring about erections.

For the young person, masturbation can be one solution for what to do when they have reached "the peak of passion." Rather than feeling embarrassed that the erection might show, or becoming sexually involved with someone for whom there is little commitment, or risking a sexually transmitted disease, the adolescent can be given the message that masturbation is natural, healthy, and self-protective. If they feel ready for intimacy with the partner, but not ready for intercourse, young people can masturbate each other. As the taboos on masturbation are lifted, it is likely that adolescents will include mutual masturbation increasingly in their repertoire of sexual behaviors.

Because adolescence is the stage of life where rapid change takes place, adolescents will probably always be vulnerable. A sound sexual education, however, will help them be less vulnerable than most are at present. Sex education can reduce vulnerability that results from withholding information from adolescents.

HOMOSEXUAL BEHAVIOR

One of the developmental tasks of adolescence is the discovery of sexual orientation. Most adolescents will move into adulthood confident of a heterosexual identity. A large minority, generally accepted as 10%, however, have lived through the difficulties inherent in being adolescent and, in addition, worry about whether or not they are lesbian or gay.

Adolescence is a crucial time in the development of a homosexual identity. The strongest predictor of an adult homosexual orientation in the study by Bell et al. (1981) was adolescent homosexual involvement, a composite of participation in homosexual behaviors and of sexual arousal by same-sex peers. These researchers concluded that adult homosexuality is a continuation of an identity that is being established in adolescence and often in childhood. These findings hold true for both females and males, although there are differences and similarities as members of each gender discover their sexual identities.

Like heterosexuals who sometimes become sexually aroused by and have sexual contact with members of their own sex, homosexuals sometimes report arousal by and sexual contact with members of the other sex. Among lesbians, almost two-thirds reported that they were sexually aroused by a male before age 19 (Bell et al., 1981). The comparable figure for heterosexual women was 81%. Gay men reported heterosexual arousal in almost the same percentages as lesbians, contrasted with 98% of the heterosexual males reporting arousal by a female. By age 19, the same percentages of lesbians as heterosexual women reported having had intercourse, mutual masturbation, and other forms of petting and necking. Gay men were less heterosexually experienced than heterosexual men. A third of the gay males as compared to two-thirds of the heterosexual males reported having intercourse by age 19.

Heterosexuals experienced more stability in their sexual orientation than homosexuals. Despite some overlapping of experiences between homosexuals and heterosexuals, homosexuals recalled many more instances of same-sex arousal and more intense pleasure in same-sex behaviors than heterosexuals. Both female and male homosexuals reported that their behavior during adolescence was more heterosexual than their feelings.

Learning to Hide

When interest in members of the same sex is intense and compelling, the young person can experience severe conflict. The culture fosters heterosexuality and stigmatizes homosexuality. Homosexual males are "sissies," "fags," "queers," and homosexual women are "lessies," "dykes," and "failed women" because they often fail to marry and have children. The adolescent who is beginning to identify the self as homosexual usually is alone in trying to deal with these issues. Martin (1982) calls the sexual socialization of the homosexual adolescent a process of learning to hide. One of the chief characteristics of the adolescent trying to come to terms with a homosexual identity is a sense of isolation.

Learning to hide can begin early. Some boys initially feel great joy as they join other boys in mutual masturbation. Finally, some deep yearnings are being fulfilled. Not knowing that most boys who participate in this activity identify as heterosexual, they can assume these other boys feel as they do. A fondly told story among homosexual males is that of the young adolescent, a future homosexual, who is engaged in mutual masturbation. Caught up in the peak of passion, he gave the other boy a big kiss. The boy responded, "Yuk. What's the matter with you? You queer or something?" Such a response leads to confusion and to a decision to hide erotic feelings for other boys.

Some gay men wait out their entire adolescence, hoping heterosexual feelings will develop. One gay male dated a girl through most of high school, although his erotic interest, but not his behavior, was directed toward other males. He said, "I thought it was a matter of time before I could make my straightness happen." This man was in his early 20s and had developed a love relationship with another man before he began to accept himself as homosexual. He reported feeling guilty about wasting his high-school girlfriend's time. He said that as an adolescent, he had no one with whom to discuss his homosexual interests, and he felt apart

from the other boys. He wasn't able to be part of their comraderie, often based on heterosexual stories of conquest.

Female Experience

Many female adolescent homosexuals have similar experiences, although same-sex genital contact is not as common as among males. They wait for years for a male to come along and stir up feelings they have experienced with close female friends. Many women who as adults identify as homosexual, however, considered themselves predominantly heterosexual during adolescence. Most of the lesbians in the report by Bell et al. (1981) described themselves in this manner. Women, raised in a love ethic as opposed to the male ethic of conquest, appear to be encouraged to have close female friends. Strong feelings of attachment are common among adolescent girls, regardless of whether they later identify as homosexual or heterosexual. Specifically, erotic feelings may be incorrectly labeled, may not be brought into awareness, or may not occur. The stigma attached to homosexuality may influence nonrecognition of attachment to other females as erotic. By such a process, the stabilization of homosexual identity may be delayed into early and, in some cases, middle and later adulthood.

The vocabulary of homosexuality is inadequate. Homosexual feelings are as sweet, intense, and delightful as heterosexual feelings. Terms like "lessie" and "queer" are antithetical to the quality of homosexual feelings. "Going out with" and "dating" may describe heterosexual behavior, but the use of these terms to describe the behavior of homosexuals is awkward, probably because of strong heterosexual connotations. Lacking an adequate vocabulary, the homosexual adolescent is unable to think clearly about sexual identity, and talking to others is very difficult. The result is confusion and sometimes self-hatred.

The Family

The adolescent needs someone with whom to talk. The family can be unavailable. For generations, mothers and fathers have been held responsible for the development of homosexuality in their children. When there is a hint of homosexuality, much less an open statement, parents go into their own homosexual panic, driven by guilt and self-recrimination. Even the most accepting of parents struggle because they know, as Freud (1951) stated so many years ago, being homosexual is no advantage in terms of the stigmatization. Several types of reactions are common, including denial (i.e., the idea the child will outgrow it), recrimination, and, sometimes, ostracism. When parents are centered on what they think are their own inadequacies and failure, they are unavailable to their children. Professionals need to be alert to parental guilt and offer empathy and guidelines for action. The temptation is strong to play into parents' guilt, by looking into their behavior for causes. No one knows what causes homosexuality. What is known is that homosexuals were probably raised by heterosexual parents.

Families and children benefit from a discussion and exploration of negative stereotypes; they need to test them against the reality of the positive aspects of the homosexual life. It is a hostile environment and not individual pathology that makes the homosexual lifestyle problematic. The process of accepting their child as homosexual, as well as self-acceptance by the homosexual, is probably somewhat easier in families where roles, tasks, behaviors, and feelings are not assigned rigidly according to gender and age but by personal style. In other words, a flexible, open family style facilitates the family's acceptance of a homosexual child, which, of course, facilitates the homosexual's self-acceptance.

The adolescent who is struggling with sexual identity would benefit from a knowledgeable adult taking the initiative in broaching the subject. Fisher (personal communication, May 2, 1985), a social worker specializing in work with gay clients, recommended an open-ended approach such as the following:

> I don't know what's going on with you, but a lot of kids have questions about sex. Sometimes they wonder about feelings for other people. They might have a special liking for someone. Sometimes the liking is for someone of the other sex, sometimes for someone of the same sex. Do you ever have these feelings?

This low-key approach begins with an honest statement of not being omniscient. The young homosexual often thinks her or his sexual feelings are transparent. Such a statement also is respectful of the young person's privacy and developing autonomy. It is important to leave the question of sexual identity open and to let the adolescent know that the process usually takes years. The adolescent may need permission to be confused.

Coming Out

Coming to terms with sexual identity involves self-acceptance and acceptance by others. The process for homosexuals is called coming out. It involves feelings, behaviors, and cognitions. Feelings often exist for 3 or more years before there is any homosexual behavior (Bell et al., 1981). Acceptance on the cognitive level may precede behavior. However, it frequently follows behavior by months and years. One gay male described a cognitive element of his coming out: "I remember standing in front of a mirror one day and saying to myself, 'Admit it. You're a homosexual.'" Of major significance is the detail of the mirror. He was looking at his own reflection and telling himself who he was sexually.

Heterosexuals have heterosexuality reflected back to them when they look out into the world. Everyday life is heterosexual. The homosexual looks out at the world, and heterosexuality, which she or he has typically tried for years, is dissonant, whereas homosexuality, when it is apparent at all, is reflected back in distorted ways. A positive gay identity is not part of what the adolescent sees as she or he looks out into the world. Looking into a mirror suggests the difficulty homosexuals have in seeing the self clearly (i.e., in undistorted ways). The person in the mirror can also be considered a substitute for significant others, whose role, in part, is to reflect back identity. In a more benevolent world, significant others would reflect a positive homosexual identity.

Coming out is both joyful and sad. The joy of coming out is complex: "I now know who I am sexually, I now am able to be open about my sexuality at least to myself and to some others, and I am now able to pursue love and acceptance." Typically done with others over time, coming out is like a birth. Supportive friends and sometimes mental health professionals serve as coaches and guides through the difficult process of examining three main areas: negative stereotypes, the positive reality, and the realistic difficulty of the homosexual lifestyle. After years of conflict, and often loneliness and lovelessness, coming out can be a tremendous relief.

The sadness relates to mourning heterosexuality and what heterosexuality implies. This could mean no heterosexual marriage, no children, limited social acceptance by the larger society, not having children and marriage in common with parents, siblings, and straight friends. This is sometimes called the loss of heterosexual privilege. Adolescents struggling with homosexuality often have serious difficulty imagining the future as a homosexual. The heterosexual script is clear. For the adolescent who is a future homosexual, the life script is either full of blanks or full of negatives. One young male, brought into counseling by his parents who found a gay magazine in his bedroom, asked his counselor, "Can I have an okay life like that?" The counselor's answer was, "You can, but it's difficult."

For young women, letting go of the heterosexual script involves a restructuring of the identity of future wife and mother, expectations directed toward little girls from the earliest years. Despite social change, females still receive strong messages that career is secondary to domestic duties, to husband and children. These roles are, of course, idealized and obviously tied to heterosexual behavior.

The young person who might be homosexual needs exposure to positive images and aspects of homosexuality. For young women, not getting married and having children allows them to pursue options other than those tied to the traditional heterosexual script. Many homosexuals maintain long-term and lifelong relationships (McWhirter & Mattison, 1984). A homosexual social network is available in most towns and cities. Slowly, the mental health professions and the general public are beginning to accept homosexuality as a lifestyle that is no less nor no more healthy than heterosexuality. Positive models of homosexuality are beginning to replace the illness model in psychotherapy (cf. Coleman, 1981/82). The *Diagnostic and Statistical Manual of Mental Disorders (DSM-III)* (American Psychiatric Association, 1980) does not list homosexuality as a mental disorder, except in cases where the person is in severe conflict about it. Gradually, the idea is spreading

that it is the social environment that is pathological, not the homosexual.

An Ideal Outcome

The ideal outcome of the development of a homosexual orientation is an understanding that sexual identity is one of an individual's many identities (cf. Cass, 1984). Indeed, many people are not exclusively homosexual or heterosexual. An individual has an identity in an occupation (mechanic, student, executive), as a family member (sibling, aunt, uncle, son, daughter, and sometimes mother and father), and in many other roles. When there is an acceptance of self as having multifaceted identities, the homosexual usually is comfortable socializing with heterosexuals and homosexuals. There is a degree of openness about sexual orientation among trusted friends (Cass, 1984; Coleman, 1981/82).

A mistrust of and denigration of heterosexuality typically precedes comfort with sexual orientation. During this time, the homosexual is working hard at building a self-concept and feels threatened by heterosexuality. For some, this is a period of separatism. Eventually, pride and tolerance develop in one's sexual orientation, and often acceptance of heterosexuality becomes possible. This degree of self-acceptance and acceptance of others is difficult to achieve and maintain in environments hostile to homosexuality. Adolescents may not be able to attain this degree of acceptance, but they need to know such openness is possible.

Like heterosexuality, there are health issues related to homosexuality. The alcoholism rate is thought to be higher than among heterosexuals (Coleman, 1981/82). Sexually transmitted diseases are as common among homosexuals as heterosexuals. Males, who typically have more sexual partners than females, are more prone to contracting these diseases. Getting treatment can be more problematic for homosexuals because of stigmatization of same-sex behavior. Acquired Immune Deficiency Syndrome (AIDS), a fatal disease which has been afflicting mainly male homosexuals, is reaching epidemic proportions. Some young homosexuals have developed a sense of fatalism about the disease. Because they frequently have multiple partners, they assume they already have been exposed to the AIDS virus. Thus, they take no precautions.

It is better to assume that it is not too late to be self-protective. Transmitted through the exchange of body fluids, AIDS is thought to be transmitted between homosexuals through sexual contact. "Safe sex" is being promoted within the gay community. This involves the use of condoms and the reduction in the number of sexual partners.

Like heterosexual counterparts, the homosexual adolescent has little reliable information about sexuality and sexually related health issues. In the few schools that offer sex education, for example, little or no attention is paid to homosexuality (Newton, 1982). Homosexual adolescents suffer severe consequences when information is withheld from them.

Bisexuality

Adolescents need information about bisexuality. Kinsey, Pomeroy, and Martin (1948) found that sexual orientation can be described as existing on a continuum, ranging from exclusive heterosexuality to exclusive homosexuality. In the midrange are individuals who experience various mixes of heterosexual and homosexual feelings, behavior, thoughts, and fantasy. Some reject the notion of bisexuality, believing it is a way of avoiding coming to terms with a homosexual orientation. Indeed, for some this might be true. Bisexuality can be a transitional stage between a heterosexual socialization and a homosexual orientation. Many adolescents experience this. There is, however, sufficient evidence to conclude that some individuals are neither exclusive heterosexuals or homosexuals. Yet, bisexual individuals frequently choose one person as the significant other. Under these conditions, some continue to relate sexually to members of both sexes, whereas others choose to be monogamous. Such information would be invaluable to adolescents who ask, "Can I have an okay life like *that*?" Being "like *that*" can actually mean a fulfilled and exciting life, when the individual is able or enabled to deal with sexual issues.

SEXUAL ABUSE OF ADOLESCENTS

There are parallels between how the contemporary heterosexual script is acted out and the conduct of individuals involved in the sexual abuse and exploitation of adolescents. In rape, incest, and molestation of adolescents, the typical configuration is the older male and the younger female. As age differences increase, power discrepancy increases. Physical strength, notions of who is in charge (the adult or the child), and knowledge, in the form of experience (and sometimes in the level of cognitive development) are some aspects of the power of the older person over the adolescent. The male typically uses deception, manipulation, and sometimes physical aggression, and is the initiator. The females feel guilty, believing they did something to cause their own victimization, a notion supported by the myths of rape. They often feel as if they are damaged goods. Some take what for them is the next logical step—promiscuity and possibly prostitution. These young women frequently know little about sexuality, consensual or nonconsensual.

When boys are raped, molested, or involved in incest, the perpetrator is almost always male. As with girls, there frequently is a large age disparity, which results in an imbalance of various forms of power. Boys, too, often feel stigmatized by the abuse, sometimes humiliated and outraged. They wonder what they did to attract the sexual attention of another male. They ask many questions that beg resolution. "Am I gay?" "Why couldn't I defend myself against another male?" "Am I a wimp?" Some become sex offenders. It is probable that when they sexually victimize younger children, they are attempting to recapture a sense of power, a sense violated by their own abuse. Rather than identifying with the victim, they take on the qualities of the persons who aggressed against them. They frequently, however, express a great deal of remorse for their own sexual offenses. Such a splitting of affect indicates a divided self.

How individuals involved in juvenile prostitution conduct themselves also has parallels with the heterosexual script. The adolescent girl almost always has a pimp, who virtually runs her life and is male. Thus, the theme of male control is salient. Customers, too, are older males whose money buys control of how the sexual act will be conducted, regardless of whether the prostitute is female or male. Neither pimp nor customer is concerned with the well-being of the young prostitute. She is a means to their own ends, an extension of the ethic of male sexual conquest, which can result in lack of caring for the partner. Ironically, however, the juvenile sees the customer as a commodity. Sex with him is work, not sex and not love.

The pimp uses deception, manipulation, and even physical violence. The first two are employed to ease her into "the life." His recruits are youngsters who have tenuous ties to their families, frequently are runaways and typically are rebelling against adult authority. Besides rather desperately wanting to be treated like adults, the recruits often have no means of support, either economic or emotional. Young adolescent runaways have the adult problems of providing themselves with shelter, food, and clothing, but are too young and untrained for self-support. The pimp begins his recruitment by playing into all of these needs. He spends a great deal of time courting her, buying her presents, telling her he loves her, supplying her with food and shelter. She feels great, having finally found the great lover and provider. When he senses that she might be dependent on him and isolated from other sources of support, he makes prostitution a condition of the continuance of their relationship. For girls who leave their families in order to get control over their lives, the degree of control by the pimp is an ironic outcome.

The young prostitute typically believes she is in love with the pimp. Self-deceptive or not, this belief can keep the young woman in prostitution for extended periods. The pimp, on the other hand, quite obviously does not behave as if he loves his "girl." She often lives with several other of his "girls," where they compete for the attention of the pimp. So strong is the attachment to the pimp for some that they consider sex with the pimp a way of showing love and sex with the customer as work. One juvenile, pregnant, said, "I don't know how I got pregnant. I didn't have sex for a month before." She did have sex with customers, but not with her pimp, whom she calls her boyfriend.

Age and Gender

A large proportion of adolescent females have been sexually abused. Russell (1983), for example, found that 38% of a sample of 930 San Francisco women stated they had experienced one or more instances of sexual abuse by age 18. About one third had been sexually abused by

age 14. Finkelhor (1979) found that 19% of the women in a survey of almost 800 New England college students described themselves as sexually victimized as children. Many studies have reported adolescence to be the peak years for the sexual abuse and assault of the female (DeJong, Hervada, & Emmett, 1983; Finkelhor, 1984; Hayman & Lanza, 1971; Herjanic & Wilbois, 1978; Jaffe, Dynneson, & ten Bensel, 1975; Massey, Garcia, & Emich, 1978; Russell, 1983).

Adolescent boys are much less likely to be victims of sexual abuse, molestation, and rape than girls. The percentages of males reported as victimized during childhood ranges from about 9% to 18% (DeJong et al., 1983; Finkelhor, 1984; Hayman & Lanza, 1971; Jaffe et al., 1975). The peak age for the reported victimization of boys is between the ages of 5 and 7 (DeJong et al., 1983; Finkelhor, 1984). At no age level does the number of victimized boys approach that of girls. Boys are increasingly less vulnerable as they approach latency and puberty. Though it is probable that abuse of boys is more frequently underreported than abuse of girls, it is fairly clear that girls are much more likely to be victimized than boys.

Perpetrators are almost always male (DeJong et al., 1983; Finkelhor, 1984; Hayman & Lanza, 1971; Jaffe et al., 1975; Landis, 1956; Tilelli, Turek, & Jaffe, 1980). Further, they typically are a generation or more older than their victims. Most offenders are known to the child, with strangers accounting for about 10% to 25% of all perpetrators (Adams-Tucker, 1981; Cantwell, 1981; Conte & Berliner, 1981; Dejong et al., 1983; Gilgun, 1984; Orr & Prietto, 1979; Peters, 1976; Tilelli et al., 1980). About 50% of perpetrators known to the child are family members. The remainder are friends of the family or acquaintances of the victim.

These studies suggest that sexual abuse of the adolescent is primarily a heterosexual event that can be considered a caricature of the behaviors supported by the heterosexual script. Sexual abuse of the adolescent is an extension far down the continuum of heterosexual behaviors.

Effects

Coming to terms with sexual abuse, regardless of who the perpetrator might have been and how long the abusive relationship continued, is, for most victims, a difficult task that requires coping skills throughout the life course. At each stage of development, affect and self-concept connected to memories must be contended with in different ways (Adams-Tucker, 1985). The severity of the effects of the abuse appear to be mediated through the family. Emslie and Rosenfeld (1983), for example, concluded that the psychiatric hospitalization of children and adolescents is not simply an effect of incest, but the consequence of severe familial disorganization, of which child sexual abuse is a part. In a similar vein, running away, suicide or attempts, promiscuity, seizures, multiple personality, and prostitution, all reported as effects of sexual abuse (Bowman, Blix, & Coons, 1985; Bracey, 1983; Browning & Boatman, 1977; Felice, Grant, & Reynolds, 1978; Gilgun, 1984; Goodwin, 1981; Goodwin, Simms, & Bergman, 1979; Gross, 1979; Silbert & Pines, 1981, 1983), appear to result from a mix of forms of abuse and neglect—sexual, physical, and emotional.

Besides these strongly overt effects of abuse, other adolescents have been found to believe the abuse was their fault. They expressed: (a) fears of abandonment, anxiety, anger, sadness, and ambivalence toward the perpetrator and the mother when the perpetrator was the father; (b) the belief that they had been damaged; and (c) school and peer problems (Boatman, Borkan, & Schetky, 1981; Browning & Boatman, 1977; Felice et al., 1978; Gilgun, 1984; Pino & Goodwin, 1982). One of the most difficult reactions occurred when there was a mixture of pleasure and these negative responses (Finkelhor, 1979). In these cases, the attribution of responsibility was especially complex.

The so-called "seductive" behavior of adolescents has frequently been cited as proof that children seek out sexual gratification with adults (see review by Gilgun, 1984). Some investigators have concluded that this is a form of testing and a means of exerting control over a situation perceived as unsafe (Krieger, Rosenfield, Gordon, & Bennett, 1980) or as counterphobic behavior (de Young, 1984). Adolescents who have been sexually abused also might have been socialized to believe that being sexual is a preferred way of attaining attention and what they hope is affection.

Systems outside the family affect how the victim and family cope with the effects of sexual abuse and its disclosure. Researchers have expressed concern that the management of child sexual abuse by the social welfare system and the courts is chaotic and harmful (Finkelhor, 1983; Furniss, 1983; Summit, 1983). Finkelhor (1983) pointed out that even experienced professionals have difficulty coping with the stories victims tell about their sexual abuse and exploitation. This difficulty has been termed "therapist's flight" (Herman & Hirschman, 1977). Gordon (1985) made a strong case for professionals to come to terms with their own sexuality before they try to help others with theirs. Although training is difficult to obtain, there has been some progress. For example, at the University of Minnesota–Twin Cities, the Program on Human Sexuality runs sexual attitude reassessment programs for professionals who are working in the area of child sexual abuse. They present numerous short courses relevant to sexual abuse. In addition, the Schools of Social Work and Public Health offer three academic courses covering different aspects of child sexual abuse.

Juvenile Prostitution

Most prostitutes enter "the life" while adolescent. For example, in a survey of 200 female street prostitutes, Silbert and Pines (1983) found that 80% became prostitutes while adolescent. Further, 70% were 20 or younger and 50% were 16 or younger at the time of the survey.

Sexual abuse frequently precedes prostitution for these juveniles. Of the Silbert and Pines (1983) sample, 60% stated that they were sexually abused by age 18, with sexual abuse defined as "sexual activity forced on a juvenile" (p. 408). Other studies have shown sexual abuse to be present in the background of about 50% (see review by Bracey, 1983). All are likely to have suffered multiple forms of abuse prior to their entry onto the street, as discussed above.

Once on the street, young prostitutes are further victimized by pimps, muggers, and customers. Because they turn their money over to the pimp, they are destitute or close to it (Silbert & Pines, 1983). The pimp may buy them clothes and give them a few dollars for candy and cigarettes, but he controls the money she makes. Any sign they might be striking out on their own could lead to violence. Some youngsters defend their pimps by saying, "He only hits me where it doesn't hurt too much, never on the face." While out "working," also called "turning tricks," they often carry large sums of money on them. They are easy prey for muggers. Customers, or "johns," sometimes beat them up, justifying their violence by telling themselves prostitutes deserve it.

Like other victims of sexual and physical abuse, the juvenile prostitute feels shame and guilt about his/her behavior. He/she often feels dirty and thinks prostitution is the only thing he/she is good for (Silbert & Pines, 1983). Groups whose purpose is to help prostitutes leave the life are called pride groups, to emphasize the importance of discovering and asserting self-worth. Juvenile prostitutes are hurting. They desperately are seeking something better. Vulnerable because of their age and history of abuse, they often have no one to turn to for help. Cycles of self-denigration, despair, depression, and loneliness set in. Alcohol and drug abuse are common.

Work with juvenile prostitutes on the street involves, first, gaining their trust, which is difficult, given their experience of exploitation by adults. Once there is some trust, the next goal is to connect them to sources of food, shelter, and medical care. Once these basic needs are met, education and treatment become possibilities. The goals of an established adolescent pride group are:

- Support in getting out or staying out of prostitution;
- Dealing with current issues, such as school, health, and employment;
- Learning about oneself in relation to one's family and others;
- Increased self-esteem. (Family and Children's Service, 1984, p. 45)

Work with families is an important aspect of the treatment of juvenile prostitution. Sometimes the family has little to offer the young person and remains unreachable with known intervention strategies. Other families, however, eventually are able to reintegrate the young person back into their lives. Adjustment to a "straight" life for the youngster often is difficult, pointing to a need for continued supportive services.

Though hardly a heterosexual event, the conduct of those involved in juvenile male prostitution is deeply connected to male sex-role socialization. There appear to be three basic types of juvenile male prostitutes: straights, drag queens, and gays (D. LeTourneau, personal communication, April 23, 1985). The straights are perhaps the most dangerous. Rageful, into chemical abuse, robbery, and assault, the prostitute who considers himself straight has obvious role conflicts. He appears to externalize shame and guilt, in contrast to the female, who tends toward self-denigration and self-blame.

Drag queens frequently are gay. Some, because of lack of support for their homosexuality, find a female role or its caricature preferable to grappling with a homosexual orientation (D. LeTourneau, personal communication, June 12, 1985). They frequently delight in fooling their customers. Part of the thrill of being in drag is the danger of johns discovering they have been tricked. At this point, the young prostitute is at risk for being beaten or killed.

The gay juvenile prostitute often seeks a sense of community on the street. Some live with their families, although others are "throw aways," on the street because they have no other place to go. Those with families perceive little or no acceptance of their sexual orientation and drift into gay areas on weekends. They are called "weekend warriors," turning a few tricks to earn extra money for a stereo or clothes. "Throw aways" typically have been scapegoated by their families to the point where they leave home or have been kicked out. Sometimes the homosexuality is the focus of the scapegoating. What is clear is that the juvenile prostitute frequently has been targeted by the family as the cause of its problems.

The male juvenile prostitute is as vulnerable as his female counterpart, except that he more often can defend himself physically. Food, shelter, clothing, and affection are among his deepest needs. Also like the female prostitute, he is desperately seeking a relationship (cf. Price, Scanlon, & Janus, 1984). Unlike the female, however, the male does not have a pimp who controls him. He is, however, easy prey for older male homosexuals who provide some basic necessities in exchange for sex. Under these conditions, the prostitute continues to hear the message that affection is connected to sex. Juveniles need a relationship with older men where affection and caring are not sexualized. Rarely does the victimization extend to the point where the boy is passed from man to man at sex "parties," but it does happen. Both male and female juvenile prostitutes are vulnerable to exploitation by individuals who produce pornography.

Outreach workers for the male juvenile prostitute offer services similar to those offered to females. Resources are even more scarce than those for girls, who have few services themselves. Gay organizations are beginning to do some outreach to juvenile prostitutes. Pride groups for males also are forming.

Sexual Abuse by Adolescents

Like prostitution, a history of sexual abuse appears to be one factor in the development of sexually abusive behaviors during adolescence. Most adolescent perpetrators report prior sexual abuse, although other forms of abuse and neglect other than sexual abuse alone appear to be antecedents. Understanding and treating the juvenile offender is in the nascent stage at this time (Thomas & Rogers, 1983).

Thus far, two types of adolescent abusers have been identified: those who are physically violent when they rape and those who are not overtly violent (see review by Mrazek, 1983). The physically violent offender may beat, stab, and even kill his victims, who may range in age from young children to old women. Victims may or may not have been known to him. The nonviolent abuser, who frequently is an older brother, cousin, babysitter, or neighbor, frequently uses bribes or threats. Peters (1976) reported, "After offering a three-year-old child sunflower seeds, two adolescent boys attempted intercourse" (p. 416). An 11-year-old interviewed by Gilgun (1984) said that after her 14-year-old babysitter licked her vulva, he told her not to tell her mother. If she told, he said, he would say she jumped on the bed.

Frequently, there is confusion over what constitutes sexual abuse. Occasionally boys in early adolescence who engaged in consensual sex with someone of the same age are considered sexual abusers. As Thomas and Rogers (1983) pointed out, such behavior may be socially unacceptable, but it doesn't constitute sexual abuse. For a juvenile to be considered a sexual abuser, the use of force, threats, and violence are present. When there is an age difference that suggests coercion, manipulation, and abuse of authority, the possibility that sexual contact was abusive is quite real.

Treatment of juvenile sex offenders appears to be carried out most frequently in groups. These provide peer support, a sense that one is not alone, and a means of testing new behaviors. In juvenile sexual abuser treatment programs, a great deal of time typically is spent on sex education and reeducation (Lutheran Social Services of Minnesota, 1984; Thomas & Rogers, 1983). Like any other adolescent, the sex abuser is not knowledgeable about sex. These programs also involve the family in treatment. Frequently, parents initially are seen separately from the juvenile perpetrators. However, the longer range treatment plan includes family therapy.

SUMMARY

Adolescents engage in a range of sexual behaviors. The incidence of intercourse and oral sex has increased over the past decade. Masturbation has become less stigmatized. Many adolescents abstain from intercourse until late adolescence and adulthood. Among those who are sexually active, some engage in sexual interaction of their own free will, in the spirit of tenderness, excitement, and experimentation. Many others, however, have sexual interaction imposed on them. Some males, more than females, engage in coercive sexual behaviors. Coercive sexuality appears to have social support in the form of the male ethic of conquest and control. Many young males believe they are supposed to be sexually aggressive.

Both homosexual adolescents and adolescents who have been sexually abused can be considered harmed by the imperiousness of the heterosexual script. So strong is the socialization to be heterosexual that homosexuality is stigmatized. Thus, the homosexual adolescent learns to hide her or his sexuality, waits to become heterosexual in many cases, and achieves a stable sexual orientation later than heterosexually oriented peers.

The conduct of those who are involved in the sexual abuse of adolescents has parallels with behaviors supported by the heterosexual script.

The abusers are typically male, and the victims are typically female. Sexually abused adolescents experience a variety of negative reactions to the abuse and typically cope with the effects of the act for the rest of their lives. Some sexual abuse victims have severe reactions to the abuse (e.g., running away, suicide or suicide attempts, psychomotor seizures, prostitution). It is likely that these reactions are mediated by other forms of physical and emotional abuse and neglect. Some males who have been sexually abused become sexual abusers during adolescence; most adolescent sex offenders report having been sexually abused.

Whether abstainers, postponers, sexually experienced of their own free will, or victims of various forms of coercion and sexual abuse, adolescents suffer from a lack of sexual information and access to contraception. Social policy and, therefore, American society are ambivalent about adolescent sexuality. Major segments of the population support the ethic of male sexual aggression, which, in interaction with other socialization practices, results in consequences few intend. Sexual abuse occurs to such a large proportion of the adolescent female population that it can be considered normative female experience. Indeed, recent research shows that social support for male sexual aggression is so pervasive as to suggest the existence of a norm.

The context in which the adolescent comes to terms with sexuality is problematic for many. Though under the best of circumstances, adolescence is a time of vulnerability, contemporary mores makes adolescence more trying and sometimes more traumatic than it need be.

Acknowledgements—The authors would like to thank Luann Gilbert, Bruce Fisher, and Donna Johnson of the Minneapolis Family and Children's Service; Ellen Solly, Don LeTourneau, and Jan Beebe of Minneapolis Youth Diversion; and the staff of Home Away, a shelter for runaway girls, located in Golden Valley, Minnesota, for their valuable discussions of many of the issues contained in this chapter. The authors assume all responsibility for content and for any errors subsequently discovered.

REFERENCES

Adams-Tucker, C. (1981). A socio-clinical overview of 28 sex-abused children. *Child Abuse and Neglect, 5*, 361–367.

Adams-Tucker, C. (1985). Defense mechanisms used by sexually abused children. *Children Today, 14*, 9–12, 34.

Alexander, S. J., & Jorgensen, S. R. (1983). Sex education for early adolescents: A student of parents and students. *Journal of Early Adolescence, 3*, 315–325.

American Psychiatric Association. (1980). *Diagnostic and statistical manual of mental disorders* (3rd ed.). Washington, DC: Author.

Bell, A. P., Weinberg, M. S., & Hammersmith, S. K. (1981). *Sexual preference: Its development in men and women*. Bloomington: Indiana University Press.

Berman, A. L. (1985). The teenager at risk for suicide. *Medical Aspects of Human Sexuality, 19*, 123–124, 129.

Boatman, B., Borkan, E. L., & Schetky, D. H. (1981). Treatment of child victims of incest. *American Journal of Family Therapy, 9*, 43–51.

Bowman, E. S., Blix, S., & Coons, P. M. (1985). Multiple personality in adolescence: Relationship to incestual experiences. *Journal of the American Academy of Child Psychiatry, 24*, 109–114.

Bracey, D. H. (1983). The juvenile prostitute: Victim and offender. *Victimology: An International Journal, 8*, 151–160.

Broderick, C., & Rowe, G. (1968). A scale of preadolescent heterosexual development. *Journal of Marriage and the Family, 30*, 97–101.

Browning, D. H., & Boatman, B. (1977). Incest: Children at risk. *American Journal of Psychiatry, 134*, 69–72.

Burt, M. R. (1980). Cultural myths and supports for rape. *Journal of Personality and Social Psychology, 38*, 217–230.

Burt, M. R. (1983). Justifying personal violence: A comparison of rapists and the general public. *Victimology: An International Journal, 8*, 131–150.

Cantwell, H. B. (1981). Sexual abuse of children in Denver, 1979: Reviewed with implications for pediatric intervention and possible prevention. *Child Abuse and Neglect, 5*, 75–85.

Carns, D. E. (1973). Talking about sex: Notes on first coitus and the double standard. *Journal of Marriage and the Family, 35*, 677–688.

Cass, V. C. (1984). Homosexual identity formation: Testing a theoretical model. *Journal of Homosexuality, 20*, 143–167.

Cassell, C. (1984). *Swept away: Why women fear their own sexuality*. New York: Simon & Schuster.

Coleman, E. (1981/82). Developmental stages of the coming out process. *Journal of Homosexuality, 7*, 31–43.

Conte, J. R., & Berliner, L. (1981). Sexual abuse of children; Implications for practice. *Social Casework, 62*, 601–606.

Cvetkovich, G., & Grote, B. (1980). Psychosocial development and the social problem of teenage pregnancy. In C. Chilman (Ed.), *Adolescent pregnancy and childbearing: Findings from research* (NIH Publication No. 81-2077, pp. 216–227). Washington, DC: U. S. Government Printing Office.

DeJong, A. R., Hervada, A. R., & Emmett, G. A. (1983). Epidemiologic variations in childhood sexual abuse. *Child Abuse and Neglect, 7*, 155–162.

de Young, M. (1984). Counterphobic behavior in multiply molested children. *Child Welfare, LXIII*, 333–339.

Eastman, W. F. (1972). First intercourse. *Sexual Behavior, 2*, 22–27.

Emslie, G. J., & Rosenfeld, A. (1983). Incest reported by children and adolescents hospitalized for severe psychiatric problems, *American Journal of Psychiatry, 140*, 708–711.

Family and Children's Service. (1984). *PRIDE: A manual for anyone interested in starting a pride group*. Minneapolis: Author.

Felice, M., Grant, J., & Reynolds, B. (1978). Follow-up observations of adolescent rape victims, *Clinical Pediatrics, 17*, 311–315.

Finkelhor, D. (1979). *Sexually victimized children*. New York: The Free Press.

Finkelhor, D. (1983). Removing the child—Prosecuting the offender in cases of sexual abuse: Evidence from the national reporting system for child abuse and neglect. *Child Abuse and Neglect, 7*, 195–205.

Finkelhor, D. (1984). *Child sexual abuse: New theory and research*. New York: The Free Press.

Forty percent of girls now 14 to be pregnant by age 29, experts say. (1985, May 1). *Syracuse Post-Standard*, p. 3.

Fox, G. L. (1981). The family's role in adolescent sexual behavior. In T. Ooms (Ed.), *Teenage pregnancy in a family context: Implications for policy* (pp. 73–130). Philadelphia: Temple University Press.

Freud, S. (1951). Letter to an American mother. *American Journal of Psychiatry, 107*, 787.

Furniss, T. (1983). Mutual influence and interlocking professional-family process in the treatment of child sexual abuse and incest. *Child Abuse and Neglect, 7*, 207–223.

Furstenberg, F. E., Jr. (1976). *Unplanned parenthood: The social consequences of teenage childbearing*. New York: The Free Press.

Gagnon, J. H., & Simon, W. (1973). *Sexual conduct*. New York: Aldine.

Gilgun, J. F. (1984). Sexual abuse of the young female in life course perspective. (Doctoral dissertation, Syracuse University, 1983). *Dissertations/Abstracts International, 45*, 3058.

Gilgun, J. F., & Gordon, S. (1983). Sex education and moral values. *Journal of Research and Development in Education, 16*, 27–33.

Gilgun, J. F., & Gordon, S. (1985). Sex education and the prevention of child sexual abuse. *Journal of Sex Education and Therapy, 11*, 46–52.

Goldsmith, S., Gabrielson, M., & Gabrielson, I. (1972). Teenagers, sex, and contraception. *Family Planning Perspectives, 4*, 32–38.

Goldsmith, S., Gabrielson, M., Gabrielson, I., Mathews, V., & Potts, L. (1972). Teenagers, sex, and contraception. *Family Planning Perspectives, 4*, 32–38.

Goodwin, J. (1981). Suicide attempts in sexual abuse victims and their mothers. *Child Abuse and Neglect, 5*, 217–221.

Goodwin, J., Simms, M., & Bergman, R. (1979). Hysterical seizures: A sequel to incest. *American Journal of Orthopsychiatry, 49*, 698–703.

Gordon, S. (1979). *You would if you loved me*. New York: Bantam Books.

Gordon, S. (1984). The case for a moral sex education. *Thresholds in Education, X*, 6–11.

Gordon, S. (1985). Before we educate anyone else about sexuality, let's come to terms with our own. *Journal of Sex Education and Therapy, 11*, 16–21.

Gordon, S., & Gordon, J. (1983). *Raising a child conservatively in a sexually permissive world*. New York: Simon & Schuster.

Gordon, S., Scales, P., & Everly, K. (1979). *The sexual adolescent*. North Scituate, MA: Dixbury Press.

Gross, M. (1979). Incestuous rape: A cause for hysterical seizures in four adolescent girls. *American Journal of Orthopsychiatry, 49*, 704–708.

Hayman, C. R., & Lanza, C. (1971). Sexual assaults on women and girls. *American Journal of Obstetrics and Gynecology, 109*, 480–486.

Herjanic, B., & Wilbois, R. P. (1978). Sexual abuse of children: Detection and management. *Journal of the American Medical Association, 239*, 331–333.

Herman, J., & Hirschman, L. (1977). Father–daughter incest. *Signs: Journal of Women in Culture and Society, 2*, 735–756.

Jaffe, A. C., Dynneson, L., & ten Bensel, R. W. (1975). Sexual abuse of children: An epidemiological study. *American Journal of Diseases of Children, 129*, 689–692.

James, J., Womack, W., & Strauss, F. (1978). Physician reporting of sexual abuse of children. *Journal of the American Medical Association, 240*, 1145–1146.

Jessor, R., Costa, F., Jessor, L., & Donovan, J. E. (1983). Time of first intercourse: A prospective study. *Journal of Personality and Social Psychology, 44*, 608–620.

Jessor, L., & Jessor, R. (1975). Transition from virginity to nonvirginity among youth: A social–psychological study over time. *Developmental Psychology, 11*, 473–484.

Jones, E. F., Forrest, J. D., Goldman, N., Henshaw, S. K., Lincoln, R., Rosoff, J. I., Westoff, C. F., & Wulf, D. (1985). Teenage pregnancy in developed countries: Determinants and policy implications. *Family Planning Perspectives, 17*, 53–63.

Kanin, E. J. (1957). Male sexual aggression in dating and courtship relations. *American Journal of Sociology, 63*, 197–204.

Kanin, E. J. (1969). Selected dyadic aspects of male sexual aggression. *Journal of Sex Research, 5*, 12–28.

Kanin, E. J., & Parcell, S. R. (1977). Sexual aggression: A second look at the offended female. *Archives of Sexual Behavior, 6*, 67–76.

Kinsey, A. C., Pomeroy, W. B., & Martin, C. E. (1948). *Sexual behavior in the human male*. Philadelphia: Saunders.

Kirby, D., Alter, J., & Scales, P. (1979). *An analysis of U. S. sex education programs and evaluation methods*. Springfield, VA: National Technical Information Service.

Kirkpatrick, C., & Kanin, E. (1957). Male sexual aggression on a university campus. *American Sociological Review, 22*, 52–58.

Korman, S. K., & Lelie, G. R. (1982). The relationship of feminist ideology and date expense-sharing in perceptions of sexual aggression in dating. *Journal of Sex Research, 18*, 114–129.

Krieger, M. J., Rosenfield, A. A., Gordon, A., & Bennett, M. (1980). Problems in the psychotherapy of children with histories of incest. *American Journal of Psychotherapy, 34,* 81–88.

Landis, J. (1956). Experiences of 500 children with adult sexual deviants. *Psychiatric Quarterly Supplement, 30,* 91–109.

Laws, J. L. (1979). *The second x: Sex role and social role.* New York: Elsevier.

Lindemann, C. (1974). *Birth control and unmarried young women.* New York: Springer.

Lutheran Social Services of Minnesota. (1984). *Personal/social awareness: A summary report (PSA).* Minneapolis: Author.

Malmuth, N., Haber, S., & Feshbach, S. (1980). Testing hypotheses regarding rape: Exposure to sexual violence, sex differences, and the "normality" of rape. *Journal of Research in Personality, 14,* 121–137.

Martin, A. D. (1982). Learning to hide: The socialization of the gay adolescent. *Adolescent Psychiatry, X,* 52–65.

Massey, J. B., Garcia, C. R., & Emich, J. P., Jr. (1971). Management of sexually assaulted females. *Obstetrics and Gynecology, 38,* 29–36.

McWhirter, D. P., & Mattison, A. M. (1984). *The male couple.* Englewood Cliffs, NJ: Prentice-Hall.

Miller, P. Y., & Simon, W. (1974). Adolescent sexual behavior: Context and change. *Social Problems, 22,* 58–76.

Mrazek, D. A. (1983). Long-term follow-up of an adolescent perpetrator of sexual abuse. *Child Abuse and Neglect, 7,* 239–240.

Nass, G. D., Libby, R. W., & Fisher, M. P. (1981). *Sexual choices.* Monterey, CA: Wadsworth Health Science Division.

Newcomer, S. F., & Udry, J. R. (1985). Oral sex in an adolescent population. *Archives of Sexual Behavior, 14,* 41–46.

Newton, D. E. (1982). A note on the treatment of homosexuality in sex education classes in the secondary school. *Journal of Homosexuality, 8,* 97–99.

Orr, D. P., & Prietto, S. V. (1979). Emergency management of sexually abused children. *American Journal of Diseases of Children, 133,* 628–632.

Ostrov, E., Offer, D., Howard, K. I., Kaufman, B., & Meyer, H. (1985). Adolescent sexual behavior. *Medical Aspects of Human Sexuality, 19,* 28, 30–31, 34–36.

Paluszny, M. J. (1984). Reasons for adolescent suicide attempts. *Medical Aspects of Human Sexuality, 18,* 13.

Peters, J. J. (1976). Children who are victims of sexual assault and the psychology of offenders. *American Journal of Psychotherapy, 30,* 398–421.

Phillips, S. (1984). Gonorrhea in adolescents. *Medical Aspects of Human Sexuality, 18,* 74, 77, 81, 84.

Pino, J. O., & Goodwin, J. (1982). What families say:

The dialogue of incest. In J. Goodwin (Ed.), *Sexual abuse: Incest victims and their families* (pp. 57–75). Boston: John Wright.

Price, V., Scanlon, B., & Janus, M. (1984). Social characteristics of adolescent male prostitutes. *Victimology: An International Journal, 9,* 211–221.

Roebuck, J., & McGee, M. G. (1977). Attitudes toward premarital sex and sexual behavior among black high-school girls. *Journal of Sex Research, 13,* 104–114.

Russell, D. (1983). Incidence and prevalence of intrafamilial and extrafamilial sexual abuse of female children. *Child Abuse and Neglect, 7,* 133–146.

Scales, P., & Beckstein, D. (1982). From macho to mutuality: Helping young men make effective decisions about sex, contraception, and pregnancy. In Stuart, I. R., & Wells, C. F. (Eds.), *Pregnancy in adolescence: Needs, problems, and management* (pp. 264–289). New York: Van Nostrand Reinhold.

Silbert, M. H., & Pines, A. M. (1981). Sexual child abuse as an antecedent to prostitution. *Child Abuse and Neglect, 5,* 407–411.

Silbert, M. H., & Pines, A. M. (1983). Early sexual experience as an influence in prostitution. *Social Work, 28,* 285–289.

Sorensen, R. (1973). *Adolescent sexuality in contemporary America.* New York: World.

Summit, R. C. (1983). The child sexual abuse accommodation syndrome. *Child Abuse and Neglect, 7,* 177–193.

Thomas, J. N., & Rogers, C. M. (1983). A treatment program for intrafamily juvenile sexual offenders. In J. G. Greer & I. R. Stuart (Eds.), *The sexual aggressor: Current perspectives on treatment* (pp. 127–143). New York: Van Nostrand Reinhold.

Thornburg, H. D. (1981). The amount of sexual information learning obtained during early adolescence. *Journal of Early Adolescence, 1,* 171–183.

Tilelli, J. A., Turek, D., & Jaffe, A. (1980). Sexual abuse of children: Clinical findings and implications for management. *New England Journal of Medicine, 302,* 319–323.

Vener, A. M., & Stewart, C. S. (1974). Adolescent sexual behavior in middle America revisited: 1970–1973. *Journal of Marriage and the Family, 8,* 335–343.

Zelnik, M., & Kantner, J. F. (1977). Sexual and contraceptive experiences of young unmarried women in the United States. *Family Planning Perspectives, 9,* 55–70.

Zelnik, M., & Kantner, J. F. (1980). Sexual activity, contraceptive use and pregnancy among metropolitan area teenagers: 1971–1979. *Family Planning Perspectives, 12,* 230–237.

CHAPTER 10

Family and Environment

Thomas S. Parish

We may not be responsible for what happens to us, but we are responsible for the way we react to what happens to us. This notion, which is consistent with William Glasser's (1984) Control Theory, suggests that we are the primary controllers of our own destinies. Notably, though, we are not the sole rudder that guides us through life. This chapter will therefore consider some of the possible ways children and adolescents can be influenced by such sources as their families, peers, teachers, and others, as well as present some possible strategies that might serve to ameliorate any negative effects these sources might have upon them.

SOME NOTEWORTHY THEORIES

As we seek to understand how the family and the environment affect youth, it might be particularly helpful to keep in mind the following three theories that attempt to explain how one's attitudes and actions are fostered through various human interactions.

Social Behaviorism

First, Social Behaviorism, as proposed by Arthur Staats (1968, 1975, 1981), suggests that classical conditioning affects both our attitudes and our instrumental (i.e., voluntary, behav-

iors). In other words, positiveness (in terms of antecedent stimuli or events) begets positiveness (in terms of consequent attitudes and behaviors), whereas negativeness (in terms of antecedent stimuli or events) begets negativeness (in terms of consequent attitudes and behaviors).

Hierarchy of Needs

Second, Abraham Maslow's (1954) Hierarchy of Needs, portrayed in Figure 10.1, proposes that our lower-level needs (e.g., physiological needs, safety and security needs) take priority over our higher-level needs (e.g., love and belonging, self-esteem needs). More specifically, one's lower-level needs must be fulfilled before one can direct his or her attention toward satisfying higher-level needs. Numerous writers (e.g., Parish, 1980; Parish, Dostal, & Parish, 1981; Simpson, 1976) have further suggested that social, emotional, and/or moral development is fostered best when one's needs are being met and may fail to develop adequately when one's needs are not met.

Attribution

Third, application of Fritz Heider's (1958) Attribution Theory utilizes the question, "Who's responsible?" For example, if a youth has en-

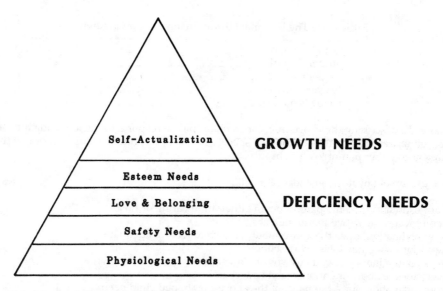

Figure 10.1. Maslow's Hierarchy of Needs. (From "The Role of Environmental Factors in the Development of Moral Judgment" by T. Parish and J. Parish, in *Contemporary Issues in Moral Development* (p. 247) edited by T. Parish and K. Kiewra, 1984, Lexington, MA: Ginn. Copyright 1984 by T. Parish and K. Kiewra. Reprinted by permission.)

countered favorable circumstances in life, those who are perceived as being responsible for creating these favorable circumstances are likely to be looked upon favorably, but if unfavorable circumstances have prevailed, then the youth will likely develop an unfavorable attitude toward those she or he holds responsible for these circumstances.

These theories cumulatively suggest that where stress and unhappiness occur, one's social, emotional, and moral development will likely be negatively affected, and blame for these circumstances will be placed on those perceived to be responsible. On the other hand, an unstressful, happy environment will generally facilitate one's development, and those perceived to be responsible for these positive circumstances will be held in high regard.

Although the message conveyed by these theories seems to be quite clear, a popular song sung by Jack Jones some years ago may say it best. The title of this song is "What the World Needs Now is Love, Sweet Love." In other words, what children and adolescents (and the rest of us) need are fully functioning support systems that can help to fulfill their needs and, in so doing, allow them to grow and develop and possibly reach their potential.

PRIMARY SUPPORT SYSTEMS

Some of the more relevant support systems that generally operate to fulfill the needs of children and adolescents are identified in the Personal History Inventory for Children (Parish & Wigle, 1985a) in Table 10.1. Basically, teachers, parents, or other individuals interested in fostering the development of children and adolescents can use this inventory to assess various support systems and ascertain whether or not they are functioning properly. If they are, then the support systems are operable, and there should be little need to be concerned. If they are not operating properly, however, then attention needs to be directed toward correcting this situation so that the child or adolescent in question can develop without experiencing undue hardships or unnecessary stress and unhappiness.

The Family as a Possible Support System

The family in general, and the parents in particular, have often been deemed to be the most important support system available to the child (Cox & Cox, 1979). Several studies (e.g., Marotz-Baden, Adams, Bueche, Munro, & Munro, 1979; Parish et al., 1981; Raschke & Ras-

Table 10.1. The Personal History Inventory for Children

Student's name _____
Student's birthdate _____
Student's grade _____
Teacher's name _____
School's name _____

Instructions: In describing the above-mentioned child, please respond to the following questions by indicating either yes or no in the appropriate spaces. You need respond to items 9–14 only if the child has experienced either parent loss or absence.

If you are unsure of any item, just leave it blank.   Yes   No

1. In your estimation, do the parents act in either an uncaring or hostile fashion toward the above-mentioned child?
2. In your estimation, does the above-mentioned child receive adequate supervision when he/she is *not* in school?
3. In your estimation, have you and your fellow teachers generally shown concern for the above-mentioned child's welfare?
4. In your estimation, have the peers of the above-mentioned child been supportive of him/her?
5. In your estimation, has the family of the above-mentioned child experienced a great deal of geographic mobility?
6. In your estimation, has the family of the above-mentioned child experienced a great deal of financial hardship?
7. Have the parents of the above-mentioned child separated or gotten a divorce?
8. Have one or both parents of the above-mentioned child died?
9. If the above-mentioned child experienced parental loss or absence, was there a stigma associated with this event?
10. If the above-mentioned child experienced parental loss or absence, did the remaining parent experience (at least for a time) a shakened sense of confidence?
11. If the above-mentioned child experienced parent loss or absence, did the remaining parent experience (at least for a time) a marked increase in their role responsibilities?
12. If the above-mentioned child experienced parental loss or absence, did the remaining parent experience (at least for a time) a task overload?
13. If the above-mentioned child experienced parental loss or absence did the remaining parent experience (at least for a time) an emotional overload?
14. If the above-mentioned child experienced parental loss or absence, did the remaining parent remarry (Note: This effect appears to be dependent upon the gender of the child, i.e., females seem to benefit more than males)? Therefore, kindly indicate the sex of the child below:

           male _____   female _____

           Today's date _____

Note. From "Discerning Functionality of Children's Support Systems through the Use of the Personal History Inventory for Children" by T. Parish and S. Wigle, 1985a, *Psychological Reports, 57,* p. 33. Copyright 1985 by *Psychological Reports.* Reprinted by permission of the publisher.

chke, 1979; Wallerstein & Kelly, 1980) have demonstrated support for the notion that familial happiness is directly associated with psychologically healthy parents and children who are involved with one another in appropriate ways.

According to Shinn (1978), it is the quality and quantity of attention given by parents to their children that is the critical factor. Seven studies of high and/or low achievement, reviewed by Shinn, showed that paternal interest and paternal encouragement were positively related to school achievement. Furthermore, children who perceived themselves as having been rejected by their fathers were more likely to be underachievers. Cox and Cox (1979) have stated that warm, loving parents tend to create a secure, unstressful environment in which the child can be more readily socialized and thus learn more appropriate behaviors. However, if the parents are hostile or uncaring, or if the family is generally perceived to be unhappy, the longer these circumstances persist the more chronically troubled the youth may become (Parish & Wigle, 1985b). To offset the effect of hostile or uncaring parents, other operable support systems—external to the family—may help.

Teachers and Peers as Possible Support Systems

In and out of school, youth need adequate supervision and the realization that those in authority actually are concerned for their welfare. In the wake of familial stress, needed attention, sympathy, and tolerance provided by teachers was reported by Kelly and Wallerstein (1977) to be sustaining to a number of the emotionally undernourished children they had been studying.

Teachers and ancillary personnel need *not* confine their efforts, however, to just meeting the needs of youth who have experienced familial turmoil. Rather, there are many who might be troubled for various other reasons and might also need an increase in love and attention as well. For instance, children who are handicapped are far too often negatively perceived by those around them. There are a number of studies (e.g., Blood & Blood, 1983; Gottlieb, 1975; Parish, Ohlsen, & Parish, 1978) and reviews of studies (e.g., Abramson, 1980; Madden & Slavin, 1983) that have reported that nonhandicapped children have tended to harbor negative attitudes toward their handicapped peers. What makes matters even worse, however, is that these handicapped children's teachers have also harbored negative attitudes toward them, as measured by self-report measures (e.g., Parish, Dyck, & Kappes, 1979) and by physiological measures (e.g., Gargiulo & Yonker, 1983).

Not only do teachers often harbor negative attitudes toward their handicapped students, but they frequently model these attitudes for all

their students to learn. Unfortunately, teachers who possess such attitudes are generally unaware of their biases. That such biases exist, however, was demonstrated by Parish and Copeland (1978). In their study they asked teachers to describe how handicapped children would evaluate themselves and found that these teachers actually projected their own negative attitudes onto their handicapped students. In actuality, however, nothing could be further from the truth. As is shown in Figure 10.2, although teachers believed that handicapped children with various disabilities may have evaluated themselves increasingly more negatively depending upon their handicap, the handicapped children themselves made no such differentiation. Rather, like their nonhandicapped counterparts, they, too, evaluated themselves—as individuals—very positively.

What these findings probably indicate is that although teachers and nonhandicapped peers (and in some instances even handicapped peers) may be failing as support systems for handicapped children, handicapped children have not given up on themselves (Parish, Baker, Arheart, & Adamchak, 1980). Perhaps other support systems or sources of love (e.g, parents, siblings) may be available to buoy them up and help them to perceive themselves positively. This is conjectural, but is in line with the idea proposed by Pines (1979) regarding "super kids." Specifically, super kids managed to thrive in impoverished environments, primarily because someone cared and attended to their needs. Without that care and attention, however, development on the part of the super kids would have been most unlikely.

Derogation + Stress = Troubled Individuals

Besides disparaging the handicapped, for whatever reason(s), many of us derogate other groups of people, too. For instance, those who have sought psychological counseling are generally found to be negatively evaluated by those who have and by those who have not sought psychological counseling. Interesting, however, is the recent finding by Parish and Grosdidier (1986) that those who have sought counseling put themselves down, too. Thus, in contrast to the handicapped children/adolescents who have maintained positive self-concepts despite

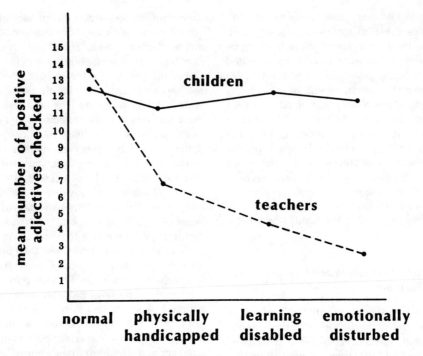

Figure 10.2. Teachers' perceptions of students' self-evaluation versus students' actual self-evaluation. (From "Teachers' and Students' Attitudes in Mainstreamed Classrooms" by T. Parish and T. Copeland, 1978, *Psychological Reports*, *43*, p. 54 (Fig. 1). Copyright 1978 by *Psychological Reports*. Reprinted by permission of the publisher.)

the derogations of their teachers, nonhandicapped, and even handicapped, peers, those who have sought counseling have actually been found to demean themselves. Why is this so? Before we attempt to answer this question, let us first examine more carefully the study by Parish and Grosdidier (1986).

Besides determining self-concepts and ratings of those who have sought counseling, this study requested that the respondents complete the Holmes and Rahe (1967) Social Readjustment Rating Scale, which assesses the number of traumatic events encountered within the past 12 months and places a stress value on each of the traumatic events. The results of this survey indicated that those who had sought counseling had a mean stress score on this scale of 304, whereas those who had *not* sought counseling had a mean stress score of 188. The highly significant difference between these two scores suggests that where a number of support systems have failed and/or when an overwhelming number of traumatic events have been encountered, the outcome may be increased feelings of insecurity and stress that, in turn, make it more

likely that individuals will give up on themselves and adopt lower self-concepts.

THE ANTECEDENTS OF DIVORCE

What everyone needs are friends. Friends are those individuals who help us to like ourselves. If everyone endeavored to be everyone else's friend, many of life's stresses would be alleviated. Of course, it may be virtually impossible to achieve the goal of becoming everyone's friend. In fact, often it is difficult to even be a friend to one's spouse. There are many reasons why this is so. Perhaps an individual may have a lack of commitment to his or her spouse or an egotistical concern for self-interests, or perhaps he or she may have been overwhelmed by some of the traumatic events listed on the Social Readjustment Rating Scale. Whatever the case, these individuals fail to attend to their spouses' needs and often actually create more stress for themselves, their spouses, and of course, their children. The situation may deteriorate even further, for marital discord is increasingly likely to end in parental divorce.

Although the divorce rate has currently stabilized to a degree, Horn (1975) reported that divorce rates had increased 700% in the past 50 years. According to Wallerstein and Kelly (1980), it is estimated that 40% of the current marriages of young adults will end in divorce and that 40% to 50% of the children born in the 1970s will spend about 6 years living in a single-parent family before they reach the age of 18. In real numbers, we are looking at 13,000,000 children/adolescents currently, and that figure is continuing to grow at an alarming rate (Parish & Nunn, 1983).

The Process of Parental Divorce

To some (e.g., Holmes & Rahe, 1967), parental divorce is considered to be an event. To others, however, it is a process that begins and ends well before and after the date on a divorce decree. More specifically, accompanying parental divorce, family members may also experience one or more of the following support system malfunctions.

Perceived Parental Neglect

In the wake of marital disruption, parents' own needs are often left unmet, and it is therefore often difficult for them to attend to their children's needs as they had done previously. Hence, the children, and others too, may construe that lack of attention as parental neglect.

Increased Financial Hardship

Children of divorce often experience what some would term a marked "contrast effect," as they might have been accustomed to living better prior to the divorce as opposed to after the divorce (Wallerstein & Kelly, 1980). Such disappointment would be less likely to occur in other familial configurations. For example, among families who have never known a father, the children might never have known financially better times. Additionally, for children in families where the fathers have died, the fathers' life insurance policies would help to cushion the financial blow of the loss.

Increased Geographic Mobility

Perhaps due partly to the financial hardships encountered, the family in transition often tries to adjust by moving either to less expensive housing or to where the remaining parent's family members reside (Brown, 1980). For what-ever the reason, such a move usually could mean that the children's schools, peers, and teachers could change, placing the children into unfamiliar environments. Following parent divorce and father loss, such a change could put even more stress on family members, particularly the children.

Stigma of Event

With parent loss through death, often extended family members, friends, and others pitch in to help get the family through the hard times. However, if the marital relationship ends leaving bitter feelings, one side of the family or the other may sever ties, and adult friends of the family—not wanting to choose sides or get involved in any dispute—may stand back, allowing the single-parent family to try and cope with its problems more or less single-handedly. Thus, children of divorce are more likely to be victimized, even though their parents' divorce may not have been of their choosing.

Notably, along with the loss of adult support can go peer support as well. According to Ellison (1979), peers can actually take the place of parents as sources of attachment, but if such peer support is unavailable it could add greatly to the woes of these children of divorce.

Increased Overload

The father in the typical intact family may be little more than a "fifth wheel" or a "spare tire," in that he may not be as fully involved as the mother in fulfilling the needs of the various family members. Nevertheless, he may fulfill certain role responsibilities needed to maintain the family. With his absence, however, these responsibilities may fall upon the mother. At least this is what one survey (Loeb, 1984) recently reported (see Figure 10.3). Combined with other duties and problems, this situation could create a myriad of stresses, such as task and emotional overloads for the remaining parent (typically the mother). This can be particularly devastating for a parent who has already experienced a shakened sense of confidence.

Two points need to be made very clear before we go any further. First, although children from divorced families (as opposed to children from other familial constellations) are less likely to have their needs met because of the various stressors noted above, these children's parents, friends of the family, extended family members, and teachers can do a great deal to help them

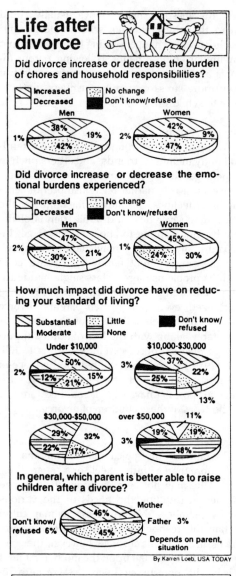

By Karren Loeb, USA TODAY

About the poll

The poll is based on interviews with 1,230 adults selected at random from across the USA by the Gordon S. Black Corp., of Rochester, N.Y., for USA TODAY. The survey has a margin of error of plus or minus 3 percent.

Figure 10.3. Changes in household responsibilities for fathers and mothers in the wake of divorce. (From "Life after Divorce" by K. Loeb, 1984, *USA Today*, Dec. 31, p. 6A. Copyright 1984 by *USA Today*. Reprinted by permission.)

overcome these problems (or at least greatly reduce their effects by continuing to operate as functional support systems). Second, the divorce process may last for weeks, months, even years. Typically, however, researchers like Hetherington, Cox, and Cox (1976) suggest that after the first year or two the most traumatic part of the divorce process is over and that things are generally improving. This may be because old support systems, such as friends, parents, and grandparents, are back in operation or because new sources of support have been found to replace the previously inoperable support systems.

One study was recently reported, however, that suggests that it might actually take from 2 to 6 years before the children of divorce can largely overcome the acute stressors often associated with this experience. This study, by Parish and Wigle (1985b), is particularly noteworthy, because it went beyond simply comparing children from existing intact with children from divorced families over a period of time. In addition, it included a group of children who were from intact families when the initial survey of self-concepts and ratings of parents took place, but who were in a divorced family situation when the follow-up survey was taken 3 years later. The findings from this group (the Intact-Divorced Group) demonstrated that their self-concepts and evaluations of parents on the follow-up survey were substantially more negative than: (a) those of children who were from intact families; (b) those of children who were from families that had been previously divided by divorce for an average of 6 years; and even (c) those of children who were from intact families but who matched with the Intact-Divorced group on pretest scores, suggesting that both groups were possibly from families that had been troubled, unhappy, and/or in conflict.

As one peruses Figures 10.4, 10.5, and 10.6, it seems—at least in terms of self-concepts and ratings of parents—that, in the wake of parental divorce and the various problems associated with it, children are negatively affected for the first few years. However, this negative effect is largely moderated for the group of children who had experienced parental divorce—an average of 6 years earlier (i.e., the Divorced-Divorced Group). Curiously, though, no such dramatic changes occurred for those who had remained in intact families, even though their

Evaluation of Self

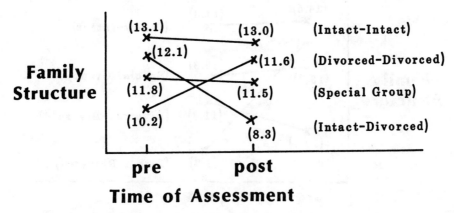

Figure 10.4. A longitudinal view of evaluations of self by children and adolescents from various family structures. (From "A Longitudinal Study of the Impact of Parental Divorce on Adolescents' Evaluations of Self and Parents" by T. Parish and S. Wigle, 1985b, *Adolescence, 20*, p. 241. Copyright 1985 by Libra Publishers. Reprinted by permission.)

original self-concepts and ratings of parents were matched with those of the Intact-Divorced Group. This finding suggests that they (i.e., the Special Group) were possibly unhappy with their familial situations, but that the many other available support systems were functioning sufficiently to sustain the Special Group's higher self-concepts and parent ratings even 3 years later.

These findings suggest that the plight of an

Evaluation of Mother

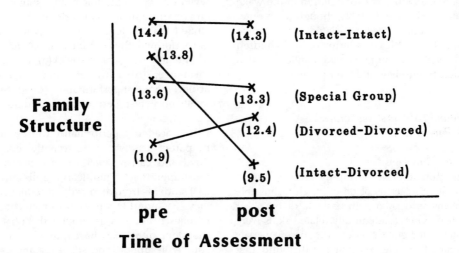

Figure 10.5. A longitudinal view of evaluations of mothers by children and adolescents from various family structures. (From "A Longitudinal Study of the Impact of Parental Divorce on Adolescents' Evaluations of Self and Parents" by T. Parish and S. Wigle, 1985b, *Adolescence, 20*, p. 241. Copyright 1985 by Libra Publishers. Reprinted by permission.)

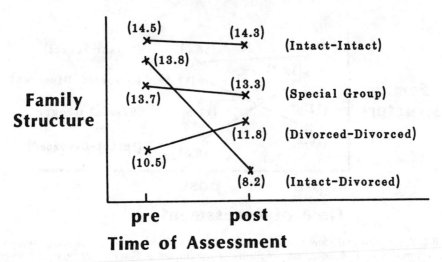

Figure 10.6. A longitudinal view of evaluations of fathers by children and adolescents from various family structures. (From "A Longitudinal Study of the Impact of Parental Divorce on Adolescents' Evaluations of Self and Parents" by T. Parish and S. Wigle, 1985b, *Adolescence, 20*, p. 241. Copyright 1985 by Libra Publishers. Reprinted by permission.)

unhappy family may not be optimal and may even have some chronic or long-term problems associated with it, but at least it avoids the acute crises of having a number of support systems potentially fail at one time, which is thought to be more likely to occur for children in the wake of parental divorce. Notably, though, with time, even the acute crises associated with divorce seem to fade, at least in terms of how children and adolescents from divorced families come to evaluate themselves and their parents.

Various Problems Associated with Parent Loss

Academic Problems

Unfortunately, we have only seen the tip of the iceberg in terms of describing the possible problems associated with parental divorce. For instance, when academically related skills were examined for children from one-parent versus two-parent families, Brown (1980) found that children from one-parent families were more likely than children from two-parent families to experience: (a) discipline problems, (b) suspensions, (c) student (geographic) mobility, (d) tru-

ancy, (e) Title I programs, (f) expulsions, and (g) dropping out. In fact, Brown (1980) was astonished to find that of the 18,000 students studied, the only ones expelled were from single-parent families. Furthermore, Shinn (1978) reviewed 28 methodologically sound studies and reported that the majority of them demonstrated that students from two-parent families outperformed those from one-parent families in the following categories: (a) reading performance, (b) arithmetic performance, (c) achievement test performance, (d) aptitude and intelligence test performance, and (e) grade-point averages.

That academic performance can be impeded by parent loss was more recently reported by Boyd and Parish (1985). This conclusion was most applicable to non-learning-disabled (non-LD) students from divorced, nonremarried families. For non-LD students from reconstituted families it appears as though the presence of the stepparent may have provided a needed source of support and some regained stability resulting in GPAs *not* significantly different from their counterparts from intact families. However, this group of students from reconstituted families, like the non-LD students from divorced nonremarried families, demonstrated deficient mathematics and reading achievement scores (as compared to their counterparts from intact families), suggesting that parental remarriage may not readily remediate all of the academic lag experienced by this group of students.

The LD students' reading and mathematics achievement scores were *not* found to vary significantly as a function of family structure. This finding by Boyd and Parish (1985) seems to suggest that the special attention these students get from their teachers may greatly facilitate them in their efforts to cope academically, regardless of what is going on at home. Interestingly, though, the LD students from divorced nonremarried families did demonstrate significantly lower grade point averages than the LD students from either intact or divorced remarried families. Boyd and Parish speculated that this finding might be reflective of teachers' perceptions of pupils from divorced families, or a kind of teacher expectation effect. "In other words, teachers may be more likely than tests to unknowingly establish limiting expectations for students from divorced families as opposed to other familial configurations" (Boyd & Parish, 1985).

Social – Emotional Problems

Beyond the classroom, other types of social-emotional difficulties have been associated with the circumstances surrounding parent loss—particularly through divorce—and being raised in a single-parent family. For instance, numerous researchers (e.g., Kalter, 1977; Sorosky, 1977; Wallerstein & Kelly, 1976) have reported that children who have experienced these circumstances, as compared to those who have not, were more likely to engage in one or more of the following behaviors:

- Acting out
- Aggressiveness
- Anger
- Antisocial behavior
- Apprehensiveness
- Behavior disorders
- Conflict with the law
- Delinquency
- Depression
- Drug abuse
- Eating disorders

- Enuresis
- Fear of abandonment
- Guilt
- Hostile relationships with parents
- Loneliness
- Loyalty conflicts
- Neurotic symptomatology
- Obsessive–compulsive behaviors
- Psychophysiological disorders
- Psychotic breakdowns
- Sense of betrayal by parents
- Shakened sense of confidence
- Schizophrenic reaction
- Sexually promiscuous behavior

As was reported earlier, it has been generally supposed that problems such as those listed above seem to be ameliorated over time and/or with the reestablishment of various support systems. That this is not always the case, however, has been attested to by a number of studies (e.g., see Wallerstein & Kelly, 1980) that have examined—in a cross-sectional fashion—adults who either had or had not experienced parent loss through divorce during their childhood. Specifically, those who had experienced parent loss through divorce and a single-parent family background (at least for a time) were more likely than their counterparts from intact families to manifest the following behaviors as adults:

- Anxiousness
- Anger
- Crying spells
- Constant worry
- Despair
- Divorce
- Fear
- Feelings of worthlessness
- Guilt
- Insecurity
- Insomnia
- Loneliness
- Marital problems
- Poor physical health
- Self-concept and self-esteem problems
- Suicide attempts

Many Factors to be Considered

These data, however, may be making a very complex problem simplistic. More specifically, the studies that have been reviewed have generally compared groups of individuals from intact families with those from divorced single-parents families. In order to gain a more complete picture of the many facets of parent loss and its associated circumstances, we will now expand our examination by also including a group of children who had experienced the loss of a parent through death. As can be seen in Table 10.2, the findings of the Nunn and Parish (1982b) study indicated that the fifth through tenth grade respondents fared best overall in terms of their personal, social, and familial adjustment if they were from intact families rather than from families where the fathers had died. Furthermore, Table 10.2 also shows that students from families where the fathers had died were, in turn, significantly better off in many respects than children from divorced families. Such findings, across so many different indices, certainly seem to suggest that the children of divorce—especially the males—are more likely to be at risk and therefore probably in greater need of new or rejuvenated support systems.

Another study by Nunn and Parish (1982a) looked beyond the single-parent family in order to consider the possible effects on children and adolescents of the remarriage of the remaining parent and the introduction of a stepparent into the family. As is shown in Table 10.3, it appears that the findings varied largely as a function of the gender of the youth involved. Specifically, it appears as though sons benefited most where the remaining parent, i.e., the mother, chose not to remarry, whereas the daughters seemed to be better off when the mothers did remarry. The explanations offered for these findings are purely conjectural, but it seems that with a mother's nonremarriage, the daughters may lose their mother's companionship because the mother may have to fulfill so many other roles (e.g., mother, homemaker, breadwinner, etc.). Effectively, then, daughters lose close contact with two parents and not just one. In contrast sons may generally be more distant from both parents all along and, with the departure of the father, would likely receive greater responsibility and autonomy, which may be appealing to them. With remarriage, however, the stepfathers may assume roles that free the mothers and make them more available for their daughters, facilitating the fulfillment of the daughters' needs. In contrast, the entry of the stepfather generally means that the sons' desire for increased control and responsibility is likely to be usurped and their needs are therefore largely left unmet.

Parish and Dostal (1980) found that when the mothers of divorced families do not remarry, they are evaluated better than when they do remarry. The reverse is true for the absent fathers. These findings may indicate that the absent fathers are held responsible for the problems associated with the single-parent family. When the mother remarries, however, the father is taken off the proverbial "hook" (children might be heard to say "Dad really wasn't such a

Table 10.2. Various Measures of the Personal, Social, and Familial Adjustment of Youth as a Function of Family Structure (Intact/Death/Divorce) and Gender of Respondent

		Self Concepts	Eval. of Mothers	Eval. of Fathers	Eval. of Family	Perc. of Home	Perc. of School	Perc. of Peers	State Anxiety	Trait Anxiety
Intact	Males	A	A	A	A	A	B	B	A	A
	Females	A	A	A	A	A	A	A	A	A
Death	Males	B	A	A	B	A	B	C	B	A
	Females	B	A	A	B	A	B	A	B	B
Divorce	Males	C	B	B	B	B	C	D	C	B
	Females	B	B	B	B	A	B	C	C	B

Key: A > B > C > D
Note. Data in this summary table from "Personal and Familial Adjustment as a Function of Family Type," by G. Nunn and T. Parish, 1982b, *Phi Delta Kappan, 64,* p. 141. Reprinted by permission of authors.

Table 10.3. Various Measures of the Personal, Social,
and Familial Adjustment of Youth as a Function of
Family Structure (Intact/Divorced Nonremarried/Divorce Remarried)
and Gender of Respondent

		Self Concepts	Eval. of Mothers	Eval. of Fathers	Eval. of Family	Perc. of Home	Perc. of School	Perc. of Peers	State Anxiety	Trait Anxiety
Intact	**Males**	A	A	A	A	A	B	B	B	B
	Females	A	A	A	A	A	A	A	A	A
Divorce NR	**Males**	B	B	B	B	B	C	B	B	A
	Females	B	B	C	C	C	C	B	C	C
Divorce R	**Males**	C	B	B	C	C	C	C	D	C
	Females	A	B	B	B	C	A	B	C	C

Key: A > B > C > D
Note. From *Children's Personal Adjustment in Intact, Single-Parent and Reconstituted Families* by G. Nunn and T. Parish, 1982a. Paper presented at the meeting of the American Educational Research Association, New York. Reprinted by permission of authors.

bad guy, was he?"), but the mother is then held responsible because the new stepfather was actually her idea and her choice.

A parallel study by Parish and Kappes (1980) indicated that fathers and mothers were actually evaluated most positively where the fathers had died, fairly positively where the children were from intact families, and very negatively when the children were raised in a divorced family.

Parish and Kappes (1980) speculated that when the fathers had died they were generally held in high regard by their wives, who most likely placed as their chief concern the raising of the children. Through such positiveness on the mothers' part and the willingness to attend to the needs of others, all (even the stepfathers) benefited from the "halo effect" that was created.

In contrast, where fathers were absent due to divorce, neither parent was likely to hold the other in very high esteem. This may have created a stigma effect rather than a halo effect. As a result, both parents (and the stepfathers, if any) were derogated by the children. Subsequent research by Ambert and Saucier (1983) and Rosendal (1983) have generally supported these conclusions, particularly with regard to evaluations of fathers across familial configurations.

These findings, reported by Parish and

Kappes (1980), were found by Parish and Kaiser (1981) to be most applicable to the first-born children rather than to the younger children. This finding suggests that the first-born child may serve as a buffer for his or her younger siblings in terms of seeing to it that their needs are met. Unfortunately, what the first-born child obviously needed was "an older brother or sister" to attend to his or her needs in the face of adversity. These findings are quite in line with previous results reported by Hetherington (1972).

That children of divorce perhaps suffer more and have their needs attended to less than children from other familial configurations can also be inferred from the findings of Parish, Hattrup, and Rosenblatt (1980). In this study respondents completed the Rokeach (1967) Values Survey. The results indicated that students from families divided by divorce placed significantly higher priority on the values "mature love," "self-respect," and "polite" than students from intact families. In turn, students from families where the father had died placed significantly *less* priority on these three values than students from either intact or divorced families.

These findings probably do not suggest that students from families where the fathers have died actually have their needs met better, but they might perceive that to be the case. As was noted earlier, family members who are subjected to a divorce might assume rather negative stances toward one another, whereas family members who have endured the death of the father tend to adopt very positive views toward one another. Parish, Hattrup, and Rosenblatt (1980) have concluded:

> As a result of the negativeness of divorce and the positiveness that surrounds the father's death, and in keeping with Rokeach's (1973) notion that individuals hold very important those values which are absent or scarce in their lives, it is easy to understand why those individuals from families broken by divorce placed greatest priority on the values "self-respect," "mature love," and "polite," while the individuals from families where their fathers had died placed least priority on these particular values. (p. 378).

As was noted much earlier regarding Maslow's (1954) Hierarchy of Needs, social, emotional, and moral judgment development could be impaired if one's needs are not adequately met. That this may be a valid conclusion is attested to by the findings of Oshman and Manosevitz (1976) as well as by Parish (1980). In the former study, it was found that students from intact families obtained significantly higher scores than students from father-absent families on five of the six subscales of the Ego Identity Scale (Rasmussen, 1964), which is believed to index the first six Eriksonian crisis stages. Students from stepfather families, in turn, outperformed students from father-absent families on two of the six subscales of the Ego Identity Scale. Interestingly, these differences held regardless of the cause of father absence and demonstrate how social development may be impaired by families that have experienced the trauma of father loss. However, this trauma may be offset somewhat by the presence of a stepfather to take his place.

In the study by Parish (1980), the D score on the Defining Issues Test (Rest, Davison, & Robbins, 1978) was used as an index of moral judgment and was correlated with the number of years the respondents had experienced father absence. A significant inverse relationship ($r = -.50$) was found between these two variables. When cause of loss was considered, however, the correlations varied markedly. Specifically, those who had undergone parental loss through divorce achieved a significant inverse relationship between years of parent loss and

level of moral development ($r = -.64$). In contrast, for those from families where their fathers had died, a nonsignificant correlation ($r = -.19$) was found between these two variables. What these findings seem to suggest is that the longer one is raised in a one-parent or fatherless home, the more likely it is that he or she will experience lower levels of moral judgment as a young adult. This conclusion only seems to apply, however, to those who have experienced father loss due to divorce. This finding, along with most of the previously reported findings noted in this chapter, seems to be saying that where support systems have failed, one's needs are not likely to be met. When this occurs, development—moral or otherwise—is likely to be impeded, and one's potential is less likely to be realized. What can we do about it?

WAYS TO PREVENT OR AMELIORATE THE PROBLEMS ASSOCIATED WITH PARENT LOSS

What we can do is stress to each family member that the family must be (or become) a happy unit, regardless of whether the family is an intact one or not. That this is so is attested to by the findings of Nunn and Parish (1983), who examined children and adolescents from intact and divorced family configurations that were deemed by the respondents as either happy or unhappy families. These individuals were surveyed across a broad range of social–emotional adjustment measures, including self-concept, perception of school adjustment, home adjustment, peer relations, state and trait anxiety, as well as evaluations of parents. In nearly every instance, the scores achieved were more positive *if* the respondents were from happy families versus unhappy families, regardless of their particular configuration (i.e., intact or divorced). Similarly, Hess and Camara (1979) and Wallerstein and Kelly (1980) found that, even in the wake of parental divorce, the children fared much better socially and emotionally if both parents pulled together to meet their children's needs and were supportive of them, as opposed to children whose parents were not inclined to be supportive of them.

Stepparents, too, need to understand that they should be supportive of their stepchildren. In fact, they should be assuming this role long before any wedding bells are rung if they wish to be well received by *all* the members in the family. Specifically, taking the children along on dates or just spending some time with the children without the parent is desirable if the future stepparent wants to avoid the role of intruder and competitor for the parent's time and to assume instead the role of friend. For more helpful hints and a handy reference source on how to cope in remarried families, the reader should refer to "*The Remarried Family: An Annotated Bibliography*," by Beatrice Berquist (1984).

As noted earlier, a friend is someone who helps you to like yourself. This being understood, it is imperative that every family member (e.g., mother, father, stepparents, sibling) works to become an effective friend. Importantly, though, we must not stop there, because we also need to provide support for those outside the family as well.

Outside the family, the school is considered the main arena of social interaction. Notably, teachers often have the power not only to become a benefactor and friend to their students, but also to orchestrate their students' interactions between one another. Teachers need to understand this position of importance and how they can most effectively bring about positive interactions between all concerned. Of course, the suggestions that follow will be directed toward helping children and adolescents from families in transition, but many of these notions are far more generalizable than that.

Teachers should probably begin by becoming more aware of their own feelings, values, and attitudes regarding divorce, seeking greater understanding by reading appropriate books, and then discussing their views with those perceived to command a degree of competence in the area. As teachers do this, they should learn to be more accepting of different lifestyles and customs that their students represent and come to understand that families in transition may be in a crisis situation and, as a result, parents may not be able to "parent" as well as they would like. Of course, children undergoing familial crises may not convey their situation to their teachers. Therefore, teachers will need to be alert for changes in their students' personalities or behaviors and also must maintain an "open door" policy as an indication of their concern for and interest in their students' well-being. Also, any learning materials should include a broad range of settings and life-styles and any

school activities that could be embarrassing for students (e.g., mother/daughter lunches, father/son outings) should be more flexible in format to avoid inadvertent discrimination against single-parent children. Teachers should also routinely offer instruction to help provide students with better coping skills. Covering the basics in food preparation, in first-aid procedures, and in dealing with emergency situations (in the comfort of the classroom) should be quite beneficial to all students, but particularly those who must take care of themselves and others.

Teachers should not try to do it alone, however, because the continuance of crisis conditions in the home may negate the teachers' efforts to handle their students' problems and to enhance their students' social–emotional and academic development. At least this was the conclusion reached by Parish and Philp (1982), who pretested and posttested fifth through eighth grade student in terms of their self-concepts and in the interim had the children's teachers work diligently at fulfilling their needs. After a month of having the teachers intensively try to fulfill students' needs and enhance their self-concepts, the posttest findings revealed that their endeavors had worked only for those children from intact families and not for those children from either divorced single-parent families or divorced remarried families. This finding suggests that if we are going to enhance children's self-concepts, then we must work to fulfill the needs of the children at home as well as in the classroom, and that limiting our efforts to the classroom simply will not do.

Basically, it seems that we need to be mindful of *all* the possible support systems of children and adolescents (such as those indicated earlier on the Personal History Inventory for Children) and not just those that operate within the walls of the school. To accomplish this end, teachers will need to work more closely with parents in order to achieve a united team effort, whereas parents are going to need to be introduced, in turn, to the use of local professionals and possibly involvement in such self-help networks as Parents Without Partners.

SUMMARY

What we have considered are some ways that teachers and parents can work together, or separately, to help fulfill children's and adolescents' needs and subsequently affect their level of development. Of course, we have only scratched the surface since there are other sources and programs available to further aid our efforts (e.g., Boy/Girl Scouts, Big Brother/ Big Sister Programs, rap sessions with peers, etc.). Once we have done what we can do for someone, however, it behooves that child or adolescent to do what he or she can for himself or herself. Only if we *all* work together, helping each other, and helping ourselves, can we really overcome adversity.

REFERENCES

Abramson, M. (1980). Implications of mainstreaming: A challenge for special education. In L. Mann & D. Sabatino (Eds.), *The fourth review of special education* (pp. 315–340). New York: Grune & Stratton.

Ambert, A., & Saucier, J. (1983). Adolescents' perceptions of their parents and parents' marital status. *Journal of Social Psychology, 120*, 101–110.

Berquist, B. (1984). The remarried family: An annotated bibliography. *Family Process, 23*, 107–119.

Blood, I., & Blood, G. (1983). School-age children's reactions to deaf and hearing impaired children. *Perceptions and Motor Skills, 57*, 373–374.

Boyd, D., & Parish, T. (1985). An examination of academic achievement in light of familial configuration. *Education, 106*, 228–230.

Brown, B. (1980). A study of the school needs of children from one-parent families. *Phi Delta Kappan, 61*, 537–540.

Cox, M., & Cox, R. (1979). Socialization of young children in the divorced family. *Journal of Research and Development in Education, 13*, 58–67.

Ellison, E. (1979). *Classroom behavior and psychosocial adjustment of single- and two-parent children.* Paper presented at the meeting of the Society for Research in Child Development, San Francisco.

Gargiulo, R., & Yonker, R. (1983). Assessing teachers' attitudes toward the handicapped: A methodological investigation. *Psychology in the Schools, 20*, 229–233.

Glasser, W. (1984). *Control theory.* New York: Harper & Row.

Gottlieb, J. (1975). Attitudes toward retarded children: Effects of labeling and behavioral aggressiveness. *Journal of Educational Psychology, 67*, 581–585.

Heider, F. (1958). *The psychology of interpersonal relations.* New York: Wiley.

Hess, R., & Camara, K. (1979). *Post-divorce family relationships as mediating factors in the consequences of divorce for children.* Paper presented at the meeting of the Society for Research in Child Development, San Francisco.

Hetherington, E. (1972). Effects of father absence on personality development in females. *Developmental Psychology, 7*, 313–326.

Hetherington, E., Cox, M., & Cox, R. (1976). Di-

vorced fathers. *Family Coordinator, 25*, 417–428.

Holmes, T., & Rahe, R. (1967). The Social Readjustment Rating Scale. *Journal of Psychosomatic Research, 11*, 213–218.

Horn, P. (1975, June). A look at the disintegrating world of children. *Psychology Today*, pp. 32–36.

Kalter, N. (1977). Children of divorce in an outpatient psychiatric population. *American Journal of Orthopsychiatry, 47*, 40–51.

Kelly, J., & Wallerstein, J. (1977). Brief interventions with children in divorcing families. *American Journal of Orthopsychiatry, 47*, 23–39.

Loeb, K. (1984, December 31). Life after divorce. *USA Today*, p. 6A.

Madden, N., & Slavin, R. (1983). Mainstreaming students with mild handicaps: Academic and social outcomes. *Review of Educational Research, 53*, 519–569.

Marotz-Baden, R., Adams, G., Bueche, N., Munro, B., & Munro, G. (1979). Family form or family process? Reconsidering the Deficit Family Model approach. *Family Coordinator, 28*, 5–14.

Maslow, A. (1954). *Motivation & personality.* New York: Harper.

Nunn, G., & Parish, T. (1982a). *Children's personal adjustment in intact, single-parent and reconstituted families.* Paper presented at the meeting of the American Educational Research Association, New York.

Nunn, G., & Parish, T. (1982b). Personal and familial adjustment as a function of family type. *Phi Delta Kappan, 64*, 141.

Nunn, G., & Parish, T. (1983). *The impact of family type and family process upon selected psychological adjustment factors in children and adolescents.* Paper presented at the meeting of the Midwestern Psychological Association, Chicago.

Oshman, H., & Manosevitz, M. (1976). Father absence: Effects of stepfathers upon psychological development of males. *Developmental Psychology, 12*, 479–480.

Parish, T. (1980). The relationship between factors associated with father loss and individuals' level of moral judgment. *Adolescence, 15*, 535–541.

Parish, T., Baker, S., Arheart, K., & Adamchak, P. (1980). Normal and exceptional children's attitudes toward themselves and one another. *Journal of Psychology, 104*, 249–253.

Parish, T., & Copeland, T. (1978). Teachers' and students' attitudes in mainstreamed classrooms. *Psychological Reports, 43*, 54.

Parish, T., & Dostal, J. (1980). Evaluations of self and parent figures by children from intact, divorced and reconstituted families. *Journal of Youth and Adolescence, 9*, 347–351.

Parish, T., Dostal, J., & Parish, J. (1981). Evaluations of self and parents as a function of intactness of family and family happiness. *Adolescence, 16*, 203–210.

Parish, T., Dyck, N., & Kappes, B. (1979). Stereotypes concerning normal and handicapped children. *Journal of Psychology, 102*, 63–70.

Parish, T., & Grosdidier, L. (1986). *Do self-concepts and GPAs vary due to stressful experiences and/or having sought psychological counseling?* Paper presented at the meeting of the meeting of the Southwestern

Psychological Association, Ft. Worth.

Parish, T., Hattrup, D., & Rosenblatt, R. (1980). Father loss and individual's subsequent values prioritization. *Education, 100,* 377–381.

Parish, T., & Kaiser, H. (1981). *College students' evaluations of themselves and their parents as a function of their birth order and familial configuration.* Paper presented at the meeting of the Rocky Mountain Psychological Association, Denver.

Parish, T., & Kappes, B. (1980). Impact of father loss on the family. *Social Behavior and Personality: An International Journal, 8,* 107–112.

Parish, T., & Nunn, G. (1983). Locus of control as a function of family type and age at onset of father absence. *Journal of Psychology, 113,* 187–190.

Parish, T., Ohlsen, R., & Parish, J. (1978). A look at mainstreaming in light of children's attitudes toward the handicapped. *Perceptual and Motor Skills, 46,* 1019–1021.

Parish, T., & Parish, J. (1984). The role of environmental factors in the development of moral judgment. In T. Parish & K. Kiewra (Eds.), *Contemporary issues in moral development* (pp. 244–248). Lexington, MA: Ginn.

Parish, T., & Philp, M. (1982). The self-concepts of children from intact and divorced families: Can they be affected in school settings? *Education, 103,* 60–63.

Parish, T., & Wigle, S. (1985a). Discerning functionality of children's support systems through the use of the Personal History Inventory for Children. *Psychological Reports, 57,* 32–34.

Parish, T., & Wigle, S. (1985b). A longitudinal study of the impact of parental divorce on adolescents' evaluations of self and parents. *Adolescence, 20,* 239–244.

Pines, M. (1979, January). Superkids. *Psychology Today,* pp. 53–54, 57–58, 61, 63.

Raschke, H., & Raschke, K. (1979). Family conflict and children's self-concepts: A comparison of intact and single-parent families. *Journal of Marriage and the Family, 5,* 367–374.

Rasmussen, J. (1964). Relationship of ego identity to psychological effectiveness. *Psychological Reports, 15,* 815–825.

Rest, J., Davison, M., & Robbins, S. (1978). Age trends in judging moral issues: A review of cross-sectional, longitudinal, and sequential studies of the Defining Issues Test. *Child Development, 49,* 263–279.

Rokeach, M. (1967). *Values Survey.* Sunnyvale, CA: Halgren Tests.

Rokeach, M. (1973). *The nature of human values.* New York: Free Press.

Rosendal, F. G. (1983). Halos vs. stigmas: Long-term effects of parents' death or divorce on college students' concepts of the family. *Adolescence, 18,* 947–955.

Shinn, M. (1978). Father absence and children's cognitive development. *Psychological Bulletin, 85,* 295–324.

Simpson, E. (1976). A holistic approach to moral development and moral behavior. In T. Lickona (Ed.), *Moral development and moral behavior* (pp. 159–170). New York: Holt, Rinehart & Winston.

Sorosky, A. (1977). The psychological effects of divorce on adolescents. *Adolescence, 12,* 123–126.

Staats, A. (1968). Social behaviorism and human motivation: Principles of the Attitude-Reinforcer-Discriminative System. In A. Greenwald, T. Brock, & T. Ostrom (Eds.), *Psychological foundations of attitudes* (pp. 33–66). New York: Academic.

Staats, A. (1975). *Social behaviorism.* Homewood, IL: Dorsey.

Staats, A. (1981). Paradigmatic behaviorism, unified theory, unified theory construction methods, and the zeitgeist of separatism. *American Psychologist, 36,* 239–256.

Wallerstein, J., & Kelly, J. (1976). The effects of parental divorce: Experiences of the child in later latency. *American Journal of Orthopsychiatry, 46,* 256–270.

Wallerstein, J., & Kelly, J. (1980, January). California's children of divorce. *Psychology Today,* pp. 67–68, 70–72, 74.

CHAPTER 11

Morals and Values in Adolescence

Rosanne Perlmutter and Ester R. Shapiro

The study of morals and values in adolescence is a very complicated area of theory and research in the already complex field of adolescent study. The establishment of moral codes and values by which the next generation will live is a process about which both the adolescents and the adults in the society have deep, heartfelt, and often conflicting opinions. In addition, the social upheaval of the 1960s and 1970s, with the catalytic civil rights and antiwar movements, emphasized through both the mass media and through painful battles in many homes the process of moral and value change through radical rejection of the previous generation's values. Nevertheless, the study of morals and values in adolescence requires that the developmental process be viewed in the light of, but independent from, the social forces of a particular historical period. The social climate needs to be seen as an influence on adolescent morals and values that varies for each cohort through historical time (Elder, 1975; Riley, 1975).

The study of morals and values is in itself two distinct areas of theory and research that have evolved in two separate fields within psychology and sociology. The study of morals has an intellectual history in the ancient Greek conceptions of objective versus relativistic ethics and in religious and philosophical debates concerning the nature of good and evil (Kurtines & Gewirtz, 1984). In the current psychological literature, the study of morality involves primarily the evaluation of moral development as an orderly progression of stages through the life span. The study of values has investigated shifting value orientations over the life span as well as over historical time and across cultures (Feather, 1975; Rokeach, 1973). Very little writing addresses the direct relationship between moral development and values (Nisan, 1984; Turiel, 1974).

Further, a limited literature in moral or values development addresses adolescence in particular. The following literature review and discussion will emphasize the conceptual trends in the literature and extract the material that is relevant for the understanding of morals and values in the adolescent developmental experience. Because the authors are an educational

184

developmental psychologist and a clinical developmental psychologist, we share an interest in the practical applications of these literatures for the development of adolescents in their families and in the classroom. The chapter, then, will include description of two educational approaches designed to enhance moral and value development. In addition, to capture the experiential flavor of adolescent thinking about morals and values, we will include data from discussions with adolescents in a high school psychology class that illustrate concepts from the theoretical literature review.

The development of morals and values in adolescence is embedded in the matrix of change that characterizes this turbulent period of the life cycle. Adolescence is a time of extraordinarily intense and visibly dramatic change in all areas of a growing child's life. The body is no longer that of a child, yet is not altogether that of an adult. Intellectual and cognitive advances are made in the capacity for abstract abilities and in the capacity to see the self with less egocentrism and more perspective. Yet, the capacity for abstract thought about the self or about close relationships continues to be, at best, erratic, as any parent or teacher of adolescents can attest. The social world is explored with more independence from parents, and yet dependence on the parents is still necessary. Emotions are intense and fluctuate erratically, partially in correspondence to physical and hormonal changes, partially in response to a growing awareness of self among others in the world outside the family.

At the center of all these changes, the adolescent is attempting to determine a unique sense of self within relationships to family, community of peers, and the larger society. The exploration of unique morals and values has often been seen as the hallmark of adolescent development. During the period of social upheaval of the 1960s and early 1970s, both the youth culture and the mass media placed emphasis on the rejection of parental values and socially accepted traditions. The current generation of adolescents in the '80s is viewed, at least anecdotally and in the mass media, as more practical, more interested in financial security, and perhaps less moral than their predecessors. Boyer (1983) uses Gallup poll data to support his argument that adolescents in the 1980s are as politically concerned as their counterparts in the 1960s and 1970s, but lack the opportunity for service. At Newton North High School, Newton, Massachusetts, where one author is a teacher and the other is a student's parent, the student speakers at the 1985 graduation frequently and proudly described their activist groups lobbying for nuclear disarmament and for response to the Ethiopian famine.

In fact, every generation of adolescents on their way to becoming adults has to establish some balance and integration of the continuity granted by established values of the previous generation with the creative discontinuity of finding their own way in the world. The adolescent's declaration of personal morals and values seems to be an important avenue for identity development in general. The criticism of established morals and values promotes the growth and development of both individuals and societies.

In this chapter, we will emphasize the developmental place of morals and values within the context of an interpersonal theory of identity or ego development in adolescence. To our minds, this orientation gives greater conceptual coherence to the present-day controversies in the study of morals and values. Is morality a unique developmental line, or is it an aspect of superordinate developmental processes? Are there significant gender differences in moral development and moral orientation? What is the relationship of moral concepts to moral action in everyday life? The chapter will review and discuss the following topics: (a) history and development in the study of morals and values; (b) two educational approaches to morals and values; (c) morals, values, and ego development; and (d) interactional morality and the interpersonal self. An interpersonal theory of identity development (Shapiro, 1985, in press), which views development as organized by transactions in relationships, will be offered as an organizing framework for understanding the development of morals and values in adolescence.

HISTORY AND DEVELOPMENT IN THE STUDY OF MORALS AND VALUES

Moral Development in Adolescence

Discussion of the nature of good and evil has been present in Western thought since the writings of Plato and Socrates, who began the written debate contrasting an absolute or objective morality with a subjective or contextual morality (Kohlberg, 1981; Kurtines & Gewirtz, 1984). The intellectual legacy inherent in this debate is still with us, in the present argument between Kohlberg's essentially classical theory of objective morality and Gilligan's (1982) contextual theory of the morality of care and response in relationships. In this century, the study of moral development has taken place in two distinct literatures: (a) the psychoanalytic literature beginning with Freud's work on superego development and (b) the cognitive developmental literature, beginning with Piaget's work on the moral judgment of the child, and continuing in the current cognitive theories of Kohlberg and others.

Psychoanalytic Theory of Morality: Superego and Identity

Psychoanalytic theory was from its beginning deeply concerned with the nature of morality. Freud's theory of unconscious psychic conflict was in Victorian times a radical acknowledgement and exploration of the internal battle waged between three psychic structures: the primitive instincts (or id), the conscious, competent self (or ego), and the mandates of conscience (or superego) (Freud, 1905, 1913, 1921, 1925). In addition to his structural theory of psychic conflict, Freud proposed a stage theory of libidinal and superego development that is relevant to the study of moral development.

According to Freud, the infant is initially dominated by instincts, which differ at different developmental phases, and is frustrated or opposed in the expression of impulses by the parents as representatives of social authority. In the oedipal phase of development, the child wishes for an unattainable sexual relationship with the parent of the opposite sex. In the process of renouncing that forbidden wish, the child internalizes the parental and social conscience in the form of the superego. According to Freud, the child's castration anxiety is the motivation for renouncing the love of the parent and for repressing the sexual drives during the latency stage, until their emergence toward appropriate objects in adolescence.

Freud's theory of oedipal development generated a theory of gender development that continues to be controversial. Because the cas-

tration fear was such a central aspect of the resolution of the oedipal complex, Freud reasoned that the girl, who was already without a penis, had less motivating anxiety and would consequently only gradually abandon the love of the father, in some , situations not at all. Freud (1925) was therefore forced to conclude that the superego in women is deficient compared to that of men:

I cannot evade the notion (though I hesitated to give it expression) that for women the level of what is ethically normal is different from what it is in men. Their super-ego is never so inexorable, so impersonal, so independent of its emotional origins as we require it to be in men. Character traits which critics of every epoch have brought up against women—that they show less sense of justice than men, that they are less ready to submit to the great exigencies of life, that they are more often influenced in their judgments by feelings of affection or hostility—all these would be amply accounted for by the modification in the formation of their super-ego which we have inferred above. We must not allow ourselves to be deflected from such conclusions by the denials of the feminists, who are anxious to force us to regard the two sexes as completely equal in position and worth; but we shall, of course, willingly agree that the majority of men are also far behind the masculine ideal and that all human individuals, as a result of their bisexual disposition and of cross-inheritance, combine in themselves both masculine and feminine characteristics, so that pure masculinity and femininity remain theoretical constructions of uncertain content. (pp. 257–259)

Many psychoanalytic and feminist writers have argued against Freud's theory of feminine and masculine development as devaluing of women. It is interesting to note, though, that when a value judgment is removed from Freud's contrast between the inexorable or "objective rules" - oriented male morality, and the subjective or emotionally grounded feminine morality, the description mirrors Gilligan's (1982) current discussion of feminine morality "in a different voice" from that of men.

In contrast to Freud's id and superego emphasis in the development of morality, more recent psychoanalytic writings in moral development have emphasized ego, ego-ideal, and identity development (Blos, 1962, 1968, 1972; Erikson, 1968; Nass, 1966; Schaefer, 1968). Psychoanalytic developmental theorists have proposed that the superego is one aspect of the developing adaptive functions of the ego, with critical developmental transitions in early infancy, during the oedipal phase, and again in adolescence (Blos, 1968, 1972; Esman, 1972; Jacobson, 1964; Nass, 1966; Schaefer, 1960). Blos (1968, 1972) describes early adolescence as a second individuation period, which parallels the toddler's cognitive discovery of self/other difference. Blos argues that the work of individuation in adolescence requires the establishment of a sense of one's self and one's beliefs that is separate from the parents, but that includes identifications with the parents.

Erikson's (1964, 1968) writing on identity development has offered another perspective on moral development in adolescence. Erikson proposes three stages of moral development: specific moral learning in childhood, adolescent exploration of ideologies in the search for identity, and ethical consolidation in adulthood. Erikson argues that the adolescent is preoccupied with the establishment of identity and that failure at this developmental task leads to identity confusion, with serious negative consequences for future development. Erikson sees adolescence as a crucial bridge between the rules-oriented morality of childhood and the deeper ethical sense that orients adult life. According to Erikson, fidelity is the ego-integrating value that is for the first time available in adolescence and that provides inner coherence in the self-organizing search for ideology. "Fidelity is the ability to sustain loyalties freely pledged in spite of the inevitable contradictions of value systems. It is the cornerstone of identity and receives inspiration from confirming ideologies and affirming companions" (Erikson, 1964, p. 125).

Erikson, like Freud, argues that masculine and feminine development of identity differs, although Erikson's discussion of gender differences focuses on adolescent identity development rather than on the oedipal phase. According to Erikson, identity development requires the establishment of an autonomous, independent self. As Erikson describes it, women form identity within their intimate relationships, especially their relationships to their husbands. From his point of view, then, women postpone identity development until the next phase, the establishment of intimacy in early adulthood. Erikson believes that women differ from men in having an "inner space" that is filled by relationships to husband and children.

> But how does the identity formation of women differ by dint of the fact that their somatic design harbors an "inner space" destined to bear the offspring of chosen men and, with it, a biological, psychological, and ethical commitment to take care of human infancy? Is not the disposition for this commitment (whether it be combined with a career, and even whether or not it be realized in actual motherhood) the core problem of female fidelity? (Erikson, 1974, p.337)

Feminist writers have argued against Erikson's formulation, because of its quality of biological imperative that anatomy is destiny. More recently, writers on the psychology of women suggest that the problem with Erikson's theory lies not in the postulation of sex differences in moral and identity development, but rather in value judgments which describe feminine development as an inferior or defective version of masculine development (Gilligan, 1982; Miller, 1976).

Psychoanalytic theory of moral development in adolescence has not generated a research literature. However, it offers valuable theory that continues to be part of the crucial conceptual foundation for current theoretical development and research.

Cognitive Theory of Moral Development in Adolescence

The cognitive theories of moral development view the development of morality, like the development of all cognitive abilities, as progressing through a series of fixed, discrete stages. Piaget (1932) and Kohlberg (1958, 1981, 1984) are the major proponents of this cognitive stage approach. Piaget proposed three stages in the moral development of children: a first premoral stage where there is no sense of obligation to rules, a second stage of moral realism or heteronomous morality, and a third stage of autonomous morality of reciprocity. In the stage of moral realism or heteronomous morality, children view rules as sacred obligations and see an action as right or wrong depending on its literal conformity to established rules. They judge right and wrong primarily in terms of the consequences of an act, either because of the magnitude of the act or the severity of the punishment that follows it. Children at this stage also believe in "immanent justice," that is, justice is seen as intrinsic to subjective reality, so that violation of the rules will automatically incur punishment by some higher authority.

The stage of autonomous morality or reciprocity is established in late childhood or early adolescence. In this more mature stage, the child or adolescent views rules as arrived at through social agreement and thus subject to multiple perspectives and modification in response to complex situations. Right or wrong is arrived at by considering intentions as well as consequences, and it becomes especially important to consider the perspective of the other. Piaget suggests that the child's egocentrism and concrete logical operations limit the capacity to make mature moral judgments. In adolescence, with diminished egocentrism, increased capacity to see multiple perspectives, and with the new capacity to use formal operations, the child can make moral judgments that are abstract and reciprocal.

Kohlberg's approach to moral reasoning has its roots in the theories of Dewey and Piaget, both of whom postulate preconventional, conventional, and autonomous levels of moral development (Kohlberg, 1958, 1975). Kohlberg's six-stage theory of moral development has generated extensive research interest. Kohlberg suggests that moral reasoning is an overall mental structure and that moral development is a thought process involving universal developmental characteristics. Whereas the content of moral reasoning may be culture-bound, according to Kohlberg, the process of moral reasoning requires reasoning, judgment, and decision-making that progresses through six stages (See Table 11.1).

In his initial research, Kohlberg (1958) proposed only these six stages. In a 1969 follow-up study of his original sample, though, he found that a number of his subjects appeared to have regressed to an earlier stage of development (Kohlberg & Kramer, 1969). These findings made it necessary to postulate transitional stages between the six stages, which are now part of the updated coding manual (Colby & Kohlberg, 1984). Relevant to adolescent moral development, Kohlberg described a quasi-stage that usually occurs during adolescence, a transitional stage between Stages 4 and 5. In this transitional stage, moral reasoning on the surface appears to be like Stage 2 reasoning. It is relativistic, egocentric, and related to selfish desires. Under closer scrutiny, however, Stage 4 1/2 individuals do not make simplistic judgments of right as being whatever the person wishes. The person recognizes socially accepted morality, which is the "official" morality, but rejects this point of view as the reason for determining right from wrong.

Kohlberg's work has stimulated an enormous body of research literature applying his stages of moral development to a variety of age groups and cultures (for reviews, see Hoffman, 1977; Kurtines & Greif, 1974; Snarey, 1985). At the same time, Kohlberg's work has been criticized on both methodological and theoretical grounds. The premise at the heart of a structural cognitive theory, that the sequence of stages is homogeneous, universal, and invariant, has been questioned by researchers attempting to replicate Kohlberg's stages (Holstein, 1976; Kurtines & Greif, 1974). Kohlberg's transitional stage between Stages 4 and 5 was developed after Kohlberg's follow-up of his original sample (Kohlberg & Kramer, 1969) found many participants who had actually regressed in their stage of moral development. Kohlberg offered the transitional stage as an explanation for the regression that would maintain the invariant sequence of his stages. Critics have argued, though, that these regressions in fact constitute a deviation from the hypothesized invariant sequence (Liebert, 1984).

In addition, while Kohlberg has stated that philosophical writing supports his theory that there are certain agreed-upon absolute principles of morality, others have pointed out that the universality of absolute moral principles continues to be debated. In a recent, extensive review of the cross-cultural research on Kohlberg's stages of moral development, including many unpublished studies, Snarey (1985) proposed that Kohlberg's description of the higher stages of moral development is philosophically incomplete. In his review of studies in 42 cultures outside the United States, Snarey found that among non-Western cultures the higher stages of moral reasoning appeared less frequently than in the Western samples. Among Kenyan village leaders, Tibetan monks, and New Guinea village leaders, groups selected for their positions of ethical leadership, no instances of moral reasoning were found beyond Stages 3 or 3/4.* In examining the responses of these participants, especially the responses that are difficult to score within the updated Kohlberg manual, Snarey found that these village leaders emphasized values of embeddedness in relationships within a community. He concluded that collective or communalistic principled reasoning is missing or misunderstood from the Kohlberg view of principled reasoning based on an individualistic sense of justice.

Social-learning theorists with an interest in moral development have argued that Kohlberg overemphasizes moral reasoning and lacks a theory of social action (Burton, 1984; Liebert, 1984; Sommers, 1984; Sommers, personal communication, May 21, 1985). From Kohlberg's cognitive developmental model, action will follow from cognitive structure. Social-learning theorists suggest that with the typical Kohlberg moral dilemma, which requires that a subject express conscious awareness of a moral problem and describe the dimensions of the conflict, Kohlberg excludes the morality of everyday life (Burton, 1984). Liebert (1984) argues that Kohlberg's theory assumes moral superiority on the part of his Stage 5 and 6 subjects, when they are more likely superior at moral justification.

Haan (1983) criticizes Kohlberg's theory on the grounds that it decides à priori the dimensions of moral situations, and she argues that the morality of everyday life is social–interactional. She proposes that the moral dialogue, in which the individual actively participates with others in self-affirming exchange, is the most productive way of understanding moral development. The dialogue can take place between two people, within a single person who is initially of several minds and who weighs the various alternatives, between people and society, and between societies. "Thus, moral tensions are ubiquitous, and moral resolutions are constantly created, instead of occasionally reproduced" (Haan, p. 234, 1983).

Haan argues that from childhood the individual is inherently motivated to act morally and to be seen as a moral person by others, but also by the self. The individual strives for equilibrium in the view of the moral self through moral dialogue, which is constantly revised on the basis of new information in relationships. According to Haan (1983):

> Interactional morality does not evolve from the child's learning fixed moral categories and then progressively integrating and reintegrating these at different stages. Instead, moral development evolves from the considerably more situationally and intersubjectively responsive skill of coming to know how to engage in exchange, to know when, why, and how much to give in terms of the other's claims and needs and one's own, when all involved are deserving and all have a future together, invariably interacting and mutually needful and committed to each other . . . more inventiveness, fluidity, and flexibility are required in moral dialogues and resolutions than can be embraced within stages, which, if not literally true, can be conceptually useful only if they represent invariant structures. Gradualism is the kind of learning involved in interactional morality. (p. 241)

Although Haan arrived at these insights through her social psychology developmental research (1978), her work has a great deal in common with the ego developmental and family therapy approaches to moral development which will be discussed later.

In its literature on prosocial behavior and prosocial action (Staub, 1978, 1984), the field of social psychology offers an alternative to the cognitive–developmental view of moral development. In that area of work, writers have studied the conditions that are required for people to act altruistically or out of concern for the well-being of others and how that capacity for altruistic action develops through childhood. Hoffman (1980, 1984) argues that the development of the capacity for empathy is the crucial variable in a theory of moral development that emphasizes social action rather than cognitive reasoning.

In addition to these methodological and theoretical critiques, other writers have argued that Kohlberg's model has an individualistic and masculine gender bias (Hogan, 1975; Peters, 1971; Simpson, 1974). The most significant re-

---

*By 3/4 is meant, for example: If a subject's reasoning was 50% at Stage 3, 45% at Stage 4, and 5% at Stage 5, the global stage score of 3/4 is given.

Table 11.1. The Six Moral Stages of Kohlberg's Theory of Moral Development

Level and Stage	Content of Stage		Social Perspective of Stage
	What Is Right	*Reasons for Doing Right*	
LEVEL I—PRECONVENTIONAL			
Stage 1—Heteronomous Morality	To avoid breaking rules backed by punishment, obedience for its own sake, and avoiding physical damage to persons and property.	Avoidance of punishment, and the superior power of authorities.	*Egocentric point of view.* Doesn't consider the interests of others or recognize that they differ from the actor's; doesn't relate two points of view. Actions are considered physically rather than in terms of psychological interests of others. Confusion of authority's perspective with one's own.
Stage 2—Individualism, Instrumental Purpose, and Exchange	Following rules only when it is to someone's immediate interest; acting to meet one's own interests and needs and letting others do the same. Right is also what's fair, what's an equal exchange, a deal, an agreement.	To serve one's own needs or interests in a world where you have to recognize that other people have their interests, too.	*Concrete individualistic perspective.* Aware that everybody has his own interest to pursue and these conflict, so that right is relative (in the concrete individualistic sense).
LEVEL II—CONVENTIONAL			
Stage 3—Mutual Interpersonal Expectations, Relationships, and Interpersonal Conformity	Living up to what is expected by people close to you or what people generally expect of people in your role as son, brother, friend, etc. "Being good" is important and means having good motives, showing concern about others. It also means keeping mutual relationships, such as trust, loyalty, respect, and gratitude.	The need to be a good person in your own eyes and those of others. Your caring for others. Belief in the Golden Rule. Desire to maintain rules and authority which support stereotypical good behavior.	*Perspective of the individual in relationships with other individuals.* Aware of shared feelings, agreements, and expectations which take primacy over individual interests. Relates points of view through the concrete Golden Rule, putting yourself in the other guy's shoes. Does not yet consider generalized system perspective.

Stage	What Is Right	Reasons for Doing Right	Social Perspective of Stage
Stage 4—Social System and Conscience	Fulfilling the actual duties to which you have agreed. Laws are to be upheld except in extreme cases where they conflict with other fixed social duties. Right is also contributing to society, the group, or institution.	To keep the institution going as a whole, to avoid the breakdown in the system "if everyone did it," or the imperative of conscience to meet one's defined obligations (Easily confused with Stage 3 belief in rules and authority; see text.)	*Differentiates societal point of view from interpersonal agreement or motives.* Takes the point of view of the system that defines roles and rules. Considers individual relations in terms of place in the system.

LEVEL III—POSTCONVENTIONAL, or PRINCIPLED

Stage	What Is Right	Reasons for Doing Right	Social Perspective of Stage
Stage 5—Social Contract or Utility and Individual Rights	Being aware that people hold a variety of values and opinions, that most values and rules are relative to your group. These relative rules should usually be upheld, however, in the interest of impartiality and because they are the social contract. Some nonrelative values and rights like *life* and *liberty*, however, must be upheld in any society and regardless of majority opinion.	A sense of obligation to law because of one's social contract to make and abide by laws for the welfare of all and for the protection of all people's rights. A feeling of contractual commitment, freely entered upon, to family, friendship, trust, and work obligations. Concern that laws and duties be based on rational calculation of overall utility, "the greatest good for the greatest number."	*Prior-to-society perspective.* Perspective of a rational individual aware of values and rights prior to social attachments and contracts. Integrates perspectives by formal mechanisms of agreement, contract, objective impartiality, and due process. Considers moral and legal points of view; recognizes that they sometimes conflict and finds it difficult to integrate them.
Stage 6—Universal Ethical Principles	Following self-chosen ethical principles. Particular laws or social agreements are usually valid because they rest on such principles. When laws violate these principles, one acts in accordance with the principle. Principles are universal principles of justice: the equality of human rights and respect for the dignity of human beings as individual persons.	The belief as a rational person in the validity of universal moral principles, and a sense of personal commitment to them.	*Perspective of a moral point of view* from which social arrangements derive. Perspective is that of any rational individual recognizing the nature of morality or the fact that persons are ends in themselves and must be treated as such.

Note. From "Moral Stages and Moralization" by L. Kohlberg, 1976, in *Moral Development and Behavior* (pp. 34-35) edited by T. Lickona, New York: Holt, Rinehart, & Winston. Copyright 1976 by Lawrence Kohlberg. Reprinted by permission.

cent critique of the gender bias in Kohlberg's writing has been offered by Gilligan (1982), whose writing on the moral development of women has questioned the universality of Kohlberg's stages, which have been elaborated exclusively from research with male subjects.

Gilligan (1982) notes that when Kohlberg's measure of moral development is applied to women, they are most often found to be at lower developmental levels. When women's responses to Kohlberg's moral dilemmas are scored by his criteria, most women attain a Stage 3, the Good Boy or Good Girl morality of maintaining good relations. Gilligan points out that when women's moral reasoning is assessed in its own right, what emerges is a coherent system of moral reasoning based on the ethics of care and response. She argues that developmental theories have emphasized increasing separation and the development of autonomy as the important processes in human development. This basically individualistic assumption is inherent in theories of identity development, such as that of Erikson, as well as in Kohlberg's theory of moral development. For this reason, women's development, which emphasizes care in relationships, has been understood as deficient or defective compared to the development of men.

Gilligan views adolescent girls as very much involved in the establishment of identity, but with a heightened awareness of the individual's embeddedness within relationships. Gilligan relates Hirschman's (1970) economic organizational model to adolescent development. She notes that in a Western market economy, the negotiation of needs within a relationship is not given adequate attention; either the relationship works, or you take your business elsewhere (Gilligan, 1985):

> The growth to full stature at puberty releases the child from dependence on parents for protection and heightens the possibility of exit as a solution to conflicts in family relationships. . . . The heightened availability of and impetus toward exit in adolescence, however, can stimulate the development of voice—a development enhanced by the cognitive changes of puberty, the growth of reflective thinking and the discovery of the subjective self. Seeing the possibility of leaving, the adolescent may become freer in speaking, more willing to assert perspectives and voice opinions that diverge from accepted family truths. But if the transformations of puberty heighten the potential for both exit and voice, the experience of adolescence also changes the meaning of leaving and speaking by creating dilemmas of loyalty and rendering choice itself more self-conscious and reflective. (pp. 3–4)

Gilligan views adolescents, especially adolescent girls, as exquisitely attuned to the communicational climate of a relationship, the capacity of a relationship to allow the individuals voice and to engage in response. She speculates that the current epidemic of anorexia nervosa and related eating disorders among adolescent girls may be a means of voicing protest against this society's failure to provide a safe environment for relationships in an age of nuclear proliferation (Gilligan, 1983).

At this time, the Kohlberg and Gilligan approaches to moral development have been viewed as representing a masculine, rules-oriented morality on the one hand, and a feminine, relationships-oriented morality on the other hand. Bakan (1966) has noted that because it is in the nature of the human psyche to polarize ideas, these dualities are often posed as if they were in opposition in human development, when in fact they are elements in dynamic counterpoint that require exploration and integration. The literature on masculinity and femininity itself has been critiqued from this point of view, with many writers arguing that a theory of androgyny that examines the balance of masculine and feminine characteristics in both men and women more accurately captures the complexity of gender (Kaplan & Sedney, 1980).

Gilligan and her colleagues have been working on research exploring the integration of a morality of care and response with a morality of justice and rules within individuals of both sexes, and across different moral situations (Gilligan, 1985; Johnston, 1985; Lyons, 1982, 1983). The field of psychology in general and moral development in particular has to be alert to the difficult but necessary task of integrating these seemingly opposite orientations.

Values in Adolescence

A vast number of studies and writings concerning values have been published during the past 50 years. However, there seems to be no definitional agreement among writers for the term value. As Kluckhohn (1951) pointed out:

> Reading the voluminous, and often vague and diffuse, literature on the subject in the various fields of learning, one finds values considered as attitudes, motivations, objects, measurable quantities, substantive areas of behaviour, affect-laden customs or traditions, and relationships such as those between individuals, groups, objects, events. (p. 390)

Baier and Rescher (1969) also wrote about the problem of defining the term value: "In fact sociologists employ a bewildering profusion of terms, ranging from what a person wants, desires, needs, enjoys, prefers, through what he thinks desirable, preferable, rewarding, obligatory to what the community enjoins, sanctions or enforces" (p. 35).

Nevertheless, there are some scholars who have noted similarities on the topic of value. According to Gabriel (1963), "values are guides to our actions." Similarly, Rokeach (1968) stated that:

> Values . . . have to do with modes of conduct and end states of existence. To say that a person has a value is to say that he has enduring belief that a specific mode of conduct or end state of existence is personally and socially preferable to alternative modes of conduct or end states of existence. Once a value is internalized it becomes, consciously and unconsciously, a standard or criterion for guiding action, for developing and maintaining attitudes toward relevant objects and situations, for justifying one's own and others' actions and attitudes, for morally judging self and others and for comparing oneself with others. (p. 16)

According to Rokeach, values serve adjustive, ego-defensive, knowledge, and self-actualizing functions. Values are the standard by which a person organizes the self, takes action in the world, and relates to others. Rokeach further distinguished between "terminal values," which relate to goals or "end states of existence" (such as a comfortable life, a world at peace, or family security); and "instrumental values," which relate to means or "modes of conduct" (such as ambitious, responsive, self-controlled). Rokeach states that the social sciences have used the concept of value with too many different meanings, and he argues for a definition of value that will distinguish it from other concepts

such as attitude, personal or social beliefs, or interests.

As in the moral development literature, a distinction is made in the study of values between values that the individual describes and values that are reflected in action. Carl Rogers (1964) pointed out that he was primarily concerned with operative or conceptualized values. He credited Morris (1956) with having made useful distinctions in regard to values, saying that "operative values" are the behaviors of organisms that show preference for one object or objective.

Raths, Harmin, and Simon (1966) define the term values "as those elements that show how a person has decided to use his life." They further suggest that values are personal in nature and tend to be a product of experience. These authors believe that because people have different experiences, they develop different values. Values are neither static nor do they function in a pure, abstract way. This view is also consistent with Rogers' (1964) observation about values:

> Values are not held rigidly, but are continually changing. The painting which last year seemed meaningful now appears uninteresting; the way of working with individuals which was formerly experienced as good now seems inadequate, the belief which then seemed true is now experienced as only partly true, or perhaps false. (p. 164)

Raths, Harmin, and Simon point out that because of the personal nature of values, "It follows that if we are to respect a person's life, we must respect his experience and his right to help in examining it for values."

The early research in the area of values and values orientation attempted to measure the relative strength of basic values. Allport, Vernon, and Lindzey (1960: earlier editions 1931, 1951) drew on Spranger's *Types of Men* to generate six basic values: theoretical, economic, aesthetic, social, political, and religious. Their studies, and those of others who used their research instrument, attempted to rank the importance of these values for individuals. (See review of these studies by Dukes, 1955.)

Another classic study of values was Kluckhohn's research on value orientations in different cultures (references). Kluckhohn and Strodtbeck (1961) generated five value orientations with three categories within each, and compared cultures by their stance on these values: (a) conceptions of the innate character of human nature: evil, neutral, or mixed, changeable or unchanging; (b) conceptions of man's relationship to nature and the supernatural: man subjugated to nature, man living in harmony with nature, or man dominant over nature; (c) time orientation in human life: focused on the past, the present, or the future; (d) view of the nature of the self: emphasis on being, on being-in-becoming, or on doing; (e) view of men's relationships to others: linear, collaborative, or individualistic.

Kluckhohn and his colleagues explored these five categories of values through interviews of participants in a variety of cultures. They contrasted Western industrialized cultures, emphasizing dominance of nature, future orientation, doing, and individualism, with Native American and other nonindustrialized cultures that emphasize harmonious coexistence with nature, a present or past orientation, a being-in-becoming view of the development of the self, and collaborative relationships with others.

Rokeach (1973) developed a Value Survey listing 18 terminal values and 18 instrumental values, in which he asked respondents to rank order the values in each group. Other researchers in the study of values have used rank ordering of a value list as a means of determining the importance of values for an individual (Bengtson, 1975; Feather, 1975; Kohn, 1969). The Rokeach Value Survey was used by Beech and Schoeppe (1974) in a study of change from early to late adolescence among New York public school students and by Feather (1975) in a study of Australian high-school students.

Beech and Schoeppe (1974) found that as both boys and girls progressed from age 11 to age 17, they increasingly valued achievement, open-mindedness, responsibility, and self-respect, while decreasing their valuing of conformity to convention and authority. At the same time, both boys and girls throughout adolescence valued highly family security and a world at peace. Feather (1975) found his Australian sample to be very similar to the Beech and Schoeppe sample. Feather (1980) notes that although values consistent with identity development, such as autonomy, responsibility, and honesty, become increasingly important in adolescence, adolescents continue to value affiliative and family connections as well.

Another group of studies of adolescent values

have involved college students. Keniston (1971) called this group "youth" rather than adolescents, arguing that this additional developmental group emerged in affluent societies that brought young people together for extensive education. As Keniston describes youth in these circumstances, they experience a period of questioning the relationship between themselves and the existing social order. Characteristic of these youth is the formation of cultures counter to the adult society's values and norms, criticism of earlier socialization and development of youth-specific identities in relationship to peers. The political activism that characterized his sample of college students may have been influenced by the social and political activism of the civil rights movement and the antiwar movement in the middle and late 1960s.

Because the predominant moral-development literature is either intrapsychic psychoanalytic or cognitive developmental, the literature has not emphasized socialization influences on adolescent moral development. In contrast, the literature on values in adolescence does discuss the importance of socialization influences on the development of adolescent values. Writers have identified the family, the school, the peer group, and the mass media as avenues through which the adolescent learns about and establishes personal values (Feather, 1980).

As Rokeach noted, values serve crucial self-organizing functions, at all stages of the life cycle. In the period of adolescence, when an independent sense of self has to be forged out of family identifications and current relationships, values become an especially important means of delineating and organizing the emerging adult self.

EDUCATIONAL APPROACHES TO MORALS AND VALUES

Until the early part of this century, instruction in morals and values was considered an essential aspect of the education of the young (Sloan, 1980). With the decline of the religious component of education and the rise of the value-free view of science, ethical education entered a long decline. During the late 1960s to the present, interest in morals and values education has reemerged. Two of the approaches that captured both professional and public attention were the educational applications of Kohlberg's research in moral development and the educational work in values clarification.

Kohlberg's six-stage theory of moral development, described above, was seen as both descriptive and prescriptive. Kohlberg suggested that it was possible to promote growth toward higher stages of moral reasoning by means of specific educational interventions. Originally, these interventions consisted of moral dilemma discussions and probes designed to promote a higher level of moral reasoning beyond the one the person was believed to be on. The dilemma discussions were thought to serve as a "pacer" to promote moral development.

Later applications of moral education involved the creation of school environments that would promote moral development. Programs such as the "Just-community school" (Cambridge, Massachusetts) and the Self-Governance at School-Within-a-School (Brookline, Massachusetts) were attempts to build positive environments and involve students in developing their own system of governance as a way to promote moral and ego development (Mosher, 1979). These programs and other similar studies in moral education tried to address the real life moral and social issues students faced in school and/or in the classroom.

Mosher is one of the principal educators who built on Kohlberg's approach and broadened its scope. He developed curricula to stimulate the personal development of adolescents, which became known as "deliberate psychological education" (Mosher, 1979; Mosher & Sprinthall, 1971). Research evaluating these programs suggests that some of these curricula have succeeded in promoting moral, ego, and personal development in adolescents (Mosher & Sprinthall, 1971; Perlmutter, 1980). Higgins, Power, and Kohlberg (1984) summarize data collected at democratically organized schools and contrast the moral atmosphere at these schools as compared to that of the regular high schools. They found that students at the democratic schools, in contrast to regular high school controls, favored prosocial responsibility and made higher stage judgments of responsibility.

An even more widely used educational program was that of values clarification originated by Louis Raths, which during the 1970s was implemented in hundreds of schools across the nation (Sommers, 1984). Raths, Harmin, and Simon (1966) state that the creative clarification of personal values is a necessary part of healthy functioning in an increasingly complex, changing society. Values clarification emerged from a humanistic educational approach that maintains that humans have the potentiality of being thoughtful and wise and that, given the opportunity, they will use their intelligence to relate to the environment in a meaningful, reasoning, and purposeful way. The theory does not advocate one set of values over another, but rather offers a process for developing values and value clarity that suits the individual's background and current situation.

According to Raths, Harmin, and Simon (1966), in order for something to become a value, it must meet the following seven criteria: (a) choosing freely; (b) choosing from alternatives; (c) choosing after thoughtful consideration of the consequences of each alternative; (d) prizing and cherishing, being happy with the choice; (e) affirming, being willing to affirm the choice publicly; (f) acting, doing something with the choice; and (g) acting repeatedly, to make a pattern in a life.

While values clarification was becoming part of the educational scene in the United States, critics of values clarification have written that values clarification is "relativistic," "superficial," and lacking in a solid theoretical base (Kohlberg, 1975; Stewart, 1975). Kirschenbaum (1977) countered that in contrast to Kohlberg's moral developmental approach, which focuses exclusively on moral questions involving the correct way one should act, values clarification focuses on the wider topic of personal values as well as broader moral issues. Evaluation research of values clarification programs is equivocal, with some studies showing no quantifiable change, whereas others show a positive change in attitudes toward school and in school functioning (Perlmutter, 1980).

MORALS, VALUES, AND EGO DEVELOPMENT

In addition to the separate bodies of literature on morals and values described previously, other writers argue that the development of morals and values is in itself an aspect of ego development (Loevinger, 1966, 1976) or the development of the sense of self (Damon, 1976, 1984). Loevinger's theory of ego development is of special interest because it integrates concepts from both the cognitive and the psychoanalytic developmental fields. Further, her theory of ego development examines moral development in the context of the individual's awareness of the boundary between self and other, and the capacity for articulated awareness of self in relation to other. For this reason, it provides an important bridge between individual and interpersonal theories of identity development.

Loevinger sees the ego as an internal process dealing with the concerns of self-organization and self-concept. She describes six stages of ego development, with transitional stages between them. In the *presocial and symbiotic stage* (I-1) of ego development, the stage of the newborn baby, the baby has a close relationship with the mothering person and is able to distinguish that person from the environment, but is not able to distinguish self from other. In the *impulsive stage* (I-2), initiated by the acquisition of language, the child begins to exercise his or her own autonomy, which confirms his or her separate existence from the mothering person. The child sees the world in concrete, egocentric terms, and interpersonal relationships are exploited as sources for gratification. Impulse control is not very dependable at this stage and is modified through reward and punishment.

Loevinger characterizes the next stage, the *self-protective stage* (Delta), as an opportunistic one. Morality is a matter of expediency, and rules are obeyed only in terms of immediate danger. There is an interpersonal shift from dependence to independence, the beginnings of impulse control, and preoccupation with having advantage and being in control in relationships. Self-criticism is not characteristic of this stage, but rather blame is externalized to other people or to situations and circumstances. In the *conformist stage* (I-3), rules are partially internalized but obeyed only because they are rules. A strong desire to win approval and love produces compliance with the majority view and a conscious preoccupation with status and material things. Genuine reciprocity and mutual trust are now possible, but usually to a limited in-group such as close friends and family, and there may be a strong prejudice against outgroups.

Loevinger considers the stage in transition from conformist to conscientious (I-3/4) to be the modal level for adults in this society. At this stage the individual is capable of seeing alternatives and exceptions in situations, but tends to see differences in terms of categories and stereotypic groupings rather than in terms of individual differences and needs. There is a new level of self-awareness but conformity to the group is still important. In the *conscientious stage* (I-4), the individual is concerned with self-evaluated standards and issues of responsibility. Morality has been internalized and group-sanctioned rules are not as important as one's inner moral imperatives. There is a conscious preoccupation with differentiated inner feelings, obligations, ideals, and achievements. The sanction against doing something wrong is the feeling of guilt. The person at this stage is capable of differentiated self-criticism, which was not possible in the conformist stage. At this stage, interpersonal relationships are characterized by feelings of responsibility and obligation for the care of others, along with a sense of privileges, rights, and fairness.

At the individualistic level, in the transition from conscientious to autonomous stages (I-4/5), the person becomes aware that the problem of dependence and independence is an emotional one rather than a purely practical one. There is also a beginning awareness of inner conflict. At this stage, interpersonal relationships may be seen as antagonistic to strivings for achievement. In the *autonomous stage* (I-5), there is a fuller capacity "to acknowledge and to cope with inner conflict, that is, conflicting needs, conflicting duties, and the conflict between needs and duties" (Loevinger, 1976). Interpersonal relationships take into consideration an awareness of interdependence and the understanding that other people also need autonomy. At this stage, the person has a deeper understanding of his or her own development and is able to recognize paradox in life. Loevinger sees the *integrated stage* (I-6) as the highest stage of ego maturity. Upon reaching this stage, a person has achieved a harmonious integration of all inner components of the self and has an integrated identity.

Although Loevinger sees ego development as a progression toward greater maturity, she cautions against idealizing any ego stage. She notes that each stage has its paradoxes, weaknesses, and opportunities, which provide for potential growth or potential maladjustment. From the point of view of Loevinger's theory, the developmental thrust is an increasingly self-aware, internally differentiated self in empathic relationships with close others. Loevinger asserts that the striving to create a more and more complex meaning of the self in the world is the outstanding characteristic of ego development.

Other psychoanalytic and developmental theorists agree with Loevinger that the crucial step in the maturation of the self is the capacity for awareness of the divided self. Jung (1933) offers a theory of individuation in the life cycle that describes a developmental progression from the "monarchic" consciousness of childhood, in which all conflict is externalized, to the "dualistic" consciousness of youth, in which desires or impulses are first seen as in conflict within the self. He suggests that adolescence and the period of youth are especially important junctures in the human life cycle, precisely because of the new developmental capacity to experience the self as capable of internal conflict.

Jung describes the wish to avoid this consciousness of the divided self and to avoid engagement with life's expanded horizons and resultant realities as a major problem in the period of youth. According to Jung, the typical adolescent relieves the turbulence generated by awareness of the complex self in internal conflict by constriction of the potential avenues for the self. Because the process of fullest personal exploration is extremely difficult and unrewarded by society, the typical young person makes socially prescribed choices that emphasize social achievement rather than the more challenging alternative, exploring "the tension inherent in the play of opposites—in the dualistic stage—and thereby to build up a state of wider and higher consciousness" (Jung, 1933, p. 102). Jung notes that those aspects of the self which could not be explored in young adulthood, often consisting of opposite-sex identifications, then recur in middle age. Research in adult development has supported Jung's clinically formulated theory of individuation, in that many writers have found that opposite-sex characteristics increase in midlife (Guttman, 1975; Lowenthal, Thurnher, & Chiriboga, 1975; Neugarten, 1964).

Jung's theory of individuation in the life cycle, combined with Loevinger's theory of ego development, has important implications for an understanding of the adolescent developmental experience in all its complex contradictions. The

adolescent is for the first time capable of viewing the self as separate from others and of understanding complex impulses and motivations within the self, many of which are in conflict with one another. As Erikson notes, the adolescent is involved in an active search for fidelity. The values of truth and integrity are vital to the adolescent, because of the importance of relational integrity in self-affirmation. Yet the challenge of self-awareness of a complex, contradictory self proves to be too much for most adolescents. Because adolescents are as unforgiving of their own personal hypocrisy as they are of the inconsistencies and hypocrisies of the adult world, they have to find some means of making sense of themselves and their own behavior. The psychological defenses that are characteristic of adolescence—intense but shifting group loyalties, agonizing self-awareness alternating with stubborn externalization, abrupt reliance on blanket denial or on impulsive action, can be seen as attempts to both explore and make peace with the contradictory self.

Interactional Morality and the Interpersonal Self

Missing from the ego development theories described above is an interpersonal theory of the development of the self within relationships. Although the theorists discussed so far have described identity development in general, and moral development in particular, as a largely internal process, other writers have suggested that the development of identity is an interpersonal, interactive process. The burgeoning clinical literatures in the areas of family systems theory and interpersonal or object-relations psychoanalysis focus on the development and treatment of psychopathology from the point of view of relationships (in family therapy, see Boszormenyi-Nagy & Spark, 1973; Framo, 1970; Green & Framo, 1981; Minuchin, 1974; in psychoanalysis see Guntrip, 1971; Searles, 1979; Winnicott, 1965). These interactional clinical literatures emphasize the vital importance in human development of relationships that are open to mutual, responsive communication. For the purpose of this discussion, we will focus on Boszormenyi-Nagy's theory of contextual family therapy, which directly discusses the ethical dimension of family relationships.

Boszormenyi-Nagy (1965, 1981; Boszormenyi-

Nagy & Spark, 1973) is a writer in the new field of family therapy who offers an interpersonal theory of development within relationships, while emphasizing the ethical dimension of family relationships. Boszormenyi-Nagy draws on the work of philosopher Martin Buber, who described the distinction between an "I–it" and an "I–thou" relationship. According to Buber, morality is not a characteristic of the individual, but a characteristic of relationships. In an I–it relationship, the individual experiences the self as the subject of interactions and relegates the other to the position of object. In an I–Thou relationship, both self and other are experienced as subjects; full, empathic respect and awareness of subjective experience is afforded both to the self and to the other. The implications of this perspective are quite profound, because from this ethical interactional point of view, an I–it relationship is limiting and potentially damaging both to the self and to the other, whereas an I–Thou relationship enhances both self and other. According to Buber, awareness of self and other in the I–Thou relationship is established through dialogue.

Beginning with Buber's work as an ethical and philosophical foundation and drawing on his work in family therapy, Boszormenyi-Nagy has formed a theory of intergenerational family relationships that emphasizes that the meeting of ethical responsibilities within intergenerational relationships is the primary resource for individual and family health and growth. According to Boszormenyi-Nagy, taking care of others is an inherently rewarding, self-affirming experience that is fundamental to human nature. For parents, the act of caring for their children is existentially rewarded by the care that their offspring in turn will give to their own children in the next generation of the family. According to Boszormenyi-Nagy, people earn credit by caretaking (in relationships) that is both self-affirming, and that entitles them in turn to care from others. Boszormenyi-Nagy finds that children are extremely loyal to their parents for this caretaking, whether they discharge their loyalty obligations through direct care and concern or whether they do so by self-punishing or self-constricting "invisible loyalties" to the parents. Often, an invisible loyalty can take the form of a physical separation from the family accompanied by a psychological failure to separate. According to Boszormenyi-Nagy's theory of individuation,

true autonomy consists of a capacity for spontaneous, independent action that includes commitment and responsible care within family relationships.

When the parents have themselves suffered trauma, mistreatment, or family deprivation, they may feel too injured to give to the next generation. Rather, according to Boszormenyi-Nagy, these parents accumulate what he calls "destructive entitlement," that is, the feeling that they are permitted to make the next generation suffer the same harms that they suffered. Children in these families may become "parentified" (i.e., expected to be the emotional caretakers for the parents). There may also be generations of resentment and emotional cutoff between parents and their children, in which the naturally existing bonds are affirmed in covert ways that restrict growth and generate psychological symptoms.

In the most disturbed families, the boundary between self and other becomes blurred. The parents use the children as extensions of their intrapsychic defenses. In these families, parents use their power and authority to restrict and control the actions and feelings of the child, in attempts to control their own emotional experience. Change becomes equated with separation and loss of family unity, and family stability is rigidly maintained. For these fused or enmeshed families, awareness of differences between self and other is experienced as so disruptive to the "undifferentiated ego mass" (Bowen, 1981) that the spontaneous, independent action of individual family members is overtly and covertly forbidden. In these disturbed families, the children will develop a variety of symptoms as a means of giving voice to the communications that are forbidden direct expression in the family.

Much of the family therapy field has moved in the direction of communications-oriented strategic or structural interventions that bypass self-awareness or insight. In therapeutic interventions based on contextual therapy, Boszormenyi-Nagy emphasizes the importance of dialogue as a vital transformational force in intergenerational relationships. He encourages family members to overtly acknowledge the merit of each person's point of view within the family. When all family members are able to engage in a full dialogue that empathically recognizes the subjective experience of each person, rigid or stagnant patterns of family relationship become available to change.

Individuation theory in itself can be an interpersonal as well as an intrapsychic theory (Shapiro, 1985, in press). From the point of view of an interpersonal individuation theory, the self is interpersonally established, maintained, and growthfully modified through transactions in family relationships. Any major developmental transition experienced by an individual will require change from the other family members. Family intimacy requires readiness and generosity on the part of family members who will—more or less reluctantly—walk or be dragged along in their own growth with an individual's moves toward growth.

Interpersonal identity changes are especially dramatic at periods of transition in the family life cycle. Both individual and family therapists have documented the intense experience of change in the family both when children reach puberty and become adolescents, and again when adolescents prepare to leave home and establish lives outside the family. Because the majority of writing on adolescent development has focused on the individual, the process of development in the parent/child relationship has not been given full attention. An interpersonal theory of individuation can illuminate the family developmental experience during adolescence from the point of view of both the parents and the child.

As Jung described adult development, the youth deals with awareness of the complex self by constricting the self and choosing particular, often stereotyped avenues of development. From the point of view of Jung's theory, the parents of an adolescent, typically in the period of early middle age, have not yet arrived at the stage of their own life cycle where the complex self is once again spontaneously explored. According to Jung, the exploration of the complex self and of the roads not taken in life, comes in later midlife after the children have left home. The entry of a child into adolescence initiates a developmental period when all values are examined and questioned and when the new self is defined in opposition to, as well as in connection with, the parental self. The adolescent develops a new image of self by communicating in close relationships and requesting a response that acknowledges the changing relationship within the family constellation.

In order to fully respond to the increasing independence and separation of the adolescent, the parents are forced to reexamine the choices in their own lives. Interactions with the adolescent compel parents to remember their old doubts and ask themselves again about the avenues they chose in their own development and the roads not taken. Parents can respond to the change in the adolescent with corresponding change in self. Parents who are too rigidly or defensively invested in their own choices during youth may respond to the challenge the adolescent presents with attempts to restrict or control the adolescent's growth or silence voice so that these disquieting, developmentally challenging interactional moves will cease.

Adolescent Values and Identity: In their Own Words

The following examples of adolescent thinking about the place of morals and values in their own development were selected from material gathered in a high school psychology class at a suburban high school near Boston, Massachusetts (Perlmutter, 1985). These particular passages were selected for their illustration of the two dimensions of adolescent moral and value development discussed in this chapter: (a) the adolescent's own striving to integrate autonomy and creative innovation with family loyalty and connection and (b) the importance of parental response to the challenge of change presented by the adolescent.

A 17-year-old girl said the following in response to a question about her own values:

> My mother's generation had it much easier in terms of values and what is expected of a person—a teenager. My mom tells me she did not sleep with any man before she got married, she was 23 years old then. She didn't even sleep with my father, before marriage, and she loved him. But nice girls didn't. And it was just like that! With us, you have all these different things—someone like my mom would be weird. Sometimes I wish I knew what I should do and not do. I can't listen to how my mother was, it does not help me. But when I listen to my friends I'm also confused.

Because of the radical generational change in sexual morals, she finds herself having difficulty establishing continuity with the morals and values of her mother's life. Without the connection to the traditions of the previous generation, the options available to the self become so complex they may become overwhelming.

A 17-year-old boy, describing his own decision-making process in establishing values to live by, illustrates the adolescent's conflict between self-interest and care for others and his careful scrutiny of the values that his parents offer:

> Decisions, decisions. Everyone is after me·and I'm totally confused. I know I like the "good life" but there are so many things which are also very important, like doing things for other people. I like a Porsche for a car and some other expensive things I see rich people have. My parents don't say I have to become rich, but the way they complain about not being able to buy this or that makes me wonder.

In his own internal process of decision-making, he is torn between materialism and altruism, both of which offer satisfactions. In the process of self-exploration, he turns to his parents' values and becomes acutely aware that his parents care more about material posessions than they are willing to let on, and these discrepancies in family values add to the burden of confusion. Parents hearing his accusation that their stated values may not be congruent with their actions may be able to respond with honest self-examination or may deny the discrepancy out of their own conflicts.

The following statement by a 15-year-old boy illustrates the detrimental effect of the failure of parental responsiveness to adolescent value change:

> When I hear some of the kids say they can talk to their parents I feel like screaming or just telling them it's a lie! I have two parents. They are married but sometimes I wish they were divorced. When we are all together at the dinner table, or such, either they fight with each other or with us. It's the truth. My father has this thing about always being right, we kids are always wrong. You do it his way even if it does not make any sense. He came here from the old country when he was 10 years old. You would think he has learned something since then. . . . Honestly, I can't wait to get out of this crazy place. Sometimes I feel guilty feeling like I do about my old man. I can't say my mother is of much help.

This boy is deeply frustrated in a family situation where there is no evidence of respectful interchange and communication. His growing ability to think independent thoughts and hold independent values appears to be discounted. His father seems to be too intent on maintaining control to affirm and acknowledge his son's development, and the conflict between his parents also makes his mother inaccessible. At the same time, his loyalty to his father compels him to mention that his father was an immigrant who failed to adjust to the different values in a new country. He feels guilty and torn between wishing to respect his father, and feeling unable to grant respect in this relationship in which he has no voice and experience no response.

Finally, this poem written by a 17-year-old girl, Stacey Strand, illustrates the growth-producing tensions between family and peer values in the adolescent's development of identity:

> I used to be . . .
>   I am . . .
>   I want to be . . .
>   me!!
>
> When I was a child, I was carefree and wild,
> anyone could see how happy I was by the way
> I smiled.
> I had a glow on my face and a flicker in my eye,
> I was like a bird flying high in the sky.
>
> I had no worries or problems bothering me,
> I had my friends and my family,
> I was as content as could be.
>
> Then something happened, I changed deep
> down inside,
> New ideas took over and feelings that I could
> not hide.
>
> All of a sudden I wanted to be away from my
> parents,
> grown up and on my own,
> but at the same time I found myself feeling
> scared and all alone.
>
> I became totally devoted to my friends,
> and thought that we'd be together until the
> world's end.
> I disobeyed my parents, did things they didn't
> approve of.
> I covered up my insecurity and mixed-up feelings by trying
> to act tough.
>
> This kind of behavior lasted for a few years,
> a period of time that was filled with many confused
> emotions and tears.

Since then I have settled down
I now know my parents aren't as bad as they
seem,
I have found that my life is a lot calmer when
my family works as a team.

This insightful and self-revealing poem documents the passages in the growth of the awareness of the divided self. This young woman describes the period of childhood bliss in which the self is in harmony with parents and peers, and protected by family dependence. The disturbing change in self and corresponding change in family relationships is described explicitly as a change in self-awareness, "new ideas took over and feelings that I could not hide." The wish to separate from family and be on her own was accompanied by intense feelings of fear and loneliness, and she sought the comfort of peer relationships that would last forever. She began to act in ways that challenged her parents' values as a means of asserting her own independence and experienced a great deal of turmoil and confusion. In the conclusion of the poem, she describes the relief at forging a connection with her parents again, describing her life as "calmer" because she has established a sense of teamwork with her parents.

These adolescents speak to the reality that there is an optimal balance for learning about morals and values. The challenge of discovering new values for the self has to be balanced by the reassurance of maintaining some congruence with family values. The integration of self in adolescence is best supported by a climate of family relationships in which the parents respond to the growing maturity and self-assertion of the adolescent with acknowledgement and recognition.

SUMMARY

Up to this point, we have discussed the current literature on morals and values in adolescence, described the current controversies in that literature, and offered a conceptual framework by which to view the development of morals and values. We have argued that moral development needs to be viewed as an aspect of interpersonal identity development embedded in the adolescent's individuation experience of attachment and separation within the family. In addition, attention needs to be given to the milieu, political climate, mass media, religious institutions, and private and public schools, all of which are value-laden. Any one of these or a constellation of these forces have the possibility to energize, educate, and help bring out the person's potentialities for ethical and moral action so as to become a personally responsible individual and a socially responsible citizen. The schools of the nation are especially uniquely equipped to teach democratic values in the tradition of responsible citizenship.

In the adolescent's development of the complex self, different moral and value orientations are given voice that are crucial to the delineation and cohesive organization of the more mature self. There is a basic human motivation for autonomy and independence, as well as a basic human yearning for attachment and connection with close others. The affirmation in relationships of both of these motivations is essential to human development at all stages of the life cycle. The interpersonal affirmation of the connected yet autonomous self is especially crucial to the adolescent, who is exploring the new experience of a self that differs from the parents, and who needs to know that his or her growing independence and eventual leaving home will not sever these crucial, life-affirming ties to family.

The importance of the study of morals and values as they emerge in the context of relationships in everyday life cannot be overstated, because the capacity for moral action is a crucial aspect of mental health for individuals, families, and societies. Considering that we live in an ever-shrinking universe in which we are becoming increasingly more interrelated as individuals and as societies, with a threat of nuclear extinction, it is even more urgent that we educate our adolescents in the development of morals and values.

REFERENCES

Allport, G., Vernon, P., & Lindzey, G. (1960). *A study of values: A scale for measuring the dominant interests in personality* (rev. ed.). Boston: Houghton Mifflin.

Baier, K., & Rescher, N. (1969). (Eds.). *Values and the future*. New York: Free Press.

Bakan, D. (1966). *The duality of human existence*. Chicago: Rand McNally.

Beech, R., & Schoeppe, A. (1974). Development of

value systems in adolescents. *Developmental Psychology, 10,* 644–656.

Bengtson, V. (1975). Generation and family effects in value socialization. *American Sociological Review, 40,* 358–371.

Blos, P. (1962). *On adolescence: A psychoanalytic interpretation.* New York: Free Press.

Blos, P. (1968). Character formation in adolescence. *The Psychoanalytic Study of the Child, 23,* 245–263.

Blos, P. (1971). The child analyst looks at the young adolescent. *Daedalus, 100,* 961–978.

Boszormenyi-Nagy, I. (1965). A theory of relationships: Experience and transaction. In I. Boszormenyi-Nagy & J. Framo (Eds.), *Intensive family therapy* (pp. 33–86). New York: Harper & Row.

Boszormenyi-Nagy, I. (1981). Contextual therapy: Therapeutic leverages in mobilizing trust. In R. Green & J. Framo (Eds.), *Family therapy: major contributions* (pp. 395–415). New York: International Universities Press.

Boszormenyi-Nagy, I., & Spark, G. (1973). *Invisible loyalties.* Hagerstown, MD: Harper & Row.

Boyer, E. (1983). *High school: A report on secondary education in America.* New York: Harper & Row.

Burton, R. (1984). A paradox in theories and research in moral development. In W. Kurtines & J. Gewirtz (Eds.), *Morality, moral behavior, and moral development* (pp. 193–207). New York: Wiley Interscience.

Colby, A., & Kohlberg, L. (1984). *The measurement of moral judgement.* New York: Cambridge University Press.

Damon, W. (1977). *The social world of the child.* San Francisco: Jossey Bass.

Damon, W. (1984). Self-understanding and moral development from childhood to adolescence. In W. Kurtines & J. Gewirtz (Eds.), *Morality, moral behavior, and moral development* (pp. 109–127). New York: Wiley Interscience.

Dukes, W. (1955). Psychological studies of values. *Psychological Bulletin, 52,* 24–50.

Elder, G. (1975). Adolescence in the life cycle: An introduction. In S. Dragastin & G. Elder (Eds.), *Adolescence in the life cycle: Psychological change and social context.* New York: Wiley.

Erikson, E. (1964). *Insight and responsibility: Lectures on the ethical implications of psychoanalytic insight.* New York: Norton.

Erikson, E. (1968). *Identity: Youth and crisis.* New York: Norton.

Erikson, E. (1974). Womanhood and the inner space (1968). In J. Strouse (Ed.), *Women and analysis.* New York: Dell.

Esman, A. (1972). Adolescence and the consolidation of values. In S. Post (Ed.), *Moral values and the superego concept in psychoanalysis.* New York: International Universities Press.

Feather, N. (1975). *Values in education and society.* New York: Free Press.

Feather, N. (1980). Values in adolescence. In J. Adelson (Ed.), *Handbook of adolescent psychology* (pp. 247–295). New York: Wiley.

Framo, J. (1970). Symptoms from a family transactional viewpoint. In N. Ackerman, J. Lieb, & J.

Pearce (Eds.), *Family therapy in transition* (pp. 125–171). Boston: Little, Brown.

Freud, S. (1905). Three essays on the theory of sexuality. In J. Strachey (Ed.), *Standard edition (Vol. 7).* London: Hogarth.

Freud, S. (1913). Totem and taboo. *Standard edition (Vol. 13).* London: Hogarth.

Freud, S. (1921). Psychology and the analysis of the ego. *Standard edition (Vol. 18).* London: Hogarth.

Freud, S. (1921). Some psychical consequences of the anatomical distinction between the sexes. *Standard edition (Vol. 19).* London: Hogarth.

Gabriel, R. H. (1963). *Traditional values in American life.* New York: Harcourt, Brace, and World.

Gilligan, C. (1982). *In a different voice.* Cambridge, MA: Harvard University Press.

Gilligan, C. (1983). *Morals, values and the life cycle.* Discussion of papers presented at a conference: Morals, Values and the Life Cycle, Cambridge Hospital, Boston, MA (Sept. 1983).

Gilligan, C. (1985). *Exit-voice dilemmas in adolescent development.* Paper presented at the Hirschman Conference, University of Notre Dame, South Bend, IN.

Green, R., & Framo, J. (1981). *Family therapy: Major contributions.* New York: International Universities Press.

Guntrip, H. (1971). *Psychoanalytic therapy and the self.* London: Hogarth.

Guttman, D. (1975). Parenthood: A key to the comparative study of the life cycle. In N. Datan & L. Ginsberg (Eds.), *Life-span developmental psychology.* New York: Academic.

Haan, N. (1978). Two moralities in action contexts: Relationships to thought, ego regulation, and development. *Journal of Personality and Social Psychology, 36,* 286–305.

Haan, N. (1983). An interactional morality of everyday life. In N. Haan, R. Bellah, P. Rabinow, & W. Sullivan, *Social science as moral inquiry* (pp. 218–250). New York: Columbia University Press.

Higgins, A., Power, C., & Kohlberg, L. (1984). The relationship of moral atmosphere to judgments of responsibility. In W. Kurtines & J. Gewirtz (Eds.), *Morality, moral behavior, and moral development.* New York: Wiley.

Hirschman, A. (1970). *Exit, voice and loyalty: Responses to decline in firms, organizations, and states.* Cambridge, MA: Harvard University Press.

Hoffman, M. (1977). Moral internalization: current theory and research. In L. Berkowitz (Ed.), *Advances in experimental social psychology* (pp. 86–135). New York: Academic.

Hoffman, M. (1980). Adolescent morality in development perspective. In J. Adelson (Ed.), *Handbook of adolescent psychology* (pp. 302–343). New York: Wiley.

Hoffman, M. (1984). Empathy, its limitations, and its role in a comprehensive moral theory. In W. Kurtines & J. Gewirtz (Eds.), *Morality, moral behavior, and moral development* (pp. 283–302). New York: Wiley.

Hogan, R. (1975). Moral development and the structure of personality. In D. Depalma & J. Foley

(Eds.), *Moral development: Current theory and research*. Hillsdale, NJ: Erlbaum.

Holstein, C. (1976). Development of moral judgment: A longitudinal study of males and females. *Child Development, 47*, 51–61.

Jacobson, E. (1964). *The self and the object world*. New York: International Universities Press.

Johnston, D. (1985). *Two moral orientations—Two problem solving strategies: Adolescent's solutions to dilemmas in fables*. Unpublished doctoral dissertation, Harvard University School of Education, Cambridge, MA.

Jung, C. (1933). The stages of life. In *Modern man in search of a soul* (pp. 95–114). New York: Harcourt, Brace.

Kaplan, A., & Sedney, M. (1980). *Psychology and sex roles: An androgynous perspective*. Boston: Little, Brown.

Keniston, K. (1971). *Youth and dissent: The rise of a new opposition*. New York: Harcourt Brace Jovanovich.

Kirschenbaum, H. (1977). *Advanced values clarification*. LaJolla, CA: University Associates.

Kluckhohn, C. (1951). Values and value orientations in the theory of action. In T. Parsons & E. Shils (Eds.), *Toward a general theory of action*. Cambridge, MA: Harvard University Press.

Kluckhohn, C. & Strodtbeck, F. (1961). *Variations in value orientations*. Evanston, IL: Row, Peterson.

Kohlberg, L. (1958). *The development of modes of thinking and choice in the years 10 to 16*. Unpublished doctoral dissertation, University of Chicago, IL.

Kohlberg, L. (1975). The cognitive-developmental approach to moral education. *Phi Delta Kappan, 56*, 670–677.

Kohlberg, L. (1981). *Essays in moral development: Vol. I. The philosophy of moral development*. New York: Harper & Row.

Kohlberg, L. (1984). *Essays in moral development: Vol. II. The psychology of moral development*. New York: Harper & Row.

Kohlberg, L., & Kramer, R. (1969). Continuities and discontinuities in childhood and adult moral development. *Human Development, 12*, 93–120.

Kohn, M. L. (1969). *Class and conformity: A study in values*. Homewood, IL: Dorsey.

Kurtines, W., & Gewirtz, J. (1984). *Morality, moral behavior, and moral development*. New York: Wiley.

Kurtines, W, & Greif, E. (1974). The development of moral thought: Review and evaluation of Kohlberg's approach. *Psychological Bulletin, 81*, 453–470.

Liebert, R. (1984). What develops in moral development? In W. Kurtines & J. Gewirtz (Eds.), *Morality, moral behavior, and moral development* (pp. 177–192). New York: Wiley.

Loevinger, J. (1966). The meaning and measurement of ego development. *American Psychologist, 21*, 195–217.

Loevinger, J. (1976). *Ego development: Conceptions and theories*. San Francisco: Jossey-Bass.

Lowenthal, M., Thurnher, M., & Chiriboga, D. (1975). *Four stages of life: A comparative study of men and women facing transitions*. San Francisco: Jossey-Bass.

Lyons, N. (1982). *Conceptions of self and morality and modes of moral choice: Identifying justice and care in judgements of actual moral dilemimas*. Unpublished doctoral dissertation, Harvard Graduate School of Education, Cambridge, MA.

Lyons, N. (1983). Two perspectives: On self, relationships, and morality. *Harvard Educational Review, 53*(2), 125–145.

Miller, J. B. (1976). *Toward a new psychology of women*. Boston: Beacon Press.

Minuchin, S. (1974). *Families and family therapy*. Cambridge, MA: Harvard University Press.

Morris, C. (1956). *Variations of human value*. Chicago. IL: University of Chicago Press.

Mosher, R. (Ed.). (1979). *Adolescents' development and education*. Berkeley, CA: McCutchan.

Mosher, M., & Sprinthall, N. (1971). Psychological education: a means to promote personal development during adolescence. *The Counseling Psychologist, 2*, 3–82.

Nass, M. (1966). The superego and moral development in the theories of Freud and Piaget. *The Psychoanalytic Study of the Child, 21*, 51–68.

Neugarten, B. (1964). *Personality in middle and late life*. New York: Atherton.

Nisan, M. (1984). Content and structure in moral judgement: An integrative view. In W. Kurtines & J. Gewirtz (Eds.), *Morality, moral behavior and moral development* (pp. 208–225). New York: Wiley.

Perlmutter, R. (1980). *The effects of the values clarification process on the moral and ego development of high school students*. Unpublished doctoral dissertation, Boston University School of Education, Boston, MA.

Perlmutter, R. (1985). *Teenagers and their feelings*. Unpublished manuscript.

Peters, R. (1971). Moral development: A plea for pluralism. In T. Mischel (Ed.), *Cognitive development and epistemology*. New York: Academic.

Piaget, J. (1932). *The moral judgment of the child*. New York: Harcourt.

Raths, L., Harmin, M., & Simon, S. (1966). *Values and teaching*. Columbus, OH: Charles Merrill.

Rogers, C. (1964). Toward a modern approach to values: The valuing process in the mature person. *Journal of Abnormal and Social Psychology, 68*, 160–167.

Riley, M. (1976). Age strata in social systems. In R. Binstock & E. Shanas (Eds.), *Handbook of aging and the social sciences* (pp. 189–217). New York: Van Nostrand.

Rokeach, M. (1968). *Beliefs, attitudes, and values*. San Francisco: Jossey-Bass.

Rokeach, M. (1973). *The nature of human values*. New York: Free Press.

Schaefer, R. (1960). The loving and beloved superego in Freud's structural theory. *The Psychoanalytic Study of the Child, 15*, 163–188.

Schaefer, R. (1968). *Aspects of internalization*. New York: International Universities Press.

Searles, H. (1979). *Countertransference and related subjects*. New York: International Universities Press.

Shapiro, E. (1985). *Change and continuity in family de-*

velopment. Unpublished manuscript.

Shapiro, E. (in press). Individual and family development: Individuation as a family process. In C. Falicov (Ed.), *Family transitions.* New York: Guilford.

Simpson, E. (1974). Moral development research: A case study of scientific cultural bias. *Human Development, 17,* 81–106.

Sloan, D. (1980). The teaching of ethics in the American undergraduate curriculum, 1876–1976. In D. Callahan & S. Bok (Eds.), *Ethics teaching in higher education* (pp. 1–57). New York: Plenum.

Snarey, J. (1985). Cross-cultural universality of social–moral development: A critical review of Kohlbergian research. *Psychological Bulletin, 97,* 202–232.

Sommers, C. (1984). Ethics without virtue: Moral education in America. *American Scholar, 53,* 381–389.

Staub, E. (1978). Positive social behavior and morality. New York: Academic.

Staub, E. (1984). Steps toward a comprehensive theory of moral conduct: goal orientation, social behavior, kindness, and cruelty. In W. Kurtines & J. Gewirtz (Eds.), *Morality, moral behavior, and moral development.* New York: Wiley.

Stewart, J. S. (1975). Clarifying values clarification: A critique. *Phi Delta Kappan, 56,* 684–688.

Turiel, E. (1974). Conflict and transition in adolescent moral development. *Child Development, 45,* 14–79.

Winnicott, D. (1965). *The maturational processes and the facilitating environment.* New York: International Universities Press.

CHAPTER 12

Intellectual Growth

Alan S. Kaufman and Jim Flaitz

To understand the process of intellectual growth, it is important to first have some clear notion of what is meant by intelligence. Unfortunately, this is not a simple matter, as there are a number of theoretical as well as psychometric approaches to the subject of defining intelligence, with only limited agreement among those who have investigated the phenomenon. To make matters worse, efforts at measuring intelligence and at theoretically defining intelligence have historically not been coordinated. More recent theorists (Guilford, 1979; Horn & Cattell, 1966; Jensen, 1972) have undertaken the development of assessment instruments to explicate the phenomena treated in their theoretical work; however, these instruments have rarely found their way into general usage. At one point, opinion regarding the nature and definition of intelligence was so diverse that the psychologist Boring (1923) suggested that intelligence is what intelligence tests measure. And although he may have intended a certain degree of cynicism in this observation, in truth, the traditional measures of intelligence have largely served both to define intelligence and to direct research into the intricacies of intellectual behavior. For this reason, it might be instructive to consider the outlook of one of the central figures in the field of assessment of intelligence: David Wechsler.

Wechsler (1975) suggested that intelligence is not a quality of the mind but is rather " . . . an aspect of behavior; it has to do primarily with the appropriateness, effectiveness, and worthwhileness of what human beings do or want to do" (p. 135). He viewed intelligence as multifaceted and most appropriately perceived as a global capacity. Further, Wechsler did not consider intelligence to be primarily a matter of mental functions or logical operations. Rather, he regarded intelligence as a relativistic concept that could not be defined in absolute terms. The dimensions within which intelligence were cast included: awareness (to distinguish intelligent behavior from instinctive behavior), meaningfulness (intelligent behavior is goal-directed), rationality (intelligent behavior should be logically deducible and consistent), and, finally, worthwhileness (to be characterized as intelligent, behavior must be deemed valuable and useful by others). Wechsler summed up his position with the following definition: Intelligence is " . . . the capacity of an individual to understand the world about him and his resourcefulness to cope with its challenges" (p.139).

Intelligence is one of the most intriguing and

investigated of subjects, yet at the same time remains one of the most intransigent and controversial in the field of psychology (Miller & Reynolds, 1984). Despite Wechsler's proffered advice, efforts have continued to link intelligence to genetic factors (Jensen, 1979, 1982, 1984) and to define intelligence either in terms of general factors or multiple abilities (Cattell, 1971; Guilford, 1967, 1979; Horn, 1968, 1970, 1972, 1976, 1979; Horn & Cattell, 1966). It would seem that as each new wave of conceptualizing human characteristics and functions arrives, a corresponding effort to apply those new concepts to intelligence quickly emerges (e.g. information-processing models).

Another focus of interest in the study of intelligence is the issue of development of intelligence across the life span. The theoretical contributions of Jean Piaget toward the understanding of cognitive development represent the most detailed and sophisticated effort to describe the developmental process to date. Most (but not all) contemporary investigators of cognitive development begin with the ideas of Piaget.

Ultimately, the value of any theory lies in its ability to generate worthwhile applications. In the case of theories of intelligence, the development of valid methods of measuring intelligence is an important goal of researchers, and yet until only recently, no major clinical assessment instruments for measuring intelligence reflected contemporary influences of theory and research. Understanding how assessment is conducted is essential to interpreting and using the results of intelligence tests.

Much of the traditional body of knowledge concerning intelligence is slowly giving way to more modern theories and methods. Future developments will almost certainly extend the recent work in neuropsychology and cognitive psychology, with an emphasis on the integration of previously unrelated research programs.

HISTORY OF
INTELLIGENCE TESTING

The history of theories of intelligence and that of intelligence testing are integrally related. It might even be suggested that modern thought concerning the nature of intelligence has evolved from efforts to measure intelligence. Interest in the intellectual qualities of man ap-
pears to go back to antiquity, with Greek philosophers contemplating the nature of man and the forces that shaped men's lives (Gould, 1981). However, being largely philosophical, such efforts provided little more than a framework for subsequent students of human nature, with specific emphasis being placed upon the concept of "individual differences." In one of Plato's works, a dialogue is presented in which a rationale was being constructed to explain why some men attained greatness while others lived lives of deprivation and hardship. The essence of the treatise was that people must be told that differences in station were due to differences in the personal qualities of the individuals. An analogy was provided that likened the differences in men to the differences in metals, with some men being cast of gold, whereas others were cast of lead. It was reasoned that only if men accepted differences in station as being a function of their own innate qualities could society's fabric be maintained (Gould, 1981).

Very little can be said to have changed in the intervening centuries with regard to the notion of individual differences, save for the considerations of how those differences originated and what attributes should be considered most significant in differentiating among men. Nevertheless, what attention was devoted to matters of individual differences and intelligence continued to be largely philosophical until the publication and dissemination of Charles Darwin's writings.

Darwin's cousin, Sir Francis Galton, is credited with devising the first measurement systems that were intended to index differences in human intelligence. Galton's methods, however, were based on techniques advocated and used by the German experimental psychophysicists (Wundt, Fechner, Weber). These researchers began by attempting to measure and define the limits and range of human sensation and judgment and to translate those measurements into mathematical functions that would be generalizable to the populace at large.

It was Galton's belief, predicated largely upon his cousin's work, that within the human species gradations of abilities would be found as a consequence of genetic variations. Galton also was a staunch supporter of the eugenics movement; methods for detecting the most genetically superior stock from among the general populace had special significance for him. Ultimately, Galton instituted widespread data collection for the purpose of documenting individual differences among people. Galton's tests of sensory motor skills were taken as evidence of intellectual potency based upon two arguments. With antecedents in the works of John Locke and David Hume, among others, it was reasoned that all knowledge of the world derived from sensation. Hence the intelligence of an individual would be foremost a function of the efficacy of the sensory apparatus.

The second argument was more empirical in nature and involved the patterns actually observed in Galton's data. Persons of obvious high intellect (those of breeding and education, clearly successful and erudite) exhibited consistently faster reaction times and sharper sensory skills, whereas those of obvious inferior intellect (those confined to jails or asylums, the poor and wretched) consistently exhibited much slower reaction times and far duller sensory skills. Galton's friend Karl Pearson provided a means of quantifying the relationship between the observational and the psychophysical with the introduction of the product moment coefficient, an index of relatedness.

Although it is possible in retrospect to offer criticisms of both Galton's methods and his reasoning, during his time his conclusions proved extremely influential and lasting in England, on the continent, and in America (where they were propagated most notably by James McKeen Cattell, a former assistant in Galton's anthropometric laboratory).

At a time when Galton was the preeminent authority on intelligence, an alternative voice was seeking to be heard in France. Alfred Binet strenuously objected to the notion that intelligence could be measured with tests of sensory and psychomotor skills, insisting instead that intelligence was a far more complicated phenomenon than Galton's scales could reflect and that more direct measures of knowledge and verbal ability were both possible and appropriate (Binet & Simon, 1905).

When the French Minister of Public Instruction commissioned Binet to develop and implement a testing program to identify the academically deficient among the children entering the public school system, Binet had his opportunity to implement his ideas concerning the measurement of intelligence. Binet devised a battery of assessment activities that tapped general fund of knowledge, verbal skills, memory, and reasoning. These activities were graduated so as to be appropriate for the various age groups and could be interpreted as an index of academic readiness. Binet himself hesitated to identify his scales as a measure of general intelligence. However, others were less reticent, and so the system of assessment that Binet devised came to be used for numerous purposes, not all of these related to academic situations, and eventually evolved into the instrument we know today as the Stanford–Binet test of intelligence.

A critical period for the testing movement came at the turn of the century when two studies were conducted and reported that appeared to undercut all of the momentum that had accrued through the efforts of Galton's American students and the introduction of the Binet scales to the United States. The first was a study by Sharp (1898–1899), conducted in Titchener's laboratory at Cornell University, which employed the Binet scales and the Galton measures with a group of students. Results showed virtually no relationship between Galton's scales and those of Binet and little association between either set of measures and academic status. Sharp's conclusions, although partially supportive of the Binet scales, were predominantly skeptical of testing in general. The second study, by Wissler (1901), employed the Galton scales with students in Cattell's lab and likewise found no significant relationship between the Galton scores and academic status.

What makes the subsequent controversy concerning the Galton and Binet measures most ironic is that in neither study were the conclusions drawn necessarily valid. In the first study, the size of the sample was seven individuals and the sampling procedure was far from random (or in any sense representative), yielding a sample comprised exclusively of graduate students. In the second study, the size of the sample also was rather small, and again the sample was extremely homogeneous with regard to academic status (being comprised this time of college students). Thus, in neither study should the results have been taken as the total negation of the validity of intelligence tests.

For a time, the testing movement was placed on the defensive; however, momentum eventually was recovered. Spearman (1904b) demonstrated that the lack of variability among the subjects in the Sharp and Wissler studies resulted in artificially depressed indices of relationship between the measures and academic indicators. Out of Spearman's work emerged the concept of restriction of range and the methodology for correction for attenuation. Nevertheless, it was Binet's work that ultimately became the bedrock of testing throughout Europe. And with such American psychologists as Kuhlmann, Goddard, Wallin, Terman, and Yerkes undertaking the task of bringing Binet's scales to the United States (Pintner & Paterson, 1925), translated versions began to appear in this country. Terman's version, which came to be known as the Stanford–Binet, eventually emerged as the accepted American version due, in large part, to the painstaking efforts of Terman to standardize and norm the instrument. It was Terman as well who popularized the term "IQ" in his 1916 scale, after Stern (1914).

The next major influence on the testing movement was World War I. For the first time, a method was needed for classifying enormous numbers of persons quickly and efficiently. Specifically, some procedure for matching enlistees and recruits with work categories was required. The most promising approach for performing such a sorting job appeared to be general intelligence. The Binet scales, which by this time had been widely adopted for research purposes in the United States, were the obvious candidate for testing. However, the method of administration, which required a one-on-one arrangement, was not suitable. A little known researcher, Otis, had devised a means of administering the Binet items in a paper-and-pencil fashion and thus provided the needed solution.

A paper-and-pencil test of general intelligence that could be used in large group testing and that preserved the validity of the measure appeared to solve the problems of the military. However, one final problem remained to be solved. Many of the army's inductees were either first generation immigrants with poor command of the English language, or persons from rural America, where illiteracy was still prevalent. These groups were not validly assessed by the instrument that had come to be referred to as Army Alpha, and thus they could not be readily classified. However, it was found that certain measures of nonverbal reasoning, which could be administered without language, did validly measure the same dimensions as were measured by Army Alpha. The group-administered nonverbal instrument came to be known as Army Beta and was routinely administered with non-English-speaking and nonreading inductees. Those people who could not be assessed validly with either the Army Alpha or Beta were given the Army Individual Performance Scale Examination (Yoakum & Yerkes, 1920).

The next significant influence on intelligence testing came when Wechsler combined the verbal tests associated with Binet and the performance tests developed during World War I (e.g., Picture Completion from the Army Beta and Picture Arrangement from the individual performance test) to produce a battery sensitive to different modes of expressing intelligence. Wechsler, who was primarily a clinician by training, believed that although intelligence was a unitary trait as suggested by Spearman, it manifested itself in diverse forms. Further, he believed that important clinical information would be obtained if a battery were available that could assess functioning differentially for verbal and nonverbal tasks.

For many years, Wechsler's instruments were eschewed in favor of the still popular Binet scales. However, this situation was reversed in time, as the clinical significance of the verbal/performance comparison came to be more fully appreciated. Acceptance was also aided by the ongoing work of Wechsler to keep his scales current and properly normed. The Binet scales, by contrast, remained largely unchanged despite the impact of technology and a rapidly changing environment on the ages at which children encounter and master certain tasks. The ultimate vindication of Wechsler's work may be the extensive body of evidence that supports the validity of a two-factor model for assessing intelligence. Since Wechsler's contribution, most of the modern history of intelligence testing has involved refinements rather than breakthroughs.

Perhaps the most puzzling aspect of the history of mental testing until the recent development of the *Kaufman Assessment Battery for Children* (K-ABC; Kaufman & Kaufman, 1983a) has been the almost total absence of theory in the formulation of measures of intelligence. At the time of the first emerging measures (Galton and Binet), it can be conceded that the psychology of intelligence was in its infancy, and no well-formulated theories of intelligence had yet emerged. Since that time, however, many developments have taken place in the understanding of human intelligence. Nevertheless, theory and research into the mechanisms of intelligence had a negligible impact on mental testing until the Kaufmans based their definition of intelligence on the theories of mental processing emerging from the neuropsychological laboratories of Sperry (1968) and Luria (1966). This assessment approach and its relevant theoretical underpinnings are treated later in this chapter. Now we will address our attention to two different avenues of intelligence theories—factor-analytic approaches (Spearman, Thurstone, Cattell-Horn, Guilford) and developmental approaches (Piaget).

FACTOR-ANALYTIC THEORIES OF INTELLIGENCE

Beginning with Galton, scientific theories have been advanced to account for the mechanisms of intelligence and the individual differences observed among persons. To provide a sense of historical continuity, as well as to serve as a basis for considering contemporary efforts at measuring and understanding human intelligence, the theoretical perspectives of Spearman, Thurstone, Horn and Cattell, Guilford, and Piaget will be reviewed in some detail.

In reaction to the studies of Sharp and Wissler noted earlier, Charles Spearman (1904b) published a paper pointing out the limitations and inconsistencies in each study and then went on to outline a general theory of intelligence (Spearman, 1904a). This was predicated on the notion that measures to assess intelligence, such as those developed by Galton and Binet, were appropriate. Spearman reasoned that, whereas on one level the various tasks called for in the diverse measures did indeed reflect unique facets of intelligence, at a higher level they all contributed to the assessment of a general factor that he took to be intelligence.

One of the most serious criticisms to emerge from both the Sharp and the Wissler studies was the finding that the separate scales of the batteries (Binet and Galton) were poorly and in some cases negatively intercorrelated. Spearman countered these criticisms by demonstrating that the phenomenon of restriction of range was responsible for the low correlation values

and reported an investigation of school achievement and sensory discrimination ability that, when corrected for attenuation, produced an astounding correlation coefficient of 1.00 (Spearman, 1904a).

Spearman's theory of intelligence (Spearman, 1927), which came to be known as a two-factor theory of intelligence, posited that each measure of intelligence would reflect two factors, a general factor that was the contribution of some unspecified mental energy to the accomplishment of the task, and a specific factor that was an inherent and unique characteristic of that particular task. Thus, within a battery of scales, the extent to which the scales were found to be interrelated would be based upon the amount of g (general factor) they possessed in common. Spearman was hesitant to identify the general factor as intelligence, but suggested that various tests and scales used for assessing intellectual abilities had this general factor in common.

Spearman's theoretical model of intelligence was far more complicated than the two-factor theory indicates. However, that aspect of the theory had the highest utility because it lent itself readily to empirical investigation. One direct implication of his theory was the law of tetrad differences (Spearman, 1927), which suggested that among any four measures of intelligence, all correlations will be positive and may be arranged hierarchically in terms of the amount of g each possesses. Thus, Spearman's theory not only provided a structure and framework for understanding intelligence; it provided a more empirical methodology for selecting scales to be included in a battery for measuring intelligence. The most serious test for Spearman's theory of intelligence came from the observation that in some cases, specific tests of ability were more closely correlated than would be predicted based upon their shared g loading. Intuitively, the reaction to such findings would be to explain the anomalies as a function of the similarity of the two measures beyond their g loading. However, if one concludes that the tests share specific (s) loadings, then the testability of the two-factor theory is lost.

It was this very problem of similarity of scales, above and beyond the shared g factor, which was predicted by the law of tetrad differences, which led Thurstone to suggest an alternative model of intelligence. Thurstone (1931) applied a statistical methodology that began with the premise that more than one factor might exist to explain the shared variance among a set of scales. This premise, in turn, stemmed from three assumptions that Thurstone made regarding the nature of mental abilities (Thurstone, 1938): (a) performance on a test of ability arose as the consequence of several fundamental abilities working together, (b) the number of fundamental abilities that would be tapped in a battery of measures would be less than the number of batteries, and (c) performance on any specific measure of ability would not depend upon the operation of all of the fundamental abilities. From Thurstone's three assumptions arose his doctrine of simple structure, which suggested that, within a battery of measures, grouping of scales would occur, such that the majority of the variance in the total battery would be explained by a smaller number of factors upon which groups of scales would load. Subsequent empirical efforts to substantiate the doctrine of simple structure led Thurstone to identify nine factors that were believed to represent primary abilities (spatial ability, perceptual ability, numerical ability, verbal relations, words, memory, induction, arithmetic reasoning, and deduction).

The apparent substantiation of two contradictory theories of intelligence—one predicated on the premise that intelligence is a unitary phenomenon, the other based upon the existence of some number of primary abilities—provided a challenge for subsequent theorists to resolve. It is instructive to note that the evidence for each theory derives from distinct methodological approaches. In the case of Spearman, it is the law of tetrad differences, which focuses upon the existence of a single superordinate g factor. With Thurstone, it is the doctrine of simple structure, which imposes a method leading to the identification of multiple factors. And, in point of fact, each of these theorists recognized the value of the other's work, although each remained steadfast to his own interpretation of the evidence. It remained the task of another theorist, Raymond B. Cattell, to attempt a reconciliation between the two great theorists.

Cattell, a student of Spearman, was interested in finding the common thread in the works of Spearman and Thurstone. Cattell proposed that although Thurstone was indeed correct in suggesting that diverse measures of ability would converge in a factor analysis to define

several dimensions that were reflective of distinct primary abilities, these factors were themselves interrelated. Horn and Cattell (1966) demonstrated that when the correlation matrix obtained from the first-order factor analysis was subjected to a further factor analysis (second-order factor analysis), the result was a further convergence of factors into a single superordinate factor. Cattell took this to be the general intelligence factor predicted by Spearman.

Cattell continued to study the abilities that were associated with intelligence. Together with Horn, he offered a theory of intelligence that attempted to model in a more dynamic fashion the development of intelligence. Specifically, Cattell and Horn suggested that each individual was possessed of a native ability, akin to the general intelligence factor described by Spearman. This served as the fundamental basis on which all subsequent skills and abilities derived. Cattell referred to this mainspring of learning as fluid intelligence (Cattell, 1963). He envisioned it to be the mechanism by which the individual confronted and solved novel problems or situations. However, as the individual mastered certain types of problems, a residue of intact skills was posited to develop. These were referred to as crystallized intelligence. Cattell (1963) offered the analogy of the coral reef, wherein fluid intelligence would be represented by the living coral organism, and the crystallized intelligence represented the inert coral structure.

Although the entirety of Horn and Cattell's theory involves considerable complexity, inasmuch as it reflects the interactive influences of personality, culture, and motivation, among others; the basic framework of fluid and crystallized intelligence is the primary emphasis of the theory (Cattell, 1971, 1979; Horn, 1970, 1976). In this theory, it is suggested that one reason for finding evidence for a single common factor for intelligence, or numerous primary abilities, was the relative absence of measures of fluid intelligence (i.e., measures that do not depend upon the by-products of intellectual activity for their indicators of ability).

One very important implication of Cattell's work involves the role of culture in influencing performance on traditional IQ measures. These measures are heavily loaded on the crystallized intelligence factor, which he suggests are directly influenced by the emphases a given culture places upon the acquisition of specific skills. As such, the findings of traditional IQ measures will confound the potential ability of the individual, which is relatively immune to the effects of culture and past learning, with an achievement-like component. Cattell distinguishes between crystallized intelligence (i.e., the ability to perform tasks that are relatively familiar) and crystallized achievement (i.e., the actual past knowledge and skills acquired). According to Cattell, this achievement-like component has been determined in part by: (a) fluid intelligence applied to past circumstances leading to crystallized intelligence, (b) the impact of culture, which selects the types of skills and abilities that will be emphasized in the learning environment, and (c) personal factors of interest and motivation. A major implication stemming from Horn and Cattell's work was that traditional IQ measures would experience problems in assessing the individual's general intelligence to the extent that fluid intelligence was undermeasured and crystallized intelligence was overmeasured in those scales.

The need for culture-free or culture-fair testing is a focal point of Horn and Cattell's theory (Cattell, 1979). A continuing issue in ability testing is that of the extent to which ability measures reflect achievement rather than some more pure form of intelligence and the extent to which ability tests should rely on achievement as a central component of intelligence.

Another aspect of Horn and Cattell's theory worthy of mention involves the dynamic nature of intelligence. Where previous theories were relatively mute on the matter of how intelligence develops, Cattell's ideas appear to parallel those of Piaget, among others, who have viewed intelligence as a process, or unfolding phenomenon. Cattell suggests that each individual initially possesses some degree of fluid intelligence, which is determined by genetic and biological factors. As the individual encounters new experiences, the fluid intelligence factor is employed, leading to learning and the acquisition of skills. The skills acquired early, in turn, become tools or aids for further learning. Thus, the generalization of skills proceeds as a combined function of the actions of fluid and crystallized intelligence. Altogether novel situations will depend upon fluid intelligence for their mastery, whereas permutations of old situations will call for either crystallized intelli-

gence, or some combination of fluid and crystallized intelligence.

The final factor-analytic theory to be considered is that of Guilford (1967, 1979). This is by far the most ambitious and encompassing, as it proposes a factor structure of intelligence that involves three dimensions (operations, content, and product). Guilford posits that there are 150 separate types of intellectual ability (1979) and that higher-order factor analyses to discover g are inappropriate. The 150 types of intelligence that Guilford's model predicts have not all been directly observed. Many are extremely unlikely to be of immediate concern to the practitioner.

Guilford derives his factors through a matrix analysis of elements of the three dimensions of intelligence. For operations, Guilford indicates that there are five: cognition, memory, divergent production, convergent production, and evaluation. In the dimension of content, which is comprised of the areas of information in which the operations are applied, there are four: figural, symbolic, semantic, and behavioral. The final dimension of abilities contains the products of operations applied to the areas of content. There are six of these: units, classes, relations, systems, transformations, and implications.

Methodologically, Guilford proceeds by first identifying, in an a priori fashion, one of the abilities from the intersection of an operation, an area of content, and a specific product, and then finding a method for operationalizing the intellectual ability that should correspond to that intersection point. Next, the measure or measures so identified are incorporated into a study along with other, previously defined ability measures, and the performances of a sample of respondents are obtained. Those results are subjected to factor analysis, and the hypothesis that the new measures are orthogonal to (uncorrelated with) the other measures is tested.

Perhaps a serious deficiency for Guilford's model to date has been the failure to demonstrate that the measures of the many discrete abilities posited in the model are truly orthogonal and, as such, do not contribute to the defining of some higher-order factors. Guilford specifically rejects the idea that the three dimensions of his structure of intellect model are hierarchically superordinate to the individual abilities found in the cells of his matrix.

Although a shift to Guilford's model as a basis for clinical or psychoeducational testing appears unlikely in the near future, certain aspects of the model should perhaps be carefully considered by test developers. Guilford's work has helped to focus attention on the complexity of mental operations, and the need to analyze the nature of tasks in terms of those operations as well as the content of the task and the manner in which the respondent will perceive and react to the task. Similarly, Guilford's work has had significant impact on the field of creativity research and has helped to clarify the relationship between creativity and intelligence. As a practical matter, attempting to operationalize all aspects of Guilford's model simultaneously in a single assessment battery would result in an unwieldy instrument. Attempts to apply Guilford's theory do exist (Meeker, Mestyanek, Shadduck, & Meeker, 1975; Torrance, 1974), underscoring the value of the theory.

PIAGET'S DEVELOPMENTAL THEORY OF INTELLIGENCE

With the exception of Horn and Cattell's work, most other theories of intelligence do not adequately address the matter of development of intellectual functioning. In part, this problem may stem from the relatively nebulous status of intelligence as a general and pervasive trait or attribute. It also may be due to the considerable difficulty associated with conducting the longitudinal research needed to study the development of intelligence over time. Finally, it should be recognized that for most of the history of theories of intelligence, the role of biology and genetics has been prominent in explaining both the trait and individual differences in the population on that trait. Going back as far as Galton (or even Plato), the premise that intelligence was primarily a function of genetics has been either implicitly or explicitly embraced by most theories of intelligence. From such a frame of reference, it is plausible to assume that the potential for learning and achievement, which is usually at the center of most theories of intelligence, exists in some relatively immutable form from birth. Its manifestation over time is little more than a direct consequence of acquiring the necessary skills for expressing that native intelligence. Thus, the focus of a theory of intelligence would not be on the development of

intelligence but rather on its nature and constitution.

Interestingly, the testing movement would seem to have given credence to such a model of intelligence in a somewhat indirect fashion. As Binet approached the problem of identifying those students who would have difficulty in school, he recognized that changes in the curriculum with age would make a single battery of tests for use with students of all ages inappropriate. Therefore he varied the tasks to correspond to the age of the student. Later, as results of the battery were interpreted, comparisons of individual scores to the typical score for students of that age led to the expression of the score in terms of mental age. Because raw scores were compared to a norm for the appropriate age group, the impression is given that intelligence is a relatively stable and unchanging trait.

The impact of the environmentalist–behaviorist perspective applied to intelligence was to suggest that intelligence was a cumulative phenomenon, influenced greatly by the environment within which the child grew. A more sophisticated model might suggest that, during certain stages of development, rapid changes in intellectual ability were manifested, due in part to physiological maturation and in part to a broader exposure to stimulation in the environment. Nevertheless, it took the work of Piaget and his colleagues, spanning more than half a century from the early 1920s to the 1970s, to formulate a theory of cognitive development that presented in a rational and well-organized fashion the stages and sequence for the development of intellectual ability (see for example, Piaget & Inhelder, 1969). Perhaps as important as the notion of stages of cognitive development proved to be, the strength of Piaget's work lies in the identification of a process whereby the development takes place.

A brief review of the stages of cognitive development and the mechanisms that Piaget offers to explain that development follows. For a more formal treatment of the theory, several excellent sources including the work of Piaget and Inhelder are recommended (Flavell, 1963; Gallagher & Easley, 1978; Neimark, 1975a; Piaget & Inhelder, 1969).

First, Piaget identifies the problem of cognitive development as one of genetic epistemology (an accounting of how knowledge accrues which emphasizes the role of the biological structure and modifications in that structure). Piaget's formal training was in biology, and it was in that context that he began to theorize on the mechanisms of change in the organism that accompanied changing demands from the environment. When he turned his attention to the understanding of cognitive development, he found what he believed to be qualitative changes occurring over the course of development, which could not be entirely explained as a function of cumulative experience. Piaget posited that in some fashion the human organism must possess a mechanism for adapting to the changing demands of the environment. He further suggested that this adaptation process occurred in an orderly sequence in which the organism modified its behavior to adapt itself to the environment commensurate with the biologically determined capabilities of the organism at any particular point in its developmental history.

Thus, the theory indicates that certain adaptations will not occur until the cognitive structure for those adaptations has developed. This notion leads to a stage model of development in which the organism experiences both qualitative and quantitative changes over time. Within a given stage, a consolidation process is taking place in which as much mastery of the environment takes place as the existing structure will allow. Movement to a higher stage requires both experience and maturation.

The two mechanisms that Piaget identified as responsible for development were assimilation and accommodation. The fundamental drive of the organism is to achieve what Piaget refers to as equilibration. This is a homeostatic-like function in which the organism strives to achieve a balance between the demands placed on it by the environment and the skills or schema that it must acquire to address those demands. Assimilation is the process whereby new demands are met using the existing schema. This process may be entirely successful, broadening the range of situations that the organism is capable of mastering, or it may be partially successful if the match between the demand and the schema is a poor one. The result of an increasing discrepancy between demands and schema may be accommodation, as new schema are required to successfully deal with those demands. Accommodation then is a process in which new or significantly modified existing schema emerge in response to the demands of the environment.

Piaget identifies three major stages of cognitive development (four, if one treats preoperations and concrete operations as separate stages). He indicates that each stage involves qualitatively different modes of reasoning. The first stage, which characterizes the behavior of the newborn infant, is the *sensory-motor period*. During this phase, the infant engages in patterns of behavior that are significantly influenced by reflex. These behavior routines, referred to as schema, are applied to all aspects of the environment in an initially indiscriminant fashion. Thus the sucking schema, which is very adaptive in securing milk if a breast or bottle is in the vicinity, is less useful when applied to other objects, such as toys, blanket, fingers, or toes. Nevertheless, the behavior is repeated, and, through the repetition, the infant learns about the environment (albeit in a relatively unsophisticated fashion). The importance of such simple learning should not be overlooked, however. It is the development of increasingly efficient schema that allows the infant to explore the immediate environment. By the end of the sensory-motor period, the infant will have developed perceptual and learning skills (e.g., the important object concept) adequate to deal with the immediate environment. However, the accomplishments of this stage are something less than true thinking, in the sense that thinking involves symbolic manipulations or operations.

Following the sensory-motor period, which is usually viewed as extending through the 2nd year of life, the child enters a period in which mental operations are first manifested and develop. This period, referred to as the *concrete operations stage*, is divided into a preoperational subperiod and a true concrete operations subperiod. During the preoperational phase, mental operations will not have appeared. However, skills in imagery and symbolization will develop through the customary activities of children of this age (2–7 years, approximately), including play and make-believe, drawing, and other similar activities. In this way, the groundwork is laid for the onset of the earliest mental operations. During the second phase, the concrete operations subperiod (approximately 7–11 years), the child begins to operate on elements of the environment symbolically. This concrete operations phase is characterized by the ability to classify objects based on their properties, perform tasks of seriation (deal with the concepts of magnitude and order), and deal with problems of conservation. Whereas in the preoperational phase, the child's thought processes dealt primarily with discrete objects and individual entities, the concrete operations phase involves mental operations that deal with the properties of objects and the relations between or among them.

One of the more dramatic changes taking place during the concrete operations phase is the diminishing influence of perception on judgment. Thus, in conservation tasks, the preoperational child tends to view manipulations that alter only shape as actually altering mass or volume. The concrete operational child is more likely to arrive at a correct judgment of the effects of such alterations by overruling the perceptual in favor of the rational or conceptual conclusion. A major factor in the thinking process operating in the child confronted with a conservation task is the ability to mentally reverse the effects of the transformation so as to verify that no change of mass, volume, or number has occurred.

The last distinct stage proposed by Piaget is the *formal operations period* (11 to adulthood), which is divided into a subperiod of organization (11–15 years) and a subperiod of achievement (15 to adulthood). The distinction between the concrete operations period and the formal operations period is not as extreme as that between the sensory-motor and the concrete operations periods. The differences are found in the level of abstraction characteristic of the formal operations stage, the elements of thought (propositions, which are combinations of properties or relations according to rules), and the structure of organization.

With regard to the level of abstraction, although the concrete operational child does operate on abstractions, these derive directly from real objects and elements of the environment. In contrast, the formal operational individual is capable of dealing with a purely abstract concept, derived from propositions rather than from experience. Further, the validity of these abstractions and properties can be tested logically rather than empirically. The reasoning of the individual can thus be characterized as de-

ductive in the formal operational period as opposed to the inductive, which is more characteristic of the concrete operational period. In practice, the type of reasoning that emerges during the formal operations period permits the individual to consider and solve problems that could not actually occur in nature. (e.g., How could humans establish communications with aliens from another world?) Put more simply, the formal operations stage involves the development of the capacity to think in terms of possibilities.

The emergent structures characterizing formal operations are the combinatory structures (viewing elements of a problem in terms of their effects on one another) and the INRC structure (the rules of formal operations, Identity transformations, Negation transformations, Reciprocal transformations, and Correlative transformations). The essence of the formal operations stage boils down to the development of a capacity for dealing with the possible and an increased flexibility of thought. Piaget posits that the individual transitions from concrete to formal operations on the basis of the acquisition of reflexive abstraction.

Although Piaget's contributions have been enormously influential, many issues remain unresolved. One aspect of Piaget's work that has been criticized is the method used to make observations. Of particular concern is the matter of individual differences among children at specific stages. In a broader sense, this has been a fundamental difference in the European tradition in psychology and the Anglo–American tradition. Similarly, the pragmatic bent of the American researcher looks to adapt Piaget's ideas to quantification methods for correctly identifying the stage of development of specific children. This is typically for the purpose of matching instructional efforts to the child's needs and level of development.

Yet another issue has to do with the evidence for the existence of a formal operations stage. In truth, the manner in which Piaget distinguishes the accomplishments of the later concrete stage from the formal operations stage offers the possibility of interpreting the transition as a quantitative rather than a qualitative one. However, the weight of research evidence appears to substantiate the qualitatively distinct formal operations stage (Neimark, 1975b). On the other hand, a problem for the theory as offered by

Piaget is the manner in which the formal operations stage is achieved. A significant body of evidence (Blasi & Hoeffel, 1974; Lawson & Blake, 1976; Lawson & Renner, 1974, 1975) has indicated that a substantial segment of the population does not appear to evidence the skills and insights characteristic of this stage of development. Reasons offered have included the suggestion that the tasks typically employed to assess the attainment of formal operations are often drawn from the physical sciences and involve materials and operations that are unfamiliar to most adolescents and even adults. Another explanation offered is that the attainment of formal operations is a very broad-based phenomenon for which consolidation may occur slowly.

In two studies (Danner & Day, 1977; Stone & Day, 1978), it was demonstrated that although many adolescents were unable to spontaneously produce solutions to formal operations problems, they did succeed in adopting and using appropriate strategies when given prompts. These studies lead to a further explanation to the effect that, early in the formal operations stage, many adolescents may be able to correctly solve formal operations problems without being able to articulate the principles or operations leading to the solution (e.g., isolation of variables). Inasmuch as some measures of formal operations attainment require the respondent to solve the problem and to state the general strategy leading to the solution, this lack of ability to articulate strategies may have led to the improper classification of students as concrete.

Piaget (1972) attempted to reconcile some of the apparently discrepant evidence that had come from studies in the United States by suggesting that the potential for formal reasoning manifested itself at a specific stage, but that the potential might not necessarily be realized where opportunity or appropriate experiences were not available. He recognized that his Geneva subjects were relatively atypical in being from upperclass and privileged homes. He offered the hypothesis that

> All normal subjects attain the stage of formal operations or structuring if not between 11–12 to 14–15 years, in any case between 15 and 20 years. However, they reach this stage in different areas according to their aptitudes and their professional specializations . . . the way in which these formal structures are used, however is not necessarily the same in all cases. (Piaget, 1972, pp.9-10)

At the heart of the problem of identifying individuals as concrete versus formal is the issue of measuring attainment of formal operations. Representing an extreme position are those researchers who refer to themselves as "constructivists" and who argue that no one-to-one correspondence exists between formal operations attainment and specific behaviors. Therefore, attempts to measure formal operations attainment are forever doomed to failure (Emerick & Easley, 1978).

In an impressive attempt at meta-analysis of research focused on formal operations and adolescent thinking, Nagy and Griffiths (1982) lament the lack of methodological rigor and theoretical consistency characteristic of the vast majority of the research they reviewed. Problems encountered included inappropriately small samples, inconsistency in interpreting the results of tests of formal reasoning, and failure to address basic questions of reliability and validity. Rather than conducting the proposed meta-analysis, the authors classifed the types of flaws and consequences of poor methodology, concluding that little of the existing research has contributed useful information to the understanding of adolescent thinking. As an avenue to better understanding the educational status and needs of students, Nagy and Griffith (1982) concluded that little evidence existed for the use of the concept of formal operations and the various measures thereof. However, they did end on a hopeful note by suggesting that some very promising directions for further research had been identified (Case, 1978; Shayer, Adey, & Wylam, 1981; Shayer & Wharry, 1974).

Some research has been directed toward the general question of factors related to formal operational thinking. Demetriou and Efklides (1979) investigated the roles of education and sex in formal operational thinking and concluded that both were important factors. Focusing on the reasoning styles of educated and uneducated adult males and females, differences were noted between them, in favor of males, confirming other findings of sex differences (Dulit, 1972). Some researchers have suggested that what appears to be a sex difference is in reality a difference in cognitive styles (Lawson, 1975; Linn, 1978). However, Flexer and Roberge

(1983) examined the relationship between field dependence–independence and formal operational thought and concluded that performance on measures of formal thought is not significantly influenced by degree of field independence. They found that differences in performance of formal operations tasks were apparently related to field independence, but that when IQ was partialled out, the differences disappeared. Thus, the conclusion of this study was that differences in formal operations task performance were more closely related to differences in intelligence.

In another investigation of intelligence and the attainment of formal operations, Webb (1974) studied children (ages 6 to 11 years) with extremely high IQs (greater than 160), using both concrete and formal operational tasks. Webb concluded that being very bright would lead to a more rapid mastery of the variety of tasks characteristic of a given stage, but would not accelerate the transition from the concrete stage to the formal operations stage.

Concerning the role of education, Piaget originally downplayed the significance of educational experiences on the attainment of formal operational thinking. However, some research has indicated an important role for education. The earlier cited research of Demetriou and Efklides (1979) showed that educational level was significantly related to performance on formal operational tasks, with educated adults exhibiting a greater degree of formal thinking than uneducated adults. Muhs, Hooper, and Papalia-Finlay (1979–80) found a similar relationship between educational level and logical concept formation in a longitudinal study.

In the course of studying cognitive functioning as a longitudinal phenomenon, researchers have drawn several tentative conclusions about functioning beyond adolescence. Several researchers (Brabeck, 1984; Commons, Richards, & Kuhn, 1982; Kitchener, 1983; Kramer, 1983; Labouvie-Vief, 1980; Papalia & Del Vento Bielby, 1974) investigating the cognitive functioning of adults have posited the existence of a stage or stages of cognitive development beyond the formal operations stage. Postformal stages are characterized by a new form of flexibility in dealing with problems having no simple and scientific solution. They also involve an ability to work with and accept partial solutions and a relativistic frame of reference. Whether such

postformal stages exist or are merely a manifestation of consolidation within the formal operational stage is still a matter of conjecture.

The major importance of Piaget's work in this country has been due to its implications for educational practices and curriculum design. If it is true that children of various ages operate on the elements of their environment in qualitatively different ways, then designing an effective educational system would appear to require an attempt to match instructional activities to cognitive processes. Efforts to address this matter of instructional/learner match have generated some controversy, however. Piaget originally appeared to be cool to the idea that instructional activity could significantly accelerate the movement from stage to stage, and that appears to be the general consensus. Nevertheless, some investigators (Brainerd, 1978; Case & Fry, 1973) have attempted to document the efficacy of teaching strategies that result in concrete operational children dealing successfully with formal operational tasks. These isolated studies, however, do not fare well with regard to generalization of acquired skills and appear to demonstrate that a formal operational task can be mastered as a concrete one when sufficient structure is provided. What is perhaps of greater concern is the matter of instructing children in transition from the concrete to the formal stage of cognitive development. For these children, it is clear that the types of experiences encountered are important as determinants of the extent and even the likelihood that formal reasoning will develop. If this causal relationship is true, then the ability to correctly identify and differentiate concrete and formal operational thinkers is critical.

Piaget's methods involving clinical interview are extremely time-consuming and require extensive training. Thus, much research has been directed toward the development of assessment batteries based on the Piagetian tasks that can be administered more efficiently and can be administered by personnel such as classroom teachers (Lawson, 1978; Shayer et al. 1981; Staver & Gabel, 1979; Tschopp & Kurdek, 1981; Walker, Hendrix, & Mertens, 1979).

However, a more serious shortcoming of the traditional Piagetian tasks may be their reliance on physical science subject matter. It has been discovered that much individual variability exists regarding the types of formal reasoning tasks that are utilized (Demetriou & Efklides, 1979, Muhs et al., 1979-1980). Also, the specific content of the task may be critical in the success of the examinee. One useful recommendation (Kuhn & Brannock, 1977) is to develop tasks for assessing the level of operations that reflect relatively commonplace experiences or "natural experiments." This suggestion is proffered in response to the predominant use of mathematical and physical science tasks in measuring reasoning.

Another problem that has been addressed involves the role of each of the components of formal reasoning: proportional logic, control of variables, and propositional logic. Some research (Lawson & Wollman, 1981) has suggested that proportional logic may be a necessary precursor of formal operations rather than a corollary manifestation of formal reasoning.

Given the relatively brief period of serious investigations of the assessment of formal reasoning, the present degree of apparent inconsistency in findings and multiple directions being taken should not necessarily be viewed as casting doubt on the validity of the efforts. Attempting to understand a very pervasive but unobservable phenomenon will be trying and will lead to many partial answers before more encompassing perspectives become possible. This has been true of research into the mechanisms of intelligence as well as the development of cognitive functioning.

CLINICAL ASSESSMENT OF INTELLIGENCE

As noted earlier, intelligence testing and theories of intelligence, although related, have not influenced one another in a symmetrical fashion. That is, although logic might suggest that measuring intelligence would necessitate first postulating and producing empirical evidence in support of a theory of intelligence, in fact the most popular and widely used measures of intelligence, the Stanford–Binet and the Wechsler scales, are not theory-based. Nevertheless, they have exerted an influence on the development of theory. As Boring (1923) contended, in the absence of any consensus as to what intelligence actually is, intelligence is best defined as what intelligence tests measure.

What then has served to sustain the popularity of these intelligence measures? Perhaps it is

simply that they do what they were originally developed to do—they predict academic achievement so well. But more significantly, it may be that psychologists, who are the primary users of intelligence tests, view these tests as direct measures of mental functioning. In any case, intelligence tests are employed extensively for purposes other than predicting academic achievement. Many of these uses in some sense involve the clinical assessment of intellectual functioning.

As a clinical instrument, the Stanford–Binet is of limited value inasmuch as it yields only one global estimate of intellectual functioning. The Wechsler scales have gained popularity as clinical instruments primarily as a consequence of the verbal/performance comparisons possible with those scales and the profile of 10 to 12 scores in separate tasks that is yielded by an administration of a complete Wechsler battery. David Wechsler did not intend to suggest that there were two types of intelligence when he introduced the Wechsler–Bellevue, precursor to the present day instruments, which featured the verbal/performance dichotomy and subscores. Rather, he meant to improve on the existing methodology for assessing intelligence, which placed undue emphasis on verbal skills. By incorporating performance tasks in equal measure, Wechsler recognized that different individuals could manifest their intelligence in different ways.

Meanwhile, research into the effects of known amounts and locations of brain injury led to the discovery that consistent discrepancies between verbal and performance scores on the Wechsler scales seemed to be associated with the nature and location of the brain injury. Two important implications derive from the research into effects of brain injury. First, it may be posited that specific mental functions are localized in identifiable areas of the brain. Second, it might be possible to interpret observed discrepancies between verbal and performance scores as evidence of actual differences in brain functioning. This would be of clinical value in assessing overall intellectual functioning. However, the research in this important area has proved to be confusing and occasionally contradictory (Matarazzo, 1972; Todd, Coolidge, & Satz, 1977).

Finally, extensive factor-analytic research using data from the Wechsler scales (Gutkin &

Reynolds, 1981; Kaufman, 1975; Swerdlik & Schweitzer, 1978; Van Hagen & Kaufman, 1975) has confirmed the existence of verbal and perceptual organization factors in the instruments for a wide range of populations. However, this evidence is tempered by the recognition that the subtests nominally identified as Verbal and Performance by Wechsler do not load in the expected fashion on the verbal and perceptual organization factors. Moreover, a third factor, freedom from distractibility, almost always emerges from the analysis of the Wechsler Intelligence Scale for Children-Revised (WISC-R) and often is observed in analyses of the other Wechsler scales (except for the Wechsler Preschool and Primary Scale of Intelligence (WPPSI), the preschool battery).

The fact that the Wechsler scales were developed independent of any single theory of intelligence may actually have served to broaden the value and usefulness of the instruments, because the information they yield about the intellectual functioning of the individual has been interpreted with success from most contemporary theoretical perspectives (Kaufman, 1979). However, significant advances have occurred in two areas of research, neuropsychology and cognitive psychology, that have served to date the traditional tests of intelligence.

In the area of neuropsychology, the work of Bogen (1969), Sperry (1968), Luria (1966, 1970), and Gazzaniga (1970) has proven invaluable in understanding the manner in which the brain functions and is integrated in those functions. Beginning with Sperry's split-brain studies, it has become evident that the brain functions in two distinct modalities. One is characterized by a sequential processing of information, and the other employs a more simultaneous processing of information. Although it has been suggested that this dichotomy represents a left brain-right brain functioning (Bogen, 1969; Sperry, 1968), Luria and his followers have offered evidence that the division may be more of a front-back split. What is of greater importance is that all of the research to date has converged on the conclusion that these two distinct methods of processing information exist and seem to operate in all individuals.

At first, it was believed that the basis for a distinction in brain function centered on the nature of the stimulus presented. That is, the left hemisphere was lateralized for verbal material, and the right hemisphere was adept at handling nonverbal stimuli. More recently, recognition has developed that the nature of the stimulus is of less consequence than the manner in which it is processed, either sequentially or simultaneously (Levy, 1972). Thus, the route for correct problem-solving may well be determined by the goal to be achieved rather than the type of information presented.

The other area of experimentation that has converged nicely with neuropsychological research is cognitive psychology, specifically information-processing theory (Das, 1973; Das, Kirby, & Jarman, 1979; Estes, 1976: Neisser, 1967; Resnick & Glaser, 1976; Sternberg, 1979). Much of the work in this field has focused on models of cognitive functioning. Many of these models feature two processing modes, such as parallel–serial or multiple–sequential. Finally, and perhaps of greatest significance to the assessment of cognitive functioning, it has been recognized that both processing modes will operate in an integrated fashion under normal circumstances (Galin, 1976).

As a clinical tool, intelligence tests have been employed most often with populations characterized by dysfunction of some sort, either as a means of confirming or disconfirming the hypothesis of dysfunction or as a mechanism for attempting to identify the source of the dysfunction. Such uses are static in that they fail to produce usable hypotheses for intervening in such a way as to defeat the prediction of future limitations due to the present dysfunction. What follows is a brief description of one approach to clinical assessment that has come to be known as "intelligent testing." A more detailed treatment may be found in Kaufman (1979) and Kaufman and Reynolds (1983).

Events of the past decade have placed significant new demands on psychologists utilizing intelligence tests. From one side come repeated calls for the abolition of testing because of abuses and questions of bias. From another direction, psychologists often are obliged to operate under unrealistic administrative rules governing placement and diagnostic decisions, rules that may serve to overemphasize the role of testing while ignoring the inherent limitations all tests possess. The conscientious practitioner must attempt to define some middle ground on which to build a reasonable and defensible use of test information. This requires the tester to be keenly aware of the strengths and limitations of the instruments employed, to use tests only for the purpose for which they were designed, and to base clinical assessments on all of the information available, not just test information. Thus, the tester assumes the role of detective and scientist. Further, the method of the tester is the development and testing of hypotheses, with the role of the test being primarily that of a tool.

To begin with, the clinical practitioner must be fully cognizant of the many theories of intelligence, cognitive functioning, and intellectual dysfunction and their implications for individual behavior and dysfunction. Having a single orientation will hamper the investigator in exploring all possible hypotheses with regard to the performance of the client. Second, the test administrator must be trained in clinical observation techniques to provide a source of valuable diagnostic information that will supplement the results of the test or tests administered. Naturally, the test administrator must be fully trained in the administration and scoring of the tests employed and must possess a breadth of training that encompasses many tests. Finally, the test administrator must be adept at interpreting the information yielded by the tests in the context of behavioral observations and background information.

These interpretations must transcend mere labeling, however. The findings of a clinical assessment must lead to some intervention that will benefit the client. Also, they must be sufficiently specific to suggest intervention strategies. Clearly, tests that yield a single piece of information (total score) are poorly suited to this task. As noted earlier, the factor-analytic research into the underlying dimensions of the Wechsler scales has revealed a legitimate structure that can and should be subjected to investigation as circumstances warrant.

One of the difficulties in clinical assessment is the initial identification of those persons needing in-depth evaluation. Particularly in the educational setting, the problem of screening is an important one. Because the process of full-scale assessment (often with multiple measures) and interviews is time-consuming and expensive, many attempts have been made to develop shortcuts to the assessment process. One of the more unfortunate shortcuts has been the introduction of brief (and often poorly normed or unidimensional) instruments that purport to be measures of intelligence. The variability in psychometric qualities of these tests is considerable. Often their use is both indiscriminate and inappropriate.

A preferred strategy for clinical screening involves the administration of selected subtests of an accepted measure of intelligence such as WISC-R. Research by Kaufman (1976) has indicated that using two Verbal subtests (Arithmetic, Vocabulary) and two Performance subtests (Block Design, Picture Arrangement) will typically yield valid indicators of intellectual functioning. Other researchers (Jeffrey & Jeffrey, 1984; Ryan, Larsen, & Prifitera, 1983) have investigated other permutations of the Wechsler subtests as short forms, usually resulting in some evidence for their use as screening instruments.

The greatest value in using selected subtests of the Wechsler scales as screening instruments is that where the screening reveals potential deficiencies, the remainder of the subtests can be administered to generate the full scale scores for the individual. When screening has revealed areas of suspected deficiency, the investigator should proceed on the assumption that the deficiencies do exist and are not a function of test error. Although short forms suffer in the area of reliability compared to the full scale forms, it usually is wise to err in the direction of assuming that test evidence of a deficiency is valid. The investigator may increase slightly the number of normally functioning individuals who are given full scale assessments, but he or she can ensure that nearly all individuals with impaired functioning are detected and fully assessed. When screening has resulted in a tentative identification of the individual as being in need of further testing, more comprehensive instruments should be administered. The most popular measures of intellectual functioning at present are the Wechsler scales.

The rationale on which the Wechsler scales are predicated serves as a useful vehicle for their interpretation. In the tradition of Spearman, Wechsler intended that the batteries be used as a stable and valid indicator of general intellectual functioning. On the other hand, the tasks are divided into verbal and performance measures, and differences in the VIQ and the PIQ may be noted. Such differences, in and of themselves, may be relatively insignificant, and attempts to impose clinical interpretations on small verbal/performance differences are inappropriate. Only when differences achieve statistical significance should the clinician be inclined to interpret those differences. Moreover, the prepared clinician will have become familiarized with base-rate data concerning the prevalence of differences within the normal population.

For too long it was unrecognized that differences of statistically significant dimensions existed within the general population, rendering clinical diagnoses of brain dysfunction or similar pathology inappropriate and certainly premature. Great care must be taken in interpreting such differences when significant, because the existence of the difference may imply a preference for one modality of reasoning, without necessarily involving organic or functional impairment. If significant differences exist between verbal and performance scales, the investigator is justified in exploring possible sources for the observed difference. Inasmuch as the verbal and performance scales are each comprised of several different measures, there may naturally arise a temptation to engage in some form of profile analysis in an attempt to identify which specific tasks account for the observed discrepancies.

There are two compelling reasons for caution in interpreting profiles. The separate verbal and performance subtests are not distinct measures of intelligence, but are found to share a great deal of common variance, as revealed in correlational and factor analytic studies. Further, constructs underlying verbal and performance abilities consistently emerge as distinct, robust factors, suggesting that these two global skills, as estimated by the verbal IQ and performance IQ, should assume primacy over the separate subtests when interpreting Wechsler profiles. Thus, it would be improper to attempt to isolate single measures and attach undue importance to what they measure apart from the battery as a whole, unless such attempts are based on a rigorous statistical approach. Moreover, as was true in interpreting verbal/performance differences, knowledge of the base rate of differences of various magnitudes between and among the subtests is crucial in attempting to interpret such differences.

Research into profile scatter found among the Wechsler scales has occurred in two phases. The first phase focused on the contention that for certain subpopulations, particularly learning-disabled children, significant amounts of scatter were consistently found within profiles. (For a discussion of this practice, see Sattler, 1982.) For a time, this "discovery" was heralded as a major breakthrough in the diagnosis of learning-disabled children and offered much promise for linking the condition to specific deficits originating in differential brain functioning. The second phase of research served to put the existence of profile scatter in perspective. These studies found that although significant scatter was found in the profiles of learning-disabled children, it also characterized a significant proportion of all profiles examined in the normal population (Kaufman, 1976; Reynolds & Gutkin, 1981). However, the existence of scatter can have clinical implications and, if interpreted with care, can contribute to the clinician's overall understanding of the client's intellectual functioning.

In assessing strengths and weaknesses in the examinee's performance, the clinician should consider the extent to which individual subtests deviate from the mean of all subtests for that scale (verbal or performance). This ipsative approach to analyzing profiles reduces the risk of overinterpreting differences, while permitting more meaningful analyses of differences relative to the level of functioning of the individual. After determining a person's significant strengths and weaknesses, the scatter in his or her profile can be examined (e.g., by counting the *number* of subtests deviating significantly from the person's own mean score, or the *range*, from the lowest to the highest subtest score). However, these indexes of scatter will only have meaning when they are compared to the indexes of scatter that characterize the normal population. No diagnosis of an abnormality should be based wholly or primarily on an amount of scatter that is within the normal range.

Employing a hierarchical approach to test interpretation, in which examination of more specific test performances is predicated on the existence of significant discrepancies between or among the superordinate components of the battery, leads the clinician toward a valid and objective assessment of the examinee's functioning. However, this approach can and should be supplemented by the externally generated information from behavioral observations conducted during testing and other forms of background information. In the case of a client referred for testing who shows little evidence of impairment in test performances, the question remains as to what might account for the behaviors or symptoms that led to referral. The thorough clinician is not going to be content with negative findings and a simple report to the effect that the intellectual functioning of the individual is within normal limits. Rather, this clinical investigator is going to attempt to generate hypotheses in which the test results as well as the background information are reconciled in some fashion which can, in turn, lead to effective intervention strategies.

As was mentioned earlier, many of the advances in cognitive psychology and neuropsychology are not reflected in the traditional measures of intelligence. More recently, a new assessment battery of intellectual functioning for children has been developed that attempts to incorporate some of the more promising new findings in these two fields. This instrument is the Kaufman Assessment Battery for Children (K-ABC; Kaufman & Kaufman, 1983a, 1983b), which is appropriate for children ages 2¹/₂ to 12 years. It was developed around the ideas of Sperry (1968) and other cerebral specialization researchers and the ideas of Luria (1966) as articulated by Das (1973, 1980) and Das, Kirby, and Jarman (1979). The theory of intelligence proposed by Horn and Cattell (1966) also relates to the organization of the K-ABC. From Luria, Sperry, and Das, the authors of the K-ABC have incorporated the concept of a simultaneous/sequential processing dichotomy.

The factor-analysis work conducted with the Wechsler scales served as an early indicator of the importance of this dual processing concept. Indeed, the loadings of individual subtests onto two of the three major factors (Perceptual Organization and Freedom from Distractibility) strongly suggested that, in fact, the common elements of the emergent factors were distinct patterns of processing. Yet, despite the suggestive evidence provided by these analyses, the Wechsler scales as published cannot truly serve as proper measures of the two modes of mental processing. This is because the subtests were developed to assess different skills and therefore only incidentally reflect simultaneous/sequential processing.

The other major theory influencing the development of the K-ABC is the work of Horn and Cattell described earlier. The fluid/crystallized

dichotomy is the underlying concept of the theory. This is manifested in the K-ABC by the separation of achievement scales from mental processing scales. The distinction between the two types of subtests rests upon the extent to which past achievement influences performances in each case and upon the degree to which the nature of the tasks is "culturally loaded."

To minimize the effects of culture and past experience, the mental processing or intelligence subtests have been developed to minimize the role of language, which has been shown to introduce a strong cultural influence in performance. The examinee is taught the procedure underlying each subtest during an unscored sample item and during the first two test items administered. The K-ABC may be unique as a global and comprehensive measure of intellectual functioning in that it is theory-based and thoroughly founded on careful psychometric research. One positive outcome of the various efforts to obtain fairer assessment of children on the K-ABC is the reduction, by about one half, of the traditional one standard deviation difference in the IQs earned by whites and blacks. This reduction was accomplished *without* a concomitant decrease in the validity of the K-ABC Mental Processing Scales as a predictor of academic achievement (Kaufman & Kaufman, 1983b).

With specific reference to the assessment of adolescent and adult intelligence, the development of measuring systems that take into full account prevailing theories of development and cognition has been slow. One advantage that the Stanford–Binet has enjoyed over the years is its applicability to a wide range of test-takers, including adults (although Form L–M of the Binet was not normed above 18 years). However, the Stanford–Binet does not necessarily provide appropriate tasks to measure aspects of intelligence beyond academic intelligence.

The Wechsler scales for adults have two primary liabilities in this same context. First, the nature of the tasks is substantially the same as that of the tasks on the children's scales. Second, the breaking point (age 16) for the two scales (WISC-R and Wechsler Adult Intelligence Scale-Revised, or WAIS-R) is not particularly well-founded in any theory. Until recently, another criticism of the WAIS was its failure to provide a revised version that would reflect advances in theory and practice, as well as address changes in norms. The WAIS-R was published in 1981; although it does provide new and generally excellent norms, it otherwise does not reflect theoretical or clinical advances (Kaufman, 1983).

Since the publication of the WAIS-R, there has been a growing body of literature concerning its psychometric properties. Inasmuch as the WAIS had been thoroughly examined for the factor validity of the verbal/performance dichotomy, it is not surprising that much of the current research on the WAIS-R also investigates the factor structure of the new instrument, with particular interest in its factor stability. Most researchers investigating the factor structure of the WAIS-R (Gutkin, Reynolds, & Galvin, 1984; Naglieri & Kaufman, 1983; Parker, 1983) have concluded that the existence of either two or three factors can be reasonably supported. These are typically defined as verbal comprehension, perceptual organization, and, in the case of a three-factor solution, freedom from distractibility. However, it is noteworthy that other factor solutions may be obtained (Naglieri & Kaufman, 1983) depending on techniques selected and decision rules applied. In interpreting WAIS-R results, consideration should be given to which factor solution (two, three, or even four factors) provides the best possible explanation of the test data for a given individual.

The other principal area of investigation has involved the degree of convergence between the WAIS and the WAIS-R (Feingold, 1984; Lippold & Claiborn, 1983; Smith, 1983). In these studies, the general conclusion has been that the revised form closely parallels the original WAIS.

FUTURE DIRECTIONS IN THE STUDY OF INTELLIGENCE

What is lacking in currently available measures of adolescent and adult intelligence is a theoretical base that integrates important dimensions of human intelligence and cognitive processing that have come to light during the past decade. Two areas in particular should be addressed in efforts to more appropriately assess adolescent and adult intelligence. First, such measures should reflect the qualitative changes in cognition that distinguish the child from the adolescent (concrete vs. formal opera-

tions in Piaget's model). Second, such measures should address the component of planning as a significant aspect of intelligent behavior.

Research on the relationship between Piagetian assessment scales and traditional measures of intelligence generally have revealed positive but moderate correlations between the two (Humphreys & Parsons, 1979; Webb, 1974). Some investigators (Humphreys & Parsons, 1979) have suggested that a mixture of traditional and Piagetian measures would provide a broader and more meaningful picture with regard to mental functioning than either taken separately. Recognition that important distinctions exist between the ways that children and adults reason should lead to more appropriate measures of cognitive functioning.

Concerning the dimension of planning, several investigators (Ashman, 1979; Atkinson & Shiffrin, 1968; Das, 1980; Das, Kirby, & Jarman, 1979) have studied the role of planning in purposive, goal-directed behavior and have established the centrality of this concept to understanding intelligent behavior. From a theoretical point of view, incorporating a planning dimension within the assessment of the intelligence of individuals who have entered the stage of formal operations is necessary, as planning stands as an important component of overall cognitive functioning.

Many of the important developments of the recent past in the area of intelligence and cognitive functioning have arisen from the work of neuropsychologists investigating the anatomy and physiology of the brain. Future developments will doubtless involve increased understanding of the physiology of intelligence. Research efforts directed toward developing a model of brain function will continue, assisted by such technological tools as CAT and PET scans. In particular, positron-emission technology has produced a crude but promising method for mapping brain function. As in the past, neuropsychological research into effects of specific and localized brain damage will assist in these same efforts.

The question of developmental changes in intellectual potency in the later adult years is one that has engendered a great deal of controversy over the past 15–20 years. The importance of the question grows as the U.S. population becomes an older one. The traditional view, based primarily on trend curves obtained from cross-sectional analyses of such instruments as the WAIS, holds that following late adolescence the intellectual function, as represented by a graph line, first plateaus and then declines in the later years. Interpretations of these trends have differed, however. Some have suggested that a true developmental trend is evidenced. Others have suggested that this represents a relatively invariant effect of aging (i.e., neurological impairment, loss of adequate vascularization of brain tissues).

More recently, however, the interpretation of intellectual decline data has tended to split into two camps. On the one hand, Horn (1970) has suggested that the important distinction drawn between fluid and crystallized intelligence in his writing serves as a conceptual tool for understanding decline in intellectual functioning. Specifically, fluid intelligence, which is determined largely by biological and genetic factors, is seen to suffer a significant decline in the later years of adulthood. Crystallized intelligence, representing many functions that have been generalized and reinforced throughout adulthood and typically are still being called on frequently, remains relatively unaffected by age. It is important to note that Horn does not dismiss the factors of health and neurological status as influential, but rather views these as typically concomitant with aging. Other researchers (Baltes & Schaie, 1976; Botwinick & Siegler, 1980; Labouvie-Vief, 1977; Schaie, 1965, 1972, 1979; Schaie & Hertzog, 1983) have suggested that evidence of intellectual decline can be explained better by reference to cohort differences in cross-sectional studies and the effects of history (specifically disease and injury effects) in longitudinal research. Attempts have been made to conduct cross-sequential investigations which are designed to minimize the artifactual influences of cohort differences. At present, no single methodology appears capable of overcoming all significant shortcomings. For this reason, the differences in interpretation may remain unresolved for some time. What is of significance is the interest in this important area and the continued efforts at overcoming the methodological problems of the past.

It may be cautiously suggested that developments of the recent past in both theories of intelligence and the measurement of intelligence will serve as powerful springboards for future research and test development. Perhaps the most important development of the near future will be an increased integration of findings and theorizing from previously disparate and independent fields of study.

SUMMARY

The past and present efforts to define and measure intelligence and research directed at substantiating the various theories of intelligence have generated much controversy. Beginning with Galton, the assessment of intelligence has evolved to its present state with an emphasis on cognitive processes. Given the extensive use of intelligence tests in this society, the clinical practitioner must be vigilant to their proper use and interpretation. Today's theories and models of intelligence can be traced to the work of Spearman and Thurstone, and the theories of Horn and Cattell and Guilford continue to influence research and measurement in intelligence. However, Piaget's extensive contributions serve as the major theoretical influence in studying cognitive development. Although certain issues remain unresolved, this theory continues to be vital and productive.

In the future, more attention should be directed toward a better understanding of the changes in cognitive development that accompany the arrival of adulthood and old age. Advances in neuropsychology and information-processing theories will continue to influence the understanding of intellectual growth and the theories and measurement of intelligence.

REFERENCES

Ashman, A. F. (1979). Planning—the integrative function of the brain: Empirical evidence and speculation. *Educational Enquiry, 2*, 78–94.

Atkinson, R. C., & Shiffrin, R. M. (1968). Human memory: A proposed system and its control processes. In K. W. Spence & J. T. Spence (Eds.), *The psychology of learning and motivation* (Vol. 2, pp. 89–195). New York: Academic.

Baltes, P. B., & Schaie, K. W. (1976). On the plasticity of intelligence in adulthood and old age: Where Horn and Donaldson fail. *American Psychologist, 31*, 720–725.

Binet, A., & Simon, T. (1905). Methodes nouvelles pour le diagnostic du niveau intellectuel des anormaux [New methods for diagnosing the intelligence standards of abnormals]. *L'Annee Psychologique, 11*, 191–244.

Blasi, A., & Hoeffel, E. C. (1974). Adolescence and

formal operations. *Human Development, 17*, 344–363.

Bogen, J. E. (1969). The other side of the brain: Parts I, II, and III. *Bulletin of the Los Angeles Neurological Society, 34*, 73–105, 135–162, 191–203.

Boring, E. G. (1923, June 6). Intelligence as the tests test it. *The New Republic*, pp. 35–37.

Botwinick, J., & Siegler, I. C. (1980). Intellectual ability among the elderly: Simultaneous cross-sectional and longitudinal comparisons. *Developmental Psychology, 16* (1), 49–53.

Brabeck, M. M. (1984). Longitudinal studies of intellectual development during adulthood: Theoretical and research models. *Journal of Research and Development in Education, 17* (3), 12–27.

Brainerd, C. J. (1978). Learning research and Piagetian theory. In L. S. Siegel & C. J. Brainerd (Eds.), *Alternatives to Piaget* (pp. 69–109). New York: Academic.

Case, R. (1978). A developmentally-based theory and technology of instruction. *Review of Educational Research, 48*, 439–463.

Case, R., & Fry, C. (1973). Evaluation of an attempt to teach scientific inquiry and criticism in a working-class high school. *Journal of Research in Science Teaching,14*, 135–142.

Cattell, R. B. (1963). Theory of fluid and crystallized intelligence: A critical experiment. *Journal of Educational Psychology, 54*, 1–22.

Cattell, R. B. (1971). *Abilities: Their structure, growth, and action.* Boston: Houghton Mifflin.

Cattell, R. B. (1979). Are culture-fair intelligence tests possible and necessary? *Journal of Research and Development in Education, 12* (2), 3–13.

Commons, M. L., Richards, F. A., & Kuhn, D. (1982). Case for levels of reasoning beyond Piaget's stage of formal operations. *Child Development, 53*, 1058–1069.

Danner, F. W., & Day, M. C. (1977). Eliciting formal operations. *Child Development, 48*, 1600–1606.

Das, J. P. (1973). Structure of cognitive abilities: Evidence for simultaneous and successive processing. *Journal of Educational Psychology, 65*, 103–108.

Das, J. P. (1980). Planning: Theoretical considerations and empirical evidence. *Psychological Research, 41*, 141–151.

Das, J. P., Kirby, J., & Jarman, R. F. (1975). Simultaneous and successive syntheses: An alternative model for cognitive abilities. *Psychological Bulletin, 82*, 87–103.

Das, J. P., Kirby, J., & Jarman, R. F. (1979). *Simultaneous and successive cognitive processes.* New York: Academic.

Demetriou, A., & Efklides, A. (1979). Formal operational thinking in young adults as a function of education and sex. *International Journal of Psychology, 14*, 241–253.

Dulit, E. (1972). Adolescent thinking á la Piaget: the formal stage. *Journal of Youth and Adolescence, 1*, 281–301.

Emerick, B. B., & Easley, J. A., Jr. (1978). *A constructivist challenge to the validity of formal operations.* Paper presented at the annual meeting of the American Educational Research Association, Toronto.

Estes, W. K. (1976). Intelligence and cognitive psychology. In L. B. Resnick (Ed.), *The nature of intelligence* (pp. 295–305). Hillsdale, NJ: Erlbaum.

Feingold, A. (1984). The effects of differential age adjustment between the WAIS and WAIS-R on the comparability of the two scales. *Educational and Psychological Measurement, 44*, 569–573.

Flavell, J. H. (1963). *The developmental psychology of Jean Piaget.* New York: Van Nostrand.

Flexer, B. K., & Roberge, J. J. (1983). A longitudinal investigation of field dependence–independence and the development of formal operational thought. *British Journal of Educational Psychology, 53*, 195–204.

Gallagher, J. M., & Easley, J. A., Jr. (Eds.). (1978). *Knowledge and development: Piaget and education* (Vol. 2). New York: Plenum.

Galin, D. (1976). Educating both halves of the brain. *Childhood Education, 53*, 17–20.

Gazzaniga, M. S. (1970). *The bisected brain.* New York: Appleton-Century-Crofts.

Gould, S. J. (1981). *The mismeasure of man.* New York: Norton.

Guilford, J. P. (1967). *The nature of human intelligence.* New York: McGraw-Hill.

Guilford, J. P. (1979). Intelligence isn't what it used to be: What to do about it. *Journal of Research and Development in Education, 12* (2), 33–46.

Gutkin, T. D., & Reynolds, C. R. (1981). Factorial similarity of the WISC-R for white and black children from the standardization sample. *Journal of Educational Psychology, 73*, 227–231.

Gutkin, T. B., Reynolds, C. R., & Galvin, G. A. (1984). Factor analysis of the Wechsler Adult Intelligence Scale-Revised (WAIS-R): An examination of the standardization sample. *Journal of School Psychology, 22*, 83–93.

Horn, J. L. (1968). Organization of abilities and the development of intelligence. *Psychological Review, 75*, 242–259.

Horn, J. L. (1970). Organization of data on life-span development of human abilities. In L. R. Goulet & P. B. Baltes (Eds.), *Life-span development psychology* (pp. 423–466). New York: Academic.

Horn, J. L. (1972). The structure of intellect: Primary abilities. In R. M. Dreger (Ed.), *Multivariate personality research* (pp. 451–511). Baton Rouge: Claitor.

Horn, J. L. (1976). A review of research and theories in the early 1970's. *Annual Review of Psychology, 27*, 437–485.

Horn, J. L. (1979). The rise and fall of human abilities. *Journal of Research and Development in Education, 12* (2), 59–78.

Horn, R. B., & Cattell, R. B. (1966). Refinement and test of the theory of fluid and crystallized ability intelligences. *Journal of Educational Psychology, 57*, 253–270.

Humphreys, L. G., & Parsons, C. K. (1979). Piagetian tasks measure intelligence and intelligence tests assess cognitive development: A reanalysis. *Intelligence, 3*, 369–382.

Jeffrey, T. B., & Jeffrey, L. K. (1984). The utility of the modified WAIS in a clinical setting. *Journal of Clinical Psychology, 40*, 1067–1069.

Jensen, A. R. (1972). *Genetics and education.* London: Metheun.

Jensen, A. R. (1979). The nature of intelligence and its relation to learning. *Journal of Research and Development in Education, 12* (2), 79–95.

Jensen, A. R. (1982). The chronometry of intelligence. In R. J. Sternberg (Ed.), *Advances in the psychology of human intelligence* (Vol. 1, pp. 242–267). Hillsdale, NJ: Erlbaum.

Jensen, A. R. (1984, December). Objectivity and the genetics of I.Q.: A reply to Steven Selden. *Phi Delta Kappan,* pp. 284–286.

Kaufman, A. S. (1975). Factor analysis of the WISC-R at eleven age levels between 6½ and 16½ years. *Journal of Consulting and Clinical Psychology, 43,* 135–147.

Kaufman, A. S. (1976). A four-test short form of the WISC-R. *Contemporary Educational Psychology, 1,* 180–196.

Kaufman, A. S. (1979). *Intelligent testing with the WISC-R.* New York: Wiley-Interscience.

Kaufman, A. S. (1983). Review of Wechsler Adult Intelligence Scale-Revised. *Journal of Psychoeducational Assessment, 1,* 309–313.

Kaufman, A. S., & Kaufman, N. L. (1983a). *K-ABC administration and scoring manual.* Circle Pines, MN: American Guidance Service.

Kaufman, A. S., & Kaufman, N. L. (1983b). *K-ABC interpretive manual.* Circle Pines, MN: American Guidance Service.

Kaufman, A. S., & Reynolds, C. R. (1983). Clinical evaluation of intellectual function. In I. Weiner (Ed.), *Clinical methods in psychology* (2nd. ed., pp. 75–125). New York: Wiley-Interscience.

Kitchener, K. S. (1983). Cognition, metacognition, and epistemic cognition. *Human Development, 26,* 222–232.

Kramer, D. A. (1983). Post-formal operations? A need for further conceptualization. *Human Development, 26,* 91–105.

Kuhn, D., & Brannock, J. (1977). Development of the isolation of variables scheme in experimental and "natural experiment" contexts. *Developmental Psychology, 13,* 9–14.

Labouvie-Vief, G. (1977). Adult cognitive development: In search of alternative interpretations. *Merrill-Palmer Quarterly, 23,* 227–263.

Labouvie-Vief, G. (1980). Beyond formal operations: Uses and limits of pure logic in life-span development. *Human Development, 23,* 141–161.

Lawson, A. E. (1975). Sex differences in concrete and formal reasoning ability as measured by manipulative tasks and written tasks. *Science Education, 59,* 397–405.

Lawson, A. E. (1978). The development and validation of a classroom test of formal reasoning. *Journal of Research in Science Teaching, 15,* 11–24.

Lawson, A. E., & Blake, A. J. (1976). Concrete and formal thinking abilities in high school biology students as measured by three separate instruments. *Journal of Research in Science Teaching, 13,* 227–235.

Lawson, A. E., & Renner, J. W. (1974). A quantitative analysis of responses to Piagetian tasks and its implications for curriculum. *Science Education, 58,* 545–559.

Lawson, A. E., & Renner, J. W. (1975). Relationships

of science subject matter and developmental level of learners. *Journal of Research in Science Teaching, 12,* 347–358.

Lawson, A. E., & Wollman, W. T. (1981). Developmental level and learning to solve problems of proportionality: Discussion. *Journal of Research in Science Teaching, 18,* 385–388.

Levy, J. (1972). Lateral specialization of the human brain: Behavioral manifestations and possible evolutionary basis. In J. A. Kiger (Ed.), *Biology of behavior.* Corvallis, OR: Oregon State University Press.

Linn, M. C. (1978). Influence of cognitive style and training on tasks requiring the separation of variables schema. *Child Development, 49,* 874–877.

Lippold, S., & Claiborn, J. M. (1983). Comparison of the Wechsler Adult Intelligence Scale and the Wechsler Adult Intelligence Scale-Revised. *Journal of Consulting and Clinical Psychology, 51,* 315.

Luria, A. R. (1966). *Human brain and psychological processes.* New York: Harper & Row.

Luria, A. R. (1970). The functional organization of the brain. *Scientific American, 222,* 66–78.

Matarazzo, J. D. (1972). *Wechsler's measurement and appraisal of adult intelligence* (5th ed.). Baltimore: Williams & Wilkins.

Meeker, M. N., Mestyanek, L., Shadduck, R., & Meeker, R. (1975). *S.O.I. Learning Abilities Test.* (Available from SOI Institute, 214 Main St., El Segundo, CA)

Miller, T. L., & Reynolds, C. R. (Eds.). (1984). Special issue . . . The K-ABC. *The Journal of Special Education, 18* (3).

Muhs, P. J., Hooper, F. H., & Papalia-Finlay, D. (1979–80). Cross-sectional analysis of cognitive functioning across the life span. *International Journal of Aging and Human Development, 10,* 311–333.

Naglieri, J. A., & Kaufman, A. S. (1983). How many factors underlie the WAIS-R? *Journal of Psychoeducational Assessment, 1,* 113–119.

Nagy, P., & Griffiths, A. K. (1982). Limitations of recent research relating Piaget's theory to adolescent thought. *Review of Educational Research, 52* (4), 513–556.

Neisser, U. (1967). *Cognitive psychology.* New York: Appleton-Century-Croft.

Neimark, E. D. (1975a). Intellectual development during adolescence. In F. D. Horowitz (Ed.), *Review of child development research* (Vol. 4). Chicago: University of Chicago Press.

Neimark, E. D. (1975b). Longitudinal development of formal operations thought. *Genetic Psychology Monographs, 91,* 171–225.

Neimark, E. D. (1979). Current status of formal operations research. *Human Development, 22,* 60–67.

Papalia, D. E., & Del Vento Bielby, D. (1974). Cognitive functioning in middle and old age adults: A review of research based on Piaget's theory. *Human Development, 17,* 424–443.

Parker, K. (1983). Factor analysis of the WAIS-R at nine age levels between 16 and 74 years. *Journal of Consulting and Clinical Psychology, 51,* 302–308.

Piaget, J. (1972). Intellectual evolution from adolescence to adulthood. *Human Development, 15,* 1–12.

Piaget, J., & Inhelder, B. (1969). *The psychology of the*

child. New York: Basic Books.

Pintner, R., & Paterson, D. G. (1925). *A scale of performance tests*. New York: Appleton.

Resnick, L. B., & Glaser, R. (1976). Problem solving and intelligence. In L. B. Resnick (Ed.), *The nature of intelligence* (pp. 205–230). Hillsdale, NJ: Erlbaum.

Reynolds, C. R., & Gutkin, T. B. (1981). Test scatter on the WPPSI: Normative analyses of the standardization sample. *Journal of Learning Disabilities*. *14*, 464–467.

Ryan, J. J., Larsen, J., & Prifitera, A. (1983). Validity of two- and four-subtest short forms of the WAIS-R in a psychiatric sample. *Journal of Consulting and Clinical Psychology*, *51* (3), 460.

Sattler, J. (1982). *Assessment of children's intelligence and special abilities* (2nd ed.). Boston: Allyn & Bacon.

Schaie, K. W. (1965). A general model for the study of developmental problems. *Psychological Bulletin*, *64*, 92–107.

Schaie, K. W. (1972). Limitations on the generalizability of growth curves of intelligence: A reanalysis of some data from the Harvard growth study. *Human Development*, *15*, 141–152.

Schaie, K. W. (1979). The primary mental abilities in adulthood: An exploration in the development of psychometric intelligence. In P. B. Baltes & O. G. Brim, Jr. (Eds.), *Life-span development and behavior* (Vol. 2, pp. 67–115). New York: Academic.

Schaie, K. W., & Hertzog, C. (1983). Fourteen-year cohort-sequential analyses of adult intellectual development. *Developmental Psychology*, *9*, 531–543.

Sharp, S. E. (1898–1899). Individual psychology: A study in psychological method. *American Journal of Psychology*, *10*, 329–391.

Shayer, M., Adey, P., & Wylam, H. (1981). Group tests of cognitive development: Ideals and a realization. *Journal of Research in Science Teaching*, *18*, 157–168.

Shayer, M., & Wharry, D. (1974). Piaget in the classroom (Part I): Testing a whole class at the same time. *School Science Review*, *55*, 447–458.

Smith, R. S. (1983). A comparison study of the Wechsler Adult Intelligence Scale and the Wechsler Adult Intelligence Scale-Revised in a college population. *Journal of Consulting and Clinical Psychology*, *51*, 414–419.

Spearman, C. (1904a). General intelligence, objectively determined and measured. *American Journal of Psychology*, *15*, 201–293.

Spearman, C. (1904b). The proof and measurement of association between two things. *American Journal of Psychology*, *15*, 72–101.

Spearman, C. (1927). *The abilities of man*. New York: Macmillan.

Sperry, R. W. (1968). Hemisphere deconnection and unity in conscious awareness. *American Psychologist*, *23*, 723–733.

Staver, J. R., & Gabel, D. L. (1979). The development and construct validation of a group-administered test of formal thoughts. *Journal of Research in Science Teaching*, *16*, 535–544.

Stern, W. (1914). *The psychological methods of testing intelligence*. Baltimore: Warwick and York.

Sternberg, R. J. (1979). Intelligence research at the interface between differential and cognitive psychology: Prospects and proposals. In R. J. Sternberg & D. K. Detterman (Eds.), *Human intelligence: Perspectives on its theory and measurement* (pp. 33–60). Norwood, NJ: Ablex.

Stone, C. A. & Day, C. M. (1978). Levels of availability of a formal operational strategy. *Child Development*, *49*, 1054–65.

Swerdlik, M. E., & Schweitzer, J. (1978). A comparison of factor structures of the WISC and WISC-R. *Psychology in the Schools*, *15*, 166–172.

Thurstone, L. L. (1931). Multiple factor analysis. *Psychological Review*, *38*, 406–427.

Thurstone, L. L. (1938). *Primary mental abilities*. Chicago: The University of Chicago Press.

Todd, J., Coolidge, F., & Satz, P. (1977). The Wechsler Adult Intelligence Scale discrepancy index: A neuropsychological evaluation. *Journal of Consulting and Clinical Psychology*, *45*, 450–454.

Torrance, E. P. (1974). *Torrance Test of Creative Thinking: Directions manual and scoring guide*. Lexington, MA: Ginn.

Tschopp, J. K., & Kurdek, L. A. (1981). An assessment of the relationship between traditional and paper-and-pencil operations tasks. *Journal of Research in Science Teaching*, *18*, 87–92.

Van Hagen, J., & Kaufman, A. S. (1975). Factor analysis of the WISC-R for a group of mentally retarded children and adolescents. *Journal of Consulting and Clinical Psychology*, *43*, 661–667.

Walker, R. A., Hendrix, J. R., & Mertens, T. R. (1979). Written Piagetian task instrument: Its development and use. *Science Education*, *63*, 211–220.

Webb, R. A. (1974). Concrete and formal operations in very bright 6- to 11-year olds. *Human Development*, *17*, 292–300.

Wechsler, D. (1975). Intelligence defined and undefined. *American Psychologist*, *30* (2), 135–139.

Wissler, C. (1901). The correlation of mental and physical tests. *Psychological Review*, Monograph (Supp.), *3* (No. 6).

Yoakum, C. S., & Yerkes, R. M. (1920). *Army mental tests*. New York: Holt.

CHAPTER 13

Research Issues

Steven Beck

With any substantive content area in psychology it is often easier to identify the methodological shortcomings and gaps of theoretical and empirical direction in a given research area than it is to articulate the gains and systematic advances made in a body of research. This fact is most evident after reviewing past and current research pertaining to adolescence. Many questions concerning the adolescence phenomenon remain unanswered. Our understanding of adolescence as a distinct developmental stage pales in comparison to the amount of scientific data presently available about infants and children. As noted by Hill (1982), a doctrinaire emphasis that early basic social and cognitive processes during the first 5 years of life determined most of later development undoubtedly played a role in the previous lack of adolescent research. On a more pragmatic note, adolescence research typically was not conducted because access to this population for laboratory-based or direct observational studies were difficult to secure, as adolescents were a more mobile and difficult population "to capture" than elementary-age children. Besides, adolescents were generally viewed as too volatile and socially, cognitively, and affectively too disorganized to study.

However, due to the growth in developmental psychology, and particularly in the life-span movement, investigators are currently more likely to employ adolescents as subjects for research and to examine adolescence as a distinctive feature of the second decade of life. Three new journals, *Adolescence*, *The Journal of Early Adolescence*, and *The Journal of Youth and Adolescence*, are now published. However, articles pertaining to adolescence still are published less frequently than are studies pertaining to infants and children in *Developmental Psychology* and *Child Development*, the two most respected journals in developmental psychology.

In addition to the life-span movement in developmental psychology, Hill (1983) speculates that the increased interest in adolescence was shaped by social forces emanating from the 1960s. Due to the increased number of adolescents from the post-World War II baby boom that interacted with the social unrest and consciousness of youth that characterized the 1960s, interest began to focus on adolescent values, education, and adjustment. This trend continues, with greater emphasis on applied research and a willingness among researchers to explore some of the softer issues in the science of psychology, such as self-esteem and parent and adolescent relationships.

Because adolescence is now considered more than a way station between childhood and adulthood, advances have been made in our understanding of this stage of development. For example, the early psychoanalytic view that adolescence is considered a time of storm and stress (Hall, 1904) has been supplanted by the finding that adolescent upheaval appears related to a more continuous, persistent quality rather than to a transitory or developmental stage (Offer & Offer, 1975). In other words, turmoil is not necessarily the universal state of adolescence that is so popularized by our mass media, but instead, adolescents generally maintain their prior levels of adjustment.

This is not to suggest, however, that adolescence as a developmental stage is not associated with a variety of critical changes. In a cross-sectional survey of nearly 2,000 school children from grades 3 to 12, Simmons, Rosenberg, and Rosenberg (1973) identified early adolescents as experiencing the most difficulty with self-esteem. In addition, although it is now understood that normal adolescent development is not characterized by psychological upheaval, this age range (between 13 and 17 years of age) is associated with sharp increases in antisocial behavior, suicide attempts, drug and alcohol abuse, eating disorders, and depression (Rutter, 1980). This is also reflected in the fact that Minnesota Multiphasic Personality Inventory (MMPI) norms are required for male and female adolescents, as their profiles tend to be elevated (Marks, Seeman, & Haller, 1974), suggesting that adolescents display wider variability in adjusting to the stress and vicissitudes of life.

Due to cognitive, biological, and social factors, not all is quiet on the adolescent front, but rebelliousness does not seem to be the common pathway to adolescence autonomy and independence. Instead, the core conceptual issue of adolescence is one of change, whereby emerging mechanisms for coping are developed, although our understanding of what the critical coping mechanisms are and how they develop is relatively uncharted (Livson & Peskin, 1980). The study of change during adolescence has become a legitimate area of research (Hill, 1983). This chapter examines one of the more obvious changes observed in adolescents, namely how they interact within their primary social network of peers, family, and school.

The purpose of this chapter is to review three seemingly divergent, yet critical, areas of adolescent research. Specifically, this chapter reviews selected studies that address changes in adolescents vis-à-vis peers, family, and school. From this review, gaps in content areas that impede our further understanding of adolescent changes will be highlighted. The first section discusses how the adolescent-relationship literature has failed to identify and treat the adolescent who has problematic peer relationships. The second section reviews the more sophisticated methodological studies in the adolescent literature that examine the changes in the adolescent–parent relationship and the potentially conflictual relationship between adolescents and mother-only and stepparent families. The third section reviews research that examines how an environmental factor, school transition, affects young adolescents. The final section discusses the merits and limitations of longitudinal and cross-sectional research and the lack of objective measures in adolescent research. Finally, suggestions for future adolescent research are proposed.

ADOLESCENCE AND PEERS

Special importance is attributed to friendships during adolescence. By early adolescence, friendship is characterized by a sense of reciprocity and equality. Peer conversations involve more sharing, explaining, and mutual understanding, whereas adolescent–parent conversations involve parents explaining their ideas even at the expense of not understanding their children's alternative views (Hunter, 1985). There is evidence that the influence of parents and friends upon adolescents varies according to types of activities and topics of conversation. For example, parents' influence seems to prevail in the future-oriented domains, such as choices of schools and career plans (Kandel & Lesser, 1972); friends' influence centers around current events and activities (Hunter, 1985). Peer discussions can provide adolescents with opportunities to express, test, and verify alternative views about interpersonal relationships, which then lead to further socialization (Youniss, 1980). It has often been assumed that same-sex friendships are closer and more intense in early adolescence than in any other phase of the life span (Douvan & Adelson, 1966). Daily friendship interactions take up a substantial portion of adolescents' free time (Crockett, Losoff, & Peterson, 1984; Montemayer, 1982). Adolescents report spending more time talking to peers than in any other activity and describe themselves as most happy when so engaged (Csikszentmihalyi, Larson, & Prescott, 1977).

The significance of friendships among adolescents has been explained by biological, social, and cognitive factors. Although reminiscent of the popular notion of adolescence as a period of storm and stress, one explanation for the strong concern for friendship among adolescents is to share with peers the difficulties associated with the biological changes that are often so troubling to this age group. Another explanation for the strong bonds between peers during adolescence concerns the unique characteristics of the adolescent's social environment. Early adolescents are not treated as children nor are they treated as adults. Sexual involvement with the opposite sex is strongly discouraged. They acquire fairly limited independence and are required to remain in school and not be employed until age 16. These conditions create a relatively stable environment of school and neighborhoods and a significant amount of time and energy to be devoted to peers. Finally, cognitively speaking, the transition from concrete, stimulus-bound to abstract, generalized thinking allows the adolescent to better understand friends' thoughts and feelings. They become more aware of the importance of mutuality and reciprocity, which can foster stable and meaningful friendships (Berndt, 1982).

The degree of similarity between adolescent friends on various broad characteristics, such as age, sex, and race has been investigated in a large number of studies. Early adolescents appear similar to their friends in two general ways. First, friends have a similar orientation to school with regard to attitudes, educational aspirations, and achievement (Ball, 1981). Second, friends are similar in their orientation towards contemporary teen culture. They like the same music, clothes, and leisure time activities (Ball, 1981).

Although research has yielded a considerable amount of theoretical and descriptive information about the importance and features of adolescent friendships, relatively little information is available about the characteristics of adolescents who are liked or not liked by peers. The interest in peer-neglected or rejected adolescents is more than academic, because young children who are judged by their first- and second-grade peers as being withdrawn and aggressive generally continue to be ignored or rejected by peers throughout their elementary and middle school careers (Moskowitz, Schwartzman, & Ledingham, 1985; Weintraub, Prinz, & Neale, 1978). Furthermore, recent research indicates that the distinction between peer-neglected and peer-rejected elementary-age children is critical, because rejected children are reported to be lonelier and at higher risk for later adjustment problems than neglected children (Asher & Wheeler, 1985).

Theorists of social-skills intervention planning (Dodge & Murphy, 1984; McFall, 1982) explain that a three-step assessment process should precede any effective treatment plan for socially incompetent adolescents. The first step is to identify the incompetent adolescent. In contrast to elementary-age children, relatively scant attention has been given to identifying adolescents with problematic peer relationships.

Future research on adolescent peer relationships could be enhanced by implementing sociometric measures as a means to identify and classify adolescents. As an example, a considerable amount of fruitful research concerning elementary-age children's peer relationships now exists that has classified these children into popular, controversial, neglected, and rejected groups according to peer sociometric ratings. This classification has allowed investigators to identify behavioral profiles among the different sociometric groups (e.g., Asher & Wheeler, 1985; Coie, Dodge, & Coppotelli, 1982; Green, Forehand, Beck, & Vosk, 1980) and assess their stability (e.g., Beck & Collins, 1985; Coie & Dodge, 1983; Newcomb & Bukowski, 1984).

Sociometric measures can consist of instruments that ask respondents to name or identify group members who satisfy a preference choice. One common sociometric measure is a scale on which subjects rate each group member (typically classmates) from 1 to 5 in terms of how much they would prefer their companionship. Two other measures, the positive and negative nomination procedures, ask subjects to identify the three group members whom they like the most and the three whom they like the least. One sociometric device, the Adjustment Scale for Sociometric Evaluation of Secondary-School Students (ASSESS), has been developed to assess the social domain of students in grades 9 through 12 (Prinz, Swan, Liebert, Weintraub, & Neale, 1978). This psychometrically sound scale consists of 41 items (e.g., acts obnoxious, has confidence in self, fails to turn in assignments on time), and requires the student to put in the name of any classmate who matches the description. Five scales are derived from the ASSESS: aggressive–disruptive, withdrawal, anxiety, social competence, and academic difficulty.

The second step in planning an effective intervention for a socially incompetent adolescent is to identify the particular social contexts, tasks, or situations in which the targeted adolescent displays the problematic behaviors. Dodge, McClaskey, and Feldman (1985) recently developed the Taxonomy of Problematic Social Situations for Children (TOPS) and identified specific social situations and tasks (e.g., peer group entry, responding to a provocation by a peer, or persuading a peer to engage in a particular behavior) as social situations that differentiate skilled from unskilled elementary-age children. However, normative behavior for adolescents in specific social situations is presently not available. Although taxonomic research cannot be expected to target the unique social situations of every adolescent with poor peer relationships (Dodge & Murphy, 1984), an empirically derived taxonomy of several relevant and problematic adolescent social situations would enhance the assessment and treatment of socially incompetent adolescents.

The third step in developing effective interventions for adolescents lacking in satisfactory peer relationships is to target the specific component skills in each of the critical social situations. Research examining elementary-age (mostly third to fifth grade) children's peer relationships has consistently identified popular children as displaying a range of prosocial behaviors towards peers (e.g., Gottman, Gonso, & Rasmussen, 1975; Green et al. 1980; Rubin & Beirness, 1983). Similarly, elementary-age children identified as rejected by peers have been found to be disruptive, impulsive, and easily provoked, to display poor interpersonal problem-solving strategies, and to have a bias towards viewing peers negatively (Beck, Forehand, Baskin, & Neeper, 1983; Coie et al., 1982; Dodge, Coie, & Brakke, 1982; Dodge & Frame,

1982). Children who are neglected by peers appear shy and withdrawn and also display poor interpersonal problem-solving strategies (Coie et al., 1982; Richard & Dodge, 1982).

Although it may seem plausible to conclude that well-liked adolescents engage in a high rate of prosocial behaviors similar to popular elementary-age children, and conversely, disliked adolescents engage in negative interactions similar to disliked elementary-age children, these conclusions await empirical verification. There is one study that suggests liked and disliked children display different peer-interactive behaviors as a function of age. Beck, Collins, Overholser, and Terry (1985) found that well-liked first-grade children engaged in positive peer and teacher interactions in the classroom and showed a positive relationship between their sociometric status and academic achievement. On the other hand, well-liked sixth-grade children displayed more positive peer interactions with peers than did disliked children, but did not show a relationship between their sociometric status and academic achievement. In addition, negative teacher and peer interactions (e.g., a teacher giving a warning to a preadolescent or the preadolescent not complying to a request) were positively correlated with sixth graders' nominations of well-liked peers.

Research is clearly needed to identify which specific skills and behaviors are observed or lacking in adolescents who are well-liked or disliked by their peers. In one study that examined social competence in adolescents, Ford (1982) found that ninth and twelfth graders judged to be socially competent were able to display empathy (defined as the ability to accurately comprehend the feelings and thoughts of others). Empathy is very similar to a referential communication skill identified by Gottman et al. (1975) that differentiated popular from unpopular elementary-age children. This skill involves the ability to take the perspective of another person. Cognitive resourcefulness, such as the ability to effectively generate strategies for resolving interpersonal conflicts, also appears to be a salient characteristic for all socially skilled children and adolescents (Richard & Dodge, 1982; Spivack, Platt, & Shure, 1976).

McFall and his colleagues (Freedman, Rosenthal, Donahoe, Schlundt, & McFall, 1978; Gaffney & McFall, 1981) are among the few investigators who have conducted a thorough and systematic analysis of the skill deficits in a group of adolescent juvenile delinquents. These researchers developed the Adolescent Problem Inventory (API: Freedman et al., 1978) for adolescent males and the Problem Inventory for Adolescent Girls (PIAG; Gaffney & McFall, 1981) for adolescent females. These instruments empirically identified those situations that are most problematic for delinquent adolescent boys and girls. McFall and his colleagues compared the performance of a matched group of delinquent and nondelinquent adolescents on both inventories. Both instruments successfully discriminated the nondelinquent from the delinquent groups, suggesting that social-skill deficits are a correlate of delinquency.

As noted earlier, empirical verification of social situations critical for establishing or maintaining positive peer relationships needs to be identified, and the ability to discriminate the performance of liked and disliked adolescents should be demonstrated. Until this is accomplished there is no way of knowing whether intervention programs focus on the most relevant problem situations for peer-rejected adolescents or whether the behaviors taught in programs represent genuine solutions to these target problems. For example, a few studies have attempted to teach social skills to adolescents (Goldstein, Sherman, Gershaw, Sprafkin, & Glick, 1978; Ollendick & Hersen, 1979a; Sarason & Sarason, 1981) without adequately determining whether the specific skills taught in their respective treatment programs represented genuine solutions to their poor peer relationships.

In summary, the fact that adolescence has often been overlooked as a distinct developmental stage is most evident when examining the amount of research and progress made in the assessment and identification of elementary-age children deficient in peer relationships contrasted to adolescents with similar deficiencies. When one considers the lack of emphasis in assessing and treating adolescents with problematic peer relationships, adolescence appears to be viewed merely as a way station between the attention given to "more vulnerable" elementary-age children and the oft-cited consequences of later adult psychopathology (e.g., Cowen, Pederson, Babigian, Izzo, & Trost, 1973). Although problematic peer relationships most likely have their roots in childhood, it is equally important to identify the behavioral characteristics of individuals who experience unsatisfactory peer relationships in adolescence. Only after this is accomplished can appropriate treatment studies be implemented and evaluated to determine the effectiveness of teaching social skills to adolescents.

ADOLESCENCE AND THE FAMILY

Although adolescence is a time of cognitive, biological, and social changes, only a handful of empirical studies have examined changes in family relationships during this period. Montemayer (1982) conducted one of the more thorough, descriptive studies examining the amount of time and types of activities adolescents spend with parents and peers, as well as the frequency and quality of adolescent–parent conflicts in Caucasian, two-parent middle-income families. He employed a time-use methodology, whereby adolescents reported a chronology of the previous day's events to interviewers who called on three randomly selected evenings during any day of the week. In this way, the amount of free time and task time, which included such activities as home chores, homework, eating, personal hygiene, and attending church services (over half of the adolescents' families were members of the Mormon church), and with whom these activities were done with, were determined. Measures of the frequency, intensity, and duration of adolescent–parent conflicts were also collected.

Results indicated that although adolescent use of time was highly variable, they spent significantly more free time with peers than with parents or alone, but, in overall time (free time plus task time), they spent equal amounts of time with parents and peers. The data revealed that parents and peers provide adolescents with contrasting social worlds. Time spent with parents mainly centered around the completion of a variety of social and household activities, whereas peer time was spent in entertainment, playing games, and talking. Free time with parents was most commonly involved watching television, a passive activity for which adolescents show little enthusiasm (Csikszentmikalyi et al., 1977). Surprisingly, the adolescents in the Montemayer study spent an approximately equal amount of time with their mothers and fathers, in contrast to mothers' spending considerably more time with their preadolescent sons and daughters than fathers.

These data suggest that for middle-class Caucasian families there is a general decrease in mothers' childcare activities and a slight increase in fathers' playtime with their adolescents. These data also show that adolescents reported three times more conflicts with their mothers than with their fathers, and females had more conflicts with their parents than did males. Conflicts with parents reported by the adolescents were about everyday occurrences of adolescent family life, including school work, chores, and general irritations. Because most arguments were about family matters, it is not surprising that more arguments took place with mothers rather than fathers. However, the picture that emerges from these studies is that between childhood and adolescence mothers become less involved with their adolescent children, yet still have squabbles with their sons or daughters about everyday home and school responsibilities.

In contrast to the psychoanalytic theorizing that conceptualizes adolescence as a time of disengaging from the parent–child bond (Blos, 1979), recent evidence supports a view of this period as one of gradual renegotiation between parents and their children (White, Speisman, & Costos, 1983). The process of how families negotiate the transition from a primarily unilateral relationship to a more mutual coalition during late adolescence has been studied. Similar to studies of parent–child rearing practices, which have taken into account the reciprocal relationship between parents and children (Bell, 1968), accounts of the changing parent–adolescent relationship requires going beyond unilateral concepts, such as parental styles, to more reciprocal relational constructs (Maccoby & Martin, 1983). The reciprocal, give-and-take process that occurs during adolescent–parent interactions has been captured in studies using observational methods. The most common method involves tape-recording families engaged in a decision-making task.

In one of the most often cited studies using an observational procedure to examine the transformation in family relations during stages of male puberty, Steinberg and Hill (1978) found that family communication patterns undergo changes as male adolescents grow older. They observed that midpubertal adolescents (as defined by the adolescent's physical maturity) deferred to their mothers less often than prepubertal peers, but that parental explanations were less and interruptions more frequent toward sons who were at midpubertal physical development. Patterns of interactions between family members appeared more rigidly structured in families with sons at midpuberty compared to families with sons at prepuberty or late puberty.

Steinberg (1981) replicated these findings with a more longitudinal focus by examining families over a period of 1 year. His findings replicated data showing that interruptions between the male adolescent and his mother increased from the onset of puberty to midpuberty and that the adolescent's deference to his mother diminished. Also, explanations between mother and the adolescent declined during this period. Steinberg's (1981) study shed additional light on the interaction patterns between fathers and male adolescents. Similar to the adolescent and his mother, the adolescent's father interrupted his son increasingly and explained himself less frequently during his son's early to midpuberty development. In contrast to the adolescent's more disruptive behavior towards his mother, however, his behavior towards his father showed more deference. Based on these two studies, a picture emerges that, by late puberty, middle-class, Caucasian male adolescents with two-parent families occupy a position in their ability to influence final family decisions above that of the mother and below that of the father. The adolescent's input in family decision-making discussions increases with age, whereas the father maintains an authoritative position and the mother's input declines. These results clearly indicate that the transformation in the male adolescent's relationships with his parents are related to changes in physical appearance.

Grotevant and Cooper (1985) examined the progressive redefinition of normal parent–adolescent relationships by comparing the adolescent's identity formation as it related to communication patterns in the family. Identity formation refers to the developmental adolescent task of formulating one's own identity with a cohesive set of values, goals, and beliefs (Erikson, 1968). These investigators argued that two important communication patterns, individuality and connectedness, would be observed in healthy family relationships. From a communication standpoint, individuality refers to the ability to express one's own views from those of others and the ability to take responsibility for communicating it clearly. Connectedness refers to the ability to be sensitive, open, and responsive to the view of others. For Grotevant and Cooper, these constructs are critical communication patterns that are observed in parent–adolescent relationships, because they involve the ability of family members to have opinions that may differ from those of others and thus foster healthy identity formation in adolescents.

Subjects in the study were middle-class two-parent families that included a male or female high-school senior and at least one sibling. Similar to the family decision-making task, both parents, the target adolescent, and one sibling were audiotaped making plans together for a fictional 2-week vacation for which the family had unlimited funds. They found that males with a strong developing sense of self (as measured by a paper-and-pencil measure) had fathers who frequently complimented and infrequently disagreed with their son's statements. They also observed that these fathers were less likely to express their own ideas, apparently to allow their sons the opportunity to contribute to the family vacation plans. These fathers, at the very least, seemed to be encouraging, or at least tolerating, their son's assertiveness.

In contrast, fathers of daughters with a strong developing sense of self commented on others' suggestions rather than expressed their own ideas, but disagreed often with their wives and daughters. In these situations mothers expressed their own ideas directly, but also served a mollifying role by attempting to be sensitive to their husbands' remarks as well as playing the role of coordinating the family discussion. This study provides information about family-interaction patterns between mid to late puberty male and female adolescents and their parents. These findings are consistent with the previous studies, which suggest that there are fewer conflicts between fathers and adolescent sons than between mothers and adolescent sons. Relationships between adolescent daughters and mothers, however, may fare better. Research suggests that daughters report more intimacy (Hunter & Youniss, 1982) and openness of communication with mothers (Kon & Losenkov,

1978; Rivenbark, 1971), and seek advice and guidance (Kandel & Lesser, 1972) more often from mothers than from fathers. Montemayer and Van Komen (1980) also report that certain mutually interesting activities may increase for mothers and adolescent daughters, such as shopping together for clothes.

Recent studies have also examined the emergence of the increasingly commonplace adolescent–single-parent family. Two methodologically rigorous studies will be reviewed that document the difficulties involved between adolescents and single-parent and stepparent families, particularly when the adolescent presents with deviant behavior. Dornbusch et al. (1985) examined a large sample of adolescents to study the interrelationships among family structure, patterns of family decision-making, and deviant behavior among adolescents. This study is noteworthy because its sample of 7,000 subjects was stratified and represented the entire United States target population with respect to age, sex, race, region population density, and population growth. Dornbusch et al. assessed families in which the biological mother was always present and the biological father was either present or absent and not replaced by a stepfather. Several measures were used as indicators of adolescent deviance, such as contacts with the law, arrests, truancy, and school discipline, from which a total deviance score was derived. After controlling for family income, parental education, and age of the adolescents, they found that single-parent households differ from two-parent households in their ability to control adolescents. Adolescents from mother-only households exhibited higher deviance patterns.

When a subgroup of mother-only households containing an additional adult (e.g., grandparents, other relatives, boyfriends) was examined, the presence of the additional adult lowered the rate of adolescent deviance. Presence of two adults, regardless of the adult affiliations, resulted in greater social control of the adolescent. However, closer inspection of the data showed that adolescent males in stepparent families had as high deviance scores as males in mother-alone families, and males in stepparent families had much higher deviance scores than males in extended mother-only families or families with two natural parents. Female adolescents in stepparent families had deviance scores that fell between mother-only families and families with two natural parents. These data suggest that male adolescents may experience specific conflicts in their relationships with their stepfathers.

Adolescent decision-making was assessed in the present study by asking parents and adolescents separately: "Who makes most of the decisions on the following topics?" These topics included such decisions as choosing adolescent clothes and curfew hours. After controlling for family income, because a previous study by Dornbusch and his colleagues (1983) had shown that higher income families are more likely to exhibit more joint (parent–adolescent) decision-making, they found that mother-only households exhibited more youth-alone and lower parent-alone decisions. The mother, faced with the problem of controlling an adolescent without a father, is less likely to make decisions without input from the youth and is more likely to allow the youth to make his or her own decisions. These data suggest that raising an adolescent is not easily accomplished by a mother alone and that the presence of any other adult in a mother-only household brings control levels closer to those found in two-parent families. As suggested by Dornbusch and his colleagues, the relation of deviance to decision-making patterns is probably reciprocal. Parents, when faced with a recalcitrant or difficult-to-handle adolescent, may reduce their attempts to confront the youth. On the other hand, the youth's deviance might be a function of the parents lack of surveillance, lack of appropriate teaching, or lack of social support for the single parent that leads to a reduction in control of adolescents.

The presence of adolescent deviance in the developing adolescent–parent relationship, particularly in the adolescent–stepparent relationship, was studied by Garbarino, Sebes, and Schellenbach (1984). These authors note that despite public and professional emphasis on child abuse and neglect, adolescent maltreatment accounts for some 47% of the known cases of abuse, although teenagers account for only 38% of the population under the age of 18. Moreover, half of these cases were chronically maltreated in childhood as well (Garbarino & Gilliam, 1980). Nonetheless, the majority of adolescent–parent relationships precipitate maltreatment only in adolescence.

Garbarino et al. (1984) recruited 62 two-parent families that contained a youth between the ages of 10 to 16. Families were recruited from schools, social service agencies, or professionals who had some concern for problematic development in the target adolescent. A research team visited the family at the home, conducted interviews, administered a battery of questionnaires, and observed structured family interactions. Based upon an adolescent self-report measure, parental behaviors were categorized into four groups: (a) physical and sexual abuse, (b) verbal or psychological abuse, (c) neglected, or (d) appropriate parenting behavior. These investigators found that high-risk parents (parents that used abusive behaviors) reported a high degree of adolescent deviance, were observed to be chaotically enmeshed, used coercive parenting styles, and were consequently more easily pushed past the threshold at which maltreatment occurs. Low-risk families, on the other hand, were characterized as having more supportive, less punishing styles of parenting, as well as important buffers (such as greater adolescent social competence), even though the adolescent displayed a fair amount of deviant behavior. These data support the notion that some families, even though the adolescent engages in disruptive behaviors, can absorb adolescent psychopathology without precipitating maltreatment.

This study also found that adolescents' pathology in the stepfamilies was greater than other adolescents in the high-risk group. A variety of studies broadly support the notion that stepparent-adolescent relationships are risky, particularly among families in which adolescents exhibit deviance (Daly & Wilson, 1981; Garbarino et al., 1984). Explanations for the potentially volatile adolescent–stepparent relationship could be attributed to less parental investment in children because of not having a genetic connection, plus the interpersonal challenge of complex, multiple, and often competing patterns of interactions in stepparent families.

To briefly summarize the parent–adolescent family relationship literature, family interaction patterns in normal, middle-class, two-parent families appear to change as males become more physically mature. Specifically, adolescent males ascend to a more dominant role in the family decision-making progress, while the mothers' input declines. The relationship between adolescent girls and two-parent families is less clear, and the specific effects of adolescent girls' physical appearance or maturity upon family interactions have yet to be studied. Preliminary data suggest that middle-class fathers from two-parent families may feel more uncomfortable with adolescent daughters than with adolescent sons. Grotevant and Cooper (1985) found that fathers of apparently well-adjusted daughters disagreed more often with them compared to fathers of adolescent sons. Several studies suggest that in healthy, two-parent families, adolescent daughter–mother relationships can become more open and intimate about issues concerning dating and future planning. There are more squabbles about everyday mundane tasks between daughters and mothers compared to sons and mothers and even fewer conflicts between sons and fathers.

The two important studies by Dornbusch et al. (1985) and Garbarino et al. (1984) indicate that mother-alone families and stepfamilies are more likely to have problematic adolescents and experience difficulty controlling them. These findings become relevant when one considers the U.S. Census Bureau (1980) report that indicates a 79% increase in the number of single-parent families between 1970 and 1980. This means that approximately one in five families raise children and adolescents with a single parent (usually the mother) with or without a foster, surrogate, or stepparent. Future research needs to unravel the causality of adolescent deviance by examining factors that are set in motion before or after family realignment occurs when one parent leaves the household. Studying families with adolescents who have adjusted satisfactory to family realignments is one way to better understand the critical parental, adolescent, and interactive characteristics that are required to increase the likelihood that adolescents make better adaptations to changing family structures.

ADOLESCENCE AND SCHOOL

Schools are complex social systems that have a profound effect upon children's socialization (Sarason & Klaber, 1985). There is little doubt that the school environment (including activities that take place within it) is a major factor in a youth's life. Indeed, the school plays a critical role in an adolescent's socialization. Surprisingly, there have only been a few empirical studies that have examined the consequences of school on adolescent adjustment and on peer socialization in particular. Blyth and his col-

leagues (Blyth, Simmons, & Bush, 1978; Blyth, Simmons, & Carlton-Ford, 1983) examined the adjustment of early adolescence to transitions in two types of school organizational patterns that presently confront most American adolescents, namely, the 8–4 or 6–3–3 school grade split. The 8–4 school split refers to the transition between schools that occurs for adolescents who go from more child-oriented protective kindergarten-through-eighth-grade (K–8) schools to a typically larger, considerably more diverse, and more departmentalized 4-year high school. By contrast, the 6–3–3 arrangement involves a first transition in the seventh grade as the students leave a relatively small homogeneous neighborhood elementary school to enter a large, more departmentalized junior high school containing grades seven through nine. After 3 years in this junior high environment, these students again make a second transition into the 10th grade, where they enter an even larger, and perhaps more prestigious, senior high school.

These school transitions, particularly the entry into junior high school, in our modern, extremely age-graded society, have been viewed as the closest American society comes to a formal right of passage for adolescence (Elder, 1968). Given the importance of these transitions, Blyth and his colleagues have examined how disruptive the transitions are from one school environment to another and whether or not the timing of the transitions in an adolescent's life course make a significant difference in how disruptive the changes will be.

In their first study, Blyth, Simmons, and Bush (1978) assessed over 600 children and considered the impact of the transition into the seventh grade for students in K–8 schools compared to students in the K–6 schools. They examined the amount of change between sixth and seventh grade in five areas of social and psychological development: parent–peer orientation, participation in extracurricular activities, early dating behavior, self-esteem, and the student's perception of his or her anonymity in the school environment. They also assessed the amount of victimization (i.e., the number of physical assaults, robberies, or thefts that occurred in and around the school during the sixth and seventh grade).

They found that the K–8 students appeared to be more influenced by their peers, as they dated more and preferred to be with their close friends more than K–6 students. The K–6 students, on the other hand, were more likely to be academically oriented and to have internalized a greater sense of responsibility as they prepared for the transition into junior high. However, in support of the K–8 schools, they found that K–8 students became increasingly more positive about themselves, participated more in school activities, and felt less anonymous in their school environment. By contrast, the seventh graders who went into junior high (and especially the girls) felt less positively about themselves, decreased their participation in activities at school, and felt a high degree of anonymity within their school environment. In addition, the junior-high students moved from a relatively safe environment to a more hostile one in which males were much more likely to experience an act of victimization.

Using the same sample of adolescents, Simmons, Blyth, Van Cleave, and Bush (1979) identified the girls who experienced the lowest self-esteem as a result of the transition from the sixth grade to the seventh grade located in a junior high. They found that these girls experienced recent multiple changes: they changed schools, reached puberty, and also started to "date." They reported that among boys with similar changes, early pubertal development increased self-esteem.

The final study by Blyth, Simmons, and Carlton-Ford (1983) was a longitudinal evaluation of the sample mentioned earlier that allowed for examination of the consequences of three different transitions occurring in the two different organizational structures. Specifically, they studied the entry of students into junior high school in seventh grade and their subsequent entry into a senior high school in tenth grade, compared to the entry of students from a K–8 school into a 4-year high school at ninth grade. While reiterating their earlier findings that the transition into seventh grade for those students entering a junior high school has some disadvantageous consequences, they also found that girls continued to experience a loss of self-esteem in ninth and tenth grade, whereas girls in the K–8 cohort gained in self-esteem over the course of the study.

Blyth and his colleagues provide data on how adolescents adjust to a universal role transition, namely from a more protected elementary school environment to a larger, more departmentalized junior high or high school setting.

Their data suggest that a transition made too early in one's development can have a relatively long-lasting negative effect, whereas transitions made at a later developmental stage may be made without serious consequences. Their conclusions also suggest that girls who have entered junior high school are at a disadvantage in comparison both to boys in general and also to those girls who do not have to change schools in the seventh grade. They also found that girls who have not only experienced the environmental discontinuity of junior high school, but also the early physiological transformations of puberty and the new social behavior of dating, are at greater risk for negative self-esteem than any other group of children. These empirical studies clearly show how environmental contexts, biological factors, and social behavior impact on the coping skills of young adolescents.

RESEARCH DIRECTIONS AND METHODOLOGICAL CONSIDERATIONS

The preceding sections identified three groups of adolescents particularly at risk for current and later adjustment difficulties. Whether the vulnerability suggested for socially incompetent adolescents, disruptive adolescent males residing in mother-alone or stepparent families, or early adolescent girls experiencing multiple changes is more of a temporary reaction or an indication of future adjustment problems can best be addressed by longitudinal or cross-sectional studies. To some developmental theorists (e.g., Erikson, 1968), certain periods of personal turmoil are beneficial to eventual adjustment because they allow an individual to develop adaptive coping skills. However, data from the New York Longitudinal Study (Chess & Thomas, 1984) indicate that a superior level of functioning in early adulthood requires a consistent, healthy, and productive developmental course from early childhood onward to early adulthood. Presence of childhood or adolescent behavior problems signalled the occurrence of a period of excessive stress and reduced the possibility of superior early adulthood adaptation.

Some researchers argue that the longitudinal method, which thoroughly assesses a single group of subjects as they age, is the best approach for disentangling developmental changes and possible origins of psychopathology in adolescence. This is the only approach that provides a complete description of the growth phenomenon (Livson & Peskin, 1980), but it is costly, attrition-plagued, and by its very nature time-consuming. The most common methodology for taking a shortcut to identifying possible age differences for a particular variable are cross-sectional studies. Cross-sectional research (which involves assessing independent samples at different ages at the same time) is probably the only feasible way to obtain large-scale normative data typifying different age groups at a particular moment in history (Achenbach, 1982). However, the cross-sectional approach (e.g., classifying subjects into pre-, mid-, or late-adolescent groups according to age or physical maturity and then assessing potential changes in self-esteem across these three age groups) does not necessarily permit inference about adolescent developmental change. Obtained differences among the adolescent groups on self-esteem can arise from many possible sources other than developmental differences. Differences among these age groups could be due to differences in the cohorts used to represent each age group. For example, declining birth rates could mean that the average birth rank of 18-year-olds differs from that of 13-year-olds; differences between these two groups could thus reflect experiential differences due to birth rank rather than age differences per se.

Besides the obvious call for cross-sectional and longitudinal adolescent research, the most glaring methodological problems in adolescent research are the lack of objective measures for assessing adolescent transactions and adjustments. As noted by Hill (1982), there presently are no valid measures of such critical adolescent phenomena as "autonomy" or "independence," even though numerous ways have been employed to assess these constructs. The majority of the adolescent studies reviewed in this chapter collected data from self-report methods, interviews, or new questionnaires of questionable reliability and validity. For example, one of the primary dependent measures in the research examining the effects of the transition from one school setting to another on adolescent self-esteem was a time-consuming, interview procedure instead of a more objective paper-and-pencil measure. Without the development of reliable and valid paper-and-pencil measures of adolescent adjustment, the ability to assess crit-

ical dimensions of adolescent adaptation is seriously hampered.

On the other hand, several studies reviewed in this chapter used structured, systematic observations of parent–adolescent communication patterns. Development of structured observations of parent–adolescent decision-making tasks has greatly augmented the understanding of changes in normal parent–adolescent relationships (e.g., Steinberg & Hill, 1978) and parenting styles of at-risk families (e.g., Garbarino et al., 1984). This analogue method is similar to the structured parent–child interactions developed by Patterson (1982) and Forehand (Forehand & McMahon, 1981), whereby parents are instructed to direct and then follow their child in play in order to assess the quality and frequency of commands and compliance between parents and young children. The structured parent–adolescent decision-making task allows similar insights into the patterns of interactions that occur in families with developmentally more advanced children.

Finally, more descriptive studies are needed to develop a wider taxonomy of adolescent peer and family transactions from a wider range of adolescents from differing socioeconomic and sociocultural backgrounds. In developmental psychology, a number of ecologically oriented psychologists have stressed the need for naturalistic research that assesses the ways family members actually speak and behave toward each other (e.g., Bronfenbrenner, 1979). Studies that have examined the everyday behavior of adolescents (e.g., Hunter, 1985; Montemayor, 1982) have used adolescents from mainly two-parent, Caucasian, middle- and upper-middle-income families. Although these studies are necessary for providing norm-referenced behaviors, field observations of adolescents from other demographic backgrounds (e.g., minority adolescents) would yield valuable additional data about the more universal qualities of parental and peer adolescent relationships. Achenbach (1982) notes that our picture of maladjusted children and adolescents has primarily been formed by a downward extrapolations of adult disorders. This problem can be partly rectified by developing an empirical taxonomy of normal and aberrant child and adolescent everyday behaviors.

Research agenda for advancing our understanding of adolescence has also been articulated by others. Hill (1983) has made several

broad recommendations for adolescence research. In his opinion, high priority research
activities should include short-term longitudinal studies of attachment, autonomy, sexuality
intimacy, achievement, and identity. He points
out that most adolescence research is cross-sectional rather than longitudinal and is done in
discrete and unrelated "chunks" rather than
programmatically. Hill also calls for relevant research focusing on the assessment and education of adolescents on a variety of critical behaviors that will impact on prevention and
social-policy programs. He argues that concentrated efforts should be made to educate and
intervene during early adolescence before life-
style habits are established on such health-relat-
ed activities as exercise, food behavior, and
smoking. Others have noted that adolescent
cigarette smoking and alcohol consumption are
more serious health risks in terms of death and
disease than marijuana abuse and other illegal
drugs, yet the latter addictions are often viewed
as more serious adolescent health problems
(Evans, 1985). Hill (1983) points out that studies
of the onset of sexual activity and early pregnancy and their determinants are relatively
nonexistent. He further advises that research be
undertaken to assess adult perception of adolescence, as this age period is typically viewed
with ambivalence.

SUMMARY

Even though adolescence brings with it the
most rapid and dramatic changes in the human
organism since infancy, this developmental
stage has historically been viewed as basically a
way station between critical childhood developments and eventual adult adjustment. No one
developmental era has a corner on contributing
to our understanding of change as does adolescence, yet, until recently, adolescence was
viewed as a global, undifferentiated period of
storm and stress. Our more recent understanding of this developmental stage is that adolescents are viewed as capable of displaying wide
variability in adjusting to the intrinsic cognitive,
biological, and social changes found in the second decade of life.

The present chapter reviewed research as to
how adolescents relate to peers, families, and
school. The importance of peer friendships during adolescence was discussed, and the relative

lack of research (with the exception of the research conducted on juvenile delinquents by
McFall and his colleagues) concerning adolescents who have problematic peer relationships
was noted. A three-step assessment procedure
for identifying socially incompetent adolescents
was outlined, and the contrast between the
amount of research conducted with elementary-
age children who have poor peer relationships
and adolescents with those difficulties was similarly noted.

The chapter also reviewed recent descriptive
studies of adolescent activities with parents and
peers and the transformation of adolescent–
parent relationships as the adolescent physically matures. Methodologically sophisticated research was also reviewed that indicates that
mother-only households have a difficult task of
raising adolescents and that stepparents who
have an adolescent who displays deviant behavior are particularly vulnerable to abusive family
interactions. The need for more descriptive adolescent studies from other than two-parent,
Caucasian, middle- to upper-middle-income families was noted, so that a more universal range
of adolescent parental and peer behaviors could
be catalogued.

The final content section of the chapter
described three studies that showed how organizational school patterns influence adolescent adjustment. In particular, young adolescent girls having to adjust to multiple changes
appeared to be the most vulnerable to lower
levels of self-esteem. These studies are noteworthy because they examine how simultaneous
variables, such as school change, puberty, and
dating habits, impact on the coping skills of
young adolescents. Yet these studies also highlight the problem of the lack of objective assessment measures in adolescent research. An
exception to the lack of reliable and valid assessment methods in adolescent research is the
promising structured, observational method of
recording adolescent–parent decision-making
tasks. These allow researchers to assess adolescent–parent interactions and communication
patterns.

The last section of the chapter discussed the
need for longitudinal and cross-sectional research that can provide a taxonomy of adolescent behaviors along the developmental continuum and also allows behavior to be viewed in
the context of change. Finally, several broad

research suggestions concerning adolescent health and sexual behavior were made.

REFERENCES

Achenbach, T. M. (1982). Research methods in developmental psychopathology. In P. C. Kendall & J. M. Butcher (Eds.), *Handbook of research methods in clinical psychology* (pp. 569–589). New York: Wiley.

Asher, S. R., & Wheeler, V. A. (1985). Children's loneliness: A comparison of rejected and neglected peer status. *Journal of Cousulting and Clinical Psychology, 53*, 500–506.

Ball, S. J. (1981). *Beachside comprehensive.* Cambridge: Cambridge University Press.

Beck, S., & Collins, L. (1985). *Children's sociometric groups: Developmental and stability issues.* Paper presented at meeting of the Midwestern Psychological Association, Chicago.

Beck, S., Collins, L., Overholser, J., & Terry, K. (1985). A cross-sectional assessment of the relationship of social competence measures to peer friendship and likeability in elementary-age children. *Genetic Psychology Monographs, 111*, 41–67.

Beck, S., Forehand, R., Baskin, C. H., & Neeper, R. (1983). An examination of children's perceptions of themselves and others as a function of popularity level. *Journal of Social and Clinical Psychology, 1*, 259–271.

Bell, R. (1968). A reinterpretation of the direction of effects in studies of socialization. *Psychological Review, 75*, 81–95.

Berndt, T. J. (1982). The features and effects of friendship in early adolescence. *Child Development, 53*, 1447–1460.

Blos, P. (1979). The second individuation process of adolescence. In P. Blos (Ed.), *The adolescent passage: Developmental issues* (pp. 141–170). New York: International University Press.

Blyth, D. A., Simmons, R. G., & Bush, D. (1978). The transition into early adolescence: A longitudinal comparison of youth in two educational contexts. *Sociology of Education, 51*, 149–162.

Blyth, D. A., Simmons, R. G., & Carlton-Ford, S. (1983). The adjustments of early adolescents to school transitions. *Journal of Early Adolescence, 3*, 105–120.

Bronfenbrenner, U. (1979). *The ecology of human development.* Cambridge, MA: Harvard University Press.

Chess, S., & Thomas, A. (1984). *Origins and evolution of behavior disorders: From infancy to early adult life.* New York: Brunner/Mazel.

Coie, J. D., & Dodge, K. A. (1983). Continuities and changes in children's social status: A five-year longitudinal study. *Merrill-Palmer Quarterly, 29*, 261–282.

Coie, J. D., Dodge, K. A., & Coppotelli, H. (1982). Dimensions and types of social status: A cross-age perspective. *Developmental Psychology, 18*, 557–570.

Cowen, E. L., Pederson, A., Babigian, H., Izzo, L. D., & Trost, M. A. (1973). Long-term follow-up of early detected vulnerable children. *Journal of Consulting and Clinical Psychology, 41*, 438–446.

Crockett, L., Losoff, M., & Peterson, A. C. (1984). Perceptions of the peer group and friendship in early adolescence. *Journal of Early Adolescence, 4*, 155–181.

Csikszentmihalyi, M., Larson, R., & Prescott, S. (1977). The ecology of adolescent activity and experience. *Journal of Youth and Adolescence, 6*, 281–294.

Daly, M., & Wilson, M. (1981). Child maltreatment from a sociobiological perspective. *New Directions for Child Development, 11*, 93–112.

Dodge, K. A., Coie, J. D., & Brakke, N. P. (1982). Behavior patterns of socially rejected and neglected preadolescents: The role of social approach and aggression. *Journal of Abnormal Child Psychology, 10*, 389–409.

Dodge, K. A., & Frame, C. L. (1982). Social cognitive biases and deficits in aggressive boys. *Child Development, 53*, 620–635.

Dodge, K. A., McClasky, C. L., & Feldman, E. (1985). Situational approach to the assessment of social competence in children. *Journal of Consulting and Clinical Psychology, 53*, 344–353.

Dodge, K. A., & Murphy, R. R. (1984). The assessment of social competence in adolescents. In P. Karoly & J. J. Steffen (Eds.), *Adolescent behavior disorders: Foundations and contemporary concerns* (pp. 61–96). Lexington, MA: Heath.

Dornbusch, S. M., Carlsmith, J. M., Bushwall, S. J., Ritter, P. L., Leiderman, H., Hastorf, A. H., & Gross, R. T. (1983). *Social class, race, and sex differences in family influence upon adolescent decision making.* Paper presented at the meeting of the Pacific Sociological Association, San Jose, California.

Dornbusch, S. M., Carlsmith, J. M., Bushwall, S. J., Ritter, P. L., Leiderman, H., Hastorf, A. H., & Gross, R. T. (1985). Single parents, extended households, and the control of adolescents. *Child Development, 56*, 326–341.

Douvan, E., & Adelson, J. (1966). *The adolescent experience.* New York: Wiley.

Elder, G. H. (1968). *Adolescent socialization and personality.* Chicago: Rand McNally.

Erikson, E. H. (1968). *Identity: Youth and crises.* New York: Norton.

Evans, R. I. (1985). *Prevention and health promotion: Has psychological research really made significant contributions?* Symposium presented at the meeting of the American Psychological Association, Los Angeles.

Ford, M. E. (1982). Social cognition and social competence in adolescence. *Developmental Psychology, 18*, 323–340.

Forehand, R., & McMahon, R. J. (1981). *Helping the noncompliant child: A clinician's guide to effective parent training.* New York: Guilford.

Freedman, B. J., Rosenthal, L., Donahoe, C. P., Schlundt, D. G., & McFall, R. M. (1978). A social-behavioral analysis of skill deficits in delinquent and nondelinquent adolescent boys. *Journal of Consulting and Clinical Psychology, 46*, 1448–1462.

Gaffney, L. R., & McFall, R. M. (1981). A comparison of social skills in delinquent and nondelinquent adolescent girls using a behavioral role-play inventory. *Journal of Consulting and Clinical Psychology, 49*, 959–967.

Garbarino, J., & Gilliam, G. (1980). *Understanding abusive families*. Lexington, MA: Lexington.

Garbarino, J., Sebes, J., & Schellenbach, C. (1984). Families at risk for destructive parent–child relations in adolescence. *Child Development, 55,* 174–183.

Goldstein, A., Sherman, M., Gershaw, N. J., Sprafkin, R., & Glick, B. (1978). Training aggressive adolescents in prosocial behaviors. *Journal of Youth and Adolescence, 7,* 73–92.

Gottman, J. M., Gonso, J., & Rasmussen, B. (1975). Social interaction, social competence and friendships in children. *Child Development, 46,* 709–718.

Green, K. D., Forehand, R., Beck, S., & Vosk, B. (1980). An assessment of the relationship among measures of children's social competence and children's academic achievement. *Child Development, 51,* 1149–1156.

Grotevant, H. D., & Cooper, C. R. (1985). Patterns of interaction in family relationships and the development of identity exploration in adolescence. *Child Development, 56,* 415–428.

Hall, G. S. (1904). *Adolescence: Its psychology and its relations to physiology, anthropology, sociology, sex, crime, religion, and education.* New York: Appleton.

Hill, J. P. (1982). Guest editorial. *Child Development, 53,* 1409–1412.

Hill, J. P. (1983). Early adolescence: A research agenda. *Journal of Early Adolescence, 3,* 1–21.

Hunter, F. T. (1985). Adolescent's perception of discussions with parents and friends. *Developmental Psychology, 21,* 433–440.

Hunter, F. T., & Youniss, J. (1982). Changes in functions of three relations during adolescence. *Developmental Psychology, 18,* 806–811.

Kandel, D. B., & Lesser, G. S. (1972). *Youth in two worlds: U.S. and Denmark.* San Francisco: Jossey-Bass.

Kon, I. S., & Losenkov, V. A. (1978). Friendship in adolescence: Values and behavior. *Journal of Marriage and the Family, 40,* 143–155.

Livson, N., & Peskin, H. (1980). Perspectives on adolescence from longitudinal research. In J. A. Adelson (Ed.), *Handbook of Adolescent Psychology* (pp. 47–98). New York: Wiley.

Maccoby, E. E., & Martin, J. A. (1983). Socialization in the context of the family: Parent-child interaction. In E. M. Hetherington (Ed.), *Handbook of child psychology: Vol. 4. Socialization personality, and social development* (pp. 1–101). New York: Wiley.

Marks, P. A., Seeman, W., & Haller, D. (1974). *The actuarial use of the MMPI with adolescents and adults.* New York: Oxford University Press.

McFall, L. M. (1982). A review and reformulation of the concept of social skills. *Behavioral Assessment, 4,* 1–34.

Montemayer, R. (1982). The relationship between parent–adolescent conflict and the amount of time adolescents spend alone and with parents and peers. *Child Development, 53,* 1512–1519.

Montemayer, R., & Van, R. (1980). Age segregation of adolescents in and out of school. *Journal of Youth and Adolescence, 9,* 371–381.

Moskowitz, D. S., Schwartzman, A. E., & Ledingham, J. E. (1985). Stability and change in aggression and withdrawal in middle childhood and early adolescence. *Journal of Abnormal Psychology, 94,* 30–41.

Newcomb, A. F., & Bukowski, W. M. (1984). A longitudinal study of the ability of social preference and social impact on sociometric classification schemes. *Child Development, 55,* 1434–1447.

Offer, D., & Offer, J. (1975). *From teenage to young manhood.* New York: Basic Books.

Ollendick, T. H., & Hersen, M. (1979). Social skills training for juvenile delinquents. *Behaviour Research and Therapy, 17,* 547–554.

Patterson, G. R. (1982). *Coercive family process.* Eugene, OR: Castalia.

Prinz, R. J., Swan, G., Liebert, D., Weintraub, S., & Neale, J. M. (1978). ASSESS: Adjustment scales for sociometric evaluation of secondary-school students. *Journal of Abnormal Child Psychology, 6,* 439–501.

Richard, B. A., & Dodge, K. A. (1982). Social maladjustment and problem solving in school-aged children. *Journal of Consulting and Clinical Psychology, 50,* 226–233.

Rivenbark, W. H. (1971). Self-disclosure patterns among adolescents. *Psychological Reports, 28,* 35–42.

Rubin, K. H., & Beirness, T. D. (1983). Concurrent and predictive correlates of sociometric status in kindergarten and grade 1 children. *Merrill-Palmer Quarterly, 29,* 337–352.

Rutter, M. (1980). *Changing youth in a changing society patterns of adolescent development and disorder.* Cambridge, MA: Harvard University Press.

Sarason, S. B., & Klaber, M. (1985). The school as a social situation. *Annual Review of Psychology, 36,* 115–140.

Sarason, I. G., & Sarason, B. R. (1981). Teaching cognitive and social skills to high school students. *Journal of Consulting and Clinical Psychology, 49,* 908–918.

Simmons, R. G., Rosenberg, F., & Rosenberg, M. (1973). Disturbance in the self-image at adolescence. *American Sociological Review, 38,* 553–568.

Simmons, R. G., Blyth, D. A., VanCleave, E. F., & Bush, D. M. (1979). Entry into early adolescence: The impact of school structure, puberty, and early dating on self-esteem. *American Sociological Review, 44,* 948–967.

Spivack, G., Platt, J., & Shure, M. (1976). *The problem-solving approach to adjustment.* San Francisco: Jossey-Bass.

Steinberg, L. D., & Hill, J. P. (1978). Patterns of family interaction as a function of age, the onset of puberty, and formal thinking. *Developmental Psychology, 14,* 683–684.

Steinberg, L. D. (1981). Transformation in family relations at puberty. *Developmental Psychology, 17,* 833–840.

U.S. Census Bureau (1980). *Statistical abstract of the United States.* Washington, DC: Author.

Weintraub, S., Prinz, R. J., & Neale, J. M. (1978). Peer evaluations of the competence of children vulnerable to psychopathology. *Journal of Abnormal Child Psychology, 6,* 461–473.

White, K. M., Speisman, J. C., & Costos, D. (1983). Young adults and their parents: Individuation to mutuality. In H. D. Grotevant & C. R. Cooper (Eds.), *Adolescent development in the family: New directions for child development* (pp. 61–76). San Francisco: Jossey-Bass.

Youniss, J. (1980). *Parents and peers in social development*. Chicago: University of Chicago Press.

PART IV

Specific Disorders

Theodore Lownik Library
Illinois Benedictine College
Lisle, Illinois 60532

CHAPTER 14

Conduct Disorders

Philip H. Bornstein, David Schuldberg, and Marcy Tepper Bornstein

Childhood conduct disorders comprise a diversity of problem behaviors. The professional literature is replete with descriptions including physical destructiveness, violation of others' basic rights, and general disregard for socially acceptable norms. Typically, these behaviors occur in conjunction with one another and can be further defined into aggressive and nonaggressive subtypes. Aggressive types focus upon violence against persons and property (e.g., vandalism and fire setting), whereas nonaggressive types tend to be more concerned with childhood rule-breaking behaviors (e.g., stealing, running away, substance abuse, truancy).

Aggression is the child behavior problem described by teachers as being most disruptive to the classroom situation. It is also the most common child referral problem presented to mental health agencies (Achenbach & Edelbrock, 1981). Surveys indicate that one third to one half of all child referrals received from both parents and teachers are concerned with conduct disorders (Patterson, Reid, Jones, & Conger, 1975; Wolff, 1961). Research indicates that early acting-out behavior is related to adult maladaptive behavior (Robins, 1966; Watt, 1978). Further, childhood aggression, truancy, substance abuse, and arrests have been shown to be precursors of adult substance abuse (Kellam, Brown, & Fleming, 1982). Thus, conduct disorders are a serious childhood behavior problem that may, in fact, lead to a variety of adult difficulties.

Given the above, the purpose of this chapter is to describe and examine conduct disorders with regard to epidemiological findings, assessment/diagnosis, treatment, and current research. In addition, an illustrative case example will be provided.

OVERVIEW OF THE DISORDER

Description of Conduct Disorders

Conduct disorders, as presented in the *Diagnostic and Statistical Manual of Mental Disorders*, 3rd edition (*DSM-III*) (American Psychiatric Association, 1980), are divided into four major subtypes. These vary according to the presence/absence of aggressive antisocial behavior and adequate social bonds (i.e., undersocialized, aggressive; undersocialized, nonaggressive; socialized, aggressive; and socialized, nonaggressive). In general, all four subtypes may present difficulties in home, school, and community. Conduct-disordered children exhibit low self-esteem and are often precocious in their sexual

245

behavior. Early smoking, drinking, and other substance use frequently occur. Irritability, temper outbursts, and attentional problems are common. Although the degree of antisocial behavior can vary from mild to extreme, the conduct-disordered youth exhibits a repetitive and persistent pattern of impaired social and school functioning.

Undersocialized Aggressive Subtype

This form of conduct disorder is characterized by regular occurrence of aggressive behavior that violates the rights of others. Manifestations may include either (a) physical violence against persons or property (e.g., vandalism, rape, breaking and entering, fire setting, mugging, assault) or (b) thefts outside the home involving confrontation with a victim (e.g., extortion, purse snatching, armed robbery). Failure to establish a normal degree of affectional bonding is characteristic of the undersocialized aspect of this disorder. This can be exhibited by the absence of guilt and remorse or the exhibition of callous disregard for others.

Undersocialized Nonaggressive Subtype

These individuals display persistent and repetitive patterns of nonaggressive behavior in which the rights of others are violated (e.g., running away from home, serious lying, stealing, truancy, substance abuse). In addition, there is again the failure to establish normal affectional bonds as exhibited by the lack of concern for friends or companions, inability to feel guilt or remorse, and callous behavior directed toward others.

Socialized Aggressive Subtype

This form of the disorder is similar to the undersocialized aggressive subtype inasmuch as the individual's behavior is aggressive and the rights of others are violated. However, differences occur with regard to the existence of social attachments. Specifically, the individual exhibiting socialized conduct-disordered behavior problems may establish peer group friendships lasting longer than 6 months, give of himself or herself to others when no immediate reward is apparent, feel genuine guilt or remorse, avoid blaming or informing on companions, and show concern for the welfare of others. Obviously, the nature of the conduct-disordered behavior, though, remains aggressive.

Socialized Nonaggressive Subtype

This form of the disorder again violates the rights of others or demonstrates disregard for age-appropriate societal rules. However, the behaviors exhibited are nonaggressive in nature and do not involve confrontation with a victim. Social attachment is also evident and may be manifest by any two of the following: (a) has one or more peer group friendships lasting at least 6 months, (b) extends self for others when no immediate reward is evident, (c) feels appropriate guilt or remorse, and (d) demonstrates concern for and avoids blaming/informing on friends or companions.

Although the *DSM-III* classifications are clearly more specific and more objective than were those of its predecessors (i.e., *DSM-I* or *DSM-II*), the reliability of the diagnostic categories is still questionable. In 1980, an American Psychiatric Association study reported .52 clinician agreement on diagnoses of conduct disorders. Subsequent investigations have indicated even lower reliabilities (Mattison, Cantwell, Russell, & Will, 1979; Mezzich & Mezzich, 1979).

There also is some controversy regarding the validity of these subtypes. Acceptable levels of predictive validity were found with adjudicated populations (Henn, Bardwell, & Jenkins, 1980), but further evidence supporting these findings is nonexistent. In fact, it has been proposed that the dimensions of variety, frequency, and seriousness might be diagnostically more useful than those currently in use. Further, socialized and undersocialized conduct disorders may simply represent distinct syndromes rather than two subtypes of the same disorder. In accord with the above, Wells (1981) and Achenbach (1982) suggest that the weakness of *DSM-III* diagnostic categories resides in their lack of empirical derivation. That is, the conduct disorders' diagnostic categories lack reliability and predictive validity because they were derived by committee (consensus/opinion of *DSM-III* committee) rather than by relevant research efforts.

Empirically Derived Subtypes of Conduct Disorders

The extent to which *DSM-III* subtypes correspond to empirically identified syndromes of childhood disorders has been reviewed by Quay (1979). Examining factor-analytic studies of childhood psychopathology, Quay identified two syndromes related to aggressive behavior: (a) Conduct Disorder and (b) Socialized Aggressive Disorder. Achenbach and Edelbrock (1978) independently found evidence supporting two corresponding syndromes that they labeled Aggressive and Delinquent. Using a cluster analysis of parent-observed behavior problems, Chamberlain (1980) described three relevant antisocial behavior clusters. These were labeled Aggressive, Unsocialized, and Immature. The aggressive and unsocialized clusters were found to be quite similar to the two aggressive syndromes identified by Quay (1979) and Achenbach and Edelbrock (1978). Lorber and Patterson (1981) examined the presenting problems of children referred to a traditional facility for aggressive youth. Their analyses revealed three progressions of behavior problems: Stealer, Social Aggressive, and Immature. All three progressions began with noncompliance as the most commonly occurring presenting problem. However, these researchers contend that although the immature subtype presently is not well understood, other subtype progressions (e.g., stealers and social aggressives) may have different causes, prognoses, and treatment outcomes. Finally, Quay (1964) also found three patterns of antisocial behavior in institutionalized boys (Socialized-Subcultural Delinquency, Unsocialized-Psychopathic Delinquency, and Disturbed-Neurotic Delinquency). These also appear congruent with the research cited above.

Thus, the empirical evidence indicates that at least two separate syndromes can be identified in conduct-disordered children. Unfortunately, these do not consistently correspond to *DSM-III* subtypes. Quay (1979) has specified the behavioral characteristics most frequently found in these studies. Reliability and validity have been more than adequate. In addition, Achenbach (1980) compared *DSM-III* and empirically derived categories (see Table 14.1). He concluded that if socialized aggressive and nonaggressive conduct disorders differ merely on the basis of gender (i.e., delinquent girls tend to be socialized nonaggressive and delinquent boys tend to be socialized aggressive), the empirical syndromes do correspond to the *DSM-III* diagnostic categories. In any case, it appears as though additional research is necessary to more adequately identify and define the various subtypes of children's conduct-disordered behavior.

ASSESSMENT AND DIAGNOSIS

This section examines the uses of psychological assessment with a conduct-disordered population. Different models of psychological assessment are discussed, focusing on stages of the assessment process where each is most useful. Descriptions of particular instruments and representative test signs are provided wherever possible.

Functions and Models of Assessment

Clinical assessment with conduct-disordered youth may serve any of the following purposes: psychological screening, differential diagnosis, classification, treatment planning, and/or establishing goals for intervention. In addition, assessment methodologies may also be employed in defining groups (and subgroups) of subjects for experimental research.

The assessment of conduct disorders presents

Table 14.1. Correspondence of *DSM-III* and Empirically Derived Categories of Aggressive Disorders

DSM-III Diagnostic Category	Empirically Derived Category
Undersocialized, Aggressive Conduct Disorder	1. Conduct disorder (Quay) Aggressive (Achenbach)
Undersocialized, Nonaggressive Conduct Disorder	2. No counterpart
Socialized, Aggressive Conduct Disorder	3. Socialized Aggressive Disorder (Quay) Delinquent (boys) (Achenbach)
Socialized, Nonaggressive Conduct Disorder	4. Delinquent (girls) (Achenbach)
Oppositional Disorder	5. No counterpart

a picture of competing philosophies, methodologies, and preferred levels of psychological measurement. Clinicians have tended to view these behavioral problems as separate from "emotional" disorders. In our opinion, this distinction is neither accurate nor useful. In addition to assessing problem behaviors, it is necessary for the clinician to garner information regarding cognitive, personality, and interpersonal variables. These have value in both differential diagnosis and treatment planning.

Different aspects of the term conduct disorder are conceptually related to various assessment methodologies. First, and directly related to the diagnosis, is a behavioral component. Intervention strategies that focus on target symptoms concentrate in this area. Next, an assessment of cognitive skills involved in learning, judgment, decision making, and problem solving are essential to the selection of therapeutic program components. Finally, there is an interpersonal aspect of the disorder involving empathy, relatedness, and the client's repertoire of appropriate/inappropriate social behaviors. Given the nature of the disorder, the usefulness of this information should be immediately apparent.

Psychological Screening

The identification of a population in need of preventive or treatment-related interventions often is a first stage in the assessment process. Specifying high-risk or "delinquency-prone" subjects has been emphasized in early research with conduct-disordered youth. Brief instruments, such as problem checklists completed by parents or teachers, represent convenient forms of clinical interview and data-gathering methods. Objective personality inventories also have been utilized in this manner. However, in actual practice, conduct-disordered children often are identified by informal observation and referred by community agencies due to the high visibility of their behavioral symptoms.

Differential Diagnosis

Once the child is identified, the clinician will be concerned with classification and differential diagnosis. An emphasis on problem behaviors, rather than categorical diagnosis, has characterized criticisms of DSM-III's approach to disorders of infancy, childhood, and adolescence. The dimensional approach concentrates on symptom clusters or behavioral factors. Other workers within the behavioral tradition emphasize specific problems or target symptoms. Decisions regarding management require information about the client's degree of aggressiveness and the possibility of self-destructive behavior.

The presence or absence of other forms of dysfunction must also be evaluated. Acting-out behavior may be secondary to psychotic impairment, affecting perception, judgment, or impulse control. Depression may be present and, in fact, may be the primary symptom with some acting-out individuals (Kashani, Cantwell, Shekim, & Reid, 1982; Puig-Antich, 1982). Yet, clinicians may fail to recognize childhood depression when it occurs in the context of provocative behavior. Self-report instruments such as the Children's Depression Inventory (CDI; Kovacs, 1981) may be useful in these situations.

Classification

Obviously, differential diagnosis and classification are highly related clinical activities. Interestingly, cognitive variables (e.g., level of empathy, role-taking ability, moral development, self-esteem) have assumed increasing importance in the classification and treatment of psychiatric disorders. For example, some practitioners have treated the behavioral symptoms of conduct disorder as secondary, attempting to deal instead with cognitive and affective etiological factors (e.g., powerlessness, inadequate social judgment, deficits in cognitive development) (Malmquist, 1978).

At a more basic level, behavioral problems in the classroom may also be secondary to sensory or learning difficulties. As a result, clinicians will want to assess individual clients' particular strengths and weaknesses. Attentional deficits, for example, may be associated features of conduct disorder or they may warrant independent and primary classification of their own accord (Safer & Allen, 1976). Consequently, for purposes of classification, standardized achievement tests and neurological evaluations may be highly appropriate adjuncts to traditional psychological assessment.

Treatment Planning and Intervention Goals

The establishment of a treatment regimen requires that the clinician learn about the client's interpersonal behavior. In the area of conduct disorders, degree of interpersonal manipulativeness and potential for attachment to others are particularly significant. An understanding of environmental and family factors will also provide hypotheses about the genesis of the client's difficulties that should be useful in treatment planning. The *DSM-III* itself requires the assessment of personality style and interpersonal behavior in classifying conduct disorders. That is, the socialized versus undersocialized distinction concerns whether the subject forms a normal degree of affectional and empathic bonding with others. This distinction has clear prognostic implications in that it begins to address issues related to the acute versus characterological dimension, resistance toward therapeutic efforts, and likelihood of change.

Further, treatment planning often will require basic operant information: identification of problem behavior (i.e., frequency, intensity, duration) and knowledge of the context in which it occurs. Thus, interpersonal, environmental, family, and descriptive operant information will all aid in planning/monitoring the effectiveness of treatment and in matching a therapeutic regime with client characteristics. Unfortunately, the clinician often is asked to also predict future behavior (e.g., parole violation, successful foster-home placement). Although testing is useful in therapeutic planning and predicting *potential* pitfalls in treatment, prognosticating beyond the power of one's instruments is a form of professional jeopardy and clearly not in the best interests of one's clients.

A final word about systems conceptualizations is warranted. Those professionals who adopt an interactional orientation (e.g., Patterson, 1976) frequently focus on assessing behavioral chains and describing sequences of aversive/coercive events that culminate in an aggressive episode. This information clearly is useful for intervention and may also shed light on issues of nosology. More importantly, however, such data influence decision making regarding the appropriateness of a family-based intervention. Behavioral assessment of family interactional sequences merges conceptually with systems-oriented family treatment programs. Therefore, the clinician will want to assess individual functioning of parents or caretakers and of the family as a whole. Consequently, individual family members' skills, deficits, and interactional patterns (particularly in such crucial areas as discipline and limit-setting) must be evaluated. Where possible, assessment should also consider the role and function of the conduct-disordered child in the family system.

In recent years, more "traditional" methods of personality assessment emphasizing dynamic or dispositional factors have been regarded with some disfavor. This chapter will not consider the relative merits of categorical, dimensional, behavioral, dynamic, or trait-measurement approaches. Rather, we will focus on instrument utility (regardless of theoretical approach), implications for assessment/treatment, and the variety of data that are likely to be obtained.

Selected Methodologies and Instruments

This section examines a number of different assessment methodologies and representative instruments. Emphasis is placed on clinical utility, diagnostic information secured, treatment planning implications, and ease of use/applicability to the clinical situation.

Clinical Interview

In its most basic form, the clinical interview provides background data and demographic information. Thus, the clinician will want to gather facts about history, family constellation, school functioning, and social supports available to the identified client and the system as a whole. Wells and Forehand (1985) discuss the value of interviewing in the home. This is especially helpful in providing in vivo observation of the client's social skills and more general family functioning.

Because the main criterion for the diagnosis of conduct disorder involves the commission of norm-violating behavior, a substantial amount of the information necessary to make the diagnosis may be obtained from the interview—unglamorous backbone of the clinical assessment process—in the initial phases of evaluation. Structured history-taking forms and interviewing formats are available (e.g., Lorei & Vestre, 1969). Many of the behavioral rating or problem checklist instruments described below can also be viewed as focused objective history-taking devices.

Within the interview itself, it is important to ascertain the occurrence of important life events or environmental stressors. This contextual information may become a focus of treatment (e.g., in family therapy or parent training programs) or aid in determining whether behavioral symptoms are an acute reaction to situational events or part of a long-standing characterological problem. In either case, careful participant-observation of the conduct-disordered client certainly is appropriate. Such observation provides information regarding the client's response to naturally occurring events. For example, in a situation that approximates the diagnostic play or analogue behavioral setting, the clinician can structure the interview to elicit information about a client's tolerance to frustration or capacity for controlling anger.

Behavioral Methods

Three different forms of behavioral assessment have been utilized in the area of conduct disorders. The first relies on rating or checklist measures of the child's behavior. The second utilizes direct behavioral observation in the naturalistic environment. Finally, behavioral assessment may employ analogue, role-play, or contrived observation.

Behavioral Ratings. This type of behavioral assessment typically consists of ratings completed by parents or teachers. Thus, these instruments often function as measures of the observer's *perception* of the child, rather than direct records of contemporaneous behavior. A large number of behavioral rating scales and checklists are available (see review by Wells, 1981). They not only provide the clinician with a list of specific problem behaviors useful in planning a focused intervention, but may also yield factor scores that locate the individual on specific behavioral dimensions.

The Behavior Problem Checklist (Quay, 1977; Quay & Peterson, 1975) serves as an example of this. Fifty-five problem behaviors are rated on a 3-point scale by parent or teacher. The instrument produces factor scores relevant to the diagnostic category of conduct disorder. Similarly, the Child Behavior Checklist (Achenbach, 1978; Achenbach & Edelbrock, 1979) is composed of 112 items plus questions in the area of social competence. The Devereaux Elementary School Behavior Rating Scale (Spivack & Swift, 1967) is a teacher rating scale consisting of 47 items that have been analyzed into 11 separate factors. The Conners' Teachers Rating Scale

(Conners, 1969) is a 39-item behavioral symptom checklist. Rutter (1967) also has developed a questionnaire for use by teachers, and Langer et al. (1976) describe a screening method for use with parent interviews. A relatively new instrument is the Eyberg Child Behavior Inventory (Robinson, Eyberg, & Ross, 1980), a 36-item scale for assessing the frequency and problematic nature of various child behaviors. Items on this instrument were specifically designed to be useful to the practicing clinician.

Behavioral rating instruments have, as a group, been subjected to extensive multivariate analyses similar to personality inventory item development procedures. Thus, both psychometric and behavioral models of assessment have influenced rating scale and checklist methodology (Korchin & Schuldberg, 1981).

Behavioral Observation. Less inferential behavioral assessment methods utilize direct observational techniques. Applications have been developed that rely on observations in a wide variety of community and naturalistic settings. These procedures often concentrate on observing target symptoms and identifying baseline rates of behavior. This information may then be used for classification, intervention, or treatment evaluation purposes. In addition to the simple observation of individual subjects, interactional observational systems also are available (Hetherington & Martin, 1979). In most instances, these represent a behavioral approach to the assessment of family or parent–child interaction.

Complex behavioral observation data collection methods frequently employ elaborate coding schemes (see Wells, 1981). These are most typically used for operant and skills-training programs in inpatient, outpatient institutional (e.g., school), and home settings. However, broad-band observational coding systems have tended to be too cumbersome for use in nonresearch-oriented clinical settings. Wells, Griest, and Forehand (1980) have attempted to deal with this problem by developing a method for parents to function as behavioral observers in the home.

Analogue Methods. Behavioral assessment also may be conducted in analogue settings or through role-playing of hypothetical situations (Bornstein, Bellack, & Hersen, 1977). With adolescents, this behavioral–analytic approach (Goldfried & D'Zurilla, 1979) is best exemplified by the work of Freedman, Rosenthal, Donahoe, Schlundt, and McFall (1978) in the development of their Adolescent Problem Inventory (API).

In addition to behavior–analytic methods, other analogue forms of cognitive assessment are useful in the psychological evaluation of conduct disorder. For example, a cognitive-behavioral approach to treatment may require knowledge of the child's strategies for deploying attention, regulating self-esteem, or controlling impulses (Little & Kendall, 1979). Knowledge about the child's self-concept, moral reasoning, and cognitive capabilities in the area of role-taking also may be useful in planning intervention strategies. Further, traditional assessment of intellectual abilities is sometimes important in the treatment of conduct-related learning disabilities. As mentioned earlier, some workers stress the primacy of cognitive or cognitive-developmental factors in the etiology of conduct disorders. Consequently, the potential importance of neuropsychological screening and testing is worth noting again here.

Objective Personality Instruments

A number of self-report personality inventories are useful for screening clients and deriving a general sense of current functioning level. Objective inventories also have been developed to be completed by others knowledgeable about the client. For example, the Personality Inventory for Children (PIC; Wirt, Lachar, Kinedinst, & Seat, 1977) is a 600-item MMPI-like instrument, completed by an informant, usually a parent. Items ask about the child's behavior, attitudes, and family relationships. Goh, Cody, and Dollinger (1984) provide evidence for the discriminant validity of the PIC in distinguishing between learning-disabled and conduct-disordered youth.

The Minnesota Multiphasic Personality Inventory (MMPI) also can be used with clients as young as 16 years (Hathaway & McKinley, 1967). In general, objective personality instruments are useful in treatment planning and the assessment of personality style. Further, extensive research has been conducted on the association of MMPI code types with delinquent behavior (Hathaway & Monachesi, 1953). Scale 4 (Psychopathic Deviant) was originally derived

using adolescents or young adults, many of whom would now fit the *DSM-III* conduct disorders diagnosis. Other relevant scales include Scale 9 (Mania) and Scale 8 (Schizophrenia). High scores on Scale 0 (Social Introversion) and Scale 2 (Depression) also have been found to be negatively related to delinquency. Overall, subtle items may be more useful with conduct-disordered populations, but it is important to note that the 4–9 code types is relatively more prevalent with adolescents. Adolescent norms for the MMPI are available in the *Handbook* (Dahlstrom, Welsh, & Dahlstrom, 1972).

The recently developed Millon Adolescent Personality Inventory (Millon, Green, & Meagher, 1982) has several scales relevant to the construct of conduct disorder. Three of these are SS (Impulse Control), TT (Social Conformity), and WW (Attendance Consistency). The California Psychological Inventory (CPI; Gough, 1969) also has been used extensively with adolescents, and Gough (1969) has indicated that the CPI has special utility for this population. The CPI Socialization scale (So) was developed within the theoretical framework of role-taking (Gough, 1960) and constructed using delinquent and nondelinquent criterion groups. The Responsibility (Re) scale is also conceptually and empirically relevant. The CPI *Handbook* (Megargee, 1972) reports lower scores on Well-being (Wb), Tolerance (To), and Achievement via conformity (Ac) for delinquent groups. The CPI can also distinguish delinquent subgroups. Finally, the 16 PF (Cattell, Eber, & Tatsuoka, 1970) and PRF (Jackson, 1974) also have been used as assessment devices with adolescents. Additional objective personality devices are described by Doke and Flippo (1983).

Projective Instruments

Projective methods are useful for assessing several aspects of the conduct-disorder syndrome. These methods are sensitive to detecting psychotic thought processes, evaluating the quality of the client's interpersonal relationships, and deciding the degree to which acting-out is a characterological versus neurotic symptom. However, attempts to link violent and aggressive projective content to overt behavior have produced contradictory results. As with adults, the role of projective instruments in the assessment of children has been controversial

(Mundy, 1972; O'Leary & Johnson, 1979). Much of the controversy over their application has focused on predictive validity issues. It is our opinion that if the constructs to be assessed are specified carefully, projective instruments have a place in the psychological battery when evaluating conduct-disordered youth.

Rorschach. The Rorschach is especially useful in differentiating between neurotic, characterological, and psychotic acting-out patterns. However, Rorschach signs must be evaluated differently depending on the age of the child under study. New norms based on the Comprehensive System are available (Exner, 1985). Prior to age 12, normal children and character-disordered acting-out children are quite similar in their Rorschach configurations (Exner & Weiner, 1982). After age 12, the neurotic group tends to show more Rorschach indices of psychological "hurting" (e.g., high scores on Achromatic Color [C'] and Vista [V]). They also are more concerned with emotional control (FC responses). In contrast, characterological youngsters appear self-centered (Egocentricity Index), unable to manage stress (Distress Index), and inadequate in the area of impulse control (e.g., preponderance of Color-dominated Color responses). In addition, the number of white space (S) responses may be elevated, indicating an oppositional and angry interpersonal style.

The quality of the child's interpersonal relationships can be ascertained both indirectly and directly with the Rorschach. The traditional use of the Rorschach as a measure of intrapsychic traits utilizes test signs linked conceptually to personality variables. The absence of pure H (human) responses can be indicative of a lack of concern for and connectedness with other people. T (texture) responses are interpreted as suggestive of the child's past experience and future expectation of positive close relationships. Quality of the subject's judgment in interpersonal situations also can be assessed through the perceptual accuracy of Human Movement responses. The developmental level of a child's responses also can serve as a measure of cognitive maturity. Research has been conducted on hostile Rorschach content (Coleman, 1967; Davids, 1973).

By contrast, a transactional approach to projective techniques (Singer, 1977) treats the testing situation as an opportunity for direct observation of the client's interpersonal style. It examines the transactions between examiner and subject, viewing this sample of interpersonal behavior as characteristic of the manner in which the client relates to others.

The importance of assessing the possibility of psychotic thought processes in children with behavior problems has been mentioned, and the Rorschach is invaluable in this area. It is very useful for detecting early schizophrenia, evaluating perceptual accuracy, and assessing judgment in both impersonal and interpersonal situations.

Thematic Apperception Test. The Thematic Apperception Test (TAT) has been used extensively in research with conduct-disordered children, and has become mired in research attempting to relate projective themes to overt manifestations of aggression. The findings here are extremely contradictory, and it is our belief that the TAT is most appropriately used as a device for eliciting information about the quality of a subject's fantasy productions. As such, it may provide clinical data regarding the client's wishes, beliefs, concerns, defenses, coping mechanisms, and expectations about the future.

Other Projective Instruments. An adolescent TAT-like instrument is available (Symonds, 1949). The Hand Test also is a projective instrument developed specifically for the prediction of overt aggressive behavior (Bricklin, Piotrowski, & Wagner, 1962). Moderately positive results have been found in validation studies using this measure. A number of sentence completion forms contain relevant items referring to family, school, emotions, and behavior. These may serve to alert the clinician to conduct problems, aid in diagnostic formulation, or explicate key areas of personal concern.

Systems Assessment

A number of clinicians favor an interpersonal, systems-oriented approach to assessment with conduct-disordered children. Basic information about the child's family environment is important for treatment planning, and the clinician may obtain this information either via history or from the reports of others. A systems assessment may proceed indirectly, through the use of interview and testing procedures with individual family members. However, if at all possible, direct observation and clinical interaction with the family or a family subsystem is recommended. Important factors to be considered include level and type of family discord, influence of extended family, community resources for support, etc. Certainly, degree of psychopathology and psychological resources of the parents or caretakers is relevant (e.g., Dean & Jacobson, 1982). Also deserving attention are patterns of childrearing, family interaction, and parental ability to discipline and command. Related to the above, Olweus (1980) has demonstrated a causal role for the family/parenting variables of: (a) mother's negativism, (b) mother's permissiveness, and (c) mother and father's use of power-assertive methods of childrearing. Obviously, parents' style of discipline and patterns of family interaction concerned with limit-setting are crucial variables.

Behavioral methods may be used for coding parent–child and spouse interaction (Hetherington & Martin, 1979). Marital discord appears to play an important role in the incidence of conduct disorders (Porter & O'Leary, 1980). Marital hostility, rather than marital dissatisfaction, appears highly predictive of behavioral difficulties in the child (Porter & O'Leary, 1980). Last, Wahler (1980) has indicated that the family's degree of social isolation may be a crucial variable. Accordingly, he has made the distinction between insular and noninsular families. This information is essential in planning a family or social-environmental intervention.

TREATMENT AND CURRENT RESEARCH

Traditional therapeutic programs for conduct-disordered youth have not demonstrated consistently positive effects (Lipton, Martinson, & Wilks, 1975). As a result, recent research has attempted to examine newer, more innovative programs aimed at a variety of prosocial behaviors across a wide diversity of treatment environments. Moreover, because research and application seem so inextricably woven together in this area, we have chosen to combine research and treatment sections in the present chapter. Further, although considerable overlap exists across intervention programs, for explanatory purposes we will discuss treatment within: (a) institutionalized and community-based settings, (b) family settings, and (c) clinical settings.

Treatment Within Institutionalized Settings and Community-Based Residential Facilities

A considerable amount of applied research has been conducted within institutionalized and community-based settings. Most of the programs examined have utilized multiple-component treatment packages with a strong operant and contingency management flavor. As a consequence, we have grouped them together for purposes of explication and didactic discussion. Rather than attempting to provide a superficial overview, however, we have chosen to discuss the most significant of these programs on an individual basis. Thus, we shall briefly detail each of the following: (a) CASE II, (b) California Youth Authority programs, and (c) Achievement Place.

CASE II

One of the first behavior modification programs for conduct-disordered youth was instituted at the former National Training School (NTS) for Boys in Washington, DC (Cohen & Filipczak, 1971). The 2-year project operated under the acronym CASE (Contingencies Applicable to Special Education) and involved a 24-hour-a-day token economy with emphasis on educational achievement and academic accomplishment. Forty-one boys, ages 14 to 18 years, participated in the program. All were high-school dropouts, who had been committed to the institution for a variety of offenses, including homicide, assault, armed robbery, burglary, etc. As might be expected, these youth had little interest in academic matters and generally were quite hostile toward any type of formal education.

The boys lived together in a converted dormitory building on the grounds of the training school. Individual, self-paced academic programs were established for each resident. Points were received for academic advancement and exemplary social behavior. As typically occurs within most token economy programs, these points were exchangeable for a variety of backup reinforcers consisting of rewards, privileges, recreational opportunities, and activities. Clearly, however, the primary goal of the CASE II program was to increase academic performance and facilitate a return to the regular public school classroom. Consequently, measures of academic performance were utilized for the purpose of evaluation. In general, standardized achievement (Stanford Achievement Test) and intelligence tests (Revised Army Beta) revealed significant improvement over time. At 3-year follow-up, high levels of achievement had been retained. Unfortunately, though, overall recidivism rate for the CASE II youths was approximately 55%. Although this figure is considerably reduced from the Training School reinstitutionalization rate as a whole, it is regrettably similar to previously published national recidivism data (Burchard & Harig, 1976).

California Youth Authority

Although there have been numerous token economy programs implemented within institutions for conduct-disordered youth, rarely have comparative investigations been undertaken. One exception, the California Youth Authority program, compared the efficacy of two substantially different treatment models—behavior modification (BM) and transactional analysis (TA). To accomplish this, Jesness and his associates (Jesness, 1975, 1976; Jesness & DeRisi, 1973; Jesness, DeRisi, McCormick, & Wedge, 1972) randomly assigned residents to one of two institutions, O. H. Close (TA) or the Karl Holton School (BM). Both schools were in the same geographical region and had similar organizational structures, physical facilities, and staffing patterns. During the time the program was in effect, 983 youths, ages 15–21 years, were involved in the study. This was quite a large-scale endeavor and, in fact, one that has not been replicated in overall comprehensiveness.

The TA program was primarily concerned with individual self-concept and residents' subjective perceptions of the world. Soon after admission, residents engaged in life-script interviews to determine broad life patterns that appeared to be in effect. Three kinds of mutually agreeable verbal contracts were then negotiated: academic, small group, and social. Individual counseling and small group therapy sessions served as important components of treatment. During these sessions, therapists and clients would analyze scripts, establish goals, explore alternative ways of dealing with the world, and structure bilateral agreements for new plans of action.

The BM program, on the other hand, dealt with specific targets of behavior change. A variety of techniques were employed, including: a token economy, behavioral contracting, systematic desensitization, assertive training, extinction, and avoidance conditioning. Three classes of behavior were the focus of treatment: (a) convenience behaviors (i.e., those related to the orderly functioning of the institution); (b) academic behaviors; and (c) critical behavior deficiencies (i.e., those related to parole success/failure). The incentive program allowed for both immediate and long-term reinforcement. Thus, immediate backup reinforcers included privileges, personal items, and special services. Major long-term reinforcers focused on the opportunity for parole hearings and eventual release from the institution.

Comparative outcome data revealed some very interesting findings. First, both programs generated rather specific treatment effects. The BM program demonstrated greater gains in behavioral ratings, whereas the TA model appeared more successful on attitudinal and self-report scales. Second, reported misconduct decreased in both programs. Indeed, there was a 60% reduction in the need to utilize detention for rule violations. Third, the TA program generally received higher consumer satisfaction ratings from residents than did the BM program. Fourth, at 12-month follow-up, 31% of both TA and BM residents had violated their parole. This was substantially lower than the 46% parole violation rate at other California Youth Authority institutions. However, at 2-year follow-up, over 50% of the youths had recidivated. Thus, it appears as though both programs improved behavior within the institution and increased the probability of successful readjustment at least for a short period of time. However, without an aftercare component, likelihood of generalization to the natural environment was apt to be of the "train and hope" variety (Stokes & Baer, 1977).

Achievement Place

Clearly, the most outstanding example of behavior modification principles applied to predelinquent youth within a community setting is that of Achievement Place (Hoefler & Bornstein, 1975). The original Achievement Place program in Lawrence, Kansas, was operated in conjunction with the Department of Human Development at the University of Kansas. Since its inception in 1967, dozens of reports have been published and the model has been replicated in over 100 group homes across the country.

The Achievement Place program is based on a number of key principles. First, it is believed that conduct disorders occur not because of an inherent psychopathology within the individual, but rather due to faulty learning histories (Phillips, Phillips, Fixsen, & Wolf, 1971, 1972). That is, youths develop skill deficits because of inadequate training, ineffective incentives, poor adult models, delinquent peer group, etc. Second, to develop more appropriate behavior patterns, these youths must be exposed to a highly structured, systematic program administered by professionally trained and caring staff members. Third, providing a residential, community-based "homestyle" program should facilitate generalization to the natural environment. Thus, the overall goals are to modify undesirable antisocial behavior, develop new appropriate ways of relating, and establish social/academic/vocational skills that will promote good citizenship and community success.

Those children and adolescents referred to Achievement Place are typically adjudicated youth with a history of poor school performance, family problems, and repeated contacts with authorities and social service agencies. The Achievement Place model provides these children with a family-style program of group foster care operated under the direction of residential "teaching parents." The program has four main areas of concentration: (a) skills training, (b) a token economy reinforcement system, (c) student government, and (d) relationship building. However, the token economy clearly serves as the central concept around which the program is organized. When an individual first enters Achievement Place, maximum feedback regarding appropriate/inappropriate behavior is provided by the daily point system. This is subsequently faded to a weekly point system and, ultimately, to a merit system (where all privileges are free). Following continued success in the merit program, the youth advances to the homeward-bound program. At this point, return to the youth's original home is coordinated by regular meetings between parents and teaching parents. Therefore, although the token

economy remains the organizing element of the program, teaching parents are the activating agents. In essence, they form the nucleus of everyday operations.

Achievement Place has been a very carefully researched program. Well-controlled investigations have examined articulation errors (Bailey, Timbers, Fixsen, & Wolf, 1971), social behaviors (Phillips, 1968), self-government (Fixsen, Phillips, & Wolf, 1973), home-based reinforcement (Bailey, Wolf, & Phillips, 1970), etc. Unfortunately, demonstrations of functional control do not address larger questions of overall program effectiveness. Although there has been a shift toward greater emphasis on outcome evaluation at Achievement Place (Kirigin, Braukmann, Fixsen, Phillips, & Wolf, 1975), successful community adjustment remains the key question. Definitive research on this issue has yet to be conducted.

Treatment Within Family Settings

Our survey of the literature indicates that four major family-based approaches have been used in treatment of conduct-disordered children and adolescents: (a) parent training, (b) behavioral contracting, (c) negotiation, and (d) family therapy. Although overlap exists across the four areas, they represent conceptually distinct avenues of intervention. Consequently, we will address them individually.

Parent Training

By far, the family treatment approach that has received the greatest attention is that of reprogramming the social environment through parent training (Wells & Forehand, 1985). Such approaches emphasize that children's deviant behavior is generated and maintained by faulty family communication and maladaptive coercive interactions. Thus, parent training programs focus on the teaching of social learning principles that have direct application to children's target behaviors. Most programs are quite operant in nature and represent a dramatic shift from traditional child therapy. In such programs, parents or caregivers are given the major responsibility for behavior change and treatment primarily is applied in the natural environment.

In the typical parent training program, parents are first provided with a written manual on child management and social learning principles. The therapist then gives instructions on the identification, observation, and recording of undesirable behaviors. Application then follows. This may occur with the child in the clinic, by home training, or role-play interaction. Parents monitor progress over time, and independent observations are usually conducted in the home to verify changes in child and/or parent behavior.

Perhaps the most extensive applied research programs in this area have occurred under the direction of Patterson (Patterson, 1974), Forehand (Forehand & McMahon, 1981), and Wahler (e.g., Wahler, Berland, & Coe, 1979). Their research and evaluative reviews of the literature generally support the efficacy of parent-training procedures in reducing a wide range of conduct-related problems (Bernstein, 1982; Griest & Wells, 1983; O'Dell, 1974; Patterson & Fleischman, 1979). In summary, parents have been taught to modify their children's noncompliance, temper tantrums, destruction of property, overall aggressiveness, stealing, etc. As indicated by O'Dell (1974), "there does not appear to be any class of overt child behaviors that parents cannot be trained to modify" (p. 421).

Behavioral Contracting

Although parent training procedures have been demonstrated to be effective with relatively young children, difficulties in administration lessen their utility with adolescent populations. As a result, clinicians have explored the use of contingency contracting with children ages 13 through adolescence. These contracts provide a means by which the adolescent may enjoy a variety of privileges in exchange for designated prosocial behaviors. In establishing a behavioral contract, adolescents and parents agree on behaviors to be emitted before a specified privilege is granted. Accordingly, negotiation and clear definition of reciprocal responsibilities are actively pursued. This is typically accomplished in conjunction with a trained therapist.

Stuart (1971) and Weathers and Liberman (1975) have discussed five issues that should be confronted in developing a good contingency contract: (a) what are the privileges to be obtained? (b) what are the behavioral responsibilities to which each party agrees? (c) what are the

penalties for failure to meet responsibilities? (d) what bonuses will be provided for contract compliance? and (e) what method of monitoring will be employed while the contract is in force? In answering questions such as these, all parties assure that contingencies will be clear, behaviorally specific, and understandable.

Although numerous applied investigations have utilized behavioral contracts as part of family-based treatment, results have not always been overwhelmingly successful (Wells & Forehand, 1981). In fact, Stuart and Lott (1972) indicate that the nature of the contract itself may be somewhat irrelevant. Rather, it is the tactical skill of the therapist in creating a climate of compromise that may be of the utmost import. Obviously, in chronically chaotic families " . . . a contingency contract is worth about as much as the paper it's printed on" (Weathers & Liberman, 1975, p. 365). Under these circumstances, thorough assessment and comprehensive family intervention strategies are required.

Negotiation

Most conduct-disordered youths experience rather intense family conflict. Naturally then, a highly appropriate treatment strategy involves training these adolescents and their families in the utilization of effective conflict resolution or negotiation skills. A number of such investigations have been conducted with results generally suggestive of improved parent–child relations and decreases in adolescent acting-out behaviors (Kifer, Lewis, Green, & Phillips, 1974; Robin, 1979, 1981; Robin, Kent, O'Leary, Foster, & Prinz, 1977).

Kifer et al. (1974) evaluated conflict negotiation skills in a multiple baseline design across parent–child pairs. During hypothetical role-play interactions, targeted negotiation behaviors included: (1) complete communication (statement of one's position and request for similar information from other party); (b) identification of issues (explicit identification of conflict areas); and (c) suggestion of options that might potentially resolve the conflict. Results indicated that negotiation behaviors of each parent–child pair increased dramatically with the introduction of training. Further, audiotaped assessments in the home revealed similar increases in cooperative communication behaviors.

Similarly, Robin (1981) developed a problem-solving communication program to train parents and adolescents in the democratic resolution of specific disputes. This model trains parent–child pairs in the D'Zurilla–Goldfried (1971) problem-solving format, remediates negative communication patterns, cognitively restructures inappropriate attitudes, and provides opportunity for in-home practice of negotiation-communication skills. Results were very promising, with significant reductions occurring in self-reported disputes and conflictual communications. Moreover, problem-solving training subjects demonstrated improvements on independently related behavioral measures of effective communication. Thus, the problem-solving program emphasizing negotiation and communication skills appeared highly effective in ameliorating parent–adolescent conflict.

Family Therapy

Although a wide variety of family therapy approaches have been employed with conduct-disordered youth (see Gurman & Kniskern, 1981), we will elaborate in this section solely on the work of Alexander and his associates. We have chosen to discuss this most laudable research program because of its demonstrated effectiveness and replicability.

Alexander and Parsons (1973) employed a family therapy and problem-solving training approach with 46 families of conduct-disordered adolescents. Using modeling and behavioral rehearsal, therapists implemented a program intended to emphasize negotiation, clear communication, and generation of alternative solutions. Treatment led to lower recidivism rates, in general, and in comparison to a wide variety of therapeutically oriented control conditions (client-centered therapy, psychodynamic theory). Moreover, a 3$^1/_2$-year follow-up revealed that the siblings of treated youth had significantly fewer court contacts than did siblings of youth in the control conditions (Klein, Alexander, & Parsons, 1977). Alexander, Barton, Schiavo, and Parsons (1976) replicated the original program and found similar results. Further, an analysis of process measures revealed that no recidivism occurred among youths whose families had significantly modified their problem-solving and interactional style. Thus, it appears that family therapy used to enhance communication skills can have substantial impact on delinquency-prone adolescents.

Treatment Within Clinical Settings

Obviously, there are a myriad of psychotherapeutic procedures that may be used with conduct-disordered youth. Many of these techniques are based upon the adult treatment literature (see Bornstein, Balleweg, & Weisser, 1985; Bornstein, Hamilton, & McFall, 1981). However, we have chosen to discuss procedures which have been explicitly employed with this chapter's population of interest. Consequently, we will briefly review the research and treatment literature in the following four areas: (a) interpersonal problem-solving, (b) modeling, (c) role-taking, and (d) self-control.

Interpersonal Problem-Solving

It has been frequently asserted that delinquent behaviors are often the result of a deficit in cognitive and behavioral skills necessary for effective functioning in interpersonal situations. The most extensive research in this area is that of Spivack and his colleagues at Hahnemann Hospital (Spivack, Platt, & Shure, 1976). Although most of this group's investigations have involved younger children, a few studies have examined the interpersonal problem-solving skills of adolescents. These have included emotionally disturbed adolescent boys (Spivack & Levine, 1963), teenage psychiatric inpatients (Platt, Spivack, Altman, Altman, & Peizer, 1974), and young incarcerated heroin addicts (Platt, Scura, & Hannon, 1973). These comparisons have consistently shown that nondelinquents score higher on tests of three different interpersonal problem-solving abilities: (a) means–end thinking, (b) alternative thinking, and (c) perspective taking. In summary, the results of the Hahnemann and related studies (e.g., Freedman et al., 1978) indicate that conduct-disordered youth may be able to discriminate adaptive from nonadaptive interpersonal problem solutions but cannot independently generate such alternative solutions.

Treatment packages attempting to remedy these deficiencies have produced improvements in both problem-solving skills and socialization behaviors. Unfortunately, because training is usually comprehensive, it is difficult to ascertain the therapeutic contribution of interpersonal problem-solving, per se.

Modeling

Sarason and his associates have devised a number of modeling programs for incarcerated youths. Specifically, Sarason and Ganzer (1973) compared modeling, group discussion, and no-treatment controls with 15- to 18-year-old delinquent boys. In the modeling condition, two graduate student group leaders demonstrated competent ways of handling interpersonal problem situations. Group participants were then asked to imitate the modeled behaviors. In the discussion condition, the boys were simply asked to examine the adaptiveness of a variety of response forms, but no actual modeling occurred. Results revealed that both treatment groups produced immediate and long-term recidivism reductions as compared to no-treatment controls. Although no differences were evident between the two treatment conditions, modeling subjects did evince greater subjective benefit than those exposed to the discussion condition. Moreover, other more recent experimental comparisons have demonstrated the superiority of modeling treatments (Ollendick & Hersen, 1979; Synder & White, 1979). In light of the discussion above, it also should be noted that Little and Kendall (1979) have suggested that the critical variable in the modeling treatment may have been the teaching of problem-solving and other cognitive-based skills.

Role-Taking

Antisocial behavior historically has been considered a violation of individuals' rights due to an inability to assume the perspective of others (Gough, 1948; Mead, 1934). However, it is only recently that empirical evidence has been accumulated to support the notion that perspective-taking deficits may lead to the development of antisocial behavior (Chandler, 1973). In fact, deficits in role-taking have been found to be most evident among delinquents and psychopathic criminal offenders (Jurkovic & Prentice, 1977). Consequently, efforts have been implemented to educate delinquents in the plight of their victim through perspective-taking training.

The most significant research in this area was conducted by Chandler (1973). In this investigation, 45 delinquent boys were randomly assigned to either a role-taking, attention-control, or assessment-control condition. Those receiving role-taking wrote brief skits about real-life situations involving characters their own age. Each skit was performed and videotaped until every subject had been given the opportunity to play each role in the production. The attention-control subjects produced films about their own neighborhood, but were not allowed to use themselves as actors. Chandler (1973) found significant improvement in perspective-taking only by those assigned to the primary experimental condition. Moreover, at an 18-month follow-up, these subjects had 50% fewer court contacts than during a similar time period prior to training.

Self-Control

A number of delinquency theories posit that antisocial behavior results from a serious deficit in impulse control (e.g., Glueck & Glueck, 1974). To remediate problems in this area, individuals have been taught to self-regulate or more effectively govern and control their own behavior.

McCullough, Huntsinger, and Nay (1977) trained a 16-year-old aggressive boy to control subvocal cursing with relaxation and a self-instructed thought-stopping procedure. Although this combined treatment had dramatic effects, systematic replication efforts by Huntsinger (1976) showed no differences between treatment and control conditions. However, Synder and White (1979) successfully trained five aggressive conduct-disordered youths to use self-instructions as a means of controlling inappropriate behavior within a residential clinical program. In addition, Seymour and Stokes (1976) and Wood and Flynn (1978) made reinforcement contingent on accurate self-recording and thereby increased and maintained work-related and room-cleaning behaviors in adolescent delinquent males and females.

Further, a number of other multiple component programs (Gross, Brigham, Hopper, & Bologna, 1980; Schwitzgebel & Kolb, 1964; Stumphauzer, 1976) have utilized self-control treatments as part of a more comprehensive therapeutic package. Results are impressive, but the independent effects of self-control training cannot be immediately evaluated. It does appear, however, that providing conduct-disordered youth with the opportunity to manage their own behavior may be an effective means of circumventing noncooperative attitudes and resistant behaviors so often encountered with this clinical population. Moreover, self-management programs hold the promise of producing superior maintenance as compared to externally managed traditionally oriented regimes.

CASE ILLUSTRATION

History and Diagnosis

Bob S. was taken into custody at age 13 for threatening to kill his mother and brother. Prior to his incarceration, there was a 4-year history of "obnoxious and abusive behavior" directed toward his mother. The first incident of physical assault occurred when Bob's mother refused to let him go outside after dinner (age 9 years). Bob struck his mother with closed fists in the arm, stomach, and face. He then proceeded to shove her against a wall and threatened to kill her with a butcher knife.

During this period of time, Bob was admitted to a variety of inpatient facilities for diagnostic purposes. His length of stay never exceeded 45 days and, upon return to the home of his natural mother, Bob's moody, belligerent, abusive behavior would recur. With increasing age, Bob's violence and aggressiveness began to extend outside the home. In addition to his mother's reports of being beaten by Bob, he was accused of breaking neighborhood streetlights and threatening other youths with a wrench and hammer.

Bob was the only child born out of a common-law marriage. His father left the household when Bob was 18 months old and never resumed contact with the family. Mrs. S. did remarry and bore two more children, but that marriage also ended shortly after the birth of the second child. Mrs. S. reports that she was able to control Bob's behavior through his childhood years by restricting his television watching. However, since age 9, her disciplinary tactics had been futile. In fact, Mrs. S. reported that she was unable to enforce any sanctions due to Bob's size and her being absent from the home for purposes of employment.

Based upon extensive clinical interview and formal psychological assessment (WISC-R, Problem Behavior Checklist, Rorschach, TAT, and Sentence Completion forms), Bob was diagnosed as Conduct Disorder, Undersocialized Aggressive subtype. Due to the perceived volatility and dangerousness of Bob's behavior, it was recommended that he be placed in a highly therapeutic structured environment. However, due to his apparent lack of affectional bonding, it was further recommended that he be court-referred to a group-home facility based upon a family treatment model.

Treatment

Bob has now been at the group-home facility for 1 year. His adjustment to date has been marginal, but improving. During the first 3 months, he broke every rule in the household. Bob quickly learned, however, that such behavior afforded him very few advantages. The home was run on a modified token economy program. As Bob continued to lose points on a daily basis, he received little (if any) of the privileges and activities awarded to others. This was discussed with him in both individual and group therapy sessions and eventually had some impact. By his 4th month in the program, Bob had started to respond in a slightly more positive manner. Consequently, he was provided with better living accommodations, increased TV time, opportunity for after-school activities, and one night per week outside the home. In addition, Bob and his family (mother and two siblings) began work in a relationship-based therapy. Although progress in all areas (home, school, family, and community) has been slow, there have been definite improvements. Behavior in the group-home has become generally acceptable, with minor losses of control occurring on an irregular and infrequent basis. School grades have improved, although Bob remains below grade level in most subject areas. Family life has shown the greatest gains. Bob has spent weekends at home on six separate occasions. Although he returned to the group-home early after his second visit, he clearly has learned more effective ways of dealing with his mother. Mother, in turn, has grown as well, learning how to discipline and appropriately demonstrate her caring. Finally, instances of fighting and vandalism did occur early in Bob's stay at the group home. However, no such reports have occurred over the course of the past 4 months.

Prognosis

Bob will remain in the group home for another 6 months to 1 year. Although the above-noted progress is certainly laudatory, this is a young man with longstanding difficulties and continuing emotional problems. As a consequence, his prognosis must remain guarded.

SUMMARY

The purpose of the present chapter was to describe and examine conduct disorders with respect to epidemiological findings, assessment/diagnosis, treatment, and current research. The four major conduct disorders subtypes (undersocialized aggressive, undersocialized nonaggressive, socialized aggressive, and socialized nonaggressive) were first presented and descriptions of their distinguishing characteristics were noted. In general, the disorder appears to be characterized by a blatant disregard for socially acceptable norms and a persistent pattern of impaired home, school, and community functioning. Empirical research has indicated that at least two separate syndromes (aggressive, unsocialized) can be identified in conduct-disordered children. Unfortunately, these syndromes do not consistently correspond to *DSM-III* classification subtypes.

Clinical assessment with conduct-disordered youth may serve a variety of functions: psychological screening, differential diagnosis, classification, treatment planning, and/or establishing goals for intervention. As a result, a wide variety of different assessment methodologies and instruments are available to the practicing clinician. These include clinical interviews, behavioral rating scales, behavioral observation, analogue methods, objective personality instruments, and projective techniques. In addition, systems-oriented assessment methods may prove invaluable.

Traditional therapeutic programs for conduct-disordered youth have not been demonstrated to be highly effective. Consequently, the present chapter attempted to review newer, more innovative treatment programs aimed at a wide variety of prosocial behaviors. These were examined within institutionalized and community-based settings, within the family, and in clinically relevant situations. Most of the programs within institutionalized and community-based settings have utilized multiple-component treatment packages with a strong operant and contingency management flavor. Most notable among these are the Case II Program, California Youth Authority, and Achievement Place. Within family settings, four major approaches were reviewed: parent training, behavioral contracting, negotiation, and family therapy. Clinically, the research and treatment literatures indicate four major therapeutic alternatives: interpersonal problem-solving, modeling, role-taking, and self-control. These clinical alternatives were discussed and treatment recommendations provided. Finally, the chapter concluded with a brief case illustration integrating history, assessment, diagnosis, and treatment functions.

REFERENCES

Achenbach, T. M. (1978). The child behavior profile: I. Boys aged 6–11. *Journal of Consulting and Clinical Psychology, 46,* 478–488.

Achenbach, T. M. (1980). *DSM-III* in light of empirical research on the classification of child psychopathology. *Journal of the American Academy of Child Psychiatry, 19,* 395–412.

Achenbach, T. M. (1982). *Developmental psychopathology* (2nd ed.). New York: Wiley.

Achenbach, T. M., & Edelbrock, C. S. (1978). The classification of child psychopathology: A review and analysis of empirical efforts. *Psychological Bulletin, 85,* 1275–1301.

Achenbach, T. B., & Edelbrock, C. S. (1979). The child behavior profile: II. Boys aged 12–16 and girls aged 6–11 and 12–16. *Journal of Consulting and Clinical Psychology, 47,* 223–233.

Achenbach, T. M., & Edelbrock, C. S. (1981). Behavioral problems and competencies reported by parents of normal and disturbed children aged four through sixteen. *Monographs of the Society for Research in Child Development, 46* (1, Serial No. 188).

Alexander, J. F., Barton, C., Schiavo, R. S., & Parsons, B. V. (1976). Systems-behavioral intervention with families of delinquents: Therapist characteristics, family behavior, and outcome. *Journal of Consulting and Clinical Psychology, 44,* 656–664.

Alexander, J. F., & Parsons, B. (1973). Short-term behavioral intervention with delinquent families: Impact on family process and recidivism. *Journal of Consulting and Clinical Psychology, 81,* 219–225.

American Psychiatric Association. (1980). *Diagnostic and statistical manual of mental disorders* (3rd ed.). Washington, DC: Author.

Bailey, J. S., Timbers, G. D., Fixsen, D. L., & Wolf, M. M. (1971). Modification of articulation errors of pre-delinquents by their peers. *Journal of Applied Behavior Analysis, 4,* 265–281.

Bailey, J. S., Wolf, M. M., Phillips, E. L. (1970). Home-based reinforcement and the modification of pre-delinquent classroom behavior. *Journal of Applied Behavior Analysis, 3,* 223–233.

Bernstein, G. S. (1982). Training behavior change agents: A conceptual review. *Behavior Therapy, 13,* 1–23.

Bornstein, M. R., Bellack, A. S., & Hersen, M. (1977). Social skills training for unassertive children: A multiple baseline analysis. *Journal of Applied Behavior Analysis, 10,* 183–195.

Bornstein, P. H., Balleweg, B. J., & Weisser, C. E. (1985). Anger and violent behavior. In M. Hersen & A. Bellack (Eds.), *Handbook of clinical behavior therapy with adults* (pp. 603–629). New York: Plenum.

Bornstein, P. H., Hamilton, S. B., & McFall, M. E. (1981). Modification of adult aggression: A critical review of theory, research, and practice. In M. Hersen, R. M. Eisler, & P. M. Miller (Eds.), *Progress in behavior modification* (Vol. 12, pp. 300–350). New York: Academic.

Bricklin, B., Piotrowski, Z. A., & Wagner, E. E. (1962). *The hand test: A new projective test with special reference to the prediction of overt behavior.* Springfield, IL: Charles C Thomas.

Burchard, J. D., & Harig, P. T. (1976). Behavior modification and juvenile delinquency. In H. Leitenberg (Ed.), *Handbook of behavior modification and behavior therapy* (pp. 405–452). Englewood Cliffs, NJ: Prentice-Hall.

Cattell, R. B., Eber, H. W., & Tatsuoka, M. M. (1970). *Handbook for the Sixteen Personality Factor Questionnaire (16PF).* Champaign, IL: Institute for Personality and Ability Testing.

Chamberlain, P. (1980). *Standardization of a parent report measure.* Unpublished doctoral dissertation, University of Oregon.

Chandler, M. J. (1973). Egocentrism and antisocial behavior: The assessment and training of social perspective-taking skills. *Developmental Psychology, 9,* 326–332.

Cohen, H. L., & Filipczak, J. (1971). *A new learning environment: A case for learning.* San Francisco: Jossey-Bass.

Coleman, J. C. (1967). Stimulus factors in the relation between fantasy and behavior. *Journal of Projective Techniques and Personality Assessment, 31,* 67–73.

Conners, C. K. (1969). A teacher rating scale for use in drug studies with children. *American Journal of Psychiatry, 6,* 884–888.

Dahlstrom, W. G., Welsh, G. S., & Dahlstrom, L. E. (1972). *An MMPI Handbook.* Minneapolis: University of Minnesota Press.

Davids, A. (1973). Aggression and thought and action of emotionally disturbed boys. *Journal of Consulting and Clinical Psychology, 40,* 322–327.

Dean, R. S., & Jacobson, B. P. (1982). MMPI characteristics for parents of emotionally disturbed and learning-disabled children. *Journal of Consulting and Clinical Psychology, 50,* 775–777.

Doke, L. A., & Flippo, J. R. (1983). Aggressive and oppositional behavior. In T. H. Ollendick & M. Hersen (Eds.), *Handbook of child psychopathology* (pp. 323–356). New York: Plenum.

D'Zurilla, T. J., & Goldfried, M. R. (1971). Problem solving and behavior modification. *Journal of Abnormal Psychology, 78,* 107–126.

Exner, J. E. (1985). *A Rorschach workbook for the comprehensive system* (2nd ed.). Bayville, NY: Rorschach Workshops.

Exner, J. E., & Weiner, I. B. (1982). *The Rorschach: A comprehensive system (Vol. 3): Assessment of children and adolescents.* New York: Wiley.

Fixsen, D. L., Phillips, E. L., & Wolf, M. M. (1973). Achievement Place: Experiments in self-government with delinquents. *Journal of Applied Behavior Analysis, 6,* 31–49.

Forehand, R., & McMahon, R. J. (1981). *Helping the noncompliant child: A clinician's guide to parent training.* New York: Guilford Press.

Freedman, B. J., Rosenthal, L., Donahoe, C. P., Schlundt, D. G., & McFall, R. M. (1978). A social-behavioral analysis of skill deficits in delinquent and nondelinquent adolescent boys. *Journal of Consulting and Clinical Psychology, 46,* 1448–1462.

Glueck, S., & Glueck, E. (1974). *Of crime and delinquency.* Springfield, IL: Charles C Thomas.

Goh, D. S., Cody, J. J., & Dollinger, S. J. (1984). PIC profiles for learning-disabled and behavior-disordered children. *Journal of Clinical Psychology, 40,* 837–841.

Goldfried, M. R., & D'Zurilla, T. J. (1979). A behavioral-analytic model for assessing competence. In C. D. Spielberger (Ed.), *Current topics in clinical and community psychology,* (Vol. I, pp. 151–196). New York: Academic.

Gough, H. G. (1948). A sociological theory of psychopathy. *American Journal of Sociology, 56,* 359–366.

Gough, H. G. (1960). Theory and measurement of socialization. *Journal of Consulting Psychology, 24,* 23–30.

Gough, H. G. (1969). *Manual for the California Psychological Inventory* (rev. ed.). Palo Alto, CA: Consulting Psychologists Press.

Griest, D. L., & Wells, K. C. (1983). Behavioral family therapy with conduct disorders in children. *Behavior Therapy, 14,* 37–53.

Gross, A. M., Brigham, T. A., Hopper, C., & Bologna, N. C. (1980). Self-management and social skills training: A study with predelinquent and delinquent youths. *Criminal Justice and Behavior, 7,* 161–184.

Gurman, A. S., & Kniskern, D. P. (1981). *Handbook of family therapy.* New York: Brunner/Mazel.

Hathaway, S. R., & McKinley, J. C. (1967). *The Minnesota Multiphasic Personality Inventory manual.* New York: Psychological Corporation.

Hathaway, S. R., & Monachesi, E. D. (1953). *Analyzing and predicting juvenile delinquency with the MMPI.* Minneapolis: University of Minnesota Press.

Henn, F. A., Bardwell, R., & Jenkins, R. L. (1980). Juvenile delinquents revisited: Adult criminal activity. *Archives of General Psychiatry, 37,* 1160–1163.

Hetherington, E. M., & Martin, B. (1979). Family interaction. In H. C. Quay & J. S. Werry (Eds.), *Psychological disorders of childhood* (2nd ed., pp. 247–302). New York: Wiley.

Hoefler, S., & Bornstein, P. H. (1975). Achievement Place: An evaluative review. *Criminal Justice and Behavior, 2,* 146–168.

Huntsinger, G. M. (1976). *Teaching of self-control of verbal and physical aggression to juvenile delinquents.* Unpublished manuscript, Virginia Commonwealth University, Richmond.

Jackson, D. N. (1974). *Manual for the Personality Research Form.* Goshen, NY: Research Psychologists Press.

Jesness, C. F. (1975). Comparative effectiveness of behavior modification and transactional programs for delinquents. *Journal of Consulting and Clinical Psychology, 43,* 759–779.

Jesness, C. F. (1976). The Youth Center project: Transactional analysis and behavior modification programs for delinquents. *Behavioral Disorders, 1,* 27–36.

Jesness, C. F., & DeRisi, W. J. (1973). Some variations in techniques of contingency management in a school for delinquents. In J. S. Stumphauzer (Ed.), *Behavior therapy with delinquents* (pp. 196–235). Springfield, IL: Charles C Thomas.

Jesness, C. F., DeRisi, W. J., McCormick, P. M., & Wedge, R. F. (1972). *The Youth Center research project.* Sacramento, CA: American Justice Institute.

Jurkovic, G. J., & Prentice, N. M. (1977). Relation of moral and cognitive development to dimensions of juvenile delinquency. *Journal of Abnormal Psychology, 86,* 414–420.

Kashani, J. H., Cantwell, D. P., Shekim, W. O., & Reid, J. C. (1982). Major depressive disorder in children admitted to an inpatient community mental health center. *American Journal of Psychiatry, 139,* 671–672.

Kellam, S. G., Brown, C. H., & Fleming, J. P. (1982). *The prevention of teenage substance use: Longitudinal research and strategy.* Chicago, IL: Social Psychiatry Study Center.

Kifer, R. E., Lewis, M. A., Green, D. R., & Phillips, E. L. (1974). Training predelinquent youths and their parents to negotiate conflict situations. *Journal of Applied Behavior Analysis, 7,* 357–364.

Kirigin, K. A., Braukmann, C. J., Fixsen, D. L., Phillips, E. L., & Wolf, M. M. (1975). *Is community-based correction effective? An evaluation of Achievement Place.* Paper presented at the meeting of the American Psychological Association, Chicago.

Klein, N. C., Alexander, J. F., & Parsons, B. V. (1977). Impact of family systems intervention on recidivism and sibling delinquency: A model of primary prevention and program evaluation. *Journal of Consulting and Clinical Psychology, 45,* 469–474.

Korchin, S. J., & Schuldberg, D. (1981). The future of clinical assessment. *American Psychologist, 36,* 1147–1158.

Kovacs, M. (1981). Rating scales to assess depression in school-aged children. *Acta Paedopsychiatrica, 46,* 305–315.

Langer, T. S., Gersten, J. C., McCarthy, E. D., Eisenberg, J. G., Green, E. L., Herson, J. H., & Jameson, J. D. (1976). A screening inventory for assessing psychiatric impairment in children 6 to 18. *Journal of Consulting and Clinical Psychology, 44,* 286–296.

Lipton, D., Martinson, R., & Wilks, J. (1975). *The effectiveness of correctional treatment.* New York: Praeger.

Little, V. L., & Kendall, P. C. (1979). Cognitive-behavioral interventions with delinquents: Problem-solving, role-taking, and self-control. In P. C. Kendall & S. D. Hollon (Eds.), *Cognitive-behavioral interventions: Theory, research, and procedures* (pp. 81–115). New York: Academic.

Lorber, R., & Patterson, G. R. (1981). The aggressive child: A concomitant of a coercive system. *Advances in Family Intervention, Assessment and Theory, 2,* 47–87.

Lorei, T. W., & Vestre, N. D. (1969). A set of factor analytically derived scales for scoring the M-B History Record. *Multivariate Behavioral Research, 4,* 181–193.

Malmquist, C. P. (1978). *Handbook of adolescence.* New York: Aronson.

Mattison, R., Cantwell, D. P., Russell, A. T., & Will, L. A. (1979). Comparison of *DSM-II* and *DSM-III* in the diagnosis of childhood psychiatric disorders. *Archives of General Psychiatry, 36,* 1217–1222.

McCullough, J. P., Huntsinger, G. M., & Nay, W. R. (1977). Case study: Self-control treatment of aggression in a 16-year-old male. *Journal of Consulting and Clinical Psychology, 45,* 322–331.

Mead, G. (1934). *Mind, self, and society.* Chicago: University of Chicago Press.

Megargee, E. I. (1972). *The California Psychological Inventory handbook:* San Francisco: Jossey-Bass.

Mezzich, A. C., & Mezzich, J. E. (1979). *Diagnostic reliability of childhood and adolescent behavior disorders.* Paper presented at the meeting of the American Psychological Association, New York.

Millon, T., Green, C. J., & Meagher, R. B. (1982). *Millon Adolescent Personality Inventory manual.* Minneapolis: Interpretive Scoring System.

Mundy, J. (1972). The use of projective techniques with children. In B. B. Wolman (Ed.), *Handbook of child psychopathology* (pp. 247–302). New York: McGraw-Hill.

O'Dell, S. (1974). Training parents in behavior modification: A review. *Psychological Bulletin, 81,* 418–433.

O'Leary, K. D., & Johnson, S. B. (1979). Psychological assessment. In H. C. Quay & J. S. Werry (Eds.), *Psychopathological disorders of childhood* (2nd ed., pp. 210–246). New York: Wiley.

Ollendick, T. H., & Hersen, M. (1979). Social skills training for juvenile delinquents. *Behaviour Research and Therapy, 17,* 547–554.

Olweus, D. (1980). Familial and temperamental determinants of aggressive behavior in adolescent boys: A causal analysis. *Developmental Psychology, 16,* 644–660.

Patterson, G. R. (1974). Interventions for boys with conduct problems: Multiple settings, treatments, and criteria. *Journal of Consulting and Clinical Psychology, 42,* 471–481.

Patterson, G. R. (1976). The aggressive child: Victim and architect of a coercive system. In E. J. Mash, L. A. Hammerlynck, & L. C. Handy (Eds). *Behavior modification and families* (pp. 267–316). New York: Brunner/Mazel.

Patterson, G. R. (1980). Mothers: The unacknowledged victims. *Monographs of the Society for Research in Child Development, 45* (5, Serial No. 186).

Patterson, G. R., & Fleischman, M. J. (1979). Maintenance of treatment effects: Some considerations concerning family systems and follow-up data. *Behavior Therapy, 10,* 168–185.

Patterson, G. R., Reid, J. B., Jones, R. R., & Conger, R. E. (1975). *A social learning approach to family intervention: Families with aggressive children.* Eugene, OR: Castalia.

Phillips, E. L. (1968). Achievement Place: Token reinforcement procedures in a home-style rehabilitation setting for predelinquent boys. *Journal of Applied Behavior Analysis, 1,* 213–223.

Phillips, E. L., Phillips, E. A., Fixsen, D. L., & Wolf, M. M. (1971). Achievement Place: Modification of the behaviors of predelinquent boys within a token economy. *Journal of Applied Behavior Analysis, 4,* 45–59.

Phillips, E. L., Phillips, E. A., Fixsen, D. L., & Wolf, M. M. (1972). *The teaching-family handbook.* Lawrence, KS: University of Kansas Press.

Platt, J. J., Scura, W., & Hannon, J. R. (1973). Problem-solving thinking of youthful incarcerated heroin addicts. *Journal of Community Psychology, 1,* 278–281.

Platt, J. J., Spivack, G., Altman, N., Altman, D., & Peizer, S. B. (1974). Adolescent problem-solving thinking. *Journal of Consulting and Clinical Psychology, 42,* 787–793.

Porter, B., & O'Leary, K. D. (1980). Marital discord and childhood behavior problems. *Journal of Abnormal Child Psychology, 8,* 287–295.

Puig-Antich, M. (1982). Major depression and conduct disorder in pre-puberty. *Journal of the American Academy of Child Psychiatry, 21,* 118–128.

Quay, H. C. (1964). Personality dimensions in delinquent males as inferred from the factor analysis of behavior ratings. *Journal of Research in Crime and Delinquency, 1,* 33–36.

Quay, H. C. (1977). Measuring dimensions of deviant behavior: The Behavior Problem Checklist. *Journal of Abnormal Child Psychology, 5,* 277–289.

Quay, H. C. (1979). Classification. In H. C. Quay & J. Werry (Eds.), *Psychological disorders of childhood* (2nd ed., pp. 289–301). New York: Wiley.

Quay, H. C., & Petersen, D. R. (1975). *Manual for the Behavior Problem Checklist.* Unpublished manuscript.

Robin, A. L. (1979). Problem-solving communication training: A behavioral approach to the treatment of parent–adolescent conflict. *The American Journal of Family Therapy, 7,* 69–82.

Robin, A. L. (1981). A controlled evaluation of problem-solving communication training with parent-adolescent conflict. *Behavior Therapy, 12,* 593–609.

Robin, A. L., Kent, R. N., O'Leary, K. D., Foster, S., & Prinz, R. J. (1977). An approach to teaching parents and adolescents problem-solving communication skills: A preliminary report. *Behavior Therapy, 8,* 639–643.

Robins, L. N. (1966). *Deviant children grown up: A sociological and psychiatric study of sociopathic personality.* Baltimore: Williams & Wilkins.

Robinson, E. A., Eyberg, S. M., & Ross, A. W. (1980). The standardization of an inventory of child conduct problem behavior. *Journal of Clinical Child Psychology, 48,* 117–118.

Rutter, M. (1967). A children's behavior questionnaire for completion by teachers: Preliminary findings. *Journal of Child Psychology and Psychiatry, 8,* 1–11.

Safer, D., & Allen, P. (1976). *Hyperactive children: Diagnosis and management.* Baltimore, MD: University Park Press.

Sarason, I. G., & Ganzer, V. J. (1973). Modeling and group discussion in the rehabilitation of juvenile delinquents. *Journal of Counseling Psychology, 20,* 442–449.

Schwitzgebel, R., & Kolb, D. A. (1964). Inducing behavior change in adolescent delinquents. *Behaviour Research and Therapy, 1,* 297–304.

Seymour, F. W., & Stokes, T. F. (1976). Self-recording in training girls to increase work and evoke staff praise in an institution for offenders. *Journal of Applied Behavior Analysis, 9,* 41–54.

Singer, M. T. (1977). The Rorschach as a transaction. In M. A. Rickers-Ousiankina (Ed.), *Rorschach psychology* (rev. ed., pp. 455–485). Huntington, NY: Krieger.

Snyder, J. J., & White, M. H. (1979). The use of cognitive self-instruction in the treatment of behaviorally disturbed adolescents. *Behavior Therapy, 10,* 227–235.

Spivack, G., & Levine, M. (1963). *Self-regulation in acting-out and normal adolescents* (Report No. M-4531). Washington, DC: National Institutes of Health.

Spivack, G., Platt, J. J., & Shure, M. B. (1976). *The problem-solving approach to adjustment.* San Francisco: Jossey-Bass.

Spivack, G., & Swift, M. (1967). *Devereaux Elementary School Behavior Rating Scale manual.* Devon: The Devereaux Foundation.

Stokes, T. F., & Baer, D. M. (1977). An implicit technology of generalization. *Journal of Applied Behavior Analysis, 10,* 349–367.

Stuart, R. B. (1971). Behavioral contracting with the families of delinquents. *Journal of Behavior Therapy and Experimental Psychiatry, 2,* 1–11.

Stuart, R. B., & Lott, L. A. (1972). Behavioral contracting with delinquents: A cautionary note. *Journal of Behavior Therapy and Experimental Psychiatry, 3,* 161–169.

Stumphauzer, J. S. (1976). Elimination of stealing by self-reinforcement of alternative behavior and family contracting. *Journal of Behavior Therapy and Experimental Psychiatry, 7,* 265–268.

Symonds, P. M. (1949). *Adolescent fantasy: An investigation of the picture-story method of personality study.* New York: Columbia University Press.

Wahler, R. G. (1980). The insular mother: Her problems in parent–child treatment. *Journal of Applied Behavior Analysis, 13,* 207–219.

Wahler, R. G., Berland, R. M., & Coe, T. D. (1979). Generalization processes in child behavior change. In B. B. Lahey & A. E. Kazdin (Eds.), *Advances in clinical child psychology* (Vol. 2, pp. 35–69). New York: Plenum.

Watt, N. F. (1978). Patterns of childhood social development in adult schizophrenics. *Archives of General Psychiatry, 35,* 160–170.

Weathers, L., & Liberman, R. P. (1975). Contingency contracting with families of delinquent adolescents. *Behavior Therapy, 6,* 356–366.

Wells, K. C. (1981). Assessment of children in outpatient settings. In M. Hersen & A. S. Bellack (Eds.), *Behavioral assessment: A practical handbook* (2nd ed., pp. 484–533). Elmsford, NY: Pergamon.

Wells, K. C., & Forehand, R. (1981). Childhood behavior problems in the home. In S. M. Turner, K. S. Calhoun, & H. E. Adams (Eds.), *Handbook of clinical behavior therapy* (pp. 527–567). New York: Wiley.

Wells, K. C., & Forehand, R. (1985). Conduct and oppositional disorders. In P. H. Bornstein & A. E. Kazdin (Eds.), *Handbook of clinical behavior therapy with children* (pp. 218–265). Homewood, IL: Dorsey.

Wells, K. C., Griest, D. C., & Forehand, R. (1980). The use of a self-control package to enhance temporal generality of a parent training program. *Behaviour Research and Therapy, 18,* 347–353.

Wirt, R. D., Lachar, D., Kinedinst, J. K., & Sent, P. D. (1977). *Multidimensional description of child personality: A manual for the Personality Inventory for Children.* Los Angeles: Western Psychological Services.

Wolff, S. (1961). Symptomatology and outcome of pre-school children with behaviour disorders attending a child guidance clinic. *Journal of Child Psychology and Psychiatry, 2,* 269–276.

Wood, R., & Flynn, J. M. (1978). A self-evaluation token system versus an external evaluation token system alone in a residential setting with predelinquent youths. *Journal of Applied Behavior Analysis, 11,* 503–512.

CHAPTER 15

Anorexia Nervosa and Bulimia

Katherine A. Halmi

Anorexia nervosa and bulimia (binge eating), with or without purging, are eating behavioral aberrations that have existed since early Western civilization. Well-documented case reports of anorexia nervosa are present in the literature describing early Christian saints. An example is the detailed case of Princess Margaret of Hungary, who had a typical anorectic premorbid personality and course of illness. She died at age 26 from the complications of emaciation (Konradyne, 1973). Other dramatic cases of anorexia nervosa present in Italian saints are described by Bell (1985). He reports St. Catherine of Sienna as not only having severe starving behavior, but also bingeing and purging episodes. He also documents the type of reed she used to self-induce vomiting and the herbal cathartics that she used for purging. The *syndrome* of bulimia, an addictive form of binge eating in normal-weight individuals, has become a common problem today. However, it is not well documented in the history of early Western civilization.

Anorexia nervosa is one of the few psychiatric illnesses that may have a course that is unremitting until death. Anorexia nervosa and the syndrome bulimia, bulimia nervosa, are behavioral eating disorders that have been studied comprehensively and with systematic methodologies only in the past 20 years. These eating-behavior conditions are entities and not diseases with a common cause, course, and pathology. They are best conceptualized as syndromes. Therefore, they are classified on the basis of the cluster of symptoms that are present.

DESCRIPTION OF THE DISORDERS

Anorexia Nervosa

Anorexia nervosa is a disorder characterized by preoccupation with body weight and food, behavior directed toward losing weight, peculiar patterns of handling food, weight loss, intense fear of gaining weight, disturbance of body image, and amenorrhea.

Anorectics' intense fear of gaining weight is reflected in their tendency to constantly think about food and how fat they are. Although these patients may deny their preoccupation with food and losing weight, one can assume that they are concerned with the slenderness of their bodies by observing their frequent mirror gazing and by listening to their incessant concerns about looking fat and feeling flabby. Collecting recipes and preparing elaborate meals for their families are other behaviors that reflect their preoccupation with food.

Peculiar handling of food also is characteristic of anorectics. They will hide carbohydrate-rich foods, such as candies and cookies, around the house. They will hoard large quantities of candies and carry them in their pockets and purses. If forced to eat in public, they often will try to dispose of their food surreptitiously to avoid eating. Further, they will spend a great deal of time cutting food into small pieces and rearranging the food on their plates. If confronted about their peculiar behavior, they usually will flatly deny it or refuse to discuss it. Their fear of gaining weight exists even in the face of increasing cachexia and contributes to their characteristic disinterest and even resistance to treatment.

Anorectics lose weight by different methods. All anorectic patients drastically reduce their total food intake and disproportionately decrease the intake of high-carbohydrate and fat-containing foods. Some anorectics will develop rigorous exercising programs, and others will simply be as active as possible at all times. The latter patients will stand instead of sit and frequently will run up and down stairs. They seem obsessed with the notion that they need to move constantly. Vomiting is another way in which anorectics attempt to lose weight. This frequently follows a binge-eating episode. Abusing laxatives and diuretics are other purging behaviors that present a danger by lowering serum potassium levels, which, in turn, can cause cardiac arrhythmias and, in rare cases, sudden death secondary to cardiac arrest. Persistent vomiting also is associated with the development of severe dental problems. (Medical complications of this disorder are described below.)

Weight loss and the refusal to maintain body weight over a minimal normal weight for age and height are the most identifying characteristics of this disorder. Most anorectic patients come to medical attention when their weight loss is obvious. Physical signs, such as hypothermia, dependent edema, bradycardia, hypotension, and lanugo often are present.

Anorectics have a disturbance in the way in which they experience their body weight, size, or shape. They often fail to recognize that their degree of emaciation is "too thin." Some regard themselves as being normal weight or even overweight. Others realize that they actually are underweight but describe the sensation of "feeling fat."

The diagnosis of anorexia nervosa frequently is missed by the gynecologist, who will see the patient because of amenorrhea. This can appear before noticeable weight loss has occurred.

Obsessive–compulsive behavior often develops after the onset of anorexia nervosa. Obsession with cleanliness, such as frequent hand washing or an increase in housecleaning activities, a more compulsive approach to studying (some patients actually have an improvement in their grades at onset of illness), and the development of other rituals not associated with food or eating are not uncommon in anorexia nervosa.

Poor sexual adjustment frequently is present in anorectic patients. Many adolescent anorectics have delayed psychosocial sexual development, and adults often have a markedly decreased interest in sex with the onset of anorexia nervosa.

Anorexia nervosa patients can be subdivided into those who binge and purge and those who merely restrict food intake in order to lose weight. Casper, Halmi, Goldberg, Eckert, and Davis (1980) and Garfinkel, Moldofsky, and Garner (1980) have shown a higher association of impulsive behaviors, such as suicide attempts, self-mutilation, stealing, and substance abuse (including alcohol abuse) present in the bingeing and purging (bulimic) anorectics. The bulimic anorectics are less likely to be regressed in their sexual activity and in fact may be promiscuous. Bulimic anorectics also are more likely to have discreet personality disorder diagnoses (Strober, 1981).

Bulimia

Bulimia is merely a term that means binge eating. This is a behavior that has become a common practice among young female students both in universities and, more recently, in high schools. Not all persons who engage in binge eating have a psychiatric diagnosis. Bulimia, as mentioned previously, also is a behavior that can occur in anorexia nervosa. Bulimia can occur in a normal-weight condition associated with psychological symptomatology. Russell (1979) coined the term bulimia nervosa. At that time, Russell conceptualized bulimia nervosa as an "aftermath of the chronic phase of anorexia nervosa" (p. 440). Only 6 of the 30 patients he studied had no history of preceding anorexia nervosa. The term bulimia nervosa implies a psychiatric impairment and therefore is a better label for the binge-eating disorder.

Bulimia Nervosa

Bulimia nervosa is a disorder in which the behavior of bulimia or binge eating is the predominant behavior. Binge eating is an episodic, uncontrolled, rapid ingestion of large quantities of food over a short period of time. Abdominal pain or discomfort, self-induced vomiting, sleep, or social interruption terminate the bulimic episode, which is followed by feelings of guilt, depression, or self-disgust. Bulimic patients often use cathartics for weight control and have an eating pattern of alternate binges and fasts. Bulimic patients have a fear of not being able to stop eating voluntarily. The food consumed during a binge usually has a high-dense calorie content and a texture that facilitates rapid eating. Frequent weight fluctuations occur but without the severity of weight loss present in anorexia nervosa.

Binge eating as a discreet eating pattern was first described in a minority of obese persons (Stunkard, 1959). Then, binge-eating behavior was noted to occur in about one-half of anorexia nervosa patients and to develop in some anorectics after weight restoration (Casper et al., 1980; Russell, 1979). Later, binge-eating behavior was found to occur predominantly in adolescent girls and young women within a normal weight range. Subsequently, the term bulimia was applied to this latter group. As mentioned above, the latest development is to separate the psychiatric disorder of bulimia nervosa from bulimia, a behavior that may occur sporadically in some individuals but not in association with other psychological symptomatology.

Bulimia nervosa usually begins after a period of dieting that may last from a few weeks to a year or longer. The dieting may or may not have been successful for inducing weight loss. Most binge-eating episodes are followed by self-induced vomiting and less frequently by use of laxatives. A minority of bulimics use diuretics for weight control. The average length of a binge-eating episode is about 1 hour. Most patients learn to vomit by sticking their fingers down their throat. After a short time they advance to vomiting on a reflex basis. Some patients have abrasions and scars on the backs of their hands (Russell's Sign) obtained from persistent efforts at vomiting. Most bulimic patients do not eat regular meals and have difficulty feeling satiety at the end of a normal meal. Also, most bulimic patients prefer to binge alone and usually in their homes. About one-third to one-fifth of these individuals are mildly overweight before the onset of their illness. In contrast to anorectic patients, many bulimics will choose a weight within a normal weight range as their ideal body weight. About one-fourth to one-third of bulimia nervosa patients will have had a previous history of anorexia nervosa.

The majority of bulimic patients have depressive signs and symptoms. They have problems with interpersonal relationships, self-concept, impulsive behaviors, and high levels of anxiety and compulsivity. Chemical dependency is not unusual in this disorder, with alcohol abuse being most common. Bulimics will abuse amphetamines to reduce their appetite and to lose weight. Impulsive stealing usually occurs after the onset of binge eating. However, about one-fourth of the patients actually begin stealing before onset of bulimia. Food, clothing, and jewelry are the most common items stolen.

Numerous medical complications are associated with bulimia. Electrolyte imbalances, such as hypokalemia and fluid depletion, are related to purging behaviors. Dental problems are frequent and include erosion of the enamel, caries, and gum erosion. Parotid gland enlargement, esophageal tears, and acute gastric dilatation also may occur. Menstrual irregularities are common, although amenorrhea for periods of 6 months or longer is extremely rare.

Taking into account the recent studies in anorexia nervosa and bulimia nervosa, the *Diagnostic and Statistical Manual of Mental Disorders, 3rd edition (DSM-III)* (American Psychiatric Association, 1980) criteria were recently revised and are presented in Table 15.1. They are called the *DSM-IIIa* criteria. It should be noted that a patient meeting criteria for anorexia nervosa who also binges and purges will be given two diagnoses on the Axis I classification. That individual will have the diagnoses of both anorexia nervosa and bulimia nervosa.

Table 15.1. *DSM-IIIa* Criteria for Anorexia Nervosa and Bulimia Nervosa

Anorexia Nervosa
   A. Intense fear of becoming obese, which does not diminish as weight loss progresses.
   B. Disturbance in the way in which one's body weight, size, or shape is experienced (e.g., claiming to "feel fat" even when emaciated; belief that one area of the body is "too fat" even when obviously under-weight).
   C. Refusal to maintain body weight over a minimal normal weight for age and height (e.g., weight loss leading to maintenance of body weight 15% below expected; failure to make expected weight gain during period of growth, leading to body weight 15% below expected).
   D. In females, absence of at least three consecutive menstrual cycles when otherwise expected to occur (primary or secondary amenorrhea).

Bulimia Nervosa
   A. Recurrent episodes of binge eating (rapid consumption of a large amount of food in a discrete period of time, usually less than two hours).
   B. Fear of not being able to stop eating during eating binges.
   C. Regular occurrences of either self-induced vomiting, use of laxatives, or rigorous dieting or fasting to counteract the effects of the binge eating.
   D. A minimum average of two binge eating episodes per week for at least three months.

Eating Disorders: Not entering criteria listed above (examples)
   A. An individual of normal weight who does not have binge-eating episodes, but frequently engages in self-induced vomiting for fear of gaining weight.
   B. All of the features of anorexia nervosa in a female except for absence of menses.
   C. All of the features of bulimia nervosa except for the frequency or duration of binge-eating episodes.

Note. Adapted from *Diagnostic and Statistical Manual of Mental Disorders* (3rd ed., pp. 69–71) by the American Psychiatric Association, 1980, Washington, DC: Author. Copyright 1980 by the American Psychiatric Association.

Causes

Psychological theories on the causes of anorexia nervosa have centered mostly on phobic mechanisms and psychodynamic formulations. Crisp (1967) postulated that anorexia nervosa constitutes a phobic-avoidance response to food resulting from the sexual and social tension generated by the physical changes associated with puberty. The resulting malnutrition leads to reduction in sexual interest, which in turn leads to greater self-starvation. Brady and Rieger (1972) also conceptualized anorexia nervosa as an eating phobia:

> Eating generates anxiety, and the failure of anorectics to eat represents avoidance. In other words, their cessation of eating after ingesting a very small portion of a meal (or removing it from the body by self-induced vomiting) is reinforced by anxiety reduction. (p. 58)

An early psychodynamic theory focused on anorectic patients rejecting through starvation a wish to be pregnant. Other early psychody-namic theories focused on fantasies of oral impregnation. Since then, dynamic formulations have included a dependent seductive relationship with a warm but passive father and guilt over aggression toward an ambivalently regarded mother. Oral deprivation and overprotection block self-concept differentiation in individualization. Unable to retain the mother or find a substitute in pubescence, preoedipal regressive forces push the patient back to an oral–anal mode of drive discharge and ego functioning.

A cognitive and perceptual developmental defect was postulated by Bruch (1962) as being the cause of anorexia nervosa. She described disturbances of body image (denial of emaciation), disturbances in perception (lack of recognition or denial of fatigue, weakness, hunger), and a sense of ineffectiveness as being caused by false learning experiences. In a recent study in which a large comprehensive battery of cognitive and perceptual tests was given to anorectic patients, nearly half of the patients had a greater than expected number of cognitive failures. The most common deficit was impaired reaction time. This was present during both pretreatment and after nutritional rehabilitation. However, fewer deficits were present after treatment. It is of interest that a greater number of cognitive deficits was associated with poor outcome.

The assessment of the "disturbance of body image" in anorexia nervosa has been controversial. To most clinicians, the disturbance in body image means that the anorectic patient feels she is overweight even when she is at a normal weight or underweight. As pointed out by Garner and Garfinkel (1981), it is very likely that this disturbance of body image can be subdivided into several components in the heterogeneous anorexia nervosa population. This topic, as well as the heterogeneity of personality disorder in psychological characteristics in anorexia nervosa, will be discussed further in the section on current research.

Physiologic and Metabolic Changes

Most of the physiologic and metabolic changes found in anorexia nervosa or bulimia nervosa also are present in starvation states or are a direct result of purging behavior. The starvation metabolic aberrations revert to normal with nutritional rehabilitation. Abnormalities in hematopoiesis, such as leukopenia (low white count) and relative lymphocytosis found in acutely emaciated anorectic patients, are a common finding (Carryer, Berkman, & Mason, 1959). These patients do not need an extensive medical workup because of the low white count, which will return to a normal level with nutritional rehabilitation. Both Silverman (1974) and Lampert and Lau (1976) reported that the hypoplasia of bone marrow in starved anorectics reverted to normal after weight gain. The incidence of leukopenia and infection in anorexia nervosa was studied by Bowers and Eckert (1978) who reviewed 68 cases of anorexia nervosa and found no more infection in the anorectics than control subjects despite frequent and often severe leukopenia in the patients. Although the risk of infection seems to be no greater in anorectics than in control subjects, there is reason to be concerned from other investigations that if the anorectic patient develops an infection, the morbidity risk will be much greater than in a healthy person because

anorectics have a reduced capacity to fight infections (Gotsch, 1975).

Both anorexia nervosa and bulimia nervosa patients who engage in self-induced vomiting or who abuse purgatives and diuretics are susceptible to developing hypokalemic alkalosis (Mitchell, Pyle, Eckert, Hatsukami, & Lentz, 1983; Rodger & Collyer, 1979; Wallace, Richards, Chesser, & Wrong, 1968; Warrent & Steinberg, 1979). Mitchell et al. (1983) showed that 49% of eating-disorder patients studied had electrolyte abnormalities that included elevated serum bicarbonate, hypochloremia, hypokalemia, and, in a few cases, a low serum bicarbonate, indicating a metabolic acidosis. The latter was particularly true in laxative abusers. It is important to remember that fasting can promote dehydration, which results in volume depletion. This in turn can cause generation of aldosterone leading to further potassium excretion from the kidneys. Thus, there can be an indirect renal loss of potassium as well as direct loss through self-induced vomiting. Patients with electrolyte disturbances have physical symptoms of weakness, lethargy, and, at times, cardiac arrhythmias.

Electrolyte changes most likely contribute to the electrocardiographic (EKG) changes, such as flattening or inversion of the T-wave, ST segment depression, and lengthening of the QT interval. These have all been noted in the emaciated state of anorexia nervosa and revert to normal with nutritional rehabilitation (Silverman, 1974). However, Thurston and Marks (1974) noted that these electrographic changes are similar to those frequently observed in patients with head injuries. In acute intracranial disease, sympathetic centers are stimulated in the hypothalamus. This results in release of catecholamines within the myocardium. These investigators postulate that a similar phenomenon occurs in anorexia nervosa and that these catecholamines may cause damage to the contractile apparatus and to the cell membrane of the myocardial cells, resulting in the changes just described. Another study (Gottdiener, Gross, Henry, Borer, & Ebert, 1978) found impaired myocardial function in undernourished anorectic patients.

Undoubtedly, there are multiple mechanisms for cardiac arrhythmias in these patients. Recent studies are showing that normal weight bulimia nervosa patients, who also have normal serum electrolytes, can have severe cardiac rhythm disturbance (Zucker, 1984). Injudicious rapid refeeding can cause heart failure in anorectic patients. Unfortunately, this fact was publicized in the lay press and led a large number of medically uneducated therapists to be dangerously cautious in seeking appropriate weight gain treatment and nutritional rehabilitation for their patients.

Both anorexia nervosa and bulimia nervosa patients who binge and purge can be diagnosed by the dentist. These patients can have severe attrition and erosion of the teeth, causing an irritating sensitivity, pathologic pulp exposures, loss of integrity of the dental arches, diminished masticatory ability, and an unaesthetic appearance (Stege, 1982).

Parotid gland enlargement associated with elevated serum amylase levels commonly is observed in patients who binge and self-induce vomiting (Mitchell et al., 1983). In fact, the serum amylase level is an excellent way to follow reduction of vomiting in eating-disorder patients who deny purging episodes. Acute dilation of the stomach is a rare emergency condition for patients who binge. Gastric emptying is delayed in emaciated anorexia nervosa patients. In one study (Dubois, Gross, Ebert, & Castell, 1981) a parasympathetic agent, bethanechol, produced only a partial restoration of gastric emptying and acid secretion in patients with anorexia nervosa. The investigators believed that the defect in gastric emptying and acid secretion reflects the presence of inhibitory influences and not just impaired parasympathetic neurotransmission.

It is not unusual for serum enzymes reflecting liver function to be elevated in anorexia nervosa. The elevation of these enzymes most likely reflects some fatty degeneration of the liver and is observed both in the emaciated anorectic phase and during refeeding (Halmi & Falk, 1981). There is a wide scatter of serum cholesterol and triglyceride levels in anorexia nervosa. Elevated serum cholesterol levels tend to occur more frequently in younger patients (Nestel, 1974). Carotenemia often is observed in malnourished anorectic patients and disappears with weight restoration. Robboy, Sato, and Schwabe (1974) hypothesized that an acquired but reversible error of metabolism of beta-carotene in vitamin A precursors occurs in anorexia nervosa.

A major diagnostic criterion for anorexia nervosa is amenorrhea. Studies on the hypothalamic–pituitary–ovarian axis in patients with anorexia nervosa will be discussed in the section on current research. Considering the fact that amenorrhea occurs in about one-third of anorectic patients before any weight loss occurs, Russell (1969) proposed that the amenorrhea is caused by a primary disturbance of hypothalamic function and that the full expression of this disturbance is brought about with psychological stress. He suggested that the malnutrition of anorexia nervosa perpetuates the amenorrhea but is not primarily responsible for the endocrine disorder, which could be attributed partly to still unknown causes. After treatment, the return of normal menstrual cycles usually lags behind the return to normal body weight. The resumption of menses is associated with marked psychological improvement (Morgan & Russell, 1975).

Most of the physical signs and symptoms of bulimia nervosa patients are related to their behaviors of binge eating and purging and were described previously. Severe abdominal pain in the bulimia nervosa patient should alert the physician to a diagnosis of gastric dilatation and the need for nasogastric suction, x-rays, and surgical consultation. The serious consequence of gastric dilatation is a potentially fatal gastric rupture. Esophageal tears are another potential hazard in bulimia nervosa when patients self-induce vomiting. A complication of shock could result subsequent to the esophageal tear, and should be treated by experienced medical and surgical personnel. Cardiac failure caused by cardiomyopathy from ipecac (emetine) intoxication is a medical emergency that is being reported more frequently and usually results in death (Friedman, 1984). Symptoms of precordial pain, dyspnea, and generalized muscle weakness associated with hypotension, tachycardia, and electrocardiogram (EKG) abnormalities should alert one to ipecac intoxication. Other laboratory findings may include elevated liver enzymes and an increased erythrocyte sedimentation rate.

At this point, the patient obviously needs to be under a cardiologist's care. An echocardiogram will show a congested type of cardiomyopathy contraction pattern. There are most likely multiple mechanisms for cardiac arrhythmias and sudden death in bulimia patients. Those already mentioned were arrhythmias associated with serum electrolyte disturbances and arrhythmias associated with bingeing behavior even when the serum electrolytes were within normal limits. Bulimia nervosa is associated with greater psychological heterogeneity than anorexia nervosa. Because psychological assessments of bulimia nervosa are recent, these will be discussed in the current research section.

EPIDEMIOLOGICAL FINDINGS

There is documented evidence that the incidence of anorexia nervosa has increased in the past 30 years both in the United States and in Western Europe. In the United States, the most methodologically sound incidence study was from Monroe County, New York. This investigation showed an average annual incident rate of 0.35 per 100,000 population between 1960–1969 with an increase to 0.64 per 100,000 in the years 1970–1976 (Jones, Fox, Babigian, & Hutton, 1980). Theander (1970) calculated the incidence of anorexia nervosa in a region in southern Sweden over a 30-year period from 1930 to 1960 to be 0.24 per 100,000 inhabitants per year. He noted a sharp increase in incidence during the three decades. In the last decade (1951–1960), the incidence was 0.45 per 100,000. However, Theander (1970) studied the incidence in women only and thus his study is not as truly representative of the population as the Monroe County effort.

A retrospective study of case histories in the canton of Zurich revealed that the incidence of anorexia increased from 0.38 per 100,000 for 1956–1958, to 0.55 per 100,000 for 1963–1965, to 1.12 per 100,000 for 1973–1975 (Willi & Grossmann, 1983). Crisp, Palmer, and Kalucy (1975) surveyed nine populations of schoolgirls (ages 12 to 18) in London during the period from 1972 to 1974. The prevalence was one severe case in about 200 girls. In those age 16 to 18, it was one severe case in every 100 girls.

The above-mentioned prevalence and incidence studies have shown this disorder to be predominantly in the upper and middle socioeconomic classes. Age of onset is most common between 12 and 30 and occurs predominantly in the white and oriental population. In the past 5 years, there have been small series of case reports of age onset over 40 and other case reports of anorexia nervosa occurring in blacks. This is

some indication that the disorder may be spreading to a wider population. It will be of interest to see if the incidence studies of the 1980s will show that to be true.

Anorexia nervosa occurs predominantly in females. In a survey of 94 patients with this illness, Halmi (1974) reported only six males (6%). The percentage of males is similar to the 5% figure reported by Decourt (1964) and the 4% found by Dally (1969).

There are no satisfactory incidence studies on bulimia nervosa. There are several reasons for this. First, bulimia nervosa emerged only in 1980 as a distinct diagnostic entity in DSM-III. In this manual, bulimia nervosa is referred to as bulimia. The criteria do not allow one to distinguish between occasional binge-eating episodes and the truly incapacitating disorder of bulimia nervosa. All of the prevalence studies on bulimia have been in special populations and are not representative of the general population. Five studies using strict *DSM-III* criteria with added restrictions for frequency and chronicity of behavior show the prevalence of bulimia among college and high school students to vary between 3.8 and 9% (Carter & Duncan, 1984; Johnson, 1982; Pyle, Mitchell, Eckert, Halvorson, Neuman, & Goff, 1983; Stangler & Printz, 1980).

Most of these studies use self-report questionnaires, and thus a diagnosis was not confirmed by personal interview. Other investigations in specialized populations, such as college students, ballet dancers, and attenders at a family-planning clinic, showed the prevalence of binge-eating behavior to vary between 20.9% for the family clinic (Cooper & Fairburn, 1983) and 90% for ballet dancers (Abraham, Mira, & Llewellyn-Jones, 1983b). Only two of these studies assess the prevalence of vomiting. Halmi, Falk, and Schwartz (1981) found vomiting present in 9.9% of college students, and Cooper and Fairburn (1983) found it to be present in 2.9% of family-planning-clinic attenders.

All of these investigations showed bulimia to be far more prevalent in women than in men. There is a suggestion that bulimia nervosa is more common in men than anorexia nervosa. Or to phrase it another way, the prevalence of males in the bulimia nervosa population probably varies between 10 and 15% compared with 4 to 6% for the anorexia nervosa population.

Average age for onset of bulimia in most studies is 18, with a range between 12 and 35. The typical bulimic patient seen in an outpatient clinic is white, single, college-educated, and in the early 20s in age with symptoms from four to six years. Nevertheless, there is evidence that this disorder has greater heterogeneity than anorexia nervosa. Two studies, Johnson (1982) and Lacey (1982) have shown a much higher representation of Social Classes 4 and 5 (semi-skilled and unskilled fathers' occupations) in the bulimia nervosa patients compared with the anorexia nervosa patients.

Family studies of anorexia and bulimia nervosa have shown a familial occurrence of these eating disorders and a high association with affective disorder. Theander (1970) found six probands with seven sisters who had anorexia nervosa. He calculated that the morbidity risk for a sister of an anorectic patient is about 6.6%, which greatly exceeds normal expectation. In studies of 30 sets of female twins in London (Holland, Hall, Murray, Russell, & Crisp, 1984), 9 of 16 of the monozygotic and 1 of 14 of the dizygotic twins were concordant for anorexia nervosa. In the monozygotic twins, there was a trend toward concordance being associated with a familial loading for psychiatric illness. The authors thought these results suggested a genetic predisposition that could become manifest under adverse conditions, such as inappropriate dieting or emotional stress. A genetic vulnerability might be a predisposition to a particular personality type, to psychiatric illness in general (and, in particular, affective disorder), to a disturbance of body image, or to a hypothalamic disorder. A monozygotic twin carrying one or more vulnerability factors would have both the potential for developing anorexia nervosa under conditions of stress in addition to a genetic loading for this disorder. In a study of 56 families with anorexia nervosa, Kalucy, Crisp, and Harding (1977) found that 16% of the mothers and 23% of the fathers had an explicit history of significant adolescent low-weight phobia.

Family studies of both anorexia and bulimia nervosa patients have shown an increased amount of affective disorders in first-degree relatives of the eating-disorder subjects compared with the first-degree relatives of normal control subjects (Gershon et al., 1984; Hudson, Pope, Jonas, & Todd, 1983; Rivinius et al., 1984; Winokur, March, & Mendels, 1980). Some of these studies are fraught with methodological problems ranging from small numbers of subjects to inconsistent methods of interviewing. Two of the better-designed family history investigations of anorexia nervosa patients (Gershon et al., 1983; Strober, 1984) showed a higher prevalence of affective disorder in the first-degree relatives of eating-disorder patients compared with a normal control sample. However, they did not find a higher prevalence of eating disorders in the first-degree relatives of affective disorder patients. Therefore, the researchers in both studies suggested that an independent predisposition to anorexia must be superimposed on a predisposition to affective disorders for anorexia to be manifest. In a controlled family study, Strober (1984) found increased rates of anorexia nervosa, bulimia nervosa, and subclinical anorexia nervosa in first- and second-degree relatives of anorectic patients compared with the relatives of nonanorectic psychiatrically ill control subjects. He proposed that the pattern of familial clustering of these disorders represents variable expressions of a common underlying psychopathology.

ASSESSMENT AND DIAGNOSIS

The diagnosis of anorexia nervosa should be obvious and easy to make. However, it is frequently missed because anorectic patients deny many of their characteristic symptoms because they are not motivated for treatment. Often it is necessary to obtain the information necessary for diagnosis from family members or friends who have observed the anorectic's behavior. Sometimes it is even necessary to hospitalize the patient for diagnostic observation. Information is necessary in eight different categories in order to make the diagnosis of anorexia nervosa. Those categories are: weight history, menstrual history, eating behavior, purging behavior, preoccupation with and fear of weight, activity, depressive symptomatology, and impulsive behavior. The latter category should include inquiries on drug abuse, alcohol abuse, and suicide attempts. In addition to information necessary for the diagnosis, it is important to inquire about the patient's family. Frequently, stressful marital conflict is present in eating-disorder families. It is important to inquire into the parent's responses to the patient's eating behavior and the patient's dependency on her parents. It also is helpful to inquire about previous treatment for the eating-disorder problem. If the patient has had several previous hospitalization treatment failures, then she will be far more difficult to treat. Knowledge of the type of previous treatments and an assessment of the patient's and family's attitudes towards previous treatment attempts should be made in order to effectively persuade the patient and family to cooperate in any future treatment plans.

All anorexia nervosa and bulimia nervosa patients should have a routine physical examination with special attention paid to blood pressure, pulse rate, evidence of dehydration, salivary gland enlargement, and dependent edema. All patients should also have a complete blood count and determination of serum electrolytes. Abnormal serum electrolytes may be the only evidence that the patient is self-inducing vomiting. A serum amylase also is useful as an indication of vomiting behavior.

The diagnosis of anorexia nervosa and bulimia nervosa should be made on the positive criteria for these disorders as outlined earlier. In rare circumstances, the patient can have both anorexia nervosa and a medical illness contributing to weight loss. In such a situation, of course, both the underlying medical condition and the anorexia nervosa must be treated.

Anorectic patients must be differentiated from those with solely depressive disorders. Depressed patients do not become preoccupied with the calorie content of food, nor do they collect recipes or spend an inordinate amount of time cooking and preparing foods. They do not deny the existence of a normal appetite but truly have a decreased appetite. It is possible that some eating-disorder patients will meet the criteria for anorexia nervosa, bulimia nervosa, and a major depression. In these cases, all three diagnoses should be made. Other cases will meet criteria for bulimia nervosa and major depressive disorder.

Somatization disorder is a diagnosis that is not frequently made in eating-disorder patients. Weight loss and vomiting can occur in somatization disorder. However, the weight loss generally is not as severe as in anorexia nervosa, and amenorrhea is seldom a persistent finding in somatization disorder.

Schizophrenic patients usually have delusions about the food they are eating but are seldom concerned with calorie content. Schizophrenic patients are rarely preoccupied with the fear of becoming obese and do not have the hyperactivity that is frequently present in anorectic patients. On occasion, however, both anorexia nervosa and bulimia nervosa patients will meet criteria for schizophrenia as well as their respective eating-disorder criteria. In this case, both conditions should be diagnosed.

TREATMENT

Both anorexia nervosa and bulimia nervosa require medical management, behavioral, individual, cognitive, and family therapy as a multifaceted treatment endeavor. There are some cases in which family therapy is not possible or advisable. However, in those cases, issues of family relationships must be dealt with in individual therapy or in brief counseling sessions with immediate family members. The only controlled treatment studies in the eating disorders have involved drug treatment or behavioral-cognitive therapies.

The first step in treatment of the anorectic patient is to obtain her cooperation in a treatment program. Most anorexia nervosa patients are disinterested and even resistant to treatment and are brought to a therapist's office unwillingly by agonizing relatives or friends. For these patients, it is important to emphasize the benefits of treatment and to reassure them that intervention can bring about a relief of insomnia, depressive symptoms, a decrease in obsessive thoughts about food and body weight that interfere with ability to concentrate on other matters, and a restoration of peer relationships. If the anorectic is extremely emaciated, she will be upset over the fact she no longer has the energy to be active. Reassurance that her previous activity level can be restored with treatment also will be helpful in persuading the patient to participate in a treatment program. The relative's support and confidence in the doctor and treatment team are essential when firm recommendations must be carried out. The patient's family should be warned that she will resist treatment and that in the first several weeks of treatment the family may get dramatic complaints from those patients who are in a hospitalized treatment program. Bulimia nervosa patients initially seem to be more motivated to cooperate in treatment. However, there may be difficulty in compliance with the program over time with this group.

For anorectic patients, the immediate aim should be to restore their nutritional state to normal. Mere emaciation or the state of being mildly underweight (15–25%) can cause irritability, depression, preoccupation with food, and sleep disturbance. It is exceedingly difficult to accomplish a behavioral change with psychotherapy in a patient who is suffering the psychological effects of emaciation. Admitting the anorectic patient to a structured environment in a hospitalization treatment program allows for an efficient nutritional rehabilitation and a more rapid recovery. Outpatient therapy as an *initial* approach has the best chance for success in adolescent anorectics who (a) have had the illness for less than 6 months, (b) are not bingeing and vomiting, and (c) have parents who are likely to cooperate and effectively participate in family therapy.

Unfortunately, there are no studies in the literature that provide evidence for the effectiveness of initial outpatient treatment programs versus initial hospitalization treatment approaches for anorexia nervosa patients. A few centers will consistently start with outpatient therapy unless the patient is in dire medical condition. Many other centers, both in the United States and Europe, emphasize immediate hospitalization with aftercare outpatient therapy. Undoubtedly, there has been a selection bias of the more ill patients going to the hospitalization treatment programs. Normal-weight bulimia nervosa patients should be hospitalized when they are in severe electrolyte imbalance, have cardiac arrhythmias, are severely depressed and suicidal, or are completely incapacitated by their binge eating and purging behaviors.

The more severely ill anorectic and bulimia patients may cause an extremely difficult medical-management problem. They may require daily monitoring of weight, fluid and calorie intake, and urine output. In a patient who is vomiting, frequent assessment of serum electrolytes is necessary. Hospitalization of anorectic patients has the advantage of isolating them from a potentially noxious environment. This factor was recognized over 100 years ago by Sir William Gull (1874) when he recommended "the patient should be fed at regular intervals, and surrounded by persons who would have more influence over them, relatives and friends being generally the worst attendants" (p. 28).

Nursing treatment programs were developed from this principle. In this type of program, the patient is put to bed and must remain there until he or she achieves a normal weight for his age and height. At that time, the patient is allowed more activity as he or she continues to cooperate and improve psychologically. Obviously, this nursing treatment program, which involves forced bedrest, uses behavioral contingencies (Crisp, 1965; Russell, 1973). Recently, a number of investigations have shown that the use of behavioral contingencies has become more sophisticated. For the bulimia nervosa patient, a well-monitored, structured hospitalization treatment setting can bring about an immediate cessation to the binge eating and purging behavior and stabilize the patient.

Behavior Therapy

Behavior therapy is most effective in the medical management and nutritional rehabilitation of the eating-disorder patients, although there are times when other target behaviors can be changed with this approach. Behavior therapy can be used both in outpatient and inpatient treatment settings. Systematic desensitization (Wolpe, 1958), a behavior therapy technique often used for treatment of phobias, inhibits anxiety by using a gradual series of imagined scenes with concurrent deep muscle relaxation. As Leitenberg, Agras, and Thompson (1968) succinctly state,

> The assumption (with systematic desensitization) is that the desired behavioral changes in the real situation will automatically occur as anxiety dissipates in therapy sessions. The conditioning strategy, on the other hand, attempts to gradually change overt behavior, the assumption being that each behavioral step forward will reduce anxiety. In essence, the systematic desensitization strategy takes care of anxiety and lets overt behavior take care of itself; while the operant strategy takes care of behavior and lets anxiety take care of itself (p. 213).

The use of systematic desensitization without operant conditioning has not been effective in treating anorectic patients (Hallsten, 1965).

The operant-conditioning paradigm has been the most efficacious form of behavior therapy for the treatment of anorexia nervosa. Positive reinforcements are employed that consist of increased physical activity, visiting privileges, and social activities contingent on weight gain. It is important to conduct an individual behavior analysis on each patient because there are some anorectic patients who are withdrawn and prefer to spend all their time isolating themselves. Obviously, for this type of patient, a negative reinforcement would be to refuse the patient access to her room during the day unless she has made her expected weight gain.

The most effective behavior therapy programs are individualized; that is, a program is set up only after a behavioral analysis of the patient is completed. The timing of reinforcements is important in this treatment approach. An adolescent needs at least a daily reinforcement for weight increase. A medically safe rate of gain would be $1/4$ lb, or $1/10$ kg, per day. Initially, weight gain, rather than eating behavior, should be reinforced. The reason for this is that the patients can eat a normal meal, earn their reward, and then go the bathroom and induce vomiting, hence never changing their weight status. Making positive reinforcements contingent only on weight gain is helpful in reducing the staff–patient arguments and stressful interactions over how and what the patient is eating, because weight is an objective measure.

Experimental control procedures have been used to study the operant-conditioning paradigm. In a series of five single-case experiments, Agras, Barlow, Chapin, Abel, and Leitenberg (1974) used the technique of systematic analysis to demonstrate a strong effect of regular feedback of information regarding weight and calorie intake on actual weight gain. Pertschuk, Edwards, and Pomerleau (1978) employed a multiple baseline design to show the efficacy of an operant-conditioning therapy in anorectics. In another study, Wulliemier, Rossel, and Sinclair (1975) compared the efficacy of an operant-conditioning form of behavior therapy with a program of strict isolation, appetite-stimulating drugs, and psychotherapy in 16 anorectic patients. The latter program was not free of behavioral contingencies, because it contained a strong negative reinforcer of strict isolation. However, results indicated that the rate of weight gain was three times as great for those patients receiving the operant-conditioning program.

The only randomly assigned controlled treatment study evaluating behavior therapy was a collaborative effort involving three hospitals (Eckert, Goldberg, Halmi, Casper, & Davis, 1979). In this study, significant differences in weight gain

were found between the behavior therapy and milieu therapy groups. Those receiving behavior therapy gained weight at the rate of 4.2 kg/month compared with a rate of 3.6 kg/month for milieu therapy. Explanations for the lack of efficacy of behavior therapy in this report were: (a) constant reinforcers were used in all patients instead of individualized reinforcers; (b) a schedule of delayed reinforcers given only every 5th day might not have been as effective as a schedule of more immediate daily reinforcers; and (c) the milieu program, which did involve some isolation, may have produced a maximal possible weight gain so that behavior therapy could not be expected to do any better. The investigators believed that if these patients had been followed until they reached their target weight in the designed protocol, there would have been a difference in the rate of weight gain in those receiving behavior therapy compared with those in the milieu therapy condition.

In addition to effectively inducing weight gain, behavior therapy can be employed to stop vomiting in both anorectic and bulimic patients. For example, response prevention is a technique that currently is being studied for the treatment of bulimia (Mizes & Lohr, 1983; Rosen & Leitenberg, 1982). In hospital-treatment programs, response prevention frequently is used when binge eating and purging patients stay in an observed dayroom area for 2 to 3 hours after every meal. Very few patients vomit in front of other people. Thus, the emesis response is prevented and after a period of time is extinguished. In outpatient programs, a response-prevention technique is utilized in a similar manner in that patients are either requested to bring in foods they wish to binge on or are provided with those foods and then instructed to go ahead and eat as much as they wish. After the eating episode, the therapist stays with the patient until her urge to vomit dissipates.

Cognitive therapy techniques are being developed for both individual and group psychotherapy. The assessment of cognition is the first step in cognitive therapy. Patients are asked to write down thoughts on an assessment form so that they can be examined for systematic distortions in the processing and interpretation of events. In an excellent paper, Garner and Bemis (1982) described the use of cognitive techniques, such as operationalizing beliefs, decentering, the "what if" technique, evaluating autonomic thoughts, prospective hypothesis testing, reinterpreting body-image misperception, examining underlying assumptions, and modifying basic assumptions.

Group therapies using both cognitive and behavioral treatment have been carefully designed but, thus far, no randomly assigned controlled treatment study has been completed (Fairburn 1981; Lacey, 1983). The above-mentioned group therapies have been used exclusively with bulimia nervosa patients. Another group format employed to treat bulimia patients is the "psychoeducational group treatment" described by Johnson, Connors, and Stuckey (1983). In actuality, there is very little difference between this format and the cognitive–behavioral approach. For the psychoeducational approach, didactic presentations were designed to inform and challenge beliefs around issues such as overevaluation of thinness and distorted ideas about food, weight, and dieting. Behavioral strategies were taught to reduce bingeing and purging and normalize eating through self-monitoring in self-graduated goal-setting. All of these behavioral and cognitive group strategies just described have had some immediate value in treating bulimia nervosa patients.

Drugs

Drugs can be useful adjuncts in the treatment of both anorexia and bulimia nervosa. The first drug used in treating anorectic patients was chlorpromazine (Dally & Sargent, 1960). This medication is especially effective in severely obsessive–compulsive anorectic patients. However, there has been no controlled double-blind study to definitely prove the efficacy of chlorpromazine in inducing weight gain in anorectics. This is surprising because it is the first drug used, as well as the drug used in the most severely ill patients or in those very severely agitated and anxious anorectic patients.

Another category of drugs frequently used in the treatment of both anorexia and bulimia nervosa is the antidepressant. Eating-disorder patients have many depressive symptoms, such as sleep disturbance, irritability, depressed mood, and difficulty concentrating. These observations have stimulated the treatment of eating-disorder patients with antidepressant medication. In a recent double-blind study in which 72 anorectic patients were randomly assigned to amitriptyline, cyproheptadine, an antihis-

taminic drug, and a placebo, it was found that both cyproheptadine and amitriptyline had a marginal effect on decreasing the number of days necessary to achieve a normal weight. Cyproheptadine had an unexpected antidepressant effect demonstrated by a significant decrease on Hamilton depression ratings (Halmi, Eckert, Labu, & Cohen, 1986). A differential drug effect was present in the bulimic subgroup of anorectic patients, with cyproheptadine significantly decreasing treatment efficiency for the bulimic patients when compared with the amitriptyline and placebo groups. The differential cyproheptadine effect on the anorectic–bulimic subgroups was the first pharmacological evidence for the validity of the subgroups.

Lithium carbonate produced no overall effect on weight gain in a 4-week double-blind study of 16 anorexia nervosa patients (Gross, Ebert, Faden, Goldberg, Nee, & Kaye, 1981). There is little justification for using lithium in treating anorexia nervosa because the risks of toxicity are high in patients who restrict fluid intake and who purge. Another double-blind cross-over investigation compared 11 anorectic patients with delta 9-tetrahydrocannabinol and 11 patients with an active placebo, diazepam. There was no overall effect of the drug on weight gain and three of eleven patients experienced adverse reactions of paranoid ideation and feelings of loss of control (Gross et al., 1983).

Gastrointestinal symptoms, such as postprandial epigastric pain, belching, vomiting, anorexia, and early satiety, were significantly improved by the drug metoclopramide in a double-blind study (Saleh & Lebwohl, 1980). Because metoclopramide crosses the blood-brain barrier, it is associated with neurological side effects. A single case report showed that domperidone, a drug that enhances gastric peristalsis and antiemetic properties and accelerates gastric emptying, but does not cross the blood-brain barrier, was effective in alleviating abdominal discomfort in an anorectic woman. This encouraging report should stimulate a double-blind study of domperidone in anorexia nervosa (Kaplan, Garfinkel, Darby, & Garner, 1983).

A new development in the psychopharmacology of eating disorders has been the use of antidepressant medications in the treatment of bulimia nervosa patients. In the past 3 years, several double-blind controlled treatment studies have shown some of the antidepressants to be effective in a select group of patients. Drug compliance can be a serious problem in bulimia nervosa patients, and these studies measuring the efficacy of antidepressant drugs do so only in patients who are obviously taking the medication. Therefore, these studies have been done in a biased and select group, and it would be of interest to compare the drug refusers or non-compliers with those who cooperate in a treatment study. In a randomly assigned double-blind study with imipramine in 22 bulimic patients, there was a drug effect that reduced frequency of binge eating, decreased intensity of binges, decreased preoccupation with food, produced greater subjective global improvement, and decreased depression as measured by the Hamilton Depression Scale (Pope, Hudson, Jonas, & Yurgelun-Todd, 1983). In a recently reported investigation, desipramine produced a significant reduction in frequency and severity of bulimic symptoms whereas the placebo produced no change with a double-blind trial in 22 bulimic patients (Hughes, Wells, & Cunningham, 1984).

The mood disturbance of patients with bulimia has been equated with that of patients with atypical depression or a depression with many symptoms of anxiety. Because of this observation, some clinicians have been treating bulimics with monoamine oxidase inhibitors. A recent double-blind study of phenylzine in 20 bulimic patients showed that the phenylzine-treated group had significantly fewer binges per week compared with the placebo group in an 8-week study. No patients experienced a hypertensive reaction, although they were carefully screened for compliance to a tryamine-free diet. Also, the effect of the monoamine oxidase inhibitor on binge eating was independent of its effect on antidepressant activity (Walsh, Stewart, Roose, Gladis, & Glassman, 1984).

It should be noted that the first controlled drug study in bulimia actually was conducted 8 years ago with the anticonvulsant drug phenytoine (Wermuth, Davis, Hollister, & Stunkard, 1977). In a double-blind cross-over trial of 19 bulimic patients, there was a significant decrease in binge eating in those subjects who received phenytoine preceding placebo. Phenytoine was effective in preventing binge eating at serum levels as low as 5 g/ml. There is no association of EEG abnormalities and response to the medication. More recently, another anticonvulsant drug, carbamazepine, was studied in 6 bulimic outpatients in a double-blind cross-over trial over 20 weeks. Five patients had no drug response, but one with a history suggestive of bipolar disorder responded with complete cessation of binge eating (Kaplan et al., 1983).

Although no controlled study has been conducted with trazadone in bulimia nervosa patients, a word of caution is warranted concerning this drug. Three bulimic patients with major depressive episodes developed delirium shortly after the initiation of trazadone treatment (Damlouji & Ferguson, 1984).

Pharmacological treatment of eating disorders often has been regarded unenthusiastically. However, recent studies such as those just discussed are proving that some antidepressant drugs and some serotonin and dopamine antagonists are useful adjunct treatments for both anorexia nervosa and bulimia nervosa. A restatement of the introduction to this treatment section is useful in summarizing this section. A multidimensional or multifaceted treatment approach is necessary for anorexia and bulimia patients. With medical rehabilitation, there is an associated improvement in psychological state. Behavioral contingencies are very useful in inducing weight gain and changing the medical condition of the patient. If an anorectic patient has a predominance of depressive symptomatology, a trial on amitriptyline or cyproheptadine is warranted. A bulimia nervosa patient with anxiety and depressive symptomatology may respond to phenylzine, imipramine, or desipramine. Further, some bulimic patients may respond with a reduction of bingeing episodes to phenytoine. Severely obsessive–compulsive, anxious, and delusional anorectic patients are likely to require chlorpromazine. All patients need cognitive individual psychotherapy, and many bulimia nervosa patients will respond well to a cognitive–behavioral group-therapy program. The more severely ill patients need hospitalization in the initial stages of their treatment and must be followed in a continued outpatient treatment program.

Case Illustrations

Case 1. Gloria

Gloria was a 15-year-old girl, who voluntarily began dieting after a competitive swimming meet when one of the girls whom she admired remarked that Gloria looked overweight. Initially, Gloria deleted high-carbohydrate foods from her meals. She gradually eliminated more and more food items until her total caloric intake was less than 600 calories a day. Gloria had her last menstrual period the month before she began to diet. At that time, she weighed 45 kg, which had been her highest weight and was a normal weight for her age and height. In a 2-month period of time, she had lost to 36 kg. Because of her rapidly progressing weight loss and the inability of the family to handle her, she was admitted to the hospital for treatment.

A month after Gloria started dieting, she developed bulimic episodes in which she would eat a large amount of ice cream or cookies. She denied ever abusing laxatives or self-inducing vomiting. Gloria expressed a marked fear of gaining weight and stated that she was doing 30 sit-ups twice a day to keep her stomach from sticking out. In the past 2 months, she had developed an interest in cooking and was collecting recipes and actually preparing most of the meals for her family. She would refuse to eat the meals she prepared and hid candies and sweets around the house. The only physical abnormalities she had on admission to the hospital other than a low weight were bradycardia and hypothermia.

Gloria was born in another country and moved here with her parents when only a few months old. She has one sibling, a younger sister with whom she was extremely competitive. When Gloria was 4 years old her parents were divorced. During the next 4 years, there was considerable dramatic fighting between the parents over the father's visiting rights. Her mother was killed in a car accident when Gloria was 8 years old, and shortly after this she and her younger sister came to live with their father. At the time Gloria was admitted to the hospital, her father was a 46-year-old general surgeon who had diabetes and followed a special diet. He was anxious, controlling, overactive, and dramatic. He issued many rules and regulations for the household, but his daughters managed to circumvent most of them. The father and daughters spent very little time together. The father had been dating casually until about 2 years ago when he began to consistently date one person. About 6 months before Gloria was admitted to the hospital, she became very jealous over her father's dating and requested he stop dating entirely. He complied with her request. Gloria was an excellent student and was

at the top of her class at the time she went into treatment for anorexia nervosa.

Gloria was treated with a multidimensional treatment program. Behavior therapy was used to promote weight gain. She had individual cognitive psychotherapy sessions 3 times a week and family session with her father and sister once a week. It was very difficult for Gloria to engage in psychotherapy seriously. She was dramatically superficial in her interactions with the staff and therapist. She constantly tested rules, exercised frequently, and tried to hoard food. She had a slow, steady weight gain while in the hospital and was discharged at 45.3 kg.

Following discharge from the hospital treatment program, Gloria continued in an outpatient program. Shortly after discharge, she lost 2 kg and maintained that weight for almost 4 months. In her weekly therapy sessions she was resistive, and her housekeeper reported that she was again engaging in unusual food handling. Initially after Gloria was discharged from the hospital, the father and sister refused to return for family therapy sessions. However, after 4 months the housekeeper called Gloria's therapist to inform her that it was very difficult to handle Gloria and that she was again doing strange things with her food. At that time, the housekeeper, father, and sister agreed to return for family therapy sessions. Shortly after, Gloria lost another 2 kg and was hospitalized for a week. During this period she was tube fed and placed on a behavior-therapy program that brought her back to her target weight. She continued with outpatient therapy. The father was unable to follow through with any of the suggestions made during family therapy sessions. He continued to engage in power struggles with the patient. Nine months after Gloria was discharged from the hospital, her outpatient therapy was discontinued because she moved to another state with her father and sister. After the move, Gloria received no further therapy. She lost about 2 kg and maintained her weight at that level. She was able to graduate from a local college and currently has a fairly responsible job with a business enterprise. She maintains her weight in a low-normal range and on rare occasions will have a binge-eating episode. She has continued to live with her father and sister and the household servants during this entire time. She dates occasionally and has made no plans to move out of the family home.

Case 2. Sue

Sue was age 21 and had been binge eating and vomiting for 8 years before she was referred for a hospitalization treatment program. She had achieved her greatest weight of 59 kg when she was a sophomore in high school and 15 years of age. Sue had several stresses during that year; she did not make the cheerleading team, her grandfather, with whom she was very close, died, and some close friends moved away. She developed a general feeling of unhappiness, loneliness, and loss. Also during that year, her pets had been given away by her parents because they were too much trouble. It was during this time that Sue decided she wanted to lose weight and soon developed the habit of self-induced vomiting. She gradually increased the amount of self-induced vomiting until her senior year in high school when she was vomiting 4 times a week. When Sue began to lose weight, she soon resorted to a series of fad diets. She refused to eat meals with her family and after about 6 months of dieting she began to get up at night for binge-eating episodes followed by self-induced vomiting, which she had perfected for the past several months.

Sue started her menses at age 14. At about age 16 she began to have irregular menses. However, she continued to menstruate until 7 months before hospitalization. Her lowest weight was 40.9 kg, and that was just a few months before her hospitalization. She had gained 5.9 kg in a local hospital before being transferred to the Eating Disorder Program. At the time of transfer, her weight was 46.8 kg.

After graduating from high school, Sue went to college for 1 year and majored in animal science. She did not like this curriculum and dropped out after the year. However, during that time her symptomatology increased. She actually wallpapered one of the walls with M & M wrappers. She then went back to live at home and had a series of jobs in food stores, such as a doughnut shop and a deli, or in clothing stores. Sue stated she wasn't able to hold a job more than a few months because of her binge eating and vomiting behavior.

Her most stable relationship was with her boyfriend, with whom she was living for a year before hospitalization. During that time, at her boyfriend's insistence, she saw a social worker weekly for several months but then stopped treatment abruptly. Her binge eating and vomiting got out of control so that her boyfriend took her to a local hospital. She was there for 3 months and then transferred directly to a special hospitalization eating-disorder program. During her 3-month hospitalization, she was allowed to come and go as she pleased and she merrily continued her binge eating and vomiting behavior. At the time of admission to the treatment program, Sue admitted to feeling depressed and having frequent crying spells. She also had difficulty falling asleep at night. She was totally preoccupied with thoughts of binge eating and thoughts about food. The most significant findings on her physical exam were a slight scoliosis and marked deterioration of her teeth. She was only 4.5 kg below her target weight of 50.9 kg.

The patient was placed on a multifaceted treatment program with twice weekly individual psychotherapy sessions and biweekly family sessions. Initially, Sue expressed considerable denial and anger and later was able to describe feelings of emptiness, loneliness, and a sense of inadequacy. Adjunctive drug treatment was attempted, but had to be discontinued because of side effects. Sue was unable to tolerate even low dosages of imipramine or phenylzine. Because of her severe agitation, she was given chlorpromazine but developed an allergic reaction. Haloperidol (Haldol®) had to be discontinued because of side effects and molindone hydrochloride (Moban®) was discontinued after 6 weeks because it did not effect any noticeable change in the patient's behavior. Response prevention was used to stop the vomiting and binge eating behavior. Sue did very well in the structured setting. She gradually gained control over her eating behavior and developed considerable insight into her problems and self-confidence. During her 4 months of hospitalization, she responded well to the gradual introduction of responsibility for her eating behavior and for other aspects of her life. Sue continued her treatment in an outpatient setting and had both individual and family therapy. She returned to live with her parents and brother, where she stayed for 6 months until she could find a supportive apartment. In the fall, she began attending a community college. Her binge eating and vomiting had stopped entirely, and she was eating normally and maintaining her weight within a normal range. However, her prognosis is guarded because of her long history of eating problems.

CURRENT RESEARCH

Current research in the areas of diagnosis, epidemiology, physical aberrations, and treatment were discussed in their respective sections. There is a great need for prospective studies of large populations during the age of risk to determine social, psychological, and biological factors that make individuals vulnerable to develop anorexia or bulimia nervosa. There also is a need for sound methodological long-term follow-up investigations of these disorders. Sound methodological requirements for obtaining meaningful information from long-term follow-up studies are as follows:

1. Adequate sample size is necessary, with all patients accounted for in the follow-up study.
2. Standardized diagnostic criteria must be used for all patients at the time of the initial assessment.
3. Data must be obtained with a systematic method by using standardized instrumentation for assessing behavior, both at the time of the initial assessment and at the follow-up.
4. Outcome investigations should be conducted at a sufficient period of time after the initial assessment (at least 5 years for the first follow-up investigation), and the outcome investigation should be conducted in a uniform time period after the initial assessment.
5. Outcome should be assessed in discrete and specific categories such as weight, eating behavior and attitudes, psychological status, medical status, sexual adjustment, social adjustment, vocational adjustment, and family relationships in order to evaluate the independence of symptoms.
6. Follow-up data should be obtained from at least one person other than the patient and by means of an interview technique in order to insure completeness and accuracy of the data.

None of the best follow-up studies on eating disorders in the literature meet a majority of these requirements. Because of the heterogeneity of the eating-disorder population (even with the use of specific criteria), it is necessary to have a substantial number of patients assessed in a follow-up study. Virtually all of the follow-up efforts have deficiencies due to failure to employ standardized instruments for assessing behavior both at the time of initial assessment and at follow-up assessment. Most follow-up studies have not evaluated outcome in discrete and specific categories covering a range from weight, eating behavior, and attitudes, to social, family, and work adjustment. A disproportionate number of these investigations do not use a systematic interview technique of the entire sample to obtain follow-up data.

In assessing the effectiveness of treatment programs, it is necessary to keep in mind that the outcome of anorexia nervosa and bulimia nervosa is related to certain prognostic factors that often override the effect of treatment. Across all follow-up research, the best indicator of good outcome is early-age onset of illness. The most consistent indicator of poor outcome is late-age onset and the number of previous hospitalizations. Such factors as childhood neuroticism, parental conflicts, bulimia, vomiting, laxative abuse, and various behavioral manifestations (e.g., obsessive–compulsive, hysterical, depressive, psychosomatic, neuroticisms, denying of symptoms) all have been related to poor outcome in some studies and have not been thought to be significant in others. It is likely that the frequency of vomiting and laxative abuse is consistently related to poor outcome (Halmi, Brodland, & Loney, 1973; Morgan & Russell, 1975; Theander, 1970). In a short-term outcome study of 43 bulimia nervosa patients, the only predictor of good outcome was the onset of binge eating before age 16 (Abraham, Mira, & Llewellyn-Jones, 1983a). A follow-up study of 100 females with anorexia nervosa (Hsu, 1979) found poor outcome associated with a longer duration of illness, older age of onset, lower weight during illness, and the presence of symptoms such as bulimia, vomiting, poor childhood social adjustment, and poor prenatal relationships.

In a prognostic study of 41 anorectic patients, Morgan and Russell (1975) reported, on a follow-up of at least 4 years or more after treatment, that an unfavorable outcome was related to late-age onset of illness, a longer duration of illness, previous admissions to psychiatric hospitals, a disturbed relationship between the patient and other family members, and premorbid personality difficulties. These investigators stress that the long-term outcome in their series depended more on factors relating to the severity of their patient's illness than on the method of treatment. Maintenance of a normal weight was associated with better scores on psychological and social indices. Morgan and Russell also emphasize that these were general statistics and that in the specific individual case it is impossible to predict outcome.

In a follow-up study of 79 patients treated for anorexia nervosa from 1920 to 1972, Halmi, Brodland, and Rigas (1975) found that 17 patients had died while severely ill with anorexia nervosa (mortality of 21.5%). The average time from onset of anorexia nervosa to death was 12 years (range from 1 to 35 years). Three patients had recovered from anorexia nervosa and died from unrelated causes. Forty-one patients had recovered, and nine were currently ill with anorexia nervosa. Of the recovered group, only 12% were obese at follow-up. All patients who were ill at the time of follow-up had a current history of vomiting and laxative abuse. In a recent 30-year follow-up study, Theander (1985) found a 20% mortality rate and also noted the association between greater duration of illness before treatment and poor outcome. Emphasis is placed here on the long-term outcome studies because the short-term follow-up efforts have been misleading and have encouraged a rather casual approach to the treatment of anorexia and bulimia nervosa.

The assessment of "disturbance of body image" in anorexia nervosa has been perplexing and controversial. To most clinicians, the disturbance in body image means that the anorectic feels that she is overweight even when she is at a normal weight or underweight state. It is very likely, as pointed out by Garner and Garfinkel (1981/1982), that this disturbance of body image can be subdivided into several components in the heterogeneous anorexia nervosa population. This disturbance has been mainly measured experimentally by a visual size estimation apparatus (Casper, Halmi, Goldberg, Eckert, & Davis, 1979; Crisp & Kalucy, 1974; Garner, Garfinkel, Stancer, & Moldofsky, 1981; Slade & Russell, 1973). All confirmed that emaciated anorectic patients overestimate the width of various body parts. However, there were no significant differences in body perception indices between anorectic patients and normal age-matched controls. Casper et al. (1979) and Button, Fransella, and Slade (1977) found large individual differences between patients in their individual body size estimates. Casper et al.

(1979) reported that those patients with greatest overestimation of body parts were also those who were most malnourished and who had experienced the most failures to respond to treatment in previous hospitalizations. Button et al. (1977) were able to determine that those patients who vomited overestimated their size more than did the nonvomiters. A greater denial of illness was associated with greater body distortion in some investigations (Crisp & Kalucy, 1974; Garner et al., 1976).

The concept of disturbance of body image seems to include both a distortion of body size and a disparagement of body image. Strober, Goldenberg, Green, and Saxon (1979) used more subjective assessments, including the image-marking procedure, the Fischer Body Distortion Questionnaire, and the Sophistication of Body Concept Scale. Their results supported previous findings of considerable heterogeneity of body-image distortion within the anorexia nervosa patient group. The repertory grid technique is another measure that has been employed to examine body-image disturbances in anorectic patients. In one study using this technique, attitudes toward weight and shape were systematically studied in a group of anorectic patients, normal control females, and a group of "neurotic" females (Fransella & Crisp, 1979). This investigation showed that the anorectic patients used the constructs in a way that was different from normal and neurotic groups. Research using this technique has not been well developed. However, it may be a more meaningful way to evaluate the body-image disturbance and disparagement present in the anorectic patients.

The identification of the psychology behind the physical symptomatology in anorexia nervosa is fraught with methodological problems, imprecision, and lack of consistency in the various studies. Perhaps this just supports the heterogeneity of the syndrome of anorexia nervosa. Bruch (1962) lists the relentless pursuit of thinness, denial of cachexia, and the general ineffectiveness of these patients as being the core psychological symptoms. Numerous self-report questionnaires have been devised to assess these areas. Results generally have confirmed Bruch's clinical statement.

Recognition of the fact that a variety of personality disorders can exist within the diagnosis of anorexia nervosa was made as far back as 20 years ago by Dally (1969). He categorized his anorexia nervosa patients into three types: (a) hysterical personality type, (b) compulsive personality type, and (c) mixed personality type. Obviously, the existence of a specific personality disorder will affect the prognosis of anorexia nervosa in that patient. Treatment strategies must take into account the underlying personality disorder. The *DSM-III* provides a descriptive structure on which personality diagnoses can be made and thus provides a modality for systematic studies of personality disorders among different investigators.

The great variety of outcome in various follow-up investigations of anorexia nervosa patients could well be explained by a biased sampling of personality disorders within the populations studied. Schizoid personality disorder, borderline personality disorder, histrionic personality disorder, and antisocial personality disorder have been diagnosed in patients with anorexia nervosa (Bram, Eger, & Halmi, 1983). Anorectic patients who have bulimia are likely to have a personality-disorder diagnosis (Strober 1981). Because a higher association of impulsive behavior, such as suicide attempts, self-mutilation, stealing, and substance abuse, are present in binge eating and purging anorectics, one may expect a higher prevalence of well-defined personality disorders in the bulimic anorectics (Casper et al., 1980; Garfinkel et al., 1980).

Because amenorrhea is a major diagnostic symptom of anorexia nervosa, extensive studies have been conducted on the hypothalamic–pituitary–ovarian axis in patients with this disorder. The controversies of whether changes seen in this axis are due to nutritional status (eating behavior and/or weight change) or stress factors are important because they represent an important etiological hypothesis of the illness; that is, whether anorectic patients have a primary impairment of hypothalamic function. Both urinary excretion and plasma levels of gonadotrophins are decreased in anorexia nervosa (Nillius & Wide, 1979).

In a study conducted by Brown, Garfinkel, Jeuniewic, Moldofsky, and Stancer (1977), only 22% of the variance for leutenizing hormone (LH) levels (a gonadotrophin necessary for normal menstruation) was accounted for by the degree of weight loss or percentage below ideal body weight. Weiner (1983) points out that if 78% of the variance in LH levels must be ac-

counted for by factors other than weight loss, then there can be no simple relationship between weight loss, LH levels, and amenorrhea. Weiner also pointed out that the amenorrheic runners in a study by Schwartz et al. (1981) had increased LH levels when compared to exercising women who retained their menses. Weiner suggests that evidence against a direct relationship between weight and gonadotrophin levels is that women who lose weight and have secondary amenorrhea, but do not develop anorexia nervosa, can have normal LH levels.

Some normal-weight bulimics have low LH and follicular stimulating hormone (FSH) levels and some patients with psychogenic amenorrhea have no weight loss but have low LH and FSH levels compared with normal controls. Post-pubertal bulimic women with a normal weight can be amenorrheic and have age-inappropriate patterns of gonadotrophin secretion. Women having full recovery of ideal body weight but with persisting symptoms of anorexia nervosa or bulimia still show age-inappropriate gonadotrophin secretion patterns (Katz, 1978).

After treatment, the return of normal menstrual cycles lags behind the return to a normal body weight and the resumption of menses in anorexia is associated with marked psychological improvement (Falk & Halmi, 1982). Research in the area of assessing hypothalamic function in eating-disorder patients continues and has expanded into different channels. One of these is examining neurotransmitter function and satiety mechanisms in anorexia and bulimia nervosa.

Neurotransmitter function is reasonable to study in the eating disorders because dopamine, serotonin, and norepinephrine (all neurotransmitters) influence appetite, satiety, and eating behavior (Hoebel, 1984). Because of the signs and symptoms of depression in the eating disorders, it is of interest to ascertain if similar dysfunctions in neurotransmitters exist in the eating disorders and in major depressive illness.

There is the serious methodological problem of how to assess neurotransmitter function in the human brain. Most commonly, plasma, urine, or CSF levels of neurotransmitters and their metabolites are measured, and an assumption is made that they reflect to some degree, what is occurring in the brain. This is probably a very tenuous assumption. Another way to assess neurotransmitter function in the brain is by specific pharmacological perturbation tests in which the pharmacological agent is known to bind to a specific receptor site and to cause a specific response.

At this time, studies of neurotransmitter metabolites in the CSF are difficult to interpret. It is not possible to put together a clear picture of the relationships of these various metabolites to each other in the disorders of anorexia and bulimia nervosa (Gerner et al., 1984; Kaye, Ebert, Raleigh, & Lake, 1984). It is not particularly helpful for the understanding of basic physiological mechanisms in the eating disorders to merely label them as affective disorders. There is, in fact, something different and unique about them biologically as well as psychologically.

Some preliminary studies of satiety responses in anorexia nervosa have shown distinct differences in satiety responses to a test-meal paradigm in anorectic patients relative to control subjects. These disparities persisted even after weight restoration and the resumption of normal eating behavior (Owen, Halmi, Gibbs, & Smith, 1985). Another report has shown distinct differences in taste preferences for sweetness and "fattiness" in restricting anorectics, bulimic anorectics, normal weight bulimics, and control subjects (Halmi et al., 1985). Further research on the identification of disturbances in the psychological processes of hunger, satiety, and taste could provide cogent clues for impaired central mechanisms.

The combination of self-report questionnaires and multivariate statistics has flooded the bulimia nervosa field with repetitive studies and information. The validity and importance of most of these efforts are questionable. Most systematic investigations of bulimia nervosa have been conducted in the past 5 years. In a comprehensive study of the clinical features of bulimia nervosa, Fairburn and Cooper (1984) found that the most commonly reported precipitant of binge eating was having adopted a rigid diet. The most frequently cited reason for beginning vomiting was a response to a gross bout of overeating. This finding may have important significance with regard to the physiological mechanisms involved in binge eating and purging. In another study of clinical features, Hatsukami, Eckert, Mitchell, and Pyle (1984) found that in a sample of 108 women with bulimia nervosa, 43.5% had affective disorder at some time in their lives and 18.5% had a history of alcohol or drug abuse. A little over half of these patients scored within the moderate to severe range of depression on the Beck Depression Inventory.

Another investigation (Hatsukami, Owen, Pyle, & Mitchell, 1982) compared bulimia nervosa women with alcohol- and drug-abusing women on the Minnesota Multiphasic Personality Inventory (MMPI) and showed that the two groups had similar profiles. Specifically, they had elevations on the scales denoting depression, impulsivity, anger, rebelliousness, anxiety, rumination, social withdrawal, and idiosyncratic thinking. Another similarity between these populations was found in the distribution of MMPI code types. For both groups, two of the three most prevalent code types were: (a) "within normal limits" and (b) a profile characterized as unpredictable, argumentative, and experiencing repeated problems with interpersonal relationships. Individuals with this profile also are characterized as basically insecure and demonstrating symptoms of depression, anxiety, and social withdrawal. Women with bulimia were also characterized by an obsessive–compulsive code type associated with symptoms of overanxiousness, rumination, difficulty in making decisions, withdrawal, and inhibition.

Two studies using the social adjustment scale reported that bulimia nervosa women were significantly worse in all areas of adjustment (work, social and leisure activities, relationship with extended family, role as spouse, role as parent, membership in the family unit) than a normal control sample (Johnson & Berndt, 1983; Norman & Herzog, 1984). These findings remained stable at a 1-year follow-up.

An excellent synthesis of the current research in bulimia and a discussion of how biological, familial, and social-cultural factors may predispose adolescent and young women to develop the disorder is provided by Johnson and Maddi (1985).

SUMMARY

The eating disorders anorexia nervosa and bulimia nervosa have become a prevalent public-health problem in the past 20 years. The process of refining the diagnosis of these disorders is still proceeding as current research gives us more information concerning the epidemiology, clinical course, and response to treatment of these disorders. Bulimia nervosa as a distinct entity has only been systematically studied in the past 5 years. Virtually nothing is known of the long-term outcome of normal-weight bulimia nervosa patients. Social, psychological, familial, and biological factors are important in producing the eating-disorder syndromes. Consequently, all of these factors must be considered in the effective treatment of the eating disorders. Hence, multifaceted treatment programs have been developed and attend to the medical needs and provide individual psychotherapy, family therapy, behavior therapy, and adjunct drug treatment if necessary. There is a special need for prospective research to determine risk factors and long-term follow-up studies so that an understanding of the course of these disorders may facilitate the development of more efficacious treatment programs.

REFERENCES

Abraham, S. F., Mira, M., & Llewellyn-Jones, D. (1983a). Bulimia: A study of outcome. *International Journal of Eating Disorders, 2*, 175–181.

Abraham, S. F., Mira, M., & Llewellyn-Jones, D. (1983b). Eating behaviors amongst young women. *Medical Journal Australia, 2*, 225–228.

Agras, S., Barlow, D., Chapin, H., Abel, G., & Leitenberg, H. (1974). Behavior modification of anorexia nervosa. *Archives of General Psychiatry, 30*, 279–286.

American Psychiatric Association. (1980). *Diagnostic and statistical manual of mental disorders* (3rd ed.). Washington, DC: Author.

Bell, R. M. (1985). *Holy anorexia*. Chicago: University of Chicago Press.

Bowers, T. K., & Eckert, E. (1978). Leukopenia in anorexia nervosa: Lack of increased risk of infection. *Archives of Internal Medicine, 138*, 1520–1523.

Brady, J. P., & Rieger, W. (1972). Behavior treatment of anorexia nervosa. In *Proceedings of the International Symposium on Behavior Modification* (pp. 57–63). New York: Appleton-Century-Crofts.

Bram, S. B., Eger, D. J., & Halmi, K. A. (1983). Anorexia nervosa and personality type: A preliminary report. *International Journal of Eating Disorders, 2*, 67–74.

Brown, G. M., Garfinkel, P. E., Jeuniewic, N., Moldofsky, H., & Stancer, H. C., (1977). Endocrine profiles in anorexia nervosa. In R. A. Vigersky (Ed.), *Anorexia nervosa* (pp. 123–125). New York: Raven.

Bruch, H. (1962). Perceptual and conceptual disturbances in anorexia nervosa. *Psychosomatic Medicine, 24*, 187–195.

Button, E. J., Fransella, F., & Slade, P. D. (1977). A reappraisal of body perception disturbance in anorexia nervosa. *Psychological Medicine, 7*, 235–242.

Carryer, H. M., Berkman, J. M., & Mason, H. L. (1959). Relative lymphocytosis in anorexia nervosa. *Staff Meetings of the Mayo Clinic, 34*, 426–432.

Carter, J. A., & Duncan P. A. (1984). Binge eating and vomiting: A survey of a high school population. *Psychology in the Schools, 21*, 198–203.

Casper, R. C., Eckert, E. D., Halmi, K. A., Goldberg, S. C., & Davis, J. M. (1980). Bulimia: It's incidence and clinical importance in patients with anorexia nervosa. *Archives of General Psychiatry, 37*, 1030–1035.

Casper, R. C., Halmi, K. A., Goldberg, S. C., Eckert, E. D., & Davis, J. M. (1979). Disturbances in body image estimation as related to other characteristics and outcome in anorexia nervosa. *British Journal of Psychiatry, 134*, 60–66.

Cooper, P. J., & Fairburn, C. G. (1983). Binge eating and self-induced vomiting in the community, A preliminary study. *British Journal of Psychiatry, 142*, 139–144.

Crisp, A. H. (1965). A treatment regimen for anorexia nervosa. *British Journal of Psychiatry, 112*, 505–510.

Crisp, A. H. (1967). The possible significance of some behavioral correlates of weight and carbohydrate intake. *Journal of Psychosomatic Research, 11*, 117–123.

Crisp, A. H., & Kalucy, R. S. (1974). Aspects of perceptual disorder in anorexia nervosa. *British Journal of Medical Psychology, 47*, 349–352.

Crisp, A. H., Palmer, R. L., & Kalucy, R. S. (1976). How common is anorexia nervosa? *British Journal of Psychiatry, 128*, 549–554.

Dally, P. J. (1969). *Anorexia nervosa*. New York: Grune & Stratton.

Dally P. J., & Sargent, W. (1960). A new treatment of anorexia nervosa. *British Medical Journal, 1*, 1770–1773.

Damlouji, N. F., & Ferguson, J. M. (1984). Trazedone-induced delirium in bulimic patients. *American Journal of Psychiatry, 141*, 434–435.

Decourt, N. (1964). Sur l'anorexie mentale de l'adolescence dans le sexe masculin [A study of adolescent males with anorexia nervosa]. *Review Neuropsychiatrica Infant, 12*, 499–512.

Dubois, A., Gross, H. A., Ebert, M. H., & Castell, D. O. (1981). Effect of bethanecol on gastric functions in primary anorexia nervosa. *Digestive Diseases and Sciences, 26*, 598–600.

Eckert, E. D., Goldberg, S. C., Halmi, K. A., Casper, R. C., & Davis, J. M. (1979). Behavior therapy in anorexia nervosa. *British Journal of Psychiatry, 134*, 55–59.

Fairburn, C. (1981). A cognitive behavioral approach to the treatment of bulimia. *Psychological Medicine, 11*, 707–711.

Fairburn, C. G., & Cooper, P. J. (1984). The clinical features of bulimia nervosa. *British Journal of Psychiatry, 144*, 238–246.

Falk, J. R., & Halmi, K. A. (1982). Amenorrhea in anorexia nervosa: Examination of the critical body hypothesis. *Journal of Biological Psychiatry, 17*, 799–806.

Fransella, F., & Crisp, A. H. (1979). Comparisons of

weight concepts in groups of neurotic, normal and anorexic females. *British Journal of Psychiatry, 134,* 79–86.

Friedman, E. J. (1984). Death from ipecac intoxication in a patient with anorexia nervosa. *American Journal of Psychiatry, 141,* 702–703.

Garfinkel, P. E., Moldofsky, H., & Garner, D. M. (1980). The heterogeneity of anorexia nervosa. *Archives of General Psychiatry, 37,* 1036–1046.

Garner, D. M., & Bemis, K. M. (1982). A cognitive-behavioral approach to anorexia nervosa. *Cognitive Therapy and Research, 6,* 1223–1250.

Garner, D. M., & Garfinkel, P. (1981/1982). Body image in anorexia nervosa: Measurement, theory and clinical implications. *International Journal of Psychiatry in Medicine, 11,* 263–283.

Garner, D. M., Garfinkel, P. E., Stancer, H. C., & Moldofsky, H. (1976). Body image disturbances in anorexia nervosa and obesity. *Psychosomatic Medicine, 38,* 227–232.

Gerner, R. H., Cohen, D. J., Fairbanks, L., Anderson, G. M., Young, J. G., Scheinin, M., Linnoila, M., Shaywitz, B. A., & Hare, T. A. (1984). CSF neurochemistry of women with anorexia nervosa and normal women. *American Journal of Psychiatry, 141,* 1441–1444.

Gershon, E. S., Schreiber, J. L., Hamovit, J. R., Dibble, E. D., Kaye, W., Nurnberger, J. I., Andersen, A., & Ebert, M. (1984). Clinical findings in patients with anorexia nervosa and affective illness in their relatives. *American Journal of Psychiatry, 141,* 1419–1422.

Gotsch, F. M. (1975). Reversible granulocyte killing defects in anorexia nervosa. *Clinical and Experimental Immunology, 21,* 244–249.

Gottdeiner, J. S., Gross, H. A., Henry, W. L., Borer, J. S., & Ebert, M. H. (1978). Effects of self-induced starvation on cardiac size and function in anorexia nervosa. *Circulation, 58,* 425–433.

Gross, H., Ebert, M. H., Faden. V. B., Goldberg, S. C., Kaye, W. H., Caine, E. D., Hawks, R., & Zinberg, N. (1983). A double-blind trial of tetrahydrocannabinol in primary anorexia nervosa. *Journal of Clinical Psychopharmacology, 3,* 165–171.

Gross, H. A., Ebert, M. H., Faden, V. B., Goldberg, S. C., Nee, L. E., & Kaye, W. H. (1981). A double-blind controlled trial of lithium carbonate in primary anorexia nervosa. *Journal of Clinical Psychopharmacology, 1,* 376–381.

Gull, W. (1874). Anorexia nervosa (Apepsia hysterica, anorexia hysterica). *Trans Clinical Society, 7,* 22–29.

Hallsten, E. A. (1965). Adolescent anorexia nervosa treated by desensitization. *Behaviour Research and Therapy, 3,* 87–91.

Halmi, K. A. (1974). Anorexia nervosa: Demographic and clinical features in 94 cases. *Psychosomatic Medicine, 36,* 18–22.

Halmi, K. A., Brodland, G., & Loney, J. (1973). Prognosis in anorexia nervosa. *Annals of Internal Medicine, 78,* 907–909.

Halmi, K. A., Brodland, G., & Rigas, C. (1975). A follow-up study of 79 patients with anorexia nervosa: An evaluation of prognostic factors in diagnostic criteria. *Life History Research in Psychopathology, 4,* 290–301.

Halmi, K. A., Drewnowski, A., Pierce, B., Gibbs, J.,

& Smith, G. P. (1985, May). *Taste differences in anorexia and bulimia nervosa.* Paper presented at American Psychiatric Association Conference, Dallas, Texas.

Halmi, K. A., Eckert, E. D., LaDu, T., & Cohen, J. (1986). Anorexia nervosa: Treatment efficacy of cyproheptadine and amitriptyline. *Archives of General Psychiatry, 43,* 177–181.

Halmi K. A., & Falk, J. R. (1981). Common physiological changes in anorexia nervosa. *International Journal of Eating Disorders, 1,* 16–27.

Halmi, K. A., Falk, J. R., & Schwartz, E. (1981). Binge-eating and vomiting: A survey of a college population. *Psychological Medicine, 11,* 697–706.

Hatsukami, D., Eckert, E. D., Mitchell, J. E., & Pyle, R. (1984). Affective disorder and substance abuse in women with bulimia. *Psychological Medicine, 14,* 701–704.

Hatsukami, D., Owen, P., Pyle, R., & Mitchell, J. (1982). Similarities and differences on the MMPI between women with bulimia and women with alcohol or drug abuse problems. *Addictive Behaviors, 7,* 435–439.

Hoebel, B. (1984). Neurotransmitters in the control of feeding and its rewards: Monoamines, opiates and brain-gut peptides. In A. J. Stunkard & E. Steller (Eds.), *Eating and its disorders* (pp. 15–38). New York: Raven.

Holland, A. J., Hall, A., Murray, R., Russell, G. F. M., & Crisp, A. H. (1984). Anorexia nervosa: A study of 34 twin pairs and one set of triplets. *British Journal of Psychiatry, 145,* 414–419.

Hudson, J. I., Pope, H. G., Jonas, J. M., & Todd, D. (1983). Family history study of anorexia nervosa and bulimia. *British Journal of Psychiatry, 142,* 133–138.

Hughes, P. L., Wells, L. A., & Cunningham, C. J. (1984, May). *A controlled trial using desipramine for bulimia.* Paper presented at the American Psychiatric Association Meeting, Los Angeles, CA.

Hsu, L. K. G. (1979). Outcome of anorexia nervosa. *Lancet, 1,* 61–65.

Johnson, C., & Berndt, D. J. (1983). Preliminary investigation of bulimia and life adjustment. *American Journal of Psychiatry, 140,* 774–777.

Johnson, C., & Maddi, K. (1985). The etiology of bulimia: A bio-psycho-social perspective. *Annals of Adolescent Psychiatry, 13,* 1–20.

Johnson, C. L. (1982). Bulimia: A descriptive survey of 316 cases. *International Journal of Eating Disorders, 2,* 3–16.

Johnson, C. L., Connors, M., & Stuckey, M. (1983). Short term group treatment of bulimia. *International Journal of Eating Disorders, 2,* 209–241.

Jones, D. J., Fox, M. M., Babigian, H. M., & Hutton, H. E. (1980). Epidemiology of anorexia nervosa in Monroe County, N.Y.: 1960–1976. *Psychosomatic Medicine, 42,* 551–567.

Kalucy, R. S., Crisp, A. H., & Harding, B. (1977). A study of 56 families with anorexia nervosa. *British Journal of Medical Psychology, 50,* 10–25.

Kaplan, A. S., Garfinkel, P. E., Darby, P. L., & Garner, D. M. (1983). Carbomazepine in the treatment of bulimia. *American Journal of Psychiatry, 140,* 1225–1226.

Katz, J. L. (1978). Weight and circadian LH secretory

pattern in anorexia nervosa. *Psychosomatic Medicine, 40*, 549–567.

Kaye, W., Ebert, M. H., Raleigh, M., & Lake, R. (1984). Abnormalities in CNS monoamine metabolism in anorexia nervosa. *Archives of General Psychiatry, 41*, 350–355.

Konradyne, G. M. (1973). *Margitsziget* [Saint Margaret]. Budapest: Kossuth Nyomda.

Lacey, J. H. (1982). The bulimic syndrome and normal body weight: Reflections on pathogenesis and clinical features. *International Journal of Eating Disorders, 2*, 59–66.

Lacey, J. H. (1983). An outpatient treatment program for bulimia nervosa. *International Journal of Eating Disorders, 2*, 209–241.

Lampert, F., & Lau, B. (1976). Bone marrow hypoplasia in anorexia nervosa. *European Journal of Pediatrics, 124*, 65–71.

Leitenberg, H., Agras. W., & Thomson, L. E. (1968). A sequential analysis of the effect of selective positive reinforcement in modifying anorexia nervosa. *Behaviour Research and Therapy, 6*, 211–218.

Mitchell, J. E., Pyle, R. L., Eckert, E. D., Hatsukami, D., & Lentz, R. (1983). Electrolyte and other physiological abnormalities in patients with bulimia. *Psychological Medicine, 13*, 273–278.

Mizes, J. S., & Lohr, J. M. (1983). The treatment of bulimia. *International Journal of Eating Disorders, 2*, 55–66.

Morgan, H. G., & Russell, G. F. M. (1975). Values of family background and clinical features of predictors of long-term outcome in anorexia nervosa. *Psychological Medicine, 5*, 355–371.

Nestel, P. J. (1974). Cholesterol metabolism in anorexia nervosa and hypercholesterolemia. *Journal of Endocrinology and Metabolism, 38*, 325–328.

Nillius, S. J., & Wide, L. (1979). Effects of prolonged leutenizing hormone-releasing hormone therapy on follicular maturation, ovulation, and corpus leutium function in amenorrheic women with anorexia nervosa. *Upsala Journal of Medical Science, 80*, 21–35.

Norman, D. K., & Herzog, D. B. (1984). Persistent social maladjustment in bulimia: A one year follow-up. *American Journal of Psychiatry, 141*, 355–340.

Owen, W. P., Halmi, K. A., Gibbs, J., & Smith, G. P. (1985). Satiety responses in eating disorders. *Journal of Psychiatric Research, 19* (2/3), 279–284.

Pertschuk, M. J., Edwards, N., & Pomerleau, O. F. (1978). A multiple baseline approach to behavioral intervention in anorexia nervosa. *Behaviour Research and Therapy, 9*, 368–376.

Pope, H., Hudson, J. I., Jonas, J. M., & Yurgelun-Todd, D. (1983). Bulimia treated with imipramine: A placebo-controlled double-blind study. *American Journal of Psychiatry, 140*, 554–560.

Pyle, R. L., Mitchell, J. E., Eckert, E. D., Halvorson, P. A., Neuman, P. A., & Goff, G. M. (1983). The incidence of bulimia in freshman college students. *International Journal of Eating Disorders, 2*, 75–86.

Rivinius, T. M., Biderman, J., Hertzog, D. B., Kemper, K., Harper, G. P., Harmatz, J. S., & Houseworth, S. (1984). Anorexia nervosa and affective disorders: A controlled family history study.

American Journal of Psychiatry, 141, 1414–1418.

Robboy, M. S., Sato, A. S., & Schwabe, A. D. (1974). The hypercarotenemia in anorexia nervosa: A comparison of vitamin A and carotene levels in various forms of menstrual dysfunction. *American Journal of Clinical Nutrition, 27*, 326–327.

Rodger, M. W., & Collyer, J. A. (1979). Anorexia nervosa with concealed hyperphasia and self-induced vomiting, hypokalemic alkalosis and normal eldosterone excretion. *Canadian Medical Association Journal, 103*, 415–418.

Rosen, J. C., & Leitenberg, H. (1982). Bulimia nervosa: Treatment with exposure and response prevention. *Behavior and Therapeutics, 13*, 117–124.

Russell, G. F. M. (1969). Metabolic, endocrine and psychiatric aspects of anorexia nervosa. *Scientific Basis of Medicine Annual Review, 14*, 236–255.

Russell, G. F. M. (1973). The management of anorexia nervosa. In *Symposium on Anorexia Nervosa and Obesity* (pp. 41–50). Edinburgh: Constable.

Russell, G. F. M. (1979). Bulimia nervosa: An ominous variant of anorexia nervosa. *Psychological Medicine, 9*, 429–448.

Saleh, J., & Lebwohl, P. (1980). Metoclopramide-induced gastric emptying in patients with anorexia nervosa. *American Journal of Gastroenterology, 74*, 127–132.

Schwartz, B., Cumming, D. C., Riordan, E., Selye, M., Yen, S. S., & Rebar, R. W. (1981). Exercise associated amenorrhea: A distinct entity? *American Journal of Obstetrics and Gynecology, 141*, 662–670.

Silverman, J. A. (1974). Anorexia nervosa: Clinical observations in a successful treatment plan. *Journal of Pediatrics, 84*, 68–73.

Slade, P. D., & Russell, G. F. M. (1973). Awareness of body dimensions in anorexia nervosa: Cross-sectional and longitudinal studies. *Psychological Medicine, 3*, 188–192.

Stangler, R. S., & Printz, A. M. (1980). *DSM-III*: Psychiatric diagnosis in a university population. *American Journal of Psychiatry, 137*, 937–940.

Stege, P. (1982). Anorexia nervosa: Review including oral and dental manifestations. *Journal of the American Dental Association, 104*, 648–652.

Strober, M. (1981). The significance of bulimia in juvenile anorexia nervosa: An exploration of possible etiological factors. *International Journal of Eating Disorders, 1*, 28–43.

Strober, M. (1984, September). *A family study of anorexia nervosa.* Paper presented at the International Conference on Anorexia Nervosa & Related Disorders, University College, Swansea, Wales.

Strober, M., Goldenberg, I., Green, J., & Saxon, J. (1979). Body image disturbance in anorexia nervosa during the acute and recuperative phase. *Psychological Medicine, 9*, 695–701.

Stunkard, A. J. (1959). Eating patterns and obesity. *Psychiatric Quarterly, 33*, 284–295.

Theander, S. (1970). Anorexia nervosa. *Acta Psychiatrica Scandinavia, 214*, 1–300.

Theander, S. (1985). Review: Outcome and prognosis in anorexia nervosa and bulimia. *Journal of Psychiatric Research, 19*, 493–508.

Thurston, J., & Marks, P. (1974). Electrocardiographic

abnormality in patients with anorexia nervosa. *British Heart Journal, 36*, 719–723.

Wallace, M., Richards, P., Chesser, E., & Wrong, O. (1968). Persistent alkalosis and hypokalemia caused by surreptitious vomiting. *Quarterly Journal of Medicine, 148*, 577–588.

Walsh, B. T., Stewart, J. W., Roose, S. P., Gladis, M., & Glassman, A. H. (1984). Treatment of bulimia with phenelzine. *Archives of General Psychiatry, 41*, 1105–1109.

Warrent, S. E., & Steinberg, S. M. (1979). Acid-base and electrolyte disturbances in anorexia nervosa. *American Journal of Psychiatry, 136*, 415–418.

Weiner, H. (1983). Hypothalamic–pituitary–ovarian axis in anorexia and bulimia nervosa. *International Journal of Eating Disorders, 2*, 109–116.

Wermuth, B. N., Davis, K. L., Hollister, L. E., & Stunkard, A. J. (1977). Phenytoin treatment of the binge-eating syndrome. *American Journal of Psychiatry, 134*, 1249–1255.

Willi, J., & Grossman, S. (1983). Epidemiology of anorexia nervosa in a defined region of Switzerland. *American Journal of Psychiatry, 140*, 564–567.

Winokur, A., March, V., & Mendels, J. (1980). Primary affective disorder in relatives of patients with anorexia nervosa. *American Journal of Psychiatry, 137*, 695–698.

Wolpe, J. (1958). *Psychotherapy by Reciprocal Inhibition*, Stanford, CA: Stanford University Press.

Wulliemier, F., Rossel, F., & Sinclair, K. (1975). La therapie comportementale de l'anorexie nerveuse [Behaviour therapy in anorexia nervosa]. *Journal of Psychosomatic Research, 19*, 267–272.

Zucker, P. (1984, April). *Disturbances in cardiac rhythm in bulimia*. Paper presented at the International Eating Disorder Meeting, New York.

CHAPTER 16

Depression and Suicide

Theodore A. Petti and Chris N. Larson

Depression in adolescence has been described poignantly by Burton and other giants of literature (Anthony, 1983). Freud's Wolf Man depicts the varying components of symptoms, predisposing factors, and dynamics of depression in adolescence. John Stuart Mill portrays himself and what he describes as "analytic depression" during his adolescence in less clinical terms (Anthony, 1970). The analytic description of the life of Virginia Woolf provides a view of an adolescent with bipolar depression and the impact of the disorder on a talented youth's growth and development (Feinstein, 1980). Clinicians have long described depressive disorders in adolescents (Campbell, 1952; Kassanin, 1931). Adolescent depression has most recently been described as the most expanding research area in adolescent psychopathology (Hodgman, 1983).

A number of classificatory schemes have been developed to aid in the diagnosis and treatment of depressed adolescents. The *Diagnostic and Statistical Manual, 3rd edition (DSM-III)* (American Psychiatric Association, 1980) provides the predominant nosologic formulation for the present. In this schema, depression in adolescents is included in the diagnostic classifications applicable to adults. Although not includ-

ed in the diagnostic criteria, certain special features pertaining to adolescents are delineated to include such age-specific associated features as negative or antisocial behavior in boys, substance abuse, failure to attend to personal appearance, increased emotionality, and school difficulties. Other features also seen in depressed adolescents include withdrawal from social activities, sulkiness, restlessness, grouchiness, aggression, reluctance to participate in family activities, and desire to leave home with accompanying feelings of not being understood. Sensitivity to rejection in a romantic relationship is also considered a feature of the adolescent picture of depression (American Psychiatric Association, 1980).

Anthony (1983) provides a concise review of the psychodynamic nosologies of adolescent depression. Anthony (1970) has described five types of mood disorders in adolescents. These include: (a) the normal moodiness of adolescents; (b) youngsters manifesting "depressive equivalents" (boredom, restlessness, stimulus chasing, and "acting out"); (c) a Type-1 depression with cyclical development, crisis in self-esteem, and predominance of shame and identity problems; (d) a Type-2 depression that is noncyclical, has a pubertal onset and predominance of guilt; and, finally, (e) borderline and psychotic depressions.

Malmquist (1971) outlines a similar system of classification that spans depression as: (a) a normal feature of development; (b) a reaction to current loss; (c) a reaction to past loss; (d) an associated feature of chronic illness or handicapping condition; (e) an extension of depression with onset during "latency" years and "depressive equivalents"; (f) "character depressions"; and (g) depressions associated with schizo-affective and manic-depressive disorders.

Additional classificatory systems adapted from Berman (1980) and Feinstein (1975) consider the perspectives of parent–adolescent transactions and psychoanalytic thinking, respectively. The previous lack of agreed-upon nosology and criteria for the diagnosis of depression has markedly hampered the development of a clear picture of suicide and suicidal behavior in adolescents as related to depression (Petzel & Riddle, 1981).

Suicide and related violent death in the adolescent–young adult years are major public health problems in the United States, Canada, Europe, and Japan (Headley, 1983). Worldwide, suicide ranks as the fourth major cause of death in this age group. In the United States, suicide is the third leading cause of death, and the rate has tripled over the past 30 years. A plethora of theories concerning suicidal behavior have been offered. The theories are far ranging, but can generally be grouped (Petti, 1985a) as: (a) Intrapsychic/Psychoanalytic, (b) Sociological, (c) Sociocultural/Familial, and (d) Biologic/Psychopathologic (Holinger & Offer, 1981; Petzel & Kline, 1978; Petzel & Riddle, 1981).

This chapter, therefore, will attempt to provide an overview of depression and suicidal behavior in adolescents and of approaches to assessment and treatment of these serious disorders.

DESCRIPTION OF DEPRESSION IN ADOLESCENTS

Depression and moodiness have been traditionally viewed as normative phenonema of adolescence. The only study comparing adults and adolescents in variability of mood (Larson in Offer & Franzen, 1983) reports adolescents demonstrating wider swings of mood. In expanding the study of normal adolescent psychological development employing standardized instruments and procedures, Offer and Franzen (1983) note a relative stability of mood in adolescents over time. Younger females perceived themselves as experiencing more negative affect during the earlier stages of adolescence by self-report. An overwhelming majority of all the youth tested were happy and believed capable of coping with their own emotional states. The study concluded that girls perceived themselves as sadder, lonelier, and more easily hurt than boys. The lower self-esteem of girls and their greater sensitivity to internal affective states were consistent findings throughout the study. Of major significance is the finding that by self-report, mood states of adolescents in a normal population are stable over time; mood swings are infrequently experienced.

The phenomenon of affective stability, however, may be dependent on the environment and culture to which the adolescent is exposed. Prince (1983) describes the "brain-fag" syndrome in African students. This work considers the transcultural aspects of affective disorders in presumably normal adolescents and the impact of social and cultural factors on affective states. The disorder affects an average of 54% of secondary students in Western-type school settings. Most observers have noted the major anxiety accompanying this disorder, but emphasize the depressive components. There is seldom a precipitating event or set of circumstances, it occurs more frequently in males and "seems to vary directly with the level of Westernization of the culture native to the student" (p. 69). Brain-fag has been reported in a number of developing countries, and, in Africa, may affect from 20 to 40% of high school and university students.

The description of the depressions in adolescence has also been conceptualized by developmental stage. Early work by McKinley and Dreisbach (1967) suggests variation in depressive symptoms with age. They found that anxious depression (sleep difficulties, somatic concerns, anxiety, and depressed mood) presents bimodally, with peaks at ages 40–49 years and then again at 70 and older. Introjection of blame (blames self, guilt feelings, expression of need for help) peaks at 20–29 years, then gradually declines. Murray (1970), in outpatient samples, notes that anxiety is more prominent in younger children and aggressive behavior more prevalent in older depressed youth ages 11–15 years.

Work detailing the cues that adolescents themselves employ in identifying or defining their peers as depressed may provide guides to classification. Siegel and Griffin (1983) studied the perceptions of depression among peers of 12- to 18-year-old students. Social isolation was identified as the important component. The questionnaires were administered in the classroom setting and consisted of forced choice and open-ended questions. A higher frequency of alcoholism and marijuana use was ascribed to depressed adolescents who were also described as crying often, being alone, not interacting with peers, parents, and siblings, and daydreaming. Thoughts of suicide were considered to be part of the depressive picture by 86% of the respondents, with 35% believing that suicidal attempts and self-destructive acts were additional components. Cause of the depression was ascribed to illness, boredom, drug problems, and so forth, as one set of factors; "inadequate family and social integration" as a second; and loneliness and rejection as a third.

Weeks, Michela, Peplau, and Bragg (1980), in contrast, have noted that loneliness and depression are correlated but differing constructs. They found that they may share common origins and high stability over time in their study of 333 undergraduate students who agreed to complete loneliness and depression measures 5 weeks apart.

Carlson (1981) suggests that adolescent depression is often masked by other disorders, such as school phobia, anorexia, some conduct disorders, and stomachaches, but that a good examination can provide sufficient material to make a satisfactory diagnosis. Moreover, some youth who deny depression and anhedonia later develop clear cut depressive episodes.

Inamdar, Siomopoulos, Osborn, and Bianchi (1979) studied 30 adolescents ages 12–18, with depressed mood as a major psychopathological feature. Overlap of symptoms with the adult depressive picture existed, but discrepancies were found. Mood-congruent hallucinations, restlessness, and pacing were not identified to the same extent as in adults; nor were feelings of persecution, delusions of guilt, or hopelessness. Hudgens (1974) also did not report such

adult symptoms in depressed youth. Most of the adolescents looked sad only when discussing their sad moods; moods were not considered transient or normative. Despite the disabling nature of the depressed mood, they did not complain of depression as a symptom. Moods lasted from a few hours to 2 days and were viewed as resulting from external events related to conflict with a significant other and hence not requiring treatment. Loss of interest, apathy, boredom, loss of pleasure, poor concentration, decreased school performance and suicidal ideation were present in less than 70%, although more than 40% had irritability, weight loss, loss of memory, subjective anergia, thought slowing, somatic symptoms, and so on.

Mitchell, McCauley, Burke, Moss, and Smith (1984) studied the phenomenology of depression in children and adolescents with affective and psychotic symptoms. They compared 40 preadolescents ages 7–12 years and 40 adolescents ages 13–17 years, from middle- to upper-middle-class families, who had received a Research Diagnostic Criteria (RDC) diagnosis of a recent or recurrent major depressive episode. All adolescents and 80% of preadolescents were referrals to an outpatient clinic; the other 20% were hospitalized. Children and adolescents presented similar depressive symptoms. Adolescents noted fatigue and hypersomnia more than preadolescents; both described the same rate of anorexia, but adolescents presented with significantly more weight loss. All other symptoms, including hallucinations and delusions, were present at the same rate. Over half of the outpatient adolescents and children reported hopelessness and psychomotor disturbance, with less than 30% in both groups reporting hallucinations of low severity. Manic behavior and delusions were reported at rates of 7.5% and 11%, respectively. These data suggest that younger patients, compared to adults, present with symptoms of a cognitive or behavioral nature (i.e., guilt, suicidal preoccupation, excessive worrying, low self-image), whereas adults report more endogenous symptoms. The similarities between preadolescents and adolescents were noted to be greater than the dissimilarities. These data are similar to those reported by Carlson (1981).

Personality dimensions are an additional factor influencing the actual clinical presentation

(Akiskal, 1983), and are described by Robins, Alessi, Yanchyshyn, and Colfer (1983) in depicting six adolescents with an endogenous major depressive disorder diagnosis. Reasons for referral for hospitalization, psychosocial stressors, personality disorder, predominant defenses, object relations, and predominant conflicts are nicely tabulated. It may be that the longitudinal characterologic factors related to school and interpersonal functioning have major implications for treatment planning.

The Bipolar Type of Major Affective Disorder may have the poorest prognosis in terms of life-threatening behavior for adolescents. The characteristics of the disorder are in the process of being clarified (American Psychiatric Association, 1980; Davis, 1979; Feinstein, 1980, 1982; Gammon, Rothblum, Millen, Tischler, & Weissman, 1983; Kestenbaum, 1980, 1982; Kron et al., 1982; Welner, Welner, & Fishman, 1979). Feinstein (1980) argues that individuals who ultimately develop a manic–depressive clinical syndrome demonstrate evidence of affective instability as early as age 1 year. The hypothesized developmental profile to explain the symptom picture includes difficulty with separation–individuation, the inability to dampen emotional responses and exaggerated responses to loss, as well as persistence of idealized self-structures and grandiosity. Family history studies of affective disorders suggests a genetic factor in this disorder (Strober & Carlson, 1982). Manic–depressive or bipolar disorder patients are often described as displaying symptoms of "intense adolescent turmoil." The bipolar pattern manifests itself as marked instability of behavior and short periods of depressed or manic affect.

Kestenbaum (1980) notes that depressive symptoms are common in childhood, but manic disorders are rare. She cites a literature supporting the view that the first history of bipolar disorder frequently occurs during adolescence, with the average age of onset of bipolar disease considered to be 30 years. However, one-third of such individuals have development of symptoms between the ages of 10 and 19 years (Kron et al., 1982; Strober & Carlson, 1982). Significant depressive symptoms may precede the initial manic episode in adolescents. Moreover, follow-up data (Strober & Carlson, 1982; Welner et al., 1979) suggest that the onset of bipolar disease in adolescence may portend an especially malignant outcome with a high incidence of suicide and recurrent mood swings. This is "presumably because uncontrollable fluctuations in the affective state have concomitant long-term effects on personality development" (Strober & Carlson, 1982, p. 300).

Strober and Carlson (1982) conducted a 3 to 4 year follow-up prospectively of 60 adolescents, ages 13–16 at the time of first hospitalization for a major depressive episode. Of these, 12 developed mania during the follow-up period. All met RDC criteria. At intake many gave histories of moodiness and irritability originating in late childhood, but only 2 (3%) were judged to have had an episode of major depression. Of this group, 47 (78%) were female; 9 were hospitalized at age 13, 16 at age 14, 21 at age 15, and 14 at age 16. The Wechsler Intelligence Scale for Children-Revised (WISC-R) assessments indicated a range of full-scale IQ from 92 to 144. History revealed that all were reared by one or both biological parents; parents of 16 (27%) were divorced. The shift to mania occurred an average of 28.4 weeks following index admission (10–76 weeks); two shifted during the index admission after resolution of the depressive episodes. All 10 of the remainder received a diagnosis of mania when readmitted. Of 48 with nonbipolar affective illness, 1 failed to recover completely from the index episode, 10 had one or more further major depressive episodes, 4 had intermittent episodes of dysphoria which failed to meet criteria for major depression, and 33 remained relatively asymptomatic through the follow-up period.

The bipolar youth were differentiated from the nonbipolar outcome group by 12 on the Schedule for Affective Disorders and Schizophrenia (SADS) at time of index admission: shorter duration of onset of symptoms, higher ratings on depressed mood, bodily concerns, diminished concentration, psychomotor retardation, and the presence of mood-congruent delusions or hallucinations. Nonbipolars received significantly higher severity ratings on: suicidal tendencies, weight gain, irritability, self-pity, and demandingness. There was much overlap in the "distinct quality of depressed mood, worry, self-negation, pessimism, sleep disturbance, anergia, appetite loss, withdrawal, loss of pleasure, nonreactivity of mood and agitation" (Strober & Carlson, 1982, pp. 306–307). The presence of any of the following five variables was found to be highly predictive of a bipolar outcome: (a) a symptom cluster of acute onset, psychotic features, and psychomotor retardation; (b) a family history of bipolar illness; (c) a three-generational history of affective disorder; (d) a loaded pedigree for affective illness; and (e) pharmacologically induced hypomania. Although induction of mania is the least sensitive, it is the surest predictor of bipolar outcome.

In a follow-up study of 77 adolescents hospitalized 8 to 10 years previously (Welner et al., 1979), 12 had been diagnosed as having bipolar disorders and were severely disabled, 11 had a long-term course, and 3 had committed suicide. Unipolar depression was diagnosed in 16 youth, 5 with one depressive episode who were well during the follow-up exam, and 1 with many episodes and complete remissions. Partial remissions and accompanying impairment of functioning related to severity of the symptoms was found in 10 of the patients, one of whom committed suicide. Those with episodic illness were considered to have a favorable prognosis, whereas the 10 with unremitting illness were considered to have a less favorable one.

EPIDEMIOLOGY OF DEPRESSION IN ADOLESCENTS

The incidence and prevalence of depression and depressed mood in adolescence have been infrequently addressed in major epidemiologic studies (Kandel & Davies, 1982). Several recent studies (Albert & Beck, 1975; Kandel & Davies, 1982; Kaplan, Hong, & Weinhold, 1984; Kaplan, Landa, Weinhold, & Shenker, 1984; Reynolds, 1984) have surveyed nonclinical populations of adolescents to determine incidence and prevalence of depressed mood and disorder. Employing a modified Beck Depression Inventory (BDI), Albert and Beck (1975) surveyed a young adolescent group of parochial school students. Surprisingly high rates of moderate to severe depression and suicidal ideation were revealed. The study suffered from lack of a proven reliable and valid measure as well as the excessively high prevalence of psychopathology.

Kandel and Davies (1982) limited their study to self-reported depressed mood and depressive symptoms rather than a depressive syndrome. The two-stage random sample consisted of 8,206 adolescents ranging in age from 14 to 18 years. The students represented the public secondary school population of New York State during 1971–1972. The proportion of youth defined as depressed varied from 15 to 28%, depending on the symptom score cut-off point employed. Sex, with the girls scoring much higher than boys, was the only sociodemographic variable upon which differences were demonstrated; meaningful differences were absent regarding social class as indexed by father's education, race, religion, or age. Youths whose family incomes were less than $3,000 were the most depressed. Analysis of factors related to self-report of depressed mood in adolescents revealed self-esteem as the most important, followed by participation in minor delinquency and strong orientation toward peers. Less involvement toward peers compared to parents (especially in girls) and the absence of delinquency predicted lower levels of depression; the greater the degree of active involvement with peers, the less the depression. Adolescents from laissez-faire or authoritarian homes were also more likely to experience depression. Those who frequently visited a physician or who had a depressed parent (particularly in mother–daughter pairs) were also more depressed. The proportion of youth experiencing delinquency and/or depression was identical for both sexes, but boys were less likely to be both delinquent and depressed.

Another New York study (Kaplan, Hong, & Weinhold, 1984) of 385 junior and senior high school students who completed the BDI, employed the standard cutoff for depression: 77.9% were considered not depressed; 13.5% scored in the mildly, 7.3% in the moderately, and 1.3% in the severely depressed range. Differences were not found between the sexes when age and socioeconomic status were controlled. Youth from lower-social-class families and older youth were more depressed than those who were from higher-class families and were younger. Major depression, defined as a BDI score greater than 16, was found in 8.6% of the youth surveyed.

In a related study of 398 high-school students (Kaplan, Landa et al., 1984), adverse health behaviors related to substance abuse exclusive of marijuana were highly correlated with BDI items of suicidal ideation and hopelessness. These findings support previous research indicating that depression in adolescents often precedes substance abuse, which may be a marker for depressed behavior. Paton, Kessler, and Kandel (1977) have reported that "the use of illicit drugs other than marijuana is related to the relief of depression for some adolescents and that these adolescents have a particularly high probability of continuing the use of these drugs compared to other users" (p. 284). Moreover, depressed mood was found to have a definite relationship to onset of marijuana use among youth who did not formerly use it and was mildly related to those who had ceased use by the follow-up. For those who were initially depressed and prior users of marijuana and of other drugs, if at follow-up they were still using the other drugs, then their depressed mood was likely to be decreased.

Reynolds (1984) reported a prevalence rate of 18% in high school students meeting Beck criteria for moderate to severe depression. The sample consisted of over 2,800 students, of whom 126 participated in a repeated assessment longitudinal study. This latter group seems to demonstrate that severe depression is relatively stable over time and consistent with a *DSM-III* dysthymic disorder diagnosis.

As might be expected, the incidence and prevalence of depression varies depending upon clinical setting and population studied. In inpatient psychiatric settings, recent data range from 20 of 30 consecutive adolescent admissions meeting depression criteria on the Kiddie-SADS (K-SADS) (Klee & Garfinkle, 1982), to an earlier report (Welner et al., 1979) that 28 of 77 adolescents with a mean age of 16 years on admission were diagnosed as unipolar or bipolar depressions on follow-up 8 to 10 years later. Reynolds (1984) notes that the prevalence of depression among clinic-referred populations ranges from 32 to 40%.

Kashani and associates (Kashani, Barbero, & Bolander, 1981; Kashani, Cantwell, Shekim, & Reid, 1982; Kashani, Lababidi, & Jones, 1982) have conducted a number of studies in clinical settings to determine the prevalence of depression. In one study, for example, of 100 pediatric patients, ages 6–18 years, who presented with chest pain and other cardiovascular symptoms, 13% were identified with major depression. Moreover, 51 of the children reported feeling unhappy most of the time (Kashani, Lababidi, & Jones, 1982).

Another vulnerable group are those adolescents involved in the criminal or juvenile justice systems. Several studies have demonstrated the increased incidence of depression in juvenile offenders. Chiles, Miller, and Cox (1980) identified 23% of 120 delinquents admitted to a correctional facility as meeting RDC criteria for a major depressive disorder. Depression was significantly predicted by history of a depressed or alcoholic family member.

The Michigan group (Alessi, McManus, Grapentine, & Brickman, 1984; McManus, Alessi, Grapentine, & Brickman, 1984) reported a variety of affective disorders in "serious" juvenile offenders, those with especially violent or dangerous behavior. Of 71 serious offenders, 11 (15%) had active major depression: 8 unipolar, and 1 each of bipolar I, II, and schizoaffective depression. Major depressive disorder in remission was identified in 6: 5 unipolar and 1 bipolar II. Minor depression was found in 11 youth. The serious delinquents had significantly higher rates of endogenous depression (one-half) than a hospital control group (one-third). If dysthymic disorders are included as an at-risk group (Kovacs et al., 1984), then 38% of serious delinquents may be at risk for a major depressive episode. Active cases of secondary depression were considered to be more frequent in the incarcerated versus the hospital group, and often related to substance abuse or alcoholism. Hollander and Turner (1985), on the other hand, do not mention depression as a significant symptom or syndrome among incarcerated delinquents.

Offspring of families with a history of depressive disorders represent another group vulnerable for depression in adolescence. Welner, Welner, McCrary, and Leonard (1977) studied children of parents who were hospitalized with depression. By means of interviews with both children and mothers, they found that the 6- to 16-year-old offspring were more likely to experience depressed mood, death wishes, fights, withdrawn behavior, unexplained headaches, and loss of interest than matched children of well controls. At least five of eight depressive symptoms were present in 11% of the children of depressed parents, and 7% met adult criteria for a depressive disorder. Neither pattern was found in any of the children of the control group.

Weissman and Paykel (1974) have reported

similar observations. Of importance is their additional finding that the irritability found in depressed mothers persisted beyond the period of their depressive episodes, rendering the children vulnerable over extended periods.

DESCRIPTION OF SUICIDE IN ADOLESCENTS

The research literature concerning adolescent suicide is comprised of studies of suicide attempters and those who have actually completed suicide. One should be cautious in drawing conclusions from this because suicide attempters are usually drawn from psychiatric or general hospitals or private practices, whereas completed suicides are likely to have never been treated or evaluated in a clinical setting (Petti, 1985a; Shafii & Shafii, 1982). Another problem is the underreporting of suicide in the U.S. Vital Statistics using coroner's reports. Estimates are that only one-half to one-third of all suicides are actually reported as such.

Description of suicidal behavior is made complex by the variety of suicidal behaviors and theories related to the act of committing or attempting suicide. "Parasuicidal" adolescents, those who contemplate, threaten, or make suicidal gestures or attempts, have generally been the focus of clinical descriptions and research. Examples of clinically useful descriptions of such youth have been provided by Glaser (1981) and Hendin (1975). Glaser describes an interesting array of dynamic subtypes of suicidal adolescents. These include: (a) those for whom the suicidal behavior is a response to depression and a coping mechanism to terminate perceived physical and psychological suffering; (b) those who are signaling a cry for help and demonstrating their depression more overtly and attempting to force a solution to their problems; (c) those who are psychotic and suffering from a schizophrenic-like disorder; and (d) those who make the gesture as an impulsive act intended to gain advantages or goals that may not be in the best interest of the teen. The latter group is most likely to deny or fail to manifest depressive symptomatology. Glaser notes that the subtypes show considerable overlap in features and, in his experience, some element of depression, past or present, is invariably found. Hendin (1975) has described another group of suicidal college students in whom "death as a

life style" is a particularly strong dynamic. A number of divergent views of suicidal teens have been summarized elsewhere (Petti, 1985a).

Teicher and Jacobs (1966) describe several developmental stages leading to adolescent suicide. *Stage 1* often occurs before adolescence and consists of long-standing family problems that are numerous and serious (e.g., broken homes, conflicts over behavior, geographical moves). *Stage 2*, escalation of problems during the preceding 5 years, follows. This stage consists of a failure of such adaptive techniques as physical aggression, withdrawal, rebelliousness, and psychosomatic illness, and progressive isolation accompanied by the feeling of nothing working. The *final stage* consists of an acute dissolution of residual relationships, including a predictably unsuccessful attempt at romance with a member of the opposite sex or exodus of siblings from the home, a conceptual justification of suicidal action because no other solution appears viable, and finally the attempt. The attempt, in retrospect, has been reported as the only perceived means to achieve resolution of problems. All the youth studied by Teicher and Jacobs felt that suicide was a solution; two thirds had a history of prior suicide attempts.

Tishler (1983; Tishler, McKenry, & Morgan, 1981) reports frequent warning signs and precipitating crises for suicidal adolescents based on a study of 108 teen attempters over a 2-year period. Rosenthal (1981) presents an enlightening discussion probing the sexual differences in suicidal behavior of our youth in an attempt to explain the disproportionate numbers of attempts by females and completed suicides by males. Peck (1981) similarly depicts the loners, particularly young white males, who are at high risk for completed suicides.

Few studies have described the adolescents who actually complete suicide. Shafii and associates (Shafii, Carrigan, Whittinghill, & Derrick, 1985; Shafii et al., 1984) have presented a retrospective reconstruction of the psychological status of 20 teens, ages 19 and younger, who committed suicide in Jefferson County, Kentucky. The common factors in these youth were listed as: (a) they were ages 17–18 years; and (b) the act was preceded by a 4- to 6-week period of physical complaints, behavioral changes, allergies, and depressive symptoms. Many of these adolescents visited a physician but their emotional states were not investigated. Breakdowns of communication with parents or friends and direct or indirect mention of suicidal intent were common. Some had made prior suicidal attempts; many had consumed large amounts of alcohol a few hours before the final act. Generally, a major confrontation with a meaningful person occurred on their last day; and many made a desperate attempt to contact a friend by phone before killing themselves.

Earlier studies by Shaffer (1974) and Jan-Tausch (1964) provide demographic data on completed teen suicides. Jan-Tausch (1964) notes the continuum between threats, attempts, and suicide, and suggests that 9 attempts are made for each completed suicide and that 10 threats are made by children for each youth who makes the attempt.

EPIDEMIOLOGY OF SUICIDAL BEHAVIOR IN ADOLESCENTS

The frequency of suicide attempts far outnumbers the number of completed suicides by as many as 50 or more times. Girls are two to three times more likely to attempt suicide, whereas males are more likely to complete suicide by a ratio of 2 to 1. The rate of completed suicide seems to increase dramatically at about age 12, suggesting that there is a somewhat protective factor for suicide before puberty (Otto, 1966; Shaffer & Fisher, 1981). Reasons for this dramatic age relationship have been hypothesized to include biological or hormonal factors related to puberty and the normal growth spurt, neurological and physical maturity of the body and nervous system, and finally, cognitive or dynamic factors.

The overall suicide rate for all ages rose 22% between 1961 and 1975, but this rise was primarily due to increases in the 15- to 24-year-old age group, which underwent a 131% increase (Holinger, 1978). This is the largest rate of increase since U.S. statistics were first recorded in 1900. The rise was highest for young adult white males, followed by white females. Between 1970 and 1978, the suicide rate for persons 15–24 years increased 41% due primarily to suicides by white males. The number and rate of suicides by 15 to 19-year-olds was half that of 20- to 24-year-olds (Centers for Disease Control, 1983). Reasons for these secular changes over time could be a reflection of many

factors, including increased availability of firearms or poisons, increases in stress, family disruption, particularly of the nuclear family, poor adult supervision, or just increased reporting related to better postmortem techniques and drug screens.

Characteristics of suicide completers outlined by Shaffer (1974) and Shaffer and Fisher (1981) are those of a pubertal adolescent, more often a male. Antisocial and affective symptoms were present in over 50% of the suicide completers, with precipitating events often related to an anticipated disciplinary crisis either at home or school. These individuals tended to be above average in IQ and tall for their age. Personality characteristics seemed to fall under either perfectionistic, uncommunicative, or impulsive styles. Previous psychiatric care was sometimes, but not always, present. The presence of psychiatric illness in the families of suicide completers is well reported in both the adult and child literature, showing higher rates of affective disorder and suicide (Barraclough, Holding, & Fayers, 1976; Robins et al., 1959; Sanborn, Sanborn, & Cimbalic, 1979; Shaffer, 1974).

In a recent study of 52 completed suicides under the age of 20, born between 1957 and 1967, Salk, Lipsitt, Sturner, Reilly, and Levat (1985) report that these individuals had a higher rate of complications and respiratory distress at birth, which without modern intensive care would have resulted in death. It may be that early medical complications or respiratory distress at birth may result in hypoxic damage to delicate nervous system tissue, possibly predisposing the person to depression or suicidal behavior. The mothers of these individuals also were described as having more chronic illness and receiving less prenatal care, compared to their control population. Although while further conclusions from these data are limited, the need for additional research in this area is clear.

Shafii et al. (1985) report a comparative study of completed suicides of 12- to 20-year-olds in Jefferson County, Kentucky, to matched controls consisting of friends of the victims matched for age, sex, race, education, socioeconomic status, and often for religion. Controls were found for 17 of the 20 suiciders. Significant differences were found regarding degree of suicidal ideation (85% vs. 18% of controls), history of suicidal threats (55% vs. 12%), prior suicidal attempts (40% vs. 6%), drug and alcohol abuse (70% vs. 29%), antisocial behavior (70% vs. 24%), inhibited personality (65% vs. 24%), and prior psychiatric treatment (45% vs. 24%). Significant differences were also found regarding exposure to suicide of a parent, siblings, relative, or friend. Suicide victims had greater exposure to parental emotional problems, parental absence, and parental abuse.

Significant differences were not found between the groups concerning poor academic performance, falling behind in school, broken homes, overcrowded home or large families, parental dependence on drugs or alcohol, or demandingness of parents.

Holinger and Offer (1981) cite data indicating that single teens have a lower rate of suicide than married teens, and that divorced teens have the highest rate of all. Moreover, adolescent rates of suicide vary from country to country and appear to be independent of methods of case detection. Several authors (Robins & Conroy, 1983; Shafii & Shafii, 1982) note the epidemic nature of suicidal behavior and its possible "contagion" quality.

Goldacre and Hawton (1985) studied hospital and record linkage data to investigate the relationship between repetition of self-poisoning and death during 1974–1978 in 2,492 youth ages 12–20 years admitted to regional hospitals for overdoses. Repeat overdosers comprised 9.5% of the group over the 4 years; 6.3% repeated within the 1st year of the index admission. The 237 repeaters made a total of 594 repeat episodes. The early teen years for girls and later years for boys bore the greatest numbers of repeat attempts. Rates were significantly higher for 16- to 20-year-old males as compared to female repeaters. The mean follow-up was 2.8 years. Ten of the youth died, with a death rate 4 times that of the national average. Suicides probably accounted for six of the deaths, but only one had a coroner's verdict of suicide.

The data of the Goldacre and Hawton study are consistent with general clinical experience that suicide is underreported for a number of social and political reasons, as well as methodological limitations, such as the absence of a specific International Classification of Diseases coding for suicide (Centers for Disease Control, 1983).

As mentioned previously, studies of suicide attempters are largely drawn from clinical populations so that the actual incidence of suicide attempts in a nonreferred population is difficult to estimate. Most studies of suicide attempters do not clearly address the issue of diagnosis, so specificity of suicide attempts with any particular diagnostic category, as has been reported for adults with depression, is unclear (Robins, 1981). However, Garfinkel, Froese, and Hood (1982) and Herjanic and Welner (1980) suggest that a number of the adolescent suicide attempters were alcohol or drug abusers as well as having some physical illness.

Garfinkel et al. (1982) reported on 505 suicide attempts in children and adolescents between 1970 and 1977 in Rhode Island and compared them to 505 emergency-room controls. Attempters were found to be 3 times as likely to be female, and 37% were found to have prior substance abuse or alcohol abuse compared to 5% of the controls. Of the suicide attempters, 51.6% had a family history of mental illness, compared to 16.4% of controls; 8.3% of the attempters had a family history of suicide or previous suicide attempts, compared to 1.1% of controls. Families of suicide attempters were also marked by family problems, with absence of a father figure in nearly one-quarter of the cases and absence of both parents in nearly one-quarter. Medical severity of suicide attempts was rated, and it was found that the less severe attempts tended to be drug ingestions compared to the more severe attempts, which tended toward more violent means, such as hanging or firearms. A suicide note was more likely to be found in the severe-attempter group. Most attempts were at home or after school in the evening, when someone else was there, but this was significantly less true of the more severe attempts, which took place in more isolated or secluded surroundings. Most of the serious attempts were made by students who were functioning at or above their grade level. Finally, the severe-suicide-attempter group was associated with a high percentage of psychiatric symptoms, estimated at 85.7%. It has been suggested (Garfinkel et al., 1982; Glaser, 1981; Shaffer & Fisher, 1981) that there is a trend for many suicide attempters to use threats and mild nonserious attempts to gain control over somewhat disruptive and disorganized family situations.

In another study of suicide attempts in Sweden (Otto, 1971), 1,727 adolescents under the age of 21 were followed-up after 10 years. Of the girls, 2.9% followed-up eventually committed suicide in contrast to 10% of boys. The maximum period of risk for completing suicide was the first 2 years after an initial suicide attempt. In 70% of the completed suicides, the same method as the initial attempt was used.

Although at least one study did not show that drug abuse was a factor in suicidal behavior (Sanborn et al., 1974), others have suggested that suicide attempts were often associated with marijuana or alcohol abuse (Crumley, 1979).

In summary, it seems that diagnostic specificity of depression has not been clearly demonstrated with suicidal adolescents as it has been for adults (Robins, Murphy, Wilkinson, Gassner, & Kayes, 1959), where 94% had a psychiatric diagnosis, of which 23% were chronic alcoholics. It has been speculated that suicidal behavior in adolescents may, in addition to a clear-cut depressive illness, represent masked depression (Carlson, 1983).

ASSESSMENT AND DIAGNOSIS OF ADOLESCENT DEPRESSIVE DISORDERS

The diagnosis of depression in children and adolescents has been a controversial as well as a clouded issue. Although most adolescents have periodic mood changes associated with normal situational events, there is no clear demarcation between normal adolescent mood changes and psychopathology that requires treatment. Often the response to a sudden loss, such as the death of a loved one, produces a significant depressive syndrome, although this is time-limited. One problem in the initial assessment of a child or adolescent is to determine the extent to which recent life events are the obvious cause for the patient's low mood, poor self-esteem, or decline in functioning.

Frequently, the history-taking process is guided by the theoretical orientation of the examiner. For example, a Freudian might inquire about early object loss as well as about the development of ego strength and defense mechanisms. A behaviorist might be interested in recording the frequency of various positive and negative reinforcing events and persons in the patient's life as it relates to his presenting complaint. Indeed, the learned helplessness model of Seligman (1975) is another example of how

operant factors in the patient's life, family, or school might combine to produce a withdrawn and depressed clinical picture. A therapist oriented toward a cognitive approach (Beck, Rush, Shaf, & Emery, 1979) might focus on patterns of depressed thinking or cognitions. Collecting history about automatic thoughts, overgeneralization, and expectations of catastrophe about situations or thoughts, and how these represent faulty or distorted ways the adolescent views himself or herself, the world, or the future might be a starting point for the therapist's clinical interview. Finally, the therapist trained in the medical model supposes that depression is a collection of signs, symptoms, and behaviors that constitute a psychiatric syndrome. Although many proponents of this model acknowledge the importance of life events, environmental factors, and cognitive development, the etiology is not necessarily known. Indeed, a great deal of research in this area points to altered physiology of the central nervous system where biochemical abnormalities, genetic influence, or predisposition have been established (Petti, 1983; Puig-Antich, in press).

In short, the key to assessing an individual patient is to begin with an open mind without dogmatic adherence to any particular theoretical model. Thus, in addition to documenting the patient's current mood and affective state, one needs to gather a complete and comprehensive history that begins with perinatal and birth information up to the present time. History should be gathered from as many sources as possible and should include parents, teachers, or others who have known the adolescent for a period of time. In this way one is able to establish previous episodes of behavior problems as well as quite carefully recording any other medical or physical complaints that may have preceded the current clinical picture. It is important to gather a family history of both first- and second-degree relatives, inquiring about psychiatric and medical illness that can produce a persistently depressed mood. These should be explored both with the patient and the family and should include any long-standing medical or hormonal problems.

A careful chronological history of signs and symptoms relating to physical as well as psychiatric symptoms is essential. Aches and pains, headaches, or frequent absence from school should be signals for the examiner to inquire more deeply about changes in mood, weight, appetite, concentration, school performance, and general behavior.

Research into mood disorders in children and adolescents has lagged behind the rest of psychiatry, largely because of the reluctance of many clinicians to acknowledge that they exist. Most of the research to date has focused on more severe cases of depression that phenomenologically appear similar to those in adults. The advantages of this are that for research purposes one is able to establish homogeneous groups that are comparable in the number and severity of depressive symptoms. In addition, the adoption of objective, operational criteria allows comparability of research between centers so that conclusions drawn on one population may be generalized to others with similar clinical characteristics. Finally, objective operational criteria do not impose any theoretical bias as to etiology. A word of caution should be noted because although unmodified adult criteria have been applied to children and adolescents in an attempt to sharpen the distinction between those who are depressed and normals, one must remember that the clinical presentation of individual patients may be at variance.

The notion of masked depression is clearly an unresolved topic. Indeed, it is possible that some youth may present with symptoms of depression but initially without subjective mood disturbance (Carlson, 1981). It has been shown in an adult general-practice setting that somatic symptoms may precede onset of depressed mood and a clinical syndrome of depression (Cadoret, Widmer, & Troughton, 1980).

The current version of the *DSM-III* is the culmination of operationally defined criteria initially applied to adults (Feighner, Robins, Guze, Woodruff, & Winokur, 1972; Spitzer & Endicott, 1978) as well as similar criteria applied to children (Ling, Oftedal, & Weinberg, 1970; Weinberg, Rutman, Sullivan, Pencik, & Dietz, 1973). *DSM-III* has attempted to modify restrictive research criteria for broader use by clinicians. Limitations of these criteria seem to be that they do not incorporate any age-specific features that may be related to developmental stages in a child or adolescent (Shaffer, 1985). Indeed, rigorously defining in operational terms the "normal adolescent" is a task that has yet to be accomplished.

STRUCTURED INTERVIEWS IN THE ASSESSMENT OF ADOLESCENT DEPRESSION

The current methods of assessment include both structured and unstructured diagnostic interviews, self-report inventories, as well as ratings by teachers, parents, and peers (Petti, 1985b). Projective techniques have been used historically in elaborating and inferring depressive themes and dynamic factors. Work is in progress to establish reliable biologic or biochemical markers that might successfully distinguish normal from depressed children and add to our understanding of state versus trait markers and how they relate to altered physiology in depression and mania (Puig-Antich, 1985).

Instruments that may be useful in the assessment of depression in children and adolescents have been reviewed elsewhere (Petti, 1985b). The following short descriptions provide a sampling of standardized instruments.

The Interview Schedule for Children (ISC) is a structured diagnostic instrument developed for use with children ages 8 through 13 years, primarily for the purpose of assessing depressive symptomatology and related behavior disturbances. The ISC is administered directly to the child or parent by a trained interviewer with clinical experience. It generally takes from one-half to three-quarters of an hour to administer. The ISC is considered to be a good instrument for the assessment of depressive symptoms.

The Bellevue Index of Depression (BID) (Petti, 1978) incorporates interviews with the child as well as the parents and others, but is restricted to ages 6 through 12. It uses a semistructured format and has also been used with adolescents (Coats & Reynolds, 1985). The interview takes from 15 to 30 minutes, depending on the extent of depressive symptoms present, and has been used as a repeated measure to assess improvement in pharmacologic studies (Petti, 1985b). The major limitation of this instrument is its inability to be translated into *DSM-III* diagnoses.

The Children's Depression Rating Scale (CDRS) by Poznanski, Cook, and Carroll (1979) and its revised form, the CDRS-R (Poznanski et al., 1984), is an adaptation of the Hamilton Rating Scale. It has been used primarily as a clinical screening instrument and to measure the change of severity of symptoms, and it is generally regarded as an easy instrument to administer in addition to giving good reliability (Petti, 1985b).

Structured interviews intended to make diagnoses by *DSM-III* suitable for epidemiologic investigations include the Diagnostic Interview for Children and Adolescents (DICA) (Herjanic & Reich, 1982) and the Diagnostic Interview Schedule for Children (DISC) (Costello et al., 1984). Both of these instruments are suitable for teenagers as well as children and provide separate forms for child and parents. However, both are undergoing the final stages of revision and testing. These instruments allow wide coverage of a great number of psychiatric symptoms and the range of *DSM-III* diagnoses with children and adolescents.

The K-SADS is a modification of the SADS adapted for use in children and adolescents. It involves a semistructured format but allows for diagnoses by both *DSM-III* as well as the RDC. As with the ISC, the K-SADS is rigorous and intended to be given by a trained clinician in a semistructured format, unlike the DISC and DICA, which are intended for epidemiologic use and may be given by a trained lay interviewer. The K-SADS provides collection of data from both the child and parent interviewed separately as well as a summary rating based on all sources. It is intended for use between the ages of 6 and 17 years and requires approximately 45 to 90 minutes to administer. Its reliability thus far seems to be fairly good (Chambers et al., 1985), and test-retest before and after drug treatment in depressed children indicates that it is also sensitive to changes in severity of depressive symptoms. A form for epidemiologic study is available (Orvaschel, Sholomskas, & Weissman, 1983).

There are a variety of self-report scales that have been used in assessing child and adolescent depression. Though not diagnostic instruments, they are often used as screening instruments or as measures of severity once the diagnosis has been established. The Children's Depression Inventory (CDI) (Kovacs, 1981) is a modification of the Beck Depression Inventory. It consists of 27 items that are rated as either absent or present, with severity rated when appropriate. Norms for this instrument have been established using both normal and psychiatric samples. Questions have been raised about whether such self-report inventories are valid measures in children and adolescents (Carlson & Cantwell, 1980). Adaptations of the CDI as well as other self-report scales are available and are reviewed elsewhere (Petti, 1985b).

Although projective tests such as the Rorschach or Thematic Apperception Test (TAT) have been used for many years to uncover presumably unconsciously repressed material, the testing is often rather time-consuming and may not necessarily yield more information than a careful clinical examination or interview.

OTHER ASSESSMENT ISSUES

Puig-Antich (1985) has summarized the state of the art of psychobiological markers in affective illness as they relate to underlying neuronal, chemical, or physiological mechanisms which regulate mood and affect. He has also explored the potential significance of biologic markers, including the blunted thyroid-stimulating hormone (TSH) response to thyroidtropin-releasing hormone (TRH), sleep abnormalities, patterns of growth-hormone release in response to an insulin-tolerance test, and growth-hormone response to other pharmacologic agents known to affect noradrenergic activity in the central nervous system. How these biologic markers relate to the patient's age, pre-or postpubertal status, as well as familial and genetic loading is likely to be useful in understanding the biologic mechanisms taking place through puberty that may be responsible for the increase in depressive disorders and suicide after age 12 and into old age (Kupfer & Foster, 1979; Poznanski et al., 1982). In addition, these types of studies will help identify underlying trait markers from those specifically associated with the depressed or manic state and perhaps aid in the diagnostic process. However, there is no clearly defined clinical use for such biological markers as the Dexamethesone Test (DST) (Hsu et al., 1983) and all-night EEG in adolescents at the present time.

Affective symptoms of depression have been reported with a variety of other psychiatric syndromes in children and adolescents. These include anxiety states, such as separation anxiety, agoraphobia, or panic disorder, as well as eating disorders and attention deficit disorders (Carlson & Cantwell, 1980; Strober, 1984). Furthermore, conduct disorders and depression are often found together (Alessi et al., 1984; Chiles et al., 1980; McManus et al., 1984; Shaffer, 1974). One must be cautious when interpreting such associations. Simply because patients have depressive symptoms associated with some other disorder, or may benefit from treatment with antidepressant medication, does not necessarily mean that they are related. Although it is possible that a final common pathway responsible for depressive symptoms exists, it is clearly too early to draw any conclusions on the pathogenesis or etiology based on treatment response.

In assessing the depressed adolescent, clinicians must be mindful that bipolar affective disorder or manic depressive illness often has its onset in adolescence (Winokur, Clayton, & Reich, 1969). Strober (1984) notes that although many adolescents with a bipolar disorder present with symptoms similar to adults, such as hyperactivity, overtalkativeness, insomnia, irritability, and grandiose delusions, many present as very paranoid and aggressive with prominent psychotic symptoms. Thus, when encountering a severely psychotic adolescent, one must be careful not to misdiagnose a patient as having schizophrenia (Carlson & Strober, 1978).

In summary, in assessing the adolescent with any behavior disorder, it is clear that one needs to engage in a careful, thorough, and exhaustive history-taking process that focuses not only on the patient's current or more recent complaint, but also examines the past for a full range of other associated symptoms that may or may not be temporally associated with affective lability, conduct problems, school refusal, or hyperactivity. Many clinicians have long suspected the significance of affective disorder in children and adolescents, and it is hopeful that future research will give them the knowledge and tools they need to appropriately diagnose and effectively treat their patients.

TREATMENT OF THE DEPRESSED ADOLESCENT

Treatment of the depressed adolescent must take into account multiple factors, suggesting a role for a biopsychosocial model. Few controlled studies have demonstrated the efficacy of therapeutic interventions with psychiatrically disturbed adolescents (Reynolds, 1984); most controlled studies have been conducted with institutionalized delinquents (Tramontana, 1980). This section will first consider psychological approaches to treating depressed adolescents and conclude with somatic interventions.

Psychological Approaches

Psychodynamic Treatment

Psychodynamic and psychoanalytic approaches have long been the accepted mode of treating depressed or suicidal adolescents in the United States. Much of the literature in this area consists of anecdotal material and case descriptions. Shaffer (1984) and Tramontana (1980) review this work.

Rossman (1982) provides a comprehensive overview of the psychotherapeutic approaches to treating the depressed, acting-out adolescent and discusses interpretive tactics and their rationale as related to etiology and clinical picture. He notes that adolescents are rarely self-referred. They often, by using denial and projection, fail to relate depressive symptoms. In this model, engagement is the primary task of therapy. The immediate goal is to engage in a treatment relationship to contain the teen's burdensome feelings of dysphoria, helplessness, and of being tormented by others. The teen is guided to find socially acceptable alternatives to express underlying thoughts, feelings, and emotions. The therapist must then offer compensatory satisfactions that are gratifying, helpful, and supportive in rapid fashion. Otherwise, underlying depressive conflicts are expected to persist and therapy to be endangered.

Rossman suggests that the initial treatment strategies and interpretive tactics must address the underlying distrust and suspiciousness and make clear that the therapist is working for the youth. Helpful techniques such as acknowledging the justification of mistrust, that is, supporting the teen's paranoia, and trying to dissipate the anger, if problematic, are offered. The need to clarify fantasies about treatment and to share the dilemma of which issues to address, the consequences of actions, and a request for no rash judgments regarding the therapist until personal observations are accumulated are also addressed.

Another aspect of psychodynamic treatment of depressed teens is to make explicit the expected benefits of treatment and the issue of disappointment. Depressed teens often have harsh consciences and resultant intolerable guilt feelings. These may be projected and the teen then acts provocatively to incur perceived deserved punishment. If the adolescent externalizes conscience "onto the therapist, the teen will likely feel increasingly persecuted, criticized, and tormented—with the result that he flees treatment" (Rossman, 1982, p. 458). It is critical to clarify goals of treatment as helping the patient to understand more about self and family, improve relationships, sense of competence, and self-esteem, feel more powerful as reflected in self-understanding and sense of choice about his life. As with other types of interventions, there is a need to provide structure to the therapy setting in order to lessen gratification through disruptive behavior.

Rossman also delineates other critical issues: (a) importance of taking a stand: (b) acknowledging the imperative of a teen's view of the world; (c) clarifying negative behaviors as successful coping mechanisms in delivering a message; (d) accepting and processing negative and narcissistic transference; (e) employing humor in fostering self-observation; (f) offering rationale for opposition to acting-out behavior; (g) considering the issue of autonomy and fear of external control; and (h) considering autonomy versus the authoritarian position of the therapist. Major aspects of adolescent depression are the conflicting feelings of being incompetent or unloveable while demanding dependent relations with powerful adults. A distinction between the adolescent being in charge of his own life and always knowing more than the therapist and the therapist knowing more about therapy is critical in this model of intervention. The aim of such therapy with the depressed adolescent, as described by Rossman, is to offer an unexpected but gratifying encounter with a powerful and significant adult. The therapeutic approach recognizes the teen's need to view the therapist as competent, powerful, interested, concerned, and able to contain disruptive behaviors. According to Rossman (1982):

It may be argued that the successful ingredients of psychotherapy with depressed adolescents center not so much on content of the treatment process as on the degree of perceived gratification in the therapist–patient interaction, and on the type of adult model that the therapist offers to the adolescent. (p. 467)

Similar approaches employing a psychodynamic model are described in the treatment of the medically ill adolescent (Schowalter, 1983) and the self-immolator (Stoddard & Cahners, 1985). Anthony (1970) distinguishes between treatment of the depression based on preoedipal, symbiotic dynamics and one based more on oedipal, masochistic, and punitive superego issues.

Cognitive and Behavioral Treatments

Bernard and Joyce (1984) provide an overview of applying rational emotive therapy strategies with depressed children and adolescents. A successful cognitive therapy approach with a prepubertal depressed male that extended into adolescence is also described (Petti, Kovacs, Feinberg, Paulauskas, & Finkelstein, 1982).

Coats and Reynolds (1984) have conducted the only controlled study employing learning theory principles in the treatment of depressed adolescents. A multistage screening process identified 36 adolescents from a pool of 800 high school students. The students met BDI and other criteria for moderate depression and were not in treatment for the depression or related disorders. Thirty of this group agreed to participate in a controlled study with random assignment to a cognitive–behavioral, relaxation, or wait-list control condition. Each of the active treatments consisted of 10 group sessions, over 5 weeks, lasting 50 minutes. Two groups for each condition were held at the high schools attended by the subjects. Each subject received reinforcement contingent on attendance and participation in treatment. The cognitive–behavioral therapy was divided into three training phases of self-control skills: self-monitoring, self-evaluation, and self-reinforcement. The relaxation-training group was presented a general introduction and the hypothesized relationship between depression and tension-related problems, taught Jacobsen's systematic relaxation, and worked at generalizing use of the procedure across stress-producing situations.

The design of the Coats and Reynolds' (1984) study included probes regarding therapist compliance with intervention format and other threats to validity. A moderate percentage of dropouts occurred at post-treatment and fol-low-up assessment. Results indicate that both active treatment groups achieved substantial and significant reductions in the symptoms of moderate depression, and that the gains persisted through the 5-week follow-up. The control group remained moderately depressed on the BDI and other measures of depression. Academic self-concept also markedly improved for the experimental groups. The study is limited by the small sample size, the drop-out rate for outcome measures, and the manner of sample selection. However, it is clear that psychologic interventions of this nature show promise for future work.

Previous case reports employing cognitive therapy (Petti et al., 1982), behavior therapy (Petti, Bornstein, Delamater, & Conners, 1980), and a study applying self-control and behavior therapy with children (Stark, Reynolds, & Kaslow, 1985) further support the potential for these types of psychologic interventions. Guidelines for the application of cognitive therapy in treating depressed adolescents are available (Emery, Bedrosian, & Garber, 1983).

Family Approaches

Family therapy is described by Emery et al. (1983) as one means of assisting in the process of altering negative cognitions in the depressed adolescent, as part of the cognitive therapy strategy. Guttman (1983) advocates family therapy as the treatment of choice when the diagnostic process reveals that the depression represents an attempt by both the adolescent and the collective family to deal with a barrier in family development. A clear depressive reaction to a chronic illness would represent another indication for a family approach rather than a solely individual approach. Rationale for such treatment of major and minor depressive disorders of adolescents with guidelines for consideration and use are provided. Goals in family therapy for treating the adolescent with a major affective disorder include facilitating acute treatment, assisting the family in understanding the phenomenon, and restoring family functioning through supportive, interpretive, cathartic, and insight-generating strategies (Guttman, 1983). In treating teens with minor or reactive depressions, the goal is the promotion of individual and family growth through insight or task-ori-ented family therapy. Family therapy is often suggested as an important component in the care of the suicidal child or adolescent (Petti, 1985a).

Psychopharmacologic Approaches

Psychopharmacologic treatments of depression have been limited to lithium carbonate and the tricyclic antidepressants. A number of studies and case reports suggest lithium as an effective treatment of bipolar-like depressions of adolescents (Berg, Hullin, Allsopp, O'Brien, & MacDonald, 1974; Coll & Bland, 1979; Davis, 1979; Dyson & Barcai, 1970; Horowitz, 1977; Kelly, Hoch, & Buegel, 1976; Wolpert, 1983). Carlson (1979) notes the absence of controlled studies and offers guidelines for lithium use. The major indication is the treatment and prophylaxis of bipolar disorders. History should be obtained from family members regarding the disorder and its treatment and systematic investigation as to its effect on mood, cognition, and psychomotor and vegetative signs should be conducted when used. Also, it should be employed as part of a total treatment program.

The National Institute of Mental Health/National Institutes of Health (NIMH/NIH) Consensus development conference statement (1985) succinctly reviews the literature and reports that though lithium and tricyclic antidepressants prevent recurrences of unipolar depression for both sexes from early adulthood to old age, few data are available for children and adolescents. Moreover, according to the NIMH/NIH statement, preventive doses of the tricyclic antidepressants have not been adequately defined. There are a number of uncontrolled studies that report the beneficial effects of tricyclic antidepressants on the depressions of adolescence and older children (Kuhn, 1963; Nissen, 1984; Staton, Wilson, & Brumback, 1982). The use of this class of drugs has also been advocated for special populations of depressed adolescents, for example, those with asthma (Kanner, Rubinstein, Gittleman, & Mascia, 1983), cancer patients (Pfefferbaum-Levine, Kumor, Cangir, Choroszy, & Rosenberry, 1983), the mentally retarded (Dosen, 1984), those with school phobia or refusal who also manifest dysphoria (Gittelman-Klein & Klein, 1973), and those with organic brain damage (Nissen, 1984).

Geller, Cooper, Farooki, and Chestnut (1985c) report the results of treating nondelusionally depressed adolescents, focusing on dose and plasma levels of nortriptyline. Of the 8 subjects, 6 cleared their depression completely and 2 partially, with 1 improved after the protocol ended and the other stopping treatment after 2 months. In the same study, delusionally depressed adolescents were treated with a combination of nortriptyline and chlorpromazine. The delusions cleared within 2 weeks in all 6 subjects, and the depression cleared in all but 1 by week 8 of the protocol. His depression cleared along with this problematic hypersomnia after the dose of chlorpromazine was lowered to 50 mg/day. Of particular interest was the finding that the combined treatment necessitated lowering the dose of nortriptyline to achieve the therapeutic plasma range of the tricyclic. No effect on plasma levels of the neuroleptic with combined therapy were noted. Geller's group also report on the preliminary pharmacokinetics and dose/plasma level parameters of nortriptyline in depressed children and adolescents (Geller, Cooper, & Chestnut, 1985a; Geller, Cooper, Chestnut, Anker et al., 1985b).

Controlled studies of tricyclic treatment of adolescent depressions have thus far yielded confusing results. Kramer and Feiguine (1981) compared the efficacy of amitriptyline, 200 mg/day, with placebo in a double-blind study. No differences between the two conditions were noted employing a modified Hamilton rating scale. The Depression Adjective Checklist, an adult self-report scale, demonstrated statistically significant differences between the groups, but a questionable bias concerning severity ratings was raised. The study has a number of methodological problems, including the absence of a placebo washout period and maldistribution of females between the groups.

Though the presence of neurovegetative signs of depression have been associated with a positive response to tricyclic antidepressants in prepubertal children and adults, recent data suggest that the response rate to tricyclics in adolescents with major depression is less favorable (N. D. Ryan, personal communication, July 10, 1985). However, Gittelman-Klein and Klein (1973), in a double-blind controlled study, report significant improvement in dysphoric symptoms of the imipramine compared to placebo groups of 6- to 14-year-old school phobics.

In an uncontrolled study, Strober and Carlson (1982) report that 24 of 45 nonbipolar depressed adolescents had unequivocally positive responses to antidepressant medication. This is in contrast to a positive response in only 2 of 12 bipolars, with no differences found in dosage levels between the groups. However, hypomanic episodes were precipitated in 2 of the bipolar patients. This is similar to an earlier report (Westman, 1965) in which youth ranging from 11 to 19 years were treated with imipramine. Those classified as endogenous depressives by adult criteria constituted the majority of positive responders, whereas those with rapid mood changes responded poorly.

Prien et al. (1984) report that lithium alone was as effective as lithium and imipramine together and superior to imipramine alone in preventing manic episodes and as effective in preventing depressive episodes in bipolar patients. In addition, carbamazepine USP (Tegretol®) may be useful in controlling adolescent bipolar disorder (Post, Uhde, Ballenger, & Squillace, 1983). In unipolar depressives, the combination of imipramine and lithium or imipramine alone were more effective than lithium and a placebo in preventing depressive episodes but the combination was no more effective than imipramine alone.

There are few reported cases of iatrogenic untoward reactions to imipramine or other tricyclic antidepressants in adolescents other than the induction of manic or hypomanic behavior. Petti (1983) summarizes the precaution related to cardiac changes, seizures, and drug-withdrawal effects. Given the lack of controlled studies supporting the superiority of antidepressants over a placebo in treating depressed youth, blood levels of the tricyclics should assume increasing importance. The Task Force on the Use of Laboratory Tests in Psychiatry (1985) comments on the increase in future utility of blood antidepressant levels and the role that differences in inpatient and outpatient populations, as well as metabolic differences between patients, might play in the confusing results reported to date.

TREATMENT OF THE SUICIDAL ADOLESCENT

Approaches to treating the suicidal adolescent with group, family therapy, individual psychotherapy, cognitive therapy, and pharmacotherapy have been described (Hochberg, 1977; Peck, 1981; Richman, 1981; Sudak, Ford, & Rushforth, 1984; Walker & Mehr, 1983). Richman (1981) provides an outline of considerations for the therapist of suicidal adolescents. Prevention, however, should be the major focus of consideration in treating the suicidal adolescent and must be aimed at the primary through tertiary levels of intervention (Petti, 1985a). The family plays a critical role in this task. Efforts must be made by medical and other human-services professionals to educate families and make them aware of stress-reducing behaviors, normal and abnormal behaviors of children, the need for more open, positively oriented communication among family members, and the need to identify and treat parents in addition to the teenager with depression. The schools also play a pivotal role in the early detection of a youth who is becoming isolated, demonstrates low self-esteem and failure to work to potential, and is considered an illicit substance or alcohol user. Greater emphasis on social and problem-solving skills, as well as health attitudes, are another component of the required involvement of the educational system.

Physicians, nurses, psychologists, and other public-health professionals must become aware of and pursue the possibility that a youth might be suicidal. This is particularly true for youngsters with chronic disorders, such as epilepsy, diabetes, asthma, cystic fibrosis, and developmental disabilities. It is necessary to convey to such professionals that they may be the only persons to whom depressed adolescents might turn. In addition, families and associates of both suicide completers and attempters should be considered as vulnerable and in need of assistance. Juveniles using or abusing alcohol and other illicit substances should be considered as possibly self-medicating a depressive disorder and should be treated accordingly.

The media, including newspapers, radio, and television, must be made responsible in addressing the impact that they may have on a youngster with suicidal potential or one who is easily swayed and could conceivably imitate a suicidal or other violent act (Petti, 1985a). Public-health organizations must make a commitment to educate all levels of government to the seriousness of suicidal and other violent behaviors in regards to public health and welfare. They must be alerted to the relationship between availability of lethal means, such as handguns and barbiturates, and suicidal behavior, as well as to the converse—that lack of a means has been correlated with decreases in suicidal behavior (Goldney & Katsikitis, 1983). Issues related to the broad spectrum of preventive efforts have been reviewed and summarized elsewhere (Holinger & Offer, 1981; Petti, 1985a; Petzel & Riddle, 1981; Richman, 1981; Shafii & Shafii, 1982; Shafii et al., 1984; Sudak et al., 1984; Tishler, 1983; Tishler et al., 1981).

Case 1. J. J.

J. J. is a 14-year-old white male eighth grader enrolled in a regular classroom who lives with his parents and two older high-school-aged brothers. J. J. has always been a bit shy but well liked by his peers and teachers. Although previously achieving B's in school, this past year his grades have fallen to D's and his frequent complaints of head and body aches were not found by the family pediatrician to have an identified cause. J. J. has also started missing school, claiming that he "feels stupid" and would rather stay home, even after mother goes to work. His brothers have been upset with J. J. because he no longer joins them in games or sports, claiming he is "too tired." They have noticed that J. J. has trouble getting his chores done and complains bitterly of being picked on. J. J. and his mother have gotten into several arguments over his not wanting to pick his clothes up off the floor, and most recently J. J. ran out of the house crying and claiming that "everyone hates me." The parents had consulted the school counselor who assured them that this was "just a phase" and they should not worry. Shortly after this, J. J. was suspended from school for fighting and then refusing to stay after school in detention to finish an assignment. That evening J. J.'s mother returned home to find J. J. sleeping in his room with an empty bottle of her sleeping pills next to him.

After medical evaluation at the local hospital emergency room, J. J. reluctantly agreed to talk with a child psychiatrist. J. J. denied being "depressed," but did admit that he "just wanted to go to sleep." He explained that he has had a several month history of difficulty falling asleep for up to 3 hours each night, with occasional early morning awakening. Despite his inability to sleep, he feels tired and irritable, especially in the morning. School work has become very "boring" and J. J. finds it difficult to concentrate and finish it. J. J. admitted that he was afraid that his parents would punish him after his suspension that day, and he felt extremely guilty about this, as no one in his family had ever been "kicked out of school." He admitted to several months of suicidal thoughts, usually after arguments at home. Family history was significant for a maternal aunt who was hospitalized in her 20s for a "nervous breakdown" when she stopped doing housework and went to bed. In addition J. J.'s mother reluctantly admits to frequent crying spells and several years of intermittent insomnia. Past medical history and physical examination were unremarkable for this healthy male with full pubertal development. Mental status examination revealed a sad, slightly sedated teenaged male with a restricted affect and psychomotor agitation, wringing his hands and ruminating about the day's events. Speech was of normal rate and elaboration. Mood was sad and anxious, admitting to suicidal ideation with intent. There was no evidence of thought disorder or cognitive dysfunction present.

The patient was admitted to the psychiatry service, a family meeting was held the next day, and the diagnosis of major depression, single episode, with melancholia was confirmed. Achievement and intellectual testing along with routine blood and thyroid function tests were normal. Individual therapy was initiated for support. The patient agreed to a trial of the antidepressant, imipramine, starting at a dose of 50 mg at bedtime, gradually increasing to 150 mg. The patient initially experienced minor side effects of dry mouth and dizziness when he stood up suddenly, but these were minimized by the gradual increases in dose. A serum imipramine (and its metabolite, desipramine) level was within the therapeutic range and an electrocardiogram showed no conduction abnormalities (which are usually associated with excessive serum levels). Within 2 to 3 weeks J. J.'s energy and mood returned to normal along with improvement in his sleep, concentration, appetite, and schoolwork. He went on to make the honor roll the following grading period. School attendance improved, and there were no further outbursts or episodes of fighting. The patient feels that both the medication and regular family meetings have improved his general outlook, as well as helped his family understand and communicate with one another. His family has also learned a great deal about depression, its treatment, and how to cope with its possible recurrence.

Case 2. M. C.

M. C. is a 16-year-old white female high-school sophomore in advanced classes who lives with her divorced mother and younger brother. Things have stabilized in the 3 years since the father left the family. At that time M. C. had become quite withdrawn and depressed for 2 months or so, but her mother felt this was certainly understandable under the circumstances. Although the school principal had urged the mother to have M. C. seen by a counselor, by the time an appointment was available M. C. seemed to "snap out of it" on her own. This spring, as the regional cheerleading finals were approaching, the patient attended practice everyday with the hope of being selected to go to the state finals. M. C. decided on her own to organize a fund-raising effort to get everyone new cheerleading outfits. Initially, M. C. had planned a bake sale for an upcoming Saturday morning, but without discussing it she announced that it had been cancelled. She explained that she had been staying up at night planning the "ultimate fund raiser." She spoke rapidly and was euphoric about her "brilliant plan" to put on a telethon to benefit all cheerleaders everywhere. M. C.'s mother noted that for the past several weeks M. C. was up late in the evening and would even play the stereo loudly at 3 a.m. Her mother also noticed that M. C. was eating large amounts of food, often not remembering to put the rest away. When her mother confronted M. C. about this, she became defensive and hostile, insisting that she was now an extremely important person who had recently been sent on a "special mission" for the benefit of mankind. By this time M. C. had stopped sleeping altogether. Her voice was hoarse from her rapid and incessant talking and singing. Euphoria alternated with irritability and paranoia, and her classmates were bewildered by M. C.'s bizarre behavior, suspecting she was on drugs.

M. C. refused to attend the psychiatric evaluation her mother had scheduled for her, stating "there's nothing wrong with me, I'm on top of the world." Indeed, she was able to calm down, but gradually she would again become more excited, making lots of long-distance phone calls. Finally, her mother contacted the police when M. C. stayed out all night with an older male she had just met. M. C. was seen in the emergency room after being escorted there by police. Mental status examination revealed an attractive but disheveled young woman with a broad affect who talked rapidly and at times incoherently, changing topics with loosening of associations. Her mood was irritable and euphoric. She stated she felt like she was "speeding," even though she denied drug abuse. Although her thoughts were racing, she was also able to admit that she was fearful and paranoid that someone might be secretly giving her "pep pills." She denied hallucinations but maintained her story of being on a "special mission." Cognitive examination showed that her memory and intellect were fully intact. Physical examination and medical history were unremarkable. Family history was significant for the father, who had at age 20 had a psychotic episode that responded to major tranquilizers for what was thought to be schizophrenia. However, he had been medication-free for the next 15 years until he became very depressed during the divorce. The diagnosis of bipolar affective disorder had been considered.

M. C. received a diagnosis of bipolar affective disorder, manic. Thyroid function tests and a drug screen were negative. She was started on lithium carbonate, 300 mg 3 times a day, and was given the neuroleptic medication, chlorpromazine, 100 mg in the morning and at bedtime temporarily to help reduce her extreme excitement and improve her sleep. The lithium dose was raised to a dose of 600 mg twice a day in order to achieve a blood level of approximately 1.0 mg/dl. She was cautioned about the signs and symptoms of toxicity, including confusion, nausea, vomiting, or physical incoordination, and cautioned to avoid becoming pregnant while taking lithium without consulting her doctor. Over the next 2 weeks M. C.'s thoughts and speech returned to normal, as did her sleep, and chlorpromazine was discontinued. Her grandiose plans and ideas subsided. However, she reported feeling quite embarrassed about her past behavior. She continues to take lithium and participates in outpatient therapy, where she is actively trying to put her social and academic life back together. After she graduates from high school, she intends to attend college.

RESEARCH DIRECTIONS

Research developments in child psychiatry and in the area of affective disorders are being made at an ever-increasing pace, such that some of the findings already described in the text of this chapter may be outdated by the time it reaches publication. The wheels of progress are turning in vitally new directions, incorporating previous knowledge and observations of various theorists and synthesizing them with the more rigorous and scientific methods of epidemiology, biochemistry, genetics, and the fundamental aspects of medicine and endocrinology.

The field is still hard at work establishing the natural history of affective illness and suicidal behavior as it begins in childhood and adolescence and continues into adult life. In this way it is also possible to determine the phenomenology of these significant public health problems as they occur in the general population. Although the majority of clinical studies are done on samples of referred-patient groups, we also need to know about affected individuals who never seek professional assistance. We can only speculate about the untold suffering and loss of productivity as many adolescents pass through their critical years of education and career development into adulthood. Major prospective studies comparing and contrasting suicide attempters and suicide completers are underway and are an important step in understanding this significant source of mortality. Furthermore, large-scale epidemiologic studies are needed to characterize and carefully describe the general adolescent population and elucidate factors that may predispose or protect against subsequent disorder. Family and twin studies have suggested already that genetics play a predisposing role (Gershon et al., 1976; Strober, 1984). Adoption studies are needed to help separate out the respective contributions of genetics and social environment as they interact together.

The areas of neurochemistry and endocrinology have already begun to offer glimpses into understanding biological mechanisms that appear to undergo significant changes during affective episodes. Recombinant genetic research is a promising technique for studying the molecular and biochemical vulnerability that seems to run in many families. Magnetic resonance imaging (MRI, NMR) and positron emission tomography (PET scans) also hold promise in unravelling altered nervous system metabolism.

In addition to direct study of affected patients and families, the animal models of learned helplessness as reviewed by Petty and Sherman (1985) and the ongoing primate separation work related to children and adolescents by McKinney (McKinney, Suomi, & Harlow, 1972) are examples of nonhuman affective disability. These show promise of being pertinent to the study of affective illness in man.

Just as rigorous research methodology is now being used to carefully study and describe affective illness, all approaches to treatment must be subjected to controlled trials to determine their efficacy. Although studies of antidepressant medication are few, and thus far somewhat disappointing compared to prepubertal and adult effectiveness, further controlled studies of psychotherapeutic and pharmacologic interventions are needed (Puig-Antich et al., 1979; N. D. Ryan, personal communication, July 10, 1985). This situation must be corrected. We must strive to train therapists in effective treatment approaches and educate patients and families with reliable facts about the illness. This knowledge is an important tool for alleviating the guilt and misunderstanding surrounding affective illness and suicidal behavior.

In this day of cost containment in health care it is apparent that third-party reimbursement in the future will be limited to only those therapists and providers who engage in proven treatment modalities. The challenge in research is clearly to document each treatment modality that is effective and to have the courage to discard those that are not. Only in this way will we move ahead toward genuine scientific knowledge and be able to offer real hope to our depressed adolescent patients.

SUMMARY

Over the past decade, depression in adolescence has been recognized as a major psychopathologic entity. Advances in our efforts in diagnostic classification and decreased reliance on psychoanalytic doctrine have provided clinicians and researchers with the required resources for more reliable diagnosis and efficacious treatment. We have been able to avail ourselves of the bountiful experience gained in the diagnosis and treatment of depression in adults as we have perceived the considerable continuity of depressive disorder through the life cycle. All of these advances, in conjunction with our increasing understanding of normal cognitive, affective, and social development, coupled with the considerable tools of epidemiology, should aid us in clarifying the longitudinal course of depressive disorders through adolescence into adulthood.

Considerable work remains to be done in clarifying those aspects of the depression diagnoses that are specific and critical in the assessment and treatment of dysphoric and depressed adolescents. Increasing attention must be given to the morbidity and ultimate mortality associated with the dysthymic-disorder (minor or neurotic depression) diagnoses (Fine, Moretti, Haley, & Marvage, 1985; Kovacs et al., 1984). Greater resources are required in conducting controlled studies of the various psychotherapeutic (behavioral, cognitive, family, psychoanalytic, psychodynamic) and psychopharmacologic modalities, employing standardized assessment instruments in clearly defined groups of youth suffering from clinically significant depressive disorders.

We must continue our efforts at understanding suicidal behavior, as well as develop methods for early identification of possibly suicidal youth and methods of prevention. We must increase our work to curb the epidemic of suicidal behavior through consultation and education efforts for schools, physicians, community agencies, and the media. The amount of knowledge we have concerning the familial and genetic contribution to depressive disorders should assist us in identifying teens vulnerable to depression and suicide and in planning for their care. The tools for rapid advancements in increasing our understanding of adolescent depression and its treatment are at hand. Mental health professionals working with adolescents must increase their efforts and commitment to the use of such instruments and information.

REFERENCES

Akiskal, H. S. (1983). Dysthymic disorder: Psychopathology of proposed chronic depressive subtypes. *American Journal of Psychiatry, 140*(1), 11–20.

Albert, N., & Beck, A. T. (1975). Incidence of depression in early adolescence: A preliminary study. *Journal of Youth & Adolescence, 4*, 301–307.

Alessi, N. E., McManus, M., Grapentine, W. L., & Brickman, A. (1984). The characterization of depressive disorders in serious juvenile offenders. *Journal of Affective Disorders, 6,* 9–17.

American Psychiatric Association. (1980). *Diagnostic and statistical manual of mental disorders* (3rd ed.). Washington, DC: Author.

Anthony, E. J. (1970). Two contrasting types of adolescent depression and their treatment. *Journal of the American Psychoanalytic Association, 1,* 841–859.

Anthony, E. J. (1983). Depression in adolescence: A psychodynamic approach to nosology. In H. Golomber & B. D. Garfinkel (Eds.), *The adolescent and mood disturbances* (pp. 151–165). New York: International Universities Press.

Barraclough, B. M., Holding, T., & Fayers, P. (1976). Influence of coroners' officers and pathologists on suicide verdicts. *British Journal of Psychiatry, 128,* 471–474.

Beck, A. T., Rush, A. J., Shaf, B. F., & Emery, G. (1979). *Cognitive therapy of depression.* New York: Guilford.

Berg, I., Hullin, R., Allsopp, M., O'Brien, P., & Mac-Donald, R. (1974). Bipolar manic–depressive psychosis in early adolescence. *British Journal of Psychiatry, 125,* 416–417.

Berman, S. (1980). The response of parents to adolescent depression. *Adolescent Psychiatry, 8,* 367–377.

Bernard, M. E., & Joyce, M. R. (Eds.) (1984). *Rational-emotive therapy with children and adolescents.* New York: Wiley.

Cadoret, R., Widmer, R., & Troughton (1980). Somatic complaints: Harbinger of depression in primary care. *Journal of Affective Disorders, 2*(1), 61–70.

Campbell, J. D. (1952). Manic–depressive psychosis in children. *Journal of New Mental Disorders, 116,* 424–439.

Carlson, G. (1979). Lithium carbonate use in adolescents: Clinical indications and management. *Adolescent Psychiatry, 7,* 410–418.

Carlson, G. A. (1981). The phenomenology of adolescent depression. *Adolescent Psychiatry, 9,* 411–421.

Carlson, G. A. (1983). Overview of masked or alternate forms of depression. In D. P. Cantwell & G. A. Carlson (Eds.), *Affective disorders in childhood and adolescence: An update* (pp. 106–108). New York: Spectrum Publications.

Carlson, G. A., & Cantwell, D. P. (1980). A survey of depressive symptoms, syndrome, and disorder in a child psychiatric population. *Journal of Child Psychology and Psychiatry, 21,* 19–25.

Carlson, G. A., & Cantwell, D. P. (1981). Diagnosis of childhood depression: A comparison of Weinberg and *DSM-III* criteria. *Journal of American Academy of Child Psychiatry, 21,* 247–250.

Carlson, G. A., & Strober, M. (1978). Manic-depressive illness in early adolescence. *Journal of the American Academy of Child Psychiatry, 17,* 138–153.

Centers for Disease Control. (1983). Violent deaths among persons 15 to 24 years of age—United States. *Journal of American Medical Association, 250,* 3147.

Chambers, W. J., Puig-Antich, J., Hirsch, M., Paez, P., Ambrosini, P. J., Tabrizi, M. A., & Davies, M. (1985). The assessment of affective disorder to children and adolescents by semistructured interview: Test–retest reliability of the K-SADS-P. *Achives of General Psychiatry, 42,* 696–702.

Chiles, J. A., Miller, M. L., & Cox, G. B. (1980). Depression in an adolescent delinquent population. *Archives of General Psychiatry, 37,* 1179–1184.

Coats, K. I., & Reynolds, W. M. (1984). *A comparison of cognitive-behavioral therapy and relaxation training for the treatment of depression in adolescents.* Unpublished manuscript.

Coll, P. G., & Bland, R. (1979). Manic depressive illness in adolescence and childhood. *Canadian Journal of Psychiatry, 24,* 255–263.

Consensus Development Panel (1985). Mood disorders. Pharmacologic prevention of recurrences. *American Journal of Psychiatry, 142,* 469–476.

Costello, A. J., Edelbrock, C. S., Dulcan, M. K. et al. (1984). *Report on the NIMH Diagnostic Interview Schedule for Children (DISC).* Unpublished report.

Crumley, F. E. (1979). Adolescent suicide attempts. *Journal of the American Medical Association, 241,* 2404–2407.

Davis, R. E. (1979). Manic-depressive variant syndrome of childhood: A preliminary report. *American Journal of Psychiatry, 136,* 702–706.

Dosen, A. (1984). Depressive conditions in mentally handicapped children. *Acta Paedopsychiatrica, 50,* 29–40.

Dyson, W. L., & Barcai, A. (1970). Treatment of children of lithium-responding parents. *Current Therapeutic Research, 12,* 286–290.

Emery, G., Bedrosian, R., & Garber, J. (1983). Cognitive therapy with depressed children and adolescents. In D. P. Cantwell & G. A. Carlson (Eds.). *Affective disorders in childhood and adolescence—An update* (pp. 445–471). New York: Spectrum.

Feighner, J. P., Robins, E., Guze, S. B., Woodruff, R. A., & Winokur, G. (1972). Diagnostic criteria for use in psychiatric research. *Archives of General Psychiatry, 26,* 57–63.

Feinstein, S. (1975). Adolescent depression. In E. J. Anthony & T. Benedek (Eds.), *Depression and human existence* (pp. 317–336). Boston: Little, Brown.

Feinstein, S. C. (1980). Why they were afraid of Virginia Woolf: Perspectives on juvenile manic-depressive illness. *Adolescent Psychiatry, 8,* 332–343.

Feinstein, S. C. (1982). Manic-depressive disorder in children and adolescents. *Adolescent Psychiatry, 10,* 256–272.

Fine, S., Moretti, M., Haley, G., & Marvage, K. (1985). Affective disorders in children and adolescents. The dysthymic disorder dilemma. *Canadian Journal of Psychiatry, 30,* 173–177.

Gammon, G. D., Rothblum, J. K., Millen, K., Tischler, G. L., & Weissman, M. M. (1983). Use of structured diagnostic interview to identify bipolar disorder in adolescent inpatients, frequency and manifestations of disorder. *American Journal of Psychiatry, 140,* 543–547.

Garfinkel, B. D., Froese, A., & Hood, J. (1982). Suicide attempts in children and adolescents. *American Journal of Psychiatry, 139,* 1257–1261.

Geller, B., Cooper, T. B., & Chestnut, E. C. (1985a). Serial monitoring and achievement of steady state nortriptyline plasma levels in depressed children and adolescents: Preliminary data. *Journal of Clinical Pharmacology, 5,* 213–216.

Geller, B., Cooper, T. B., Chestnut, E. C., Anker, J. A., Price, D. T., & Yates, E. (1985b). Child and adolescent nortriptyline single dose kinetics predict steady state plasma levels and suggested dose: Preliminary data. *Journal of Clinical Psychopharmacology, 5,* 154–158.

Geller, B., Cooper, T. B., Farooki, Z. Q., & Chestnut, E. C. (1985c). Preliminary data on dose and plasma levels of nortriptyline and chlorpromazine in delusionally depressed adolescents and nortriptyline in depressed adolescents. *American Journal of Psychiatry, 142,* 346–348.

Gershon, E. E., Bunney, W. E., Ledeman, J. F., Van Eerdewegh, M., & DeBausch, B. A. (1976). The inheritance of affective disorders: A review of data and hypotheses. *Behavioral Genetics, 6,* 227–261.

Gittelman-Klein, R., & Klein, D. F. (1973). School phobia: Diagnostic considerations in the light of imipramine effects. *Journal of Nervous and Mental Disease, 156,* 199–215.

Glaser, K. (1981). Psychopathologic patterns in depressed adolescents. *American Journal of Psychotherapy, 35,* 368–382.

Goldacre, M., & Hawton, D. (1985). Repetition of self-poisoning and subsequent death in adolescents who take overdoses. *British Journal of Psychiatry, 146,* 395–398.

Goldney, R. D., & Katsikitis, M. (1983). Cohort analysis of suicide rates in Australia. *Archives of General Psychiatry, 40,* 71–74.

Guttman, H. A. (1983). Family therapy in the treatment of mood disturbance in adolescence. In H. Golomber & B. D. Garfinkel (Eds.), *The adolescent and mood disturbance* (pp. 263–272). New York: International Universities Press.

Headley, L. A. (Ed.) (1983). *Suicide in Asia and the Near East.* Berkeley: University of California Press.

Hendin, H. (1975). Student suicide: Death as a life style. *Journal of Nervous & Mental Disease, 160,* 204–219.

Herjanic, B., & Reich, W. (1982). Development of a structured psychiatric interview for children: Agreement between child and parent on individual symptoms. *Journal of Abnormal Child Psychology, 10,* 307–324.

Herjanic, B., & Welner, Z. (1980). Adolescent suicide. *Advances in Behavioral Pediatrics, 1,* 195–223.

Hochberg, R. (1977). Psychotherapy of a suicidal boy: Dynamics and interventions. *Psychotherapy: Theory, Research and Practice, 14,* 428–433.

Hodgman, C. H. (1983). Current issues in adolescent psychiatry. *Hospital and Community Psychiatry, 34,* 514–521.

Holinger, P. C. (1978). Adolescent suicide: An epidemiologic study of recent trends. *American Journal of Psychiatry, 135*(6), 754–756.

Holinger, P. C., & Offer, D. (1981). Perspectives on suicide in adolescence. *Research in Community and Mental Health, 2,* 139–157.

Hollander, H. E., & Turner, F. D. (1985). Characteristics of incarcerated delinquents: Relationship between development disorders, environmental and family factors, and patterns of offense and recidi-

vism. *Journal American Academy of Child Psychiatry, 24,* 221–226.

Horowitz, H. A. (1977). Lithium and the treatment of adolescent manic depressive illness. *Diseases of the Nervous System, 38,* 480–483.

Hsu, L. K. G., Molcan, K., Cashman, M. A., Lee, S., Lohr, J. & Hindmarsh, D. (1983). The dexamethasone suppression test in adolescent depression. *Journal of the American Academy of Child Psychiatry, 22,* 470–473.

Hudgens, R. W. (1974). *Psychiatric disorders in adolescents.* Baltimore: Williams & Wilkins.

Inamdar, S. C., Siomopoulos, G., Osborn, M., & Bianchi, E. C. (1979). Phenomenology associated with depressed moods in adolescents. *American Journal of Psychiatry, 136,* 156–159.

Jan-Tausch, J. (1964). *Suicide of children 1960–63.* Trenton, NJ: New Jersey Public Schools, Division of Curriculum & Instruction, Office of Special Education Services, Department of Education.

Kandel, D. B., & Davies, M. (1982). Epidemiology of depressive mood in adolescents. *Archives of General Psychiatry, 39,* 1205–1216.

Kanner, A. M., Rubinstein, B., Gittleman, R., & Mascia, A. (1983, October). *The use of imipramine in intractable asthmatic children: A preliminary report on its effect on the psychiatric and asthmatic disorders.* Paper presented at the meeting of the American Academy of Child Psychiatry, San Francisco.

Kaplan, S. L., Hong, G. K., & Weinhold, C. (1984). Epidemiology of depressive symptomatology in adolescents. *Journal of the American Academy of Child Psychiatry, 23,* 91–98.

Kaplan, S. L., Landa, B., Weinhold, C., & Shenker, I. R. (1984). Adverse health behaviors and depressive symptomatology in adolescents. *Journal of the American Academy of Child Psychiatry, 23,* 595–601.

Kasanin, J. (1931). The affective psychoses in children. *American Journal of Psychiatry, 10,* 897–926.

Kashani, J. H., Barbero, G. J., & Bolander, F. D. (1981). Depression in hospitalized pediatric patients. *Journal of American Academy of Child Psychiatry, 20,* 123–134.

Kashani, J. H., Cantwell, D. P., Shekim, W. O., & Reid, J. C. (1982). Major depressive disorder in children admitted to an inpatient community mental health center. *American Journal of Psychiatry, 139,* 671–672.

Kashani, J. H., Lababidi, A., & Jones, R. S. (1982). Depression in children and adolescents with cardiovascular symptomatology. The significance of chest pain. *Journal of the American Academy of Child Psychiatry, 21,* 187–189.

Kelly, J. T., Hoch, M., & Buegel, D. (1976). Lithium carbonate in juvenile manic–depressive illness. *Diseases of the Nervous System, 37,* 90–92.

Kestenbaum, C. J. (1980). Adolescents at risk for manic–depressive illness. *Adolescent Psychiatry, 8,* 344–366.

Kestenbaum, C. J. (1982). Children and adolescents at risk for manic–depressive illness: Introduction and overview. *Adolescent Psychiatry, 10,* 245–255.

Klee, S. H., & Garfinkel, B. D. (1984). Identification of depression in children and adolescents: The role of the dexamethasone suppression test. *Jour-*

nal of Child Psychiatry, 23, 410–415.

Kovacs, M. (1981). Rating scale to assess depression in school-aged children. Acta Paedopsychiatra, 46, 305–315.

Kovacs, M., Feinberg, T. L., Crouse-Novak, M., Paulauskas, S. L., Pollack, M., & Finkelstein, R. (1984). Depressive disorders in childhood: II. A longitudinal study of the risk for a subsequent major depression. Archives of General Psychiatry, 41, 643–649.

Kramer, A. D., & Feiguine, R. J. (1981). Clinical effects of amitriptyline in adolescent depression: A pilot study. Journal of the American Academy of Child Psychiatry, 20, 636–644.

Kron, L., Decina, P., Kestenbaum, C. J., Farber, S., Gargan, M., & Fieve, R. (1982). The offspring of bipolar manic-depressives: Clinical features. Adolescent Psychiatry, 10, 273–291.

Kuhn, R. (1963). The occurrence and treatment of endogenous depression in children. Schweizerische Medizinische Wachenshrift, 93, 86–90.

Kupfer, D., & Foster, F. G. (1979). EEG and sleep depression. In R. L. Williams & I. Karacan (Eds.), Sleep disorders: Diagnosis and treatment (pp. 163–203). New York: Wiley.

Ling, W., Oftedal, G., & Weinberg, W. (1970). Depressive illness in childhood presenting as a severe headache. American Journal of Diseases of Children, 120, 122–124.

Malmquist, C. P. (1971). Depressions in childhood and adolescence. New England Journal of Medicine, 284, 887–893, 955–961.

McKinley, C. K., & Dreisbach, L. K. (1967). Variations in depressive symptomatology as a function of age. Texas Reports on Biological Medicine, 25, 179–185.

McKinney, W. T., Suomi, S. J., & Harlow, H. F. (1972). Repetitive peer separations of juvenile-age Rhesus monkeys. Archives of General Psychiatry, 27, 200–203.

McManus, M., Alessi, M. E., Grapentine, W. L., & Brickman, A. (1984). Psychiatric disturbance in serious delinquents. Journal of Child Psychiatry, 23, 602–615.

Mitchell, J., McCauley, E., Burke, P., Moss, S., & Smith, E. (1984, October). Phenomenology of depression in children and adolescents I: Affective and psychotic symptoms. Poster presented at the meeting of the American Academy of Child Psychiatry, Toronto.

National Institute of Mental Health/National Institutes of Health. (1985). Mood disorders: Pharmacologic prevention of recurrence, consensus development panel (conference statement). American Journal of Psychiatry, 142, 469–476.

Nissen, G. (1984). Somatogenic depression in children and adolescents. Acta Paedopsychiatrica, 50, 21–28.

Offer, D., & Franzen, S. A. (1983). Mood development in normal adolescents. In H. Golomber & B. D. Garfinkel (Eds.), The adolescent and mood disturbance (pp. 23–36). New York: International Universities Press.

Orvaschel, H., Sholomskas, D., & Weissman, M. (1983). The assessment of psychopathology and behav-

ioral problems in children. A review of scales suitable for epidemiological and clinical research (1967–1979) (DHHS Publication No. ADM 83-1037). Washington, DC: National Institute of Mental Health.

Otto, U. (1966). Suicidal attempts made by children and adolescents because of school problems. Acta Paediatrica Scandinavica, 54, 348–356.

Otto, U. (1971). Suicidal attempts in childhood and adolescence: Today and after ten years. A follow-up study. Depressive states in childhood and adolescence: Proceedings of the 4th Union of European Pedopsychiatrists Congress (pp. 357–366). Stockholm: Almquist & Wiksell.

Paton, S., Kessler, R., & Kandel, D. (1977). Depressive mood and adolescent illicit drug use: A longitudinal analysis. Journal of Genetic Psychology, 131, 267–289.

Peck, M. L. (1981). The loner: An exploration of a suicidal subtype in adolescence. Adolescent Psychiatry, 9, 461–466.

Petti, T. A. (1978). Depression in hospitalized child psychiatry patients: Approaches to measuring depression. Journal of the American Academy of Child Psychiatry, 17, 49–59.

Petti, T. A. (1983). Imipramine in the treatment of depressed children. In D. Cantwell & G. Carlson (Eds.), Affective disorders of childhood and adolescence (pp. 375–415). New York: Spectrum.

Petti, T. A. (1985a). Policy implications of adolescent suicide. Unpublished manuscript.

Petti, T. A. (1985b). Scales of potential use in the psychopharmacologic treatment of depressed children and adolescents. Psychopharmacology Bulletin, 21, 951–977.

Petti, T. A., Bornstein, M., Delamater, A., Conners, C. K. (1980). Evaluation and multimodality treatment of a depressed pre-pubertal girl. Journal of the American Academy of Child Psychiatry, 19, 690–702.

Petti, T. A., Kovacs, M., Feinberg, T., Paulauskas, S., & Finkelstein, R. (1982, October). Cognitive therapy of a 12-year-old boy with atypical depression: A pilot study. Paper presented at the meeting of the American Academy of Child Psychiatry, Washington, DC.

Petty, F., & Sherman, A. D. (1982). Neurochemical differentiation between exposure to stress and the development of learned helplessness. Drug Development Research, 2, 43–45.

Petzel, S. V., & Kline, D. W. (1978). Adolescent suicide: Epidemiological and biological aspects. Adolescent Psychiatry, 6, 239–266.

Petzel, S. V., & Riddle, M. (1981). The interlocking psychologies of suicide and adolescence. Adolescent Psychiatry, 9, 343–398.

Pfefferbaum-Levine, B., Kumor, K., Cangir, A., Choroszy, M., & Rosenberry, E. A. (1983). Tricyclic antidepressants for children with cancer. American Journal of Psychiatry, 140, 1074–1076.

Post, R. M., Uhde, T. W., Ballenger, J. C., & Squillace, K. M. (1983). Prophylactic efficacy of carbamazepine in manic-depressive illness. American Journal of Psychiatry, 140, 1602–1604.

Poznanski, E. O., Carroll, B. J., Banegas, M. C., Cook, S. C., & Grossman, J. A. (1982). The dexamethasone suppression test in prepubertal depressed children. *American Journal of Psychiatry,* *139,* 321–324.

Poznanski, E. O., Cook, S. C., & Carroll, B. J. (1979). A depression rating scale for children. *Pediatrics,* *64,* 442–450.

Poznanski, E. O., Grossman, J. A., Bucksbaum, Y., Banegas, M., Freeman, L., & Gibbons, R. (1984). Preliminary studies of the reliability and validity of the children's depression rating scale. *Journal of the American Academy of Child Psychiatry, 23,* 191–197.

Prien, R. F., Kupfer, D. J., Mansky, P. A., Small, J. G., Tuason, V. B., Voss, C. B., & Johnson, W. E. (1984). Drug therapy in the prevention of recurrences in unipolar and bipolar affective disorders. *Archives of General Psychiatry, 41,* 1096–1104.

Prince, R. (1983). Transcultural aspects of affective disorders in adolescents: The brain-fag syndrome in African students. In H. Golomber & B. O. Garfinkel (Eds.), *The adolescent and mood disturbance* (pp. 53–71). New York: International Universities Press.

Puig-Antich, J. (in press). Effects of age and puberty on psychobiological markers of depressive illness. In M. Rutter, C. Izard, & P. Read (Eds.), *Development of affect.* New York: Blackwell Scientific.

Puig-Antich, J., Perel, J. M., Lupatkin, W., Chambers, W. J., Shen, C., Tabrizi, M. A., & Stiller, R. L. (1979). Plasma levels of imipramine (IMI) and desmethylimipramine (DMI) and clinical response in prepubertal major depressive disorder: A preliminary report. *Journal of the American Academy of Child Psychiatry, 18,* 616–627.

Reynolds, W. M. (1984). Depression in children and adolescents: Phenomenology, evaluation and treatment. *School Psychology Review, 13,* 171–182.

Richman, J. (1981). Family treatment of suicidal children and adolescents. In C. F. Wells & I. R. Stuart (Eds.), *Self-destructive behavior in children and adolescents* (pp. 274–291). New York: Van Nostrand Reinhold.

Robins, D., & Conroy, R. C. (1983). A cluster of adolescents suicide attempts: Is suicide contagious? *Journal of Adolescent Health Care, 3,* 253–255.

Robins, D. R., Alessi, N. E., Yanchyshyn, G. W., & Colfer, M. (1983). Psychodynamic and characterological heterogeneity among adolescents with major depressive disorders. *Journal of the American Academy of Child Psychiatry, 22,* 487–491.

Robins, E. (1981). *The final months.* New York: Oxford University Press.

Robins, E., Murphy, G. E., Wilkinson, R. H. Jr., Gassner, S., & Kayes, J. (1959). Some clinical considerations in the prevention of suicide based on a study of 134 successful suicides. *American Journal of Public Health, 49,* 888–899.

Rosenthal, M. J. (1981). Sexual differences in the suicidal behavior of young people. *Adolescent Psychiatry, 9,* 422–442.

Rossman, P. G. (1982). Psychotherapeutic approaches with depressed, acting-out adolescents. Interpretive tactics and their rationale. *Adolescent Psychiatry, 10,* 455–468.

Salk, L., Lipsitt, L. P., Sturner, W. Q., Reilly, B. M., & Levat, R. H. (1985). Relationship of maternal perinatal conditions to eventual adolescent suicide. *Lancet, 1,* 624–627.

Sanborn, D. E., Sanborn, C. J., & Cimbalic, P. (1974). Two years of suicide: A study of adolescent suicide in New Hampshire. *Child Psychiatry and Human Development, 3,* 222–234.

Schowalter, J. E. (1983). Mood disturbance and physical illness in adolescence. In H. Golomber & B. D. Garfinkel (Eds.), *The adolescent and mood disturbance* (pp. 123–134). New York: International Universities Press.

Seligman, M. E. P. (1975). *Helplessness: On depression, development and death.* San Francisco: Freeman.

Shaffer, D. (1974). Suicide in childhood and early adolescence. *Journal of Child Psychology and Psychiatry, 15,* 275–291.

Shaffer, D. (1984). Notes on psychotherapy research among children and adolescents. *Journal of Child Psychiatry, 23,* 552–561.

Shaffer, D. (1985). Depression, mania, and suicidal acts. In M. Rutter & L. Hersov (Eds.), *Child and adolescent psychiatry: Modern approaches* (2nd ed. pp. 698–719). London: Blackwell Scientific Publications.

Shaffer, D., & Fisher, P. (1981). The epidemiology of suicide in children and young adolescents. *Journal of the American Academy of Child Psychiatry, 20,* 545–565.

Shafii, M., Carrigan, S., Whittinghill, J. R., & Derrick, A. (1985). *Psychological autopsy of completed suicide in children and adolescents: A comparative study.* American Journal of Psychiatry, 142, 1061–1064.

Shafii, M., & Shafii, S. L. (1982). Self-destructive, suicidal behavior, and completed suicide. In M. Shafii & S. L. Shafii (Eds.), *Pathways of human development* (pp. 164–180). New York: Thieme-Stratton.

Shafii, M., Whittinghill, J. R., Dolen, D. C., Pearson, V. D., Jr., Derrick, A., & Carrigan, S. (1984). In H. S. Sudak, A. B. Ford, & N. B. Rushford (Eds.), *Suicide in the young* (pp. 271–294). Boston: John Wright & Sons.

Siegel, L. J., & Griffin, N. J. (1983). Adolescents' concepts of depression among their peers. *Adolescence, 8,* 965–973.

Spitzer, R. L., & Endicott, J. (1978). *The schedule for affective disorders and schizophrenia.* New York: New York State Psychiatric Institute.

Stark, K. D., Reynolds, W. M., & Kaslow, N. J. (1985, March). *A comparison of the relative efficacy of self-control and behavior therapy for the reduction of depression in children.* Paper presented at the Fourth National Conference on the Clinical Application of Cognitive Behavior Therapy, Honolulu.

Staton, R., Wilson, H., & Brumback, R. A. (1982, October). *Differential effects of amitriptyline versus imipramine upon childhood psychological functioning.* Paper presented at the meeting of the American Academy of Child Psychiatry, Washington, DC.

Stoddard, F. J., & Cahners, S. S. (1985). Suicide attempted by self-immolation during adolescence. II. Psychiatric treatment and outcome. In H. Golomber & B. D. Garfinkel (Eds.), *The adolescent and mood disturbance* (pp. 266–280). New York: International Universities Press.

Strober, M. (1984). *Family study of adolescent psychopathology*. Paper presented at the University of Pittsburgh, Dec. 7, 1984, Pittsburgh, Pa.

Strober, M., & Carlson, G. (1982). Predictors of bipolar illness in adolescents with major depression: A follow-up investigation. *Adolescent Psychiatry, 10,* 299–319.

Sudak H. S., Ford, A. B., & Rushforth, N. B. (1984). *Adolescent suicide: An overview. American Journal of Psychotherapy, 38,* 350–363.

Task Force on the Use of Laboratory Tests in Psychiatry. (1985). Tricyclic antidepressants—Blood level measurements and clinical outcome. *American Journal of Psychiatry, 142,* 155–162.

Teicher, J. D., & Jacobs, J. (1966). Adolescents who attempt suicide: Preliminary findings. *American Journal of Psychiatry, 122,* 1248–1257.

Tishler, C. L. (1983). Making life meaningful for youth: Preventing suicide. In L. E. Arnold (Ed.), *Preventing adolescent alienation* (pp. 97–105). Lexington, MA: Lexington Books.

Tishler, C. L., McKenry, P. C., & Morgan, K. C. (1981). Adolescent suicide attempts: Some significant factors. *Suicide and Life-Threatening Behavior, 11,* 86–91.

Tramontana, M. G. (1980). Critical review of research on psychotherapy outcome with adolescents. *Psychological Bulletin, 88,* 429–450.

Walker, B. A., & Mehr, M. (1983). Adolescent suicide—A family crisis: A model for effective intervention by family therapists. *Adolescence, 18,* 285–292.

Weeks, D. G., Michela, J. L., Peplau, L. A., & Bragg, M. D. (1980). Relation between loneliness and depression: A structural equation analysis. *Journal of Personality and Social Psychology, 39,* 1238–1244.

Weinberg, W. A., Rutman, J., Sullivan, L., Pencik, E. C., & Dietz, S. G. (1973). Depression in children referred to an educational diagnostic center: Diagnosis and treatment. *Journal of Pediatrics, 83,* 1065–1072.

Weissman, M. M., & Paykel, E. S. (1974). *The depressed woman: A study of social relationships.* Chicago: University of Chicago Press.

Welner, A., Welner, Z., & Fishman, R. (1979). Psychiatric adolescent inpatients—Eight- to ten-year follow-up. *Archives of General Psychiatry, 36,* 698–700.

Welner, Z., Welner, A., McCrary, M. D., & Leonard, M. S. (1977). Psychopathology in children of inpatients with depression: A controlled study. *Journal of Nervous and Mental Disease, 164,* 408–413.

Westman, M. (1965). Tofranil treatment of depressions in adolescence. *Lakartidningen* (Supplement II), *62,* 87–92.

Winokur, G., Clayton, P. J., & Reich, T. (1969). *Manic-depressive illness.* St. Louis: Mosby.

Wolpert, E. A. (1983). The treatment of manic-depressive illness in adolescence. In H. Golomber & B. D. Garfinkel (Eds.), *The adolescent and mood disturbance* (pp. 179–187). New York: International Universities Press.

CHAPTER 17

Substance Abuse in Adolescence

John J. Horan and Lawrence K. Straus

One's first puff of a cigarette can be terribly unpleasant, producing, for example, feelings of dizziness and nausea. Why do many adolescents persist and eventually subject themselves to what is clearly the foremost preventable cause of death in America (Califano, 1979)? Alcohol is likewise an acquired taste, ultimately responsible for up to 25,000 traffic fatalities in the United States each year. A tenth of our population consumes half of the alcohol sold; why are there 3 million teenage problem-drinkers in this country (National Institute on Alcohol Abuse and Alcoholism [NIAAA], 1981), and what can be done about it?

We have chosen the words "substance abuse" in our chapter title rather than "drug abuse," because cigarettes and alcohol are rarely referred to as drugs. Yet, their adverse consequences to the individual and to society may be every bit as devastating as those attributable to the chronic consumption of illegal substances. In our opinion, the drug abuse field has been inappropriately preoccupied with the products used by "impolite" society; we hope to provide less arbitrary coverage.

Our chapter is divided into six sections of somewhat uneven length. We open with a description of the problem, noting definitional difficulties and various etiological factors. Our second section on epidemiology provides information on the frequency of consumption of the various substances over the past decade. Section three focuses on assessment and diagnosis, and section four examines the various intervention modes. Most substance abuse work with adolescents is prevention-based. Our final section identifies a number of current complementary approaches to the problem of adolescent drug use.

DESCRIPTION OF THE DISORDER

Definitional Difficulties

Drug abuse, as a professional specialty area, exists because of widespread public consensus that the consumption of certain substances by our nation's youth constitutes a major social problem. Unfortunately, the concept of "abuse" is not at all clear. Zinberg (1976) suggested that

313

various professions have defined the term in a manner consistent with their own best interests. For example, lawyers define abuse as "violation of a particular statute," physicians as "use without a prescription," and pharmacists as "not following the directions on the label."

Some civil libertarians have argued that the problem is largely one of our own making. By restricting the availability of a given substance, we increase its market value, create an underground culture of users not amenable to help and suppliers not subject to taxation, and damage our law enforcement structure by draining its resources and exposing its personnel to overwhelming lucrative, but corrupt, alternatives. Rhetoric pertaining to freedom of choice—including that of self-destruction—occasionally is meshed with the libertarian perspective.

We can offer no beacon of light here. Although the civil libertarian case is not without merit, it is important to note that in a compassionate society the potential costs of self-abuse are not born entirely by the abuser. Motorcycle-helmet laws, for example, are frequently the targets of free-choice polemics. However, in truth, the hundreds of thousands of dollars that may be required to rehabilitate the head trauma of a single cyclist are inevitably paid not by the faulty decision-maker, but by society at large. Similarly, the costs of drug abuse to our nation's economy are truly staggering. Cigarette smoking alone represents an annual drain of $5 to $6 billion in health care expenses, plus an additional $12 to $18 billion due to declines in productivity, losses in wages, and increased absenteeism caused by smoking-related illness (Califano, 1979).

Given the mores of current society, our own definition of abuse would be inextricably entwined with the frequency, quantity, and variety of adverse physical and social consequences of consumption experienced by the individual. Unfortunately, the experience of being arrested may be more hazardous on a number of dimensions than the actual act of consumption. In a society of our own making, we would prefer to define abuse strictly in terms of tissue damage and sustained psychological dysfunction (the latter needing thorough operationalization). In so doing, it might surprise the reader to learn that maximum chronic use of alcohol may be more harmful than similar use of heroin (S. Irwin, personal communication, 1973). On the other hand, the hazard potential of most drugs taken infrequently at a very low dosage level has not been clearly established. In view of these definitional difficulties, we won't distinguish between use and abuse, preferring to let readers define for themselves the boundary between these two concepts, if indeed one can be drawn.

Etiological Factors

There are several reasons why most responsible discussions about the etiology of drug use appear rather speculative and laden with qualifications. In the first place, much of the data on drug users are gathered (often long) after drug use has begun. Thus, it is difficult to sort out the potential causes for taking drugs from the possible effects of having consumed them. For example, when heavy cocaine users are contrasted with abstainers on biological and psychological indices, it is likely that the user group will display higher rates of perforated nasal septums and greater quantities of some untoward psychological variable. No one would mislabel the perforated septum as a reason for taking up the habit; neither can one assuredly claim that some trait or type of emotional lability produced the cocaine preoccupation.

A second difficulty in the construction of etiological theory derives from our previous discussion on distinguishing use from abuse. Some researchers define drug use as any contact whatsoever, including, for example, a single exploratory puff of a marijuana cigarette. Others employ the high-consumption frequencies of chronically addicted populations as operational criteria. In terms of etiology, it is likely that those who cease and desist after slaking their curiosity may be quite unlike those who use drugs on a periodic basis. The latter, in turn, may have little in common with chronic users.

Yet another obstacle to the formation of a concise, consensually validated, etiological explanation stems from the manner in which drugs are classified. Some researchers study only one kind of drug; other researchers may study more than one drug but categorize them in idiosyncratic ways. Given related issues, such as the differing availabilities of certain drugs and the disparate social sanctions their use may engender (e.g., tobacco vs. heroin), useful etiological theory may need to be drug-specific. Moreover, polydrug users may require an entirely separate facet of a comprehensive theory.

Because of the foregoing difficulties, our goals in this section are rather modest. We will open with a brief description of behavioral variables which, at least theoretically, contribute to the initiation and maintenance of drug use. We will then move on to the perspective offered by classical decision theory before concluding with the more ambitious formulations of Lichtenstein and Marlatt and their associates.

Behavioral Variables

Of all the psychosocial correlates of drug use, perhaps the most convincing are the relationships between an individual's use of drugs and the drug-taking behavior of peers, older siblings, and parents. Reported correlations are conspicuous and convincing across all drug categories, including smoking (Borland & Randolph, 1975; Levitt & Edwards, 1970; Wohlford, 1970), drinking (Kandel, Kessler, & Margulies, 1978), and the consumption of illegal substances (Kandel, 1974a, 1974b). These data lend themselves well to etiological hypotheses involving modeling and social reinforcement. Indeed, the power of these principles has been experimentally demonstrated on alcohol consumption (Dericco & Garlington, 1977) and in the formation of expressed drug attitudes (Shute, 1975; Stone & Shute, 1977).

There are, of course, potentially powerful modeling influences beyond the peer group and family. Commercial television, for example, is saturated with themes of "a pill for every ill," and the leaders of many prominent musical groups openly acknowledge their use of drugs. Although modeling and social reinforcement undoubtedly play a role in the initiation of drug use, maintenance of a drug-taking habit is probably more complex. Several theoretical models exist. Pomerleau (1979), for example, offered a complex operant analysis in which cigarette smoking eventually provides a wide variety of positive and negative reinforcers independent from those which elicited exploration with the drug.

Other sources of reinforcement for the taking of drugs have been catalogued by Cahoon and Crosby (1972), Horan (1973), Miller (1973), and Miller and Barlow (1973). In addition to the positive physiological reinforcement (euphoria) resulting from drug use, positive social reinforcement may occur as well. Many readers will remember the status conferred on their adolescent peers who were able to master cigarette inhalation without coughing. In the current youth culture, speaking from personal experience about the effects of other drugs may produce similar social benefits.

Positive reinforcement may act alone or in conjunction with negative reinforcement. In other words, one might use drugs because of the "reward" that follows or the "pain" that precedes such use, or both. As with positive reinforcement, the sources of negative reinforcement may be physiological or social. Examples of the former include chronic drug users' seeking to avoid or ward off the imminent discomforts of a withdrawal reaction by continued ingestion and medically mismanaged "normal" individuals who rely on prescription drugs to escape chronic pain. Similarly, one can find relief from noxious social situations, such as a miserable home, school, marital, or vocational life, by taking drugs. The probabilities of a vicious cycle developing are high, because continual use of drugs usually triggers a worsening of the physical and social situation, which then may be followed by more and more relief-seeking (drug-taking) behavior—hence, the stereotypical alcoholic who drinks to forget the problems precipitated by previous drinking.

Classical Decision Theory and Drug Use

The behavioral variables underlying drug use fit rather comfortably into a classical decision-theory framework (see Broadhurst, 1976; Bross, 1953; Horan, 1979; Mausner, 1973). In its simplest form, classical decision theory posits that our choice of a given activity rests on the cornerstone concepts of value and probability.

Subjective values are known as utilities and may be positive or negative in nature (cf. positive reinforcements vs. punishment). Indulging in or abstaining from drugs, for example, will result in a variety of utilities. Depending on the particular peer group, drug abstinence might be met with approval or ridicule. Similarly, the physical effects of drug consumption might be perceived as pleasant or aversive. Utilities can be quantified in such a way as to imply that one alternative may be far more desirable than another. If peer approval is important to us and our peer group eschews the use of drugs, and if we perceive the effects of a particular drug to be rather unpleasant, our choice is obvious. Our choice is much less obvious if our peer group advocates drug use. In this case, our decision would rest on the difference between the utility magnitudes we attach to peer approval and physical comfort.

The foregoing example presumes that the probabilities of the relevant utilities are certain (i.e., equal to 1.0). In many decisions, however, the probabilities of the various utilities accruing are much less than inevitable. For example, "getting caught" with drugs by parents or police might be perceived as quite horrible. However, in a given situation, the odds of this occurring might be judged as very slight. Moreover, except in simple repeatable events, such as rolling a pair of dice, there is no way to "objectively" arrive at a given probability estimate. In fact, all a priori probability estimation must be considered "subjective" (see Savage, 1954).

Classical decision theory thus suggests that in choice situations we select the alternative with the highest subjectively expected utility (SEU) value. In other words, we qualify our utilities with an estimation of how likely they are to be realized should a considered alternative be implemented. To illustrate, in deciding whether or not to smoke a marijuana cigarette, we would: (a) identify the possible positive and negative utilities; (b) weight them (e.g., on a 1 to 10 scale); (c) multiply each utility score by each probability "guesstimate"; and finally (d) select the alternative with the highest perceived payoff (total SEU value).

It is important to realize that classical decision theory does not proclaim that everyone purposefully goes through the foregoing mental gymnastics prior to choosing. However, the mathematical relationships involved are good predictors of which alternative we eventually will select. In a longitudinal study, Bauman (1980) found such to be true with adolescent decisions about the use of marijuana.

Curiously enough, classical decision theory not only accounts for what we in fact do; it also has strong implications for what we ought to do. Whenever the former does not correspond with the latter, factors such as irrational (maladaptive) utilities or inaccurate probability information can usually be found lurking in the background. Several implications of classical decision theory for drug abuse prevention programming will be discussed later in this chapter.

The Lichtenstein Model

Lichtenstein (1982) and his associates (Danaher & Lichtenstein, 1978; Lichtenstein & Brown, 1980) have developed a four-stage "natural history" model of a smoker's career and suggested various factors thought to be responsible for each stage. *Starting* to smoke primarily is determined by psychosocial factors, such as availability, curiosity, rebelliousness, and modeling influences. *Continuing* the habit, however, can be linked to the pharmacological effects of nicotine as well as to psychosocial and cognitive variables. *Stopping*, or at least the decision to quit, is determined by psychosocial factors (e.g., health, expense, aesthetics, and social support). Finally, *resuming* or relapsing can be brought about by the appearance of physiological withdrawal symptoms, alcohol consumption, stress, social pressure, and what Marlatt has described below as the "abstinence violation effect."

The Marlatt Model

Marlatt and his associates (e.g., Marlatt, 1978; Marlatt & Donovan, 1981) have developed a cognitive–social learning model of the addiction process that accounts for the acquisition, maintenance, and relapse of substance-abuse behavior. As with Lichtenstein, social factors, such as availability, modeling, and peer pressure, contribute to the initiation of drug use. Marlatt argues that a "predisposition" for continuing to use drugs, however, is linked to social-skills deficits that produce a "perceived loss of control." The reinforcement (euphoria) derived from heroin, for example, then becomes a personally controllable alternative to reinforcement not attainable from complex social situations that typically spawn stress and frustration.

Maintenance of the habit occurs when the pharmacologically reinforcing properties of the drugs begin to supplant the social factors. Marlatt's concept of the "emotional paradox," however, extends our earlier discussion of relevant behavioral variables. At low doses, alcohol, for example, leads to increased arousal subjectively labeled by the drinker as excitement, euphoria, energy, and power. As consumption increases over time, however, dysphoria sets in. Unfortunately, this negative affective feedback occurs too late to exert any influence on subsequent drinking. Instead, the individual continues to drink under the mistaken belief that doing so will reduce the unpleasant feelings.

Marlatt's concept of an "Abstinence Violation Effect" addresses the relapse problem. If after a prolonged period of voluntary abstinence, a substance abuser has a subsequent drug experience, the likelihood of continued use (loss of control) increases because of two cognitive processes. First, *cognitive dissonance* occurs when beliefs ("I am an abstainer") and behavior ("I have consumed alcohol") are not consistent. The subsequent dissonance (e.g., guilt, depression) in itself may trigger drinking and will ultimately erode the initial belief concerning one's abstinence into something like "once a junkie, always a junkie" (cf. Ray, 1976). Second, *personal attribution* plays a corollary role in that the initial break with abstinence is perceived as being due to internal weakness and personal failure (rather than to situational factors). The subsequent dysphoria and loss of perceived self-efficacy rekindle beliefs about the drug as a means of coping and enhancing personal control.

EPIDEMIOLOGICAL FINDINGS

The prevalence of the substance abuse problem is typically established through survey research. Two ongoing nationwide projects are most noteworthy. The first, conducted by J. D. Miller and associates, has gathered data every 2 years since 1971. Miller's most recent effort was based on interviews of 1,581 youths in various age brackets between 12 and 17, young adults (18 to 25), and those over 25 (Miller et al., 1983). The second project, performed annually since 1975 by L. D. Johnston and his associates, derives its information exclusively from high-school seniors. Their 1983 sample included 16,300 students from 134 schools (Johnston, O'Malley, & Bachman, 1984). Publication of data gathered on the 1984 graduating class is imminent (University of Michigan, 1985).

In addition to the national panoramas provided by Miller and Johnston, several statewide studies exist, including, for example, Maryland (Mills & Noyes, 1984), New Jersey (Fisher, 1984), and New York (Spencer, Pitkin, Lee, & Clarke, 1984). Finally, there are surveys on adolescent use of individual substances, such as alcohol (Hawkins, 1982; Milgram, 1982), cigarettes (United States Department of Health, Education, and Welfare [USDHEW], 1976), and PCP (Davis, 1982). Information gathered over the past few years by Johnston and his associates seems most representative and relevant to this chapter. Readers interested in the use of particular substances in specific geographical locales may consult the other citations.

According to the Johnston data, overall drug use by adolescents can probably be said to have peaked in 1978. At that time, experimentation with cigarettes, alcohol, and marijuana appeared to be the norm (Johnston, Bachman, & O'Malley, 1979). Approximately 60% of all high school students had smoked at least one marijuana cigarette prior to graduation, and similar contact with alcohol and tobacco was almost universal.

Conspicuous minorities of the high-school population also had experimented with hallucinogens (14%), cocaine (13%), inhalants (12%), amphetamines (23%), and sedatives and tranquilizers (16%). (The percentages attached to the latter three drugs do not include medical prescription usage.) Experimental use of opiates was less common (10%), and only 1.6% of the sample had specifically tried heroin.

Further inspection of these 1978 data, however, underscores the importance of distinguishing among various levels of use. Although the percentages of students who have had one experience with a given drug may seem extremely high, these numbers decline rather dramatically if a criterion of 20 or more times in the past year (i.e., once or twice per month) is applied. Figures for such usage are 2.6% for amphetamines and less than 1% for all other drugs (except cigarettes, alcohol, and marijuana). Moreover, the percentages of students involved in higher levels of chronic use show continued substantial decrements.

Certainly these percentages, however small, amount to large numbers of drug-involved youth when extrapolated across the entire population. Nevertheless, the usage-distinction data temper the erroneous but popular impression that experimentation with drugs inevitably implies habit formation.

More recent epidemiological findings indicate some cause for optimism. The current survey by Johnston and his associates (University of Michigan, 1985) on the 1984 graduating class shows that overall substance abuse among adolescents has evidenced a gradual but consistent decrease since 1980. Daily and monthly use of marijuana, for example, have respectively dropped from 11% to 5% and 37% to 25% over the past few years. Cocaine is apparently the only substance exempt from this downward trend. Sharp increases in cocaine usage were evident between 1976 and 1979. Since 1979, however, consumption rates have remained relatively stable at 16% in one's lifetime, 12% annually, and 6% monthly.

This gradual decline in substance abuse by our nation's youth is hardly grounds for complacency. Large numbers of adolescents currently are involved with illegal drugs, and the percentages of those who abuse alcohol and/or cigarettes are serious indeed. For example, the Johnston data indicate that 5% of 1984 high school seniors drink daily and 39% acknowledge having five or more drinks on one occasion during the past 2 weeks (University of Michigan, 1985).

Moreover, the Surgeon General's Report (United States Public Health Service [USPHS], 1979) provides especially troubling data on adolescent tobacco use; 4.9% of males aged 12–14, 18.1% of males aged 15–16, and 31% of males aged 16–17 smoked cigarettes at least weekly in 1974. Female rates for these age brackets were, respectively, 4.2%, 20.2%, and 25.9%. Two thirds of the males and more than half the females exceeded half a pack daily. These figures represent staggering increases since 1968 for young women in the 12–14 and 15–16 age categories (up 816% and 210%, respectively). Given that deaths from lung cancer in women now exceed breast cancer and are accelerating at nearly double the rate of increase for men (United States Department of Health and Human Services [USDHHS], 1984), the morally repugnant Virginia Slims advertisement fails to interpret what "You've come a long way, baby" really means. We in the substance abuse field have a long way to go. Johnston's 1983 data indicate that 21% of high school seniors continue to smoke cigarettes on a daily basis, with 13.8% exceeding the half-pack per day criterion (Johnston et al., 1984).

ASSESSMENT AND DIAGNOSIS

Facilities that treat adolescent drug abusers (Owen & Nyberg, 1983) frequently claim use of the *Diagnostic and Statistical Manual of Mental Disorders, 3rd edition (DSM-III)* (American Psychiatric Association, 1980). The *DSM-III* distinguishes between adult substance abuse and substance dependence, but does not make separate provisions for these problems when they occur in childhood or adolescence.

Substance abuse is defined as a pattern of pathological use that causes an impairment in social or occupational functioning that lasts at least 1 month. *Substance dependence*, on the other hand, requires physiological involvement as evidenced by either tolerance or withdrawal. This means that increased doses are required to maintain the effect and that discontinuance of the drug produces unpleasant physical symptoms. Interestingly, tobacco is excluded from the abuse category. However, one can abuse and/or depend on all other drugs. Finally, the *DSM-III* describes the possible courses of the disorder as continuous, episodic, in remission, or unspecified.

Despite its widespread adoption, the *DSM-III* is not particularly helpful for assessing the possible goals or various approaches to intervention. These goals can be crudely classified along three dimensions, namely, *relevance, assessment mode*, and *success criteria*.

Relevance

The "bottom line" for professionals in the substance abuse field is drug abuse behavior. Has consumption frequency, quantity, and/or variety decreased as a result of our intervention? Several other variables frequently are mentioned in the literature, although their relevance falls along a wide-ranging continuum.

Some substance abuse intervention programs, for example, attempt to modify drug attitudes or drug knowledge in addition to drug behavior. The general rationale for this activity is presumably that both antidrug attitudes and increased knowledge about drugs ultimately will manifest themselves in lowered levels of substance-abuse behavior. Because attitude scales are typically more malleable than usage indices, they offer a potential consolation prize for the evaluator when no changes are registered in the actual behavioral data.

Similarly, gains in drug knowledge are relatively easy to effect. However the relationship between drug knowledge and drug use is extremely complex. For example, the inhibiting effects of drug knowledge on drug use have not yet been clearly established. Moreover, some subsets of the knowledge variable either result from or covary with drug use (see Horan & Harrison, 1981).

Although the need to reduce actual drug-abuse behavior in chronically addicted populations is obvious, there are a number of methodological difficulties involved with extrapolating that goal to projects seeking the prevention of future substance abuse. For instance, two junior-high-school classes exposed to experimental and control drug education programs will in all probability show no immediate differences on a behavioral use scale. In fact, eyeballing the data often will reveal that, on a short-range basis, actual drug-taking behavior is negligible (if not nonexistent) among all subjects. Moreover, the interval between program completion and posttesting is so short that a majority of subjects could not be expected to even have access to many of the substances. In such cases, the project evaluator must wait several years after conducting the program, when the seducing influences of history and maturation have taken their toll, before collecting behavioral data capable of being analyzed in a meaningful manner.

Recognizing the need for some sort of preliminary feedback, Horan and Williams (1975) suggested changing the wording of posttest usage questionnaires so that respondents could indicate whether they would try a particular substance if given the opportunity. Further verbal embellishments could presumably tap desired usage beyond the exploratory level. On the other hand, because all of this consumption activity is hypothetical, whatever is being assessed may be more indicative of transient attitudes than drug abuse behavior.

In addition to the literature on assessing drug knowledge, attitudes, and behavior, there is a growing body of evidence that social skill deficiencies play a causal role in the development of substance abuse and that increasing one's interpersonal competence can contribute to the amelioration or prevention of a drug problem (e.g., Marlatt & Donovan, 1981; Van Hasselt, Hersen, & Milliones, 1978). Thus, measures of social skill appear highly appropriate to drug abuse assessment and program evaluation.

Unfortunately, many of the instruments that have been used in the evaluation of drug abuse prevention projects are empirically irrelevant to the drug problem. The typical drug education program of the past decade, for example, is more likely to have been evaluated with a measure of self-acceptance than a survey of subsequent drug use. We believe that pursuits of popular humanistic goals should be supported on the basis of their own merits, rather than with redirected drug abuse prevention resources. Although such measures certainly could supplement a drug use assessment battery in order to examine possible covariations, it is unfortunate that many drug abuse prevention programs have abandoned their primary purpose.

Assessment Mode

In addition to the dimension of relevance, drug abuse assessment variables can be examined from the standpoint of assessment mode. For example, data may be derived from self-report, other report, unobtrusive observations, and/or physiological monitoring. Although any drug-related outcome, including social-skills improvement, can be viewed through these channels, our primary concern here is with drug abuse behavior.

Self-reported drug use is the most common form of assessment. Yet, this data collection mode is inherently vulnerable to questions of validity. Might not subjects "fake good," for example, in order to avoid even the slightest possibility of eventual legal harrassment or criminal prosecution? Researchers who do not secure a priori legal guarantees may be subject to subpoena of their records or their knowledge of an individual's use of illegal drugs. Thus, respondent suspiciousness is adaptive, not paranoid!

Even when confidentiality is guaranteed by the experimenter, different self-report assessment procedures per se may exert systematic influence on outcome. In one study, for example, only 18% of a group of interviewed subjects admitted to using or experimenting with drugs "harder" than marijuana and hashish, whereas 46% of an equivalent group acknowledged doing so on anonymous questionnaires (Horan, Wescott, Vetovich, & Swisher, 1974).

Although inclusion of items, such as "How often have you taken curare?" (a little known drug causing paralysis) can assist in identifying protocols of the "faking severe" variety (Horan, 1972; Horan & Swisher, 1973), self-report offers no way of determining how many individuals deny or minimize their drug-taking activity.

Attempting to confirm self-report data by questioning individuals residing with the subject (other report), can increase one's confidence in the data, or even provide an alternate measure. However, significant others also are quite capable of distorting the truth. The validity of their answers depends on whether they have a pipeline to the subject's private consumatory behavior.

Unobtrusive behavioral measures of the sort described by Webb, Campbell, Schwartz, and Sechrest (1966) would undoubtedly resolve some of the problems with self-report. Present Orwellian speculation includes urinalysis via clandestine taps into institutional (or even residential) plumbing systems and the use of dogs trained in marijuana detection surreptitiously sniffing at experimental and control student lockers during the night. It goes without saying that such devices are, at least, costly and cumbersome and, at most, repugnant and illegal (see Flygare, 1979). At present, the art of unobtrusive drug-behavior assessment remains impractical.

Chemical Verification of Self-Report:
An Extended Digression

Chemical analyses of bodily products, such as breath, saliva, blood, or urine, are highly touted methods for verifying self-reported drug use. For example, smoking behavior can be objectively checked by noting the level of expired air carbon monoxide (CO) contained in a sample of a subject's breath (see Horan, Hackett, & Linberg, 1978; Lando, 1975). Nonsmokers rarely exceed a few parts per million (ppm) CO. Smokers, on the other hand, typically range from 20 to 80 ppm CO, depending on the severity of their habit. Smoking behavior also can be detected by noting the level of thiocyanate in the blood (Brockway, 1978) or nicotine in the urine (Paxton & Bernacca, 1979).

Similarly, alcohol consumption is readily discernible from analysis of a subject's breath, blood, or urine. Indeed, when prosecuting drunk drivers, law enforcement personnel frequently rely on legal definitions of intoxication expressed in terms of blood alcohol concentration (Miller, Hersen, Eisler, & Watts, 1974). Finally, urine tests exist for detecting morphine, barbituates, amphetamines, and other drugs. In fact, the Food and Drug Administration requires such testing on a regular basis for addicts enrolled in methadone maintenance programs (Edwards, 1972; Goldstein & Brown, 1969; Trellis, Smith, Alston, & Siassi, 1975).

The limitations of chemical assays for drug use have not received widespread publicity. In the first place, they are not foolproof. We know of one enterprising subject, for example, who wore a rubber bulb filled with his nondrug-involved roommate's urine in the pit of his arm. During assessment periods, he simply squeezed the bulb and forced the fluid through a pliable tube (concealed beneath his shirt sleeve) into the test receptacle.

Other limitations may be much more serious. One problem emerges when the half-life of the substance being monitored is relatively brief. For example, in the test for verifying a smoker's self-report described above, the amount of CO in a smoker's breath actually reflects the quantity of carboxyhemoglobin (COHb) in the smoker's blood. COHb has a half-life of about 5 hours. This means that if a heavy smoker registering 80 ppm CO abstains for 5 hours, the reading will drop to 40 ppm, then to 20 ppm after another 5 hours, and so forth. A smoker abstaining for a day or even less might not be detected with this technique. Ironically, the existence of a long half-life poses its own set of problems. Thiocyanate, for example, has a half-life of 14 days, which means that traces may be present nearly a month after subjects validly report that they stopped smoking.

Each chemical assay procedure has its own set of limitations. Some tests can easily be confounded by the dietary habits of subjects or by their legitimate use of patent or prescribed medication. No test is fully reliable even when conducted by closely supervised, highly competent personnel. However, unacceptable low reliability is only one of a host of problems that can occur when the researcher-therapist relies on commercial laboratories to conduct the analyses (see Trellis et al., 1975). If researchers choose not to delegate control, they face equipment costs that may run quite high. For example, an Ecolyzer,* which measures only CO, currently costs $1,045. The capital costs of gas-liquid chromatography (glc) equipment often used in urinary analyses ranges from $4,000 to $6,000 (Paxton & Bernacca, 1979). Technical skill requirements also vary. The Ecolyzer mandates little more than literacy; glc equipment, on the other hand, demands a fair degree of laboratory savvy.

---

*Energetics Science, Inc., Hawthorne, New York.

The obtrusiveness of chemical assays poses two sets of problems. First, subject resistance fluctuates with the nature of the bodily product being assayed. Breath and saliva tests routinely pose no problem. Urine specimen requests are occasionally refused. Many subjects, however, will balk at having blood samples drawn, especially if such monitoring is required on a regular basis. Second, the generalization potential of treatment programs evaluated with chemical assays is difficult to determine. The pretest is undoubtedly a highly reactive event. Therefore, complex Solomon-type experimental designs may be required to adequately sort out treatment effects from those attributable to testing-treatment interface (Campbell & Stanley, 1966).

In spite of the fact that the foregoing commentary might be construed as pessimistic, we strongly believe that chemical collaboration of self-report data is of utmost importance in the context of research on addictions treatment. Apart from the utility of biological assays in their own right, their use undoubtedly increases the accuracy of self-report measures. Most work with adolescents, however, is school-based and prevention-oriented. Although chemical assays can be routinely embedded in medical, military, or penal settings, their application to school populations, for example, may elicit objections grounded on the U.S. Constitution and Bill of Rights. Thus, except for a few recent endeavors targeting smoking behavior, no drug-education program, to our knowledge, has ever been evaluated with chemically verified self-report data.

Success Criteria

The final assessment dimension is the definition of program success, which presumably ought to be the mirror image of what constitutes a clinical problem. Decreased consumption frequency (evidenced by self-report and/or lowered quantities of targeted biological compounds) is a consensually validated objective.

In the case of cigarette smoking, we would further argue that abstinence provides the most meaningful test of treatment efficacy. Complete elimination of the habit is the goal sought by most smokers undergoing treatment. This is a wise choice, as those who simply reduce their consumption level eventually return to baseline (Lichtenstein & Danaher, 1976). Moreover, abstinence represents the ultimate reduction of health hazard. For research purposes, abstinence data generate the most confidence. In the first place, subjects can discriminate whether they are smoking or not with greater accuracy than rate estimation allows. Likewise, a person in the environment nominated by the subject to confirm the self-report can more readily do so with abstinence rather than with rate-reduction criteria. Finally, abstinence is easier to verify than lowered consumption level with biological assays.

Perfect abstinence (e.g., zero consumption over time) is readily understood, but researchers do not treat "blemished" abstinence (e.g., a single consumption episode in a follow-up period) with consistency. Moreover, given the previously discussed difficulties of distinguishing use from abuse, and the epidemiological normalcy of experimentation with some substances, it is difficult to argue that perfect abstinence from all other drugs is either desirable and/or attainable. The concept of "controlled drinking," for example, has been frequently defended as a viable outcome in the treatment of alcoholism (Lloyd & Salzberg, 1975; Lovibond & Caddy, 1970; Pattison, Sobell, & Sobell, 1977), albeit not without controversy (Miller & Caddy, 1977).

INTERVENTION

Practitioners in the drug abuse field typically function in one of three roles: (a) prevention, (b) crisis intervention, or (c) treatment of the addicted. These three enterprises also are known respectively as primary, secondary, and tertiary prevention (see Swisher, 1979). However, given that substance abuse already is occurring in the latter two cases, use of the term *prevention* is probably a misnomer.

The majority of drug abuse work with adolescents falls within the strictly defined *prevention* category. Drug education and drug abuse prevention are essentially interchangeable descriptors for intervention activities directed toward general audiences who are not (yet) using drugs. The accent is on avoidance of future abuse rather than on reduction of present consumption levels.

The *crisis intervention* enterprise usually occupies a very short period between that point in time when prevention has failed and treatment begins. Crisis intervention includes specific activities, such as "telephone hotline" work with highly anxious callers and emergency room management of barbiturate comas. This subset of the drug abuse field is largely outside the scope of our chapter.

Most of the *addictions treatment* literature involves adults, or at least older adolescents. Although the problem of youthful addiction may seem ubiquitous, published accounts of specific treatment programs are rare. There also may be conceptual difficulties with extrapolating the logic and data implications of adult treatment downward to the youthful addict.

Prevention Programming

There is an enormous body of literature written in the name of drug education (see Blum, 1976; Evans, D'Augelli, & Branca, 1976; Goodstadt, 1974; Ostman, 1976; Shain, Riddell, & Kelty, 1977). Horan and Harrison's (1981) review, however, indicated that only 26 published references were to intervention endeavors that included drug-related outcome measures. Further, only a third of the studies cited met the main requirement of true experimentation, namely random assignment to experimental conditions. Moreover, some projects apparently were conducted in the absence of a coherent theoretical base. Most were not replicable due to the undefined or undefinable nature of the independent variable, and data analysis errors seemed to be the norm rather than the exception. Schaps, DiBartolo, Moskowitz, and Churgin (1981) were able to locate 75 citable projects (of which 69% were unpublished) and expressed similar dismay about the lack of design quality in this literature.

Drug abuse prevention programs are typically directed at fostering one or more of the following objectives: (a) increasing knowledge about drugs, (b) promoting healthy attitudes about drugs, and (c) decreasing potential drug-abuse behavior in the general population (Horan, Shute, Swisher, & Westcott, 1973; Warner, Swisher, & Horan, 1973). Unfortunately, serious conceptual and methodological problems are inherent in these goals (Horan, 1974; Horan & Harrison, 1981). For example, there is a lack of professional consensus on just what constitutes a "healthy" drug attitude. Moreover, prevention by definition implies a reduced probability of future substance abuse. Yet, only 4 of the 26 projects in the Horan and Harrison (1981) review included any sort of follow-up evaluation effort.

Information-based programming is the most common prevention modality. Its logic ultimately can be traced to classical decision theory (see Bauman, 1980; Broadhurst, 1976; Bross, 1953; Horan, 1979; Mausner, 1973). However, such linkage is rarely articulated. Recall that, according to this perspective, our choice between two or more alternatives (e.g., the taking of or abstaining from drugs) depends on the utilities inherent in each alternative and their probabilities of occurrence. Essentially, we act to maximize subjectively expected utility (SEU), that is, we pick the alternative with the greatest likely payoff.

The logic of information-based programming is thus fairly clear: if we provide our youth with an awareness of the dangerous consequences of drug use (negative utilities) and indicate to them that their consequences are indeed highly probable, the drug avoidance option is virtually assured. No rational human being would select an alternative with a comparably low SEU value! Indirect support for such a rationale was provided by Halliday (1976), who demonstrated that drug attitudes can be manipulated by varying the kind of information supplied to the individual.

Unfortunately, information-based approaches to prevention frequently get tangled up in yarn of their own making. Drug educators, however well-intentioned, often distort the facts about drugs to such an extent that the potential user is apt to find more correct information about drugs in the drug culture than in the classroom. Most accompanying instructional materials—films, posters, pamphlets, etc.—likewise attempt to miseducate (see National Coordinating Council on Drug Education [NCCDE], 1972; Globetti, 1975).

Current drug educators who wish to wipe the slate clean, to begin anew with dispassionate portrayals of factual information, will find it difficult to overcome the stereotypes fostered by their predecessors. In fact, the perceptual set of the consumer audience may now be a highly reactive obstacle to drug education program evaluation.

From an empirical standpoint, Horan and Harrison's (1981) review indicated that, compared to no-treatment control groups, information-based drug education curricula can raise drug knowledge levels (as measured by achievement tests keyed to the particular program). Such findings are not especially noteworthy, however, given that we might expect parallel outcomes from any high-school course in geometry or civics. Information-based programming is not likely to meaningfully alter attitudes or drug-use behavior until its implementation corresponds to the decision-making framework on which it ought to be based (e.g., the information needs to be perceived as accurate and relevant to the consumption decision). Data confirming that possibility have yet to be collected.

Two additional approaches to prevention also were reviewed by Horan and Harrison (1981), namely, induced cognitive dissonance and behavioral group counseling. The former derives from extrapolations of Festinger's (1957) work by Rokeach (1971), who showed that decreases in racial prejudice could be affected by pointing out the inconsistency between certain values claimed by the subjects and the holding of a bigoted attitude. Behavioral group counseling evolved from the work of Krumboltz and his students (see Krumboltz & Baker, 1973), who found that modeling and verbal reinforcement procedures could facilitate vocational information-seeking. Drug educators presumed that similar procedures could foster the development of attitudes and behaviors incompatible with the taking of drugs. Unfortunately, the implementation of these techniques can be unwieldy (e.g., student models may model the wrong behavior). Also, the empirical stature of both approaches is equivocal at best.

The exhaustive review by Schaps et al. (1981) categorizes the literature into 10 intervention strategies: information, persuasion, affective–skill, affective–experiential, counseling, tutoring/teaching, peer group, family, program development, and alternatives. They note that several of the strategies are relatively unused, whereas many others were deployed in various combinations. Only 10 studies met their minimal criteria for design quality and service delivery intensity. Of these, only two showed an impact on drug use. Given that the compilation by Schaps et al. (1981) began with 75 published and unpublished documents that contained 127 evaluated programs, the fact that 2 should emerge as promising is not surprising and indeed might be expected by chance alone. Unfortunately, their review does not provide a reference list, thus precluding closer inspection of the database.

Against this pessimistic backdrop, there is emerging evidence in support of social skills approaches to prevention (see Pentz, 1983). We illustrate with one of our own projects on assertion training.

Case Example: Assertion Training as a Drug Abuse Prevention Strategy

Assertion training is an extremely popular and thoroughly documented vehicle for enabling individuals to do "what they really want" in particular social situations (e.g., Alberti, 1977; Galassi, Galassi, & Litz, 1974; Heimberg, Montgomery, Madsen, & Heimberg, 1977; McFall & Marston, 1970). As a drug abuse prevention strategy, assertion training rests on the assumption that many youths, who would otherwise opt to abstain from taking drugs, reluctantly participate because they lack the interpersonal skills necessary to extricate themselves from social situations where drug use is imminent.

Recall that, in terms of classical decision theory, the probable role of peer approval as a utility (or disapproval as a negative utility) accruing from drug abstinence or consumption is difficult to overstate. However, SEUs other than those pertaining to the likelihood of peer approval/disapproval also are relevant to drug decisions. For example, the potential user may additionally estimate (however crudely) the probabilities of euphoric and adverse physiological consequences. Thus, the role of assertion training as a drug abuse prevention strategy is limited to simply shoring up the possibility of free choice. Following such training, youths could still decide to take drugs (on the basis of other SEUs), but in so doing they would not be capitulating to peer pressure, as they would have the competence necessary to finesse themselves away from the drug consumption option without losing face.

In order to evaluate the efficacy of this approach, Horan and Williams (1982) randomly assigned 72 nonassertive junior-high students to either assertion training (in which one third of the training stimuli involved drug-use peer pressure), placebo discussions focused on similar topics, or no treatment at all. The experimental and placebo treatments were delivered in the context of five small group counseling sessions of 45 minutes duration over a 2-week period. Each treatment group was composed of three same-sex subjects plus the counselor.

The assertion treatment was based on the intervention model of Galassi et al. (1974), ten general assertiveness (nondrug) training stimuli borrowed from McFall and Marston (1970), and five additional training situations involving peer pressure to use drugs. Essentially, the sessions began with the counselor's instructing about assertiveness and live modeling of an assertive response to a particular training stimulus. Subjects rotated twice in the roles of speaker, listener, and responder for each stimulus. The counselor provided feedback plus additional instruction and modeling, when appropriate, after each subject's role-played response. Three training stimuli (one involving drugs) were used in each counseling session. Typical examples are as follows:

General Assertiveness Training Stimulus

Picture yourself just getting out of class on any old weekday morning. Hmm. You're a little hungry, and some candy or some milk would taste good right about now, so you walk over to the machines and put your money in. You press the button . . . and . . . out it comes. You open it up. Mmm. Whatever it is you just bought, it sure tastes good. It's a good break, right after class. . . . Oh, oh. Here comes your mooching friend again. This person is always borrowing "just a dime" from you. He's getting closer now, and as he gets closer your relaxation sort of changes to irritation. Oh, here he comes. Moocher: "Hey, I don't have any money and I'm hungry. How 'bout loaning me a dime for a candy bar?"

Drug-specific Assertiveness Training Stimulus

You are out for the evening with a group of close friends. While eating some food at a drive-in restaurant, you notice a friend whom you have not seen for awhile and invite him or her over to talk. During the conversation he or she says: "I just got back from the greatest vacation. I was up in the mountains with some friends of my older brother. We really had a wild time!

Hey! You should have been there. I got a chance to try a lot of different drugs that some of the other kids had. I've got some stuff at home. My family isn't home. Come on over and I'll give you some. You all will have the greatest time! Are you coming?"

The results of this study were very promising. At posttest, experimental students showed highly significant gains on behavioral and psychometric measures of assertiveness, as well as decreased willingness to use alcohol and marijuana in comparison to control subjects. At a 3-year follow-up, these students continued to display higher levels of assertiveness and less actual drug use behavior.

Addictions Treatment

Given that exploratory use of cigarettes and alcohol is virtually universal, the foregoing paragraphs on prevention interventions are still relevant. Although consummatory behavior has occurred, there is no real evidence of a clinical problem and interventions more intensive than say, providing information and modeling social skills, may not be cost-beneficial. We would *cautiously* extend this suggestion to include trial episodes of marijuana and some other illegal substances as well. Despite the potentially devastating penal consequences, such behavior does not in and of itself imply psychopathology. Moreover, exploratory forays with several illegal substances occur at sufficient population percentages to be considered within the bounds of statistically normal behavior.

Chronic use of drugs, however, is another matter. Addictions treatment requires a far more extensive scope and budget than is the case with drug education. The classic comprehensive approach to addictions treatment (e.g., Miller & Eisler, 1976) includes three generic objectives: (a) decrease the immediate reinforcing properties of drugs, using, for example, aversion therapies and medications such as Methadone; (b) teach alternative behaviors (e.g., assertiveness); and (c) rearrange the environment so that reinforcement occurs for being "off" drugs. Marlatt's model (e.g., Marlatt & Donovan, 1981) also implies the need for problem-solving skills and cognitive restructuring (the latter to challenge erroneous beliefs about the effects of drugs).

Other theoretical perspectives on addictions treatment also exist. Some of these include: family systems therapy (e.g., Bry, 1983; Reilly, 1984; Reuger & Liberman, 1984), Pentecostal Protestantism (USDHHS, 1980), and self-help derivatives of Alcoholics Anonymous. Although behavioral principles are rarely if ever articulated in this literature, they are nevertheless easily discernable:

> A behavioral analysis shows that these groups provide a potently reinforcing group atmosphere which does not tolerate drug or alcohol abuse. New, more adaptive patterns of behavior are encouraged and reinforced through group approval and increased status within the group. Drinking buddies and addicted friends are replaced with more appropriate role models exhibiting complete abstinence. The fact that the "helping agents" were once abusers of drugs or alcohol and therefore represent successful coping models may foster imitation of their behavior and enhance their reinforcing value. (Miller & Eisler, 1977, p. 392)

Regardless of its theoretical basis, most of the addictions treatment literature involves adults or at least older adolescents. Although the problem of youthful addiction may seem ubiquitous, except for occasional reports of individual cases, published accounts of specific treatment programs are rare. Those that have been published frequently suffer from methodological difficulties. The Teen Challenge Program, for example, reports striking differences between graduates of their facilities and comparison groups on substance abuse indices (USDHHS, 1980). However, because their program requires that participants be heterosexual, free of emotional disturbance, willing to give up TV, radio, and recordings, and become "born again" Christians, and because the comparison groups were made up of drop-outs of their program, their data are difficult to interpret. Conventional canons of evaluation, for example, require that drop-outs and success stories be combined and contrasted against alternative or control treatments initially formed by random assignment of subjects.

On the other hand, there is a growing body of treatment literature specific to cigarette addiction that has been subjected to reasonably rigorous empirical scrutiny. What follows is a synopsis and illustration of the rapid-smoking technique and its alternatives. Unfortunately, most of the supporting data have been derived from adult or older adolescent populations; extrapolations downward may be tenuous.

Rapid Smoking

The single most effective treatment technique to appear in the literature over the past decade is an aversion-conditioning strategy known as rapid smoking. This technique was first mentioned by Lublin (1969). However, Lichtenstein and his associates are credited with most of the procedural refinement and validation (Lichtenstein, Harris, Berchler, Wahl, & Schmahl, 1973; Schmahl, Lichtenstein, & Harris, 1972). Rapid smoking essentially consists of having cigarette users take a normal inhalation every 6 seconds until they are no longer able to do so. Each trial usually lasts about 5 minutes, during which time an average of four or five cigarettes are smoked. Two or three trials punctuated by 5-minute rest periods are given in each of 8 to 12 treatment sessions. Subjects are instructed not to smoke between sessions, and initial sessions are scheduled daily. Early studies found that rapid smoking alone produced 60% abstinence rates (verified by independent informants) 6 months after termination of treatment. However, multiple-year follow-ups of these investigations have shown some disappointing relapse rates (Lichtenstein & Rodrigues, 1977). Current investigations also have produced less impressive results. Danaher's (1977) comprehensive review points out that many of the failures to replicate may be due to changes in the standard treatment format.

The principal drawback of the rapid-smoking procedure involves a controversy concerning medical risk. Rapid-smoking is specifically designed to induce physiological discomfort. It does so through bodily absorption of greatly increased quantities of tobacco smoke, which contains particularly reactive ingredients like nicotine and carbon monoxide. Because larger doses of these compounds can severely strain one's cardiovascular system, the rapid-smoking procedure is absolutely unsuitable for individuals with coronary or pulmonary diseases. Although the technique is probably safe for normal smokers, the question of which screening criteria are adequate for routine clinical practice has not been satisfactorily answered, and consultation with a cardiologist is highly recommended (e.g., see Linberg, Horan, Hodgson, & Buskirk, 1982).

Risk-Free Alternatives to Rapid Smoking

Normal-paced aversive smoking (NPAS) (Danaher & Lichtenstein, 1978) and focused smoking (Hackett & Horan, 1978, 1979) are highly promising risk-free alternatives to the rapid-smoking procedure. Although both procedures were independently conceived and developed, they continue to evolve in the same direction. NPAS was distilled from an attention-placebo treatment involving Bantron (a nicotine chewing gum). Focused smoking initially resembled an in vivo form of covert sensitization (i.e., horror images pertaining to the potential consequences of smoking experienced during the act of smoking). However, over the course of several unpublished pilot investigations, realistic images and experiences began to be emphasized. Both NPAS and focused smoking are now sufficiently similar to permit the following common description.

The general rationale and context are similar to rapid smoking. Subjects sit facing a blank wall and smoke at their normal rate while being cued by the experimenter to focus on the discomforts of smoking. These include, for example, a bad taste in the mouth, a burning in the throat, and feelings of light-headedness and nausea. As treatment progresses, other negative sensations reported by subjects are incorporated (e.g., shakiness, sweating, dull headaches, difficulty in breathing, and an uncomfortable, heavy, tired feeling). Reminders to concentrate only on the effects of smoking are repeatedly provided. Hackett and Horan (1978, 1979) report that the procedure is comparable to rapid smoking in terms of reported discomfort and treatment success (verified abstinence 40 to 60% after 6 months). Yet, all of the medical risks associated with rapid smoking are avoided.

CURRENT APPROACHES

The role of assertion training as a drug abuse prevention strategy (in the case example described earlier) was limited to that of fostering the competence to say "no" in peer pressure situations focused on drug use. More fully developed social skills programs currently are being designed and evaluated with promising preliminary results (cf. Botvin, 1983; McAlister, 1983; Pentz, 1983).

Although social skills are critical to adaptive decisions about drugs, other competencies also seem relevant. Thus, we would opt for a comprehensive programming approach. At the core of such a program we would envision an instructional unit conforming to the implications of classical decision theory; namely, accurate information regarding the utilities of drug use and abstinence along with their probabilities of occurrence (including synopses of dissenting opinions). We find the misinformation contained in most drug prevention endeavors to be educationally and ethically abhorrent.

Classical decision theory is, however, woefully inadequate to the task. For example, it assumes that all alternatives are known and that all utilities are rational. Consequently, we would hope that when developing their curricula, drug educators pay close attention to the expanding problem-solving and decision-making literatures, which include strategies to help students: (a) define their choice problems, (b) enlarge their response repertoires, (c) identify pertinent information, and (d) implement their desired alternative (Horan, 1979; Moskowitz, 1983).

The foregoing research foci are quite consistent with traditional perspectives on dealing with substance abuse. In addition to primary, secondary, and tertiary prevention, a fourth professional role is beginning to emerge, namely that of public policy formation. At least three phenomena evidence the birth of this role.

Media Interventions

In an attempt to reach large audiences, the National Institute on Drug Abuse (NIDA) has recently sponsored the "Just Say No" advertising campaign, geared towards arming youths with refusal skills similar to those targeted by assertion training programs. Moreover, The National Broadcasting Corporation (NBC), borrowing a NIDA slogan, has aired public service announcements featuring popular actors as role models exclaiming "don't be a dope" when it comes to using drugs. Finally, the Department of Transportation has produced a television campaign featuring the music of Michael Jackson directed at discouraging teenagers from drinking and driving.

Although such efforts await empirical validation, it is important to note that they have a coherent theoretical base in the social skills and vicarious-learning literatures, that they are replicable and easily refinable, and that their cost–benefit potential may prove to be vastly superior to labor-intensive traditional interventions. (However, see Flay & Sobel, 1983, for a thorough critique of previous work in this area.)

Political Action Groups

Recently, the continuing national tragedy of alcohol-related automobile fatalities has received enormous national attention. This is largely due to the efforts of grass-roots organizations, such as Mothers Against Drunk Driving (MADD), Students Against Driving Drunk (SADD), and Remove Intoxicated Drivers (RID). Their influence is felt in at least two ways. First, they have pressured legislators to changes in law and judges to respond in a consistent manner. Second, they have contributed to the development of a media-supported social ethic in which having "one for the road" is increasingly viewed as irresponsible, if not criminal, on the part of both host and driver.

Legislative Policy

In response to the youth movement of the late 1960s and early 1970s ("We can die in Vietnam, but we can't vote or drink"), 29 states lowered their minimum legal drinking age. This legislative action led to an increase in alcohol-related traffic fatalities that did not occur in other states (Smart & Goodstadt, 1977; Williams, Rich, Zador, & Robertson, 1975). In a recent study of nine states that raised the minimum age, traffic fatalities showed a corresponding decline. The investigators (Williams, Zador, Harris, & Karpf, 1983) estimate that if all states raised their minimum drinking age to 21, there would be more than 700 fewer young drivers involved in fatal nighttime crashes each year.

Research findings such as these have been presented at congressional hearings (e.g., *Congressional Record*, 1984, June 26). In July of 1984, legislation urging states to comply with a nationwide minimum drinking age of 21 was passed. States that do not comply by 1987 could lose between $2 and $90 million in Federal highway construction funds. The bill also offers incentive grants to states that (a) enact tough laws against driving under the influence of alcohol and/or other drugs, (b) computerize traffic records to determine accident locations and identify problem drivers, and (c) create research and rehabilitation programs.

Tobacco also has been the target of increased legislative activity. In 1984, cigarette manufacturers were required to rotate four new and harsher warnings on cigarette packs about the specific hazards of cigarette smoking. Similar action taken in Sweden apparently resulted in a significant decline in smoking, especially among teenagers (Bayh & Neumeyer, 1984).

SUMMARY

Cigarettes and alcohol often are inappropriately excluded from discussions of drug abuse. The concepts of "use" and "abuse" are difficult to differentiate. We prefer to view the latter in terms of tissue damage and sustained psychological dysfunction. Behavioral variables, classical decision theory, and comprehensive models by Lichtenstein and Marlatt provide insights into the etiology of substance abuse, including, for example, the need to differentiate initiation from maintenance. Epidemiological work supports this distinction and further indicates that although the problem of substance abuse probably peaked in 1978, large numbers of our nation's youths are involved with drugs. Diagnostic devices and treatment goals can be crudely classified along the dimensions of relevance (e.g., consummatory behavior, social skills), assessment mode (e.g., self-report, biochemical assays), and criteria for success. Interventions are similarly classified in terms of prevention, crisis management, and addiction treatment. Social skills training, particularly the enhancement of assertiveness, has proved to be an effective prevention mode. Addictions treatment, however, is quite complex. Rapid smoking and its less hazardous alternatives are quite appropriate for adult smokers, but extrapolations downward to adolescence may be tenuous. Current intervention activity reflects a comprehensive programming perspective that includes, for example, (accurate) drug information, expanded social skills enhancement, and problem-solving training. Additional efforts by the media, political action groups, and legislators are evident.

REFERENCES

Alberti, R. (1977). *Assertiveness: Innovations, applications, issues*. San Luis Obispo, CA: Impact.

American Psychiatric Association. (1980). *Diagnostic and statistical manual of mental disorders* (3rd ed.). Washington, DC: Author.

Bauman, K. E. (1980). *Predicting adolescent drug use: The utility structure and marijuana*. New York: Praeger.

Bayh, B., & Neumeyer, D. B. (1984, September 10). Four-warninged is forearmed. *The New York Times*, A21.

Blum, R. H. (1976). *Drug education: Results and recommendations*. Lexington, MA: Brooks.

Borland, B. L., & Randolph, J. P. (1975). Relative effects of low socio-economic status, parental smoking, and poor scholastic performance on smoking among high school students. *Social Science and Medicine, 9*, 27–30.

Botvin, G. J. (1983). Prevention of adolescent substance abuse through the development of personal and social competence. In T. J. Glynn, C. G. Leukefeld, & J. P. Ludford (Eds.), *Preventing adolescent drug abuse: Intervention strategies*. NIDA Research Monograph Series 47 (pp. 115–140). Washington, DC: U.S. Government Printing Office.

Broadhurst, A. (1976). Applications of the psychology of decisions. In M. P. Feldman & A. Broadhurst (Eds.), *Theoretical and experimental bases of the behavior therapies*. London: Wiley.

Brockway, B. S. (1978). Chemical validation of self-reported smoking rates. *Behavior Therapy, 9*, 685–686.

Bross, I. D. J. (1953). *Design for decision: An introduction to statistical decision-making*. New York: Macmillan.

Bry, B. H. (1983). Empirical foundations of family-based approaches to adolescent substance abuse. In T. J. Glynn, C. G. Luekefeld, & J. P. Ludford (Eds.), *Preventing adolescent drug abuse: Intervention strategies*. NIDA Monograph Series 47 (pp. 154–171). Washington, DC: U.S. Government Printing Office.

Cahoon, D. D., & Crosby, C. C. (1972). A learning approach to chronic drug use: Sources of reinforcement. *Behavior Therapy, 3*, 64–71.

Califano, J. A. (1979). The secretary's foreword. In U.S. Public Health Service, *Smoking and health: A report of the Surgeon General* DHEW, USPHS Publication No. 79-50066). Washington, DC: U.S. Government Printing Office.

Campbell, D. T., & Stanley, J. C. (1966). *Experimental and quasi-experimental designs for research*. Chicago: Rand McNally.

Congressional Record. (1984, June 26). *Congressional Record-Senate. Proceedings and debates of the 98th Congress, Second session. Hearings on motor vehicle safety programs*. Washington, DC: U.S. Government Printing Office.

Danaher, B. G. (1977). Research on rapid smoking: Interim summary and recommendations. *Addictive Behaviors, 2*, 151–166.

Danaher, B. G., & Lichtenstein, E. (1978). *How to become an ex-smoker*. Englewood Cliffs, NJ: Prentice Hall.

Davis, B. L. (1982). The PCP epidemic: A critical review. *International Journal of the Addictions, 17*, 1137–1155.

Dericco, D. A., & Garlington, W. K. (1977). The effect of modeling and disclosure of experimenter's intent on drinking rate of college students. *Addictive Behaviors, 2*, 135–139.

Edwards, C. C. (1972). Conditions for investigational use of methadone for maintenance programs for narcotic addicts. *Federal Register, 35*, 9014–9015.

Evans, K., D'Augelli, J., & Branca, M. (1976). *Decisions are possible*. University Park, PA: Addictions Prevention Laboratory, The Pennsylvania State University.

Festinger, L. (1957). *A theory of cognitive dissonance*. Evanston, Il: Row, Peterson.

Fisher, W. S. (1984). *Drug and alcohol use among New Jersey high school students, 1984*. Trenton, NJ: New Jersey Department of Law and Public Safety, Division of Criminal Justice.

Flay, B. R., & Sobel, J. L. (1983). The role of mass media in preventing adolescent substance abuse. In T. J. Glynn, C. G. Leukefeld, & J. P. Ludford (Eds.), *Preventing adolescent drug abuse: Intervention strategies*. NIDA 47 (pp. 5–35). Washington, DC: U.S. Government Printing Office.

Flygare, T. J. (1979). Detecting drugs in school: The legality of scent dogs and strip searches. *Phi Delta Kappan, 61*, 280–281.

Galassi, J. P., Galassi, M. D., & Litz, M. C. (1974). Asssertion training in groups using video feedback. *Journal of Counseling Psychology, 21*, 390–394.

Globetti, G. (1975). An appraisal of drug education programs. In R. J. Gibbins, Y. Israel, H. Kalant, R. E. Popham, W. Schmidt, & R. G. Smart (Eds.), *Research advances in alcohol and drug problems*. New York: Wiley.

Goldstein, A., & Brown, B. W. (1969). Urine testing schedules in methadone maintenance treatment of heroin addiction. *Journal of the American Medical Association, 214*, 311, 315.

Goodstadt, M. S. (Ed.). (1974). *Research on methods and programs of drug education*. Toronto: Alcoholism and Drug Addiction Research Foundation.

Hackett, G., & Horan, J. J. (1978). Focused smoking: An unequivocally safe alternative to the rapid smoking procedure. *Journal of Drug Education, 8*, 261–266.

Hackett, G., & Horan, J. J. (1979). Partial component analysis of a comprehensive smoking program. *Addictive Behaviors, 4*, 259–262.

Halliday, G. W. (1976). Effect of fact valence on drug attitude. *Journal of Drug Education, 6*, 89–95.

Hawkins, R. D. (1982). Adolescent alcohol abuse: A

review. *Journal of Developmental and Behavioral Pediatrics, 3,* 2, 83–87.

Heimberg, D. G., Montgomery, D., Madsen, C. H., & Heimberg, J. S. (1977). Assertion training: A review of the literature. *Behavior Therapy, 8,* 953–971.

Horan, J. J. (1972). *An improved scale for quantifying drug abuse behavior.* Unpublished research instrument, The Pennsylvania State University, University Park.

Horan, J. J. (1973). Preventing drug abuse through behavior change technology. *Journal of the Student Personnel Association for Teacher Education (SPATE), 11,* 145–152.

Horan, J. J. (1974). Outcome difficulties in drug education. *Review of Educational Research, 44,* 203–211.

Horan, J. J. (1979). *Counseling for effective decision making. A cognitive behavioral perspective.* North Scituate, MA: Duxbury Press.

Horan, J. J., Hackett, G., & Linberg, S. (1978). Factors to consider when using expired air carbon monoxide smoking assessment. *Addictive Behaviors, 3,* 25–28.

Horan, J. J., & Harrison, R. P. (1981). Drug abuse by children and adolescents: Perspective on incidence, etiology, assessment, and prevention programming. In B. B. Lahey & A. E. Kazdin (Eds.), *Advances in clinical child psychology,* (Vol. 4, pp. 283–330). New York: Plenum Press.

Horan, J. J., Shute, R. E., Swisher, J. D., & Westcott, T. B. (1973). A training model for drug abuse prevention: Content and evaluation. *Journal of Drug Education, 3,* 121–126.

Horan, J. J., & Swisher, J. D. (1973). The Pennsylvania State University Drug Education Evaluation Scales, Part IIIB. In A. Abrams, E. Garfield, & J. D. Swisher (Eds.), *Accountability in drug education: A model for evaluation* (pp. 94–96). Washington, DC: Drug Abuse Council.

Horan, J. J., Westcott, T. B., Vetovich, C., & Swisher, J. D. (1974). Drug usage: An experimental comparison of three assessment conditions. *Psychological Reports, 35,* 211–215.

Horan, J. J., & Williams, J. M. (1975). The tentative drug use scale: A quick and relatively problem-free outcome measure for drug abuse prevention projects. *Journal of Drug Education, 5,* 91–94.

Horan, J. J., & Williams, J. M. (1982). Longitudinal study of assertion training as a drug abuse prevention strategy. *American Educational Research Journal, 19,* 341–351.

Johnston, L. D., Bachman, J. G., & O'Malley, P. M. (1979). *Drugs and the class of '78: Behaviors, attitudes, and recent national trends* (DHEW, USPHS Publication No. [ADM] 79–877). Washington, DC: U.S. Government Printing Office.

Johnston, L. D., O'Malley, P. M., & Bachman, J. G. (1984). *Highlights from drugs and American high school students, 1975–1983.* Rockville, MD: NIDA.

Kandel, D. B. (1974a). Inter- and intra-generational influences on adolescent marihuana use. *Journal of Social Issues, 30,* 107–135.

Kandel, D. B. (1974b). Interpersonal influences on adolescent illegal drug use. In E. Josephson & E. E. Carroll (Eds.), *Drug use: Epidemiological and socio-logical approaches.* Washington, DC: Hemisphere.

Kandel, D. B., Kessler, R. C., & Margulies, R. Z. (1978). Antecedents of adolescent initiation into stages of drug use: A developmental analysis. In D. B. Kandel (Ed.), *Longitudinal research on drug use: Empirical findings and methodological issues.* Washington, DC: Hemisphere.

Krumboltz, J. D., & Baker, R. D. (1973). Behavioral counseling for vocational decisions. In H. Borow (Ed.), *Career guidance for a new age* (pp. 235–284). Boston: Houghton Mifflin.

Lando, H. A. (1975). An objective check upon self-reported smoking levels. *Behavior Therapy, 6,* 547–549.

Levitt, E. E., & Edwards, J. A. (1970). A multivariate study of correlative factors in youthful cigarette smoking. *Developmental Psychology, 2,* 5–11.

Lichtenstein, E. (1982). The smoking problem: A behavioral perspective. *Journal of Consulting and Clinical Psychology, 50,* 804–819.

Lichtenstein, E., & Brown, R. A. (1980). Smoking cessation methods: Review and recommendations. In W. R. Miller (Ed.), *The addictive behaviors* (pp. 169–206). Oxford: Pergamon.

Lichtenstein, E., & Danaher, B. G. (1976). Modification of smoking behavior: A critical analysis of theory, research, and practice. In M. Hersen, M. Eisler, & P. M. Miller (Eds.), *Progress in behavior modification* (Vol. 3, pp. 79–132). New York: Academic.

Lichtenstein, E., Harris, D. E., Birchler, G. P., Wahl, J. M., & Schmahl, D. P. (1973). Comparison of rapid smoking, warm smoky air, and attention placebo in the modification of smoking behavior. *Journal of Consulting and Clinical Psychology, 40,* 92–98.

Lichtenstein, E., & Rodrigues, M. P. (1977). Long-term effects of rapid smoking treatment for dependent cigarette smokers. *Addictive Behaviors, 2,* 109–112.

Linberg, S. E., Horan, J. J., Hodgson, J. E., & Buskirk, E. R. (1982). Some physiological consequences of the rapid smoking treatment for cigarette addiction. *Archives of Environmental Health, 37,* 88–92.

Lloyd, R. W., & Salzberg, H. C. (1975). Controlled social drinking: An alternative to abstinence as a treatment goal for some alcohol abusers. *Psychological Bulletin, 82,* 815–842.

Lovibond, S. H., & Caddy, G. R. (1970). Discriminated aversive control in the moderation of alcoholics drinking behavior. *Behavior Therapy, 1,* 437–444.

Lublin, I. (1969). Principles governing the choice of unconditioned stimuli in aversive conditioning. In R. D. Kubin & C. M. Franks (Eds.), *Advances in behavior therapy 1968.* New York: Wiley.

Marlatt, G. A. (1978). Craving for alcohol, loss of control, and relapse: A cognitive-behavioral analysis. In P. E. Nathan, G. A. Marlatt, & T. Loberg (Eds.), *Alcoholism: New directions in behavioral research and treatment.* New York: Plenum.

Marlatt, G. A., & Donovan, D. M. (1981). Alcoholism and drug dependence: Cognitive social-learning factors in addictive behaviors. In W. E. Craighead, A. E. Kazdin, & M. J. Mahoney (Eds.), *Behavior* modification: Principles, issues, and applications (2nd ed., pp. 264–285). Boston: Houghton Mifflin.

Mausner, B. (1973). An ecological view of cigarette smoking. Journal of Abnormal Psychology, 81, 115–126.

McAlister, A. L. (1983). Social–psychological approaches. In T. J. Glynn, C. G. Leukefeld, & J. P. Ludford (Eds.), Preventing adolescent drug abuse: Intervention strategies. NIDA Research Monograph 47 (pp. 36–50). Washington, DC: U.S. Government Printing Office.

McFall, R. M., & Marston, A. R. (1970). An experimental investigation of behavioral rehearsal in assertion training. Journal of Abnormal Psychology, 76, 295–303.

Milgram, G. G. (1982). Youthful drinking: Past and present. Journal of Drug Education, 12, 289–308.

Miller, J. D., Cisin, I. H., Gardner-Keaton, H., Harrel, A. V., Wirtz, P. W., Abelson, H. I., & Fishburne, P. M. (1983). National survey on drug abuse: Main findings 1982. Rockville, MD: NIDA.

Miller, P. M. (1973). Behavioral treatment of drug addiction: A review. International Journal of the Addictions, 8, 511–519.

Miller, P. M., & Barlow, D. H. (1973). Behavioral approaches to the treatment of alcoholism. Journal of Nervous and Mental Disease, 157, 10–20.

Miller, P. M., & Eisler, R. M. (1977). Assertive behavior in alcoholics: A descriptive analysis. Behavior Therapy, 8, 10–20.

Miller, P. M., Hersen, M., Eisler, R. M., & Watts, J. G. (1974). Contingent reinforcement of lowered blood/alcohol levels in an outpatient chronic alcoholic. Behaviour Research and Therapy, 12, 261–263.

Miller, W. R., & Caddy, G. R. (1977). Abstinence and controlled drinking in the treatment of problem drinkers. Journal of Studies on Alcoholism, 38, 986–1003.

Mills, C. J., & Noyes, H. L. (1984). Patterns and correlates of initial and subsequent drug abuse among adolescents. Journal of Consulting and Clinical Psychology, 52, 231–243.

Moskowitz, J. M. (1983). Preventing adolescent substance abuse through drug education. In T. J. Glynn, C. G. Leukefeld, & J. P. Ludford (Eds.), Preventing adolescent drug abuse: Intervention strategies. NIDA Research Monograph 47 (pp. 233–249). Washington, DC: U.S. Government Printing Office.

National Coordinating Council on Drug Education. (1972). Drug abuse films. Washington, DC: Drug Abuse Council.

National Institute on Alcohol Abuse and Alcoholism. (1981). Fifth special report to the U.S. Congress on alcohol and health (DHHS Publication No. ADM 81-1080). Washington, DC: U.S. Government Printing Office.

Ostman, R. E. (1976). Communication research and drug education. Beverly Hills, CA: Sage.

Owen, P. L., & Nyberg, L. R. (1983). Assessing alcohol and drug problems among adolescents: Current practices. Journal of Drug Education, 13, 249–254.

Pattison, E. M., Sobell, M. B., & Sobell, L. C. (1977).

Emerging concepts of alcohol dependence. New York: Springer.

Paxton, R., & Bernacca, G. (1979). Urinary nicotine concentration as a function of time since last cigarette: Implications for detecting faking in smoking clinics. Behavior Therapy, 10, 523–528.

Pentz, M. A. (1983). Prevention of adolescent substance abuse through social skill development. In T. J. Glynn, C. G. Leukefeld, & J. P. Ludford (Eds.), Preventing adolescent drug abuse: Intervention strategies. NIDA Research Monograph 47 (pp. 195–232). Washington, DC: U.S. Government Printing Office.

Pomerleau, O.F. (1979). Why people smoke: Current psychological models. In P. Davidson (Ed.), Behavioral medicine: Changing health styles. New York: Brunner/Mazel.

Ray, M. B. (1976). The cycle of abstinence and relapse among heroin addicts. In R. H. Coombs, L. J. Fry, & P. G. Lewis (Eds.), Socialization in drug abuse. Cambridge, MA: Schenkman.

Reilly, D. M. (1984). Family therapy with adolescent drug abusers and their families: Defying gravity and achieving escape velocity. Journal of Drug Issues, 14, 381–391.

Reuger, D. R., & Liberman, R. P. (1984). Behavioral family therapy for delinquent and substance-abusing adolescents. Journal of Drug Issues, 14, 403–418.

Rokeach, M. (1971). Long range experimental modification of values, attitudes, and behaviors. American Psychologist, 26, 453–459.

Savage, L. J. (1954). The foundations of statistics. New York: Wiley.

Schaps, E., DiBartolo, R., Moskowitz, J., & Churgin, S. (1981). A review of 127 drug abuse prevention program evaluations. Journal of Drug Issues, 1, 14–44.

Schmahl, D. P., Lichtenstein, E., & Harris, W. E. (1972). Successful treatment of habitual smokers with warm, smoky air and rapid smoking. Journal of Consulting and Clinical Psychology, 38, 105–111.

Shain, M., Riddell, W., & Kelty, H. L. (1977). Influence, choice, and drugs. Lexington, MA: Heath.

Shute, R. (1975). Impact of peer pressure on the verbally expressed drug attitudes of male college students. American Journal of Drug and Alcohol Abuse, 2, 231–243.

Smart, R. G., & Goodstadt, M. S. (1977). Effects of reducing the legal alcohol purchasing age on drinking related problems: A review of empirical studies. Journal of Studies on Alcohol, 38, 1313–1323.

Spencer, D. J., Pitkin, O., Lee, J., & Clarke, P. (1984). School health assessment, planning, and evaluation project—New York City. Morbidity and Mortality Weekly Report, 33, 489–491.

Stone, C. I., & Shute, R. (1977). Persuader sex differences and peer pressure effects on attitudes toward drug abuse. American Journal of Drug and Alcohol Abuse, 4, 55–64.

Swisher, J. D. (1979). Diagnosis and treatment of substance abuse. In K. W. Hylbert & K. W. Hylbert, Jr. (Eds.), Medical information for human service workers. State College, PA: Counselor Education Press.

Trellis, E. S., Smith, F. F., Alston, D. C., & Siassi, I.

(1975). The pitfalls of urine survellience: The role of research in evaluation and remedy. *Addictive Behaviors, 1,* 83–88.

United States Department of Health, Education, and Welfare. (1976). *Teenage smoking: National patterns of cigarette smoking, ages 12 through 18, in 1972 and 1974* (DHEW Publication No. NIH 76–931). Washington, DC: Author.

United States Department of Health and Human Services. (1980). *An evaluation of the teen challenge treatment program* (NIDA Services Report). Washington, DC: U.S. Government Printing Office.

United States Department of Health and Human Services. (1984). *The health consequences of smoking: Chronic obstructive lung disease. A report of the Surgeon General.* Rockville, MD: USDHHS Public Health Service, Office on Smoking and Health.

United States Public Health Service. (1979). *Smoking and health: A report of the Surgeon General* (DHEW, USPHS Publication No. 70–50066). Washington, DC: U.S. Government Printing Office.

University of Michigan. (1985, January). *Drug study press release.* (Available from News and Information Services, The University of Michigan)

Van Hasselt, V. B., Hersen, M., & Milliones, J. (1978). Social-skills training for alcoholics and drug addicts: A review. *Addicitive Behaviors, 3,* 221–233.

Warner, R. W., Swisher, J. D., & Horan, J. J. (1973). Drug abuse prevention: A behavioral approach. *National Association of Secondary School Principals Bulletin, 57,* 49–54.

Webb, E. J., Campbell, D. T., Schwartz, R. D., & Sechrest, L. (1966). *Unobtrusive measures: Non-reactive research in the social sciences.* Chicago: Rand McNally.

Williams, A. F., Rich, R. F., Zador, P. L., & Robertson, L. S. (1975). The legal minimum drinking age and fatal motor vehicle crashes. *Journal of Legal Studies, 4,* 219–239.

Williams, A. F., Zador, P. L., Harris, S. S., & Karpf, R. S. (1983). The effect of raising the legal minimum drinking age on involvement in fatal crashes. *Journal of Legal Studies, 12,* 169–179

Wohlford, P. (1970). Initiation of cigarette smoking: Is it related to parental behavior? *Journal of Consulting and Clinical Psychology, 34,* 148–151.

Zinberg, N. (1976). *What is drug abuse?* Unpublished report, Drug Abuse Council, Washington, DC.

CHAPTER 18

Anxiety

Cyd C. Strauss and Benjamin B. Lahey

Anxiety disorders are found throughout the human life span, with the period of adolescence being no exception. However, anxiety disorders of the adolescent differ from those of other developmental periods in that both childhood and adult forms of the disorder are experienced. In this chapter, the anxiety problems of adolescence will be described and related to age, sex, and other demographic variables. The methods of assessment and diagnosis of anxiety disorders will be summarized, and current concepts of treatment will be described. This information will be illustrated in two case examples, and current topics for research will be briefly discussed.

DESCRIPTION OF THE DISORDERS

Anxiety disorders are heterogeneous and multifaceted problems that affect persons of all ages. Numerous subtypes have been distinguished in current diagnostic classification systems, including the *Diagnostic and Statistical Manual of Mental Disorders, 3rd edition (DSM-III)* (American Psychiatric Association, 1980). However, they all are characterized by intense subjective distress (anxiety or fear) and are generally accompanied by maladaptive patterns of

cognition and behavior. As noted above, adolescents may be affected by either anxiety disorders that are characteristic of children or by adult forms of maladaptive anxiety. In describing these various types of anxiety disorders, the nomenclature of the *DSM-III* will be followed.

Anxiety Disorders of Childhood and Adolescence

Three types of anxiety problems that occur primarily before adulthood have been distinguished in *DSM-III*. These are overanxious disorder, separation anxiety disorder, and avoidant disorder. Children diagnosed as having overanxious disorder display marked worries about the future, ruminate about their past behavior, are overconcerned about their competence, show an excessive need for reassurance from others, are often unable to relax, and are markedly self-conscious. Their anxiety is generalized in the sense that it is not related to specific environmental events.

Children given the label of separation anxiety disorder manifest excessive distress when separated from attachment figures (usually parents), worry about harm to those attachment figures or harm coming to them, refuse to separate

332

from the attachment figure to attend school, have difficulty sleeping away from the attachment figure, and tend to follow the attachment figure. Because refusal to attend school is frequently the event that leads to referral of the child for psychological evaluation, this disorder usually was referred to as school refusal or school phobia in the past.

Avoidant disorder is characterized by persistent avoidance of social interactions with persons who are unfamiliar, in a youth who enjoys normal social relationships with relatives and other familiar persons. These children often appear shy, timid, and are socially unassertive.

All three childhood anxiety disorders may occur in adolescents, but the great bulk of published research is on adolescents who refuse to attend school. This is probably due to the importance of school attendance, as well as the fact that onset of this aspect of separation anxiety disorder is believed to be common at two periods, early elementary-school age and early adolescence.

In addition to those anxiety disorders that are typical of childhood, the adolescent may be diagnosed as having almost all of the adult anxiety disorders. By convention, persons under the age of 18 cannot be given the *DSM-III* diagnosis of generalized anxiety disorder. However, they are given the apparently similar diagnosis of overanxious disorder. Yet, the actual relationship and continuity of these two disorders is currently unknown.

Adolescents may qualify for all other *DSM-III* adult anxiety diagnoses. Simple phobias, in which the individual excessively fears and avoids a specific object or situation, are common in both children and adolescents. Social phobias, in which the adolescent fears and avoids social encounters that involve scrutiny and evaluation, not only occur during adolescence, but have their peak period of onset after puberty (Marks & Gelder, 1966). The avoidance of leaving one's home or other limited familiar surroundings, or agoraphobia, has been thought to be rare before early adulthood. However, Sheehan, Sheehan, and Minichiello (1981) found that the age of onset was before age 20 in 26% of a large sample of adult agoraphobics, with 22% of the cases onsetting between 10 to 19 years of age.

Panic disorder is characterized by sudden attacks of intense anxiety, marked sympathetic autonomic arousal, and fear of dying or going insane. This disorder is uncommon before puberty, but often onsets during adolescence, at least when the panic attacks are accompanied by agoraphobia (Sheehan et al., 1981). Obsessive–compulsive disorders involve recurrent and distressing thoughts or urges to engage in repetitive and irrational behaviors that create considerable anxiety when resisted. Obsessive–compulsive disorders are more common in adolescence, but are found before puberty (Hollingsworth, Tanguay, Grossman, & Pabst, 1980; Rapoport et al., 1981). Thus, it is clear that the adolescent may experience a broad range of anxiety disorders.

EPIDEMIOLOGICAL FINDINGS

A growing corpus of research gives us some understanding of the epidemiology of adolescent anxiety disorders. However, extensive gaps in our database exist. In particular, virtually nothing is known about the epidemiology of overanxious disorder, social phobia, avoidant disorder, obsessive–compulsive disorder, and panic disorder. The primary focus of epidemiological research to date has been on school phobia (related to but not synonymous with separation anxiety disorder), simple phobias, and subclinical fears and worries.

Prevalence

Exceedingly little is known about the prevalence of adolescent anxiety disorders. The Isle of Wight epidemiological study (Graham & Rutter, 1973) classified 3.2% of 14- and 15-year-old children as having "emotional disorders" and an additional 1.9% as having mixed emotional and conduct disorders. The combined figure of 5.1% can be taken as a rough estimate of the combined prevalence of all anxiety disorders in young adolescents, but it must be severely qualified in two ways. First, the figure is inflated somewhat by the fact that a small percentage of the adolescents in the emotionally disordered group manifested depression and an unknown percentage manifested other types of neurotic disorders. Second, not all of the 14- and 15-year-old group had reached puberty and can be considered to be adolescents. Rutter (1976) reports that 93% of the females had reached puberty, but only 27% of the males were pubertal.

Agras, Sylvester, and Oliveau (1969) found that the prevalence of all clinically significant phobias during the adolescent period was about 60 per 1,000. The prevalence of subclinical, but often uncomfortable, fears and worries in adolescents is much higher, however (Abe & Masui, 1981; Simon & Ward, 1974, 1982).

Sex Differences

Information on sex ratios for adolescent anxiety disorders is sparse, contradictory, and generally not directly applicable to current classifications of subtypes. Weiner and Del Gaudio (1976) reported that neuroses were more prevalent in females than males aged 12–18 (15.4% versus 11.7%). In contrast, Graham and Rutter (1973) found no sex differences in emotional disorders among their 14- and 15-year-old sample. The discrepancy may be due to sample differences (Rochester, New York, vs. the Isle of Wight), differences in age range, and disparities in diagnostic criteria.

According to a study by Abe and Masui (1981), female adolescents were more likely to report fears of lightning, going outdoors alone, and of blushing, whereas males were more likely to report fear of talking. Females generally reached the peak age of reporting each fear earlier than males, a finding that may be related to the earlier age of puberty in females.

Simon and Ward (1974) found that females aged 12–14 had more total worries than males of the same age. An investigation by Croake and Knox (1971) similarly showed that ninth-grade females reported a greater number of fears than male ninth graders. In a more detailed analysis, Simon and Ward (1982) found that 12- to 14-year-old females admit to more frequent and intense family, social, and imaginary worries than males. No sex difference was evident for worries regarding personal adequacy, animals, economic factors, or health. Overall, the most common worries of adolescents, in descending rank order, concern family, school, and social relationships.

The relative prevalence of test anxiety among male and female adolescents in normal populations was reported by Entwisle and Greenberger (1972) and Payne, Smith, and Payne (1983). These studies consistently found that girls reported significantly higher levels of test anxiety than boys.

Fewer sex differences apparently exist in the reactions of male and female adolescents to specific stressful events. Le Baron and Zeltzer (1984) reported no sex differences in measures of anxiety during painful medical procedures in a sample of adolescents with cancer. Similarly, a self-report study by Abe and Masui (1981) showed no sex differences in a variety of anxious reactions to specific stress, except that boys reported a higher frequency of micturition.

It is not clear that studies of subclinical fears and worries are relevant to diagnosed anxiety disorders. Further, few data are currently available on adolescents assigned these diagnoses. *DSM-III* states that there is no sex difference in obsessive–compulsive disorder, although 20 of 26 postpubertal cases now described in the literature are males (Holingsworth et al., 1980; Rapoport et al., 1981). No sex difference is ascribed to separation anxiety disorder and the sex ratio of social phobia is stated to be unknown in *DSM-III*. Females are believed to exhibit simple phobia, agoraphobia, and panic disorder more commonly, whereas males are considered more likely to qualify for a diagnosis of overanxious disorder. However, there is apparently no published research concerning the sex ratios of these diagnoses in adolescent populations.

Age and Development Course

Studies of subclinical fears and worries indicate a general decline in these anxiety-related features from childhood to early adolescence. For example, 80% of 5- and 6-year-olds were found to express fear of animals, whereas 23% of 13- and 14-year-olds report this fear (Maurer, 1965). Similar decreases are indicated for fears of the dark and monsters (Maurer, 1965) and bedtime fears (Bauer, 1976). Similarly, Simon and Ward (1974) found a decline in total self-reported worries from ages 12 to 14. However, realistic fears (e.g., physical danger, natural hazards, school achievement, loss, and social-relationship problems) are infrequent in young children, but become more common by early adolescence (Bauer, 1976; Maurer, 1965). The epidemiological study of Agras et al. (1969) substantiated this latter finding. From childhood to adulthood, there was a sharp increase in the prevalence of subclinical fears of snakes, crowds, injections, and other realistic fears. However, most of these *began* in childhood and persisted into adolescence; the increased prevalence of realistic fears in adolescence reflects an accumulation of fears over age rather than a peak onset during the adolescent period. This fact casts doubt on the suggestion that the increased prevalence of realistic fears in adolescence reflects concurrent cognitive development (Bauer, 1976).

Age of onset of phobic levels of fear is apparently related to their stability over time. Agras, Chapin, and Oliveau (1972) found that phobias for persons under age 20 were far less persistent than for adults. Indeed, 100% of the phobias of children and adolescents had remitted within 5 years. More global classifications of anxiety symptoms present a similar picture. Gersten, Langner, Eisenberg, Simcha-Fagan, and Mc-Carthy (1976) reported that a measure of neurotic anxiety was significantly less stable over time when the child was first assessed in childhood than in adolescence. The large-scale Berkley Growth Study indicated that measures of child anxiety were not predictive of young adult anxiety, but that adolescent measures of anxiety were predictive over a 5-year period (Block, 1971; Livson & Peskin, 1967). Similarly, Weiner and Del Gaudio (1976) provide evidence that adolescent neurosis tends to continue into adulthood.

The persistent and serious nature of adolescent-onset anxiety disorders can best be seen in a large-scale study of school phobia cases (Berg, Butler, & Hall, 1976) that began in adolescence and were followed over a 3-year period. One-third showed no remaining symptoms, one-third had changed little, and the remaining third showed other neurotic symptoms. Fully one-half still had serious school-attendance problems and 6 of the 125 patients had developed definite agoraphobia.

Rutter's (1976) summary of the Isle of Wight study suggests that a substantial minority of adolescent anxiety disorders have persisted since childhood; nearly 50% of children diagnosed as exhibiting emotional disorder at ages 10–11 were given the same diagnosis at ages 14–15. The majority of diagnosed cases of emotional disorder at ages 14–15 were new since ages 10–11. However, except for an increase in depression and school refusal, there were no notable changes in types of emotional problems in adolescence.

Studies of age differences in anxious reactions to pain and other specific stress show an interesting age-related trend. Le Baron and Zeltzer (1984) and Katz, Kellerman, and Siegel (1980)

found that adolescents were less likely to scream, cry, and verbally express anxiety during a painful cancer-treatment procedure. However, Finch, Kendall, Dannenberg, and Morgan (1978) found that adolescents reacted with more state anxiety to a difficult learning task than an easy one, whereas children showed no difference between the tasks. Although additional data certainly are needed, these findings suggest that although adolescents have more control over the expression of anxiety during stress than children, they may actually experience greater subjective anxiety.

The importance of age in our understanding of anxiety disorders of adolescence can be seen further in studies of adults with clinical phobias. The less disabling simple phobias tend to have an earlier onset than more disabling ones. Sheehan et al. (1981) reported that 31% of adults with simple phobias reported an onset before 9 years of age and 26% reported onset between ages 10 and 19. In contrast, they found that only 4% of adult agoraphobics reported the onset of their disorder before age 9, but 26% reported onset between 10 and 19 years of age. Marks and Gelder (1966) similarly found that adult patients with specific animal phobias reported a mean age of onset of 4.4 years, whereas most adults with specific situation phobias, social anxieties, and agoraphobia reported an onset in adolescence or later. A substantial minority of all types of phobias begin in adolescence; less disabling phobias are more likely to begin in childhood.

Other investigations of adult agoraphobics have suggested that school phobia may be a significant precursor. Klein (1964) and Berg (1976) provided evidence that agoraphobia that begins in late adolescence or early adulthood is often preceded by school phobia in early adolescence. However, two other studies indicate that the relationship between adolescent school phobia and adult anxiety disorder is not a specific one. Berg, Marks, McGuire, and Lipsedge (1974) found that about one-fourth of both adult agoraphobics and adults with other neurotic disorders reported adolescent school phobia. Similarly, Tyrer and Tyrer (1974) found that school phobia was more common in the developmental histories of phobic, anxious, and depressed adults than normal adults, although the three psychiatric groups did not differ in this respect. However, they did find that the risk of later neurotic disorder was greater for female than male school phobics (even though most school phobics become normal adults).

Family and Other Factors

Relatively little is known about the family characteristics of adolescents with anxiety disorders. The Isle of Wight study (Graham & Rutter, 1973; Rutter, 1976) showed that emotional disorder was not related to marital intactness in young adolescents, but was related to the presence of psychiatric disorder in the mother. Hersov (1960) found that the parents of school phobics were more overprotective than parents of control children. In contrast, Berg, Butler, Fairbairn, and McGuire (1981) reported that parents of school-phobic adolescents did not differ from controls on a variety of measures of family life, including parental involvement in the adolescent's decision-making.

Socioeconomic status was not found to be related to the prevalence of emotional disorders in young adolescents in the Isle of Wight study (Graham & Rutter, 1973; Rutter, 1976). However, socioeconomic status does seem to be associated in understandable ways with subclinical worries. Simon and Ward (1974) found that higher socioeconomic-status adolescents worry significantly more about school achievement and economic matters than lower socioeconomic-status adolescents, whereas the reverse is true for imaginary and health worries.

ASSESSMENT

The modes of assessing motor, physiological, and cognitive aspects of anxiety in adolescents have included structured clinical interviews with adolescents and parents, self-report questionnaires, direct observations, parent and teacher ratings, and physiological techniques. Most of the available assessment strategies and instruments for evaluating anxiety in adolescents have been adopted from child and adult procedures. Research and clinical experience to date suggest that a multimethod assessment approach should be taken in assessing an adolescent's need for treatment.

Structured Clinical Interviews

Several structured clinical interviews have been devised recently to determine the presence and severity of psychopathology in children and adolescents. These are: the Diagnostic Interview Schedule for Children (DISC) (Costello, Edelbrock, Kalas, Dulcan, & Klaric, 1984); the Diagnostic Interview for Children and Adolescents (DICA) (Herjanic & Reich, 1982); the Schedule for Affective Disorders and Schizophrenia for School-Age Children (KIDDID-SADS) (Puig-Antich, Orvaschel, Tabrizi, & Chambers, 1978); and the Interview Schedule for Children (ISC) (Kovacs, 1983). Each of these involves interviewing children or adolescents and their parents individually with a standard set of questions covering all symptoms of psychopathology in children and adolescents. Anxiety disorders are assessed by portions of each of these interview formats.

The reliability and validity of anxiety diagnoses using these instruments have not yet been clearly established. Preliminary studies have found acceptable interrater reliability of separation anxiety, overanxious, and simple phobic symptoms using the DISC (Edelbrock, Costello, Dulcan, Kalas, & Conover, 1985) and ISC (Kovacs, 1983). On the other hand, poor concordance between parent and child or parent and adolescent reports of anxiety symptoms have typically been found (Edelbrock, Costello, Dulcan, Kalas, & Conover, in press; Herjanic & Reich, 1982; Kovacs, 1983), with children and adolescents tending to report more anxiety features than parents. These latter findings may merely reflect the fact that children and adolescents have greater awareness of their own internal emotional states than do parents. The validity of these interviews has only begun to be examined, although one preliminary investigation suggests that this approach shows promise in assessing anxiety in adolescents (Costello et al., 1984).

Self-Report Measures

Children's and adolescents' self-reports have been viewed as critical in assessment of anxiety or fearfulness. Despite their wide acceptance and use, there are several features of self-report measures that limit the conclusions that can be derived from them. These include: (a) the child's or adolescent's potential unwillingness or inability to reveal negative characteristics (Glennon & Weisz, 1978); (b) the small number of empirical studies researching psychometric properties of many scales (Barrios, Hartmann, & Shigetomi, 1981); and (c) the lack of specificity of situations that induce anxiety in the items included in most measures (Barrios et al., 1981). Several self-report questionnaires have been developed that are used to identify anxious adolescents and to measure the effectiveness of interventions. The Children's Manifest Anxiety Scale-Revised (RCMAS) (Reynolds & Richmond, 1978) is one of the more widely employed instruments. This 37-item scale has been shown to have construct (Reynolds & Richmond, 1978), concurrent (Reynolds, 1980), content (Reynolds & Richmond, 1978), and predictive (Reynolds, 1981) validity. In addition, national normative and reliability data have been obtained for the RCMAS for children and adolescents between 6 and 19 years of age (Reynolds & Paget, 1982). Through factor analysis, three factors have emerged for the measure, including physiological, worry/oversensitivity, and concentration factors (Reynolds & Richmond, 1979).

A second self-report questionnaire, derived from the Wolpe–Lang Scale for adults, is the Fear Survey Schedule for Children (Scherer & Nakamura, 1968). Children or adolescents can rate their degree of fearfulness on a 5-point scale for each of the 80 items, which represent specific objects or situations. A factor-analysis yielded the following factors for this measure: fear of failure/criticism, major fears (e.g., fire, sight of blood), minor fears (e.g., travel), medical fears, fear of death, fear of the dark, home-school fears, and miscellaneous fears. Investigations regarding the psychometric properties of this instrument have been limited to reports of high internal consistency and a moderate relationship with another self-report measure of anxiety (Scherer & Nakamura, 1968). Subsequently, Ollendick (1983) provided data supporting the internal consistency, test–retest reliability, and the convergent and discriminative validity of a slightly modified version of the Fear Survey Schedule for Children (FSSC-R). The Fear Survey Schedule (Wolpe & Lang, 1964) for adults has also been used in assessing adolescent fears.

The State–Trait Inventory for Children (STAIC) (Speilberger, 1973) is a third frequently employed self-report measure. Two 20-item scales comprise the inventory, which attempts to measure separately anxiety that varies across situations and anxiety that is stable across time and situations. However, studies generally have failed to support the validity of the state–trait

distinction (Johnson & Melamed, 1979). High split-half and moderate test–retest reliabilities have been reported for both scales of the STAIC (Morris & Kratochwill, 1983). Additional self-report measures have been devised to assess anxiety in specific situations. For example, the Test Anxiety Scale for Children (Sarason, Davidson, Lighthall, Waite, & Ruebush, 1960) is used to evaluate examination anxiety in both children and adolescents. The Fear of Negative Evaluation Scale and Social Avoidance and Distress Scale (Watson & Friend, 1969) assess interpersonal anxiety associated with social situations.

Self-monitoring (Kazdin, 1974) has been used to obtain an ongoing account of the adolescent's level of anxiety in problematic situations. Self-monitoring can range from frequency counts to diaries in which the adolescent indicates internal emotional states, anxious avoidant behaviors, and situational factors that are related to anxiety-provoking stimuli or situations. One notable disadvantage of self-monitoring in research is that it has reactive effects (i.e., behavior changes often occur in response to self-observation) (Kazdin, 1974). On the other hand, this approach is useful in providing an assessment of behavior as it occurs in the natural environment. Further, it allows for gathering data on private emotional states or cognitions (Morris & Kratochwill, 1983).

Direct Observations

The most commonly employed direct observation procedure for assessing anxiety in children and adolescents is the Behavioral Avoidance Test (BAT) (Lang & Lazovik, 1963). This observational approach involves instructing the adolescent to enter a room in which the feared object is placed and to approach and touch or pick up the object. The adolescent's latency to respond, distance traveled toward the object, and time spent handling the feared object are recorded. This procedure can be used to assess adolescents' fears of dogs, physical examinations, water, and snakes, as well as other anxiety-provoking situations or objects. Despite the fairly extensive use of the BAT in examining adolescents' fearful reactions, several features of this approach currently limit its usefulness. As noted by Barrios et al. (1981), the BAT has not been standardized in terms of types of instructions provided and number of tasks presented.

Kelley (1976) has shown that variations in instructions and demand characteristics can significantly influence approach responses. Also, the BAT is somewhat restricted in its application, in that it cannot be implemented to assess certain fears, such as separation anxiety and overanxious features. In addition, the reliability and validity of the BAT as an assessment device for adolescents have not been studied sufficiently.

Observer rating scales have also begun to be implemented to observe overt anxious mannerisms and behaviors in adolescents. Several rating scales have been developed to observe anxiety in particular situations or settings, such as reactions to painful medical procedures (Katz et al., 1980), dental treatment (Melamed, Yurcheson, Fleece, Hutcherson, & Hawes, 1978), public speaking (Paul, 1966), and hospitalization (Vernon, Foley, & Schulman, 1967). Generally, reliability and validity data concerning these coding systems are quite promising, although investigations of psychometric properties have been few in number.

Parent and Teacher Ratings

Parent and teacher ratings and checklists have figured less prominently in evaluating anxiety than other adolescent psychopathology. Despite their infrequent use, numerous behavior rating scales are available that contain an anxiety or withdrawal dimension, including the Conners' Teacher Rating Scale (Conners, 1969), the Child Behavior Checklist (Achenbach & Edelbrock, 1983), and the Revised Behavior Problem Checklist (Quay & Peterson, 1983). The validity and reliability of these indices of anxiety have been supported (Quay, 1979).

Several rating scales have been designed specifically for parents or teachers to provide evaluations of children's or adolescents' anxiety or fearfulness. For example, the Louisville Fear Survey Schedule (Miller, Barrett, Hampe, & Noble, 1972b) can be completed by parents or teachers, as well as by the adolescents themselves. This measure assesses three factors of fear of physical injury, natural events, and psychic stress.

Physiological Measures

A virtually unexplored area in the behavioral assessment of anxiety disorders in children and adolescents is physiological measurement. Assessment of heart rate and electrodermal responses has been utilized most frequently with children and adolescents. Physiological responses associated with anxiety can be monitored prior to and concurrently with the presentation of anxiety-provoking stimuli in vivo, through imagery, via audiotapes or films, or pictorially (Barrios et al., 1981).

An advantage of this assessment modality is that physiological responses are not under the voluntary control of participants for the most part. Therefore, they are less susceptible to subject bias. Also, measurement of physiological responses can be conducted reliably (Bellack & Lombardo, 1984). Disadvantages of physiological assessment are the expense of equipment, level of expertise required for measurement, and limited generalizability beyond assessment conditions (Bellack & Lombardo, 1984).

TREATMENT

A full range of treatment approaches has been applied to anxiety disorders in adolescence, including behavioral procedures, brief psychotherapy, and, more recently, pharmacological interventions. However, rigorous evaluation of the efficacy of these therapeutic procedures is strikingly absent. Literature on behavioral interventions is more extensive than for other treatment modalities, although the paucity of methodologically controlled studies, the narrow range of anxiety disorders treated, and the inclusion of nonclinical samples with only mild to moderate fears seriously limit the conclusions to be drawn even regarding behavioral strategies for treating anxious adolescents. Further, the majority of empirical studies assessing the utility of behavioral treatments for anxiety disorders apply to either child or adult populations, with the generalizability of these findings to anxious adolescents being highly questionable. Nonetheless, preliminary results that pertain to adolescents are encouraging in showing that anxiety can be successfully treated in this population.

Behavioral Strategies

The primary behavioral methods for reducing anxiety in adolescents include systematic desensitization, flooding or implosion, cognitive approaches, operant procedures, and modeling. The application of these strategies to children and adolescents has been reviewed by Carlson, Figueroa, and Lahey (in press), Morris and Kratochwill (1983), and Ollendick (1979b).

Systematic Desensitization

Systematic desensitization, formally developed by Wolpe (1958), is the most widely used approach in treating anxiety in children and adolescents (Ollendick & Cerny, 1981). The procedure consists of gradually exposing the adolescent to the fear-evoking situation while the adolescent engages in an activity incompatible with fear. Although the theory underlying this approach has been quite controversial, there is considerable empirical evidence supporting its effectiveness with adults and, to a lesser extent, with adolescents.

The current research literature examining the efficacy of systematic desensitization with anxious adolescents consists primarily of clinical case studies and analogue studies that include nonclinic samples of adolescents with relatively mild fears. One controlled single-case study and one methodologically sound group-comparison study have been presented that evaluate the utility of this treatment method for clinically anxious adolescents.

There have been a number of case reports of successfully treated clinically referred adolescents with phobias or other anxiety disorders using systematic desensitization or slightly modified versions of this approach. In particular, imaginal and/or in vivo desensitization has been associated with clinically significant reductions in school phobias and separation anxiety in adolescents (Croghan, 1981; Le Unes & Siemsglusz, 1977; O'Farrell, Hedlund, & Cutter, 1981; Phillips & Wolpe, 1981; Taylor, 1972). Systematic desensitization has also been used to reduce car phobias (Kushner, 1965; Saunders, 1976) and dream-induced anxiety (Cavior & Deutsch, 1975) in single case studies. In addition to the problems generally associated with the case-study approach in drawing valid conclusions regarding treatment effectiveness (Kazdin, 1981), these clinical case studies often included multiple treatment techniques in conjunction with systematic desensitization, thus making it more difficult to evaluate the specific contributions of the systematic desensitization procedure to positive treatment outcomes.

Ollendick (1979a) presented a controlled single-case investigation of the efficacy of systematic desensitization in the treatment of a 16-year-old anorexic male who had intense fears of gaining weight and accompanying peer criticism. Using an ABAB reversal design, Ollendick (1979a) demonstrated that weight gain was related to institution of the desensitization procedure. However, weight loss accompanied withdrawal of the procedure, so that an adjunctive approach was needed to enhance maintenance of most treatment gains over a 2-year follow-up period. Several analogue studies have further shown that systematic desensitization has been effective in reducing test anxiety or anxiety related to reading in adolescents (e.g., Kondas, 1967; Mann & Rosenthal, 1969).

The only controlled clinical group outcome study was less clearly supportive of the usefulness of systematic desensitization with adolescents. In this study, Miller, Barrett, Hampe, and Noble (1972a) compared imaginal desensitization, psychotherapy, and a waiting-list control condition in the treatment of 6- to 15-year-old clinically referred children and adolescents with various phobias. Overall, both treatments produced significantly greater improvement in parent report measures relative to no treatment, with no differences found between the two treatment approaches. On the other hand, clinicians' evaluations showed no overall effects of treatment. Moreover, when assessed using clinicians' ratings, these authors found that age was significantly related to outcome, in that both forms of therapy were shown to be effective in younger phobic children (ages 6-10), but not in older phobic groups (ages 11-15). Hampe, Noble, Miller, and Barrett (1973) reported that during a 2-year follow-up, the younger group had shown substantial improvement immediately following treatment and continued to maintain these changes. In contrast, the older and control groups demonstrated gradual improvement over the 2-year follow-up period.

In sum, these clinical case studies, analogue studies, and controlled investigations provide preliminary evidence that systematic desensitization may be useful and should be studied further in clinically anxious adolescents. However, present findings must be considered tentative due to contradictory evidence and to the small number of empirically sound investigations evaluating systematic desensitization in the treatment of clinically anxious adolescents.

Flooding and Implosion

Flooding and implosive procedures involve presentation of the feared stimuli for an extended period at intense levels, either in vivo or imaginally. Rather than providing the adolescent with an anxiety-inhibiting response to reduce fearfulness as in systematic desensitization, the adolescent is required to remain in the situation until the anxiety response is extinguished. Although implosive therapy and flooding are similar techniques, implosion is restricted to the imaginal presentation of anxiety-provoking stimuli, so that both psychodynamic themes of conflict (e.g., rejection, guilt, expression of fear of aggression) and descriptions of the phobic stimuli can be presented (Stampfl & Levis, 1967). In flooding, actual exposure to fear-eliciting stimuli is typically used, rather than having the adolescent visually imagine the phobic object.

Evaluation of flooding or implosion in the treatment of anxious adolescents again has been limited primarily to case reports. Although these can be valuable in identifying potentially useful techniques, they do not provide the methodological rigor necessary to assess adequately the effectiveness of treatment procedures. Nonetheless, numerous case studies have reported positive findings employing these forced exposure techniques with adolescents (Bolton, Collins, & Steinberg, 1983; Bolton & Turner, 1984; Hersen, 1968; Kennedy, 1965; Ong & Leng, 1979; Smith & Sharpe, 1970). In these descriptive case studies, flooding or implosion was used to treat school phobias or obsessive–compulsive disorders. Kolko (1984) presented an interesting adjunct to facilitate in vivo exposure to phobic stimuli in the treatment of a 16-year-old agoraphobic girl. Treatment consisted of paradoxical instruction to embellish subjective anxiety and to produce the anticipated negative consequences during prolonged exposure to feared stimuli. This procedure was associated with elimination of avoidance responses, as well as decreased self-reported anxiety and anxiety ratings during actual exposure. Treatment gains were maintained and enhanced at 3- and 9-month follow-up assessments.

One group investigation has been reported in which an in vivo treatment approach was compared individually to inpatient hospitalization and home tutoring with psychotherapy in the treatment of school phobia (Blagg & Yule, 1984). Subjects were mostly in the 11- to 16-year-old age group and were compared on multiple outcome measures, including school attendance, self-reports of self-concept and personality, and parent and teacher ratings of child behavior. Evaluation at greater than 1-year following treatment suggested that the group receiving in vivo flooding demonstrated superior outcome compared to the other two groups in terms of school attendance. In addition, subjects in this group showed accompanying improvements on other measures of psychological adjustment.

Although these findings suggest that in vivo flooding can be applied relatively successfully to adolescent school phobia, several features of the treatment design prevented the drawing of firm conclusions. These features included: (a) the absence of random assignment to treatment conditions (although comparisons on multiple relevant variables prior to treatment suggested similarity of subjects in the three groups) and (b) an inability to isolate active elements in the in vivo treatment package that incorporated additional behavioral methods. Nonetheless, this study provides the best available evidence that a behavioral treatment package including in vivo flooding can be efficiently and successfully employed to treat adolescent school refusal.

Cognitive Approaches

Cognitive strategies for the treatment of anxiety disorders are predicated on the assumption that thoughts and cognitions mediate anxious behavior. Consequently, cognitive therapies have been based on the notion that modification of thoughts can lead to behavior change. Various cognitive strategies have been applied to the treatment of adolescent anxiety, including a cognitive modification approach (Meichenbaum, 1971), cognitive restructuring (Beck & Emery, 1985), and cognitive attentional training (Holroyd, 1976). These interventions have been employed to treat test anxiety, agoraphobia, compulsions, and multiple phobias in adolescents.

As is characteristic of investigations regarding the application of behavioral strategies to the treatment of adolescent anxiety disorders, research supporting the use of cognitive therapy approaches consists exclusively of clinical case descriptions (Ownby, 1983) and treatment analogue studies. Barlow and Seidner (1983) presented case examples of cognitive treatment of adolescent agoraphobia. Treatment consisted of 10 weekly group-therapy sessions incorporating cognitive restructuring, self-initiated exposure, and panic management, with mothers also participating in therapy. Two of the three adolescents treated demonstrated improvement on their agoraphobia, as well as in their relationships with their mothers, at posttreatment and at a 6-month follow-up. Although promising in suggesting that cognitive approaches may be useful in treating adolescent anxiety disorders, the same cautions discussed previously regarding uncontrolled case studies apply to these findings.

Warren, Smith, and Velten (1984) reported the successful application of rational–emotive therapy in an analogue study including nonclinical adolescents. Fifty-nine adolescents, between 12 and 16 years of age, who volunteered to participate in treatment for interpersonal anxiety were randomly assigned to one of four treatment conditions: (a) rational–emotive therapy (RET); (b) rational–emotive therapy plus a coping imagery procedure (REI), in which subjects practiced substituting rational self-verbalizations for irrational self-talk while imagining anxiety-provoking situations in conjunction with the procedures used in the RET group; (c) relationship-oriented counseling (ROC); and (d) a waiting-list control group (WLC). Sociometric measures, completed by teachers and peers at post-assessment, revealed that the RET and REI groups were less interpersonally anxious than the WLC group, although self-report measures did not differentiate among groups at post-assessment. Also, both the RET and REI groups showed greater reductions in irrational thinking than did the other two groups. There was some evidence that the REI treatment was superior to the RET approach, as well.

In a second analogue study evaluating the efficacy of a cognitive strategy, Little and Jackson (1974) employed an attentional and relaxation training approach to treat test-anxious students. The attentional component consisted of training seventh- and eighth-grade students who demonstrated high test anxiety and general anxiety, relative to their peers, to direct their attention away from irrelevant cognitions interfering with performance and to focus instead on the actual task at hand. Students receiving attentional training were compared to students in one of the following four treatment conditions: (a) attentional training plus training in deep muscle relaxation, (b) relaxation training alone, (c) placebo expectancy, and (d) no treatment. At postassessment, only subjects in the attention plus relaxation treatment condition showed significant reductions in both test and general anxiety.

Clearly, there is inadequate empirical evidence to support strongly the use of cognitive procedures with adolescents who demonstrate clinically significant anxiety disorders. However, the outcomes of clinical case studies and two analogue studies are sufficiently positive to suggest that this approach has promise and warrants further investigation.

Operant Procedures

The goal of operant procedures is to strengthen approach behaviors and reduce fear responses. Various operant procedures have been employed effectively, including positive reinforcement, shaping, extinction, or some combination of these approaches. Positive reinforcement involves providing praise or a tangible reward following the occurrence of an approach behavior to increase the frequency of that behavior. Positive reinforcement has been used in conjunction with other contingency management procedures to eliminate school phobia (e.g., Vaal, 1973) and a toilet phobia (Luiselli, 1977) in clinical case reports.

Shaping is used when the targeted approach behavior is likely to be unresponsive to positive consequences because it is either too difficult or complex for the child to perform. A shaping procedure involves providing praise or material rewards following successive approximations to the desired behavior. For example, shaping has been found helpful in alleviating school phobia (Tahmisian & McReynolds, 1971) exhibited by a 13-year-old girl. In this clinical case description, the girl was reinforced for gradually spending greater amounts of time walking around school either with her parents or alone. She subsequently was able to attend one class and finally all classes by herself. This 3-week shaping procedure resulted in regular school attendance that was maintained at a 4-week follow-up assessment. Interestingly, systematic desensitization had previously been ineffective in reducing the child's school-related anxiety.

Extinction involves the removal of reinforcing

consequences for avoidance responses. Through careful evaluation, the therapist identifies and controls these reinforcing consequences. Parental attention can often contribute to the continuation of avoidance behaviors, so that asking parents to withdraw attention to fearfulness sometimes can lead to discontinuation of the adolescent's anxious behavior. Most typically, extinction is used in combination with positive reinforcement for nonfearful behavior. A clinical case example was provided by Hersen (1970) in the treatment of a 12½-year-old-boy with school phobia. In addition to requiring the adolescent to remain in school, as in in vivo flooding, Hersen (1970) altered the contingencies in the home and school settings by (a) instructing the parents and a school guidance counselor to reduce attention for the boy's crying and other avoidant behaviors and (b) having the parents praise the child for coping with school-related activities. In addition, during therapy sessions the therapist extinguished inappropriate school-related responses by withdrawing attention and praised coping responses related to school. At the end of treatment and 6 months following therapy, the adolescent was regularly attending school and showed improved academic performance.

Reinforced practice, an anxiety-reduction procedure that combines a number of successful operant components, has been developed by Leitenberg and Callahan (1973). Using this approach, avoidance responses are treated by reinforcement for graduated approach responses to the feared stimulus. Components of reinforced practice are: (a) repeated and graduated in vivo practice in approaching the phobic stimuli, (b) social reinforcement for small improvements, (c) trial-by-trial feedback on performance, and (d) the therapist's communication to the child of expectations of gradual success. Although the utility of this procedure has been supported by an analogue study of young nonclinic children who were fearful of the dark (Leitenberg & Callahan, 1973) and several investigations conducted with adults (see review by Leitenberg, 1976), only one uncontrolled case study has been reported using this approach with an adolescent. In this report, a procedure approximating reinforced practice was successfully employed to treat a 15-year-old mentally retarded adolescent's toileting phobia (Luiselli, 1977).

Overall, the systematic empirical evaluation of an operant approach in the clinical treatment of anxious adolescents has been extremely meager. In particular, controlled investigations of operant techniques applied to clinic adolescents with anxiety disorders are lacking.

Modeling

Modeling has been applied to the treatment of adolescent anxiety by having adolescents observe models approach the feared object or engage in the anxiety-producing behavior. The modeling procedure is believed to teach the adolescent new approach behaviors or to extinguish anxious responses by having the adolescent witness other people's behavior, the affective reactions of the model, and consequences for the approach behavior (Bandura, 1968, 1969). Several types of modeling have been distinguished, including symbolic, live (or vicarious), and participant modeling.

In symbolic modeling, the adolescent observes a model approach the feared situation or object on videotape or film. One advantage of this approach is that the therapist has greater control over the behavior of the model and the phobic object. Symbolic modeling also permits repeated presentations of the gradual-approach sequence (Ross, 1981). In live modeling, adolescents watch a "live" model interact with the feared object or engage in the feared behavior, without the adolescent actually participating in the activity associated with the phobic object. Participant modeling involves the adolescents actively making approach responses following observations of a model (Rosenthal & Bandura, 1978). The anxious adolescent first watches a model approach the feared object in a graded sequence. Then, the model guides the adolescent through the sequence with gentle prompting and praise. Finally, the adolescent performs the approach responses unassisted.

As is true for the other behavioral treatments for adolescent anxiety, evidence supporting the modification of adolescent anxiety disorders through modeling is fairly weak. Several analogue studies have been conducted of nonclinic children with relatively mild specific fears (see review by Ollendick, 1979b). One controlled single-case design adopting a multiple baseline strategy has been presented to demonstrate the effectiveness of a participant modeling approach in the treatment of a 13-year-old male adolescent's obsessional slowness manifested in multiple situations, such as dressing and washing (Clark, Sulgrim, & Bolton, 1982). No studies have been conducted of the appropriateness of modeling for other types of anxiety disorders, such as separation anxiety or overanxious disorders.

Ollendick (1979b) reviewed three analogue studies that employed adolescents with fears of snakes and heights as subjects. These studies showed that each of several different versions of modeling was superior to no treatment in reducing these fears. However, these studies indicate that the particular type of modeling procedure used influences the outcome of treatment. Participant modeling frequently has been found to be superior to modeling alone (Ollendick, 1979b). Similarly, exposure to models who interact fearlessly with the stimulus has sometimes, but not always, been found to be less effective than fearful models who "cope" with their fears (Ginther & Roberts, 1983).

Brief Psychotherapy

Long-term psychotherapy has generally been replaced during the past 25 years by various forms of brief psychotherapy. This is a result of the absence of demonstrated effectiveness and the high cost of the longer intensive therapy approaches (Gittelman, 1985). Although many types of psychotherapy have been applied to the treatment of adolescent anxiety disorders, few have been evaluated empirically. In the most notable examination of the efficacy of brief psychoanalytically oriented therapy, Miller et al. (1972a) compared a 24-session psychotherapy approach to behavior therapy and to a waiting-list control group in the treatment of a variety of child and adolescent anxiety disorders. As was described previously, treated children and adolescents were judged by parents as significantly improved relative to subjects on the waiting list, with no differences appearing between children and adolescents receiving behavior therapy versus psychoanalytic psychotherapy. These differences between treated and untreated subjects were not obtained when the professional staff rated change. Of particular note, separate analyses conducted for younger and older subjects revealed that psychotherapy did not seem to improve the outcome of 11- to 15-year-old subjects when compared to untreated subjects.

Clearly, additional systematic evaluations of the usefulness of brief psychotherapy approaches are needed before discounting their efficacy for treating adolescent anxiety disorders.

Psychopharmacology

More recently, the utility of pharmacological interventions has been evaluated in the treatment of school-phobic children and adolescents, most of whom were diagnosed as displaying separation anxiety (Gittelman-Klein & Klein, 1973). In this double-blind study, children and adolescents between the ages of 6 and 14 were treated with a multidiscipline treatment program concurrently with either imipramine or placebo. After 6 weeks of treatment, subjects receiving the treatment package including imipramine showed significantly greater improvement than children and adolescents receiving a placebo. Subjects on imipramine more frequently returned to school, demonstrated reduced separation anxiety, were more often rated globally by psychiatrists, mothers, and themselves as improved, and were free of physical symptoms before going to school, relative to children and adolescents in the placebo group.

A investigation employing chlomipramine in the treatment of similar subjects did not obtain differences in outcome in drug and placebo groups (Berney et al., 1981). Both groups demonstrated low rates of school return and little change in anxiety. As pointed out by Gittelman (1985), however, small doses of chlomipramine may have been insufficient to effect a positive change in the chlomipramine group. A third study compared chlomipramine treatment to a placebo in a group of children and adolescents between the ages of 6 and 18 (mean age 14.5 years), with severe obsessive–compulsive disorder (Flament et al., in press). A double-blind, controlled trial of chlomipramine was associated with significant improvement in observed and self-reported obsessions and compulsions, relative to a placebo condition. Throughout the study, all subjects received individual supportive psychotherapy, and parents were given counseling as needed.

Overall, there is some evidence that pharmacological intervention may be an important adjunct to other forms of therapy in the treatment of this population. Clearly, further investigation of the use of drugs to treat adolescent anxiety disorders is indicated.

Case 1. Obsessive–Compulsive Disorder

Morelli (1983) reported the successful use of a simple response consequence procedure to eliminate compulsive tapping in threes by a 13-year-old adolescent male. The well-substantiated response prevention method recommended by Meyer, Robertson, and Tatlon (1970) was not used in this case because of the high degree of parental cooperation and persistence required.

The patient had a 3-year history of frequently tapping his hands, arms, feet, or head on other parts of his body or other objects in sequences of three taps. In addition, he bounced in sequences of three when walking, entering a room, sitting down, and going to bed. This compulsive pattern of behavior occurred at both home and at school, but was more flagrant and problematic at home. The rituals were a source of considerable discord among family members and were considered to be significantly impairing the patient's adjustment.

The therapist judged that the mother would not be able to implement any form of home-based treatment due to her excessive levels of anger towards her son and his compulsive rituals. For this reason, he devoted eight weekly sessions to modifying the mother's emotions and cognitions prior to treating the boy's tapping behavior. A cognitive restructuring program (Beck, 1980; Ellis, 1962) was used with the mother that emphasized reduction in her catastrophizing and "should" statements concerning the rituals. During the last 2 weeks of this treatment, the mother was instructed to ignore her son's tapping rituals. She reported that no angry outbursts had occurred on her part.

On the 9th week, a 7-day baseline period was begun during which the mother unobtrusively counted the number of tapping sequences each day between 6:00 p.m. and 9:00 p.m. The number of rituals ranged from 20 to 40 per day and showed a level slope.

The treatment procedure involved an alteration in response consequences. The mother and the boy's sister were instructed to continue to ignore his rituals except for a prescribed response by the mother. Each time the boy engaged in a tapping sequence, the mother gently asked him to engage in another behavior that would be appropriate to the stimulus situation. This simple strategy was based on Guthrie's (1935) classic method of habit reversal.

No reduction in frequency of tapping rituals was observed during the first 2 days. However, on the 3rd day, the frequency dropped dramatically. After 2 weeks of treatment, the number of rituals fluctuated between one and five per observation interval; they fell to zero during the 4th week and remained at that level. Follow-up observations conducted 9 months after termination showed no return of the tapping rituals. In addition, the mother reported less family disturbance.

Case 2. Separation Anxiety Disorder

Rob was a 12-year-old boy referred to the behavior therapy unit of Temple University Medical School following 2 years of unsuccessful psychoanalytic treatment (Phillips & Wolpe, 1981). He had not attended school, or had been forced to attend and fled from the school, for 2 years and 5 months at the time of referral. Assessment determined that Rob was not more anxious in school than in other settings, but was markedly anxious when separated from his parents. Rob could only be away from his parents when playing in his backyard with friends; at all other times he became anxious if at least one parent was not in view. For this reason, the case was not conceptualized as a phobia of school, but rather as separation anxiety disorder. Rob also engaged in a variety of motor rituals: kicking things, waving his head or arms, doing things in threes, and telephoning his father in a stereotyped manner many times each day. He explained that he did these things to prevent catastrophes from happening to his parents. This pattern of behavior, which was performed approximately 50 times per day before treatment, led to the additional diagnosis of obsessive–compulsive disorder.

Rob's father was alcoholic, and his mother exhibited agoraphobia. In addition, Rob's grandmother reportedly interfered with the family in a manner that was described by the therapists as "tyrannical." His mother had been fearful about Rob's safety when away from her and had frequently not allowed him to leave her for this reason. His father had had a series of nonfatal heart attacks, his mother had had an operation when he was 5 years old, and Rob himself had had an operation when he was 4. When Rob was 6, his grandfather had died, and when he was 9, his father had had heart surgery. These catastrophic events apparently led to fears of the death of his father and fears of being abandoned by his parents.

Treatment involved the use of multiple behavioral techniques: relaxation training, in vivo desensitization, and imaginal desensitization. The entire intervention was quite lengthy, requiring 88 sessions over a 2-year period to complete.

Rob was first taught deep muscle relaxation using a reward system for home practice. He received points for three daily practice sessions that could be accumulated and used to purchase parts of his minibike and time on his minibike. He received larger numbers of points for practicing relaxation when his parents were out of the house taking a walk or a ride and when his father was driving home from work and could not be reached by telephone.

In vivo desensitization began by having Rob's parents move farther and farther away in the office situation. At first they sat in the waiting room when he was in the office with the door open so that he could see them. In gradual steps, the parents eventually moved outside of the waiting room where they could not be seen by Rob. In other series of graduated steps, the parents progressed from riding in their car with Rob following in a car driven by the therapist to taking timed rides out of Rob's sight. Similarly, they took increasingly longer walks and car rides at home. These exposures to separation elicited fear of being abandoned by his parents that gradually extinguished.

Next, Rob was encouraged to begin doing things involving separation that would be fun and that he had not previously done because of his separation anxiety. Rob went for a haircut with an uncle, rode his bike to a store 10 blocks from home and bought ice cream, visited relatives, and the like. Because these steps were difficult for Rob, he was given additional points for completing them.

After the success in desensitization around the home, a gradual in vivo desensitization program for school attendance was implemented. Initially, his mother sat in the car where she could be seen by Rob outside his classroom window. Then, she began coming at specified times each morning that were progressively later until she was finally not coming at all. When not outside the school, Rob's mother stayed at home so that he could reach her by telephone. Rob was given points for remaining in school and for reading. To support the school desensitization program, Rob was encouraged to think of pleasant images while at school (playing basketball, riding his minibike, etc.) and to engage in coping self-statements (e.g., "I'm in school, it's going well, I'm feeling comfortable.").

In addition to in vivo desensitization conducted at home and school, imaginal desensitization was concurrently carried out at the therapist's office. This progressed slowly, with Rob requiring many presentations of anxiety-provoking scenes while maintaining relaxation. Four hierarchies were used over approximately 60 sessions. These included separation from parents, traumatic events from the past (e.g., his father's medical crises), having to wait before going home from school or another location, and other dangerous or upsetting themes, such as his father being out drinking or being in a train wreck.

Within 4 months of the initiation of therapy, Rob was attending nonschool functions (e.g., roller skating races) alone. After 6 months he was spending full days in school. His parents were able to leave him for brief periods of time and his father was able to take business and fishing trips.

The compulsive rituals were treated by asking him to substitute muscle relaxation when he became anxious. He was able to reduce the frequency gradually and was given rewards that had been promised when he reached zero frequency for each part of the multiple rituals. Two years after treatment, follow-up information arrived in an unusually convincing form. Rob sent his therapists a postcard saying that he was traveling in Europe with friends.

CURRENT RESEARCH

Current research in adolescent anxiety disorders is taking many different directions. In large part, ongoing work reflects the obvious need for basic information about these disorders during this phase of development. Clearly, much remains to be learned about the epidemiology, prognosis, etiology, and treatment of adolescent anxiety disorders.

Other current trends reflect broader new directions in psychological and psychiatric research. Increasingly, etiological research is focusing on biological variables. One significant recent example is a study of neurological functioning in 16 adolescents diagnosed as having obsessive–compulsive disorder (Behar et al., 1984). Computerized tomography and a battery of neuropsychological tests revealed that the anxious patients had significantly higher ventricular-brain ratios and showed more evidence of frontal lobe dysfunction. These findings suggest that brain dysfunction may play a part in this disabling type of anxiety disorder.

Another new area of investigation in adolescent anxiety reflects the trend for psychologists to seek solutions for psychological problems that arise from medical problems. For example, adolescents with some forms of cancer are frequently subjected to painful medical procedures that result in anxiety and resistance to treatment. Bone marrow aspiration is one of the most painful diagnostic procedures that cancer patients must frequently and repeatedly endure. Katz et al. (1980) and LeBaron and Zeltzer (1984) developed and evaluated the reliability and validity of behavioral rating scales that can measure anxiety and pain sensation in adolescent cancer patients during aversive medical procedures. These innovative studies suggest that anxiety associated with medical procedures can be reliably and validly assessed using behavioral rating scales, in conjunction with self-report measures of distress. The development of objective measures of situation-specific anxiety such as these is vital for identifying the need for treatment aimed at reducing anxiety that arises during medical procedures and for assessing the efficacy of anxiety-reduction procedures.

SUMMARY

Adolescents with anxiety disorders may be afflicted by either anxiety disorders characteristic of children or by adult forms of maladaptive anxiety. Thus, adolescents may experience a broad range of anxiety disorders, including overanxious disorder, separation anxiety disorder, avoidant disorder, simple phobia, social phobia, agoraphobia, panic disorder, and obsessive–compulsive disorder.

The specific study of adolescent anxiety disorders lags far behind research with adults and children, such that our understanding of the epidemiology, assessment, and treatment of adolescent anxiety is very limited. The primary focus of research to date has been on adolescent school phobia, simple phobias, and subclinical fears and anxiety.

The prevalence of clinically significant phobias during adolescence is estimated to be about 6%, with girls outnumbering boys in their reports of fearfulness. However, no information regarding the epidemiology of overanxious disorder, social phobia, avoidant disorder, obsessive–compulsive disorder, and panic disorder is yet available. There appears to be a change in content of fears from childhood to adolescence, as well as a decline in the number of worries reported over this period. Anxiety disorders whose onset is in adolescence appear to be more persistent than those beginning in childhood, but less stable than those originating in adulthood. Further, investigations of the onset of adult anxiety disorders suggests that less disabling phobias begin in childhood, whereas more serious forms of anxiety disorders tend to originate in adolescence or adulthood.

Assessment methods have not been designed specifically for evaluating adolescent forms of anxiety disorders. Instead, assessment approaches developed for child or adult populations have been employed with adolescents. It appears that assessment of adolescent anxiety disorders is best accomplished via multimethod approaches that integrate information from adolescent self-reports, observations and ratings by adults, and physiological arousal.

A variety of behavior therapy approaches have been applied effectively in the treatment of anxiety disorders in adolescence, although systematic evaluation of these treatment methods is lacking. Nonetheless, preliminary investigations are suggestive that systematic desensitization, flooding or implosion, cognitive, and modeling approaches can be useful in reducing adolescent anxiety. The database on operant procedures is more limited. Investigations of pharmacological intervention for school phobias and obsessive–compulsive disorder indicate that drugs may serve to enhance the outcome achieved using other therapeutic modalities. Although the treatment outcome research generally supports the use of behavioral and pharmacological techniques, serious shortcomings in our database limit the conclusions that can be drawn.

REFERENCES

Abe, R., & Masui, T. (1981). Age-sex trends of phobic and anxiety symptoms in adolescents. *British Journal of Psychiatry, 138*, 297–302.

Achenbach, T. M., & Edelbrock, C. (1983). *Manual for the Child Behavior Checklist and Revised Child Behavior Profile*. Burlington, VT: University of Vermont, Department of Psychiatry.

Agras, W. S., Chapin, H. H., & Oliveau, D.C. (1972). The natural history of phobia. *Archives of General Psychiatry, 26*, 315–317.

Agras, S., Sylvester, D., & Oliveau, D. (1969). The epidemiology of common fears and phobia. *Comprehensive Psychiatry, 10*, 151–156.

American Psychiatric Association. (1980). *Diagnostic and statistical manual of mental disorders* (3rd ed.). Washington, DC: Author.

Bandura, A. (1968). A social learning interpretation of psychological dysfunctions. In P. London & D. Rosenhan (Eds.), *Foundation of abnormal psychology* (pp. 293–344). New York: Holt, Rinehart & Winston.

Bandura, A. (1969). *Principles of behavior modification*. New York: Holt, Rinehart & Winston.

Barlow, D., & Seidner, A. (1983). Treatment of adolescent agoraphobics: Effects on parent–adolescent relations. *Behaviour Research and Therapy, 21*, 519–526.

Barrios, B. A., Hartmann, D. P., & Shigetomi, C. (1981). Fears and anxieties in children. In E. J. Mash & L. G. Terdal (Eds.), *Behavioral assessment of childhood disorders*. New York: Guilford.

Bauer, D. H. (1976). An exploratory study of developmental changes in children's fears. *Journal of Child Psychology and Psychiatry, 17*, 69–74.

Beck, A. T. (1980). *Cognitive aspects of marital interactions*. Paper presented at the meeting of the Association for the Advancement of Behavior Therapy, New York.

Beck, A. T., & Emery, G. (1985). *Anxiety disorders and phobias: A cognitive perspective*. New York: Basic Books.

Behar, D., Rapoport, J. L., Berg, C. J., Denckla, M. B., Mann, L., Cox, C., Fedio, P., Zahn, T., & Wolfman, M. G. (1984). Computerized tomography and neuropsychological test measures in adolescents with obsessive–compulsive disorder. *American Journal of Psychiatry, 141*, 363–368.

Bellack, A. S., & Lombardo, T. W. (1984). Measurement of anxiety. In S. M. Turner (Ed.), *Behavioral theories and treatment of anxiety* (pp. 51–89). New York: Plenum.

Berg, I. (1976). School phobia in children of agoraphobic women. *British Journal of Psychiatry, 128*, 86–89.

Berg, I., Butler, A., Fairbairn, I., & McGuire, R. (1981). The parents of school phobic adolescents: A preliminary investigation of family life variables. *Psychological Medicine, 11*, 79–83.

Berg, I., Butler, A., & Hall, J. (1976). The outcome of adolescent school phobia. *British Journal of Psychiatry, 128*, 80–85.

Berg, I., Marks, I., McGuire, R., & Lipsedge, M. (1974). School phobia and agoraphobia. *Psychological Medicine, 4*, 428–434.

Berney, T., Kolvin I., Bhate, S. R., Garside, R. F., Jeans, J., Kay, G., & Scarth, L. (1981). School phobia: A therapeutic trial with clomipramine and short-term outcome. *British Journal of Psychiatry, 138*, 110–118.

Blagg, N. R., & Yule, W. (1984). The behavioural treatment of school refusal: A comparative study. *Behaviour Research and Therapy, 22*, 119–127.

Block, J. (1971). *Lives through time*. Berkeley: Bancroft Books.

Bolton, D., Collins, S., & Steinberg, D. (1983). The treatment of obsessive–compulsive disorder in adolescence: A report of 15 cases. *British Journal of Psychiatry, 142*, 456–464.

Bolton, D., & Turner, T. (1984). Obsessive–compulsive neurosis with conduct disorder in adolescence: A report of 2 cases. *Journal of Child Psychology and Psychiatry, 25*, 133–139.

Carlson, C. L., Figueroa, R. G., & Lahey, B. B. (in press). Behavior therapy for childhood anxiety disorders. In R. Gittelman (Ed.), *Anxiety disorders of children*. New York: Guilford.

Cavior, N., & Deutsch, A. (1975). Systematic desensitization to reduce dream-induced anxiety. *Journal of Nervous and Mental Disease, 161*, 433–435.

Clark, D. A., Sulgrim, I., & Bolton, D. (1982). Primary obsessional slowness: A nursing treatment programme with a 13-year-old male adolescent. *Behaviour Research and Therapy, 20*, 289–292.

Connors, C. K. (1969). A teacher rating scale for use in drug studies with children. *American Journal of Psychiatry, 126*, 884–888.

Costello, A. J., Edelbrock, C., Kalas, R., Dulcan, M. K., & Klaric, S. H. (1984). *Development and testing of the NIMH Diagnostic Interview Schedule for Children (DISC) in a clinic population: Final report*. Rockville, MD: Center for Epidemiological Studies, NIMH.

Croake, J. W., & Knox, F. H. (1971). A second look at adolescent fears. *Adolescence, 6*, 279–284.

Croghan, L. M. (1981). Conceptualizing the critical elements in a rapid desensitization to school anxiety: A case study. *Journal of Pediatric Psychology, 6*, 165–170.

Edelbrock, C., Costello, A. J., Dulcan, M. K., Kalas, R., & Conover, N. C. (1985). Age differences in the reliability of the psychiatric interview of the child. *Child Development, 56*, 265–275.

Edelbrock, C., Costello, A. J., Dulcan, M. K., Kalas, R., & Conover, N. C. (in press). Parent–child agreement on child psychiatric symptoms assessed via structured interview. *Journal of Child Psychology and Psychiatry*.

Ellis, A. (1962). *Reason and emotion in psychotherapy*. New York: Lyle Stuart.

Entwisle, D. R., & Greenberger, E. (1972). Questions about social class, internality-externality, and test anxiety. *Developmental Psychology, 7*, 218.

Finch, A. J., Kendall, P. C., Dannenberg, M. A., & Morgan, J. R. (1978). Effects of task difficulty on state–trait anxiety in emotionally disturbed children. *The Journal of Genetic Psychology, 133*, 253–259.

Flament, M. F., Rapoport, J. L., Berg, C. J., Sceery, W., Kilts, C., Mellstrom, B., & Linnoila, M. (in press). Clomipramine treatment of childhood obsessive compulsive disorder: A double-blind controlled study. *Archives of General Psychiatry*.

Gersten, J. C., Langner, T. S., Eisenberg, J. G., Simcha-Fagan, O., & McCarthy, E. D. (1976). Stability and change in types of behavioral disturbance of children and adolescents. *Journal of Abnormal Child Psychology, 4,* 111–126.

Ginther, L. J., & Roberts, M. C. (1983). A test of mastery versus coping modeling in the reduction of children's dental fears. *Child and Family Behavior Therapy, 4,* 41–51.

Gittelman, R. (1985). Anxiety disorders in children. In B. B. Lahey & A. E. Kazdin (Eds.), *Advances in clinical child psychology* (Vol. 9). New York: Plenum.

Gittelman-Klein, R., & Klein, D. (1973). School phobia: Diagnostic considerations in the light of imipramine effects. *The Journal of Nervous and Mental Disease, 156,* 199–215.

Glennon, B., & Weisz, J. R. (1978). An observational approach to the assessment of anxiety in young children. *Journal of Consulting and Clinical Psychology, 46,* 1246–1257.

Graham, P., & Rutter, M. (1973). Psychiatric disorder in the young adolescent: A follow-up study. *Proceedings of the Royal Society of Medicine, 66,* 58–61.

Guthrie, E. R. (1935). *The psychology of learning*. New York: Harper & Row.

Hampe, E., Noble, H., Miller, L. C., & Barrett, C. L. (1973). Phobic children one and two years posttreatment. *Journal of Abnormal Psychology, 82,* 446–453.

Herjanic, B., & Reich, W. (1982). Development of a structured psychiatric interview for children: Agreement between child and parent on individual symptoms. *Journal of Abnormal Child Psychology, 10,* 307–324.

Hersen, M. (1968). Treatment of a compulsive and phobic disorder through a total behavior therapy program: A case study. *Psychotherapy: Theory, Research, and Practice, 5,* 220–225.

Hersen, M. (1970). Behavior modification approach to a school-phobia case. *Journal of Clinical Psychology, 26,* 128–132.

Hersov, L. A. (1960). Persistent nonattendance at school. *Child Psychology and Psychiatry, 1,* 130–136.

Hollingsworth, C., Tanguay, P., Grossman, L., & Pabst, P. (1980). Long-term outcome of obsessive-compulsive disorder in childhood. *Journal of the American Academy of Child Psychiatry, 19,* 134–144.

Holroyd, K. A. (1976). Cognition and desensitization in the group treatment of test anxiety. *Journal of Consulting and Clinical Psychology, 44,* 991–1001.

Johnson, S. B., & Melamed, B. G. (1979). Assessment and treatment of children's fears. In B. B. Lahey & A. E. Kazdin (Eds.), *Advances in clinical child psychology* (Vol. 2, pp. 111–134). New York: Plenum.

Katz, E. R., Kellerman, J., & Siegel, S. E. (1980). Behavioral distress in children with cancer undergoing medical procedures: Developmental considerations. *Journal of Consulting and Clinical Psychology, 48,* 356–365.

Kazdin, A. E. (1974). Self-monitoring and behavior change. In M. J. Mahoney & C. E. Thoresen (Eds.), *Self-control: Power to the person* (pp. 218–246). Monterey: Brooks/Cole.

Kazdin, A. E. (1981). External validity and single-case experimentation: Issues and limitations. *Analysis and Intervention in Developmental Disabilities, 1,* 133–143.

Kelley, C. K. (1976). Play desensitization of fear of darkness in preschool children. *Behaviour Research and Therapy, 14,* 79–81.

Kennedy, W. (1965). School phobia: Rapid treatment of 50 cases. *Journal of Abnormal Psychology, 70,* 285–289.

Klein, D. F. (1964). Delineation of two drug-responsive syndromes. *Psychopharmacologia, 3,* 397–408.

Kolko, D. J. (1984). Paradoxical instruction in the elimination of avoidance behavior in an agoraphobic girl. *Journal of Behavior Therapy and Experimental Psychiatry, 15,* 51–57.

Kondas, O. (1967). Reduction of examination anxiety and "stage fright" by group desensitization and relaxation. *Behaviour Research and Therapy, 5,* 275–281.

Kovacs, M. (1983). *The interview schedule for children (ISC): Interrater and parent–child agreement.* Unpublished manuscript, University of Pittsburgh.

Kushner, M. (1965). Desensitization of a post-traumatic phobia. In L. P. Ullmann & L. Krasner (Eds.), *Case studies in behavior modification.* New York: Holt, Rinehart & Winston.

Lang, P. J., & Lazovik, A. D. (1963). Experimental desensitization of a phobia. *Journal of Abnormal and Social Psychology, 66,* 519–525.

LeBaron, S., & Zeltzer, L. (1984). Assessment of acute pain and anxiety in children and adolescents by self-reports, observer reports, and a behavior checklist. *Journal of Consulting and Clinical Psychology, 52,* 729–738.

Leitenberg, H. (1976). Behavioral approaches to treatment of neuroses. In H. Leitenberg (Ed.), *Handbook of behavior modification and behavior therapy* (pp. 124–167). Englewood Cliffs, NJ: Prentice-Hall.

Leitenberg, H., & Callahan, E. (1973). Reinforced practice and reduction of different kinds of fears in adults and children. *Behaviour Research and Therapy, 11,* 19–30.

Le Unes, A., & Siemsglusz, S. (1977). Paraprofessional treatment of school phobia in a young adolescent girl. *Adolescence, 12,* 115-121.

Little, S., & Jackson, B. (1974). The treatment of test anxiety through attentional and relaxation training. *Psychotherapy: Theory, Research and Practice, 11,* 175–178.

Livson, N., & Peskin, H. (1967). Prediction of adult psychological health in a longitudinal study. *Journal of Abnormal Psychology, 72,* 509–518.

Luiselli, J. K. (1977). Case report: An attendant-administered contingency management program for the treatment of toileting phobia. *Journal of Mental Deficiency Research, 21,* 283–288.

Mann, J., & Rosenthal, T. L. (1969). Vicarious and direct counterconditioning of test anxiety through individual and group desensitization. *Behaviour Research and Therapy, 7,* 359–367.

Marks, I. M., & Gelder, M. G. (1966). Different ages of onset in varieties of phobia. *American Journal of Psychiatry, 123,* 218–221.

Maurer, A. (1965). What children fear. *Journal of Genetic Psychology, 106*, 265–277.

Meichenbaum, D. (1971). A self-instructional approach to stress management: A proposal for stress innoculation training. In C. D. Spielberger & I. Sarason (Eds.), *Stress and anxiety* (Vol. 1, pp. 237–263). Washington, DC: Hemisphere.

Melamed, B. G., Yurcheson, R., Fleece, E. L., Hutcherson, S., & Hawes, R. (1978). Effects of film modeling on the reduction of anxiety-related behaviors in individuals varying in levels of previous experience in the stress situation. *Journal of Consulting and Clinical Psychology, 47*, 1357–1367.

Meyer, V., Robertson, J., & Tatlow, A. (1970). Home treatment of an obsessive-compulsive disorder by response prevention. *Journal of Behavior Therapy and Experimental Psychiatry, 1*, 319–321.

Miller, L. C., Barrett, C. L., Hampe, E., & Noble, H. (1972a). Comparison of reciprocal inhibition, psychotherapy, and waiting list control for phobic children. *Journal of Abnormal Psychology, 79*, 269–279.

Miller, L. C., Barrett, C. L., Hampe, E., & Noble, H. (1972b). Factor structure of childhood fears. *Journal of Consulting and Clinical Psychology, 39*, 264–268.

Morelli, G. (1983). Adolescent compulsion: A case study involving cognitive–behavioral treatment. *Psychological Reports, 53*, 519–522.

Morris, R. J., & Kratochwill, T. R. (1983). *Treating children's fears and phobias.* Elmsford, NY: Pergamon.

O'Farrell, T. J., Hedlund, M. A., & Cutter, H. S. (1981). Desensitization for a severe phobia of a fourteen-year-old male. *Child Behavior Therapy, 3*, 67–78.

Ollendick, T. H. (1979a). Behavioral treatment of anorexia nervosa: A five year study. *Behavior Modification, 3*, 124–135.

Ollendick, T. H. (1979b). Fear reduction techniques with children. In M. Hersen, R. Eisler, & P. Miller (Eds.), Progress in behavior modification (Vol. 8, pp. 127–168). New York: Academic.

Ollendick, T. H. (1983). Reliability and validity of the Revised Fear Survey Schedule for Children (FSSC-R). *Behaviour Research and Therapy, 21*, 685–692.

Ollendick, T. H., & Cerny, J. A. (1981). *Clinical behavior therapy with children.* New York: Plenum.

Ong, S. B. Y., & Leng, Y. K. (1979). The treatment of an obsessive-compulsive girl in the context of Malaysian Chinese culture. *Australian and New Zealand Journal of Psychiatry, 13*, 255–259.

Ownby, R. L. (1983). A cognitive–behavioral intervention for compulsive handwashing with a thirteen-year-old boy. *Psychology in the Schools, 20*, 219–222.

Paul, G. L. (1966). *Insight vs. desensitization in psychotherapy.* Stanford, CA: Stanford University Press.

Payne, B. D., Smith, J. E., & Payne, D. A. (1983). Grade, sex, and race differences in test anxiety. *Psychological Reports, 53*, 291–294.

Phillips, D., & Wolpe, S. (1981). Multiple behavioral techniques in severe separation anxiety of a 12 year old. *Journal of Behavior Therapy and Experimental Psychiatry, 12*, 329–332.

Puig-Antich, J., Orvaschel, H., Tabrizi, R. N., & Chambers, W. J. (1978). *Schedule for affective disorders and schizophrenia for school-age children.* New York: New York State Psychiatric Institute.

Quay, H. C. (1979). Classification. In H. C. Quay & J. S. Werry (Eds.), *Psychopathological disorders of childhood* (2nd ed., pp. 1–42). New York: Wiley.

Quay, H. C., & Peterson, D. R. (1983). *Interim manual for the Revised Behavior Problem Checklist.* Coral Gables FL: University of Miami.

Rapoport, J., Elkins, R., Langer, D. H., Sceery, W., Buchsbaum, M. S., Gillin, J. C., Murphy, D. L., Zahn, T. P., Lake, R., Ludlow, C., & Mendelson, W. (1981). Childhood obsessive-compulsive disorder. *Americn Journal of Psychiatry, 138*, 1545–1554.

Reynolds, C. R. (1980). Concurrent validity of What I Think and Feel: The Revised Children's Manifest Anxiety Scale. *Journal of Consulting and Clinical Psychology, 48*, 774–775.

Reynolds, C. R. (1981). Long-term stability of scores on the Revised Children's Anxiety Scale. *Perceptual and Motor Skills, 53*, 702.

Reynolds, C. R., & Paget, K. D. (1982). *National normative and reliability data for the Revised Children's Manifest Anxiety Scale.* Paper presented at the annual meeting of the National Association of School Psychologists, Toronto.

Reynolds, C. R., & Richmond, B. O. (1978). What I Think and Feel: A revised measure of children's manifest anxiety. *Journal of Abnormal Child Psychology, 6*, 271–280.

Reynolds, C. R., & Richmond, B. O. (1979). Factor structure and construct validity of "What I Think and Feel": The Revised Children's Manifest Anxiety Scale. *Journal of Personality Assessment, 43*, 281–283.

Rosenthal, T. L., & Bandura, A. (1978). Psychological modeling: Theory and practice. In S. L. Garfield & A. E. Bergin (Eds.), *Handbook of psychotherapy and behavior change* (2nd ed., pp. 621–658). New York: Wiley.

Ross, A. O. (1981). *Child behavior therapy: Principles, procedures, and empirical basis* (pp. 251–289). New York: Wiley.

Rutter, M. (1976). Research report: Isle of Wight studies, 1964–1974. *Psychological Medicine, 6*, 313–332.

Sarason, S. B., Davidson, K. S., Lighthall, F. F., Waite, R. R., & Ruebush, B. K. (1960). *Anxiety in elementary school children.* New York: Wiley.

Saunders, D. G. (1976). A case of motion sickness treated by systematic desensitization and in vivo relaxation. *Journal of Behavior Therapy and Experimental Psychiatry, 7*, 381–382.

Scherer, M. W., & Nakamura, C. Y. (1968). A fear survey schedule for children (FSS-FC): A factor analytic comparison with manifest anxiety (CMAS). *Behaviour Research and Therapy, 6*, 173–182.

Sheehan, D. V., Sheehan, K. E., & Minichiello, W. E. (1981). Age of onset of phobic disorders: A reevaluation. *Comprehensive Psychiatry, 6*, 544–553.

Simon, A., & Ward, L. O. (1974). Variables influencing the sources, frequency, and intensity of worry in secondary school pupils. *British Journal of Social and Clinical Psychology, 13*, 391–396.

Simon, A., & Ward, L. O. (1982). Sex-related patterns

of worry in secondary school pupils. *British Journal of Clinical Psychology, 21,* 63–64.

Smith, R. E., & Sharpe, T. M. (1970). Treatment of a school phobia with implosive therapy. *Journal of Consulting and Clinical Psychology, 35,* 239–243.

Speilberger, C. (1973). *Manual for the state trait inventory for children.* Palo Alto, CA: Consulting Psychologists Press.

Stampfl, T., & Levis, D. (1967). Essentials of implosive therapy: A learning theory-based psychodynamic behavioral therapy. *Journal of Abnormal Psychology, 72,* 496–503.

Tahmisian, J., & McReynolds, W. (1971). The use of parents as behavioral engineers in the treatment of a school phobic girl. *Journal of Counseling Psychology, 18,* 225–228.

Taylor, D. W. (1972). Treatment of excessive frequency of urination by desensitization. *Journal of Behavior Therapy and Experimental Psychiatry, 3,* 311–313.

Tyrer, P., & Tyrer, S. (1974). School refusal, truancy, and adult neurotic illness. *Psychological Medicine, 4,* 416–421.

Vaal, J. J. (1973). Applying contingency contracting to a school phobic: A case study. *Journal of Behavior Therapy and Experimental Psychiatry, 4,* 371–373.

Vernon, D., Foley, J. L., & Schulman, J. L. (1967). Effect of mother–child separation and birth order on young children's responses to two potentially stressful experiences. *Journal of Personality and Social Psychology, 5,* 162–174.

Warren, R., Smith, G., & Velten, E. (1984). Rational–emotive therapy and the reduction of interpersonal anxiety in junior high school students. *Adolescence, 19,* 893–902.

Watson, D., & Friend, R. (1969). Measurement of social-evaluative anxiety. *Journal of Consulting and Clinical Psychology, 33,* 448–457.

Weiner, I. B., & Del Gaudio, A. C. (1976). Psychopathology in adolescence. *Archives of General Psychiatry, 33,* 187–193.

Wolpe, J. (1958). *Psychotherapy by reciprocal inhibition.* Stanford: Stanford University Press.

Wolpe, J., & Lang, P. J. (1964). A fear survey schedule for use in behavior therapy. *Behaviour Research and Therapy, 2,* 27–30.

CHAPTER 19

Schizophrenia: An Evolving Construct

Michael F. Pogue-Geile and Martin Harrow

The term *schizophrenia* is generally applied to persons experiencing severe delusions and/or hallucinations without definite affective symptoms or any clear organic pathology. Difficulties often first arise during adolescence and become severe enough to warrant the diagnosis of schizophrenia most frequently during young adulthood. In addition to these disturbing experiences, persons diagnosed as schizophrenic often suffer disabilities in other domains of their lives, such as social relationships and instrumental work performance, which may have enduring consequences for their quality of life. Schizophrenia not only often entails great personal and family suffering, but is also a major public-health problem. Approximately 1% of the general population will at some time be diagnosed and treated as schizophrenic (Gottesman & Shields, 1982). Further, estimates of treatment expense and costs due to lost productivity range in the billions of dollars per year in the United States alone (Andrews et al., 1985; Gunderson & Mosher, 1975).

Despite the enormity of this personal suffering and public expense and intensive research efforts since the turn of the century, much remains to be known concerning schizophrenia and effective treatment for it. Controversy abounds and even the quite general description presented above is not unanimously agreed upon. For these reasons, schizophrenia has been termed the "cancer" of psychopathology, both for the extent of the suffering that is engendered and the complexities involved in understanding its causes and treatment. The goals of the present chapter are to survey what we do know about this difficult problem, what we need to learn, and what appear to be promising theoretical models of schizophrenia.

Before discussing the particulars of the definition of schizophrenia and its clinical description, some more general comments are in order concerning the formal characteristics of the diagnosis of schizophrenia. First, the nature of the term schizophrenia itself requires consideration. Schizophrenia may be usefully considered as an open construct rather than as a specific entity (Neale & Oltmanns, 1980). For example, although there is much that is not known about tuberculosis, there is general agreement regarding its definition. In contrast, the definition of schizophrenia is itself open to considerable debate and a major goal of research is to improve our nosological system. Thus, the term schizophrenia may be taken to indicate our current (and subject to change) theoretical structure, through which we view the behavior and experiences of certain persons.

We also need to consider what *kind* of information is utilized in any current definition of schizophrenia. Schizophrenia is currently defined using behavioral and experiential information— no classification based on pathology or etiology is available. Thus, the current construct of schizophrenia is formally more akin to the diagnosis of general mental retardation, which is made on a behavioral basis, than it is to the diagnosis of trisomy-21 (i.e., Down's syndrome), which is defined by the presence of an extra, 21st chromosome.

A potential consequence of using a definition based solely on behavioral and phenomenological information is that of underlying biological heterogeneity. Complex behavior tends to be multidetermined, with the result that similar behavioral patterns may arise for a multitude of reasons. Thus, a diagnosis of schizophrenia based on behavioral criteria probably includes individuals with differing pathophysiologies and etiologies. However, behavioral definitions need not necessarily be such invalid reflections of biological variation. For example, the diagnosis of Huntington's disease was initially made solely on behavioral criteria (i.e., certain characteristic motor abnormalities). This behavioral description was successful enough in reflecting biological determinants to allow the identification of a disorder with a homogeneous etiology, the description of its mode of genetic transmission, and the location of its gene on chromosome 4 (Gusella et al., 1983). Thus, considerable advances have occurred, even though there still remains no specific pathophysiological indicator of vulnerability to Huntington's disease.

Another formal characteristic of most current definitions of schizophrenia is that they are generally categorical. That is, one may be diagnosed as schizophrenic or not, but there is no diagnosis of "a small amount" of schizophrenia. In contrast, a dimensional approach emphasizes continuous variation, with less focus on qualitative differences and putative entities. Assessments of blood pressure and intelligence

follow a more dimensional diagnostic model. Although considerable research has been conducted on dimensional models of psychopathology (e.g., Blashfield, 1984), there is currently no generally accepted dimensional assessment of schizophrenia. Therefore, most research reviewed in the following sections has been based on the assumption of a categorical diagnostic model of schizophrenia, although it is by no means certain that this will eventually prove to be the most valid approach (cf. Gottesman & Shields, 1967; Rosenthal, 1975).

In summary, schizophrenia is perhaps best described as an evolving construct whose most useful definition remains to be determined. In addition, current diagnostic practices rely on behavioral and phenomenological information that is most frequently organized using a categorical format within which pathological or etiological heterogeneity are definite possibilities.

DEFINITION OF SCHIZOPHRENIA

Early History of the Construct

Because our current definitions of schizophrenia are not fixed or final, it is important to appreciate their historical origins. During the latter half of the 18th century, psychopathological classifications modeled themselves after the detailed biological taxonomy proposed by Linnaeus. These systems produced many diagnoses, each based on the presence of a single symptom, with different diagnoses being assigned depending on subtle symptomological distinctions (Zilboorg, 1941). Developments in the latter half of the 19th century may be seen as reactions to these systems, with an effort toward fewer, broader diagnoses.

Within this tradition, several symptom syndromes relevant to our current diagnosis of schizophrenia were described in the early 19th century (Neale & Oltmanns, 1980; Zilboorg, 1941). Phillipe Pinel, although best known for his humane treatment approaches toward the insane, included *la démence* as a diagnosis in his nosology. These patients were characterized by madness without the emotional excitement or melancholia that was present in other patients. Benedict Morel later applied a modification of this term, *démence précoce*, to such a patient who developed his madness at an early age. Similarly, the syndrome of catatonia was described by Kahlbaum and hebephrenia by Hecker during this period.

The most direct historical origins of our current description of schizophrenia derive from the work of the German psychiatrist, Emil Kraepelin, who in 1896, in the fifth edition of his textbook of psychiatry, included a chapter entitled, "Dementia Praecox." In this textbook and in his later writings, Kraepelin (1919/1971) grouped the multitude of diagnoses described by these earlier writers into two broad classes: dementia praecox and manic–depressive illness. Within the diagnosis of dementia praecox, Kraepelin included the earlier syndromes of hebephrenia, catatonia, and paranoia. His term, dementia praecox, emphasized what he saw as two important aspects of the syndrome: progressive cognitive decline (dementia) and an early onset (praecox). However, in later editions of his text, Kraepelin acknowledged that the term was somewhat inappropriate in that some patients did recover, and a number had a late onset of symptoms. Although he acknowledged individual differences in symptomatology within the diagnosis of dementia praecox (paranoid, catatonic, and hebephrenic subtypes were recognized), Kraepelin believed that all the syndromes within dementia praecox were due to the same basic organic process. For Kraepelin, a perceived similarity in course and end-state suggested a similarity in organic pathology. Therefore, given this orientation, in order to best reflect underlying biological processes, he accordingly based his classification on longitudinal considerations rather than solely on cross-sectional symptom presentation. Following this principle, Kraepelin distinguished dementia praecox, which he believed had a downhill course, from manic–depressive insanity, which he felt was characterized by a cyclical course and a prominent involvement of the emotions, especially manic excitement and depressive stupor.

Eugen Bleuler, a Swiss psychiatrist and a contemporary of Kraepelin, is the second figure who had a substantial impact on our present definitions of schizophrenia. He coined the term "schizophrenia" (E. Bleuler, 1911/1950) to replace Kraepelin's dementia praecox. Bleuler felt (as Kraepelin did later) that the term no longer accurately described the disorder; there were too many exceptions to both the "dementia" and the "praecox." In its place, Bleuler proposed the term schizophrenia (i.e., splitting of the mind) because he felt that the basic psychological process underlying all of the various secondary symptoms (e.g., delusions and hallucinations) involved a "breaking of the (mental) associative threads," which resulted in a fragmentation of mental and emotional functions. Thus, we see a change in classification method. Kraepelin united patients with a variety of symptom presentations under one construct based on the perceived commonality of a deteriorating course. Bleuler's unifying principle was an inferred psychological abnormality, although he also believed that a biological pathology was responsible for the overt psychopathology.

Bleuler's diagnostic approach differed from Kraepelin's in two fundamental ways. First, Bleuler's diagnostic scheme considerably broadened the diagnosis of schizophrenia; more patients were now diagnosed as schizophrenic. Second, where Kraepelin was content to classify based on observed characteristics, with the hope that course would accurately reflect biological factors, Bleuler's description of schizophrenia was more theory-driven. Classification depended upon broad constructs, such as his "fundamental" (i.e., necessary and sufficient) symptoms: associative disturbance; autism (withdrawal from external reality); affective disturbance (flat or incongruous emotions); and ambivalence. These two general approaches by Kraepelin and Bleuler toward the diagnosis of schizophrenia continue to influence current conceptions of the disorder, sometimes defining the opposite ends of a diagnostic pendulum's swing.

Current Diagnostic Systems

Although official classification systems of mental disorders that included schizophrenia have existed since the beginning of the 20th century (see American Psychiatric Association, 1968), it is only relatively recently that efforts to provide uniform definitions have been made. One of the earliest official diagnostic definitions of schizophrenia appeared in the *Diagnostic and Statistical Manual, 1rst edition (DSM-I)* of the American Psychiatric Association (1952). The *DSM-I* gave a general description of the "schizophrenic reactions" that emphasized disorders of thinking and affect that reflected Bleuler's influence.

This general description was little modified, with the exception of the omission of the term "reaction" in the next edition, or *DSM-II* (American Psychiatric Association, 1968), which was in use until 1980. The actual diagnostic definition of schizophrenia provided by the *DSM-II* is presented in Box 19.1. In addition to this general description, 11 different subtypes of schizophrenia were also described.

Several characteristics of the *DSM-II* definition are noteworthy. First, in the definition of schizophrenia, one can clearly recognize the influence of Bleuler, with his notion of loose associations. Abnormal behavior and experiences were "attributable primarily to a *thought* disorder," which was marked by "alterations of concept formation."

Second, the individual terms, or "symptoms," were quite vague. For example, how might one recognize "misinterpretation of reality," "inappropriate emotional responsiveness," or "loss of empathy with others"? The vagueness of these basic terms contributed to lack of agreement between diagnosticians and to the broadness of the diagnosis. In their mild form, many of these symptoms could even appear to be quite common in the general population.

In addition to the vagueness of the elementary terms, the structure itself of the definition was unclear. Aside from the necessary presence of an inferred "thought disorder," none of the previously described symptoms were clearly required for the diagnosis. This ambiguity in relationships among symptoms similarly contributed to a broad definition, with many persons qualifying for the diagnosis of schizophrenia. Note also that psychotic symptoms, such as hallucinations and delusions, were *not* required to be diagnosed as schizophrenic under *DSM-II*, although it was stated that some schizophrenics would show such symptoms.

Further complicating this vagueness concerning inclusion criteria for schizophrenia was the ambiguity of the exclusion criteria. The relationship between schizophrenia and major affective illness was particularly problematic. Thus, although major affective illnesses "are dominated by a *mood* disorder," schizophrenic schizo-affective subtype diagnoses were allowed "for patients showing a mixture of schizophrenic symptoms and pronounced elation or depression." Thus, patients with schizophrenic and affective symptomatology could be included under schizophrenia if it appeared that their mental status was attributable primarily to a *thought* disorder rather than to a *mood* disorder. Obviously, this might be a difficult distinction to make and contributed to the broadness of the diagnosis and lack of diagnostician agreement.

In summary, the *DSM-II* definition of schizophrenia was a broad one that was patterned more on a Bleulerian than on a Kraepelinian tradition. It was maximally inclusive; subsuming both nonpsychotic disorders, such as latent schizophrenia, and affective symtomatology. In addition, the vagueness of the definition made diagnostic disagreements based on differing interpretations likely.

During the 1960s and 1970s, dissatisfaction grew among researchers with the *DSM-I* and *DSM-II* definitions of schizophrenia. These criticisms involved two general points, one meth-

Box 19.1. Official American Definitions of Schizophrenia: *DSM-II* (1968)

Schizophrenia
This large category includes a group of disorders manifested by characteristic disturbances of thinking, mood and behavior. Disturbances in thinking are marked by alterations of concept formation that may lead to misinterpretation of reality and sometimes to delusions and hallucinations, which frequently appear psychologically self-protective. Corollary mood changes include ambivalent, constricted and inappropriate emotional responsiveness, and loss of empathy with others. Behavior may be withdrawn, regressive, and bizarre. The schizophrenias, in which the mental status is attributable primarily to a *thought* disorder, are to be distinguished from the *Major affective illnesses* (q.v.) which are dominated by a *mood* disorder. The *Paranoid states* (q.v.) are distinguished from schizophrenia by the narrowness of their distortions of reality and by the absence of other psychotic symptoms.

Note. From *Diagnostic and Statistical Manual of Mental Disorders* (2nd ed., pp. 33) by American Psychiatric Association, 1968, Washington, DC: Author. Copyright 1968 by American Psychiatric Association. Reprinted by permission.

odological and one theoretical. First, a number of studies reported unacceptable levels of inter-diagnostician agreement for the *DSM-I* and *DSM-II* diagnosis of schizophrenia (see summary by Kendell, 1975). Some investigations suggested that much of this unreliability could be attributed to the vagueness of the diagnostic "criteria" (Ward, Beck, Mendelson, Mock, & Erbaugh, 1962). Therefore, considerable interest was shown in altering the diagnostic description of schizophrenia (along with other diagnoses) to improve interrater reliability.

The second, more theoretically oriented criticism of *DSM-II*, concerned the breadth of the schizophrenic diagnosis. For example, the Cross-National Project (Cooper et al., 1972), which compared diagnostic practices in New York and London, found that schizophrenia was diagnosed approximately twice as frequently in the United States as in the United Kingdom. In contrast with the generally Bleulerian diagnostic tradition here, the British employed a narrower concept of schizophrenia (*A Glossary of Mental Disorders*, 1968). Although it is desirable that there be comparability in diagnostic practices across countries, such efforts shed little light on whether the broader or the narrower view is actually the more valid definition of schizophrenia in terms of reflecting pathology.

Nevertheless, for a variety of reasons, current definitions of schizophrenia in the United States evolved toward a narrower, more Kraepelinian conception. This shift toward a more conservative definition of the disorder was influenced by: (a) efforts at improving reliability, which emphasized easily defined psychotic signs and symptoms; (b) the introduction of lithium and effective antidepressants, which improved treatment of affective disorders; and (c) the desire for consistency with European practices.

A most timely alternative to the *DSM-II* diagnosis of schizophrenia was proposed by Feighner and his Washington University colleagues in an often-quoted article in 1972 (Feighner et al., 1972). In it they outlined the "Feighner criteria" for schizophrenia. This definition differed from the *DSM-II* in both form and content. The Feighner definition enumerated definite inclusion and exclusion criteria. Specifically, definite psychotic symptoms (hallucinations, delusions, or severe incoherent speech) of at least 6 months duration were required for the diagnosis. In addition, the presence of definite affective symptoms ruled out a diagnosis of schizophrenia. The definition also included several optional nonsymptomatic criteria, such as being single, having a family history of schizophrenia, or having a poor work history prior to hospitalization. As can be seen, the Feighner criteria represented a marked departure from *DSM-II*. They considerably narrowed the definition of schizophrenia, and their specificity offered the promise of improved interrater reliability. The Feighner criteria remain a frequently used definition of schizophrenia among researchers and are the basis for many of the most recent definitions of schizophrenia.

Based on the Feighner criteria and their modifications, such as the Research Diagnostic Criteria (RDC) (Spitzer, Endicott, & Robins, 1978), the *DSM-III* was adopted as the official American nomenclature in 1980 (American Psychiatric Association, 1980). Box 19.2 presents the *DSM-III* criteria for schizophrenia. The *DSM-III* employs a formal structure similar to the Feighner criteria, with specific inclusion and exclusion criteria. However, the range of required psychotic experiences is somewhat narrower in the *DSM-III*; only certain types of delusions and hallucinations contribute to the diagnosis. To some extent, the emphasis on these specific psychotic experiences is due to the influence of the first-rank symptoms approach proposed by Kurt Schneider. Schneider, a German psychiatrist, proposed a definition of schizophrenia based on the presence of 11 first-rank symptoms that he felt were pathognomonic of schizophrenia (Schneider, 1959). The *DSM-III* also incorporates 6-month duration of symptoms and decline in functioning criteria. Similar to Feighner criteria, the *DSM-III* also rules out the diagnosis of schizophrenia in the presence of a definite affective syndrome.

A comparison of Tables 19.1 and 19.2 highlights the change in the definition of schizophrenia that has occurred. This change has led to improved diagnostic agreement. A number of studies have found improved reliability using the *DSM-III* (e.g., Spitzer, Forman, & Nee, 1979). The newer definition is also clearly narrower than the *DSM-II*, with fewer patients being diagnosed as schizophrenic (e.g., Silverstein, Warren, Harrow, Grinker, & Pawelski, 1982; Stephens, Astrup, Carpenter, Shaffer, &

Box 19.2. Official American Definitions of Schizophrenia: *DSM-III* (1980)

Diagnostic Criteria for a Schizophrenic Disorder

A. At least one of the following during a phase of the illness:
1. bizarre delusions (content is patently absurd and has no possible basis in fact), such as delusions of being controlled, thought broadcasting, thought insertion, or thought withdrawal
2. somatic, grandiose, religious, nihilistic, or other delusions without persecutory or jealous content
3. delusions with persecutory or jealous content if accompanied by hallucinations of any type
4. auditory hallucinations in which either a voice keeps up a running commentary on the individual's behavior or thoughts, or two or more voices converse with each other
5. auditory hallucinations on several occasions with content of more than one or two words, having no apparent relation to depression or elation
6. incoherence, marked loosening of associations, markedly illogical thinking, or marked poverty of content of speech if associated with at least one of the following:
   (a) blunted, flat, or inappropriate affect
   (b) delusions or hallucinations
   (c) catatonic or other grossly disorganized behavior

B. Deterioration from a previous level of functioning in such areas as work, social relations, and self-care.

C. Duration: Continuous signs of the illness for at least 6 months at some time during the person's life, with some signs of the illness at present. The 6-month period must include an active phase during which there were symptoms from A, with or without a prodromal or residual phase.

D. The full depressive or manic syndrome (criteria A and B of major depressive or manic episode), if present, developed after any psychotic symptoms, or was brief in duration relative to the duration of the psychotic symptoms in A.

E. Onset of prodromal or active phase of the illness before age 45.

F. Not due to any organic mental disorder or mental retardation.

Note. From *Diagnostic and Statistical Manual of Mental Disorders* (3rd ed., pp. 188–190) by American Psychiatric Association, 1980, Washington, DC: Author. Copyright 1980 by American Psychiatric Association. Reprinted by permission.

Goldberg, 1982). It remains an open question, however, whether this narrower *DSM-III* conception of schizophrenia more validly reflects pathology and etiology than the broader *DSM-II* approach.

As a testimony to the unknown validity of the official *DSM-III* definition of schizophrenia, a number of alternative operational diagnostic criteria also have been proposed. Although these will not be discussed in detail, they include the New Haven Schizophrenia Index (Astrachan et al., 1972), the Flexible System (Carpenter & Strauss, 1973), and the Taylor and Abrams' Criteria (Taylor & Abrams, 1978), in addition to the Feighner Criteria (Feighner et al., 1972) and the RDC (Spitzer et al., 1978). In general, all of these newer operational definitions provide for satisfactory interrater reliability, although they differ markedly in the number and characteristics of persons diagnosed as schizophrenic (Endicott et al., 1982; Fenton, Mosher, & Matthews, 1981; Helzer, Brockington, & Kendell, 1981; Kendell, Brockington, & Leff, 1979; McGlashan, 1984; McGuffin, Farmer, Gottesman, Murray, & Reveley, 1984).

A major research strategy therefore has evolved in which patients are diagnosed with these multiple criteria. The different diagnostic systems are then compared in terms of the relative strength of their associations with various validating criteria, such as course, response to treatment, family history of disorders, biological, and psychological characteristics (Robins & Guze, 1970). Such studies should contribute to the evolution of our definition of schizophrenia and eventually result in a more valid *DSM-IV*.

THE DISTRIBUTION OF SCHIZOPHRENIA

Frequency of Schizophrenia

One might expect, given the complexities involved in the definition of schizophrenia, that the answer to the question, "How frequent is schizophrenia?" is not a simple one. The answer most certainly depends on the broadness of the definition of schizophrenia that is used. As most of the best epidemiological investigations of schizophrenia have been carried out in

Europe, where a generally narrow definition has been employed, estimates reported here *probably* parallel those that might be found using *DSM-III*, although few data are directly relevant to this issue (cf. Robins et al., 1984).

Other factors affecting the answer involve how the frequency of schizophrenia is expressed (Gottesman & Shields, 1982). One initial issue is the potential difference between treated (person affected ever contacted mental health services) and untreated cases of schizophrenia. For example, there appears to be a substantial number of severely depressed persons who do not contact treatment services. Therefore, the difference between the frequency of total depressions (treated plus untreated) is much different from that which would be estimated from treated cases alone (Weissman, Myers, & Thompson, 1981). To the best of our current knowledge, the situation is different for narrowly defined schizophrenia. Dohrenwend et al. (1980) report that 83.3% of persons diagnosed as schizophrenic in six cross-sectional community surveys had been hospitalized at some time. Similar conclusions were reached by Gottesman and Shields (1982) based on other studies. In addition, some number of these as-yet-untreated schizophrenics may seek treatment in the future, thus raising the treated/total ratio even higher. Consequently, it appears that most narrowly defined schizophrenics eventually come in contact with mental health services in Western cultures. This finding implies that epidemiological estimates of the rate of schizophrenia based on mental-health-service contacts may not be overly conservative.

There are a number of different statistics used to express the frequency of schizophrenia in a given population, depending on study methodology and purposes (MacMahon & Pugh, 1970). Point prevalence refers to the number of current cases of schizophrenia that are identified at any certain time divided by the total living population. Lifetime prevalence is the same measure, except that an attempt is made to determine (generally through retrospective recall) the number of persons who have *ever* experienced schizophrenia by a certain date. Dohrenwend et al. (1980) have computed a conservative median true prevalence of schizophrenia of .59% derived from 14 European community surveys. Higher estimates were reported by Gottesman and Shields (1982) and Robins et al. (1984).

Although useful for administrative purposes, prevalence rates are difficult to compare across populations that may differ in age structure and other factors. A more useful statistic, the lifetime morbid risk (MR), is the probability that a person who survives the period of risk (e.g., age 15 to 45) will develop schizophrenia (see Gottesman & Shields, 1982, for further description). Estimates of the morbid risk for schizophrenia generally average slightly less than 1%, with .85% being a commonly accepted figure (Slater & Cowie, 1971; Zerbin-Rüdin, 1972).

Association with Demographic Factors

Given this lifetime expectancy for schizophrenia of approximately 1%, we will next examine whether certain person-characteristics are associated with increased risk. The traditional view has been that gender is not associated with risk for schizophrenia (Dohrenwend et al., 1980; Slater & Cowie, 1971). This observation has held in community-based, hospital-based, European, and American samples. However, there is some recent evidence that suggests that the more recent narrow American criteria may diagnose more males than females (Lewine, Burbach, & Meltzer, 1984) in treated samples. Further research is required on this issue.

Schizophrenia has a variable age of onset. Although the extremes of the range are subject to debate, the ages of risk for the onset of schizophrenic symptoms are generally accepted to be between 15 and 45 or 55 years old. New cases with schizophrenia-like symptoms do appear for the first time after age 55, although they are rare. The risk for schizophrenia is not equal throughout this age range, but rather tends to peak dramatically in the 20s for men and in the late 20s or early 30s for women. This sex difference in the peak age of onset for schizophrenia is one of the most replicated results in schizophrenia research, and yet its origin remains unclear (Lewine, 1981). Thus, for many males, florid schizophrenia is a disorder of late adolescence, but for females this is less often the case. These age of onset statistics are generally based on first hospitalization or appearance of psychotic symptoms. However, as will be discussed later, a variety of difficulties often predate hospitalization.

TREATMENT

Over the years, an extraordinary range of procedures has been applied to schizophrenic patients in the name of treatment. However, most have never been found to be effective and are thus primarily of historical interest. Rather than describe these historical developments, the present brief survey will emphasize current treatments for schizophrenia that have demonstrated some utility. In addition, this survey will focus on the treatment of relatively acute schizophrenic patients as opposed to the rehabilitation of more chronic, long hospital-stay individuals.

At present, one of the most frequent courses of schizophrenia consists of symptomatic exacerbations with interepisode residual difficulties. This course presents the clinician with two somewhat different treatment problems: (a) the reduction of acute symptomatology, and (b) the improvement of interepisode functioning. As these two aspects of schizophrenia appear to require different treatment approaches, they will be discussed separately.

Acute Treatment

The administration of the various specific treatments described next all necessarily occur within some administrative/environmental context that may itself exert a beneficial or iatrogenic influence on the course of treatment. Since the deinstitutionalization movement of the 1960s, the role of the inpatient hospital facility in the treatment of schizophrenia has been closely questioned and severely limited. A number of studies have suggested that longer hospitalizations are no better for most schizophrenic patients than shorter stays (e.g., Caffey, Galbrecht, & Klett, 1971). Due to these empirical, economic, and social influences, a model of the institutional management of schizophrenia has evolved in which acute episodes are most often treated within a limited-stay inpatient hospital environment (generally of 2 to 10 weeks duration). Follow-up care is then delivered on an outpatient basis of some nature. Thus, most of the specific treatments for the described acute episodes are routinely administered and were evaluated within an inpatient hospital context.

Pharmacological Treatments

The development of the phenothiazine, chlorpromazine, by the Frenchman Paul Charpentier in the early 1950s, and its administration to psychiatric patients by Delay and Deniker in 1952, may mark one of the most significant and serendipitous advances in our knowledge of schizophrenia. Since that time, thousands of studies have investigated these substances, and dozens of different antipsychotic medications have been developed. Although differing somewhat in chemical structure, potency, and side-effects, these various drugs all seem to be equally effective with similar pharmacological effect and thus will be considered together.

It is by now clear that adequate doses of antipsychotic medications, such as chlorpromazine and haloperidol, are more effective than a placebo in reducing psychotic symptoms in most schizophrenic patients during an acute episode. Many controlled studies during the 1960s have demonstrated this conclusion beyond any reasonable doubt (Klein & Davis, 1969). As the name implies, these drugs are not schizophrenia-specific. Rather, they appear generally effective for the treatment of most psychotic episodes. However, antipsychotic medications are not effective for all schizophrenic patients. In a major National Institute for Mental Health (NIMH) collaborative study, 75% of broadly diagnosed schizophrenics showed substantial improvement during a 6-week in-hospital controlled drug trial (Cole, Goldberg, & Klerman, 1964). Although impressive, approximately 25% of the patients did not respond to the medication. Similarly, about 25% of the placebo group showed substantial improvement. Thus, although antipsychotic medications are effective during acute episodes for many schizophrenic patients, there remains a substantial subgroup of patients who appear medication-resistant and a subgroup who would improve without medications. Unfortunately, no consistent predictors of medication nonresponse have been identified to date (Davis, Schaffer, Killian, Kinard, & Chan, 1980).

Note should also be made concerning the quality of improvement shown in those patients who do respond to antipsychotic medication. Although marked improvement may take place, return to complete normal functioning is not the most common result. Thus, although definitely improved over their condition on admission, many patients are discharged with diminished psychotic symptoms rather than no symptoms at all (Harrow, Carone, & Westermeyer, 1985; Harrow, Silverstein, Lazar, &

Pogue-Geile, in press). Delusions and hallucinations may be attenuated and less insistent, but they may still be present in many patients after drug treatment. Antipsychotic medications also are not equally effective for all schizophrenic symptoms. They appear to be most effective against the positive psychotic symptoms of delusions, hallucinations, and formal-thought disorder. Although initial reports found them also to improve the negative symptoms of flat affect and psychomotor retardation (Cole et al., 1964), more recent studies have suggested that these negative symptoms are often medication-resistant (Angrist, Rotrosen, & Gershon, 1980).

Antipsychotic medications also produce a range of frequent acute side-effects. These extrapyramidal symptoms (EPS) include akathisia (motor restlessness), dystonias (loss of muscle control and muscle stiffness), sedation, and other side effects, which may occur in approximately 40% of patients during the early course of treatment (Lipton & Burnett 1979). However, some of these side-effects are short-lived and can be treated using anticholinergic medications. Nevertheless, these unpleasant aspects of antipsychotic medications contribute to frequent patient noncompliance with the treatment regimen.

Despite these drawbacks, antipsychotic medications represent a marked advance in the treatment of schizophrenia. Because we cannot predict beforehand who will respond to them, a trial of antipsychotic medication is clearly justified for any acute episode of schizophrenia or other psychotic disturbance. These antipsychotic medications have now become the standard against which other potential treatments are compared.

In addition to the traditional antipsychotic medications just discussed, a number of other pharmacotherapies have been investigated in treating acute schizophrenic episodes (Donaldson, Gelenberg, & Baldessarini, 1983). Most attention has focused on the potential efficacy in schizophrenia of lithium carbonate, which is the treatment of choice in bipolar affective disorder. Contrary to some theories, controlled trials have found that perhaps between one-third and one-half of schizophrenic patients may benefit from lithium (Delva & Letemendia, 1982). In addition, among patients with schizophrenic symptoms, the presence of affective symptoms does not appear to predict response to lithium (Donaldson et al., 1983). Thus, it ap-

pears unlikely that lithium-responsive schizophrenic patients are merely "misdiagnosed" bipolar patients. Rather, lithium response may be greatest (as is response to antipsychotic medication) in "good prognosis" schizophrenics who are characterized by a good premorbid history and acute onset (Donaldson et al., 1983).

Psychosocial Therapies

Traditional individual psychotherapy alone has generally been found to be less effective in the inpatient treatment of acute schizophrenic episodes than antipsychotic medication (May, 1968). A more useful question, then, is whether various psychosocial therapies in conjunction with medication provide an increment in effectiveness over medication alone during the acute inpatient period. Of the few studies that have investigated this question, it generally appears that traditional individual psychotherapy delivered along with medication during the inpatient stay contributes relatively little compared to medication alone (e.g., May, 1968). Similar findings are generally reported in studies comparing group therapy plus medication versus medication alone (Mosher & Keith, 1980). Most investigations of traditional psychosocial therapies with acute schizophrenic inpatients find little effect of such interventions relative to pharmacotherapy. However, these studies present a number of methodological complications and have often not employed outcome measures that might be more appropriate to psychosocial interventions than symptom reduction alone. Nevertheless, the current orientation toward brief hospital stays suggests that extensive psychosocial programs directed toward improving social functioning may be more useful during the posthospital period, after some measure of symptom reduction has been achieved using antipsychotic medication.

Posthospital Aftercare

Pharmacological Treatment

In addition to the treatment of acute symptoms, antipsychotic medications have been used with relatively asymptomatic patients after hospital discharge in order to prevent relapse. To date, over 20 controlled studies of maintenance antipsychotic medication during the posthospital period have provided strong evidence of its effectiveness compared to a placebo (Davis et al., 1980). In a compilation of these studies comprising 3,519 patients, Davis et al. estimate a relapse rate after 1 year of 19% for maintenance medication *versus* 55% for a placebo, although others find higher relapse rates for medicated patients (Hogarty et al., 1979). Although impressive, these results are similar to those for the treatment of acute symptoms in that some patients appear treatment-nonresponsive and others appear able to function without maintenance medication. To date, no patient characteristics have been identified that will reliably predict response to maintenance medication. In addition, no controlled studies have investigated the efficacy of maintenance medication over longer than 2 years. Therefore, the benefit of extended multiyear maintenance treatment has yet to be empirically demonstrated.

The identification of patients who do not require maintenance medication is particularly important given the risks involved in long-term maintenance medication. In addition to the acute side-effects mentioned above, more disturbing side-effects also appear later in the course of treatment (American Psychiatric Association, 1980). Most concern has focused on tardive dyskinesia, which involves a loss of muscular control, with patients displaying involuntary buccal movements, truncal swaying, and repetitive hand movements. At present, there is no treatment for this disabling neurological condition. Although some patients improve after withdrawal from antipsychotic medications, for many the condition is irreversible. The prevalence of clinically significant symptoms of tardive dyskinesia has been estimated as approximately 10–20% of schizophrenic patients who have been exposed to antipsychotic medications for at least 1 year, with higher prevalences in elderly patients. Tardive dyskinesia appears strongly linked to antipsychotic use, although its associations with specific dosages and duration of treatment are not entirely clear. Nevertheless, there is some evidence that extended treatment and high doses may increase the risk for the condition.

The risks of tardive dyskinesia must therefore be balanced against the demonstrated benefits of maintenance antipsychotic medication. In addition to efforts at identifying patients who do not relapse off medication, two newer strategies have evolved in an effort to decrease the risk of tardive dyskinesia. The first approach

attempts to identify the minimal dose of antipsychotic medication that is sufficient to prevent relapse. Preliminary results suggest that doses one-tenth of those usually employed still provide significant protection from relapse (Kane, 1983). Another approach has been termed the targeted medication strategy, in which patients are maintained off medication until the onset of prodromal signs of a relapse is detected, at which time medication is promptly administered. Preliminary data suggest that such a targeted approach may be as effective as traditional maintenance medication (Carpenter & Heinrichs, 1983). However, targeted medication requires that a patient's disorder be episodic rather than chronic, that it show sufficient prodromal signs, and that a system for close monitoring of clinical state be available. Although these newer strategies require further research, they represent important attempts at decreasing the exposure of schizophrenic patients to the potential hazards of antipsychotic medications.

Psychosocial Therapies

Given the demonstrated effectiveness of maintenance medication, most studies of outpatient psychosocial interventions have investigated whether these treatments in combination with medication provide an increment in functioning over antipsychotic medication alone. This survey will emphasize specific therapies rather than more community-oriented interventions.

The major outpatient study by Hogarty and his associates comparing individual therapy plus medication with medication alone found little additional value for psychosocial therapy in the first year after discharge in reducing relapse rates (Hogarty & Goldberg, 1973). However, a positive effect of the psychosocial treatment did begin to emerge in the second year after discharge (Hogarty, Goldberg, Schooler, & Ulrich, 1974). A second study by this group found similar results, although they did not achieve statistical significance (Hogarty et al., 1979). The individual therapy (labeled major role therapy) employed in these studies was not a traditional supportive or dynamic therapy, but was rather directed toward the patients' daily difficulties in employment and social adjustment. A recent study comparing psychodynamic therapy plus medication with a similar social therapy plus medication also found some slight advantages favoring the more reality-oriented approach (Gunderson et al., 1984). Thus, it appears that an individual therapeutic approach may provide some additional late-appearing benefit with maintenance medication, and that structured practically oriented interventions may be preferable to more traditional therapies.

Several studies have also examined the efficacy of group therapy in the aftercare of schizophrenic patients (Mosher & Keith, 1980). This form of treatment offers the potential advantages of being efficient in terms of therapist time and of focusing on the improvement of social functioning. Studies comparing group therapy plus medication with medication alone have generally found no additional effect of the treatment in preventing relapse. However, there is some evidence for a small positive effect on social functioning (Mosher & Keith, 1980). In addition, research comparing group therapy plus medication with individual therapy plus medication generally has shown little difference between the two. Given this equivalence, group therapy would appear to have some advantage from a cost–benefit perspective.

Family treatment with schizophrenic outpatients has been receiving increasing attention in light of the findings that schizophrenic patients who are discharged to hostile and critical families are more likely to relapse than those returning to more supportive families (e.g., Vaughn, Snyder, Jones, Freeman, & Falloon, 1984). To date, all three studies of family therapy with schizophrenic outpatients have found generally positive results comparing family therapy plus medication with medication alone (Falloon et al., 1982; Goldstein, Rodnick, Evans, May, & Steinberg, 1978; Leff, Kuipers, Berkowitz, & Sturgeon, 1985).

Although such treatment is only applicable to patients who are not living alone, it appears to be an extremely promising area in the psychosocial treatment of schizophrenic outpatients.

In summary, although great advances have been made in the treatment of schizophrenia, it still remains a disorder with an all too grave prognosis. Work needs to be done in developing more effective medications without the serious side-effects of tardive dyskinesia. Also, alternative treatments for medication-resistant patients need to be devised. In the interim, the emphasis on decreasing medication to the minimum level and shortening hospitalizations should serve to reduce some of the iatrogenic effects of our current treatments. As it is clear that medications do not provide comprehensive care, more research into psychosocial interventions is also needed. Although the results for the psychosocial therapies to date have not been impressive, we are beginning to see the development of some innovative treatments specifically tailored for the schizophrenic patient that focus on family- and reality-oriented issues rather than traditional psychotherapy (e.g., Hogarty et al., 1986). Such innovations in both psychosocial and pharmacological areas are clearly needed, as our current treatment of schizophrenia is not ideal.

CASE DESCRIPTION

In order to add human detail to this discussion of diagnostic criteria and treatment strategies, a brief case history of a person meeting DSM-III criteria for schizophrenia will be presented. Although no single patient can be representative of such a heterogeneous diagnostic category, this patient presents some of the common features of schizophrenia discussed here. He is selected from the sample of the Chicago Follow-up Study, which is a prospective follow-up study of schizophrenia and other major psychopathology (Grinker & Harrow, in press; Harrow & Quinlan, 1985). This patient entered the study at the time of his second hospitalization and has been reinterviewed 5 times, at approximately 2-year intervals, covering a span of 12 years. Names and details of the history have been altered to ensure confidentiality.

John's florid symptoms first began at age 18 following his high school graduation. After high school he started work as a clerk in a local department store. However, shortly after beginning work he began to experience difficulties. He felt that he knew a girl at work, but she did not acknowledge him. He became increasingly anxious around her, and after lunch one day he noted that things had begun to look different—they had lost their dimensions and looked plastic. These experiences eventually became so anxiety-inducing that John ceased going to work.

Following this incident, he looked for work and continued to have increasingly bizarre experiences. One day after being rejected for a job, John thought that the radio was beginning to refer directly to him. In anticipation of a visit to the city by the president of the United States, a radio report had mentioned that a suspicious man had been seen near the president's hotel. John believed that this referred to him and that people were beginning to follow him while he was driving. He also heard his own thoughts coming over the radio.

At this time, John's mother left on a trip to California. John became increasingly agitated and thought that voices were speaking to him from the furnace. Eventually he began dismantling the furnace, until his father discovered him. After escaping his father and running to various neighbors, John was finally subdued and taken to a local psychiatric hospital.

John's first hospitalization lasted 1 month, during which time he was treated with high doses of chlorpromazine resulting in a reduction of his psychotic symptoms. He was discharged to his parents' home, but after 1 week his bizarre behavior increased and his parents felt that they could not handle him. John therefore was admitted for his second hospitalization and was enrolled in the Chicago Follow-up Study.

John's second hospitalization lasted 4 months, during which time he responded well to antipsychotic medication and appeared to benefit from practically oriented individual psychotherapy. He was again discharged to his parents on maintenance medication with continuing outpatient psychotherapy. At this time he was asymptomatic and was functioning well. He began to attend a community college part-time.

However, after several months he increased to a full-time school load, and his bizarre experiences began to return. He believed that during class all his classmates were crying and that the teacher was making strange signs to him. He heard voices talking to him and believed that people were following him. After a number of arguments with his father, he became increasingly withdrawn from his family until he finally presented himself at a local police station and asked to be hospitalized.

Between the time of his first hospitalization at age 18 until his last research interview 12 years later, John has been hospitalized a total of 10 times for 22 months in all and has lived in four halfway houses for a total of 36 months. He has also been involved in years of outpatient maintenance medication and periodic outpatient therapy. He has held a number of unskilled jobs, although often only for a few months each.

At his last follow-up interview at age 31, John reported no florid psychotic symptoms in the past year, although he appeared distracted and preoccupied. He had not worked for the past 2 years, was living alone in a rooming house, was taking chlorpromazine and lithium carbonate, and was involved in individual psychotherapy. He reported few social contacts and no dating. His most frequent activity was watching television alone. He was rated as showing moderate flat affect and poverty of speech.

CURRENT RESEARCH

Research on schizophrenia continues to be an increasingly vigorous area of inquiry. Methodological advances in diagnosis and measurement techniques along with substantive innovations have increased our knowledge of schizophrenia in recent years. In the following sections, we will selectively survey the current state of this knowledge as it pertains to several basic questions about schizophrenia. Limitations of space make a comprehensive and critical review impractical, and instead references to key reviews have been provided where possible. Several recent books are also available that provide general reviews of research on schizophrenia (see Gottesman & Shields, 1982; Neale & Oltmanns, 1980).

Early Characteristics of Schizophrenic Patients

A number of studies have attempted to describe characteristics of schizophrenic patients *prior* to their onset of severe symptoms and subsequent hospitalization. Such information has potential value for prediction, prevention, and understanding pathological processes. At this point, however, we usually cannot determine whether such prior characteristics, if identified, might reflect early manifestations of pathological processes, or might be independent factors that contribute to the risk for schizophrenia. Although identification of early characteristics that might be predictive of schizophrenia is an extremely valuable goal, it should be remembered that it may not necessarily be possible. For example, consider the difficulty of trying to predict, from childhood characteristics alone, adult baldness, in which the relevant genetic factors are not overtly expressed until relatively late in development.

The investigation of the precursors to some infrequent condition with a late and variable age of onset, such as schizophrenia, presents many methodological difficulties. Because it is generally impractical to follow a cohort of 10,000 persons from birth to age 55 in the hope of identifying the early characteristics of the 1% who will develop schizophrenia, research has usually employed one of two general strategies—the follow-back or the prospective design (Garmezy & Streitman, 1974; Pogue-Geile & Harrow, 1984b). Follow-back designs have generally begun with hospitalized adult patients and then attempted to retrospectively recreate their past history either through subjective recall or the use of archival sources (e.g., school or child-clinic records). Such studies have the advantage of relative efficiency, because each subject has eventually developed the condition of interest. However, subjective recall has obvious potential biases, and often archival records do not contain all of the necessary information.

A number of follow-back studies have examined the childhood intelligence of schizophrenics (see review by Aylward, Walker, & Bettes, 1984), with one of the most comprehensive being that by Lane and Albee (1963; 1970). Preschizophrenics showed significantly lower intelligence scores recorded during elementary school than peers from the same neighborhood (Albee, Lane, & Reuter, 1964) and their own siblings (Lane & Albee, 1965; Schaffner, Lane, & Albee, 1967). Other studies using follow-back designs also have found similar results (Offord, 1974; Pollack, Woerner, & Klein, 1970). Although consistent, these deficits in tested intelligence generally are not large, however. The interpretation of these findings has emphasized either lowered intelligence as a consequence of some early pathological process (Lane & Albee, 1965) or as an independently transmitted factor that increases the risk for the expression of schizophrenia (Jones & Offord, 1975).

With regard to preschizophrenic interpersonal behavior, some of the best follow-back information comes from a large study by Watt, Fryer, Lewine, and Prentky (1979) that investigated teachers' recorded comments about children who were later hospitalized for schizophrenia. Essentially, the findings suggested that there were few differences between preschizophrenics and matched normal controls during elementary school (Watt, 1978). However, by high school, preschizophrenic girls were rated as significantly more socially introverted than the normal control girls, whereas preschizophrenic boys were rated by teachers as more disagreeable than the normal control boys (Watt, 1978). However, these sex interactions were not apparent in a larger sample, when ratings were averaged across all grades (Lewine, Watt, Prentky, & Fryer, 1978). Overall, Watt's study suggests that some schizophrenics show behavioral disturbances during adolescence that teachers generally perceived as disagreeable and immature. It is also important to note that not all preschizophrenics showed such interpersonal difficulties, and that not all children with similar problems became schizophrenic.

In order to surmount some of the difficulties inherent in such retrospective studies, prospective studies of cohorts of children selected to be at risk for schizophrenia, termed "high-risk" studies, have been undertaken. Being an offspring of a schizophrenic parent is one of the most common selection criteria for high-risk studies. This is because such children are at an approximately 10-fold increased risk for schizophrenia compared to the general population (Mednick & McNeil, 1968; Pearson & Kley, 1957). Putative high-risk groups of children also have been selected based on adolescent and family characteristics (Goldstein, Judd, Rodnick, Alkire, & Gould, 1968) and hypothesized psychometric indexes (Chapman, Edell, & Chapman, 1980). The clear advantage of such prospective designs over follow-back studies is the variety of measures that can be obtained. However, there are potential problems in generalization from such selected groups to other schizophrenics who did not experience the particular risk factor (e.g., the 90% of schizophrenics who do not have a schizophrenic parent). Although such designs are more efficient than an unselected birth-cohort design, the final yield of schizophrenic cases may still be quite low (e.g., potentially 10 cases from 100 offspring of schizophrenic parents). In addition, the variable age of onset for schizophrenia may mean that final comparisons will have to wait until the cohort has passed through the majority of the period of risk, with the potential of considerable sample attrition.

The high-risk methodology based on the offspring of schizophrenic parents, was initially proposed by Pearson and Kley (1957) and was first utilized by Mednick and Schulsinger (1968) in Denmark. It has since been employed in a number of projects. A recent progress report of high-risk studies conducted to date included 15 major ongoing projects (Watt, Anthony, Wynne, & Rolf, 1984). Any survey of this growing area must be preliminary at best, as few of the subjects in these studies have yet passed through the age of risk for schizophrenia. Therefore, most results to date concern cross-sectional comparisons of high-risk children with controls. Such analyses most directly address the consequences of having a schizophrenic parent, rather than identify the precursors of schizophrenia (McNeil & Kaij, 1979).

Consistent with the follow-back data presented in the previous paragraphs, many (but not all) high-risk studies have found lower childhood intelligence scores in offspring of schizophrenic parents than in offspring of normal control parents (e.g., Mednick & Schulsinger, 1968; Watt, Grubb, & Erlenmeyer-Kimling, 1982; Winters, Stone, Weintraub, & Neale, 1981; cf. Hanson, Gottesman, & Heston, 1976). However, no significant differences generally have been found in childhood intelligence between the offspring of schizophrenic parents and the offspring of other psychiatric patients (e.g., Winters et al., 1981). Thus, mild deficits in general intellectual functioning may be a nonspecific consequence of severe parental psychopathology.

Like follow-back research, high-risk studies have also assessed the social behavior of children in school settings. Several investigations have found that high-risk children were rated as generally less socially competent and more aggressive by teachers and peers than were normal controls (e.g., Fisher, Schwartzman, Harder, & Kokes, 1984; Watt et al., 1982; Weintraub & Neale, 1984). However, the children of parents with psychiatric diagnoses other than schizophrenia also often appear as deviant in school behavior as the children of schizophrenic parents (e.g., Weintraub & Neale, 1984; cf. Fisher

et al., 1984). Thus, again, lowered childhood competence and increased aggressiveness may represent relatively nonspecific consequences of parental psychopathology.

A number of high-risk studies have focused on various measures of cognitive functioning, particularly attentional measures, that discriminate between adult schizophrenic patients and controls. The offspring of schizophrenics have been found to be more distractible on a short-term memory task than children of psychiatric controls (Harvey, Winters, Weintraub, & Neale, 1981) and to show deficits in sustained attention on the Continuous Performance Test (CPT) compared to normal controls (e.g., Cornblatt & Erlenmeyer-Kimling, 1984; cf. Asarnow, Steffy, MacCrimmon, & Cleghorn, 1977). Although the results in this area appear promising, more information is needed concerning the specificity of these deficits to the offspring of schizophrenic parents compared to the offspring of other psychiatric groups.

The prospective high-risk methodology has also made possible psychophysiological and neurological assessments. Event-related cortical potentials (ERP) have been assessed in Erlenmeyer-Kimling's New York High-Risk Study (Friedman, Vaughan, & Erlenmeyer-Kimling, 1982) with high-risk children having been found to have decreased late positive components of their ERPs. A number of studies have also reported higher rates of neurological softsigns in high-risk children (Fish, 1984; Hanson et al., 1976; Marcus, Hans, Mednick, Schulsinger, & Michelsen, 1985; McNeil & Kaij, 1984) compared to normal controls.

This research attempting to characterize the "preschizophrenic," although incomplete in specifics, provides some general points for consideration. First, it appears that at least *some* schizophrenics show clear behavioral deviance a number of years prior to the development of clinical symptoms. However, at this time we do not know whether these characteristics reflect some early schizophrenic process or are independent contributing factors. It also seems unlikely from behavioral data alone that preschizophrenics will be able to be identified a priori. The behavioral characteristics ascribed to them are not specific enough and the base rate of schizophrenia is too low. Too many children with similar behavioral styles never subsequently develop schizophrenia. Another important point is the number of preschizophrenics who do *not* show any early behavioral abnormalities, which is further evidence of the range of individual differences among schizophrenics. Although by no means certain, perhaps the most enlightening findings regarding prediction and pathology *may* come from the more biologically oriented assessments of high-risk children. Measures such as evoked potentials and CT scans appear to hold more promise for specificity and information regarding pathology than broad behavioral descriptions. Follow-up results from high-risk studies will show the extent to which this promise may be fulfilled.

The Posthospital Course of Schizophrenia

Description of the Courses of Schizophrenia

Although a topic of interest since the time of Kraepelin, much current research has focused on the description of the longitudinal characteristics of schizophrenia following onset of marked symptoms and hospitalization. One of the hallmarks of this posthospital course of schizophrenia appears to be variation—both variation over time within the same individual and variation among schizophrenic patients in the severity of their course. Although he initially attempted to define a syndrome based on a homogeneous poor outcome, Kraepelin recognized this variation and all of the recent major long-term (e.g., M. Bleuler, 1972/1978; Ciompi, 1980; Huber, Gross, Schüttler, & Linz, 1980; Tsuang, Woolson, & Fleming, 1979) and short-term follow-up studies (e.g., Harrow, Grinker, Silverstein, & Holzman, 1978; Strauss & Carpenter, 1977; World Health Organization [WHO], 1979) of schizophrenia also document these marked individual differences in the course of the disorder. Some patients show fairly complete recovery and others suffer chronic symptoms and disabilities. Although agreeing on this overall picture, the recent follow-up investigations vary somewhat in the proportion of schizophrenic patients that they find recovered or incapacitated.

One of the most comprehensive and optimistic of the recent long-term follow-up studies of schizophrenia was performed in Switzerland by Manfred Bleuler, the son of Eugen Bleuler. He personally followed 208 schizophrenics for over

20 years after their index hospitalization (M. Bleuler, 1972/1978). Bleuler reported that complete symptomatic recovery lasting 5 years or more occurred in 16% of his first admission cohort, compared to 24% showing moderate/severe chronic psychosis. The majority of patients showed some outcome between these extremes—most often with an episodic course consisting of alternating periods of relative remission and exacerbation. Although findings depend somewhat on the control group employed, studies also report that although there is often considerable overlap, the course of schizophrenia is generally more severe than that of other psychiatric disorders, especially that of depression. In addition to this tendency toward persisting symptomatology and social disability, another important aspect of the posthospital course of schizophrenia is the increased risk for suicide, which is estimated to be approximately 10% (Drake, Gates, Whitaker, & Cotton, 1985). Although not quite as high as the long-term risk for suicide in depression, this rate is dramatically higher than that found in the general population.

Prognostic Research

A large number of older and more recent studies have investigated correlates of these individual differences in the course of schizophrenia. The concept of "premorbid" adjustment, which includes interpersonal relations and occupational functioning prior to first hospitalization, has been particularly important in this research (Kokes, Strauss, & Klorman, 1977). Overall, these measures of prehospital social and instrumental functioning appear to be moderately effective in predicting later posthospital measures of functioning in schizophrenia (Stoffelmayr, Dillavou, & Hunter, 1983; WHO, 1979), although more recent investigations that have controlled for the extent of previous chronicity generally find somewhat weaker predictive power for these characteristics (e.g., Westermeyer & Harrow, 1984). In addition, each prehospital characteristic tends to predict best the similar characteristic at followup; that is, prehospital social functioning best predicts posthospital social functioning (Strauss & Carpenter, 1977). The few studies that have examined the prognostic value of prehospital adjustment in other diagnostic groups have reported mixed results (Strauss, Kokes, Carpenter, & Ritzler, 1978; cf. Bromet, Harrow, & Kasl, 1974). Consequently, although it generally appears that levels of prehospital adjustment have some prognostic importance, this may not be specific to schizophrenia.

The investigation of the prognostic value within schizophrenia of specific symptoms occurring at onset has focused predominantly on the importance of affective symptoms, such as depression and manic mood in better predicting later functioning. Results of such early studies have been a major influence on the current diagnostic practice of having the presence of definite affective symptomatology as exclusion criteria for the *DSM-III* diagnosis of schizophrenia (e.g., Pope & Lipinski, 1978). Previous research by Vaillant (1962), Stephens (1970), Astrup and Noreik (1966), and others suggested that the occurrence of affective symptomatology was related to improved outcome within schizophrenia. However, more recent and methodologically sophisticated studies do not corroborate this result (e.g., Bland, Parker, & Orn, 1978; Carpenter, Bartko, Strauss, & Hawk, 1978; Gift, Strauss, Kokes, Harder, & Ritzler, 1980) and thus question the previous consensus that, within a broad diagnosis of schizophrenia, the presence of definite affective symptomatology is moderately predictive of better outcome functioning (see review by Harrow & Grossman, 1984).

The negative-symptom syndrome, which includes flat affect and poverty of speech, also has received considerable recent attention as a potential sign of poor prognosis within schizophrenia (Andreasen & Olsen, 1982; Crow, 1980; Pogue-Geile & Harrow, 1984a; Strauss, Carpenter, & Bartko, 1974). Crow (1980) had initially speculated that negative symptoms might represent the behavioral manifestation of structural brain abnormalities that might define a subgroup of schizophrenic patients with poor outcome (cf. Owens et al., 1985). Further, prospective studies have found that negative symptoms do predict poor outcome functioning within schizophrenia (Carpenter et al., 1978; Pogue-Geile & Harrow, 1985).

Other aspects of symptomatology that have been investigated for their prognostic importance include the rate of onset of florid symptoms, and patient age at their onset. Although inconsistent, studies generally have found that an earlier age at first hospitalization and a gradual onset of symptoms are associated with poorer outcome functioning in schizophrenia (e.g., Westermeyer & Harrow, 1984). In addition, schizophrenic males often have been reported to have poorer outcomes than females (Salokangas, 1983; Westermeyer & Harrow, 1984).

In summary, a large literature has investigated the prognostic value of various prehospitalization characteristics of schizophrenia. The findings are by no means uniform and are often vitiated by methodological difficulties, particularly the inclusion of already chronic patients in the follow-up sample. Although there is evidence for significant prognostic importance of the previously mentioned factors, these characteristics, alone or in combination, rarely predict a majority of the variation of outcome within schizophrenia (WHO, 1979). In addition, major questions remain concerning the specificity of such prognostic factors to schizophrenia. These results suggest that much of the variation in schizophrenic posthospital functioning may be due to either unmeasured person characteristics (e.g., biological variation) or to the influence of factors operating *during* the posthospital period.

Posthospital Environment

Research that has sought to explain the variability in the course of schizophrenia in terms of concurrent posthospital environment generally has utilized the global concept of stress. As stressors, most studies have investigated the potential influence of life events or family social environment. Representative of the research on life events (Rabkin, 1980) is a follow-up study by Leff, Hirsch, Gaind, Rhode, and Stevens (1973) in which stressful life events assessed retrospectively were found to be somewhat more frequent among relapsed patients than among those who did not relapse. However, many patients relapsed without reporting any previous life events. Thus, although the occurrence of stressful events may increase the likelihood of relapse, discrete life events probably do not explain most of the variation in schizophrenic outcome.

Considerably more recent research has examined the potential role of the more chronic ongoing stressors of family social environment on schizophrenic relapse. Originating with the work of Brown and colleagues at the University of London (Brown, Monck, Carstairs, & Wing, 1962), a systematic program of research has evolved, in which four major independent studies have investigated these issues (Brown et al., 1962; Brown, Birley, & Wing, 1972; Leff & Vaughn, 1981; Vaughn & Leff, 1976; Vaughn et al., 1984). These studies have focused on the role that expressed emotion (EE) in family members plays in predicting relapse among schizophrenic patients who return to a family home following discharge from the hospital. Expressed emotion is primarily defined as the extent of critical and hostile comments made by family members about the patient and the degree of emotional overinvolvement of the family members with the patient. All of these investigations have found an association between high family EE and relapse in schizophrenia at 9-month to 2-year follow-ups after hospital discharge. A major innovation of this work has been to evaluate the amount of personal contact that the discharged patient had with family members. This is crucial in order to attribute the occurrence of relapse to the immediate noxious effect of returning to a high-EE family. Consistent with the hypothesis, the deleterious "effect" of high EE tends to be lessened by decreased face-to-face contact between the patient and family members. In addition, the most recent replication of this work in California showed that the effect of contact with low-EE families was mildly helpful (Vaughn et al., 1984). Nine percent of schizophrenics from high-contact low-EE homes relapsed, in contrast with 29% of those from reduced-contact low-EE families. Results of these correlational studies have encouraged several controlled treatment studies in which discharged schizophrenic patients are randomly assigned to interventions designed to reduce family EE (e.g., Falloon et al., 1982; Leff, Kuipers, Berkowitz, Eberlein-Vries, & Sturgeon, 1982; Leff et al., 1985). As discussed above, these controlled investigations have found such family treatment helpful in reducing relapse among schizophrenic patients who were also taking antipsychotic medication.

In summary, although Kraepelin initially intended that his concept of dementia praecox would unite a variety of symptom syndromes that all had a deteriorating course, from his day to the present, a range of posthospital courses for schizophrenia has been found. Despite this variation, however, the posthospital course for schizophrenic patients is most frequently unfavorable, compared to what might be looked forward to by most young adults without psychiatric symptomatology. The presence of such variation in course and the possibility of numerous social influences suggests that schizophrenia, as it is currently diagnosed, may be less similar to a disorder like measles, with a relatively fixed progression of symptoms and outcome, and more similar to a multifactorial disorder such as hypertension, which shows great variation in course and is susceptible to a variety of ameliorative and negative influences.

Cognitive Psychopathology of Schizophrenia

The goal of much recent research on the cognitive psychopathology of schizophrenia has been to identify aberrant psychological processes that might lead to, or reflect, the predisposition to schizophrenia, and/or overt schizophrenic symptomatology. A distinction is often made in this research between those psychological processes that might underlie the vulnerability to schizophrenia and those that might be associated with overt symptomatology (Zubin & Spring, 1977). Indicators of vulnerability to schizophrenia are hypothesized to be: (a) present prior to clinical symptom onset, (b) persistent throughout the course of the disorder, (c) present in nonsymptomatic relatives, and (d) not necessarily correlated with fluctuations in overt symptomatology. In contrast, episode indicators have been theorized to be closely correlated with the presence of overt symptoms and to be within the normal range prior to onset and during remission. Most current research has attempted to identify indicators of vulnerability, with less interest being shown in the processes that might be most related to specific symptoms (cf. Neale, Oltmanns, & Harvey, 1985). Although perhaps heuristic, this distinction may be overly artificial, as it is likely that those processes underlying a vulnerability to schizophrenia are also intimately involved in the occurrence of overt symptomatology.

Although a broad range of tasks have been studied (see reviews by Chapman, 1979; Nuechterlein & Dawson, 1984), much current research has investigated the role that disordered attentional processes might play in the cognitive psychopathology of schizophrenia. Based on earlier reports that some schizophrenic patients report subjective experiences of decreased selective attention early in the course of the disorder (e.g., McGhie & Chapman, 1961), a number of information-processing tasks have been designed to index this complex construct. Most efforts have focused on various dichotic listening tasks (e.g., Pogue-Geile & Oltmanns, 1980), digit span performance (e.g., Oltmanns, 1978), span of apprehension (e.g., Neale, 1971), and reaction-time tasks (e.g., Nuechterlein, 1977) as measures of selective attention, and the continuous performance task (e.g., Kornetsky & Orzack, 1978) as a measure of sustained attention. Schizophrenic inpatients have consistently been shown to evidence deficits on these various tasks compared to normal controls. Although considerably less research has addressed the important question of the specificity of these deficits to schizophrenia compared to other diagnostic groups, studies have reported such specificity for some tasks (e.g., Pogue-Geile & Oltmanns, 1980), but not for others (e.g., Oltmanns, 1978; Strauss, Bohannon, Stephens, & Parker, 1984). However, it appears likely that, during the acute phase, many manic patients may show cognitive deficits that are difficult to distinguish from those of schizophrenic patients, although more research is needed on this issue.

In terms of the longitudinal persistence of such attention deficits, the few investigations that have assessed schizophrenics following the inpatient phase generally have reported the presence of continuing cognitive deficits (e.g., Asarnow & MacCrimmon, 1978, 1981, 1982; Frame & Oltmanns, 1982; Strauss, Bohannon, Kaminsky, & Kharabi, 1979), although it is possible that these abnormalities reflect the disrupting effect of continued psychosis in these schizophrenic patients.

As discussed above, a number of researchers have also examined the presence of such attentional deficits in the high-risk offspring of schizophrenic parents in an attempt to ascertain whether these cognitive abnormalities might predate the clinical onset of schizophrenia. Although the preliminary cross-sectional reports have often revealed differences between children at risk for schizophrenia and normal controls, the offspring of parents with other diagnoses also frequently appear to show such

cognitive abnormalities. The eventual follow-up of these high-risk offspring should provide more resolution of this issue.

To date, an enormous amount of research has attempted to identify attentional abnormalities that might serve as indicators of the predisposition to schizophrenia. Enough positive findings have been reported to suggest that this continues to be a viable approach. However, more multivariate studies are needed to investigate the convergent validity among the various putative attentional tasks. Thus far, correlations among these tasks, all of which aim to index attentional dysfunction, have been disappointingly low (e.g., Asarnow & MacCrimmon, 1978). In addition, the establishment of discriminant validity for such tasks is also fraught with potential psychometric difficulties (Chapman & Chapman, 1978). Further emphasis on other psychopathic control groups is required to determine whether these deficits are specific to schizophrenia, or are more related to overall upset and psychosis in general. Although results appear promising, much more research along these lines is required to implicate with certainty a role for attentional dysfunction in the cognitive psychopathology of schizophrenia.

Another potential behavioral indicator of the predisposition to schizophrenia may be an abnormality of smooth-pursuit eye-tracking (see review by Lipton, Levy, Holzman, & Levin, 1983). First documented by Diefendorf and Dodge (1908), recent work by Holzman and colleagues (e.g., Holzman, Proctor, & Hughes, 1973; Holzman, Solomon, Levin, & Waternaux, 1984) and others (e.g., Iacono & Koenig, 1983) have consistently reported greater eye-tracking abnormalities in schizophrenic patients than normal controls. Although the prevalence of these abnormalities appears to be greatest in schizophrenic patients, there is evidence that they also are present in excess in other psychotic patients, particularly manic patients. A recent study has suggested that these abnormalities in manic patients may represent side-effects of the administration of lithium carbonate (Levy et al., 1985). Few data exist, however, concerning the long-term stability of eye-tracking abnormalities.

Considerable research has investigated the prevalence of eye-tracking abnormalities in first-degree relatives of schizophrenics and other patient groups (e.g., Holzman et al., 1974; Holzman et al., 1984; Levy et al., 1983) and the co-twins of schizophrenic probands (Holzman, Kringlen, Levy, & Haberman, 1980; Holzman et al., 1977). These studies have reported a prevalence of deviant eye tracking in approximately 50% of the parents of schizophrenics, whereas the rates in parents of manic and depressed probands did not differ from normal values. In addition, monozygotic co-twins of schizophrenic probands who were discordant for psychosis also tended to show abnormal eye-tracking patterns. In these studies, there was a trend for concordance of eye-tracking abnormalities within families of schizophrenics. However, this was not complete; deviant eye-tracking was found in parents and co-twins of schizophrenic probands who themselves did not show pursuit abnormalities. Holzman et al. (1984) have recently interpreted these data as indicating the genetic transmission of a latent trait that may manifest itself as overt schizophrenia, deviant eye-tracking, or both, depending on other factors.

Research on deviant eye-tracking as a potential indicator of vulnerability to schizophrenia represents an impressive and promising body of evidence. It would be particularly interesting to integrate this work with the previously discussed measures of attentional dysfunction and with the high-risk studies of the offspring of schizophrenic parents. In addition, more longitudinal study of the stability of eye-tracking dysfunction would be valuable. Although empirically promising, the potential theoretical link between deviant eye-tracking and the manifestation of schizophrenic symptomatology has not been examined as thoroughly (cf. Holzman, 1978).

Pathophysiology

Neurochemical Aspects

The dopamine hypothesis is the current dominant theory concerning the potential biochemical pathophysiology of schizophrenia (Haracz, 1982; Meltzer & Stahl, 1976), although other possibilities have also been proposed (Bowers, 1980). In its most general form, the dopamine hypothesis proposes that the overt signs of schizophrenia are caused by a functional excess of central dopaminergic neural transmission, perhaps due to a supersensitivity of postsynaptic dopamine receptors. To date, the major evidence supporting this hypothesis remains indirect. Drugs that decrease dopamine activity, such as the phenothiazines, generally possess antipsychotic properties. In addition, there is a high correlation between a drug's ability to inhibit dopaminergic transmission and its antipsychotic potency (Snyder, Banerjee, Yamamura, & Greenberg, 1974). In contrast, drugs that increase dopamine activity, such as amphetamine, may induce psychosis.

However, more direct investigations have generally produced only equivocal support. Studies of the levels of dopamine, its precursors, metabolites, and receptors in cerebrospinal fluid, postmortem brain, blood, and urine of schizophrenic patients report a variety of conflicting findings (see review by Haracz, 1982). The ambiguity of these more direct tests of the dopamine hypothesis, as well as the existence of clinical phenomena that it explained poorly (e.g., the extended time-lag between administration of antipsychotic medication and its effect), suggest that some revision of the hypothesis is probably required. The existence of extensive and complex interconnections between dopaminergic neuronal tracts and pathways mediated by other transmitter substances (both known and currently unknown) has recently been taken to indicate that dopamine may be only part of the explanation of the pathogenesis of schizophrenia and that it may merely reflect other more central abnormalities (Haracz, 1982). In addition to such neurochemical elaborations of the dopamine hypothesis, other recent theorists have offered that dopamine abnormalities may be important, but only for a subgroup of currently diagnosed schizophrenics. Crow (1980) has further proposed an association between putative dopaminergic abnormalities and a specific group of "positive" symptoms, such as hallucinations and delusions. However, few mechanisms linking an abnormality in dopaminergic transmission with the symptoms of schizophrenia have been proposed.

Although a global dopaminergic overactivity appears unlikely to be the entire story of the pathogenesis of schizophrenia, the dopamine hypothesis has provided the invaluable heuristic function of stimulating an immense amount of both basic and clinical neurochemical research. The resulting advances in basic neurosciences and characterization of other neurotransmitters are likely to provide the framework for more sophisticated neurochemical hypotheses of schizophrenia and theory relating neurochemical abnormalities to the symptomatology of schizophrenia.

Neuroanatomical Aspects

In addition to neurochemical investigations, neuroanatomical research on schizophrenia has received renewed interest in recent years (Weinberger, Wagner, & Wyatt, 1983). Although the histological examination of postmortem brain is experiencing a revival as well (e.g., Stevens, 1982), most recent research has employed methods, such as the computed tomography (CT) scan and magnetic resonance imaging (MRI), that allow in vivo examination of macrobrain structures. Despite major methodological controversies (Luchins, 1982; Maser & Keith, 1983), beginning with the work of Johnstone, Crow, Frith, Husband, and Kreel (1976), most CT scan studies have reported increased abnormalities in schizophrenics compared to normal controls (Reveley, 1985). Ventricular enlargement and cortical atrophy are the abnormalities most commonly reported. However, these are nonspecific signs that occur in a variety of neurological disorders. They only occur in a minority of schizophrenic patients, and most schizophrenics show no CT scan abnormalities. Mild cortical atrophy also has recently been reported to occur in a similar proportion of bipolar affective patients (e.g., Rieder, Mann, Weinberger, VanKammen, & Post, 1983). In both schizophrenic and affective patients, CT abnormalities appear to be correlated with impairments in functioning and poor clinical course (e.g., Pearlson, Garbacz, Moberg, Ahn, & DePaulo, 1985). Consequently, it is possible that these general CT scan abnormalities may represent relatively nonspecific risk factors for psychopathology that also contribute to the severity of its manifestation. Within the normal population, variation in ventricular size appears to be predominantly under genetic control (Reveley, Reveley, Chitkara, & Clifford, 1984). However, twin (Reveley, Reveley, Clifford, & Murray, 1982) and family (Weinberger, DeLisi, Neophytides, & Wyatt, 1981) studies suggest that, within schizophrenia, ventricular enlargement may also reflect some environmental etiology. Clearly, more research along these lines is needed to better understand the significance and origins

of ventricular enlargement within schizophrenia and other disorders.

Neurophysiological Aspects

Recent advances in technology, such as positron emission tomography (PET), have for the first time allowed a noninvasive three-dimensional view of in vivo central neuronal activity (Phelps & Mazziotta, 1985). Studies using PET, along with other surface techniques, such as regional cerebral blood flow (RCBF) (e.g., Gur et al. 1985) and advanced brain electrical activity mapping (BEAM) (e.g., Morihisa, Duffy, & Wyatt, 1983), have begun to investigate regional brain activity abnormalities in schizophrenics, both at rest and during specific cognitive tasks. Several of the PET studies have thus far found a decreased anteroposterior activity gradient relative to normal controls, although similar findings have recently been reported for affectively disordered patients (Buchsbaum et al., 1984). Given the early stage of research with these techniques, solid conclusions must await further replication and study. As promising as these techniques appear, additional technological advances may have even greater impact on the study of schizophrenia. One particularly intriguing method employs PET to measure the activity of biochemical reactions other than the usual glucose metabolism, such as dopamine binding (Wagner et al., 1983). This next generation of techniques should allow the integration of neurochemical hypotheses of schizophrenia with those involving anatomical localization (e.g., Farde, Hall, Ehrin, & Sedvall, 1986).

Etiology

Genetic Influences

It is generally acknowledged that genetic influences play a role in the etiology of most schizophrenias. Building upon the positive findings of the early family and twin studies, the more methodologically rigorous twin and adoption studies of the 1960s have made this conclusion one of the most certain facts that we currently possess about schizophrenia. A comprehensive review of this evidence can be found in Gottesman and Shields (1982).

Recent genetic investigations have tended to focus on more specific questions concerning the nature of these genetic influences on schizophrenia. Although not new, one of the areas of recent active research has been the attempt to identify the mode of genetic transmission of schizophrenia. A number of recent investigations, using pedigree-segregation analysis (e.g., Tsuang, Bucher, & Fleming, 1982) or path analytic techniques (O'Rourke, Gottesman, Suarez, Rice, & Reich, 1982) with either single (e.g., Tsuang, Bucher, & Fleming, 1983) or aggregated data sets (e.g., McGue, Gottesman, & Rao, 1983) have evaluated a variety of different transmission models for schizophrenia (see recent review by Faraone & Tsuang, 1985). These studies concur in rejecting any simple fully penetrant Mendelian model for the genetic transmission of schizophrenia, although more complex multiple-loci models are difficult to reject. Instead, multifactorial models (e.g., Gottesman & Shields, 1982) that allow for both polygenic and environmental influences have received the most support to date. This apparent absence of simple major gene effects has profound implications for the direction of research in schizophrenia. It implies that schizophrenia, as it is currently diagnosed, may be heterogeneous, in some sense, with a number of different etiological pathways to the final syndrome.

Such findings have stimulated other recent genetic research attempting to better define the "phenotype" of schizophrenia. These studies have either sought to define other syndromes that might be genetically related to currently diagnosed schizophrenia or have attempted to identify genetically distinct subsyndromes within our current concept of schizophrenia.

Although it has a long history (e.g., Slater & Cowie, 1971), the notion of a spectrum of genetically related schizophrenic disorders gained considerable empirical support with the Danish adoption studies (e.g., Kety, Rosenthal, Wender, Schulsinger, & Jacobsen, 1978). In these investigations, the diagnostic categories of borderline and uncertain schizophrenia were found to be significantly elevated in the biological, but not the adoptive, relatives of schizophrenic adoptees. This clinical diagnosis has since been operationalized and incorporated within the *DSM-III* under the term schizotypal personality disorder (Spitzer, Endicott, & Gibbon, 1979), which includes such characteristics as magical thinking, ideas of reference, social isolation, recurrent illusions, and other mild

psychotic phenomena. This operationalized diagnosis of schizotypal personality disorder has been found to be associated with chronic schizophrenia in a reanalysis of the Danish adoption studies (Kendler, Gruenberg, & Strauss, 1981) and in an independent family study (Baron et al., 1985).

Efforts to identify distinct genetic subsyndromes within schizophrenia based on symptomatology have been less successful. Family studies of the tendency of schizophrenic subtypes (e.g.,paranoid, disorganized, catatonic) to "breed true" within families have produced mixed results (e.g., Kendler & Davis, 1981), whereas twin studies have found substantial (but not complete) homotypia (Gottesman & Shields, 1982). This discrepancy may be due to the tendency of symptomatology to change over the course of the disorder and the fact that co-twins are age-matched (Kendler, Gruenberg, & Tsuang, 1985). In addition to subtyping based on traditional cross-sectional symptomatology, some recent reanalyses of twin studies have used alternative schemes, suggesting that schizophrenics with negative symptoms (Dworkin & Lenzenberger, 1984) and those with poor premorbid histories and chronic courses (Farmer, McGuffin, & Gottesman, 1984; Gottesman, 1968) may represent more severe genetic forms that are nonetheless genetically related to other schizophrenias. The genetic studies investigating these issues suggest that, at least based on observable, behavioral characteristics, the heterogeneity of schizophrenia may be more a matter of quantitative differences in multifactorial liability than a reflection of the presence of several genetically distinct syndromes.

Environmental Risk Factors

Recent research on environmental factors that increase risk for schizophrenia, either independently or through an interaction with genetic vulnerability, has focused on several different areas. One promising area appears to be that of obstetrical complications. Although relatively few studies have investigated the question, chronic schizophrenic patients appear to have somewhat increased rates of obstetrical complications at birth compared to normal controls (McNeil & Kaij, 1978). It must be recognized of course that obstetrical complications may also be the result of the child's genotype and not an independent environmental factor. In any case, because obstetrical complications are not infrequent in normal adult outcomes and because relatively few schizophrenic patients appear to experience them, it is unlikely that they contribute to the etiology of most schizophrenias.

A number of studies have investigated the possibility that schizophrenic patients show an excess of winter births compared to normal controls. Such a potential season-of-birth effect in schizophrenia has been hypothesized to reflect some harmful effect that tends to be associated with winter births, such as increased frequency of perinatal viral infections. Although a number of studies report such an excess of winter births for schizophrenic patients (e.g., Pulver, Stewart, Carpenter, & Childs, 1983), some have suggested that these results may be due to statistical artifacts (e.g., Lewis & Griffin, 1981). In any case, the number of excess winter births that is generally reported is relatively small and, if in fact present, would appear to be relevant to only a minority of schizophrenic patients as they are currently diagnosed.

More specific viral hypotheses of the etiology of schizophrenia are attractive and have been proposed by a number of investigators (e.g., Crow, 1983). For example, other disorders have been identified in which viral infection leads to disease onset, but only in genetically vulnerable individuals. In addition, a number of known viruses are neurotropic (i.e., selectively migrate toward the nervous system. Also, some viruses have long latency periods with episodic exacerbations. However, in spite of these theoretically attractive aspects of viruses as an etiologic agent, research investigating the actual presence of viral antigens in schizophrenia has been quite disappointing (e.g., Stevens, Langloss, Albrecht, Yolken, & Wang, 1984). Nevertheless, much remains to be investigated in this area, and it is certainly too early to rule out some role for viral infection in the etiology of schizophrenia.

A final area of active research on environmental risk factors for schizophrenia emphasizes psychological influences that are transmitted culturally within the family. The notion of the psychogenesis of schizophrenia is an old one, and a number of studies have examined the characteristics of parents of schizophrenic patients (e.g., Hirsch & Leff, 1975). Many of these studies have reported increased communication abnormalities among parents of schizophren-

ics. However, such family research does not allow the relative weights of family genetic influences and family rearing practices to be distinguished. To date, two studies have investigated the family communication patterns of adoptive parents of schizophrenic patients, with one yielding positive results (Wynne, Singer, & Toohey, 1976) and another finding no difference (Wender, Rosenthal, Rainer, Greenhill, & Sarlin, 1977). Further, replications of this type of work are needed. Yet, even such designs cannot fully resolve the direction of causality (i.e., do faulty communication patterns contribute to the onset of schizophrenia, or does life with a schizophrenic offspring produce parental communication abnormalities?) Although not conclusive, path models of twin and family data suggest that relatively little of the variation in liability to schizophrenia is accounted for by shared family environment. Instead, environmental influences that are idiosyncratic to the individual and not shared within families may be more important (McGue et al., 1983). If accurate, such data would suggest that if family-rearing factors are important, then they must be focused on some offspring and not others or they must interact with some offspring's vulnerability and not his or her siblings'. Investigation of such hypotheses is a difficult task that has received relatively little research attention to date.

In summary, although the importance of genetic factors seems clear, their specific characterization is not. The picture with regard to contributory environmental influences is considerably less complete. To date, the best evidence for some role of environmental factors is the fact that genetic influences do not appear to completely account for the etiology of schizophrenia as it is currently diagnosed. The identification of definite environmental risk factors has not been achieved. Some factors may hold promise, but it may also be that no specific environmental influences can be identified. It may be that a number of relatively common nonspecific experiences that most persons weather without difficulty interact with some persons' genetic vulnerability to lead to the onset of schizophrenia (Gottesman & Shields, 1982).

SUMMARY

From this survey, it should be apparent that some advances are being made in our understanding and treatment of schizophrenia.

Despite this, many important aspects of schizophrenia remain poorly understood. This lack of basic understanding is not due to any lack of research. On the contrary, a tremendous amount of study has focused on schizophrenia. Nevertheless, when compared with many physical disorders, such as cancer and cardiovascular disease, research funding has been considerably less. One potential reason for the recalcitrance of schizophrenia may be that an understanding of the disorder is intimately tied to our state of knowledge in a number of basic areas, such as neuroscience, genetics, and psychology. Advances in these general areas should shed new light on our investigations in schizophrenia, just as research on schizophrenia has stimulated basic investigations.

One theme of this chapter has been that schizophrenia is an evolving construct. The current diagnostic classification of schizophrenia is not fixed—its boundaries with other syndromes are not resolved, and divisions within the current classification are possible. Research on the psychological and biological correlates of a fallible classification will almost certainly result in confusing findings. A major challenge is, therefore, the improvement of our current nosology.

A second major and related theme of this chapter has been that of the question of heterogeneity. Schizophrenia, as it is currently conceived, is probably not a simple disorder. The methods used to investigate schizophrenia thus far probably would have been able to identify any simple etiology, at least a simple genetic etiology. Although a simple, single cause cannot be completely ruled out, particularly as concerns environmental factors, it is likely that the etiology of schizophrenia is multifactorial, probably both genetically and environmentally. At the level of pathology, it is also likely that variation in pathogenesis is present, although this is less certain. Clearly, no biochemical, anatomical, or psychological characteristic has been found to date that is abnormal in all schizophrenic patients and normal in other persons. Of course, this may be because we have looked in the wrong places. However, it is also consistent with the notion that no homogeneous pathology of schizophrenia may exist. It is apparent that variation is also a hallmark of schizophrenia at the behavioral phenotypic level. Marked variation in behavioral characteristics exists both among schizophrenic patients, and within patients over time. Again, although this phenotypic variation does not necessarily imply etiological or pathological heterogeneity, it is certainly consistent with individual differences in cause and biology. Another major challenge, therefore, is to understand the nature of this potential heterogeneity and, as important, to develop strategies to investigate it.

Although this review of our current knowledge about the construct of schizophrenia has highlighted the questions that remain unanswered, it should be apparent that advances have been made and a number of promising research leads exist. Increased methodological sophistication, creative hypotheses, and a questioning of old assumptions have improved the state of research on schizophrenia in recent years. Advances in neuroscience and genetics should also stimulate new theories and allow current ones to be more thoroughly evaluated. Although major questions remain concerning schizophrenia, the means, both technical and conceptual, of addressing them are beginning to emerge.

Acknowledgements—The writing of this chapter was supported in part by grant MH-26341 from the National Institute of Mental Health and grants from the John D. and Catherine T. MacArthur Foundation and the Carnegie Corporation. The authors also wish to thank Ms. Nancy Koeber for preparation of this manuscript.

REFERENCES

Albee, G. W., Lane, E. A., & Reuter, J. M. (1964). Childhood intelligence of future schizophrenics and neighborhood peers. *Journal of Psychology, 58,* 141–144.

American Psychiatric Association. (1952). *Diagnostic and statistical manual: Mental disorders* (lst ed.). Washington, DC: Author.

American Psychiatric Association. (1968). *Diagnostic and statistical manual of mental disorders* (2nd ed.). Washington, DC: Author.

American Psychiatric Association. (1980). *Diagnostic and statistical manual of mental disorders* (3rd ed.). Washington, DC: Author.

American Psychiatric Association. (1980). Tardive dyskinesia: Summary of a task force report of the American Psychiatric Association. *American Journal of Psychiatry, 137,* 1163–1172.

Andreasen, N. C., & Olsen, S. (1982). Negative positive schizophrenia: Definition and validation. *Archives of General Psychiatry, 39,* 789–794.

Andrews, G., Hall, W., Goldstein, G., Lapsley, H., Barthols, R., & Silove, D. (1985). The economic costs of schizophrenia. *Archives of General Psychiatry, 42,* 537–543.

Angrist, B., Rotrosen, J., & Gershon, S. (1980). Differential effects of amphetamine and neuroleptics on negative vs. positive symptoms in schizophrenia. *Psychopharmacology, 72,* 17–19.

Asarnow, R. F., & MacCrimmon, D. J. (1978). Residual performance deficit in clinically remitted schizophrenics: A marker of schizophrenia? *Journal of Abnormal Psychology, 87,* 597–608.

Asarnow, R. F., & MacCrimmon, D. J. (1981). Span of apprehension deficits during the post-psychotic stages of schizophrenia: A replication and extension. *Archives of General Psychiatry, 38,* 1006–1011.

Asarnow, R. F., & MacCrimmon, D. J. (1982). Attention/information processing, neuropsychological functioning and thought disorder during the acute and partial recovery phases of schizophrenia: A longitudinal study. *Psychiatry Research, 7,* 309–319.

Asarnow, R. F., Steffy, R. A., MacCrimmon, D. J., & Cleghorn, J. M. (1977). An attentional assessment of foster children at risk for schizophrenia. *Journal of Abnormal Psychology, 86,* 267–275.

Astrachan, B. M., Harrow, M., Adler, D., Brauer, L., Schwartz, A., Schwartz, C., & Tucker, G. (1972). A checklist for the diagnosis of schizophrenia. *British Journal of Psychiatry, 121,* 529–539.

Astrup, C., & Noreik, R. (1966). *Functional psychoses: Diagnostic and prognostic models.* Springfield, IL: Charles C Thomas.

Aylward, E., Walker, E., & Bettes, B. (1984). Intelligence in schizophrenia: Meta-analysis of the research. *Schizophrenia Bulletin, 10,* 430–459.

Baron, M., Gruen, R., Rainer, J. D., Kane, J., Asnis, L., & Lord, S. (1985). A family study of schizophrenic and normal control probands: Implications for the spectrum concept of schizophrenia. *American Journal of Psychiatry, 142,* 447–455.

Bland, R. C., Parker, J. H., & Orn, H. (1978). Prognosis in schizophrenia. *Archives of General Psychiatry, 35,* 72–77.

Blashfield, R. K. (1984). *The classification of psychopathology.* New York: Plenum.

Bleuler, E. (1950). *Dementia praecox or the group of schizophrenias.* (J. Zinkin, Trans.). New York: International Universities Press. (Original work published 1911)

Bleuler, M. (1978). *The schizophrenic disorders: Long-term patient and family studies.* (S. Clemens, Trans.). New Haven, CT: Yale University Press. (Original work published 1972)

Bowers, M. B. (1980). Biochemical processes in schizophrenia: An update. In National Institute of Mental Health, *Special report: Schizophrenia 1980* (DHHS Publication No. ADM 81-1064). Washington, DC: U. S. Government Printing Office.

Bromet, E., Harrow, M., & Kasl, S. (1974). Premorbid functioning and outcome in schizophrenics and nonschizophrenics. *Archives of General Psychiatry, 30,* 203–207.

Brown, G. W., Birley, J. L. T., & Wing, J. K. (1972). Influence of family life on the course of schizophrenic disorders: A replication. *British Journal of Psychiatry, 121,* 241–258.

Brown, G. W., Monck, E. M., Carstairs, G. M., & Wing, J. K. (1962). The influence of family life on the course of schizophrenic illness. *British Journal of Preventive and Social Medicine, 16,* 55–68.

Buchsbaum, M. S., DeLisi, L. E., Holcomb, H. H., Cappelletti, J., King, A. C., Johnson, J., Hazlett, E., Dowling-Zimmerman, S., Post, R. M., Morihisa, J., Carpenter, W., Cohen, R., Pickar, D., Weinberger, D. R., Margolin, R., & Kessler, R. M. (1984). Anteroposterior gradients in cerebral glucose use in schizophrenia and affective disorders. *Archives of General Psychiatry, 41,* 1159–1166.

Caffey, E. M., Galbrecht, C. R., & Klett, C. J. (1971). Brief hospitalization and aftercare in the treatment of schizophrenia. *Archives of General Psychiatry, 24,* 84–86.

Carpenter, W. T., Bartko, J. J., Strauss, J. S., & Hawk, A. B. (1978). Signs and symptoms as predictors of outcome: A report from the International Pilot Study of Schizophrenia. *American Journal of Psychiatry, 135,* 940–944.

Carpenter, W. T., & Heinrichs, D. W. (1983). Early intervention, time-limited, targeted pharmacotherapy of schizophrenia. *Schizophrenia Bulletin, 9,* 533–542.

Carpenter, W. T., & Strauss, J. S. (1973). Flexible system for the diagnosis of schizophrenia: Report from the WHO International Pilot Study of Schizophrenia. *Science, 182,* 1275–1278.

Chapman, L. J. (1979). Recent advances in the study of schizophrenic cognition. *Schizophrenia Bulletin, 5,* 568–580.

Chapman, L. J., & Chapman, J. P. (1978). The measurement of differential deficit. *Journal of Psychiatric Research, 14,* 303–311.

Chapman, L. J., Edell, W. S., & Chapman, J. P. (1980). Physical anhedonia, perceptual aberration and psychosis proneness. *Schizophrenia Bulletin, 6,* 639–653.

Ciompi, L. (1980). The natural history of schizophrenia in the long-term. *British Journal of Psychiatry, 136,* 413–420.

Cole, J. O., Goldberg, S. C., & Klerman, G. L. (1964). Phenothiazine treatment in acute schizophrenia. *Archives of General Psychiatry, 10,* 246–261.

Cooper, J. E., Kendell, R. E., Gurland, B. J., Sharpe, L., Copeland, J. R. M., & Simon, R. J. (1972). *Psychiatric diagnosis in New York and London: A comparative study of mental hospital admissions.* London: Oxford University Press.

Cornblatt, B., & Erlenmeyer-Kimling, L. (1984). Early attentional predictors of adolescent behavioral disturbances in children at risk for schizophrenia. In N. F. Watt, E. J. Anthony, L. Wynne, & J. E. Rolf (Eds.), *Children at risk for schizophrenia* (pp. 198–211). New York: Cambridge University Press.

Crow, T. J. (1980). Molecular pathology of schizophrenia: More than one disease process? *British Medical Journal, 280,* 1–9.

Crow, T. J. (1983). Is schizophrenia an infectious disease? *Lancet, 1,* 173–175.

Davis, J. M., Schaffer, C. B., Killian, G. A., Kinard, C., & Chan, C. (1980). Important issues in the drug treatment of schizophrenia. In National Institute of Mental Health, *Special report: Schizophrenia 1980* (DHHS Publication No. ADM 81-1064). Washington, DC: U. S. Government Printing Office.

Delva, N. J., & Letemendia, F. J. J. (1982). Lithium

treatment in schizophrenia and schizoaffective disorders. *British Journal of Psychiatry, 141,* 387–400.

Diefendorf, A. R., & Dodge, R. (1908). An experimental study of the ocular reactions of the insane from photographic records. *Brain, 31,* 451–489.

Dohrenwend, B. P., Dohrenwend, B. S., Gould, M. S., Link, B., Neugebauer, R., & Wunsch-Hitzig, R. (1980). *Mental illness in the United States: Epidemiological estimates.* New York: Praeger.

Donaldson, S. R., Gelenberg, A. J., & Baldessarini, R. J. (1983). The pharmacologic treatment of schizophrenia: A progress report. *Schizophrenia Bulletin, 9,* 504–527.

Drake, R. E., Gates, C., Whitaker, A., & Cotton, P. G. (1985). Suicide among schizophrenics: A review. *Comprehensive Psychiatry, 26,* 90–100.

Dworkin, R. H., & Lenzenweger, M. F. (1984). Symptoms and the genetics of schizophrenia: Implications for diagnosis. *American Journal of Psychiatry, 141,* 1541–1546.

Endicott, J. E., Nee, J., Fleiss, J., Cohen, J., Williams, J. B. W., & Simon, R. (1982). Diagnostic criteria for schizophrenia. *Archives of General Psychiatry, 39,* 884–889.

Falloon, I. R. H., Boyd, J. L., McGill, C. W., Razari, J., Moss, H. B., & Gilderman, A. M. (1982). Family management in the prevention of exacerbations of schizophrenia: A controlled study. *The New England Journal of Medicine, 306,* 1437–1440.

Faraone, S. V., & Tsuang, M. T. (1985). Quantitative models of the genetic transmission of schizophrenia. *Psychological Bulletin, 98,* 41–66.

Farde, L., Hall, H., Ehrin, E., & Sedvall, G. (1986). Quantitative analysis of DZ dopamine receptor binding in the living human brain by PET. *Science, 231,* 258–261.

Farmer, A. E., McGuffin, P., & Gottesman, I. I. (1984). Searching for the split in schizophrenia: A twin study perspective. *Psychiatry Research, 13,* 109–118.

Feighner, J. P., Robins, E., Guze, S. B., Woodruff, R. A., Winokur, G., & Munoz, R. (1972). Diagnostic criteria for use in psychiatric research. *Archives of General Psychiatry, 26,* 57–63.

Fenton, W. S., Mosher, L. R., & Matthews, S. M. (1981). Diagnosis of schizophrenia: A critical review of current diagnostic systems. *Schizophrenia Bulletin, 7,* 452–476.

Fish, B. (1984). Characteristics and sequelae of the neurointegrative disorder in infants at risk for schizophrenia: 1952–1982. In N. F. Watt, E. J. Anthony, L. C. Wynne, & J. E. Rolf (Eds.), *Children at risk for schizophrenia* (pp. 423–439). New York: Cambridge University Press.

Fisher, L., Schwartzman, P., Harder, D., & Kokes, R. F. (1984). A strategy and methodology for assessing school competence in high-risk children. In N. F. Watt, E. J. Anthony, L. C. Wynne, & J. E. Rolf (Eds.), *Children at risk for schizophrenia* (pp. 355–359). New York: Cambridge University Press.

Frame, C. L., & Oltmanns, T. F. (1982). Serial recall by schizophrenic and affective patients during and after psychotic episodes. *Journal of Abnormal Psychology, 91,* 311–318.

Friedman, D., Vaughan, H. G., & Erlenmeyer-Kimling, L. (1982). Cognitive brain potentials in children at risk for schizophrenia: Preliminary findings. *Schizophrenia Bulletin, 8,* 514–531.

Garmezy, N., & Streitman, S. (1974). Children at risk: The search for the antecedents of schizophrenia. Part I. Conceptual models and research methods. *Schizophrenia Bulletin, 8,* 14–90.

Gift, T. E., Strauss, J. S., Kokes, R. F., Harder, D. W., & Ritzler, B. A. (1980). Schizophrenia: Affect and outcome. *American Journal of Psychiatry, 137,* 580–585.

A glossary of mental disorders. (1968). London: General Register Office.

Goldstein, M. J., Judd, L. L., Rodnick, E. H., Alkire, A. A., & Gould, E. (1968). A method for the study of social influence and coping patterns in families of disturbed adolescents. *Journal of Nervous and Mental Disease, 147,* 233–251.

Goldstein, M. J., Rodnick, E. H., Evans, J. R., May, P. R. A., & Steinberg, M. R. (1978). Drug and family therapy in the aftercare treatment of acute schizophrenia. *Archives of General Psychiatry 35,* 1169–1177.

Gottesman, I. I. (1968). Severity/concordance and diagnostic refinement in the Maudsley–Bethlem schizophrenic twin study. *Journal of Psychiatric Research, 6,* 37–48.

Gottesman, I. I., & Shields, J. (1967). A polygenic theory of schizophrenia. *Proceedings of the National Academy of Sciences, 58,* 199–205.

Gottesman, I. I., & Shields, J. (1982). *Schizophrenia: The epigenetic puzzle.* New York: Cambridge University Press.

Grinker, R. R., & Harrow, M. (in press). *A multidimensional approach to clinical research in schizophrenia.* Springfield, IL: Charles C Thomas.

Gunderson, J. G., Frank, A. F., Katz, H. M., Vannicelli, M. L., Frosch, J. P., & Knapp, P. H. (1984). Effects of psychotherapy in schizophrenia: II. Comparative outcome of two forms of treatment. *Schizophrenia Bulletin, 10,* 564–598.

Gunderson, J. G., & Mosher, L. R. (1975). The cost of schizophrenia. *American Journal of Psychiatry, 132,* 901–906.

Gur, R. E., Gur, R. C., Skolnick, B. E., Caroff, S., Obrist, W. D., Resnick, S., & Reivich, M. (1985). Brain function in psychiatric disorders: III. Regional cerebral blood flow in unmedicated schizophrenics. *Archives of General Psychiatry, 42,* 329–334.

Gusella, J. F., Wexler, N. S., Conneally, M. P., Naylor, S. L., Anderson, M. A., Tanzi, R. E., Watkins, P. C., Ottina, K., Wallace, M. R., Sakaguchi, A. Y., Young, A. B., Shoulson, I., Bonilla, E., & Martin, J. B. (1983). A polymorphic DNA marker genetically linked to Huntington's disease. *Nature, 306,* 234–238.

Hanson, D. R., Gottesman, I. I., & Heston, L. L. (1976). Some possible childhood indicators of adult schizophrenia inferred from children of schizophrenics. *British Journal of Psychiatry, 129,* 142–154.

Haracz, J. L. (1982). The dopamine hypothesis: An overview of studies with schizophrenic patients.

Schizophrenia Bulletin, 8, 438–469.

Harrow, M., Carone, B. J., & Westermeyer, J. F. (1985). The course of psychosis in early phase of schizophrenia. *American Journal of Psychiatry, 142,* 702–707.

Harrow, M., Grinker, R. R., Silverstein, M. L., & Holzman, P. (1978). Is modern-day schizophrenic outcome still negative? *American Journal of Psychiatry, 135,* 1156–1162.

Harrow, M., & Grossman, L. S. (1984). Outcome in schizoaffective disorders: A critical review and re-evaluation of the literature. *Schizophrenia Bulletin, 10,* 87–108.

Harrow, M., & Quinlan, D. M. (1985). *Disordered thinking and schizophrenic psychopathology.* New York: Gardner Press.

Harrow, M., Silverstein, M., Lazar, B., & Pogue-Geile, M. F. (in press). Psychotic symptoms and first rank symptoms in the post acute phase of schizophrenia. In R. R. Grinker & M. Harrow (Eds.), *A multidimensional approach to clinical research in schizophrenia.* Springfield, IL: Charles C Thomas.

Harvey, P., Winters, K., Weintraub, S., & Neale, J. M. (1981). Distractibility in children vulnerable to psychopathology. *Journal of Abnormal Psychology, 90,* 298–304.

Helzer, J. E., Brockington, I. F., & Kendell, R. E. (1981). Predictive validity of *DSM-III* and Feighner definitions of schizophrenia. *Archives of General Psychiatry, 38,* 791–797.

Hirsch, S. R., & Leff, J. P. (1975). *Abnormalities in parents of schizophrenics.* New York: Oxford University Press.

Hogarty, G. E., Anderson, C. M., Reiss, D. J., Kornblith, S. J., Greenwald, D. P., Javna, C. D., & Madonia, M. J. (1986). Family psychoeducation social skills training and maintenance chemotherapy in the aftercare treatment of schizophrenia. *Archives of General Psychiatry, 43,* 633–642.

Hogarty, G. E., & Goldberg, S. C. (1973). Drug and sociotherapy in the aftercare of schizophrenic patients: One-year relapse rates. *Archives of General Psychiatry, 28,* 54–64.

Hogarty, G. E., Goldberg, S. C., Schooler, N. R., & Ulrich, R. F. (1974). Drug and sociotherapy in the aftercare of schizophrenic patients: II. Two-year relapse rates. *Archives of General Psychiatry, 31,* 603–608.

Hogarty, G. E., Schooler, N. R., Ulrich, R. F., Massure, F., Ferro, P., & Herron, E. (1979). Fluphenazine and social therapy in the aftercare of schizophrenic patients: Relapse analyses of a two-year controlled study of fluphenazine decanoate and fluphenazine hydrochloride. *Archives of General Psychiatry, 36,* 1283–1294.

Holzman, P. S. (1978). Cognitive impairment and cognitive stability: Towards a theory of thought disorder. In G. Serban (Ed.), *Cognitive defects in the development of mental illness* (pp. 361–376). New York: Brunner/Mazel.

Holzman, P. S., Kringlen, E., Levy, D. L., & Haberman, S. J. (1980). Deviant eye tracking in twins discordant for psychosis. *Archives of General Psychiatry, 37,* 627–631.

Holzman, P. S., Kringlen, E., Levy, D. L., Proctor, L. R., Haberman, S. J., & Yasillo, N. J. (1977). Abnormal pursuit eye movement in schizophrenia: Evidence for a genetic indicator. *Archives of General Psychiatry, 34,* 802–805.

Holzman, P. S., Proctor, L. R., & Hughes, D. W. (1973). Eye-tracking patterns in schizophrenia. *Science, 181,* 179–181.

Holzman, P. S., Proctor, L. R., Levy, D. L., Yasillo, N. J., Meltzer, H. Y., & Hurt, S. W. (1974). Eye-tracking dysfunctions in schizophrenic patients and their relatives. *Archives of General Psychiatry, 31,* 143–151.

Holzman, P. S., Solomon, C. M., Levin, S., & Waternaux, C. S. (1984). Pursuit eye movement dysfunctions in schizophrenia. *Archives of General Psychiatry, 41,* 136–139.

Huber, G., Gross, G., Schüttler, R., & Linz, M. (1980). Longitudinal studies of schizophrenic patients. *Schizophrenia Bulletin, 6,* 592–605.

Iacono, W. G., & Koenig, W. G. R. (1983). Features that distinguish the smooth-pursuit eye-tracking performance of schizophrenic, affective-disorder, and normal individuals. *Journal of Abnormal Psychology, 92,* 29–41.

Johnstone, E. C., Crow, T. J., Frith, C. D., Husband, J., & Kreel, L. (1976). Cerebral ventricular size and cognitive impairment in chronic schizophrenia. *Lancet, 2,* 924–926.

Jones, M. B., & Offord, D. R. (1975). Independent transmission of IQ and schizophrenia. *British Journal of Psychiatry, 126,* 185–190.

Kane, J. M. (1983). Low-dose medication strategies in the maintenance treatment of schizophrenia. *Schizophrenia Bulletin, 9,* 528–532.

Kendell, R. E. (1975). *The role of diagnosis in psychiatry.* Oxford: Blackwell Scientific Publications.

Kendell, R. E., Brockington, I. F., & Leff, J. (1979). Prognostic implications of six alternative definitions of schizophrenia. *Archives of General Psychiatry, 36,* 25–31.

Kendler, K. S., & Davis, K. L. (1981). The genetics and biochemistry of paranoid schizophrenia and other paranoid psychoses. *Schizophrenia Bulletin, 7,* 689–709.

Kendler, K. S., Gruenberg, A. M., & Strauss, J. S. (1981). An independent analysis of the Copenhagen sample of the Danish adoption study of schizophrenia. II. The relationship between schizotypal personality disorder and schizophrenia. *Archives of General Psychiatry, 38,* 982–984.

Kendler, K. S., Gruenberg, A. M., & Tsuang, M. T. (1985). Subtype stability in schizophrenia. *American Journal of Psychiatry, 142,* 827–832.

Kety, S. S., Rosenthal, D., Wender, P. H., Schulsinger, F., & Jacobsen, B. (1978). The biologic and adoptive families of adopted individuals who became schizophrenic: Prevalence of mental illness and other characteristics. In L. C. Wynne, R. L. Cromwell, & S. Matthysse (Eds.), *The nature of schizophrenia* (pp. 25–37). New York: Wiley.

Klein, D. F., & Davis, J. M. (1969). *Diagnosis and drug treatment of psychiatric disorders.* Baltimore, MD: Williams & Wilkins.

Kokes, R. F., Strauss, J. S., & Klorman, R. (1977).

Measuring premorbid adjustment: The instruments and their development. *Schizophrenia Bulletin, 3,* 186–213.

Kornetsky, C., & Orzack, M. H. (1978). Physiological and behavioral correlates of attention dysfunction in schizophrenic patients. *Journal of Psychiatric Research, 14,* 69–79.

Kraepelin, E. (1971). *Dementia praecox and paraphrenia.* (R. M. Barclay, Trans.). Huntington, NY: Krieger. (Original work published 1919)

Lane, E. A., & Albee, G. W. (1963). Childhood intellectual development of adult schizophrenics. *Journal of Abnormal and Social Psychology, 67,* 186–189.

Lane, E. A., & Albee, G. W. (1965). Childhood intellectual differences between schizophrenic adults and their siblings. *American Journal of Orthopsychiatry, 35,* 747–753.

Lane, E. A., & Albee, G. W. (1970). Intellectual antecedents of schizophrenia. In M. Roff & D. F. Ricks (Eds.), *Life history research in psychopathology* (Vol. 1, pp. 189–207). Minneapolis: University of Minnesota Press.

Leff, J., Hirsch, R., Giand, R., Rhode, P., & Stevens, B. (1973). Life events and maintenance therapy in schizophrenic relapse. *British Journal of Psychiatry, 123,* 659–660.

Leff, J., Kuipers, L., Berkowitz, R., Eberlein-Vries, R., & Sturgeon, D. (1982). A controlled study of social intervention in the families of schizophrenic patients. *British Journal of Psychiatry, 141,* 121–134.

Leff, J., Kuipers, L., Berkowitz, R., & Sturgeon, D. (1985). A controlled trial of social intervention in the families of schizophrenic patients: Two-year follow-up. *British Journal of Psychiatry, 146,* 594–600.

Leff, J., & Vaughn, C. (1981). The role of maintenance therapy and relatives' expressed emotion in relapse of schizophrenia: A two-year follow-up. *British Journal of Psychiatry, 139,* 102–104.

Levy, D. L., Dorus, E., Shaughnessy, R., Yasillo, N. J., Pandy, G. N., Janicak, P. G., Gibbons, R. D., Gaviria, M., & Davis, J. M. (1985). Pharmacologic evidence for specificity of pursuit dysfunction in schizophrenia: Lithium carbonate associated with abnormal pursuit. *Archives of General Psychiatry, 42,* 335–341.

Levy, D. L., Yasillo, N. J., Dorus, E., Shaughnessy, R., Gibbons, R. D., Peterson, J., Janicak, P. G., Gaviria, M., & Davis, J. M. (1983). Relatives of unipolar and bipolar patients have normal pursuit. *Psychiatry Research, 10,* 285–293.

Lewine, R. R. J. (1981). Sex differences in schizophrenia: Timing or subtypes? *Psychological Bulletin, 90,* 432–444.

Lewine, R., Burbach, D., & Meltzer, H. Y. (1984). Effect of diagnostic criteria on the ratio of male to female schizophrenic patients. *American Journal of Psychiatry, 141,* 84–87.

Lewine, R. R. J., Watt, N. F., Prentky, R. A., & Fryer, J. H. (1978). Childhood behavior in schizophrenia, personality disorder, depression, and neuroses. *British Journal of Psychiatry, 132,* 347–357.

Lewis, M. S., & Griffin, P. A. (1981). An explanation for the season of birth effect in schizophrenia and certain other diseases. *Psychological Bulletin, 89,* 589–596.

Lipton, M. A., & Burnett, G. B. (1979). Pharmacological treatment of schizophrenia. In L. Bellak (Ed.), *Disorders of the schizophrenic syndrome* (pp. 320–352). New York: Basic Books.

Lipton, R. B., Levy, D. L., Holzman, P. S., & Levin, S. (1983). Eye movement dysfunctions in psychiatric patients: A review. *Schizophrenia Bulletin, 9,* 13–32.

Luchins, D. J. (1982). Computed tomography in schizophrenia. *Archives of General Psychiatry, 39,* 859–860.

MacMahon, B., & Pugh, T. F. (1970). *Epidemiology: Principles and methods.* Boston: Little, Brown.

Marcus, J., Hans, S. L., Mednick, S. A., Schulsinger, F., & Michelsen, N. (1985). Neurological dysfunctioning in offspring of schizophrenics in Israel and Denmark. *Archives of General Psychiatry, 42,* 753–761.

Maser, J. D., & Keith, S. J. (1983). CT scans and schizophrenia—report on a workshop. *Schizophrenia Bulletin, 9,* 265–282.

May, P. R. A. (1968). *Treatment of schizophrenia.* New York: Science House.

McGhie, A., & Chapman, J. (1961). Disorders of attention and perception in early schizophrenia. *British Journal of Medical Psychology, 34,* 103–116.

McGlashan, T. H. (1984). Testing four diagnostic systems for schizophrenia. *Archives of General Psychiatry, 41,* 141–144.

McGue, M., Gottesman, I. I., & Rao, D. C. (1983). The transmission of schizophrenia under a multifactorial threshold model. *American Journal of Genetics, 35,* 1161–1178.

McGuffin, P., Farmer, A. E., Gottesman, I. I., Murray, R. M., & Reveley, A. M. (1984). Twin concordance for operationally defined schizophrenia. *Archives of General Psychiatry, 41,* 541–545.

McNeil, T. F., & Kaij, L. (1978). Obstetric factors in the development of schizophrenia. In L. C. Wynne, R. L. Cromwell, & S. Matthysse (Eds.), *The nature of schizophrenia: New approaches to research and treatment* (pp. 401–429). New York: Wiley.

McNeil, T. F., & Kaij, L. (1979). Etiological relevance of comparisons of high-risk and low-risk groups. *Acta Psychiatrica Scandinavica, 59,* 545–560.

McNeil, T. F., & Kaij, L. (1984). Offspring of women with nonorganic psychoses. In N. F. Watt, E. J. Anthony, L. C. Wynne, & J. E. Rolf (Eds.), *Children at risk for schizophrenia* (pp. 465–481). New York: Cambridge University Press.

Mednick, S. A., & McNeil, T. F. (1968). Current methodology in research on the etiology of schizophrenia. *Psychological Bulletin, 70,* 681–693.

Mednick, S. A., & Schulsinger, F. (1968). Some premorbid characteristics related to breakdown in children with schizophrenic mothers. In D. Rosenthal & S. S. Kety (Eds.), *The transmission of schizophrenia* (pp. 267–291). Elmsford, NY: Pergamon.

Meltzer, H. Y., & Stahl, S. M. (1976). The dopamine hypothesis of schizophrenia: A review. *Schizophrenia Bulletin, 2,* 19–76.

Morihisa, J. M., Duffy, F. H., & Wyatt, R. J. (1983). Brain electrical activity mapping (BEAM) in schizophrenic patients. *Archives of General Psychiatry, 40,* 719–728.

Mosher, L. R., & Keith, S. J. (1980). Psychosocial treatment: Individual, group, family, and community support approaches. In National Institute of Mental Health, *Special Report: Schizophrenia 1980*. (DHHS Publication No. ADM 81-1064). Washington, DC: U. S. Government Printing Office.

Neale, J. M. (1971). Perceptual span in schizophrenia. *Journal of Abnormal Psychology, 77,* 196-204.

Neale, J. M., & Oltmanns, T. F. (1980). *Schizophrenia*. New York: Wiley.

Neale, J. M., Oltmanns, T. F., & Harvey, P. D. (1985). The need to relate cognitive deficits to specific behavioral referents of schizophrenia. *Schizophrenia Bulletin, 11,* 286-291.

Nuechterlein, K. H. (1977). Reaction time and attention in schizophrenia: A criticial evaluation of the data and theories. *Schizophrenia Bulletin, 3,* 373-428.

Nuechterlein, K. H., & Dawson, M. E. (1984). Information processing and attentional functioning in the developmental course of schizophrenic disorders. *Schizophrenia Bulletin, 10,* 160-203.

Offord, D. R. (1974). School performance of adult schizophrenics, their siblings, and age mates. *British Journal of Psychiatry, 125,* 12-19.

Oltmanns, T. F. (1978). Selective attention in schizophrenia and manic psychoses: The effect of distraction on information processing. *Journal of Abnormal Psychology, 87,* 212-225.

O'Rourke, D. H., Gottesman, I. I., Suarez, B. K., Rice, J., & Reich, T. (1982). Refutation of the general single-locus model for the etiology of schizophrenia. *American Journal of Human Genetics, 34,* 630-649.

Owens, D. G. G., Johnstone, E. C., Crow, T. J., Frith, C. D., Jagoe, J. R., & Kreel, L. (1985). Lateral ventricular size in schizophrenia: Relationship to the disease process and its clinical manifestations. *Psychological Medicine, 15,* 27-41.

Pearlson, G. D., Garbacz, D. J., Moberg, P. J., Ahn, H. S., & DePaulo, J. R. (1985). Symptomatic, familial, perinatal, and social correlates of computerized axial tomography (CAT) changes in schizophrenics and bipolars. *Journal of Nervous and Mental Disease, 173,* 42-50.

Pearson, J. S., & Kley, I. B. (1957). On the application of genetic expectancies as age specific base rates in the study of human behavior disorders. *Psychological Bulletin, 54,* 406-420.

Phelps, M. E., & Mazziotta, J. (1985). Positron emission tomography: Human brain function and biochemistry. *Science, 228,* 799-809.

Pogue-Geile, M. F., & Harrow, M. (1984a). Negative and positive symptoms in schizophrenia and depression: A follow-up. *Schizophrenia Bulletin, 10,,* 371-387.

Pogue-Geile, M. F., & Harrow, M. (1984b). Strategies for psychopathology research. In A. S. Bellack & M. Hersen (Eds.), *Research methods in clinical psychology* (pp. 179-207). Elmsford, NY: Pergamon.

Pogue-Geile, M. F., & Harrow, M. (1985). Negative symptoms in schizophrenia: Their longitudinal course and prognostic significance. *Schizophrenia Bulletin, 11,* 427-439.

Pogue-Geile, M. F., & Oltmanns, T. F. (1980). Sentence perception and distractibility in schizophrenic, manic, and depressed patients. *Journal of Abnormal Psychology, 89,* 115-124.

Pollack, M., Woerner, M. G., & Klein, D. F. (1970). A comparison of childhood characteristics of schizophrenics, personality disorders, and their siblings. In M. Roff & D. Ricks (Eds.), *Life history research in psychopathology* (pp. 208-225). Minneapolis: University of Minnesota Press.

Pope, H. G., & Lipinski, J. F. (1978). Diagnosis in schizophrenia and manic-depressive illness. *Archives of General Psychiatry, 35,* 811-828.

Pulver, A. E., Stewart, W., Carpenter, W. T., & Childs, B. (1983). Risk factors in schizophrenia: Season of birth in Maryland, U. S. A. *British Journal of Psychiatry, 143,* 389-396.

Rabkin, J. G. (1980). Stressful life events and schizophrenia: A review of the research literature. *Psychological Bulletin, 87,* 408-425.

Reveley, A. M., Reveley, M. A., Chitkara, B., & Clifford, C. (1984). The genetic basis of cerebral ventricular volume. *Psychiatry Research, 13,* 261-266.

Reveley, A. M., Reveley, M. A., Clifford, C. A., & Murray, R. M. (1982). Cerebral ventricular size in twins discordant for schizophrenia. *Lancet, 1,* 540-541.

Reveley, M. A. (1985). CT scans in schizophrenia. *British Journal of Psychiatry, 146,* 367-371.

Rieder, R. O., Mann, L. S., Weinberger, D. R., VanKammen, D. P., & Post, R. M. (1983). Computed tomographic scans in patients with schizophrenia, schizoaffective, and bipolar affective disorder. *Archives of General Psychiatry, 40,* 735-739.

Robins, E., & Guze, S. B. (1970). Establishment of diagnostic validity in psychiatric illness: Its application to schizophrenia. *American Journal of Psychiatry, 126,* 107-111.

Robins, L. N., Helzer, J. E., Weissman, M. M., Orvaschel, H., Gruenberg, E., Burke, J. D., & Regier, D. A. (1984). Lifetime prevalence of specific psychiatric disorders in three sites. *Archives of General Psychiatry, 41,* 949-958.

Rosenthal, D. (1975). The concept of subschizophrenic disorders. In R. R. Fieve, D. Rosenthal, & H. Brill (Eds.), *Genetic research in psychiatry* (pp. 199-208). Baltimore, MD: Johns Hopkins University Press.

Salokangas, R. K. R. (1983). Prognostic implications of the sex of schizophrenic patients. *British Journal of Psychiatry, 142,* 145-151.

Schaffner, A., Lane, E. A., & Albee, G. W. (1967). Intellectual differences between suburban preschizophrenic children and their siblings. *Journal of Consulting Psychology, 31,* 326-327.

Schneider, K. (1959). *Clinical psychopathology*. (M. W. Hamilton, Trans.). New York: Grune & Stratton. (Original work published 1959)

Silverstein, M. L., Warren, R. A., Harrow, M., Grinker, R. R., & Pawelski, T. (1982). Changes in diagnosis from *DSM-II* to the Research Diagnostic Criteria and *DSM-III*. *American Journal of Psychiatry, 139,* 366-368.

Slater, E., & Cowie, V. (1971). *The genetics of mental disorder*. New York: Oxford University Press.

Snyder, S., Banerjee, S. P., Yamamura, H. I., &

Greenberg, D. (1974). Drugs, neurotransmitters, and schizophrenia. *Science, 184,* 1243–1253.

Spitzer, R. L., Endicott, J., & Gibbon, M. (1979). Crossing the border into borderline personality and borderline schizophrenia. *Archives of General Psychiatry, 36,* 17–24.

Spitzer, R. L., Endicott, J., & Robins, E. (1978). *Research Diagnostic Criteria (RDC) for a selected group of functional disorders* (3rd ed.). Available from New York State Psychiatric Institute.

Spitzer, R. L., Forman, J. B. W., & Nee, J. (1979). DSM-III field trials: I. Initial interrater diagnostic reliability. *American Journal of Psychiatry, 136,* 815–817.

Stephens, J. H. (1970). Long-term course and prognosis in schizophrenia. *Seminars in Psychiatry, 2,* 464–485.

Stephens, J. H., Astrup, C., Carpenter, W. T., Shaffer, J. W., & Goldberg, J. (1982). A comparison of nine systems to diagnose schizophrenia. *Psychiatry Research, 6,* 127–143.

Stevens, J. R. (1982). Neuropathology of schizophrenia. *Archives of General Psychiatry, 39,* 1131–1139.

Stevens, J. R., Langloss, J. M., Albrecht, P., Yolken, R., & Wang, Y. N. (1984). A search for cytomegalovirus and herpes viral antigen in brains of schizophrenic patients. *Archives of General Psychiatry, 41,* 795–801.

Stoffelmayr, B. E., Dillavou, D., & Hunter, J. E. (1983). Premorbid functioning and outcome in schizophrenia: A cumulative analysis. *Journal of Consulting and Clinical Psychology, 51,* 338–352.

Strauss, J. S., & Carpenter, W. T. (1977). Prediction of outcome in schizophrenia: III. Five-year outcome and its predictors. *Archives of General Psychiatry, 34,* 159–163.

Strauss, J. S., Carpenter, W. T., & Bartko, J. J. (1974). Speculations on the processes that underlie schizophrenic symptoms and signs. *Schizophrenia Bulletin, 11,* 61–69.

Strauss, J. S., Kokes, R. F., Carpenter, W. T., & Ritzler, B. A. (1978). The course of schizophrenia as a developmental process. In L. C. Wynne, R. L. Cromwell, & S. Matthysse (Eds.), *The nature of schizophrenia* (pp. 617–630). New York: Wiley.

Strauss, M. E., Bohannon, W. E., Kaminsky, M. J., & Kharabi, F. (1979). Simple reaction time crossover occurs in schizophrenic outpatients. *Schizophrenia Bulletin, 5,* 612–615.

Strauss, M. E., Bohannon, W. E., Stephens, J. H., & Parker, N. E. (1984). Perceptual span in schizophrenia and affective disorders. *Journal of Nervous and Mental Disease, 172,* 431–435.

Taylor, M. A., & Abrams, R. (1978).The prevalence of schizophrenia: A reassessment using modern diagnostic systems. *American Journal of Psychiatry, 135,* 945–948.

Tsuang, M. T., Bucher, K. D., & Fleming, J. A. (1982). Testing the monogenic theory of schizophrenia: An application of segregation analysis to blind family history study data. *British Journal of Psychiatry, 140,* 595–599.

Tsuang, M. T., Bucher, K. D., & Fleming, J. A. (1983). A search for schizophrenia spectrum disorders: An application of a multiple threshold model to blind family study data. *British Journal of Psychiatry, 143,* 572–577.

Tsuang, M. T., Woolson, R. F., & Fleming, J. A. (1979). Long-term outcome of major psychoses. *Archives of General Psychiatry, 36,* 1295–1301.

Vaillant, G. E. (1962). The prediction of recovery in schizophrenia. *Journal of Nervous and Mental Disease, 135,* 534–543.

Vaughn, C. E., & Leff, J. P. (1976). The influence of family and social factors on the course of psychiatric illness: A comparison of schizophrenic and depressed neurotic patients. *British Journal of Psychiatry, 129,* 125–137.

Vaughn, C. E., Snyder, K. S., Jones, S., Freeman, W. B., & Falloon, I. R. H. (1984). Family factors in schizophrenic relapse: Replication in California of British research on expressed emotion. *Archives of General Psychiatry, 41,* 1169–1171.

Wagner, H. N., Burns, D., Dannals, R. F., Wong, D. F., Langstrom, B., Duelfer, T., Frost, J., Ravert, H. T., Links, J. M., Rosenbloom, S. B., Lukas, S. E., Kramer, A. V., & Kuhar, M. J. (1983). Imaging dopamine receptors in the human brain by positron tomography. *Science, 221,* 1264–1266.

Ward, C. H., Beck, A. T., Mendelson, M., Mock, J. E., & Erbaugh, J. K. (1962). The psychiatric nomenclature: Reasons for diagnostic disagreement. *Archives of General Psychiatry, 7,* 198–205.

Watt, N. F. (1978). Patterns of childhood social development in adult schizophrenics. *Archives of General Psychiatry, 35,* 160–165.

Watt, N. F., Anthony, E. J., Wyne, L. C., & Rolf, J. E. (1984). *Children at risk for schizophrenia: A longitudinal perspective.* New York: Cambridge University Press.

Watt, N. F., Fryer, J. H., Lewine, R. R. J., & Prentky, R. A. (1979). Toward longitudinal conceptions of psychiatric disorder. In B. Maher (Ed.), *Progress in experimental personality research* (Vol. 9, pp. 199–282). New York: Academic.

Watt, N. F., Grubb, T. W., Erlenmeyer-Kimling, L. (1982). Social, emotional, and intellectual behavior at school among children at high risk for schizophrenia. *Journal of Consulting and Clinical Psychology, 50,* 171–181.

Weinberger, D. R., DeLisi, L. E., Neophytides, A. N., & Wyatt, R. J. (1981). Familial aspects of CT scan abnormalities in chronic schizophrenic patients. *Psychiatry Research, 4,* 65–71.

Weinberger, D. R., Wagner, R. L., & Wyatt, R. J. (1983). Neuropathological studies of schizophrenia: A selective review. *Schizophrenia Bulletin, 9,* 193–212.

Weintraub, S., & Neale, J. M. (1984). Social behavior of children at risk for schizophrenia. In N. F. Watt, E. J. Anthony, L. C. Wynne, & J. E. Rolf (Eds.), *Children at risk for schizophrenia* (pp. 279–283). New York: Cambridge University Press.

Weissman, M. M., Myers, J. K., & Thompson, D. (1981). Depression and its treatment in a U. S. urban community, 1975–1976. *Archives of General Psychiatry, 38,* 417–421.

Wender, P. H., Rosenthal, D., Rainer, J. D., Greenhill, L., & Sarlin, M. B. (1977). Schizophrenics' adopting parents: Psychiatric status. *Archives of General*

Psychiatry, 34, 777–784.

Westermeyer, J. F., & Harrow, M. (1984). Prognosis and outcome using broad (*DSM-II*) and narrow (*DSM-III*) concepts of schizophrenia. *Schizophrenia Bulletin, 10,* 624–637.

Winters, K., Stone, A., Weintraub, S., & Neale, J. (1981). Cognitive and attentional deficits in children vulnerable to psychopathology. *Journal of Abnormal Child Psychology, 9,* 435–453.

World Health Organization. (1979). *Schizophrenia: An international followup study.* New York: Wiley.

Wynne, L. C., Singer, M. T., & Toohey, M. L. (1976). Communication of the adoptive parents of schizophrenics. In J. Jorstad & E. Ugelstad (Eds.), *Schizophrenia 75: Psychotherapy, family studies, research.* Oslo: Universitetsforlaget.

Zerbin-Rüdin, E. (1972). Genetic research and the theory of schizophrenia. *International Journal of Mental Health, 1,* 42–67.

Zilboorg, G. (1941). *A history of medical psychology.* New York: W. W. Norton.

Zubin, J., & Spring, B. (1977). Vulnerability—A new view of schizophrenia. *Journal of Abnormal Psychology, 86,* 103–126.

CHAPTER 20

Mental Retardation

Edward S. Shapiro and Jeffry Friedman

Mental retardation is not specifically a problem related to adolescence. Indeed, the definition of mental retardation as specified by the American Association on Mental Deficiency (AAMD) notes that mental retardation must occur during the developmental period. Although the developmental period would include adolescence, it is highly unusual to find an individual who has not been identified as mentally retarded prior to the teen years. Typically, children are first diagnosed as mentally retarded either in the preschool years or at school entrance.

In further examination of the definition of mental retardation, the AAMD manual on classification requires that any individual so diagnosed must show significant deficits in both intellectual capacity and adaptive behavior. Intellectual capacity is usually measured via a standardized intelligence test. Deficiencies in adaptive behavior are likewise measured using instruments designed to provide a norm-based comparison of the individual to nonhandicapped persons. The degree of deficiency has been defined by the AAMD as two standard deviations below the mean. Although others have suggested alternative strategies for classifying mental retardation (see Bijou, 1966), the AAMD standard is the generally accepted definition.

Although mental retardation is usually identified prior to adolescence, the issues and concerns of normal adolescent development still prevail for the mentally retarded person (Cleland, 1978). Learning the appropriate means of social interaction, morals, sexual development, and other events of adolescence must be considered when understanding the adolescent mentally retarded individual. Additionally, issues such as educational curriculum and future planning are particularly important. It would make sense, therefore, that efforts be devoted to studying how adolescent development in the mentally retarded individual compares to that of nonhandicapped adolescents.

Given the rising interest in the area of adolescence as an important subdiscipline within developmental psychology over the past 30 years (e.g., Lerner & Spanier, 1980; Long & Cobb, 1983; Rice, 1984), it was quite surprising to find so little research specifically related to understanding the development of the mentally retarded adolescent. The paucity of research in this area is apparently longstanding and was noted by Hutt and Gibby (1976) and Blodgett (1971).

In the present chapter, we examine each of six areas and attempt to review literature that has addressed the adolescent in some way. Specifically, we will examine physical growth, social behavior, intellectual changes, sexuality, family issues, and educational/vocational issues. One should note that these areas represent general issues of normal adolescent development and are covered in detail in chapters 7 through 12 and 23 through 25 of this text. Our coverage will specifically address how each of these issues relates to the mentally retarded adolescent.

SPECIFIC ISSUES OF ADOLESCENCE AND MENTAL RETARDATION

Physical Growth

One of the most dramatic events of adolescent development is the physical growth and maturation of the individual. During this period, significant hormonal changes occur, which result in the excessive growth in height, body weight, and secondary sexual characteristics. Indeed, much attention is given to physical growth and maturation in every textbook on adolescent development (e.g., Lerner & Spanier, 1980; Long & Cobb, 1983; Rice, 1984). Detailed discussion on these issues is also included in chapter 17 of this volume.

Despite the extensive effort and interest in understanding the physical growth and maturation of adolescent individuals, there is a paucity of literature that has explored similar issues with mentally retarded adolescents. This is surprising, because it would be anticipated that mentally retarded adolescents may face a somewhat different set of issues related to physical maturation than do nonhandicapped adolescents.

In this section of the chapter, we will address three areas related to physical growth and maturation: (a) general developmental changes in adolescent mentally retarded individuals, (b) posture and physical appearance, and (c) weight control. Other areas related to physical growth, such as sexual maturation, will be covered in a later section.

Developmental Changes

Few studies have actually examined the pattern of development of the mentally retarded individual through the adolescent period. Schlottmann and Anderson (1982) examined the results of the Developmental Record, a behavior rating scale providing data on self-care

skills, perceptual–motor skills, social skills, communication skills, and self-direction. Data were obtained on 200 mentally retarded individuals between the ages of 5.9 and 19.0 years (mean = 13.1 years) who were residents at a state institution. The scale had been collected annually. Results plotted across the chronological age range (5–19 years) showed clearly that, when the children were divided by their classified levels of mental retardation, growth across the age range appeared to be linear. In other words, the data suggested that during the adolescent period developmental changes in each of the assessed areas progressed at rates equivalent to younger years.

Posture and Physical Appearance

Nonhandicapped adolescents have frequently been found to place a strong emphasis on physical appearance. This includes complexion, body build and fitness, strength, and maturity. Additionally, body posture may be important. Sherrill (1980) reported that mentally retarded individuals have more postural problems than nonmentally retarded individuals. In some studies, up to 75% of those mentally retarded clients screened showed difficulties, including flat feet, protruding and sagging abdomen, sway back, too little arm swing when walking, uneven gait, forward tilt of the trunk, and so forth. These problems may present difficulties when the individual is attempting normalization because these characteristics often are noticed by others and may cause ridicule. Although no studies have specifically addressed these issues with adolescent mentally retarded individuals, these are the types of problems that may result in peer rejection (Gottlieb & Budoff, 1973). As such, it would be important to design strategies to modify these problems.

Sherrill (1980) recommends incorporating training in appropriate posture within the context of the physical education program. This could be accomplished by using game-like activities designed to improve muscle tone, relaxation training, use of videotape feedback, and behavior management programs.

Related to posture problems is the area of physical fitness. Mentally retarded individuals display distinct deficiencies in all areas of physical fitness (Campbell, 1973; Coleman & Whitman, 1984; Rarick, Widdop, & Broadhead, 1970). Studies attempting to improve physical fitness have been reported with adult mentally retarded populations (e.g., Allen & Iwata, 1980; Coleman & Whitman, 1984; Wysocki, Hall, Iwata, & Riordan, 1979), as well as with children (Chasey & Wyrick, 1971; Corder, 1966; Funk, 1971). Continued investigations into the prevalence and remediation of deficits in physical fitness are particularly important for the mentally retarded adolescent given the importance physical appearance can play in adolescent development.

Weight Control

Among the areas related to physical growth and maturity that affect mentally retarded adolescents, weight control is probably one of the most well researched. Anthony Rotatori and Robert Fox have provided the majority of studies investigating weight control with mentally retarded individuals. Again, although their studies are not specifically related to adolescents, their findings are equally applicable.

Fox and Rotatori (1982) examined the prevalence rates of obesity among 1,152 mentally retarded individuals between the ages of 18 and 77. Using a standard formula for determining overweight and obesity based upon the ratio of excess body weight to standards for height (Bray, 1979), Fox and Rotatori (1982) found that between 12.5 and 23.9% of their sample were overweight and between 6.9 and 38.2% of the sample were obese. Their results suggest a prevalence rate equivalent to the nonhandicapped population. Unfortunately, data that examine similar problems in adolescent mentally retarded persons are not available.

Rotatori, Switzky, and Fox (1981) reviewed studies that attempted to implement weight-control programs with mentally retarded individuals. All of these programs were based on principles of behavior modification and had varying degrees of success. Interestingly, of the 12 studies reviewed, 8 were done with adolescents. This suggests that the difficulties reported by Fox and Rotatori (1982) are equally applicable for adolescents.

Numerous strategies were employed among these studies. Foxx (1972) reported a 79-pound weight loss in a mildly mentally retarded adolescent as a result of having the individual earn a weekly trip to the facility canteen contingent upon a 1½-pound loss each week. Buford (1975) used self-monitoring of weight, energy expenditure, and an external reinforcement procedure. Altman, Bondy, and Hirsch (1978) employed self-monitoring of food intake and weight with a reinforcement procedure in obtaining an average 31-pound loss in two Prader–Willi syndrome children. Gumaer and Simon (1979), also using a self-monitoring procedure combined with external reinforcement, found an average loss of 7.9 pounds across 11 adolescents. Others have used similar procedures and found comparable results (Rotatori & Fox, 1980; Rotatori, Fox, & Switzky, 1979; Rotatori & Switzky, 1979).

Clearly, the research suggests that weight control is a significant problem for a proportion of mentally retarded adolescents. Further, behavior management strategies used with nonhandicapped individuals appear to be equally effective with mentally retarded persons (Rotatori & Fox, 1981). It is important to note, however, that maintenance and generalization of the effects found in these studies have not often been reported. Future efforts toward establishing strategies and programs to maintain losses are important. Additionally, studies that examine the interrelationship between weight loss and improved fitness with mentally retarded adolescents are also needed. Finally, studies have not reported the relationship between weight problems in mentally retarded adolescents and peer acceptance and self-perception. It is anticipated that as with nonhandicapped adolescents, mentally retarded adolescents who are overweight may be rebuked by their peers and feel awkward in social situations. Future studies should address these issues.

Social Issues: Companionship, Dating, Peer Acceptance

One of the most dramatic changes evident during the adolescent period is the increased importance of the peer group. Throughout these years, nonhandicapped adolescents begin to become interested in the opposite sex, to establish long-term friendships, and to reduce their dependency on parents. Peer acceptance in this period is crucial and may directly influence much of the adolescent's behavior.

For the mentally retarded adolescent, these same issues are prevalent. It is surprising, however, to find no published studies that have addressed issues of companionship and/or dating behavior with the adolescent mentally retarded individual. There has, however, been substantial research examining the acceptance of mentally retarded *children* by nonhandicapped peers.

Over the past 10 years, the concept of mainstreaming has become increasingly popular. Mainstreaming involves the integration and education of handicapped pupils in classes for nonhandicapped individuals. As mandated by Public Law 94–142 (Education for all Handicapped Children Act, 1975), handicapped children must be educated in the least restrictive alternative. This law has resulted in large numbers of mildly handicapped pupils being returned to classes for nonhandicapped children and has provided an opportunity to examine changes in peer acceptance as a result of direct interaction among handicapped and nonhandicapped children.

Early studies showed that mildly mentally retarded students placed into classes of nonhandicapped pupils are rejected more often than nonmentally retarded peers and that mainstreamed mentally retarded children are rejected more often than those mentally retarded children educated in segregated classes (Goodman, Gottlieb, & Harrison, 1972; Gottlieb & Davis, 1973; Iano, Ayers, Heller, McGettigan, & Walker, 1974). Other studies, however, have shown that after about 1 year mainstreamed pupils feel more readily accepted by their classmates (Gampel, Gottlieb, & Harrison, 1974; Gottlieb & Budoff, 1972). Still other studies exploring peer acceptance among mainstreamed mentally retarded children found that acceptance was influenced by teacher attitude (Foley, 1979), academic ability of the handicapped students (Budoff & Gottlieb, 1976), social class of the nonhandicapped peers (Bruininks, Rynders, & Gross, 1974; Gottlieb & Budoff, 1973), and whether or not the child is actually known by his classmates to have been identified as mentally retarded (Budoff & Siperstein, 1978). This last point is interesting because many argue that labeling results in stigmatizing the child among his peers (e.g., Hobbs, 1975). What may actually be occurring is that, without the known label, the child's atypical behaviors are seen as unexplainable by his or her peers, who may then reject the child. Knowing the child is mentally retarded provides an "excuse" in the eyes of peers and thus results in greater acceptance.

Although these findings are relevant to children, there have been few attempts to specifically examine peer acceptance among adolescent mentally retarded individuals. Stager and Young (1981) examined the "contact hypothesis" among mentally retarded adolescents who were mainstreamed for at least one regular class but not for the whole day. The contact hypothesis assumes that intergroup contact over time reduces initial prejudice and fosters greater understanding and acceptance by nonhandicapped peers.

In their study, Stager and Young (1981) examined whether simply mainstreaming retarded adolescents resulted in nonretarded classmates viewing them as more positive and socially acceptable following a full school year with the handicapped pupils in their same class. The authors also examined whether or not the mentally retarded pupils viewed their classmates more favorably. Using peer nomination and questionnaire measures, results showed no significant changes over time. The mentally retarded adolescents were rated as significantly more competent and likeable by mentally retarded peers but were not viewed as such by their nonretarded peers. Further, intergroup contact did not increase social interaction among classmates either in the classroom or after school.

The results of studies in mainstreaming led Gottlieb (1981) to suggest that the entire concept of mainstreaming be reconsidered. He cites the extensive literature evaluating academic achievement, life adjustment, and social adjustment. What is clear, however, is that just placing mildly mentally retarded children or adolescents into regular classrooms is not sufficient. In contrast to the findings of Gottlieb and his associates (1981), Johnson, Johnson, De Weerdt, Lyons, and Zaidman (1983) examined the use of a specific intervention strategy to effect acceptance of handicapped pupils by nonhandicapped pupils in mainstreamed settings. In a review of the research, Johnson, Johnson, and Maruyama (in press) suggest that moderately and mildly mentally retarded individuals are more successfully mainstreamed when cooperative learning procedures are employed than when "traditional" competitive or individualistic learning procedures are implemented. Johnson et al. (1983) integrated nine severely handicapped, mildly mentally retarded pupils into two classrooms of seventh-grade pupils. Five of the handicapped youths were assigned to the cooperative condition and the other four to the individual condition.

In the cooperative condition, students were instructed to work together to solve problems and perform tasks as a group. Students in this condition were required to produce one product representing group effort. In the individual condition, similar tasks were used by students to produce individual products.

Measures of achievement, interpersonal attraction, verbal interaction, and sociometric peer acceptance were collected. Results showed that achievement of the nonhandicapped students was unaffected by the presence of the handicapped pupils in the cooperative condition. Further, the mentally retarded adolescents freely interacted with the nonhandicapped peers. Measures of interpersonal attraction uniformly showed that greater interpersonal attraction and peer acceptance was evident in the cooperative condition than in the individual condition.

The results of this and other studies by Johnson, Rynders, Johnson, Schmidt, and Haider (1979) and Rynders, Johnson, Johnson, and Schmidt (1980) strongly suggest that Gottlieb's (1981) message about mainstreaming may only reflect the poor quality of service delivery that often occurs when mainstreaming is implemented. Unless substantial efforts are made to increase peer acceptance, it is inevitable that mentally retarded students will remain isolated and unaccepted by their peers and will continue to have difficult social adjustments. Continued efforts like those of Johnson and his colleagues are needed in all attempts to mainstream handicapped pupils.

Cognitive Changes

Much has been written on the intellectual development of the mentally retarded individual. Study after study has explored various aspects of memory processing, degree of abstract thinking, conceptual development, language, and so forth. Likewise, with adolescents, intellectual development has also been carefully studied (see chapter in this volume). Unfortunately, with mentally retarded adolescents, little research has actually been conducted.

Snart, O'Grady, and Das (1982) examined the cognitive processing of mentally retarded individuals between the ages of 9 and 22 years. Using the information-processing model of Das, Kirby, and Jarman (1979), mentally retarded youth diagnosed as either brain damaged of known origin, Down's syndrome, or retardation with "unknown cause" were asked to perform a series of tasks designed to examine their abilities in successive and simultaneous processing.

Results showed that moderately mentally retarded youths relied more on coding functions than nonmentally retarded youths when solving complex tasks. Additionally, although the subgroup of mentally retarded individuals with retardation of unknown origin had superior IQ scores to the Down's syndrome group, IQ level could not discriminate the groups on the tasks administered. Analyses of the tests administered found that the brain-damaged and unknown origin group performed better in successive processing than the Down's syndrome group.

Overall, the study by Snart et al. (1982) suggests that any differentiation of mentally retarded individuals on the basis of etiology alone may not provide an effective means of discriminating learning styles among children. Likewise, their findings must be interpreted cautiously because the educational implications from information-processing models are presently questionable (Bracken, 1985). It is important to note, however, that treating all moderately mentally retarded adolescents similarly in cognitive processing is misleading.

Other studies involving cognitive processing in mentally retarded adolescents have concentrated specifically on impulsivity in responding. Peters and Davies (1981) used the self-instruction procedures developed by Meichenbaum and Goodman (1971) to increase latency and decrease errors on the Matching Familiar Figures test (MFFT) (Kagan, 1966). One group of adolescents received self-instruction training and the other group received modeling alone. Both groups performed the same tasks and received the same prompts for slowing down and checking alternatives. Groups were also matched on length of sessions and frequency of feedback. Results showed that, after training, the self-instruction group made significantly fewer errors and had significantly longer alternatives compared to the modeling-alone group.

Meador and Rumbaugh (1981) investigated whether or not severely mentally retarded adolescents are capable of using cognitive mediational processes in a discrimination task. Results of their study found that these subjects did use these techniques despite the fact that they were never explicitly taught to use them. The discrimination-reversal hypothesis holds that associational learning is indicated by superior performance on two reversal conditions as compared with a standard reversal task, but that mediational learning is indicated if performance in all three cases is equivalent. Meador and Rumbaugh (1981) found the latter to be the case.

Burger, Blackman, and Clark (1981) examined three types of cognitive-strategy training with mentally retarded children and adolescents. One group was taught to correctly name, identify characteristics of, and describe likenesses of sets of three similar items using a relevant attribution training program, in which subjects were required to detail attributes of pictures, were praised for correct responses, and were corrected for incorrect responses. When subjects were asked to describe how items in a triad were alike, correct answers were again praised and incorrect answers were corrected by the experimenter and repeated by the subject. In the modeling condition, subjects watched other subjects perform but did not use it themselves. A third group was taught to use self-instruction training derived from Meichenbaum and Goodman (1971) when performing the task. A no-training control group was also included. Measures of performance were obtained at pretraining, posttraining, maintenance, and on a new set of items (generalization).

Results showed that all three treatment groups had significantly higher posttest scores than the control. No treatment differences among groups were evident. These findings were also identical for the generalization assessment, whereas maintenance assessment found the self-instruction and modeling groups to be superior to the relevant attributes and control conditions.

Several important findings arise from these studies with regard to cognitive impulsivity of mentally retarded adolescents. Relationships typically expected between measures of impulsivity and mentally retarded persons are evident. Compared to nonmentally retarded persons, mentally retarded individuals display shorter latencies and more errors on the MFFT. Second, a developmental lag may exist in the cognitive style of mentally retarded adolescents because they become more reflective with age.

When matched with nonmentally retarded children of the same mental age, however, mentally retarded children tend to show more impulsivity than their nonhandicapped counterparts. Thus, mentally retarded adolescents may still be as impulsive as young children and may take longer to become reflective.

Finally, cognitive-based training procedures, such as self-instruction training, can effectively be used by moderately mentally retarded adolescents to improve skills. This suggests that these pupils are capable of modifications in cognitive styles. This has been clearly advocated and demonstrated in the work of Feuerstein (1979).

Sexuality

Among the many important topics for understanding the adolescent, sexual behavior is often the most important. This is not surprising, given that the sexual development of a person clearly is centered during the adolescent development period. With mentally retarded individuals, this is equally true. Much has been written about the sexual behavior of adolescent mentally retarded individuals. Specifically, a fairly large amount of research has centered around issues related to sex-role identity, attitudes about sexual behavior, knowledge and education of sexuality, and actual sexual behavior per se.

Sex Roles

Sigelmann, Ater, and Spanhel (1978) examined the sex role stereotypes of mentally retarded and nonhandicapped persons. Children and young adults (N = 328) were assessed in regard to the degree of their participation in typically male or female tasks. Male tasks included repairs, mowing the lawn, and taking out the garbage. Female tasks involved meal preparation, cleaning, and day care. A survey was completed by caretakers who rated each activity in regard to the amount of participation in the task of each person relative to the number of times the task was done in the home or institution. Results showed that mentally retarded subjects had sex role stereotyping patterns similar to nonhandicapped persons.

Attitudes and Knowledge

The attitudes of mentally retarded adolescents toward sexual behavior were addressed by Hall, Morris, and Barker (1973). The authors surveyed 61 noninstitutionalized, moderately and mildly mentally retarded adolescents using a questionnaire that was read to them if they could not read independently. Items on the questionnaire concerned knowledge of sexual behavior, ethics and socially appropriate sexual behavior, and self-concept. Parents were asked to predict their adolescents' scores on the measure. Results indicated that adolescents from higher socioeconomic groups had more sexual knowledge, but no more liberal attitudes or better self-concepts than adolescents from other groups. Additionally, age of puberty onset did not correlate with any of the scores on the measure. Mildly mentally retarded adolescents were found to have more knowledge of sexual behavior overall, but lacked knowledge about conception, contraception, and venereal disease.

Comparisons with parental predictions found no significant differences between the adolescents' actual scores and parental predicted scores on sexual knowledge and self-concept. Discrepancies between parent and adolescent scores increased as the adolescent's self-concept score increased. Less discrepancy was evident if the adolescent had had some sex education. The authors noted that both the adolescents and parents expressed concern that further sex education was needed.

In a follow-up to this study, Hall and Morris (1976) compared the results of these noninstitutionalized adolescents with 61 institutionalized adolescents. A new form of the survey was also administered to the noninstitutionalized group so that direct comparisons could be made between the two groups. As expected, the noninstitutionalized participants attained higher scores on all measures than the institutionalized group. However, significant differences were found only for scores on knowledge. Results also showed that the amount of sexual knowledge significantly decreased with increasing time in the institution. Those adolescents living in coeducational quarters had significantly more knowledge than those in same-sex quarters. Participants in both groups showed a lack of knowledge in areas similar to those in the Hall et al. (1973) study, such as masturbation, pregnancy and intercourse, menstruation, and sterilization.

Goodman, Budner, and Lesh (1971) examined parental attitudes about adolescent sex, marriage, and childrearing. Interviews with 11 par-

ents of adolescent mentally retarded individuals were conducted. Most parents greatly restricted their adolescent's travel and activities for fear of sexual aggression against them. Acknowledgment of their teen's sexuality was also difficult. Some parents welcomed the physical maturation of their adolescent, but others were apprehensive about the changes. Masturbation was considered normal and accepted if done privately, and all parents agreed to their children's wishes to be married.

Alcorn (1974) discussed the parental views and attitudes of trainable mentally retarded individuals and traced the attitude and knowledge of the mentally retarded individual to the parents' own knowledge of sexuality. Parents expressed concerns about their adolescent's stated wishes to marry and the ability of their sons/daughters to use birth control. They had strong reservations about the ability of their moderately mentally retarded children to effectively manage their own children. In general, parents displayed a significant amount of concern about the sexual future of their children.

Sexual Behavior

Although surveys of parents of mentally retarded adolescents as well as the adolescents themselves suggest significant deficits in the degree of sexual knowledge, the question may be raised whether the sexual behavior per se of the mentally retarded adolescent reflects lack of knowledge. Gebhard (1973) compared 84 moderately and mildly mentally retarded adult males with 477 males attending elementary school or high school regarding their sexual behavior. Of the 84 mentally retarded participants, 57 were in penal institutions, 26 were institutionalized, and one was not. The comparison group had not been convicted of crimes nor institutionalized.

Results of his survey found that mentally retarded males reported reaching puberty at a mean age of 13.3 years, whereas the comparison group reported puberty beginning at 13.8 years. Masturbation among the mentally retarded group was similar to the comparison group—92% of the mentally retarded population and 83% of the nonhandicapped group. The mentally retarded individuals indicated that as adolescents they engaged in masturbation on the average of 1.3 times per week, below the average of 1.75 for the nonmentally retarded group. Regarding fantasies during masturbation, the mentally retarded group reported 57% heterosexual fantasies and 24.5% homosexual compared to 99% and 8%, respectively, for the nonhandicapped group. This is not surprising given the nature of the mentally retarded group (mostly institutionalized). The mentally retarded group reported premarital petting and intercourse as adolescents at just below 70% and 51%, respectively, compared to incidence rates of 75% and 44% in the comparison group.

Although the data gathered by Gebhard (1973) suggest that mentally retarded and non-mentally retarded individuals progress equally in regard to sexual behavior, his subject selection procedures are atypical of the mentally retarded population. Mulhern (1975), in his survey of sexual behavior of individuals in institutionalized settings, provided a more typical sample of mentally retarded persons. Questionnaires were mailed to 82 institutions, and 85% were returned. Masturbation was reported to have occurred in 81% of the institutions, 70% reported occurrence of heterosexual intercourse, 75% noted homosexual behavior between males, and 69% reported homosexual behavior between females.

Again, questions are raised about whether these results are representative of most mentally retarded individuals in general. Additionally, the generalizability of these results to mentally retarded adolescents is questionable. Edmonson, McCombs, and Wish (1979) compared institutionalized mentally retarded adults with those living in the community. Their results showed that institutionalized females tended to be more permissive than males and that this trend was echoed in the community setting. Women in the noninstitutionalized group were most negative in attitudes regarding dating, marriage, intercourse, pregnancy, and intimacy. Both institutionalized men and women were more positive about marriage compared to those living in the community. Males living in the community were also more favorable toward intercourse, intimacy, and dating than their female counterparts.

Across groups, mentally retarded adults were most knowledgeable about community risks and hazards (i.e., rape), but less so about dating. They reported knowing little about venereal disease, alcohol and drugs, masturbation, and intercourse. Women were more knowledgeable than men about menstruation, birth control, and childbirth.

In general, although few surveys have examined the sexual behavior and attitudes of mentally retarded adolescents, it appears that mentally retarded individuals are lacking in sexual knowledge but have levels of desire and interest similar to nonhandicapped persons. Edgerton and Dingman (1964), for example, examined dating behavior and found that mentally retarded adults made complex arrangements for private meetings, adhered to proper rules for conduct on dates, and displayed substantial impulse control when in social situations. Clearly, inclusion of sex-education programs for mentally retarded individuals is critical for teaching effective and appropriate skills regarding sexual behavior. Obviously, the time for this to occur is during the adolescent period when sexual desires are just emerging. A significant amount of literature has described such programs.

Sex Education

One of the earliest reported programs for sex education was described by Kratter and Thorne (1957). In their program, which was conducted at a state residential facility, instruction was implemented in a group and on an individual basis for all residents. The major emphasis in their program was on personal and mental health. Menstruation was explained to the girls along with appropriate menstrual care during periods. Development of secondary sex characteristics was discussed with the boys. Additional information provided in the instruction included the physical changes associated with adolescence, dating behavior, appropriate male–female relationships, sexual attraction, pregnancy and motherhood, and the limitations of mentally retarded persons as parents.

Thorne (1958), in a follow-up article, discussed the progress of the program described by Kratter and Thorne (1957) for the adolescent girls and women included in their sex-education program. Although no data are provided, Thorne (1958) notes that teachers reported the girls to be natural and appropriate regarding sexual behavior.

Although these two reports are obviously lacking in any empirical data or description, they are noteworthy in the historical context that concern about the sex education of mentally retarded individuals has been a long-standing issue. Others have similarly reported concern and described programs that have attempted to teach the mentally retarded adolescent and adult appropriate sexual behavior. Kempton (1975) emphasized the cooperative effort needed between teachers and parents in teaching these skills. Likewise, Bass (1974) notes that the current efforts at deinstitutionalization make sex education even more important. Both authors particularly note the need for teaching birth control. Shapiro and Sheridan (1985) reported an assessment and training program for teaching reproductive health care to a mentally retarded woman.

Several reports of sex education programs have appeared in the literature. Bloom (1969) found that individuals between the ages of 11 and 14 had reduced fears regarding sexual behavior following a course in sex education. Fischer and Krajicek (1974) found that moderately mentally retarded adolescents had more knowledge and ability to understand sexual behavior than their parents. Regarding birth control, Coleman and Murphy (1980) reported that 95% of institutions surveyed reported provision of social activities or dances, which encourage heterosexual interaction, but that only 66% provided contraceptive counseling. Goodman (1973) noted that mentally retarded adolescents are very receptive to birth-control training programs and are willing to talk about their sexuality openly.

Conclusions

It is quite apparent that the degree of sexual behavior of mentally retarded adolescents is not matched by the amount of sex education they receive (Murphy, Coleman, & Abel, 1983). Yet, numerous studies reported that mentally retarded adolescents are very receptive to learning about sexual behavior and accepting of the limitations they may have regarding parenting. Interestingly, surveys of parents of mentally retarded adolescents show that the degree of concern about sexuality is high.

Despite the apparent need for sex-education programs, few empirically documented effective programs have been developed for teaching mentally retarded adolescents. Future efforts should be devoted toward the development of training packages that can be replicated across programs. These training programs need to provide empirical evidence that increases in knowledge and understanding of sexual behavior are evident. Shapiro and Sheridan (1985) recently described such a program for assessing

sexuality knowledge in a moderately mentally retarded woman. Richman, Reiss, Bauman, and Bailey (1984) described a similar program for teaching menstrual care. These are examples of procedures with demonstrable results. More investigations of this type are clearly needed.

Family

Given the number of social and psychological events affecting the adolescent, the influence of one's family obviously plays a large part in facilitating the adjustment made by the adolescent. As with many other areas of research examined in this chapter, there appear to have been few investigations specifically aimed at understanding the familial relationship with mentally retarded adolescents. Instead, it is assumed that the issues and concerns of nonhandicapped youth apply to the mentally retarded adolescent as well.

An exception was a study reported by Nihira, Meyers, and Mink (1983). In a longitudinal analysis over a period of 3 years with 112 moderately mentally retarded young adolescents, the home environment was assessed annually for characteristics reflecting interactions between the parents, home variables, and environmental influences. Specifically, assessments were conducted to examine educationally related stimuli and opportunity for the child, type of parental reinforcement used to change behavior, psychosocial climate of the home (cohesion vs. conflict, expressiveness, achievement orientation, moral-religious, etc.), environmental status variables such as father-figure presence, mother's level of education, and number of children in the family. The social competency and psychosocial adjustment of the youth over the 3-year period was also assessed.

Results showed that a reciprocal relationship exists and that the most important environmental variables facilitating development (defined as increases in personal self-sufficiency, psychological adjustment, and social adjustment, and decreases in social maladaptation and personal maladaptation) included language stimulation, cohesion versus conflict at home, physical environment, stimulation of academic behavior, stimulation through toys, games, and reading materials, and behavioral control of the parents over the child. The most important variables affecting the home environment include mothers' educational level, social adjustment, personal maladaptation, subject's IQ level, personal–social responsibility, and presence of father at home.

In general, the results of the Nihira et al. (1983) study leave little question regarding the influence of the home environment on the adjustment of the mentally retarded adolescent. Likewise, the mentally retarded adolescent has a reciprocal influence on the home environment. Adjustment of the youth directly influences the adjustment of the parents in terms of the use of physical punishment and of showing pride, affection, and warmth toward the child. These findings are not surprising and are consistent with those found for nonhandicapped youth (e.g., Lerner & Spanier, 1980; Long & Cobb, 1983; Rice, 1984).

Vocational and Educational Issues

Among the topics covered in this chapter, researchers seem to have devoted most of their attention to the study of vocational and educational issues with the mentally retarded adolescent. This is appropriate given the importance of these years for establishing the possibility of adolescent mentally retarded youth emerging into adulthood with the full capacities to live a successful and independent life.

One of the major shifts in emphasis during the adolescent period occurs within the educational curriculum. Throughout the elementary-school years, much effort was devoted toward teaching the mentally retarded individual basic academic skills in reading, math, spelling, and other areas of education. Those being educated in classrooms for the mildly handicapped followed the academic instructional curriculum for a longer period. Others in classes for the moderately mentally retarded were being instructed in basic academic skills but were also being taught functional skills that would aid them in moving toward prevocational and vocational areas during adolescence. Individuals in the classes for severely/profoundly handicapped most likely were not being taught academic skills at all but instead concentrated on learning daily living and self-help skills.

As mentally retarded children move into the adolescent years, emphasis in the educational curriculum at all levels shifts toward teaching vocational and functional living skills (Cegelka & Prehm, 1982). The teaching of these skills can be accomplished in a variety of ways. In some curricula, personal and community self-sufficiency are taught directly as objectives in the instructional process. Brolin (1982) provides an excellent example of such a curriculum. Individuals responsible for implementing such a curriculum would include teachers in home economics, physical education, special education, school counselors, vocational educators, employers, and vocational counselors.

In contrast, other curricula that have similar goals of achieving community and personal self-sufficiency place more emphasis on academic skills as the initial basis for learning vocational and functional living skills. Bluhm (1977) described a curriculum in which two levels of secondary education are identified. The first level, prevocational skills, included concentration on reading, language, and number skills but also taught personal–social and home-living skills. At the second level, an evaluation of work potential is performed, individuals are trained in work adjustment programs, and are placed into competitive employment settings during their training. Bluhm (1977) notes that prevocational training should occur during the early adolescent period in the junior-high or middle-school level, whereas vocational training occurs at the high-school age.

Payne and Patton (1981) described a curriculum that emphasized vocational skills alone. They noted five phases in their program, which included vocational exploration, vocational evaluation, vocational training, vocational placement, and follow-up. At the exploration stage, the nature of different occupations and their respective skill requirements are discussed with the students. An initial assessment and analysis of varying jobs is developed in an attempt to aid the adolescent in selecting an appropriate career goal.

The second level requires evaluation. It is important for mentally retarded adolescents to actually experience specific jobs in the course of their evaluation. Thus, vocational assessment that relies only on paper-and-pencil measures is clearly inappropriate for these pupils. Typically, vocational assessment should be conducted using work-sample methods where individuals actually work on simulated jobs and are assessed based on their abilities to complete these jobs. It is important to remember that the purpose of the work sample assessment with these individuals is not job placement but career se-lection, where some potential for success is evi-dent. The vocational assessment should pro-vide information regarding whether individuals have any possibility of being successful in their preferred occupation.

Once the evaluation is completed and the ad-olescent has selected a job goal, training of the necessary skills in that job are begun. This in-cludes on-the-job experience, initially in simu-lated settings and eventually in competitive em-ployment. Helping the individual actually locate a job is the next step, followed by ongoing follow-up to aid the adolescent in dealing with difficulties as well as providing further training.

Kolstoe (1975) described a high school work–study program for mentally retarded adoles-cents. During the first year, the first half of the student's day was spent in learning basic aca-demic and community skills. The second half of the day involved practical instruction in analyz-ing jobs and a vocational assessment. In the second year, students concentrated on complet-ing job applications, job-interview skills, and the development of vocational skills based on the assessment. Finally in the third year, stu-dents spent one-half of their day in school and one-half of their day in competitive employ-ment.

In general, it is clear that the curriculum for adolescent mentally retarded students includes strong shifts toward vocational-skills training. However, continuation of academic skills is also important because these skills underlie many of the requirements of jobs. Despite the student's interest, exclusion of certain job areas would not be unusual if certain basic academic skills were missing. Numerous programs have been de-scribed for mentally retarded adolescents that have demonstrated the types of academic and vocational skills that need to be emphasized.

Academic Skills

These skills function as prerequisites to many occupational tasks. Most academic skills for ad-olescent mentally retarded individuals, howev-er, are functional. For example, although it is important to teach math skills, the skills taught must relate to actual problems the individuals will face (Snell, 1981). Bellamy and Buttars (1975) taught moderately mentally retarded ad-olescents to count by 1s, 5s, 10s, and 25s by using cards with prices from $.01 to $1.00. Indi-viduals were taught to label price cards and identify coins corresponding to the appropriate prices. They were then instructed to count out money to match the prices on the cards. Using praise and points for correct performance along with modeling and physical guidance when necessary, all subjects learned counting and could count out any amount of change under $1.00.

Wheeler, Ford, Nietupski, Loomis, and Brown (1980) used prompting and correction procedures to teach use of a calculator, recogni-tion of food items and price tags, and other shopping skills to mentally retarded adoles-cents. Teaching took place in a simulated super-market in the classroom and later in a real su-permarket. All students reached criterion in most skill areas. The skills further generalized from teachers to parents. When parents dictat-ed shopping lists to students, the students were able to write down the items and independently shop for them within 30 minutes.

In another study, Beattie and Algozzine (1982) compared a traditional and game-like for-mat for teaching math to mentally retarded ado-lescents. Results showed that students in the game conditions did significantly better on a posttest of math achievement than those using standard math worksheets teaching the identi-cal skill areas. In addition, students in the game conditions spent more time attending to their task than those in the traditional condition.

Learning of vocabulary is another important functional skill. Hanley-Maxwell, Wilcox, and Heal (1982) compared use of a direct instruction approach (prompting, feedback, and reinforce-ment) to an incidental teaching technique in which words were presented but not directly instructed. Pretests revealed that none of the words that were taught were known by the sub-jects. Of the six individuals in the study, three learned 100% of the target words and three learned 47% of the target words under the di-rect teaching approach. The higher group also learned 40% of those words presented to their peers, whereas low group members learned on-ly about 5%. The study shows that, at least for some individuals, incidental learning will have a great effect in improving vocabulary, but for others direct instruction on all words taught is important. The implication of the study is that the teaching of functional vocabulary words needs to be considered through direct instruction methods to assure that even the low performers will learn the words.

Numerous other studies have concentrated on teaching different aspects of reading behavior to mentally retarded adolescents. For example, Lally (1981) used computer-assisted instruction to improve the sight-word vocabulary of mentally retarded children and adolescents. Worrall and Singh (1983) taught word recognition to moderately mentally retarded children using embedded picture cues. Bos and Tierney (1984) investigated whether young mentally retarded adolescent readers are capable of producing inferences of equal quality to those produced by nonmentally retarded elementary-school students.

In addition to traditional and functional academic skills, other skills that have been taught to mentally retarded adolescents within the school setting could be conceptualized as skills in personal self-sufficiency. For example, Crain, McLaughlin, and Eisenhart (1983) described a program to teach dance skills to mildly mentally retarded adolescents. Goals of the program included teaching movement, coordination, and rhythm, as well as improving social interaction. The authors also hoped to increase the leadership, cooperation, and peer teaching among their students. Results of their program indicated that: (a) one group improved in both social and physical skills; (b) another group improved in physical skills only; (c) one group improved in social skills only; and (d) one group showed no change.

Longhi, Follett, Bloom, and Armstrong (1975) described a program to teach mildly mentally retarded adolescents about the legal consequences of underage drinking and driving after drinking. Following a pretest on knowledge regarding issues related to drinking and driving, subjects were shown a film telling a story about two adolescent boys and their experiences with underage drinking and driving. Posttesting showed a gain of 18% in correct responses on information.

As is apparent, the range of issues covered in the curriculum of the adolescent mentally retarded student is quite wide and varied. Although some educators advocate strict adherence to a vocational curriculum, others suggest incorporation of functional academic skills along with the vocational training. Wimmer (1979) expressed some concern about the amount of academic content in the career-education curriculum of mentally retarded adolescents. A scale was developed consisting of questions taken from several curricula and administered to mentally retarded and nonmentally retarded children and adolescents. The total population showed 77% mastery, with nonmentally retarded subjects failing to master four areas and mentally retarded subjects not mastering 12 areas. Wimmer (1979) notes the importance of starting career education earlier and the need for teaching more direct knowledge of jobs and job skills.

Zetlin and Gallimore (1980) called for the incorporation of more cognitive skills into the curriculum of the moderately mentally retarded student. They felt that the focus on self-care, community, and other functional skills, although important, needs to be supplemented by more basic academic training. A study was conducted with three moderately mentally retarded individuals, who met as a group with a teacher 3 times a week and attempted to improve reading comprehension skills. After the training program, students showed substantially better inferential skills and improved cognitive abilities.

Vocational Skills

Despite the obvious importance of academic skills as prerequisites for learning vocational skills, the curriculum of the mentally retarded adolescent is clearly focused upon vocational skills. Typical methods employed include the use of work–study, split-days, and simulated work environments.

Bucci and Hansen (1980) described a prevocational training model in which surveys of sheltered workshops were first conducted in order to determine the types of jobs being completed in those settings. Tasks similar to those in workshops were analyzed and taught using a prompting procedure combined with praise. When criterion levels were reached, students began working independently and in small groups with minimal teacher support, again to simulate the workshop and competitive employment environments. Reinforcement was made contingent on production and error rates and was faded as proficiency was achieved.

Fleres (1975) described a program designed to facilitate vocational readiness in adolescent mentally retarded students. Individuals had opportunities to spend time in different professions, including health services, offset printing, auto mechanics, cosmetology, electronics, and any other area in which they might be competitively employed. Behavioral objectives were developed and students were paid "school dollars" based on performance. Money earned was deposited in student accounts and could be used to purchase items at the school store. Training was conducted by in-class discussion about job responsibilities and actual vocational training. Other aspects of job skills, such as grooming and social skills, were taught.

Results of this project indicate that students became excited about working and began calling themselves workers rather than students. Students preferred actual work to talking about or viewing filmstrips about work. When surveyed, 90% said that they were happy about participating and 60% indicated that they had found an occupational area of interest. Social-work behaviors such as grooming showed great improvements.

One of the goals of many vocational programs is to place mentally retarded workers into competitive employment environments. Although this goal is most often met with mildly mentally retarded populations (Cegelka & Prehm, 1982), it is not impossible with more impaired populations. Frith and Edwards (1982) note that providing on-the-job experience is critical for achieving this goal. In their program, students begin by spending some of their time in classrooms and part of their time in supervised work experiences. As their skills improve, students are afforded more opportunities to work independently. Such on-the-job training can also begin to prepare mentally retarded adolescents for the realities of competitive employment. For example, Holvoet, Keilitz, and Tucker (1975) found that mentally retarded adolescents in vocational settings received more demands than nonmentally retarded workers. Although the mentally retarded adolescents seemed to respond to these demands and no specific consequences were administered by supervisors, it is important for mentally retarded adolescents to be accustomed to such working environments.

A particularly surprising omission from the literature is the discussion of training programs for mentally retarded adolescents housed in vocational–technical training schools. It seems logical that institutions that train job skills for nonmentally handicapped youth should be able to provide the best training for mentally retarded adolescents (Sitlington, 1979). Although these programs clearly exist, the literature provides almost no empirical evidence regarding the effectiveness of such programs.

One reason why the vocational–technical programs may not be used is the need for special assistance in training mentally retarded youth. It may be unrealistic to expect mentally retarded individuals to be capable of learning in the environment in which nonmentally retarded individuals learn. Inclusion of mentally retarded adolescents in vocational–technical schools therefore requires additional resources and curriculum adaptation. At the present time, the degree to which mentally retarded youth are incorporated into the vocational–technical school setting is unknown.

A particular problem that often arises during the vocational training of mentally retarded adolescents is their problems in social interaction. Students who may possess adequate skills for competitive employment fail to achieve such employment due to their inappropriate social skills in the work environment. LaGreca, Stone, and Bell (1982) attempted to identify and define the levels of inappropriate responses that prevent effective community work placements of mentally retarded adolescents. Using a behavioral-assessment approach, a Vocational Problem Behavior Inventory was developed. Both the frequency and seriousness of each behavior was rated by workshop supervisors. Concurrent validation of the scale was done by administering the Behavior Problem Checklist, selected AAMD–Adaptive Behavior Scale subscales, and a Vocational Competency Scale. Results showed moderate to strong correlations among these measures and the Vocational Problem Behavior Inventory.

SUMMARY

It is clear from the review of the literature that the adolescent period for mentally retarded individuals has not been investigated or treated in the same way that it is for nonhandicapped persons. This is particularly true for areas other than vocational/educational where the bulk of effort has been given. Whereas much attention has been given to understanding the nonmentally retarded adolescent in relation to such issues as drugs, suicide, increasing needs for independence, sexuality, social issues, and so forth, relatively little effort has been devoted to how these issues affect the mentally retarded adolescent.

Although there may be a tendency to assume that mentally retarded adolescents respond to and must deal with the same issues as their nonhandicapped peers, there is no empirical support for such a position. Conceptually, one could raise significant arguments against such similarity. Beside the obvious differences in intellectual abilities and academic achievement, the mentally retarded adolescent must face concerns related to peer acceptance, uncertain futures, and parental interactions, as well as the typical concerns of adolescents. Additionally, the mentally retarded adolescent, like most mentally retarded persons, must be specifically taught many of the skills that their nonhandicapped counterparts learn by observation. Clearly, research efforts need to be directed toward a better and thorough understanding of mentally retarded adolescents.

The establishment of adolescence as a stage of development separate from childhood and adulthood is a relatively recent phenomenon (e.g., Lerner & Spanier, 1980; Long & Cobb, 1983; Rice, 1984). In a similar way, it is time for researchers to begin a thorough investigation of this stage of development for the mentally retarded adolescent. Issues related to family, personality, and other individual/social characteristics are critical to furthering the study of mental retardation.

REFERENCES

Alcorn, D. A. (1974). Parental views on sexual development and education of the trainable mentally retarded. *Journal of Special Education, 8,* 119–130.

Allen, L. D., & Iwata, B. A. (1980). Reinforcing exercise maintenance using existing high-rate activities. *Behavior Modification, 4,* 337–354.

Altman, K., Bondy, A., & Hirsch, G. (1978). Behavioral treatment of obesity in patients with Prader–Willi Syndrome. *Journal of Behavioral Medicine, 1,* 403–412.

Bass, M. S. (1974). Sex education for the handicapped. *Family Coordinator, 23,* 27–33.

Beattie, J., & Algozzine, R. (1982). Improving basic academic skills of EMR adolescents. *Education and Training of the Mentally Retarded, 17,* 255–258.

Bellamy, T., & Buttars, K. L. (1975). Teaching trainable level retarded students to count money: Toward personalized independence through academic instruction. *Education and Training of the Mentally Retarded, 10,* 18–26.

Bijou, S. W. (1966). A functional analysis of retarded development. In N. R. Ellis (Ed.), *International review of research in mental retardation* (Vol. 1, pp. 1–18). New York: Academic.

Blodgett, H. E. (1971). *Mentally retarded children.* Minneapolis: University of Minnesota Press.

Bloom, J. L. (1969). Sex education for handicapped adolescents. *Journal of School Health, 39,* 363–367.

Bluhm, H. (1977). A vocational delivery system for the mildly retarded. In C. J. Drew, M. L. Hardman, & H. P. Bluhm (Eds.), *Mental retardation: Social and educational perspectives* (pp. 216–229). St. Louis: Mosby.

Bos, C. S., & Tierney, R. J. (1984). Inferential reading abilities of mildly mentally retarded and nonretarded students. *American Journal of Mental Deficiency, 89,* 75–82.

Bracken, B. A. (1985). A critical review of the Kaufman Assessment Battery for Children (K-ABC). *School Psychology Review, 14,* 21–36.

Bray, G. E. (Ed.). (1979). *Obesity in America* (National Institutes of Health Publication No. 79–359). Washington, DC: U.S. Department of Health, Education, and Welfare.

Brolin, D. (1982). *Vocational preparation of persons with handicaps* (2nd ed.). Columbus, OH: Merrill.

Bruininks, R. H., Rynders, J. E., & Gross J. L. (1974). Social acceptance of mildly retarded pupils in resource rooms and regular classes. *American Journal of Mental Deficiency, 78,* 377–383.

Bucci, J. R., & Hansen, C. L. (1980). A classroom-based pre-vocational program for the severely handicapped. *Education and Training of the Mentally Retarded, 15,* 278–283.

Budoff, M., & Gottlieb, J. (1976). Special-class EMR children mainstreamed: A study of an aptitude (learning potential) × treatment interaction. *American Journal of Mental Deficiency, 81,* 1–11.

Budoff, M., & Siperstein, G. N. (1978). Low-income children's attitudes toward mentally retarded children: Effects of labeling and academic behavior. *American Journal of Mental Deficiency, 82,* 474–479.

Buford, L. M. (1975). Group education to reduce overweight: Classes for mentally handicapped children. *American Journal of Nursing, 75,* 1994–1995.

Burger, A. L., Blackman, L. S., & Clark, H. T. (1981). Generalization of verbal abstraction strategies by EMR children and adolescents. *American Journal of Mental Deficiency, 85,* 611–618.

Campbell, J. (1973). Physical fitness and the mentally retarded: A review of the research. *Mental Retardation, 11,* 26–29.

Cegelka, P. T., & Prehm, H. J. (1982). *Mental retardation: From categories to people.* Columbus, OH: Merrill.

Chasey, W. C., & Wyrick, W. (1971). Effects of a physical development program on psychomotor ability of retarded children. *American Journal of Mental Deficiency, 75,* 565–570.

Cleland, C. C. (1978). *Mental retardation: A developmental approach.* Englewood Cliffs, NJ: Prentice-Hall.

Coleman, E. M., & Murphy, W. D. (1980). A survey of

sexual attitudes and sex education programs among facilities for the mentally retarded. *Applied Research in Mental Retardation, 1,* 269–276.

Coleman, R. S., & Whitman, T. L. (1984). Developing, generalizing, and maintaining physical fitness in mentally retarded adults: Toward a self-directed program. *Analysis and Intervention in Developmental Disabilities, 4,* 109–128.

Corder, W. O. (1966). Effects of physical education on the intellectual, physical, and social development of educable mentally retarded boys. *Exceptional Children, 32,* 357–364.

Crain, C., McLaughlin, J., & Eisenhart, M. (1983). The social and physical effects of a 10-week dance program on educable mentally retarded adolescents. *Education and Training of the Mentally Retarded, 18,* 308–312.

Das, J. P., Kirby, J., & Jarman, R. F. (1979). *Simultaneous and successive processes.* New York: Academic.

Edgerton, R. B., & Dingman, H. (1964). Good reasons for bad supervision: Dating in a hospital for mentally retarded. *Psychiatric Quarterly Supplement Part 2,* 221–223.

Edmonson, B., McCombs, K., & Wish, J. (1979). What retarded adults believe about sex. *American Journal of Mental Deficiency, 84,* 11–18.

Feuerstein, R. (1979). *The dynamic assessment of retarded performers.* Baltimore, MD: University Park Press.

Fischer, H. L., & Krajicek, M. (1974). Sexual development in the moderately retarded child: Level of information and parental attitudes. *Mental Retardation, 12,* 28–30.

Fleres, C. N. (1975). An experiment in the pre-occupational education of mentally retarded students on the junior high school level. *Education and Training of the Mentally Retarded, 10,* 26–28.

Foley, J. M. (1979). Effect of labeling and teacher behavior on children's attitudes. *American Journal of Mental Deficiency, 83,* 380–384.

Fox, R., & Rotatori, A. F. (1982). Prevalence of obesity among mentally retarded adults. *American Journal of Mental Deficiency, 87,* 228–230.

Foxx, R. M. (1972). Social reinforcement of weight reduction: A case report on an obese retarded adolescent. *Mental Retardation, 10,* 21–23.

Frith, G. H., & Edwards, R. (1982). Competitive employment training for moderately retarded adolescents. *Education and Training of the Mentally Retarded, 17,* 149–153.

Funk, D. C. (1971). Effects of physical education on fitness and motor development of trainable mentally retarded children. *Research Quarterly, 42,* 30–34.

Gampel, D. H., Gottlieb, J., & Harrison, R. H. (1974). A comparison of the classroom behavior of special class EMR, integrated EMR, low IQ, and non-retarded children. *American Journal of Mental Deficiency, 79,* 16–21.

Gebhard, P. H. (1973). Sexual behavior of the mentally retarded. In F. F. de la Cruz & G. D. LaVeck (Eds.), *Human sexuality and the mentally retarded* (pp. 29–49). New York: Brunner/Mazel.

Goodman, H., Gottlieb, J., & Harrison, R. H. (1972). Social acceptance of EMR's integrated into a nongraded elementary school. *American Journal of Mental Deficiency, 76,* 412–417.

Goodman, L. (1973). The sexual rights of the retarded—A dilemma for parents. *The Family Coordinator, 22,* 472–474.

Goodman, L., Budner, S., & Lesh, B. (1971). The parents' role in sex education for the retarded. *Mental Retardation, 9,* 43–45.

Gottlieb, J. (1981). Mainstreaming: Fulfilling the promise? *American Journal of Mental Deficiency, 86,* 115–126.

Gottlieb, J., & Budoff, M. (1972). Attitudes toward school by segregated and integrated retarded children: A study and experimental validation. *Proceedings of the American Psychological Association, 7,* 713–714.

Gottlieb, J., & Budoff, M. (1973). Social acceptability of retarded children in non-graded schools differing in architecture. *American Journal of Mental Deficiency, 78,* 15–19.

Gottlieb, J., & Davis, J. E. (1973). Social acceptance of EMRs during overt behavioral interaction. *American Journal of Mental Deficiency, 78,* 141–143.

Gumaer, J., & Simon, R. (1979). Behavioral group counseling and schoolwide reinforcement program with obese trainable mentally retarded students. *Education and Training of the Mentally Retarded, 14,* 106–111.

Hall, J. E., & Morris, H. L. (1976). Sexual knowledge and attitudes of institutionalized and noninstitutionalized retarded adolescents. *American Journal of Mental Deficiency, 80,* 382–387.

Hall, J. E., Morris, H. L., & Barker, H. R. (1973). Sexual knowledge and attitudes of mentally retarded adolescents. *American Journal of Mental Deficiency, 77,* 706–709.

Hanley-Maxwell, C., Wilcox, B., & Heal, L. W. (1982). A comparison of vocabulary learning by moderately retarded students under direct instruction and incidental presentation. *Education and Training of the Mentally Retarded, 17,* 214–221.

Hobbs, N. (1975). *Issues in the classification of children.* San Francisco: Jossey-Bass.

Holvoet, J. F., Keilitz, I., & Tucker, D. J. (1975). Mand interactions in retarded adolescents: An observational study in vocational settings. *Education and Training of the Mentally Retarded, 10,* 237–244.

Hutt, M. L., & Gibby, R. G. (1976). *The mentally retarded child* (3rd ed.). Boston: Allyn & Bacon.

Iano, R. P., Ayers, D., Heller, H. B., McGettigan, J., & Walker, V. S. (1974). Sociometric status of retarded children in an integrative program. *Exceptional Children, 40,* 267–271.

Johnson, R., Johnson, D. W., DeWeerdt, N., Lyons, V., & Zaidman, B. (1983). Integrating severely adaptively handicapped seventh-grade students into constructive relationships with nonhandicapped peers in science class. *American Journal of Mental Deficiency, 87,* 611–618.

Johnson, D. W., Johnson, R., & Maruyama, G. (in press). Interdependence and interpersonal attraction among heterogeneous and homogeneous individuals: A theoretical formulation and a meta-analysis of the research. *Review of Educational Research.*

Johnson, R., Rynders, J., Johnson, D. W., Schmidt,

B., & Haider, S. (1979). Producing positive interaction between handicapped and nonhandicapped teenagers through cooperative goal structuring: Implications for mainstreaming. *American Journal of Educational Research, 16,* 161–168.

Kagan, J. (1966). Reflection–impulsivity: The generality and dynamics of conceptual tempo. *Journal of Abnormal Psychology, 57,* 359–365.

Kempton, W. (1975). Sex education—A cooperative effort of parent and teacher. *Exceptional Children, 41,* 531–535.

Kolstoe, O. P. (1975). Secondary programs. In J. M. Kauffman & J. S. Payne (Eds.), *Mental retardation: Introduction and personal perspectives* (pp. 312–334). Columbus, OH: Merrill.

Kratter, F. E., & Thorne, G. D. (1957). Sex education of retarded children. *American Journal of Mental Deficiency, 62,* 44–48.

LaGreca, A. M., Stone, W. L., & Bell, C. R., III. (1982). Assessing the problematic interpersonal skills of mentally retarded individuals in a vocational setting. *Applied Research in Mental Retardation, 13,* 37–43.

Lally, M. (1981). Computer-assisted teaching of sight-word recognition for mentally retarded school children. *American Journal of Mental Deficiency, 85,* 383–388.

Lerner, R. M., & Spanier, G. B. (1980). *Adolescent development: A life-span perspective.* New York: McGraw-Hill.

Long, J. S., & Cobb, N. J. (1983). *Adolescence and early adulthood.* Palo Alto, CA: Mayfield.

Longhi, P., Follett, R., Bloom, B., & Armstrong, J. R. (1975). A program for adolescent educable mentally retarded. *Education and Training of the Mentally Retarded, 10,* 104–109.

Meador, D. M., & Rumbaugh, D. M. (1981). Quality of learning of severely retarded adolescents. *American Journal of Mental Deficiency, 85,* 404–409.

Meichenbaum, D. H., & Goodman, J. (1971). Training impulsive children to talk to themselves: A means of developing self-control. *Journal of Abnormal Psychology, 77,* 115–126.

Mulhern, T. J. (1975). Survey of sexual behavior and policies characterizing residential facilities for retarded citizens. *American Journal of Mental Deficiency, 79,* 670.

Murphy, W. D., Coleman, E. M., & Abel, G. G. (1983). Human sexuality in the mentally retarded. In J. L. Matson & F. Andrasik (Eds.), *Treatment issues and innovations in mental retardation* (pp. 581–644). New York: Plenum.

Nihira, K., Meyers, C. E., & Mink, I. T. (1983). Reciprocal relationship between home environment and development of TMR adolescents. *American Journal of Mental Deficiency, 88,* 139–149.

Payne, J. S., & Patton, J. R. (1981). *Mental retardation.* Columbus, OH: Merrill.

Peters, R. D., & Davies, K. (1981). Effects of self-instructional training on cognitive impulsivity of mentally retarded adolescents. *American Journal of Mental Deficiency, 85,* 377–382.

Rarick, G. L., Widdop, J. J., & Broadhead, G. D. (1970). Physical fitness and motor performance of educable mentally retarded children. *Exceptional Children, 36,* 509–519.

Rice, F. P. (1984). *The adolescent: Development, relationships, and culture* (4th ed.). Boston: Allyn & Bacon.

Richman, G. S., Reiss, M. L., Bauman, K. E., & Bailey, J. S. (1984). Teaching menstrual care to mentally retarded women: Acquisition, generalization, and maintenance. *Journal of Applied Behavior Analysis, 17,* 441–451.

Rotatori, A. F., & Fox, R. (1980). A comparison of two weight reduction programs for moderately retarded adolescents. *Behavior Therapy, 11,* 410–416.

Rotatori, A. F., & Fox, R. (1981). *Behavioral weight reduction program for mentally handicapped persons: A self-control program.* Baltimore, MD: University Park Press.

Rotatori, A. F., Fox, R., & Switzky, H. (1979). A parent–teacher administered weight reduction program for obese Down's Syndrome adolescents. *Journal of Behavior Therapy and Experimental Psychiatry, 10,* 339–341.

Rotatori, A. F., & Switzky, H. (1979). Successful behavioral weight loss with moderately mentally retarded individuals. *International Journal of Obesity, 3,* 223–228.

Rotatori, A. F., Switzky, H. N., & Fox, R. (1981). Behavioral weight reduction procedures for obese mentally retarded individuals: A review. *Mental Retardation, 19,* 157–161.

Rynders, J., Johnson, R., Johnson, D. W., & Schmidt, B. (1980). Effects of cooperative goal structuring in producing positive interaction between Down's Syndrome and nonhandicapped teenagers. *American Journal of Mental Deficiency, 85,* 266–273.

Schlottmann, R. S., & Anderson, V. H. (1982). Developmental changes of institutionalized mentally retarded children: A semilongitudinal study. *American Journal of Mental Deficiency, 87,* 277–281.

Shapiro, E. S., & Sheridan, C. A. (1985). Systematic assessment and training of sex education for a mentally retarded woman. *Applied Research in Mental Retardation, 6,* 307–319.

Sherrill, C. (1980). Posture training as a means of normalization. *Mental Retardation, 18,* 135–138.

Sigelmann, C., Ater, C., & Spanhel, C. (1978). Sex-role stereotypes and the homemaking participation of mentally retarded people. *Mental Retardation, 16,* 357–358.

Sitlington, P. (1979). Vocational assessment and training of the handicapped. *Focus on Exceptional Children, 12,* 1–11.

Snart, F., O'Grady, M., & Das, J. P. (1982). Cognitive processing by subgroups of moderately mentally retarded children. *American Journal of Mental Deficiency, 86,* 465–472.

Snell, M. E. (1981). Daily living skills. In J. M. Kauffman & D. P. Hallahan (Eds.), *Handbook of special education* (pp. 530–551). Englewood Cliffs, NJ: Prentice-Hall.

Stager, S. F., & Young, R. D. (1981). Intergroup contact and social outcomes for mainstreamed EMR adolescents. *American Journal of Mental Deficiency, 85,* 497–503.

Thorne, G. D. (1958). Sex education of mentally retarded girls. *American Journal of Mental Deficiency,* *63,* 460–463.

Wheeler, J., Ford, A., Nietupski, J., Loomis, R., & Brown, L. (1980). Teaching moderately and severely handicapped adolescents to shop in supermarkets using pocket calculators. *Education and Training of the Mentally Retarded, 15,* 105–111.

Wimmer, D. (1979). An investigation of the cognitive content of career education for the mildly mentally retarded. *Education and Training of the Mentally Retarded, 14,* 42–49.

Worrall, N., & Singh, Y. (1983). Teaching TMR children to read using integrated picture cueing. *American Journal of Mental Deficiency, 87,* 422–429.

Wysocki, T., Hall, G., Iwata, B., & Riordan, M. (1979). Behavioral management of exercise: Contracting for aerobic points. *Journal of Applied Behavior Analysis, 12,* 55–64.

Zetlin, A. G., & Gallimore, R. (1980). A cognitive skills training program for moderately retarded learners. *Education and Training of the Mentally Retarded, 15,* 121–131.

PART V

Special Topics

CHAPTER 21

Adolescent Culture and Subculture

Robert J. Havighurst

For purposes of this chapter, we shall define adolescence as the age period from 12 to 18. We shall also use the term youth to refer to the 10-year group from 15 through 24 years of age.

Because our topic is subcultures of adolescents, we need a clear definition of the key terms *culture* and *subculture*. A culture is a set of common and standard behaviors and beliefs shared by a group of people and taught by them to their children. Different nations have different cultures. Also, within a complex society, there are always a number of subcultures. A subculture is a culture shared by a subgroup in a complex society and different from the subcultures of other subgroups in that society. For example, the American society has a number of subcultures, including those of Italian-Americans, Mexican-Americans, Japanese-Americans, American Indians, Puerto Ricans, Appalachian whites, New Englanders, Midwesterners, Southerners, Texans, blacks, Catholics, Jews, Protestants. From this list it should be clear that any given American takes part in a number of subcultures, as well as in the common culture shared by all or nearly all citizens of the United States. Thus, a subculture does not include all the learned behaviors and beliefs of its members. Another form of subculture is that of *social class*, which we will describe and discuss later in this chapter. Still another form of subculture is that of *sex*—male or female.

Thus, we shall see the American adolescent subcultures varying according to ethnicity, social class, and sex. In describing or discussing any particular subculture we should specify the ethnicity, social class, and sex of the adolescents who are in it.

THE ADOLESCENT PEER CULTURE

It is well known that a given age group has its own somewhat truncated culture. Although the members of this age group participate in the culture of the larger society, they also have common and standardized ways of behaving and believing that are pretty much limited to their own age group. For instance, the 8-year-old boys of a community are likely to have their own game culture—a set of games with rules handed from one age cohort of 8-year-old boys to the next: rules for games of marbles, hide-and-seek, cops and robbers, and so on. To this extent, the 8-year-old boys have a peer culture, that is, a culture of a group who are approximately equal in age. There is a culture of 12-year-olds, one of 14-year-olds, 16-year-olds, 18-year-olds, and one such culture for boys with a different one for girls.

There may also be a more generalized peer culture for teenagers, into which the 12-year-olds enter slowly and unsurely, while the 18-year-olds are dropping their participation in their *adolescent peer culture* in favor of the culture of young adults. The adolescent peer culture is the set of ways of behaving and believing of the age group from 12 to 18, which they pass on to their successors. This is the kind of definition to be found in a modern democratic society, where teenagers are allowed to be "adolescents" with a minimum of control by the adult society.

In a few societies, the adolescent peer culture actually opposes the adult culture at points, and there is a long drawn-out contest between adults and adolescents. The adolescent peer culture may have certain values and interests that conflict with the values and interests of the adults. In this case, the adult society may seek to put down the adolescent peer culture. This was clearly the case in the United States in the late 1960s, when the adolescent peer culture encouraged boys to let their hair grow long and girls to shorten their skirts. There were a number of conflicts between the adolescent peer group and the adult generation, which was usually represented by teachers and school principals.

More generally, the adolescent peer culture has its own existence more or less outside the ken of adults.

In the United States, there has been something of a controversy over the question of whether an adolescent peer culture actually opposes some of the educational values of the high schools, encouraging athletics and social activities at the expense of academic study. In an influential book entitled, *The Adolescent Society*, Professor James S. Coleman (1961) reported his study of students in several Midwestern high schools. This study appeared to show that adolescent boys and girls in high school were more influenced by their peers than by their parents and teachers.

A critical analysis of Coleman's study and other studies has been written by Gottlieb and Reeves (1963). They concluded that there is a vaguely defined adolescent peer culture, made of varying peer cultures from various groups of adolescents and that this peer culture has a common basis of disagreement with the adult culture at some points. However, there is no solid monolithic adolescent peer culture that is common to all adolescents in a modern society.

SOCIAL CLASS AND SOCIAL MOBILITY

Perhaps the most widespread ambition of adolescents and their families in modern societies during the past century has been the desire to move up the socioeconomic ladder—to rise in social status, to get a higher income, to get more prestige. And it was evident that the widest road to upward mobility lay through achievement in adolescence and early adulthood. This achievement might take the form of educational progress that opened the way to higher status occupations, of hard work and cleverness in a series of ever-improving jobs, or of marriage (for girls) to a man of higher status. To be upwardly mobile, to move from one social class or socioeconomic level to a higher level, means a change from one subculture to another, or a change of life style.

Research by social anthropologists and sociologists has discovered that social classes exist as crudely defined subcultures in a number of modern societies. Although most of this research has been done in the United States, there is confirmation of the social-class phenomenon from research of the past 20 years in Sweden, Canada, Australia, New Zealand, Brazil, and England.

A social class is defined as a group of people who share certain values and attitudes and who believe themselves to be similar to each other. It may also be seen as a group of people who share a particular life style. There is much intermarriage within a social class and much informal social relationship. When a social scientist studies a particular community, he observes the various social groupings and economic groupings and he asks people in the community about the "social structure" of the community. Invariably, if the community is as big as several thousand and if it contains a population with a range of income and occupation, the residents of the community report that there is a hierarchy of social groups, or social classes, with the highest group having the highest prestige and power in the community. The metaphor of vertical distance is used by the residents, who speak of "our upper class, our middle class or classes, and our lower class or classes."

The number of visibly different social classes depends on the size and complexity of the community. It may be as many as seven or as few as three. The American community studies tend to settle on a five-class structure, named as follows: upper, upper-middle, lower-middle, upper-lower, and lower-lower. These five classes can be found in any cross-sectional community of 5,000 or more. The placing of an individual in the class system depends on his or her social relationships, occupation, income, and educational level, as well as the type of house and area of the community in which he or she lives and the clubs or church to which he or she belongs. All these social characteristics are judged by people in the community in terms of social prestige.

A democratic society has an open class system, with people moving into and out of a given social class on the basis of their performance in various sectors of socioeconomic life. Hence, there are always some people at the margin between two classes; and, therefore, some people cannot be placed as exactly as others in the class structures.

Social mobility is defined as movement within a lifetime by an individual from one class to another. Generally the move is up or down one step on a five-class scale, but sometimes a person moves two or more steps. The degree of social mobility in a society is usually measured by comparing the social class of adult sons and daughters with their fathers. Often the measurement is limited to sons and fathers, because the occupations of males can be easily determined; and occupational level is a very good indicator of social class position all over the world in complex societies.

The proportions of people in the various social classes are substantially as follows in the United States: upper, 3%; upper-middle, 10%; lower-middle, 27%; upper-lower, 45%; and lower-lower, 15%. In effect, the white-collar occupations are middle class and the blue-collar occupations are lower class or working class, with significant exceptions. Some highly skilled handworkers, such as electronic technicians and interior decorators, would be placed by their incomes and their associations in the lower-middle class. Also, owners of substantial farms who work their own farms would be placed in one of the middle classes.

ETHNIC AND SOCIAL SUBGROUPS OF ADOLESCENTS

As we look for atypical groups of adolescents, we may place them in Table 21.1, which gives the numbers of youth (age 15-24) in various ethnic subcultures. For the sake of brevity, and because there is not sufficient research on some groups, we will discuss only a few of them. Also, we will designate them by social class as well as ethnicity. The following groups will be described: Mexican-American—lower-middle class; Puerto Rican—working class; Japanese-American—middle class; American Indian—multitribal; and black middle class.

In addition, we will describe two subcultures that are not primarily ethnic, but are isolated from the mainstream of adolescents. They are: street culture males (in slums of big cities), and teenage mothers.

Table 21.1. Youth in Ethnic Subcultures

	1970		1980	
GROUP	NUMBERS OF YOUTH, 15–24 (THOUSANDS)	% OF YOUTH	NUMBERS OF YOUTH, 15–24 (MILLIONS)	% OF YOUTH
Caucasians	31,700	87.0	34.2	80.5
Blacks	4,300	11.8	5.7	13.5
Orientals	241	0.7	0.6	1.4
American Indians and Eskimos	157	0.4	0.3	0.8
Others (mainly Hispanics)			1.6	3.8

Hispanic Adolescents

A 1972 census publication reports somewhat over 9 million persons of Spanish descent, falling into five categories as shown in Table 21.2. They are living mainly in four areas: the Southwest (Texas, Arizona, New Mexico, and California); the Northeast (New York, Massachusetts, New Jersey, and Pennsylvania); Florida; and the Northcentral industrial area. We will direct special attention to the Mexican-Americans and the Puerto Ricans.

Mexican-Americans of the Southwest

What is now the southwestern corner of the United States was a part of Mexico until the Mexican War of 1848. After that war, which resulted in annexation of Texas and the southwestern territory to the United States, the Spanish and Mexican settlers who remained there became American citizens. Thus, there is an American population of Spanish origin that has as long a history of residence in this country as the New England colonists. Some of these people became business and professional leaders and legislators, so that Spanish surnames figure prominently in the history of the past 100 years in the Southwest. Cities such as Albuquerque, Santa Fe, San Antonio, El Paso, Los Angeles, and San Diego indicate by their names the Spanish influence. Also, many Spanish surnames are carried on the rosters of the Chamber of Commerce, the upper-middle-class service clubs, and the country clubs. In New Mexico, Spanish and English are both official languages.

By far the largest group of Spanish-Americans are those who identify themselves to the census taker as being of Mexican origin, although 83% of them were born in the United States. Over 5 million strong, they provide more than 40% of the children in Los Angeles public schools. Almost all of them are legally American citizens, although a few have come across the Mexican-American border illegally and are liable to deportation if they should get in trouble with the law and be found to lack citizenship papers.

The Mexican-Americans present a variety of life styles, and they are so heterogeneous in status and racial ancestry that the one thing they have in common is their Mexican heritage. They range in economic status from affluent professionals and businessmen to migrant farm workers and people on welfare in big city barrios.

The period since 1965 has seen the younger "members of the post-World War II Mexican-American" generation develop a new political consciousness and pride in their cultural heritage. The youth cohort has emerged from a fusion of Hispanic offspring, who are establishing strong cultural links to Mexican and Indian culture, and dispossessed barrio youth, who are facing "prospects of economic marginality and limited realization of aspirations. The politically conscious adolescents call themselves *Chicanos*, a word presumed to be derived from the colloquial speech of northern Mexico but in fact of unknown etiology" (Thornburg & Grinder, 1975, p. 345).

The Chicano is a product of Spanish-Mexican-Indian heritage and Anglo influence. "The new dignity of Chicano youth is manifested in the concept of Aztlán, a symbolization for the ethnic unity of the mestizo Mexican-American

Table 21.2. United States Population of Spanish Origin, 1972
(Numbers in Thousands)

ORIGIN	TOTAL	% OF U.S. POPULATION	% OF POPULATION OF SPANISH ORIGIN
Mexican	5,254	2.6	57
Puerto Rican	1,518	.7	17
Cuban	629	.3	7
Central or South American	599	.3	6
Other Spanish	1,178	.5	13
Total	9,178	4.5	100

Note. The data in this table are from U.S. Bureau of Census, *Current Population Reports, Series P-20, No. 238: Selected Characteristics of Persons and Families of Mexican and Other Spanish Origin: March 1972.* Washington, DC: Author.

and a rallying point for proclaiming the righteousness of the Mexican-American heritage" (Thornburg & Grinder, 1975, p. 345).

Thornburg and Grinder (1975) describe the rise of "Chicago power" in the 1960s as a response of Mexican-American youth to the civil rights movement. Their consciousness was stimulated by Mexican-American reform leaders, especially Cesar Chavez, who organized California farm workers, Reies Tijerina who founded the *Alianza Federal de Mercedes*, an organization of New Mexico heirs to old Mexican land grants who claimed ownership of land taken over after the Mexican-American war by the United States government, and Rodolfo "Corky" Gonzales, a youth worker in Denver who organized the Crusade for Justice, a Chicano civil rights organization. In 1969, the Crusade for Justice created the Chicano Youth Liberation Conference, when 2,000 young Chicano delegates from over a hundred Chicano youth groups called for a revival of traditional cultural values, a rebirth of Chicano nationalism, and the creation of a new political party.

Mexican-American adolescents organized two major school boycotts in East Los Angeles (1968) and Crystal City, Texas (1969). In Los Angeles, they demanded reduction of class size, bilingual counselors, expanded library and industrial arts facilities, reduction of intelligence testing, and more attention by teachers to community problems. In Crystal City, the high school enrollment was 85% Mexican-American, but cheerleaders, elected by a predominantly Anglo faculty panel, were usually Anglo. The Chicanos asked to have cheerleaders and homecoming queen elected by the student body. When the school board refused, a local Chicano leader, Jose Angel Gutiérrez organized a political campaign that resulted in his election and that of two other Chicanos to the school board. He was elected president of the school board, and significant school reforms were instigated.

These Chicano youth activities may have served to increase the attention paid by the United States Commission on Civil Rights to problems of Chicano education. That commission has held several hearings and issued several reports bearing on Mexican-American education. One of these was a 1973 report by the commission entitled *Teachers and Students: Differences in Teacher Interaction with Mexican-American and Anglo Students*. The report contains the following conclusions:

The basic finding of this report is that the schools of the Southwest are failing to involve Mexican-American children as active participants in the classroom to the same extent as Anglo children. On most of the measures of verbal interaction between teacher and student, there are gross disparities in favor of Anglos. . . . It is the schools and teachers of the Southwest, not the children, who are failing. They are failing in meeting their most basic responsibility—that of providing each child the opportunity to gain the maximum benefit of education and develop his capabilities to the fullest extent. In the Commission's view, the schools of the Southwest will continue to fail until fundamental changes are made. Changes are needed in the way teachers are trained and in the standards by which they are judged, and changes are needed in educational programs and curriculums so that all children may be reached. (p. 44)

Puerto Rican Lower Class Adolescent Subcultures

Puerto Ricans represent in the industrial North and Northeast what Chicanos represent in the Southwest—a supply of unskilled and semiskilled labor, a growing middle class with political power, and a set of problems and challenges to the schools. Puerto Ricans make up 17% of the population of Spanish descent, slightly over half of whom were born in Puerto Rico. They form a relatively youthful population and have the lowest amount of schooling among Spanish-surname groups.

Puerto Ricans come and go freely between the mainland of the United States and the island of Puerto Rico. (The number residing on the mainland is about half the number residing on the island.) Puerto Rico is a United States commonwealth and not a state. However, its citizens have the rights of United States citizens, although they are voting citizens only if they reside on the mainland.

More than half of the mainland Puerto Ricans live in the New York City metropolitan area, and there are large populations in Philadelphia, Washington, DC, and Chicago. Twenty percent of the males have white-collar jobs, very few are farm laborers, and the largest occupational group are factory and transport workers.

Of the New York City public school enrollment, approximately 250,000, or 23%, are Puerto Rican and 35% are blacks.

A considerable proportion of Puerto Rican immigrants have prospered in the United States. Therefore, the Puerto Rican population of the New York metropolitan area is dispersed between middle-class and lower-class residential areas. Two areas of lowest-income residents are the South Bronx and Spanish Harlem. Those are the areas northeast of Central Park and extending north into the Bronx.

Here there is a street culture that takes charge of the life of a boy in spite of efforts by his parents and the school and the church to direct him into morally acceptable early adult roles. This process is described vividly in the 1967 autobiography of Piri Thomas, *Down These Mean Streets*. His Puerto Rican parents did their best to control him, but they lost him to the life of the streets. It started with street games, such as stick ball, and moved on into smoking marijuana, organizing weapons and strategy to fight the gang in the next neighborhood, "making out" with girls on the tenement rooftops, and on into various forms of delinquency.

Piri Thomas summarizes:

> Ranging around on the block is a sort of science. You have a lot to do and a lot of nothing to do. In the winter there's dancing, pad combing, movies, and the like. But summer is really the kick. All the blocks are alive, like many-legged cats crawling with fleas. People are all over the place. Stoops are occupied like bleacher sections at a game, and beer flows like there's nothing else to drink. The block musicians pound out gong beats on tin cans and conga drums and bongos. And kids are playing all over the place—on fire escapes, under cars, over cars, in alleys, back yards, hallways. (p. 14)

The story of his adolescence is dated of course, because he was born in 1928 and the events he describes took place in the 1940s. But the goal has not changed. He concludes: "It was all a part of becoming *hombre*, of wanting to have a beard to shave, a driver's license, a 'stoneness' which enabled you to go into a bar like a man."

Thomas took the route through drugs to robbery, when he was sent to prison. After 6 years he was paroled and went into drug rehabilitation work. He continues his writing and a variety of community projects in New York City.

Asian-American Adolescents

The Asian-Americans were the fastest growing immigrant group during the 1970s, and they exhibit a great diversity. Only three groups were visible in the census in 1970—Japanese, Chinese, and Philipinos. But the past 20 years have seen a rapid growth in three other Asian groups—Koreans, Pacific Islanders (Guam and Samoa), and Vietnamese. In 1975, there were an estimated 215,000 Koreans living in the United States.

We do not yet know enough about the life-styles or even the number of adolescents in the newer groups to be able to describe their adolescent subcultures. Consequently, we will limit ourselves to one group, the Japanese-Americans. Also, we will omit the residents of Hawaii, where the Japanese and Chinese make up a majority of the population, with Philipinos (formerly called Filipinos), Native Hawaiians, and Anglos in the minority. What we know about the Japanese-Americans on the mainland may not describe accurately the residents of Hawaii.

Adolescents of Chinese or Japanese origin are found in practically every big city. Although their grasp of the English language is generally good, most of them were raised in a subculture in which family influence and family loyalty are very strong. This has tended to preserve their separate ethnic cultures. The Japanese-Americans are somewhat more integrated into the Anglo life-style than are the Chinese-Americans. These two groups do very well in school, on the average, and make great use of educational opportunities. Of those males who were 16 years of age and over, the 1970 census indicated that 70% of the Japanese, 62% of the Chinese, and 49% of the Philipinos had completed high school, compared to 32% of blacks and 28% of Mexican-Americans.

The Japanese immigration commenced about 1890 and consisted largely of farm workers and shopkeepers. They rented and then bought small farms in the western states, and the shopkeepers joined them to market their products and to help form mutual aid groups in small and large cities of the West. The "gentlemen's agreement" of 1907 between the American and Japanese governments bound the Japanese government to withhold passports from Japanese laborers. This was followed by the Japanese Exclusion Act of 1924, and the Japanese-American population grew very little between 1920 and 1950. Meanwhile, the Japanese-American population was improving its educational and economic status.

The *Sansei* (third generation) Japanese group is essentially a post-World War II population group. The adolescents of 1980 were born between 1962 and 1968. They have had educational and occupational opportunities, and they have had general social acceptance in the communities where they live.

A subgroup of the Sansei youth have become active politically, although they split into two groups with respect to a liberal capitalist versus a Marxist ideology. Another major subgroup does not express a political ideology but works for personal educational and economic success. This analysis has been made by Minako Maykovich based on interviews with a nonrepresentative sample of Sansei college students in California about 1970.

Liu and Yu (1975), in their study of Asian–American youth, see the contemporary Japanese–American youth as a *sweet and sour* generation that is creating new social expectations and a new identity.

American Indian Adolescents

There are about 100,000 American Indian and Eskimo adolescents, aged 12–18, scattered in 30 or more tribal groups and living in considerable numbers in about 20 states. About 90% are enrolled in school. About 15,000 are in boarding schools, mostly maintained by the federal government's Bureau of Indian Affairs. Another 45,000 are in public schools on or near Indian reservations where Indians make up more than 50% of the students. The remaining 30,000 are in public schools where they are a minority of students. A growing number of this group live in big cities.

In the social anthropological sense, Indian youth do not constitute a subculture, because they belong to a number of different tribes, each having its own tribal culture and language. Only one tribal group—the Navaho—is large enough and residentially concentrated enough to provide a clear-cut cultural base for an adolescent subculture. Two others, the Sioux and the Cherokee, have several thousand adolescent members, but they are so widely dispersed, and so many of them live in cities, that they do not find themselves associating with fellow tribal members enough to form nuclei of

an adolescent tribal subculture. Further, the young Indians living in the cities and out of contact with their tribal elders are losing their native languages and growing up without knowledge or experience of their tribal religious practices and beliefs. Also, there is a growing number of marriages with non-Indians.

At the same time, during the decade of the 1970s there has risen a strong movement for Indian self-determination in economic and educational affairs. This has resulted in the passage by Congress of the Indian Education Act (1972), the Indian Self-Determination and Educational Assistance Act (1975), and the Indian Policy Review Commission Act (1975). These acts of Congress have been expedited by the growing strength of several Indian rights organizations, which have been led by young adults.

An activist action was undertaken by a multi-tribal group who in 1977 commenced a cross-country march starting from the Pacific Coast. They called this "the longest walk" and arrived in Washington, DC, on July 15, 1978. Several thousand Indians marched into Washington and held a peaceful mass meeting, which was attended by a number of congressmen. The Indian leaders announced their opposition to some bills pending in Congress, which they claimed would abrogate some Indian treaty rights and weaken tribal cultures. Thus, there has arisen during the 1970s a kind of pan-Indian nationalism, which might lead the American Indians to think of themselves less as members of different and separate tribes and more as *Indian Americans*.

It will be a matter of interest and importance to educators to observe and to react to the development of American Indian adolescents' behavior with respect to their diverse tribal identities and to their pan-Indian issues and values.

Black Adolescent Subcultures

The largest easily visible minority group are the blacks, who comprise about 11% of the population of the United States. Whether this group, under 1980 conditions, has a significant subculture is a question that will probably be debated by the sociologists for some time to come. The blacks do not have a separate language or even a separate English dialect. They are distributed through the social-class structure, in all five classes, although they have a larger proportion of poor people and therefore of lower-class people than does the majority white group. There is no cultural characteristic that is common to all or nearly all blacks and absent in whites, unless it is the experience of being black and elements of ideology that flow from that experience.

In spite of some prejudice against blacks in certain occupations, the proportion of black men and women in middle-class occupations has been increasing since 1940. Professor William Julius Wilson, Chairman of the Department of Sociology at the University of Chicago and a black, authored a book published in 1978, entitled *The Declining Significance of Race: Blacks and Changing American Institutions*. He concluded that a substantial and growing proportion of blacks have become middle class and share middle-class attitudes and behavior with white middle-class people. However, the economic structure of the society has changed so as to create a vast underclass of blacks living in poverty-stricken ghettos. Consequently, there are two contrasting black subcultures—one middle class and one characteristic of people below the lower-working class, which he calls an *underclass*. He writes,

> A history of discrimination and oppression created a huge black underclass, and the [recent] technological and economic revolutions have combined to insure it a permanent status. As the black middle class rides on the wave of political and social changes, benefitting from the growth of employment opportunities in the growing corporate and government sectors of the economy, the black underclass falls behind the larger society in every conceivable respect. (p. 21)

The United States Office of Education reported on racial enrollments in public schools for 1974. In the 100 largest school districts, 68% of the black students were in schools with 80% or more minority enrollments. It is safe to assume that the black underclass to which Wilson refers is mainly in these ghetto schools in large cities.

On the other hand, the growing number of black middle-class students are mostly in schools with substantial numbers of Anglo students. We will describe this middle-class black adolescent subculture, relying heavily on the chapter entitled "Black Youth" by Doris Wilkinson (1975) in the *Yearbook on Youth* of the National Society for the Study of Education.

The Black Middle-Class Subculture

This group now graduates from high school and enrolls in college to almost as great an extent as do white youth. For example, in 1977, 26% of black youth aged 18 through 21 were enrolled in college, compared with 34% of white youth. Among all black youth, 68% graduated from high school.

The efforts and concerns of middle-class black youth reflect the belief that blacks must continue to confront racial discrimination and to make active protest against various forms of racial injustice. They are caught up in the Black Power movement that developed in the 1965–1970 period. They favor the various forms of "black studies" that have developed in college and secondary school curriculums.

These youth see themselves as pioneers in a new set of social and political roles as well as middle-class occupations. Wilkinson (1975) concludes her analysis as follows:

> These youth are unlike their white counterparts not only with respect to placement in the social structure and their definitions of the dynamics of interracial relations, but also with respect to the type of attitudinal orientation which emerges from their cultural experiences. They are different in their collective symbolism and self-oriented definitions of who they are and what they wish to become. For they still must contend with social issues that never confront white youth. Because of this and the prevailing differential treatment they experience and the negative myths about their identities, young blacks will not acquiesce passively in the future. (p. 305)

STREET CULTURE ADOLESCENT SUBCULTURES

The slums of big cities present a way of life that is forced on people because of the physical situation in which they live—crowded housing, absence of local neighborhood adult leadership or church influence, and low income.

When the youth are unemployed and out of school they are practically forced out on the streets. Life on the streets of the neighborhood constitutes a *street culture*. The adolescents create a subculture for themselves.

We will present a picture of the adolescent subculture of a Chicago slum area, which was observed and recorded by Gerald Suttles (1968) in 1962–1965. Another example is the Puerto

Rican subculture of East Harlem in New York City, which was described by Piri Thomas (1967) in his autobiography.

Adolescent Subculture in a Chicago Slum

The area just southwest of Chicago's downtown district has been a home for immigrant working-class people for a century. Jane Addams established Hull House to serve this area. Since 1965 this area has been changing, due to the fact that the University of Illinois at Chicago has been located on a new campus carved out of the slums.

In the period from 1962 to 1965, this area was a fairly typical Chicago slum, known as the Addams area. Suttles was a sociologist, who took residence in this area. He became acquainted with the adolescents who lived there and collected data from various available sources. In a section of his book, called "The Boys' World," he describes the life of the 12- to 18-year-olds, which centered around certain street corners in the area of about one square mile.

There were 32 boys' street corner groups with names, examples being the Erls, the Gallants, the Rapids, the Gutter Guys. The average membership was 12 to 15 boys, with about a 2-year age spread. There were three different age grades, from about 12 to about 18. There were also six girls' street corner groups.

Among the boys, there were three ethnic groups. One was entirely black, with six or eight street units. One was almost entirely Mexican, with a few Italians, and a dozen street corner units. A third was mainly Italian, with a few Mexicans, and a dozen street corner units. The three ethnic groups each lived in a separate territory, but separated only by streets.

There were four group activities:

1. *Hanging*—This consisted of loitering around the particular street corners that constituted the "turf" of the club.
2. *Fighting*—This was mainly a matter of guerrilla warfare, although each group had a secret cache with guns and other weapons. Boys who strayed into strange territory would be "jumped" by the group that "owned" the area.
3. *Stealing*—This was sometimes organized with expeditions to a target store or warehouse

outside of the area and was sometimes a matter of shoplifting in local stores or robbing local adults who had no connection with the group.
4. *Drinking*—This was mainly sharing cans of beer or bottles of wine. Only the beginning of marijuana smoking was visible at this time. That came later and was a central characteristic of the equivalent subcultures of the 1970s.

Police Encounters

A record was made of the 357 cases in which boys below age 17 were arrested during 2 years, commencing July 1963. The main categories were:

- Theft, burglary, purse-snatching (54%)
- Fighting and carrying weapons (15%)
- Malicious mischief (property destruction, false fire alarm, opening a fire hydrant) (14%)
- Drinking, glue sniffing, disorderly conduct (7%)
- Breaking curfew rules (7%)
- Sex misdemeanors (3%)

Social Surveillance

During this period, there were perhaps a dozen male social workers assigned to this area by the Chicago Youth Development Project, supported by the Ford Foundation.

Street Gangs

An article in the *Chicago Tribune* for August 13, 1978, commences:

"Street gangs. They have been around almost as long as there have been cities—roaming the streets of poor neighborhoods, broken kids from broken homes seeking sustenance from their peers. Their members call them 'youth clubs'." Thus the situation has not changed much since Suttles' study. Police estimate that in Chicago there are at least 150 active street gangs with 5,000 members. There are black gangs, white gangs, and even Chinese gangs. But the largest number are in Chicago's Latino neighborhoods.

Female Subcultures

The discussion and description of adolescent subcultures is almost certain to pay less attention to girls than to boys. This is true of this chapter, and it is unfortunate. Girls and women have different roles from boys and men in the several social classes. This is particularly true of the lower classes and of the one we have called the underclass.

There is certainly a considerable difference between male and female subcultures among Mexican-Americans and Asian-Americans. We do not as yet have much available research on adolescent women's subcultures in the several ethnic groups.

Black Families Headed by Women

The United States Commission on Civil Rights issued a report in the Fall of 1984 entitled *New Perspectives*. Among a variety of articles is one authored by Blanche Bernstein with the title "Since the Moynihan Report." Daniel Patrick Moynihan, currently U.S. Senator for the state of New York, authored a report entitled *The Negro Family: The Case for National Action* in March 1965. At that time, Moynihan was head of the Office of Planning and Research in the United States Department of Labor.

The contemporary article by Blanche Bernstein deals with the increase in the number of poor black families headed by women. Bernstein states that:

> Between 1969 and 1975 the number of poor black families headed by women soared by 64 percent, accounting for all the increases in the number of poor black families. . . . Dr. Robert Hill of the National Urban League pointed out that the number of poor black families rose by 19% between 1969 and 1975 due to the sharp rise of black families headed by women. . . .
> A study published by the Urban Institute of Washington, D.C. in 1981 found that women who were teenagers at the birth of their first child account for more than half of total AFDC expenditures in the country and comprise an astounding 71% of all AFDC mothers under 30 years of age.

Perhaps even more revealing than the data on births to teenagers are the trends in teenage sexual activity and its outcome. Between 1971 and 1979, whereas the number of teenagers 15 to 19 rose by 6%, the number who were sexually active almost doubled, from 2.5 to 4.7 million. Among whites, the figure went from 41 to 65%; among blacks, from 78 to 89%. Further, the number of teenagers who conceived a child was about double the number who gave birth out of wedlock. In other words, according to Bernstein, about half the conceptions "terminated

in an abortion or miscarriage, mainly the former."

Moreover, "what was overlooked during this period was the enormous growth in female-headed families because of lack of male family heads as a result of teenage child-bearing."

Some individual black voices were saying that in effect the blacks needed to concern themselves about the structure of the black family and particularly with teenage pregnancy.

A major breakthrough came with the publication of a pamphlet in June 1983, entitled *A Policy Framework for Racial Justice*, issued by 30 liberal black leaders (known as the Tarrytown Group) and members of the Black Leadership Forum. On the subject of teenagers, they say, "Teenagers and young men and women need to be encouraged to pursue training, work, and personal development while they delay pregnancy and family formation," and further, that: "for young people there is a special need for sex education and education about the importance of delaying sex, pregnancy and marriage."

According to Bernstein:

> The issuance of *A Policy Framework for Racial Justice* served to galvanize the black community to action on a national scale. It was followed within a year by a Black Family Summit Conference called by the National Association for the Advancement of Colored People and the National Urban League. The news release issued at the end of the conference, May 5, 1984, contains language not heard for many years. For example, John Jacobs, president of NUL, warned that "some of our problems may be self-inflicted, that we may have allowed our just anger at what America has done to obscure our own need for self-discipline and strengthened community values."
> It is urgent that the effort to postpone teenage sexual activity succeed if we are to avoid the heavy costs to society of teenage childbearing and the even heavier costs to the teenager, her child, and the black community, as well as the costs of continuing conflict between blacks, whites and other ethnic groups over the distribution of the nation's product.

Teenage Pregnancy in Illinois

As an illustration of the problem of teenage pregnancy and efforts to deal with it at multiple levels, information from the state of Illinois is noteworthy.

The Illinois State Board of Education paid special attention to the problem of teenage pregnancy, as can be seen in the description of the Agenda of the Equal Educational Opportunity (EEO) Task Force for meetings in January, 1985. A staff report presented to the EEO Task Force on December 13, 1984, contains the following:

> Teenage pregnancy and childbirth in the United States rank among the highest in the world. . . . According to the Alan Guttmacher Institute, teenage mothers raise one out of every six children born annually in the United States. From 1977 to 1982, adolescent mothers in Illinois gave birth to 232,026 children (see Table 21.3 for breakdown by year). At present, in the state, approximately 130,000 teenage mothers—two-thirds of whom are under the age of 17—are raising 150,000 children under the age of five. In addition, many other children have mothers who were teenagers when they had their first child.

Most adolescent mothers face adverse and long-lasting social and economic consequences because of serious problems in the areas of health, finance, education, and social development. Usually these problems occur because young mothers lack the preparation for parenthood. Studies show that most teenage pregnancies are unplanned.

The State Board of Education has been involved in several programs that assist prospective teenage parents, teenage parents, and students at risk to become teenage parents. Following is a brief description of those programs.

Parents Too Soon. This is a program initiated by Governor Thompson in April 1983. It is a multiagency cooperative program funded with Human Services Block Grant money. It is a complex statewide effort with a clear consistently implemented emphasis on prevention of un-

wanted teenage pregnancy, inadequate parenting by teenage mothers and fathers, and unemployment and poverty in families headed by an adolescent. The goals of the program are to: (a) reduce the incidence of teenage pregnancy; (b) reduce the health risks associated with children having children, with an emphasis on reducing infant mortality; and (c) assist teenage parents to adapt to their new responsibilities. These goals are being accomplished through integrated, cooperative efforts that provide critical medical, social, nutritional, educational, and vocational services to young persons under the age of 21.

Illinois Caucus on Teenage Pregnancy (ICTP). The ICTP began in 1977 as a private, nonprofit organization to share experiences and pool resources to assist pregnant teenagers and adolescent parents. In 1982, Governor Thompson recognized the caucus's reputation as a knowledgeable and practical resource and advocacy group. He charged the caucus to implement the comprehensive plan of his Statewide Task Force on Adolescent Parent Support Services. State agencies with adolescent programs were mandated to become involved with the caucus, and their representatives serve as ex officio members of the Board of Directors.

In August of 1983, the State Board of Education directed the State Superintendent to participate in a program of the Council of Chief State School Officers called "Adolescent Pregnancy/ Parenting—Persistent Barriers for Young Women: A State Level Approach." This project addresses important sex-equity issues involving adolescent pregnancy and policy-making activities in state departments of education. It focuses on the education programs for these students and the economic and social consequences of adolescent pregnancy. It provides opportunities for state education staff to interact with state health and human-services agencies in order to exchange information and facilitate cooperative, coordinated approaches to solving problems.

Table 21.3. Births to Teenage Mothers in Illinois

YEAR	NUMBER OF BIRTHS
1975	31,120
1976	29,778
1977	29,886
1978	28,634
1979	29,800
1980	29,783
1981	27,460
1982	25,566
Total	232,026

SUMMARY

The present chapter examined adolescent culture and subculture. These terms were defined, and a number of issues relevant across adolescent subgroups were discussed. Some of these included the adolescent peer culture, social class and mobility, and teenage pregnancy. Further, characteristics of the following ethnic and social subgroups of adolescents were described: Hispanics (Mexican-Americans and Puerto Ricans), Asian-Americans, American Indians, and blacks. Attention also was directed to street-culture adolescent subcultures and to issues concerning black families headed by women. Data pertaining to the problem of teenage pregnancy, using information from the state of Illinois were examined.

REFERENCES

Bernstein, B. (1984). Since the Moynihan Report. In *New perspectives* (Vol. 16, No. 2, pp. 2–7). Washington, DC: U.S. Commission on Civil Rights.

Coleman, J. S. (1961). *The adolescent society*. New York: Free Press.

Gottlieb, D., & Reeves, J. (1963). *Adolescent behavior in urban areas*. New York: Free Press.

Liu, W. T., & Yu, E. S. H. (1975). Asian-American youth. In R. J. Havighurst & P. E. Dreyer (Eds.), *National society for the study of education: Youth, seventy-fourth yearbook*. Chicago: University of Chicago Press.

Moynihan, D. P. (1965). *The Negro family: The case for national action*. Washington, DC: U.S. Department of Labor, Office of Planning and Research.

Suttles, G. D. (1968). *The social order of the slum*. Chicago: University of Chicago Press.

Thomas, P. (1967). *Down these mean streets*. New York: Knopf.

Thornburg, H. D., & Grinder, R. E. (1975). Children of Aztlan: The Mexican-American experience. In R. J. Havighurst & P. E. Dreyer (Eds.), *National society for the study of education: Youth, seventy-fourth yearbook*. Chicago: University of Chicago Press.

Wilkinson, D. Y. (1975). Black youth. In R. J. Havighurst & P. E. Dreyer (Eds.), *National society for the study of education: Youth, seventy-fourth yearbook*. Chicago: University of Chicago Press.

Wilson, W. J. (1978). *The declining significance of race*. Chicago: University of Chicago Press.

CHAPTER 22

The Handicapped Adolescent

Robert T. Ammerman, Vincent B. Van Hasselt, and Michel Hersen

INTRODUCTION

There has been a recent burgeoning of interest in the psychological functioning of developmentally and physically handicapped adolescents (e.g., Anderson, Clarke, & Spain, 1982; Jan, Freeman, & Scott, 1977). This is, in part, due to numerous clinical reports that demonstrate social, emotional, and behavioral problems in many of these individuals. In addition, a variety of empirical investigations have found increased psychological maladjustment in many disabled children and preadolescents (see reviews by Ammerman, Van Hasselt, & Hersen, 1986; Matson & Helsel, in press), which may continue to be manifested in adolescence and young adulthood. Despite the increased attention directed to the functioning of handicapped adolescents, there is a paucity of controlled research in this area. Thus, although the literature suggests that impaired adolescents are at risk for maladjustment and dysfunction, the precise nature and characteristics of these problems remain speculative.

Another reason for the heightened activity in this area is the growing population of disabled adolescents. For example, it is estimated that there are approximately 65,500 visually impaired (Rapin, 1979) and 90,000 hearing impaired (Adler & Williams, 1974) individuals under age 19 in the United States. There are significantly large populations of persons with other disabilities as well.

Third, it appears that the difficulties experienced by developmentally and physically disabled adolescents are qualitatively different from those in childhood and adulthood. Given the limitations imposed by their impairment, normal developmental issues of adolescence (e.g., dating, sexuality, vocational planning) are particularly difficult for the handicapped. Indeed, Greenspan (1976) has pointed out that handicapped adolescents "will have more overt and forceful expressions of their normal developmental conflicts" (p. 189).

The handicapped adolescent also is exposed to an environment that may not be conducive to normal development. Lindmann (1981) has identified four problem areas that complicate the handicapped individual's development. The first is *ignorance*, which refers to the tendency of others to be unaware of what can be expected from the handicapped person. Consequently, they may expect little, thus fostering dependence and a failure to learn important skills. On the other hand, there may be unrealistic expectations, thus increasing the likelihood that the handicapped person will fail. The second problem area is *expedience*. This refers to the practice of failing to provide challenging experiences for the handicapped individual because it is too time-consuming or difficult. This also fosters dependence. The third area is *psychological overprotection* (i.e., when the handicapped individual incorporates the attribution of being ineffectual and having low standards). This stance elicits overprotectiveness from others. Finally, *unsophisticated benevolence* pertains to excessive and unfocused sympathy directed towards the handicapped. Devoid of respect or realism, such an attitude provides handicapped persons with unrealistic views of their own skills and limitations. Partly because of the above-mentioned areas, the handicapped adolescent is at high risk for psychological maladjustment.

When studying the handicapped adolescent, it must be noted that this population is diverse and heterogeneous. Individuals may differ in terms of type of handicap. They may have orthopedic, mental, neurological, or sensory impairments. Different modes of functioning (e.g., cognitive, physical) may be affected. In addition, there is considerable heterogeneity within handicapping conditions, such as differences in etiology and severity of the disorder. For example, visual impairment may range from some light perception to total blindness. Similarly, an adolescent with spina bifida may be nonambulatory or may walk with the assistance of braces. The impairment may be congenital or acquired, degenerative or stable. Although there appear to be some psychological problems and difficulties that cut across most handicapping conditions (e.g., social isolation and withdrawal), there also may be aspects of maladjustment that are unique to specific disorders.

The purpose of this chapter, therefore, is to review the literature on psychological functioning in developmentally and physically handicapped adolescents. The literature on personality characteristics, psychopathology and behavioral disturbance, and social adjustment is reviewed. Also, relevant treatment interventions are discussed. Finally, recommendations for future research in the area are presented.

PERSONALITY CHARACTERISTICS

The impact of physical and mental disability on adolescence can be pervasive. The handicapped adolescent may be unable to participate in a variety of age-appropriate activities. In addition, there is evidence to suggest that handicapped children and youth are at risk for peer rejection (Young & Cooper, 1944). Therefore, it would be expected that handicapped adolescents would display more maladaptive and dysfunctional personality characteristics when compared to nonhandicapped peers. Although the literature tends to corroborate this hypothesis (i.e., handicapped adolescents appear to be more dependent, to have low self-esteem, and to be more anxious), a variety of methodological shortcomings make it difficult to identify the: (a) specific personality traits exhibited by handicapped adolescents, (b) prevalence of these characteristics, and (c) relationship between these traits and everyday functioning. Methodological problems in this area of research include inadequate subject size, failure to match index and control subjects on relevant demographic variables, failure to employ control groups, heterogeneity of handicapped subjects (in terms of etiology of disorder, severity of impairment, etc.), unclear definitions of personality characteristics, use of instruments with questionable psychometric properties, and use of instruments that have not been standardized or validated on handicapped populations.

Frequently cited traits in handicapped adolescents are dependency and passivity. In describing visually impaired adolescents, Jan et al. (1977) state that:

> [They] are at risk for problems of dependency, passivity, and lack of initiative. It is all too easy for them to depend upon other people, who frequently become impatient when it takes more time to teach them or explain things. The feeling of competence and mastery of the environment, which is so powerful a force in developing motivation, may be impaired . . . (p. 209)

However, it is difficult to separate dependency that is realistic and necessary, given the constraints imposed by disability, from that which is exaggerated and maladaptive.

Several investigators have noted increased dependency in handicapped adolescents. Petrucci (1953) administered the Benreuter Personality

Inventory to visually impaired adolescents. Scale scores were compared to national norms from a sighted population. Results showed that, when compared to sighted norms, 22% of the visually impaired sample were more submissive and 73% less self-sufficient. However, little information was provided regarding subject characteristics or statistics employed, thus making it difficult to interpret these data. Similar findings of dependency have been noted in the hearing impaired (Moores, 1982).

Anderson et al. (1982) examined dependency in orthopedically impaired adolescents as part of a comprehensive assessment of functioning in this population. Specifically, they administered a semi-structured interview, self-report inventories, and interviewed significant others (parents and teachers) in a study of 119 adolescents (aged 15–19 years) with spina bifida and cerebral palsy. Handicapped subjects were compared to 33 nonhandicapped controls. Results indicated that 40% of the mothers of physically impaired adolescents viewed their children as being overly dependent. Mothers also displayed concern and worry about their child's future and questioned whether or not their child would be able to function independently. The extent to which this dependency is dysfunctional, however, is unclear.

Another consistently reported personality characteristic in the handicapped is lack of confidence and low self-esteem. This is not too surprising, given that many handicapped adolescents have difficulty impacting upon their environment due to realistic or societal limitations. Anderson et al. (1982), using Rutter's (Rutter, Graham, & Yule, 1970) Malaise Inventory, found that 72% of the orthopedically handicapped sample exhibited a marked lack of confidence and fearfulness. In a study of self-concept in visually handicapped children and adolescents, Land and Vineberg (1965) administered a test measuring locus of control. Visually handicapped subjects (from both residential and mainstreamed public school settings) exhibited less internal locus of control relative to sighted peers. In another investigation, blind adolescents were asked to sort through cards containing statements about themselves and were given a semi-structured interview. When compared to sighted controls, no differences were noted on the card-sorting task. However, interview responses revealed that blind adolescents were more unsure about the future. Cooper (1976) also has reported increased levels of feelings of inferiority in deaf children and adolescents.

Several investigations have identified increased prevalence of anxiety and nervousness in disabled adolescents. For example, in an early study, Brown (1939) administered the Clark–Thurstone Personality Schedule to blind students aged 16–22 years. When compared to controls, visually impaired subjects were higher on the neuroticism subscale. In addition, females had higher scores than males in the handicapped group.

Hardy (1968) developed an instrument specifically designed to measure anxiety in visually handicapped populations. The Anxiety Scale for the Blind was standardized on 122 subjects (aged 13 to 22 years) exhibiting a variety of visual impairments. Results indicated that the instrument correlated highly with the Taylor Manifest Anxiety Scale, although it had low correlations with teacher observations. Hardy (1968) also found that level of trait anxiety increased with age.

Anderson et al. (1982) reported a high degree of excessive worrying and anxiety in spina bifida and cerebral palsy populations. Specifically, 25% of the cerebral palsy children and 43% of the spina bifida children viewed themselves as fearful and anxious. These results were corroborated by parent and teacher reports. In particular, orthopedically impaired adolescents were concerned about engaging in interpersonal interactions. They worried about possible incontinence in social situations, rejection, embarrassment, speech defects, and (in certain cases) epileptic seizures. In general, there was a positive relationship between anxiety level and severity of impairment.

There also are personality characteristics that may be unique to specific disabilities. For example, it has been suggested that the deaf tend to be paranoid, suspicious, and emotionally immature (see Matson & Helsel, in press). In addition, use of primitive defense mechanisms, such as denial, has been posited to be more frequent in the hearing impaired (Boyd & Young, 1981). However, little empirical research has been conducted to adequately address these issues in the deaf.

In brief, data have been accrued that suggest that handicapped adolescents exhibit certain dysfunctional personality characteristics. The extent to which these may be viewed as "abnormal" for the handicapped has yet to be ascertained. In addition, the impact of these traits on the impaired adolescent's daily functioning is unclear. Additional research employing more adequate experimental designs clearly is warranted.

PSYCHOPATHOLOGY AND BEHAVIORAL DISORDERS

Investigations of the incidence of psychopathology in handicapped populations are relatively recent. Earlier efforts concentrated on personality characteristics and traits, often ignoring diagnostic syndromes and behavioral disturbance. The few studies examining psychopathology demonstrate a higher rate of disturbance in handicapped adolescents. However, here again methodological problems limit the conclusions that can be drawn from the data. Design flaws are similar to those evident in research on personality characteristics. Some of these are the use of inadequate control groups and the administration of instruments not standardized or validated with disabled populations. In addition, much of the literature on psychopathology in handicapped adolescents suffers from unclear definitions of diagnostic criteria. Thus, although it appears that many handicapped adolescents exhibit a high rate of behavior problems and psychopathology, the types of diagnostic syndromes represented by this group are undetermined.

Several reports have documented general maladjustment and emotional disturbance in handicapped adolescents. Minde (1978) reported results of an 8-year follow-up investigation of severely handicapped cerebral palsy subjects 10–14 years of age. Assessment involved parent, child, and teacher interviews, and a psychiatric-symptom checklist administered to parents. Psychiatric interviews revealed that 18% of the sample exhibited "definite" psychopathology. Both conduct and neurotic disorders were represented. Interestingly, interviewer judgments of severe family discord correlated highly with psychiatric ratings ($r = .68$). Unfortunately, no control group was employed. Also, information was not provided concerning diagnostic criteria or reliability of ratings.

Maladjustment has been found in other handicapping conditions as well. For example,

Gillberg (1984) suggests that a subset of autistic children experience an exacerbation of emotional difficulties (e.g., deterioration in functioning, depression) in adolescence. A high incidence of emotional disturbance and behavior problems also have been found in deaf children and adolescents (Meadow & Schlesinger, 1971). However, in one of the few controlled investigations with visually handicapped adolescents, Cowen, Underberg, Verrillo, and Benham (1961) reported no differences in adjustment between visually handicapped and sighted adolescents. There was a tendency for partially sighted adolescents to exhibit more difficulties than their totally blind peers.

A variety of investigations have examined behavioral disturbance using parent and teacher inventories. For example, Schnittjer and Hirshoren (1981) administered the Behavior Problem Checklist (BPC) to teachers of 104 visually handicapped children and adolescents ranging in age from 6 to 21 years. Factor analysis yielded three separate factors, all of which are found in similar factor analyses of the BPC with sighted populations: (a) conduct problems, (b) personality problems (anxious-withdrawn), and (c) inadequacy–immaturity. Unfortunately, the age range employed is too wide to determine if these factors are peculiar to visually handicapped adolescents as contrasted to children and young adults. These factors also emerged in a similar study using deaf children and adolescents (Hirshoren & Schnittjer, 1979). In addition, a fourth factor (passivity–inferiority) was found. This factor reflected shyness, passivity, low self-confidence, and hypersensitivity.

Van Hasselt, Kazdin, and Hersen (1986) used the Child Behavior Checklist (CBCL: Achenbach & Edelbrock, 1978) to examine behavior problems in visually handicapped adolescents. Subjects consisted of residential visually handicapped, mainstreamed visually handicapped, and sighted male students 13 to 19 years of age. They were matched on age, IQ, and teacher's ratings of physical attractiveness. The CBCL is a factor-analytically derived instrument measuring social competence, school performance, and internalizing and externalizing behavior problems. Both parent and teacher versions were administered in this study. In addition, subjects were asked to complete the Youth Self-Report Form (YSRF: Edelbrock, 1981). The YSRF is similar to the CBCL and allows for examination of convergence of data from teacher, parent, and child reports. Results on the mother's form of the CBCL revealed elevated scores for residential visually handicapped students on the uncommunicative, obsessive–compulsive, and hostile–withdrawal subscales when contrasted with mainstreamed blind and sighted subjects. Likewise, teachers reported higher total problems in the residential group when compared to the other groups. Finally, using the YSRF, visually handicapped adolescents in residential settings had higher total problem behaviors than the mainstreamed visually impaired. These, in turn, were higher than sighted students. Thus, results suggest a higher incidence of behavior problems in the visually impaired, particularly in students in residential settings. Note that it should not be inferred from the data that residential students display more psychopathology because of their residential placement. It is quite possible that students are placed in residential settings *because* of their disruptive backgrounds and greater maladjustment (Simon, 1978).

As part of a comprehensive assessment of social and emotional adjustment in handicapped adolescents and their families, Van Hasselt, Hersen, Moore, and Ammerman (1985) used CBCL ratings by mothers (CBCL-M) and fathers (CBCL-F) to compare spina bifida, visually handicapped, and nonhandicapped adolescents. Groups consisted of 15 subjects each aged 10–18 years. Both parents were asked to complete the CBCL. Results revealed lower social-competence and higher behavior-problem scores for the spina bifida adolescents as compared to the visually impaired and nonhandicapped controls on the following subscales: Activities (CBCL-M), Social (CBCL-M), Total (CMCL-M and F), School (CBCL-F), and Schizoid (CBCL-F). Also, when contrasted with controls, spina bifida adolescents scored higher on the Schizoid (CBCL-M), School (CBCL-M), Activities (CBCL-F), and Social (CBCL-F) subscales. Further, visually handicapped adolescents had higher scores for Somatic Complaints (CBCL-M and F) than the other groups. These findings underscore the social and behavior problems exhibited by many orthopedically handicapped adolescents. Interestingly, the visually handicapped had relatively fewer elevated scores relative to nonhandicapped controls.

Research on the extent of psychiatric disorder in handicapped adolescents has shown higher prevalence rates than normal controls. Several of these investigations (e.g., Anderson et al., 1982; Jan et al., 1977) have utilized evaluation methods similar to Rutter's classic Isle of Wight study (Rutter, Cox, Tupling, Berger, & Yule, 1975). In their investigation, Rutter et al. (1975) examined incidence of psychiatric disturbance in 10–11 year olds. Results indicated a 6% incidence of psychiatric disturbance in the general population, 9% for the physically impaired, and 24% for the neurologically impaired. Similar findings were reported in another study of 5- to 15-year-olds in London (Seidel, Chadwick, & Rutter, 1975).

Depression is a commonly reported disorder in many handicapped adolescents in general and orthopedically disabled adolescents, in particular. For example, Dorner (1976) and McAndrew (1979) evaluated the psychological functioning of spina bifida adolescents. Using semi-structured interviews of parents and adolescents, Dorner (1976) found that 66% of his sample had frequent episodes of "misery" and dysphoria. Similarly, McAndrew (1978) noted low self-esteem and depression in his sample of spina bifida adolescents. These studies must be interpreted with caution due to: (a) overreliance on interview data and (b) use of ambiguous definitions of "misery" and depression.

In their assessment of spina bifida and cerebral palsy adolescents, Anderson et al. (1982) employed parent and teacher interviews, a teacher observation inventory, and the Malaise Inventory to measure psychiatric symptomatology. When compared to nonhandicapped controls, impaired adolescents had a higher global rating of maladjustment (52% versus 15%). Further, the physically handicapped subjects had a higher mean score on the Malaise Inventory than controls. Specifically, this group was viewed as unhappy, miserable, hopeless, and lonely. They also reported a greater occurrence of suicidal ideation than controls. Interestingly, cerebral palsy teenagers indicated more serious problems with depression compared to the spina bifida group. Finally, Anderson et al. (1982) found that parents and teachers were relatively unaware of their children's depression. This corroborates previous findings of Dorner (1976).

Jan et al. (1977) conducted an extensive evaluation of 92 visually handicapped children and their families. Subjects were matched with a nonhandicapped control group on gender, age, and neighborhood. Fifty-three percent of the visually impaired sample had an additional mental or physical handicap. Assessment instruments included semi-structured interviews of parents, children, and teachers, psychiatric interviews, and home observations. Visually impaired subjects were found to be more irritable, fearful, and worried when compared to controls. They were also more solitary and disliked by peers. Global ratings of psychological dysfunction revealed that 45% of the handicapped sample exhibited moderate to severe disorders. Fifty-seven percent were diagnosed as having one of the following psychiatric disorders: mental retardation (18.6%), developmental disorder (15.1%), adjustment reaction (10.5%), personality disorder (8.1%), behavior disorder (7.0%), organic brain syndrome (5.8%), psychosis (3.5%), neurotic reaction (3.5%), and special symptom reaction (2.3%). No data on diagnosis and overall adjustment were presented for controls. Also, diagnostic criteria were not provided. However, this study does constitute one of the most thorough examinations of visually handicapped adolescents to date, and documents the high incidence of psychiatric disturbance in this population.

SOCIAL ADJUSTMENT

Social functioning in developmentally and physically handicapped adolescents is one of the most widely investigated areas with these groups. Indeed, disruptions in social development appear to begin as early as infancy with the formation of mother–infant attachment. Stone and Chesney (1978) found that handicapped infants often fail to emit behaviors (e.g., smiling, responsiveness, maintaining eye contact, etc.) requisite to secure mother–infant attachment. Instead, they were described by mothers as being unresponsive, hypotonic, with few smiles or vocalizations. Visually handicapped infants, in particular, have been found to evince decreased smiling and poor eye contact in infancy (Freedman, 1964). More sophisticated assessment of the quality of mother–infant attachment has indicated a greater incidence of insecure attachment in Down's syndrome children (Cicchetti & Serafica, 1981). This may have profound implications for the social development of handicapped children, given that studies with the nonhandicapped

have demonstrated that insecure mother–infant attachment is predictive of socialization difficulties in preschool (Sroufe, 1983).

In addition to being a high risk for disruptions in attachment, handicapped children and adolescents encounter other difficulties in social development. It has been observed that physically impaired children have fewer social interactions than their nonhandicapped peers. In addition, they tend to interact solely with other handicapped children or low-status nonhandicapped peers (Fundis, 1982). Handicapped children also may be likely to experience peer rejection and social isolation because of physical unattractiveness (Johnson, 1950). For example, one study found that children give lower desirability ratings to pictures of peers with braces, crutches, etc. (Richardson, Goodman, Hastorf, & Dornbusch, 1961). Further, due to their physical limitations, handicapped children are unable to participate in a variety of age-appropriate activities (e.g., games and sports) that are requisite to normal social development (Gottman, Gonso, & Rasmussen, 1975). All of these factors combine to disrupt the socialization process in the handicapped. Specifically, they prevent the child from observing, modeling, and rehearsing appropriate social interactive skills.

Upon entering adolescence, the handicapped child may have had a history of peer rejection and social ineffectiveness. Indeed, several investigations have documented social difficulties and withdrawal in handicapped adolescents. For example, Dorner (1973, 1977) conducted two survey studies on the social adjustment of spina bifida adolescents. In the first study (1973), 37 families of adolescents with this disorder were administered an unstructured interview. Results of self-report assessment indicated that this population is severely socially restricted with minimal peer contacts and few close friends. Parent responses corroborated these findings. A separate study on peer relations in adolescents with spina bifida also revealed extensive isolation (Lorber & Schloss, 1973). In the second investigation, Dorner (1977) used interview techniques to examine the heterosocial adjustment of 63 spina bifida adolescents (mean age = 16.4 years). Contacts with the opposite sex were infrequent in both boys and girls. Also boys with mild to moderate handicaps had more extensive heterosocial contact than their more severely disabled peers.

This was partly related to their comparatively greater mobility and independence. Subjects appeared to lack basic knowledge of sexual processes when compared to nonhandicapped adolescents. They reported anxiety and worry over the prospects of sexual contact and marriage, which was associated with realistic concerns about inadequate sexual functioning due to central nervous system damage. Dorner (1977) suggests that such worries impede the disabled adolescent's initiation of heterosocial contact.

Anderson et al. (1982) compared their physically disabled sample to a nonhandicapped control group as well as to normative data from Rutter's Isle of Wight study (Rutter et al., 1975). In general, findings indicated that physically disabled adolescents are socially isolated relative to controls. When compared to nonhandicapped peers, handicapped subjects had fewer peer contacts and close friends and engaged in fewer social activities. Further, they rarely visited others, and peers almost never visited them. Teachers described the handicapped adolescents as "disliked" and "isolated." Many subjects reported that they were lonely and that their isolation was most acute during holidays. Most of their social activities were with parents or other handicapped peers (in adult-organized activities). Finally, subjects stated that they felt timid, depressed, anxious, and lacked self-confidence. Several factors mediated the extent and severity of social maladjustment. First, residential school students were more restricted than "mainstreamed" students. Second, less severely disabled adolescents were more mobile and thus had more peer contacts. However, these subjects were still isolated and friendless in comparison to their nonhandicapped counterparts.

Similar findings of poor peer relations and social maladjustment have been found in visually handicapped adolescents. As with other handicapping conditions, there is evidence of socialization problems in preadolescence. For example, use of the Vineland Social Maturity Scale and its derivatives have demonstrated social immaturity in the visually handicapped relative to sighted populations (Bradway, 1937; Maxfield & Buchholz, 1957). Most investigations in this area, however, have relied on global measures of social competence or interview data. Other investigations also have found social competency deficits in visually handicapped adolescents. Using the Benreuter Personality Inventory, Petrucci (1953) reported that 78% of the visually handicapped students felt the "need for sociability" more than sighted students, based on comparisons with normative scores. Similarly, Brieland (1950), using the Bell Adjustment Inventory, found that visually handicapped children and adolescents were more likely to evidence social adjustment problems than sighted youths.

In response to the lack of specificity characteristic of most research on social adjustment in the blind, Van Hasselt, Kazdin, Hersen, Simon, and Mastantuono (1985) developed a role-play test of social skill for visually handicapped adolescents. The role-play procedure allows for sampling of interpersonal behaviors across a variety of social situations. Role-played interactions are videotaped and retrospectively rated on a variety of social skill components. This assessment yields performance levels on those molecular behaviors constituting interpersonal effectiveness.

Van Hasselt, Kazdin, Hersen, Simon, and Mastantuono (1985) employed a 39-item role-play test to compare 21 visually handicapped adolescents and 22 sighted controls. Subjects ranged in age from 14 to 19 years. Several verbal and nonverbal categories were rated. Global ratings of overall social skill were carried out as well. Results indicated that the visually handicapped group exhibited longer speech durations and response latencies and tended to have more speech disruptions. However, several component strengths relative to sighted controls were noted. Specifically, the visually handicapped group had less hostile intonation and more expressions of appreciation. Also, they were rated more socially skilled on the overall performance measure. Although the investigators raise questions about the utility of global measures in evaluating social performance, the data appear to suggest that: (a) social dysfunction in the blind may be highly specific, involving only certain response componen s and (b) even when deficits are observed, they may have little impact on others' perception of the blind adolescent's performance.

In another study, Van Hasselt, Hersen, and Kazdin (1985) compared visually handicapped adolescents from both residential and public-school settings with sighted controls. Subjects were administered a role-play test composed of conversational and negative assertion situations. Results showed that visually handicapped adolescents displayed fewer open-ended questions than sighted students, whereas residential blind students had longer speech durations than blind and sighted public-school students. These data support the contention that social maladjustment in visually handicapped adolescents may be related more to specific response deficits than to pervasive interpersonal dysfunction.

The limited data on social development in handicapped children suggest that they are at risk for later maladjustment. Social withdrawal, limited peer contact, and peer rejection are prevalent in these populations. However, most work in this area has relied heavily on self-report or interview data. Thus, few data are available on the nature of dysfunction or the processes mediating social development in handicapped adolescents.

TREATMENT

There is a paucity of research evaluating the effects of psychosocial and psychiatric interventions with handicapped adolescents. This is not surprising given that assessment efforts are in the nascent stage. Although there is a lack of controlled outcome studies evaluating treatment efficacy, several recommendations for potentially useful intervention strategies have been offered. Psychodynamic treatments, emphasizing the intrapsychic mechanisms that play a role in depression and low self-esteem, have been suggested for these individuals (Greenspan, 1976). Jan et al. (1977) discussed the value of counseling for both the visually handicapped child or adolescent and his or her parents. In particular, parents of the handicapped require appropriate education as to what to expect from their child. Jan et al. (1977) emphasize the importance of establishing a "trusting" therapeutic relationship in treatment. Other clinicians and researchers stress the use of multidisciplinary interventions, combining psychological, medical, and rehabilitative services in the handicapped adolescent's treatment (see Lindeman, 1981).

A greater amount of investigative effort has been expended on the ameliorating of social maladjustment in handicapped adolescents.

For example, social skills training has been implemented with both visually handicapped and mentally retarded adolescents. The social skills model posits that handicapped adolescents are deficient in those response components requisite to normal social adjustment. Skills training typically consists of direct instructions, modeling, role-playing, and performance feedback and behavior rehearsal (see Bellack & Hersen, 1979). For work with handicapped individuals, certain adaptations in traditional skills interventions have been made. For example, Ammerman, Van Hasselt, and Hersen (1985) and Van Hasselt, Hersen, Kazdin, Simon, and Mastantuono (1983) included manual guidance in skills treatment of visually handicapped children and youth to facilitate learning of certain interpersonal behaviors (e.g., direction of gaze, posture, expressive physical gestures). In addition, individuals are required to practice what they have learned in their natural environment to encourage generalization of response. "Booster" sessions (i.e., reviews of previously trained materials) are provided following termination of formal training to promote maintenance of newly acquired skills.

Van Hasselt et al. (1983) used a social skills training package to increase assertive behavior in four visually handicapped female adolescents. Subjects exhibited deficits on at least three response elements of assertions (e.g., gaze, requests for new behavior, posture, voice tone). The skills treatment was administered over a 4-week period, with five 15- to 30-minute sessions per week. A series of multiple baseline analyses across behaviors consistently showed improvement in all behaviors as a function of training. Some performance deterioration was noted at a 1-month follow-up. Implementation of booster sessions, however, resulted in a return of behavioral components to posttreatment levels. Similar outcomes have been found in social skills training of mentally retarded adolescents (see Andrasik & Matson, 1985).

Several investigators have examined the utility of adaptive living skills programs with handicapped adolescents. They suggest that developmentally and physically disabled adolescents often do not have the knowledge and skills necessary to live independently. This has been related to their dependency on others during childhood, as well as a lack of exposure to adaptive living situations (especially with residential handicapped students). Adaptive living skills programs emphasize teaching adolescents how to function in the community. Stewart, Van Hasselt, Simon, and Thompson (1985) described the Community Adjustment Program (CAP), an adaptive living skills intervention for visually handicapped adolescents. CAP combines social skills training, mobility instruction, daily living skills, food preparation, recreational planning, and apartment-living experiences. Visually handicapped adolescents were taught these skills and were required to practice them in a supervised apartment setting. Parents reported significant improvement in their adolescent's independent living skills following such participation in the 3-month program (Stewart et al., 1985). Similar programs have also been widely applied with mentally retarded individuals.

SUMMARY

The extant data suggest that developmentally and physically handicapped adolescents are at risk for psychological maladjustment and dysfunction. Difficulties include personality deviance, psychopathology, and socialization problems. Their precise nature, however, is uncertain. Etiologies also are speculative at this point. Further, this is related to methodological problems that obfuscate clear interpretations of most of the research in this area. Some of these include: (a) inadequate sample sizes, (b) lack of control groups, (c) failure to match handicapped and control groups on relevant demographic characteristics, (d) overreliance on semi-structured and unstructured interview assessments, (e) employment of measurement instruments with questionable psychometric properties, and (f) utilization of assessment devices that have not been standardized or validated for use with handicapped populations. Also, age ranges of subjects included in many investigations often are too broad (i.e., they incorporate children, preadolescents, and young adults.)

Given the aforementioned shortcomings, a number of recommendations are offered. First, there is a need for increased research with more homogeneous handicapped populations. Groups consisting of a single handicapping condition rather than combinations of impairments would help to determine the population-specific nature of problems or issues under examination. Also, narrower age ranges should be employed. Third, more precise information about the nature of psychological dysfunction could be provided by the use of more widely used diagnostic systems (e.g., the *Diagnostic and Statistical Manual of Mental Disorders*, 3rd edition, American Psychiatric Association, 1980. Finally, comparisons between and among separate handicapping conditions would provide useful information regarding those difficulties that underlie the disorders.

REFERENCES

Achenbach, T. M., & Edelbrock, C. S. (1978). The classification of child psychopathology: A review and analysis of empirical efforts. *Psychological Bulletin, 85*, 1275–1301.

Adler, E. P., & Williams, B. R. (1974). Services to deaf people in the seventies. In R. E. Hardy & J. C. Cull (Eds.), *Educational and psychosocial aspects of deafness*. Springfield, IL: Charles C Thomas.

American Psychiatric Association (1980). *Diagnostic and statistical manual of mental disorders* (3rd ed.). Washington, DC: Author.

Ammerman, R. T., Van Hasselt, V. B., & Hersen, M. (1985). Social skills training for visually handicapped children: A treatment manual. *Psychological Documents, 15*, No. 2684.

Ammerman, R. T., Van Hasselt, V. B., & Hersen, M. (1986). Psychological adjustment of visually handicapped children and youth. *Clinical Psychology Review, 6*, 67–85.

Anderson, E. M., Clarke, L., & Spain, B. (1982). *Disability in adolescence*. London: Methuen.

Andrasik, F., & Matson, J. L. (1985). Social skills with the mentally retarded. In L. L'Abate & M. A. Milan (Eds.), *Handbook of social skills training and research* (pp. 418–454). New York: Wiley.

Bellack, A. S., & Hersen, M. (Eds.). (1979). *Research and practice in social skills training*. New York: Plenum.

Boyd, R. D., & Young, N. B. (1981). Hearing disorders. In J. E. Lindemann (Ed.), *Psychological and behavioral aspects of physical disability: A manual for health practitioners* (pp. 375–409). New York: Plenum.

Bradway, K. P. (1937). Social competence of exceptional children: III. The deaf, the blind, and the crippled. *Exceptional Children, 4*, 64–69.

Brieland, D. M. (1950). A comparative study of the speech of blind and sighted children. *Speech Monographs, 17*, 99–103.

Brown, P. A. (1939). Responses of blind and seeing adolescents to a neurotic inventory. *Journal of Psychology, 7*, 211–221.

Cicchetti, D., & Serafica, F. C. (1981). Interplay among behavioral systems: Illustrations from the study of attachment, affiliation and wariness in young children with Down's Syndrome. *Develop-*

mental Psychology, 17, 36–49.

Cooper, A. F. (1976). Deafness and psychiatric illness. *British Journal of Psychiatry, 129,* 216–226.

Cowen, E. L., Underberg, R. P., Verrillo, R. T., & Benham, F. G. (1961). *Adjustment to visual disability in adolescence.* New York: American Foundation for the Blind.

Dorner, S. (1973). Psychological and social problems of families of adolescent spina bifida patients: A preliminary report. *Developmental Medicine and Child Neurology, 15*(Suppl. 29), 24–26.

Dorner, S. (1976). Adolescents with spina bifida— How they see their situation. *Archives of Diseases in Childhood, 51,* 439–444.

Dorner, S. (1977). Sexual interest and activity in adolescents with spina bifida. *Journal of Child Psychology and Psychiatry, 18,* 229–237.

Edelbrock, C. S. (1981). *The behavioral assessment of children.* Unpublished manuscript, University of Pittsburgh School of Medicine.

Freedman, D. G. (1964). Smiling in blind infants and the issue of innate vs. acquired. *Journal of Child Psychology and Psychiatry, 5,* 171–184.

Fundis, A. T. (1982). Social interaction with peers: A developmental perspective on exceptional children's social isolation. In P. S. Strain (Ed.), *Social development of exceptional children* (pp. 1–12). Rockville, MD: Aspen Systems Corporation.

Gillberg, C. (1984). Autistic children growing up: Problems during puberty and adolescence. *Developmental Medicine and Child Neurology, 26,* 125–129.

Gottman, J., Gonso, J., & Rasmussen, B. (1975). Social interaction, social competence, and friendship in children. *Child Development, 46,* 709–718.

Greenspan, L. (1976). Neurological and orthopedic handicaps. In A. D. Hofmann, R. D. Becker, & H. P. Gabriel (Eds.), *The hospitalized adolescent: A guide to managing the ill and injured youth* (pp. 188–195). New York: Free Press.

Hardy, R. E. (1968). A study of manifest anxiety among blind residential school students. *New Outlook for the Blind, 62,* 173–180.

Hirshoren, A., & Schnittjer, C. (1979). Dimensions of problem behavior in deaf children. *Journal of Abnormal Child Psychology, 7,* 221–228.

Jan, J. E., Freeman, R. D., & Scott, E. P. (1977). *Visual impairment in children and adolescents.* New York: Grune & Stratton.

Johnson, G. D. (1950). A study of the social position of mentally handicapped children in the regular grades. *American Journal of Mental Deficiency, 55,* 60–89.

Land, S. L., & Vineberg, S. E. (1965). Locus of control in blind children. *Exceptional Children, 31,* 257–260.

Lindemann, J. E. (1981). General considerations for evaluating and counseling the physically handicapped. In J. E. Lindemann (Ed.), *Psychological and behavioral aspects of physical disability: A manual for health practitioners* (pp. 1–18). New York: Plenum.

Lorber, J., & Schloss, A. L. (1973). The adolescent with myelomeningocele. *Development Medicine and Child Neurology, 15* (Suppl. 2a), 113.

Matson, J. L., & Helsel, W. J. (in press). Psychopathology of sensory-impaired children. In B. B. Lahey & A. E. Kazdin (Eds.), *Advances in clinical child*

psychology (Vol. 9). New York: Plenum.

Maxfield, K. E., & Buckholz, S. (1957). *A social maturity scale for blind preschool children: A guide to its use.* New York: American Foundation for the Blind.

McAndrew, I. (1979). Adolescents and young people with spina bifida. *Developmental Medicine and Child Neurology, 21,* 619–629.

Meadow, K. P., & Schlesinger, H. S. (1971). The prevalence of behavioral problems in a population of deaf school children. *American Annals of the Deaf, 115,* 346–348.

Minde, K. K. (1978). Coping styles of 34 adolescents with cerebral palsy. *American Journal of Psychiatry, 135,* 1344–1349.

Moores, D. (1982). *Educating the deaf: Psychology principles in practice* (2nd ed.). Boston: Houghton Mifflin.

Petrucci, D. (1953). The blind child and his adjustment. *New Outlook for the Blind, 47,* 240–246.

Rapin, I. (1979). Effects of early blindness and deafness on cognition. In R. Katzman (Ed.), *Congenital and acquired cognitive disorders* (pp. 189–245). New York: Raven.

Richardson, S. A., Goodman, N., Hastorf, A. H., & Dornbusch, S. M. (1961). Cultural uniformity in reaction to physical disabilities. *American Sociological Review, 26,* 241–247.

Rutter, M., Graham, P., & Yule, W. (1970). A neuropsychiatric study in childhood [monograph]. *Clinics in Developmental Medicine, 35/36.*

Rutter, M., Cox, A., Tupling, C., Berger, M., & Yule, W. (1975). Attainment and adjustment in two geographical areas: I. The prevalence of psychiatric disorder. *British Journal of Psychiatry, 126,* 493–509.

Schnittjer, C. J., & Hirshoren, A. (1981). Factors of problem behavior in visually impaired children. *Journal of Abnormal Child Psychology, 9,* 517–522.

Seidel, V. P., Chadwick, O. F. D., & Rutter, M. (1975). Psychological disorders in crippled children. A comparative study of children with or without brain damage. *Developmental Medicine and Child Neurology, 17,* 563–573.

Simon, J. (1978). *Historical perspective regarding the education of the visually handicapped.* Unpublished manuscript, Western Pennsylvania School for Blind Children, Pittsburgh, Pennsylvania.

Sroufe, L. A. (1983). Infant–caregiver attachment and patterns of adaptation in preschool: The roots of maladaptation and competence. In M. Perlmutter (Ed.), *Minnesota symposium on child psychology* (Vol. 16, pp. 41–83). Hillsdale, NJ: Erlbaum.

Stewart, I. W., Van Hasselt, V. B., Simon, J., & Thompson, W. B. (1985). The Community Adjustment Program (CAP) for visually impaired adolescents. *Journal of Visual Impairment and Blindness, 79,* 49–54.

Stone, N. W., & Chesney, B. H. (1978). Attachment behaviors in handicapped infants. *Mental Retardation, 16,* 8–12.

Van Hasselt, V. B., Hersen, M., & Kazdin, A. E. (1985). Assessment of social skills in visually handicapped adolescents. *Behaviour Research and Therapy, 23,* 53–63.

Van Hasselt, V. B., Hersen, M., Kazdin, A. E., Simon, J., & Mastantuono, A. K. (1983). Training blind adolescents in social skills. *Journal of Visual Impairment and Blindness, 77,* 199–203.

Van Hasselt, V. B., Hersen, M., Moore, L. E., & Ammerman, R. T. (1985, August). *Assessment of social competence in visually handicapped adolescents.* Paper presented at the Annual Convention of the American Psychological Association, Los Angeles.

Van Hasselt, V. B., Kazdin, A. E., & Hersen, M. (1986). Assessment of problem behavior in visually handicapped adolescents. *Journal of Clinical Child Psychology, 15,* 134–141.

Van Hasselt, V. B., Kazdin, A. E., Hersen, M., Simon, J., & Mastantuono, A. K. (1985). A behavioral-analytic model for assessing social skills in blind adolescents. *Behaviour Research and Therapy, 23,* 395–405.

Young, L. L., & Cooper, D. H. (1944). Some factors associated with popularity. *Journal of Educational Psychology, 35,* 513–535.

CHAPTER 23

Adolescent Pregnancy and Marriage

Lewayne D. Gilchrist and Steven Paul Schinke

Pregnancy and marriage are important topics in adolescent psychology. Adolescent pregnancy, often unplanned and unwanted, is reported by 1 in 10 U.S. women each year. Teenage pregnancy can bring immediate and lasting consequences. Regardless of its resolution, early pregnancy affects young women and their children, families, and partners. Adolescent marriage—lower in incidence than pregnancy—is associated with just as serious consequences. Relative to their older counterparts, married adolescents more often experience divorce, educational setbacks, and welfare dependence. Children of parents who conceived or married young are themselves likely to be adolescent parents. The problems of pregnant and married teenagers consume many professional resources. In a tragic irony, the happy events of pregnancy and marriage can, for those who are young, lead to sad, unfulfilled lives. This chapter reviews state of the art research on adolescent pregnancy and marriage in America.

PREGNANCY

The scope of adolescent pregnancy in America is easier understood when seen from global and then national perspectives.

Global Perspective

The United States has one of the largest adolescent fertility rates in the industrial world (Westoff, Calot, & Foster, 1983). Of all developed countries, only Hungary has a higher teenage pregnancy rate. Definitive explanations for high rates of pregnancy, abortion, and childbearing among young Americans are not possible. Together, the young science of comparative international demography and obstacles to studying minors' sexual behavior defy precise explanations for fertility rates (Kar & Cumberland, 1984; Rodgers, Billy, & Udry, 1982). But the available data can rule out some reasons for this country's inordinately high rate of teenage pregnancy (Benussi, Barbone, & Gasperini, 1985; Pascoe & Berger, 1985).

One easily ruled-out reason is that American adolescents are unusually sexually active. American teenagers are no more sexually active than youth in Canada, Denmark, England, France, the Netherlands, and Sweden—countries with lower rates of adolescent fertility (Lincoln, 1983). Public assistance for young mothers can also be eliminated as a reason for America's high adolescent fertility rates. Many European countries with lower teenage fertility rates are more financially supportive of adolescent mothers (Adler, Katz, & Jackson, 1985; Burden & Klerman, 1984).

More plausible reasons for comparatively lower adolescent pregnancy rates outside the U.S. have also been advanced. Brown (1983) identified the following variables as contributing to reduced teenage pregnancy rates in Sweden:

> A close partnership between the schools and the family-planning services; easy access to contraceptive services; the widespread use of such services by young people; . . . sexual decisions equally shared by young men and young women; a general cultural acceptance of sexuality as a part of intimate relationships . . . ; supportive professional attitudes and roles . . . ; and politically secure legislation on contraceptive and abortion services which makes them legally and easily available. (p. 95)

Generalizability aside, these variables note the multiple determinants of adolescent fertility. Neither facile explanations nor single solutions seem warranted to understand and to change adolescent pregnancy rates in the United States.

National Perspective

The following paragraphs review the scope, sequelae, and correlates of adolescent pregnancy in the United States.

Scope

About 30% of 15- to 17-year-old females and 57% of 18- and 19-year-old females in this country have had premarital coitus (Dryfoos, 1985). For the latest reporting year, U. S. teenagers experienced 1.15 million pregnancies and 537,000 births. That number of births, though hardly insignificant, is smaller than in past years. American women between the ages of 10 and 19 years delivered 656,460 babies in 1970 and 562,330 babies in 1980 (Ventura, 1984). Explanations for a downward trend in births to teenagers—not unlike explanations for differential adolescent fertility rates—are easier to rule out than to definitively assert.

Smaller reported numbers of births to adolescents for recent years cannot be explained by reductions in sexual activity, increases in contraceptive use, lower incidence of unprotected coitus, or greater male responsibility for birth control. Neither can fewer recent births to teenagers be explained by increased school-based sex education, more widespread and accessible family-planning services, legislated and government support for birth-control programs, or stepped-up family involvement in pregnancy prevention efforts (Dryfoos, 1984; Hogan & Kitagawa, 1985; Jekel & Klerman, 1982; Nestor, 1982; Orr, 1983).

Instead, recent reductions in births among adolescents are more likely due to demographic changes. Past adolescent cohorts represented the children of America's baby-boom generation. As these adolescents grow out of the teen years and are not replaced in equal numbers, their number of births decreases (Ventura, Taffel, & Mosher, 1985). Another reason for adolescents' declining number of births is their greater use of abortion (Ezzard, Cates, & Schulz, 1985; Henshaw, Forrest, & Blaine, 1984; Henshaw & O'Reilly, 1983). In 1973, legal abortions were reported for 23 of every 1,000 U.S. women aged 15 to 19 years (Moore, 1985). The abortion rate (per 1,000 females) for U.S. adolescents was 38 in 1977 and 43 in 1981.

Annually, about 500,000 American adolescents obtain legal abortions. Fetal loss because of miscarriage is reported for about 150,000 teenagers each year. Adolescent women thereby account for 15% of all births in this country, 28% of all abortions, and 19% of all fetal deaths. Few adolescents who carry their babies to term relinquish them for adoption (Barth, Schinke, & Maxwell, in press; Gilchrist & Schinke, 1983c). Most pregnant teenagers and teenaged mothers do not marry. Expectedly, the percentage of adolescents who raise their children outside of marriage changes with the prevailing social mores. In 1960, 15% of all adolescent mothers were single; by 1970 this figure had doubled; by 1982 it was 51% (Moore, 1985).

Regional Variations

The multifaceted nature of adolescent fertility is borne out by regional teenage pregnancy rates in the U. S. During the latest reporting period the fertility rate (number of pregnancies per 1,000 females) for all American women was 112 (National Center for Health Statistics, 1985). For women aged 15 to 19 years, the total U.S. fertility rate was 110. By state, the adolescent pregnancy rate ranged from a low of 75 in North Dakota to a high of 200 in the District of Columbia. Geographic differences in fertility rates are also apparent. According to Bureau of Census descriptors, the lowest rates are reported in New England, Middle Atlantic, and South Atlantic regions; the highest rates occur in the western Central and Mountain regions; and rates close to the national mean are reported in the eastern Central and Pacific regions.

American cities with young and growing populations expectedly show greater adolescent pregnancy rates than more demographically stable urban areas. Also not surprisingly, rural America largely has lower rates of teenage fertility relative to urban areas. Geographic variations in adolescent pregnancy rates are partly explained by the extreme mobility of young Americans, including those with teenaged children (National Center for Health Statistics, 1984b). Still, generalities about regional differences in U. S. adolescent fertility rates cannot ignore religious and ethnic–racial factors. For instance, Utah's residents, many affiliated with the pronatalist Church of Latter Day Saints, have a mean fertility rate twice that of their Nevada neighbors (Taffel, 1984). Racial–ethnic factors are illustrated by data from Illinois, where the birth rate for black teenagers is 7 times the rate for white teenagers (National Center for Health Statistics, 1985).

Sequelae

The consequences of adolescent pregnancy are significant. Pregnant adolescents, their children, and their children's children are at risk for heightened morbidity and mortality (Hackman, Emanuel, van Belle, & Daling, 1983; Lawrence & Merritt, 1981; Roosa, Fitzgerald, & Carson, 1982a, 1982b; Scholl, Decker, Karp, Greene, & De Sales, 1984; Turk, Litt, Salovey, & Walker, 1985). Educational, emotional, social, and economic consequences of teenage pregnancy are well documented (Elster, McAnarney, & Lamb, 1983; Gruber, 1984; McAnarney & Thiede, 1981; McGee, 1982). Pregnant teenagers commonly drop out of school. Alternative schools notwithstanding, few adolescent parents regain their lost years of education. Pregnant and parenting adolescents often present with depression, social isolation, and poor interpersonal skills (Gilchrist & Schinke, 1983a; Kellam, Ensminger, Branch, Brown, & Fleming, 1984).

Of necessity, young single mothers and their babies are often dependent on public assistance (Dillard & Pol, 1982; Hofferth & Moore, 1979). Protracted unemployment and underemployment are not atypical among adolescent parents (Gilchrist, Lodish, Staab, & Schinke, 1983). Children born to teenagers not only experience the effects of their parents' educational and economic deprivation, but these children also suffer academically and behaviorally relative to children of older parents. Moreover, children of adolescent mothers are likely to grow up in single-parent households (Schinke, 1984). Compared with children of older parents, teenagers' children frequently later experience a teenage pregnancy.

Correlates

Demographic, developmental, and social factors influence adolescent pregnancy. Children and siblings of adolescent parents have heightened teenage pregnancy rates (Barth, Schinke, & Maxwell, 1983). The younger the age of first intercourse, the higher the risk of unplanned adolescent pregnancy (de Anda, 1983; Koenig & Zelnik, 1982; Philliber, Namerow, & Jones, 1985; Rogel, Zuelke, Weiss, Petersen, & Shelton, 1980; Zelnik & Shah, 1983). Pregnancy risk positively correlates with teenagers' alienation from their parents, lack of communication with their sexual partners, preferences for risk-taking, conservative opinions about abortion, low self-esteem, and external locus of control (Chilman, 1978; Fisher, 1984; Fox & Inazu, 1982; Freeman, Rickels, Huggins, & Garcia, 1984; Jessor & Jessor, 1984; Kastner, 1984; Lewis, Siegal, & Lewis, 1984).

Adolescents' attitudes about birth control further affect their pregnancy risk. Gilchrist and Schinke (1983a) found that adolescents who highly rated their ability to avoid pregnancy later acted in a consonant manner. Clark, Zabin, and Hardy (1984) discovered that among the 19% of sexually active male adolescents who agreed with the statement, "Any kind of birth control gets in the way of sex, so I wouldn't want me or my girlfriend to use it," 25% had never contracepted. Among the 31% of those males who agreed, "It is hard to talk to my girlfriend about using birth control," 37% had never contracepted. Yet, of the 81% of male adolescents who agreed, "I would understand if my girlfriend said 'no' to sex until we had some kind of birth control," 83% had contracepted and 85% had done so the last time they had coitus.

The availability of family-planning services inversely affects teenage pregnancy risk (The Alan Guttmacher Institute, 1978; Furstenberg, Shea, Allison, Herceg-Baron, & Webb, 1983; Gilchrist, Schinke, & Blythe, 1979; Kisker, 1984). Besides having access to birth-control services, teenagers can benefit from counseling tailored to their needs. Nathanson and Becker (1985) report data that, "provide strong support for the hypothesis that the quality of interaction between a family planning clinic's staff and clients does make a difference in the level of contraceptive use over time achieved by the clinic's teenage clients" (p. 36).

MARRIAGE

Adolescent marriage, unlike pregnancy, is mostly a cultural event. Time and regional variations thus give perspective to national rates of adolescent marriage.

Time and Regional Variations

Marriage rates for the United States, calculated per 1,000 persons in the population, vary with time. Illustrative are U.S. marriage rates of 12.2 in 1940, 11.1 in 1950, and 8.5 in 1960. Beginning with the 1968 rate of 10.4, the percentage of Americans who marry has been stable. Regional differences in marriage rates mirror the country's shifting young adult population. In the latest reporting period, the Middle Atlantic United States had an overall marriage rate of 8.5 (National Center for Health Statistics, 1984a). The comparable rate for the western part of the South Central United States was

13.0, and, the Mountain states, including the Southwest, had an average marriage rate of 19.9. By state, Pennsylvania's marriage rate of 7.8 was the lowest in the country, and Nevada's rate of 123.9 was the highest.

National Perspective

The following paragraphs describe the scope, sequelae, and known consequences of adolescent marriage in the United States.

Scope
The U.S. median age at marriage, ascending for several decades, has risen quickly in recent years. In 1963, the median ages of first marriage for women and men were 20.3 and 22.5 years, respectively. Ten years later, women and men were marrying at median ages of 20.6 and 22.5 years, respectively. In the latest reporting period, median marriage ages for women and men were 22.3 and 24.4 years, respectively. Of course, young people account for most first marriages, with many young women marrying just after the teen years. Among U.S. women, current marriage rates for 15- to 17-year-olds and 18- and 19-year-olds are 19.2 and 83.9, respectively, per 1,000 members of the age group (National Center for Health Statistics, 1985). Comparable marriage rates for men are 3 and 37. Each year, 362,600 teenage women and 144,900 teenage men marry.

Sequelae
Divorce rates inversely correlate with age at marriage. Thus, according to Spanier and Glick (1981):

> Women who marry at ages 14 to 17 are twice as likely to divorce as women who marry at ages 18 or 19, and three times as likely to divorce as women married at ages 20 to 24. . . . Men who marry in their teens are about twice as likely to divorce as men who marry at ages 20 to 24; and more than twice as likely to divorce as men who marry at ages 25 to 29. (p. 333)

Because many adolescents have children soon after marriage, heightened divorce rates affect multiple family members (Bachrach & Horn, 1985; Marini, 1981; Marini & Hodsdon, 1981). Problems that typically attend marriage for adolescent parents were summarized by McGee (1982):

Early marriage confers few advantages to the teen parent. Marriage during the teen years—especially during the school-age years—means a greater likelihood of dropping out of school, of having a large family and an unstable marriage, of welfare dependency, and of being a single head of household for a prolonged period. (p. 15)

The dimensions of single-parenthood are seen in the changing demography of American households. Between 1960 and 1983, the number of single- and two-parent households with children under 18 years increased 175% and 4%, respectively (Glick, 1984).

Adolescent marriages that start with or that shortly include children are particulary troublesome (Moore & Burt, 1982; Moore & Wertheimer, 1984). O'Connell and Rogers (1984) found that relative to couples who began childbearing after marriage, those who had a premarital conception or a child reported subsequently more marital dissolution, less educational attainment, lower levels of employment, poorer chances of job advancement, and reduced family income. The investigators concluded, "Overall, the data portray a difficult beginning for families in which the woman has experienced an out-of-wedlock pregnancy or birth" (p. 158).

Correlates

Correlates of early marriage share commonalities with influences on adolescent pregnancy. Chilman (1983) noted these correlates of adolescent marriage:

Being premaritally pregnant; dating early and frequently; going steady; "falling in love" at an early age; having premarital intercourse at an early age (for girls); coming from families of lower socioeconomic status; having domestic interests, a traditional view of the female sex role, and a low achievement drive (in the case of girls); and coming from either an unusually happy or unusually unhappy family situation. (p. 179)

Of equal interest are factors associated with negative outcomes for early marriages. Some suggest data that adolescence—though perhaps not the optimal time for marriage—has a marginal impact on marital outcomes relative to other factors (cf. Barth & Schinke, 1984; Philliber & Graham, 1981; Roosa, 1984). These other factors—maturity; experience with heterosexual relationships; reconciliation of personal preferences, goals, and sex roles; stability of living residence; continuity of employment; and financial security—affect marital outcomes for all couples (cf. Corder & Stephan, 1984; Espendshade, Kamenske, & Turchi, 1983; Lewis, 1985; McAnarney, Lawrence, Aten, & Iker, 1984).

But because each influential factor autocorrelates with the teen years, marital outcomes for adolescent couples are inherently confounded by many variables. Bahr and Galligan (1984) disentangled some of these confounds to better explain high divorce rates among adolescent couples. The researchers first summarized empirical support for the effects of economic and educational factors on adolescent's marital outcomes:

(1) Those who marry in their teens are substantially more likely to separate or divorce than nonteenage marriers, even after economic variables are controlled; (2) The effects of economic variables on marital disruption appear relatively small. . . . [but] a stable income and the absence of debt decrease the probability of marital disruption and . . . the wife's income has a modest, positive association with marital dissolution; (3) Higher levels of education increase the probability of a stable marriage. (p. 390)

Analyzing data from a large sample of young men, Bahr and Galligan then found, "Those who married later, had more education, and did not experience unemployment were more likely to remain in a stable marriage. Income level of neither the husband nor the wife was significantly related to marital instability" (p. 397).

A last commentary on the status of marriage in America is provided by national survey results from mothers and their 18-year-old children (Thornton & Freedman, 1982). Responding to the statement, "It's better for a person to get married than to go through life being single," 68% of the mothers and 66% of the children agreed. In response to the statement, "All in all, there are more advantages to being single than to being married," 87% of the mothers and 70% of the children agreed.

COMMENT

Adolescent pregnancy and marriage in the United States are social phenomena of considerable scope. The sequelae of pregnancy and marriage during the teen years encompass multiple, serious, and often irreversible problems. Many of these problems command the attention of behavioral and social scientists. Correlates of early pregnancy and marriage share commonalities and differences. A main commonality is that early pregnancy and marriage are frequently linked. Though at smaller rates than in the past, adolescent mothers-to-be and new mothers often marry. These marriages are not always beneficial for wives, husbands, and children.

A major difference between teenage pregnancy and marriage is that the former nearly always has negative consequences and that the latter is problematic only when other conditions coexist. Armed with this information, investigators and clinicians respectively can proceed to study and to deliver interventions for preventing unplanned adolescent pregnancy. Given the present state of the art, however, researchers and clinicians will be well served to focus on preventing concomitant problems of early marriage rather than to focus on preventing teenage marriage per se.

HISTORY AND DEVELOPMENT

Early pregnancy and marriage have not always been defined as problems in the United States. Secular trends over the past century shed light on current concerns about premature pregnancy and marriage. Eighty years ago, reproductive maturity was usually complete at age 17. Many youth married at this age. The agrarian economy provided jobs for youth and allowed young couples financial self-sufficiency. Today's technical society demands a longer preparation for employment and self-sufficient adulthood. Marriage is usually postponed until the early 20s. At the same time, because of improved nutrition and life-style changes, Americans enter and complete puberty younger than ever before (Petersen, 1979; Tanner, 1972, 1974). The gap between sexual maturation and social adulthood places adolescents at risk for problematic pregnancies. Early marriage is no longer regarded as ideal in many parts of America. Society's view of adolescent pregnancy and marriage have thus shifted over time. The following discussion traces such major shifts in recent years.

Early Attitudes and Responses

Western culture sanctions sexual activity only within matrimony. Coitus and pregnancy outside of marriage were, until recently, moral problems. So unwed, pregnant young women

have been ostracized or pitied for their "great mistake" (Teichman, 1982). In recent times, aided by psychoanalytic theory, adolescent pregnancy was explained in psychological rather than strictly moral terms (Schinke, 1984). Clinical reports, nearly all with female subjects, advanced psychodynamic factors that apparently caused early pregnancy and marriage. These causal factors included young women's underdeveloped superegos, low self-esteem, unresolved oedipal rivalries, and conflictual family relationships (cf. Abernethy, 1974; Brandt, Kane, & Moan, 1978; Cobliner, Schulman, & Smith, 1975; Hertz, 1977; Meyerowitz & Malev, 1973; Zongker, 1977).

Clinicians therefore treated the underlying, unconscious motivations that led young women to become pregnant. With abortion not an option, and mindful of the illegitimacy stigma, most unmarried young mothers elected to relinquish their babies for adoption. Social services at this time largely sheltered young women during the pregnancy and assisted with adoption (Aries, 1980). No consensus emerged from attempts to find psychological malfunctions that led to teenage pregnancy and marriage. Many early studies were badly flawed. Usually retrospective and without comparison or control groups, these studies could not establish that a young mother's psychological state caused her pregnancy (Mindick & Oskamp, 1979). Whenever alleged psychological prodromes for pregnancy-susceptible young women emerged, clinicians selected long-term psychotherapy as the treatment of choice.

Later Attitudes and Responses

Heightened social consciousness in the 1960s and early 1970s yielded economic analyses of adolescent pregnancy and marriage (Gilchrist & Schinke, 1983c). According to one such analysis:

> During the sixties the problem of adolescent pregnancy [was] redefined as a result of growing Black protest and the policy of the Great Society. It was no longer the stigma of illegitimacy which concerned the social planners, but rather the contribution of adolescent parenthood to the poverty cycle and the inability of the service system to meet the needs of the population at risk. (Aries, 1980, p. 141)

Researchers and policy makers thereby linked early pregnancy and marriage with poverty and welfare dependence (Fischman & Palley, 1978; Johnson, 1974; Klerman, 1975). Adolescent pregnancy and marriage were viewed as public welfare problems. Teenagers' sexual experimentations per se were seen as less important than the untoward and socially expensive results— pregnancy and childbearing. Adolescent marriage at this time was considered a private matter; but married youths' educational deficits and lack of economic self-sufficiency were public welfare concerns (Chilman, 1983; Furstenberg & Crawford, 1978).

Social movements of the early 1970s brought legislation to broaden family-planning options for adolescents. Though not expressly aimed at adolescents, new laws allowed teenagers access to birth control services, contraception, and abortion. Federally funded clinics gave inner-city adolescents free perinatal care, sex education, and birth-control devices (Dickens, Mudd, Garcia, Tomar, & Wright, 1973; Goldsmith, Gabrielson, & Gabrielson, 1972; Littlewood, 1977). Pregnancy prevention activities during this time reflected the assumption that lack of information and of access to contraceptives were major reasons for teenage conceptions. Information and birth-control services were therefore hoped-for solutions.

These solutions fell short of their goals to delay pregnancy and marriage. Evaluative data on programs of this era found that contraceptive services were used by but a fraction of sexually active adolescents (Chamie, Eisman, Forrest, Orr, & Torres, 1982; Jekel, Harrison, Bancroft, Tyler, & Klerman, 1975; Nathanson & Becker, 1985; Urban and Rural Systems Associates, 1976; Zabin, Kantner, & Zelnik, 1979; Zelnik, Kantner, & Ford, 1981).

Further, information about birth control and knowledge of contraceptive providers were not strongly related to adolescents' family-planning-clinic attendance or their use of contraception (McAnarney & Schreider, 1984; Schinke, 1984). Finally, sex education classes appear to have little impact on adolescents' initiation of sexual activity, contraceptive use, or marriage rates (Byrne & Fisher, 1983; MacDonald, 1981; Zelnik & Kim, 1982). Such data indicate that early pregnancy and marriage cannot be explained by youths' inadequate information or their poor access to family-planning services (Baizerman, 1977; Gilchrist & Schinke, 1983c; Herrold, 1981; Kriepe, 1983; Mindick, 1979).

Recent Attitudes and Responses

Recent efforts to delay pregnancy and marriage among adolescents recognize multifaceted developmental factors (Chilman, 1983; Jorgensen, 1983; McAnarney & Schreider, 1984; McGee, 1982; Petersen & Boxer, 1982; Schinke, Gilchrist, & Small, 1979). These efforts view adolescence per se as the genesis of youths' sexual and interpersonal experiments. Recent societal attitudes and responses thus explain adolescent pregnancy and marriage with such factors as social, cognitive, and behavioral competence and developmental maturity. Against this backdrop, the authors examine contemporary issues germane to adolescent pregnancy and marriage.

CONTEMPORARY ISSUES

Learning to interact and sexually function adaptively are major tasks of adolescence. Mastery of these tasks reduces a youth's risk of early pregnancy or marriage. To avoid pregnancy, for example, adolescents must either postpone coitus or use contraception. Contemporary theory within a developmental perspective of adolescent pregnancy and marriage has thus posed such questions as: What component skills and capacities are required to postpone sexual activity and marriage? What skills and capacities are required for successful contraception and adaptive interpersonal functioning? What opportunities are available to help adolescents acquire these requisite skills? What kind of ecological contexts affect adolescent interpersonal and sexual behavior? How are interpersonal and sexual behavior integrated into adolescents' biopsychosocial development? How does acceptance of self as capable of sexual behavior evolve?

Recent studies on adolescent pregnancy and marriage have attempted to answer these questions. Data from correlational and controlled research indicate that responsible—i.e., nonexploitative, nonharmful—sexual and interpersonal behavior requires affective, cognitive, social, and physical skills. In adolescence, biological maturity occurs before young people have acquired skills to manage their behavior. This lag in skills acquisition leaves adolescents vulnerable to unexpected consequences of precocious interpersonal and sexual experiments.

Such vulnerability can be discussed in terms of societal mores, adolescent development, and person–environment relationships.

SOCIETAL MORES

Sexual and marital mores in America are paradoxical. Magazines, movies, television, song lyrics, newspapers, and books explicitly extol sexual activity. Over a decade ago, Hoyman (1967) observed, "We have changed . . . to an openly sex-seeking culture. Sex is becoming larger than life itself: one of the new half-gods in America today" (p. 54). Contemporary mores nearly propel young people toward intercourse. Sexual relationships are glamorized. Adolescents often have inflated estimates of the magnitude of sexual activity among their peers (D'Augelli & D'Augelli, 1977; Stevens-Long & Cobb, 1983). An abundance of teenage and adult models demonstrate the physical and pleasurable aspects of intimate relationships.

Absent, however, are societal models showing the seriousness, commitments, and costs of sexual and marital behavior. Adolescents in this country receive a skewed image of what sexual and interpersonal responsibility entails. Babies, contraception, financial hardships, in-laws, and divorce seldom appear in the sexual and intimacy scenarios that adolescents derive from the popular culture. Americans in fact may be far less realistic and open about sexual and interpersonal behavior than are other Westerners. "What distinguishes American culture," according to one international study, " . . . is not that it is sex-obsessed, but that it is prudish: intolerant of premarital sexual activity and unwilling to deal with sexual topics openly" (Adler et al., 1985, p. 90).

Societal ambivalence about sex and intimacy may explain the lack of relevant, factual information for adolescents. American youth have few opportunities to see and practice responsible, nonexploitative, and nonharmful sexual and intimate interactions. Formal socialization processes for such interactive behavior are not widely accessible to American adolescents. Schools teach the mechanisms of human reproduction. Relationship building, interpersonal communication, and preparation for intimacy and marriage are rarely included in school-based curricula. Methods for controlling fertility and for obtaining relationship or family planning counseling are usually regarded as outside the bailiwick of school curricula (Sonenstein & Pittman, 1984).

Parents are frequently implicated by schools and by policy makers as the appropriate conduits for information about sexual and personal intimacy. Yet, the data consistently document the inability or unwillingness of most American families to share such knowledge with their children (Chilman, 1983; Fox, 1980; Laws & Schwartz, 1977; Lindemann, 1974; Rothenberg, 1980; Scales, 1979; Schinke, 1984; Swan, 1980; Thornburg, 1981; Yankelovich, Skelly, & White, 1979). That many parents are suited to educate their children about sex, contraception, and intimacy is indeed questionable. As Gilchrist and Schinke (1983c) noted,

> Most parents . . . came of age in sexually conservative times. . . . Parents are very often afraid to share their values about sex. . . . [and] parents may be uncertain whether they dare impose values on their child that they do not observe in their own sexual relationships. (p. 315)

Parents also seem poor sources for teaching children about appropriate marital behavior. Parents may lack credibility with their children. Adolescents, beginning to detach themselves from parents, may be disinclined to intentionally mimic their mothers' and fathers' marital behavior.

ADOLESCENT DEVELOPMENT

Pregnancy and marriage cannot be separated from the larger context of adolescent development. Developmental maturity affects youths' self-images, their facility in applying abstract information to themselves, and their skills for responsibly guiding their actions. Gaps in developmental areas, as noted before, increase adolescents' vulnerability for unwanted pregnancy and for precocious marital commitments. For present purposes, these developmental gaps are divided into emotional, cognitive, and behavioral areas.

Emotional Gaps

Understandably, adolescents are sometimes confused about intimacy and sexual matters (Schinke, 1984; Stevens-Long & Cobb, 1983).

Ambiguous societal standards may leave adolescents anxious about their sexual feelings and behavior. A particularly troublesome emotional gap may result from standards implying that sexual expressions by young men are normal, healthy, and acceptable; but the same expressions by young women are deviant, risky, and unacceptable (Elkind, 1978; Jorgensen & Sonstegard, 1984). Besides creating dissonance and denial for young women, such standards for young men may discourage intimacy and sexual responsibility. Stuart and Wells (1982) observed, "The socialization of young males continued to be based upon myths that restrict 'acceptable' male behaviors in sexual decision-making, and perpetuate a macho orientation to relationships" (p. 264).

Emotions rooted in myths about acceptable male roles in intimate and sexual matters are, at best, not productive and, at worst, insidiously damaging to heterosexual relationships. These myths include the notions that: (a) men erode their masculinity by expressing such emotions as compassion, trust, caring, and tenderness; (b) men always want and are always ready for sex; (c) once aroused, men need sexual release; (d) men must take charge of and orchestrate sexual behavior; (e) physical, athletic sexual performance connotes love and affection; (f) the true expression of love is sexual intercourse; and (g) sexual encounters must include intravaginal ejaculation to be successful and satisfying to both partners (Zilbergeld, 1978). Little wonder that many data paint images of confused adolescents, at once drawn toward new levels of intimacy and sexual enjoyment, yet anxious about engaging in forbidden pleasures (Byrne, Jazwinski, DeNino, & Fisher, 1977; Fisher, 1978, 1980; Fisher, Byrne, Edmunds, Miller, Kelley, & White, 1979; Fisher, Fisher, & Byrne, 1977; Scales & Beckstein, 1982; Sorensen, 1973).

The image of young women and young men not fully understanding their ambivalent attraction and discomfort in new relationships may partly explain high rates of contraceptive noncompliance among adolescents. According to one report,

> Adolescents find it more comfortable to bridge the values gap by being "swept away" or "overwhelmed" into "spontaneous" sex, thus avoiding the negative implications of "premeditated" sex. By not dealing consciously with the possible outcomes of their actions, they are able to remain acceptable both to their peers

and, on some conceptual level, to their parents. (Office for Family Planning, 1979, p. 40)

Fisher, Byrne, and White (1983) similarly posited that the adolescent,

> While excited about the prospect of having sex . . . is also somewhat anxious and uneasy about this subject. We would predict that this teenager will not be anxious enough to avoid intercourse, but he or she may well be anxious enough to avoid any of the prerequisite contraceptive behaviors. (p. 210)

Fisher et al. (1983) further predicted that anxious teenagers are less likely to:

> Possess accurate information about conception and contraception, . . . to acknowledge the possibility that they may have intercourse in the near future, . . . to engage in public behaviors to acquire needed contraceptives, . . . to communicate about contraception with their sexual partners, and . . . to use contraception consistently. (p. 210)

Cognitive Gaps

Adolescence is a time of transition in cognitive capacities. In Piagetian terms, the transition between concrete, childhood cognitions and abstract, adult reasoning occurs throughout the teen years (Berzonsky, 1981; Neimark, 1970). Abstract adult reasoning includes operations of deduction, conceptualizing intangibles, understanding the difference between reality and possibility, and seeing the multivariate nature of problems, situations, and solutions (Berzonsky, 1978). One consequence of abstract reasoning is a future-time perspective. This perspective enables the adult to anticipate and plan for events that have not yet happened (Dembo & Lundell, 1979). Major decisions surrounding intimacy, sexual behavior, contraception, and marriage require a future time perspective. Typically, adolescents are not ready to think within such a perspective.

Some data suggest that interpersonal intimacy and sexual decisions are inordinately resistant to adolescents' reasoning processes (Blum & Resnick, 1982; Dembo & Lundell, 1979; Gilligan, Kohlberg, Lerner, & Belenky, 1970; Gilchrist & Schinke, 1983a, 1983b; Jurich & Jurich, 1984; Rogel, Zuelke, Petersen, Tobin-Richards, & Shelton, 1980; Schinke & Gilchrist, 1984; Smith, Weinman, & Mumford, 1982). Regarding birth-control planning and decisions,

Cvetkovich, Grote, Bjorseth, and Sarkissian (1975) noted, "Adolescents are being required to make a decision about contraceptive use at a time when they are sexually undifferentiated and perhaps unprepared for such analytical thinking" (p. 266).

Another aspect of gaps in cognitive development is many teenagers' seeming inability to grasp probabilities around pregnancy risk (Baizerman, 1977; Schinke & Gilchrist, 1984). Among a teenaged sample, Zelnik (1979) found that only 36% of those who had menstrual cycle instruction could identify the time of month with highest fertility risk. Herz et al. (1984) likewise reported that less than 10% of adolescents receiving a sex-education program could specify the pregnancy-risk period in the menstrual cycle. Finally, adolescents are often reported as having considerable difficulty in resolving inconsistencies between cognitions and sexual behavior. For example, Jones and Philliber (1983) related the following disclosure from one young female subject: "I don't want to hurt my parents by becoming pregnant . . . and I want to finish school. I can't take care of a baby right now" (p. 251). Yet this same young woman had never contracepted during 18 months of regular coitus.

Behavioral Gaps

Responsible intimacy and sexual functioning require behavioral competence. An essential area of behavioral competence for adolescents is interpersonal communication skill (Gilchrist, 1981; Schinke, Blythe, Gilchrist, & Burt, 1981; Schinke, Gilchrist, & Blythe, 1980). Communication skill is necessary to establish mutually beneficial relationships, to abstain from opportunities for intercourse with a desirable partner, to resolve interpersonal conflicts, and to refuse unwanted advances and sexual attention (Adams, Fay, & Loreen-Martin, 1984; Elkind, 1984). To obtain contraceptives, adolescents must interact with health-care providers and retailers. For some contraceptive methods, youths need to communicate and negotiate with sexual partners (Jorgensen, King, & Torrey, 1980; Urberg, 1982). Adolescents have few avenues for learning verbal and nonverbal communication elements related to intimate, sexual, and contraceptive tasks (Adams & Gullotta, 1983; Gagnon & Simon, 1973; Laws & Schwartz, 1977).

Gaps in behavioral maturity related to sexual and interpersonal intimacy may also be exacerbated by gender-role expectations. Most often, males behaviorally control the nature of heterosexual relationships and assume little responsibility for the consequences of their control (Peplau, Rubin, & Hill, 1977; Scales & Beckstein, 1982). Such consequences include pregnancies, babies, abortions, divorces, and child care—all principally female responsibilities. Illustrative are data from a young male sample indicating that 9 in 10 respondents understood their equal role in preventing pregnancy; but that fewer than one-half of those men were willing to use birth control (Clark et al., 1984). Though not always in positions of power in intimate relationships, adolescent women, not unlike their adult counterparts, must be skilled enough to advocate for, obtain, and use contraceptives, to raise topics of intimacy and sexuality for discussion when problems occur, and to deal with the outcomes of broken marriages. Because less traditional and more assertive women are more apt to use birth control, recent advances toward greater gender equality may foreshadow a better distribution of future marital and sexual responsibilities (Fox, 1977; Gilchrist & Schinke, in press; Jorgensen et al., 1980).

CLINICAL IMPLICATIONS

"A focus on the person alone, or the demands of the situation alone," according to Lerner, Baker, and Lerner (1985), "will not suffice in understanding adaptive performance" (p. 114). Following this assumption, adolescent pregnancy and marriage cannot be analyzed as personal pathologies or as sheerly demographic or situational artifacts. Pregnancy and marriage, among adolescents and among adults alike, are products of interactions between individuals and environments. This perspective has implications for educational and service delivery systems aimed to prevent unplanned pregnancy and precocious and problem marriages. For instance, early efforts to prevent adolescent pregnancy regarded lack of information and services as causal factors. When sex education and contraceptive services were made available, subsequent pregnancies were seen as evidence of youths' irrationality or psychopathology (Gruber, 1984).

An enlightened view, reflecting person–environment relationships, could regard all adolescents at risk for unintended pregnancy and for early marriage (Gilchrist & Schinke, 1983c). Adolescent development does not afford most youths the cognitive and behavioral skills to convert knowledge and intentions into action. Preventive intervention must therefore be directed toward all youth. Such intervention would then help adolescents acquire cognitive and behavioral skills before the dating and sexual experimentation years. Within the context of intimate and contraceptive situations, youths must be able to process sexual information and apply it to themselves (Resnick & Blum, in press). They also must have the skills to planfully anticipate and prepare for sexual encounters and to problem-solve around obstacles to such preparation (Mindick & Oskamp, 1980; Schinke, Blythe, & Gilchrist, 1981).

Adolescents also need behavioral communication skills to request information, to refuse unwanted demands, to request desired changes, to disclose feelings and preferences, to give and receive feedback, to negotiate, and to compromise (Rubin, 1974; Zuengler & Neubeck, 1983). Finally, behavioral stress-reduction skills may be necessary for youths to deal adaptively with sexual and interpersonal intimacy (Gilchrist & Schinke, 1983a, 1983b). Research by several groups bears out the empirical wisdom of teaching such cognitive–behavioral skills in preventive interventions (Adler, 1982; Gerrard, McCann, & Fortini, 1983; Gilchrist & Schinke, 1983a, 1983b; Schinke, Blythe, & Gilchrist, 1981; Zuehlke & Rogel, 1981, 1982). To be sure, any preventive intervention for adolescents that involves intimacy and pregnancy matters is complicated by social and political factors.

The provision of sex education and heterosexual-relationship counseling for youth is a controversial area (cf. Dryfoos, 1985; Gilchrist & Schinke, 1983b, 1983c; Rodman, Lewis, & Griffith, 1984). American parents largely favor such efforts, although mothers and fathers hardly ever give their children relevant and timely assistance in sexual and marital arenas (McAnarney & Schreider, 1984; Parcel & Coreil, 1985; Shapiro, 1981). Government mandates for sexual and relationship instruction are a far way off in this country. So, despite the empirical, philosophical, and humanitarian reasons for professional interventions to prevent unplanned pregnancy and troubled marriages, questions remain before such activities are feasible. Such questions include: When should professionals intervene in adolescents' sexual and interpersonal development? How can parents be encouraged to teach their children about sex and marital roles? Who should be involved in these efforts if not parents?

FUTURE DIRECTIONS

Recent years have seen scientific progress in the analysis of adolescent pregnancy and marriage. To continue this progress, new research and clinical programs are needed.

Research Needs

Future research can profit by focusing on four areas of adolescent pregnancy and marriage: cognitive operations, dyadic interactions, male roles, and contraceptive technology. Adolescents who postpone sexual activity and marriage tend to have better developed problem-solving and decision-making skills and future time orientations (Blum & Resnick, 1982; Mindick & Oskamp, 1980; Resnick & Blum, in press; Steinlauf, 1979). Moreover, youth who experience heterosexual and contraceptive problems appear to have a limited sense of options, poor self-understanding, lack of insight into what motivates their behavior, and strong denial that pregnancy is a possible consequence of their behavior (Allgeier, 1983; Blum & Resnick, 1982; Herz, Goldberg, & Reis, 1984; Jones & Philliber, 1983; Rogel et al., 1980).

More research is needed on cognitive operations in sexual decision-making and behavior. Controlled and retrospective studies could examine developmental stages in adolescents' acquisition of future time perspective, sexual self-concept, problem-solving abilities, moral reasoning, and decisions about commitments to interpersonal relationships (cf. D'Augelli & D'Augelli, 1977). Longitudinal data would be especially helpful in these areas. Results from studies on cognitive operations could inform theory, measures, and preventive interventions related to adolescent pregnancy and marriage.

Dyadic interactions are a second area for research on the analysis and appropriate professional response to adolescent pregnancy and marriage. Some data suggest that heterosexual partners may be the only direct social influence on adolescents' birth-control use (Cohen & Rose, 1984). Accordingly, avenues for new studies could be guided by such questions as the following: What are the models for adolescents' normative behavior around dating, coital activity, and contraception for various age groups? What variations in these patterns exist for different socioeconomic and cultural groups? Under what conditions and for what reasons are marriage and intercourse postponed? What are the relationship consequences of abstaining from coital activity? Who initiates discussions around sexual abstinence and marital postponement? Here again, longitudinal research on patterns in adolescent heterosexual relationships would yield data for further study and programs to reduce unintended pregnancies and premature marriages.

Understanding of male roles in adolescent pregnancy and marriage will certainly benefit from additional research (cf. Andres & Gold, 1983; Finkel & Finkel, 1983; Gold & Berger, 1983; Rappaport, 1981; Resnick & Blum, in press; Scales, 1977; Shapiro, 1980). Though often depicted as coercive and exploitative, male partners can contribute to sexual responsibility and marital enhancement. Kastner (1984) noted the role of male support in female contraceptive use:

> While the relationship between boyfriend support and contraceptive use may be interpreted as an indication that males pressure their girlfriends to take responsibility for contraception, another possible explanation is that they facilitate rational decision-making regarding contraception, support girlfriends in acquiring the most reliable methods . . . and help girlfriends face the real but frequently denied risks of pregnancy. (p. 84)

Careful additional research is warranted on adolescent male roles in contraceptive behavior in adolescence. Little is known about the male role in early marriages. What attitudes lead males to marry early? What behavior patterns are characteristic of married adolescent males? Answers to these and similar questions could improve strategies for engaging the partners of adolescent females in counseling and service delivery programs about intimacy and sexuality.

Finally, research on better contraceptive methods for adolescents is sorely needed. Current birth-control methods do not suit adolescents (Hatcher et al., 1980). Many adolescents avoid diaphragms, possibly because of the operations involved. Intrauterine devices, al-

though relatively effective, are contraindicated for most nulliparous young women. Condoms, vaginal spermacides, and oral contraceptives are often not used correctly, greatly reducing their effectiveness. Promising efforts have been undertaken to improve contraceptive technology for youth, including research on the design, synthesis, and testing of male methods (National Institutes of Health, 1985). Still, much remains to be done in developing contraceptives for adolescents.

Program Needs

New research on adolescent pregnancy and marriage will provide a theoretically sound, empirical base for improved public policies and programs. The present authors agree with Byrne and Fisher (1983) who, relative to adolescent pregnancy, asserted: "The problem of adolescent pregnancy will require political as well as pedagogical solutions" (p. 273). Work in political and policy arenas is necessary to stimulate and support research, educational efforts, and public-health, social services, and mental-health programs for adolescents. The public and human costs of unplanned adolescent pregnancy justify a greater investment in prevention. Preventive intervention programs could begin by removing barriers to sex education and services for youth (Fisher, 1983).

Prevention could also be facilitated by the erosion of institutional, philosophical, and moral impediments to programs around adolescent pregnancy and marriage. For instance, a large impediment to aggressive public efforts to prevent unplanned teenage pregnancies is the belief that only parents can take responsibility for sex education. A similar impediment is the objection that sex-related education leads youth into promiscuity. Here, the data show that access to contraception neither increases nor decreases teenagers' sexual activity (Allgeier, 1983; Gilchrist & Schinke, 1983c).

Advocates for better programs related to adolescent pregnancy and marriage, however, must go beyond simply removing barriers and impediments. Advocacy efforts must also seek legislative and community commitments to favor preventive intervention and counseling programs for young people. Such advocacy could follow three arguments (cf. Vinovskis, 1981). A first argument is that adolescents in our society have a democratic right to be fully informed and prepared to deal with issues that markedly affect their lives. A second argument is that economics favors efforts to reduce unintended pregnancies and unhappy, broken marriages. And, a third argument is that providing youth-oriented counseling and services programs can benefit other aspects of adolescent health. For example, such programs may lower rates of sexually transmitted diseases.

Future programs to prevent and intervene with unintended pregnancies and premature, troubled marriages among adolescents, therefore, will begin with a solid research base. Through creativity, imagination, and initiative, policy makers and program planners can then carry research findings into clinical and service delivery programs.

SUMMARY

This chapter reviewed current theory and empirical research on adolescent pregnancy and marriage in the United States. Introductory material summarized the scope, sequelae, and correlates of adolescent pregnancy and marriage in America. The chapter traced the history and development of Western societal attitudes and responses to adolescent pregnancy and marriage. Secular trends over recent years have seen adolescent pregnancy and marriage defined in moral, economic, pathological, and psychosocial terms. Next discussed were relevant contemporary issues of socialization for contraception and marriage and cognitive and behavioral requisites for responsible sexual and interpersonal functioning. The authors then examined early pregnancy and marriage in the context of adolescent development.

Particular attention was given to emotional, cognitive, and behavioral gaps that affect adolescents' sexual and intimate relationships. After noting interactions of developmental and environmental forces on today's youth, the authors suggested future directions for research on adolescent pregnancy and marriage. Needed areas of research include studies on cognitive operations, dyadic interactions, male roles, and contraceptive methods. Last, the authors called for new research and programs responsive to adolescent pregnancy and marriage.

Acknowledgements—The authors thank Wendy Baldwin, Melinda Fujiwara, Cheryl Kelso, Virginia Senechal, Deane Sutcliffe, and Sunnie Tasanasanta. Funding was by the W. T. Grant Foundation of New York and by Grant DH 11095 from the Center for Population Research Branch, National Institute of Child Health and Human Development.

REFERENCES

Abernethy, V. (1974). Illegitimate conception among teenagers. *American Journal of Public Health, 64,* 662–673.

Adams, C., Fay, J., & Loreen-Martin, J. (1984). *No is not enough: Helping teenagers avoid sexual assault.* San Luis Obispo, CA: Impact.

Adams, G. R., & Gullotta, T. (1983). *Adolescent life experiences.* Monterey, CA: Brooks/Cole.

Adler, J., Katz, S., & Jackson, T. A. (1985). A teen-pregnancy epidemic. *Newsweek, 105,* 90.

Adler, N. (1982, August). *Adolescent contraceptive decision making.* Paper presented at the 9th meeting of the American Psychological Association, Washington, DC.

The Alan Guttmacher Institute. (1978). *Contraceptive services for adolescents: United States, each state & country, 1975.* New York: Author.

Allgeier, E. R. (1983). Ideological barriers to contraception. In D. Byrne & W. A. Fisher (Eds.), *Adolescents, sex, and contraception* (pp. 171–206). Hillsdale, NJ: Erlbaum.

Andres, D., & Gold, D. (1983). Selected psychosocial characteristics of males: Their relationship to contraceptive use and abortion. *Personality and Social Psychology Bulletin, 9,* 387–396.

Aries, N. (1980). Historic trends in the delivery of services to teenage parents. *Journal of Sociology and Social Welfare, 7,* 137–146.

Bachrach, C. A., & Horn, M. C. (1985). Marriage and first intercourse, marital dissolution, and remarriage: United States, 1982. *Advance Data, 107,* 1–7.

Bahr, S. J., & Galligan, R. J. (1984). Teenage marriage and marital stability. *Youth & Society, 15,* 387–400.

Baizerman, M. (1977). Can the first pregnancy of a young adolescent be prevented? A question which must be answered. *Journal of Youth and Adolescence, 6,* 343–351.

Barth, R. P., & Schinke, S. P. (1984). Enhancing the social supports of teenage mothers. *Social Casework, 65,* 523–531.

Barth, R. P., Schinke, S. P., & Maxwell, J. S. (1983). Psychological correlates of teenage motherhood. *Journal of Youth and Adolescence, 12,* 471–487.

Barth, R. P., Schinke, S. P., & Maxwell, J. S. (in press). Coping skills training for school-age mothers. *Journal of Social Service Research.*

Benussi, G., Barbone, F., & Gasperini, V. (1985). The effect of legal abortion on teenage fertility in Trieste, Italy. *Family Planning Perspectives, 17,* 23–24.

Berzonsky, M. D. (1978). Formal reasoning in adolescence: An alternate view. *Adolescence, 13,* 279–290.

Berzonsky, M. D. (1981). *Adolescent development.* New York: Macmillan.

Blum, R. W., & Resnick, M. D. (1982). Adolescent sexual decision-making: Contraception, pregnancy, abortion, motherhood. *Pediatric Annals, 11,* 797–805.

Brandt, C. L., Kane, F. J., Jr., & Moan, C. A. (1978). Pregnant adolescents: Some psychosocial factors. *Psychosomatics, 19,* 79–93.

Brown, P. (1983). The Swedish approach to sex education and adolescent pregnancy: Some impressions. *Family Planning Perspectives, 15,* 90–95.

Burden, D. S., & Klerman, L. V. (1984). Teenage parenthood: Factors that lessen economic dependence. *Social Work, 29,* 11–16.

Byrne, D., & Fisher, W. A. (1983). *Adolescents, sex, and contraception.* Hillsdale, NJ: Erlbaum.

Byrne, D., Jazwinski, C., DeNinno, J. A., & Fisher, W. A. (1977). Negative sexual attitudes and contraception. In D. Byrne & L. A. Byrne (Eds.), *Exploring human sexuality.* New York: Harper & Row.

Chamie, M., Eisman, S., Forrest, J. D., Orr, M. T., & Torres, A. (1982). Factors affecting adolescents' use of family planning clinics. *Family Planning Perspectives, 14,* 126–139.

Chilman, C. S. (1978). *Adolescent sexuality in a changing American society: Social and psychological perspectives.* Washington, DC: U.S. Government Printing Office.

Chilman, C. S. (Ed.). (1983). *Adolescent sexuality in a changing American society.* New York: Wiley.

Clark, S. D., Jr., Zabin, L. S., & Hardy, J. B. (1984). Sex, contraception and parenthood: Experience and attitudes among urban black young men. *Family Planning Perspectives, 16,* 77–82.

Cobliner, W. G., Schulman, H., & Smith, V. (1975). Patterns of contraceptive failures: The role of motivation re-examined. *Journal of Bio-social Science, 7,* 307–318.

Cohen, D. D., & Rose, R. D. (1984). Male adolescent birth control behavior: The importance of developmental factors and sex differences. *Journal of Youth and Adolescence, 13,* 239–252.

Corder, J., & Stephan, C. W. (1984). Females' combination of work and family roles: Adolescents' aspirations. *Journal of Marriage and the Family, 46,* 391–402.

Cvetkovich, G., Grote, B., Bjorseth, A., & Sarkissian, J. (1975). On the psychology of adolescents' use of contraceptives. *Journal of Sex Research, 11,* 256–270.

D'Augelli, J. F., & D'Augelli, A. R. (1977). Moral reasoning and premarital sexual behavior: Toward reasoning about relationships. *Journal of Social Issues, 33,* 46–66.

De Anda, D. (1983). Pregnancy in early and late adolescence. *Journal of Youth and Adolescence, 12,* 33–43.

Dembo, M. H., & Lundell, B. (1979). Factors affecting adolescent contraception practices: Implications for sex education. *Adolescence, 14,* 657–664.

Dickens, H. O., Mudd, E. H., Garcia, C. R., Tomar, K., & Wright, D. (1973). One hundred pregnant adolescents, treatment approaches in a university hospital. *American Journal of Public Health, 63,* 794–800.

Dillard, K. D., & Pol, L. G. (1982). The individual economic costs of teenage childbearing. *Family Relations, 31,* 249–259.

Dryfoos, J. G. (1984). A new strategy for preventing unintended teenage childbearing. *Family Planning Perspectives, 16,* 193–195.

Dryfoos, J. G. (1985). A time for new thinking about teenage pregnancy. *American Journal of Public Health, 75,* 13–14.

Elkind, D. (1978). Understanding the young adolescent. *Adolescence, 13,* 127–134.

Elkind, D. (1984). *All grown up and no place to go: Teenagers in crisis.* Menlo Park, CA: Addison-Wesley.

Elster, A. B., McAnarney, E. R., & Lamb, M. E. (1983). Parental behavior of adolescent mothers. *Pediatrics, 71,* 494–503.

Espenshade, T. J., Kamenske, G., & Turchi, B. A. (1983). Family size and economic welfare. *Family Planning Perspectives, 15,* 289–294.

Ezzard, N. V., Cates, W., & Schulz, K. F. (1985). The epidemiology of adolescent abortion in the United States. In P. Sachdev (Ed.), *Perspectives on abortion* (pp. 73–88). Metuchen, NJ: Scarecrow.

Finkel, M. L., & Finkel, D. J. (1983). Male adolescent sexual behavior, the forgotten partner: A review. *Journal of School Health, 53,* 544–547.

Fischman, S. H., & Palley, H. A. (1978). Adolescent unwed motherhood: Implications for a national family policy. *Health and Social Work, 3,* 30–46.

Fisher, W. A. (1978). *Affective, attitudinal, and normative determinants of contraceptive behavior among university men.* Unpublished doctoral dissertation, Purdue University, Lafayette, IN.

Fisher, W. A. (1980). *Erotophobia—Erotophilia and performance in a human sexuality course.* Unpublished manuscript, University of Western Ontario, London, Ontario.

Fisher, W. A. (1983). Adolescent contraception: Summary and recommendations. In D. Byrne & W. A. Fisher (Eds.), *Adolescents, sex, and contraception* (pp. 273–300). Hillsdale, NJ: Erlbaum.

Fisher, W. A. (1984). Predicting contraceptive behavior among university men: The role of emotions and behavioral intentions. *Journal of Applied Social Psychology, 14,* 104–123.

Fisher, W. A., Byrne, D., Edmunds, M., Miller, C. T., Kelley, K., & White, L. A. (1979). Psychological and situation-specific correlates of contraceptive behavior among university women. *Journal of Sex Research, 15,* 38–55.

Fisher, W. A., Byrne, D., & White, L. A. (1983). Emotional barriers to contraception. In D. Byrne & W. A. Fisher (Eds.), *Adolescents, sex, and contraception* (pp. 207–239). Hillsdale, NJ: Erlbaum.

Fisher, W. A., Fisher, J. D., & Byrne, D. (1977). Consumer reactions to contraceptive purchasing. *Personality and Social Psychology Bulletin, 3,* 293–296.

Fox, G. L. (1977). Sex role attitudes as predictors of contraceptive use among unmarried university students. *Sex Roles, 3,* 265–283.

Fox, G. L. (1980). The mother-adolescent daughter as a sexual socialization structure: A research review. *Family Relations, 29,* 21–28.

Fox, G. L., & Inazu, J. K. (1982). The influence of mother's marital history on the mother–daughter relationship in black and white households. *Journal of Marriage and the Family, 44,* 143–152.

Freeman, E. W., Rickels, K., Huggins, G. R., & Garcia, C. R. (1984). Urban black adolescents who obtain contraceptive services before or after their first pregnancy. *Journal of Adolescent Health Care, 5,* 183–190.

Furstenberg, F., & Crawford, A. (1978). Family support: Helping teenage mothers to cope. *Family Planning Perspectives, 10,* 322–333.

Furstenberg, F. F., Jr., Shea, J., Allison, P., Herceg-Baron, R., & Webb, D. (1983). Contraceptive continuation among adolescents attending family planning clinics. *Family Planning Perspectives, 15,* 211–217.

Gagnon, J., & Simon, W. (1973). *Sexual conduct: The social sources of human sexuality.* Chicago: Aldine.

Gerrard, M., McCann, L., & Fortini, M. E. (1983). Prevention of unwanted pregnancy. *American Journal of Community Psychology, 11,* 153–167.

Gilchrist, L. D. (1981). Group procedures for helping adolescents cope with sex. *Behavior Group Therapy, 3*(2), 3–8.

Gilchrist, L. D., Lodish, D., Staab, S., & Schinke, S. P. (1983). Learning the ropes: Job-seeking skills for teenage mothers. In S. E. Davidson (Ed.), *The second mile: Contemporary approaches in counseling young women* (pp. 1–32). Tucson, AZ: New Directions for Young Women.

Gilchrist, L. D., & Schinke, S. P. (1983a). Coping with contraception: Cognitive and behavioral methods with adolescents. *Cognitive Therapy and Research, 7,* 379–388.

Gilchrist, L. D., & Schinke, S. P. (1983b). Counseling with adolescents about their sexuality. In C. S. Chilman (Ed.), *Adolescent sexuality in a changing American society* (pp. 230–250). New York: Wiley.

Gilchrist, L. D., & Schinke, S. P. (1983c). Teenage pregnancy and public policy. *Social Service Review, 57,* 307–322.

Gilchrist, L. D., & Schinke, S. P. (in press). Helping adolescents cope with sex. In R. A. Feldman & A. R. Stiffman (Eds.), *Advances in adolescent mental health* (Vol. II). Greenwich, CT: JAI.

Gilchrist, L. D., Schinke, S. P., & Blythe, B. J. (1979). Primary prevention services for children and youth. *Children and Youth Services Review, 1,* 379–391.

Gilligan, C., Kohlberg, L., Lerner, J., & Belenky, M. (1970). Moral reasoning about sexual dilemmas. *Technical Reports of U.S. Commission on Obscenity and Pornography, 1.*

Glick, P. C. (1984). American household structure in transition. *Family Planning Perspectives, 16,* 205–211.

Gold, D., & Berger, C. (1983). The influence of psychological and situational factors on the contraceptive behavior of single men: A review of the literature. *Population and Environment, 6,* 113–129.

Goldsmith, S., Gabrielson, M., & Gabrielson, I. (1972). Teenagers, sex and contraception. *Family Planning Perspectives, 4,* 32–38.

Gruber, E. (1984, August). *Rational and developmental approaches to the study of adolescent sexuality.* Paper presented at the 92nd meeting of the American Psychological Association, Toronto, Canada.

Hackman, E., Emanuel, I., Van Belle, G., & Daling, J. (1983). Maternal birth weight and subsequent pregnancy outcome. *Journal of the American Medical Association, 250,* 2016–2019.

Hatcher, R. A., Stewart, G. K., Stewart, F., Guest, F., Schwartz, D. W., & Jones, S. A. (1980). *Contraceptive technology 1980–1981* (10th ed.). New York: Irvington.

Henshaw, S. K., Forrest, J. D., & Blaine, E. (1984). Abortion services in the United States, 1981 and 1982. *Family Planning Perspectives, 16,* 119–127.

Henshaw, S. K., & O'Reilly, K. (1983). Characteristics of abortion patients in the United States, 1979 and 1980. *Family Planning Perspectives, 15,* 5–16.

Herrold, E. S. (1981). Contraceptive embarrassment and contraceptive behavior among young single women. *Journal of Youth and Adolescence, 10,* 233–242.

Hertz, D. G. (1977). Psychological implications of adolescent pregnancy: Patterns of family interaction in adolescent mothers-to-be. *Psychosomatics, 18,* 13–16.

Herz, E. J., Goldberg, W. A., & Reis, J. S. (1984). Family life education for young adolescents: A quasi-experiment. *Journal of Youth and Adolescence, 13,* 309–327.

Hofferth, S. L., & Moore, K. A. (1979). Early childbearing and later economic well-being. *American Sociological Review, 44,* 784–815.

Hogan, D. P., & Kitagawa, E. M. (1985). The impact of social status, family structure, and neighborhood on the fertility of black adolescents. *American Journal of Sociology, 90,* 825–855.

Hoyman, H. S. (1967). Sex and American college girls today. *Journal of School Health, 37,* 54–62.

Jekel, J. F., Harrison, J. T., Bancroft, D. R. E., Tyler, N. C., & Klerman, L. V. (1975). A comparison of the health of index and subsequent babies born to school-age mothers. *American Journal of Public Health, 65,* 370–374.

Jekel, J. F., & Klerman, L. V. (1982). Comprehensive service programs for pregnant and parenting adolescents. In E. R. McAnarney (Ed.), *Premature adolescent pregnancy and parenthood* (pp. 295–310). New York: Grune & Stratton.

Jessor, R., & Jessor, S. L. (1984). Adolescence to young adulthood: A twelve-year prospective study of problem behavior and psychosocial development. In S. A. Mednick, M. Harway, & K. M. Finello (Eds.), *Handbook of longitudinal research* (pp. 34–61). New York: Praeger.

Johnson, C. L. (1974). Adolescent pregnancy: Intervention into the poverty cycle. *Adolescence, 9,* 391–406.

Jones, J. B., & Philliber, S. (1983). Sexually active but not pregnant: A comparison of teens who risk and teens who plan. *Journal of Youth and Adolescence, 12,* 235–251.

Jorgensen, S. R. (1983). Beyond adolescent pregnancy: Research frontiers for early adolescent sexuality. *Journal of Early Adolescence, 3,* 141–155.

Jorgensen, S. R., King, S. L., & Torrey, B. A. (1980). Dyadic and social network influences on adolescent exposure to pregnancy risk. *Journal of Marriage and the Family, 42,* 141–155.

Jorgensen, S. R., & Sonstegard, J. S. (1984). Predicting adolescent sexual and contraceptive behavior: An application and test of the Fishbein model. *Journal of Marriage and the Family, 46,* 43–56.

Jurich, A. D., & Jurich, J. A. (1984). The effect of cognitive moral development upon the selection of premarital sexual standards. *Journal of Marriage and the Family, 46*, 141–155.

Kar, S., & Cumberland, W. (1984). Impacts of behavioral intentions, social support, and accessibility on contraception: A cross-cultural study. *Population and Environment, 7*, 17–31.

Kastner, L. S. (1984). Ecological factors predicting adolescent contraceptive use: Implications for intervention. *Journal of Adolescent Health Care, 5*, 79–86.

Kellam, S. G., Ensminger, M. E., Branch, J., Brown, C. H., & Fleming, J. P. (1984). The Woodlawn Mental Health Longitudinal Community Epidemiological Project. In S. A. Mednick, M. Harway, & K. M. Finello (Eds.), *Handbook of longitudinal research* (pp. 197–207). New York: Praeger.

Kisker, E. E. (1984). The effectiveness of family planning clinics in serving adolescents. *Family Planning Perspectives, 16*, 212–218.

Klerman, L. V. (1975). Adolescent pregnancy: The need for new policies and new programs. *Journal of School Health, 45*, 263–67.

Koenig, M. A., & Zelnik, M. (1982). The risk of premarital first pregnancy among metropolitan-area teenagers: 1976 and 1979. *Family Planning Perspectives, 14*, 239–247.

Kriepe, R. E. (1983). Prevention of adolescent pregnancy: A developmental approach. In E. McAnarney (Ed.), *Premature adolescent pregnancy and parenthood*. New York: Grune & Stratton.

Lawrence, R. A., & Merritt, T. A. (1981). Infants of adolescent mothers: Perinatal, neonatal, and infancy outcome. *Seminars in Perinatology, 5*, 19–32.

Laws, J. L., & Schwartz, P. (1977). *Sexual scripts: The social construction of female sexuality*. Hinsdale, IL: Dryden.

Lerner, J. V., Baker, N., & Lerner, R. M. (1985). A person–context goodness of fit model of adjustment. In P. C. Kendall (Ed.), *Advances in cognitive-behavioral research and therapy* (Vol. 4, pp. 111–136). Orlando, FL: Academic.

Lewis, B. Y. (1985). The wife abuse inventory: A screening device for the identification of abused women. *Social Work, 30*, 32–35.

Lewis, C. E., Siegel, J. M., & Lewis, M. A. (1984). Feeling bad: Exploring sources of distress among pre-adolescent children. *American Journal of Public Health, 74*, 117–122.

Lincoln, R. (1983). Teenage pregnancy and childbearing: Why the difference between countries? *Family Planning Perspectives, 15*, 104.

Lindemann, C. (1974). *Birth control and unmarried young women*. New York: Springer.

Littlewood, T. B. (1977). *The politics of population control*. Notre Dame, IN: University of Notre Dame.

MacDonald, R. (1981). Adolescent sexuality: Whose responsibility is it? In T. J. Coates, A. C. Petersen, & C. Perry (Eds.), *Promoting adolescent health* (pp. 269–276). New York: Academic.

Marini, M. M. (1981). Effects of the timing of marriage and first birth on fertility. *Journal of Marriage and the Family, 43*, 27–46.

Marini, M. M., & Hodsdon, P. J. (1981). Effects of the timing of marriage and first birth on the spacing of subsequent births. *Demography, 18*, 529–548.

McAnarney, E. R., Lawrence, R. A., Aten, M. J., & Iker, H. P. (1984). Adolescent mothers and their infants. *Pediatrics, 73*, 358–362.

McAnarney, E. R., & Schreider, C. (1984). *Identifying social and psychological antecedents of adolescent pregnancy: The contribution of research to concepts of prevention*. New York: William T. Grant Foundation.

McAnarney, E. R., & Thiede, H. A. (1981). Adolescent pregnancy and childbearing: What we have learned in a decade and what remains to be learned. *Seminars in Perinatology, 5*, 91–102.

McGee, E. A. (1982). *Too little, too late: Services for teenage parents*. New York: The Ford Foundation.

Meyerowitz, J. & Malev. J. (1973). Pubescent attitudinal correlates antecedent to adolescent illegitimate pregnancy. *Journal of Youth and Adolescence, 2*, 251–258.

Mindick, B. (1979). Teenage pregnancies: Psychiatric or educational problem? *Psychiatric Opinion, 16*, 32–36.

Mindick, B., & Oskamp, S. (1979). Longitudinal predictive research: An approach to methodological problems in studying contraception. *Journal of Population, 2*, 259–276.

Mindick, B., & Oskamp, S. (1980). *Contraception use effectiveness: The fit between method and user characteristics*. Washington, DC: Center for Population Research, National Institute of Child Health and Human Development.

Moore, K. A. (1985, January). *Facts at a glance*. Paper presented at Training Conference on Adolescent Pregnancy Prevention, Chicago, IL.

Moore, K. A., & Burt, M. R. (1982). *Private crisis, public cost*. Washington, DC: The Urban Institute Press.

Moore, K. A., & Wertheimer, R. F. (1984). Teenage childbearing and welfare: Preventive and ameliorative strategies. *Family Planning Perspectives, 16*, 285–289.

Nathanson, C. A., & Becker, M. H. (1985). The influence of client–provider relationships on teenage women's subsequent use of contraception. *American Journal of Public Health, 75*, 33–38.

National Center for Health Statistics. (1984a). Advance report of final marriage statistics, 1981. *NCHS Monthly Vital Statistics Report, 32*(11), 1–12.

National Center for Health Statistics. (1984b). Births, marriages, divorces, and deaths for February 1984. *NCHS Monthly Vital Statistics Report, 33*(2), 1–12.

National Center for Health Statistics. (1985). Births, marriages, divorces, and deaths for October 1984. *NCHS Monthly Vital Statistics Report, 33*(10), 1–12.

National Institutes of Health. (1985). *NIH guide* (p. 5). Washington, DC: Author.

Neimark, E. D. (1970). A preliminary search for formal operations structure. *Journal of Genetic Psychology, 116*, 223–232.

Nestor, B. (1982). Public funding of contraception services, 1980–1982. *Family Planning Perspectives, 14*, 198–230.

O'Connell, M., & Rogers, C. C. (1984). Out-of-wedlock births, premarital pregnancies and their effect on family formation and dissolution. *Family Planning Perspectives, 16*, 157–162.

Office for Family Planning. (1979). *A decision-making approach to sex education* (Publication No. [HSA] 79-5608). Washington, DC: Government Printing Office.

Orr, M. T. (1983). Impact on state management of family planning funds. *Family Planning Perspectives, 15*, 176–184.

Parcel, G. S., & Coreil, J. (1985). Parental evaluations of a sex education course for young adolescents, *Journal of School Health, 55*, 9–34.

Pascoe, J. M., & Berger, A. (1985). Attitudes of high school girls in Israel and the United States toward breast feeding. *Journal of Adolescent Health Care, 6*, 28–30.

Peplau, L., Rubin, Z., & Hill, C. (1977). Sexual intimacy in dating relationships. *Journal of Social Issues, 33*, 86–109.

Petersen, A. C. (1979). Can puberty come any earlier? *Psychology Today, 12*, 604–616.

Petersen, A. C., & Boxer, A. (1982). Adolescent sexuality. In T. J. Coates, A. C. Petersen, & C. Perry (Eds.), *Promoting adolescent health: A dialog on research and practice* (pp. 237–253). New York: Academic.

Philliber, S. G., & Graham, E. H. (1981). The impact of age of mother on mother-child interaction patterns. *Journal of Marriage and the Family, 43*, 109–115.

Philliber, S. G., Namerow, P. B., & Jones, J. E. (1985). Age variation in use of a contraceptive service by adolescents. *Public Health Reports, 100*, 34–40.

Rappaport, B. M. (1981). Helping men ask for help. *Public Welfare, 39*(2), 22–27.

Resnick, M. D., & Blum, R. W. (in press). Developmental and personalogical correlates of adolescent sexual behavior and outcome. *International Journal of Adolescent Medicine and Health*.

Rodgers, J. L., Billy, J. O. G., & Udry, J. R. (1982). The rescission of behaviors: Inconsistent responses in adolescent sexuality data. *Social Science Research, 11*, 280–296.

Rodman, H., Lewis, S. H., & Griffith, S. B. (1984). *The sexual rights of adolescents: Competence, vulnerability, and parental control.* New York: Columbia University.

Rogel, M. J., Zuehlke, M. E., Petersen, A. C., Tobin-Richards, M., & Shelton, M. (1980). Contraceptive behavior in adolescence: A decision-making perspective. *Journal of Youth and Adolescence, 9*, 491–506.

Rogel, M. J., Zuehlke, M. E., Weiss, C., Petersen, A. C., & Shelton, M. (1980, August). *Female adolescents: Factors differentiating early-, middle-, late-, and never-contraceptors.* Paper presented at the 88th meeting of the American Psychological Association, Montreal.

Roosa, M. W. (1984). Maternal age, social class, and the obstetric performance of teenagers. *Journal of Youth and Adolescence, 13*, 365–374.

Roosa, M. W., Fitzgerald, H. E., & Carson, N. A. (1982a). Teenage and older mothers and their infants: A descriptive comparison. *Adolescence, 17*(65), 1–17.

Roosa, M. W., Fitzgerald, H. E., & Carson, N. A. (1982b). Teenage parenting and child develop-

ment: A literature review. *Infant Mental Health Journal, 3*, 4–18.

Rothenberg, P. B. (1980). Communication about sex and birth control between mothers and their adolescent children. *Population and Environment, 3*, 35–50.

Rubin, Z. (1974). Lovers and other strangers: The development of intimacy in encounters and relationships. *American Scientist, 62*, 182–189.

Scales, P. (1977). Males and morals: Teenage contraceptive behavior amid the double standard. *The Family Coordinator, 26*, 211–222.

Scales, P. (1979). The context of sex education and the reduction of teen-age pregnancy. *Child Welfare, 58*, 263–273.

Scales, P., & Beckstein, D. (1982). From macho to mutuality: Helping young men make effective decisions about sex, contraception, and pregnancy. In I. R. Stuart & C. F. Wells (Eds.), *Pregnancy in adolescence: Needs, problems, and management* (pp. 264–289). New York: Van Nostrand Reinhold.

Schinke, S. P. (1984). Preventing teenage pregnancy. In M. Hersen, R. M. Eisler, & P. M. Miller (Eds.), *Progress in behavior modification* (Vol. 16, pp. 31–64). Orlando, FL: Academic.

Schinke, S. P., Blythe, B. J., & Gilchrist, L. D. (1981). Brief reports: Cognitive–behavioral prevention of adolescent pregnancy. *Journal of Counseling Psychology, 28*, 451–454.

Schinke, S. P., Blythe, B. J., Gilchrist, L. D., & Burt, G. A. (1981). Primary prevention of adolescent pregnancy. *Social Work with Groups, 4*, 121–135.

Schinke, S. P., & Gilchrist, L. D. (1984). *Life skills counseling with adolescents.* Baltimore: University Park Press.

Schinke, S. P., Gilchrist, L. D., & Blythe, B. J. (1980). Role of communication in the prevention of teenage pregnancy. *Health & Social Work, 5*, 54–59.

Schinke, S. P., Gilchrist, L. D., & Small, R. W. (1979). Preventing unwanted adolescent pregnancy: A cognitive-behavioral approach. *American Journal of Orthopsychiatry, 49*, 81–88.

Scholl, T. O., Decker, E., Karp, R. J., Greene, G., & De Sales, M. (1984). Early adolescent pregnancy: A comparative study of pregnancy outcome in young adolescents and mature women. *Journal of Adolescent Health Care, 5*, 167–171.

Shapiro, C. H. (1980). Sexual learning: The short-changed adolescent male. *Social Work, 25*, 489–493.

Shapiro, C. H. (1981). *Adolescent pregnancy prevention—school-community cooperation.* Springfield, IL: Charles C Thomas.

Smith, P. B., Weinman, M. L., & Mumford, D. M. (1982). Social and affective factors associated with adolescent pregnancy. *Journal of School Health, 52*, 90–93.

Sonenstein, F. L., & Pittman, K. J. (1984). The availability of sex education in large city school districts. *Family Planning Perspectives, 16*, 19–25.

Sorensen, R. C. (1973). *Adolescent sexuality in contemporary America: Personal values and sexual behavior ages thirteen to nineteen.* New York: World.

Spanier, G., & Glick, P. (1981). Marital instability in the United States: Some correlates and recent changes. *Family Relations, 30*, 329–338.

Steinlauf, B. (1979). Problem-solving skills, locus of control, and the contraceptive effectiveness of young women. *Child Development, 50,* 268–271.

Stevens-Long, J., & Cobb, N. J. (1983). *Adolescence and early adulthood* (1st ed.). Palo Alto, CA: Mayfield.

Stuart, I. R., & Wells, C. F. (Eds.). (1982). *Pregnancy in adolescence: Needs, problems, and management.* New York: Van Nostrand Reinhold.

Swan, R. W. (1980). Sex education in the home: The U.S. experience. *Journal of Sex Education and Therapy, 6,* 3–10.

Taffel, S. (1984). *Birth and fertility rates for states, United States 1980* (Series 21, No. 42). Hyattsville, MD: U.S. Department of Health and Human Services.

Tanner, J. M. (1972). Sequence, tempo and individual variation in growth and development of boys and girls aged twelve to sixteen. In J. Kagan & R. Coles (Eds.), *Twelve to sixteen: Early adolescence* (pp. 1–24). New York: Norton.

Tanner, J. M. (1974). Sequence and tempo in the somatic changes in puberty. In M. M. Grumbach, G. C. Grave, & F. E. Meyer (Eds.), *Control of the onset of puberty* (pp. 448–470). New York: Wiley.

Teichman, J. (1982). *Illegitimacy, a philosophical examination.* Oxford: Basil Blackwell.

Thornburg, H. D. (1981). The amount of sex information learning obtained during early adolescence. *Journal of Early Adolescence, 1,* 171–183.

Thornton, A., & Freedman, D. (1982). Changing attitudes toward marriage and single life. *Family Planning Perspectives, 14,* 297–303.

Turk, D. C., Litt, M. D., Salovey, P., & Walker, J. (1985). Seeking urgent pediatric treatment: Factors contributing to frequency, delay, and appropriateness. *Health Psychology, 4,* 43–59.

Urban and Rural Systems Associates. (1976). *Improving family planning services for teenagers.* Washington, DC: Office of the Assistant Secretary for Planning and Evaluation.

Urberg, K. A. (1982). A theoretical framework for studying adolescent contraceptive use. *Adolescence, 17,* 527–540.

Ventura, S. J. (1984). *Trends in teenage childbearing, United States 1970–81* (Series 21, No. 41). Hyattsville, MD: U.S. Department of Health and Human Services.

Ventura, S. J., Taffel, S., & Mosher, W. D. (1985). Estimates of pregnancies and pregnancy rates for the United States, 1976–1981. *Public Health Reports, 100,* 31–40.

Vinovskis, M. A. (1981). An "epidemic" of adolescent pregnancy? Some historical considerations. *Journal of Family History, 6,* 205–230.

Westoff, C. F., Calot, G., & Foster, A. D. (1983). Teenage fertility in developed nations: 1971–1980. *Family Planning Perspectives, 15,* 105–110.

Yankelovich, Skelly, & White, Inc. (1979). *The General Mills American family report, 1978–79.* Minneapolis, MN: General Mills.

Zabin, L. S., Kantner, J. F., & Zelnik, M. (1979). The risk of adolescent pregnancy in the first months of intercourse. *Family Planning Perspectives, 11,* 215–222.

Zelnik, M. (1979). Sex education and knowledge of pregnancy risk among U.S. teenage women. *Family Planning Perspectives, 11,* 355–357.

Zelnik, M., Kantner, J. F., & Ford, K. (1981). *Sex and pregnancy in adolescence.* Beverly Hills, CA: Sage.

Zelnik, M., & Kim, Y. J. (1982). Sex education and its association with teenage sexual activity, pregnancy and contraceptive use. *Family Planning Perspectives, 14,* 117–126.

Zelnik, M., & Shah, F. K. (1983). First intercourse among young Americans. *Family Planning Perspectives, 15,* 64–70.

Zilbergeld, B. (1978). *Male sexuality.* Boston: Little, Brown.

Zongker, C. E. (1977). The self-concept of pregnant adolescent girls. *Adolescence, 12,* 477–488.

Zuehlke, M. E., & Rogel, M. J. (1981, August). *Adolescent peers as facilitators of contraceptive use.* Paper presented at the meeting of the American Psychological Association, Los Angeles.

Zuehlke, M. E., & Rogel, M. J. (1982, November). *Adolescent contraceptive use: A model intervention.* Paper presented at the meeting of the Academy of Psychosomatic Medicine, Chicago.

Zuengler, K. L., & Neubeck, G. (1983). Sexuality: Developing togetherness. In H. I. McCubbin & C. R. Figley (Eds.), *Stress and the family, Volume I: Coping with normative transitions* (pp. 41–53). New York: Brunner/Mazel.

CHAPTER 24

Educational Influences

John Murphy

Education for Homo sapiens has been part and parcel of existence. The processes of transmitting ideas, images, and language, of sharing behaviors and values, of leading others into patterns of thought, of training individuals to decision-making, have been argued, fought about, analyzed, studied and researched.

This chapter is about what education does to the adolescent, that phase of human development that this handbook has been defining, describing, and exploring. These pages will look at educational influences, both in their common place and cosmic dimensions, to give another focus on the many factors affecting adolescence. Education in the form of schooling has become one of the primary adolescent experiences, even though schooling was unknown to 90% of our population at the beginning of this century.

What is the meaning of influence? The word includes positive and negative aspects, so that perhaps the absence of education may be negative, or some of the actual processes of education may cause negative influences. If we are aware of the major critiques of American high schools, we may believe that much of the education for adolescents is less than praiseworthy. Positive influences may be seen in increased literacy, greater opportunities for learning for all

levels of society, and especially improved possibilities for adolescents considered in the disadvantaged minorities (e.g., the handicapped, members of certain racial and ethnic groups, and women).

We direct our attention to the term "educational." The writings of major American education historians, such as Lawrence Cremin (1966) and Bernard Bailyn (1960), have shown the multiplicity of forces and institutions that constitute education—an extremely important factor because access to schools for most of the population was rare in the 17th, 18th, and even 19th centuries. Rightfully considered, the church, the family, and the community all were educational influences, each with rules and traditions, crafts and trades, values and systems. In our day, we have added visual and audio tools of transmission, profoundly altering the receptions of ideas, images, and values unknown to any civilization before. Moreover, today we have another educational institution—widely available and generally required—formal schools for most adolescents. And they are actually a new and critical factor to our life's experiences. Schools are an integral part, in a way never experienced before, of the universal passage of adolescents from childhood to adulthood. A society in which the major portion of adolescents will not experience the rites of passage within some type of school/educational control is becoming increasingly rare. Importantly, this widespread educational influence on adolescent development is only occurring in the past 50 years of the history of humankind.

ADOLESCENT LEARNING: A SEARCH

What do young people learn in the adolescent years? Perhaps one way to look at this phenomenon is to refer to the historical experiences given us in many ways (e.g., through literature, religious expressions, and cultural rites). A recalling from our own knowledge of myths, fables, epics, and religious narratives will confirm that the adolescent experience has frequently been considered an exploration and examination of the world by a rapidly developing individual. It is a story about someone soon to be, in the process of attaining independence from nurturing roots.

Erik Erikson (1968) has made the "identity crisis" a part of our general vocabulary and has introduced many of us to the concept of "conflict resolution" in stages of development necessary to move forward to human growth. In the adolescent period, it is interesting to think in terms of the adolescent being educated by new and separate experiences not explained or referred back simply to father or mother. There are new, and as yet uncertain, directors and directions. There is trial and error. In the adolescent struggles of yore, the conflict was more easily identified with the world outside the self, but it was necessary for the person to go out, to seek, to conquer. Of course, on the contemporary issue, the role of the young women in fable and myth was less sung about, but there were some similarities. Ruth in the Bible must go away, must leave her own people; the woman in marriage must break away from her own family, albeit to another one, but she will learn from the new society. In the Grimm's tales, the young girl is subjected to forests, wolves, outside evil, but is more frequently the rescued rather than the rescuer. This is an area that needs to be explored more fully as contemporary educational influences change the perception of sexual differences.

The idea of the young person as seeker who moves away to find self is fascinating, because it also indicates the need for personal choice, for alternatives, for possibilities of success and fail-

ure, and for challenge. Today, curiously enough, our American secondary school adolescent experience is very frequently challenged because it is educationally or academically unchallenging or inflexible.

EVOLUTION OF THE SCHOOL

What of the more structured intellectual or religious formation or education of the past for adolescents? For all ages, most people were unschooled, most frequently unlettered, and accessibility to formal schooling was probably limited to 1% of the world's population up to our age. As we know, the transmission of a culture's ideas and values occurred through many modes, such as architecture, drama, religious ritual, festivals, and rites of passages that gave meaning to existence and that educated. However, the idea of formal education in some set place with a period of extended study, apart from the day-to-day existence of work and survival, was restricted to very few. And if we believe the limited documentation of daily existence throughout man's history, it was only the ruling, propertied, or religious class or castes. Perhaps, if it had been left to Plato, education would be only for those capable of high moral and intellectual achievement.

In our Western society, the growth of more widely based schooling, outside the monastic traditions, began with the advent of printing, with the accessibility of reading materials, and with the growth of a mercantile class to whom some formal learning was essential. Add to that, the religious fervor of the Reformation with a call to some of the Christian community to look more personally and individually at the scriptures. However, even as the number of "colleges" grew in England and on the continent, there was not a great thrust to reach out to the bulk of the population, whose needs were not considered in terms of academic time and study. Ciphering and some writing might be needed, but education that moved the common man to that level of the propertied, noble, or clerical classes was not a consideration.

THE AMERICAN APPROACH

In our own country, new elements were to become operative in the late 18th and early 19th centuries to prepare for what would be the radical idea of popular-based education—education for all the worthy common men. The early colonial heritage of schooling had begun with the establishment of Harvard, Yale, and Princeton to carry on the divinely ordered work of salvation. By the mid-1700s, other forces more economically and politically directed were moving through our new society. Two major American figures, noted principally for their work in politics, gave a thrust to what would become American education's radically new direction. These men were Benjamin Franklin and Thomas Jefferson.

Benjamin Franklin

Franklin, born in 1706, ended his formal education at 10 because the schools of the day offered very little to a young man of Franklin's background and interest. The high price to a family of his class and means was also a discouraging factor, but even more of a deterrent was the formal structure of instruction and the distinct emphasis on the classical and the clerical. As Best (1962) wrote, "Franklin's recognition of some of these difficulties led to his effort to reform and redirect the educational establishment of his time" (p. 3).

One of Franklin's major efforts was the foundation of an academy based on his own design, created with a curriculum that would be directly useful to preparing young men for any trade or profession, a major breakthrough for its day. It was a utilitarian revision of the schooling of his day because it placed the students' needs at the center of the school. The academy program was to be equal to the classical offering, both within the same walls—almost a precursor of our contemporary comprehensive high school. In Franklin's thinking, this academy would not only prepare young men for college, but it would also offer a complete secondary education for the trades and the professions, and the instruction would be in the vernacular, English. This would set the tone for this new society and for the need for an education that could be achieved on time and with practicality.

Jefferson to Dewey

With Thomas Jefferson, we have the other major direction. It was he who first articulated "the inextricable tie between education and the politics of a free society" (Cremin, 1966, p. 5). By 1816 he had proposed a state education system that would provide 3 years of public schooling to every free white child of the Commonwealth of Virginia and then provide, for the brightest students, grammar (or elementary) school and college, free of charge.

In both these seminal thinkers, there are the roots of American secondary education today; roots that go to the immediate needs of society, to the political and social values; roots that touch as many members of the community as possible. It was not to be an elite world of tradition or wealth alone.

Importantly, in the American approach, this radical direction needed a practical solution of financing and public support. This breakthrough comes with Horace Mann's solution for a statewide system that began at a local level and that provided a public institution at the elementary or grammar-school level available to all citizens, and basically paid for by all as a common good.

What emerged was then an institution, a formal school. The path from Jefferson to Horace Mann to John Dewey was an unbroken line that goes on to our time. Cremin's (1966) words are critical:

> There is a subtle shift of emphasis when the idea (of Jefferson) gets to Dewey, however, that is worth discussing, since it highlights certain crucial elements in the American theory of popular education. Jefferson was a great believer in schooling, but it never occurred to him that schooling would be the chief educational influence on the young. . . . Public education was to be only one part of the education of the public, and a relatively minor part of that. (p. 6)

Dewey believed that all of life educates and, of course, that "deliberate" education was only one part of the education of a person. As Cremin writes, Dewey advanced "the characteristic complaint of early twentieth-century progressives: industrialism is destroying the traditional home, shop, neighborhood; they are no longer performing their educational functions." Who or what can step in? "Public education would become co-extensive with the education of the public" (pp. 8–9). It was a significant move and one that, if you consider the secondary school today, should cause us to reflect on the role of the teacher, the adviser, the work of social reform, the school as desegregator, as the place for special education, for moral values.

THE HIGH SCHOOL

While the theoreticians and movers were basically creating a new model, the work of creating the actual form of secondary education evolved slowly and fascinatingly. Officially, the first high school comes in 1821, the Boston English School, with 100 boys enrolled during its first years. This was basically established because of a feeling that the existing grammar schools were inadequate for the day and because most people could not afford to send their children to private academies. The work of extending the support that Horace Mann garnered by the midcentury for elementary education then needed the support of the courts to give an emphasis for secondary education at tax payers' expense throughout the country.

The idea of public-supported secondary education did not come as an automatic given after the general establishment of elementary education. To many, it was a question of legality. Was the state free to utilize tax funds and make attendance requirements for this form of education, which in the history of man had been available only to a few by the right of birth or money? Were the laws for elementary school to be applied to secondary? Through a series of state court cases during the 1870s—the most famous, the Kalamazoo Decision of the Supreme Court of Michigan in 1872—it was decided that it was legal for communities to tax themselves for the support of public high schools. And what had evolved by then was an American institution—a comprehensive school, an institution for the college-preparatory student, the vocational-preparation student, and the student who fitted into neither category.

The Committee of Ten: 1893

This high school, by the turn of the century, enrolled approximately 10% of our adolescent population, and, although now legally a part of our American system, in practice had still not resolved its own mind about what was to be valued. In 1893, a Report of the Committee of Ten sponsored by the National Education Association caught the ambiguity of the day. Although the committee recommended a liberalization and expansion of course sequences at the secondary level, it took a conservative stance regarding the purposes of high-school educa-

tion, interestingly enough, a position not in accord with the "education for the common man" movement of the previous decades. This report influenced secondary-school curricula and college-entrance standards for many years. Some of the words of the report indicate the problem facing American secondary education in those years, and that would continue to our time:

> Secondary schools, taken as a whole, do not exist for the purposes of preparing boys and girls for colleges. . . . Their main function is to prepare for the duties of life that small proportion of all the children in the country—a proportion small in number, but very important to the welfare of the nation—who show themselves able to profit by an education prolonged to the eighteenth year, and whose parents are able to support them while they remain so long at school . . . the preparation of a few pupils for college should in the ordinary secondary school be the incidental and not the principal object. At the same time, it is obviously desirable that the colleges and scientific schools should be accessible to all boys and girls who have completed creditably the secondary school course. (Hillsheim & Merrill, 1971, p. 357)

We were to have a common school, with an uncommon problem of curricula for different futures.

The Cardinal Principles: 1918

By 1918, another view became more publicly acceptable, reflecting in practice the more pragmatic and democratic viewpoints that were implicit in the idea of American secondary education. Moving away from the more rigid curricula recommendations of 1893, "The Cardinal Principles of Secondary Education" gave the following as the main objectives of education:

1. Health
2. Command of fundamental processes
3. Worthy home-membership
4. Vocation
5. Citizenship
6. Worthy use of leisure
7. Ethical character

A new perception of life in the 20th century provides this significant description under the objective, "Command of fundamental processes": "Much of the energy of the elementary school . . . is to teaching, reading, writing, arithmetical computation. . . . The facility that a child of 12 or 14 may acquire in the use of these tools *is not sufficient* [italics added] for the needs of modern life" (Hillsheim & Merrill, 1971, p. 374). Another significant comment, adding to a new dimension of education, is under "Worthy use of leisure":

> The school was failed . . . to organize and direct the social activities of young people as it should, . . . the school . . . has a unique opportunity . . . because it includes in its membership representatives from all classes of society and consequently is able through social relationships to establish bonds of friendship and understanding that can not be furnished by other agencies. (Hillsheim & Merrill, 1971, p. 376)

With this document we have the school ideal as developed by Dewey, that institution conceived of in *Democracy and Education* and *Schools of Tomorrow*, the institution of social change. It is a statement that logically leads to George S. Counts' 1932 work *Dare the School Build a New Social Order?* Fascinatingly enough, 22 years late, the Supreme Court then gives a description of education, perhaps surpassing what the educators might ever have dreamed about:

> Today, education is perhaps the most important function of state and local governments. Compulsory school-attendance laws and the great expenditures for education both demonstrate our recognition of the importance of education to our democratic society. . . . It is the very foundation of good citizenship . . . is a principal instrument in awakening the child to cultural values . . . for later professional training and in helping him adjust normally to his environment. (Beckner & Dumas, 1970, p. 202)

These words of the court are a far cry from the private academy and the Latin school, with their limited availability to the common men. We now call for full support of an institution that encompasses all or most of life's preparation. The above quotation is from the 1954 court decision on segregation, *Brown vs. Board of Education*. It would seem that education, in its own way, could rebuild the social order. This institution of schooling, the form that education has taken in our day, would be primary experience of life and its values, now from ages 6 through 18.

By the 1960s all states required attendance to at least 16 years of age (although hardly all students were enrolled), and some required attendance even to the age of 18. By the 1970s over 97% of adolescents aged 14–17 were enrolled either in public or private schools.

Two charts give the best overview of the amazing growth of "the educational influence" on adolescents of the American high school, especially in the public sector.

Figure 24.1 is the public-high-school enrollment from 1900 through 1981.

Figure 24.2 gives another view of the data, equally impressive in terms of adolescents completing high school.

The Comprehensive High School

The school was becoming more and more comprehensive. By the late 1950s, another major document by James B. Conant (1959), *The American High School Today*, was describing and defining the unique American situation. Significantly, in the foreword, the president of the Carnegie Corporation of New York (related to the 1983 sponsor of *High School* by Boyer) gives us the clearest view of this idea:

> The comprehensive high school—a peculiarly American phenomenon . . . because it offers, under one administration and one roof, secondary education for almost all the high-school-age children of one town or neighborhood . . . for educating the boy who will be an atomic scientist and the girl who will marry at eighteen; . . . in sum, for providing good and appropriate education, both academic and vocational, for all the young people within a democratic environment which the American people believe serves the principles they cherish. (Conant, 1959, pp. ix–x)

Conant's own words, about the effectiveness of the approach, are in another work in 1967. He noted that these schools provide the opportunity for students from different backgrounds to get along with one another. He wrote, "If this ideal had been overriding in all states and all communities a century ago, there would have been no segregated schools" (p. 8).

TODAY'S IMAGES

The statistics, questions, and issues of the 1980s remind us that the institution of schools for adolescents is now an experience for most

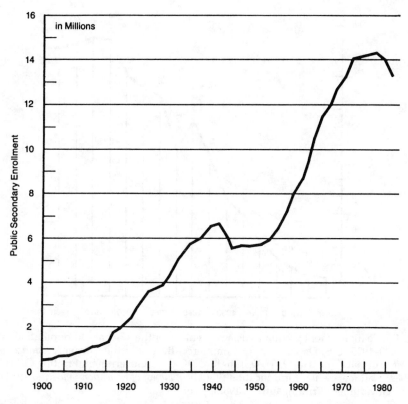

Figure 24.1. Public high school enrollment, 1900–1961. (Data from: 1900–1916: U.S. Department of Commerce, Bureau of the Census, *Historical Statistics of the United States: Colonial Times to 1970.* (Washington, DC: Government Printing Office, 1975), pp. 368–69; 1917–1954: Unpublished data, National Center for Education Statistics; 1955–1961: National Center for Education Statistics, *Digest of Education Statistics: 1966,* (Washington, DC: Government Printing Office, 1966), p. 24; 1962–1973: *Digest of Education Statistics: 1973,* p. 31; 1974–1981, *Digest of Education Statistics: 1982,* p. 38.)

Americans alive today. And this experience has its own images in our minds. We all have personal images and popular images produced by another experience and institution—media, whether it be radio, film, television, VCR, newspaper—and, for an increasingly few—literature. These images and concepts are part of the input data for the educational influence on adolescents. Frequently, we are informed that the "medium is the message," or we become what we are told we are. It is not within the scope of this work to consider the full data, but questions about what students believe about education and the expected behavior in school and what messages the students are receiving from the media need to be addressed.

There has been a progression of images about education, teachers, students, and schools. The simplicity of learning in the one-room school house is exemplified by *Little House on the Prairie,* the book and the television program. As the experience of schooling grew, and more and more adolescents went on to secondary learning, it is curious that the high schools were the place for other experiences (e.g., growing up socially, class/cast distinctions, sport rivalries, romance). In the United States, Andy Hardy was the early popular high-school boy. For many of us, the first film depicting nonromantic or comedy setting for schools was *Blackboard Jungle,* the indictment of the urban problem schools. These were followed by *To Sir With Love,* and *If. Welcome Back Kotter,* a popular television program, created a situation comedy based on problems of urban youth in a classroom situation. The typical adolescent in school

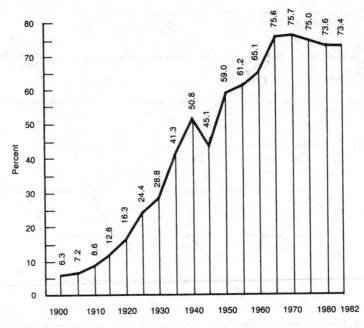

Figure 24.2. Public high school graduates as a percentage of the 17-year-old population, 1900–1982. (Data from: 1900–1935: U.S. Department of Commerce, Bureau of the Census, *Historical Statistics of the United States: Colonial Times to 1970* (Washington, DC: U.S. Government Printing Office, 1975), p. 379; 1940–1982: National Center for Education Statistics, *Digest of Education Statistics: 1982* (Washington, DC: U.S. Government Printing Office, 1982), p. 65.)

was depicted as anti-establishment and totally uninvolved with the planned course of studies. The school is the background for adolescent growth (e.g., *Happy Days, American Graffitti, Lords of Flatbush*). By the 1980s, the type of adolescent experience in film has changed (e.g., *Ridgemont High, Porky's Risky Business,* and *Angel*: high school honor student by day, prostitute by night.)

In all, the school is rarely depicted as the setting for success stories in learning or as an effective institution. Teachers, particularly teachers and tutors in American culture, are more lightly or comically presented. The image of doctors and lawyers in the media, on the other hand, has been one of general competence, for the most part. The family, as institution, has been positive, although perhaps innocuous. Education and schooling have had a mixed reception. The high school has not achieved a strong role in the popular mind and experience.

The popular image is hard to measure. It is easier to call upon the statistics available, to review the many reports on schooling in America,

and to compare our work here with other countries and cultures. We do need, of course, to see what information is available today to help us understand the adolescents' world at school and to hear the critics.

Two Critics: Goodman and Friedenberg

Let us start with the critics of American secondary education. Although there have been four major reports or studies in the 1980s alone that touch upon secondary education, two voices popular in the early 1960s need to be reheard as preliminary to the general criticism of today.

Although James Conant's thinking on high schools was prominent in 1959, another writer was asking different questions, a forerunner of many of the challenges of the 1960s and our day. Most important to some were Paul Goodman's (1956) questions and issues in *Growing Up Absurd*. Some are very prophetic still in the 1980s. He called Conant's report "superficial," and commented on teacher burnout, which he characterized by "despair and deep resignation." There is the perennial problem of inadequate financing, and the "academic curriculum . . . mangled by the demands of reactionaries, liberals, and demented worriors" (Goodman, 1956, pp. 25–26). He also made an important statement that "education is not life," in contrast to the ideal that education is more dominant than family and church and community today.

Another voice about American educational influences in 1963 was Edgar Z. Friedenberg (1967) in *Coming of Age in America*. He stressed the idea that the school affects society. "It alters individuals, their values, their sense of personal worth, their patterns of anxiety and sense of mastery and ease in the world. . . . The school endorses and supports values and patterns of behavior of certain segments of the population" (p. 49). These questions are still being examined, and by many other disciplines, as we redefine our "habits of the heart," in the last half of this century.

The 1980s

By the 1980s, we had reports: The National Commission on Excellence in Education, *A Nation at Risk*; the National Research Center of Chicago report authored by Coleman, *High School and Beyond: A National Longitudinal Study for the 1980's*; a major statement on the intellectual life—Mortimer Adler's *The Paideia Proposal*; and the Carnegie Foundation for the Advancement of the Teacher report authored by Boyer, *High School—A Report on Secondary Education in America*. This latter work, based on studies in the field and including assistance of major American education spokespersons from the 1950s through the 1980s is a significant statement and one that can provide a base for the issue of educational influences.

The document is valuable in its data about current curriculum approaches, time actually utilized in the school, teacher training, students, values, and national aims. Its primary thrust was to look for ways of developing a core curriculum, with a centrality of language and the development of critical thinking. It starts with the assumption that "all our future depends on public education," a strong charge for a relatively new institution.

The first listed conclusion is to clarify the goals of education, followed by a return to centrality of language and the relationship of curriculum to a changing national and global context, a move away from the simpler American citizenship role of the Cardinal Principles of 1918. The topics show the traditional areas— goals, teachers, structure, leadership—and some new topics in our day—teaching/learning, technology, and connections beyond the campus.

How many students are in what number of schools in America? In the report we find about 10% (roughly 2.9 million) of the students are in the cities. Fifty-six percent (4.5 million students) are in rural areas, with school districts sometimes extending hundreds of miles. Thirty-four percent (6.3 million students) are in the suburbs. Slightly more than half, almost 82,000, are 4-year institutions. About 4,400 combine junior and senior high, and another 32,000 are 3-year schools, beginning at 10th grade. And most of these public high schools have fewer than 30% minority enrollment.

Troubled Institution

The choice of the words "the troubled institution" (not too far removed from David Elkind's chapter "Schools for Scandal," in *All Grown Up and No Place to Go*, 1984) gives the general viewpoint of most critics. Boyer's (1983) findings are basically that we are not satisfied with our performance, as recorded by testing. In fact, we have been shocked and disappointed by reports of continuously failing test scores. Yet, as Boyer points out, these past decades were also a period of major social unrest, reevaluation, and restructuring of some basic institutions, such as family life. The overall performance, however, is not healthy, because "our schools are surviving, not thriving" (p. 38).

High School (Boyer, 1983) makes a provocative statement about the raison d'être in one purpose of the school that is extraordinary. "High school *is* home for many students. It also is one institution where it is all right to be young. Here, teenagers meet each other, share hopes and fears, start love affairs, and experiment with growing up" (p. 38). How comprehensive has the institution become? The school, following the direction set for social development in 1918, is now called upon to provide the services and transmit the values we used to expect from the community, home, and church. But it has even exceeded the idea that the school should direct social activities. For some of our adolescents, it is *the* activity of their years.

Boyer (1983) asks: What do Americans want high school to accomplish? Quite simply, "we want it all." And yet, consider the words of Arthur Bestor in 1953: "The idea that the school must undertake every need that some other agency is failing to meet regardless of the suitability of the school room to the task is a preposterous delusion that in the end can wreck the educational institution" (p. 75).

If we think we want it all, do we understand what the schooling of today means to the students, have we measured in any significant way what "all" this does to adolescence? What about those who cannot cope with all we offer or demand or who reject some part of the experience by dropping out?

American society, of course, needs a trained people, as well as a nation with cohesive values. Some of the students in our high schools are succeeding well in the process of education. In spite of all the major complaints, some students thrive. It seems fascinating that many of us learn to survive, and achieve as well, but we are uncertain as to what happened to us in process and how it happened. Frequently, for example, in my graduate classes, I ask my students to recall positive learning experiences. It is perhaps a minor commentary on all of the research data that my generally achieving students have difficulty recalling many, if any, learning experiences that were memorable at the secondary level.

What is Happening?

In a recent study, *Being Adolescent* by Csikszentmihalyi and Larson (1984), the authors examined the problem of "coping with classes" and suggested that we do not yet have major data as to "what the educational process does to the self as a whole, not just to its cognitive dimensions" (p. 199). From the researchers' perspective the schools are essentially machines for providing negative feedback. These writers, in the direction of Friedenberg (1967), argue that a community "needs people who are self-confident, motivated to achieve yet respectful of others, who are adaptable, original, and at peace with their own selves, more than it needs

students who score high on tests" (p. 199). The traits listed above are difficult to measure; on the other hand, academic performance would be considered easy in comparison. Therefore, these researchers point out that schools are evaluated in terms of what can be measured and the rest is ignored. "It is impossible to tell how much harm or good schools do until the total impact of formal education can be assessed, not only its most obvious cognitive results" (p. 199). In placing the emphasis on the total person in the school setting, the authors are reinforcing the quotation they use from Friedenberg: "What is learned in high school, or for that matter anywhere at all, depends far less on what is taught than on what one actually experiences in the place" (Friedenberg, 1966, p. 89).

AN AMERICAN SOLUTION

In each stage of our educational history, we have chosen a particularly unique thrust. Often, however, we looked elsewhere and argued that European and (now) Oriental schooling was more demanding and produced more than our popular American approach with its high schools called "people's colleges." Frequently, the private schools utilized the English or European model of upper and lower forms, with a traditional classical curriculum.

Americans have generally known little about other models of education, and most of the immigrants of the late 19th or early 20th century came from among the less educated populations of their own counties. We did not pay much attention, in our comparisons with the results in other countries, of the role of early selection or determination of life by testing or screening, common in the European model, which eliminated many students from advancement through what we call the comprehensive school. We, however, have the largest percentage of students in secondary education, we are a popular-based form of schooling, and we allow mobility and failure up through the age of 18 for all.

An example of the differences between the major industrial nations (Figure 24.3) will be evident by seeing the proportions of adolescents in the 15–18 range who were enrolled in school in 1970 (Van Til, 1978, p. 129).

The lower figure for what we term secondary

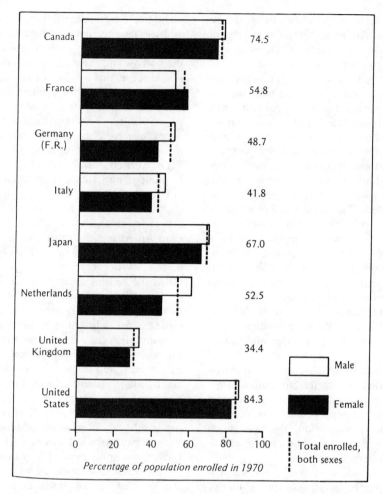

Figure 24.3. Population aged 15–18 enrolled in education. The education enrollment of U.S. teenagers of both sexes is higher than that of other countries. (From: *The Condition of Education* (p. 170), 1976, U.S. Government Printing Office, Washington, DC.)

education is due mostly to tracking and earlier release into the working force of many adolescents. We, in our "comprehensive approach" for the larger population, avoided the dual system of education that had characterized secondary education in Europe. In the words of Van Til (1978),

> The democratic ideal was furthered through avoiding one set of schools for the prosperous who were destined for college attendance and another set of schools for the people who could not afford to attend college and would, at first, enter the job market much earlier. (p. 128)

THE JAPANESE CHALLENGE

One country, Japan, has attracted considerable attention in our concern today about economic superiority or survival. It is argued that a superior economic and educational approach has made the Japanese nation a major force, and that our own system of schools, especially the high school—"the troubled institution," "the school for scandal"—could look to the East for a more efficient and satisfactory model.

A widely distributed series of essays on schooling in Japan in *Education Week* (Ranbom, 1985) documented the many aspects of similarities and contrasts in the American and Japanese school systems. An interesting title, in view of our comprehensive approach, is "The Total System," which described Japan's precollege curriculum designed to produce a "high minimum of learning in all students and at the same time to imbue with them the historic moral and social values of the culture" (p. 19). It would seem we both want it all, but actually the American and Japanese systems, according to this report, are antithetical, mirror images of one another, designed with different goals in mind. At the heart of the matter, two fundamental differences are present: The broad scope of Japanese schooling—beyond any similar institutional bond in America—grows out of the Japanese's historical search for harmony and social order, "producing strong family ties, clear lines of authority, and planned group-mobilized efforts toward common goals" (p. 20). Quickly it comes to mind that we have a very different heritage and direction: We are a frontier people stressing the individual's freedom and search for the new.

The unity of the Japanese system and the power and efficiency of its curriculum come from strong, centralized planning. The national government is in control of the aims, content, form, and pace of education. We have yet to decide whether there should be a powerful federal arm of education.

In the Japanese school system, there is a merit-ordered hierarchy of schools and students, determined principally by test scores. In many eyes, it has worked with success, providing the Japanese economic system with assembly-line workers and corporate executives through a type of quality education that has provided the world's most literate and highly skilled population. We ask the question: What impact does the Japanese system have on adolescent development? What type of influence is that? Do we have a value system that would call some of their approaches unacceptable to our hierarchy of values, our sense of human development?

In Ranbom's second essay, "High School— Cultural Values in Conflict," a chart is offered on values as seen by the students from the two countries (Table 24.1). The list is worthwhile from the standpoint of the similarities and the contrasts.

Questions of self-esteem and control of one's own life are significant values in American life, and we have created an educational institution where adolescents seem comfortable about themselves and their ability to perform at some point. Yet, is this a value for an educational institution, or should the product or outcome be of paramount importance? Many people supposedly think of the good old days when students "received" a good education. One does not get the impression from *The Republic* that Plato worried about individual happiness or fulfillment, and a state in life was assigned rather than chosen.

Other areas need to be noted briefly in the report on Japan. Many school systems, other than American, use testing to separate, eliminate, and select out, rather than just to report on the state of everyone's progress. The key article in the second essay on Japanese schooling begins with "Examination Hell." Being accepted by the right university assures success, but the struggle for admission dominates students' lives and distorts, many argue, the content and purpose of high school. Americans worry about SAT scores, and there are some for whom the right college is very critical, but we have not produced such trauma in the academic field, nor created such a tension. Surprisingly, in the report, the question arises whether, in assessing the psychological tool of testing, the meritocracy has gone awry. "Many in Japan . . . attribute their country's alarming increase in incidents of school violence—particularly assaults against teachers—to the psychological toll taken by examination hell" (Ranbom, 1985, p. 16).

The school system, also, is touched by other problems more familiar to our scene (e.g., the classroom rebel) and by the call for moral education, the question of permissiveness, and the change in family life. Less noted generally by many commentators, but discussed by Ranbom, is the role of women in Japanese society, a major interest in assessing any educational influences today. In the rapid increase of women's studies here in some universities, the civil rights issue of women as a privileged minority, the legislation of discrimination in athletics, we have an area of concern and study. Both societies in all these areas are raising new questions about the meaning of education suitable for the 20th century.

Table 24.1. Attitudes of 1980 Japanese and American High-School Seniors

VARIABLE	JAPAN			UNITED STATES		
	ALL SENIORS	MALES	FEMALES	ALL SENIORS	MALES	FEMALES
Self-esteem (agree):						
I'm a person of worth	30%	37%	19%	90%	90%	89%
I'm satisfied with myself	28	32	24	79	80	79
At times, I think I'm no good	59	49	71	46	41	51
I have the ability to complete college*	39	49	27	81	80	81
Locus of control (agree):						
Good luck is more important than hard work for success	25	28	21	11	13	9
What happens is my own doing	59	60	59	77	79	76
Plans hardly ever work out	74	70	78	23	20	25
Life values (seen as very important):						
Success in line of work	84	89	78	88	89	88
Marriage and happy family life	81	80	82	81	78	84
Lots of money	28	35	19	31	40	23
Strong friendships	92	91	94	81	81	82
Finding steady work	69	68	71	84	86	83
Being a community leader	8	13	2	10	12	7
Giving my children better opportunities	43	43	44	67	67	66
Living close to parents and relatives	13	14	10	14	13	15
Getting away from this area of country	27	30	23	14	15	14
Correcting social and economic inequalities	22	24	18	13	12	14
Having children	55	55	54	39	34	44
Having leisure time	67	72	61	70	72	69
Work choice values (seen as very important):						
Previous experience in the area	26	29	22	31	30	32
Good income to start	22	24	20	46	48	43
Job security and permanence	70	64	77	58	58	58
Important and interesting work	89	89	89	86	81	89
Freedom to make own decisions	55	61	47	62	47	53
Meeting and working with friendly people	72	69	76	66	58	73

*The Japanese question uses "enter" instead of "complete" because the dropout rate from college is negligibly small in Japan.
Note. From: National Center for Education Statistics, 1983.

TWO MAJOR INFLUENCES

The earliest major argument or rationale for education in our Western world is found in Plato's view of the problem of society and stability in *The Republic*. In looking at the "just" society, Socrates dialogues about the meaning of existence and what would have to be done to achieve a just and lasting world. Important to his operation of the world would be the choice of material to be studied, who should study, and those "guardians" who should be entrusted with the transmission of that body of knowledge. We are still asking the same Platonic questions, and the answers are still so complex.

Who should be educated has been solved in our view, even though everyone may not choose to use the service. What, as human beings, we decide is worth handing over to other persons, and how to do it, are still in question. This leads us to two major educational "influences" today: the curriculum and the teachers—topics in every report, every suggestion, every recommendation on schooling and education today.

Curriculum

Curriculum involves the idea of a course, a race, a pattern to be followed that has a "determined" end. For most societies, meaning of life and values and behaviors were worked out in a definite pattern, learned and accepted, if not fully understood. The idea of progression in stages of life, of matching ideas and actions to intellectual and physical development, or of selecting out important principles, was part of charting this course. Plato's first concern, after selecting the students, was what material was suitable to achieve the goals he had set. It is still valuable for us today to read the material suitable and acceptable and the unsatisfactory subjects (e.g., role models described in fable who are strong and show no weaknesses or martial-type music used to avoid the inculcation of weak or "romantic" feelings). Plato is firm in the narrowness of his curriculum because he understands how easy it is to be distracted or to miss the carefully designed goal.

In exploring this early model, it is easier to call for the inclusion of some contemporary words used in the educational literature such as creativity, imagination, freedom, or electives, motivation, consensus, future thinking. However, even with the use of new terminology, we still have to resolve the basic problems in curriculum—How much freedom is suitable for a student in choosing the materials to be learned? Do we want creative problem-solving individuals in our society? Is it necessary for us to agree on a common view of life and to have our adolescents today be secure in their assigned roles?

The earlier curriculum decisions for our high schools in the 1893 statement of the Committee of Ten and the 1918 Cardinal Principles represent more direct and perhaps narrower statements on social policy. The students received direction about what courses to take, and the definitions of expected behavior were, in the minds of the authors, easier to formulate. Generally, in those years, we did not have to face decisions about 90% of the adolescent population in schools. The greater the number involved, with the wider range of abilities, decisions, interests, and suitabilities, the greater the number of curriculum decisions we thought we had to make. If the content or meaning of present life is uncertain, it becomes more difficult to create a working plan for a curriculum that now encompasses all of life for adolescents. Ambiguity for many in our society is frightening, because many feel a need for some canopy ("sacred" or otherwise) that will give meaning to the universe. Others have suggested that we have meaning, but that its contemporary is searching for a new language.

Language Values

Robert Bellah and a team of researchers (Bellah, Madsen, Sullivan, Swidler, & Tipton, 1985) have recently explored, in *Habits of the Heart*, the equation of individualism and commitment in American life, two terms that are also critical to American education. These writers note that success, freedom, and justice are found in all central strands of our culture. Importantly, these concepts have characterized the underlying ideas for American education from its roots in Franklin and Jefferson, to Dewey, and to Conant's hope that our schools would be the instrument of social reform. It is under the umbrella of justice in civil rights that education has moved to assist the minorities and the handicapped to an extent never before attempted on such a broad base.

How Americans understand and verbalize these concepts is critical also to our clarification of goals in education. Bellah et al. write:

> The common difficulties . . . different people face in justifying the goals of a morally good life point to a characteristic problem of people in our culture. For most of us, it is easier to think about how to get what we want than to know what exactly we should want. . . . are confused about how to define such things such as the nature of success, the meaning of freedom, and the requirements of justice. (p. 21)

As our educational commentators are calling for goal setting, we are faced with the need of a suitable language, a means of articulating what we feel, our "habits of the heart." Bellah's thrust is provocative. In the team's conversations with Americans on the meaning of our tradition, they came to realize that:

> Although we have to rely on our traditions to answer those questions (about justice, freedom, success), we will have to probe those traditions much more critically than we are used to doing if we are going to make sense of the challenges posed by the rapidly changing world in which we live. (p. 22)

In that context, one of the reports, Boyer's (1983) *High School*, calls for a "core of common learning" for the American high school, a curriculum that should be a study of those "consequential ideas, experiences, and traditions common to all of us by virtue of our membership in the human family at a particular moment of history" (p. 95).

The curriculum is spelled out briefly in the following categories: Literature, United States History, Western Civilization, Nonwestern Civilization, Science and the Natural World, Technology, Mathematics, Foreign Language, The Arts, Civics, Health, Work. To that are added a Senior Independent Project, a transition period between work and learning.

What becomes evident is that our curriculum, with its consequent impact on human growth, has expanded in scope almost as much as the number of our students. We not only want it all, but all may have to know it all, by the age of 18. (Note that Boyer's report makes no major study of the media a part of the curriculum.)

The Teacher

The final component of educational influences in this chapter is the teacher, the immediate transmitter, contact, and instrument of schooling. If we now have historically an extraordinary number of adolescents in this process of schooling, we need a comparable number of adults to take leadership or supervisory roles. This requires a look at the relation of teacher to curriculum, and the training of teachers.

The question of teacher freedom in the classroom is old. How freely we lead students was a question faced by Socrates. Plato realized that it would be important to educate certain individuals to see the truth, a process of great rigor and discipline that did not allow for deviation from the known truth. As you read *The Republic*, with its sections on the training of the guardians, the importance of understanding the common good, and the control of the emotions, each calls for educators who do not seek their own truth, but rather transmit the truths entrusted to them. *The Republic* provides an insight into teaching methods that remained very constant for most of mankind's history. One brief passage about the poet, who gives truth, will bear out the paradox of being a teacher:

> We shall employ the poets and story-tellers of the more austere and less attractive type, who will reproduce only the manner of a person of high character and, in the substance of their discourse, conform to those rules we laid down . . . (Plato, 400 B.C./1941, p. 85)

In our society, everyone is calling for a renewal of the teaching profession, but the question of the role of the teacher has not been clarified. We mentioned that the image of teacher in the media was not strong, but part of the teacher's problems has always been the instrument/servant type of role expectation. There have always been traditions of behavior that teachers were bound to in terms of their marital status, dress, and public conduct, because these people were the "guardians" of the young and had to be above reproach. Although the school was to be considered "in loco parentis," it was also presumed that the teachers would represent what was best in the community and would be the faithful transmitter of this knowledge. Now that the school, and, in our view, the high school, has become the primary educational influence of the adolescent, the teachers seemingly bear the burden of the primary role models and developers of values (intellectual, social, etc.).

Who are these persons of such great significance and importance to our society, and how do we prepare them to be the educational influence? The development of teaching is a formal skill and as a profession is very new. There were always great teachers, persons who profoundly influenced others, but moving from the art of teaching to the development of a replicable skill for many is a basically 20th-century practice. Without a major digression, the beginnings of teacher education run rather closely with the growth of the student population, and only by the late 19th century do we have the beginning of a systematized body of knowledge about learning and the process of teaching. The educators William James and G. Stanley Hall, for two examples, are the pioneers of contemporary educational psychology. Schools for teaching came slowly, perhaps because of the idea that we learn in spite of our schooling. The data for teachers about human behavior have come more slowly than is popularly realized. It may be suggested that much of what was done as an educational influence was based on what limited knowledge we had of adolescent learning patterns. In many cases, teachers were not given any data on psychological aspects of learning, because such data were not considered critical to schooling's effectiveness.

How we select teachers and with what tools we prepare them to teach depends ultimately on what *we* want them to do. The "we" is critical to any discussion. In our country, it is primarily the individual states, mostly in connection with the universities, that set the requirements for teacher training and for specific course content. To understand what our society thinks about the approaches to adolescent learning, it is necessary to find out what an individual state *requires* of a person who wants to be an "influence" in the classroom as a teacher. We have a multiplicity of teacher preparation and certification requirements in this country. It is significant, however, that frequently at the high-school level it is only necessary to have a bachelor's degree in the subject area to be taught and any other educational requirements

are kept to a minimum because they can be learned on the job, if necessary. Importantly, we are now suggesting that a knowledge of the learning processes of the students is not as critical as the information possessed by the teacher. It is the content that is significant. Perhaps it is because we have not resolved the meaning of the interaction or perhaps because the impact of a teacher cannot be considered important enough that legislators have recently approved this move that goes against all the suggestions of the universities involved in teacher training.

Role of Psychology

Those of us involved in secondary-level teacher training have for many years looked for further development from educational psychology research for curricula decisions. There has always been evidence that we needed to know much more about adolescent learning so that our curricula would be geared not only to the intellectual needs, but also would be presented by teachers with the best understanding of the level of receptivity of the adolescent. In review of the standard texts used in educational psychology courses at my campus, it is evident that much of the material on the psychology of learning has been directed to the early childhood. The work in this handbook itself will be critical to our further knowledge of how adolescents learn. To speak of an educational influence, such as a teacher who does not have the data needed for communicating with an adolescent, is to raise questions about the types of influence we are intending.

In Boyer's (1983) report, there is a call for renewal of teaching, for its professional growth, while acknowledging also that "teaching has never been a haven for the most gifted students" (p. 171).

An examination of the problem of who can teach and how to train those persons can only be answered when we know how effectively adolescents can be served by this 20th century institution. If school is a holding pattern for young persons to act out their transitions, in spite of what we do, the school will not attract gifted people dedicated to the special fields of study needed to help the adolescent move with most effectiveness in all aspects of growth.

SUMMARY

The school seems to be the given instrument of our day for the journey of this stage of human growth. We need to watch it with care and with all the knowledge and understanding that we can give it. In a book that touches on the mystery of human life, *Seasons That Laugh or Weep* (1983), the author, Walter Burghardt, writes a paragraph that combines the promise and the problem of adolescents and includes a final phrase from Erik Erikson that could be a model of "educational influence" for this day:

> *The* adolescent virtue, Erik Erikson insists, is fidelity. He defines this as "the ability to sustain loyalties freely pledged in spite of the inevitable contradictions of value systems." How does fidelity reveal itself in youth? In a high sense of duty, in truthfulness, in genuineness, in loyalty, in fairness, in "all that is implied in devotion—a freely given but binding vow, with the fateful implication of a curse befalling traitors." Such fidelity "is the cornerstone of identity." Nevertheless, it is not realized in a context of self-sufficient independence, it calls for "confirming adults and affirming peers." (pp. 14–15)

Our work must acknowledge the adolescent in search, in movement, alone and with others, which calls for "confirming adults and affirming peers."

REFERENCES

Adler, M. (1982). *The paideia proposal*. New York: Macmillan.

Bailyn, B. (1960). *Education in the forming of American society*. New York: Vintage.

Beckner, W., & Dumas W. (Eds.). (1970). *American education—Foundations and superstructures*. Scranton, PA: International Textbook.

Bellah, R. N., Madsen, R., Sullivan, W. M., Swidler, A., & Tipton, S. M. (1985). *Habits of the heart*. Berkeley: University of California Press.

Best, J. H. (Ed.). (1962). *Benjamin Franklin on education*. New York: Teachers College Press.

Bestor, A. E. (1953). *Educational wastelands: The retreat from learning in our public schools*. Urbana: University of Illinois Press.

Boyer, E. L. (1983). *High school. A report on secondary education in America*. New York: Harper & Row.

Burghardt, W. J. (1983). *Seasons that laugh or weep*. New York: Paulist Press.

Coleman, J. (1980). *High school and beyond: A national longitudinal study for the 1980's*. Washington, DC: U.S. Government Printing Office.

Conant, J. B. (1959). *The American high school today*. New York: McGraw-Hill.

Conant, J. B. (1967). *The comprehensive high school*. New York: McGraw-Hill.

Counts, G. (1932). *Dare the schools build a new social order?* New York: The John Day Co.

Cremin, L. A. (1966). *The genius of American education*. New York: Vintage Books.

Csikszentmihalyi, M., & Larson, R. (1984). *Being adolescent*. New York: Basic Books.

Dewey, J. (1916). *Democracy and education*. New York: Macmillan.

Elkind, D. (1984). *All grown up and no place to go*. Reading, MA: Addison-Wesley.

Erikson, E. H. (1968). *Identity youth and crisis*. New York: Norton.

Friedenberg, E. Z. (1966). *The dignity of youth and other atavisms*. Boston: Beacon.

Friedenberg, E. Z. (1967). *Coming of age in America*. New York: Vintage Books.

Goodman, P. (1956). *Growing up absurd*. New York: Vintage Books.

Hillsheim, J. W., & Merrill, G. D. (Eds.). (1971). *Theory and practice in the history of American education: A book of readings*. Pacific Palisades, CA: Goodyear.

The National Commission on Excellence in Education. (1983). *A nation at risk: The imperative for educational reform*. Washington, DC: U.S. Government Printing Office.

Plato. (1941). *The Republic* (F. M. Cornford, Trans.). London: Oxford University Press. (Original work ca. 400 B.C.)

Ranbom, S. (1985, February 20). Schooling in Japan. *Education Weekly*, pp. 11–34.

Van Til, W. (1978). *Secondary education: School and community*. Boston: Houghton Mifflin.

CHAPTER 25

Career Planning

B. Geraldine Lambert and Nancy Bradford Mounce

The factors that influence career choice probably have not changed during the past half century; however, the factor entities have expanded and become more complex during each decade. The basic factors of home and family environment, church and community environment, and education and educational opportunities have always been influential in the selection of an occupation. An array of varied stimuli projected by these factors confront today's adolescent.

SOCIAL THEORIES OF OCCUPATIONAL CHOICE

Theorists who support the sociological bases of occupational choice contend that persons are influenced by the social systems of their environment. These theorists include Super and Bachrach (1957), Roe (1957), and Crites (1958). Their theories are outlined in Table 25.1.

According to Super and Bachrach (1957), the individual is affected in descending order by the following social systems: (a) family, school, and church; (b) peer group, neighborhood, and ethnic group; (c) geographical region, social class, and racial background; and (d) the general American and Western culture of free enterprise, values, and mores.

Roe (1957) theorized that the individual's perception of his parents, home, and family environment shaped his selection of an occupation. According to her theory, if the child perceived the parents to be loving, accepting, protecting, and demanding, he would choose a "toward persons"–oriented occupation. On the other hand, if he viewed the parents as casual, rejecting, avoiding, and neglecting, he would select a "toward nonpersons" occupation. Roe categorized occupations into eight areas, with six levels in each area. The areas relating to "toward persons" included service, arts and entertainment, general culture, business contacts, and business organizations. The areas of science, technology, and outdoors were categorized as "nonperson" orientations.

Crites (1958) found that the school was second only to the family in its influence on "vocationalization." According to him, the school offered the student an opportunity to acquire a system of values that could be instrumental in the choice of careers.

DEVELOPMENTAL THEORIES

Ginsberg, Ginsberg, Axelrod, and Herma (1951) believe the family is fundamental in shaping an occupational choice. However, their

458

Table 25.1. Social Theories of Occupational Choice

AUTHOR	THEORY
Crites	School (furnishes system of values)
Roe	Family (Perception of treatment by parents)
Super and Bachrach	Family, school, church
	Peer group, neighborhood, ethnic group
	Geographical region, social class, racial background
	General culture (Western)

theory is developmental in that they believe that as the child matures and gains knowledge by various methods of exposure, he passes through the fantasy stage, the tentative stage, and the realistic stage of occupational choice (see Table 25.2).

The stage of fantasy occurs up to about age 11. From 11 through 18 years of age, the adolescent passes through four periods of the tentative stage. Here, the individual does not imagine jobs without considering relevant traits and abilities but begins to: (a) become interested in certain areas, (b) become aware of personal abilities, (c) become aware of personal values and integrate these with abilities, and (d) assume a transition period from tentative to realistic choices. Last, around the age of 18, when the individual begins to explore, crystallize (commit self to an occupation), and specify (choose a specific aspect) occupations, he reaches the realistic stage.

In 1972, Ginsberg reformulated the theory by stating that some persons are occupationally mobile throughout life and that the upper classes have more choices than the minority races and the economically disadvantaged.

Super's self-concept theory (1967) is similar to a developmental theory. The stages he proposes are crystallization (ages 14–18) specification (ages 18–20), implementation (ages 21–24), and stabilization (ages 25–35). These include: (a) crystallizing work with self-concepts, (b) choosing an occupation, (c) entering an occupation, (d) accepting the choice, and (e) attaining status and advancement.

Havighurst (1972) defines a developmental task as:

> A task which arises at or about a certain period in the life of an individual, successful achievement which leads to his happiness and to success with later tasks, while failure leads to unhappiness in the individual, disapproval by the society, and difficulty with later tasks. (p. 2)

Lambert, Rothchild, Atland, and Green (1978) stated, "These developmental tasks have been defined as the skills, knowledge, functions and attitudes that must be acquired at certain points in life and are mastered through physical maturation, social learning, and personal strivings." Correlating vocational development with other aspects of the development of the adolescent,

Table 25.2. Developmental Theories of Occupational Choice

AUTHOR	THEORY
Ginsberg	Fantasy stage (ages to 11)
	Tentative stage (ages 11–18)
	Realistic stage (ages 19+)
Havighurst	Identification with significant others (ages 5–10)
	Acquisition of work habits (ages 10–15)
	Identification with a work setting (15–25)
	Become productive worker (ages 25–40)
Super	Crystalization (ages 14–18)
	Specification (ages 18–20)
	Implementation (ages 21–24)
	Stabilization (ages 25–35)
	Consolidation (after age 35)

Havighurst's stages would include: (a) by identification with parents and other significant persons, a concept of work becomes essential to the ego ideal (ages 5–10); (b) by acquisition of habits related to work versus play, one learns to organize time and energy (ages 10–15); (c) by identification in an actual work setting one acquires experience and prepares for a career (ages 15–25); and (d) by becoming a productive worker one masters skills and earns promotion (ages 25–40) (Rice, 1978).

TRAIT-FACTOR THEORIES

Holland (1972) believes that occupations are selected based upon personality types, and that a person selects a career that matches his personality type (see Table 25.3). Holland lists six types:

1. *Realistic*—person chooses careers that are practical and that require few social skills (e.g., farming, construction);
2. *Intellectual*—individual chooses career that requires abstract thinking (e.g., scientist and mathematician);
3. *Social*—person chooses career that utilizes verbal and interpersonal relation skills (e.g., teaching and social work);
4. *Conventional*—person chooses career that has structured activities (e.g., clinical and bank teller);
5. *Enterprising*—individual chooses career that utilizes verbal persuasion and leadership (e.g., politics and salesmen);
6. *Artistic*—person chooses career in which one can express self without social interaction (e.g., writing and painting).

Holland has devised a self-directed search system which measures six personality types that can be used in vocational counseling (Rice, 1978).

Cattell (1967) measures 32 factors of personality with the 16 Personality Factor Inventory. By testing persons in occupations, he has been able to identify average personality profiles of persons who are successful in the different occupations. Many personnel managers and school counselors use his instrument for selection, placement, and guidance of adolescents.

THEORIES OF MOTIVATION AFFECTING CAREER PLANNING

A highly motivated person may not perform well; the reason is that, in theory, performance is the product of motivation times ability. Ability is the individual's capabilities for performing certain tasks. They are necessary but not sufficient precursors of performance. Motivation is the individual's *desire* to demonstrate the behavior and reflects willingness to expend effort. (Muchinsky, 1983, p. 358)

The factors theorized as the bases of occupational choice can be correlated to Maslow's (1970) hierarchy of needs and other motivational theories. Maslow's basic needs (physiological and safety) would be fulfilled during the tentative period of Ginsberg et al. (1951) and the specification and implementation periods of Super (1967). Maslow's higher order needs (social, self-esteem, and self-actualization would be fulfilled by the theories of Roe (1957), Super and Bachrach (1957), and Havighurst (1972) (see Table 25.4).

Alderfer (1969, 1972) theorized that three

Table 25.3. Trait-Factor Theories of Occupational Choice

AUTHOR	THEORY (PERSONALITY TYPES)
Holland	Realistic
	Intellectual
	Social
	Conventional
	Enterprising
	Artistic
Cattell	Reserved vs. Outgoing
	Concrete logic vs. Abstract logic
	Emotional vs. Calm
	Accommodating vs. Assertive
	Serious vs. Impulsive
	Expedient vs. Conscientious
	Timid vs. Uninhibited
	Self-Reliant vs. Sensitive
	Trusting vs. Skeptical
	Practical vs. Imaginative
	Open vs. Calculating
	Self-Assured vs. Apprehensive
	Conservative vs. Liberal
	Follower vs. Self-sufficient
	Undisciplined vs. Compulsive
	Composed vs. Tense
Myers–Briggs	Extraversion vs. Introversion
	Sensing vs. Intuition
	Thinking vs. Feeling
	Judging vs. Perceptive

Table 25.4. Motivational Theories of Work

AUTHOR	THEORY	NEEDS
Maslow	Need Hierarchy	Physiological Safety Social Self-esteem Self-actualization
Alderfer	ERG Theory	Existence Relatedness Growth
Adams	Equity Theory	Person Others Inputs Outcomes
Vroom	Expectancy Theory	Job outcomes Expectancy
Locke	Goal-setting Theory	Bases for motivation Direct motivation

types of needs, existence, relatedness, and growth motivate people to work (ERG theory). This theory, also, is similar to the "choice" influences presented by family, peers, community, race, and ethnic groups.

Adams (1965) presented an equity theory that stated that the worker is motivated by social comparison of self to others. The individual compares his inputs and outcomes to the inputs and outcomes of others. If the person perceives an inequitable situation or an unfair situation, he feels tension and is motivated to reduce the tension. This reduction of tension can be done by increasing or decreasing productivity and/or the quality of work. Career planning could also be based on this theory.

The expectancy theory of Vroom (1964) states that individuals expend effort (or are motivated) when they see a relationship among desired outcomes based upon reward for performance and effort related to that performance.

The goal-setting theory of Locke (1968) is based on the premise that there is a relationship between conscious goals, intentions, and task performance. The basic premise is that conscious ideas regulate a person's actions (Muchinsky, 1983). The basis of career planning is contained in their theory.

Motivational theories imply that there is something external and/or internal that directs the behavior of an individual. They also imply that there are extrinsic and intrinsic stimuli, reinforcers, and rewards.

Realistic career planning should include knowledge of one's abilities, personality traits, interests, and motivational desires.

VOCATIONAL AND CAREER EDUCATION

The past two decades have seen vast changes in all areas of education, and vocational education is no exception. "No area of education is more complex and none has changed as greatly as vocational education has in the past two decades" (Bottoms & Coppa, 1983, p. 348).

A 1973 U.S. Office of Education career education model was presented that required the cooperative efforts of all segments of an adolescent's environment—school, family, business, and community (Lambert et al., 1978). The model emphasized the value of providing career information in order to enhance vocational choice. "Career education guidelines required that academic subjects should: (1) be structured around career development; (2) include extensive counseling for decision making and, (3) prepare students for a career of their choice or for advanced education" (Lambert et al., 1978). There were over 100 career education pilot projects with almost 750,000 students enrolled during 1973, and by 1974 about 5,000 of the 17,000 school districts in the United States had instituted career education programs (Lambert et al., 1978). The decade of the 1980s has brought a decline in federal funds available for such programs and for vocational education as a whole (Passmore & Welch, 1983). The 1980s have also seen an increase in the number of adolescents in the work force, increase in the unemployment rate, and a change in the career opportunities available to adolescents in the United States.

The National Commission on Excellence in Education (Gardner et al., 1983) reported in *A Nation at Risk* that American high schools graduate 75% of the nation's young people. About 11% of all of these high-school students were enrolled in six or more vocational courses. Seventy-eight percent took at least one vocational course (Boyer, 1983). Available data reflect that, in general, graduates of vocational programs do not do any better in the job market than students who graduate from a nonspecialized curriculum (Boyer, 1983). However, other research indicates that vocational educational programs are associated with higher unemployment (Bottoms & Coppa, 1983). An extensive study of the public American secondary school system funded in part by the Carnegie Foundation for the Advancement of Teaching recommended in 1983 that high schools eliminate the vocational track from the curriculum while maintaining some vocational courses. The study also proposed that all high-school students be required to take a seminar on work (Boyer, 1984).

Currently, more than 10 million vocational students are 18 years or younger and attending school; 24% of the total enrollment in vocational programs is made up of minority students; 51.6% of all students in vocational education programs are female, and 48.4% are male (Bottoms & Coppa, 1983). Vocational programs offered in a wide variety of institutions range from those dealing with basic and employability-skills training to those dealing with occupationally specific instruction.

Perhaps those in the best position to judge the effectiveness of the preparation of adolescents for the world of work are the employers to whom they apply for jobs. There seems to be a vast discrepancy between the skills demanded by business and industry and those demonstrated by secondary-school graduates in the areas of writing, speaking, listening, reasoning, mathematics, and science (Junge, Daniels, & Karmos, 1984). Additionally, many employers reflect the need for some specific occupational preparation (Bottoms & Coppa, 1984). A 1983 poll indicated that, for those students ending their education with high school, the public would require both vocational training and business courses (Gallup, 1983).

The concept that "competent workers must first of all be educated, competent human beings" (Herr & Long, 1982, p. 60) seems to be prevalent in both the educational and business communities. To be successful, the vocational education instruction of the future must maintain high levels of academic preparation while broadening programs to meet the needs of a vacillating economic and diverse occupational structure.

VOLUNTARISM AND VOCATIONAL EXPERIENCE

The importance of volunteer work for the adolescent, particularly the younger adolescent unable to obtain remunerative employment, is irrefutable in terms of providing valuable vocational experience. Volunteer work can provide the adolescent with feelings of adequacy and status (Lambert et al., 1978). Volunteer participation can also help the adolescent develop positive work habits, establish contacts, gain self-confidence, learn job-search techniques, and often acquire specific skills useful in future employment (Beale, 1984).

The value of the volunteer sector has been vitally reinforced by the current administration. Public Law 96-114, the Congressional Award Act, provides for the recognition of volunteers ages 14 through 23. The volunteer efforts of adolescents take a wide variety of forms. Perhaps their earliest involvement is the scouting programs available in cities throughout the country (Lambert et al., 1978). These programs are often sponsored through schools or church organizations.

The educational institutions at the secondary level provide a wide array of volunteer opportunities in the extracurricular programs. Students interested in music often have the opportunity to participate in community symphony and orchestra programs. Those involved in high-school newspapers and yearbooks learn the valuable skills of team work, individual responsibility, meeting deadlines, writing, editing, and photography that may prove useful in careers in advertising, journalism, and public relations. Some organizations unite the school and community in an effort to foster voluntarism and civic responsibility in adolescents. These include: Key Clubs, sponsored by Kiwanis; Leo Clubs, sponsored by the Lions Club; Interact, sponsored by Rotary; and 4-H, sponsored by county or parish agents. These programs afford the adolescent exposure not only to voluntary activities that enhance their level of occupational information, but also exposure to career role models within their community. In many schools, National Honor Society and Beta Club students serve as peer tutors. Project Lead, a current project of the Association of Junior Leagues and the Quest Foundation, has trained 8,000 youth volunteers in 12 states to conduct programs varying from the development of relationships between the adolescent and the elderly to the development of safety programs for elementary-school children. Service organizations within school and church settings allow the adolescent to work with such groups as the Salvation Army. These groups are also called upon to serve as ushers or parking attendants for large community functions. Adolescents are also able to serve as peer counselors in hot-line programs ranging from suicide prevention to health information. Hospitals often involve adolescents in their volunteer programs, thus providing the adolescent with exposure to the numerous career fields available in medicine. City libraries and museums also frequently establish programs utilizing adolescent volunteers.

Considering the fact that the typical worker changes jobs between 5 and 7 times in his lifetime (Herr & Long, 1982), and in view of the current crisis in the U.S. workplace (Bottoms & Coppa, 1983), it would seem that at least a partial solution to the problem of providing adolescents with extensive occupational information could be found in the volunteer sector of communities throughout the country.

COMPUTERS AND CAREERS

Recent developments in computer technology have been found valuable in enhancing career-development concepts (Pyle, 1984). Numerous systems, both informational and complete guidance, are available to many of today's adolescents. A 1983 study revealed that 24% of public secondary schools operated computer-assisted career guidance systems (Haring-Hi-dore, 1984). These computer systems provide a variety of services, including the announcement of job vacancies, the matching of employers with student employees, computer-assisted testing, and skill-building techniques as decision making, resume preparation, and interviewing (Pyle, 1984).

A 1984 study by JoAnn Harris-Bowlsky found the vocational choice theories of Roe and Holland quite adaptable to computers because they "both prescribe step-by-step, potentially one-time processes." On the other hand, she found that the developmental theories of Super and Teideman were less adaptable to computerization, indicating that the computer could only serve to provide informational resources or to act as a sort of monitor in the process of career development (Harris-Bowlsky, 1984).

The selection of an appropriate system seems to be made difficult by the numerous systems available in today's market. Of assistance are the standards set by the Association of Computer-Based Systems for Career Information (Mc-Kinlay, 1984).

These systems should:

1. Cover 90% of the total employment in the systems' service area;
2. Have an empirical base;
3. Cover standard occupational topics ranging from job duties to factors influencing projected supply and demand;
4. Be demonstrably understandable in format, style, and language level and avoid racial, sexual, and status references;
5. Be based on current data and documented by the research staff;
6. Be validated and updated at least yearly;
7. Be able to demonstrate an empirical relationship between user and occupational characteristics in any sorting mechanism;
8. Cover all significant instructional programs;
9. Describe educational program objectives, specialties, degrees conferred, sample courses, and institutions;
10. List only licensed and accredited educational institutions;
11. Cover admissions, housing costs, financial aid, and student services in school information; and
12. Enhance comparisons among schools.

Chapman and Katz (1982) indicated weaknesses in many of the available systems. They found that the system's treatment of such necessary variables as interests and attitudes was inconsistent and often overly simplified. An additional frailty was the almost complete lack of attention to values. Evidence also indicates that in many of the schools that have computer-assisted career information systems less than 50% of the students avail themselves of the system's potential (Chapman & Katz, 1982; Haring-Hidore, 1984).

EMPLOYMENT

In 1982, 7.7% of the entire labor force in the United States was between the ages of 16 and 19. There were 4.5 million males and 4.1 million females between the ages of 16 and 19 employed in 1982 (U.S. Department of Commerce, 1984). This is a marked increase from the 2.8 million males and 2.1 million females between the ages of 16 and 19 reported in 1960 as members of the civilian labor force (see Table 25.5).

These adolescents are entering a world of work that is in a constant state of fluctuation. "The trends toward urbanization and consolidation in business and farming, along with the rise in technology, all combine to produce significant shifts in employment patterns" (Atwater, 1983). Where do they begin?

Many adolescents begin with part-time employment. Over 30% of 16- to 19-year-olds were employed part-time in 1982 (U.S. Dept. of Labor, 1984). Many of these students worked in service and fast-food industries, which provide

their own on-the-job training (Boyer, 1983). The Junior Achievement Clubs, organized in secondary schools throughout the country, introduce students to the free-enterprise system. (Lambert et al., 1978). The adolescent involved in part-time work has an advantage in having begun to increase his level of occupational information, to develop vocational values, and to learn skills related to work (Manaster, 1977).

Part-time employment at the high-school level is more common among girls than boys. The employment of high-school girls is associated with a higher socioeconomic family status and slightly higher academic achievement; this is not true of boys (Gade & Peterson, 1980).

The selection of part-time employment can have a significant effect on an adolescent's future career opportunities (Dunn, 1984). Nevertheless, there may be some detrimental effects of part-time employment that could affect the adolescent. These include increasing the adolescent's impatience with the high-school program, increasing a preexisting desire to leave school, and alienating the adolescent from his peers (Lambert et al., 1978). With the current trend to strengthen academic requirements in secondary schools, some adolescents may find it difficult to meet the stringent requirements of both work and school.

The employment picture in the United States is colored with change and new demands, and the adolescent must be able to deal with the changes and meet the demands. During the next decade young people will face the problem of finding fulfillment of self at work and with

Table 25.5. Youth Labor Force Participation
(Percentage of Youth Employed)

	1960	1965	1970	1975	1980	1982
Female						
16–17 years	29.1	27.7	34.9	40.2	43.5	41.0
18–19 years	50.9	49.3	53.5	58.1	61.9	61.2
20–24 years	46.1	49.9	57.7	64.1	68.9	69.8
Male						
16–17 years	46.0	43.9	47.0	48.6	50.1	45.4
18–19 years	69.3	65.9	66.7	70.6	71.3	67.9
20–24 years	88.1	85.8	83.3	84.5	85.9	84.9
Totals						
16–17 years	37.1	35.8	41.9	42.4	46.8	43.2
18–19 years	60.1	59.6	60.1	64.4	66.6	64.6
20–24 years	67.1	67.9	70.5	74.3	77.4	77.4

Adapted from U.S. Department of Commerce, Bureau of Census, *Statistical Abstract*, 1984, p. 407.

family. Data reflecting adolescent employment can be found in Table 25.6

PRACTICAL CAREER PLANNING

Each adolescent is an individual who may or may not have been influenced by one or more of the theories of occupational choice. Psychologists would agree that there are external and internal influences that motivate behavior. Whatever the motivation for selection of an occupation and then a career, the adolescent needs to be aware of his or her capabilities, personality traits, interests, and values. School counselors and teachers or private counselors and psychologists can help the individual identify these traits and characteristics. Additionally, the students must be aware of the criteria or performance dimensions of a job (Muchinsky, 1983), a procedure that is called a job analysis.

The *Dictionary of Occupational Titles* (U.S. Department of Labor, 1977), the *Guide to Occupational Exploration* (U.S. Department of Labor, 1979), the *Worker Trait Group Guide* (Appalachia Educational Laboratory, Inc., 1978), and the *Occupational Outlook Handbook* (U.S. Department of Labor, 1984) all contain unlimited information pertaining to job requirements, qualifications, duties, and future employment outlook on thousands of jobs that have been classified by the U.S. government.

Businesses and industries attempt to "fit" individuals with jobs by correlating the tasks performed with the abilities and interests of the person selected. It is necessary for adolescents to be realistic about their abilities and liabilities in order to plan to pursue an occupation in which they will succeed and one in which they will be happy and content.

Because tests of mental ability have been and still are used for personnel selection, the adolescent needs to become test-wise in the method of taking paper and pencil tests. Among the mental ability tests commonly used in industry are the Otis Self-Administering Tests of Mental Ability (Otis, 1967), the Wonderlic Personnel Test (Wonderlich & Howland, 1939), and the Adaptability Test (Tiffin & Lawshe, 1942) (Muchinsky, 1983). Additionally, the state employment counselors administer the General Aptitude Test Battery (GATB) or selected aptitude tests from the battery to many applicants. This test measures G—general intelligence, V—verbal ability, and N—numerical ability, in addition to eight specialized aptitudes: spatial, form perception, clerical perception, motor coordination, finger dexterity, manual dexterity, eye-hand-foot coordination, and color discrimination.

Other aptitude tests include the Differential Aptitude Test (Bennett, Seashore, & Wesman, 1964), the Bennett Test of Mechanical Comprehension (Bennett, 1940), the Minnesota Spatial Relations Test (Patterson, 1930), and the Minnesota Paper Form Board Test (Likert & Quasha, 1948).

Ability tests, other than mental ability tests, measure or assess sensory and learning sensitivity, perceptual accuracy, and motor abilities. Standardized tests in these areas include: Snellen Eye Chart, Purdue Pegboard (Tiffin, 1941), Crawford Small Parts Dexterity Test (Crawford & Crawford, 1946), and the SRA Test of Mechanical Concepts (Stanard & Bode, 1976).

Table 25.6. Percentage Distribution of Youth Employed, Ages 16–19 and 20–24

	1960	1965	1970	1975	1980	1982
AGES 16–19 YEARS						
Female	8.8	9.6	10.3	10.8	9.6	8.5
Male	6.0	7.0	7.8	8.5	8.1	7.2
Totals	7.0	7.9	8.8	9.5	8.8	7.7
AGES 20–24 YEARS						
	1960	1965	1970	1975	1980	1982
Female	11.1	12.8	15.5	16.5	16.1	16.0
Male	8.9	10.1	11.2	13.4	14.0	13.8
Totals	9.6	11.1	12.8	14.7	14.9	14.6

Adapted from U.S. Department of Commerce, Bureau of Census, *Statistical Abstract*, 1984, p. 407.

Personality Inventories, which measure personality characteristics of the individual, include the 16 Personality Factor Test (16PF) (Cattell, 1964) and the Minnesota Multiphasic Personality Inventory (MMPI) (Hathaway & McKinley, 1943).

Interest tests, which reveal the selected areas of interests of the person, are the Interest Check List (U.S. Dept. of Labor, 1979), Strong–Campbell Interest Inventory (Strong & Campbell, 1974), the Vocational Preference Inventory (Holland, 1965), The Kuder Occupational Interest Survey (Kuder, 1974), and the Self-Directed Search (Holland, 1972).

Allport, Vernon, and Lindzey's (1970) Study of Values, the Myers-Briggs Type Indication (Briggs & Myers, 1983), and the FIRO Awareness Scales (Schutz, 1978), all reveal to the adolescent traits, values, and attitudes about him or herself that are important in career selection (see Table 25.7).

Biographical information is also important to the individual when selecting a job or career. The subjects pursued in high school, GPA, extracurricular activities, and work experience (volunteer and remunerative) all imply abilities, attitudes, values, and interests, and to some extent personality traits (see Table 25.8).

If the adolescent is aware of his special and unique traits and if he is exposed to the "world of work" through participating in self-assessments and tests and by reading about or being presented materials pertaining to job requirements, he can begin to prepare for occupation and career selection.

Because his self-concept and ego strength are closely related to his career and because he will most often identify himself by what type of work he does for a livelihood, it is necessary that he realize that all jobs and occupations are worthwhile and that his evaluation of self can be a positive one.

JOB SATISFACTION

When preparing for a career, the adolescent must become knowledgeable about the factors that contribute to job satisfaction or the lack of job satisfaction. Herzberg (1959) researched the area of work satisfaction and found two factors, content and context, into which he has classified many other factors. Content factors are those to which he refers as *satisfiers*. These include achievement recognition, advancement, and responsibility. Context factors relate to the context of the job, such as company policy, supervising salary, and working conditions. He refers to these as *dissatisfiers* (Muchinsky, 1983).

The adolescent needs to realize that his job will have satisfiers and dissatisfiers; and, whether he has carefully selected a career or haphazardly stumbled into one, he will not always be satisfied with the global aspect of his job. Additionally, research indicates that the age, the race, and the sex of the individual are variables that cause satisfaction or dissatisfaction.

Some of the perceived satisfiers have been identified in a recent survey (Sakell, 1985) of 182,000 college freshmen. Two surveys were conducted; one in 1966 and one in 1984. In the 1984 survey, 71% of those surveyed want to be financially well off, and only 44.6% believe they need to develop a philosophy of life. This is in contrast to a survey by Yankelovich (1974) that listed the following top five criteria: (a) pay that is good (61%); (b) work that is interesting (70%); (c) opportunity to use your mind (65%); (d) work results that you can see (62%); and (e) friendly, helpful coworkers (70%).

Table 25.7. Interest Areas Measured for Job Selection and Placement

Interest Check List
    Artistic
    Scientific
    Plants and animals
    Protective
    Mechanical
    Industrial
    Business detail
    Selling
    Accommodating
    Humanitarian
    Leading and influencing
    Physical performing

The Self-Directed Search and
The Strong Vocational Interest Blank
    Realistic
    Investigative
    Artistic
    Social
    Enterprising
    Conventional

FIRO Awareness Scales
    Wanted behavior
    Expressed behavior

Table 25.8. Vocational Profile Checklist

TRAITS & ABILITIES	NONE	SOME	INDIVIDUAL'S AVERAGE	ABOVE	AVERAGE	AMOUNT NEEDED FOR DESIRED JOB
Verbal communication	___	___	___	___	___	___
Verbal reasoning	___	___	___	___	___	___
Numerical reasoning	___	___	___	___	___	___
Mechanical reasoning	___	___	___	___	___	___
Perception						
Spacial	___	___	___	___	___	___
Clerical	___	___	___	___	___	___
Dexterity						
Finger	___	___	___	___	___	___
Manual	___	___	___	___	___	___
Coordination						
Motor	___	___	___	___	___	___
Eye–hand–foot	___	___	___	___	___	___
Color discrimination	___	___	___	___	___	___
Interest (Work with)						
People	___	___	___	___	___	___
Things, objects, data	___	___	___	___	___	___
Ideas	___	___	___	___	___	___
Temperaments						
Routine tasks	___	___	___	___	___	___
Creative tasks	___	___	___	___	___	___
Influence others	___	___	___	___	___	___
Help others	___	___	___	___	___	___
Working conditions						
Inside	___	___	___	___	___	___
Outside	___	___	___	___	___	___
Hot	___	___	___	___	___	___
Cold	___	___	___	___	___	___
Physical abilities						
Light work	___	___	___	___	___	___
Heavy work	___	___	___	___	___	___
Sedentary	___	___	___	___	___	___
Active	___	___	___	___	___	___
Education						
10 years	___	___	___	___	___	___
H.S. Diploma	___	___	___	___	___	___
College	___	___	___	___	___	___

Adapted from *Job Analysis Form*, Council for Independent Relations, VDARE Service Bureau, Inc., Athens, GA, 1980.

Only 1.6% of the students in the 1984 Sakell survey were interested in a career in fine arts, whereas a total of 18% were interested in areas of business and business administration and 6.2% were interested in engineering.

A comparison between the students' answers on the 1966 and 1984 surveys is shown in Table 25.9.

THEORY OF WORK ADJUSTMENT

Of importance to any study of careers is the degree to which an individual is suited to the work he performs in relation to the degree to which that worker meets the requirements of the job he is performing. Theoretically, the higher the degree of correspondence between these two need factors, the needs of the individual and the needs of the job, the greater the adjustment to the world of work.

Foremost among theories dealing with adjustment to the world of vocations is the theory of work adjustment proposed by the Industrial Relations Center at the University of Minnesota (Industrial Relations Center, 1968), the major precepts of which are summarized in the following paragraphs.

Work adjustment is, in essence, the workers'

Table 25.9. Students' Answers in
1966 and 1984

	1966 %	1984 %
Worried about finances	43.8	71.2
Helping others	68.0	
Being an authority on a subject	66.0	
Keeping up with politics	56.8	
Raising a family		68.5
Being successful in business		51.6
Professed to be liberal	19	21.5
Professed to be conservative	15.0	25.0
Above average math skills	35	
Above average writing skills	27	
Would need remedial math		24.6
Would need remedial English		12.1
Father with college education	16.9	35
Mother with college education	15.3	24
Chose business major	14.3	18
Chose education major	10.6	6.2
Chose fine arts major	8.4	1

Adapted from UCLA/American Council in Education
Survey as reported in *Guidepost*, 27(13), March 2, 1985.

ability to adapt to his vocational environment. This process of adaptability is measured by two components in the Minnesota study, *satisfaction* and *satisfactoriness*. The first component used to judge the degree of adjustment, satisfaction, is person-oriented, whereas the second component, satisfactoriness, is job-oriented. The greater the correlation between these two variables, satisfaction and satisfactoriness, the greater the harmony between worker and work. The satisfaction experienced by an individual as a result of his work environment depends on the extent of correlation between his needs and abilities and the reinforcers granted by the job he is performing. The level of satisfactoriness is dependent upon the correlation between the workers' set of abilities and the abilities demanded by the work setting. Thus, the successful adaptability or adjustment to the world of work is verified by the degree of correlation between ability and ability requirements inherent, respectively, in the worker and his work, as well as by the degree of correlation between needs and reinforcers inherent, respectively, in the worker and his work. The Minnesota study further elaborates that, the higher the degree of satisfaction, the less likely an individual is to voluntarily leave his chosen employment. Additionally, the higher the level of satisfactoriness, the less likely that the worker would be forced to leave his chosen employment. Thus, the stability of a worker's remaining in his chosen field of employment is a direct result of a high degree of both satisfaction and satisfactoriness.

An excellent publication, the *Minnesota Occupational Classification System II (MOCSII)* (Dawis, Lofquist, Henly, & Rounds, 1979), delineates individual requirements and job reinforcers. The needs of the worker are defined by the correlates of the *Dictionary of Occupational Titles* (i.e., data, people, and things). The requirements of the jobs are defined by a variety of reinforcer "clusters." Included as individual reinforcers that are combined in a variety of methods to form reinforcer groups are the following variables (Dawis et al., 1979; pp. xiv–xv):

1. Ability Utilization
2. Achievement
3. Activity
4. Advancement
5. Authority
6. Company policies and practices
7. Compensation
8. Co-workers
9. Creativity
10. Independence
11. Moral values
12. Recognition
13. Responsibility
14. Security
15. Social Service
16. Social Status
17. Supervision—human relations
18. Supervision—technical
19. Variety
20. Working Conditions
21. Autonomy

These variables are combined by the authors to form reinforcer groups. It is these groups that are assembled in a variety of ways to form the clusters used to define the various reinforcer systems provided by various jobs. The reinforcer groups are (Dawis et al., 1974, pp. xv–xvi):

    I. Safety
        Company policies and practices
        Supervision—human relations
        Supervision—technical
    II. Comfort
        Activity
        Independence
        Variety

III. States
    Compensation
    Security
    Working conditions
III. States
    Advancement
    Recognition
    Authority
    Social states
IV. Altruism
    Co-workers
    Moral values
    Social service
V. Achievement
    Ability utilization
    Achievement
VI. Autonomy
    Responsibility
    Creativity
    Autonomy

The implication of the usefulness of a theory of vocational adaptability to the adolescent is apparent. Considering the rather high degree of vacillation inherent in the life of the developing adolescent, it would seem crucial that the professional working in the field of vocational preparation be cognizant of the variety of needs and abilities, the diversity of reinforcers, and the correlation between them. Computer-assisted programs are invaluable in establishing such an awareness of the diversity of factors affecting successful, satisfying vocational placement.

SUMMARY

The world of work is a world foreign to many an adolescent, but his successful introduction to it has far-reaching implications. The making of choices seems to dominate this developmental period, and vocational choice is certainly no exception. Of necessary consideration in a study of adolescents and vocations are those theories that set forth principles relevant to both the stage of development and the work environment. These theories include social theories, trait-factor theories, and theories of motivation. None of these can be considered exclusively, but must be viewed in combination with one another to form an accurate profile of the adolescent.

Because the majority of adolescents are participants in some form of educational process, career/vocational education and its computer component are additional factors inherent in an understanding of the process of the "vocationization" of the adolescent. As is true of most educational programs, the career/vocational program is in a state of constant flux and endless, continuous evaluation. Voluntarism as a means of deriving valuable vocational experience should also be considered as a tool to further the adolescent's concept of opportunities available to him in the world of work.

The selection of a vocation by the adolescent must be based on the most comprehensive and extensive knowledge. To this end, practical career planning should be considered. The plan, to be effective, should include available testing instruments and cognizance of the factors inherent in a theory of vocational adaptability or work adjustment.

REFERENCES

Adams, J. S. (1965). Unequality in social exchange. In L. Berkowitz (Ed.), *Advances in experimental social psychology.* New York: Academic

Alderfer, C. P. (1972). *Existence, relatedness & growth: Human needs in organization settings.* New York: Free Press.

Allport, G., Vernon, P. E., & Lindzey, G. (1970). *Study of values* (3rd ed.). New York: Houghton Mifflin.

Appalachia Educational Laboratory, Inc. (1978). *Worker trait group guide.* Bloomington, IL: McKnight.

Atwater, E. (1983). *Adolescence.* Englewood Cliffs, NJ: Prentice-Hall.

Beale, A. H. (1984). Exploring careers through volunteerism. *The School Counselor, 32,* 68–71.

Bennett, G. K. (1940). *Test of mechanical comprehension.* New York: Psychological Corp.

Bennett, G. K., Seashore, H. G., & Wesman, A. G. (1962). *Differential aptitude tests.* New York: Psychological Corp.

Bottoms, G., & Coppa, P. (1983). A perspective on vocational education today. *Phi Delta Kappan, 64,* 348–354.

Boyer, E. L. (1983). *High school. A report on secondary education in America.* New York: Harper & Row.

Boyer, E. L. (1984). Vocational education (Annual report). *Today's Education,* 44–45.

Briggs, K. C., & Myers, I. B. (1983). *Myers–Briggs type indicator.* Palo Alto, CA: Consulting Psychologists Press.

Cattell, R. (1964). *Sixteen personality factor test.* Champaign, IL: Institute for Personality and Ability Testing.

Chapman, W., & Katz, M. (1982). Career information systems in secondary schools: A survey and assessment. *Vocational Guidance Quarterly, 31,* 165.

Crawford, J. E., & Crawford, D. M. (1946). *Small parts dexterity test.* New York: Psychological Corp.

Crites, J. O. (1958, March). *Vocational maturity and vocational adjustment.* Paper presented at the meeting of the American Personnel and Guidance Association, St. Louis, MO.

Dawis, R., Lofquist, L. H., Henly, G. A., & Rounds, J. B. Jr. (1974). *Minnesota occupational classification system II*. Minneapolis: University of Minnesota.

Dunn, D. (1984). Steering graduates to the right job. *Business Week*, No. 2842, 174–176.

Gade, E., & Peterson, L. (1980). A comparison of working and nonworking high-school students on school performance, socioeconomic status, and self-esteem. *Vocational Guidance Quarterly, 29,* 65–68.

Gallup, G. H. (1983). Fifteenth annual Gallup poll of the public's attitude toward the public schools. *Phi Delta Kappan, 65,* 33–48.

Ginsberg, E. (1972). Toward a theory of occupational choice: A restatement. *Vocational Guidance Quarterly, 20,* 169–176.

Ginsberg, E., Ginsberg, S. W., Axelrod, S., & Herma, J. L. (1951). *Occupational choice: An approach to a general theory*. New York: Columbia University Press.

Haring-Hidore, M. (1984). In pursuit of students who do not use computer for career guidance. *Journal of Counseling and Development, 63,* 137–140.

Harris-Bowlsky, J. (1984). The computer and career development. *Journal of Counseling and Development, 63,* 145–148.

Hathaway, S. R., & McKinley, J. C. (1943). *Minnesota multiphasic personality inventory* (rev. ed.). New York: Psychological Corp.

Havighurst, R. J. (1972). *Developmental tasks and education* (3rd ed.). New York: McKay.

Herr, E. L., & Long, T. (1982). Vocational education. *Today's Education, 71,* 60–62.

Holland, J. L. (1965). *Manual for the vocational preference inventory*. Palo Alto, CA: Consulting Psychologists Press.

Holland, J. L. (1972). *Professional manual for the self-directed search*. Palo Alto, CA: Consulting Psychologists Press.

Industrial Relations Center. A theory of work adjustment. In *Minnesota studies on vocational rehabilitation*. Minneapolis: Author.

Junge, D., Daniels, M., & Karmos, J. S. (1984). Personnel managers' perceptions of requisite basic skills. *Vocational Guidance Quarterly, 32,* 138.

Kuder, G. F. (1974). *The Kuder occupational interest survey*. Chicago, IL: Science Research Associates.

Lambert, B. G., Rothschild, B. F., Atland, R., & Green, L. B. (1978). *Adolescence: Transition from childhood to maturity*. Belmont, CA: Wadsworth.

Likert, R., & Quasha, W. H. (1948). *Revised Minnesota paper form board test*. New York: Psychological Corp.

Locke, E. H. (1968). Toward a theory of task motivation and incentive. *Organizational Behavior and Human Performance, 3,* 157–189.

Manaster, G. J. (1977). *Adolescent development and the life tasks*. Boston: Allyn & Bacon.

Maslow, A. H. (1970). *Motivation and personality* (3rd ed.). New York: Harper & Row.

McKinlay, B. (1984). Standards of quality in systems of career information. *Journal of Counseling and Development, 63,* 149–152.

Muchinsky, P. M. (1983). *Psychology applied to work*. Homewood, IL: Dorsey.

Otis, A. S. (1967). *Otis self-administering tests of mental ability*. Tarrytown, NY: World.

Passmore, D. L., & Welch, F. G. (1983). Relationship between preferences for part-time work and characteristics of unemployed youth. *Adolescence, 18,* 181–192.

Patterson, D. G. (1930). *Minnesota spatial relations test*. Chicago: Stoelting.

Pyle, R. K. (1984). Career counseling and computers: Where is the creativity? *Journal of Career Counseling and Development, 63,* 141–144.

Rice, P. F. (1978). *Development, relationships, culture*. Boston: Allyn & Bacon.

Roe, A. (1957). Early determinant of vocational choice. *Journal of Counseling Psychology, 4,* 212–217.

Sakell, T. (1985, March 7). Today's students seek financial security: ACE/UCLA survey. *Guidepost, 27,* 6.

Schutz, W. (1978). *FIRO awareness scales*. Palo Alto, CA: Consulting Psychologists Press.

Stanard, S. J., & Bode, K. W. (1976). *SRA test of mechanical concepts*. Chicago: Science Research Associates.

Strong, E. K., & Campbell, D. P. (1974). *Strong–Campbell interest inventory*. Stanford, CA: Stanford University Press.

Super, D. E. (1967). *The psychology of careers*. New York: Harper & Row.

Super, D. E., & Bachrach, P. B. (1957). *Scientific careers and vocational therapy*. New York: Teachers College Bureau of Publications.

Tiffin, J. (1941). *Purdue pegboard*. Chicago: Science Research Associates.

Tiffin, T., & Lawshe, C. H., Jr. (1942). *The adaptability test*. Chicago: Science Research Associates.

U.S. Department of Commerce. (1984). *Statistical abstracts of the United States*. Washington, DC: U.S. Government Printing Office.

U.S. Department of Education. (1983). *A nation at risk. Report of the National Commission on Excellence in Education*. Washington, DC: U.S. Government Printing Office.

U.S. Department of Labor. (1979). *Guide to occupational exploration*. Washington, DC: U.S. Government Printing Office.

U.S. Department of Labor. Bureau of Labor Statistics. (1984). *Occupational outlook handbook*. Washington, DC: U.S. Government Printing Office.

U.S. Department of Labor. Employment and Training Administration. (1977). *Dictionary of occupational titles* (4th ed.). Washington, DC: U.S. Government Printing Office.

U.S. Department of Labor. Employment and Training Administration. (1979). *Interest check list*. Washington, DC: U.S. Government Printing Office.

Vroom, V. H. (1964). *Work and motivation*. New York: Wiley.

Wonderlich, E. F., & Hovland, C. I. (1939). The personnel test: A revision of the Otis S. A. test for business and industrial use. *Journal of Applied Psychology, 23,* 685–702.

Yankelovich, R. (1974). Turbulence in the working world: Angry workers, happy grads. *Psychology Today, 8,* 80–82.

PERMISSIONS

Chapter 2

Excerpts from: Piaget, J. (1960). *The child's conception of physical causality* (M. Gabain, Trans.). Atlantic Highlands, NJ: Humanities Press International. (Original work published 1927). Reprinted with permission of Humanities Press International.

Chapter 4

Excerpts from: Winnicott, D. (1958). Transitional objects and transitional phenomena. In D. Winnicott (Ed.), *Collected papers: Through pediatrics to psychoanalysis*. New York: Basic Books. (Original work published 1951). Reprinted with permission of Basic Books.

Chapter 6

Excerpts from: Alapack, R. J. (1984). Adolescent first love. In C. M. Aanstoos (Ed.), *Studies in the social sciences: Vol. 23. Exploring the lived world: Readings in phenomenological psychology* (pp. 101–107). Carrollton: West Georgia College. Reprinted with permission of West Georgia College.

Chapter 11

Poem "I Used To Be." Reproduced with permission of the author, Stacey Strand.

Author Index

472

Subject Index

About the Editors
and Contributors

THE EDITORS

Michel Hersen, PhD, is Professor of Psychiatry and Psychology at the University of Pittsburgh. He is a past president of the Association for Advancement of Behavior Therapy. He has co-authored, edited, and co-edited 46 books, including *The Clinical Psychology Handbook, Handbook of Psychological Assessment*, and *Handbook of Child Psychopathology*. He is co-editor and co-founder of the *Clinical Psychology Review, Behavior Modification, Progress in Behavior Modification, Journal of Family Violence, Journal of Anxiety Disorders*, and the *Journal of the Multihandicapped*. In collaboration with his colleagues, he has received numerous grants from funding agencies, including the National Institute of Mental Health, the National Institute of Handicapped Research, the Department of Education, and the March of Dimes.

Vincent B. Van Hasselt, PhD, is Research Supervisor at the Western Pennsylvania School for Blind Children and Assistant Professor of Psychiatry at the University of Pittsburgh School of Medicine. He is the recipient of grants from the March of Dimes Birth Defects Foundation, National Institute of Handicapped Research, Handicapped Children's Early Education Program, and Special Education Programs (U.S. Department of Education) for research projects focusing on the social and emotional adjustment of developmentally and physically disabled children and youth. He is the author of numerous scientific journal articles and book chapters concerning psychological assessment and treatment approaches for disabled persons. He is also co-editor and co-founder of the *Journal of Family Violence* and the *Journal of the Multihandicapped*.

THE CONTRIBUTORS

Richard Alapack, PhD, is Associate Professor of Psychology at the University of St. Jerome's College, Waterloo, Ontario. Most of his published research is in the area of adolescent/young adult development. He is consulting editor for the *Journal of Phenomenological Psychology, The Humanistic Psychologist, Duquesne University Press*, and *Humanities Press*. His major area of interest is the cross-fertilization of phenomenology and psychoanalysis as it pertains to a development approach to social relations.

Robert T. Ammerman, PhD, is a Research Associate at the Western Pennsylvania School for Blind Children. He has published in the area of social and emotional adjustment in handicapped children, as well as child maltreatment. His current research interest is child abuse and neglect of handicapped children.

Steven Beck, PhD, is Assistant Professor of Psychology in the Clinical Psychology program at the Ohio State University. He received his PhD from the University of Georgia in 1981. He has published articles and book chapters on a wide range of behavioral disorders and therapies. He is currently on the editorial board of *Behavior Modification, Applied Research in Mental Retardation*, and *Behavioral Medicine Abstracts*, as well as serving as editorial consultant for other journals.

Marcy Tepper Bornstein, MA, The University of Montana, is presently serving a 1-year internship at the University of Arizona Health Sciences Center. Her major areas of interest currently include treatment programs for children of divorce, eating-related disorders (anorexia and bulimia) and techniques of marital/family therapy. Ms. Bornstein's most recent publications have appeared in *Behavior Therapy, American Journal of Family Therapy*, and the *Journal of Child and Adolescent Psychotherapy*. In addition, she has co-contributed chapters to the *Handbook of Behavioral Assessment* and *Child Behavioral Assessment: Principles and Procedures*. Ms. Bornstein is also the co-author, with Philip Bornstein, of the newly published book, *Marital Therapy: A Behavioral Communications Approach*.

Philip H. Bornstein, PhD, is Professor of Psychology at the University of Montana. His major interests involve research and clinical practice activities with couples, adolescents, and families. He is the co-author (with Marcy Tepper Bornstein) of *Marital Therapy: A Behavioral Communications Approach* and co-editor (with Alan E. Kazdin) of the *Handbook of Clinical Behavior Therapy with Children*.

Jeanne Brooks-Gunn, PhD, is a Senior Research Scientist in the Division of Education Policy Research and Services at the Educational Testing Service. In addition, she is the Director of the Adolescent Study Program at the St. Luke's–Roosevelt Hospital Center and Educational Testing Service. She holds clinical appointments in pediatrics at Columbia University, College of Physicians and Surgeons, and University of Pennsylvania Medical School. Her current research is on the psychosocial and physical development of adolescent females. Within this area she is presently conducting longitudinal studies of pubescent girls and teenagers who have become pregnant. Her two most recent books are *Girls at Puberty* and *Adolescent Mothers in Later Life*.

Constance T. Fischer, PhD, is Professor of Psychology at Duquesne University. She has published regularly in her major interest areas: applying a human science approach to qualitative research and to clinical psychology. She is a consulting editor for the *Journal of Phenomenological Psychology* and is on the editoral board of *The Humanistic Psychologist*. She is President of APA's Division of Theoretical and Philosophical Psychology (1985–1986), author of *Individualizing Psychological Assessment*, and Director of the Pittsburgh Assessment and Consultation Center.

Jim Flaitz, PhD, is an Associate Professor of Measurement and Evaluation at the University of Southwestern Louisiana. His academic training is in psychology and educational research and his research interests are focused primarily on the areas of effective teaching and the development of cognitive functioning in learners.

Jeffry Friedman, MEd, is a Doctoral Candidate in School Psychology at Lehigh University. His major applied and research interests include behavioral assessment and remediation of academic deficits, self-management, and developmentally disabled populations.

Lewayne D. Gilchrist, PhD, is Research Assistant Professor at the School of Social Work, University of Washington. Her research interests and publications are in the areas of health promotion and disease prevention with children, adolescents, and women.

Jane F. Gilgun, PhD, is Assistant Professor in the School of Social Work, University of Minnesota, Twin Cities, and Adjunct Assistant Professor at the Hubert H. Humphrey Institute of Public Affairs,

University of Minnesota, Twin Cities. Her current research projects are an investigation into the transition from victim to perpetrator in child sexual abuse and research and evaluation at a rural incest treatment program. Her publications have been in the areas of sex education, child sexual abuse, and the use of qualitative methods in research and evaluation.

Sol Gordon, PhD, is Professor Emeritus at Syracuse University's College for Human Development. He was recognized for his creative work in the field of sex education by receiving the Annual American Association of Sex Educators, Counselors, and Therapists Award in 1982. Dr. Gordon is the author of many books, including *Raising a Child Conservatively in a Sexually Permissive World* (with Judith Gordon).

Alan M. Gross, PhD, is Associate Professor of Psychology at the University of Mississippi. His research interests include self-management, child behavior therapy, and behavioral pediatrics. He is the recipient of several grants from NIH. Currently he serves on the editorial board of three journals and is the Editor-elect of *The Behavior Therapist*.

Katherine A. Halmi, MD, is Professor of Psychiatry at Cornell University Medical College, New York Hospital-Westchester Division. She is the Director of a 12-bed inpatient unit for the treatment of anorexia nervosa and bulimia patients. Her extensive publications on topics concerning anorexia nervosa and bulimia include treatment, follow-up, and endocrine and epidemiological studies.

David J. Hansen, PhD, is an Assistant Professor in the Department of Psychology at West Virginia University. His major clinical and research interests are social skills assessment and training with children and adolescents, assessment and intervention with abusive and neglectful parents and their children, and problem-solving assessment and training. His research includes procedures for assessing and improving generalization and social validity of skills training.

Martin Harrow, PhD, is Director of Psychology at Michael Reese Hospital and Medical Center in Chicago, and Professor in the Department of Psychiatry and the Department of Behavioral Sciences at the University of Chicago. A former chess master, he has engaged in extensive research on long-term adjustment and thought disorder in schizophrenia and affective disorders. He has published over 140 articles in these and related areas, and is on the editorial board of several major psychology journals.

Robert J. Havighurst, PhD, is Professor Emeritus of Human Development at the University of Chicago. He has published a number of essays on adolescence and on the transition from adolescence to adulthood. He has described *The School as a Socializing Agency*, and also as a source of delinquency. A chapter on "The High School in the Big City" carries the proposition that the staff contributes to social urban renewal.

John J. Horan, PhD, is Professor and Director of the Counseling Psychology Program at Arizona State University. Much of his research has involved the experimental evaluation of cognitive–behavioral interventions applied to health psychology outcomes. He is on the editorial board of the *Journal of Counseling Psychology* and has served as a consultant to a number of other journals.

Alan S. Kaufman, PhD, is Professor and University Research Fellow at the University of Alabama. He is author of *Intelligent Testing with the WISC-R* and co-author (with Nadeen L. Kaufman) of the Kaufman Assessment Battery for Children (K-ABC) and Kaufman Test of Education Achievement (K-TEA). He has written numerous chapters and professional articles on intellectual assessment and serves on numerous editorial boards.

Jeffrey A. Kelly, PhD, is Professor of Psychiatry (Psychology) and Chief of the Division of Psychology at the University of Mississippi Medical Center. He major interests involve applications of behavior therapy and skills-training interventions to clinical populations. The author of several behavior therapy books, he also serves on the editorial boards of *Behavior Therapy*, *Behavior Modification*, the *Journal of Family Violence*, and the *Journal of Applied Behavior Analysis*.

Benjamin B. Lahey, PhD, is Professor of Psychology at the University of Georgia. He is Director of the Georgia Children's Center for Psychological Assessment and teaches in the Clinical Psychology Training Program. He is co-editor with Alan E. Kazdin of *Advances in Clinical Child Psychology* and is involved in biobehavioral research on attention deficit and conduct disorders in children.

B. Geraldine Lambert, PhD, is a Professor of Psychology at the University of Southwestern Louisiana. She served as Department Head of the Psychology Department for over 10 years. She was senior author of the textbook *Adolescence: Transition from Childhood to Maturity*. She has served as consultant to the Acadiana Mental Health Center and the Iberia Parish Schools. Her research interests are in personality and occupational choice of adolescents.

Chris N. Larson, MD, is an Assistant Professor of Child Psychiatry at the University of Pittsburgh School of Medicine. He holds an MS degree in Preventive Medicine and Environmental Health and is interested in Psychiatric Epidemiology and diagnostic issues in children and adolescents, particularly in the area of affective and anxiety disorders.

Howard D. Lerner, PhD, is Assistant Professor of Psychology in the Department of Psychiatry at the University of Michigan Medical School. After receiving a BA and MA from the University of Illinois and a PhD in Clinical Psychology from Rutgers University, he was a postdoctoral fellow at Yale University. He is a member of APA, a Fellow in the Society of Personality Assessment and a Diplomate in Clinical Psychology. He is presently a candidate at the Michigan Psychoanalytic Institute. His areas of interest include adolescent psychopathology and psychotherapy. His research focus has been on the borderline diagnosis, the assessment of defensive structure and object relations in borderline adolescents, and the complex interaction between theory, clinical practice, and research. He has co-edited two books on psychodiagnostic testing and has published articles on the borderline diagnosis, eating disorders, and contemporary psychoanalytic theory. He serves as editorial consultant for a number of journals in psychiatry and psychology.

Renee B. Levin, PhD, is a Postdoctoral Fellow at the Medical University of South Carolina. Her research interests include the development of social competence and behavioral medicine. Her most recent publications appear in *Behavior Modification; Behaviour, Research, and Therapy*; and *Biofeedback and Self-Regulation*.

John Paul McKinney is Professor of Psychology at Michigan State University. He is coauthor of *Developmental Psychology*, a series of three texts in that field. His main interests include adolescence, the development of values, and family psychotherapy.

Nancy Bradford Mounce, MS, is currently employed by the Lafayette Parish Schools, where she teaches English and Honors Courses at Lafayette High School. Her interests include psychology of work and counseling with focus toward the adolescent. Her MS degree in Rehabilitation Counselor Education was earned at the University of Southwestern Louisiana, Lafayette, Louisiana.

John F. Murphy received his PhD from Columbia University in the area of Religion and Education. He is an Associate Professor of Education at Brooklyn College of the City University of New York. His major studies and publications have been in the value concerns of adolescents, in the training of secondary school teachers and administrators, and most recently with his wife, Arlene Wrigley Murphy, in religious education of children and adolescents.

Thomas S. Parish, PhD, is Professor of Human Development at Kansas State University. His primary research endeavors have been in providing insight regarding the assessment and amelioration of social and emotional problems in children and adolescents. He is currently on the editorial board of the *Journal of Genetic Psychology* and *Genetic Psychology Monographs* and serves as an editorial consultant for a number of other journals.

Rosanne Perlmutter, EdD, teaches psychology at Newton North High School in Newton, Massachusetts, and has a private clinical practice. She has lectured and presented papers on adolescent development, morals and values in adolescence, and on identity and self-esteem, both in the United States and in Europe. For the last 12 years, she has been co-chair of an Annual Conference on Psychological Education.

Anne C. Petersen, PhD, is Professor of Human Development and Head of the Department of Individual and Family Studies at The Pennsylvania State University. Her research interests are in biopsychosocial development in adolescence and factors influencing gender differences. She has published three books on adolescence and one on gender differences, as well as numerous articles and chapters in each area.

Theodore A. Petti, MD, MPH, is an Associate Professor of Child Psychiatry, Western Psychiatric Institute and Clinic, University of Pittsburgh. He has been awarded the J. Franklin Robinson Award from the American Academy of Child Psychiatry for his work in childhood depression, has edited a book on depression in children, and has published articles and book chapters on a wide range of topics, including childhood depression, psychopharmacology, and the moderate psychopathologies of childhood and adolescence. His recent interest has involved delivery of services to rural areas.

Michael F. Pogue-Geile, PhD, is Assistant Professor in the Department of Psychology and the Department of Psychiatry at the University of Pittsburgh. He has published on longitudinal and individual difference perspectives on schizophrenia, behavior genetics, and methodology in psychopathology research. He also serves as editorial consultant for several major journals.

Maryse H. Richards, PhD, is Assistant Professor of Psychology at Loyola University of Chicago. Her major interests are in early adolescence, pubertal development, and body image, with a special focus on sex differences and the psychology of women.

Steven Paul Schinke, PhD, is Professor of Social Work at Columbia University. He has published extensively on social and health topics related to children, youth, and families. He is Associate Editor of *Children and Youth Services Review*. He is a member of the editorial boards of *Journal of Social Service Research* and the *Journal of Family Violence*, and is a Consulting Editor for *Behavioral Medicine Abstracts*.

David Schuldberg, PhD, is Assistant Professor of Psychology at the University of Montana. His research interests include family functioning, particularly in divorce, and the assessment of creativity and positive mental health. He is also interested in the integration of behavioral and play approaches to the assessment and treatment of children.

Edward S. Shapiro, PhD, is Associate Professor of Education and Coordinator, School Psychology Programs, at Lehigh University. He has previously held academic appointments at the University of Pittsburgh School of Medicine and the University of Arizona. He has published numerous articles in the areas of behavioral assessment of academic skills, behavioral interventions for school-based behavior problems, behavioral approaches to delivering school psychological services, and self-management with developmentally disabled children and adults. Additionally, he is Associate Editor of *School Psychology Review*.

Ester R. Shapiro, PhD, is a child and family therapy supervisor at Cambridge Hospital, instructor at Harvard Medical School, and psychological consultant to the Family Support Center–Judge Baker Guidance Center in Boston. Her research and writing interests are in the area of family development and family life-cycle transitions. She is in private clinical practice, with a special interest in family development during adolescence.

Lori A. Sisson, MS, is a doctoral candidate in clinical psychology at the University of Pittsburgh and a graduate student researcher at Western Psychiatric Institute and Clinic, University of Pittsburgh School of Medicine. Her major research interests are in the areas of behavior modification and behavioral assessment with mentally retarded and other handicapped children and adolescents.

Lawrence K. Straus, MS, is a Doctoral Candidate of Counseling Psychology at the Pennsylvania State University. He is currently completing a clinical internship under the direction of Aaron T.

Beck, MD, at the Center for Cognitive Therapy, University of Pennsylvania. He is coauthor with Dr. John Horan on another chapter on adolescent substance abuse and is a contributing author of a book, in preparation at the Center for Cognitive Therapy, about the cognitive therapy of personality disorders.

Cyd C. Strauss, PhD, is an Instructor in the Department of Psychiatry at the University of Pittsburgh School of Medicine, Western Psychiatric Institute and Clinic. Her major research interests are in the etiology, development, and treatment of anxiety disorders in children and adolescents.

Juliet M. Vogel, PhD, received her doctorate in developmental psychology from Harvard University. She has held faculty positions at Rutgers University and Kalamazoo College. Her interests include cognitive and perceptual development and clinical applications of developmental psychology.